Gun Digest®

1986/40th Annual Edition

EDITED BY KEN WARNER

DBI BOOKS, INC.

ABOUT OUR COVERS

We are indeed proud to have Firearms Import & Export (FIE) products featured on the front and back covers of this, the 40th Annual Edition of GUN DIGEST.

On our front cover you'll find a trio of Single Action rimfires from FIE. On the left and right are a pair of FIE Texas Ranger rimfires chambered for 22 Short, Long and Long Rifle (22 Mag. combo also available). These guns all feature a hammer-block safety, walnut grips and fixed sights. Barrel lengths include 4¾, 6½ and 9 inches.

The new FIE single action revolver in the center of our front cover was designed by GUN DIGEST's Editor-in-Chief Ken Warner. Ken, as you can see, enjoys the graceful shape of birds-head style grips and short (3-inch) barrels. Dubbed, "The Little Ranger," this S/A rimfire has all the standard features of the full-size Texas Ranger, including a functional ejector rod.

The beautifully scrimshawed ivory polymer grips are optional and available in a number of styles; the Texas Ranger grips are shown.

Our back cover features three FIE long guns. On the left is FIE's Hamilton & Hunter single-barrel shotgun. It's available in 12 or 20 gauge or .410 bore—all having 3-inch chambers, button-break actions, automatic ejectors and hardwood stocks. In the center is FIE's GR-8 "Black Beauty" semi-auto rimfire. Chambered in 22 Long Rifle, the Black Beauty features a structural Nylon stock, checkering and adjustable sights. It also weighs in at a light 64 ounces and comes grooved for tip-off scope mounts.

To the right is FIE's newest offering, the Hamilton & Hunter Model 122 bolt action, clip-fed rimfire. Chambered for 22 Shorts, Longs and Long Rifles, the Model 122's receiver is also grooved for tip-off mounts. It comes with a selected "Imbuia" wood stock, has fully adjustable sights and tips the scales at 5½ pounds. Photos by John Hanusin

A Little More About Our Covers: A Personal Note

It is not often the case that a gun writer directly establishes a new firearm pattern, but this unusual lightning struck in the case of FIE's new Little Ranger. Your faithful Editor actually cut and pasted catalog pictures to describe—3 years ago—to FIE's Ron Vogel what is now on our covers, a delightful variation on the single-action theme. So, though I haven't shot the little gem yet, I like it a lot.

Ken Warner

GUN DIGEST STAFF

EDITOR-IN-CHIEF
Ken Warner
ASSISTANT TO THE EDITOR
Lilo Anderson
SENIOR STAFF EDITOR
Harold A. Murtz
ASSOCIATE EDITOR
Robert S. L. Anderson
PRODUCTION MANAGER
Pamela J. Johnson
CONTRIBUTING EDITORS
Bob Bell
Dean A. Grennell
Rick Hacker
Edward A. Matunas
Layne Simpson
Larry S. Sterett
Hal Swiggett
Ralph T. Walker
D. A. Warner
J.B. Wood
EUROPEAN CORRESPONDENT
Raymond Caranta
EDITOR EMERITUS
John T. Amber
GRAPHIC DESIGN
Jim Billy
Mark Goldstein
Stephen Johnson
PUBLISHER
Sheldon L. Factor

DBI BOOKS, INC.

PRESIDENT
Charles T. Hartigan
VICE PRESIDENT & PUBLISHER
Sheldon L. Factor
VICE PRESIDENT — SALES
John G. Strauss
TREASURER
Frank R. Serpone

The views and opinions contained herein are those of the authors. The editor and publisher disclaim all responsibility for the accuracy or correctness of the authors' views.

Manuscripts, contributions and inquiries, including first class return postage, should be sent to the Gun Digest Editorial Offices, 4092 Commercial Ave., Northbrook, IL 60062. All material received will receive reasonable care, but we will not be responsible for its safe return. Material accepted is subject to our requirements for editing and revisions. Author payment covers all rights and title to the accepted material, including photos, drawings and other illustrations. Payment is at our current rates.

CAUTION: Technical data presented here, particularly technical data on handloading and on firearm adjustment and alteration, inevitably reflects individual experience with particular equipment and components under specific circumstances the reader cannot duplicate exactly. Such data presentations therefore should be used for guidance only and with caution. DBI Books, Inc. acceptes no responsibility for results obtained using this data.

Arms and Armour Press, London, G.B., exclusive licensees and distributors in Britain and Europe; Australia; Nigeria, South Africa and Zimbabwe; India and Pakistan; Singapore, Hong Kong and Japan.

ISBN 0-910676-88-7 Library of Congress Catalog #44-3588

Some Up; Some Down; Some Sideways

Beretta is riding high in the saddle over the military contract for their 9mm pistol; High Standard is gone, the office closed, the parts sold; Harrington & Richardson is at this writing in Chapter 11 status, under the protection of the court and USRAC and Savage are talking merger as we go to press.

The gun business has not been easy, this twelve-month past, but that SHOT Show reported nearby seemed to indicate the climate is looking better. Certainly, a lot of people in the business are counting on it.

SHOT SHOW: Too Big or Not Too Big?

The extraordinarily successful string of SHOT Shows put on by the National Shooting Sports Foundation have finally given rise to complaint. Of the 1985 Show, held in Atlanta and once more a new record in number of exhibitors, square feet, visitors, business transacted or any other unit of measurement applicable, the trade press said it was too big. One fellow calculated that only the most industrious show-goer could spend as many as 90 seconds at 50% of the booths. Some exhibitors said there was such a crowd of buyers they couldn't really talk.

If a national trade show must have problems, those are the problems to have. Since all else has been solved, it is likely these will be, too. We shall see in January in Houston.

Grits Gets A Gun

Grits Gresham, Gun Editor of *Sports Afield*, was named 1984 Gunwriter of the Year by Anschutz. Shown presenting the solid bronze award is E. Alan Johnson, President of Precision Sales International. Dieter Anschutz, President of Anschutz, has Grits's 1422D Custom Rifle.

NRA: Once Again, Fracas

Well, they went around and around in Seattle. Neal Knox came up short again, something like 2 to 1 the votes ran this time. The assembled Life Members and other voting members didn't want Neal and they didn't want the hassle of the election, so they voted it back to the Board of Directors.

They did want Ray Arnett, President Reagan's friend and shooter and hunter, to be the chief operating officer, so he is now NRA's Executive Vice-President, at a reported $150,000 a year. If NRA didn't have a $50,000,000 annual budget, that would sound like a lot of money.

Harlon Carter? Happily back where he chose from all the world to be the last time he retired—Arizona. He's rich in accomplishment, in memories, and in his marriage. And the pension probably ain't bad, either.

A. M. Wynne, Jr. 1907-1984

Better known to his good friends as Breezy Wynne, this long-time companion and hunting partner of John Amber, died on October 29th, 1984, at Fayetteville, Arkansas, after a prolonged series of heart problems.

He is survived by his widow and two daughters, who have our deep sympathy, as does our Editor Emeritus.

Employees Buy DBI Books, Inc.

Since the 39th Edition of GUN DIGEST came off the printing press, DBI Books, Inc., was sold by its parent company to two of DBI's key employees, Charles T. Hartigan, DBI's President, and John G. Strauss, Vice-President of Sales & Marketing.

"We all had invested so much time in this company," Hartigan says, "that, given the opportunity, choosing to work harder and own it ourselves seemed the only thing to do."

Few visible changes are planned, but one has come along. DBI's offices have moved. The new address is:

4092 Commercial Avenue
Northbrook, IL 60062.

Army Re-Ups Flayderman

E. Norman Flayderman, quite trim in his cammies, is out on the hustings as Civilian Aide to the Secretary of the Army for Connecticut in the nearby picture. Flayderman, the well-known author and dealer in antique arms of New Milford, has begun his second term in this advisory staff function.

"It's the most challenging and rewarding position I have yet filled," Flayderman notes, "and I'm very much looking forward to the next two years."

CONTENTS

FEATURES

DEPARTMENTS

THE M16A2: New World Standard For Infantry Rifles . . .

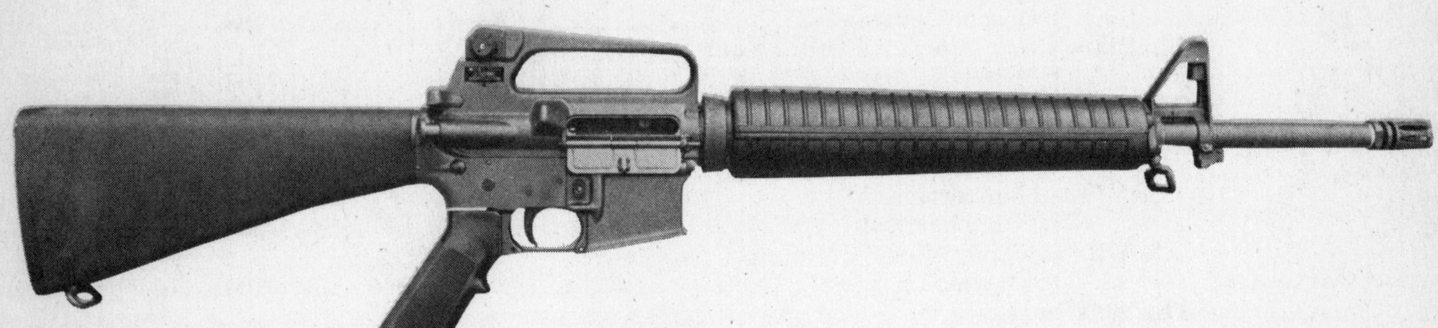

. . . out-penetrates the M1 rifle shooting M2 ball at 800 yards.

M16A2 barrel marking gives caliber and twist as "1/7."

THE M16A2 is the new standard to which past and future military rifles will be compared. This second-generation 5.56mm rifle is the product of co-operation between industry and U.S. forces to develop, test and field a product-improved rifle which should meet their needs to the end of this century. The M16A2, standardized in November, 1983, is a wonderful example of how the military development and procurement system is *supposed* to work. The efficiency with which this work proceeded from concept to production and fielding is a tribute to military-industrial cooperation.

When the M16A1 rifle was first adopted by U.S. troops in 1967, the Marines were the most vocal opponent of a "small caliber" rifle. At that time there were valid complaints about the reliability of the M16 and its M193 ammunition and its range and lethality. Although changes in the rifle and ammunition corrected the functional problems, by 1970 it was apparent the sights and the ballistics of the 55-gr. M193 cartridge reached their limits in combat at

by C.E. HARRIS

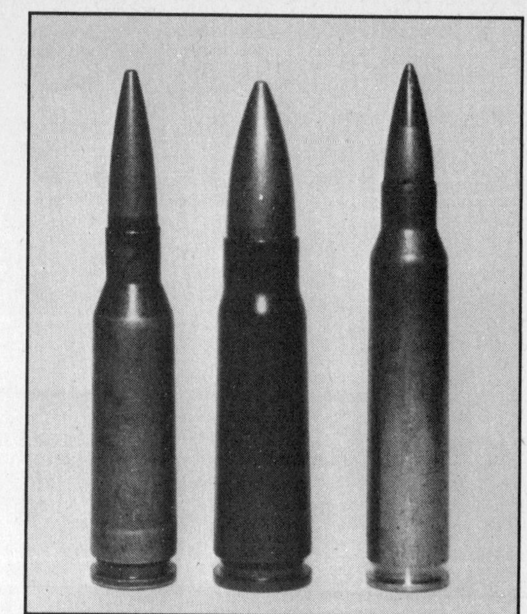

The AK74 5.45mm cartridge and the AK47 7.62mm cartridge—the competitors—are shown to the left of the 5.56mm NATO M855 cartridge, our new standard.

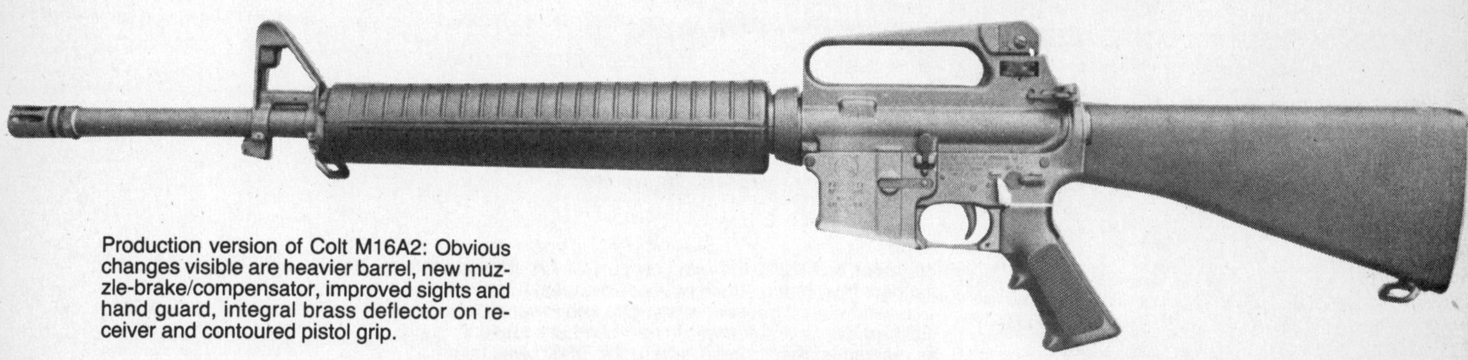

Production version of Colt M16A2: Obvious changes visible are heavier barrel, new muzzle-brake/compensator, improved sights and hand guard, integral brass deflector on receiver and contoured pistol grip.

about 500 yards. To many critics, even 500 yards pushed credibility.

Adopting the 5.56mm NATO SS109/M855 cartridge in 1977 brought ammunition effective to well beyond 600 yards in lethality and accuracy and penetration. Standardization of this NATO cartridge brought a need to adapt the M16 rifle to it, and provided the opportunity to correct the known tactical deficiencies in the M16A1. The USMC Firepower Division, at Quantico, VA, was tasked with this development in cooperation with Colt Industries, under supervision of the Joint Services Small Arms Program (JSSAP).

The product-improved rifle was identified as M16A1E1 during operational testing which preceded formal type classification. Operational testing of 30 M16A1E1 rifles served to evaluate the changes and provide input for further refinements which would be incorporated in the production version of the M16A2. The Modified Operation Test (MOT) began on November 23, 1981, and was completed on December 11, 1981. Supplemental tests continued through August, 1982, to confirm the validity of some proposed improvements and to confirm their production feasibility.

The M16A2 is now in full production, having been adopted by the U.S. Marines to replace their entire complement of M16A1 rifles within the next five years. The Army has also decided to adopt the M16A2. The Canadians are also adopting it, but without the new sights or burst control, as the C7.

The test findings summarized in the MOT Final Report conclude the M16A2 performs as well or better than the M16A1 in all areas. The advantages of the M16A2 over the M16A1 are listed below:

- *Increased effectiveness*: higher hit probability, greater lethality and penetration, improved range through use of NATO standard SS109/M855 ammunition.
- *Better durability and handling* with improved, stronger handguard, and buttstock, longer buttstock, new buttcap, contoured pistol grip.
- *Reduced barrel jump and muzzle climb* during full automatic or sustained semi-automatic fire with new muzzle-brake-compensator.
- *Reduced dust signature* as well when fired over sandy or dusty ground.
- *Heavier, stronger barrel*, to resist bending, with 7-inch twist to exploit advantages of new NATO ammunition.
- *Better sights*: improved contrast and less glare with square post front sight, faster target acquisition of moving targets, better detection of targets in low light, and improved accuracy at long range by use of two optimized rear sight apertures.
- *Better fire control* and more effective use of ammunition with 3-shot burst option.

Operational firepower effectiveness was evaluated by comparing the M16A1 and M16A2 in tactical scenarios. These included base of fire, assault and counterattack, ambush, long range and mid-range defensive fires, final protective fires, defense against ambush, area target suppression, and night firing.

Right side of receiver shows the integral brass deflector on the receiver behind the ejection port which prevents left-handers from being struck by ejected cases. Aluminum device sandwiched between pistol grip and lower receiver inhibits inadvertent automatic in non-combat situations, such as marksmanship training, where this photo was taken.

There was no appreciable difference in base of fire effectiveness between the M16A1 and M16A2, but in the assault and counterattack, test results from the Small Arms Remoted Target System (SARTS) showed the A2 obtained a significantly greater percentage of hits in burst fire. When fired semi-automatic on the field range and Infantry Tactical Training (ITT) course simulations, no significant difference was noted. In the ambush scenario, using high volume semi-automatic fire no appreciable difference was noted. Firing in the burst mode at night the data were inconclusive, but when the same course of fire was fired in daylight on the area target suppression test, the A2 delivered 7 percent more hits at 100 meters than did the M16A1.

When firing in the burst mode at multiple targets at 100 meters the A2 gave a significantly higher number of hits, but at 50 meters this difference was not apparent. All persons firing the M16A1 used for comparison were firing short bursts of 2 or 3 rounds, which may or may not be what would happen in the high stress of actual combat. In the simulation of a patrol being ambushed, requiring quick reaction, immediate action and firing in bursts or automatic fire, the A2 obtained 19 percent hits, compared to only 12 percent for the M16A1.

The A2's increased ruggedness was evaluated through user assessments and inspection of rifles for damage after an exercise in which several squads conducted an operation clearing seven buildings in "combat town." Rifles were used as steps and to gain access to second stories of buildings. Each participant attacked a rubber dummy stabilized by ropes, executing the vertical butt stroke, smash, parry and horizontal butt stroke, in the same sequence with each weapon. Participants also fixed bayonets and attacked a simulated enemy, bayonetting and slashing it twice. The handguards of the A2 were more durable and appeared to offer better control in close combat, and for urban or built-up area operations.

Portability of each weapon was compared for tactical and non-tactical methods of carry, including the manual of arms while marching. Test par-

The contoured pistol grip is intended to provide more secure grasping; backstrap is deeply grooved, and frontstrap has deep finger groove to provide secure hold. Selector lever offers choice of semi-auto or 3-shot bursts. Rear sight has minute of angle clicks for windage and elevation, matched to M855 or SS109 ammunition.

ticipants marched to and from the range with both weapons, and carried them through the combat town course, day movement course and other subtests which included a forced march. User comments indicated no preference for carrying either the M16A1 or A2.

Vulnerability of the weapons to detection and countermeasures were assessed by comparing the noise generated when being carried, and while being operated, as well as the muzzle flash and/or dust signature produced when each weapon fired in day or night conditions. Photographic presentations of the muzzle flash or dust produced were obtained to provide an accurate assessment. Personnel in the butts also answered questionnaires assessing their ability to identify which weapons were being fired based on sounds heard in the butts.

Conclusions indicated no difference in the amount of noise generated by either weapon when being carried or operated. No difference was indicated in muzzle flash in day or night conditions. No significant dust signature was noted due to cold weather conditions, although when firing over new snow less disturbance was noted under the muzzles of the A2s. No essential difference in shape that could be used as a characteristic to identify units can be noted at any distance without the aid of binoculars or a telescope. Personnel in the butts could distinguish which ammunition was being fired at ranges beyond 600 meters, because the NATO SS109 and M855 ammunition remains supersonic to a far greater range, producing a distinct crack as it passes overhead, whereas the 55-grain M193 bullet goes subsonic shortly beyond 600 meters, producing only a muffled pop.

A limited test compared the M16A1 and the new A2 as to any interference generated while carrying the weapons caused by changes in center of gravity, or methods of carry when engaged in airborne, amphibious or helicopter operations. Participants carried both rifles in operation scenarios wearing full combat gear. There was no meaningful difference between weapons regarding their compatibility or suitability while entering or exiting landing craft, vehicles or air-

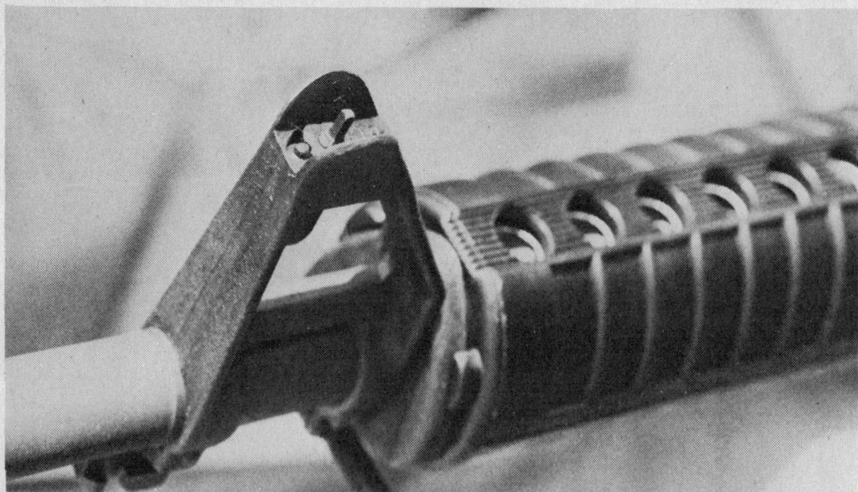

M16A2 front sight is square in cross-section with parallel sides to provide a more distinct sight picture. After first zero adjustment, rear sight offers all adjustments normally required.

The small aperture leg is used for precision daylight fire at ranges beyond 200 meters. The large aperture is used for snap shooting at ranges less than 200 meters and for low light level use near dawn or dusk. Elevation drum moves sight in minute of angle clicks.

craft.

The human factors evaluation, or "man-machine interface" characteristics of the two rifles were compared as they might affect operating safety (including hot or sharp parts), useability and adjustability of sights and controls in terms of speed, accessibility, and accuracy of adjustment; and recoil, as it affects recovery time, in burst fire or sustained rapid semiautomatic fire, accuracy in precision fire, comfort and confidence. The effects of the redesigned handguard and buttstock were also evaluated as they affected accuracy, control in automatic fire and hand to hand combat.

Test participants preferred the sights on the M16A2 to those on the M16A1 because they were easier to adjust and provided a greater range of adjustment, which effectively doubles the useful engagement range of this rifle with SS109/M855-type ammunition compared to the M16A1 with M193-type ammunition. The sights on the A2 are safer to adjust when the weapon is loaded than those on the M16A1, because the front sight is not used for routine sight changes. Ranging adjustments are made on the elevation dial of the rear sight after the front sight is initially adjusted to obtain a battlesight zero. Refinements were made in the size of the front sight post and rear sight apertures based on these tests to optimize precision of fire in daylight conditions, and target acquisition for close range snap shooting and firing in morning or evening nautical twilight conditions.

The M16A2 production sight is adjustable from 300 to 800 meters and has indexing marks on the dial and receiver which align when the sight is turned all the way down or within one click. The 300- and 800-meter settings are co-located on the same position, marked with an indexing line on the top of the dial. Remaining ranges are marked on the dial in 100m increments: i.e., 4, 5, 6, 7. Range markings on the elevation dial align with the following detents 8/3 (800/300 meters) at 0 or 25th click, 4 - 3rd click, 5 - 7th click, 6 - 12th click, 7 - 18th click. The short range rear sight aperture is used for ranges up to 200m, has an outside diameter of .375-in. and an inside diameter of .20-in. It is marked "0-2" at the base and has a windage reference point at the top which is used for precision fire with the long range aperture.

The long range aperture is used for firing beyond 200m and has an outside diameter of .375-in. with an in-

Table I
Accuracy Comparison of M16A2 vs. AK-74

Weapon/Ammunition	Range (yds.)				
M16A2 with 55-gr. M193	100	300	600	800	1000
Mean Radius (ins.)	1.87	4.18	13.2	18.3	no hits
Extreme Spread (ins.)	5.25	13.4	31.4	46.5	no hits
Hits On "E" Silhouette 39" high x 19" wide	20x20	20x20	11x20	10x20	no hits
Score on NRA decimal target SR and MR	99-6X	93-1X	81-1X	79	no hits
M16A2 with M855/SS109					
Mean Radius (ins.)	1.95	5.22	10.98	11.78	15.95
Extreme Spread (ins.)	5.5	15.75	32.75	43.0	73.9
Hits on "E" Silhouette	20x20	20x20	15x20	12x20	6x10
Score on NRA decimal target SR and MR	99-5X	90-1X	91-2X	82-1X	79-1X
AK-74 with 5.45 mm PS					
Mean Radius (ins.)	1.87	8.47	15.9	20.3	no hits
Extreme Spread (ins.)	7.25	21.6	44.0	74.5	no hits
Hits on "E" Silhouette	20x20	17x20	9x20	7x20	no hits
Score on NRA decimal target SR and MR	99-6X	79-0X	69-0X	57	no hits

side diameter of .070-in. It is marked "3-8" at the base. The rear faces of both sight apertures are concave and heavily phosphated to reduce glare. One quarter-revolution (one movement/detent) of the front sight moves point of impact approximately 1.4 moa, one click of the elevation dial on the rear sight moves point of impact approximately 1 moa, and one click of the windage knob on the rear sight moves point of impact approximately ½ moa. Firing tests indicate that point of impact is not significantly different with M193 or SS109/M855 ammunition when using the same sight settings at ranges less than 500 meters.

Accuracy and penetration of the M16A1 with M193, the A2 with M193 and SS109/M855 and the Soviet AK-74 with 5.45mm Type PS ammunition were compared at ranges from 100 to 900 meters. The Soviet AK-74 was found to be reliable and accurate at short ranges, but its sights were a limiting factor beyond about 200 meters—it has a short sighting radius, open rear notch sight and no windage adjustments. The M193 ammunition was found most accurate at ranges less than 300 meters, but the SS109 most accurate at ranges beyond 500 meters. The most accurate rifle overall was the M16A2 with SS109 ammunition; the next most accurate was the M16A2 with M193, followed by the M16A1 with M193 and finally the AK-74 with Type PS ammunition. Accuracy results for the various weapons and types of ammunition tested are summarized in the accompanying tables.

In penetration tests the M16A1 rifle with M193 ammunition, the M16A2 with SS109, M855, M193 and Olin Penetrator (commercial approximation of the SS109), and the AK-74 with Type PS ammunition were fired against 3.5mm thick mild steel plates at various ranges. In addition, the 7.62mm M40A1 Remington sniper rifle with M118 Special Ball (Match, 175-2.0 gr. bullet at 2575 fps) and M80 standard Ball (148.0-2.0 bullet at 2750 fps) were fired for comparison. Maximum ranges at which penetrations of the test plate occurred were 500 yards for the M193, 600 for the AK-74 and 7.62mm M80, and 800 for the 7.62mm M118, 5.56mm SS109, M855 and Olin Penetrator. Results are summarized in an accompanying table.

The question of lethality and effectiveness of the M193 cartridge fired from the fast twist rifling in the M16A2 was of concern because existing stocks of M193 ammunition will

Familiar M16A1 features such as take-down mechanism and bolt-assist knob coexist with new things like brass deflector at right on M16A2.

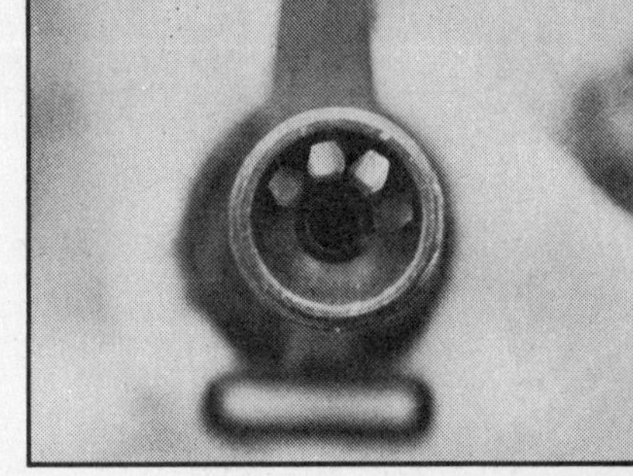

New muzzle-brake/compensator has closed bottom to reduce dust signature produced when rifle is fired from prone position. It also dramatically improves hit probability in burst fire by reducing muzzle climb.

Table II

Performance Of Typical Military Rifles Against NATO 3.5mm Thick Mild Steel Test Plate

Weapon	Cartridge	Range (yds.)	Performance*
Carbine, M1	Ball, M1	100	CP
		200	FP
AKM	7.62x39 PS (steel core)	300	CP
		400	50% CP, 50% PP
M16A1	Ball, M193	400	CP
		500	50% CP, 50% PP
		600	FP
M16A2	Ball, M855	600	CP
		700	CP
		800	50% CP, 50% PP
		1000	FP
AK-74	5.45x39 PS	600	CP
		800	FP
Rifle, M1	Ball M2	500	CP
		600	FP
Rifle, M14	Ball M80	700	CP
		800	FP
Rifle, M21/M40	Ball M118	800	CP
		900	50% CP, 50% PP
		1000	FP

*Explanation of terms:

CP - complete perforation in which major portion of the projectile exits the armor

PP - partial penetration in which a hole is generated but the major portion of the projectile does not exit the armor

FP - failure to penetrate, the plate may be dented but is intact

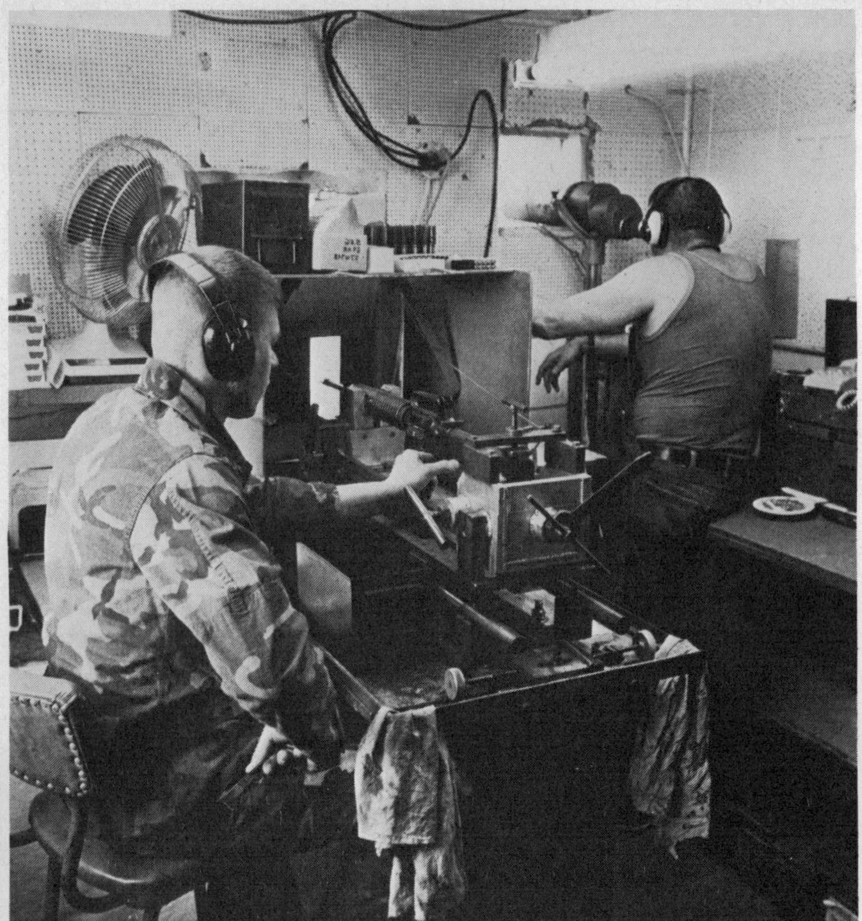

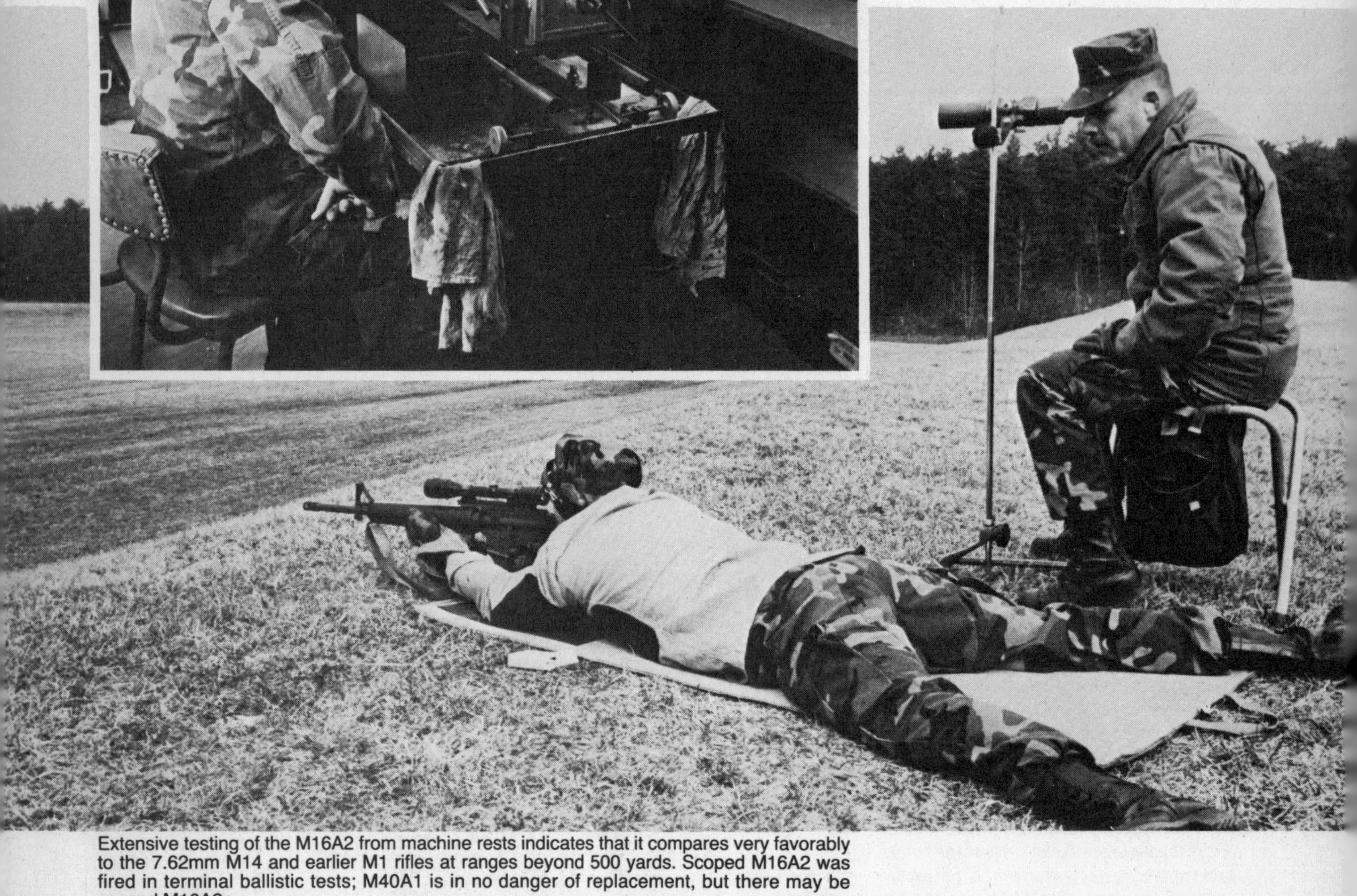

Extensive testing of the M16A2 from machine rests indicates that it compares very favorably to the 7.62mm M14 and earlier M1 rifles at ranges beyond 500 yards. Scoped M16A2 was fired in terminal ballistic tests; M40A1 is in no danger of replacement, but there may be scoped M16A2s.

Writer Harris is well-known as a shooter who will shoot all of what's handy anytime there's a chance. Here he shoots an Egyptian AKM; he has fired the AR15 and the various M16 options in about all the variations there are and created some of them himself. Indeed, the USMC officially commended Harris for his work with them on the M16A2.

be used until sufficient supplies of type M855 ammunition can be produced to replace it. Previous testing had already established there was no loss of precision when M193 ammunition was fired in the M16A2. However, since some nations had adopted faster twists of rifling for supposed humanitarian reasons, this factor had to be investigated. Test firings were conducted with M193 ammunition in both the M16A2 and M16A1 at ranges of 100, 300 and 500 yards, shooting into 20 percent gelatin blocks of U.S. DoD standards, 50cm thick. Testing indicated there was no significant difference in the lethality of M193 ammunition in the M16A2 as compared to the M16A1 at any range fired. The SS109/M855 was equivalent to the M193 at ranges up to 300 yards, and it was significantly more effective at longer ranges, such as 500 yards.

Brief tests were conducted to determine the compatibility of the M16A2 barrel with 22 rimfire ammunition used in the M261 Conversion Unit. This sub-caliber training device is used by Army and Air Force units for preliminary training and by reserve units not having year-round ranges. The conversion unit replaces the standard bolt carrier assembly and converts the weapon to blowback operation, firing 22 LR ammunition from 10-round magazine inserts which are loaded into standard M16 magazines. The device is made under contract to the U.S. Army by Saco Defense Systems, Inc., Saco, Maine, USA.

The normal accuracy expected of 10-shot groups with 22 rimfire ammunition fired from the M16A1 with M261 Conversion unit is about 4 MOA at ranges up to 50 meters. Although this is about twice the dispersion of M193 or SS109 type ammunition, it is deemed adequate for training purposes. Side-by-side comparisons with two M16A2 and M16A1 upper receivers, used alternately on the same lower receivers, firing the same M261 unit showed no significant difference in precision, the mean extreme spread of ten consecutive 10-shot groups with each being 2.25-in. and 2.37-in., respectively, at 50 yards.

Testing to date indicates that the M16A2 preserves the strong points of the M16A1 system, while correcting most, if not all of its deficiencies. Since the M16A2 has been adopted by the U.S. Army and U.S. Marine Corps, as well as by the Canadian Forces, it is sure to become a new standard against which future generations of small caliber weapons will be compared. ●

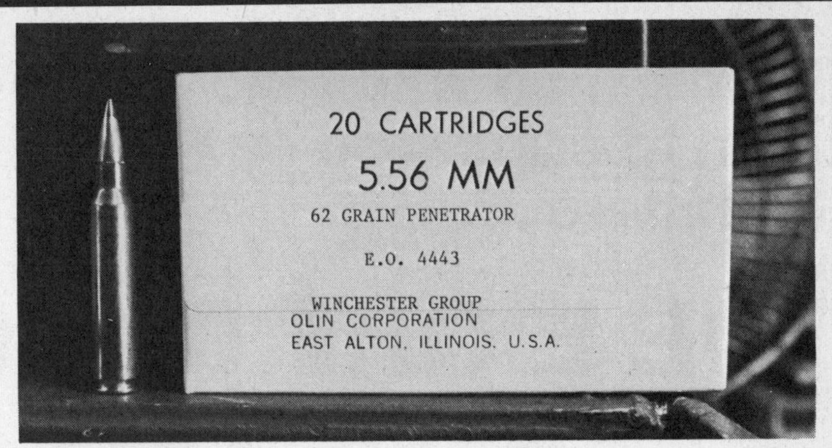

NATO 5.56mm ammunition is made in the U.S. by Olin Corp. and by Lake City Ammunition Plant. FN production is the standard by which others are compared. Ballistics are approximately 3100 fps for a 62-gr. steel core bullet from the M16A2, capable of perforating a 3.5mm steel plate at 700 yards, and capable of defeating soft body armor to 1000 yards. Accuracy of this ammunition from the M16A2 is approximately 2 minutes of angle at ranges less than 300, and about 3 minutes to 1000 yards.

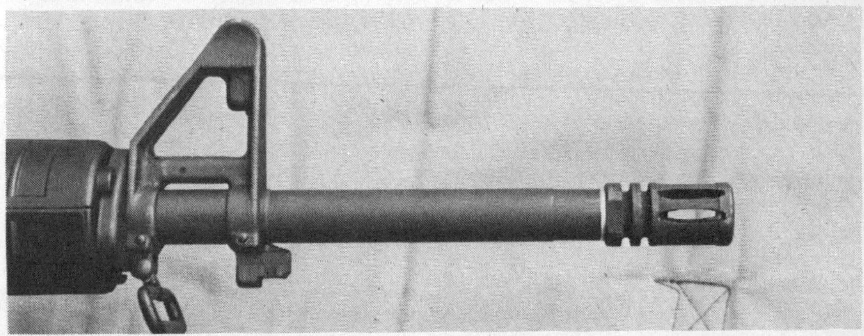

All the old infantry hardware is present—sling swivel and bayonet lug—on the M16A2 but the barrel is noticeably heavier than the M16A1 and the new muzzle brake is a boon.

From a man who teaches them to cops, you can learn here . . . .

THE EIGHT DANGEROUS MYTHS OF SELF-DEFENSE

by MASSAD AYOOB

WHEN PEOPLE feel a compelling need to know something and those in position to give the information don't want to share it, people turn to back alley myths and bad things will typically result. Until 1981, only cops were teaching judicious use of deadly force, and if you weren't a policeman yourself, you'd be told, "Sorry, but that's privileged information. Just use common sense and don't shoot anybody and you'll be all right."

In that informational vacuum, inevitably, half-truths and outright myths flourished. Let's look at some of those old saws, and get them out of your system before they get you into trouble.

Myth #1: "You can shoot any trespasser you find in your home." This weird distortion of the English common law doctrine that "a man's home is his castle" has been unwittingly reinforced by some of the well-intentioned pro-gunners who've pushed through bills like the "castle law" in Massachusetts. Intended to ratify the civilian's right to use deadly force to protect himself and his family from danger without having to retreat in his home, these laws have often been misread and construed as a license to kill any outsider found within the walls. In fact, every such law I've ever seen states clearly that the homeowner may shoot *only if he reasonably perceives danger* at the hands of an intruder he has confronted.

In Pennsylvania, one of the first subsequent householders to shoot an intruder had misread that state's then-new "castle law." He shot a fleeing teenage burglar in the back and he went to prison for it.

I've had two situations where I've drawn guns on people who had illegally entered my domicile and was very glad I did not fire. In the September, 1981 incident, the two intruders I placed at gunpoint (and "dog-point") turned out to be two bozos from the gas company who thought the basement door had been left open for them. In February, '85, I was asleep in a midwestern motel room when the sound of a key slipping into my door lock snapped me awake. I looked over, saw the door shoved suddenly open and reacted. I rolled out of bed, scooped up the Colt autoloader from the floor, and covered the two people in the doorway with the command, "Don't move!"

They turned out to be a nice young couple from Missouri who had been given a key to the room by a dimwitted clerk who thought I'd checked out. Technically, they were illegal intruders into my domicile, but had I shot them on those grounds alone, I would now be singing jailhouse blues instead of writing this article.

Myth #2: "If you shoot an intruder who turned out not to have a weapon, stick a kitchen knife in his hands and be sure to drag the body inside the house before you call the police." This has to be the most common of the armed defense myths, and may well be the most dangerous.

Why did you shoot him? Because he placed you in what a reasonable and prudent man would consider to be immediate and otherwise unavoidable danger of death or grave bodily harm. Your altering of the evidence will be seen by judge and jury as proof that you're lying about the circumstances of the situation, and what was originally a justifiable homicide has now become a charge of murder that will probably stick.

And, you *will* be found out. Do you know the fingerprint pattern consistent with a man who had picked up a knife before being shot, as opposed to a fingerprint pattern consistent with a man having a knife put in his hand *after* being shot? The detectives know. They'll also find out if you moved the body through microscopic fiber evidence, and traces of blood you thought you'd wiped up, and now, having lied to police, you are the little boy that cried wolf. The jury will no longer believe you when you say you had to shoot. You can discuss the injustice of it all with the other inmates in the prison exercise yard.

Myth #3: "If you shoot a bad guy, make sure he's dead, or the resultant lawsuits will ruin you." It's true that in California, for instance, a man you've wounded can sue you for punitive damages in addition to real damages, while the estate of a dead man cannot. Consider, however, that in three out of four shootings by trained police, the wounded suspect survives. Consider, too, that once the man you've wounded has given up the fight, you're guilty of murder if you finish him off with a *coup de grace*. The investigators will be able to determine if this was the case by bullet track angles and other evidence.

In short, if you try to follow that advice, you'll probably end up in prison. And, frankly, if you can look down at a wounded man who has thrown his gun away and is begging for his life and say, "Sorry, but I'm going to shoot you in the head to silence you and keep you from suing me," you *belong* in a cage.

Myth #4: "After you've shot down the mugger, look both ways for witnesses and if you don't see any, leave. That way, you save all the legal hassle." Folks, the prisons are full of people who looked both ways for witnesses and didn't see them until they appeared in court to testify against them.

Never forget that in the mind of judge and jury, *flight equals guilt!* In the Magliato case in New York, the defendant was a businessman who shot and killed a vicious junkie who attacked him on the street with a club. The shooting itself was justified; I testified on the stand that I would have shot him down myself; but when the junkie fell, Magliato panicked and fled, and hid out for a few days before he came to his senses and turned himself in. Even one of the best trial lawyers in New York couldn't overcome the jury's innate belief that only a guilty man flees the scene of his actions. They found him guilty of murder.

The irony is that virtually everyone involved with the case agrees that if Magliato had simply stayed at the scene, handed his Detective Special and his carry permit to the first responding officer, and said, "He said he was going to kill me, and he was coming toward me with a deadly weapon, and I shot him," the grand jury would almost certainly have returned a "no true bill," in effect finding him innocent by reason of justifiability.

Myth #5: "Guns are useless for a woman in rape defense, since most rapists don't have deadly weapons and it's illegal to shoot an unarmed man." It's amazing how often I hear this from feminists; ironically, fear of

In the state of Washington, Ayoob taught law officers advanced tactical know-how on the range and advanced legal awareness in the classroom. Photo by Rich Mootham, Kelso, WA police dept.

Massad Ayoob is director of the Lethal Force Institute, P.O. Box 122, Concord, NH 03301, and offers 40-hour courses for civilians at locations around the country that are designed to take the student to police level and beyond in terms of tactics and legality of defensive deadly force. There is a rigid screening process for prospective students.

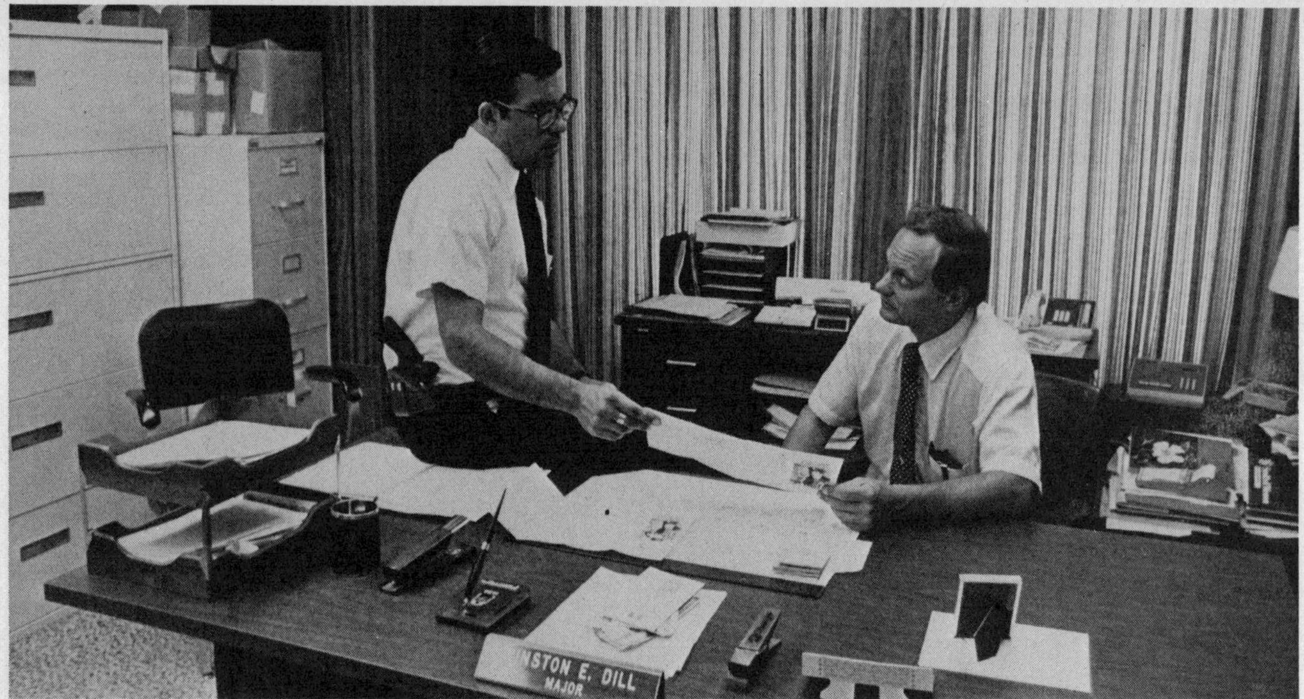

Ayoob developed his own awareness of the special new problems of self-defense in courtrooms, on the street, and in the confidence of police executives like Major Winston Dill of the Athens, GA, police department. (Photo courtesy *Police Product News* magazine.)

guns seems to be the last bastion of "Suzy Housewife Mentality" in the feminist movement.

In fact, the three criteria that determine a deadly jeopardy situation that warrants lethal defensive force are *ability, opportunity,* and *jeopardy*. *Ability* is the power to kill or cripple; *opportunity* means that the attacker(s) are close enough to use their ability to kill or cripple; and *jeopardy* means they are acting in such a manner that a reasonable and prudent person would assume they were *going* to kill or cripple an innocent individual.

Women more than men can take advantage of a legal concept called "disparity of force." That is, one or more unarmed men far stronger than you in size and strength, or in numbers, are recognized to be so much more capable of killing or maiming you that their greater or combined strength is a "weapon" equal to a gun or knife, a weapon that justifies your own resort to a loaded gun in self-defense.

Ironically, many "macho" men still believe in the philosophy voiced by one of the first jurors in the Inez Garcia trial who, after voting to find her guilty in the shooting death of her rapist, said, "You can't kill someone for trying to give you a good time." Largely as a result of that statement, the guilty verdict was overturned, and Garcia was properly found not guilty in her second trial.

The justification for using deadly force in self-defense is, "Immediate and otherwise unavoidable danger of death or grave bodily harm." Why did any rape victim in history ever submit to her assailant? Because he made it clear that she was "in immediate and otherwise unavoidable danger of death or grave bodily harm." As one who has taught both self-defense and rape prevention, I find that these concepts mesh rather neatly.

Myth #6: "I don't think I could really shoot anybody; I just have this gun to scare burglars away." There is enough truth in this dangerous myth to make it believable to those who do not fully understand the dynamics of violence.

A California study found that in 13 out of 14 incidents where citizens drew guns against criminal suspects, they did not have to shoot their antagonists. A Florida criminologist has done studies that place that figure higher: he found that only once in 34 encounters was the civilian likely to have to blow his attacker away.

Does this mean that you can use the gun merely as a scare tactic? NO! An adult lifetime spent in study of the dynamics of violent encounters has convinced me that *criminals do not fear the gun, they fear the resolute man or woman holding it on them!* A gun they don't believe will be fired at them is not something they fear, but a man or woman prepared to shoot them to death if they transgress one step further is an occupational hazard that makes criminals shiver.

Thus, ironically, the gun's great power is its deterrent capability as opposed to its ability to kill, but that deterrent power only works in the hands of someone who can project the fact that they *are* prepared to kill, if they must, in self-defense.

Myth #7: "The key to armed self-defense is having the right gun. If you've got a largebore revolver/15-shot 9mm/45 automatic (pick one) you'll be almost unbeatable in a gunfight." It's amazing how many gun writers believe that a certain sidearm will be a "magic sword Excalibur" and how many of their readers desperately want to believe it, and insure their invulnerability with the purchase of the "right" gun.

Certainly, the defensive handgun of choice is the most powerful one you can control in rapid "stress shooting." Still, the ability to hit center is far more important than the ability to hit anyplace *hard.* I am helping defend a woman in court who shot her attacker three times with a 22 revolver; he staggered out of her house and collapsed and died within 20 feet. Some 18 months ago, I was retained to defend a police officer who had to shoot a suspect eight times with his Colt 45 auto before the felon stopped trying to kill a second officer with his Llama 32. Many of the 45 hits were peripheral; only when the sergeant steadied down and shot the felon through the heart did he solve the problem.

In my extensive studies of street gunfights, I've found that the best of the 38 Special +P loads—the all-lead 158-grain semi-wadcutter hollow point known colloquially as the "FBI load"—is roughly the equal in stopping power to 230-grain round nose, jacketed hardball 45 auto ammunition. Of course, the Federal and Super Vel hollow points I carry in my own 45 are proportionally more authoritative, but I'll tell you frankly, the reason I carry a 45 auto is less stopping power than the tactical advantages of the gun (very high hit potential under stress, great likelihood of bullets staying in the offender's body with hollow point loads, and low muzzle flash at night), coupled with the fact that since I was 12 years old I've simply shot the 45 auto better under pressure than any comparable sidearm.

Do not be misled by "stopping power statistics" formulated on slide rules and ballistic gelatin. In recent months, two reputable gun writers touted the new 32 Magnum as an effective manstopper, and a third wrote that the 10mm (40-caliber) Bren Ten round was the *ultimate* manstopper. This was amusing to those of us aware of the fact that no human being had yet been shot with either round.

It comes back to skill. I recall talking with a seasoned black cop in a major city who had used a single 158-grain round nose 38 slug to kill an offender armed with a 45 automatic. When I asked if he felt outgunned, he said (really), "My man, shootin' straight with my thirty-eight beats him givin' me jive with his forty-five."

Myth #8: "Don't draw a gun unless you're going to pull the trigger." No, little grasshopper, the rule is don't pull the gun unless you're *prepared* to pull the trigger. There is a marked difference.

I've never had to shoot a man, but I've pulled guns on well in excess of twenty violators and made it clear to them (sometimes verbally, sometimes non-verbally) that I would shoot them dead if they did not halt their transgressions. Lawyers tell me that I could have killed maybe four of them right there, without it going any farther. However, you already know about the two gas men and nice couple from Missouri who did something stupid but with no criminal intent, and would have died if I'd been a believer in Myth #8.

To say that you won't draw until it's time to kill is to say that you want an excuse to take a life and aren't willing to draw against danger and pre-empt the other man's potentially lethal movement. In *Florida v. Officer Luis Alvarez*, a manslaughter trial stemming from a video arcade incident where an officer killed an armed suspect and triggered a major riot, the prosecution said that the cop was wrong for shooting the deceased when the latter moved toward the gun the cop knew he had, and that the officer should have waited to *see* the gun. I testified that if the officer had waited to see the gun, he would have seen what came out of it, and showed the jury how quickly the suspect could have killed the officer and his partner if the cop had not fired when he did. The jury apparently agreed, since they found Officer Alvarez not guilty.

After the trial, I reflected on situations I'd been involved in, and what might have happened if I'd waited to draw the gun until the point where I was *going* to shoot instead of merely prepared to. I would have had to kill the man who was reaching under his arm where he carried his 380 when I outdrew him with my 45 and froze him in mid-reach. I would have had to kill the man who pulled a knife on me on a city street, instead of drawing my 38 when his knife came out and wordlessly convincing him to put his knife away and stop trying to mug tourists from New England.

Like many of the dangerous myths, #8 was formulated by people who had fantasized about killing but had never been in a position to learn the real-life dynamics of "threat management." See Myth #6.

Forget the myths, and seek out the truth. The bottom line is: if you have a gun for self-defense and don't know how or when to use it, what you thought was your salvation may very well get you into more trouble than it gets you out of. ●

LEARNING WHEN TO USE DEADLY FORCE

Most of those reading this article won't have $400 tuition and 40 hours to take one of the Lethal Force Institute courses offered around the country. To get a better understanding of when you can and can't resort to the gun, follow this study guide:

LOCAL LIBRARY: In the reference section you want to see the RSA (Revised Statutes Annotated) and the Penal Code or Criminal Code of your state. Study anything listed under "Firearms," "Weapons," "Assault," "Homicide," "Justifiable Homicide," and "Use of Force."

LEGAL LIBRARY: You'll find a legal library open to the public in the courthouse of any city that's a County Seat. Study anything under the above-listed headings in the CJS, the Corpus Juris Secundum (translated from Latin, "the Body of the Law"). Follow the references you'll find and, with the librarian's help, look up citations for case law (cases where the court has ruled and created a precedent) in situations involving the above subjects. Begin with case law in your own state, and then look up that of others; in higher courts, case law doctrine from any state may be used as precedent.

ATTORNEY CONSULTATION: After making notes and formulating your questions, seek out one of the most reputable *criminal trial attorneys with experience in deadly force cases* in your state. An hour's consultation will cost you $50 to $300, and will be worth it. Be asking about "the mood of the courts" in your jurisdiction. Ask *his* advice on when you can use lethal force in self-defense, and if at all possible, get a signed, written memo from him on this and place it somewhere safe. Something you've done "on advice of legal counsel" is extremely defensible in court, one reason so few lawyers will commit themselves specifically on the subject.

Remember to consult a specialist attorney with deep experience in trying deadly force cases; the subtleties of lethal force law are seldom addressed in law school, and the average attorney knows little more about it than you do, and may have fallen victim to some of the Myths himself.

—Massad Ayoob

The unbelievably efficient Baker BB 84 12-gauge muzzle on the left is huge, yet normally gives more velocity and tighter patterns with the same shells than a standard 12.

BAKER BORES 'EM BIG

by DON ZUTZ

Bored out to take 10-gauge chokes, 12 bores shoot tighter than ever.

ON MY bookshelf is a thin tome entitled *Shooting on The Wing,* which was written by someone who styled himself An Old Gamekeeper. Published in 1884, it isn't only a treatise on wingshooting theory, but discusses the mechanical and performance aspects of shotguns as well. At one point in this early Yankee sporting book, the author recorded that, ". . . to increase the closeness with which the gun throws its shot, it is usual for gunsmiths to enlarge the diameter of the barrels (bore) for about one third of their length next to the muzzles. This is technically called *freeing, . . .*"

Thus far, that 1884 reference to improved patterns via enlarged bore diameters is the earliest I've uncovered in stateside literature. When the British used the same concept of bore expansion with muzzleloaders, they employed a tapered enlargement that opened as it neared the muzzle, and they termed it "tight behind" or "relieved." Famous British game shots and gunmakers like Colonel Peter Hawker and Joe Manton experimented with and studied seriously the relationship of bore size and shape relative to patterns, and they endorsed the practice of relieving bore diameters. On breechloaders, however, the British modified their geometry and made the taper a parallel expansion.

Since those days, the technique of enlarging shotgun bores beyond established industry standards has popped up periodically, although it has never — until now — attracted much public attention. Waterfowlers and trap shooters have generally continued to equate snug patterns with long, lean, tightly-choked barrels; the idea that relaxing bore diameters could actually enhance downrange shotshell performance didn't appeal to those who measure scattergun muzzles with dimes and who own guns that "shoot like rifles."

Contrary to popular mythology, however, it has been proved repeatedly that increasing the bore diameter of any given shotgun gauge begets meaningful pattern improvement and, for any given load, recoil reduction. On the other hand, scrunching down the bore diameter and choke constriction increases recoil sensation and leads to an "overchoke" condition that ruins both density and distribution. Thus, tightening chokes and bores can be counterproductive, whereas work with relieved dimensions has shown improvement. *("Improvement," in this discussion, means a gun will shoot tighter patterns. Both the writer and the editor know a tighter pattern is not necessarily an improvement, except when that's what you want. K.W.)*

In the 20th century, shotguns with enlarged bores became known as "overbored." Do *not* confuse that with over*choked*. Over*choke* means that the choke constriction is made *narrower;* over*bore* means that the lengthy cylindrical bore is made *wider* than established by industry standards.

Shotgun bores have always been made—more or less—according to a systematic "gauge" system predicated upon the number of lead spheres of a given diameter it takes to weigh 16 ounces. For example, it takes ten 0.775-inch lead balls to make a pound; consequently, a 0.775-inch-diameter bore is a 10-gauge. For a 12-gauge, the diameter is 0.729-inch. And so on, to provide reasonable uniformity in a developing and then a mature industry on several continents.

The system is in a little trouble. Shotshells have become progressively more powerful, and the original bore diameters are no longer suited to the high-velocity, magnum-charged concentrations of 2s, BBs, and buckshot hunters now insist on launching. Those original bore diameters until recently handled considerably lighter loads than we have today. The 10-bore, for instance, reached pre-World War I maximum with 5 drams of black powder under just 1¼ ounces of shot. The 20's best black powder load has 2¾ drams of powder and the ⅞-ounce shot charge. The 16 gauge seldom topped 1 ounce, and the 12 gauge used a lot of 1⅛-ounce loads. At those levels, the basic bores worked reasonably well. Indeed, the standard 12 gauge will still pattern 1-ounce target loads beautifully, generally outshooting short magnums with coarse shot by 10-20 percent through the same full-choke barrel.

But today, our "more is better" syndrome finds us cramming significantly heavier loads through those same bore diameters, and being kicked excessively while getting indifferent to poor patterns in the process. We now expect the 10-gauge bore to handle 2-2¼ ounces of shot. The 12 gauge is being stuffed with 1⅞- and 2-ounce charges. And we expect the narrow 20-gauge bore to handle 1¼ ounces of shot, which is the equivalent of the former 10 gauge!

Despite the excellence of our modern slow-burning propellants which permit the use of these obese payloads, our penchant for heavier and heavier loads has turned out to be counterproductive. Experimental shooting has proved that there's just so much stuff we can shove through a given bore without encountering excess recoil, deteriorating patterns, and poor pressure/velocity ratios.

That's why the overbored shotgun made its first serious *blip* in American gunmaking during the 1920s and 1930s when high-velocity hunting loads and the 3-inch 12 came along. Sophisticated shotgun technicians quickly learned that these new cartridges performed better in overbored barrels at about 0.740-inch, meaning about a 0.010- to 0.012-inch enlargement. The A. H. Fox Gun Co. of Philadelphia put this overboring to work in some long-range guns like the Super Fox or HE, although to what extent all the Super Foxes were overbored I don't know. A leader in this practice was Burt Becker, an A. H. Fox employee, who eventually became famous as the gunmaker who built the

The cavernous muzzle of a Baker "Big Bore 84" is roughly the size of a 10-gauge muzzle and is easy to spot.

Compared to the standard Winchoke tube on the left, the choke tubes for Stan Baker's BB 84 are gigantic. They are, in effect, 10-gauge choke tubes applied to the enormous 0.800-inch bore.

tight-shooting 3-inch 12s used by Nash Buckingham, the popular outdoor writer. In the 1930s Remington also offered an overbored barrel for the humpbacked Model 11 autoloader and the Model 31 pump, then the hottest selling waterfowl guns.

A casual hunter or shooter might cock a skeptical left eyebrow at opening out a shotgun bore; those who took more than a passing interest in the shotgun and who bothered to test the concept felt that the overbored barrel was a definite improvement. Its strengths then, as now, were deemed to be threefold: (1) the larger-than-standard bore permitted easier, smoother payload passage to reduce pellet deformation; hence, patterns were enhanced by the presence of a higher percentage of shot still round after exit; (2) recoil was lowered because quicker and easier payload slippage tempered the recoil-causing pressure peak otherwise needed to ram the shot/wad tandem into and through the normally abrupt forcing cone and tighter bore of a conventionally-dimensioned barrel; and (3) the wider bore produced a somewhat shorter shot string.

From the inception of the 3-inch 12 to the summer of 1983, a 0.010-inch overbore was deemed maximum in gunning and gunmaking circles. Rule-of-thumb theorists argued that opening shotgun bores beyond that would reduce velocities, and even advanced scattergun folks doubted the advisability of enlarging the bore of a 12 gauge by 0.015-inch. Along with ballistics considerations, of course, there's always the matter of safety: machining a conventional barrel with an overbore greater than 0.010-inch might leave the walls so thin that the pressures from slow-burning powders could potentially cause a burst ahead of the beefy chamber area.

But, as in any other sport or business, there is always a radical element. In this case, some early experimenters produced what became known in the 1920s as the chamber*less* shotgun barrel, in which the bore was basically an extension of the wide chamber diameter. There was no forcing cone. In the 12 gauge, the bore was a gigantic tube roughly 0.800-inch in diameter. Apparently the originators of this experiment thought that if some bore relief were effective, virtually total relief would be tremendous. However, the project gained no popular acceptance whatsoever. Most sportsmen scoffed at it, and, at the time, they were probably right in doing so; for the chamberless bore was undoubtedly victimized by the poor gas-sealing qualities of the contemporary card/filler wad stacks.

The chamberless shotgun was simply ahead of its time. For now it's back with us, known as the "Baker Bore 84" and performing in a most unbelievable fashion. Not only are patterns superbly tight with heavy magnum charges of coarse pellets or buckshot, but velocities are actually *higher* than those for the same loads in conventional bores of the same gauge.

This newest venture into radically overbore shotgun barrels was made by Stan Baker, the respected barrelsmith who plies his craft at 5303 Roosevelt Way N.E., Seattle, WA 98105.

BASICS

Gauge	Standard Bore Dia. (Ins.)
4	1.052
6	0.919
8	0.835
10	0.775
12	0.729
14	0.693
16	0.662
20	0.615
24	0.579
28	0.550
32	0.526

For years, Baker had contentedly overbored trap, Skeet, live pigeon, and magnum-grade hunting guns for advanced shooters, always sticking relatively close to the conservatve figures of 0.005- to 0.010-inch with just occasional forays into wider bores of 0.015- to 0.020-inch.

Baker changed the nomenclature of barrel work by dropping the word "overbore" in favor of the term "backboring" to describe an enlarged shotgun bore. His reason: "The term 'overboring' seems to indicate that something has been overdone."

To eliminate this negative connotation, then, Baker began stressing backboring as the word to define bore enlargement, and others in his field picked it up. Since this is the term now in vogue, we'll use it for the remainder of this article. In theory and practice, however, it's still the same as the former designation, namely, overboring.

In the early 1980s, Stan Baker began an experiment to learn how far he could go with backboring before performance suffered significantly. He began with a production-grade Model 1200 Winchoke barrel which had a relatively heavy wall and a 0.730-inch bore diameter as it came from the factory. Testing started with a reboring of 0.005-inch, and thereafter velocity tests were scheduled for each additional 0.005-inch increment. At the 0.735-inch diameter, the largest point at which a standard Winchoke tube could be used, Baker reamed and threaded the M1200 barrel to accept his own magnum screw-in choke tubes. During these initial steps, Baker found very little velocity change, and what he did learn was contrary to popular belief that velocities would drop; his velocities increased, however slightly.

Eventually, Baker tired of cutting and testing every 0.005-inch, and he jumped to increments of 0.010-inch. In fact, other business plus the absence of any startling discovery prompted him to lose interest, and he set the project aside for almost a year. When he picked it up again, he had to install his 10-gauge screw-in choke, as the bore was running about 0.780-inch.

The experiment continued until the bore was as wide as the 12-gauge chamber, meaning about 0.800-inch, which is a whopping 0.020- to 0.025-inch larger than a nominal 10-gauge bore. Despite that seemingly excess diameter, however, Baker got a velocity 60 fps, on average, higher than that for the same control ammo in the original 0.730-inch bore! This was substantiated in the well-equipped lab of a major ammo maker (one who wishes to remain nameless).

Wanting further confirmation of the 0.800-inch-diameter bore's surprising performance, Stan Baker supplied this writer with a "Baker Bore 84" barrel, the likes of which, I note, he has been advertising recently as the Baker "Big Bore." This sample was a 30-inch job with a lofted competition rib for the Remington Model 1100 12-gauge trap gun. It was tapped for the Baker 10-gauge screw-in choke tubes.

Unlike the Winchester M1200's heavy barrel, the Model 1100's barrel can't handle a full backboring to 0.800-inch bore diameter; that would leave the walls too thin. Thus, an entirely new tube is fitted to the M1100's breech segment in a manner that the British call "sleeving." The original M1100 barrel is cut three inches ahead of the very back line of the chamber, and the original chamber is then opened so that an extension of the new barrel can be inserted in male/female fashion. These are soldered, and a thin gold ring marks the juncture. All such spacious 0.800-inch-diameter barrels are plainly marked "STAN BAKER BB 84."

My first move was to chronograph the cavernous bore alongside a conventional 12-gauge of the same basic length but with the more common bore diameter of 0.725-0.729-inch. This I found in a Perazzi MX-8 with 29½-inch barrels. My loads were standard trap loads. All chronographing was done at the same time over an Oehler Model 33 teamed with Skyscreens set three feet apart. I employed a baffle to eliminate muzzle blast and was able to establish a 4½-foot instrumental situation. Here is how the final averages read:

Load	MX-8	BB-84
Peters trap (3 - 1⅛)	1,241	1,283
Federal trap (2¾ - 1⅛)	1,156	1,196
ACTIV trap (3 - 1⅛)	1,224	1,266
Peters target (2¾ - 1)	1,172	1,211

How can we explain this seemingly crazy performance? By a combination of two factors: first, the BB-84 gives powder gasses more wad area—from the same wad—on which to push; hence, there's a greater transfer of chemical energy to kinetic energy.

As shot charges have gotten heavier, shotgun experimenters have learned that the original bore diameters are no longer efficient. Enlarging the bores was once termed "overboring" but now is called "backboring."

Secondly, the wider BB-84 offers far less friction to standard wads than do standard bores, and the energy from powder gasses can go into velocity rather than being wasted overcoming wad/bore friction.

Of course, all this is made possible by the efficiency with which modern plastic wads seal gasses. Put pressure on the base of most such wads, and their peripheral flanges will indeed spread to at least 0.800-inch and prevent power-robbing, pattern-spoiling seepage. It is this technological advance—improved gas sealing—which makes the backboring and Baker's BB-84 a success. The chamberless guns of the 1920s would have revolutionized shotgun performance then had such wads been available.

What does this mean in practical terms? It means that a trap shooter can get about 3 dram equivalent velocities from 1⅛ ounces of shot (roughly 1,200 fps) with lighter-recoiling 2¾ dram equivalent loads. To a competitor who fires 200-300 trap loads a day, that means a lot. The difference in recoil between a 2¾ and a 3 drams equivalent load is quite noticeable for just a single 25-target round. If one wishes the speed of 3-dram ammo, one can get the exterior ballistics of a 3-dram trap load with the interior ballistics and recoil of a 2¾-dram load.

The system can improve the velocity of hunting loads, but I did not work enough with them to determine a rule-of-thumb velocity advantage except to say that it's at least the level reachable with trap loads. My tests were run under summery conditions, and ballistics and the flexibility of plastic wads can change under cold conditions. I know of one instance where cold wads became stiff and did not expand sufficiently to seal the big 0.800-inch bore, and the results were weak, squib-type performances as gas seeped past the wad.

We do have something yet to learn about the backbored barrel and its optimum dimensions relative to wad performance and temperatures. My own feeling now is that the backbore job which brings a 12-gauge barrel to 0.740-0.745-inch is useful for cold weather hunting to permit gas sealing, while the larger 0.800-inch bore is ideal for warm-weather trap, Skeet, live pigeon, and hunting guns.

My patterning was done mainly over 40 yards to match my results against industry standards. The control load was 3 dram-equivalent Peters Blue target ammo with 1⅛ ounces of No. 7½ shot. Tubes supplied me had diameters of 0.720-, 0.740-, 0.750-, 0.760, 0.770-, and 0.780-inch.

The tube stamped .720 was a revelation. A conventional 12-gauge full choke has 0.035- to 0.045-inch of constriction, with anything tighter being deemed overchoke and likely to open patterns rather than tighten them. The Baker .720 tube, however, has about 0.080-inch of constriction from the .800-inch bore—double that of a standard full-choked 12. But did it pattern! For a 5-shot string at 40 yards, it averaged 86 percent with extremely tight center densities. The .720 tube put nearly as many pellets into the 15-inch-diameter core circle of the patterning sheet as it did into the annular ring of the 30-inch-diameter patterning circle, which promises greatness for long-yardage trap handicap and live pigeon events. There was nothing "overchoked" about the .720 tube at all.

On a percentage basis, from .740-inch through .770-inch, *all* threw averages well above the 70 percent level needed to call it full choke. However, there were subtle differences in the way they distributed their pellets throughout the 30-inch ring. The more open the tubes became, the fewer pellets that appeared in the 15-inch center. The .740 tube, for example, averaged 78 percent, but it put 40 fewer pellets into the core and 20-25 more into the annular ring than did the .720 tube. The relatively open .770 tube still averaged 78 percent, but stuck still more shot into the annular ring. It was not until the .780 tube that percentages hovered about the 70 percent level, which is still full choke despite just a 0.020-inch constriction! Indeed, it was difficult to make the BB 84 do anything but full choke regardless of the tube. The main variation among the tubes was distribution between center and ring.

I ran some cursory patterns with the BB 84 using the newest 1½-ounce short magnums and the results were tremendous. Remington's Nitro Mags with black 2s and buffering did 84 percent at 40 yards; Winchester's Super Double-X with copper-plated 4s and buffering ran 89 percent. It would be interesting to learn how Federal's new 2-ounce load for the 3-inch 12 performs in such a spacious bore. It might just obsolete the Magnum 10 if gas sealing is accomplished. But patterns of 84-89 percent with coarse shot are exceptional; a standard 12 with conventionally narrow bore might do well to give 75 percent with the same loads, as standard 12-bore dimensions do not have a history of handling coarse shot well.

Backboring, therefore, is a way to improve shotgun performance with the modern, heavy loads the standard bore diameters were never meant to handle. And the industry has already utilized the concept. Remington's Model 870 Competition single shot pumpgun has an overbored barrel around 0.740-inch, and I understand that the relatively new MX-3 Perazzi also has its bore enlarged by about 0.010-inch. The .800-bore concept may not catch on universally, but Stan Baker's radical step should definitely point the way for a change in bore diameters for improved patterning, efficiency, and less recoil. ●

Zutz shot his own patterns with the back-bored barrels. His trap grade Model 1100 was equipped with Baker's BB 84 barrel. There is a release trigger, which explains the trigger finger's position.

UP THE SPOUT

WITH JOHN AND KEN

. . . or how paper wadding could save your day as once it did in Blighty.

by ROGER BARLOW

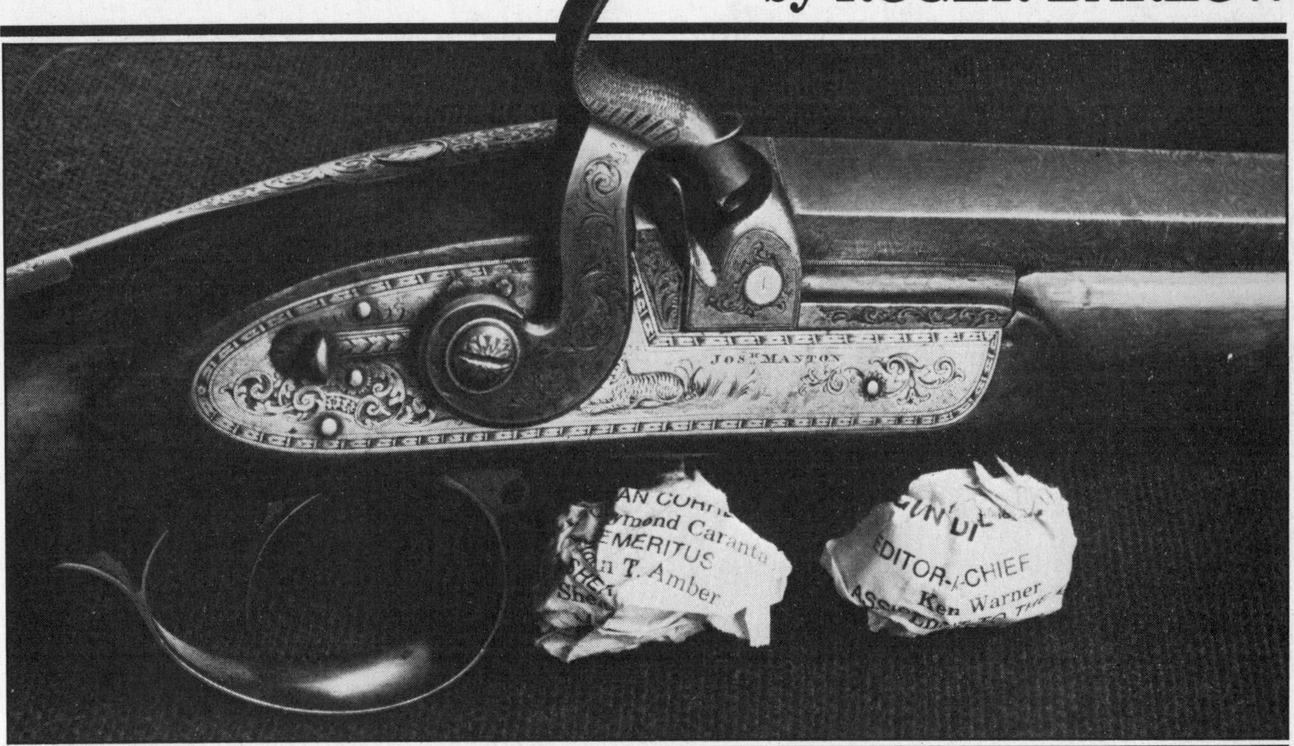

These crumpled paper wads made from the first page of the GUN DIGEST not only carried the names of Editor-in-Chief Ken and Editor Emeritus John, but proved the publication's scope in serving its readers.

WHEN RELOADING after bagging a bird on the first covey rise of the morning, an English partridge shooter afield, alone one day in the 1790s with his brace of setters and Durs Egg muzzleloader, discovered his entire supply of felt wadding, carried in the right hand pocket of his jacket, had been lost through a rent in the fabric. Now, with the day's shooting just under way, was his sport to be terminated so ignominiously . . . with both dogs pointing singles a hundred yards away?

Of course not. The solution to this Englishman's predicament was, as usual, to be found in the pages of *The London Times*. His copy, still unread, had fortuitously been dropped into his game bag as he left his breakfast table. Our Squire, in this instance, was not to benefit from specific editorial guidance or comment, but from the pages *themselves*—crumpled up and rammed down firmly on top of each powder charge.

English sporting literature contains so many versions of this tale that today it might very well be considered apocryphal. However, I was so

Some of the test shooting of the 150-year old Manton with the crumpled paper wads was done by the author's 11-year old stepson; neither gun nor boy were damaged.

Pattern shot with the usual Manton loading of a thick card over the powder, a ⅜-in. Feltan filler wad and a thin over-shot card at 30 yards. That's 1⅛ oz. of #7½ shot.

certain that it not only could have happened but *did* that I recently carried out these photo-documented tests utilizing my 12-bore percussion Joseph Manton shotgun.

To establish normal patterns for this gun and load, some test shots were let off using my normal wad column of a thick over-powder card, a ⅜-inch Feltan cushion wad and a thin over-shot card. With that established, I then set out with my substitute wadding:

First, a crumpled but well compressed rough cylinder (about an inch long) made from a portion of the front page of *The Times*, kindly sent on to me by David Baker, was started down the muzzle and then rammed home directly on top of a normal charge of black powder. I slammed away with repeated blows in hopes of insuring enough radial pressure and friction to get the powder burning properly before the shot charge was half-way up the barrel. This also provides a firm surface for the shot charge. Then, in lieu of either card or felt, a smaller wad of *The Times* was pushed down the barrel and my first test shot with this emergency wad column let off.

Recoil was about normal, so it was not surprising to find the pellets well buried in the hardwood behind my paper target. The pattern certainly looked every bit as effective as those just produced by the normal wad column and had I been that 18th century Englishman shooting at a partridge, I would have had a handsome bird to drop into my game bag beside the rest of *The Times*.

I had rather expected the *Times* wadding to be set alight by the flaming powder charge as it went up the barrel, but not so. Neither were any pellets so deeply embedded or entangled in the upper face of the crumpled-paper wadding that they remained stuck there. Further test shots merely repeated these gratifying results. However, subsequent shooting revealed that such crumpled-paper wadding will not provide enough initial resistance *in a clean and slightly oily* barrel to enable the black powder charge to burn properly and recoil and velocity will be well below normal. Best to dirty the bore before going after game by first firing off a powder charge with or without a shot charge. Also remember that a small wad of crumpled paper, even well rammed, is not very effective in retaining the shot charge if the gun is carried muzzle-down for very long. And, of course, in a double barreled gun, such wadding ought definitely to be rammed again if the second barrel is not fired right after the first one.

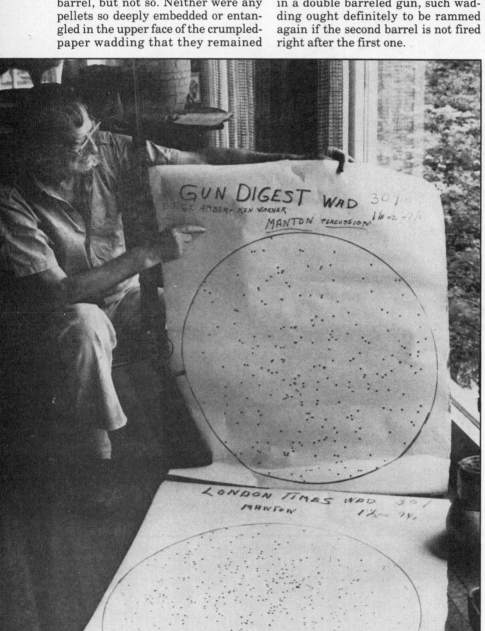

An amused Barlow examines the magical game-getting pattern produced by the Ken Warner wad of balled-up paper. This, of course, was an editorial contribution.

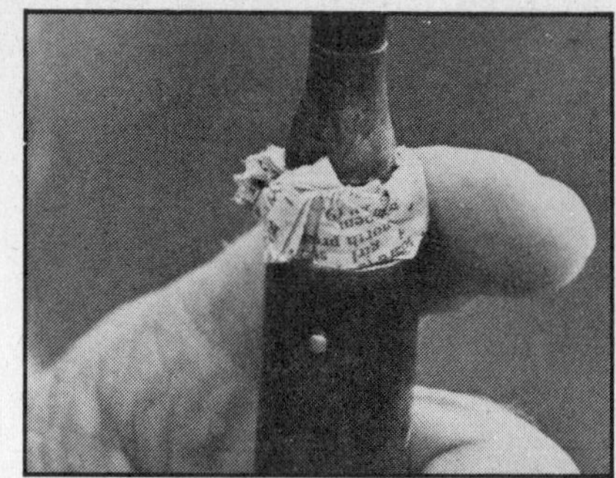

The knack of paper wadding is that it works best in a dirty bore, rammed tight. Over-shot wadding? Just roll another ball and carry on.

It occurred to me that if my report on this 18th century newspaper wadding was to appear not in *The London Times* but in our own GUN DIGEST, the least I could do would be to establish the efficacy of *its* pages in such an emergency! As you can see by the photos of the first of these GUN DIGEST wads, both Editor Ken Warner and Editor Emeritus John Amber participated by, in effect, going up the spout with those wads and both produced excellent patterns! I plan to again have these two amiable gentlemen with me in this form as part of my pocket of wadding next fall when I hope to hunt with the Manton for partridge and pheasant in South Dakota.

Envisioning a situation where I might want to load some special shotshells but find that I am unexpectedly out of 12-gauge filler wads, I ran off a batch of shells using nitro powder (Red Dot), a thick over-powder card, a filler wad made from a page torn from an L.L. Bean catalog, a thin card on top of that, and closed with the usual folded crimp—all with the aid of my versatile Hornady 266 reloader. As expected, these seemed to shoot every bit as well as store-bought ammo on clay targets and the pattern board. No doubt modern one-piece plastic wads will produce the best possible ballistics, which might be needed if you try 40-yard shots at ducks or pheasants, but for most of our shooting at upland game (20 to 30 yards) this 18th century wadding is more than adequate. It is truly satisfactory and amusing.

It has pleased me enormously to prove to my own satisfaction that a scrap of newspaper, a page of the Gun Digest or even the wrapping of a Hershey bar can keep the fire in my muzzleloaders from melting down the shot charge, enabling me, like that Englishman in 1790, to overcome a bad situation and return home with birds in the game bag along with the remains of *The Times* (or Gun Digest) and a story to pass on down the years. ●

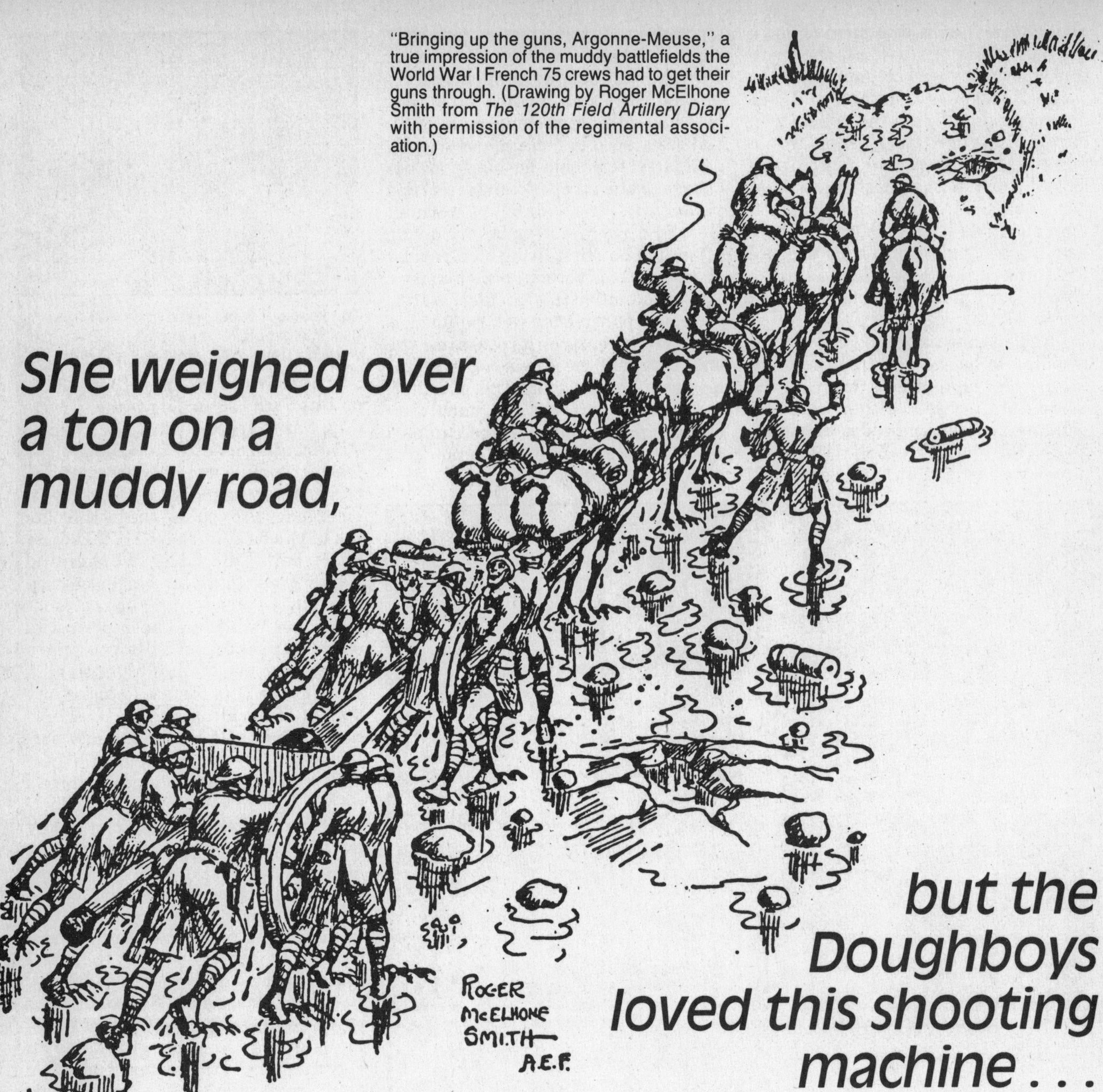

"Bringing up the guns, Argonne-Meuse," a true impression of the muddy battlefields the World War I French 75 crews had to get their guns through. (Drawing by Roger McElhone Smith from *The 120th Field Artillery Diary* with permission of the regimental association.)

She weighed over a ton on a muddy road,

but the Doughboys loved this shooting machine . . .

The Legendary FRENCH 75

by KONRAD F. SCHREIER, JR.

This French 75 fired the first American cannon shot in WW I from this position near Bathlemont in Lorraine, on October 23, 1917. (U.S. Army Signal Corps photo)

AFTER April, 1917, the Doughboys of the American Expeditionary Force in France made some pretty famous lady friends.

The best known was the "Mademoiselle from Armentieres" they loved to sing about. Parlez vous?—remember?

Another named "Mademoiselle Soixante Quinze" was also very popular. She was already a legend when the Doughboys got there for she was the famous "French 75" field gun. Her proper French name was *Canon de 75mm, Modele 1897,* and in the U.S. Army she was the *75mm Field Gun, Model 1897 (French)*.

While the French Army had made its *soixante-quinze* (seventy-five) a redoubtable field piece in the early battles of World War I, the Field Artillerymen of the A.E. F. were able to teach her a whole new bag of tricks. There is no record they managed to teach the mademoiselles of Armentieres anything.

The story of the Doughboys' affair with Ma'mselle Saucy Cans—many Yanks pronounced it that way—began soon after the United States got into the war. The first troops of the A.E.F. arrived in France within weeks, and the U.S. Army began expanding as fast as it could. The two kinds of combat troops Gen. John J. "Black Jack" Pershing needed most were Infantry and Field Artillery,

This Yank French 75 crew is laying the gun, including getting the trail dug in, before their next fire missions in the Argonne-Meuse in 1918. (Drawing by Roger McElhone Smith)

"The Pirate Gun," an impression of a lone French 75 firing in front-line Infantry support in France in 1918. (Drawing by Roger McElhone Smith)

This schematic shows the French 75's hydropneumatic recoil system, the most advanced of its day and the key factor which made the French 75 the best field gun of World War I. (U.S. Army drawing)

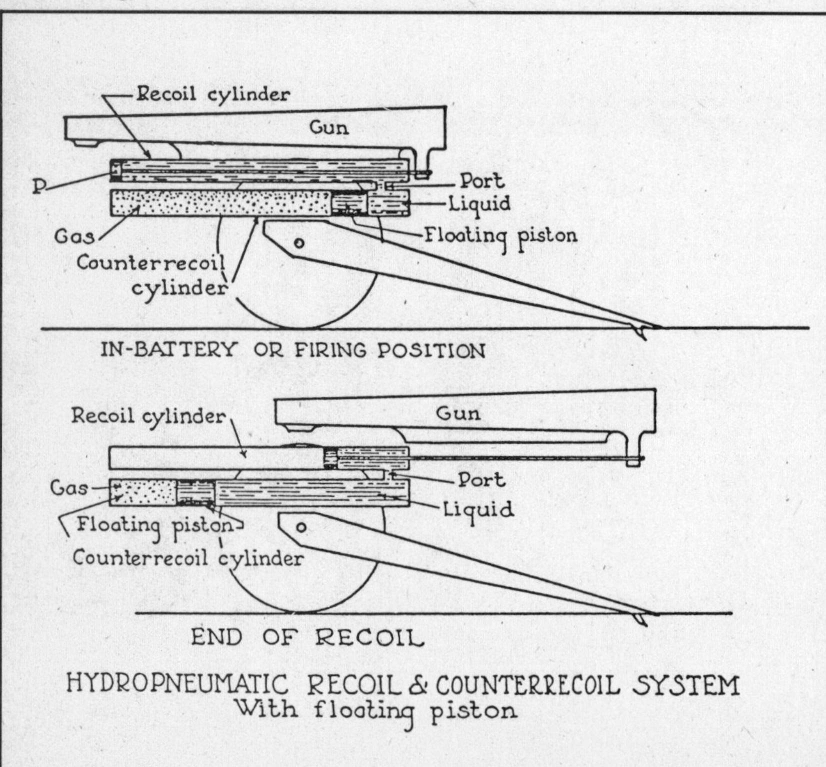

and men and weapons for both these arms were scarce. The U.S. Army did not have enough field gunners or guns to fill the requirement. And there was no chance either could be turned out in America in sufficient numbers soon enough to meet the need.

The French came to the rescue in the matter of guns. They had enough 75s, the capacity to build more, ammunition, and training camps sufficient to equip and instruct the Field Artillery of the A.E.F. It wasn't long before Doughboys were chasing their French 75s "Over hill, over dale, along the muddy trail."

In many respects, the French 75 was a typical World War I field gun: Ready to march, the gun and a limber of ammunition weighed some 4,500 pounds, which was figured to be the load a good six-horse gun team could handle. The cannon and recoil system were mounted on a steel carriage, and rolled on heavy duty wooden wheels. There was a shield on the gun to protect its crew from small-arms fire.

Its 75mm—2.95-inch—bore was very close to the 3-inch bore of most World War I field guns. It fired a "fixed cartridge" similar to a huge centerfire rifle cartridge with projectiles weighing 12 or 13 pounds depending on type. Its normal muzzle velocity was about 1,900 feet per second. Since its projectile was somewhat lighter than most others of its time, this was faster and perhaps a little flatter shooting than most contemporary field guns.

Like all World War I field guns, the 75 had an "on-carriage recoil system" to absorb its kick and avoid the need to re-lay (aim) the gun after every shot. The recoil system was a hydropneumatic type which used controlled oil flow to absorb the recoil and a compressed gas "spring" to push the gun back into battery. This recoil system was the "secret" of the French 75, and a very closely guarded French military secret before, during and even after World War I. It was such an efficient system that similar systems are still used on most cannon to this day. It is also the same system automobile hydraulic shock absorbers use.

In many ways the French 75 was substantially different from the U.S. Army's field gun, so the Field Artillery was sent to school to learn it. These gunners were collected from the regular U.S. Army, the National Guard, and from among volunteers and draftees. Many of the National Guardsmen and some of the regulars were Cavalry "galvanized" into the

Rear view of a French 75 in firing position, showing its unique breech system which revolves around the barrel. (U.S. Army Chief of Ordnance photo)

Field Artillery. Pershing needed artillery, not cavalry. He figured cavalry troops could handle the gun-team horses, and could be taught to use the field guns.

The A.E.F. Field Artillery School set up at a French military post called *Coetquidan*—a name hardly any of them ever learned to pronounce properly. There was classroom instruction in the care and feeding of the French 75, and there was practical marching training on the muddy roads of France, and they shot on even muddier firing ranges.

The Yanks did not adopt the French methods of handling the gun, but used U.S. Army drills they believed were better. The U.S. Army gun drill, a system familiarly called "the cannoneers' hop," had been perfected from the drill used for Civil War muzzleloaders, and was faster and more precise than the French system. It is still the basic gun drill in the U.S. Army.

When the Doughboys finally got Saucy Cans on the firing ranges, they fell in love with her. They had a little trouble getting used to her unique rotary breech mechanism which was unlike any used on any other field gun. The sighting system was different, but they adapted it to the system used on U.S. Army field guns.

It didn't take much firing for the Doughboys to find the French 75 was as accurate as any field gun of its

This is the Doughboy-manned French 75 in action in mid-1918. They are in rapid fire—note the shell being loaded into the breech and the fired case in the air. (U.S. Army Signal Corps photo)

This front view of a U.S. Army French 75 shows the unusual rollers for the recoil system on the gun's muzzle, the trademark of the French 75. (U.S. Army photo)

time. Artillery aiming techniques of the time required as high a degree of mathematical skill as they still do, and the A.E.F. found men to master them. Many had been civilian school teachers or engineers, selected and sent to The Field Artillery School to learn "fire control and direction."

It didn't take the Doughboys long to learn to get better accuracy out of the gun than French Field Artillerymen had come to expect. They could nail any target within the gun's regular 7,000 yard—four mile—range with the first salvo.

At 6:05 a.m. on October 23, 1917, a U.S. Army French 75 fired the A.E.F.'s first cannon shot in World War I—just five months after the U.S.A. had entered the war. The gun was one from U.S. Army Battery C, 6th Field Artillery, commanded by Capt. Idus R. McLendon. The gun was in the Lunneville Sector some 450 yards east of Bathelemont. This specific gun survived the war, and it is now in the museum of the United States Military Academy at West Point.

Once their first shot was fired, Doughboy-manned French 75s kept up a constant barrage for the remaining twelve and a half months of World War I. For that last year of the war, the Allies' artillery fire was something right out of a Hollywood movie special effects sequence. Doughboys who were there said the Allied shelling literally never stopped night or day—something was always popping off. And the French 75 was used to fire in every kind of situation.

There were barrages of thousands of shells to irritate "The Boche," as the Germans were called. Often enough, a mess of poison gas was mixed in with the high explosives. Interdiction fire into the enemy's rear areas botched up his lines of supply. This fire was "by the map," a form of mathematically triangulated indirect

When the Infantry attacked "over the top," the 75s fired a "lifting barrage" of shells landing just in front of their advance. When the enemy attacked, a "lowering barrage" was into their advancing troops. When friendly positions came under attack a "box barrage" could be fired with shells landing on all sides of the friendly troops, and thus among the attackers.

All this firing shot up thousands and thousands of rounds of French 75 ammunition every day. The rate per gun got so high that barrel life became a real concern. Fortunately the French 75s was pretty darn good. It was excellent to about 10,000 rounds, and adequate to as many as 15,000. The barrel life of the excellent 1903 Springfield rifle was excellent to 5,000 rounds, and adequate to about 7,500. So a French 75 barrel lasted twice as long as a darn good rifle's would.

The French began supplying five 75s a day on August 1, 1917, with necessary ammunition and other equipment. When that first A.E.F. battery went into action in late October, the U.S. Army had some 270 guns—enough for 64 gun batteries. A new battery was added every day, seven days a week!!

There were always enough guns for the Yank Field Artillery, and enough A.E.F. artillery for anything except major offensives. Major offensives were always cooperative efforts, and

A battery of four M2 French 75s being prepared for inspection about 1940. (U.S. Army photo)

in them Saucy Cans was called on to support both the French and British.

The A.E.F. had only five complete combat divisions in action by the end of 1917. In early 1918, troops training in the U.S.A. were ready, and American divisions began streaming to France. By mid-summer, 1918, there were 30 American divisions over there, and on August 10, 1918, the U.S. 1st Army was formed to fight the first big A.E.F. offensive—St. Mihiel.

St. Mihiel set a record for barrage artillery preparation which wasn't broken until World War II. On September 12, 1918, a million artillery rounds were fired in a four-hour barrage. It took 3,000 guns, fully half of them French 75s. The 75s fired two-thirds of the total. It was a shoot to be remembered.

The St. Mihiel offensive gave the Doughboys' a chance to test their own ideas of how to use the French 75 in an All-American fight. They began the regular practice of putting the 75s trail in a pit to give it more elevation. This gave it both more range and the "plunging fire" of a howitzer.

Since the A.E.F. had been warned the Germans might use tanks, the job of fighting as anti-tank guns was also given to French 75 outfits. Guns were usually detailed for this front line duty in pairs—"by the section" in Field Artillery parlance.

There was also a Doughboy artilleryman scheme in which one gun—a "half-section"—was sent into the front lines to fight Boche machine-guns. One of the first of these was from National Guard Battery F, 149th Field Artillery, of the legendary 42nd "Rainbow" Division, and its actions are described in *A Bug's Eye View Of The War* by the late playwright Charles MacArthur and published in 1919.

One gun and a crack crew were selected to be an advanced "Pirate Gun." The gun's horses took it as close to the front lines as possible. Then, with the help of the Infantrymen in the area, the 2,660-pound Saucy Cans was manhandled up to right behind the front line trenches, and hidden. The Infantry helped with no complaint.

The Pirate Gun remained silent during the tremendous opening barrage, and through the Boche counter-battery fire, but it was hot for action when the Infantry went over the top. As machine gun nests began opening fire, the gun crews had no trouble spotting them. Firing with the simple open sights on the 75s barrel, they sniped them. Some were only a couple hundred yards away, and one 75 shell was about all it took to scratch one nest. They took out the closest ones first, and kept picking them off out to about a thousand yards.

Then the gun was manhandled further forward, but the Boche were in flight and there were no targets. That night they hauled the gun further forward to take a strong point. At first light, the fortified farm house was quickly reduced to rubble. Nobody kept score, but this single gun reduced enough Boche positions to let its Infantry advance with minimal casualties.

One other thing that made the French 75 a Doughboy legend was how fast the gun could be made to fire. The French rated the gun at 10 rounds per minute regularly, and at 15 in emergency situations. When the Doughboys cranked up, they could, and often did, get off 30 rounds per minute!! That's one shot every two seconds, and to do it the gun has to be reloaded as it returns to battery. It recoiled about 44 inches after each shot.

A battery of four 75s firing at this rate can get off some 120 rounds per minute, almost a machine gun rate of fire. With 13-pound high explosive 75 shells, that's over 1,500 pounds of sudden devastation a minute.

The Doughboy gunners found they could fire up to 300 well-aimed shots

This is a high explosive round for the French 75 of the type the French supplied for the gun and the kind of shell the Doughboy gunners fired most. (U.S. Army Ordnance Dept. drawing)

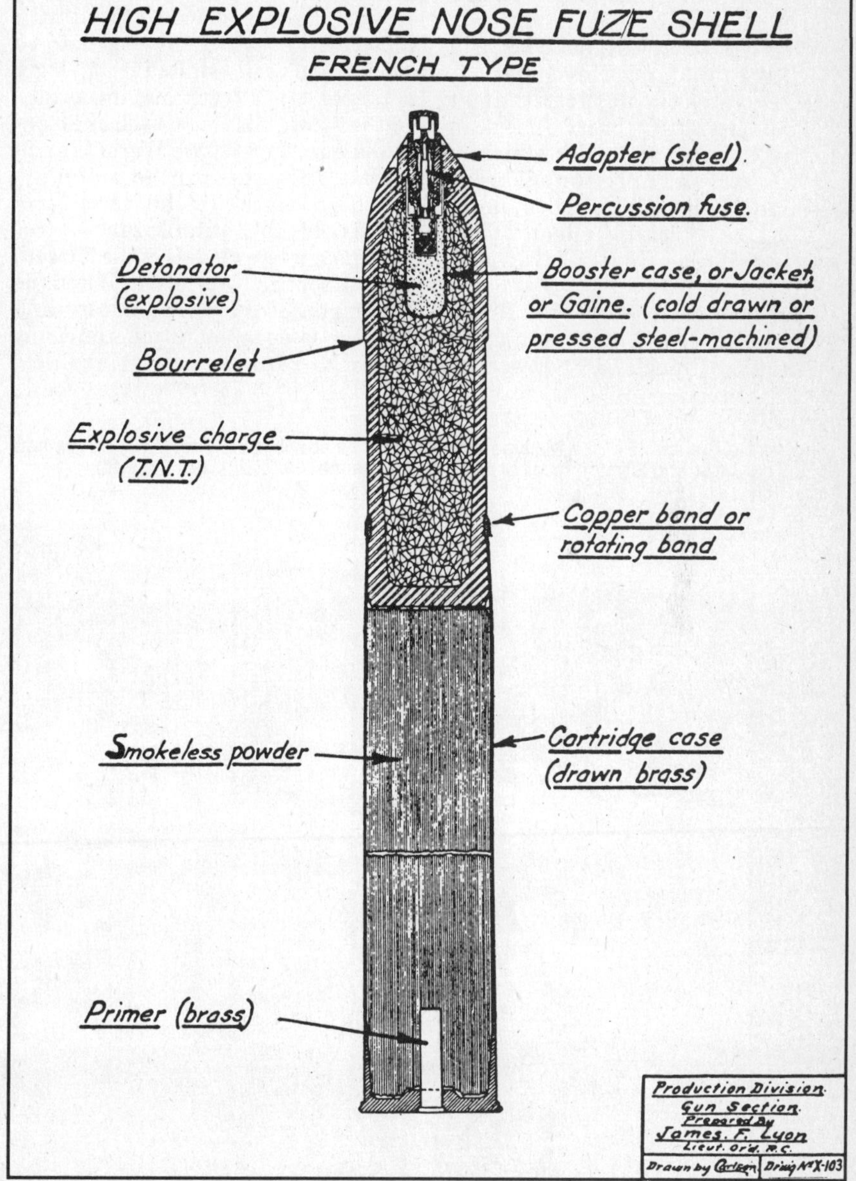

an hour, five per minute, but only at the cost of burning the paint off the barrel, despite cooling it with buckets of water. It didn't seem to hurt the guns, but the recommended rate of fire was still only 150 rounds per hour. At the 300-round rate a four-gun battery could pour out seven tons of shells in an hour.

In all, the A.E.F. fired over six million rounds of Saucy Cans ammunition in combat in World War I—over 80,000,000 pounds of them. Most of this ammunition was supplied by the French, since the American production didn't really get to the front lines in quantity until the war was nearly over, and most was high explosive shells—probably two-thirds of the rounds fired. The rest were mostly gas shells or shrapnel. The shrapnel was fired with a time fuse set so it burst over the enemy and showered them with 270 half-inch lead balls. The HE and gas shells detonated on impact.

When the Armistice ended World War I at 11:00 a.m., November 11, 1918, it was only natural that at 10:59:59, practically every American 75 fired one last shot. For almost a full minute, the only sounds were those last shells falling. Then, nothing but a bit of deathly silence. Then cheering. It was finally "over over there."

From then until World War II, the veterans of the A.E.F. sang the praises of the French 75. They went so far as to invent a devastating brandy-champagne cocktail they christened The French 75, and an equally dangerous French 75 Punch.

By the time the figures were totaled, the U.S. Army had acquired over 3,000 Saucy Cans from the French, along with their equipment. The Doughboys thought the gun was the cat's pajamas, and official U.S. Army reports rated it an excellent field gun, so the 75-mm Field Gun, Model 1897 (French) remained the standard until the early 1930s. Then it was improved by equipping it with pneumatic rubber-tired wheels so it could be truck towed and thus march 30 miles per hour, ten times as fast as the team of horses could move it.

In the mid-1930s, an extensively modified and improved French 75 was adopted—the 75 mm Field Gun M2. This new model featured a split trail carriage which allowed the 75 to fire at high angles of elevation, and with wide traverse which allowed it to be quickly and easily shifted from target to target. Or to track moving tanks, for the 75 was also to be used as an antitank gun. Just before World War II, the M2 75 was mounted on an armored half-track to make it a self-propelled field and antitank gun.

Although late models of the 75 were used all through World War II and the 75mm gun of the Sherman M4 tank fired the same ammunition, the Army began to replace it with its new 105mm Howitzer M2 in 1940. The new 105 was a completely modern field gun firing a shell over twice the weight of the 75s, and by the end of the war the 105 had made the 75 completely obsolete.

But the new 105 howitzer had some French 75 blood. Although it was arranged differently, the 105s recoil system was mechanically identical to the French 75s. Now the 105 is no longer first-line standard in the U.S. Armed Forces, but a number of foreign armies still use it, and rate it an excellent field gun.

The heart and secret of the French 75 was its hydropneumatic recoil system. This ancient system invented way back in the 1890s—nearly a century ago—is still in wide use today. In one form or another, it works in even the most modern field guns. Pretty good for a French lady with a cute name. ●

NOTE ON SOURCES: Much information was drawn from the World War histories of the 120th, 149th and 151st Field Artillery Regiments of the A.E.F. In addition, the official World War I reports of the U.S. Army Ordnance Department and the periodical *The Field Artillery Journal* were consulted. And additional information from the author's files on the 75 as well as the official U.S. Army manuals on the gun. The author began collecting information on the French 75 during World War II, and still does.

A modernized French 75 of the M2 type firing on a range about 1937. The gun is on the new split trail carriage, and is in full recoil of 44 inches. Note the dust. (U.S. Army photo)

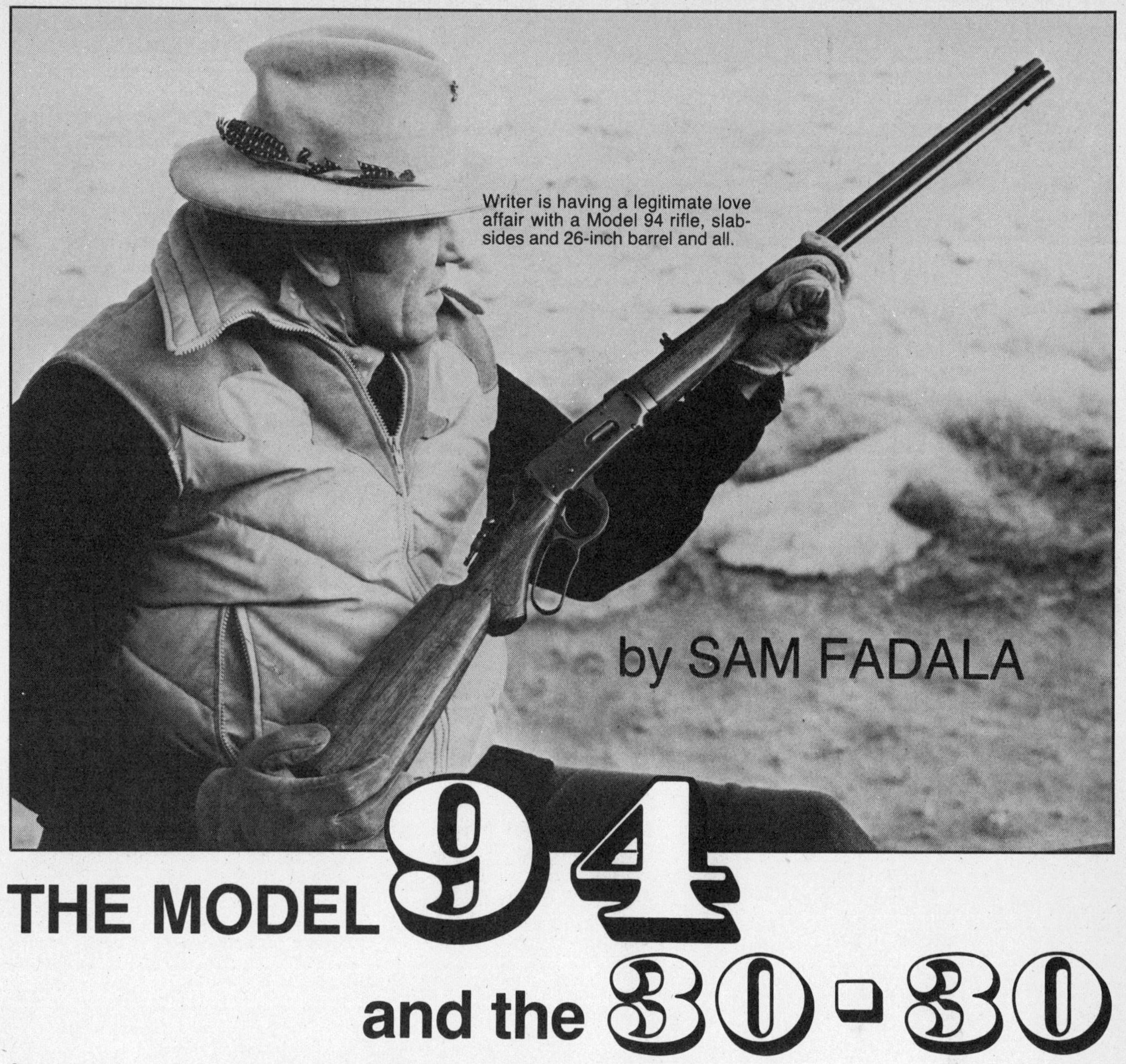

Writer is having a legitimate love affair with a Model 94 rifle, slab-sides and 26-inch barrel and all.

THE MODEL 94 and the 30-30

It was a marriage made in Winchester and it works today as few have since.

I WANTED a very special rifle in a very special caliber to do a lot of work for me. My needs were specific: a trim, easy-to-carry, easy-to-store, rugged and reliable firearm with sufficient accuracy and power for close-range to modest-range shooting of game from varmints and small edibles all the way to deer, and even larger than deer under some circumstances. Bullets would have to penetrate well, break a shoulder blade if called upon to do so, and yet avoid the shrapnel effect. The rifle would have to be at home under many circumstances, including tough late season Western black timber hunting, where snow would be the rule.

I had a beautiful 6.5 DGS Improved built by Dale Storey, a lightweight beauty, and certainly a lot of punch out of a smallish case, but I needed something else. One day I was resting against a red boulder in a tight little draw, catching my breath before heading deeper into deer territory when by my foot I noticed a spent round. The half-tarnished case lay in a small drift of sand which surrounded my resting rock. I rolled it in my fingers, shaking silt from the inside. Anybody who shoots would recognize it, but I brushed the headstamp against my denim pants anyway to be sure it wasn't a 32 Winchester Special fooling me. I smiled and chuckled. "Used to have one," I said softly. "The old 30-30."

I had gotten rid of my 30-30 a very long time ago. "Outgrew it," I used to say. Strangely enough, I traded Slab-Side away while living on the Mexican border in fine whitetailed deer country and now I remembered why I had gotten rid of mine.

It was the end of a deer season which saw me miss several decent bucks. I missed all of them with Slab-Side, jumping some pretty good ones at no more than 30 or 40 paces, but missing all the same. I was pretty young and blamed my artillery for my lack of success, so I got a 270 Winchester with a 4x scope. I worked all summer to buy it and I just knew my luck was going to change the first time I tried her out at long range after sighting in. A man could hit a tomato can at 300 yards with that 270 if he had a good rest.

I was right about the luck. I got a fine buck that made the bottom of the Boone & Crockett book the very first season I carried the 270. I jumped that buck in a grassy draw, maybe as far as 30 paces off. I had a terrible time finding him in the scope. The first hit did not drop the deer. I had to fire four times, I think, before he stayed down.

After finding the 30-30 case, I went home and pondered my situation again. I still needed a sidekick rifle. I decided to call a gunwriter friend of mine and chew the fine points of the dilemma with him. He cut me short. "There's not a thing I can say about the 30-30 that would be good," said he.

That was that. Maybe I had forgotten how bad the 30-30 is, I said, for the same opinion seemed to be found in quite a bit of the literature I came across. Modern writing seemed to disfavor the round. Oldtime literature was just the opposite. One modern writer claimed the 30-30 was no good on deer beyond 50 yards.

I suppose a streak of obstinacy took over. I had to take a good look at the 30-30 all over again, as well as the Model 94 slab-side. After reading that the 30-30 wounded more deer than any other cartridge in Christiandom, the verdict of one modern writer, I concluded that I had to see just how true, ballistically speaking, this could be. On the other side of the fence, there were some pretty smart writers saying that the 30-30, especially with the softer bullets that expanded well, took deer cleaner than a mountain breeze with any well-placed hit. One of the better-written manuscripts on the old round was found in GUN DIGEST, the 34th 1980 edition. The author, H. V. Stent, said, on page 13, "In a whitetail deer survey taken by the *American Rifleman* in 1947, the 32 Special scored slightly better than the 30-06/220-gr. when it came to dropping a deer in its tracks with a hit in the heart area. The 30-30 170-gr. scored about 15% less. What were the only two calibers which scored 100% when all the others made only about 50%? The 300 Magnum and—wait for it—the 30-30 150-gr.!"

Warren Page had made a similar report with the same results. Now, to be sure, I'm not suggesting that the 30-30 is better on deer or anything else over a 30-06, but defunct is defunct, gentlemen, and the 30-30 has plenty of punch to take a deer out with one shot at modest range with a correct hit, every time, not just now and again. I already knew that. I don't know why I was having to re-learn what I had known years ago. But relearning I was.

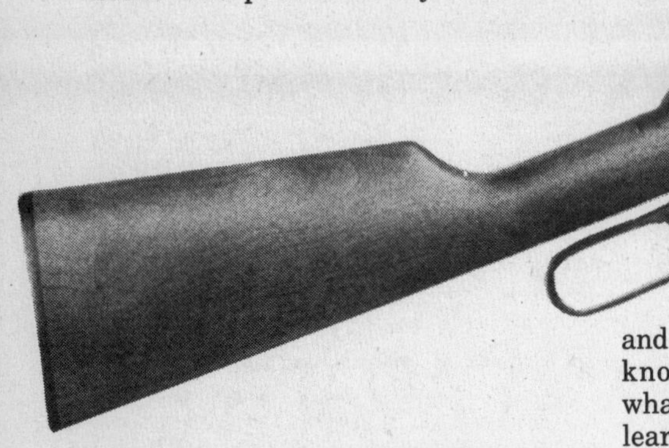

This is the editor's USRAC 94 Trapper, a good gun in every sense Fadala writes of. Receiver sights are a concession to myopia.

Some say that the 30-30 was designed as a black powder round. If so, it was a mighty poor choice and a step backwards, because there were plenty of black powder cartridges which were better *with black powder*. I just don't believe it. I think Winchester had a smokeless round up its sleeve from the start. At any rate, Catalogue No. 53, in 1894, touted the Model 94 rifle (not carbine). It was chambered for the 32-40 Winchester round and the 38-55 Winchester. But in August of 1895, a nickel steel barrel was announced and so were two new cartridges, both using smokeless powder. One was the 25-35 and the other was our 30-30.

Some say a 170-grain bullet was offered early on, but most writers agree that the bullet probably weighed 160 or 165 grains, and that it took off at around 1970 fps from the muzzle. The actual ballistics are academic at this point. The 30-30 caught on. So did the rifle and later the carbine. Caught on? I should say so. By 1927, President Calvin Coolidge was presented with a Model 94 Winchester, serial number 1,000,000! President Truman got one, too, back in 1948. His was number 1,500,000. The old 30-30 was gaining in popularity during the working lives of many "superior" rounds. Still, the 30-30 was the first *sporting* cartridge to use smokeless powder.

From the start, American hunters, as well as hunters in Mexico and Canada, had a love affair with the Model 94 and the 30-30 chambering. In *Outdoor Pastimes of an American Hunter*, by Theodore Roosevelt, the Scribner's 1923 text, President Teddy summed it up nicely. The President was antelope hunting in 1896. "I was using for the first time one of the new small-calibre, smokeless-powder rifles, with the usual soft-nose bullet," Roosevelt said on page 196.

Roosevelt used to like to pace things off, or have other people do it for him, so we get some solid guesstimations as to how far away he downed some of his game. In this case, the 1896 antelope hunt, he said "The band had just reached the ridge crest about 220 yards from me across the head of the valley, and had halted for a moment to look around. They were starting as I raised my rifle, but the trajectory is very flat with these small-bore smokeless-powder weapons, and taking a coarse front sight I fired at a young buck which was broadside to me."

Teddy got him. And later on he got another buck at what was judged 180 yards.

"The buck was rear-most, and at him I aimed; the bullet struck him in the flank, coming out of the opposite shoulder, and he fell in his next bound. As we stood over him, Joe (Joe Ferris, Roosevelt's hunting companion) shook his head and said, 'I guess that little rifle is the ace;' and I told him I guessed so too." (p. 201)

I remembered back on my own 30-30 days. While I was none too good with mine, my friends were. When I lived in Patagonia, Arizona, for a brief time, my host, John Bradsher, a man who settled in that area long before I was born, did all of his hunting with a Model 94 30-30 carbine. He was entirely successful. Mr. Bradsher hunted for meat. And the meat was important to him. Had his 30-30 failed him, he would have dropped it like a hot rock. His sons Robert and Richard had no problem bringing venison home with the same rifle. As I look back now, I can see where my shortcomings lay with old Slab-Side. I figured you had to snapshoot at your game with that rifle. Of course, that's nonsense. Later on, I took a good number of game animals in four countries with muzzleloaders, and I did not snapshoot. I aimed. Call it snapshooting if that means *taking aim quickly*.

My natural love for things old has lately brought me to a rifle that was probably manufactured in about 1899, a Model 94 take-down with a 26-inch octagon barrel and a full-length magazine, semi-pistol grip with checkering on grip and forearm. The rifle was in retirement, but for sale, by the Elmira Arms Company of Elmira, NY. A telephone call later, it belonged to me. I also took possession of the old standby, the Model 94 carbine, this one put out in the late 1950s, from what I can gather by the serial number. And I had to try a new Model 94 as well.

I wanted to try both factory and handloaded ammo in my two 30-30 Model 94s. My first surprise came when I studied reloading die sales by RCBS, for shooters were hard at work refilling 30-30 cases. The old 30-30 was ranked sixth in sales in 1977 by RCBS, and fifth in 1978. It was fifth, sixth, fifth, seventh in succeeding years. Only the 30-06, the 357/38 Special, lately the 223 and sometimes the 44 Magnum are consistently ahead of the 30-30 in this compilation.

I tried a good many 30-30 loads for myself. If there is a problem with 30-30s, it is that requirement for blunt pointed bullets in tubular magazines. One round being behind the other, a pointed bullet can detonate a primer and what happens after a cartridge goes off in the magazine is very expensive and dangerous. Therefore, it's flat nose or round bullets for the Model 94, Marlin 336 and others like them.

A 30-30 can be loaded with a pointed bullet in the old Model 54 bolt-action rifle, or the Savage Model 340 rifle, or a single shot model. Out of a 26-in. barrel I have chronographed 165-grain spire points or spitzers at over 2500 fps. I could zero this load between 2.5 and 3.0 inches high at 100 yards and the bullet would be right on the money at 200 yards. Out of the carbine, a 3.0-in. high sighting at 100 yards would also be close to on at 200 yards. The flat point 170-grain load would be on at about 150-165 yards with a 3.0-in. high 100-yard sight-in.

But I wasn't finished yet. I learned that out of the carbine or the rifle, the old 190-grain 303 Savage Silvertip bullet could earn a flat 2000 fps MV. You have to pull this bullet from factory-loaded 303 Savage ammunition, but it's just the thing for a close-range shot on a game animal of larger-than-deer dimensions. I would not hesitate to go—at decent range—for the shoulder area of an elk with a 190-grain Silvertip out of the 30-30.

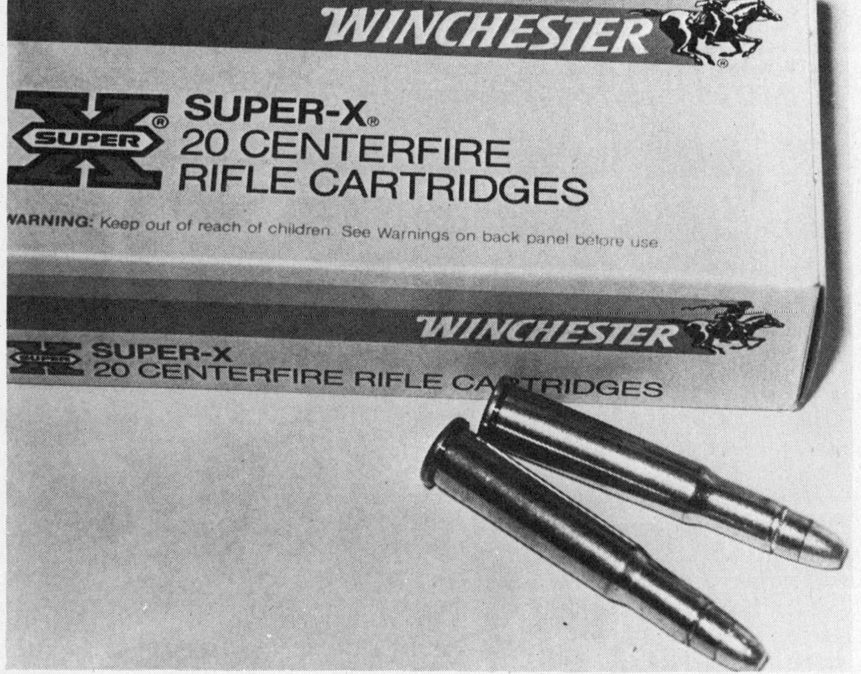

Nearly everybody loads a lot of 30-30s. Winchester's 170-grain Silvertip load chronographed at about 2100 fps MV in the 26-inch barrel and about 2035 fps in the 30-inch carbine barrel, either entirely adequate for big game with well-placed shots since the Silvertip penetrates well.

And there was more to come. I could push a 100-grain Speer Half-Jacket bullet at 2875 fps MV from the 26-in. barrel and 2671 fps MV from the 20-in. barrel, chronographed. Using 33.0 grains of H4198 powder, these loads showed no case head expansion in my two test rifles and the standard deviation from the mean velocity was only 9 fps up to a maximum of 19 fps in my tests.

My handloading was bringing versatility to the old 30-30. A squib load with a cast bullet was my next experiment. Using *Lyman Reloading Handbook*, 44th Edition, I found a load of 19.0 grains of IMR-4198 with the 131-grain cast bullet, No. 311410, No. 2 Alloy, for only 1658 fps MV. This would be just right for some small game hunting and also for a mountain load. Where I live, it is perfectly legal to harvest mountain grouse with a rifle, and I could take a few of these fine-eating birds with my 30-30.

The versatility factor improved again. I now had a fairly far-reaching load in the 165-grain bullet for a rifle with non-tubular magazine, a good 175-yard hold-right-on load with the 170-grain Speer bullet in the Model 94 or Model 336, and a 190-grain thumper for close-up work. Then I had my cast bullet squib for small game

The handloader with a real yen to use the 190-grain Silvertip bullet (left) must buy 303 Savage ammo and pull the bullets; deer bullets for the 30-30 should be a little bit more fragile and the 170-grain Sierra bullet at right is ideal.

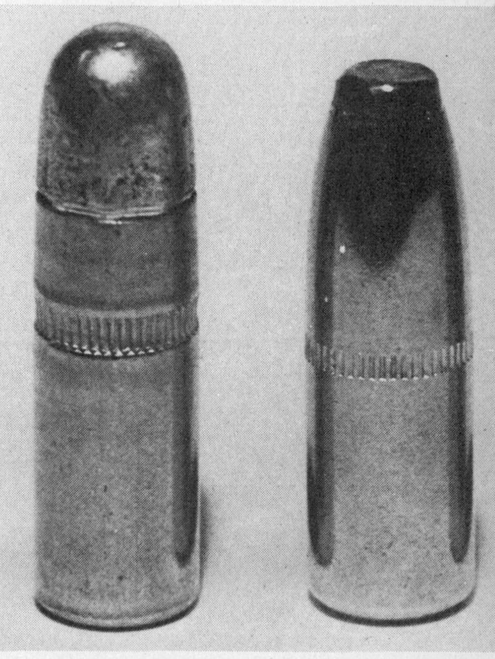

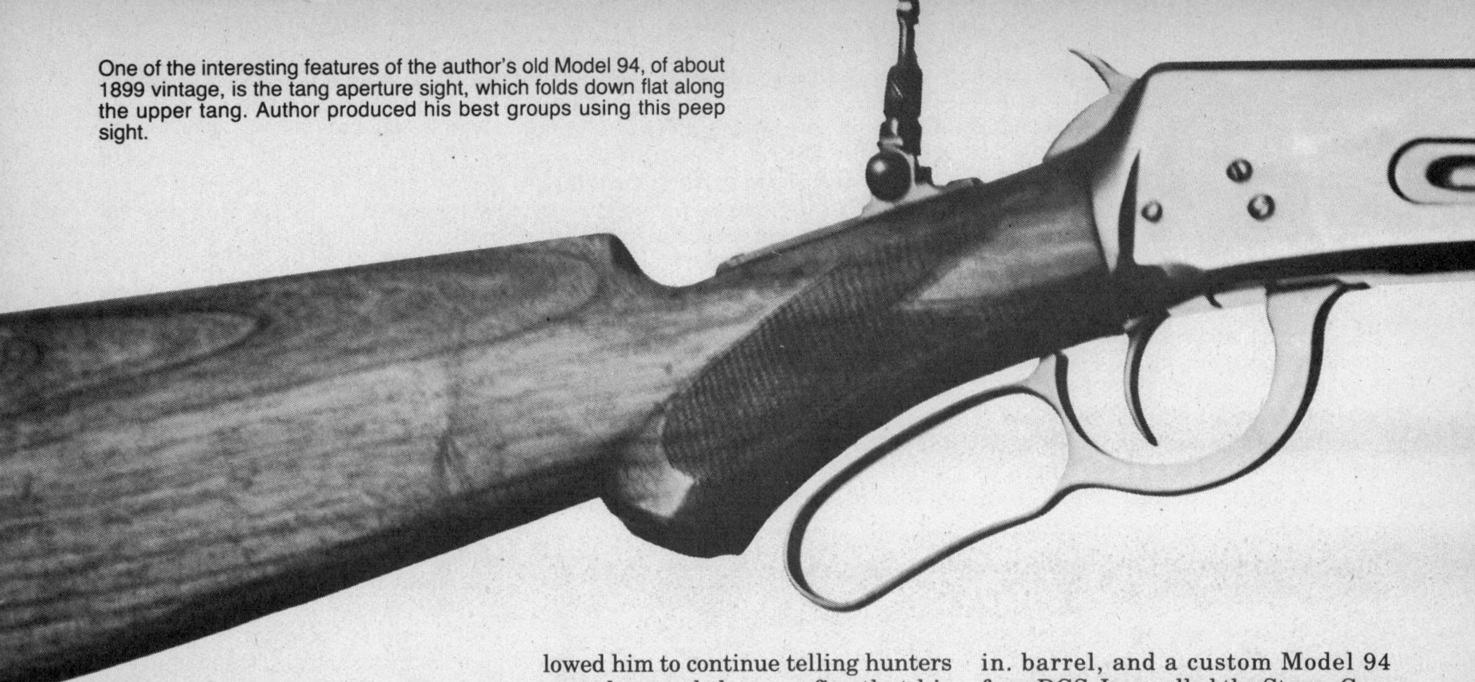

One of the interesting features of the author's old Model 94, of about 1899 vintage, is the tang aperture sight, which folds down flat along the upper tang. Author produced his best groups using this peep sight.

and mountain grouse. And a varmint load was also possible using the 130-grain Speer bullet or the 125-grain Sierra hollow point bullet. (I know. Varmint hunting is always supposed to be done at 300 yards—plus with a scope-sighted rifle firing hotrock smallbore pills at eyewatering scintillating velocity. A lot of ranchers and farmers drop varmints with the rifle they have with them, often a handy 30-30 carbine. They don't know any better.)

The ballistics with the 165-grain bullet, though fired from a non-tubular magazine rifle, did give me some fuel to pour on the fires of the anti-30-30 boys. I had the most fun with a certain fellow who is a fan of the 6mm class of rounds for deer. Had he left my little 30-30 untarnished and not called her names, I would have allowed him to continue telling hunters seated around the campfire that his 6mm rounds knocked the sauce out of deer at 300 yards.

The facts were, I enjoyed telling everyone: The 6mm Remington or 243 Winchester will push a 100-grain handloaded pill out at 3100 fps MV. The muzzle energy here is 2134 fp (foot pounds), a shade under my pet 30-30 load with the 165-grain bullet and a bit more than my 170-grain load. At 100 yards, his 100-grain bullet would be worth 1770 fp, but the 165-grain 30-30 load was still worth 1957 fp.

That does not make my 30-30s long range firearms. They wear iron sights and I prefer to shoot at close range. As I write this, I have three Model 94s in use, the two mentioned above, a standard carbine with 20-in. barrel, the nice old Model 94 rifle with its 26-in. barrel, and a custom Model 94 from DGS, Inc., called the Storey Conversion, a handsome and accurate rifle in 30-30 Improved caliber.

The Storey Conversion drives a 150-grain bullet at just shy of 2700 fps chronographed muzzle velocity with a rather standard loading, and case extraction is perfect. Even so, all three of my Model 94s are for short-range work because I use them that way. I enjoy stalking for a close shot and I find much of my game with my 8×40 glasses first, thus allowing a calculated stalk. I even carry a "smoke bag" of powder to keep the wind current patterns in check.

My 30-30s are rugged, even the handsome Storey Conversion. They have those fit-anywhere flat sides, and I can carry them with ease. On backpack trips, these are my trail companions. There's a Trapper model

Just six rounds of factory made this 2¼-inch (o.c.) group with iron sights and a Model 94. Anderson fired two from 25, two from 50 and two from 100 yards.

Just Six Shots

The reasoning was simple. The brush was going to be thick and the shots short. I didn't even need a scope. The old pre-WW II Model 94 carbine in 30-30 should be just about right. The timing was bad as I only had five days to get ready, so no reloads this time.

I grabbed a box of 150-grain soft points and headed for the range. I had bought 20 boxes of that ammo for $1.99 per 20 rounds some three years ago while wandering through the local "Monkey Wards." It was one of their "Blue-Light" (unannounced) sales. (Got to the counter too darn late— missed the 30-06 stuff by about five minutes. Same price. Lousy timing.)

When I arrived at my friend's house I had a cup of coffee, did some talking, and then got out to the range. Nothing unusual. I sat down at the 25-yard bench, loaded up and proceeded to sight the carbine in. No sandbags, just the elbows. With the help of a nylon-headed drift, a B-Square hammer and five rounds of ammo I managed to get bullet impact about where I wanted it.

I put up a new target and, as I walked back to the bench I realized I only had about two good handfuls of ammo left. Should be enough. Only needed a 6-inch group at 50 yards anyway. No big deal. Things were

Even with gloves on, one can feed the Model 94 30-30. Although this seems to be very open terrain, Fadala took a turkey with this carbine in the draw behind him an hour after this shutter clicked.

on the way, which may earn a spot in the outback, with its 16-in. barrel. On photo safaris in the wild places one of the little slab-sides will go along, too. In fact, when in the field for just about any reason, one of my Model 94s will often be there, doing its thing without fanfare, but thoroughly.

Some of the cognoscenti still downgrade the 30-30, while millions—not thousands, but millions—of shooters continue to use it. Why would they do this? The answer is simple. They use the 30-30 cartridge and lever-action guns because they both work. I often hear that the 30-30 is not a "bad kicker," and that it is all right as a beginner's rifle. But I wonder. Sure, the light, easy-to-handle Model 94 is pleasant to manage. But I think of the Model 94 and its 30-30 chambering as a *specialized* combination, a very special animal indeed.

I find myself hunting 30-30 style with the old rifle and round, meaning a careful walk in the wild, working for that closer shot. Hopping along one side of the canyon while trying to push something out on the other side of that canyon is out of the picture. Looking and moving carefully is more correct. Even in the thicker places, maintaining intelligent field position which is likely to produce a good shot is my way of using the 30-30, not that this technique is out of place with any caliber or firearm.

Perhaps the 30-30 is, after all, specialized. It comes up fast. It is reliable as the setting of the sun. One can take aim—notice that I said *aim*—quickly with a Model 94. We tend to snapshoot with it, which is all right if that term means "aim quickly," but if it means "up and fire," the heck with it. You aim a 94 the same as you aim any other firearm. It's not a shotgun.

I carry the 94 on those everyday treks. As this is written I am 24 hours past harvesting an antelope with my older Model 94 rifle, hunting in a somewhat broken area and taking the shot at 200 paces—about 125 to 150 yards, since the ground was not all that flat. One shot did it, the 170-grain Speer bullet smacking hard and harvesting clean.

Few rifles in the land load up faster than a 94, and it can be carried in the field with an empty chamber, because one flick of the wrist will have a cartridge home and ready to be fired. And I also like to carry the carbine into places I would not necessarily tote a fancier rifle.

---

running smoothly.

Sat down. Stuffed one handful of ammo through the loading gate. Fired two rounds—just the elbows as the only rest. Two bullet holes appeared in the center of the target—$^9/_{16}$-inch edge-to-edge. Cute. Had to be luck. Decided to try again.

I walked back to the 50-yard mark and sat down on the edge of a little bridge, crossed my legs casually, shouldered the 94 and rested my left elbow on my left knee. I looked like I was sitting in my living room. Fired two more rounds at the same target. The spread was just under 1⅛ inches edge-to-edge, the impact low and left, less than an inch away from the first two shots.

The 100-yard bench was only 50 yards away. Why not? Didn't have much else to do that day. Sat down. Fired two rounds. The spread was 1¾-inch edge-to-edge, about an inch and a quarter away from the 25-yard holes.

There we have it. Not a complicated story, nor an involved test. Those three, 2-round groups all fell into 2½ inches, edge-to-edge. Iron sights. No sandbags. I'll be the first to admit that six rounds of 30-30 ammo isn't a lot of testing, but I wish all of my "testing" was this easy.

My shooting pal Bob Loftus was beside himself. "Go back and tack that one up in your office. That's super shooting. Iron sights, too."

Well, I never did make the deer hunt—too busy. But I did tack the target up. I don't think it's so much a testimony to good shooting. It's a better commentary on the gun and cartridge combo. I talked to a handful of other gunwriters about my success. To a man they were all enthusiastic about the results. They *all* had one other thing to say. It went something like, "I've had a 94 for years but never benched the darn thing. Didn't know it could do *that* well."

Then I called Sam Fadala. Told him my story. His comment was a patient, "I know, Bob, *I know*."

—Robert S. L. Anderson

As for the round, it's no powerhouse by modern standards, but you don't need a sledge hammer to drive a tack. At close range, where the 30-30 is at home, it is plenty for deer. Its factory ammo, which I have tested at length, is rather remarkably well loaded. Nothing I have tested seems better put together than 30-30 fodder. For example, 170-grain Frontier ammo showed a standard deviation hovering around the 9 fps mark. The same brand with the 150-grain bullet went as low as 6 fps in standard deviation from the mean velocity. Winchester 170-grain Silvertips did as well with a rating of 7 fps standard deviation, and Federal did, too, with a mere 8 fps mode for its 125-grain load. Remington's Core-Lokt earned a low of 5 fps standard deviation with its 170-grain bullet, and so forth. That is good ammo.

Bad weather doesn't bother a Model 94 carbine. Whitetails shelter along this stream bottomland, and the little 94 is a perfect rifle for these conditions.

If I were starting a new shooter with a deer rifle for western hunting in the mountains, I would probably go with a bolt-action model with a high-intensity cartridge and a good scope sight. If I were starting a deer hunter in brush country, I might use a an Angle-Eject so I could still mount a scope. Personally, I would want more than a 30-30 for grizzlies and for serious varmint hunting, give me a rifle with flat-shooting accuracy.

All that leaves is that broad area of heavy use by *practical* hunters who are willing to hunt and who are willing to strive for good shot placement. This brand of successful hunter has taken to the 30-30 and stayed with it. Even in the face of super-velocity modern cartridges, this type of hunter keeps his faith in the old 30-30.

The Model 94 and the 30-30 changed American hunting forever. The round proved that smokeless powder was viable in sporting ammunition, and that higher velocity meant flatter trajectory. The 30-30 proved something else, though we may not often think about it. It proved that a cartridge can have considerable punch in a small case, providing a much smaller firearm.

But most of all, the reason for the 30-30 and its Model 94 staying with us so long is the fact that the combination is supremely fine in pairing good ballistics with a very manageable firearm, especially for that hunter who has worked long and has gained "expert" status. As Harold McFarlane, gun expert, said in *The American Rifleman*, January, 1949, "Usually, I tote a modern bolt gun with the latest in hunting scopes when rambling in the wood, but . . . when the larder is empty . . . I reach for the old 30-30 carbine. I know it's obsolete and the shell is a has-been, but for some reason deer die just as dead whether hit in the center or the edge of the heart with it. Too, most deer in timber country are killed within 50 yards. The point that interests me is the speed of handling of the little carbine. By the time the deer makes two jumps, I can perforate his hide with it . . ." (quote from GUN DIGEST, 1980, 34th edition, p. 12).

The Model 94 in 30-30 is the most successful sporting outfit to ever come down the pike. That isn't because the round and its rifle will "get you by." It's because the round and its rifle are *just right* for some very special tasks. And the modern hunter who wants to extend the usefulness of that package can do so by handloading, as well as by using the fine factory ammo available over the counter in 30-30 loading. One of my Model 94s goes with me often when I take to the hills. I have a pretty good idea that this relationship is going to last a long, long time. I won't be able to drop a deer in the next county with the 30-30, nor do I want to try that. But one thing is sure—when I do call upon the old gun to do its magic for me, she'll not balk nor complain. She'll just bark with her modest report and rear back enough to let me know that the job is done, and in her modest way, she will harvest the game before me, if I do my part half-way as well as she does hers. ●

ACCURACY TESTS

30-30 Winchester Model 94 rifle with 26-inch barrel and iron sights (fine bead). All fired at 50 yards, benchrest, in 3-shot groups measured center to center.

Notes:

Using a total of only 9 shots, the reliability factor of these accuracy demonstrations is not as high as it would be with 5-shot groups and at least 15 individual shots fired with each load. However, the data does give a very good and reasonable accuracy figure for the load and the rifle.

A Model 94 carbine, manufacture date *circa* 1955, was fired with a few of the more accurate loads and groups were very close to those obtained with the 26-inch barrel rifle, manufacture date *circa* 1899.

Lower velocity loads seemed less accurate than medium to higher velocity loads. With only 3-shot groups in strings of three, we cannot draw conclusions concerning the accuracy of any given bullet. Groups fired at 50 yards to hold best iron sight picture.

Bullet (grs.)	MV/fps (avg.)	Smallest (in.)	Largest (in.)	Average (in.)
100 Speer half jacket	2878	.80	1.12	.96
100 Speer half jacket	2717	.86	1.05	.96
100 Speer half jacket	1312	1.77	2.14	1.96
100 Hornady round nose	2671	.78	1.12	.95
110 Speer round nose	2862	.82	1.09	.96
110 Hornady full metal jacket	1700	1.06	1.12	1.09
125 Sierra flat nose	2709	.89	.99	.94
130 Speer flat nose	2683	.57	.59	.58
150 Hornady round nose	2425	1.22	1.31	1.27
170 Sierra flat nose	2368	.66	.87	.77
180 Speer round nose (single-loaded only)	2062	1.19	1.42	1.30
190 Winchester Silvertip	2012	.67	.71	.69

My Pet 30-30 Loads

Introduction

CONTRARY to what many of us have heard or read, the 30-30 Winchester round is a very fine candidate for reloading. Some claim a shooter can't strain more from the 30-30 case than the factory already puts into it. This is not quite so, although factory 30-30 ammunition is among the best ammo of all. Handloading makes the 30-30 a surprisingly versatile cartridge, so reloading for the 30-30 is worthwhile.

These loads are geared toward options. This is why there is such a variety. One surprise may be the lack of 150-grain loads. In many tests, we found the 150-grain bullet gained very little velocity over the 170-grain bullet. Also, we did considerable work with the 165-grain boattail bullet but decided not to present it in detail because one ought not use this bullet in tubular magazines.

The blunter bullets, however, are not always without decent ballistic shape. As an example, we have the 170-grain Speer bullet. It has a ballistic coefficient of .304, which is not bad. In fact, the profile of the 170-grain Speer bullet for the 30-30 is sharper than the profile of the Speer 180-grain bullet.

100-grain Speer 308-in. Plinker (half-jacket)/33.0 grains of H-4198 rifle powder

Average MV (5 Shots)	Standard Deviation
2878 fps	9 fps 26-in. barrel
2672 fps	19 fps 20-in. barrel

Comments:
This is an accurate load, and a very useful varmint load.

110-grain Hornady round nose soft point/37.0 grains of BL-C-2 rifle powder

Average MV (5 Shots)	Standard Deviation
2671 fps	17 fps 26-in. barrel
2609 fps	12 fps 20-in. barrel

Comments:
Here is another good varmint load for the 30-30 for those who carry a rifle on a daily or near daily basis. This load will handle any varmint from prairie dog to coyote with no trouble about as far as one can count on hitting them.

110-grain Speer round nose/31.5 grains of RX-7 rifle powder

Average MV (5 Shots)	Standard Deviation
2862 fps	9 fps 26-in. barrel
2800 fps	11 fps 20-in. barrel

Comments:
In our rifles, this was an accurate load, capable of two-inch groups at 100 yards from a benchrest, and very pleasant to shoot. It is one of our better "high speed" loads for the 30-30.

110-grain Hornady FMJ/11.0 grains of H-4227 rifle powder

Average MV (5 Shots)	Standard Deviation
1700 fps	24 fps 26-in. barrel

Comments:
This load was worked up especially for wild turkey hunting where it is legal to employ a full metal jacket bullet. It would also be a fine load for anyone on a trap line.

150-grain Hornady round nose/38.5 grains of W-748 rifle powder

Average MV (5 Shots)	Standard Deviation
2425 fps	16 fps 26-in. barrel
2371 fps	17 fps 20-in. barrel

Comments:
One can see why we have left the 150-grain bullet on the back burner in the case of the 30-30 cartridge. The 150-grain bullet in the 30-30 was given much devotion and praise by many deer hunters who said, and rightfully, that it dispatched deer faster than the 170-grain and as well as just about any hunting rifle at close range. Yes, this was true and in some cases would still be true, but not because of the 150-grain bullet *per se*. It was and is due to the fact that *some* of the 170-grain bullets were constructed too hard to expand on deer with 30-30 velocities, while the 150-grain bullets were fragile enough to give good expansion. Today, however, there are many good 170-grain bullets on the market which will expand properly on deer and one can see that these 170-grain bullets come close enough to the 150-grain in muzzle velocity to recommend them. The 170 is our choice over the 150-grain bullet, then, due to the better penetration of the former.

170-grain Sierra flat nose Pro-Hunter/37.0 grains of W-748 rifle powder

Average MV (5 Shots)	Standard Deviation
2368 fps	15 fps 26-in. barrel
2295 fps	9 fps 20-in. barrel

Comments:
The ever-famous 170-grain bullet is still a fine choice for the 30-30. We found several good loads using various powders, all propelling the 170-grain bullet at or over 2200 fps MV in the 20-in. barrel, and at or over 2300 fps MV in the 26-in. barrel. Our fastest 170-grain load to date was with 39.0 grains of W-748; however, we found that 37.0 grains was sufficient to produce the ballistics we wanted out of the 30-30 and recommend it. Other 170-grain bullets also delivered the same MV with the above charge.

190-grain Silvertip 303 Savage bullet/31.0 grains of W-748 rifle powder

Average MV (5 Shots)	Standard Deviation
2012 fps	12 fps 26-in. barrel
1999 fps	21 fps 20-in. barrel

Comments:
The 190-grain bullet was used in 303 Savage factory loads in the heyday of the 30-30 and similar rounds, and some hunters felt that the 303 Savage was a better hunting cartridge than the 30-30. William Hornaday, hunter-naturalist, used the 303 Savage for collecting grizzly bear specimens, as an example. However, the 303 Savage is no more than a 30-30. So we pulled 190-grain Silvertip bullets from the 303 Savage and here duplicate the 303 Savage load.

—Sam Fadala

by E. B. MANN

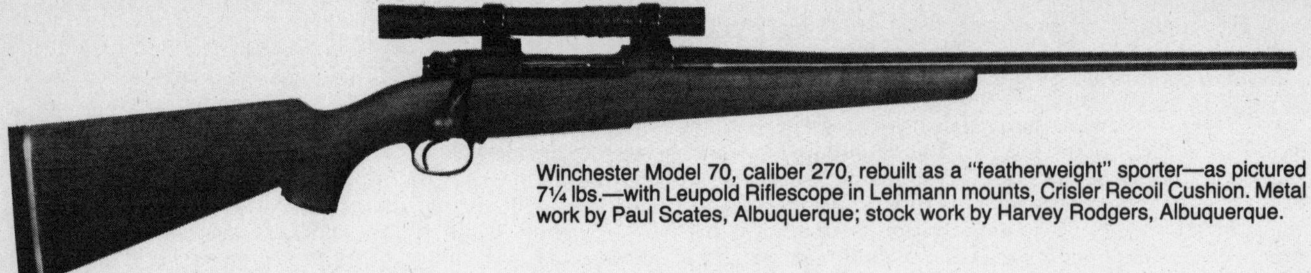

Winchester Model 70, caliber 270, rebuilt as a "featherweight" sporter—as pictured 7¼ lbs.—with Leupold Riflescope in Lehmann mounts, Crisler Recoil Cushion. Metal work by Paul Scates, Albuquerque; stock work by Harvey Rodgers, Albuquerque.

When Bev Mann wanted to go light and hunt happy, way back when, he came up with . . .

A FIRST FEATHERWEIGHT

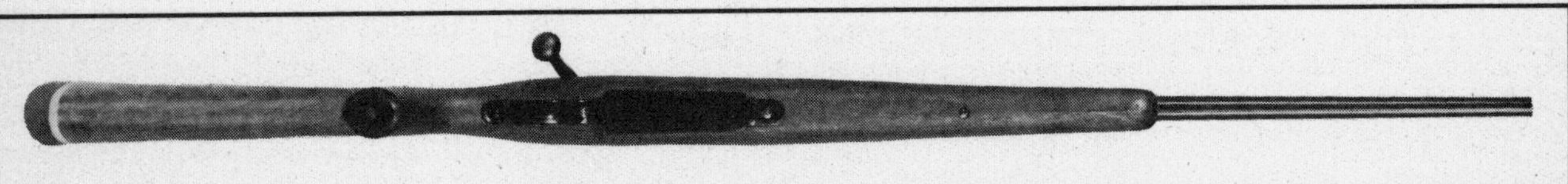

This sort of slimming is as important as profile changes when it comes to losing ounces and gaining feel in a hunting rifle.

IT ALL BEGAN in the mid-1940s at one of those Seminars in which certain firearms manufacturers showed off their new or improved products to such gun writers and editors as Elmer Keith, Charley Askins, Jack O'Connor, Warren Page, John Amber, and other similarly interested parties. We learned a lot in those sessions, both from our hosts and from each other. Differences of opinion were common enough, but we were usually tolerant of each other, and friends notwithstanding.

It takes some remembering, but there weren't any lightweight rifles for big game then, and on this occasion I was complaining about having had to tote some 11 pounds of artillery for nearly a week over some of New Mexico's roughest country. I didn't see why, I said, a rifle couldn't be whittled down to where, even with telescopic sights and a sling, it would weigh approximately the same as a lever-action 30-30 and still get the job done on anything smaller than, maybe, moose; and we didn't see many moose in New Mexico.

O'Connor's snort of derision was utterly lacking in tolerance! First, it couldn't be done. Second, if it were done, the rifle would be ruined: short of both range and accuracy; too much recoil; too much muzzle blast. And, anyway, hell's bells, if a man ain't man enough to carry a big game rifle, he shouldn't hunt big game!"

Somebody, I think it was Page, answered him: "Wouldn't make those 500-yard-plus shots you write about, eh, Jack?," and the laughter that followed prevented any comment I might have offered.

But the question was right on target. At an earlier Seminar, I had made some derogatory remarks about long range shooting being poor fodder for magazine articles which would be read by less expert hunters who would take them as excuses for shooting at anything they could see through a 4x scope.

But O'Connor's words rankled. What if I could prove him wrong? Having a rifle customized would cost something, but maybe I could write an article about it and get some of the money back. I knew the people who could do the work for me: Paul Scates, a fine gunsmith who had done work for me on rifles sent me for testing; and Harvey Rodgers, one of the best stockers in the country—so good that Ellis Christian Lenz had devoted half a chapter to him in his excellent book, *Muzzle Flashes*. So I talked it over with Scates and Rodgers, and bought a Winchester Model 70, caliber 270.

Next, I chose a Leupold scope, for several reasons. I had tried several of them, and liked them. Optically excellent and mounted low in rigid ring mounts, with a dot reticle subtending three minutes of angle, it would be perfect. And it weighed only 6¼ ounces.

Recoil in a hunting rifle is mostly in the mind of the shooter, but O'Connor had mentioned it specifically, so I chose Crisler Cushion Pads; pads plural because they came in pairs, one thick and one thin to adjust for the difference in "reach" caused by summer or winter clothing. I don't think they are on the market now, which is too bad. They were good looking, effective—and they weighed only 4¼ ounces; a trifle less in fact, when trimmed to fit my slimmer stock.

Meanwhile, Scates was working on the rifle. New, it had weighed 8¼ pounds, as advertised. First, he cut 4 inches off the barrel. That disposed of the front sight and sight ramp, so we discarded the rear sight too. The scope would be the only sight I wanted or would need. Then Scates lathed what was left of the barrel (20 inches) in a long taper from the receiver forward. The rear sight bulge disappeared and the barrel, finished and crowned, looked like something designed for space travel.

We discussed slimming the action, too, cutting magazine capacity by one cartridge. But Rodgers objected. "You won't gain much in weight, and it would spoil the lines of the rifle, making it look weak in the middle." There was no use begging Harvey to do something that would spoil the lines of the rifle, so we bowed to wisdom.

Meanwhile also, Rodgers was re-bedding the barrel, shortening and tapering the forearm, thinning and shaping the stock, lifting the curve behind the trigger guard to produce a full pistol grip, and finally, believe it or not, drilling half-inch holes deep from the butt forward and covering the holes with a white liner and one of the black Crisler butt cushions. When we seated the metal into the wood, it looked—well, as pretty as a picture, and here are pictures so you can see for yourself.

The question now was: will it shoot?

We did some sighting-in shots at 25 yards. Then we moved out to 100 yards and adjusted blanket and bedrolls for prone shooting. I asked Scates to shoot first; I had buck fever, and Scates was a better rifleman than I was.

His first three shots centered at one o'clock, two inches above point of aim, measuring a hair under an inch, center to center. The ammunition was 130-grain Western Silvertip Expanding Super X.

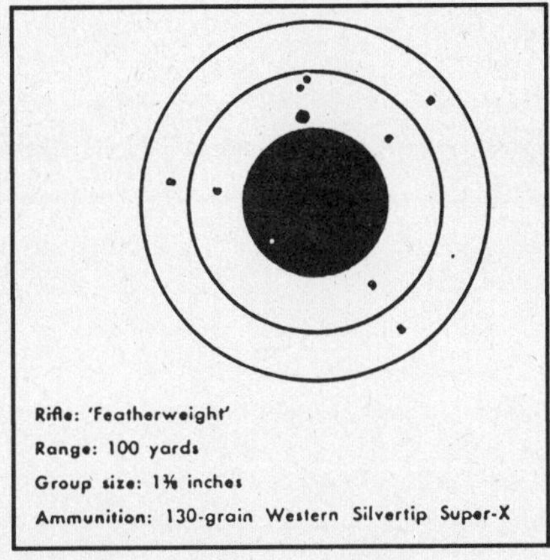

Here's how *The American Rifleman* showed off Mann's new rifle's potential.

I let my fingers come unclinched.

"I'd like it centered, 3½ inches high at 100, Paul," I said. "That will keep them within a 4-inch rise or fall out to around 300 yards, and that's as far as I will ever shoot it. Move it over one click and up one, and try three more."

He made the adjustments. The next two shots were where I had requested, 3½ inches high, centered, with ⅜ of an inch between them. When the third was fired Scates called it "Low, damn it. Just a little low, but centered." His call was correct: the group measured 1⅜ inches.

I did some shooting then, to make sure that Paul and I were seeing alike. We were not; my groups were low and left, about seven o'clock, due to my funny vision. My three best groups were 1½ inches.

(I have been asked, "Why did you fire only three-shot groups?" My answer: "When did you ever get more than three shots, if that many, at a game animal? If three shots don't get him, ten to one it wasn't because of the rifle!")

We shot it later at 200 and 300 yards, prone, with rest. Our best groups at 200 were around 2½ inches; at 300, just under 4 inches. Good enough, we thought, for a hunting rifle. Neither muzzle blast nor recoil were noticeably worse than those of standard rifles fired for comparison.

I carried the "shorty" on a couple of hunts, then wrote my article. *American Rifleman* bought it. When it was published I got a letter from Winchester: "We enjoyed your article. It was of particular interest in the matter of design, and many of the points brought out deserve further study. Would it be possible for us to examine the rifle?"

Needless to say, I sent them the rifle. Considerably later it came back to me with their verdict: "It will do everything you said it would do."

I sent a stat of that letter to Jack O'Connor. It came back to me with a question scrawled across it: "But what will it do at 500 yards?"

The question was hardly worthy of Jack; given the data furnished, any ballistics table would tell him what it would do at other ranges. I simply scrawled my answer under his: "Who the hell cares?"

I carried that rifle over a lot of miles and it did everything I asked it to do; no spectacular 500-yard kills, but who needs them? I did put a variable-power scope on it for a time, and the gunsmith who mounted it did, as a favor to me, some other work that I hadn't asked for; a favor that cost me a day of re-testing to make sure the rifle had lost none of its accuracy. It hadn't. But I had to replace the old mounts and scope when I sold it; the buyer demanded that the rifle come to him in exactly its original condition, matching his copy of the "Rifleman" article.

There are many "featherweight" rifles today. The Winchester Model 70 ("The Rifleman's Rifle") is now offered as "The Rifleman's Carbine,"—20-inch barrel, weighing as little as six pounds. A scope sight and sling would add at least a pound to that, but the comparison is obvious. New materials have made it easier to produce a light rifle; fiberglass stocks, for example. They have advantages; but I still like walnut better!

No, I did not invent the featherweight hunting rifle; I only happened to build one of the earlier ones. The trend was already in process. My rifle cost me $373.95. It was a profitable venture, dollar-wise. But most valuable to me was its dozen years or more of impeccable performance. ●

EDITOR'S NOTE

You can find, if you look, the name E. B. Mann high on the mastheads of gun magazines back a long way. He delighted me 20 or more years ago by buying photography and even articles from me, and not so long ago by being my roommate at some of those seminars he mentions.

So, like another fellow we both knew, if Bev Mann tells you he was there, he was there. And if he tells you it shot, it shot. No doubt about it—even if it was all the best part of 40 years ago. *K.W.*

LAST CHANCE BUFFALO

Sometimes it's more difficult than other times; sometimes you don't even get a chance; sometimes you get all you need.

IT WAS LATE in the afternoon. We had just begun our sundowners in Frik's mess tent, a pleasant place with its wicker settee and small wood stove to chase the chill and keep our morning tea warm. Bols brandy seared a path through the dust trail in my throat. One can't be too choosy in the African bush, especially in a country fighting one of those "dirty little wars" advertised daily in international newspapers.

The lack of popular booze—Scotch, in particular—was my first realization of what dirty little wars are about. When we arrived in then Salisbury (now Harare) ten days earlier, I had innocently announced to Frik that I needed to pick up a few bottles of Dewars before we headed in. He told me that it just might be available from an "importer" he knew on the other side of town at probably somewhere in the neighborhood of $60 a fifth. That was my first introduction to trade sanctions. The Bols brandy cost three bucks and it worked.

The distant rattling of a Land Rover now broke the silence of late afternoon. It was a new sound for that time of day. There wasn't much traveling between sundowners and breakfast. The terrorists preferred to move under the cover of darkness. Those who defended against them just as practically preferred to remain behind security fences, or at least within the confines of a camp perimeter.

"That must be Andy," Frik said. "I told him to stop in for a beer. He's been out in the area for a couple of days, too, and may have a bit that's helpful for our buffalo."

That was one thing I had come to like in Frik. He was an optimist. "Our buffalo?" We had spent the last eight days hunting as hard as I know for "our buffalo," and spent the remainder of the 21 days on our sable, and the other lesser "our" animals I wanted from this first safari.

I had already taken our kudu. Of course, I was buffalo hunting when it happened. We had staged a late afternoon hunt near the river. Like the other hunts, it had been a close encounter of the buffalo kind. The big black forms had vanished as easily as UFOs, too. We had gotten into their dust, literally. I had even seen their shadows moving through the thick bush, had heard the hooves moving away from me, but no buffalo.

Then on the way back in, Frik had seen the kudu horns showing above the growth of African bush. I had taken the shot through a hole at some 40 yards. Frik told me the kudu should be a good one because it stood so tall. So I shot, seeing no more of him than the horn tips and a patch of skin through the leaves. It was the luckiest shot I'll ever make.

He *was* a good one. Both horns right at 50 inches, with good mass (12-in. circumference at the base) and a 36-in. spread. Frik sent the boys to get help from the nearest kraal to load him. We celebrated the kudu with a slug or two of Bols and my first cigarette in six months.

Before the boys returned, several things happened. First, the Rhodesian moon set the scene all silver and the kudu looked beautiful lying there. Secondly, I started smoking two packs a day again. Thirdly, I felt that, with a little luck, I could take African game from the wheelchair if we continued to put in long hunting days.

Now after eight days, some of the latter confidence was wearing off. We were in good buff country. I knew that. Doc had taken his first after only two days. It was a trophy bull in the classic manner. He was a massive old

by SPENCE DUPREE

Dupree and his buffalo. The rifle is a Whitworth 375. The chair is a standard lightweight folding model for easy auto travel, and works well over rough ground when carried by muscular others.

buff and had even put up a partial charge before Doc's second round put him down for keeps. But it had all been done on foot.

Our hunts—Frik's and mine—were from the back of the Land Rover. We were hoping to stumble over a buffalo that could be taken from the vehicle. Frik's license would be revoked if the authorities found that he had allowed a hunter in a wheelchair to shoot a buffalo from the ground.

But here he was, all confident because Andy was rattling down the road to tell us where "our" buffalo might be found. After eight days, I didn't think we could ambush a buffalo from a vehicle. He was too sharp. He had all his sensibilities—hearing, sight, and smell. I had seen enough of buffalo to know that much.

Maybe in the open savannah country of Kenya it could be done. My 375—a poor man's fusil imported by Interarms, stocked by Sile in Italy, action built in Czechoslovakia, and proofed in England, impressively branded a "Whitworth"—religiously put three handloads in 1½ inches at 100 yards. It wasn't built by Holland & Holland, but I will still put it up against their doubles at longer ranges.

A long-range rifle doesn't do much extra in Zimbabwe's lowveld. Buffalo prefer the thick country of Mopani and pangara thorn where 50 yards is a long shot. When they hear a vehicle coming, their next move is to get the hell out of Dodge. People had been hunting hard in the area allegedly to aid in the control of domestic cattle diseases. A more probable reason was that biltong, dried strips of meat similar to jerky, was selling for two dollars a pound in Rhodesian cities. The heavy hunting pressure had made buffalo as wild as New York whitetails hereabouts.

Frik was pouring a second round as Andy's ancient Land Rover bumped to a stop in front of our tent. Judging from his appearance, Andy would be fitting company for sundowners. Wearing kneepants and a highneck sweater, his eyes crinkled when he smiled through his beard. He looked every inch a man at home in the bush. His right arm was bandaged from wrist to elbow.

"Andy had a go with a leopard, I believe. Didn't you, chap?" Frik asked.

I was all ears. Here was someone who had actually been mauled. I had only used that word once or twice when quoting from a book. Now I was talking to a man who had undergone the process known as mauling and was still alive to talk about it.

He nodded and began to tell his story. A leopard had taken several calves from a nearby livestock paddock for a month. Hunting from blinds over kills had failed to produce even a sighting of the leopard. That's when Andy and Hilton, another professional hunter in the area, decided to put a dog pack on the leopard's tail.

A few days later the leopard struck again and soon the dogs were on a hot trail. The cat came to bay in a small thicket.

"The dogs closed in and I could see the leopard pacing back and forth," Andy explained. "But I couldn't shoot for fear of hitting one of the pups.

"It was a smallish female and she was getting madder by the minute. You can tell when they're really mad. They will slick their ears back on their head.

"Finally, she'd had enough. She came through the dogs and headed for me, flattened against the ground and weaving back and forth as she ran. I raised the FN and fired," Andy said, referring to the FAL combat rifle that was standard issue in Rhodesia.

"I had the selector on full auto and that was a mistake. My first shot struck her right foot, the second grazed her side doing no damage, and the next six went high.

"Then she hit me, but I didn't go down. She tried to hold behind my neck so she could rake my belly with her back feet, but the broken right foot from the first shot kept her from getting a good grip. All the time, she was chewing on my arm. Next I knew there was an explosion right in my face. Hilton had shot her point blank in the ear with his 44 Magnum Smith & Wesson.

"It all happened so fast, I didn't realize my arm was a bit chewed until after she was dead. It hurt like bloody hell then," Andy said.

"The worst has been the infection. I've been back to Chiredzi Hospital twice with the thing and taken enough pills to disinfect an army latrine. It's still giving a bit of trouble," he finished as Frik poured another round and gave Andy a fresh Lion lager.

Guide Frik Nel and author admire the first bushbuck. There was also kudu, and much driving.

Andy's leopard weighed only 75 pounds. A good bull Cape buffalo would go somewhere in the neighborhood of a ton. I guessed that one probably didn't hear too many firsthand stories of buffalo poundings. There was no one around to tell them.

According to Andy, there were now good numbers of buffalo along the Mkwasine River on a government tract known as the Potential. It got its name because it was potentially tillable. Frik had rights to hunt it for buffalo only.

"The buff are moving to the river to drink at night. Some are staying near the river as much as two days before going back to the grazing. As dry as everything is, you can drive along the riverbed and may find an old bull getting himself a drink or rolling in the mud. You can see down the straight stretches and may be able to take a long shot before he spots you," Andy said.

We all agreed it was worth a try. Frik and I would hunt buffalo two more days before giving up. By then, we would have to concentrate on sable, eland and waterbuck as well as some of the lesser trophies if I hoped to round out a good bag before heading home.

I was awake the next morning before the old one-cylinder Lyster generator began pumping its steady cadence through the silent bush. I was making mental kills on imaginary buffalo when the tent light began to pulse with the sound of the generator. The smell of Johnny Ngozoh's coffee brought me to the side of my bed. Buffalo hunting sure beats working for a living.

After a light breakfast, we were off to the area just as the sun shone its first pink rim on the eastern horizon. We were traveling down little more than footpaths through heavily wooded forests of mopani and other species I could not identify. Suddenly Frik stopped the Land Rover and cut the engine. He pointed with his eyes and whispered, "There's a good bushbuck. He's going away so take him fast as you can."

I could just make him out in the early shadows. He had trotted across our trail and was moving behind the trees glancing at us with every other step. I barely made out his horns and wondered how Frik could tell if he was a good buck with no more light. When I looked through the Kahles scope, I realized why they are so expensive. It was like turning on a stage light. I found the buck easily and squeezed the shot moving with him as I fired. He was down before I recovered from the recoil.

My 375 handload of IMR 4350 behind a 300-grain Hornady solid was hardly what I call ideal for animals like the bushbuck. It caught him right in the boiler though and he succumbed with scarcely a flinch. We celebrated the kill quickly as the boys caped him on the spot and hung the meat for pick up that afternoon. I regretted the time lost, but was proud of the trophy which Frik felt would easily make the book. (He measured 14½ × 14¼ dry and registered 19th in the Safari International Book of Big Game Records.)

Sable fell to author's handload—IMR 4350 behind a 180-grain Nosler Partition in his light rifle, a 300 Magnum.

As it turned out, the bushbuck was the highpoint of that day. Shortly after we entered the Potential, Frik put the Land Rover down the sandy river course of the Mkwasine. During the winter months of July and August, the river is little more than a stream, leaving most of its sandy bed exposed. At ten o'clock, the bottom dropped from under the vehicle and we became hopelessly stuck—crusty on top, and ooze just under the surface of the crust. When the boys stepped out, they were up to their knees. It was midafternoon before they got back with Land Rover number two and it was my longest day in Africa.

The other Land Rover was a controlled wreck, fenders held with bailing wire, valves ground as thin as communion wafers. She proudly ground to a halt just above our predicament in the sand. Her lower sides were blown out by land mines and she huffed and puffed to pull us from the muck and she did it. I could have kissed her rear tyre and patted her South Hall sides. We headed back to camp and I was looking forward to Bols like never before.

At camp, I found it had been Doc's best day. He and Hilton had gone for kudu in an area not far from camp. Roy (Doc's other name) had dropped his 300 Winchester the day before and had decided to take the 375. He was shooting an identical load to mine in it. We both had become confident with the solid bullets on smaller game.

Luck was with Doc. Three large rocks lying under an old baobab didn't get his attention until one rock flicked its tail. When a tickbird perched on the largest rock and began to eat its dinner, Doc and Hilton started a stalk. The biggest bull put his head up when they were 70 yards out and Doc gave him one in the throat. All three buff were up and on the move. The blood trail was heavy and shortly the wounded buff was left behind.

When Roy told his tale that evening at sundowners, I couldn't help but feel a little envy. The old bull was up and looking him dead in the eye when it came time to administer the coup-de-grace. The buff had started his charge when Doc let him have it right in the nose. That was all it took and he went down, still alive but unable to fight anymore.

So we celebrated Doc's bull that night around our camp and discussed possibilities for tomorrow's hunt. Frik was not only undaunted about our hunt, he was enthusiastic: "We will find buffalo tomorrow along the river. The spoor was too heavy and fresh. They are there and one is ours."

I didn't share his enthusiasm. I wasn't too disappointed either. We had hunted hard for a Cape buffalo for nine days. We had covered miles of bush in very decent buff territory, had smelled their dust, and seen the shadows through the trees. In short, Frik had done just about everything short of trying a cow call to get me a shot at a bull. It was like the time I went out for pitcher on the Little League baseball team. The first kid laid a perfect bunt down the third base line and I realized quickly that the wheelchair and I were better suited for other sports. It wasn't that big a disappointment, just a new fact of life.

When I loaded the big 375 rounds in the semi-darkness that morning, I noticed that they were worn and scarred from dozens of trips through the magazine. This would be the last time.

When we reached the slope of the Mkwasine basin, Frik sent Banda and Robin, our two best trackers, ahead. "We are going to give them time to see what is along the river," he said.

Half an hour later, we proceeded along the river bank, this time staying on higher ground out of the sand. Soon we were again crossing buffalo sign. Their tracks were everywhere and chunks of dung lay on the trail. Occasionally, Frik would stop the Land Rover to break open one of the huge pellets and check its freshness. We traveled as quietly as the Land Rover would allow and spoke only in whispers.

Whitworth 375 H&H shows off some of the better features of more expensive English magazine rifles. This one is equipped with a Jaeger QD mount; the hat is equipped with sweat and memories.

During one of our stops, I heard padding feet coming our way from the river. Soon Banda's black face mingled with the shadows of the bush. His face was inscrutable, but there was a tinge of excitement in his whisper as he reported to Frik in Shona. It was unintelligible to me except the word "inyati" and the tracker's hand gestures pointing downriver. Maybe this was the chance I had been waiting for.

Frik returned to the vehicle and explained, "The boys spotted three bulls moving from the river on an old trail. Banda thinks the trail crosses ne an opening a mile further down. We are going to try to set up there before the buff arrive. You will have to try it from the ground, but I will be behind you with the 458."

We took a short run on our backtrail and then turned through the bush to circle the animals at a distance we hoped would not disturb them. Soon we stopped and began to move on foot. I was in the wheelchair, moving by the strong arms and legs of African black power as the boys literally carried me and my chair through the bush. And soon we were set up on the edge of a clearing some 100 yards wide.

If the ambush were to work, the buffalo would enter the clearing from the opposite side. I had a slight height advantage, which should allow for a shot up to 60 yards. All contingent, of course, on the whims and meanderings of 6,000 pounds of wild flesh that might be on the other side of the river for all we really knew.

Half an hour passed and with the exception of several flocks of squeaky little yellow birds, the opening in the bush lay as quietly as a rural cemetery. The sun was now up full and creating suspicious black spots in the bush around the perimeter. Occasional wisps of air stirred the foot-high grass. I was relieved they fell flush on my face and not on my back.

My stare had become blank and my mind drifted as I felt Frik's hand go tight around my forearm.

"Easy now," he said. "They're not ready yet. Wait on them. They're doing just right. The big boy is in the rear."

They were not the only ones who weren't ready. I didn't even see them. Furthermore, I was suddenly out of breath and suffering my first bout of palsy.

Then I saw. Cautiously, they came onto the open terrace. They held their heads out and at a slight upward angle testing each breeze. Then they stopped and just stood there looking stupid, confident, and in total control. What a tenderfoot! I realized that I was holding my breath again and getting all trembly. A comic picture of a wheelchair bumping through the bush with a ton of buffalo in hot pursuit flirted across the mental picture window. I glanced at Frik and the 458 and felt more settled.

The buffalo began to move slowly, plodding a quartering path across the opening. Seventy yards, then sixty.

"Take him in the shoulder," Frik whispered. "Don't try anything fancy," he added, referring to earlier conversations over sundowners regarding neck shots.

The thought had never entered my mind as I lowered the Whitworth and found the rear bull in the scope. It was black on black as the crosshairs settled on the spot. There was no noise, no recoil from the rifle that kicked the hell out of me on the bench. Just motion, as the lead bulls headed for the bush and I pumped another round down the chamber.

Up again with the rifle; this time I looked at a changed animal. His head was low on the ground and he was looking back at me. I went for a spot halfway down his neck that would rake him all the way through due to the angle. This time he went down and I felt Frik slap my back. I said something very unprintable. The buffalo still had his head up postured like a resting Jersey chewing its cud.

"How do you kill him?" I asked Frik.

"He's ours now. Just put one through his right ear flap and that should do it," he replied.

It did. The big head went limp against the ground and I felt the high that belongs to us tenderfeet when we kill a buffalo. We aren't the coolheaded super hunters that I read about in the old British hunting stories. We are just the ones who have fun and talk like magpies when the deed is done.

I had my buffalo and had realized a dream that started about the time I aspired to be a baseball pitcher. You lose some and win others. That night sundowners lasted long, well into moonlight. ●

Editor's Note

This writer tells of a Cape buffalo hunt where nothing really went wrong, nothing unusual happened. He fired three shots at reasonable range—not "close" on buffalo, but not far, either—and the buffalo died. Still, I find the circumstances special and hope you will, too.

Mr. Dupree sadly reports that his companion here, Frik Nel, was taken by terrorists some time later and reportedly died in a camp in a neighboring African nation. Thus, we have not to worry if we reveal any possible technical violations of the hunting regulations. Personally, I feel Mr. Nel did just fine. So did Mr. Dupree.

K.W.

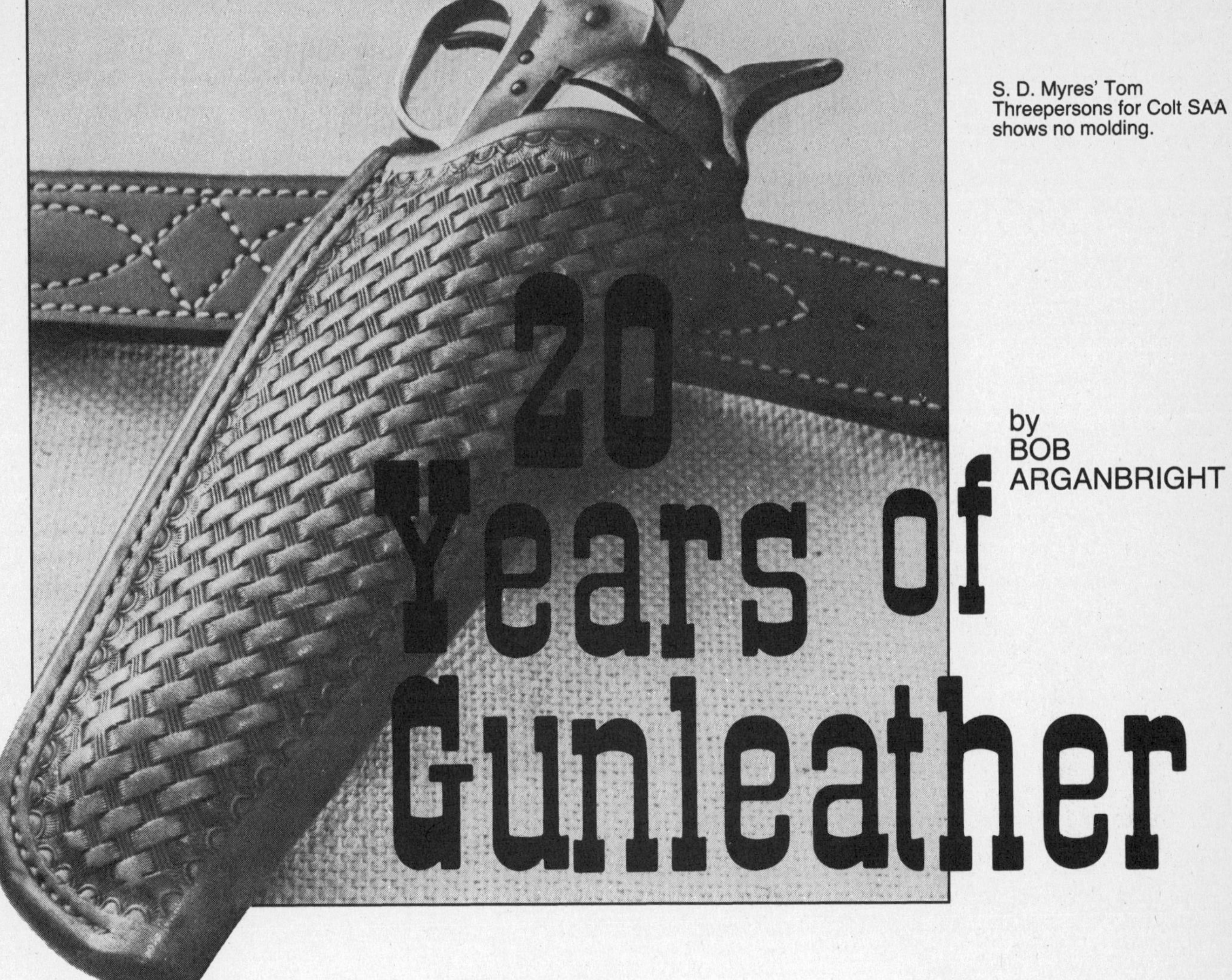

S. D. Myres' Tom Threepersons for Colt SAA shows no molding.

20 Years of Gunleather

by BOB ARGANBRIGHT

MY FIRST GUN DIGEST, the 1959 issue, was a major influence on my shooting activities since. I bought it specifically for the article "Hollywood Gunmen" by Charles MacDonald Heard. On the infant sport of Western Fast Draw, this article included information on the special holster rigs used by Hollywood Western stars. It impressed me with the importance of the correct holster for different handgun uses.

I went on to take up leathercraft in order to produce my own custom holsters. Many of my early endeavors ended up in the trash can, but I eventually turned out holsters as fine as any money could buy. With a competition Fast Draw rig of my own design and manufacture, I won the 1980 National Fast Draw Championship. I think it is appropriate that I should now be writing about handgun leather for the GUN DIGEST.

In this article about holsters, we will look at where we were approximately 20 years ago, where we are today, and where we are going in the future.

In 1958, when "Hollywood Gunmen" was written, there were three giants of the holster industry, H. H. Heiser of Denver, S. D. Myres of El Paso and George Lawrence of Portland. All three were originally frontier saddle makers who added a line of holsters. They all offered Border Patrol and swivel holsters for the uniformed police officer and the Threepersons' hip holster and shoulder holsters for the plainclothes detective. Holsters for sportsmen tended to all be hip holsters of the traditional style or the popular western buscadero rig.

All three makers were known for top quality. Their holsters were made of heavy saddle leather, with thick full length welts, and each was hand blocked for the gun it was to carry. Blocking is the shaping of the wet holster around a form to provide the proper fit for the gun.

In addition, there was the Hunter Co. of Denver and Brauer Brothers Mfg. of St. Louis producing full lines of economy holsters.

Of the Big Three, Heiser was purchased by Keyston and no longer produces holsters; Myers sold their company and name and they are currently a small volume custom operation; and only the George Lawrence Co. continues with a full line of holsters.

The only specialty holster of this era to have a lasting influence was the Berns-Martin, the first of the break-front designs. Though no longer available, the Berns-Martin was a major influence on holster design with both the front break "Speed" hip holster and the upside down "Lightning" shoulder holster.

About the mid-1950s, we saw the emergence of Western Fast Draw. Three major new holster makers emerged, specializing in steel-lined competition fast draw rigs. These were Arvo Ojala with his Hollywood Fast Draw Holster, Andy Anderson with his Gunfighter line, and Alfonso Pineda of Alfonso of Hollywood. Today, Ojala and Anderson are retired and Alfonso has a holster shop in North Hollywood. It is interesting to note that of the three, only Andy Anderson was formerly a saddle maker, and it was his designs that blazed the trail for today's leading holster makers. Andy was the first to offer the full contoured gunbelt, the muzzle forward safety holster, the steel-lined hip plate and the adjustable tension holster. He personally preferred a high hip carry, which is standard today. All of these features are found on many of today's best rigs.

At the same time, there was a need for a different type of holster. A small group of professional gun carriers such as the Secret Service, undercover police officers and members of certain clandestine government agencies, needed maximum concealment holsters that were light weight, comfortable, fast and secure. These men were soon beating a path to the New York City shop of Chic Gaylord. Chic's holsters were very different. They were made from a minimum of lightweight leather, they didn't have welts (the thick piece of leather running down the seam of the holster pouch) and they used a very tight friction fit for retention of the handgun. It was Gaylord who introduced the thumb break keeper strap and the extensive wet fitting that we take for granted today. In his shop, wet fitting was done by hand by forming the wet leather around an actual gun, working it into all of the contours. For all but the most extreme cases, this perfect fit would retain the gun without any kind of strap. Gaylord also worked extensively with the shoulder holster, offering the first horizontal carry.

The Gaylord tradition was carried on by Seventrees after Chic passed away. Seventrees offered an extensive line of special concealment holsters and added such refinements as offering them in horsehide, which wears much longer than the traditional cowhide. I have been told of a Seventrees horsehide holster which returned from a full tour of duty in Vietnam looking like new.

While Seventrees established a reputation for uncompromising quality, they had management problems which caused them to go out of business. I was very fortunate in obtaining a Colt 45 hip holster out of horsehide by Seventrees. A local police officer brought this holster into a gun shop and traded it for a full flap hip holster due to his department regulations. Like trading a Cadillac for a Ford Pinto!

Today, we have such makers as Alessi, Galco (formerly Jackass), and De Santis offering concealment holsters. In addition, there is the K. L Null Co. which completed Seventrees unfilled orders under contract to them and then developed their own line of specialty concealment holsters. Ken Null offers the most extensive line available today. He was kind enough to make me a friction fit high hip carry Gaylord-style holster for my favorite Ruger 4⅝" Blackhawk.

The original Big Three have been replaced by a new Big Three. Emerging within the last 20 years have been Bianchi Gunleather and Safariland, with Roy's Custom Leather Goods emerging as a major maker within the past 10 years. Roy's currently offers a full line of holsters, but started with the original Roy Baker Pancake holster. Don Hume makes very good leather, but specializes in police holsters.

Bianchi Gunleather is undoubtedly the leader. Headed by John Bianchi, a former California police officer who made holsters as a hobby, Bianchi offers the most extensive line in the industry. They adopted the wet fit as pioneered by Gaylord and refined it to a process using an aluminum gun form and a hydraulic press to shape the holster exactly to the gun it is to carry. Recently, they have pioneered the use of a lighter weight high quality leather tanned specially for this molding process.

Safariland's line isn't as extensive as Bianchi's. However, they offer their

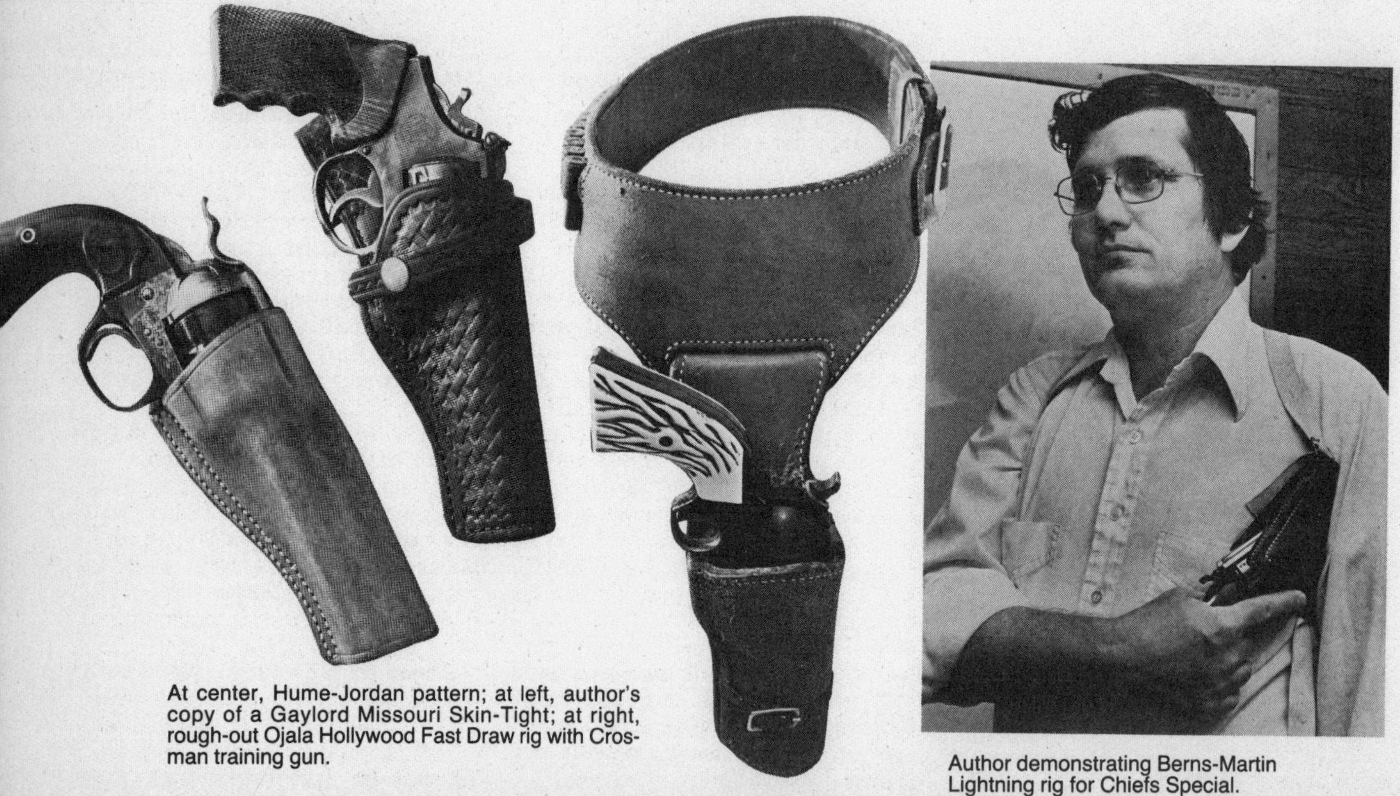

At center, Hume-Jordan pattern; at left, author's copy of a Gaylord Missouri Skin-Tight; at right, rough-out Ojala Hollywood Fast Draw rig with Crosman training gun.

Author demonstrating Berns-Martin Lightning rig for Chiefs Special.

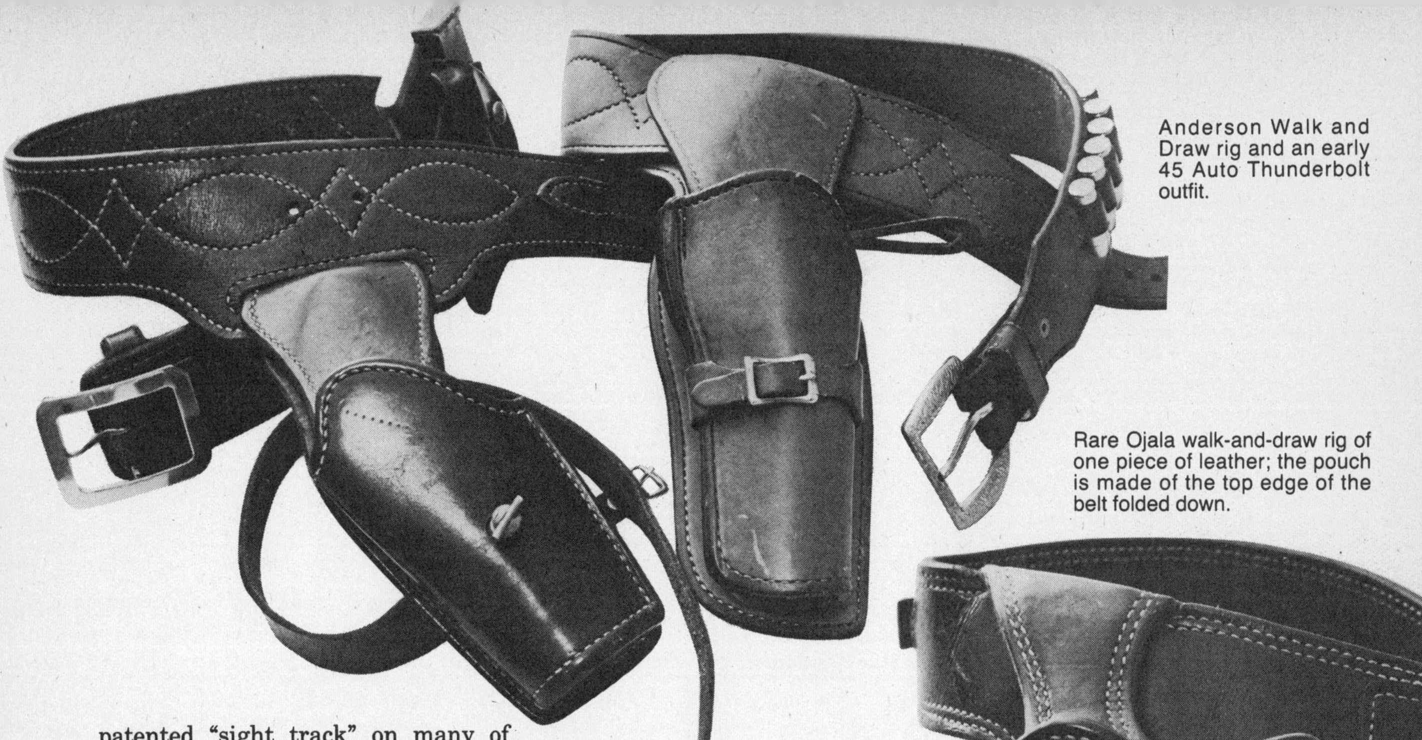

Anderson Walk and Draw rig and an early 45 Auto Thunderbolt outfit.

Rare Ojala walk-and-draw rig of one piece of leather; the pouch is made of the top edge of the belt folded down.

patented "sight track" on many of their holsters. This is a strip of vinyl running down the front of the holster pouch. It has a groove cut in it to provide a track for the front sight to ride in. This is a great improvement over its predecessors for the target sighted handgun. Most makers now offer some type of sight channel in their top of the line holsters.

As previously mentioned, Roy's is the maker of the original Pancake holster. The Pancake is two oval pieces of leather sewn together at the front and back edges to form a pocket to hold the handgun. In place of a belt loop, there are slots in the leading and trailing edges. The belt is threaded through these slots to support the holster. All major makers offer some form of Pancake today. They all differ from Roy's in that his multiple slots in the leading edge allow the one holster to be worn as a strong side hip holster or a cross draw. This feature is protected by a U.S. patent.

The major advantage of the pancake-style holster is its comfort. Designed to be worn on a 1¾-inch waist belt, the distance between the front and back belt slots distributes the weight over a larger area than a conventional hip holster. This can be important when wearing a large, relatively heavy handgun for long periods of time. The pancake style holsters are popular with both police officers and sportsmen. I have an early Roy Baker Pancake for a 5½-inch Colt SAA revolver which is one of my favorites. Interestingly, Roy Baker was an apprentice under Andy Anderson before Andy's move to Hollywood.

Recently, many makers have offered belt slide holsters. These are hip holsters cut off just below the be loop. Many of them are chopped o pancakes. These are meant to be low profile holsters, as with the gun removed, they don't appear to be holsters. Personally, I find this to be of questionable merit and I don't care for the belt slides.

Today's economy holsters are furnished by Hunter and Bucheimer and Brauer. There are a lot of holsters of this type made for the Red Head label as well. Apart from bare-bones gun pouches, these companies attempt more sophisticated designs as well.

As previously shown, the police market has caused a flurry of activity in the development of concealment holsters. In addition, the police uniform holster has undergone numerous changes. Bianchi Gunleather is the leading manufacturer of break front police holsters. In 1975, Bianchi announced the purchase of the Berns-Martin company. They currently produce four different front-break revolver holsters, an improved version of the Berns-Martin "Lightning" upside-down shoulder holster and a front-break hip holster for the Colt 45 auto pistol.

Considerable design effort has gone into producing break-front holsters which offer a maximum of gun security, making it difficult for an assailant to snatch the weapon. It is a sad commentary on our times that many police officers are shot with their own handguns. Unfortunately, there are no snatchproof holsters, and no less an authority than Jeff Cooper has stated that this is a tactical problem rather than a holster design problem. I tend to agree.

I find it interesting that while the original Berns-Martin holster was designed in order to draw a long barreled SA revolver comfortably from a high ride hip holster, there are currently no break-front SA holsters. A break-front would be an excellent holster for the man who prefers a hip holster for his 10½-inch Super Blackhawk.

The last few years have seen two additional major influences on the holster industry. The first of these was the formation of the International Practical Shooting Confederation (IPSC) in 1976. The second is the large number of handgun hunters who need holsters to carry their handguns in the field.

The holsters seen in IPSC competition have changed a great deal since its inception. The popular rigs of four to six years ago were the so-called full race rigs. These were very similar to the earlier Hollywood fast draw rigs, being low-hung steel-lined muzzle-forward (muzzle-raked) holsters on 2½ to 3-inch contoured gun belts worn below the waist. With the stress on practicality, we have seen these rigs slowly disappear. The later IPSC holster rule said that the holster must be worn on a belt around the waist and the belt must run through the trouser belt loops. In addition, the gun butt could not be below the belt.

A number of new makers have appeared who cater mainly to the IPSC shooter. These include Milt Sparks, Gordon Davis and Ted Blocker. While Cobra Gunskin offers a full line of holsters, they include a line of Andy Anderson designed IPSC holsters.

An interesting trend in the IPSC leather is the appearance of signature holsters. The first was Sparks' "Hackathorn Special," named for Ken Hackathorn who was the top shooter at the IPSC founding conference. This was the first of the high-ride, muzzle-raked adjustable tension holsters. Bianchi followed with their "Chapman Hi-Ride" designed in conjunction with first World Combat Champion Ray Chapman. Gordon Davis makes the "Usher International" designed for world-class shooter Jerry Usher. Ted Blocker makes the "Jayhawker" named for my Jayhawker Custom Holsters and has just introduced a slightly modified "Jayhawker" called the "ISI" rig, for Mickey Fowler of International Shootists Inc. Mickey was the 1981 World IPSC Championship runnerup.

An interesting trend in IPSC competition is the popularity of the cross-draw holster. While 25 years of SA fast draw competition have biased me toward the strong-side hip holster, the cross-draw has some advantages for the IPSC competitor. These include easier access to the weak hand when a weak hand draw is needed, and not being in the way when one needs to use the rollover prone shooting position. It also is very fast when one is sitting, which some matches require.

Two things have brought the shoulder holster to an all time peak in popularity. One was the Clint Eastwood movie "Dirty Harry" in which he carried a long-barreled S&W Model 29 in a shoulder holster. The other is the popularity of handgun hunting today. Many handgun hunters select the shoulder holster for their long barreled handguns.

The most important improvement has been the new harnesses which support the holster. The elastic strap running across the back and around the off side arm has been replaced with a second support which carries accessories, such as extra ammo, handcuffs, pistol magazines or a folding hunting knife. These have been designed to distribute the weight evenly which reduces the previously objectionable discomfort of wearing a shoulder holster.

In these times of high inflation, the price of a top quality holster is equally inflated. In addition, the U.S. is one of only a few major producers of commercial cowhide. Much of the U.S. production is exported, forcing the

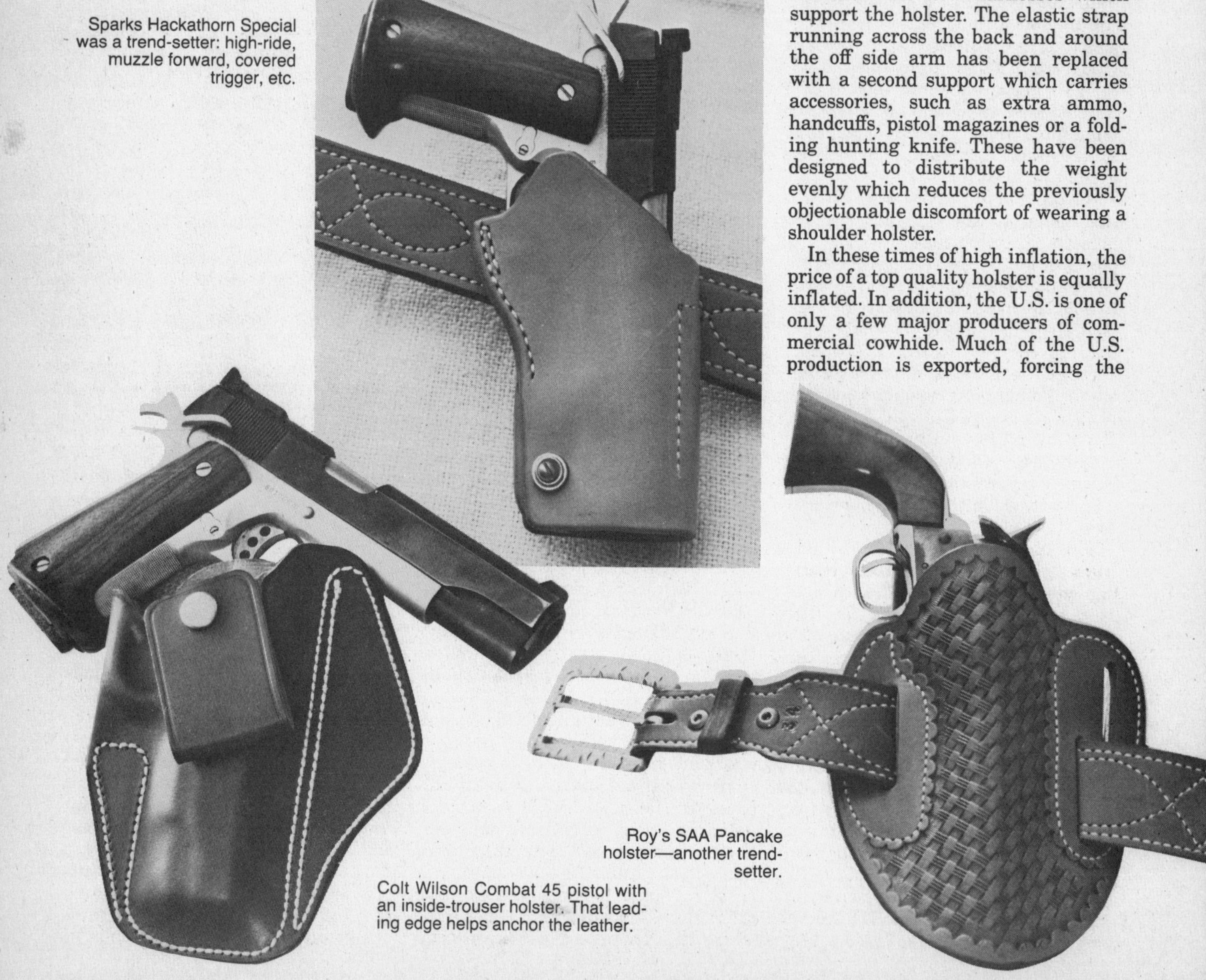

Sparks Hackathorn Special was a trend-setter: high-ride, muzzle forward, covered trigger, etc.

Roy's SAA Pancake holster—another trend-setter.

Colt Wilson Combat 45 pistol with an inside-trouser holster. That leading edge helps anchor the leather.

Rick Bachman of Kalispell, MT crafts handsome period rigs like this to order.

Bob Angell worked for Chic Gaylord; now his Active Leather Corp. makes these minimum-leather, maximum-speed shoulder rigs.

Cobra Gunskin Sidewinder with swiveling loop lets wearer choose angle.

price to the holster makers ever higher. One should expect to pay $40 - $60 for a top quality holster and one can easily spend $100 - $150 on an IPSC competition rig. But in these days of $600 Colt SAs, $400 Colt 45 autos and $600 - $1000 IPSC guns, $40 - $150 for leather gear isn't unreasonable.

Finally, the last few years has seen the introduction of holsters made from synthetic materials. These include the Snik break-front 45 auto holster and a line of Police holsters by Rogers Holsters. These don't seem to have made much of an inroad in the holster industry. I find it interesting that when Rogers made a very limited number of Ken Hackathorn Signature IPSC holsters, they were of leather.

A very recent development is the introduction of the Commemorative rig. John Bianchi is producing 3000 John Wayne Commemorative gunbelt and holster rigs which are duplicates of the rig used by Wayne in most of his more recent Western movies. El Paso Saddlery and Ted Blocker's Custom Holsters offer similar rigs called the "Duke," and Gordon Davis has a "Rooster" rig. El Paso Saddlery produced very limited numbers of Pat Garrett and O.K. Corral Gunfight Centennial commemorative rigs during 1981. These are authentic replicas of an actual holster used by Pat Garrett and an 1880s-era holster from a Tombstone, Arizona Territory, gunshop. Arvo Ojala advertised briefly a replica of the Hollywood Fast Draw Holster used by Richard Boone as Paladin in the TV series "Have Gun, Will Travel," complete with sterling silver chess knight on the side of the holster. It will be interesting to see if this trend of producing new collectors rigs continues.

Gunmakers are furnishing holsters as well now. Smith & Wesson has built a plant to make their leather and has the most complete line. Ruger contracts to have flap holsters made for their guns; and Bianchi works directly with Heckler & Koch on holster designs.

I feel this is an accurate picture of the major holster developments of the past 20 years. Just as one thinks that the ultimate holster has been designed and produced, something new appears. Cobra Gunskin recently introduced their "Sidewinder" inside the pants holster with a unique patented swivel belt loop which allows the user to position the holster at whatever angle he chooses. I have found this to be an excellent holster, with the gunbelt providing the needed tension to secure my 45 auto while shooting in IPSC matches.

I believe the future will bring new holsters for the IPSC revolver shooter. Bianchi makes a thumbreak cross draw holster that is state of the art, with Sparks, Davis and Blocker offering high ride, muzzle raked revolver holsters. It seems that IPSC is swinging more to the practical in match design with fewer of the mad dash, shoot and reload, 12 shots or better stages. This lets the revolver shooter once again be competitive. I think we will see more revolvers in IPSC, and therefore we will see new leather for them.

The U.S. holster industry offers the finest holsters in the world today, whatever your holster requirements. I am confident they will continue to do so. ●

EDITOR'S NOTE

This article is on gun leather, and it does not examine the unleather rigs so popular over the past couple of years. *That* discussion will come in due course.

K.W.

Gun Digest Discussion No. 3

When weather and hunting get tougher, Matunas wants a rifle that will help correct a mistake, like this Remington 700 Classic in 300 H&H Magnum.

I WON'T HUNT WITH SINGLE SHOT RIFLES

by E. A. MATUNAS

This pronghorn is but one of several trophies taken by "Old Deadly Shorty," Simpson's Ruger Number 1A in 30-06. He has yet to feel a need for more firepower.

I DO HUNT WITH SINGLE SHOT RIFLES

by LAYNE SIMPSON

THERE WAS A time when single shot rifles fascinated me. To hunt with a single shot was the ultimate challenge. One shot, carefully placed at exactly the right moment, would get the job done. No shots at running game, no shots through heavy cover; just a single round left unfired until the quarry had been carefully stalked for a 100% guaranteed effective shot. This indeed was the highest level of sportsmanship and the maximum thrill of hunting.

Who could question such an undertaking? If I spooked the quarry as I approached, then it was left unmolested as it ran off. After all, spooked game, according to my strict code of hunting ethics, was not successfully hunted. And for the animals that were successfully stalked, who would ever require a second shot? One carefully placed round through the heart was all that was needed. Or so I thought in years gone by!

But as in all things that we repeat often enough, the biggest lessons are not always learned at the beginning. Often it takes a great number of repetitions of nearly the same occurrence to bring out all of the variables. A few downed deer or other big game animals prove little as to what one can expect over a great number of similar happenings. Perhaps the relating of some experiences will illustrate a few of the faults in employing a single shot rifle for hunting.

It was just about daybreak on top of Weldon's Mountain as I cautiously moved across the meadow and entered the timber. The time to load my rifle quickly arrived. As I paused to do so, I noticed a bit of movement off to my left. I froze and carefully watched. In the early light, another movement showed me a doe that had obviously just gotten up from her grassy bed; and then another and still another. Hoping to see a buck, my thoughts went back to loading my rifle. I carefully removed a round from my pocket and eased it into the chamber. In order to prevent it from going "KERPLUNK" as it dropped, I held the gun somewhat horizontal as I pushed the shell into place.

While so doing, I saw what I had been searching for; still another deer. This one, however, had a fine rack, perhaps one of the best I had ever seen on a Vermont buck; eight points but large and well-formed, I guessed. The buck was still unaware of my presence despite the fact that the doe nearest to me was at least concerned about my silhouette. When he looked directly away from me I began to close my action. But the cartridge I had so carefully placed in the chamber had slid slightly to the rear, obviously due to the fact that the muzzle was somewhat elevated, and the breech block stopped against the protruding cartridge. I looked down, saw what was wrong and I dropped the muzzle downward. I opened the action fully and allowed the shell to drop back into place. When I closed the lever, I looked up only to find the buck had evaporated into the morning mist. I wish I could say that the hunt later proved successful, but in four days of hard hunting I never again saw a deer with horns.

A dark rainy day with black bear as the target: I had been on my stand for about two hours when I saw the shadow of black moving toward the bait. It wasn't a big bear, as blacks go, but then it's not every day one even gets to see a bear. Bears always look big. With the crosshairs steady, I squeezed a shot off while the bruin's head swayed left and right testing the wind. That black knew something was amiss but wasn't certain of what was out of place.

Perhaps it was the poor light com-

IF YOU ARE a lousy hunter and satisfied to be a lousy shot on big game, stop reading immediately because what I'm about to say about single shot rifles won't interest you. The same goes if you lack familiarity with your rifle and confidence in yourself because you're just too lazy to learn better and especially those of you who believe firepower makes up for lack of practice with a rifle.

However, if you believe as I do that a well-aimed first shot is worth far more than spraying lead with great abandon, you're my kind of people. Read on.

While writing this opus, I'm not aware of what the other fellow has to say about single shot rifles, but won't be a bit surprised if his worn-out song is the same one hummed by those who have criticized the one-shooter ever since Bill Ruger brought it back into style. The tune goes about like this:

1. Single Shots Have Snob Appeal

On more than one occasion it has been written that snob appeal sells more single shot big game rifles than any other factor and, as the story continues, many who choose this type rifle are more than a bit limp of wrist and wear monogrammed boxer shorts. Bull puckey. Generally, hunters carry single shots simply because they are willing (and able) to sacrifice firepower for lightness and portability. My first Ruger Number One, a 1A in 30-06, is a good example. The first time it showed up, my two elk hunting buddies took great joy in putting down such a little "peashooter." Two seasons later, they dubbed it "Deadly Little Shorty" and showed up in camp with Number Ones of their own. They had been converted not by my defense of the rifle, but by its performance in the field, meaning it always brought home the meat and horns.

I bought "Deadly Little Shorty" strictly for rough country elk hunting and there is where it shone brightest. In those days all my elk chasing was done afoot and I needed a light rifle that wouldn't collapse the old arches during a day's tough hike. Also, I needed a short rifle for maneuvering through black timber and over blowdowns when the bulls were shy, as well as one that packed enough punch for shots across canyons and meadows. The Ruger loaded with 180-grain Nosler partitions to 2,800 fps filled the bill quite nicely.

Before I retired old Shorty it accounted for seven elk, eleven mule deer, five pronghorn, four whitetails and two porcupine. If a more practical big game rifle than a single shot 30-06 with 22-inch barrel was ever built, I've certainly not found it.

Now let's listen to the next stanza sung by most single shot detractors:

2. Single Shots Ain't Accurate

What this part of the melody says if we listen closely enough is this: single shot rifles are not as inherently accurate as bolt actions, which because of their more rigid lockup and the manner in which their barreled actions are mated to a stock, are theoretically more accurate than single shots. All of this means something more than a hill of beans in a demanding sport such as benchrest shooting, but is worth between nothing and zilch when talking about big game hunting under typical field conditions.

While we all love to talk about our minute-of-angle big game rifles, the truth is, few (if any) of us are capable of maintaining such accuracy when

All the author's favored hunting guns are good turn-bolt scoped rifles. Here, he's shown with his most favored 270—the 270 being probably his favorite cartridge.

If every shot looked like this, maybe a single shot might be enough, Matunas thinks. But they're not.

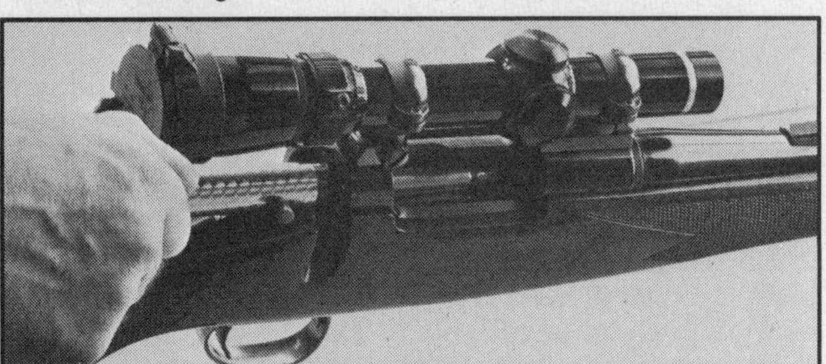

Follow-up shots are sometimes necessary and managing a repeater is easy, so Matunas leaves the single shot rifles home.

When fed good clean ammunition, a single shot rifle is just as dependable as any other. Simpson shot a few thousand rounds to find that out.

Big game rifles are carried much more than they are shot. The TCR '83 shown here carries well.

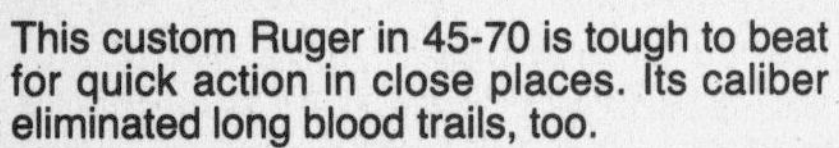

This custom Ruger in 45-70 is tough to beat for quick action in close places. Its caliber eliminated long blood trails, too.

bined with a dark bear and the rain on my scope lens. Whatever the reason, my perfect shot wasn't. When the gun went off, the bear howled, fell, got up and headed downhill—fast. I loaded quickly, but the bear was out of sight long before I started to close the action. In fact, he was gone before I had transferred the shell from my pocket to the chamber. With my single shot finally reloaded, I was aghast at the sudden silence. The bear was gone; even out of hearing range.

I followed a long trail that was lost several times. But before I could catch up to that bear it had stumbled into another hunter in its panic and pain-filled escape. The hunter emptied his semi-automatic's four shots into the bear since, as he explained afterward, he felt he was being charged by the bear. In any event, it was difficult to pin-point which of the five holes in that bear was the result of my shot. But I suspect I was responsible for the one well to the rear of the vitals. I can only guess that the bear was in a contorted position and that what I thought was the shoulder simply was not. Bear fever? Poor light? Contorted bear? A combination of all three factors? It matters not. I had lost any chance of anchoring that hit bear because I did not have a quick follow-up shot available.

On still another occasion, a single shot proved less than ideal. A hunting companion missed a very long shot on a caribou, hitting it low on a rear leg. Unlike most caribou, this bull attempted to travel after being wounded. It was a scant 25 yards to the crest of a hill and if the bull reached it he would be hidden from sight. With no quick way to cover the distance and fumbling with a dropped cartridge, my partner resorted to shouting "Finish him! Finish him!" It took two shots from my bolt action 270 to drop that bull.

Another acquaintance told me of "nearly having my butt chewed off by an irate grizzly." His problem: A single shot that didn't get the job done quickly enough at an extremely short range. The story had a happy ending, however, with the guide controlling everything quite nicely with a bolt-action rifle. "Bang, Bang" and it was over.

A single shot simply doesn't allow for the unexpected. And even the most experienced and careful hunter falls upon the unanticipated from time to time. If there were not unexpected situations, hunting would quickly become less appealing. OK, but what about the appeal of a successful stalk and one well-placed shot? It's just as great when that well-placed shot is fired from a repeating rifle. Now, don't you conscientious single shot owners go getting indignant. I don't take offense to your reasoning and enjoyment of a single shot. I just find a one-shot-gun's faults not to my liking.

No animal in the world knows if you have the potential of a backup shot. If you are human and can make a mistake, the second shot may save the day. A hunter's respect for his quarry demands that no needless suffering occur. And I'm proof to myself that the most carefully placed shot may not be all that it was thought to be. When this occurs, the most sporting condition is a fast second shot to terminate any suffering inflicted upon the quarry with the first shot. Would you like to say "I'm a careful sport hunter who uses a single shot and only once have I ever let an animal escape wounded, if only for a short while." Or, would you rather be able to say "No animal has ever gone more than a few feet or a few seconds after my first shot was fired."

I remember well one deer that I shot through the neck with a 140-

---

afield. There's a whale of a lot of difference between how accurately we can hold a rifle when calmly squeezing them off at benchrest compared to holding her steady under field conditions. If you can't hit deer-size and larger game with a two-m.o.a. rifle, you won't hit it with a real tack-driver.

Actually, all this is purely academic because, on average, single shot rifles chambered to cartridges suitable for shooting big game are just as accurate as the typical off-the-shelf rifle of any other persuasion—including bolt action sporters of like caliber. I'm not exactly without company in this opinion either; several shooters whom I know opine the same thing.

According to the chap at Ruger who is in charge of testing all firearms, every rifle must meet a certain accuracy standard before it's shipped out. Now, tamp this in your pipe and smoke it over awhile—the accuracy requirement for Ruger's Number One is identical to that for their Model 77 bolt-action rifle. I expect I've said enough on this subject so we'll now see what other criticisms the fellows who wear black hats have to spout about single shot rifles:

3. Single Shots Lack Firepower

It's in rather poor taste to boast about the total number of big game animals brought to bag during one's years of tromping through the boonies but I must risk talking about exactly 29 of them in order to make an important point. Those two dozen-plus animals came in assorted sizes and shapes; moose, pronghorn, elk, mule deer, greater kudu, bear, whitetails, wart hog, feral hog, zebra, etc., etc. Some were taken from afar in mountain and plains country, while others dropped in thick brush only a few steps from the muzzle of my rifle. A few were running, most were standing still. All have one thing in common—they were taken with a single shot rifle.

More important than anything else, I've never fired at a big game animal with a single shot rifle that I didn't kill dead as a doornail. Sure enough, a very few took more than one shot but I've yet to wound and lose an animal when hunting with a single shot rifle. In fact, not once while hunting with a one-shooter have I ever felt a need for greater firepower nor have I stood helplessly as that trophy of a lifetime bounded away because my rifle only held one cartridge.

Among the all-time great fallacies dreamed up years ago is this "need" for great firepower in wooded terrain. As the old chestnut goes, in order for a rifle to be suitable for woods hunting it must be capable of pouring on follow-up shots with great rapidity. Friends, I'll let you in on a little secret; when hunting in thick country and timber, you can count on having one shot for getting the job done. Failing that, all others will likely be in vain even though they do serve to keep the ammunition makers happy.

More important than firepower for woods hunting is a short, handy rifle that fits you like a glove and comes to shoulder in a flash. It should also smite game with enough power to down it right there or at least punch on through for an easy-to-follow blood trail. I've just described one of my favorite woods rifles. Ruger built the action and Bob Cassetty carved out its stock and forearm to my specifications. It's in 45-70 and a quicker, deadlier rifle you'll not find for shooting big game in close places.

Some years back, just to prove my point, I ran a little experiment along grain bullet that failed to expand. In and then out; leaving only a pencil-sized hole from which blood gushed profusely. A second round smashed a shoulder and pulverized a lot of bone. As the deer attempted to get its feet under itself once again, a third shot brought the matter to a conclusion. Total elapsed time from first shot to last: about 8 to 10 seconds. I had done everything right except to know beforehand that the first bullet would fail to expand causing little energy transfer to the animal. In fact, the effect of the first shot was less than if I had put an arrow through the deer's neck. With a single shot rifle, I may have recovered that deer after a long or short tracking session, or another hunter may have claimed it, or the worst of all scenarios, it could have eluded me to die a slow and useless death.

I'm not advocating the replacement of good, accurate shooting with firepower. In fact, I'm as opposed to using a semi-automatic as I am to using a single shot. Too many semi-automatic users try to make up for poor marksmanship with rapid and successive pulls on the trigger. A deer shot poorly three or four times will suffer a great deal more than if it was shot cleanly a single time. About that there can be no argument. If a semi-automatic is used prudently, it can be an acceptable hunting rifle, but rapid fire is too often a means to cover up poor shooting capability.

Aside from its lack of a prompt follow-up shot or two, the single shot rifle is less than easy to load especially if it is equipped with a scope. It sounds easy; just drop in a cartridge and close the action. But in reality the cartridge must be started directly into the chamber. For most of us this means looking at the gun somewhat more or less intently while directing the shell into place. It also means muzzle down until the breech block has slid past the shell. And it's not easy, especially with a gloved hand, to start a shell into the chamber (and under the scope) as compared to loading perhaps a bolt action rifle where shells can be snapped into the magazine with little or no attention to the gun. Even when scope-equipped, most bolt guns are a breeze to load.

Too, the single shot is usually carried with a round in the chamber. Anything less and the rifle is unloaded. But for many types of hunting I find it convenient and an added safety precaution to leave the chamber of a bolt gun empty with a full complement of cartridges carried in the magazine. I work a shell into the action only after I have spotted my game and after I have decided I want the particular animal. This works fine for antelope, sheep, goat and caribou. I've yet to have to take a very hurried shot during such hunting. And knowing my chamber is empty prevents any quick reaction shots. I therefore get fewer less-than-perfectly-placed shots or dropped game that really wasn't up to my expectations with regard to size or the worth of the trophy. Of course, for hunting game such as deer, moose or elk, not to mention bear, I always hunt with one in the chamber because frequently shots on these animals are offered only for a few short seconds.

I have also found that not every scope can be mounted on a given single shot and get the eye relief correct. Often the scope will still be too far from the eye even when mounted as far to the rear as possible. I found my Zeiss 6x scope impossible to use on a once-favored single shot 30-30 rifle. I don't like having to choose a scope on the basis of it "fits" the rifle, preferring rather to select my optical sights for their ability to help me see and cleanly kill game.

---

the firepower line. During most of two whitetail seasons I hunted with an old Remington Model 81 autoloader in 300 Savage. Whether hanging off the side of a tall pine in a tree stand or tiptoeing through the brush jump-shooting bucks, my strategy was the same; squeeze off a carefully aimed first shot, then even if my first shot found meat, immediately pour on the coal as fast as the old trigger finger could twitch. Now, either I'm one of the best at connecting with the first shot or one of the worst with follow-up shots but one thing is certain: after the first trigger squeeze, I wasted a lot of lead. If I didn't kill it with the first shot, I didn't kill it at all. If I hit it with the first shot, additional shots served no purpose other than ventilating the scenery.

In studying human nature for a year or two, I've come to another conclusion too; if all big game hunters, particularly those of little to no experience were restricted to the use of single shot rifles, I'm betting they would enjoy much greater success in the game fields and would leave less wounded game rotting in the woods. Far too many hunters draw a bead on an animal with one thought in mind—if the first shot doesn't do the job those that follow surely will. Baloney! My dad started me out at a ripe young age with a single barrel shotgun and a single shot 22 rimfire. Later, I horsetraded for my first deer rifle, a trapdoor Springfield carbine in 45-70. With this modest battery of single-shooters I could hold my own when after game, not only with friends of my age who shot fast-shooters but with most grown-ups as well. I made the first shot count for two good reasons; I had no choice and ammunition was hard to come by for a farm lad. Those old guns taught me a valuable lesson, one I'd like to see taught to youngsters today.

Something else I like about single shot rifles is their thinness through the receiver at the balance point. Take my TCR '83; its receiver is only slightly thicker than that of the Winchester Model 94, one of the best carrying rifles ever built. And, since big game rifles are carried much more than they are shot, I like this in a rifle. The single shot is also made to order for hunting from horseback because it can be carried in a saddle scabbard in any position without gouging the horse in the ribs with various projections and protuberances.

Back any student of the lead-slinging school into a corner and confront him with what I've already said in defense of single shots and he'll likely turn pale around the gills and spout these final words with quivering voice:

4. Single Shots Ain't Dependable

Wow, I wonder how those chaps who cleared the plains of bison would have reacted to such a statement. Same goes for the professional hunters who bumped off various and sundry African game back before the turn of the century. According to this old wive's tale, single shot actions lack the camming power to chamber dirty ammunition or to extract less than squeaky clean cases. Come now, guys, you can do better than that. Admittedly, single shot actions aren't tops in camming power, but who loads dirty ammunition into sporting rifles? I certainly don't and if you do then your problem is a topic discussed in journals about subjects other than guns and has nothing to do with what we're talking about here.

Another factor I chose to overlook when I was enamored of single shots was accuracy. A good single shot is an accurate rifle, but not nearly so as a good bolt gun. As evidence I offer that, gun for gun, Ruger bolt action Model 77 rifles are more accurate than Ruger No. 1 single shot rifles, a fact even the good folks at Ruger would hesitate to dispute. If you need further convincing, look at the accuracy requirement of benchrest guns. Not many single shots, other than bolt actions, show up at the range.

One-piece stocks are simply easier to hang on a barrelled action and have the resulting combination prove extremely accurate. Also, most shooters will find that a bolt gun often balances better and hence makes the easier offhand shooting. I count myself among those riflemen who find the Remington 700 Classic bolt action rifle the easiest production gun with which to hit. I have yet to shoot a single shot of hunting configuration and weight (8¾ pounds or less) that was an easy rifle with which to hit. And if you are prone to shoot running game, the short, stubby length (when barrels are of equal measurement) of a single shot is no asset.

What, then, are the advantages of a single shot rifle? Ease of loading? No way. Accuracy? Less than a good bolt gun. Beauty? Not unless you prefer two-piece stocks. Ease of scope mounting? Not on your life! The thrill of one well-placed shot being the total summation of your hunt? Perhaps, but you can make one well-placed shot even with a semi-automatic. Handling and balance for easy shooting? No sir!

On the other hand, a good turn-bolt rifle offers easy loading, maximum accuracy, beauty, easy scope mounting and the thrill of one well-placed shot. And they are usually easier to shoot. Additionally, if you run into an insufficiently sized cartridge or a bullet seated to an overly long length, there's a good chance you'll be able to jam it up into the chamber and get the action closed with a bolt gun; not so with a single shot. And on those occasions when, despite everything seeming right, the first shot fails to get the job done, a bolt gun can bring in swift end. And that, to me at least, is really what sportsmanship is all about; one well-placed shot backed up by still another because, sometimes, our human shortcomings do get the best of us.

Lest you think I speak from lack of experience, I still own several single shots that I use somewhat frequently. However, their use is relegated to shooting, not hunting. My respect for my quarry and my understanding of my shortcomings has led me to state proudly that I won't hunt with a single shot. Any game animal deserves a noble and quick death. Repeaters only, please! ●

Show me a good, modern single shot rifle, like the TCR '83, Ruger Number One and Browning Model 78 and I'll show you a dependable rifle, assuming it's fed equally good ammunition. I know this to be true because I've fired literally thousands of rounds through single shot rifles with no complaint about their dependability.

Now let's look at some other good things about single shot rifles.

First of all, pound for pound and inch for inch, a single shot is more powerful than, say, the typical bolt action rifle. How can this be? It's quite simple, my dear Cedric. A Ruger Number 1B in 7mm Remington Magnum, for example, weighs only a few ounces more than a Model 77 in the same caliber; however, the comparison stops right here. The short single shot action allows the use of a 26-inch barrel for an over-all length two inches less than the bolt action with a 24-inch barrel. All else being equal the more compact 1B will produce 80 to 100 fps more velocity than its shorter-barreled cousin.

Looking at another comparison, my Ruger 1A in 30-06 measures 38½ inches with its 22-inch barrel, or, 3½ inches shorter than a Model 77 with like barrel length in the same caliber. In fact, my 1A in 30-06 is the same length over-all as my Model 77 International in 308 and that cutie has an 18½-inch barrel. Have I made my point?

Even though I'm obviously most fond of single shot rifles, my practical side forces me to remove this type rifle from consideration for hunting dangerous game at close quarters. Here is where greater firepower is needed simply because of the need for stopping power. If a lungshot whitetail or elk covers 40 or 50 yards before expiring, it's no big deal, but there's a whole new deal when game such as the Big Five over in Africa are on the menu. For this slice of the big game hunting pie, a good bolt action has it over the single shot, although it is a tiny piece at that.

And now I rest my defense of single shot rifles. But, before I go I must make one final clarification lest you misunderstand my drift. The use of single shot rifles for hunting big game really doesn't need defending among those who have actually tried it, only among arm chair theorists. And another thing: I like all types of sporting rifles and should we ever meet in the game fields I'm liable to be toting most anything—bolt action, lever action, slide action or even an autoloader. Yep, I like them all.

But I'd just as soon be hunting with a single shot. ●

EDITOR'S NOTE

If there were no disagreements, there'd be little need for discussions, and we could all march into the sunset holding hands. However, that is not the way it works.

These two gentlemen hold contrary views. Theirs are not the only views on properly arming oneself for the hunt. Indeed, on most things they agree—both use high-velocity cartridges and telescopic sights, for instance.

You'll have to make up your own mind, but I'll tell you something else these two share: You could start now and work very hard at it and you are unlikely in the time left to you in this life to pull the trigger on as many live rounds as either one has fired.

As for which is right—well, neither one even mentions the double rifle, for one thing; for another, I usually hunt with whatever adequate rifle I can get if I can find a few cartridges to fit it.

K.W.

GUNS WE NEVER

PETZAL . . . a 222, a 270 and a 378 to cry over

BARRETT . . . a Zoli 28-ga. Extra Lusso

DEEP IN THE dark recesses of every shooter's mind dwells a secret and terrible sorrow, a nightmare memory worse than a Gene Hill dying-dog story. What is this chimera? It is the recollection of the guns you should never ever have let go. Every shooter has, in a blinding burst of idiocy, sold or traded a gun he would give anything to have back.

Since misery loves company, I thought it might be worth talking to some shooters and gun fanciers of note and see what haunted their dreams. Some of these conversations were short. It is no fun to see a grown man cry. I'll try to ease into it with my own story:

DAVID PETZAL, Executive Editor, *Field & Stream*:

There are three cases that cause me profound mental anguish:

The first is a Ruger Number One 222 I bought in 1970. It had a short (22-inch) barrel and the full forearm. The serial number was very low—in the 800s, I think. In addition to being extremely rare, it shot beautifully. A better walking-around varmint rifle you couldn't find. I sold it to Abercrombie & Fitch after a couple of years for something like $200.

The second was a 270, a left-hand Remington 700 barreled action Russell Carpenter stocked in English walnut. When we first saw the blank, it looked like a good, but unspectacular hunk of wood. But when the carving began, it turned gorgeous. What emerged was a light, dead-reliable rifle that shot a screaming-hot Nosler handload into an inch.

In 1978, possessed by devils, I sold the gun to Ed Zern. A month later, I begged him to sell it back, and made such a disgusting scene that he did. But in 1981, I sold it on consignment through a local dealer, and now it is

WOOTTERS . . . please send Model 88 No. 5303, a 308

CARMICHEL . . . all of them, without exception

SHOULD HAVE SOLD

by DAVID PETZAL

NELSON . . . a plain but beloved Winchester 24

HAGEL . . . a Krag from Keith

gone. That rifle accompanied me from Vermont to Montana to Texas, and I pray to be reunited with it in a better world than this.

The third is a Weatherby 378 that was re-done by Griffin & Howe in 1971. It was stocked in the darkest, heaviest piece of French walnut I've ever seen. The barrel was cut to 24 inches, and the rifle wore a G&H ramp front sight, a Lyman 48 rear, and a G&H side mount. Not only was it handsome, but it could actually cut cloverleafs at 100 yards.

I sold it because it scared the hell out of me. If I had it today I'd rebarrel it in 416 Rigby and have a buffalo gun *par excellence*.

JOHN WOOTTERS, Shooting Editor, *Hunting Magazine*:

"Where do I start? O.K., I'll give you two:

"The one I took the worst licking on was a mint DWM Artillery Model Luger, complete with all matching serial numbers, the original holster, and all the tools. The Luger was literally unfired; it still had the factory cosmoline caked on the corners, and there was no casehead mark on the bolt face. I bought it for about $45 and sold it for $90. But that one doesn't hurt; if I had kept it I would have shot it and ruined its collector's value.

"The one that hurts is a Winchester Model 88 lever-action 308. I traded it more than 20 years ago and I still remember the serial number—5303. I ordered it in Korea when I was stationed there in 1955, the year the gun came out. Saw it advertised in the *American Rifleman*. Believe me when I tell you that the thought of that rifle pulled me through my hitch.

"It was the first rifle I ever bought with my own money. I installed a Stith 4× Bear Cub scope on it—the old one with the 26mm tube. Then I

BRISTER . . . not one, but two Merkels

WARNER . . . an old '97 and a Savage 32

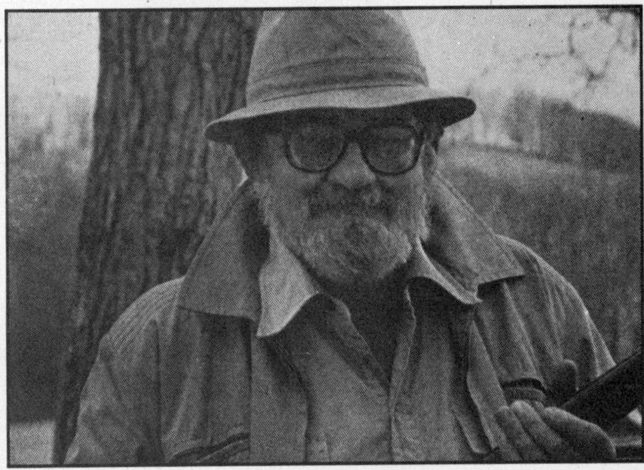

tinkered with the bedding and the stock, and that gun would *shoot*. It was so effective as a deer rifle that my friends nicknamed it 'Jumper.' They said I could prop it up against a fence and go to sleep, and if a deer came by the gun would just jump up and get the buck by itself.

"I shot the hell out of it—about 6,500 rounds, not counting factory ammo. Finally, its groups widened from 1½ to 3 inches, and I saw that the throat was starting to go.

"About that time I was getting set to go on my first elk hunt, and decided I needed a 7mm Remington Magnum. I found one—a banged-up 700 ADL—and traded the pirate of a gun store owner the Model 88 for it. The 700 was a good gun, but after a while I started to miss that 308.

"By that time, the quality of the Model 88 had gone way down. I haunted gun shows looking for another, a used one, but they were all in 243 or 284. Finally, I bought an early 88 in 243, and I'm going to have it rebarreled to 308.

"I just had an emotional involvement with that gun. It was the most effective rifle I've ever owned. Every animal I pointed it at went down. I've mentioned the serial number several times in my articles, hoping that whoever owns it now would sell it back. Believe me, I'll buy it."

PETER BARRETT, Fishing Editor, *Field & Stream*:

"It was a trade. I swapped three guns. Two were Beretta S03-EL over-unders in 12 gauge. That was the next-to-top-of-the-line model years ago. Both were sidelocks. But the third—the one that really hurts—was a Zoli Extra Lusso 28-gauge side-by-side that I got at Abercrombie & Fitch. I went in there to buy a sling swivel and they had just gotten a shipment of Zolis in. This one had the best wood in the bunch. God, it was a pretty gun.

"I swapped all three—would you mind if I wiped this tear away—for a Holland & Holland Badminton Model 12-gauge with 2-inch chambers. It's a nice gun; weighs only 5½ pounds. But I think about that Zoli all the time. I should have my butt kicked from here to Yonkers every day of the year."

JIM CARMICHEL, Shooting Editor, *Outdoor Life*:

"Guns I sold? You got all afternoon? There must be fifty like that, but I'll tell you about two:

"The first was a Paul Jaeger-built bolt-action 243 varmint rifle with a Bausch & Lomb Balvar 6×24 variable scope. I got that gun in the early '50s very cheap for some reason, and I sold it very cheap in college 'cause I was broke! If I had it today it would be worth a lot of money.

"The other one that hurts a lot was an Artillery Model Luger, the long-barreled one. It was browned, not blued, and had checkered ivory grips and an ivory fore-end. On either side of the grips were two black swastikas on a red background. I got the Luger in the late '50s and paid $15 for it. And I'm pleased to say that when I sold it, I doubled my investment.

"I'm not kidding when I say that I've done fifty deals like that. And you know what? Now I don't sell any guns for any reasons."

BOB HAGEL, Shooting Editor, *The Rifle*:

"Only one gun, an Infantry Krag with a 30-inch barrel. Elmer Keith got it for me through the N.R.A. back in 1931. I had that Krag for 15 years and shot a ton of game with it: black bear, mountain goats, elk, antelope, mule deer—everything.

"When I got into restocking, I put a piece of Circassian walnut on it, but kept the long barrel intact. For most of its life I used the issue iron sights, but later on mounted a 330 Weaver scope.

"My nephew wanted it, so I finally gave it to him, and he sold it. I don't suppose I'd use it now, but I'd like to have it back for the sentimental value."

BOB BRISTER, Shooting Editor, *Field & Stream*:

"When I started shooting pigeons seriously, I got hold of a pre-war Merkel 303E sidelock with double triggers. It was the best gun I'd ever used for thrown birds; you could just get on them with no effort at all. At one point, I had a run of 78 birds without a miss, and I think that may be a record.

"A friend of mine said that if I was that good with two triggers I'd be a lot better with a single trigger, and when I got married, he gave me a check made out to Al Miller (of the Miller Trigger Co.) as a wedding present. So, naturally, I sent the gun to Miller.

"He put in a single trigger and sent it back to me Air Express. But the Merkel never arrived. We tried to trace it, but no luck.

"It broke my heart, and I looked for another Merkel. I found a pre-war 203E, and I could really shoot that gun, too. To give you an example, at that time, no one had ever won three thrown-bird championships. I won two, and tied for first in the third. I got to be a real hot shooter on the circuit, and was approached by Garcia, who was then importing Beretta shotguns.

"They built me a beautiful set of SO-5 sidelocks, and I figured what the hell, I didn't need the Merkel anymore, so I sold it to a fellow in Florida. Naturally, I couldn't shoot the Berettas as well. I tried to buy the Merkel back, but no dice.

"Ten years later, I was at a shoot and met a pal of mine from Florida. He said, 'I've got something here that might interest you.' It was the 203E. The guy who I'd sold it to was getting divorced and needed the money. The price was twice what I'd sold it for. I bought it so damn quick . . ."

NORM NELSON, free-lance writer and photographer:

"It's hell to be poor. You're led to do some terrible things, like selling or trading off guns. The vulture beaks of later remorse tearing at your liver will be all the sharper when you find those regretted golden oldies almost non-existent on the secondhand market, and also high-priced.

"In my impecunious college days under the GI bill, I unloaded a fine-condition Winchester 24 double 12 gauge. This was a well-made, nice-handling, modestly-priced double and the first smoothbore I ever shot confidently well with. For more duckhunting firepower, I sold the 24 to buy a pump gun. Should have kept the 24 and gotten the pump, too, benefitting from the sacrifice of beer, cigarettes, and some totally unreliable co-eds in the process. Ah, the sins of our youth."

KEN WARNER, Editor-in-Chief, GUN DIGEST:

"There are two guns that would mean a lot to me if I could retrieve them from the past. One is a shotgun, the other a pistol.

"The shotgun was my first shotgun purchased from Marshall Field & Co. in the mid-'40s for $35. It was a military guard gun, a Model 97 Winchester. The salesman was very likely John T. Amber; certainly, the gunsmith who forthwith added a Cutts Compensator was John L. Smith, my Scoutmaster and Marshall Field's gunsmith.

"I fell into bad company years later at a gun show and traded my first pheasant-buster and cottontail gun and pride and joy off on an Ithaca double barrel that proved to have blued Damascus barrels. I learned a lot about guns and life that day, but it didn't sour me much.

"The handgun was my Dad's, and it went to war with a fighter pilot cousin and never came back. One day I'll own my own Savage 32 Auto, hopefully one some fellow brought back from the ETO." ●

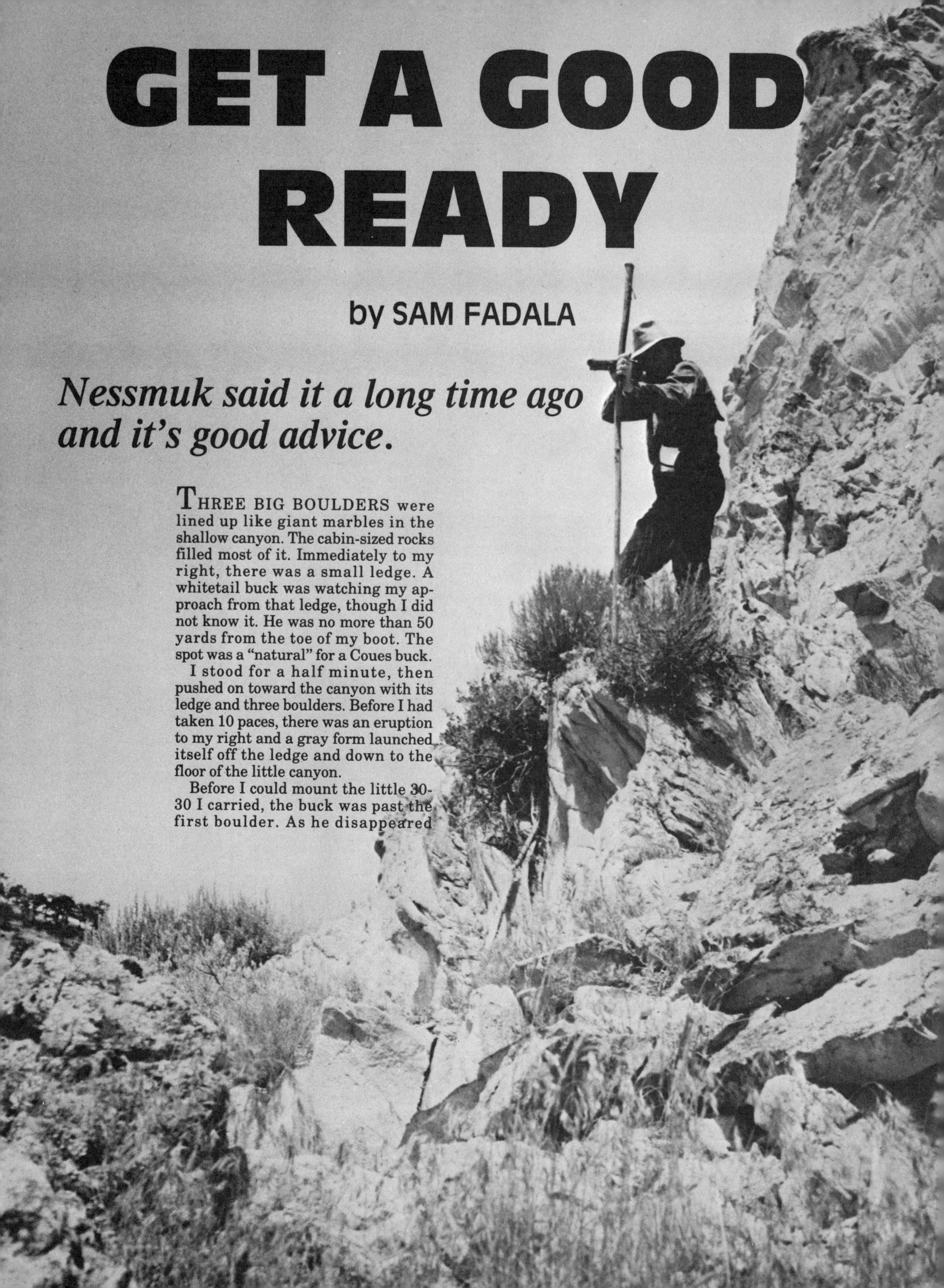

GET A GOOD READY

by SAM FADALA

Nessmuk said it a long time ago and it's good advice.

THREE BIG BOULDERS were lined up like giant marbles in the shallow canyon. The cabin-sized rocks filled most of it. Immediately to my right, there was a small ledge. A whitetail buck was watching my approach from that ledge, though I did not know it. He was no more than 50 yards from the toe of my boot. The spot was a "natural" for a Coues buck.

I stood for a half minute, then pushed on toward the canyon with its ledge and three boulders. Before I had taken 10 paces, there was an eruption to my right and a gray form launched itself off the ledge and down to the floor of the little canyon.

Before I could mount the little 30-30 I carried, the buck was past the first boulder. As he disappeared

Author works through the bottom of a draw, which is poor field position. Traveling along this route means that the hunter and the game will be on the same level, not making a "good ready."

This buck was taken through getting a good ready, for the deer was located through binoculars at a great distance and then stalked to only five yards. The stalk was so long and intense author had to gain full control over his breathing before he jumped the buck for a shot. (Nancy Fadala photo)

around the second boulder, the carbine was at my shoulder. Between the second and third boulder, there was a good 20 yards of open space. I had my shot. At the crack of the 30-30, the buck toppled. But he wasn't hit, not directly. Instantly back on his feet, he vanished as only the Coues can do, disappearing in brush and broken country that seemed inadequate to hide a small dog.

For a second, I was puzzled. My mind, as they say, spaced out the event. I did not know how I had missed a 40-yard shot. In a few seconds, however, the scene came back to me as if a movie projector were playing in my head. My bullet had struck the deer's antler, breaking a tine. I walked to the three boulders. Bits of antler were scattered in the clean sand. I had missed a very good buck and a very easy shot, one seldom offered in quite that way, for an important reason, one which plagues countless hunters every season, and which can be overcome: I had failed to get a "good ready."

Getting a good ready—the term is associated with Nessmuk. Nessmuk was George W. Sears, a grand old hunter and backwoodsman and writer of the 19th century. Although he lived into the era of the metallic cartridge and the repeating firearm, he stayed with a fine muzzleloader for his personal deer rifle a long time.

"My rifle was a neat, hair-triggered Billinghurst," said Nessmuk, "carrying sixty round balls to the pound [about 42 caliber], a muzzle-loader, of course, and a nail-driver."

Nessmuk prided himself on getting a good ready, on firing but once and having a prime buck to show for it. On one long excursion into the woods, he ". . . made just three shots in ten days, and each stood for a plump young deer in the 'short blue';" (from *Woodcraft*).

Nessmuk knew what all shooters must know—in order to be a deadly game shot, an outdoorsman must get a good ready.

There are many aspects to getting set. And all of these aspects fit together like a jigsaw puzzle. Leave a part out and the picture is incomplete. Perhaps the most basic of all of these little pieces is hunter position, both his pose and his location in the landscape. I missed that Coues buck because I failed in the first. I was not balanced to shoot. I stopped in my tracks, upped the rifle and fired, paying no regard to my personal stance. That's a sure way to miss game. I have seen hunters snap rifle or shotgun to the shoulder and fire with their bodies twisted like pretzels. They fear that if they don't fire instantly an opportunity will be gone forever.

Firing out of position is little better than having no shot at all. In a split second, a man can get a good ready with his body, maneuvering for a steady shot. Even a hunter in midstride with right leg forward might try it.

I defy anyone to shoot accurately without both feet planted firmly on the ground. Taking a shot with the right leg extended, for a right-handed shooter, or left leg outward for a left-handed shooter, may be tougher.

But hunters do shoot at game that way, and sometimes they don't even know it. Getting a good ready means taking that split second to insure that both feet are planted firmly, spread apart a bit, with the body angled maybe 45° off to the right of the intended target for a right-handed shooter. This is for riflemen. Shotgunners can afford to point their toes more toward the target, provided they bend their knees. Are there exceptions? Of course there are. My wife faces her rifle targets somewhat squarely and hits the mark. On the whole, however, better balance and proper body angle mean a great deal to a game shot.

Offhand shooting is much improved in steadiness by using the walking staff as in a rifle rest. Even though the staff is in use, all other tenets of good shooting position are observed. At right, the unsupported offhand shot should be taken with feet and face planted, the body in balance.

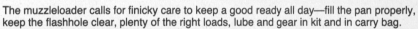

The sling can help an offhand shot, above, but there is simply nothing to beat a convenient rock benchrest as at right.

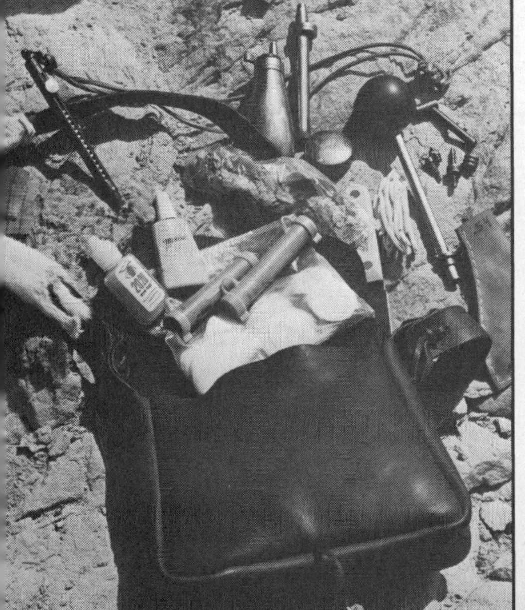

The muzzleloader calls for finicky care to keep a good ready all day—fill the pan properly, keep the flashhole clear, plenty of the right loads, lube and gear in kit and in carry bag.

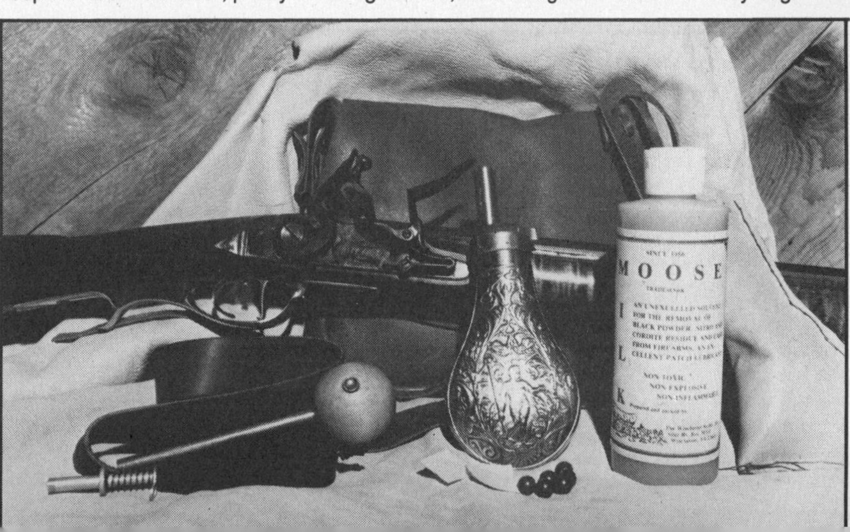

The larger sense of position involves the hunter's location as part of the environment. This is field position. Hunters should be consciously aware of how they fit into the terrain because how they move through the countryside can determine the shot they set. Often, I have crossed in the wrong place, taken the lower ground when a small rise would have given me superb vision of the cover I was approaching. And how many times does a hunter weave his way through a tangle instead of maintaining his field position so that he can see into the tangle by using the highest possible ground? Field position may include hunters in tandem, too. Instead of two men busting through a thicket, one might skirt it to stay in better position should they flush game. Getting a good ready in field position means staying highly aware of the lay of the land.

There is also a mental attitude to consider: "I wasn't ready!"

I have said those words before. So have you. Why weren't we ready when that buck jumped or the bird flushed? What we are really saying is that we were not mentally prepared for the event. Staying alert is sometimes difficult. The woods are beautiful, dark and deep (to steal from Frost) and the serenity of the scene lulls us into an overly relaxed state of mind.

I was hunting in Mexico one year, simply dropped off on a very remote ranch for 10 days. The first three days I literally found no game large or small. I was on the wrong side of the river. By the time I got into game, I found myself almost complacent about it. I was not sharp. I was not ready.

The good hunter is thinking all of the time, not only about sign, but about what he will do if a chance presents itself. Often, I project a scenario in my mind as I work country, planning visually what I will do if an opportunity suddenly arises in front of me. Does such an on-your-toes hunting style take away from the enjoyment of the sport? Concentration does not have to be tense; *relaxed* concentration is the goal of the hunter. The mind is cleared; it is prepared.

And the same is true at the end of the stalk. Very often, my group finds its game at a distance because we believe intensely in using optical aids, where possible, to locate feeding or bedded game. This allows for a careful stalk, when the game is sighted before it sees the hunter. But I have seen shots badly blown because the hunter did not have a good ready. He gets up

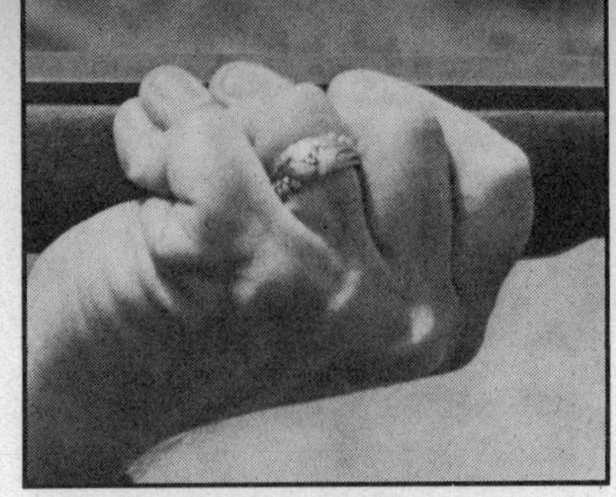

Above all, don't develop the white-knuckle grip. This death-grip is exciting, but not part of a good ready.

on the game and suddenly it is time to shoot. He has been unnerved by the excitement of the stalk and he misses the shot.

Getting a good ready is also a matter of calculating the range, and knowing the size of the game. I think most hunters grossly overestimate the height of deer. Even very large bucks are not nearly as tall as we think they are.

Range estimation is so important to shooting that one serious hunter I know has marked off, in his mind, the ranges between landmarks in his favorite open western deer country. From a given ridge, he can tell you how far a particular landmark is. He calculated all of these ranges in the off-season using a rangefinder. Often, in this expansive terrain, he takes a buck cleanly at long range because he has a good ready on range.

Earlier, we spoke of fast-moving game. Where there is a chance to take a rest before firing we have one of the best ways in the world to get a good ready. There are many natural rests in the field—tree limbs, downed timber, rocks. A hat or hand under the rifle's forearm is a good idea. I also carry a walking staff and have used it as a rest many times. I don't fire from the standing position at standing game. I will sit down take a rest or even sometimes shoot prone. If a rest is appropriate, the hunter who fails to use one is handicapping himself.

There is a great deal of emotion in hunting, and when that long-awaited shot is suddenly there, a special self-control must take over. It is possible to be excited and under control at the same time, I think, up to a point. I force myself to take a deep breath, let half of it out, and maintain a true sight picture. When I fail to do this, I don't have a good ready and I can miss.

A hunter should ask himself after a miss, "Why didn't I hit the mark?"

Often, the reason will be this lapse of emotional control, and a consequent failure to take and *hold* a sight picture. At the instant the rifle goes off, the sight picture must be planted firmly upon the target as if pasted there. Iron sights make the task a little more difficult, since it is harder to pick out just one particular spot, but it can be done.

Getting a good ready at the shot means maintaining control over emotions and consciously aiming at the game instead of throwing a shot at it. Hold a precise sight picture, take that breath, relax, and squeeze the trigger. I have enjoyed starting several friends and family members in the hunting field and I always teach them to remain under control until after they shoot.

"It's only a target," I say, "just a tin can, a paper bull's eye. Hold for one specific hair behind the shoulder and squeeze the trigger; don't jerk it."

Handling the gun or gear also affects the ready. On stand, we should get ready before the buck we hear coming breaks cover. When we swing the gun up just in time to turn the buck back before we can get a shot off, that's bad.

Gear has to be ready. I have taken more game with a muzzleloader than with a modern arm over the past decade. I know positively that when a rifle is not truly prepared, checked out, sighted in, a miss is in the making. Before I learned how to load a flintlock properly, I had misfires. I have few to no misfires in the field now. I have a hunch all our gear is that way. How do you get a good ready when your hunting clothes are all wrong? All gear has to fit us.

When thinking about Nessmuk's good ready, a hunter has to dwell on raw basics, and that is difficult. We sometimes are so involved in the more advanced aspects of the hunt—figuring our ballistic trajectories, trying to find that hot deer spot—we tend to forget the little things that actually account for bagged game. Success in hunting is the same as success in any other endeavor: It is never enough to perfect only one phase. Great shots who can't find game are not successful hunters; great hunters who can't bag game after they find it have only "track soup" to eat.

Therefore Nessmuk is my model. He would abide only an accurate rifle. He studied the ways of the game, and he learned how to locate his quarry. He practiced his shooting skill, honing his ability to a razor edge, but he never forgot the basics. When his opportunities came, he made the most of them. He got a good ready. So should we all. ●

A Challenge This Size Calls For
Remington Country
Model 700 short action BDL

The Strength Of Remington.

North American big game can present some of the world's most challenging hunting. That's where the strength of our experience and equipment can really complement yours.

Our Model 700 bolt action rifle has become legendary. As experienced big game hunters, bench rest and silhouette champions can attest, it's regarded as the strongest, most accurate out-of-the-box bolt action rifle you can buy.

The bolt face, barrel, and milled receiver surround the cartridge head with three rings of solid steel, providing an integrated system that only Remington can give you. No extractor cut weakens the bolt, as in most other rifles.

From the least costly ADL to top-of-the-line BDLs and "Custom" models, the 700 has one of the crispest triggers of any centerfire on the market. It comes with today's longest list of calibers, including the popular 7mm Mag. and the traditional 270 and 30-06. Also the widest choice of styles, including the traditional "Classic" and several left-hand versions.

For smaller-framed shooters and anyone spending extended time in the field, Remington developed the first compact bolt action rifle, designed from the ground up. We call it the Model Seven and it weighs only 6¼ pounds.

But there's more to the Remington legacy out there than guns alone. Our "Core-Lokt" ammunition delivers the consistent velocities, energies and flat trajectories needed for extended range performance.

Remington
Core-Lokt

Wherever you are, whatever you hunt, you'll find no one offers you more ideal combinations of accuracy and strength. So next time you saddle up in high country, feeling good about your equipment and about yourself... remember, you're in Remington Country.

Call 1-800-THE-GUNS for your nearest Remington ProLine™ dealer. And pick up your free catalog of the world's largest line of sporting arms and ammunition.

Model 700 "Classic" Model Seven

Remington. DUPONT

Remembering Clyde . . . .

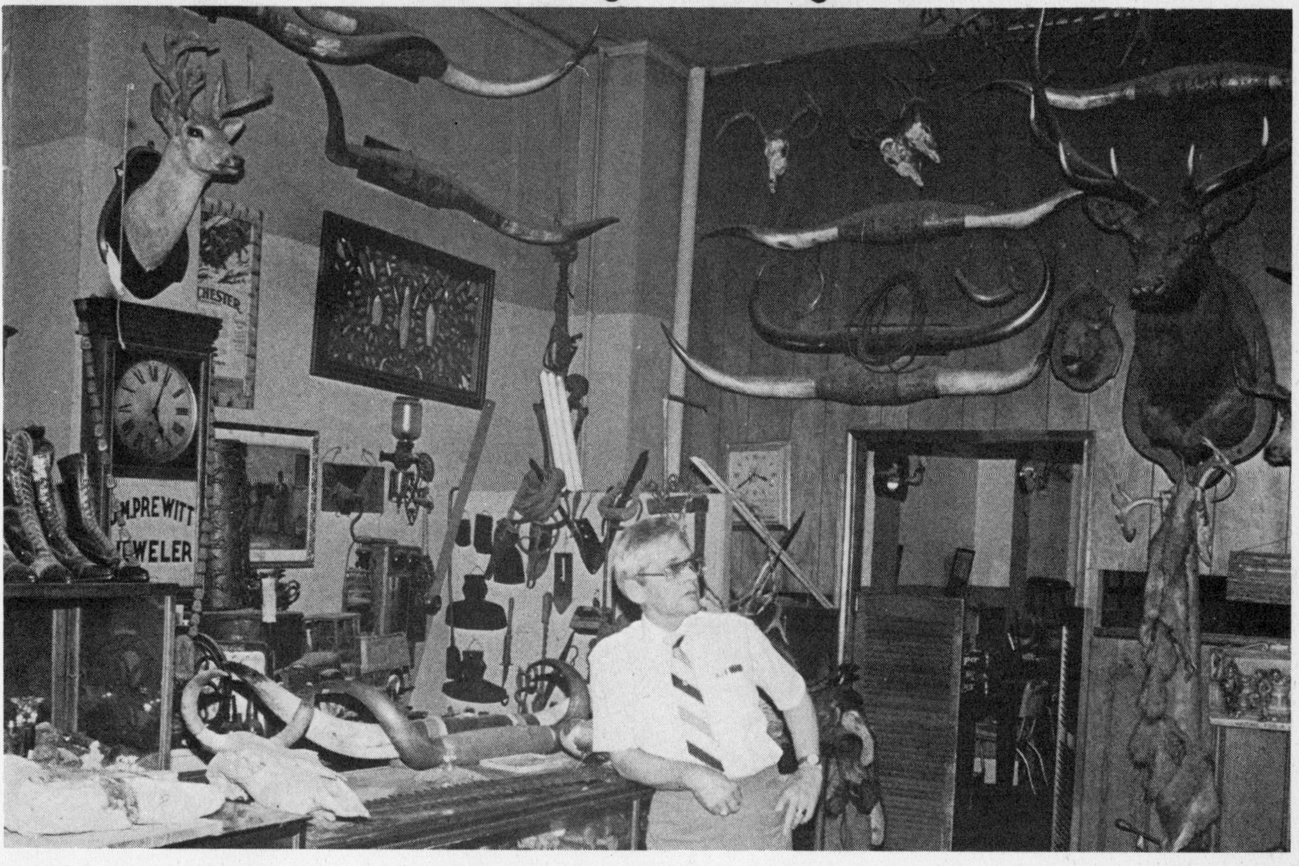

by DICK EADES

Rooms like this hold special fascination for writer Eades. They remind him of Clyde, whose place was even better.

THERE MUST BE a special place for guys like Clyde O'Neal. He wouldn't be happy in a conventional heaven. He's been gone for a lot of years now and should have it reorganized to suit himself. His special place is probably a trifle cluttered and smells faintly of Hoppes #9. Unless he's changed, there's most of a Colt Single Action Army on a table and scraps of rifle stocks in the corner.

You see, Clyde was the first gun fancier I ever met who had any real knowledge of firearms. He infected me with the gun bug when I was too young to know any better. Almost before I knew it, I was hooked on the sight and touch of blued steel, oiled walnut and polished brass.

Maybe I should start at the beginning: just about the middle of the knickers age (if you don't know what knickers are, ask your old man) my family migrated to Waco, Texas. Our first house there had a basement and since I had never seen a basement, I was fascinated. I quickly installed my livestock, including a crippled fox, one chicken snake in good condition, and a few mice. The latter, of course, were groceries for the snake.

One corner of my retreat was unfloored, and the earth exposed for a couple of square yards. I believed any exposed dirt was bound to be for digging, and had made it down about a foot when I struck something solid. The dirt flew fast until I uncovered a battered metal box just under a foot long and about six inches wide and deep. It opened easily and revealed a pair of brass-sheathed, bone-gripped daggers with wickedly curved blades. They were rather crudely made but bore markings in what I told my father "must be Chinese."

As soon as I announced my discovery, the daggers were confiscated by my parents until the actual owner could be located. The next two weeks took two lifetimes as I sweated out the search. At last, no one had claimed the daggers and they were returned with the warning I'd better not be carving on anything with them.

Scrubbing the brass sheaths until they shone was not much amusement, but I was certain that my daggers were worth a fortune and wanted them to look their best before I sold them for enough money to buy everything I'd ever imagined. Once they were buffed to their best, I set out to find someone who might possess enough money to purchase them from me.

After several false starts, I was directed to Clyde O'Neal's, the town's only antique shop. Most folks doubted he would ever amount to much since he spent money so foolishly. Why, just the week before, he had paid ten dollars for an old brass-framed Winchester that used some sort of odd ammunition that wasn't even made anymore. The local sharpie who sold him that 66 was passing the word that he had located a fool with money. Obviously, O'Neal was the man I was looking for.

O'Neal's store was another world, one populated by cigar store Indians, chunks of medieval armor, a clothing store dummy swathed in a rusty suit of chain mail and, as a centerpiece to the whole hodgepodge, the entire bowsprit from a small ship, carved elaborately to represent a bosomy female wearing little but a smile. I was so impressed I stood and stared for several moments after the owner asked what I wanted. He wasn't accustomed to customers who barely came up to his belt buckle in need of a bit of soap and water. Nevertheless, his greeting was cordial and there was only a hint of sarcasm when he asked what he could show me.

Recovering enough to extend my cherished metal box, I muttered something about hearing that he might be a buyer for some high-priced antiques.

Soberly accepting the box, Clyde formally introduced himself and extended his hand. Until then, most grownups had always smiled and patted me on the head. Being treated to a handshake made me feel I had really arrived. At that moment, Clyde won himself a warm spot in one youngster's heart, for whatever good it might do him.

My prized box was opened gently and the daggers withdrawn for his inspection. I was impressed by his hands during his investigation. He handled those battered pieces of brass and steel as if they were made of the most delicate porcelain. Within a few minutes, he had satisfied himself that they were indeed old and not something turned out by the corner blacksmith. His next few questions were to establish the fact that they were my property and not something that had been purloined from the family closets.

He then asked what I wanted for them. The question blocked my thought processes for several moments. For weeks I had daydreamed of the fantastic price the daggers would bring and of all the things I would buy, but not once had I actually tried to formulate an idea of exactly how much money I expected for them. Several seconds must have elapsed before my brain got the message to my jaws and vocal cords but I finally managed to stutter, "Wadlya give?"

This evoked a chuckle that seemed to start somewhere around his boot tops and then bubbled unevenly from his lips. Clyde murmured, "Wow! The horsetrader shows early in these kids."

That comment meant little to me at the time, and it was several years before I really understood what he was saying. At any rate, Clyde told me he would pay $3.00 for the pair of daggers in cash or would allow me $4.00 in trade on any item in his store.

My dreams had come true. Three whole cash American dollars to do with as I pleased! Until then, the greatest amount of uncommitted cash I had ever possessed at one time was 50¢.

Extending my grimy hand, I grunted, "Gimme the cash."

I knew a store just down the street that sold 22 Shorts for 14¢ per box. Three dollars worth of 14¢ 22 shells was beyond my mathematical comprehension but I knew it was plenty. For once in my life, I was going to have *all* the 22 ammo I wanted.

I must have told Clyde what I proposed to do with my riches because he next was asking about my 22 rifle and what I knew about other types of guns.

I had never touched any other gun, but I wasn't about to admit I knew almost nothing about guns. After all, I knew how to slip a cartridge into the ramp of my single shot bolt action and just how to hold the open sights for sure hits at 25 yards or so. When I assured him that my interest extended to all types of guns, Clyde led me to another room in his store and my chin must have clicked as it bounced off the floor.

Surely, this room was the depository for every handgun and rifle that had been made since the discovery of gunpowder. There must have been hundreds of rusted, pitted and battered revolvers, carbines, muskets, and other assorted firearms dangling from wires in the ceiling, nailed to the walls and heaped one on top of the other in every corner. In glass cases, deeply ornamented with streaked dust, were the better specimens.

As the day passed, I was introduced to Oriental matchlocks, a mid-Eastern snaphance and flintlock muskets from the American Revolution and the War of 1812. I was allowed to handle an ornate mid-European wheel-lock rifle and, then, the biggest revolver imagination could produce. (I later learned that this revolver was a very fine Colt Walker.)

Guns were the big thing in Clyde's place, the one Eades swamped out as a kid to get guns, ammo and know-how.

Pistols kept appearing as if by magic, and, with each, I was given a brief history of its design, use and unusual features. That day, I must have handled more engraved, inlaid, ivory-gripped pistols than most people see in a lifetime. My $3.00 cash was long forgotten and I knew there had to be some way to own at least a few of the fascinating guns I had fondled all day.

Clyde knew many of his guns should never be fired but he also knew shooting (and the cleaning required before and after) wouldn't harm a goodly number of them. He made me an offer: I could shoot any of his blackpowder guns if I would clean them before and after firing and get his approval as to the type of powder and ball that was to be used before leaving the store. This privilege was to extend to any gun not kept in the glass cases.

In addition to this magnificent gesture, he was willing to allow me $4.00

trade on my daggers toward a very shootable Colt Navy Revolver priced at $6.50. When I told him that there was simply no way I could ever come up with the $2.50 difference, he offered me a job. For cleaning guns and helping sort incoming purchases and other odd jobs around the store, he would pay me 50¢ each Saturday if I worked from opening time (8:00 A.M.) to closing time (6:00 P.M.)

As further evidence of his good faith, I could take the Colt with me if I was willing to make the deal.

Whatever resistance lingered in my mind disappeared like wisps of fog as the brass backstrap and smooth walnut grips settled themselves in my palm. Clyde threw in a handful of 36-caliber balls, a half box of caps and a small flask of powder. Before I left the store that evening, I was well schooled in loading of the revolver and proper handling of powder and caps. The next day was Sunday and I would have the entire afternoon to blast away with my new/old relic.

My tardy arrival at home set off a family discussion that included whether or not I should be permitted to keep the Colt and who was to supervise my experimental shooting. Whatever gods watch over the antics of small boys must have been in an unusually good humor that night. It was decided that I could not only keep the Colt but that I would be allowed to demonstrate my shooting prowess the following day. If I passed the test, I would be allowed unconditional retention of the revolver and its fodder and could, thereafter, shoot it when and as much as I liked, so long as I earned the money to pay for powder and caps. Lead, naturally, was free in unlimited supply from the local plumbing shop.

A gravel pit near our house offered a safe shooting area and was the site selected for the great shooting test. I collected most of the boys for several blocks around to show off my charcoal burner. Some of their fathers also elected to witness the event since few had ever seen a blackpowder revolver fired. During that depression era, guns were for one thing: hunting for edible game. Sport shooting for the sake of shooting was unknown in my neck of the woods.

I charged the cylinder of the Colt with meager loads of black powder, topped each chamber with a ball and a blob of water pump grease, then seated caps on the nipples with as much care as if I were fusing a quarter ton of dynamite. With both eyes closed, I touched off the first shot at a large can sitting atop a rock about 15 yards away. The wind was blowing gently in my face and when the gun belched a cloud of smoke, fire and bits of unburned powder, most of it drifted right back into my eyes. As soon as I was able to see again, I examined the gun (it was still intact), my hand (it was smoke-blackened but still held five fingers) and the can (it remained just where it had been placed).

The second shot was better than the first and removed the can from its roost. Encouraged, I emptied the cylinder at other bits of rubble scattered along the gravel backstop. Since I had survived, several others decided to try the front-loading revolver. As it passed from hand to hand, I became more expert in loading it and soon found I could fill its chambers in something less than four minutes, timed by the one witness who owned a watch. Speedy loading such as this served to do away with my entire supply of caps in a remarkably brief time.

Through the ensuing weeks, most of my after school hours (and quite a few during school) were spent in silent admiration of the old Colt, cleaning its bore to a mirror surface, dreaming about being able to shoot it again and talking guns to Clyde O'Neal at every opportunity. At the time, I was convinced that Clyde knew all that was to be known about every type of firearm in the world's history. He spoke with authority regarding hand cannons, wheel-locks, centerfire rifles and even machine guns. Memories of his teachings are clouded by time but he seemed to relish imparting even the tiniest scrap of knowledge in the gun field to me. During our long relationship, he must have been wrong in some of his statements but I was never aware of it and cannot recall a specific instance of error even now.

Few things beside love would have induced me to spend my days scrubbing rust off pitted metal, pouring vile smelling solvent into corroded springworks and hand-rubbing gallons of linseed oil into thirsty wood. Each day's work ended with me looking as if I had been greased lightly then shaken in a bag mixed with dirt, rust and sawdust and smelling like the dregs of a refinery with a touch of sperm oil thrown in. I wouldn't have traded my job for the easiest one in town. In fact, I was offered more money to answer the telephone at the corner pharmacy and without a moment's hesitation refused the offer.

My agreement to work for Clyde until the Colt was paid for stretched out to include payment for a Kentucky rifle, a trapdoor Springfield and several other guns. With the acquisition of each, I received a nutshell history lesson and additional odds and ends of firearms lore. This relationship lasted through my second year of high school and the addition to my collection of more than 20 shootable guns.

My last purchase from Clyde was made for cash. I had long admired a handsome Colt Single Action Army revolver that nestled in one of his glass cases. It was rigged out with one-piece ivory grips and showed absolutely no wear along its 7½ inch barrel. The "U. S." marking stood out clearly on the frame and every numbered part matched. He told me that the gun was apparently never issued but had been sold several years earlier to a friend of his who replaced the original grips with the ivory that so attracted me. The price of this pistol was more than any I had obtained up to that point. Including the beautiful grips, I paid $12.50 for the big 45.

Since that day I've bought, sold and traded several hundred guns. I've shot most of them, made money on many and lost on a few. I've hunted lots of game, tried most of the shooting sports and continued my love affair with guns in general. I've met a lot of men in the firearms field that I genuinely like. Several have become very close friends and business associates. When I think of these things, I remember Clyde O'Neal, the guy who took his time for a boy who had no money and no knowledge of guns and gave that time to develop in the boy that same love of fine guns he had himself.

At other times, when I sit in a freezing drizzle in a duck blind, crouch until I am stiff on a deer stand or lose my shirt in a gun trade, I also recall Clyde O'Neal. I could have taken up a peaceful hobby like stamp collecting or bird watching. When I feel that way, I remind myself I'm there because I want to be and because moments like that are the spice which makes every day life palatable.

I'm sure Clyde has his special place; Olympus, Valhalla, Nirvana or call it what you will. It's a place where coveys flush straight away and gobblers respond to the very first call. All the Colts are unfired and have 100% original blue; the Henrys sparkle with mint silver plate. He's there now, watching me and muttering to himself, "You're hooked, son, you're hooked."

May it always be so and may I also be able to inflict this same addiction on at least one more boy who might otherwise never know the love of the outdoors or the appreciation of fine workmanship in wood and metal that go into the making of a gun. He'll never regret it. I haven't. ●

Early PUMP GUNS

by JOHN MALLOY

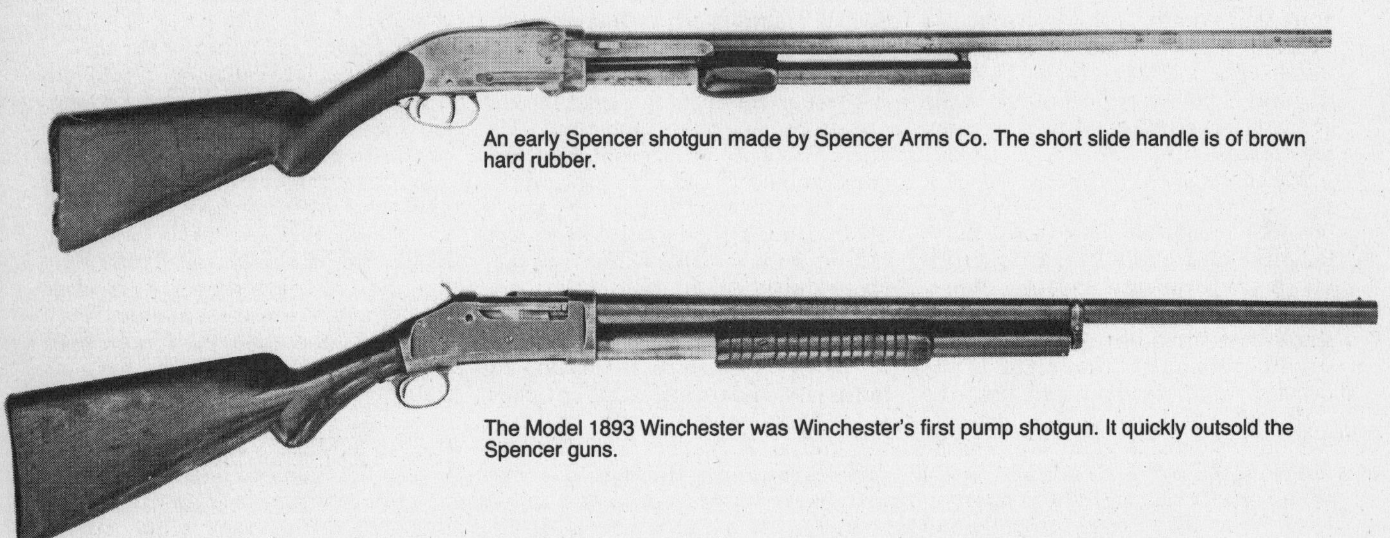

An early Spencer shotgun made by Spencer Arms Co. The short slide handle is of brown hard rubber.

The Model 1893 Winchester was Winchester's first pump shotgun. It quickly outsold the Spencer guns.

These contraptions met the double gun's challenge and beat it. And some are still shooting.

WITHOUT MUCH question, the slide action "pump gun" is the traditional American shotgun. The repeating shotgun is characteristically American, and probably more of us hunt and shoot with slide-action smoothbores than with all other types together. As tradition might demand, the first really successful repeating shotgun manufactured in this country was a slide action.

Today's pumps are dependable and strong and deserve their popularity. They are not outrageously expensive and probably cannot be equalled for value and usefulness per dollar invested. They are good looking; all have pleasing streamlined contours, which once prompted a friend to remark that on a dark morning, all pump guns look alike across the width of a duck blind. It was not always so. Early pump guns had mechanisms and shapes that were very different from the sleek guns of today.

There were earlier repeaters that reached the production stage, but they had disadvantages. The Colt revolving shotgun spewed flame at the shooter's arm forward of the cylinder, and so could not be used successfully for wingshooting. The Roper gun used special steel cartridge cases which did not seal well in its long, cumbersome action.

It took the common availability of brass-cased ammunition for the repeating shotgun to become practical, and the first gun that achieved that status was the Spencer slide action. It was the first gun to give the shooter a decided advantage over a double.

The Spencer was the development of Christopher Spencer, the young inventor and manufacturer of the famous Civil War Spencer rifles and carbines. After the War, surplus guns were available more cheaply than the new offerings of the Spencer Company. The company went brankrupt in 1869. Its assets were acquired by Winchester, and manufacture of Spencer rifles was discontinued.

After the failure of his rifle company, the 36-year-old Spencer devoted most of his time to developing and producing machine tools and parts. Only once more was a firearm bearing his name to be manufactured.

Spencer and Sylvester Roper, the designer of the short-lived Roper shotgun were friends. Spencer realized that, with the taming of the West, improved shotguns would occupy a greater proportion of the gun market. Working with Roper, he designed a new shotgun using a sliding forearm to operate the mechanism. A patent on the design was granted jointly to Spencer and Roper in 1882, and a new Spencer Arms Company was formed. Production of the new guns began, probably in late 1883 or 1884, at Windsor, CT.

The early Spencer shotguns were handsome arms. They were well made of the best materials then available.

The legend on the barrels read, "SPENCER ARMS CO, WINDSOR, CT, U.S.A. PAT. APR. 1882." Contrary to general practice, this legend was applied so as to be read from the right side of the gun. Serial numbers were stamped on the lower receiver tang, and no other marks are visible. The sliding forearm of hard rubber is short by modern standards, just three inches long.

The Spencer shotgun worked well, but its unfamiliar action did not find immediate acceptance. The company ran into financial difficulties in 1889, after making only a few thousand guns, and the mortgage was foreclosed. Spencer, then 56 years of age, never again entered into firearms manufacture. The company's assets were bought by Francis Bannerman, the well-known military goods dealer.

Bannerman moved the machinery from Windsor to Brooklyn and resumed manufacture of the Spencer guns with only a few changes. Bannerman-made guns differ in markings from the early Spencers. Barrel legend reads from the left of the gun and reads: "SPENCER RPTG. SHOT GUN PAT. APL. 1882." On the left side of the receiver, Bannerman added a two-line legend identifying himself as manufacturer and giving a model designation. Serial numbers continued to be placed on the lower tang.

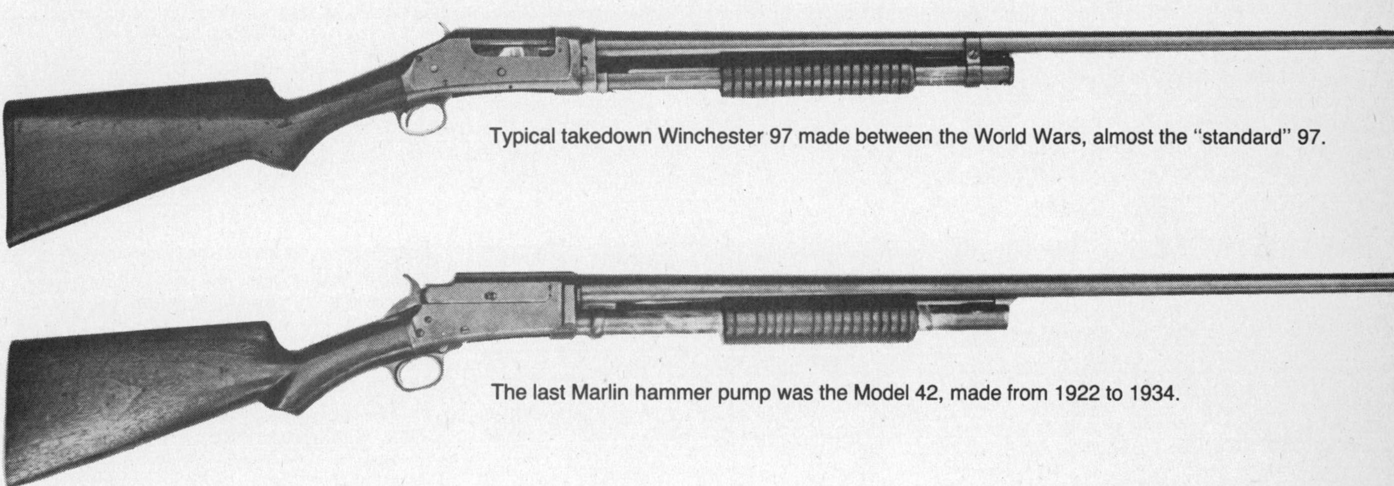

Typical takedown Winchester 97 made between the World Wars, almost the "standard" 97.

The last Marlin hammer pump was the Model 42, made from 1922 to 1934.

The Spencer mechanism was ingenious. It was the only pump shotgun manufactured that had a vertical rather than horizontal movement of the breech block. The lower portion of the breech block is bored out to hold a shotshell, pushed from the magazine into the recess by a spring-loaded magazine follower. As the sliding forearm moves back, two action bars cam the pivoted breech block down and extract the shell from the chamber.

The upper surface of the breech block is a trough onto which the fired shell is drawn. At the rearward position of the slide handle, the breech block springs upward, flipping the empty up and clear of the action. This upward motion of the block aligns the hollow holding the new shell with the chamber. Forward motion of the slide handle chambers the new round. As the slide bars continue forward, the block is cammed to its central position, locking the action closed. The central part of the block contains the firing pin, which is now aligned with the primer of the chambered round.

This action was used on no other shotgun. Still, the Spencer was a true pioneer. It introduced the tubular magazine to shotgun use. It was the first shotgun to operate the mechanism by means of a forearm sliding backward and forward on the magazine tube. The concealed hammer made its first appearance in the Spencer. It introduced loading directly into the magazine through a port in the bottom of the receiver. All these features are used on today's modern pump guns.

The Spencers were reliable guns and were moderately popular; about 20,000 were eventually made. It was the first gun to really give a shotgunner an advantage over a double, yet most shooters continued to use single or double shotguns, and many were unaware of the Spencer. It was ironic that much of the publicity about the gun came from a dramatic lawsuit that spelled the kiss of death for the Spencer and firmly placed the product of a rival company in control of the market.

The 1893 Winchester shotgun was the brainchild of a young Utah gunmaker, John M. Browning, who had supplied Winchester with most of its new models for a decade. Browning's 1890 patent for this sliding-forearm hammer gun, issued when he was 35, was assigned to Winchester; the Model 1893 was introduced in June, 1893.

Winchester's first repeating shotgun—the Browning-designed Model 1887 lever action—had been well received and sales were fairly good. Still, the lever action was not so well suited for shotgun use. Hence, Winchester had made the decision to offer another type for the growing shotgun market, and the new pump was put into production.

Browning's new design was a simple and clever one.

The Winchester 1893, somewhat like the Spencer, used a vertical movement of a major part to feed shells and lock the action, but the breechbolt moved horizontally. As the slide handle is drawn to the rear, the vertically moving part—the carrier—

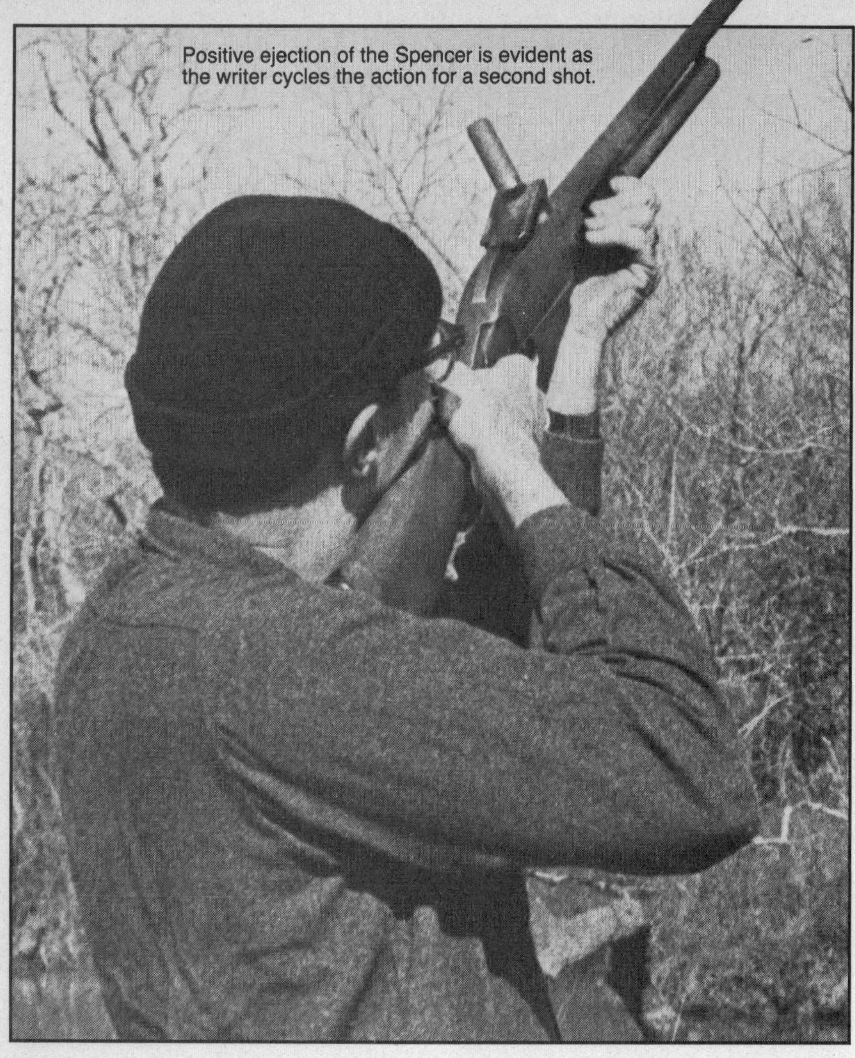

Positive ejection of the Spencer is evident as the writer cycles the action for a second shot.

moves down slightly to unlock the breechbolt, which then moves to the rear. An extractor on the bolt draws the empty case from the chamber back against a fixed stud, which deflects the case out the ejection port.

As the bolt reaches its rearward position, the carrier drops down further to allow a new shell to spring from the magazine onto the carrier's upper surface. Pushing the slide handle forward draws the bolt forward and chambers the new round. At the end of the forward stroke, the carrier rises behind the lug on the bolt, locking the action closed. It is a strong action.

Initial sales of the 1893 Winchester were fairly good. The outside hammer was familiar to most shooters and, coupled with the Winchester name and marketing system, the reception of the '93 cut into Spencer sales.

Bannerman owned, along with the other assets of the Spencer company, an 1885 Roper patent that very broadly covered any sliding-forearm firearm. He filed a suit for patent infringement against Winchester's New York agent. The suit, filed in October, 1894, gave notice that any one selling or using Winchester's slide guns would be held responsible.

Winchester immediately guaranteed its customers against any loss from the suit, continued to turn out 1893 shotguns, and prepared to defend itself in court. The best defense seemed to be to disavow infringement of Bannerman's patent by proving a similar mechanism antedated it.

With this in mind, Winchester searched patents in the U.S. and Europe. Somewhat to their surprise, they found four prior European patents covering sliding-forearm firearms; one had even been manufactured. Winchester obtained one of the manufactured guns and set about to make working models of the other three from the patent drawings. They succeeded with two.

When the patents were introduced at the trial, Bannerman's attorneys responded that they were not workable. Winchester then triumphantly produced the three functioning guns and the case was decided in Winchester's favor. Ironically, the decison was based on Bannerman's 1885 patent being antedated by the 1882 Spencer and Roper patent, which somehow was not under his control.

Winchester's grandstand play in producing the other guns was for naught, but now they were free to continued to make the Model 1983.

However, the winning of the case proved to be the end of the Model 1893. The Model 1893 was a strong and generally satisfactory gun, but its early use pointed out some problems. Hence, Winchester's decision to replace it when the case had been settled. The company had been confident as to the outcome of the trial, and had been preparing a new model—the Model 1897.

The 1893 had been a pioneer in its own right. It contributed the horizontal sliding breechblock with attached extractor to the pump shotgun. It used, as did the Spencer, an opening at the bottom of the receiver to load the tubular magazine, but permitted loading with the action closed. This feature allowed replacing shells while the gun was kept ready for action.

These characteristics, first introduced with the '93—horizontal movement of the breechbolt with an attached extractor, and loading in the closed-action position—are used in all modern pump guns today.

The 1893 had been fairly popular. In the four years of its production, over 34,000 had been manufactured. It was, however, to be completely overshadowed by its replacement, which was introduced in November, 1897.

The Winchester 1897 was a real milestone in shotgun development. It was the gun that made American shooters prefer repeaters, and the first one designed specifically for smokeless powder. It became one of the most popular hunting guns of all time, yet was also an early modern combat shotgun, seeing front-line service in World War I.

Production spanned six decades; throughout much of that time, it was the standard of performance and reliability by which other designs were judged. Production was finally stopped in 1957, and the last '97, serial number 1024700, was shipped in September of that year. Almost a million were made, a record that has been surpassed by few other shotguns. (Because 1897 serial numbers were a continuation of the 1893 sequence, late production guns will have numbers of over a million.)

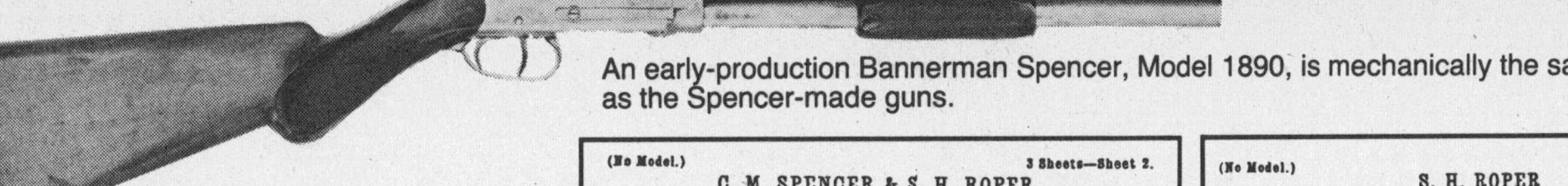

An early-production Bannerman Spencer, Model 1890, is mechanically the same as the Spencer-made guns.

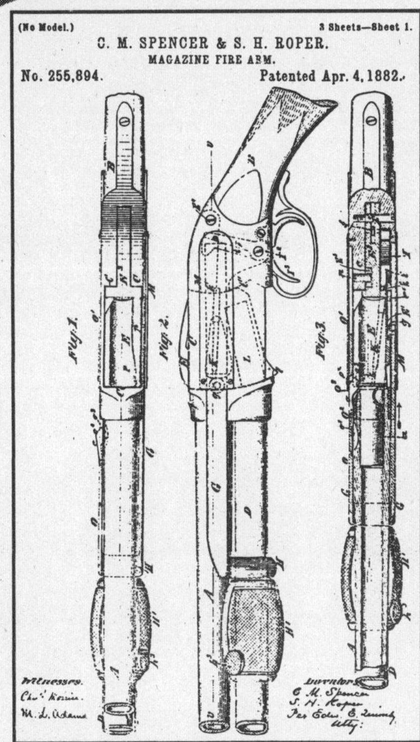

This patent started the team of Spencer and Roper off on a business that lasted about six years.

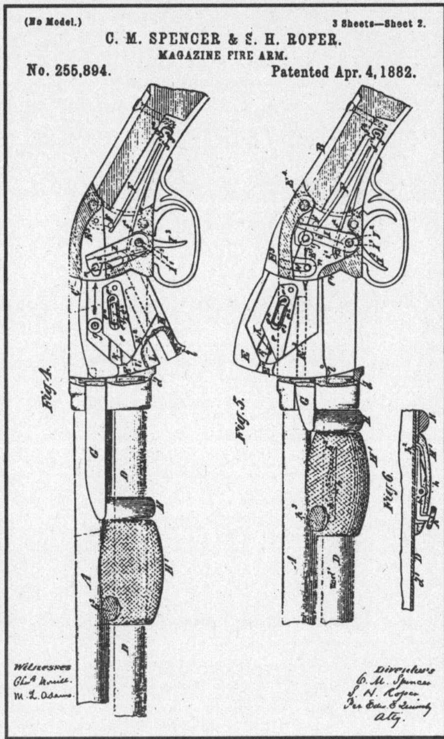

Only a few thousand guns were made before Spencer and Roper had to quit, but somehow Bannerman didn't get these patents.

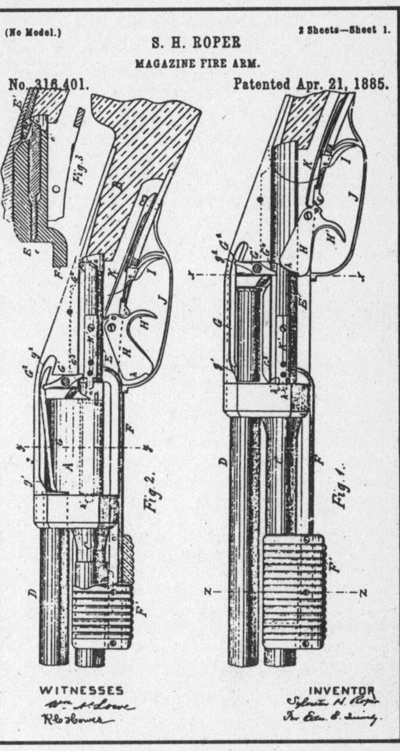

This was clearly Bannerman's patent, and he made a lot of guns, but he lost his suit against Winchester on the timing of the patent rights.

As the Spencer slide handle starts back, breechblock is cammed down and empty is extracted. Next shell to feed is in lower recess of the breechblock.

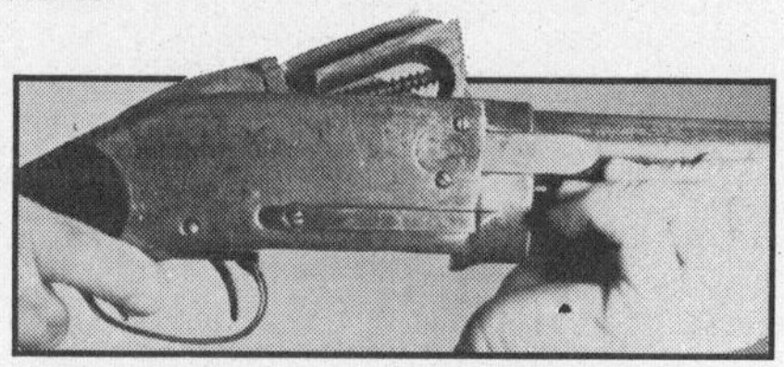

At rearward position, breechblock springs upward, throwing empty shell clear and aligning next shell with chamber. Hammer is now cocked, as shown by forward position of front "trigger."

As forearm goes forward, new shell is pulled into chamber. Then breechblock rotates down to lock action and align firing pin. Gun is now ready to fire.

Bannerman's Spencer manufactory once was identified by this sign. It now hangs in the Deep River Armory in Houston, Texas. (Courtesy James B. Hughes)

Receiver legend of early-production Bannerman Spencer, Model 1890. Original Spencers were not marked here.

Late-production Bannerman-made Spencers, such as this Model 1899, incorporated some mechanical changes and used wood forearms.

The '97 introduced the inertia lock, which kept the action locked until the chambered round had been fired. The importance of this feature cannot be overstated. Hangfires were not uncommon with the early harder-to-ignite smokeless powders, and shells going off as the action opened would have dampened the popularity of the new repeaters. The inertia lock kept the shell safely chambered until the gun was unlocked by a slight forward pull on the forearm either by the recoil of a firing round, or by a conscious movement by the shooter.

In conjunction with this feature, an action release was added. A button on the receiver allowed the action to open without being fired. (The '93 shooter had to push the end of the firing pin with his finger.)

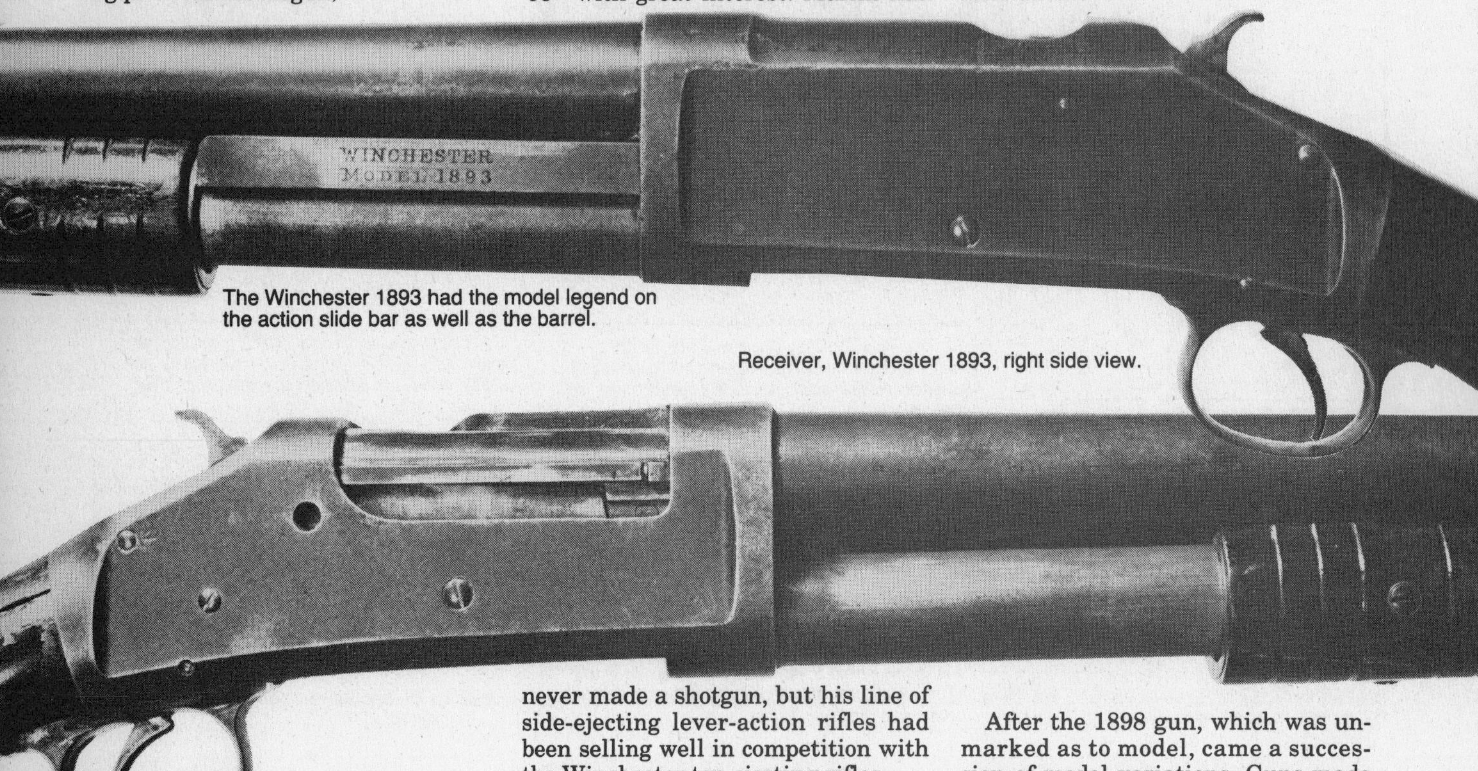

The Winchester 1893 had the model legend on the action slide bar as well as the barrel.

Receiver, Winchester 1893, right side view.

The first takedown version was introduced in 1898. It was the first takedown pump shotgun.

A few years later, a modification to allow easy pushbutton unloading of the magazine was incorporated. No longer was it necessary to work rounds through the action.

These features—inertia lock, action release, takedown mechanism and magazine unloading device—are still used on modern pump guns.

One of the competitors of the '93 and '97 had been the Burgess repeating shotgun. The inventor, Andrew Burgess, had worked on lever-action and sliding-forearm guns for some time. He began his manufacturing effort, though, with a novel design that operated by means of a pistol grip sliding backward and forward. The Burgess shotgun was introduced in 1893, the year the first Winchester pump was marketed. Although Burgess sales were relatively small, Winchester wanted to eliminate guns that were in direct competition with their offerings. In 1899, they bought the company from the ailing 62-year-old inventor and discontinued the Burgess gun.

John M. Marlin, founder of the Marlin Firearms Company, had watched the progress of the Bannerman lawsuit—and the sales of the '93—with great interest. Marlin had never made a shotgun, but his line of side-ejecting lever-action rifles had been selling well in competition with the Winchester top-ejecting rifles.

With an eye to entering the shotgun market, the Marlin Company began development work and received patents in 1894 and 1896. Their first shotgun—the Model 1898—was introduced shortly after Winchester's new 1897 gun entered the market. It was the only shotgun with which John Marlin was directly involved. He died three years later, in 1901, at the age of 65.

The Marlin gun featured a locking system that was clever, but not as strong as that of the '97. This interesting design locked at the rear of the receiver. A horizontal breechblock and vertically moving carrier were used, as in the Winchester. The breechblock, however, was hollow and open at the bottom. It contained a locking bolt pivoted in its center. Forward motion of the slide handle tipped the front of the locking bolt up. This pivoted the rear end down into a recess in the receiver.

This method took some of the direct stress of the action bar, resulting in an action that was somewhat smoother than Winchester's, but not as strong.

Unlike Winchester's system of continuing all variations under the same model designation, Marlin introduced a new model number for different gauges and slight mechanical variations. This led to a confusing series of Marlin shotguns, all with the same general appearance and same basic mechanism.

After the 1898 gun, which was unmarked as to model, came a succession of model variations. Guns made between 1906 and 1915 might be Model 16, 17, 19, 21, 24, 26 or 30, depending on gauge, takedown, inertia lock or other minor variations. After WW I, the Model 42 became standard and remained in the line until 1934.

Only one other hammer model variant was produced. Marlin had gone bankrupt in 1924 and the new owner, New Haven businessman Frank Kenna, had a unique idea for getting financial support during reorganization. A cheaper version of the Model 42, with plain wood and without a magazine unloader, was produced. This variation was probably the first use of pressed checkering. These guns were dubbed Model 49 and were given

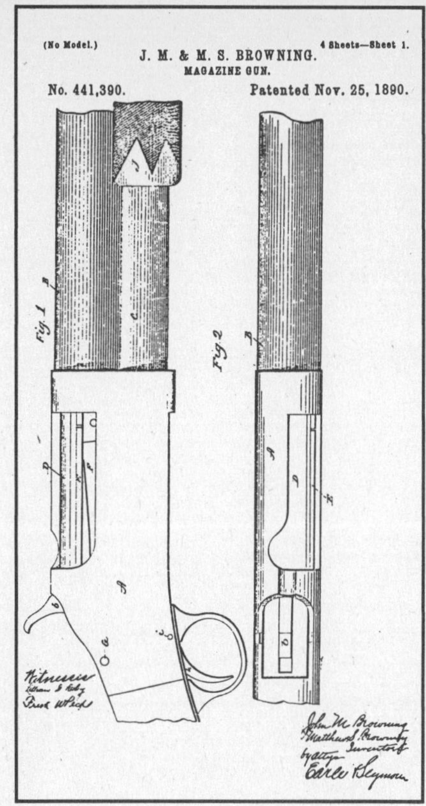

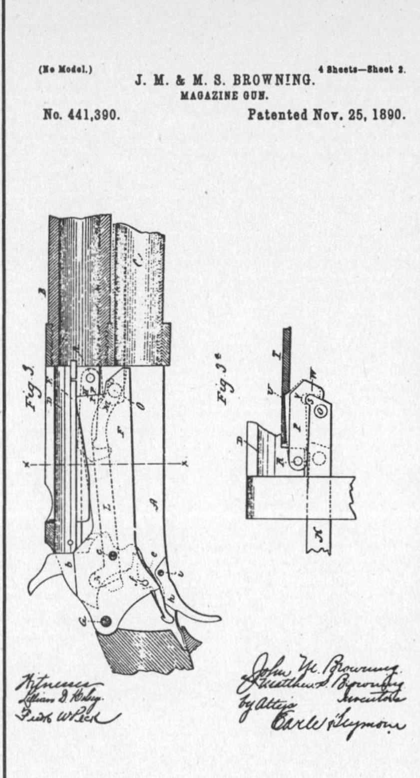

Though it didn't last long before being replaced, the Winchester Model 1893's patents were real milestones in repeating shotgun history, offering the reciprocating breech block, its attached extractor, and loading while closed, along with a now familiar general layout.

(No Model.) 4 Sheets—Sheet 3.

J. M. & M. S. BROWNING.

MAGAZINE GUN.

No. 441,390. Patented Nov. 25, 1890.

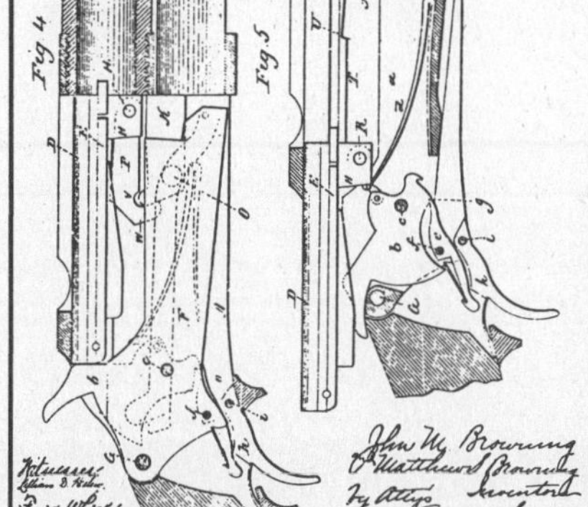

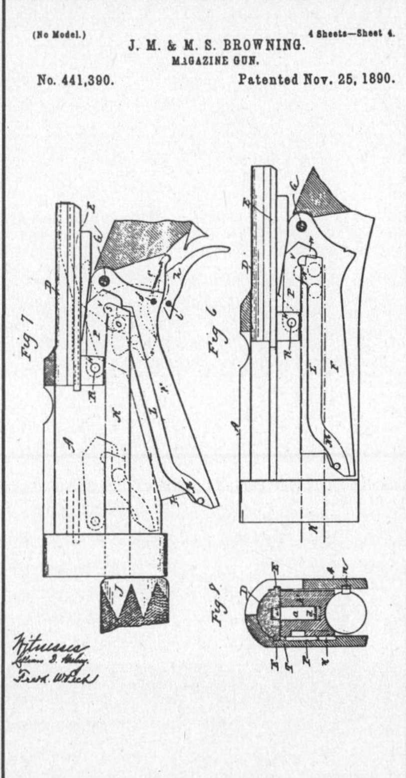

away as premiums to investors buying four or more shares of Marlin preferred stock. About 3000 were made between 1925 and 1928.

Even though the Marlin hammer guns were visually similar, each model variation apparently was numbered with a separate sequence of serial numbers. This has led to a confusing overlapping of numbers, and the total production of Marlin hammer guns is in some doubt. The number may approach 200,000. It is almost certainly not more and may be tens of thousands less.

The main contribution of the Marlin was in showing ways of performing functions other than those used by the front-running Winchesters. The Marlin, using similar horizontal breechbolt and vertical carrier motions, used different methods for locking, takedown and inertia lock.

With these four guns—the Spencer,

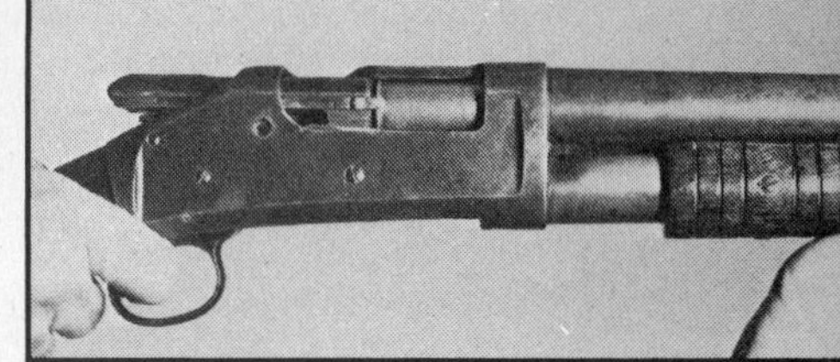

As the Winchester 1983 slide handle starts back, the carrier drops to unlock the bolt, which draws the empty from the chamber and cocks the hammer.

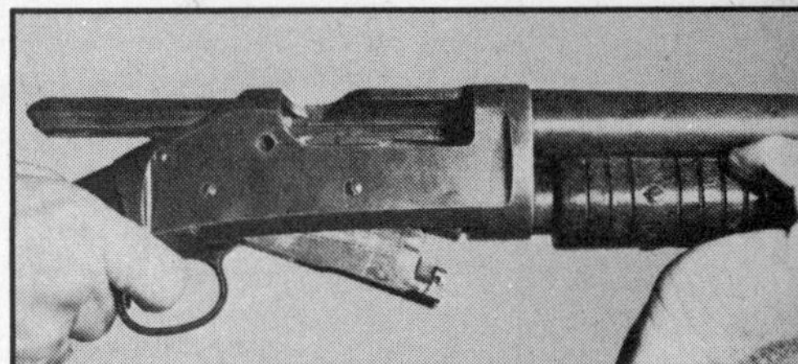

At rearward position, the empty is ejected. Carrier drops further to receive the next shell, which springs from the magazine.

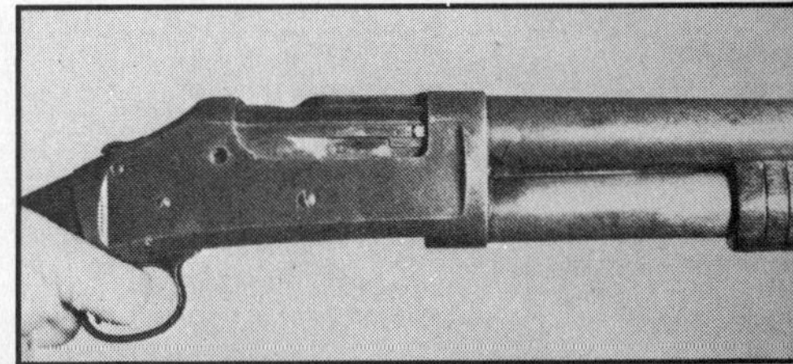

As forearm goes forward, new shell is pushed into the chamber by the bolt. Carrier rises behind the bolt lug to lock the action. Gun is now ready to fire.

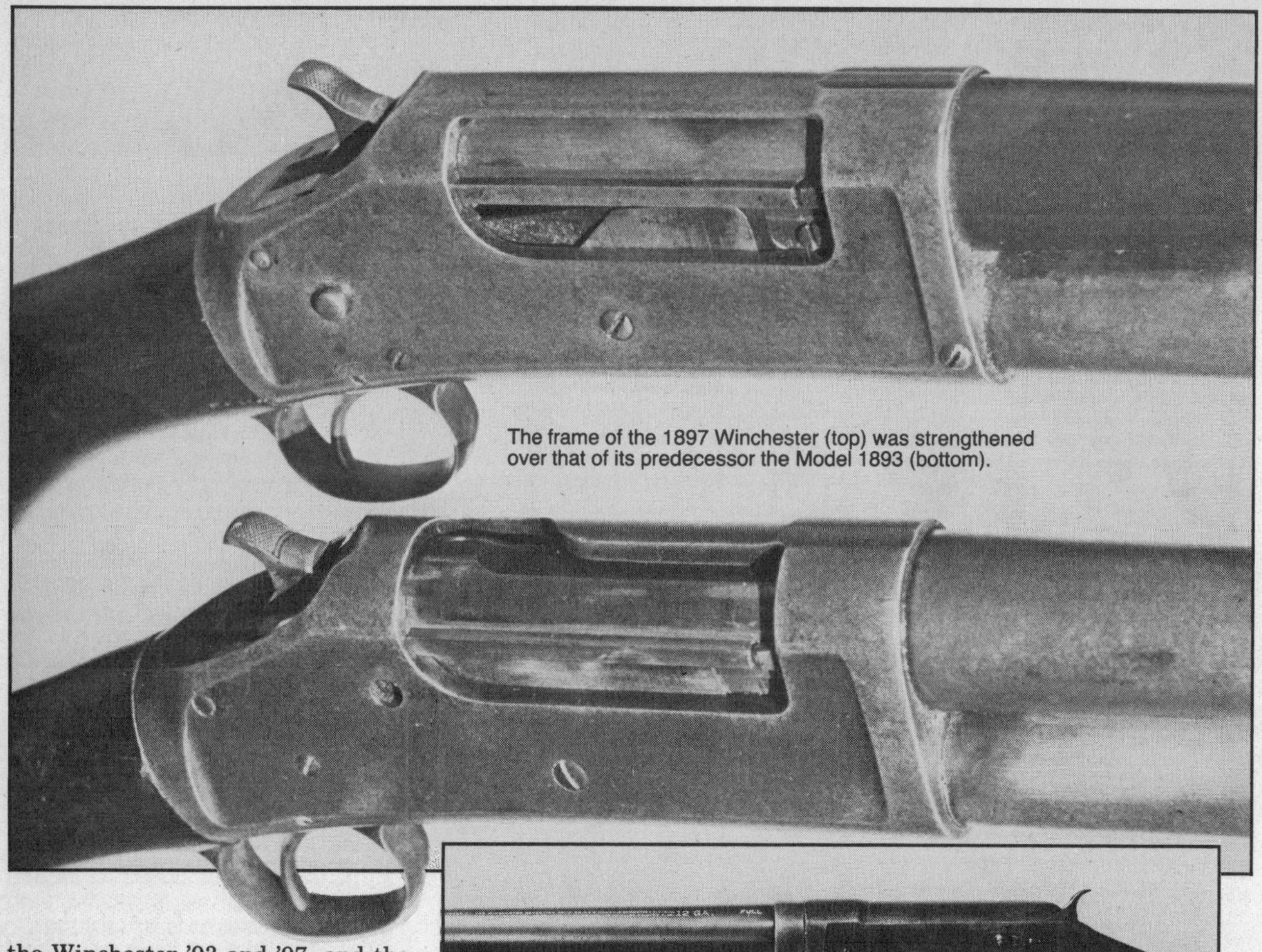

The frame of the 1897 Winchester (top) was strengthened over that of its predecessor the Model 1893 (bottom).

Those 1897 Winchesters made prior to 1918 had the model legend only on the action slide bar.

the Winchester '93 and '97, and the Marlin—an American tradition was begun. The slide action "pump" shotgun became the favored American smoothbore and those early pump shotguns provided many productive days afield for turn-of-the Century sportsmen.

Can these old guns provide a productive day afield today or would shooting them be more in the nature of a stunt? Should they be shot at all?

The first consideration, of course, is safety of the shooter. One should understand thoroughly how the gun works. If there is any doubt that the gun is in safe shooting condition, it should be checked by a knowledgeable gunsmith.

The second consideration is preservation of the gun itself. The shooter should realize that he is the custodian of a part of American history. Replacement parts for the old guns are likely to be expensive if they are available. More likely, they may be difficult or impossible to find.

Still, it is possible to enjoy shooting these old guns without allowing their condition to deteriorate. A gun that is fired at least occasionally with proper loads is more likely to receive proper

After World War I, model designation was changed from 1897 to 97 and appeared on the barrel.

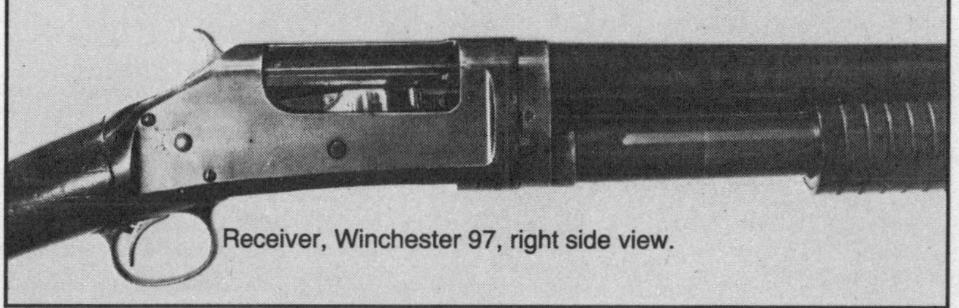

Receiver, Winchester 97, right side view.

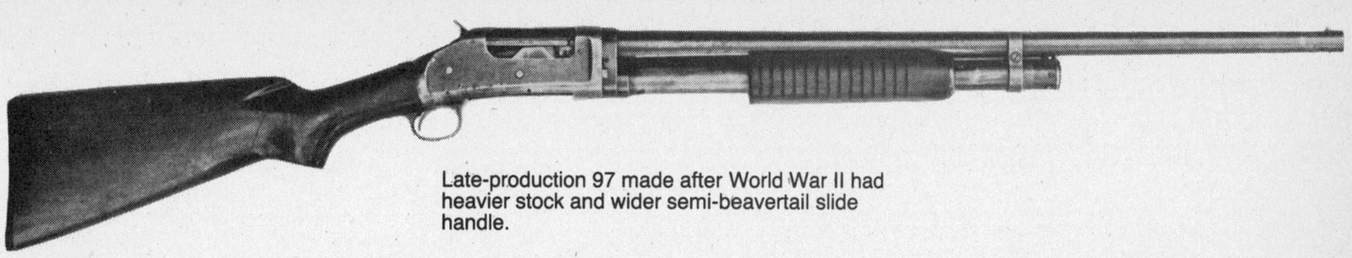

Late-production 97 made after World War II had heavier stock and wider semi-beavertail slide handle.

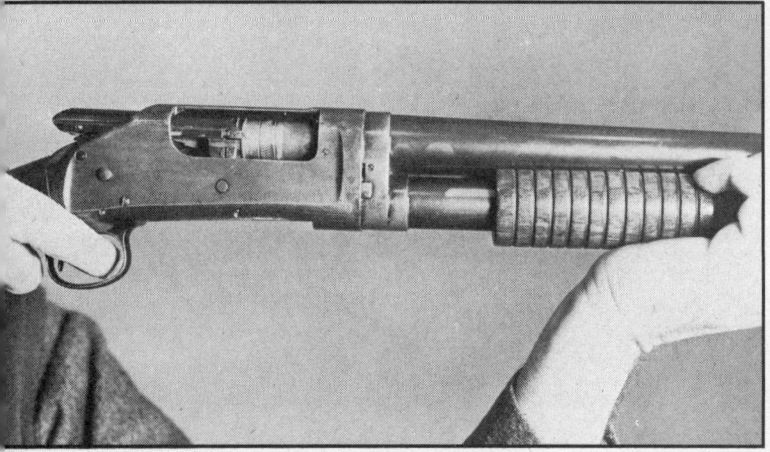

As the Winchester 97 slide handle starts back, unlocking and extraction proceed as in the 1893.

As in the 1893, ejection is accomplished at rearward position. The new shell is on the carrier.

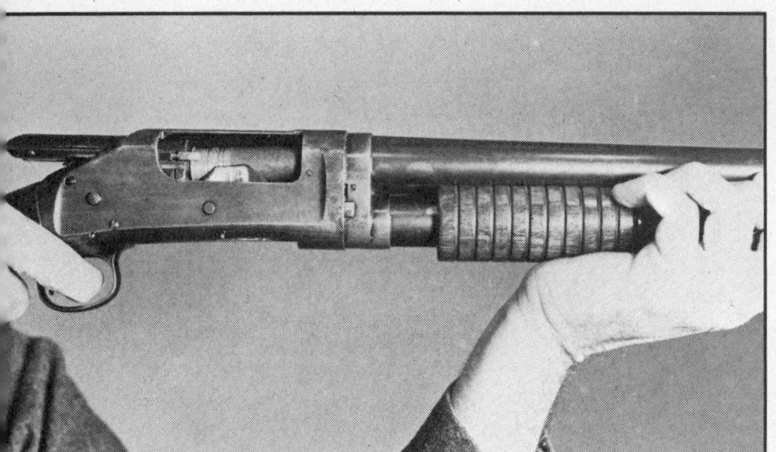

A new feature of the 97 was the cartridge guide, which rises at the beginning of the forward stroke to align the shell with the chamber.

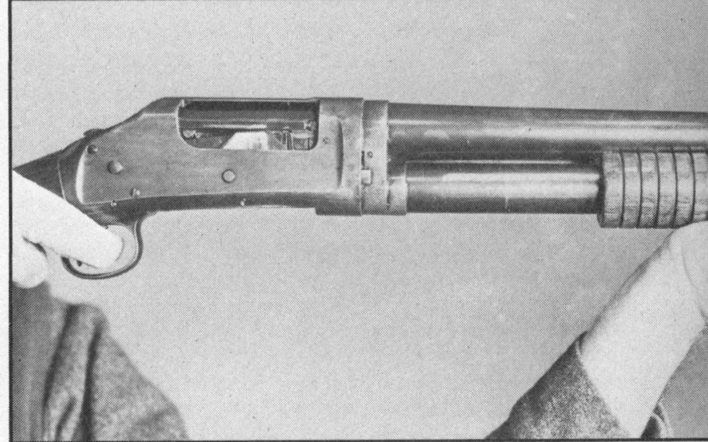

With the bolt forward and locked by the carrier, the gun is ready to fire.

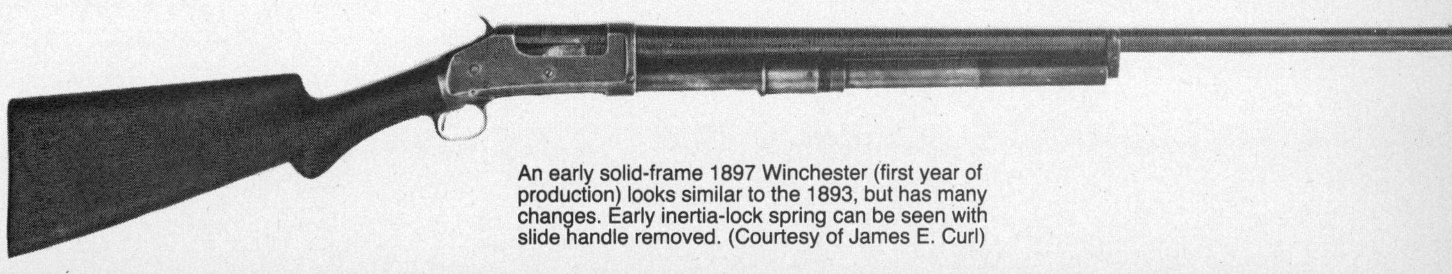

An early solid-frame 1897 Winchester (first year of production) looks similar to the 1893, but has many changes. Early inertia-lock spring can be seen with slide handle removed. (Courtesy of James E. Curl)

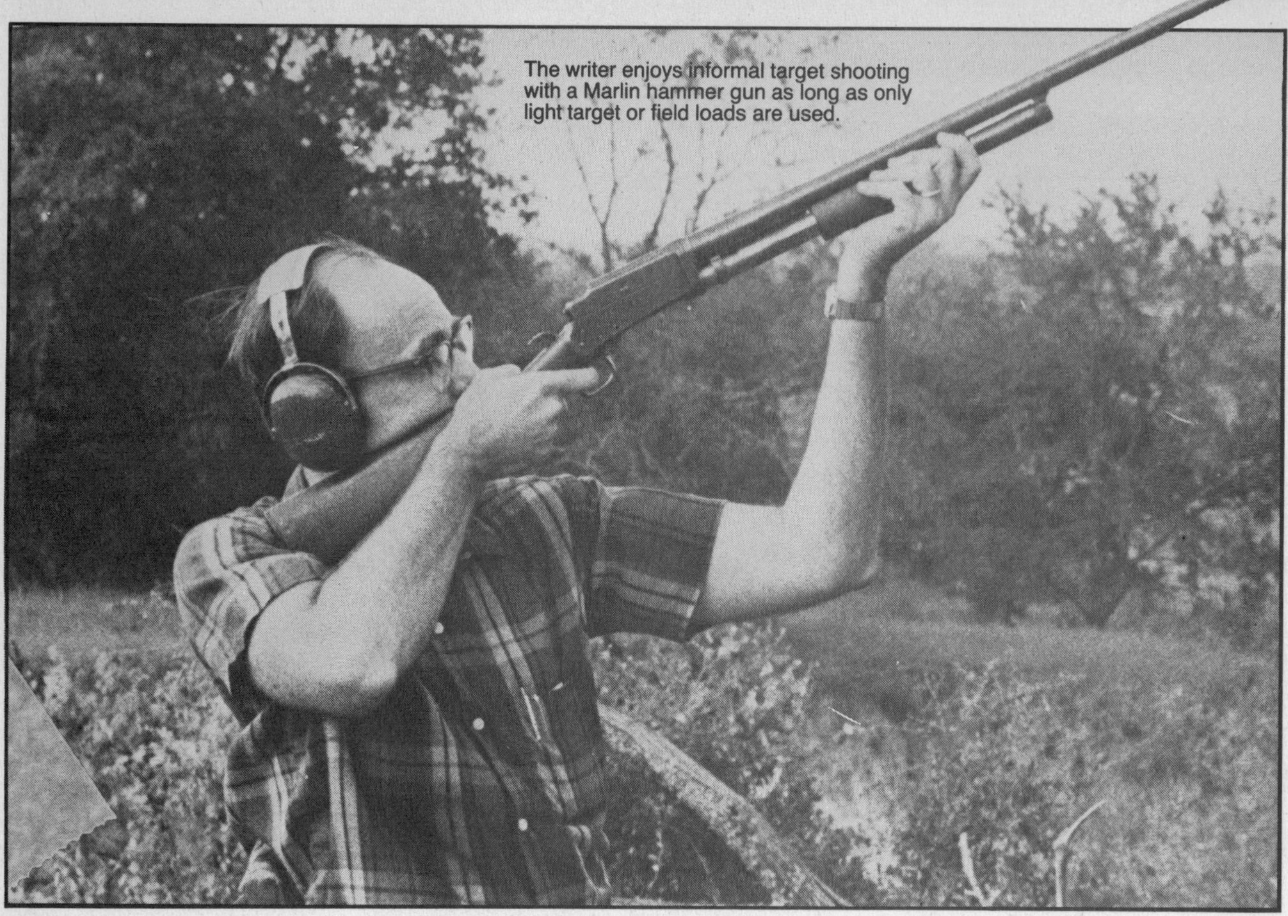
The writer enjoys informal target shooting with a Marlin hammer gun as long as only light target or field loads are used.

maintenance than one just left in the rack.

In the end, common sense should rule as to whether an old gun should be used. No one should take a chance on ruining a collectors item in a saltwater duck marsh. From the other side, the results of a long-planned hunt should not depend on an old gun for which no replacement parts are available. With these considerations in mind, if you are lucky enough to own one of these early pumps, you may want to shoot it occasionally.

I believe black powder loads are indicated for the Spencer and the 1893 Winchester. The action designs of both are strong enough, but their short chambers and the fact that the steel is the better part of a century old suggest the lower pressure of black powder. Besides, these guns were born in the black powder days—if one is going to recreate history, he may as well go all the way. Just be sure to clean thoroughly. Black powder should also be used in the small number of 1897 Winchesters made with damascus barrels.

Black powder shells are available but expensive. Fortunately, they can be loaded with simple hand tools in modern cases that have been trimmed to 2⅝ inches. The old muzzleloader's rule of "equal volumes of powder and shot" seems to work well.

A Spencer in good condition is a smooth, fast-working gun. It is easy to load, although more awkward to unload. The forward "trigger" cannot be easily cocked with the trigger finger (everyone used his thumb). The stock has too much drop, but that was usual for all shotguns in the days of its birth. A Spencer is fun for casual hunting or informal clay birds.

The 1893 Winchester was the first repeater that allowed snapshooting. The hammer location may look strange, but it is well designed to allow natural and effortless cocking when the gun is snapped up from a "ready" position. It is fun to use for hunting or informal clay bird games.

One curious thing about the '93 is its stock dimensions. Shotguns of the period had considerable drop, and the '93 was no exception. The shortness is surprising, though. At 13 inches, it had the shortest standard length of the four early pumps. Surely John Browning, over six feet tall and an accomplished wing-shot, did not specify those dimensions.

The Marlin was advertised as suitable for any smokeless powder load, but the action is not as strong as its contemporary rival, the Winchester '97. Wear in the action is more critical and tends to increase headspace. Stay away from maximum heavy loads. In good condition, the Marlin hammer pump is suitable for modern low-base target or field loads, and provides a fast-handling, smooth-working gun for field use, trap or Skeet.

The Winchester 97 stands apart from the other early pumps. Eighty-five years after its introduction, the 97 may still be found in regular use. Even today, some old-timers refer to it as the "Winchester pump gun," as if there had not been any others.

In good condition, the great strength of the action will handle any modern 2¾-in. shells. It is not really smooth, but no other repeater has ever fed, chambered, extracted and ejected shotgun shells more reliably.

The short, low stock of the '93 had been corrected. The '97 came with a longer, straighter stock that placed the hands in direct line with the

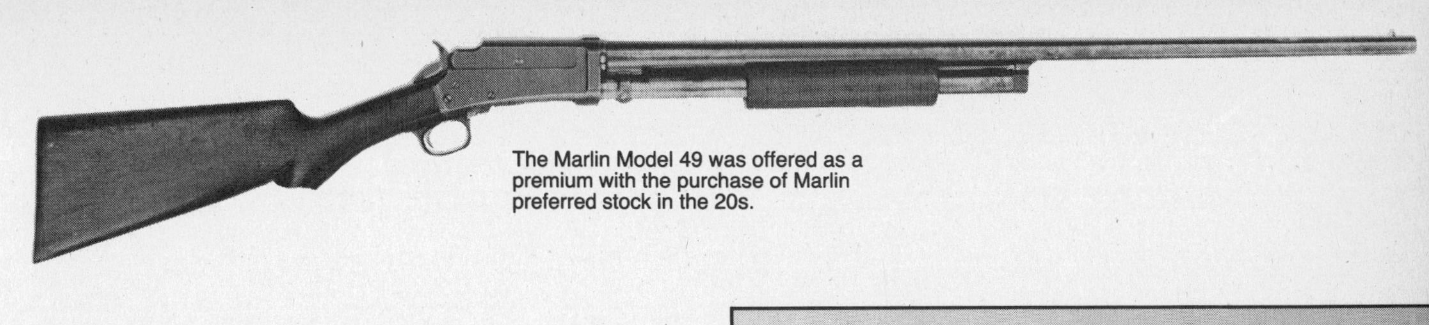

The Marlin Model 49 was offered as a premium with the purchase of Marlin preferred stock in the 20s.

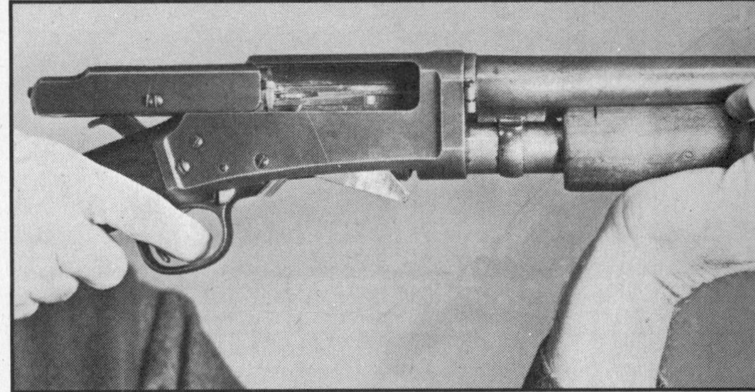

At rearward position, empty is ejected. A new shell springs onto the carrier.

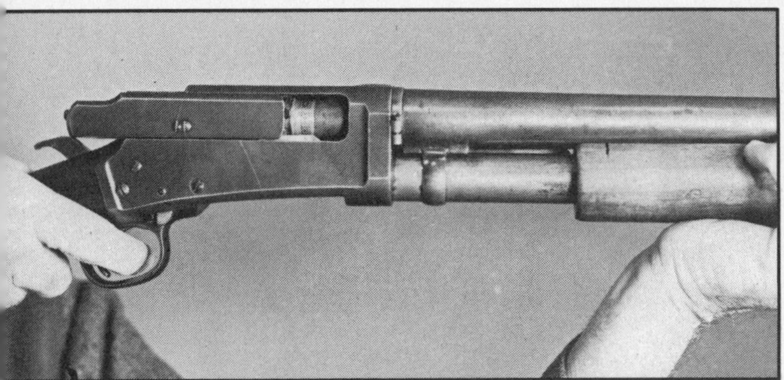

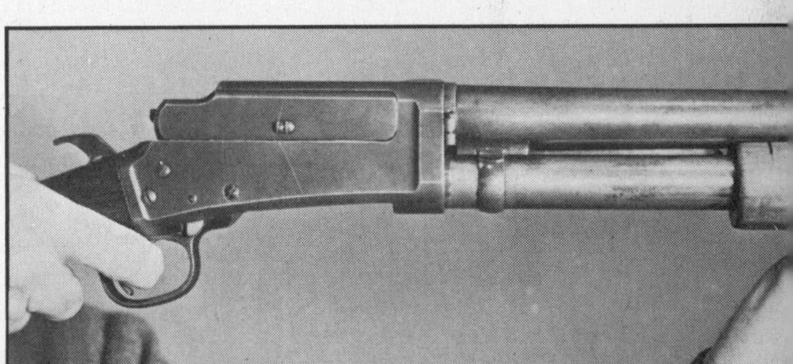

As the Marlin slide handle starts back, the concealed locking bolt inside the hollow breechblock is pivoted up from its recess at the rear of the receiver. Breechblock moves rearward, extracting shell from chamber and cocking hammer.

Running the handle forward chambers the new shell and cams the locking bolt down into its receiver recess, locking the action. Gun is now ready to fire.

Receiver, Marlin Model 49, right side view.

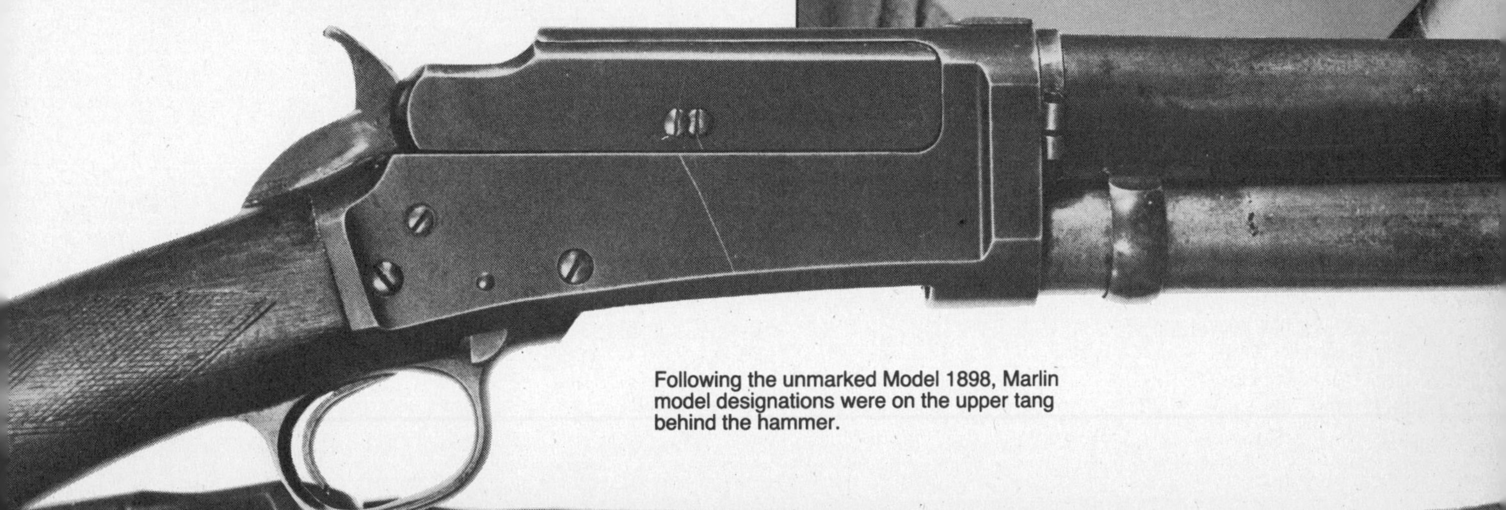

Following the unmarked Model 1898, Marlin model designations were on the upper tang behind the hammer.

You still see Model 97 Winchesters out there often enough to be unremarkable. They remain very reliable.

The Model 97 put shooters' hands in new places, and it was a natural pointer compared to the rest of them.

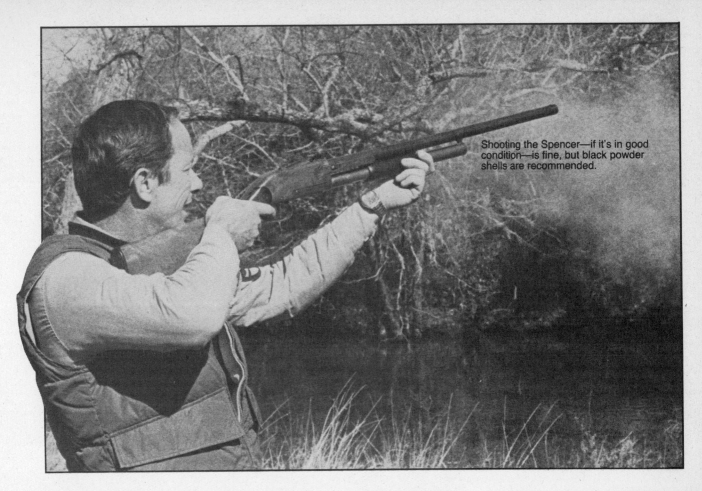

Shooting the Spencer—if it's in good condition—is fine, but black powder shells are recommended.

shoulder. The '97 soon earned a reputation for natural pointing, a characteristic emphasized by Winchester ads until the model was dropped.

Now as then, the Winchester 97 is a suitable choice for any type of hunting, and—with appropriate barrel and choke—for Skeet or trap. It is the only one of the early pumps for which parts are generally available.

The early pump guns dominated the shotgun scene into the early years of the twentieth century, but in 1904, a new era in slide action shotguns began. The Browning-designed Stevens Model 520 was introduced as the first of the modern "hammerless" pumps. The gun utilized many of the best ideas of the early pumps, but had the entire mechanism enclosed within its steel receiver.

The idea caught on. In 1907, Remington introduced its Model 10. In 1912 Winchester brought out its famous Model 12. A year later, Marlin announced its hammerless gun, the Model 28. The modern pump shotgun had arrived!

The old-timers just didn't go away, of course. But their manufacture amounted to a smaller and smaller portion of the market. The Winchester 1893 had already been supplanted by the 1897. In 1903, Bannerman offered the Spencer factory for sale; production ceased in 1907.

The Marlin hammer guns stayed in production through 1934, but their sales did not compare to the far stronger hammerless models.

Only the Winchester 97 was able to defy the trend. It remained in the line until 1957, and is still found in regular service. But its appearance in the field or on the range now is cause for curiosity.

Although the early pumps are seldom seen, their heritage lives on in the numerous design features they bequeathed to today's modern pump guns. The modern guns inherited not only many of their design characteristics, but their very popularity. For, long before today's sleek slide-actions arrived on the scene, an American tradition had been started by the early pump shotguns. ●

Picture from the past: a 97 Winchester and a limit of teal. The early pump shotguns made the slide-action repeater the traditional American shotgun—for good reasons.

Pump Guns In The Real World . . .

they shoot when it ain't easy.

by PETER NELSON

CLOUDS blotted out the moon and swallowed the last traces of dusk to the west. We in the canoe were bone-numbed and weary after a long day's duck hunt. We were also alert. The creek that carried us home was swift, and we shot through the inkiness with uncomfortable speed. I back-paddled at the stern; the bow man was steady. The passenger in the middle, however, was new and nervous.

We cut for the landing as it zipped past, the canoe straddling the current, when our passenger leaned wrong—upstream instead of down—and the canoe shipped water.

The resulting melee was over in seconds. We were ashore, wet but safe. The canoe was full of water. And my Browning autoloader was no longer with us.

The immediate lesson was that valuable objects in canoes need to be *tied* in. A more important lesson took years to assimilate, but it began the next week with my purchase of a 12-gauge Magnum Remington 870 pump shotgun.

My marriage—yes, we came that far together—to that gun has been delightful. If I notched the stock for every mallard or goose it dropped stone-like, there would be no wood left, only the stock screw at the butt of the receiver. I once used it to paddle myself home (unloaded) in lieu of a paddle that broke. It didn't whimper. I loaned it to friends, not all of whom cleaned it.

It was a cheap gun that paid dividends with each trigger pull. It loved my even cheaper and sometimes downright disreputable handloads during the days I worked through college. In thousands of shells fired at game, it has jammed once. On that day, a primer fell out of an over-used and senile handload, jamming the bolt. After a quick field-strip, the 870 was back in action that day. It has never met a gunsmith.

Today, my pumpgun looks like the blue-collared, red-blooded warrior that it is. The bluing is battered. The walnut is bare and raw, but still strong. It still slams *any* 12-gauge shell home with authority and zings the empties out.

It can shoot faster than the eye can switch target. The long 30-inch barrel tames muzzle blast and saves my ears for enjoying my grandkids someday.

Well, 870 shotguns bring a better

Ashore or afloat, waterfowl blinds are messy places, particularly with lots of cattail chaff ready to jam an autoloader.

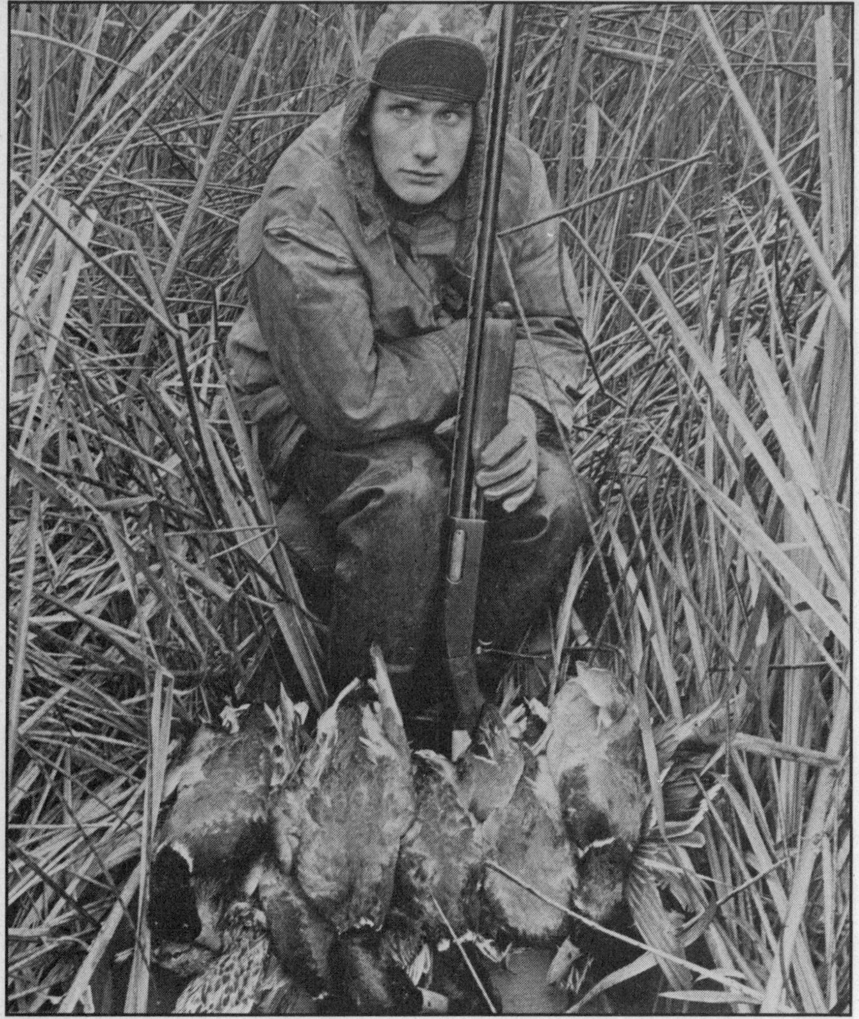

In the real world of play-it-as-it-lays waterfowling, author says a pump, preferably a long-barreled model like the Remington 870 used by this young hunter, beats any and all autoloaders.

Field gunning like this can be tough, too, on autoloading shotgun reliability. These pit gunners in wheat stubble are using pump guns.

price today, but compared to some shotgun prices, they're still bargains, boys. The better news is, there are still plenty of them and a lot of other good brands in the blue-collar price range. All put game in the freezer.

This isn't a list of brands to buy or avoid for waterfowling. This is an iteration of shotgun principles learned in duck and goose blinds.

The first thing I say to raise the ire and blood pressures of many readers is that automatic shotguns are relatively useless in the real-world duck blinds I use. I hear howls of consternation and can even envision a lynch mob now, but my phone number is unlisted, and my Spokane home is far from where most of you live. You'll cool off by the time you get here.

But you automatic fans need to face reality. A duck blind or goose pit is for most of us a nasty place. A widely-read outdoor writer once thought he needed an exorcist. Every automatic shotgun he bought jammed when the two of us went hunting on the rough-and-tumble public hunting grounds. I'm not talking about heated blinds with sharp-eyed guides and dry retrievers. I'm talking about grass-roots duck hunting, on public land, getting our buns wet, and getting our guns packed with sand, mud, cattails, coot feathers, and worse. Ditto for the ammo, which is never dry. Heck, nothing else is dry—why should the ammo be?

In any event, this outdoor writer thought the Red Gods surely against him. His autoloaders invariably jammed. He was convinced he couldn't hit with a muzzle-light pump, and he kept hoping to find an automatic that would work fine when stuffed with cattail fuzz.

Eventually, of course, he switched to a pump after a newly-acquired auto had a *grand mal* seizure in one of our muddy duck blinds and had to be put to bed. He picked up his spare shotgun, a cheap High Standard pump with no bluing left. A gun bought solely for home defense, with plenty of change from a C-note, you can bet. He eyed the cheap gun mistrustfully, shucked in some gritty loads of fours, and generally looked like a priest sneaking into a bordello.

You know the rest of the story. Two mallards swung his end of the blind. *Bam-bam. Splash-splash.* The light muzzle didn't seem to matter. Later that week, the next nine shells brought identical results. Not until the twelfth duck did he waste a shell. And that bird went down after a fast follow-up shot. The outdoor writer grinned. When you miss the first time, it is nice to know the gun will fire the next time you pull the trigger. Cops have at least as much interest in knowing that, and you'll note prowl cars carry more pumps than anything.

That outdoor writer has not fired an automatic shotgun since. His percentage with the muzzle-light pump about doubles his autoloader's score from the days he couldn't be sure the gun would fire three times. Not trusting your gun is worse than flinching.

I hear the indignant rejoiners now. "My gun has never jammed!" sputter the lovers of autoloaders.

That statement, translated, really says, "I haven't done much tough duck or goose hunting at all!"

I have seen it many times. I take a number of friends waterfowling who do more pheasant or chukar hunting or know more about wiring my house than I do. In turn, they help me shoot pheasants or chukars or keep from burning my house down. It seems they always bring automatics on our first trip, and when I suggest that autos sometimes have it rough, the reply is predictable: "This baby's never jammed!"

I know that in the course of our first duck hunt, I will drag these guys and their shiny automatics through muck, snow, owl dung—plus the nasty stuff. They usually manage to step on their own frozen shells while the boat lurches about chasing cripples. And during the course of that first hunt, their automatics jam. Always. I know it's coming, of course, but no one believes me.

I don't gloat about that. There is little point in gloating about something as predictable as sunrise. By the end of the first day, my wet and muddy guests are penitent. I tell them about the hordes of good new and used pump shotguns on the market. I tell them that in new guns they should look for ones that swing amiably to the cheek and don't cost more than about two months' worth of groceries. For used guns, I tell them to shuck the actions until they find one that is silky with age. I tell them to look for a gun with the bluing worn off—that is usually one that has given good service and will continue. I tell them to avoid buying any gun they would hesitate to use to paddle home in lieu of a broken canoe paddle.

Happily, pumps are cheap and plentiful. The pump represents the essential beauty of firearms—that blend of form and function, the sturdiness, the inherent usefulness, the lack of glitter. What is more pleasing to the eye than its plain, walnut stock, the grip

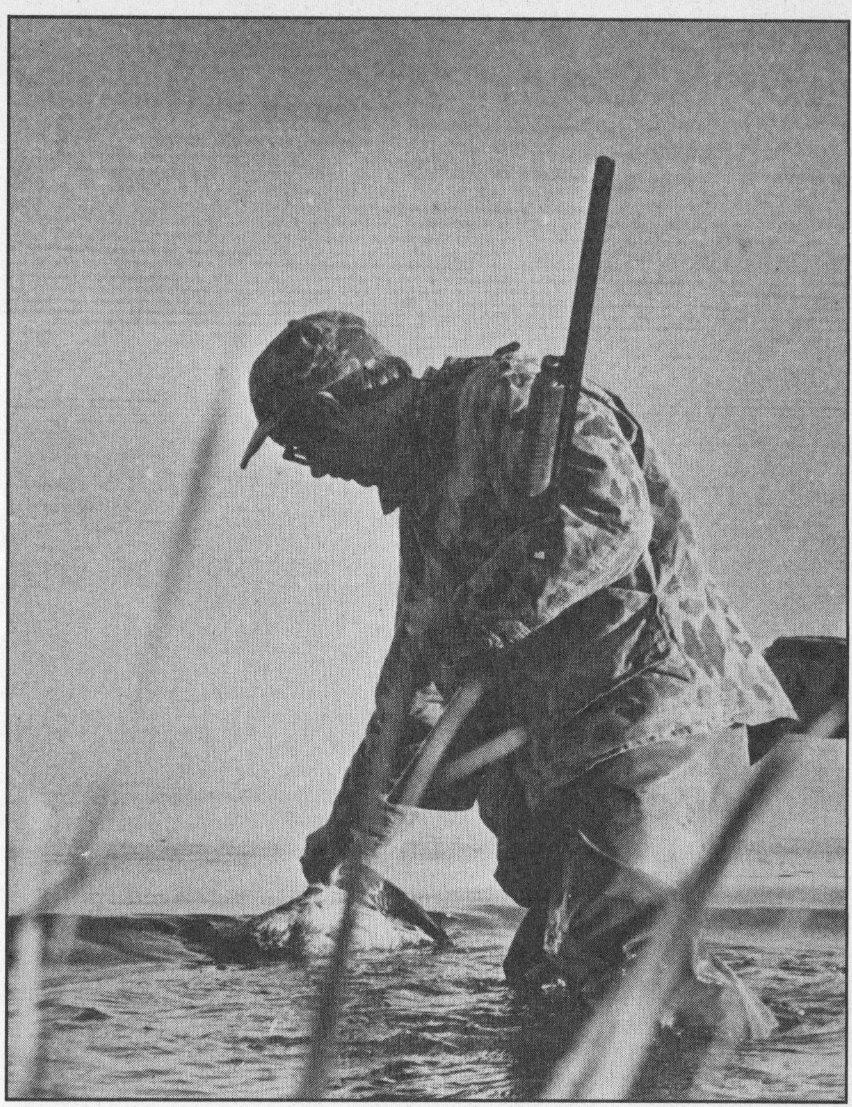

Author says that since much waterfowling is under sloppy conditions, the only worthwhile shotgun is one that handles those conditions, and for him that's a pump.

In weather and blind conditions like this, a pump gun provides sure-fire reliability too many autoloaders can't produce when wet, dirt-contaminated, or half-frozen.

dark after years of contact with a human palm? Or the dull receiver, which seems to soak up memories as it loses its bluing over the years?

Now, there is another gun type not quite as bad for duck and goose hunting as an autoloader and that's the high-priced double or over-under. The double cannot do the complete job on ducks and geese, because the job requires a three-shooter. To explain why takes a minute.

Ordinarily, you see, waterfowling doesn't demand fancy shooting. It requires only steadiness, discipline, and fire-control in the blind. And some practice. It doesn't require speed. In fact, the slow, deliberate shooter who takes a breath between shots will drop the most game.

But there is one shot in waterfowling that is as tough as any on this continent. It requires quickness and judgment, timing and accuracy. It is most easily made with a repeater. This is when you have to shoot a wing-tipped duck that has hit the water at long range and is flapping for heavy cover.

Now, if you hit a flying duck at 40 yards, it is usually 50 or 60 yards away when it hits the water. Man, you can't hesitate then, because if the bird is lively and streaking for cover, you may have no more than one second to flatten it. Otherwise, you and the pooch will be busy for a couple of hours, likely getting yourself wet in the process. That is the time for an accurate, center-of-the-pattern shot on a nimble, distant target. It is tougher by far than knocking a bird down over the decoys. If you miss, you won't have another chance.

Shooting at a flock of ducks or geese, I save that third shell for any bird going down lively. A little practice, and you know instantly whether a bird you hit is dropping stone-dead or alive. And if one of my first two shots has sent a lively bird down, I'm ready by the time it hits the water to flatten it before it even points its beak toward the tulies.

This saves game, it saves time, and it fills my limit quicker. If the duck is a diving species instead of a puddler, it will head for open water rather than the weeds. Swimming low, the bird is out of range in seconds and makes an even tougher shot than the puddle duck that heads for cover. If you miss, it means a long and potentially dangerous retrieve for your dog, or gunning the outboard to chase the bird with the boat. Usually the boat snags a half-dozen decoys each way. It is never fun.

Accordingly, I never save old, doubtful shells as "cripple loads." You need your best shells and a sharp eye to nail that cripple.

Hipboots are a compromise with the mud and water and snow and ice. So is a pump gun, better than any other.

Now to come to the point. Nothing is worse than an empty, smoking gun when wounded game takes cover. When I hunt with fanciers of the two-pipe, I usually wind up shooting their cripples with my third shot. Once a Greater Canada folded nicely at the second roar of a friend's twin-tube. It smacked water at 65 yards. Its head popped up and it was lively, perhaps only stunned. My own goose was out cold. So I swung for the cripple as Bill fumbled for shells. The goose seemed to know it too, for he was suddenly airborne, showing us his tail feathers. I have seen that happen a dozen times. A load of two's centered him at 70 yards—a providential shot that I wish I could always make.

Bill knew my three-shooter saved the goose. Yes, we might have caught him with the 70-horse outboard at wide-open throttle, but it would have been miles down the reservoir when we did. Bill now reserves his double for the uplands.

If you do insist on using a double gun, you need to practice quick reloading. The gun must have ejectors, and you need two heavy shells in your pocket that you grab reflexively after shooting. Always reload without taking your eyes off the birds, and practice until you do it fast. Then, your double is almost as good as a pump if you don't mind the mud and ice and sand on it. And *it* doesn't.

A few final comments. The long barrels commonly found on pumps are best. Muzzle blast is an inverse-square function of distance, which means 26-inch barrels are markedly louder at your ear than 30-inchers. Similarly, doubles and over-under guns are louder than repeaters with barrels of the same length, thanks to their short actions. Someone said the new 26-inch, full-choke barrels are nice for crowded blinds, but the opposite is true. Nothing is louder than the bark of your partner's gun in your ear. Urge him to get a long barrel.

Also, long barrels swing nice and may even help keep you from shooting too fast. Deliberation wins every time in waterfowl shooting, except for those pesky cripples. The bead on a long-barreled gun subtends less of your target. That helps for a maximum-range shot. My 870 has made a few of those.

The main thing though is that my 870 pump gun has made a lot of all kinds of shots in my real world hunting. That's because it's the best kind of duck gun there is. ●

THE TRUTH ABOUT THE CAVALRY

by G. N. "TED" DENTAY

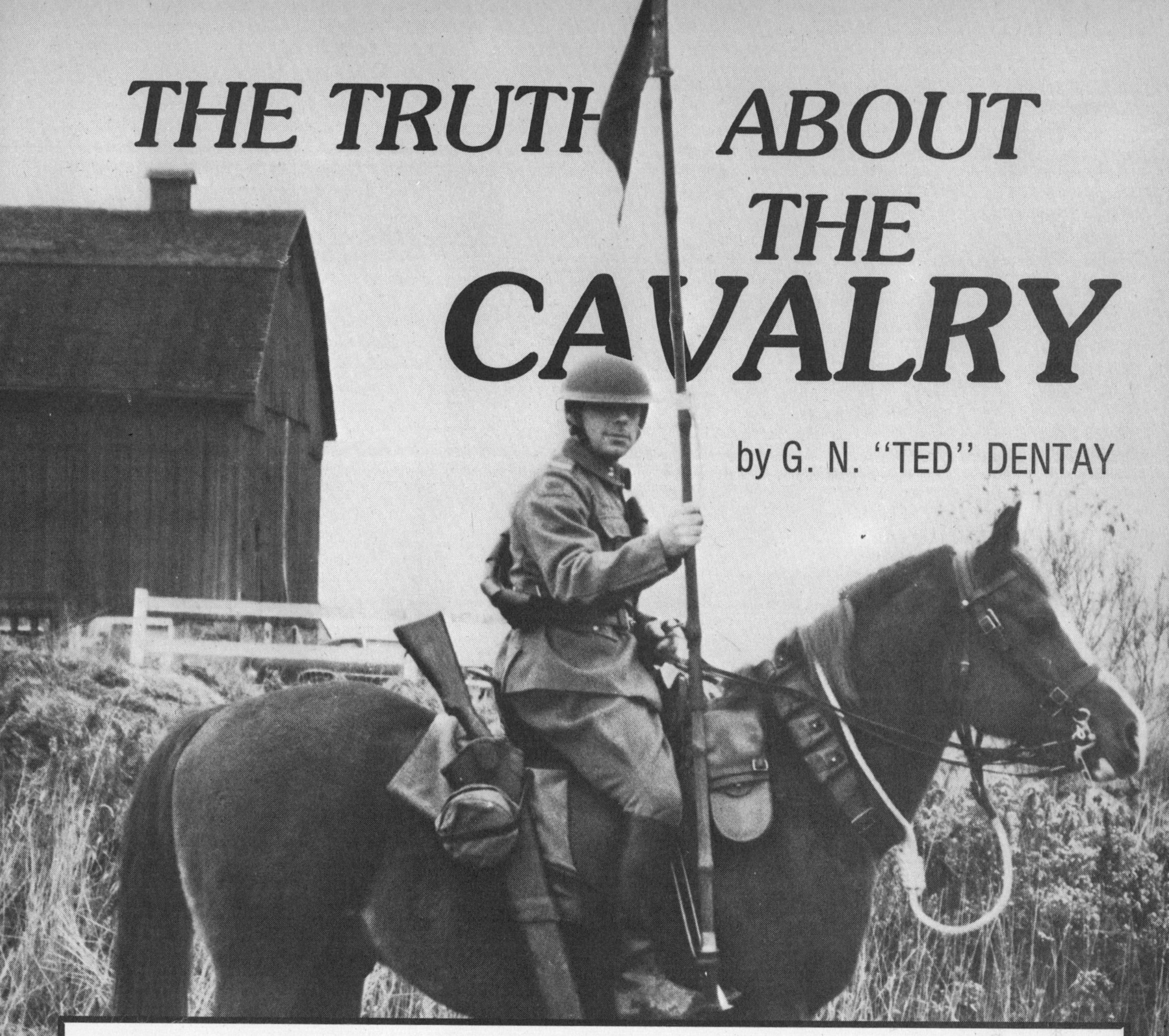

PEOPLE HAVE the strangest romantic notions of the historical kind. And I'm guiltier than the average person in my romances. You see, I indulge them. My discoveries have been both enlightening and hurtful. My wife thinks I'm nuts.

A few years ago, for instance, I was a maroon-bereted, World War II paratrooper—Canadian, of course. I carried it to the point of jumping out of airplanes with all the original 1940s equipment and guns. When our club of like-minded people disbanded, romance disappeared until I got the horse. In short order, I then stumbled across one of the only complete Boer War/World War I Canadian Army cavalry sets in private hands—romance again. In retrospect, I should have stuck with jumping out of airplanes. It was so much safer and more sensible.

Being a gun enthusiast and outdoorsman poses some terrible dilemmas. There's always this compelling urge to spend every available moment outside shooting, hunting or plain relaxing, especially in a bright summer sun (in Canada). There's more to life and hobbies than guns and hunting, so I added horses to them.

The cavalry set neatly took care of any eastern or English versus western riding style question. Cavalry riding, I found, is a happy combination of both worlds—and nobody knows a thing about it so they can't laugh too much. The two books that came later seemed to be just the tickets to learn by: *Cavalry Drill Manual - 1896* and *Cavalry Drill Manual - 1898*, both issued by the Queen's Printer (London). They are filled chock-a-block with relevant information, but no diagrams or pictures.

On the surface of things, cavalry techniques look like a fairly simple proposition to master. When you refer back to the early years of this century, you can discover that British Empire cavalry troopers were so dim no one saw fit to issue training or field manuals. They couldn't read, for the most part. The deeper truth is different. At the rate I've been going, it's going to take years to become a decent horseman, much less a competent cavalryman. But, I have had to find out the hard way that there's more to this than any books say.

Of primary interest, naturally, were the weapons that came with the collection. Some were familiar to me as a shooter and collector. Some weren't, most particularly the Pat-

The tattered copy on left must be the only volume of *Cavalry Drill 1898* still in active, everyday use. Neither book offers pictures or diagrams.

. . . troopers were dim . . .

All this goes on the horse—tack, pouches, hobbles, SMLE and bayonet, pointing sword, steel helmet, bandoliers for both and, as many ads say, more. Horse also carries the man.

tern 1908 "Pointing" sword and Pattern 1868 Lance. They looked simple enough to a fellow who used to throw a javelin and take fencing lessons in high school; it turns out they are a lot more dangerous than the guns.

Right off the bat, the sensible thing to do appeared to be to gun train my horse, a spirited Arabian. This would lead to being able to carry the standard-issue 303 "Smelly" (S.M.L.E.—Short Magazine Lee Enfield No. 1 Mk. III) and the 455 Colt New Service revolver. Fortunately, I was under no illusions about firing from horseback, especially from my horse's back. I knew that the horse's acute sense of hearing can be more easily damaged than that of a human's by gunfire. Then there's the matter of sitting six feet off the ground without a seatbelt. So I expected to do most of my shooting dismounted, somewhere close to the horse, however.

Since the object of all this was to combine plinking and hunting with horses, the logical first solution was quick in coming. Every time I went out, I took my Browning 22 T-Bolt with me, slinging it into the Hunter Gun-Loc leather scabbard, which was then attached to my "working" saddle (an Icelandic military pattern saddle). We proceeded to terrorize the countryside, and me, and every once in awhile I managed to consume a box of rimfire ammo.

It turns out he didn't like guns. Not one bit. Eventually, I prevailed and we came to a compromise.

To properly train the critter, I theorized you had to shoot something mild from a distance, then move it closer over a period of time until you were shooting from right next to the horse. The 22 proved to be no problem. What was most difficult was convincing him to stay put when he was picketed.

Every time I walked away to take a shot, I would turn around to check one last time. And every time it was only to see his south end retreating northwards, usually trailing shrubs, small trees and, once, my original 1915 oak-and-steel picketing stake. No one ever mentioned that you have to start off by training the horse to stay tied up when you tie it up.

Eventually, we got to the point where he would tolerate the 22 being fired by his side. Holding the reins and the forestock in one hand proved to have only one flaw, one I'm still working on—I could never hit the target. Every time my finger began to squeeze the trigger, he would give a mighty jerk which yanked the barrel skywards, usually as the bullet was exiting the muzzle.

The first few times this happened, the bandages on my palms gave some measure of protection. He used to jump to such an extent that the double-reins went smoking through my clenched palm. It took awhile for them to heal so after the bandages came off, I used gloves.

Eventually we came to another working arrangement. Although I've never dared fire the 303 near him, he grudgingly accepts the Colt 455 loaded with mild handloads.

Many of the problems inherent in this sort of training are so basic they're often overlooked. One was the business of placing a scabbarded rifle in the right place. While it took a few weeks to come up with a satisfactory arrangement of suspending the unit, it took another week to figure out why he bucked and kicked so much when I urged him into a canter or gallop. Since I didn't want to be seen in public with a death grip on his neck, my heels digging furrows into the ground at 25 miles an hour, I practiced in the solitude of the forest

The problem, and solution, were really quite simple. The Browning's butt, which was stable at a walk or trot, would describe wild gyrations in the air when we changed to a quicker pace. Each gyration would terminate with a smack across his flank. And at each smack he would buck. Readjusting the scabbard did the trick and he calmed right down. Sort of.

Then it came time for sword and lance work, nasty sharp instruments that, I concluded, were just accidents looking for a place to happen. It didn't help matters much when a friend, out for an afternoon's entertainment, mentioned a passage he had read in one of Rudyard Kipling's works. Something, he said, having to do with the condition of cavalry horses' ears. I think the words he used were ". . .tattered. . ." and "...ragged stumps. . . ." Somehow that punctured my illusions of flying down a grassy field, wind blasting across my face, leaning forward over that splendid streaming Arabian mane with my sword arm outstretched, point flashing ahead.

We got to the point where he didn't object too strenuously to having the sword suspended to his British Universal Military saddle, but he took exception to the slither of steel-on-steel when I went to withdraw it. Later experimentation proved more successful but I still only narrowly missed skewering myself on the weapon when my mount and I parted company.

The Pattern '08 pointing sword is an interesting piece which many

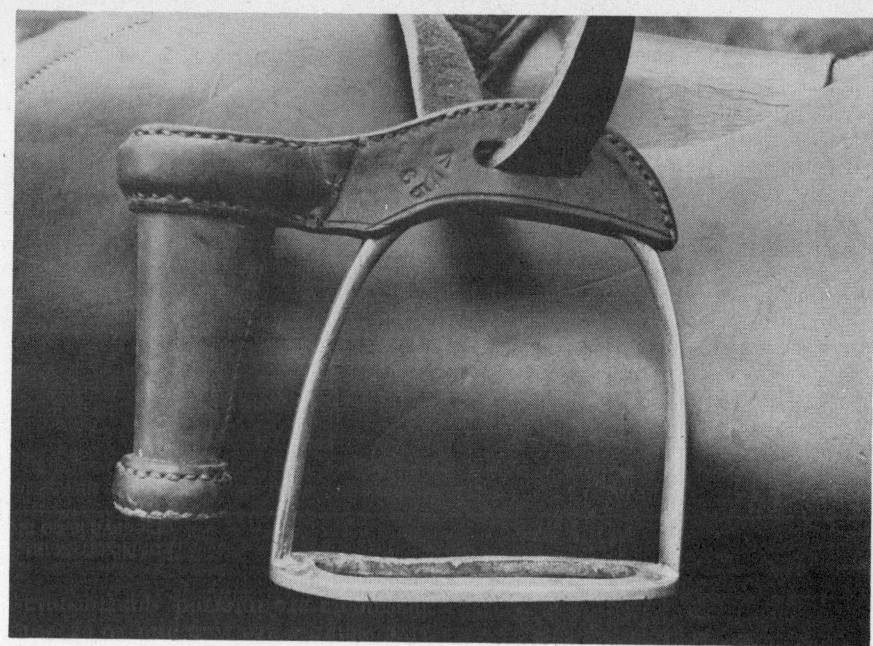

The right-hand stirrup iron has this heavy leather lance bucket, which shows that even in a world of machine guns, the cavalry knew what was important.

The left side of the horse, ready for the road, is a bit raggle-taggle, what with forage nets, feed bags, sabers and the like.

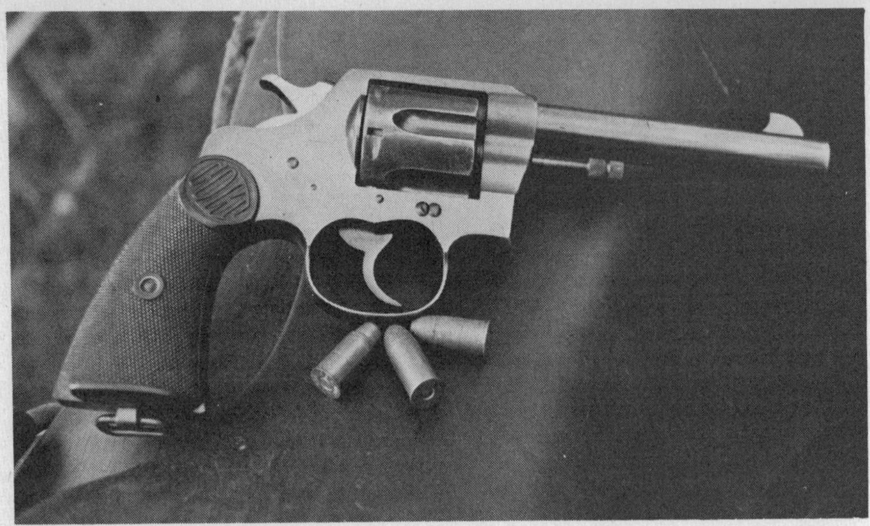

The New Service 455 was also tucked about the trooper somewhere. Mounted, he had quite a lethal array: lance, saber, pistol, rifle, bayonet, and a lot of cartridges.

made every attempt to flee when he heard that first, snarling rush and clack of jaws. Throwing a hasty look over my shoulder, I noted there was a large purebred accompanied by a scungy mutt of some sort. Kneeing the horse around, we stood fast and kept turning to face the dogs' circling strategy. Meanwhile, I reached over to the left side of the saddle with my right hand, underneath the reins, and grasped the pommel of that grand sword.

Foot by foot the naked steel emerged until I ran out of arm and suddenly found myself in a most distressing position. The point had come to rest under my left armpit and was stuck in a fold of my jacket. Now, I couldn't push back for fear of puncturing myself or ripping my jacket. I also couldn't deploy the sword any further since my rein hand was as high as it

sword aficionados will tell you was the last, and greatest, combat sword ever made. Designed in England during the early years of the 20th century by the then-Inspector of Gymnasia, the pointing sword is a different concept to the sabre we normally think of when considering cavalry.

Instead of being a slashing and cutting weapon, it's a thrusting, stabbing design. The grip is deliberately canted downwards and there's a thumbprint groove just in front of the basket. Both these aid in correctly holding the sword so that your wrist is straight and it literally becomes a straight-line extension to your arm. The sword illustrated here is unusual for what is an otherwise-common sword. The scabbard and basket are still sporting their dung brown front line colors. This is unusual because pretty well all the Pattern '08s were taken out of service shortly after World War I, then polished and chromed. Ever since, they have been used for ceremonial services. This one is actually a combat sword.

That being the case, it only seemed sensible to get to know it by using it. For months, riding around miles of countryside, I was plagued with a wide variety of nasty dogs who usually sprang out of bushes snarling and snapping at the horse's fetlocks. Naturally, his first impulse was to flee.

Using a gun on someone's beloved pet seemed to be a bit too final and also perhaps socially unacceptable. A sword, on the other hand, has more cachet and is equally useful in parrying a set of canine choppers. In my own mind, the sequence looked dramatic. When the dogs leaped out, the horse would rear and turn to face his attackers. As his forelegs were pawing the air, I would fluidly unsheath the sword and, as we came down to meet the dogs, stab and thrust with gusto thus keeping them at bay. The reality was embarrassingly different. No one witnessed it, so I can leave the really bad parts out here.

It was in early spring, an evening sojourn, when the first anti-canine opportunity came. As usual, the horse could go, while still maintaining some degree of control over the horse. I had run out of pull.

By this time, the horse gave in to his previous notion, turned on his hindquarters and bolted. The situation resolved itself. The jacket lost the contest and I lived to tell the tale.

It was, you can understand, with a great deal of suspicion that the horse viewed the nine-foot bamboo lance.

It took less time for this trooper to learn how to attain this pose than it took the horse to learn to put up with it.

The wicked three-edged tip wasn't a problem, nor even the white leather sling half way down its length. No. His primary objection was to the red-and-white cloth pennon which dropped from its end. It was an understandable objection. When the lance butt was in its leather bucket, attached to the right stirrup iron, he could see the flapping red cloth just at the extreme limit of his peripheral vision. They say that horses can't distinguish colors but there may be something about a red flag that no one has yet discovered.

We never really did come to a meeting of the minds. So, as is usual in horse training, you go back to the very basics. I parked the lance in his stall as a permanent house guest, then went out to take lancing lessons. Fortunately, there was a nearby equestrian center that still held on to a remembrance of cavalry. They taught musical riding, similar to that displayed by the famed RCMP Musical Ride. Lances, minus pennons, are both carried and used.

According to the 1898 Cavalry Drill Manual, there are a number of games that can be turned into competitions using the lance and sword. You get a latter-day equivalent of jousting. And thus you see how the weapons were supposed to be used properly.

Two of the games, tent-pegging and pig-sticking, employ the lance and sword respectively. Tent pegging, while thundering down a field at full tilt, demands you put the lance-tip through a loop of rope atop a peg hammered into the ground. Being a pessimist, I immediately considered the worst: what happens when you misjudge and bury the bobbing, swaying tip fully into the turf? The consequences appear to be as plain as the nose that was on your face.

Truth is, such an incident need not spoil your entire day. The white leather sling is there for just that eventuality. If the point does contact the ground, the lance will naturally come to an abrupt halt. But while it's doing so, you are continuing past. At this time, the point becomes a hinge and the butt will describe an overhead arc. As you go on, the butt is now parallel to your arm, thus disengaging the point from the ground. What remains is to regain your grip so that the lance is in the correct carrying position. It's at this point that the instructions become a tad vague. You are traveling, still, at over 30 miles an hour which makes any attention drawn from staying upright in the saddle décidedly fleeting.

Both my books—*1896 Cavalry Drill Manual* and *1898 Cavalry Drill Manual*—were remarkably mute on how the rest of the trooper's kit was placed on the horse and saddle. There *is* a passage which at least tells what bits and pieces are SOP, but it's up to the reader to put it all into perspective. It probably helped to have a knowledgeable sergeant.

So I was off on a clanging and banging lurch of a start. After days of head-scratching and input from "friends," I managed to get all the equipment on there. The result once launched in motion, looked more like an equine dry goods store than any classic impression of a cavalryman.

The book said it this way:

Order of Dress: MEN. MARCHING ORDER:

On the horse: Saddle and bridle complete with head rope and wallets, packed.

Breast Plate; breast harness, pioneer equipment (Regulation proportion); hoof picker; nosebag; small corn sack; forage net; mess tin; heel rope.

Carbine in bucket; sword in frog on shoe case, edge to rear; lance (for services in possession); cape (in front of wallets); cloak, rolled, in rear of saddle; surcingle pad; cape protector.

What the book didn't mention was how to pack these "wallets"—two small withers bags—with: two iron picketing pegs with rings (or two wooden pegs and rope); horse brush and curry comb; horserubber(?); sponge; one pair socks; one shirt; hold-all (complete); towel and soap; spare bootlaces; tin of grease (for the horse rubber?); emergency ration and woolen cap.

The Empire's last combat sword, the Pattern 1908, can be said to bear a considerable resemblance to the U.S. Army's last saber, which is understandable since the U.S. sword is the Model 1913.

The picketing stakes have been illustrated with this article. The long one, made of oak and edged with iron, is over two feet long and weighs about ten pounds. Of course, there's got to be a hammer of some sort to whack them into the ground, which means a large wooden mallet has also got to be stowed and carried.

Overall, trying to learn the finer points of things cavalry is comparable to getting involved in guns. It's a never-ending learning process that gets you into far fields of endeavor. As the years rush by, you are constantly learning new things while forgetting what you learned in the past.

Guns get you interested in simple gunsmithing, and horses and cavalry lead you to blacksmithing, a far more arcane art. This was spurred (ahem) by my discovery of a secret compartment in the leather sword frog—the one the manual calls a shoe case—which contained a hand-made, period horseshoe plus shoeing nails. Evidently, the cavalry trooper was expected to be able to replace and adjust his mount's shoes when necessary. Today's eastern rider, I found, hasn't the faintest notion of how it's done.

So, like any serious shooter and collector, I've started to learn the basics. And you thought guns were tough!

There's more. You must learn how the museums preserve (conserve) old leather and cloth. It doesn't last as long as the metal and wood of an antique gun. Still, like an antique gun, it's nice to trot out once in awhile and use.

Now. If only they could work out some kind of ejection seat arrangement, complete with parachute, for that saddle. ●

And Now Nikon

by BOB BELL

IN THE FIELD of optics, the name Nikon has long been a name to reckon with. The company known as Nippon Kogaku K.K. dates from 1917, when three of Japan's leading optical manufacturers merged. Glass research laboratories, glass factories, refraction telescopes, military optical equipment, microscopes, and, of course, Nikon cameras came out of this organization. The popularity and quality of these cameras in a sense changed the name of the company itself to Nikon.

With such a background, perhaps it was inevitable that Nikon would get into the rifle scope business. Two models have been announced, a straight 4x and a 3-9x variable. Not a very lengthy line, but when all is said and done, enough to cover most big game situations and routine varmint shooting. I don't know how supply is at the moment, but expect it's reasonable.

Joe Strear was kind enough to send along a sample of each model for testing, and these Nikons are impressive scopes. They are built on one-inch tubes, of course, and each has a 40mm clear objective. This results in an outside tube diameter of 48mm at the front end, which isn't a lot under 2 inches. Ultra-low mounting isn't in the cards for such a scope, but that doesn't seem to bother most riflemen.

Other specs include a field of 28+ feet for the 4x, 37-12+ with the variable. Eye relief is about 3½ inches for both. The 4x is just under 12 inches long, the variable just over. Respective weights are 13.5 and 16 oz. Adjustments are internal, quarter-minute clicks, with maximum movement of ± 40 MOA in the 4x, ± 15 MOA in the 3-9x. Outside diameter of the ocular lens unit is 42mm, or about 1.66 inches, which means you should check out scope ring height carefully. Some bolt handles might not clear enough for use with a gloved hand if low rings are used.

Nobody doubts the quality of Nikon camera lenses, so we can probably assume similar quality in these scope lenses. Light transmission and image quality are aided by multiple layer coating. Tubes are nitrogen filled and are said to be dustproof, waterproof and fog-free. It's also stated that the variable does not change point of impact when magnification is shifted, and that even after firing numerous rounds of the heaviest calibers these scopes retain their accuracy. I put it that way because, in a practical sense, it isn't possible to do enough test firing with any scope to shake it apart—though I don't doubt that any scope

For Nikon 4x on Ruger Ultra Light 308 in Ruger mounts, the large objective is no problem. Ruger rings are fairly high.

ever made, if solidly mounted, will let go if subjected to enough shots. That's not a criticism. Anything built by man will eventually fail under stress.

Big game season was over when these Nikons arrived in late December, so I couldn't use them hunting. We did put them on rifles—the 4x on a Ruger Ultralight 308 using Ruger mounts, the 3-9x on a M700 7mm Magnum in Redfield Jr. mount—to get a feel for them and do a little shooting. Both gave brilliant sharp images. The variable seemed right at home on the magnum, just clearing the barrel and bolt handle in the low Redfield rings. The objective unit of the 4x had a bit more clearance, due to the slightly higher Ruger rings, but there wasn't much room to spare between the bolt handle and ocular.

A 40mm objective isn't necessary, in my opinion, on a 4x scope, though it's just about right on the 3-9x. It gives a 10mm exit pupil with the 4x, and the human eye cannot absorb a pupil that large, no matter how poor the ambient light. It does make for fast aiming, of course, even when the rifle is rapidly aligned.

On an extremely accurate varmint or bench rifle, it's possible to check click value by group shooting. This isn't as easy on a hunting rifle. This Ruger and Remington normally put three shots into 1½ MOA or so, which is fine for hunting but not too reflective of a quarter-minute adjustment. So we checked the Nikon adjustments against a collimator grid having 4-minute squares. These should require 16 clicks per square. Both scopes came very close.

Running the variable through its complete power range showed no discernible movement against the grid—which means there would be no point of impact change that could be blamed on changing magnification.

Aimpoint electronic sights have been gathering themselves a host of users, especially among specialists such as combat handgunners. A red, parallax-free dot serves as an aiming point, seemingly plastered right on the target. It's powered by two mercury batteries and is exceedingly useful when darkness makes conventional sights almost useless—as in a lot of law enforcement shooting. Two new versions are available this year—the Mini at 5 oz., intended primarily for handgun use; and the Maxi an ounce heavier, threaded to take a 3x or a new 1.5-4x attachment.

American Import Co. has added a rubber-armored line of scopes to its traditional L.M. Dickson Signature models. The Dickson Armor scopes are offered in 10 models, including fixed powers, wide-angles, and both conventional and wide-angle variables. Special ring mounts that conform to the ridged contours of the armor are available, but standard one-inch rings can also be used.

A.R.M.S. (Atlantic Research Marketing Systems) now supplies a scope base for the H&K weapon family. Called the Swan G3 Universal Scope Base, it was developed to eliminate the requirement for various adapters. Using it, most military and civilian scopes can be installed, including night vision scopes.

Armson, Inc. offers the Armson OEG (Occluded Eye Gunsight) and several new Trijicon Riflescopes. Both eyes must be open to use the OEG. The one behind the sight sees a bright red dot against a black background, while the other eye sees the target area. The brain merges the dot and the target into one image for shooting. Such sights are intended for use in fast-firing situations—plinking or combat shooting say, rather than precision shooting. Eye relief is no problem, so the OEG can be used on handguns as well as long guns.

The Trijicon Riflescopes, scheduled for availability in May, 1985, are essentially conventional models in 4x40, 6x56, 1.5-5x32, 2-7x40 and 3-9x56 sizes. One difference is that the reticles have a red glow in poor light. This aids their visibility without impairing night vision.

Armsport, Inc. has a full line of centerfire scopes, several for rimfires, and an unusual—or "old-fashioned"—small diameter, 32-inch 4x black powder model. This one should go well with many replica rifles. Armsport's "Forever" high power scopes feature multi-coated lenses for maximum light transmission and glare elimination. Eye pieces are locked for reticle protection.

B-Square has added a number of no-gunsmithing mounts for the do-it-yourselfer who doesn't want to add any holes to his pets. There's a side mount for top-ejecting Winchester, Rossi and Browning lever guns; an over-the-bore model for the 94 Winchester Angle Eject; a shotgun mount for installing Aimpoint/Tascorama or Weaver type rings on the Mossberg 500, Ithaca 37 and Mag 10, Remington 870/1100, and Smith & Wesson 1000/3000; a design for the Savage 340 that permits iron sight use; a unit for the HK 91/93/94 pseudo-military rifles with Aimpoint/Tascorama; a mount for installing an Aimpoint on any model Ruger 22 autoloading pistol. These are easily installed units that slide on or clamp fast without drilling or tapping. Often, conventional sights are not interfered with. In some cases, the 94AE, say, scope position is higher than ideal, but that's part of the cost that must be paid for convenience. During the past year I had occasion to use a B-Square mount for putting a scope on an 870 Remington slug gun, and there's no doubt it was installed in minutes and performed with full satisfaction.

The 3-9x Nikon on a long M700 using Redfield Jr. mount, low rings, has limited eye relief option due to objective bell near the front ring. Bob Wise found it no problem.

Bausch & Lomb covers the rifleman's needs with four scopes these days, the ever-practical 4x40 and three variables that handle all ranges from brush busting to way over yonder: 1.5-6x20, 3-9x40, and 6-24x40. Note that two of these give a 4:1 power spread. B&L was the first to do this, I believe, with the long-gone 6-

24x target model. Don't see many of those anymore—probably because the shooters who have them keep 'em under lock and key. These new B&L scopes have multi-coated lenses and every variable I've tested has shown constant reticle position on the collimator grid all the way through the power range.

Beeman is best known as a supplier of precision airguns, so has received little coverage here in the past. However, they do offer a line of Blue Ribbon scopes fitted with lenses from the factory that makes Nikon camera lenses. These have Speed Dials—silhouette-type knobs—that are finger adjustable rather than requiring a coin or screwdriver. Their dials can be set at zero after sighting-in, which permits easy in-the-field changes for other ranges without losing the basic zero.

Of special interest to me were the Beeman SS (Short Scopes) announced a couple of years ago. Primarily intended for assault rifles, these models offered acceptable optics in extremely small packages. The SS-1 is a $2\frac{1}{2}$x that's only $5\frac{1}{2}$ inches long and weighs less than 7 oz. with mounting clamp; the SS-2 is available in either 3x or 4x with 21mm objective, compared to the SS-1s 16mm. The SS-2 is a bit bigger—6.8 inches and $13\frac{1}{2}$ oz. with clamp. New at this writing is the SS-3, a 1.5-4x16mm.

I don't have a lot of interest in assault rifles, but it seemed to me that the SS approach offered a way to get a scope on a 94 Winchester carbine—the original top-ejecting 94. I had tried for years to get various manufacturers to produce a scope for the 94. Make it low power and short, I said, and mount it right on the bolt. That way it will move back and forth when the lever is worked, getting out of the way of the top-popping empty.

No one was interested. Why make a scope for a single model, they asked, even though five million of that model are floating around the backwoods of this continent?

There'd be too much slop in the bolt to permit accuracy from a scope mounted right on it, some said. I pointed out that caused no problem with the aperture sight that was integral on many Model 71 Winchesters. Still, no one was interested, and eventually I quit bugging people.

Then I saw the Beeman SS-1, and the idea came back full force. And, a few days later I was at gunsmith Al Wardrop's place with an SS-1 and a rattletrap 94, a fanatic's fervor no doubt gleaming in my eyes.

Al smiled patiently, sorted through his junk box, and soon had a base that would accept the Beeman's clamp installed on the 94's bolt. A groove gave the extractor clearance, and two inline holes at the rear held things together.

A short time later I was at the range. At 50 yards, three of Remington's 170-gr. factory loads made a line $1\frac{3}{8}$ inches high, a quarter-inch wide. I went to the 100-yard target. The first two shots almost touched, the third one opening the group to $2\frac{1}{2}$ inches. The next three bullets went into $2\frac{5}{16}$ inches. I then fired five shots into $4\frac{5}{8}$ inches, four of those measuring $2\frac{9}{16}$. Actually, those first eleven shots at 100 yards went into the same $4\frac{5}{8}$-inch group.

I had some 165-gr. Speer RN bullets, so loaded them ahead of 31 grs. Winchester 748 powder and $9\frac{1}{2}$ Remington primers, after neck-sizing the brass. Three consecutive 3-shot groups measured $\frac{11}{16}$, $1\frac{7}{8}$ and $2\frac{1}{2}$ inches at 100 yards. A 5-shotter went $2\frac{1}{2}$ inches.

I've been shooting this little outfit for months now, as time permits, and 3-shot groups of $2\frac{1}{2}$ inches or so are not at all unusual at 100. I don't suppose I have to say I enjoy it. I hold the carbine in both hands, as in hunting, resting the back of my left hand on a sandbag, so results—and zero—should be close to what I'll get in the field.

Nobody needs more accuracy for whitetail hunting in the woods. There certainly is little of the predicted "slop" in this old 94. It's a real delight to have the benefits of a scope on this popular carbine—one that isn't offset or so far forward that field is greatly diminished. And unlike the conventional open sights, zeroing is precise and easy.

The SS-1s field is 32 feet, which is equivalent to that of a conventional 4x—enough for most woods use but maybe on the small side for brush hunting. One of these days I might replace it with the SS-3, which has a 44-foot field at $1\frac{1}{2}$x. A 94 Winchester carbine was my first "big" gun. It's

Bob Bell with Beeman SS mounted on bolt of old style M94 Winchester, looking as if it belonged.

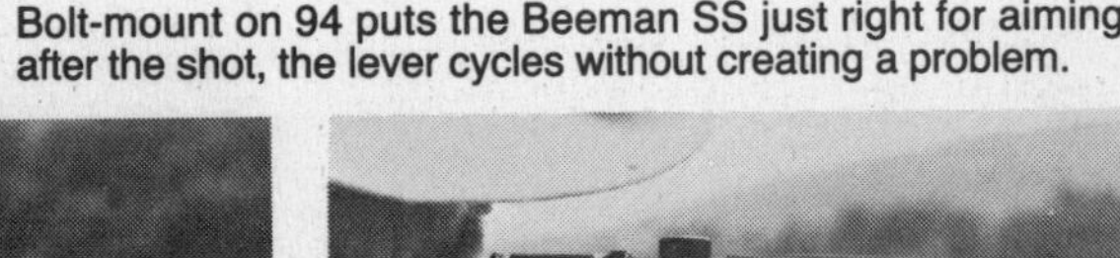

Bolt-mount on 94 puts the Beeman SS just right for aiming; after the shot, the lever cycles without creating a problem.

fun to have one again . . . fitted with a good scope.

Browning, in years past, had their own line of scopes, but discontinued them. They do still have one-inch rings in three heights and bases for Browning rifles, including some 22 rimfires. New this year are mounts for the recently introduced Browning A Bolt centerfire and for the 1885 single shot. Both have two-piece bases.

Maynard P. Buehler, Inc. has for decades been supplying all-steel bridge type and two-piece mounts for most any firearm that anyone would want to shoot. Rings are lined with micro-thin (less than .001-in.) oil-resistant synthetic rubber, which gives a positive grip on the scope tube and at the same time protects its finish. Long one-piece bases support the scope by placing the front ring beyond the action, even on magnum lengths. Conversely, extension bases permit mounting short scopes farther to the rear, for proper eye relief. Several two-piece extension bases have been added this year, and 30mm split rings for some imported scopes. The M83 no-drill, no-tap pistol mount, fabricated of high tensile aircraft aluminum alloy, is now available in either black or silver finish, to fit many calibers up through the 357 Magnum.

Burris Co. has added a pair of scopes to its already extensive line. For open country hunters, there's a 4-12x ARC (Automatic Range Compensating), while for those who work at shorter ranges and want a small scope, an adjustable objective has been added to the 4x Mini. The initials "PA" are added to the name, indicating parallax adjustment. The objective unit permits sharp focusing from 10 meters to 100 yards and beyond with only one revolution of the unit. At 9.2 inches and 10 oz., this is a neat little scope that will take the pounding of even a magnum cartridge.

Bushnell offers three rifle scope lines these days, the Scopechief, Banner and Sportview, and they have several models for rimfires, handguns and air rifles. The Banner offers conventional fixed powers from 2½x to 10x, while the only straight power in the others is 4x. All lines have numerous variables, and several Banners are made with Lite-Site reticles—switch-operated battery-powered red dots superimposed on the reticle intersection. I believe Bushnell was the first to produce this reticle, though many others have something similar now. Its advantages in gloomy woods or for early morning/late afternoon shooting are obvious.

Conetrol has for some time had the goal of being a single source of mounting hardware for any firearm which will take a scope mounted low over the receiver. Another step has been added with the recent addition of a one-piece base to fit all Ruger No. 1 Single Shots having a quarter-rib. This base replaces the Ruger rib, utilizing the factory holes. Its design places the rear scope ring farther to the rear, eliminating excessive scope overhang and making it easy to get proper eye relief with hunting scopes. The new base is offered with Huntur, Gunnur or Custum finish, to match the rings of your choice. Conetrol gives "the NRA Percent"—an automatic 1% discount to NRA members.

Davis Optical's top man, Myron Davis, says he has semi-retired. The only scope he is still manufacturing is the 1½-inch SPOT SHOT in powers from 10x to 30x. He still offers repair service.

Heckler & Koch, Inc. is well known for high-quality autoloading rifles and handguns. They also are a source for at least some models of the Schmidt & Bender scope sights, the 1.5-5x Zeiss, and mounts to attach same to various H&K rifles. Although neither of these scope lines is exactly common in U.S. gamefields, both have excellent reputations on a worldwide basis. Their optics are outstanding and both are known for their durability.

J. B. Holden Co. has adapted its Ironsighter mount to a number of rifles this year. The popular Marlin 39A lever action rimfire can now be fitted with the See-Thru mount which gives instant choice between glass and iron sights, as can Browning's new centerfire A-Bolt. Furthermore, assorted Ruger rifles now have the Ironsighter option—the 77/22 rimfire, the Number One, the Ranch Rifle, and the increasingly popular Model 77. Of interest to all Ruger fans is the fact that these new Ironsighter mounts fit the integral bases on the Rugers. All new mounts mentioned here will accept scopes of any power,

The Shepherd 3-9x on this Remington 541-S—an accurate outfit—follows the helm as advertised.

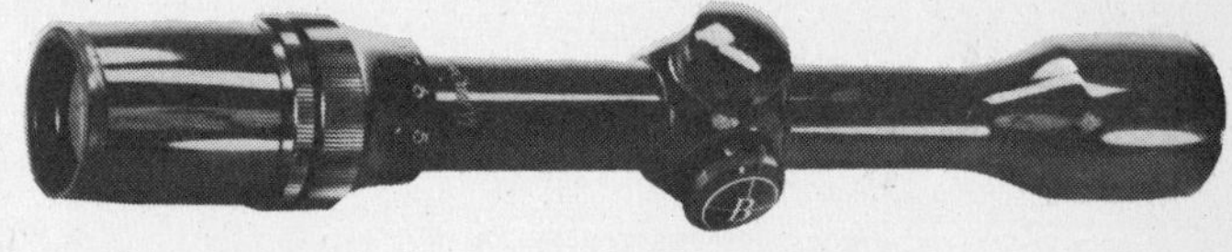

From the top, we have the Schmidt & Bender 2½-10x56mm; the Swarovski single-tube 6x36; Bushnell's 2.5-8x ScopeChief.

Bell put the Swift 3-9x40mm on his homemade 21-in. Model 52—very impressive looking.

including the rangefinder models with large objective units. Also, they are of Holden's "wide" design which offers a 34 percent wider field of view when using iron sights than the first Ironsighters. The Ironsighters, which were designed by Jerry Holden and have been available since 1967, are available for most centerfire rifles, popular muzzleloaders, rimfires having grooved receivers, many handguns and shotguns.

Paul Jaeger, Inc. still supplies their side mount for hunters steeped in tradition, but also has the popular European-style EAW quick detachable top mount, which pivots to supply windage adjustment, EAW steel rings for Redfield, Leupold and Burris bases, rings for Weaver bases, and even German claw mounts. Also, for those who want a top quality European scope to go with their classic hunting rifle, Jaeger has a full line of **Schmidt & Bender** models. Available with either steel or lightmetal tubes are the 1½x15, with a field of over 90 feet, 4x36, 6x42 and 8x56 straight powers. For varmint shooters there's a 12x42 steel model, and there are three S&B variables—1¼-4x20, 1½-6x42, and 2½-10x56. Obviously, these cover the field for any kind of hunting. All have centered reticles and a choice of numerous reticles. Reticles are located in the focal plane of the objective, which means they appear larger (though they actually subtend no more of the target) when power is boosted. However, this also means there can be no change in point of impact with any power shift.

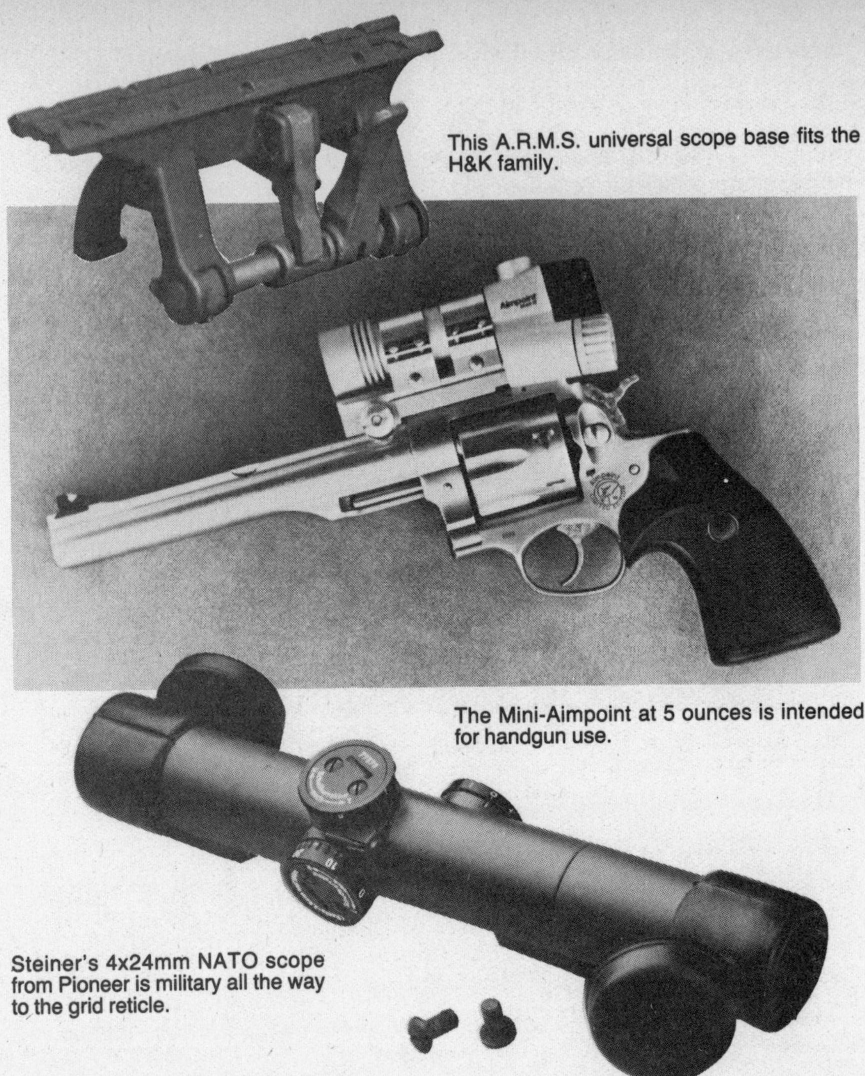

This A.R.M.S. universal scope base fits the H&K family.

The Mini-Aimpoint at 5 ounces is intended for handgun use.

Steiner's 4x24mm NATO scope from Pioneer is military all the way to the grid reticle.

Jasmar Shooting Accessories, Inc. now supplies a scope mount which replaces the left grip of military-style 22-cal. High Standard pistols. An aluminum one-piece moulding, it will accept an Aimpoint or Tascorama, or a conventional scope in Weaver-type rings.

Kimber of Oregon has for some time been supplying the neat double lever QD mount designed by the late Len Brownell. For those who want to use this mount on a non-standard outfit, Ross Billingsley of Dayton, Wyo., who worked with Brownell for years, can probably do the job. He can fit them on quarter-ribs, doubles, combination guns . . . whatever.

Kwik-Site Corp., long known for their see-thru mounts, recently added a super-low model for those who have no interest in near-simultaneous use of iron sights. The aluminum alloy split rings are extremely thin at the bottom, positioning the scope so low on Weaver-style bases that large eyepieces might not clear bolts. In such cases, a higher version is available. Personally, I like small scopes sitting right down on the receiver. This KS-WEV mount makes that possible. Also new is a version which combines the bottom half of each split ring with an integral base that's contoured to fit the action. Allen screws attach the units using factory holes.

T. K. Lee Co., maker of the famous Lee Floating Dot reticle, has for many years been owned and operated by a fine gentleman named Dan Glenn. I'm not certain how many Lee Dots I've had through the years, the first one installed by T.K. himself, the others by Dan. I've always thought it was a great reticle, fast and easy to use. Anyway, Dan tells me he was in and out of the hospital three times in '84, and he's ready to wrap it up. At age 72, he doubtless deserves some time to relax. Chances are good the Lee Dot business will continue in the hands of another shooter, but no specifics are available at this writing. We'll tell you next year.

Leupold has such an extensive line of scopes that it's hard to fit a new one in, but they managed this year with a couple of Compacts. For big game hunters, there's a Vari-X 2-7x and for the growing number of sophisticated rimfire hunters, there's a 4xRF Special. Leupold has been a leader in providing smaller than normal scopes to go with the shorter, slimmer rifles now available, and this new pair continues the trend. The 4xRF is essentially the standard Compact except that it is adjusted to be parallax-free at 75 yards rather than 150. It is therefore a perfect complement to a high-grade rimfire rifle. Its Duplex reticle also has finer than normal crosswires to permit easy quartering of a squirrel's head at woods ranges.

The new 2-7x Compact is an inch shorter and 2 oz. lighter than its full size brother, which means an awful lot of optical efficiency is wrapped up in a tiny package. I haven't used either of these scopes yet, so can't give a personal report, but it sure would be

T/C's Recoil-Proof pistol scope is here as a 1.5x with target knobs.

There are other ways to scope a 94; this is Orchard Park's Saddle-Proof for the Angle-Eject models.

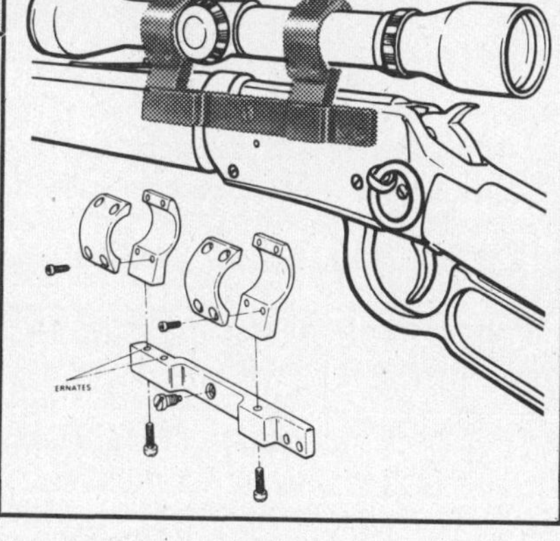

You can also try the Holden off-set mount, which fits in the factory holes.

nice to latch the 2-7x onto my Model Seven Remington 7mm-08 and head for the deer woods. Maybe next fall . . .

For handgunners with stainless steel pets, Leupold's Extended Eye Relief 4x is now offered with silver finish, to make a matching unit. In the mount area, two-piece Dual Dovetail versions for the 700 Remington and 70 Winchester are new, adding strength at the cost of windage in the mount. To go with these are new Super Low rings which put the scope $\frac{1}{10}$-inch closer to the gun than conventional low rings.

Lyman does not list any scopes in their 1985 product catalog, but does carry nine models in their trade price list—the Silhouette model in 6x, 8x and 10x, the LWBR in 20x, 25x and 35x, and hunting scopes in 4x, 2-7x and 3-9x. Lotsa other stuff in the catalog, but it's sad not to see the scopes there. I don't know if the absence signifies anything or not.

Orchard Park Enterprises has adapted their Saddle-Proof mount to the Winchester 94AE, making a low, strong and handsome rig. Designed for the Marlin lever guns, it can now be used to install a straight-tube scope on the side-ejecting Winchester.

Pioneer & Co. now is supplying the 4x24 Steiner scope for various military-type rifles. Sighting controls include a drop compensation adjustment in 100-meter units to 600 meters. Reticle is a military style, which incorporates a lateral grid that's useful in determining range. 9.2 inches, 12.3 oz., 30 foot field, water/weatherproof, multicoated lenses.

Redfield has seen no need for new scopes this year, opting to go with their extensive line of Traditional (round eyepiece), Widefield Low Profile and Tracker models. There's no doubt that one or another of these will handle any shooting situation that's likely to occur.

The 3-9x Illuminator is considered the top Redfield. As with all Redfields, it has a one-piece outer tube for strength and to reduce the possibility of leakage. Its big selling points are an airspaced triplet objective lens and five-element erector lens system, designed for optimum resolution, color correction and contrast, and flatness of field across the full diameter. The Illuminator also has a "zero tolerance" nylon cam follower and thrust washers to maintain an unshifting point of impact through the entire magnification range. With its unusual objective lens design and its large diameter, 42mm, there's no doubt the Illuminator is an effective scope at any power when ambient light is bad. Such efficiency doesn't come for free—this scope alone weighs 17 oz. and a mount will add 4 or 5 more—but there are many times when a hunter will figure that a small price to pay.

S&K Mfg. Co. continues to add mounts to their popular line. New this year is an unusual two-piece design for bolt guns. The unusual feature is the method of uniting the rings to the bases. Each ring is split vertically and has a round stud at the bottom which enters an oblong hole in the top of the base. The stud is relieved around its circumference to accept the points of two Allen screws. Working against each other from the sides, they provide windage adjustment in the mount as they move the stud in the oblong base hole.

SSK Industries—the place where handgun fanatic J. D. Jones hangs out—constantly faces the problem of keeping scopes on handguns chambered for loads that make the 44 Magnum seem like a kindergarten plaything. Jones says the T'SOB (that means Tough you-know-what) provides the strongest joining of gun and optics available. Normally, three or four rings are used. Besides keeping the scope on the gun, the extra rings provide structural support to the tubes, reducing the flexing which often leads to scope failure.

Any handgun exerts unusual recoil effect on a scope. The bigger calibers—and especially Jones's Hand Cannons—are far more destructive to scopes than even the 375 H&H Magnum rifle. Anyone thinking of getting into these had best consider J.D.'s advice on scopes and mounts.

Shepherd Scope Ltd. has made some changes in their highly unusual Dual Reticle System scope (see GD 38, 1984, for complete coverage). A significant one is the substitution of four thin glass surfaces, cemented into a hollow square, for the difficult-to-manufacture glass cube which formed the basis for the Secondary Reticle in the original. The cube had to be held to dimensions beyond the ability of a mechanical micrometer to measure. The change reduces production costs considerably. On some scopes it also was noted that magnum recoil might revolve the cube out of its locking detents, so a screw was added in the forward face of the turret to prevent this.

The military applications of the Shepherd DRS were obvious, so there have been movements in that direction. One of these is a 6x40 model which attaches to the M16-A2 with a one-piece mount rail and utilizes a reticle calibrated for the 5.56mm NATO loading. Dan Shepherd says that two civilian versions of the 6x40—a standard and a widefield—will soon be available. For rimfire shooters, a 4x20 and a 4x40 are expected out by late summer, and a 6-18x is in the works, though no availability date can be announced.

Wally Siebert continues to please countless accuracy buffs by converting Lyman, Leupold and Unertl scopes to higher powers. Along with this boosting, he can install superfine crosshairs for most precise bullet placement, or supply Lee Dots in ⅛ or ¼ minute diameter. For handgunners, he also halves the magnification of most Leupolds and the 12x Redfield, to give 10-20 inches of eye relief.

Simmons Outdoor Corp.—four generations of the shooting Simmons family, led by Ol' Ern himself, of shotgun ventilated rib fame—have jumped fullbore into the scope business. The line was introduced at the NRA show in Phoenix in 1983, Ernie Simmons III being the prime mover. His background as sales and marketing manager for Tasco for seven years provided the experience, and the availability of the Japanese-built line, designed by an American scopemaker who then withdrew, provided entry into the field.

Simmons scopes have one-piece aluminum tubes and their top models feature multi-coated lenses. All conventional powers are available, and there are wide angles, compacts, silhouette and target models, a short roof prism illuminated 4x for big game, several rimfire scopes, and camo rubber armored versions. Many have binocular-type ocular adjustments, which are far easier to use than the fine-thread eyepiece adjustment commonly seen.

For some months we've been shooting a 3-9x40 with good results. Our only criticism is that this model, a wide angle, has the extended field only in the horizontal dimension though it has the full round eyepiece. Seems to me if you're going to put up with the large ocular unit, you might as well have the full field vertically too. Optically it's fine and the adjustments are accurate.

Recently, Simmons introduced a new bridge mount, made in Australia. It's unusual in that the horizontally split rings are secured to the base by means of flat-topped cones which go through holes in the base from below. Transverse Allen screws in the riser portion of each ring engage a recess in the cone and bind everything together. The unit gives the impression of sturdiness, and we've been using it and the 3-9x Simmons on a Remington 7mm Magnum with good results. Simmons offers assorted other mount rings and bases to fit many centerfire and rimfire rifles too.

Swift Instruments Inc. currently lists nine rifle scopes, one for rimfires, the rest for bigger calibers. For the centerfires there's a 4x32 standard and wide angle, a 4x40WA, 3-9x32, 3-9x40WA, 6x40, 1.5-4.5x32, and a new 3-7x20. It's been some years now since I've hunted with a Swift scope, but I still remember how brilliant the field seemed on the one I used. Weaver-type mounts also are available.

Swarovski Optik introduced a new line of fixed and variable power scopes at the '85 SHOT Show. Included were a 4x32, a 6x36, and a 3-9x36. Scheduled for later availability are a 2-6x32 and a 10x40 with parallax adjustment.

These Swarovski scopes are built on one-inch aluminum alloy tubes, have multiplex reticles and internal quarter-minute adjustments. Focusing for the user's eyesight is via binocular-type adjustment, and the rear of the ocular has a built-in recoil system to protect against accidental impact.

Swarovski also offers several military-type scopes for use on weapons such as the M16 and various H&K rifles. These include the ZFM 6x42 with quick setting click-stop mechanical bullet drop compensator, and the 1.5x14 Cobra, intended for use on 7.62mm NATO assault rifles.

Tasco has one of the most extensive scope lines anywhere, a good size catalog full. A half-dozen World Class Wide Angles cover the usual powers from 1.7-5x20 to 3-9x32, and there are others with illuminated reticles, rubber covering, Trajectory-Range reticles, variables with a 4-1 power spread (3-1 is the accepted norm), handgun and varmint scopes, dull and brushed aluminum finishes, etc. There is also the red dot reticle Tascorama for handguns, assault weapons, etc., and scopes for air rifles, rimfires and shotguns.

Thompson/Center now has an Electra Dot reticle in both rifle and handgun scopes, four of the former introduced to complement the popular TCR 83 single shot rifle. Use of the Electra Dot is optional. It's battery powered and switch operated. When turned on, a 2-inch center dot and portions of the horizontal and vertical crosswires are illuminated to permit accurate aiming under bad light conditions.

T/C still offers the Recoil Proof and Lobo handgun scopes developed some years back to extend the usefulness of their Contender pistols. Each RP scope is tested in a unit which creates a force of approximately 1400 G's; the Lobo scopes do not have this construction.

Weatherby, Inc. is celebrating its 40th anniversary this year, doubtless one of the best known names in hunting rifles. Not bad for a feller who shortly after WW II started a gun business in a South Gate, Calif., garage. Weatherby scopes might not be quite as well known as Weatherby magnum rifles, but one line or another has been around since 1953. First were the Imperials. They were excellent scopes, but could not be adapted to the image-moving principle, so the Premiers were introduced about 1971. A little over a year ago, the Premiers were replaced by the Weatherby Supreme line, a 1.7-5x20, 2-7x34, 4x34, 4x44, and 3-9x44. Weatherby has always used large objectives, arguing, perhaps correctly, that they give better resolving power than small ones. Personally, I'll sacrifice the ultimate in definition to save weight and bulk on a hunting gun, so I like the two smaller Supreme variables best. Have been using both since before they were announced publicly and have nothing but praise for them. Wonder what goodies the Weatherby people will turn out for shooters in the next 40 years?

Williams' Twilight scope line now includes a pair of long eye relief handgun models, a 1.5x and a 2x. Both have 20mm objectives in inch tubes, eye relief of 18-25 inches, and are parallax corrected at 50 yards. Fields are 19 and 17½ feet respectively. They have 6-lens construction, internal quarter-minute adjustments, and weigh 6½ oz. Can also be used on bows, if archery is your bag.

Four Twilight rifle scopes are still available—the best in the medium price field, according to Williams, and of course they have an infinite variety of fine mounts. ●

The Ansley H. Fox Gun

THERE IS NO clear winner among makers of American double barrel shotguns. The Parker guns, Smith guns, Lefever and Baker guns all had their following, but the double produced by the A. H. Fox Gun Company of Philadelphia also had die-hard enthusiasts feeling that Ansley Fox's claim, "Finest Gun in the World," was justified.

One might wonder how a latecomer in the field of American hammerless doubles could have become so popular in such a short time as did the A. H. Fox doubles. Probably the biggest reason was the simplicity of its design, and the clean lines of the gun did much to recommend it to the sportsman. Additionally, the gun opened and closed easily, even when equipped with automatic ejectors, and the fast lock time and crisp trigger action was an aid to good shooting.

The guns have always performed well, especially with heavy waterfowl loads, and are still performing for the shooter who is fortunate enough to own a Fox double. Possibly Ansley Fox's experience as a market hunter and a professional shooter resulted in the styling of a "good shooter."

Among the admirers of the Fox double was Theodore Roosevelt, who took a Fox double on his hunts and wrote, "No better gun was ever made." Nash Buckingham, a well-subscribed outdoor writer of the 1920s and 1930s, was fond of Fox shotguns and had at least one custom "overbored" model which was a superior instrument in high pass-shooting of waterfowl where Buckingham had few peers.[6]

by DON HARDIN

Ansley H. Fox was a gun designer and inventor born in Atlanta, Georgia in 1876.[15] Fox was a fine shot, an ex-markethunter and a winner of the Grand American at live birds in 1900 and 1901. In 1901 and 1902 he was a professional shooter for the Winchester Repeating Arms Co.[15] Fox was at this time associated with the Baltimore Arms Gun Company. The Baltimore Arms Gun Co., (one of the first to make hammerless doubles) was established about 1895 and went to receivership by 1903.[7] It is known that Ansley Fox owned several of the patents used in the Baltimore Arms doubles.[12] When Fox left the Baltimore Co. because of business differences, he became associated with the Philadelphia Arms Company for its three-year existence from 1904-1906.[14] Ansley Fox, however, should not be mistaken for a George H. Fox, who had patents on doubles made by the American Arms Company of Boston and was accepted as an able gunmaker of a slightly earlier period.[7]

The Philadelphia Arms Company advertised that they were the makers of the Ansley H. Fox shotgun. These Philadelphia Arms Co. guns appearing in a 1905 edition of *National Sportsman* seem to be very much like the A. H. Fox shotguns to come later, differing externally in the recessed hinge pin and a projection on the extension rib, and in the cocking mechanism. Even the prices and seven grade designations paralleled the A. H. Fox guns to come from the same plant at Bristol and Wayne St. a year later.

At its beginning in 1906, the A. H. Fox Gun Co. employed about 100 craftsmen and turned out about $500 worth of guns each day.[15] The company was immediately successful and captured a large share of sales. Ansley Fox was actually an officer of the A. H. Fox Gun Co. for only a few years. In 1911, a Clarence A. Godshalk became president of the company and it was moved to 4600 North 18th St. in the same city. If Fox was a major stockholder, or an officer in the company is not known, but he continued to take pride in being the inventor of the "best gun in the world."

The A. H. Fox Gun Company under Godshalk's new management (1911) and in its new location quickly negotiated some manufacturing contracts to take advantage of the need for arms in the impending conflict (World War I) that seemed certain to come. First, a contract through England to produce rifle barrels for Serbian Mausers

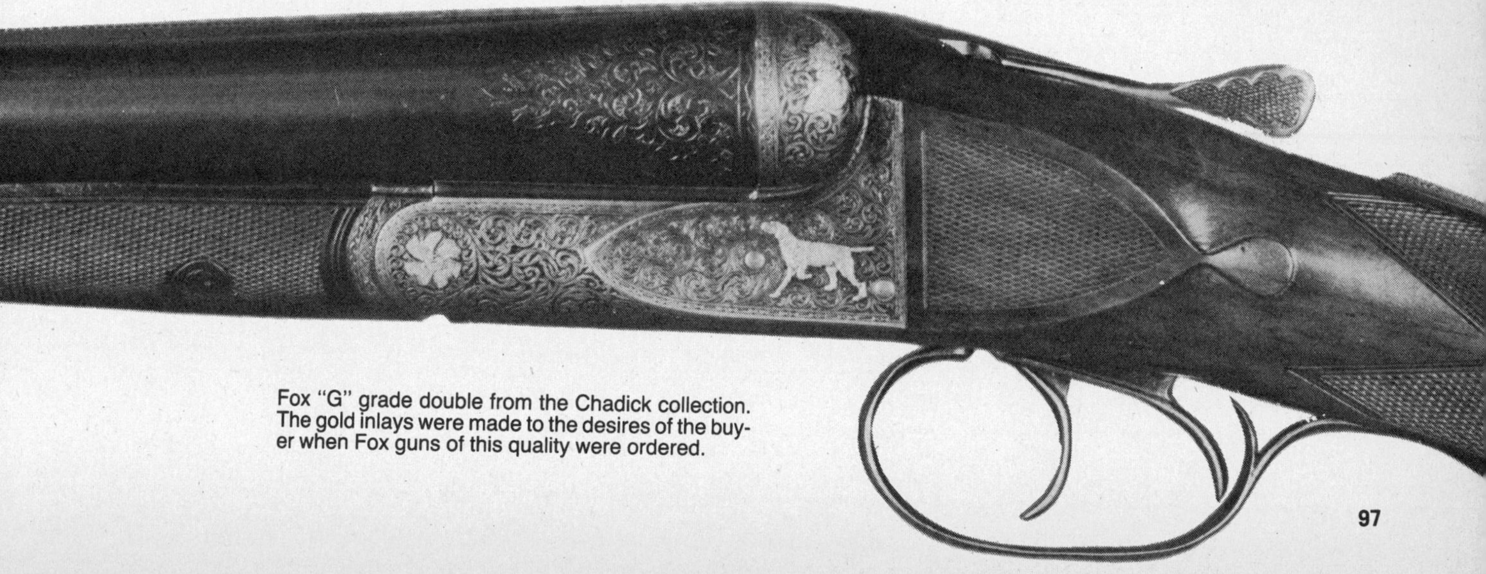

Fox "G" grade double from the Chadick collection. The gold inlays were made to the desires of the buyer when Fox guns of this quality were ordered.

was arranged. Serbia was soon to give in to Austria, leaving Fox with a large reserve of prime barrel steel. Secondly, Westinghouse subcontracted rifle barrels for Russian rifles, a project that was also of short duration and left more good steel. The company finally landed a contract and built Very flare pistols for the U.S. war effort.[13,14] When the 1914-1918 war ended, the company had a large surplus of good steel, machinery, and a trained labor force, putting the company in good position to produce quality guns.

The new work force was effective and the company produced a full line of doubles and single barrel trap guns until 1930 when they were sold to Savage Arms and moved to Utica, New York. After Fox sold out to Savage Arms in 1930, the factory in Philadelphia became the Godshalk Company handling lamps and metal. The Utica-made guns were identical to the Philadelphia-made guns in design and grade; probably most of them assembled from a large parts inventory brought from Philadelphia.

Ansley Fox remained in the Philadelphia area after leaving the company, and continued to be recognized as a "champion" live bird shot while staying active as an inventor. Fox also developed a machine gun during WW I that was not brought into production.[13] Surprisingly, in 1921, he was the maker of a luxury automobile. The car was a large, air-cooled model that sold for $3900.00. The ads claimed the car to be "as good as his shotguns."[5] This venture was short-lived and it is not known how many of the 50 hp, 132-inch wheelbase limousines were produced or have survived. In 1948, at the age of 73, Ansley Fox died in Atlantic City, New Jersey, and his obituary in the *New York Times* stated he was the designer of the A. H. Fox shotgun.

One of the Fox gun production practices that differed from other double barrel shotgun makers of the period was a conservative list of offerings regarding frame sizes and gauges. Ansley Fox simply limited manufacture in terms of frames and fittings. There were two frames—12- and 20-gauge—and 16 gauges were made on the 20-bore frame. The Baltimore Arms Co. and Philadelphia Gun Company made only 12- and 16-gauge guns while the A. H. Fox Gun company limited production to 12, 16, and 20-gauge doubles, which seems surprising to this collector as the 10-gauge was a popular choice at the turn of the century. Most likely, the demand for 28-gauge and 410-bore guns was low at all times and the cost of retooling machinery for slow-selling smaller gauge guns would not allow a profit.

Though gauge choice was limited, all Fox guns could be made to order at no extra charge within the standard of each grade. A buyer always had a choice as to barrel length and choke combination. Stocks were fitted in full pistol grip, half pistol grip and straight grip at no extra charge. The length of pull and drop of comb could be altered from standard dimensions if desired, again at no extra cost to the buyer. If extra engraving or a single trigger was requested, the customer was charged depending on the grade of gun purchased.

In all of the double guns made on the Ansley Fox design, a common basic mechanism was apparent, apart from boxlock design: the cocking slide

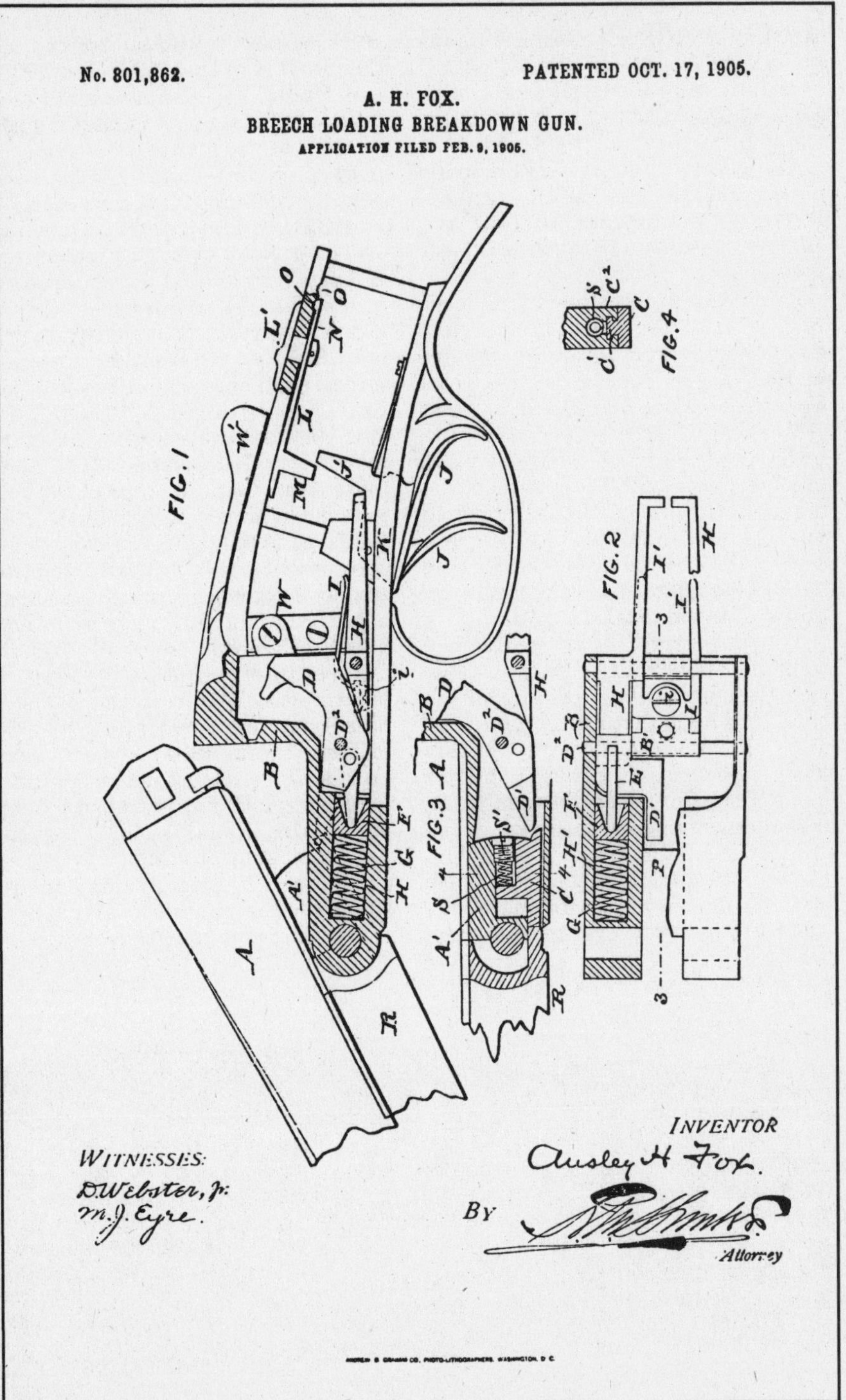

The Fox patent describes the gun made. Simplicity and strength and a line restricted to good sellers made a lot of difference.

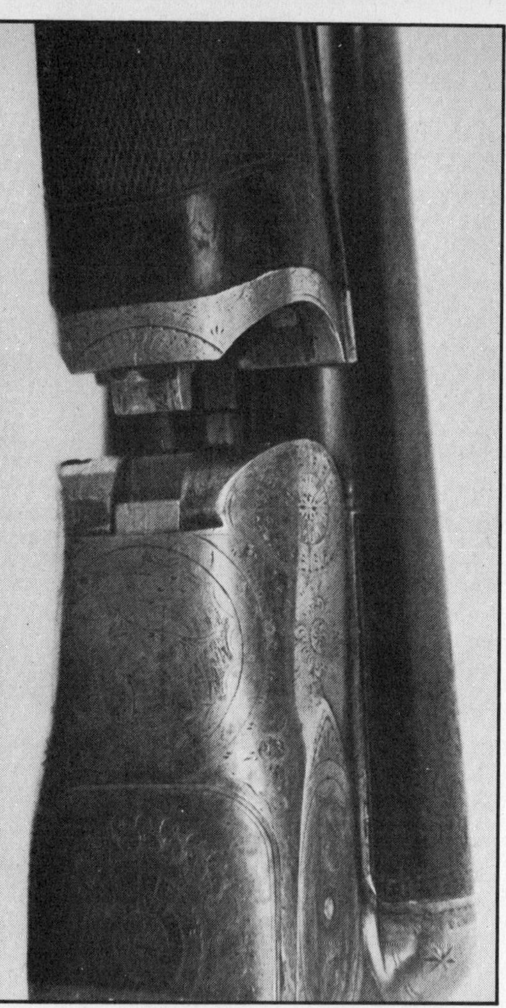

Fox action showing the dovetailing of cocking slide from forearm to receiver; this relationship of parts and distribution of work made Fox guns easy opening and closing.

carried by the bottom barrel lug lifted the hammers to full cock, and the rotary tapered bolt fastened the barrels to the frame. All A. H. Fox Co. guns used coil springs. All Fox-designed guns used a hammer and sear direct-line cocking system. The cocking slide engaged the toes of the hammer and lifted them to full cock as the gun was opened, using the weight of the barrels to accomplish the cocking. At the same time the triggers were automatically locked. This arrangement was strong and the short watertable gave the barrels a good mechanical advantage as they turned on the hinge pin. This advantage made the gun easy to open and close.

The firing pin was a part of the hammer, and according to the ads of the A. H. Fox Gun Co., dry firing would not harm the gun. Some shooters felt this to be a disadvantage however, as occasionally the gun might be difficult to open if the firing pin was still engaged against the primer. The tapered rotary bolt allowed the gun to be free of lugs locking in the frame and allowed a heavier frame which the Fox catalog claimed increased the strength of the gun.

Fox guns were indeed strong and the development of the HE grade Fox to shoot "magnum" loads was an innovation in the industry. In 1923, Western Cartridge Co., under the direction of John Olin, introduced a 3-inch cartridge, "The Super X Record," which contained a 1½-oz. load of shot. The HE grade "Super Fox" gun was introduced at the same time, having 3-inch chambers and increased weight to offset the added recoil. These heavy loads and guns did much to boost Fox sales as well as Western shell sales in the 1920s and 1930s.[6,10]

Philadelphia Arms Co. guns could be purchased with Damascus barrels as could the Baltimore Arms Co. doubles. The A. H. Fox Co., however, did not produce any guns with Damascus or twist barrels; Fox guns produced in both Philadelphia and Utica had fluid steel barrels. Prior to 1915, the barrels were labeled Krupp Fluid Steel. After WW I, however, many Americans disliked the "Krupp" label, and the Fox guns after WW I sported Chromox Fluid Steel labels. All barrels were subjected to an overload proof before being fitted to the action of the gun.

The barrels were usually bored to full choke and then opened up to shoot the pattern selected by the customer. On higher grade doubles, the boring was done by a mechanic named Burt Becker, who was considered one of the best shotgun barrel borers of all time. Nash Buckingham was extremely pleased with the barrel performance of his Becker-bored "Super Fox" magnum which helped achieve his legendary accuracy on the duck marsh. Most of Buckingham's "Becker" guns were just that—Becker specials made with Fox parts. The "over bored" Becker barrels undoubtedly were instrumental in the development of the magnum shotgun, as were similar developments by Charles Askins.

Most Fox guns were engraved; primarily with a short, deep engraving stroke that possibly would not rank with the best done on American doubles. However, on the early A. H. Fox gun and on all D, F, and G grades the engraving was of superior quality. One renowned engraver known to have worked on the better Fox guns was W. H. Gough. Gough, although associated with the A. H. Fox Co. and later Savage Arms, also did custom engraving for other gun makers.

The grades of guns produced by the three companies associated with Ansley Fox followed closely in terms of a similar letter grading system.

The Baltimore Arms Company guns initially were offered as:

1900 Catalogue[3]

Grade A	$35.00
Grade B	45.00
Grade C	80.00

1903 Catalogue[4]

Grade A	$33.00
Grade B	46.50
Grade C	92.50
Trap Gun	125.00
Grade D	175.00

The three highest grades could be purchased with fluid steel barrels. The A and B grades were of twist and Damascus respectively. The guns could be ordered with a choice of weight, barrel lengths, percentage of pattern wanted in each barrel and type of stock with dimensions to fit. The guns were offered in 12 gauge and 16 gauge.

The Philadelphia Arms Company guns were advertised as being available in seven grades ranging in price from $50 to $500 list. A complete list of grades of the Philadelphia Arms Co. guns is not available to this writer, but it is known that the Grade "C" double with Krupp Field steel barrels would cost the buyer $100.00. Very likely there were "D," "E," and "F" grade guns produced on special order.

The Philadelphia Gun Co. guns looked very much like an A. H. Fox Gun Co. gun with the exception of a hinge pin in a recess and a projection on the rib extension.

The earliest Ansley Fox doubles were offered in the following grades (with ejectors); (Fox patented his ejector in 1907 and produced ejector guns from 1908):

A	$ 65.00
B	90.00
C	115.00
D	215.00
F	515.00

Each grade gun without ejection $15 less.

The first A. H. Fox Gun Co. catalog listed the guns in 12 gauge and 16 gauge as well. Extra barrels were available at 40% of the new price of the gun. All grades featured Krupp Fluid steel tubes.[1]

Some guns sold through the H & D Folsom Arms Company of New York were of Fox manufacture. In the 1914 H & D Folsom catalog, A. H. Fox guns and Sterlingworth Company guns were advertised on the same sheet of the flyer. The Sterlingworth Co. doubles looked a great deal like the Philadelphia Arms double with the recessed hinge pin. The barrels were labeled "Sterlingworth fluid steel" and "Sterlingworth Co. Philadelphia, Pennsylvania." These guns were offered at $25 with extractors, and $32.50 if equipped with ejectors.[8]

A few years later a Sterlingworth grade double was offered by A. H. Fox Gun Co., but it was a Fox gun in all respects. The Sterlingworth was added at the bottom of the line, as a sales leader. This practice was adopted sooner or later by all of the makers of quality double guns. Prior to the addition of the Sterlingworth, the "B" grade was removed from the Fox line. At this time (about 1915) the XE grade and GE grades were added to the Fox listings, and later (early 1920s) the HE grade, a heavy gun developed for long range waterfowl, was added to the lineup.

In 1918, the Kautzky single trigger, the product of an Iowa inventor, was developed and was made available as the Fox-Kautzky single trigger at an additional charge of $31.00 on a new gun.[10] This trigger was superior to most trigger systems and was a definite asset to the prestige of the A. H. Fox Company.

Later yet, at the time of the sale of the company to Savage Arms, special double models were added for the trap and Skeet shooter. They were little changed in terms of manufacture except for a beavertail forearm and the appropriate boring.

In the early 1920s single barrel trap guns were offered in four grades but were discontinued shortly after the sale of the company to Savage Arms. These guns were well received as effective competition but served a very limited market and few were manufactured.

The 1923 Philadelphia-made A. H. Fox listings were:

Sterlingworth	$ 48.00
Sterlingworth ejector	60.00
A grade	62.00
AE (E indicates an ejector)	74.50
HE	100.00
CE	115.00
XE	185.00
DE	275.00
FE	500.00
GE	1000.00

The single trap Models:

J	at	$135.00
K	at	180.00
L	at	250.00
M	at	500.00

By 1935, the offerings of Fox guns produced by Savage Arms Corporation in Utica were modified, primarily offering a larger selection to the buyer at lower prices in order to bolster sales. At this time the offerings were:

Sterlingworth	$ 39.50
Sterlingworth ejector	52.50
Sterlingworth Deluxe	43.00
Sterlingworth Deluxe ejector	56.00
Sterlingworth Skeet and Upland Game Gun	44.50
Sterlingworth Skeet and Upland Game Gun ejector	57.50
SP Grade	57.00
SP Grade with ejector	70.00
SP Grade and Upland Game	70.00
SP Grade and Upland Game with ejectors	83.00
A Grade	57.00
AE Grade	70.00
HE Grade	72.00
CE Grade	110.00
Trap Grade	135.00
XE Grade	185.00
DE Grade	275.00
FE Grade	500.00
J Grade single trap	135.00
M Grade single trap	500.00

The only significant design change made in Utica was with the SP Grade guns streamlined with all the sharp angles on the frame removed but retaining the action common to all A. H. Fox doubles. The SP guns had a solid blue-black receiver similar to the Winchester Model 21 double which was becoming well received at this time.

The single barrel guns offered by the Utica Company were assembled from Philadelphia-made actions and were reduced in offerings to Grades J and M.

Savage Arms also added the A. H. Fox "Skeeter" to the offerings with a ventilated rib and ejectors and Skeet boring; the gun was sold at $108.00.

The production of sporting guns was resumed following World War II, but Savage Arms Co. didn't continue the A. H. Fox line of doubles. Instead, it introduced the Fox Model B, a much plainer gun using the same actions as the Stevens Model 311 (carrying the Fox name, but not designed by Ansley Fox). Although not an elegant gun, it would be safe to estimate that more double guns of this design have been sold than any other double in the world. The Fox Model B has been offered with single trigger and ejectors in recent years, but it remains predominantly a machine-made gun.

There were approximately 202,000 A. H. Fox guns produced prior to WW II and more than three quarters of this total was accounted for in production of the Sterlingworth guns. It became evident that the marketing of a sales leader at the lower-priced end of the line kept at least one double gun maker in business.

The A. H. Fox Co. produced a fine gun and claimed that less than 20% of the labor in producing the doubles was done by machine. The high cost of hand labor had become too much of a burden for the production of double guns in the United States.

The collector or sportsman who is blessed with an A. H. Fox gun of high grade is usually agreeable with the claim of Ansley H. Fox that "It is the Finest Gun in the World." ●

The Fox guns were produced in the following serial numbers:

	Serial number range	Number produced
12 ga. A-F	1 to 50,000	35,000
12 ga. Sterlingworth	50,000 to 200,000	110,000
16 ga. A-P	300,000 to 350,000	3,800
16 ga. Sterlingworth	350,000 to 400,000	28,000
20 ga. A-F	200,000 to 250,000	4,000
20 ga. Sterlingworth	250,000 to 300,000	21,000
Single Trap Gun	400,000 to 450,000	550

Footnotes

1. A. H. Fox Gun Co., Catalogue of 1907, Philadelphia, Pa.
2. A. H. Fox Gun Co., Catalogue of 1923, Philadelphia, Pa.
3. Baltimore Arms Co., Catalogue of 1900, Baltimore, Md.
4. Baltimore Arms Co., Catalogue of 1903, Baltimore, Md.
5. Clymer, Floyd, *Historical Motor Scrapbook*. Floyd Clymer Publishing Co., Vol 7, pp. 180, 1954.
6. Evans, George B., *The Best of Nash Buckingham*. Winchester Press, 1973.
7. Gardner, Robert, *Small Arms Makers*. Bonanza, 1963.
8. H & D Folsom Arms Co., *Catalogue #11*, 1914, p. 15.
9. Hinman, Robert, *The Golden Age of Shotgunning*. Winchester Press, 1971.
10. McIntosh, Michael, "Great American Guns," *Conservationist* State of Missouri.
11. Savage Arms Co., Catalogue of 1935, Utica, New York.
12. U.S. Patents: 714688, 796119, 801862, 810046, 921220, 563153.
13. Wallack, L. R. "The Fox Tale", *Gun Week*, Oct. 5, 1979, p. 7.
14. Williams, Mason, "The Shotguns of Ainsley H. Fox," *Guns and Ammo*, Jan. 1973.
15. Wright, M. H., "History of the A. H. Fox Gun Company," from the Series "History of American Arms and Ammunition," *Field and Stream*, 1908.

Book Excerpt

This 1000-yard stare belongs to CPL Erland Johnson, Co. L, 58th Infantry, 4th Division. It was October 2, 1918. His rifle has its bayonet on board.

(Left) This USAHI photo shows the 4th U.S. Infantry arriving in France, Springfields in hand.

The Springfield 1903 Rifles

by Lt. Col. William S. Brophy, USAR, Ret.

This is Victor Vandermerek, 168th Infantry, 42nd Division. The U.S.A.H.I. says this Doughboy killed a German with the butt of this rifle May 18, 1918.

In the Phillipines in happier times, the very sharp rifle team of Company I, 31st Infantry won the Chief of Infantry combat squad competition.

Victorious, the Doughboys and their Springfields marched massed as battalions in a lot of parades.

Now it's 1942 and a new generation of soldiers board a boat, toting Springfields.

In the Solomon Islands the Marines still carried the Springfield 1903 rifle. This is a straggler hunt. (USMC Museum photo)

Brophy's involvement with the Springfield includes a lot of match shooting. He's here (at left) with his good friend Col. Jim Crossman when both were younger.

The Illustrated, Documented Story of the Design, Development, and Production of All the Models, Appendages, and Accessories.

Today, Brophy works for Marlin and has become one of those anonymous "industry figures" so often quoted in the firearms press.

With the permission of the author and Stackpole Books, we present here two sections from:

The Springfield 1903 Rifles

CARBINE

During the period that the Krag was the standard U.S. arm, there were both long barrel rifles and short barrel carbine models. The long-barrelled rifle was the arm of the infantry, and the carbine was for the horse-mounted cavalry.

During the period 1900 to 1902, when trials were being conducted to find a new high velocity flat shooting magazine arm, it was still the opinion of some military leaders that both a carbine and a rifle were needed. However, the excellent performance of the newly developed caliber .30 cartridge did so well in twenty-four-inch-barrelled experimental arms that the final decision and selection was for one arm to be used by all services. The Model 1903 rifle was the result.

The 1920 Ordnance Technical Notes indicate that the Cavalry at Fort Riley wanted to again explore the development of a carbine, and the modification of a Springfield rifle into a cavalry carbine was authorized for test.

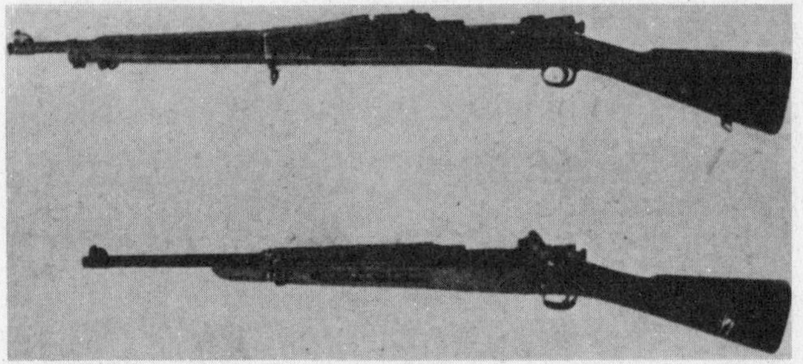

Published Springfield Armory photograph of a caliber .30 experimental carbine. *(AO)*

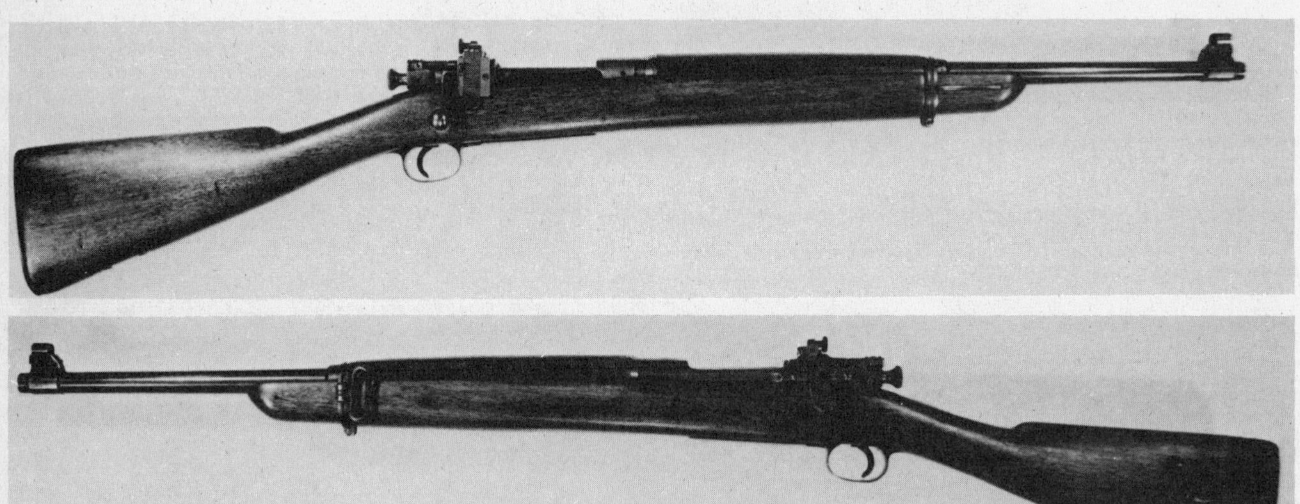

Springfield Armory experimental Model 1903 carbine serial number 2. *(Kellerstedt collection)*

Right side view of Model 1903 carbine. Note the specially marked Lyman No. 48 rear sight.

Special band of experimental carbine. The lugs on the side of the band were originally from a Model 1917 lower band.

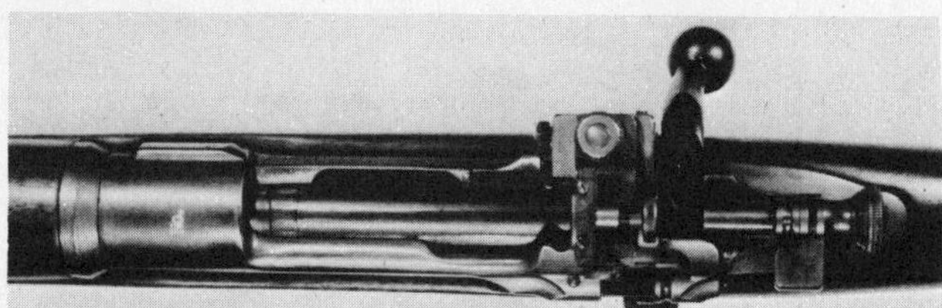

Top view of Model 1903 carbine.

Star gauge mark on the muzzle of the experimental carbine.

Special markings were handstamped into the experimental carbine floorplate identifying the promoter of the idea and the date.

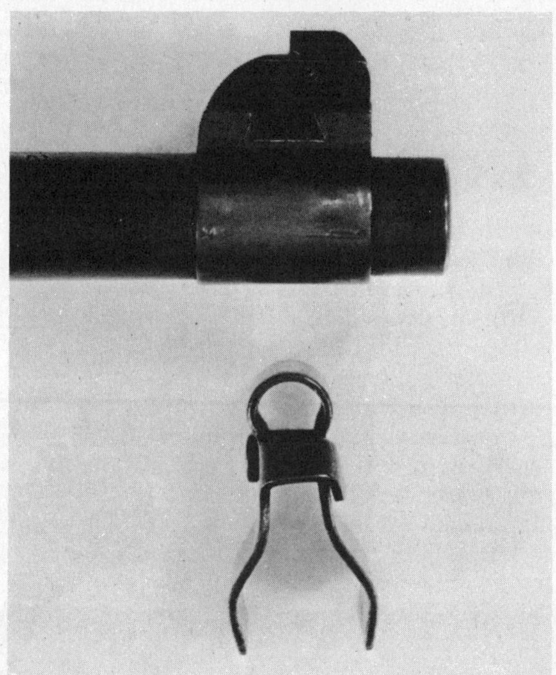

Shown in this photograph are the modified front sight and front sight cover of the experimental carbine.

The shortened standard stock of the experimental carbine had the sling swivels mounted on the left side of the stock. The original lower swivel recess was filled with a machined-down, swivel base.

Springfield Armory photograph of caliber .45 Model 1903 carbine having a 20-inch barrel made at Springfield in 1921. The carbine would shoot the standard Model 1911 caliber .45 pistol cartridge. The targets were fired at 60 feet by Mr. A. L. Woodworth and Maj. J. S. Hatcher.

The cavalry did not use the bayonet; therefore, they could eliminate the extra weight of the long stock and upper band. They were also not completely happy with the method of carrying the rifle in a scabbard when mounted on a horse, and felt they should re-evaluate the method of carrying the rifle across the back of the cavalryman. They also considered that the potential combat ranges did not require a twenty-four-inch barrel.

Springfield Quarterly *NOTES* for the first quarter of 1921 included the following description of the experimental cavalry carbine:

> Springfield Armory has completed an experimental cavalry carbine and shipped it to the President of the Cavalry Board at Fort Riley for test. The carbine has a 20-inch barrel with a short stock. It is fitted with special sling swivels on the left side in order that it may be carried slung across the cavalryman's back in such a position that the bolt handle will be away from the man's back.
>
> The carbine is fitted with a Lyman No. 48 sight modified so as to show graduations in yards instead of minutes. Each turn of the elevation screw equals five minutes. The knurled head on top of the elevation screw is divided into five divisions, each of which is equivalent to one minute. One turn of the windage screw is equivalent to four minutes or approximately one point of windage. Both the windage and elevation screws click for each minute of adjustment.
>
> It is found that the reduction in length of the barrel to 20 inches, instead of 24, reduces the muzzle velocity approximately 100 feet. The standard muzzle velocity is 2,700 feet per second while the muzzle velocity of the new weapon is 2,600 feet per second.
>
> Shortening the barrel had the effect of noticeably increasing the muzzle flash, especially when firing the rifle in a dim light.

The United States Army Historical Institute caption of this photograph in their Signal Corps collection of photographs states: "Modified U.S. Rifle, Cal. .30 M1903 designed for experiment by cavalry 3/27/40." However, this author does not believe any serious consideration for military use was given this rifle.

> It is found that the rifle handled very easily and is exceptionally well balanced. The recoil is not noticeably greater than that of the service rifle. The accuracy of the sample was found to be excellent.

It appears that only two of these experimental carbines were assembled, and that because of the austerity of the period after WW I, and because Ordnance thinking was being directed toward a semiautomatic rifle, monies to manufacture another model arm did not become available.

General Julian Hatcher in his *Hatcher's Notebook* illustrates an experimental carbine that was chambered for the .45 caliber service pistol cartridge. Made at Springfield Armory, it had a twenty-inch barrel and looked to be just a shortened '03 having a short forend and hand guard. The Armory has no information about this carbine except for having a negative of the same picture as that used by General Hatcher. The purpose and results of any tests are unknown. The targets illustrated in the photograph were shot by A. L. Woodworth and J. S. Hatcher.

A carbine that General George Patton was supposed

to have had something to do with is a modified '03 rifle that was stocked in the "Bull Pup" manner used by some sportsmen who wanted a short rifle. It is difficult for me to believe that any serious consideration of this rifle was made by cavalry or Ordnance personnel; the added cost and weight of the stock and attachment system, complicated latch-up of the trigger mechanism, and the exceptionally high front sight and obsolete Krag rear sight would all be negative factors. The photograph included here of this rifle was found in the U.S. Army Historical Institute collection of U.S. Army Signal Corps photos. No details about the rifle were available.

BUSHMASTER RIFLE

Frequently brave souls in the military perform unauthorized modifications to standard equipment. However, the fear of the discipline meted out, and the possible attachment of pay for the cost of the item, prevented many worthwhile and inventive ideas from being tried. The red tape, paperwork, and usually negative attitude of Command Personnel also prevented prospective inventors from obtaining authority to modify, alter, or experiment with equipment. However, if high authority blessed a project, it was not uncommon for ideas to be tried and, in some cases, put to use.

A good example of equipment being modified for a particular use in a specific area is the Bushmaster '03 rifle.

By order of Major General Robert H. Lewis, Commanding General of the Panama Mobile Force Command in 1942, Model 1903 rifles were shortened six inches for use by the Jungle Security Platoon while conducting missions in heavy jungle foliage.

A Bushmaster trooper aiming his rifle from the ruins of an old Spanish fort during 1942 training exercise.

World War II picture of Bushmaster officer during training exercises in the Panama Canal Zone. *(US Army)*

Enlarged photo of Bushmaster '03 that had an 18" barrel and was used during War II by the 158th Infantry Jungle Security Platoon in Panama.

Permission for the alteration of the rifle was granted by the Army Chief of Ordnance, but the work was done in the Ordnance shops at Couozal, Canal Zone.

These altered '03's were used by men of the 158th Infantry of the Oklahoma National Guard who were called into Federal service and were then stationed in the Canal Zone. They were named "Bushmasters" after the local snake—a deadly tropical pit viper.

The Ordnance shops in Panama did not have a Parkerizing capability. Thus, the barrels were blued after the shortening alteration.

DOUBLE-ACTION semi-automatic pistols had been long in the making before they became generally accepted as the excellent defensive tool they are. The first double-action pistol, the Mannlicher Model of 1894, was a double-action-only design, thereby combining the disadvantages of the revolver (heavy trigger pull when used in rapid, double-action fire) with the probable low reliability of the infant selfloader.

Kaisertreu (probably the pen name of the arms designer Karel Krnka) writes in "Danzer's Armee Zeitung" (Danzer's Army Journal) which appeared in Vienna, on October 31st, 1901:

"Considering what has just been written a double-action hammer-lockwork according to the Roth system which is described in the Austrian Patent No. 4420—effective date February 2nd, 1900—is to be preferred to the so-called automatic safeties. The essence of this ingenious invention is that by adding a special part to a double-action hammer-lockwork the pistol becomes completely self acting, whereby the double-action is only used to fire the first shot, while under continued fire the hammer is cocked by the rearward motion of the bolt, in that the hammer is thrown into cocked position after every shot and retained there until being released again."

Kaisertreu ends his paper with this remark: "I close these explanations with a resumé: For automatic pistols one should only chose a hammer-lock with a Roth-System double-action."

It should be noted here that Kaisertreu most likely describes his own invention which had been assigned to the G. Roth Company in Vienna.

The first double-action pistols were rather large and aimed at the military market. Among them was the Roth-Steyr pistol adopted by the Austrian army in 1907. The gun is equipped with a striker (semi-) double-action mechanism. However, the striker must be semi-cocked for the first shot manually. A long pull on the trigger then completely cocks and finally releases the striker, which returns to the ready position (semi-cocked) automatically after the shot has been fired. This type of functioning falls somewhat in between single-action semi-automatics, double-action-only autos, and the combined single- and double-action pistols.

Kaisertreu's double-action mechanism is partly described in the German patent No. 144,755 issued to G. Roth Company on May 3, 1902. Where the design of the Roth-Steyr deviates from the patent or from Kaisertreu's original demands, it is for the worse. The positive safety feature of the long trigger pull may have appealed to the Imperial Army's Acquisition Board more than to the young officer trying to improve his skill with the pistol. The step from this and similar contemporary designs to the 1914-introduced first double-action-only pocket pistol, the Le Francais, was not big.

By that time, however, work on the first double-action pocket pistol was well under way. On March 7, 1908 Alois Tomischka, who lived at that time at Mödling near Vienna, had applied for an Austrian patent. A little later he also filed an application in Germany where a patent was granted with the effective date of February 23rd, 1909. It describes the double-action mechanism of a pistol which later became known as "Little Tom." Production was started in Vienna around 1920 and later, probably in 1925, moved to Pilsen in Czechoslovakia. (See J.B. Wood: The Little Tom Pistol of Alois Tomischka. GUN DIGEST 34 [1980], pp. 130-134). The gun enjoyed a fair success, as approximately 40,000 were produced before its demise in 1929. The Little Tom was not made from high grade materials and the design had a few shortcomings as well. It therefore did not contribute

THE NAZIS' GUSTLOFF PISTOL:

Not even zinc alloys and cheap construction got it off the ground.

much to the propagation of the double-action pocket pistol as we know it today. In the year of Little Tom's end, however, there appeared the early star of the modern double-action pocket pistol, the Walther PP (PP = Polizei-Pistole = police pistol). Its immediate success can be attributed to the apparent properties of reliability, high grade workmanship, pleasing lines and double-action capability.

The design feature which put the PP in a class by itself and the importance of which was obviously not quite appreciated by all imitators was the automatic safety linked to the position of the trigger. This safety blocks the hammer and prevents it from touching the firing pin until the trigger has been pulled all the way back close to the release point. This lack of appreciation, which we will also meet in the Gustloff pistol, is all the more surprising since similar safeties had been used in revolvers for a long time. (The principle had been invented by Iver Johnson. He used it in his Safety Automatic Model of 1892. Similar designs are presently found in Colt, Dan Wesson, Ruger, and Smith & Wesson revolvers.) The other German manufacturers of pocket pistols soon felt the increased competition from the new Walther models and some of them designed advanced guns to improve their position in the market.

These activities resulted in two well known double-action pocket pistols—Mauser's HSc and Sauer's 38H models. Two more pistols of this type were designed and made in Germany at this time. Both have interesting features, are quite rare and definitely collectors' pieces. One of them, the Menz-Spezial-Modell, was manufactured before the war and sold commercially. It was also called PB-Modell (PB = Polizei und Behörden = Police and Authority) and sold under the trade name of Bergmann. *(Commercial sales may have been limited; but some were marked Bergmann Erben Spezial. Ed.)* Approximately 1000 pistols were sold. The distinguishing feature of this exposed hammer gun is the trigger mechanism. For the first shot the hammer can be cocked in the normal way or by pulling the trigger once. This will not release the hammer, which will only fall when the trigger is pulled a second time. For subsequent shots the pistol operates like any other blowback semi-automatic.

Interesting and innovative as the Mauser, Menz, Sauer, and Walther double-action pocket pistols may be, the rarest one in this class is the Gustloff-Pistole. Although of unusual design, it is not the hardware which sets the Gustloff apart. The circumstances, however, under which this pistol came into being are most unusual and throw some light on a time which worked great changes in the world.

Suhl in Thuringia and neighboring Zella-Mehlis were the center of German small arms manufacture during the 19th and the first half of the 20th century. In 1865 Moses Simson, Zacharias Simson and Karl Luck founded a gun factory which later became somehow connected with the Gustloff-Pistole. The company was renamed Simson & Co. in 1899 and produced hunting guns and bicycle parts. Under the provisions of the Versailles treaty, Simson & Co. became the only German manufacturer of military small arms after the 1914-1918 war. In the '20s the company

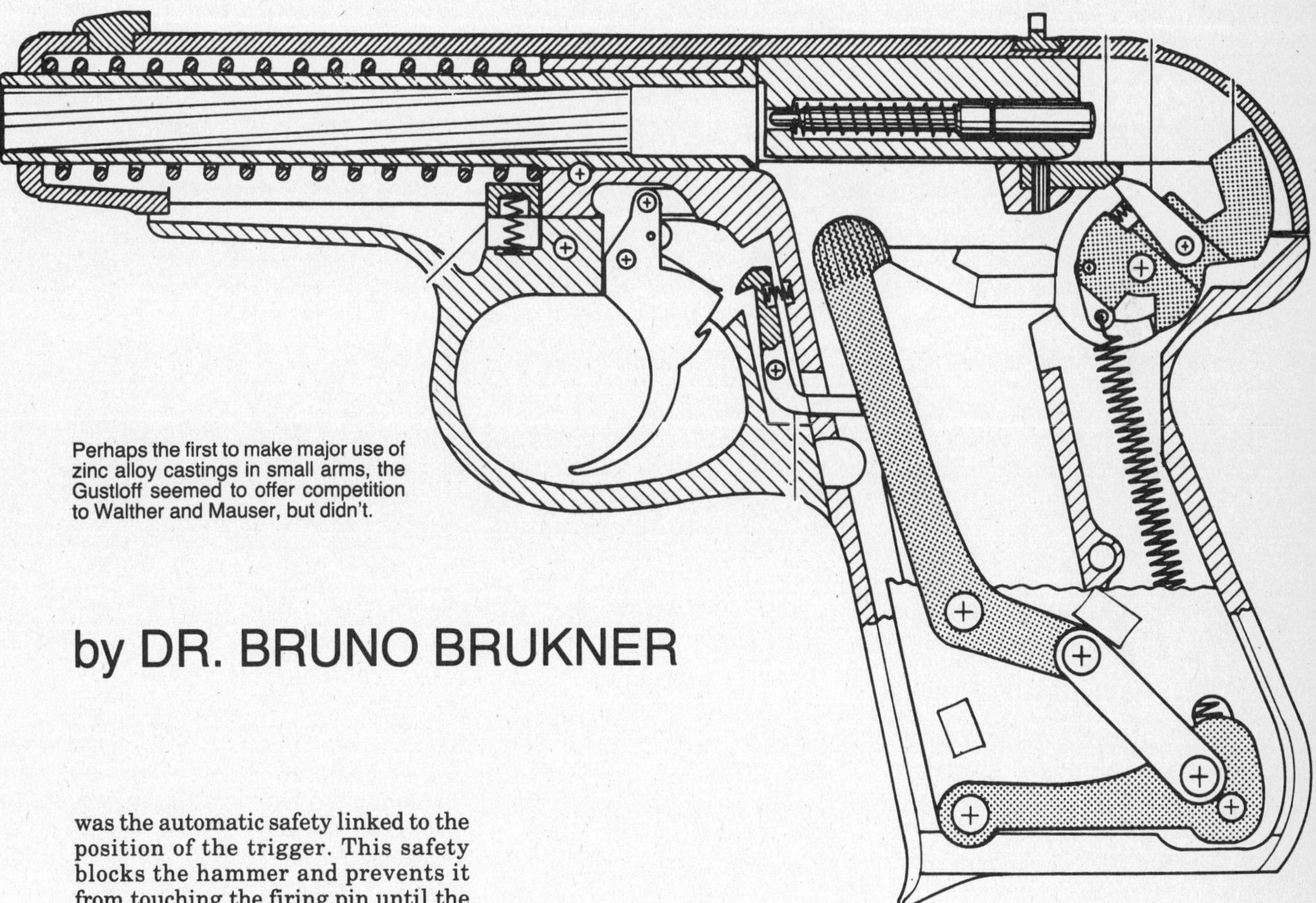

Perhaps the first to make major use of zinc alloy castings in small arms, the Gustloff seemed to offer competition to Walther and Mauser, but didn't.

by DR. BRUNO BRUKNER

produced its first pistol of its own design. This 25 ACP-caliber auto is very similar to many of its contemporary competitors. Although well made and finished, and gun laws quite liberal, production was discontinued in 1927.

Work on pistols was, however, not abandoned, as is documented by tool room models and German patents. Patent No. 621,898 with an effective data of August 18, 1934, e.g., describes a double-action mechanism reminiscent of Alois Tomischka's design. The patent is assigned to Berlin-Suhler Waffen- and Fahrzeugwerke Simson & Co. in Suhl. The change in name marked the influence of Hitler's Nationalsozialistische Deutsche Arbeiterpartei (National Socialist German Workers' Party, which we will just call party here since no misunderstanding can occur). As early as 1934 the Simson family had lost nearly all control over their company, even if they still received part of the revenues. To gain full control, the party put Arthur Simson and his managers on trial. No verdict was reached but Simson preferred to leave Germany in 1936 for obvious reasons. He went to Switzerland and later to California where he lived for the rest of his life.

Now that the party had reached its goal, the Simson Co. was amalgamated with the Wilhelm-Gustloff-Stiftung (Wilhelm Gustloff Foundation). The "honorary leader" of the foundation was Fritz Sauckel, head *(Gauleiter)* of the party in the province of Thuringia, where the plants of the foundation were located. It was named after the leader of the Swiss party section, Wilhelm Gustloff, who had been shot early in 1936 by David Frankfurter, a Yugoslavian student living in Bern, Switzerland. Gustloff's death was exploited by party propaganda and his name was not only used for the foundation but also for a cruise ship of the party's workers' welfare organization.

Simson & Co. had not only experimented with vest pocket and pocket pistols but also with a 9mm Parabellum caliber military-selfloader, of which probably one model survived. The adoption of Walther's Heeres-Pistole in 1938 as the official sidearm of Germany's armed forces, however, practically closed the market for high-power pistols in Germany, where at that time pocket pistols of 7.65mm Browning or 9mm Short caliber were generally considered sufficient for self-defense purposes. These may have been the reasons why the designers at Gustloff-Werke turned their interest to pocket pistols.

The Walther PP and PPK models were well established, Menz had put the Spezial-Modell on the market in 1936, and from the patent applications of Mauser and Sauer it was obvious that new double-action pistols were in an advanced design state. Amidst so many new ideas it must have been quite difficult to find truly competitive solutions without infringing patents. The designers at Simson/Gustloff obviously followed these directions:

1. To meet the trend the pistol had to be equipped with a double-action lock.
2. Considering the Walther and Sauer pistols the new gun should have an effective safety as well.
3. As the competitors offered well built and finished products in the higher price range, the new design should stress ease of manufacture in order to get a price advantage over the established market leaders.

Sauckel took great interest in the pistol and, as head of the Gustloff foundation, claims to have ordered its development (Waffen Revue Nr. 42 [1981], pp. 6635-6661). As patents for double-action designs had been granted to the company prior to Sauckel gaining control (patent numbers 621,898 and 801,129), one can only conclude that Simson & Co. had for some time been aware of the potential of the new development, and had considered producing a modern pocket pistol. Obviously Sauckel became interested in the project and tried to bring it to the production stage.

What was the gun like which finally was produced, if only in small quantities? I have had the opportunity to examine a pistol with the serial number 1249 from the Fichtelmann collection. Apart from minor points the gun was obviously designed for mass production. Pictures show this Gustloff from the right and left side, respectively. Unlike others, this one shown above has Bakelite grip panels. As evidenced by the serial number 1249, it is of more recent production than those whose numbers have been mentioned.

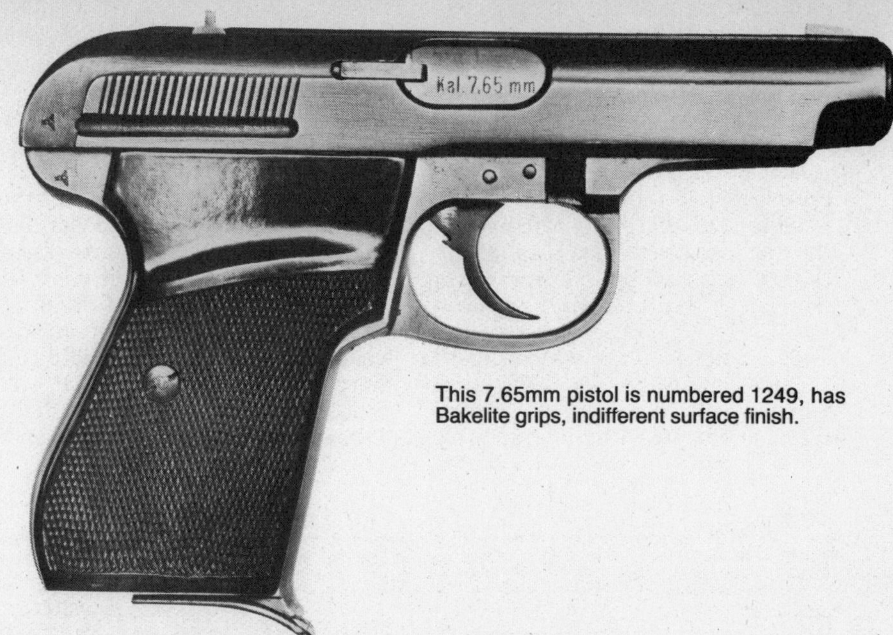

This 7.65mm pistol is numbered 1249, has Bakelite grips, indifferent surface finish.

The frame and the trigger guard sub-frame are die cast from zinc alloy. At the rear of the grooves in which the slide travels, steel lugs are cast into the frame because stress at this point is greatest during recoil. The trigger guard is connected to the frame by a tongue and groove joint and two pins. Die cast zinc alloy frames were used for the first time in these guns. *(Some authorities state Erma was using zinc alloys this way in 1936. Ed.)* After the war the Erma company in Germany made extensive use of die cast pistol frames, and High Standard in the U.S. and Weihrauch in Germany have been using the same material and technique for their 22-caliber revolver frames.

The Gustloff slide is made of a heavy sheet metal stamping into which a barrel bushing and a machined breech are welded. Presently, Heckler & Koch are making slides and other parts for some of their pistols from sheet metal stampings, not to mention the many military rifle and submachine gun designs relying on such parts.

The safety devices are shown here

They got the name—and to a diehard Nazi, Gustloff was special—big enough. Note the long arc provided for the safety button.

as well. When the safety lever is moved to the rear the main-spring is not tensioned even if the hammer is in the cocked position. At the same time, the trigger safety is ready to engage a notch at the back of the trigger and so would prevent the trigger from being moved enough to release the hammer.

To remove the slide from the frame for cleaning or inspection, a takedown plunger is pulled downwards and held in this position while the slide is pulled backwards and lifted clear of the frame in the same way as would be done with a Walther PP and many others. The hammer is an intricate piece of machined steel. The sear is mounted on the hammer by means of the sear pin. In most other pistols the sear is mounted in the frame, and the hammer has the familiar sear notch into which the sear falls to keep the hammer cocked. Here the sear bears against a steel rest plate when the hammer is cocked. The rest plate is mounted in the frame by tongue and groove and is secured against sliding by a small pin.

Similar sear-connected-to-hammer designs have been used by C.P. Clement of Belgium at the beginning of this century in his pocket pistols, and by Smith & Wesson in their 35- and 32-caliber autos (which were based on the Clement design). J.H. Wesson added an interesting disconnector to the hammer-mounted sear which is described in the German patent No. 247,668 dated January 10, 1911, and, no doubt, in a U.S. patent.

Similar double-action systems were at that time used by Mauser and Sauer. Providing a very smooth double-action pull while using only few and simple parts, this design is now employed in most of the modern DA pistols, among them the Berettas, SIGs and Smith & Wessons. Even Walther, having used a hammer latch design in their double-action pistols since 1929 when the PP was introduced, recently converted to this system when designing their new P6 9mm Luger police pistol.

When were the Gustloff pistols made? We have a reproduction of a letter (copy) from Sauckel to the aide-de-camp of the Wehrmacht (German Army) to Hitler, Hauptmann (Captain) Engel, which reveals some interesting details, as the following translation shows.

Copy

NSDAP Weimar, April 23rd, 1940
Province of Thuringia

The Leader of the Province

To the
Aide-de-Camp of the Army to the Führer
Captain Engel
Berlin W 8

Vossstr. 4

Dear Captain!

Acknowledging the receipt of your letter dated April 4, '40, I should like to inform you that you will as soon as possible get a pistol of the type the Führer has received. May I mention that it was not a Walther pistol but a completely new development of the Gustloff Works. So it is a Gustloff pistol and I am very glad that you recognize the advantages the new pistol doubtlessly boasts. The pistol received by the Fuehrer is the firstling, after several of the newly developed pistols had been tried and proven for an appropriate time and in all directions.

When we are now trying to start a modest production, besides the Führer's pistol, an allocation from the ordnance department of the army is urgently required so that the necessary equipment, etc., can be made. I myself am convinced of the urgent necessity of pistol production, as shortage prevails on all sides.

The Reichsführer SS, too, tries in vain to get a number of these pistols, because the total production - of Walther pistols also - has been requisitioned by the army. One of the biggest advantages of the pistol is - besides its quick readiness to fire - the very advantageous position in the fist and the therewith connected lowest possible recoil. I therefore beg you kindly to observe especially, when recommending the pistol, that this is not a Walther but a Gustloff pistol. For all that rivalry and competition always lead to improvments.

Furthermore, I should like to finally ask you cordially to help us make production possible, because only then can I fill the even now numerous requests.

With the best wishes and
Heil Hitler!
I remain your devoted
(signed) Fritz Sauckel

As the letter shows, only toolroom samples of the pistol had been made until April, 1940. And one year later, there was still no production, as is evidenced by a letter from Sauckel to Himmler. Here is the translation of this letter:

Fritz Sauckel Weimar, July 17, 1941

To
The Reichsführer of the SS and Head of Police
Com. Heinrich Himmler,
Berlin

Very esteemed and dear Comrade Himmler!

As you know I had ordered the Gustloff-Works to design a new semi-automatic pistol which had to have some advantages over the excellent Walther pistol. The designers of the Gustloff-Works succeeded in turning out a really outstanding, new pistol which boasts quite some advantages. The greatest are the simplicity of its safety and ease of handling, also the simplicity of its mechanism.

The pistol itself will be known to you through the information which I was able to give you. Unfortunately we did not succeed up to now to start production of this excellent weapon because of the natural demands of the war towards the Gustloff-Works. Only very few guns have been made by hand, so e.g. for the Führer and the Duce. I am now glad to be able to present to you herewith in the name of the Gustloff-Works such a one, made by a master gunsmith, hand engraved, as a token of our affection.

I very much hope that you will enjoy this pistol and that it finds your interest also.

With the best wishes and regards
Heil Hitler!
Yours,
Fritz Sauckel (signed)

Without knowing more about Fritz Sauckel than what these letters show, he at least was a hustling salesman. Comparing the rather unspecific but high claims for "his" pistol with reality shows that Sauckel either did not know much about pistols (which is quite likely) or that he hoped that those who could help him in starting production were not really handgun specialists.

Let us briefly discuss his claims for the gun: 1. a simple safety; 2. easy handling; and 3. simple mechanical design.

As can be seen here, the safety is by no means easier to operate, nor more effective, than other designs which require a lever to be moved by the thumb. The advent of the Walther PP with its automatic, trigger-actuated hammer-block safety had outmoded the Gustloff's safety before it was designed.

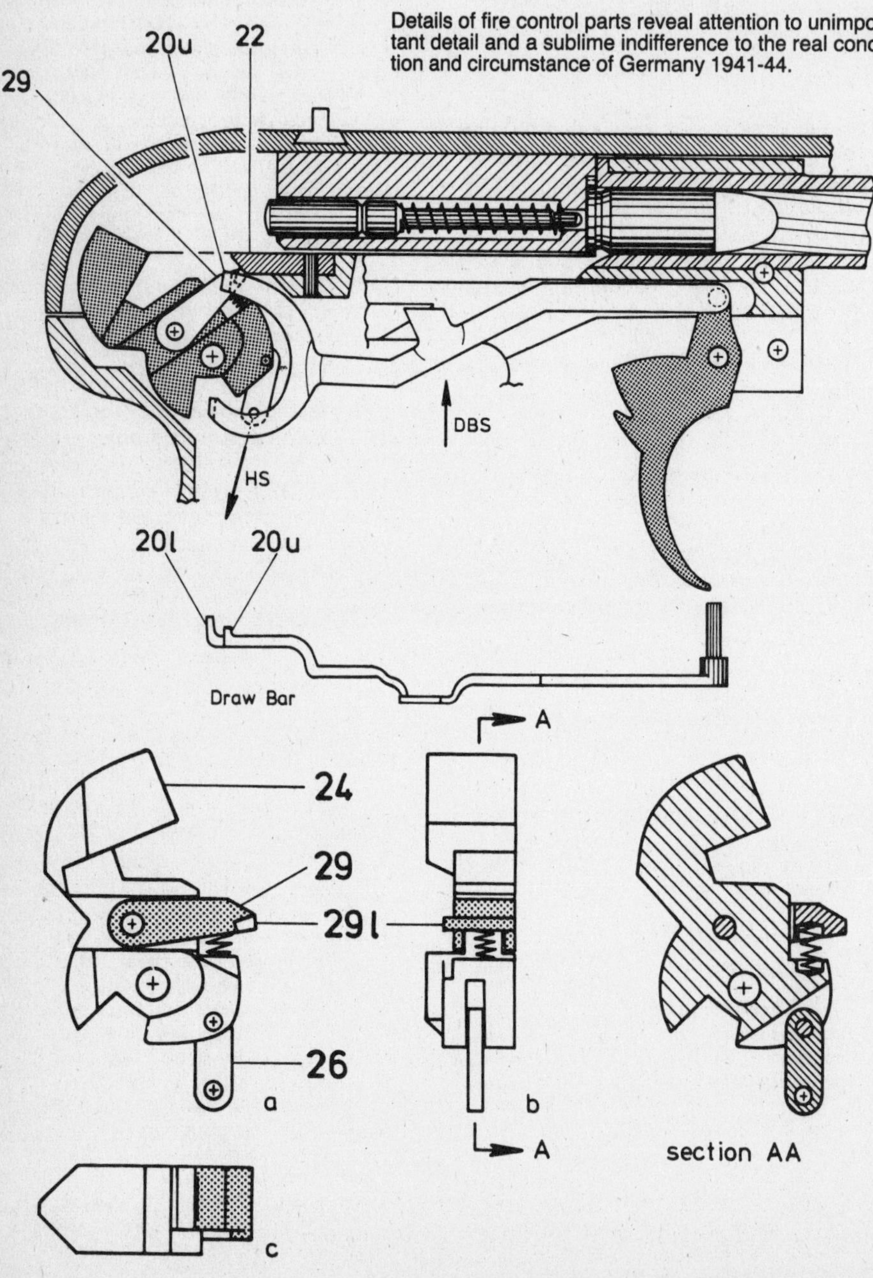

Details of fire control parts reveal attention to unimportant detail and a sublime indifference to the real condition and circumstance of Germany 1941-44.

There is very little difference in the handling qualities of the available pocket pistols of sound design in 1940. Shape and size of grips of the larger models was very good, starting at least from the Colt Model of 1903 Pocket Pistol and exemplified by such guns as the Remington Pocket Pistol Model 51, the Walther PP, and Sauer & Sohn's Model 38 Pistol. Mechanical design had been perfected to a high degree, and the better German guns were very reliable and highly accurate (in spite of the common contention that a good revolver is more accurate than a good pocket pistol, the contrary is true). If a good design has (or had) more parts than another, then only because it has more or different features. If the simplicity of the mechanism claimed by Sauckel could be measured by the number of parts, the Gustloff Pistol is by no means better than its contemporaries.

Table 1

Model	Number of Parts
Gustloff Pistol	53
Mauser HSc	36
Sauer & Sohn 38	53
Walther PP	46

The 1941 letter shows that at that time the Gustloff-Works were not ready to mass-produce their gun. Work on the project went on and in April, 1943, a 4-color owner's manual was printed.

As no further written information on the gun could be found I tried to get into contact with people who had worked for Simson/Gustloff and still could remember what had happened during that time. Since Suhl is located in the former Province of Thuringia which now belongs to the communist part of Germany, it took some perseverance to get the first useful answer to my letters. From the German patent, No. 726,624 protecting the principle of the Gustloff's safety from July 23, 1937 on (issued only on September 10, 1942), I knew that Erich Ladicke and Karl Barnitzke were connected with the design of the the gun. From my contact I now received some interesting information on the inventors and the final production of the pistol. Barnitzke was head of the department responsible for the design of small-arms and handguns at Simson/Gustloff, while Ladicke was an engineer working under Barnitzke, specializing in welded and stamped sheet metal.

During the development of the pistol probably five variations were designed and, after standardization, 28 toolroom models were built. After testing was finished, engraved models for Hitler, Sauckel, Himmler, Bormann, and others were made. From the cited letter, it follows that mass production could have by no means been started before 1942.

The information I received sets further limits to the production time. According to my source, shop was set up at Buchenwald directly beside the ill-famed concentration camp. Approximately 45 people were employed in the assembly shop alone. Just as production got under way the shop was practically completely destroyed by an Allied air raid, on August 24, 1944. It is estimated that hardly more than 2,000 pistols *(Some authorities feel only a small percentage of 2,000. Ed.)* had been assembled and delivered at that time. Where all the different parts for the pistol had been produced is no longer known, except for the diecast zinc alloy frames and trigger guards which were made by the then-König Co. at Benshausen near Suhl. Attempts to resume production after the destruction of the shop were not successful as the general conditions became more and more difficult towards the end of the war.

The production capacity of the shop prior to its destruction must have been considerable, judging by the number of people employed, and by the design characteristics of the pistol. If only 2,000 guns had been made they must have been produced during the summer of 1944, excepting the machined toolroom samples.

Where did the 2,000 pistols go? Most of those not handed over to the occupation forces were quite likely buried in the ground long enough to corrode beyond redemption. Quite a few might have found their way into the U.S. because Suhl and Buchenwald were at first occupied by American forces (this part of Germany was later handed over to the Soviets). Ladicke had one pistol made and engraved for himself which might well be in the United States now. Should the present owner of that or of any Gustloff pistol be among my readers I would really appreciate hearing about the gun. Perhaps it is not yet too late to glean more details which might throw light on the history of this interesting pocket pistol.

When I said at the beginning that the Gustloff pistol never quite made it, I should perhaps now modify my early verdict. The gun is certainly an interesting and desirable collectors item. ●

Fig. 3 shows an exploded view of the pistol.

1 Frame
2 Trigger Guard Sub-Frame
3 Barrel
4 Slide
5 Sub-Frame Pin
6 Barrel Pin
7 Trigger Pin
8 Recoil Spring
9 Firing Pin Spring
10 Firing Pin
11 Transfer Pin
12 Firing Pin Stop
13 Extractor
14 Extractor Plunger
15 Extractor Spring
16 Rear Sight
17 Trigger
18 Trigger Spring
19 Trigger Spring Pin
20 Trigger Bar
21 Trigger Bar Spring
22 Rest Plate
23 Rest Plate Pin
24 Hammer
25 Hammer Pin
26 Hammer Link
27 Link Pin
28 Mainspring
29 Sear
30 Sear Spring
31 Sear Pin
32 Trigger Safety
33 Safety Spring
34 Safety Pin
35 Takedown Plunger
36 Plunger Pin
37 Magazine Catch
38 Magazine Catch Spring
39 Magazine Assembly
40 Slide Stop
41 Slide Stop Spring
42 Grip Panel (left)
43 Grip Panel (right)
44 Grip Panel Screw
45 Grip Panel Nut
46 Mainspring Tensioning Assembly

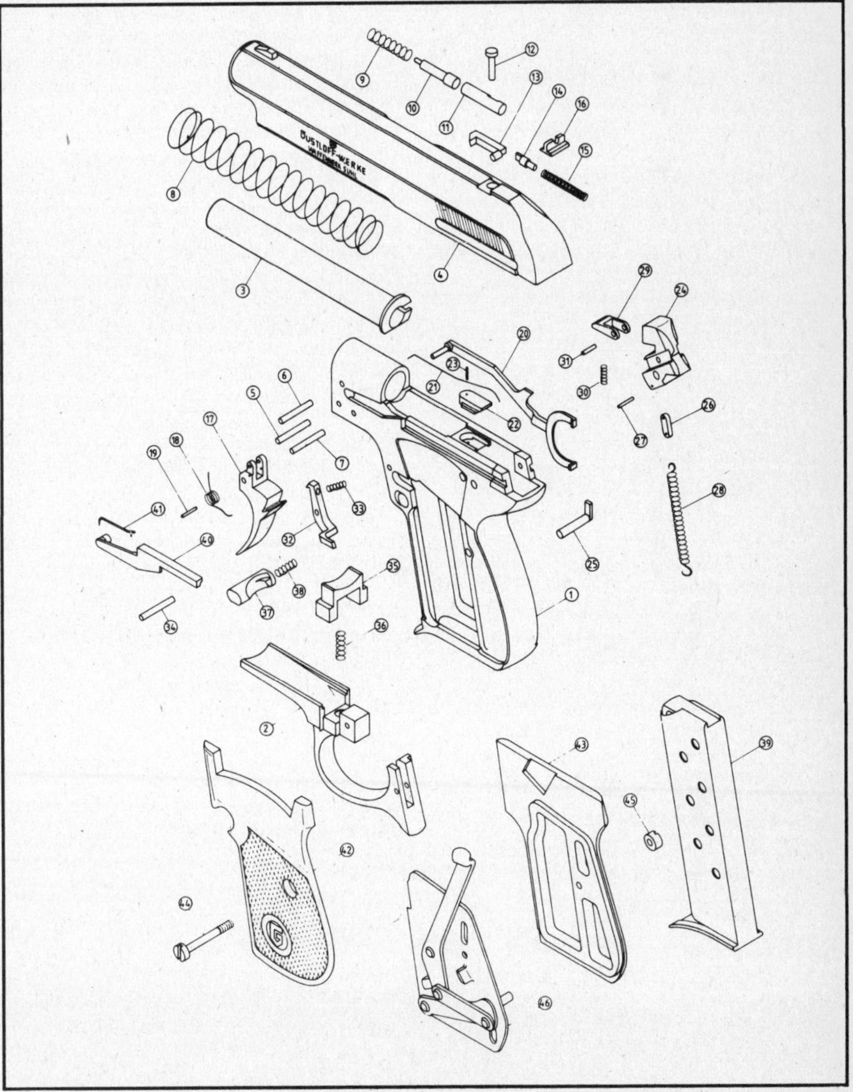

SING A SONG OF BULLETS

A SHORT STORY

by REGINALD BRETNOR

PETER MacCririck looked out of his open workshop window, where his big marmalade tomcat, Audubon, was busily bird-watching. The late afternoon sun shone down on his mountain meadow, on the gravel road that ran from the main highway half a mile off, back along the banks of Muleshoe Creek, past any number of small holdings like his own—five acres, ten, twenty—and then a few much larger spreads, five miles back to the Muleshoe Creek store and post office. Far beyond forests of fir and pine, snow-capped mountains shone in the sunlight.

MacCririck sighed, turned off the machinery, turned back to the young deputy. "Tim Griffin," he said, "you should be ashamed of yourself. This is much too nice a day for a murder." His deep, slow voice betrayed a touch of Scotland and Nova Scotia.

Ed Samuelson and old Doc Travers, sitting on the gossip bench where they couldn't get under foot when he was working, grunted their agreements.

Tim Griffin grinned. "Too bad the murderer didn't see it that way," he answered; "but murderers do get sort of inconsiderate. We want you to take a look at this bullet that did the job."

He took a self-seal plastic envelope out of his shirt pocket, removed a bullet; and MacCririck, frowning, took it delicately in his huge craftsman's hand.

He examined it closely, and his frown deepened. "It was fired from one of my barrels," he growled, "and chances are it was a 300 H&H. But murder's not what I make barrels for."

"You're sure the barrel was one of yours?"

"I'd swear to it. I ought to know the way I cut lands and grooves."

"Well," Griffin nodded, "that cinches it. We already were pretty sure about the rifle because we've got it and its owner down at Patonville." He retrieved the bullet. "When State's ballistics people get it all confirmed, we'll have an open-and-shut case."

Ed Samuelson and Doc Travers were sitting up now and taking notice. Ed pushed his grubby Stetson back on his bald head. "Okay, who the hell got killed?" he asked, before MacCririck could put the question.

"Tom Milgram," Griffin answered. "You know how every morning he always rode that roan horse down to the store to get his mail? Well, he'd dismounted at that old cattle-guard on his way home—you know, right by Cossley's place—and he'd just opened the side-gate to lead through. The bullet caught him right over the belly-button, and it really messed him up inside. Tore up his liver, among other things. He must've died just about instantly."

Doc Travers let out a laugh like a cawing crow. "No loss to the community, that s.o.b.! What public benefactor did it, Tim?"

"Dawson Banning. Cossley found the body—we figure about an hour after he was shot—because he saw a couple of Milgram's steers coming through the open gate when he took his pickup down to that old barn he keeps it in, after a trip to the co-op. He walked over to try and haze them back, and called us right away, and it didn't take us but a minute to figure it out, what with Banning's house up there on the hill about six hundred yards away."

"That barn would've been a fine place to shoot a man from," MacCririck said. "Did you think to check it out?"

"We surely did. All there was was Cossley's tracks all over, and the pickup, some old tools, and the junk he sprays flowers with—smelly stuff. Anyhow, after that we went on up to Banning's, me and Sheriff Sidgeley, and there he was, him and that big rifle, and no one can deny he had a motive, what with Milgram taking that woman of his away two-three years back."

"That," said MacCririck, keeping his sudden anger under control, "is fool nonsense. Milgram did him a favor, and however he felt then, he knows it now—Madeleine is an easy woman to get over. Anyhow, Dawson's no murderer. I doubt not he could kill a man if he was being attacked, and he'd have no trouble hitting one at six hundred yards, but he'd never use that lovely rifle on anything like Milgram. It has my barrel on a Schultz-Larsen action, and my boy stocked it specially for him. Hell, he won the Wimbledon at Perry with it two years running."

"Anyhow," put in Ed, "ain't nobody in this county didn't have a motive for killing Milgram. Guy himself was a walking motive. Even Cossley—that wimp—hated his guts. You hear how Milgram slapped him around that night down to the country club dance?"

"That was sometime last winter," said Griffin. "Milgram must've figured he'd been messing around with Madeleine. Could be—at least Cossley didn't press any charges."

"Gossip is they got something goin'. I wouldn't put it past either of 'em. But even if not, lately there's been more bad blood between Tom and Cossley, mostly about fence lines and water rights."

"Well, okay, Milgram was as popular as a skunk at a garden party, but none of that cuts any ice. Cossley doesn't even own a gun, except that way-back-when muzzle-loader hanging over his fireplace, and nobody except Dawson around here has the right kind of rifle. That right, Mr. MacCririck?"

"Yes, it's true enough—nobody who'd even have known Milgram, anyhow." MacCririck spoke very slowly, deep in thought. "You said that bullet really messed him up. It shouldn't have. With its full jacket, it should have delivered a clean, penetrating wound, unless it struck bone. Did it?"

"No," answered Grifin, "but it keyholed."

"*What?* That's more nonsense! Bullets from my barrels don't tumble, Tim, not unless they hit something on the way, and if I remember rightly there's nothing between Dawson's house and that cattle-guard for a bullet *to* hit."

Griffin shrugged. "Nobody liked Milgram. Most everybody likes Dawson. But murder's murder. Well, thanks muchly, Mr. MacCririck." He turned to go. "We may be in touch with you."

He nodded to Ed and Doc as he went out; and MacCririck, back at the window, watched him drive away. Dawson Banning was more than just a customer. He was a close friend, a hunting companion, a good loser in competition, modest when he won. A surveyor by profession, he ran a few head of cattle on his acreage, and spent most of his spare time working up match loads and polishing his shooting skills on his own range, which extended three hundred yards from his front porch to a target directly across the shallow valley opposite. He'd been going with a sweet Patonville girl, Polly Merrill, and all their friends were sure they'd marry. No, it just didn't wash.

Ed and Doc were wrangling over whether anybody had heard the shot. They decided that in that country nobody would have paid attention anyhow; someone was always shooting varmints or plinking or even poaching deer.

MacCririck, his face grim, paid no attention to them. To himself he said, *Dawson didn't kill Tom Milgram. He couldn't have. He wouldn't have. But then who did?* Brant Cossley, he told himself, would have been a prime suspect—a weak man, a spiteful man, a man to let his grudges fester in him, but one who had inherited enough to live on and play at being a playboy, all very smooth and smarmy. Not a man who'd own a bull-gun with a MacCririck barrel. Definitely not.

Still and all, for Banning there'd be the ballistics people to contend with, and their

POLI
2

report alone might convict him. No jury could be expected to believe the rifle had taken off on its own, shot Milgram, and run home again.

MacCririck shook his head in frustration, and Audubon meowed. MacCririck scratched behind his ears. Then he saw Adrienne, his trim little daughter-in-law from France almost dancing her way across the meadow toward the house, 150 yards from his, where she and Pete Junior lived and where Pete had his own shop. Her gleaming brown hair was flying, and she was singing her delight in the lovely day.

It was a song MacCririck hadn't heard before, a simple song, and it caught at a corner of his mind. He was sure his French would be adequate to understanding it, and he told himself he'd have to ask her to sing the rest of it.

He kept thinking about the murder during the remaining hour or two of the afternoon, and always he kept coming up against that dead end. Tomorrow morning, he told himself, he'd drive into Patonville and have a word with Sheriff Sidgeley.

MacCririck made his own breakfasts, and he always had dinner with Pete and Adrienne, so when he quit for the night, he and Audubon strolled over to their house. His son took one look at him, brought out a bottle, poured two good bourbons and handed him one. "Have a seat, dad," he said. "Audubon's already taken Adrienne's lap, so that's out." He grinned under his sandy moustache. "But anywhere else."

MacCririck sat down.

"And now," said Pete, "suppose you tell me what's been happening. First a deputy comes around and spends a half hour with you. Then you show up looking as if you're trying to solve the riddle of the sphinx. Are you?"

"I am," MacCririck said slowly, "in a manner of speaking." And he proceeded to fill them in, in detail.

They were good listeners and their expressions told him they agreed with his opinions of the actors in the drama. "There's *got* to be an answer," he finished, frowning.

"Yeah," Pete said, "but I'm afraid it'll be the ballistics people who'll be giving it. I feel sorry for Polly Merrill."

Adrienne coaxed Audubon into the kitchen for a plate of leftovers. "Ah, don't feel too sorry for her," she said, returning. "She is a fighter, that one. It is Dawson I am more sorry for. She will fight, but he? He is not one to give up, no, but he simply will not know what to do. He will be like lost, *euh*?"

"Well, he'll have lots of friends standing by him," said MacCririck, "for all the good that'll do."

She patted his shoulder. "Come, I cannot allow a little murder to spoil my dinner, cooked especially for you. While we eat, let us speak of more pleasant things. I shall tell you of my Uncle Jean-Pierre and how, so many years ago, he stole the sixteen sheep and was rewarded for it."

She was a natural storyteller, and the account of her uncle and the sheep took up almost the whole dinner, for it was full of involved family relationships, and who had married a mad Basque, and the intricacies of French law. Between it and the dinner and a good wine, MacCririck's melancholy was forced into abeyance, and he determined not to allow it to return.

After coffee had been served, he smiled at her. "This afternoon," he said, "you were singing a little song as you crossed the meadow. I caught just a bit of it—*En passent par la Lorraine*. Would you sing the rest of it for me?"

"But it's nothing very fine!" she protested. "Just a—how do you say?—a country song, very simple, about a girl and love and wooden shoes. But if you want . . ." She shrugged, sang the first verse softly, looked at him to make sure he wanted more.

"Please," he said.

So she went on, verse after simple French verse, chorus after chorus.

As both MacCriricks applauded her performance, "Ah," she said, "it is both sad and funny, *non*?" And it was then the phone rang.

Pete answered it. "Just a second," he told it. "He's here." He held the phone out to his father. "It's Polly Merrill, for you."

Polly, mad clear through, came directly to the point. "You've heard what they're trying to do to Dawson, haven't you? Yes? Well, Daw doesn't quite appreciate the fix he's in; he's just too decent to understand people like that. That blasted woman, that Madeleine, she already has her own lawyers in, and she's been telling the media that time after time Daw threatened Milgram's life after she ran off."

"That, of course, is an outright lie," declared MacCririck. "And if any reporters ask me, I'll tell them so."

"They've not gotten to you yet? Well, maybe you and I could get together before they do and see if we can come up with something."

MacCririck caught the anxiety in her voice, and he didn't say they'd have a rough time coming up with anything to contradict unfavorable ballistics findings on top of opportunity and a faint excuse for motive. Instead, he told her he'd meet her for lunch at The Cattleman, around the corner from the courthouse, and report on whatever Sidgeley told him.

The phone rang in both Pete's house and his own, so he asked them to take all the calls and he went home and shut down his phone and went to bed. For a while, he lay there trying to think, but Adrienne's song kept intruding. He went to sleep playing it over to himself, and next morning it was still with him as he drove the twenty miles to Patonville. *Dondaine, Oh! Oh! Oh! Avec mes sabots. Avec mes sabots. Avec . . .*

He had to wait half an hour before Sidgeley called him in.

"Sorry, Mac," he grunted, pointing to a chair, "but the newspapers have been bugging me, almost since we picked Milgram off the ground. The press, and Madeleine Milgram and her lawyers, and a couple of anti-gun columnists, and Polly Merrill, and now . . ." He broke off with another grunt, slumped into his own chair, lighted a cigar.

"And now me," said MacCririck with a smile. He and the sheriff had always been on good terms, and obviously Sidgeley was trying to be polite.

"That's right," Sidgeley told him, "and I know exactly what you're going to say. You're going to tell me Dawson Banning wouldn't hurt a fly, and that it's not true he threatened Milgram, and that anyway even if he'd flipped enough to kill him he wouldn't ever have insulted that rifle you made for him by using it. And furthermore *your* bullets don't keyhole. Have I got it straight?"

"You have," said MacCririck. "Tim Griffin has a good memory."

Sidgeley stood. "Mac, it's no good. I myself still can't quite *believe* Dawson killed that bastard, but even good men go ape sometimes. Our criminalist says there's only one rifle could've fired that bullet; so does the city's man. And when we get the report from State, you and I know they'll say the same thing. There's nothing I can do for Dawson except be nice to him while he's in my jailhouse."

"What about Cossley?" MacCririck asked.

"What about him? Okay, he had a motive like all sorts of others in these parts, and I'd a hell of a lot sooner it was him than Dawson. But look at the guy—he's even written letters to the papers yelling for gun control. Anyhow, there's no way he or anybody else could have gotten at that rifle. Dawson admits neither he nor it left the house yesterday morning. If you can show me some way except the way it was—voodoo, maybe—I'll listen."

MacCririck saw the interview was over, thanked Sidgeley, shook his hand and went out into the street again. There wasn't going to be much encouraging he could tell Polly, and he still had an hour to kill. He looked up at the courthouse and the jail, wondered if he ought to go up and see Dawson, decided not to. Slowly, he started for The Cattleman, whistling absentmindedly. He had walked half a block before he realized what he was whistling:

En passent par la Lorraine . . .

Then he stopped, stock still. To himself, he whispered the chorus that followed every verse. The idea that had come to him was not too clearly formulated, not yet. He headed for the nearest public phone and called the Patonville Police Department.

"This is Peter MacCririck," he told the desk man. "I'd like a word with Captain Botha, please . . . What? No, I'm a friend of his. It's personal."

Seconds later, Botha was on the line. "Good to hear from you Peter," he said. "What can I do for you?"

"I'd like a few mintutes of your time. I want to ask a favor of you, a confidential favor."

Botha chuckled. "Well, I know you aren't trying to sell me another gun, and I know that clunker you drive can't make it over forty-five, so I guess you aren't asking me to fix a speeding ticket. All right, come on over to the station."

In Botha's office, MacCririck got down to business. "Jake," he said, "I'll tell you what I want, and I'll give my word it'll go no further without your say-so."

Botha cocked an eyebrow.

"I want a complete rundown on Brant Cossley, FBI if you can manage it. Can do?"

Botha frowned. "Sure I can," he answered. "But should I? Can you tell me why?"

"I think," MacCririck answered, "that you can guess. I may have something big, but it's pretty tenuous, pretty far out. Let me keep it to myself for just a bit. I guarantee you'll get no repercussions." He grinned. "I'll even fix those claw-mounts on that Mauser for you."

"Bribery! Bribery!" Botha shook his head dismally. Then he, too, grinned. "Well, guess I can't resist it. I'll call you when I hear. I hope the news is what you're waiting for."

MacCririck walked slowly over to The Cattleman, sat down at its 1880s bar, ordered a dark beer, and watched the other customers while he waited. Abstractedly, he started singing softly to himself.

Joe, the bartender, snapped him out of it. "How's that? Come again, Mr. Mac."

"It's a French country song Adrienne's been singing," he replied, abashed. "Can't seem to get it out of my head."

"That's how it goes when you're workin' out a problem. Happens to me all the time."

Then Polly Merrill walked in, her progress marked by the turning of male heads. A tall redhead, she walked as queens ought to, her tailored figure far more feminine than frills might have made it. As she strode, she smiled at one or two friends, then spotted MacCririck, stopped, bent to kiss his ear.

She ordered an old-fashioned, took it and led the way to a table.

"I just saw Daw," she declared. "He still doesn't know what has hit him." Anxiety came back into her voice. "Do you have anything good to tell me?"

"Well, yes and no. My visit to Sidgeley came to not much. There's nothing for us there. But then an idea came to me . . ." He broke off. "Tell me, Polly," he said, "you're not much younger than Dawson, are you?"

"That's not a nice question to ask a lady, but being as it's you I'll tell you. Five years. He's forty-two. I'll be thirty-seven next Fall."

"So you're mature enough to handle a situation coldly, calmly, and that's what I'm going to ask you to do. I have a glimmering and I've started working on it. Tell Dawson exactly what I've said, and as soon as there's anything definite you'll be the first to know."

She looked at him intently and then, in a much smaller voice, she said, "You're serious, aren't you?"

"Dead serious," replied MacCririck. The waiter was standing there, ready to take their orders.

"All right," she said. "It's a deal. I'll fill you in on what's been happening."

Dawson, she told him, had his own lawyer, Andy Anderson, another shooter and an old friend, but she'd been wondering if they shouldn't get some big name down from Denver. After all, Madeleine would certainly have seen to it that Milgram's will left everything to her, and she already had legal talent around. What did he think?

MacCririck said he didn't think the time had come for that; first he'd like a few days to follow up his own idea. Besides, Madeleine would be busy getting at the estate. The state had its own prosecutors.

The rest of what she had to say was mostly about how Madeleine had told the press Daw had threatened not only Milgram, but her, too. He'd done it several times, by telephone, and she'd wanted to swear out a complaint against him, but Tom was such a good old boy—Polly snorted as she said it—he simply wouldn't hear of it, just laughed it off. The media ate it up—pictures in the papers, even a TV interview.

"Speaking of which," she said, her voice suddenly tense. "Look who's here!"

Brant Cossley had just entered, accompanied by another, smaller man. He looked as if he'd been decorated by magazine editors—clothes younger than his age, chosen with style-consciousness but poor taste; even his tan had an artificial look. His companion, dressed more soberly, had graying hair, rimless glasses on a narrow nose. Their table was far enough away so there was no hope of overhearing them.

Polly leaned forward, touched MacCririck's hand. "You know who that is he's with?"

MacCririck shook his head.

"That's Dunstan, the columnist, the guy who's so hot on what he calls gun control. He'll probably get a feature story out of this, maybe with a picture of lover boy there with his old muzzleloader—you know the line, there was a time when people needed guns, but now we're civilized and that time's long past."

Disgustedly, she changed the subject, telling MacCririck that she had decided to marry Dawson right away. "In the jail, if we have to." After all that'd show everybody where *she* stood.

Then she went on to report some gossip whispered to her in the office—she worked for Triple A—which claimed Madeleine and Cossley had been seen in a motel at Ellsburg, 40 miles away, while Milgram was out of town.

Things, thought MacCririck as they stood up to leave, *are beginning to add up. That explains the "lover boy."* Aloud he said, "Polly, you tell that man of yours I'm coming up to see him tomorrow. Just tell him what I told you, and to keep his chin up."

MacCririck did not stop at home, but went on toward the Muleshoe Creek store and the side road on which Milgram had died. When he reached the cattle-guard, he pulled off the road and looked the scene over. The guard marked Milgram's fence line, where his property met Cossley's few acres west of the road and Banning's east of it. Cossley's entrance was further down, Banning's a hundred yards beyond that on the other side.

MacCririck sat there thinking. On the corner of Cossley's property, only a few yards from Milgram's fence and perhaps a hundred feet from MacCririck, was Cossley's small, dilapidated barn. Cossley was making no use of his land; a lot of smaller trees had been allowed to grow, some shrubbery, and a few flowers. He got someone a couple of times a year to keep the smaller growth down, and the area around the barn looked as if it had been cleared not too long before.

MacCririck nodded to himself, drove home, and phoned Polly at her office. "Can you get off?" he asked. "I'd like to go up to Dawson's place and snoop around, and I'd like you with me. If I find what I'm looking for, it'll be downright interesting . . . What's that? Sure, I'll wait while you ask your boss."

Moments later, she was back. Yes, she could meet him up at Dawson's in half an hour. MacCririck hung up, buzzed young Pete to report what had been happening, then drove back up the Muleshoe Creek road. Dawson Banning's long, low house, half plank, half fieldstone, overlooked the valley and the cattleguard. At the access road, MacCririck shooed a couple of horses away from the gate, opened it and drove in. When Polly's small red wagon came in sight, he opened the gate again and she rode with him up to the house.

"I don't need to go in," he told her. "Let's have our look around."

Banning's shooting bench was permanently installed on his front porch, on the opposite side of the house, under cover so he could shoot rain or shine. His target frame stood level with it on the gentle hill 300 yards away. Together, they walked over to it.

MacCririck explained, "Daw didn't set this up on the true crest, but on what's called a military crest. The true crest's another 40 yards on and a good 30 feet higher, and there's this deep gully in between. The true crest makes a fine backstop."

They continued on, MacCririck carefully examining the ground. "Ah!" he said, as they reached the gully's further side, "I *thought* so." Kneeling, he picked something up. A few feet further on, he did it again. And again. He showed her what he'd found, smiling at her. "In a day or two," he said, "I hope we'll be showing these to the sheriff, you and I. I won't say now why they're so important, but just in case you're guessing, let's keep it to ourselves. We've not won the battle, not yet."

"I think I have guessed, sort of, maybe," she answered, wide-eyed, "and I promise you I won't say a blessed word, though I'd like to run right back to that awful jail and let Daw in on it."

The gunsmith drove home again and tried to work, but found he couldn't keep his mind on it what with thinking about the gaps that still existed in his theory and whether he could fill them, and Adrienne's song, just wouldn't go away. Audubon jumped onto his lap, didn't get petted, and went off to sulk on his cushion by the fireplace.

Finally, MacCririck drove to Patonville to spend his 20 minutes visiting Dawson Banning in the County Jail. Obviously, Banning was getting special treatment; the custodial deputy left the two of them alone and didn't even lock the door.

Everyone who met Banning was impressed by his evident strength and his imperturbability, and these the events of the past two days had not shaken. He was a big man, but not out to impress anyone. His sense of humor still showed, and there was no tension in his grip when he shook hands with his friend. MacCririck realized Polly had been right—Dawson didn't really appreciate his fix.

"Did Polly come up again this afternoon?"

"She sure did," Banning answered. "Trying to get me to have the wedding right away, right here in the calabozo." He grinned. "I told her that no way was she going to marry a jailbird—that there'd be plenty of time, and properly in a church, when I get out of here."

"And she gave you my message?"

"She did indeed, and made me promise not to pester you with questions . . ."

Good girl! thought MacCririck.

". . . and then she told me all about what Madeleine's been up to, and what the media people have been doing. I just can't understand how these ballistics characters think it was my rifle did it. Peter, I didn't leave the house all morning. I was in my workshop making up a big new bookcase for the livingroom. Even that creep Cossley knows that; he heard me telling Jerry at the store when I was buying screws. I'll bet that when they get an opinion down from State they'll find it was another gun entirely."

MacCririck didn't argue with him, and when Banning said, "Oh hell, let's talk about something cheerfuller!" he went along. They chatted about friends and shooting and books and the deputy came back to tell them it was time to close up shop and MacCririck left.

Abruptly, he realized he hadn't let Adrienne know he'd not be back for dinner. He phoned, and she pretended to be hurt, told him he could go and eat a three-pound steak for all she cared, and threatened never to sing to him again. That started the song going again in his head. He wandered back to The Cattleman, took a table in an obscure corner, had a drink while he waited for a full dinner, centering around a steak.

Home again, he found a note from Adrienne. Captain Botha had phoned from the police department; he wanted MacCririck to call him first thing in the morning. On the news, he got somebody quoting Madeleine, so he turned it off again. For a while, he watched TV, then tried reading, picking up a copy of *Shogun* at one of its goriest and most exciting parts, but his thoughts wouldn't leave him be. "Damn!" he said to Audubon. "I'll just have to possess myself in patience."

"Mrreow!" said Audubon.

MacCririck gave up and went to bed.

At the earliest possible moment in the morning, he called Botha.

"Well, Mac," the Captain told him, "you lucked out—or I guess you did. Take a run down here and you can have a copy of the print-out."

"Pay-dirt?" MacCririck asked.

"Dirt it is," Botha answered. "Whether it's pay or not I'll leave up to you."

Half an hour later, he was sitting across from Botha. The print-out was very much to the point. Brant Cossley's real name was Bert Ferris, and he had changed it shortly before inheriting and moving West. Cossley had been his mother's maiden name. After minor juvenile problems, he'd made it through high school with a high enough average to enter college. He'd had two and a half years there, majoring in mechanical engineering, then dropped out. Vietnam was going strong, and the army had drafted him immediately and put him into ordnance instead of infantry.

At that, MacCririck looked up. *"Ordnance?"*

Botha nodded grimly. "That's right, guns and stuff. But keep going."

Cossley had done well enough. In a couple of years, he'd made buck sergeant and married. That lasted another year and a half. Then things fell apart. His wife, heavily insured, had been suffering considerable pain from a back injury, and he'd fixed her up with an "accidental" overdose of sleeping pills, complete with alibi for himself—only the wrong people, relatives of hers, had phoned at just the wrong time. Disturbed by her incoherence, they'd driven over in a hurry and forced their way in. They were just in time, and Cossley was indicted for attempted murder. His lawyer plea-bargained and he'd served four years, then been released on probation. Since then, he'd kept his nose clean, working at petty jobs until he'd fallen into clover when his aunt died and he inherited.

"So *that's* it!" MacCririck commented. "That tells us why he owned no firearms—convicted felons aren't allowed to, and he was taking no chances. I guess his yammering against guns was a red herring, especially here in gun country. I'm going over to visit Sheriff Sidgeley. Mind if I show him this?"

"Not a bit," Botha answered. "Just don't tell him yet where you got it."

"Jake, thank you. I'll make it up to you."

He phoned Polly and told her to get right down; then he walked over to the sheriff's office and stood outside till she arrived.

Again, Sidgeley kept them waiting, and when he admitted them he was not as affable as he'd been the day before.

"Come on, Mac," he demanded, "what *is* this? We went over the whole thing yesterday, and you're flogging a dead horse. It's like I told you—it's an open-and-shut case."

"Well, sir," said MacCririck slowly, but with a touch of steel in his voice, "I'm here to spoil it for you."

"The hell you say!" Now Sidgeley was fuming. "Are you trying to tell me that bullet didn't kill Milgram, and that it didn't come out of your rifle?"

"No," said MacCririck. "The bullet *was* fired from that rifle—I've no doubt about it. And Dawson Banning fired it. But he didn't kill Milgram with it. Brant Cossley—or maybe I ought to say Bert Cossley—did that."

"You mean it's been fired twice or something?"

"Precisely."

"Look, if it had been, there'd have been two sets of land and groove marks on it. Any fool knows that!"

"It was fired first out of Dawson's bull-gun. The second time was out of Cossley's muzzleloader."

"It wouldn't have fit. That old gun must be bigger than a forty-five!"

"There are ways."

"Anyhow, where'd he get a fired bullet as fresh as that? He couldn't've dug it out of a backstop; it'd be all beat up."

"Not necessarily," MacCririck told him. "You know Dawson's home range, don't you? That long gully behind the military crest where his target stands? You also know he shoots in the winter. Well, in wintertime, that gully catches snow and holds it. The winds drift it in and back it up, packed tight. You can be shooting into thirty, forty foot of tight-packed snow. All you have to do is wait until the melt." From his pocket, he took three bullets identical to the one that had killed Milgram. "Polly and I went out yesterday. We had no trouble finding these, and you could probably find a bunch more."

Sidgeley was frowning uncertainly. He sat down. He touched the bullets. "Okay," he growled, "tell me more. What's this about *Bert* Cossley?"

MacCririck reached into his jacket pocket, took out his print-out, handed it over without a word.

Sidgeley glanced at it. "You didn't get this from *my* office," he muttered.

"No," said MacCririck, "I thought I'd better get it from someone who didn't have an open-and-shut case." He said nothing more until the sheriff had read it through.

They looked at each other across the desk. "Now let's let Polly read it," MacCririck suggested.

Sidgeley pushed it over to her. "Mac," he said, "I admit that if you'd asked me to bug the FBI for you I'd have asked you what for? Everybody around here respected Cossley's aunt and uncle; none of us ever thought any nephew of theirs might have that kind of record."

"And—?" MacCririck asked.

"I think we'd better have a talk with the D.A. You don't have hard evidence, but you've shown we have some reason to go looking for it. Maybe we won't need a search warrant, but I'd feel a lot happier with one."

"When it's issued, I'll show you where to search. I'd like to come along as an expert witness. It'll be interesting to see how the man reacts."

The District Attorney, Avery, was surprisingly easy to convince. So was the judge who still had not granted Banning bail. By three in the afternoon, the warrant was issued, and by three-thirty, Sidgeley, MacCririck, Polly, Tim Griffin, and a second deputy had arrived at Cossley's place. He wasn't in, but came driving up while they were knocking at his door.

"Hi, Sheriff!" he called as he strode up. "You have news for me?" All very friendly, open, man-to-man.

"I have a search warrant for your place," the sheriff answered coldly.

"You *what?*" Cossley's tan suddenly seemed to pale, to turn yellow. "What th' hell d'you expect to find here?"

"Mr. MacCririck thinks we'll find evidence you shot Milgram. Because of what he's already shown us and your past record, we—that's me and the D.A. *and* the judge—figured there's at least a chance of it."

Cossley started to bluster, shouted about stupidity, threatened suit.

"That's your privilege," Sidgeley said. "And you can make all the noise you like, but we search just the same." He turned to MacCririck. "Where do we start?"

"Let's go down to that old barn," MacCririck answered. "I'll show you how I think it was."

"Okay, you and I and Tim'll go on down there. Rodriguez, you stay here with Cossley; keep him company. Miss Merrill, maybe you'd best wait for us back in the car."

On the way down the slope, MacCririck said, "The way I figure is he got up early, put that long rifle, probably already loaded, in his rig, and drove into the barn. He could stand in the bed and use the cab as a rest and shoot through the open top of that Dutch door. Being inside would help muffle the sound of the shot, too. Anyhow, he'd probably tried out a few test shots, and it's only thirty, maybe thirty-five yards. Afterwards he scuttled home, cleaned the gun, and drove on down to the store. Remember, this is just a side road, and he already knew that Dawson planned to be in his workshop all morning. He could make it to the store in fifteen-twenty minutes. There'd be no real risk."

The barn's doors were wide open, and Cossley's pickup was standing there. "Let's draw a mental line from here to the spot where Milgram fell. I'll stay back because if there's anything to be found I want you two to find it. You'd better go over the ground with a fine-tooth comb, too, because what you're looking for's not very large."

"And what *are* we looking for?"

"Well, I'd guess a piece of wood, or maybe plastic, about half to three-quarters of an inch long, hollowed out almost to the base to about 30 caliber, and probably cut from a dowel about as big around as that muzzleloader's bore, then cut in half vertically."

"Hey," exclaimed Griffin. "I get the picture. And it'd work! Not too accurate, I'd guess, but at this range it wouldn't have to be. The two halves fall away, and the bullet keeps on going, right?"

"Exactly," said MacCririck. "The bullet would be badly balanced, certainly—that's why it keyholed, but with the right load it probably left the muzzle at, say, eleven or twelve hundred feet per second, quite fast enough to do its work."

Then he watched patiently while Sidgeley and Griffin went over the strip of ground slowly, inch by inch. It took them the better part of fifteen minutes before they found it, and then they only found one half, made from a drilled wooden rod and with rifling marks clearly visible.

"Let's say nothing until we see what else we find," Sidgeley told them on the way back, "then give it to him all at once. Maybe he'll say enough to hang himself."

They paid no attention to Cossley and to his strident questions as he opened the front door. Then, "Mac," Sidgeley said, "I want you to take a good look at that long rifle. See if you think it's been shot recently, and whatever else can tell us something."

MacCririck took the rifle from its pegs. It was a cap-lock, made by Johnston in St. Louis probably in the 1850s, and about 50 caliber. It was a fine piece, he reflected, historic and still in excellent condition. He looked it over carefully, point by point.

"It's been cleaned recently—I'd say very recently—and very thoroughly, but it seems to me I can still smell a bit of powder round the nipple." He opened up the patchbox, found half a dozen caps. "These are brand new," he said.

He replaced the rifle, took down the powderhorn hung about it, sifted a little into his palm. "And this powder is absolutely fresh."

"Let's see that thing we found," said Sidgeley, and Tim griffin brought it out in its plastic envelope.

Brant Cossley saw it—and something in him gave way abruptly. "H-how did you *know?*" he almost screamed. "Did Madeleine . . .?

Then he broke off. While the sheriff read him his rights, he wept hysterically.

Polly Merrill, of course, took the news to Banning, along with the judge's order releasing him, and Peter MacCririck phoned it to Pete and Adrienne, who immediately insisted that they all celebrate by coming there to dinner. "The sheriff too," she said. "I insist. I shall perform a miracle, me, the French chef! It will be a great trouble, but it makes me happy, *non?*"

They had their drinks; they gathered round the table. They had spent a good hour talking the whole thing over.

Adrienne stood up, and started singing:

En passent par la Lorraine,
Avec mes sabots,
En passent par la Lorraine,
Avec mes sabots,
Rencontrai trois capitaines,
Avec mes sabots,
Dondaine, Oh! Oh! Oh!
Avec mes sabots.

And she went on gaily all through its nine verses, finishing finally to enthusiastic applause.

"But I don't get it." Polly wrinkled her freckled nose.

"Well," MacCririck explained, "it's an old, old song, probably going back to Marlborough's time. It's about a little French country girl going through Lorraine in her wooden shoes. She meets three captains, and they call her ugly, with her wooden shoes. She tells them she isn't ugly, that the king's son loves her, that he's given her for a remembrance a bouquet of marjoram, and that if it flowers she'll be queen, but that if it dies her pains will be for nothing—and always *'Avec mes sabots!* With my wooden shoes."

"Ah," put in Adrienne, *"la pauvre petite!"* She giggled. "That 'remembrance,' that bouquet of *marjolaine*. Did you understand the double meaning?"

"I did indeed," answered MacCririck, "but there's a second double meaning that's more important. *Avec mes sabots."*

"I *still* don't see," said Polly. "I know *sabots* are wooden shoes, like on little Dutch boys with their finger in the dike. But so what?"

MacCririck saw understanding beginning to dawn on Dawson's face and on Pete's. "They're that indeed," he said. "But they're something more. Back in the last century, a *sabot* was also a sort of wooden boot that acted as a gas-check around the base of a cannon shell, designed to fall away after firing. Smaller ones were used on bullets, then, and these days there are both rifle and shotgun sabot loads on sale. Cossley picked up the know-how in the Army. It took a 200-year-old song to remind me." (Whereupon Adrienne sang it all over again.) ●

One of these four go-along guns will meet virtually any need for remote country roamings: S&W Kit gun; Model 94 30-30 Trapper; Ruger Blackhawk 357 Magnum; H&R Topper 20-gauge.

PICKING YOUR

THE BEAR was heading for me, that much was sure.

I was examining the remains of a wolf-killed caribou when I looked up to see a sizeable brown bear shuffling onto the scene some 100 yards away. Since a wet wind was at my back, I fully expected him to scram as soon as he got a noseful of me, but bears are hard to figure. This one kept coming upwind, closing the distance rapidly with his rambling gait.

I was in a remote valley beyond Alaska's Chigmit Mountains. There were no trees to climb. The nearest stunted spruce was a day's hike away. Perhaps that bear had never whiffed a human before or maybe my scent was simply masked by the odor of the caribou carcass. Whatever the reason, he was starting to make me feel decidedly uncomfortable.

The bear was 20 yards away now. I guessed he was an eight-footer weighing over 500 pounds. I'd seen bigger, but this one was beginning to look enormous. You don't run from a situation like that. It can trigger an attack. You try to talk it over.

"That's far enough!" I said in the same tone I'd use to admonish my springer spaniel.

I raised my left hand like a traffic cop. My right hand dropped to the 357 holstered on my hip. The bear didn't break stride. It seemed intent on trampling me into the tundra. And it was still 30 feet away when I fired a warning, holding well over its back.

The bear stopped, rolling its head from side to side as if listening to the echoes from the surrounding slopes. Its eyes, small in that massive head, studied me with no apparent expression. Then on he came. I would have to kill him. If I could.

I was gripping the cocked revolver with both hands, holding it close. I was determined that it would not be knocked away before I sent a bullet to the brain via the mouth or an ear. I had little confidence otherwise, in stopping that bear. He would be on me in another three or four steps.

Then anger welled up, overwhelming my rising fear. The bear was surely going to hurt me. He was going to foul up all of the plans I'd so painstakingly made for the summer. It was an irrational thought, but it made me mad.

"GET OUT OF HERE YOU S.O.B!" I raged.

The bear showed expression for the first time. It looked surprised, almost as if it had just awakened from sleepwalking. It halted, one paw upraised, holding the pose for two or three seconds. It seemed like a very long time.

Then that big bear wheeled and ran away. It really ran. Spray spurted from under those huge paws each time they pounded the rainsoaked tundra. My fingers trembled as I reloaded the fired chamber of the Ruger Blackhawk. My knees still felt wobbly as I shrugged the pack back onto my shoulders and headed down the valley.

That was in July of 1976. Dennis Harms of Chugiak had flown me into the region only a couple of days earlier, using his nimble little Super Cub to land on a tiny lake in a high valley. My plan was to camp in the summer range of the Mulchatna caribou herd, hoping to photograph the wolves which followed the cows to the snowfields at calving time.

Upon leaving, I would backpack to the headwaters of the brawling Chilikadrotna River less than 20 miles distant. There Dennis had dropped a rubber raft for me. I would raft more than 100 miles down the Chilikadrotna to the Mulchatna River; then ride the

Author pausing on a portage trail on Alaska's Kanai Peninsula—bear country, for sure.

Surprised in a blueberry patch on a snowy summer morning, this grizzly glared at the author hiking in the Alaska range.

GO-ALONG GUN

by DON L. JOHNSON

Mulchatna's currents some 50 miles to a point above the mouth of the Koktuli River. There Dennis could again land on floats to pick me up. Meanwhile, I was on my own in some of the most remote and breathtaking country left in Alaska.

The gun was not my idea. While packing and repacking for the trip I had decided not to take it. I wanted to minimize the weight I'd be carrying across rugged terrain and by deleting the handgun from the list I felt I could add another camera lens or two.

Dennis, a master Alaskan guide and outfitter, had vetoed that idea. He'd known me a long time and knew I was no novice to wilderness travel, but he'd said he would not set me down in that country without a firearm. The 357 was his minimum.

Other bears were met on that trip and I also had a brief run-in with a hostile mother moose, but that ineffectual shot over the bear's back was the only one I fired. So did I really need a gun?

In retrospect, I think I did. Without it I would still have stood my ground—I really had no alternative—but there would have been more fear. My voice, and probably my odor, would have communicated that. Bears, like dogs and many other animals, surely can sense when we are fearful. They act accordingly. I have never shot any animal in self-defense, but I've had a few other close encounters when the presence of a gun made me feel much more resolute and therefore less vulnerable to attack.

Still, I do not recommend a 357 on every camper's belt. The question of what to carry is complicated by several factors. To illustrate, I'll describe some guns I've chosen to go along with me on wilderness assignments as an outdoors writer-photographer. My choices are not the only appropriate ones, but my reasons may help you decide what's best for you.

I ought to emphasize that I am not a real gung-ho backpacker. I don't savor struggling over rugged terrain, burdened like a burro and spending all my time watching my feet so I won't break a leg. Given a choice, I'll travel by horse, canoe, raft, or dogsled, and I've logged quite a few miles on all of them. However, I've also worn out lots of boots on treks where there were no alternatives. In the final analysis, whatever the main mode of travel, hiking and packing usually constitute some part of a back-country trip. Therefore, the gun which meets the needs of the backpacker well should serve well for all wilderness travel.

We are discussing travelling when hunting is not the primary purpose. On a hunting trip, you carry the appropriate gun for the game you're after. On the other hand, when your basic aim is fishing, photography, prospecting—or just poking around in the wilds for whatever other reason—you want a gun for defense and/or foraging. The choice can be far different from the hunter's.

Let's face it, defense is a consideration whether or not you're in bear country. Even a small handgun in camp can be a comfort, dissuading all kinds of intruders. When laws permit, a good 22 handgun also can put fresh meat in the pot.

To those ends, I have carried a four-inch S&W Kit Gun on many a trail during the past 25 years. It has potted a variety of small game and dispatched a few undesirables, including an aggressive (and probably rabid) skunk which invaded camp one night.

I don't recommend a handgun for serious foraging unless you're good with it. Back when I wrote "Handguns for Hunting" (GUN DIGEST, 1960) I was shooting my sidearms almost daily. I was pretty proficient with that little S&W then. Today, having gotten somewhat rusty, I'm sure I'd eat much better on a camping/foraging trip if I depended upon a 22 rifle instead.

Foraging adds fun and challenge to a wilderness trip. Fish and game have supplemented my rations on treks ranging from Alaska's mountains to the Amazon jungle. A simple 22 rifle is a good choice. It can be an inexpensive single shot, carried on a sling, barrel trimmed to 18 or even 16 inches and the buttstock bored out to reduce weight further. Iron sights should suffice. In real wilderness country, long shots are seldom necessary.

There are many other possibilities. Remington's light, rugged Nylon 66 autoloader is excellent. More specialized is the Charter Arms AR-7 Explorer which stows in its own durable plastic stock and floats, assembled or taken down. I've carried one of those quite a bit in recent years. It's a bit bulky (though not heavy) for backpacking, but it's a dandy for canoe trips.

I want a gun which can be holstered or slung for ready access on the trail. A rifle or a shotgun should be light, short, and just plain rugged. Don't take a fancy gun; it's bound to take a beating.

An old trail buddy of mine favors the Savage Model 24-VS Camper model in 22 and 20 gauge. Another possibility is the Springfield Armory M6 survival gun. The fact is a 22 will suffice virtually anywhere except in bear country. A major advantage is the light weight of the ammo. Even 100 rounds are hardly noticeble in the pack.

So where does the big handgun come in? In North America, the answer ought to be anywhere you might have to deal with aggressive bears. No doubt about it, a handgun is the handiest answer for someone who is carrying loads over long wilderness trails or portages. If you carry a magnum, you can take along some re-

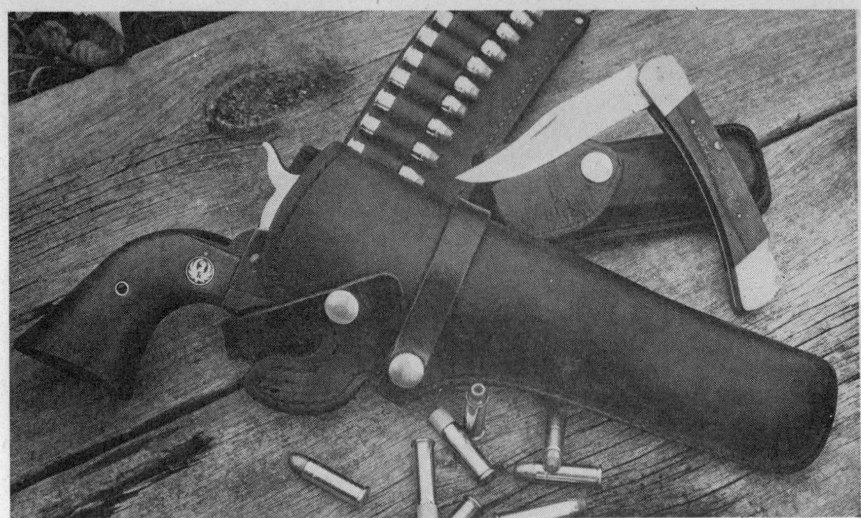

Basic belt equipment on many of author's wilderness treks—a sturdy knife and a Ruger Blackhawk 357 with assorted ammo, including 38 Special loads and Speer shotshells.

Compact Model 94 Trapper nestles neatly along pack frame; provides ample firepower for emergencies and beats any handgun for bear work.

Equipped with sling swivels, H&R Topper makes a handy and versatile trail companion; Johnson carries both slugs and shot when he goes.

Charter Arms Explorer has many features recommending it as an all-around camping gun, but is at its best on canoe trips—it's waterproof and it floats and is just right on stream-side small game.

duced loads for small game. Shot cartridges, such as the Speers, also can be used to take grouse or ptarmigan at close range.

If any handgun can be recommended for stopping bears, it would be one of the long-barreled Thompson Contenders in a big-rifle caliber. With a sling and Pachmayr grip, they make an appealing package. The single shot aspect doesn't bother me because one good shot is all you're apt to get. I'm not going to start poking at a bear with a handgun while there's a chance he'll change his mind and go the other way.

The problem with handguns is that there's a whole lot of wilderness—all of Canada—where they are taboo. A powerful sidearm may be a good choice in Alaska, but if you plan to drive there, ship your handgun ahead.

It used to be quite easy to carry a handgun through Canada. It would be sealed at the border and checked again upon leaving the country. There might be some circumstances where that is still possible, but I don't recommend trying it. I also urge you not to carry a handgun into Canada undeclared. If you are discovered, it will ruin your day and then some.

Anyway, there are many hundreds of miles of bear country between Alaska and the Lower 48. You'll probably want to camp along the way, perhaps doing some fishing and hiking. You'll want a long gun then.

If I were choosing a gun simply for survival in wild country, it would be an "all-around" rifle in the 30-06 class. Powerful enough to handle any species on the continent, such a rifle can also be used to take small game. I've used reduced loads successfully in a variety of big bores. However, I've also found that I can get by with the same loads for large and small game if a good controlled-expansion bullet is used. You want to hit the little critters in the head or neck anyway. With a good rifle sighted in for 200 to 300 yards you ought to be able to pop a blue grouse or snowshoe hare in the skull at 25-30 yards.

There are good reasons why my 280 doesn't go on non-hunting wilderness excursions. Built on a pre-64 Model 70 action with a stiff 24-inch barrel, it is too heavy and cumbersome. Also, the stock is a creation of the late great Len Brownell. It bears the marks of many hunts, but it's still too pretty to be banging against a pack frame all day.

There are some big-bore rifles better suited for travel though; Ruger's 44 Magnum carbine *(Now discontinued: Editor)* seems almost ideal. It is short, lightweight, and has few obtrusive parts. I regard the cartridge as marginal, so I would regard it as a point-blank weapon. Better, in my opinion, would be a lightweight Ruger 77, Winchester Model 70 or Remington Model Seven in 308. Drawbacks are that bolt rifles do stick out awkwardly in places and those are pretty nice rifles to knock around.

The best big-little bolt action ever made for backpacking in bear country was the Remington Model 600. It was introduced in 1964 and was offered in assorted calibers ranging from 222 to 35 Remington—the latter a pretty fair bear stopper. But, my, it was ugly. I found it easy to resist. Two years later, there was a magnum version which, incredibly, was even uglier. It was chambered for two stubby, belted cases. The 6.5mm Magnum didn't interest me, but the 350 was something else.

That spring of 1967 I was packing for a long assignment which would take me to Kodiak Island and the Aleutians; then into Alaska's interior. For the first part of the trip, which included some hunting, I chose a 300 Winchester Magnum. For my solo trek into the Brooks Range which was to follow, I wanted something handier and the 350 Magnum looked like the answer. It sounded and felt like it, too, when I got hold of one and took it to the range.

I carried the Model 600 on that trip, but never fired it again. I decided not to keep it. I really wish I had. Remington didn't make many and there is nothing else quite like them around. Less than 37 inches long and weighing only 6½ pounds, they were a lot of rifle in a small package. Alaskan bush pilots and other savvy types latched on to most of them. I saw one a couple of years ago in a cabin in Alaska's Kantishna Hills. The owner, an old trapper-miner, said he treasured it because it was handy to take up the creek to work. He added that it also was highly respected by the local bears.

The light Topper 20-gauge is the writer's last-ditch choice—the best compromise he's found.

I've arrived at a compromise when I want to carry something handy and reasonably potent. A few years ago I settled on none other than the venerable Model 94 Winchester 30-30 carbine. In the 16-inch-barreled Trapper version it is just 34 inches long. Fully loaded and equipped with swivels and sling it weighs six pounds. Its slab-sided receiver makes for easy carrying and the time-tested design is reliable. With a Williams aperture rear sight and a Redfield bead in front, I can consistently hold it to four-inch groups at 100 yards.

Never mind telling me about the inadequacies of the 30-30. I know the caliber pretty well, having fooled around with lots of rifles and loads in that number over the years. I've seen a heap of deer taken with 30-30s. Devotees of the caliber also still haul quite a few black bears out of the woods of Wisconsin where I live.

Some people think that magnum handguns are good bear insurance, but believe it's foolhardy to face a grizzly with a 30-30. The facts are different. Ballistically the 30-30 is 'way ahead of a 44 Magnum in carbine or handgun. I won't go grizzly hunting with a 30-30, but if one comes hunting me I think he'll come out second best.

But the most indispensable of my go-along guns is none of the above. The one which I think can do it all is an inexpensive H&R Topper single shot 20-gauge. Mine is a Model 98, a somewhat gussied up version with a nickel-plated receiver and a black-enameled stock. I bought it originally because of its three-inch chamber and a modified choke—just what I needed for field testing some 20-gauge steel shot loads since marketed by Federal Cartridge Co.

Later, I mounted detachable sling swivels to buttstock and barrel and took a rasp to the stock to give it a straight grip. The result was a light (5½ pound), reliable and versatile wilderness companion. It has since made several trips. I carried it across British Columbia, Yukon Territory and much of Alaska in 1980. Snowshoe hares, ptarmigan and grouse were abundant that year and I could easily have survived, if necessary, on small game taken with the Topper.

I also carried some Brennecke slug loads. I have as much bear-stopping confidence in them as in any handgun load. In a GUN DIGEST article way back in 1963 ("A Twenty's Plenty") I made a case for the 20-gauge slug for deer. I've taken large whitetails with both the standard Foster type and the Brennecke slug in that gauge. The penetration of the latter looks pretty persuasive. For that matter, at point-blank range, even an ounce of fine shot is devastating.

Even better than my Topper would be a newer version of the model—the H&R Handy Gun II combo, available in electroless nickel finish. Its 22-inch modified barrel gives the gun an overall length of 37 inches (four inches shorter than mine) and there's a matching 30-30 barrel to boot.

One drawback I can see to carrying any kind of firearm while hiking in bear country is that guns may make some people too bold. They may crowd a bear to take pictures and may shoot (and probably wound) a bear which is only bluffing. People and bears are then needlessly hurt. The gun should be regarded the same as a life insurance policy. You don't really want to use either one.

Avoid taking Old Griz by surprise. In parks where firearms aren't allowed it's an especially good idea to travel noisily through bear country, jingling bells, whistling, or talking. There is usually safety in numbers, too. The average bear is more likely to yield to two or three hikers than to one. Just don't get pushy.

To sum up, the decision on which gun to tote on back country treks depends upon what measure of protection is required and whether or not it will be used to provide provisions. If you're traveling with a companion, the choice gets easier. One of you can carry a pot gun and the other a bear buster without anybody being overburdened.

My choices are based on experience and they work well for me. On the catalog pages in this issue of GUN DIGEST you may find something more exactly tailored to your particular needs.

Personally, if I had to settle on one gun for all such wilderness adventures I guess it would be the 20-gauge single shot. It's rugged and lightweight. It's a good good game-getter and packs a pretty good punch in a pinch. If you think about it, those are all the criteria a good go-along gun has to meet. ●

HANDGUNS TODAY: SIXGUNS AND OTHERS

by HAL SWIGGETT

NEVER HAS there been so much to include on these pages. Though the immediate past 365 days were a disaster for a few handgun companies and a tremendous hardship on others, optimism for the future abounds everywhere. There is sincere enthusiasm for the days to come among handgun folks at least and I love it.

This year there are new guns; one a monster sixgun weighing six pounds, a shotgun derringer, a couple of *must* books on our subject, a new stockmaking company, a pistol-to-rifle conversion, mini-big bores, a foreign-made masterpiece of the gun makers art, a 58-caliber pistol cartridge, and more, more, more.

SSK Industries

About that 58-caliber pistol cartridge: SSK has it. J.D. Jones uses the 577 Nitro Express case shortened a bit and stuffed with the B.E.L.L. 750-grain soft point jacketed bullet over 95 grains of rifle Pyrodex. This is a black powder cartridge, obviously, since Pyrodex is a black powder substitute, which makes it handleable. There's a mighty push but no bone-crushing sharp recoil. It's devastating to whatever gets in the way with its 1,150 fps muzzle velocity.

Heritage I 45-70

If there has ever been a handful of single action the huge Heritage 45-70 revolver has to be it. It chambers half a dozen 45-70 rifle cartridges; the muzzle measures $^{25}/_{32}$-inch in diameter. GD's test revolver wears an 8-in. barrel and balanced the scale at an even six pounds. It doesn't kick at all with factory loads and you can see why—it weighs as much as many rifles.

My only problem with the Heritage is its size. Small hands have plagued me all my life. With everything about the Heritage traditional, it's a long way from the grip to that eight-pound trigger. I can reach it but not with a proper grip on the sixgun. Be that as it may, it's been fun shooting the big

Blue wildebeest taken in South Africa by Swiggett and his SSK 45-70 Hand Cannon with 4x Leupold scope.

Heritage I 45-70 single action revolver and three factory loads tested: Federal 300-grain and Remington and Winchester 405-grain.

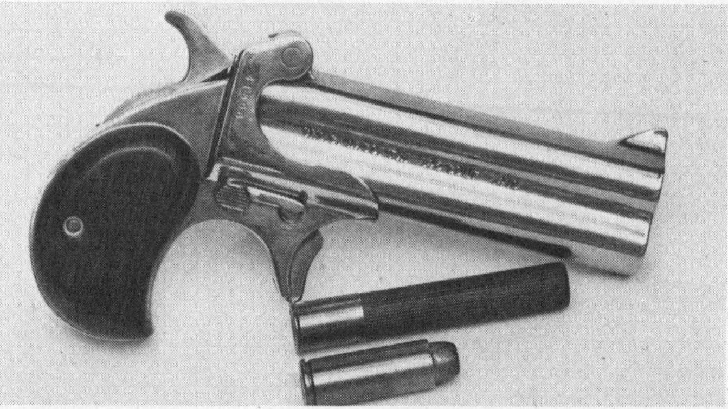

American Derringer 45 Colt/410 with Federal 300-grain HP and 3-inch 410 shotshell.

Heritage.

The Heritage is well-made, seemingly strong enough for heavy loads, more than accurate enough for anything a hunter might want to undertake. A hunter can handle both it and stout loads.

No danger of shooting the wrong cylinder in NAA's big magnum (opposite). The 45 Winchester Magnum disappears in the Express cylinder and the 450 Magnum Express cartridge won't seat in 45 Magnum cylinder.

Freedom Arms

Freedom Arms' 454 Casull single-action revolver is, beyond the shadow of any doubt, the finest built handgun sold today—anyplace. It is also the hardest kicking, most deadly at either end, when fully loaded. Absolutely no one will stand up and declare it a "fun" gun to shoot when loaded the way Dick built it to be shot. Still, it is a great one for the individual capable of handling a full charge under a 300-grain or even heavier bullet.

Smith & Wesson Model 24 Special Combat—a special run for Lew Horton Distributing in 44 Special.

Rusty Condra is only a little bigger than the 357 Super Mag Dan Wesson but he had a ball shooting it.

North American Arms 45 Win. Mag./450 Mag. Express

Announced on these pages last year, the North American Arms 450 Magnum Express is now a reality. Single action, stainless steel, five-shot, walnut stock, Millett white-outlined rear sight, red/orange front blade: that takes care of most details.

Barrel lengths are 7½ inches and 10½ inches. Finishes are three: high polish, semi-matte and black chrome. Weight of our test 7½-inch N.A.A.-SAS (for single action-stainless) is 50½ ounces—an ounce and a half less than spec sheet figures. Trigger pull is a bit heavy at six pounds with only a little creep.

Ammunition comes from two sources. Winchester-Western, of course, loads the parent 45 Winchester Magnum with a 230-grain FMJ bullet. N.A.A. supplies a longer case, their 450 Magnum Express in two bullet weights: 185-grain jacketed hollow point and 260 jacketed hollow point. No figures are supplied for either bullet, but copies of the H.P. White Laboratory report showed an average velocity for the 260-gr. load of 1,768.1 fps with an average pressure of 50,600 pounds, right in there with modern rifle pressures.

The N.A.A. 450 Magnum Express is easy to shoot with their loads. Recoil is there but it isn't going to hurt anyone. If a shooter can handle heavy loaded 44 Magnums, the 450 Magnum Express is only a step up.

American Derringer Corp.

There are derringers and then there are *derringers*. Bob Saunders and his American Derringer Corp. make the latter—hand-filling, attention-getting, big-bored over/under short guns equal to whatever any individual feels up to undertaking. These are little handguns, honest-to-goodness hideouts, but in calibers such as most anything you can name between 22 rimfire and 45 Winchester Magnum to include 223 rifle, 30-30 rifle, 45-70 rifle (as a single shot only) and now 410 shotgun shells. American Derringers wear 3-in. barrels in all but this new creation.

The 45 Colt/410 barrels are 4.1 inches in length with an over-all length of 6 inches and weigh 16 ounces—an even pound. My shooting was with the 3-in. 410s and I still have five fingers and a thumb on that right hand. I do believe, however, that 45 Colt guns are intended to be fired with 2½-in. and 45-70 with the longer shell.

Near as I can tell, it would be deadly on rattlesnakes at 10 or 12 feet. The pattern is, shall we say, wide to be kindest. I shoot a 45 Colt American Derringer often as Bob made up one of the first for me. The 410 is a mite harder to hold, but not at all a problem for anyone used to firing heavy recoiling guns.

Smith & Wesson

Smith & Wesson, many moons back, dropped the 44 Special Model 24 from their line. There was the Model 29 and company thinking assumed the lesser, meaning lighter, gun was no longer needed.

Skeeter Skelton eventually went to bat for the old-timer and was successful in getting 7,500 Model 24's built a couple of years ago. They sold out almost overnight and no more were

North American Arms big 45 with two cylinders (opposite page) has slim look for a bulky sixgun.

Terminator 44 Magnum round-butt mini-six, built from a full-sized Astra for Interarms.

Texas Border Special shows Texas Longhorn Arms' right-hand sixguns—loading gate is on the left, naturally.

planned. Again, Skeeter jumped into the fray and he won again.

S&W brought the Model 24 44 Special back and upgraded it to Model 624—stainless steel. It's cataloged!

Another addition to S&W's line is the Model 649 38 Special Bodyguard. The "6" in front of 49 means it is also stainless steel. It's a 5-shot, satin-finished, 2-in. barrel, 20-ounce revolver designed for pocket carrying—the hammer is protected so it can't hang up on clothing with only enough protruding for it to be cocked should the need arise. The intention is for double-action shooting.

Terminator (Jovino)

"Come over and get this thing, it's the ugliest gun I've ever seen." Jim Pacheco was on the other end of the phone. He's my FFL dealer. His description and mine do not agree.

The Terminator is a no-nonsense double-action 44 Magnum. It came from an Astra, made in Spain and imported by Interarms, as is plainly visible on the right sideplate. It has been nicely tuned. It's from Jovino International, designed to put a stop to tense situations. It shoots fine and I like it.

Allen Fire Arms

This Santa Fe, New Mexico company imports a fine line of black powder and centerfire handguns made by Aldo Uberti and Co., Brescia, Italy. Replicas of the first order is probably the best way to say it since the name of the company was Replica Arms until it was decided to use the family name some years back.

This meeting will stick to centerfires. First there is the 1873 Stallion. It's a rimfire convertible with cylinders for Long Rifle and Magnum. This looks like the 1873 Frontier but just a tad smaller—to fit the cartridge. The target model has a fully adjustable rear sight with a serrated ramp up front. Then there is the conventional fixed-sight sixgun. These can be had as blue guns with color case hardened frame or as all stainless steel. Barrel length is 5½ inches.

Next in line is the Cattleman. Calibers here include 45 Colt, 44-40, 357 Magnum, 38 Special and 22 LR/Magnum. As with the Stallion, this model comes in both blue with color case hardened frame or stainless steel.

A beefed up single action, blue only, with color case hardened frame, is the Buckhorn. Would you have guessed it as chambering the great 44 Magnum round? Barrel lengths are 4¾, 6 and 7½ inches. Traditionalists are accommodated with a fixed sight model though I'll never understand why.

Finally, for the '73, there is a 3-in. Sheriff's Model. Blue, color case hardened frame, fixed sights, of course.

The 1875 Army single action revolver is included in Allen's catalog with a pair of models: the Outlaw is 7½ inches of barrel, blue, color case hardened frame and brass trigger guard. Calibers are 44-40 , 45 Colt and 357 Magnum. Nickel-plated versions are available in those same calibers.

Lew Horton

Lew Horton is a distributing company deep into special order handguns. Currently they list three Smith & Wessons and one Colt that can't be purchased any place but through their company.

New for this year is the Model 624 stainless Special Combat Smith & Wesson. This is S&W's new gun for the year modified to Horton's specifications. It is an "N" frame revolver but with a "K" frame round butt grip, three-inch barrel, and it's a 44 Special. There is also the M686 Compact—the L frame S&W in round butt configuration with 2½-in. barrel and 357 Magnum, stainless steel. S&W's earlier blue Model 24 44 Specials are long gone but Horton had a special run just like the Model 624, but in blue.

Last but far from least is Horton's Colt BOA 357 Magnum. Specially serial numbered from BOA1 to BOA1200 (now you know how many were made). This is the Colt Mark V with a Python barrel and rosewood grips.

Texas Longhorn Arms

We've all heard about right-hand monkey wrenches and know the story, but here is one I'll bet you didn't know about—a right-hand single action. It's for real. There really is a right-hand single action. It's made by Bill Grover in his Texas Longhorn Arms shop and the patent has been applied for.

Described by Bill, in his brochure, as "The Rolls Royce of Sixguns" each gun is hand-built from a solid block of 4140 steel. Each part is built to fit the other until a gun is completed. All springs are handmade of music wire and are coiled. Each grip is cut from a log of dried walnut and handmade to fit each gun. The grip strap is $^3/_{16}$-in. longer than a Colt to provide a place for the shooter's little finger.

The trigger guard is round like prewar Colts. The trigger sits all the way back allowing more finger room and is shaped like a shotgun trigger to better fit the curve of a finger. The trigger is also adjustable for tension and over travel.

Only one thousand of these guns will be made, in each of three models: Texas Border Special, South Texas Army, and West Texas Flat Top Target.

Birdshead grip and 3½-in. barrel single out the Border Special. It can be either 45 Colt or 44 Special.

South Texas Army sixguns wear 4¾-in. barrels and offer a choice of 45 Colt, 44 Special, or 357 Magnum.

Flat Top Target single actions are 7½-in. with adjustable rear sight. Calibers include 45 Colt, 44 Magnum, 44 Special, 357 Magnum, and 32-20.

As mentioned, only one thousand of each will be made. Texas Longhorn Arms sixguns are delivered in deluxe Texas-grown walnut cases oil-finished with velvet lining. Each with a factory letter and lifetime warranty to the original owner. You've probably already figured out they aren't inexpensive. The price is $1,500 each.

O.K . . . so what makes them right-handed sixguns? The loading gate is on the LEFT side. Texas Longhorn Arms single actions can be loaded, fired, emptied and reloaded, without ever removing them from the right hand.

Ruger Single-Six 32 H&R Magnum has Bushnell's Magnum Phantom 2.5x scope in B-Square mount—kills rabbits to 100 yards.

Korth Target double-action revolver with interchangeable cylinder. Note cylinder latch under hammer.

Dan Wesson

Dan Wesson revolvers took over production gun silhouette shooting even before the advent of the 357 Super Mag (Remington introduced it as 357 Maximum but silhouette shooters dreamed it up and had already tagged it Super Mag). They did it with their fine 44 Magnum double-action revolver.

Once Super Mag became available, it became *the* cartridge most often seen in the winners circle. Then along came another Super Mag—the 375—based on a 375 Winchester case shortened sufficiently to be used in the same length cylinder as the 357. One of the single action companies is turning out a few guns so chambered, but the big one again is Dan Wesson.

The only way one can be purchased is through the International Handgun Metallic Silhouette Association (P.O. Box 1609, Idaho Falls, ID 83401).

Charter Arms

Charter Arms has done a bit of design improving here and there. I've been shooting a Police Bulldog 32 Magnum several months but we will get into that a bit later.

The Off Duty, Charter's non-glare matte-black finished 38 Special makes its way to consumers for a bit less money because of the savings in finishing. The Bulldog Tracker 2½-in. blue 357 Magnum now sports a full-length ramp front sight as does the 2½-in. Bulldog 44 Special. The 44's hammer has been bobbed—they call it snag-free—but is serrated for easy cocking and single-action shooting.

My Police Bulldog was outfitted with Pachmayr's great neoprene grip before ever a shot was fired. Listed at 19 ounces, weighing was neglected be-

Charter Police Bulldog 32 Magnum with Pachmayr grip as Swiggett shoots it—heavier, but easier, this way.

Texas Ranger single-action 22 revolvers from FIE are made here in the United States.

fore the grip change but now it is a much heavier 25¾ ounces. The 4-in. bull barrel, along with the Pachmayr grip, make it very easy to hold steady. Single action trigger pull is a mite heavy at 4½ pounds but so crisp the weight of pull is hardly noticeable. Double-action pull is a very smooth 11½ pounds.

Accuracy is maybe the best of the four 32 Mags I've been shooting. It's hard to say—and be fair—because H&R guns have such a horrible trigger pull there is no way to really find out how accurate they might be. The Ruger is now scoped which gives it an advantage but on a good day groups with the Charter equal those turned in by the Single Six, scope and all.

Colt

No new guns from Colt but there are a couple of modifications. The stainless Python is now offered as the Ultimate—a highly polished version. Blue Pythons are still with us. It's been said, "You can't teach an old dog new tricks." I know it categorizes me but blue guns and recurved bows will always hold a warm spot in my heart.

In keeping with the trend towards "popular pricing" Colt offers the Peacekeeper 357 Magnum. If, in your opinion, it looks like a MK V Trooper you aren't being misled. Red insert front sight, white outlined rear, vent rib and all. The only difference is a non-reflective matte blue finish and a "gripper" round bottom rubber grip.

Korth

Korth is not a familiar name to American handgunners. Throughout Europe it ranks highest in double-action revolvers. The reason—it is a limited production firearm—no more than 600 have been made in a year and this number only the past two or three years.

More than 70% of each Korth is hand work. There are no buffing wheels to ruin profiling. It is all grinding wheels and meticulous craftsmanship. There is so much hand work no parts are interchangeble. A perfectionist's revolver.

Built in two models, combat and target, three barrel lengths—3, 4 and 6-in. Rear sights are fully adjustable. Triggers can be adjusted, from the outside with a screwdriver, for both pull and over-travel.

Calibers are: 22 Long Rifle, 32 S&W Long, 32 H&R Magnum, 38 Special and 357 Magnum. Cylinders can be removed in an instant so 22 LRs and 357s can be fitted with 22 Magnum and 9mm Parabellum cylinders for those desiring interchangeability.

Korth has been in the United States in a very limited way but now they will be available to all who want them. As this is written Marty Mandall at Mandall Shooting Supplies and Robert A. Kleinguenther, at his new company Kleinguenther Firearms, will be importers. Mandall will be stocking regulation Korths. Kleinguenther is planning to have most of his engraved by the famous Austrian engraver Josef Aichholzer.

Taurus

Imported from Brazil, Taurus revolvers are shaking up the handgun industry with their widely advertised LIFETIME REPAIR POLICY. Taurus agrees to repair or replace any firearm for the life of the firearm.

Taurus revolvers are double action with barrel lengths of 2, 3, 4, and 6 inches. There are fixed and adjustable sight models in 22, 32, 38 and 357 Magnum calibers with checkered Brazilian walnut grips, blue or satin-nickel finish, or stainless steel.

Taurus' new gun for this year is the Model 85 38 Special, a 5-shot, 2 or 3-in. barrel, 21 ounce, stainless steel, fixed sight double action with Brazilian hardwood grip.

Rossi (Interarms)

It has to come from outside the United States but at least one company expanded their line of handguns. Not only have they expanded the line but, over the past few years, have upgraded quality to the point their guns are comparable to any and better than many. Maybe most.

The Rossi double-action revolver line lists eight new handguns. All are 38 Specials and things of beauty. Five are stainless. Seven are on a new medium-sized frame and one an added barrel length.

The new medium-sized frame has an integral full-length raised ventilated rib and an integral full-length ejector rod shroud on the medium weight barrel. Fixed sight service models have the same full-length rib only it isn't ventilated. The ejector rod shroud is identical. Vent rib guns have a fully adjustable rear sight with a serrated ramp red-orange insert up front.

Grips are Brazilian hardwood and described by Rossi as combat style but my description would be, for lack of a better word, magna. Not big but handfilling, of excellent grain and color, and nicely checkered.

Interarms sent a M851 for testing—the 4-in. vent rib version. It weighs 30¾ ounces. Single-action trigger pull is a sweet 46 ounces, slightly less than three pounds. Double action is like cutting through melted butter, smooth really beyond description, and an even 10 pounds. Fit and finish is very good. Care obviously went into each step of building and putting together this gun.

I am not a 38 Special shooter, but I fired four boxes in one afternoon. First 100 wadcutters then some Nyclads. That was enough to tell me the M851 shoots good—very good in fact—handles well, downright comfortable (maybe that comes from shooting lots of hot 44s and bigger), and locks up tight as a drum.

Harrington & Richardson

Harrington & Richardson, like many other gun companies, has experienced tough going. They are still in business and the catalog is thinner, but there are new listings: 32 Magnum in models 732 (2½-inch) and 733 (2½-inch). Actually these are the same gun only 732 is blue and 733 electroless matte nickel. Action is single and double, sights fixed, with swing-out cylinder and round butt.

H&R's Model 504 has been out since shortly after the 32 H&R Magnum was announced. With a year of shooting gone by let's talk about it. My M504 has a 6-in. barrel, weighs 33½ ounces, blade front and adjustable rear sight, and a 6 pound single-action trigger pull. In double action, the hammer drops at 14 pounds. The grip is just right for my size 7 Cadet hand which means it might be small for many shooters.

It does better with Federal's newer 85-grain load than with the heavier 95-grain lead bullet. Two-inch 25-yard groups are easy to the point I'm convinced they could be bettered with a decent trigger. Six pounds doesn't do a lot for tight groups.

Ruger

Ruger was the announcing gun company—but now it's gone . . . gone . . . g o n e—from their catalog. Remington and Ruger teamed up on the 357 Maximum then shortly, very shortly, after the announcement—with only a few guns out—the Southport, Connecticut, company threw in the towel. Last year it was still listed, but no guns were produced. Their 1985 catalog makes it real conspicuous by its absence.

The company, however, is alive and well. With the addition of 357 Mag and 41 Magnum to their mighty double-action Redhawk line it now well covers the field for handgunners seeking magnum power.

Brand new for this year are the Ruger Bisley Single Six and Blackhawk. The New Model Single Six is styled after the classic Bisley "flattop" configuration with the longer grip frame and lower hammer. The dovetail rear sight is adjustable for windage. Up front the base accepts interchangeable square front sight blades of various heights and styles. The cylinder is unfluted and rollmarked with a classic foliate engraving pattern along with an old-time Bisley marksman and a Bisley trophy. Calibers: 22 Long Rifle and 32 Magnum. Barrel length: 6½ inches.

Ruger's New Model Bisley Blackhawk wears the same grip style, lowset hammer and cylinder markings. Other than that it is, in fact, a Ruger Blackhawk with adjustable rear sight, ramp front and all the other Ruger niceties. Barrel length is 7½ inches and calibers include 357 Magnum, 41 Magnum, 44 Magnum and 45 Colt. You read it right—the catalog says 44 Magnum and it is a Blackhawk.

More interesting at the moment, because it is in hand and has been for many months, is the Ruger Single Six 32 Magnum. Mine is 5½-in. barreled but there are, for those desiring other lengths, 4⅝, 6½ and 9½ lengths available. The rear sight is fully adjustable with a traditional Ruger ramp up front. Mine went through several hundred Federal 95-grain lead semi-wadcutters with surprising results. Surprising because I had heard from other shooters the accuracy of that particular load wasn't all that great. I quickly determined the gun and ammo was shooting better than me, so I scoped it. It is sighted in about an inch and a half high at 50 yards which makes 100-yard jackrabbits dead rather easily.

FIE

Most times a "Yellow Rose" would be worn as a corsage or displayed in a vase but with FIE involved one has to be careful. There is now a "Yellow Rose" that can be worn on a hip—or maybe under an arm. It's made in Brescia, Italy, by Fratelli Tanfoglio S.p.a., has a 4¾-in. barrel, weighs 33¼ ounces with the magnum cylinder and a tad more when firing Long Rifle cartridges. It is single action with a blade front sight and fixed rear. Grip panels are walnut. There is a manually operated safety. Its family name is Buffalo Scout and most members are blue or chrome. The "Yellow Rose" comes by its name through its finish which is 24 kt gold. Everyone ought to own a gold-plated revolver and now it's possible because this "Yellow Rose" lists at only $124.95.

It shoots better than inexpensive revolvers have a right to, on cloudy days. The heavier those clouds are the better it shoots. On bright sunny days, forget it. On the other hand who, in his right mind, would want to shoot a gold-plated "Yellow Rose" other than to be able to say, "I own a gold-plated single action and have shot it!"

Thompson/Center

Thompson/Center's great Contender single-shot pistol continues to roll along, always on top, and they do it so quietly few folks know what is happening. I couldn't begin to list changes in the Contender since it was first introduced, yet never has there been a formal announcement. Changes are slipped into production and show up on dealer counters. That's it. That's all.

For instance, T/C recently changed the hammer making it quicker and easier to change from rimfire to centerfire, but that fact was not publicized nor featured in any way. Yet, and this is the really fantastic thing about the company, the very first frames and barrels put out will function with current production. ●

RESPONSIBILITY HAS ITS OWN REWARDS

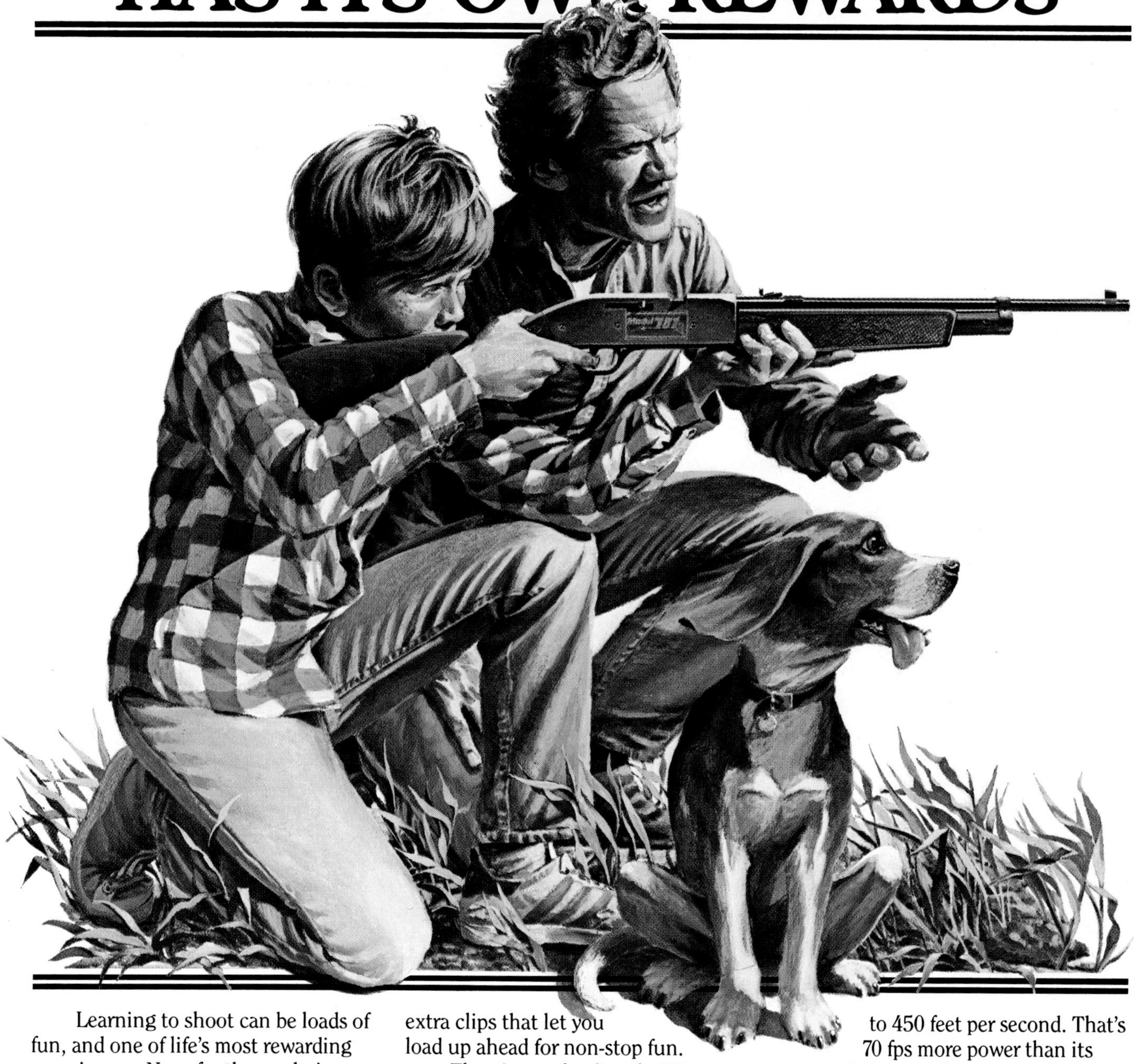

Learning to shoot can be loads of fun, and one of life's most rewarding experiences. Now, for those who've proven themselves ready, Crosman offers the perfect first gun—the new 781 Single Pump airgun.

You'll like the easy pumping. The unique four-shot pellet clip. And the extra clips that let you load up ahead for non-stop fun.

There's easy loading for BBs, with combined storage for 195 of 'em in the magazine and reservoir.

Whichever you shoot, BBs or pellets, the 781 has a quick, smooth repeating action with a velocity of up to 450 feet per second. That's 70 fps more power than its closest single-pump competitor.

See what fun responsibility can be. Now, and for years to come. Reward yourself with the Crosman 781 Single Pump at your nearby sporting goods dealer.

The New 781 Single Pump

Crosman® AirGuns

#1 IN AMERICAN AIR POWER! A Coleman Company

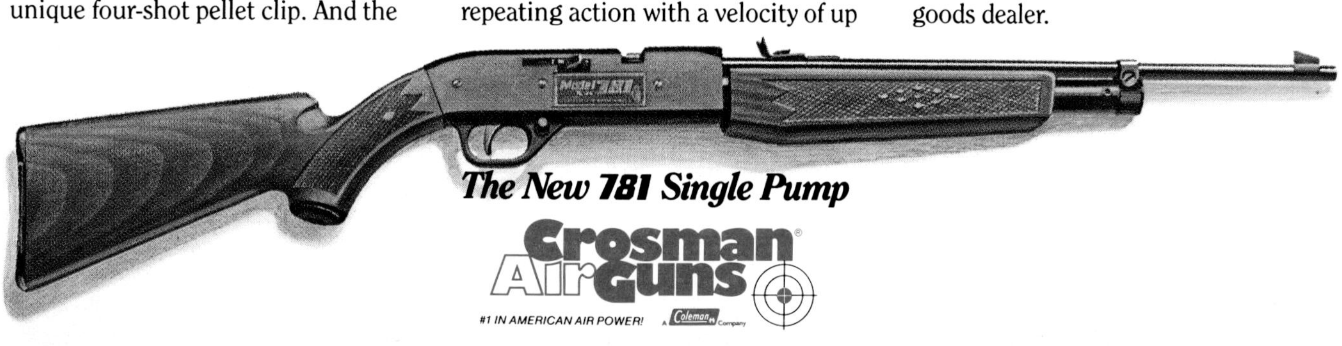

THE NEW 4x4™ FROM RCBS.

A versatile, progressive press for rifle and pistol.

■ *Five-minute caliber changeover. Just switch dies, shellplate, and adjust your powder measure.*

■ *Strong, cast-iron block "0" frame won't stretch or fatigue like many "pot metal" presses.*

■ *26 interchangeable shell-plates allow you to load thousands of different calibers.*

■ *Rotating walnut-grip "D" handle follows your natural arm motion. Compound leverage multiplies your strength.*

■ *With operator indexing, nothing advances to the next station until you want it to. Inspect and fill your cartridge boxes as you go.*

■ *Uses standard dies and powder measures.*

Spring-loaded detent allows you to easily remove a cartridge at any of four stations.

Spent primer catcher bottle —a small touch, but a handy extra any experienced reloader can appreciate.

Reliable primer feed system. Uses standard RCBS feed tubes.

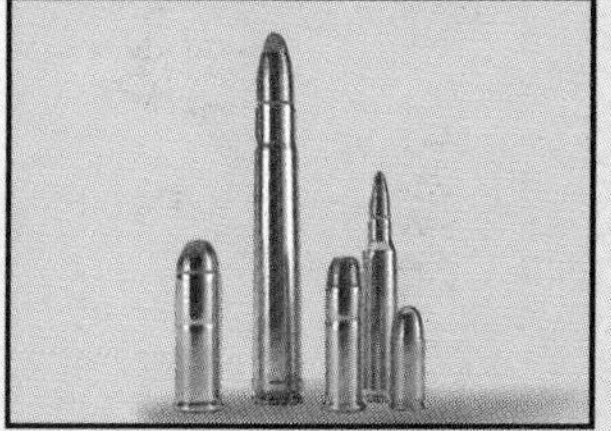

Versatile 3¾" stroke lets you load most rifle and pistol ammo from 32 auto to 375 H&H Magnum.

The new 4x4 isn't the only popularly-priced, progressive reloader in the world.

But any handloader who appreciates quality, value, and performance will instantly know it is the best.

It is so simple and reliable, a novice can use it. Yet it can easily turn out 350 precision rounds an hour.

So it's sure to appeal to those who demand both quality and quantity.

Your local dealer will be happy to show you how it works. And, remember, he's always there with parts, supplies and advice when you need them.

Try your hand at the new 4x4 today. And see why most reloaders swear by RCBS.

RCBS
OMARK INDUSTRIES

GET THE WHOLE SHOOTIN' MATCH
FROM THE GOOD OL' BOYS.
CCI, Speer, RCBS, Outers & Weaver

P.O. Box 856, Lewiston, ID 83501

BEYOND COMPARISON!

NORTH AMERICAN ARMS

450 MAGNUM EXPRESS

Single Action Revolver

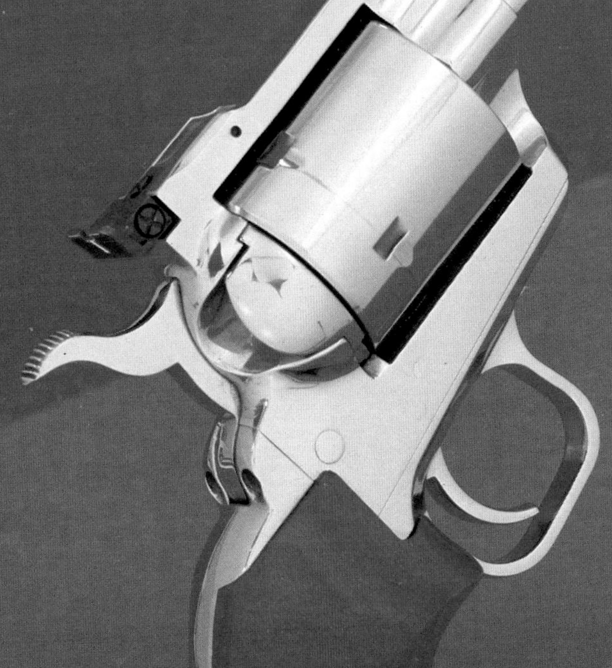

Compare the following features with any competitive revolvers:

POWER—

- Over 2100 fps with factory loaded ammunition
- 185-260 grain bullet weights

QUALITY—

- 17-4 stainless steel construction
- Manufactured to aerospace standards

SAFETY—

- 3 years testing, engineering and evaluation
- Patented hammer safety

VERSATILITY—

- Interchangeable cylinder for 450 Winchester Magnum

PO Box 280
Spanish Fork
Utah 84660
(801) 798-9893

RIGBY'S

a pursuit of excellence for over 250 years

A BEST QUALITY double rifle made in London, is, and always has been, the supreme manifestation of gun making skill and expertise. When such a rifle has *John Rigby & Co.* engraved on the sidelocks and barrel rib, then it is immediately known that a truly superior rifle is at hand.

John Rigby and Company, now managed and directed by D.G.L. Marx at 13 Pall Mall, London, is a gun and rifle making business steeped in history and tradition. The business was started in Dublin, Ireland, in 1735 and is probably the oldest independent firm of rifle and gun makers in the world today. Rigby pistols and rifles were well known in the flintlock period. The first London branch was opened in 1865 and in 1888 the Dublin premises were closed when the John Rigby of the day was appointed Superintendent of the Royal Small Arms Factory at Enfield. While John Rigby concerned himself with the production of military weapons, his son, Ernest John Rigby assumed management of the family business. Ernest John had worked at Birmingham Small Arms for several years and John Rigby thought him qualified to direct the family enterprise.

Prior to Ernest John Rigby's assumption of management, his father had invented the forming of cartridges from coiled brass sheets and had developed five-groove rifling in which the lands and grooves were of equal width. This improvement on

This is a highly refined, fully decorated Rigby double rifle in 470 Nitro caliber.

by JERRY EVANS

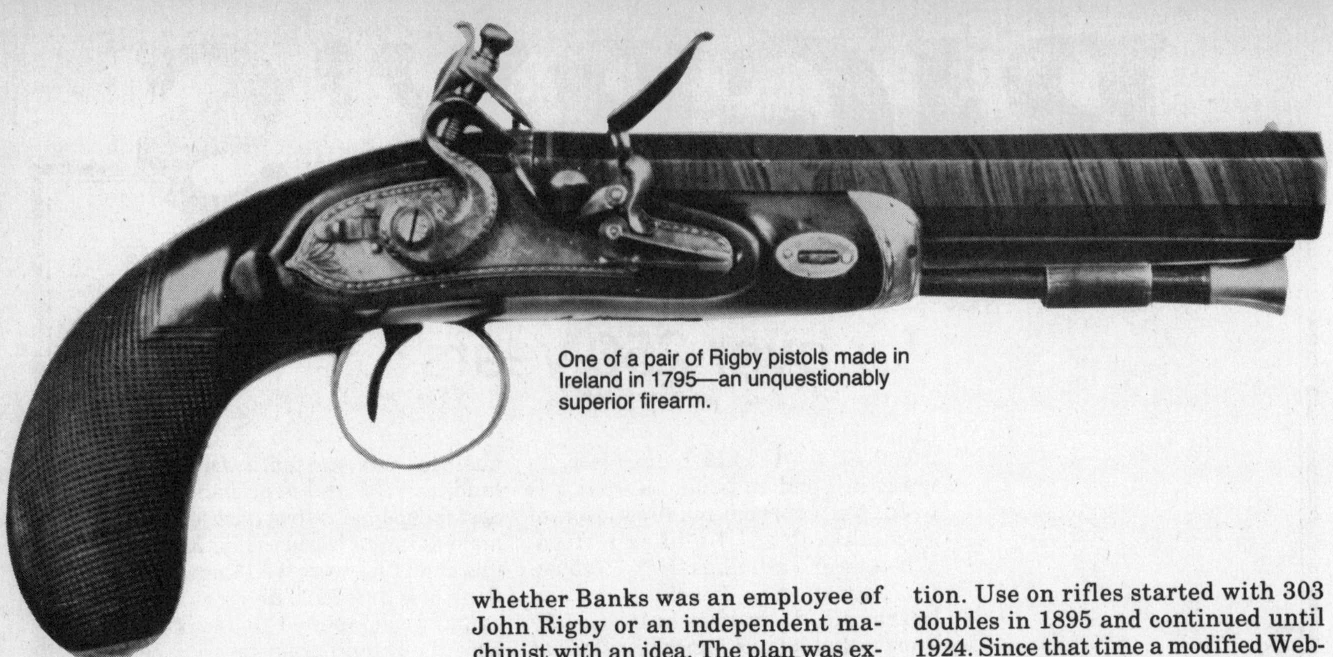

One of a pair of Rigby pistols made in Ireland in 1795—an unquestionably superior firearm.

Metford rifling was made necessary when Cordite was introduced. Metford rifling would not stand the wear from Cordite for service use. Rigby rifling was also used for 303-caliber sporting rifles. Ernest John Rigby immediately distinguished himself as a rifleman by winning honors shooting for the Irish Eight at Bisley.

Although John Rigby produced fine flintlock pistols and best quality shotguns, the company has always been best known for the excellence achieved in the making of sporting rifles. Rigby patents for use on double guns and rifles were highly regarded also.

The most notable of the Rigby patents was granted in 1887 and known as the Rigby & Banks rising vertical bolt. It is not known at this time whether Banks was an employee of John Rigby or an independent machinist with an idea. The plan was excellent and basically consisted of an extension of the top rib of the double gun. This extension had a rectangular hole that fit over a protuberance rising from the rear of the action. When the top lever was moved one fourth of the protuberance dropped down and the action could then be opened, and the chambers exposed. When the gun was snapped closed the vertical bolt rose and everything locked into firing position. A double gun with such an action is able to stand the shooting of countless rounds without loosening the fit of barrels to breech face. All best quality shotguns by Rigby between 1887 and 1910 had such an action. Use on rifles started with 303 doubles in 1895 and continued until 1924. Since that time a modified Webley doll's head rib extension has been used as the rising vertical bolt became too expensive to produce.

John Rigby & Company had two other patents that were used for many years. One was a lever-release forearm and the other a top safety on which a small square button must be depressed before the rifle could be taken off safety and fired. That mechanism was made necessary for safety reasons should the sportsman have an

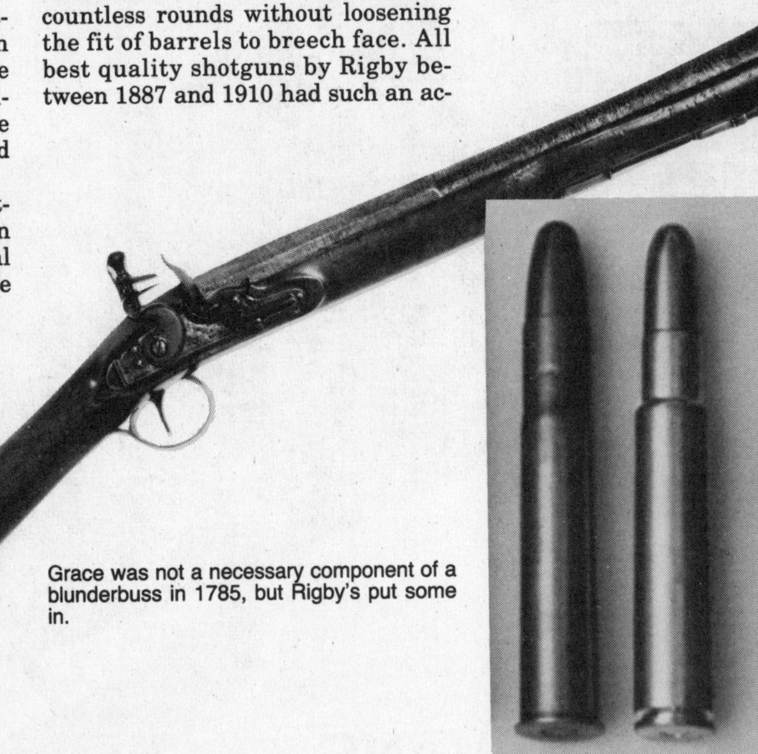

Grace was not a necessary component of a blunderbuss in 1785, but Rigby's put some in.

The cartridges were as important as the guns at Rigby's in London. These are the 470, the 416 and the 400/350, all successes.

inexperienced gun bearer.

Rigby cartridge development added another claim to fame, because in 1897 they really gave their competitors something to consider. Immediately following the introduction of the smokeless propellant called Cordite for use in 303 caliber military weapons, Rigby pioneered the modern high velocity Nitro Express cartridge. John Rigby & Company took the popular 450 Express rifle cartridge that fired lead bullets of 270, 310, 325, or 365 grains propelled by 120 grains of black powder with velocities from muzzle of 1700 to 1975 fps and loaded a 480-grain bullet pushed by 70 grs. Cordite. That loading produced a velocity of 2150 fps and the nearly 5000 foot-pounds of energy proved this cartridge to be more than adequate for any game animal that would be shot anywhere in the world. The excellence of Rigby's bullet design was another factor in the immediate acceptance of such a new cartridge.

The 450 Nitro enjoyed great popularity for several years amongst big bore shooters. Holland & Holland took their 500/450 Black Powder Express and used 70 grains of Cordite originally in 1897, then went to 75 grains behind the 480-grain bullet to compete with the Rigby straight 450. Eley Bro. developed a longer 3½-in. case and called it a 450 No. 2. Those three 450 rifles enjoyed acceptance with the big game hunters and really were no different in ballistic performance.

Rigby decided in 1899 that a smaller cartridge was needed by the hunting world and so the 400 Express case was necked down to 350. It was thusly that the Rigby 400/350 Nitro was made for doubles, single shots and bolt rifles. Again, Rigby gave close attention to bullet design and the 400/350 at once became the most popular and most widely used medium bore rifle in Africa.

The various 450 Nitros were very popular throughout the British Colonial Empire until about 1905 when the British government decided to ban cartridges of 45 caliber in India and the Sudan. That decision was made because of the great number of 577/450 caliber military rifles still in use. The British officialdom wanted to prevent components from being used by rebellious inhabitants of those areas.

While it was certainly a very remote possibility that a Sudanese tribesman or Hindu Sepoy could reload a fired 577/450 brass case using salvaged components from an unfired

Maharaja of Surguja, India, with a white tiger shot with 416 Rigby—the magazine rifle, in this case. Eventually, this prince had a 416 Rigby double.

J. J. Fenykovi with his 416 Rigby and the giant elephant now in the Smithsonian.

Jerry Evans with Lord Derby Eland and a 416 Rigby rifle—he knew Rigby guns personally.

This is what the Rigby patent rising bolt looked like.

This is an early 450 Rigby with the rising bolt and typical finish.

This 416 Rigby double rifle is the only double Rigby ever built in its celebrated proprietary cartridge designed to be used in their magazine guns.

450 Nitro, nevertheless the ban was enforced. Its principal effect may have been to stimulate the rifle and cartridge designers of the United Kingdom.

The years from 1906 through 1912 saw great accomplishments by the gun trade in developing cartridges that would achieve the results that the Rigby 450 accomplished in 1897. Holland & Holland took their 500/450 and necked it up a bit to form a 500/465. Joseph Lang brought out a 470; Westley Richards had a 476; and someone took the long 450 No. 2 and created a 475 No. 2. John Rigby & Company concentrated on the 470 Nitro and probably produced more of that persuasion than all the other rifle makers combined.

The Rigby Company didn't devote all their expertise toward the building of fine quality double 470-caliber rifles, however. In 1908 they introduced a proprietary improvement of the 400/350. This cartridge was called a 350 Rimless Magnum and was made for bolt action magazine rifles. This was a very fine cartridge and was accepted in Africa and India with great enthusiasm. A flanged version was also made for single or double rifle use. That round was called the 350 No. 2 Rigby. In performance, by American standards, the 350 Rigby would rank with a 35 Whelen whereas in Europe a 9.3 x 62 would be comparable. Because the 350 Rigby was a proprietary cartridge and available only from Rigby, the firm was able to maintain quality control of its bullets. The well designed bullet was probably a big reason for the success of the 350 Rigby. John Rigby & Company always believed that a properly designed and constructed bullet was paramount in the successful use of the cartridge.

In 1911, Rigby's again came forth with a winner. The proprietary 416 Rigby was introduced then. It was made for use in Rigby magnum Mauser-actioned rifles and was immediately successful. Again the success of the cartridge was due greatly to the design of the bullet, particularly the thickness and taper of the steel jacket used in the 410-grain solids. The 416 established an enviable reputation for use on all dangerous game under any conditions.

ABOUT THE AUTHOR

Sad to relate, but this is the last of Jerry Evans' articles. He died of a massive stroke in August, 1984.

He was a collector; he was a shooter; he was only sometimes a writer. I wish he had written more.

K.W.

Users and fans of the 416 Rigby are legion, amongst both professional African hunters, the experienced American and European big game hunters, as well as African Safari novices. The late great Jack O'Connor shot his best lion with his 416 Rigby. Fred Huntington, of RCBS fame, used a 416 while on safari with O'Connor. George Dove, a former professional hunter in Tanganyika told me that he had used all calibers for everything, but his favorite was the 416 Rigby. He had two of them. Commander David Blunt used a 416 for dangerous game and particularly elephant control work. He would recommend no other.

While hunting rhino in Angola in 1954, a sportsman named J.J. Fenykovi discovered elephant tracks that measured 24 inches. Knowing that the beast making such tracks had to be huge, he postponed the rhino hunt, returned home to Spain and got organized for a special expedition to get that elephant. The following year he returned and put his safari together. The rifle selected by Mr. Fenykovi for this special safari was his 416 Rigby. On November 13, 1955, after an 11-hour stalk, Fenykovi downed the elephant. The monstrous beast weighed

This 275 Rigby was presented to Jungle Jim Corbett by the provincial government for killing a man-eater in 1907. Plate at left was inlaid in stock.

an estimated 8 tons and stood 13 feet, 2 inches. The tusks weighed 96 pounds each. After laboriously skinning the elephant in one piece, which weighed 2 tons, he transported the hide, skull and tusks by truck and rail to the seaport of Lobito, thence to Lisbon, on to Madrid and from there to the Smithsonian Institution in Washington, D.C. The Smithsonian taxidermists spent 16 months mounting the animal where it has been displayed since 1959, the largest elephant on record.

John Taylor, writer and elephant poacher, mentions the reliability of Rigby rifles in his book *African Rifles*

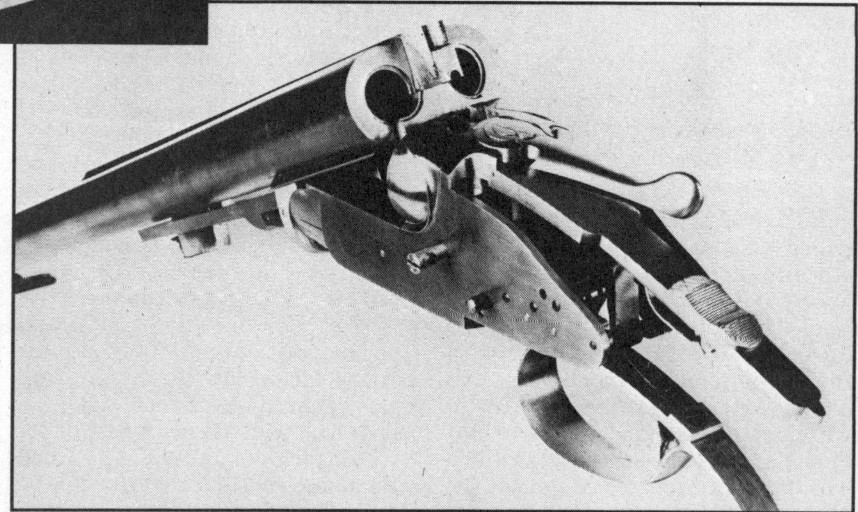

A 470 Rigby double rifle made by Paul Roberts looks like this during assembly.

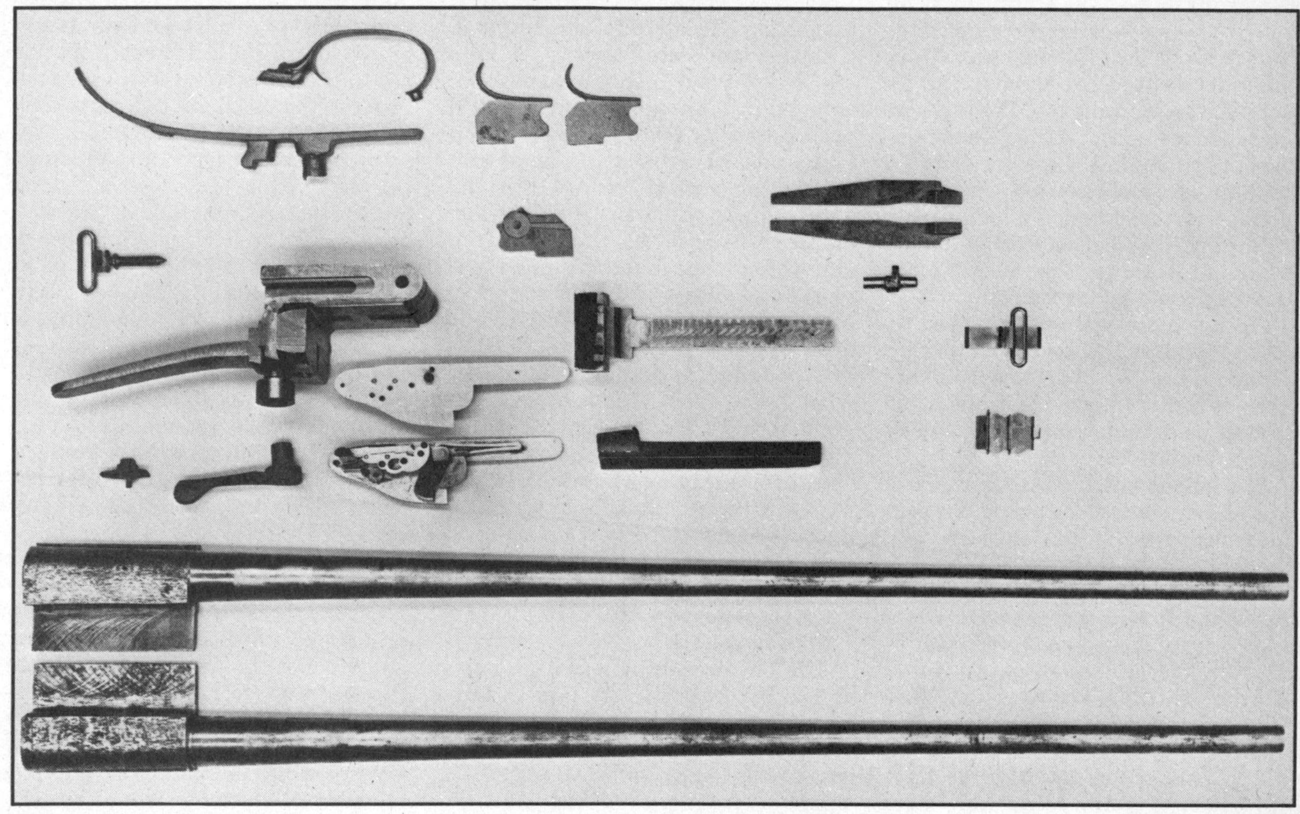

There's some filing yet to do, but these parts will make a 470 double rifle in the J. Roberts & Son shop.

This is the Roberts shop in Covent Gardens, London.

and Cartridges. Taylor was not enamored with bolt rifles and goes on to state that he would be completely happy if John Rigby could be persuaded to make a 416 Rigby double rifle for him. The Maharaja of Rewa in India, who propagated the white tigers, convinced Westley Richards in Birmingham, England, to build a best quality double sidelock ejector rifle in 416 Rigby in 1928. His neighbor, the Maharaja of Surguja, had reportedly poached a few Rewa white tigers with a 416 Rigby bolt rifle and when he saw the Rewa Westley Richards double, decided that he must have one, only he wanted his to be made by John Rigby & Company. Endless correspondence and visits to London ensued, until June, 1939, when Surguja took delivery of the only 416 Rigby double rifle ever made by John Rigby, a best quality sidelock ejector double, stocked by Shelley, barrels by Lane and engraved by Harry Kells. Those were the top workmen employed by Rigby at that time. (See *Guns and Ammo*, January 1975, "The Rifle that Rupees Built.") Rigby made about 700 magazine and that one double 416 rifles 1911 to 1979.

The golden years of African safaris and shikars to India are past, the popularity of the 416 has not lessened. Some years past Rigby had Norma Projektilfabrik in Sweden make brass cases and bullets for the 416. Those components were sent to Kynoch in England to be loaded using Nobel powder. A total of 50,000 rounds were loaded and were sold out in two months. The design of the Norma full metal jacket bullets did not meet Rigby criteria and so no more were produced. Hornady recently produced an excellent copper-clad steel jacketed 410-grain bullet that is available to handloaders and Brass Extrusion Laboratories in Bensenville, Illinois, should have brass for 416 handloaders.

A couple of years back, I sectioned a Hornady, a Norma and a Rigby-Kynoch full patch bullet for comparison of steel thickness and taper. From that examination, I would place the Hornady as number one, Kynoch at two and Norma a far distant third. On my 1983 safari in Cameroon, I used my 416 Rigby bolt rifle to collect a fine Lord Derby eland and a roan antelope. Unfortunately, we did not see any shootable elephant, so I was not able to test the Hornady solids. Barnes Bullets in American Fork, Utah, make solids and soft point bullets. They also make a 300-grain soft point. Barnes can hardly keep up with the demand for both 400-grain and 300-grain 416 bullets, although most of those bullets are used in a shortened case called a 416 Taylor.

Today, with hunting in India gone and the political problems in many parts of Africa, the rifle making business of John Rigby & Co. London certainly isn't what it once was. The cost of having a best quality London-made rifle made, added to the cost of a full African safari to use the rifle, would approach an astronomical number.

At the present time, D.G.L. Marx, Managing Director of John Rigby & Company, and Paul Roberts of J. Roberts & Son London Gunmakers, have entered into an agreement to build both best quality double rifles on Rigby sidelock actions and Rigby bolt rifles. Magazine rifles in 416 Rigby will be made when the B.E.L.L. ammunition is produced and when suitable actions are found. The now and then availability of Brevex Magnum Mauser actions is not reliable and most English rifle makers, Paul Roberts included, were never impressed with Brevex actions. John Wilkes, London riflemaker, described the Brevex as a "mechanical abortion that should have been outlawed in the British Empire." At this writing, the team of Rigby-Roberts are testing an action from Fred Wells, Arizona, a Genneco, made in California, and a BRNO semi-square bridge from Czechoslovakia.

The business known as J. Roberts & Son is comparatively new as London gunmakers. In the late 1930s, J. Roberts started selling antique used guns acquired in India. His business operated from a warehouse in London. The business known as J. Roberts & Son was actually started as gunsmiths in 1958 on St. Martins Lane, London. Paul Roberts, the son, was an ardent hunter. He had an interest in safari outfitters in Tanganyika and Kenya, and regularly hunted in India. When an opportunity to purchase a good rifle or gun occurred, Paul would buy. The weapons would be refurbished and sold. Paul Roberts was very attentive to the quality of restoration and refinishing of used weapons.

In 1972, J. Roberts & Son qualified as London Gunmakers. Within a few years Paul Roberts had established a reputation as a maker and purveyor of quality arms in addition to being very fair and honest in his business dealings. Faced with an ever-increasing business, in September, 1978, Paul Roberts moved to 5 King Street, Covent Gardens, London. J. Roberts & Son now occupy three floors for gunmaking, refurbishing and sales. Paul has been able to seek and employ workmen who are able to produce best quality work and take pride in doing so. Such work has been the hallmark of the London gunmakers for two centuries and Paul Roberts insists that such quality be maintained in his shop.

Apart from the work bearing their own name, J. Roberts & Son also help John Rigby & Company complete their orders for rifles and shotguns. Rigby has some tools and equipment available to Paul Roberts and it is hoped that this spirit of cooperation between the two firms can perpetuate the making of the traditional quality London-made weapons. Production of the Rigby-Roberts rifles is limited and the prices are not cheap. Since the double rifle production started early in 1980, orders have been received for about 12 rifles in calibers 458 Winchester, 470 and 577. Depending on amount of engraving and gold inlay, by Ken Hunt, the price is from 10,000 to 18,000 pounds sterling, including case and tools. It is doubtful that any of those fine rifles, or those produced in the future, will be used for elephant, rhino or Cape buffalo. All have been sold to collectors in America.

The John Rigby & Co. double-barreled rifles produced with the cooperation of J. Roberts & Son are works of art. They have also passed inspection and proof at the London Proof House. The barrels are regulated to fire either barrel with acceptable accuracy. In short, the same care in rifle making procedure is followed now as was followed 80 years ago when the same rifle was made for daily use for the most dangerous game in the world. ●

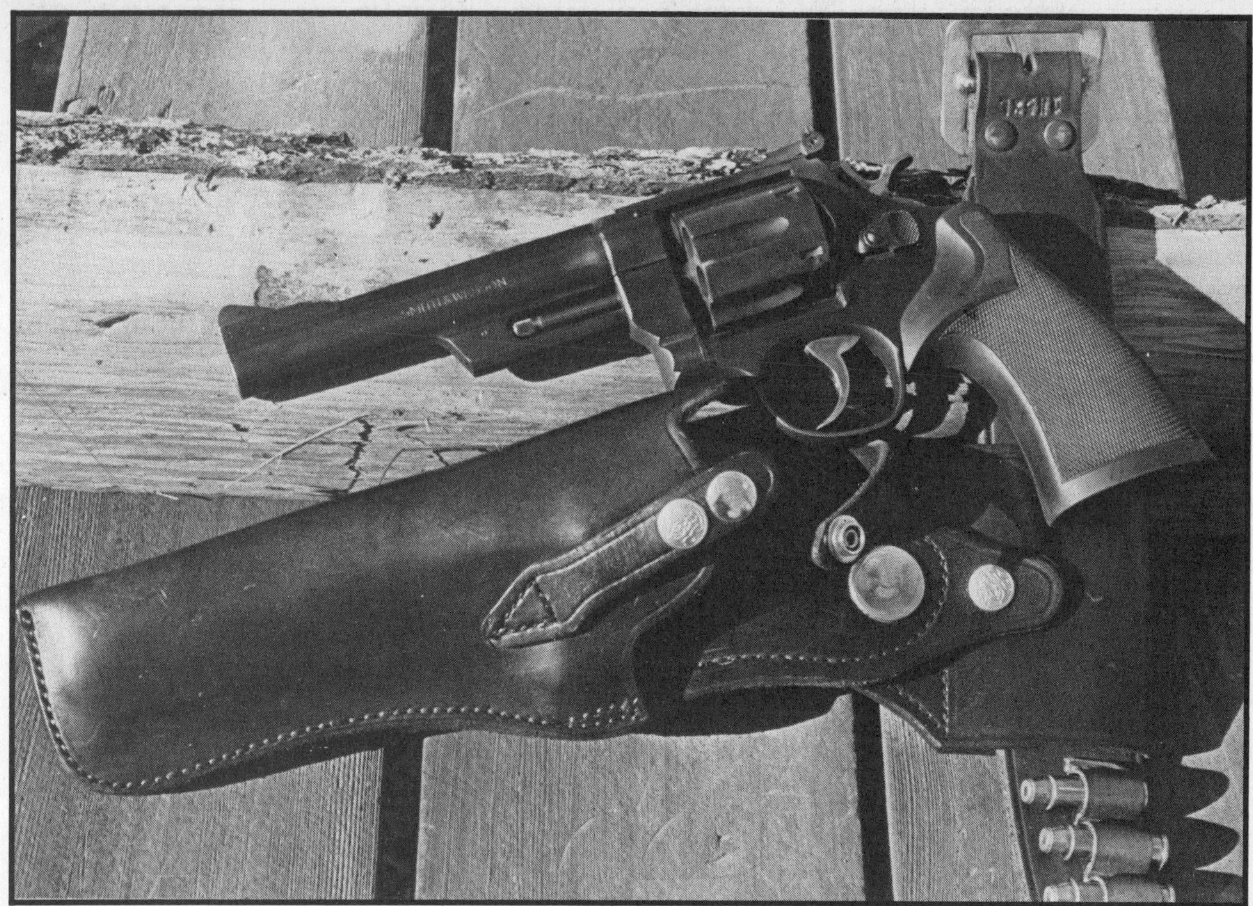

S&W Model 28 converted to 41 Magnum is a plain working revolver of great versatility. Pachmayr grips help control recoil.

The **Cautious** Converter

Making big ones out of little ones is fun, but also serious.

by RUSS GAERTNER

CONVERSION of a handgun to a new caliber has always struck me as the hard way to get the gun/cartridge combination you want. For the magnum revolver I had in mind, however, it was the only way to get my ideal all-around handgun. In the process, I learned that the job of converting a revolver is not as simple as it may sound.

Frankly, conversion has everything against it. The practice is frowned upon by the big factories. Your decision to convert says, in effect, that you know something the manufacturers don't. On the other hand, some of our greatest handguns and cartridges evolved from earlier models and older cartridges, somewhat converted, you might say.

All authorities seem to agree that hot loads are not suitable for big bore conversions. As one expert puts it, "If you want 44 Magnum performance, buy a 44 Maggie."

As the owner and shooter of several 44 Magnum revolvers, including the Super Blackhawk and the Model 29, I agree with that advice, but I didn't want 44 Magnum performance and I couldn't stand 44 Magnum recoil. A personal illness, rheumatoid arthritis, had put an end to my handgunning for almost a year. This is the crippling type of arthritis, but I was lucky and my treatment put the disease in check. As I began to recover, I found full-power ammo caused swelling and stiffness in my hands, wrists and elbows. I began thinking about guns with less recoil.

There was only one possibility. I acquired both a Ruger Blackhawk and a Smith Model 57 in 41 Magnum. Both are fine guns. The Blackhawk was easier for me to handle at first, but soon I was doing very well with the Smith. I could manage fullhouse factory ammo or handloads. It seemed to me the 41 was a caliber which could take the punishment out of magnum handgunning without much sacrifice in performance. If a recovering ar-

(Text continues Page 138)

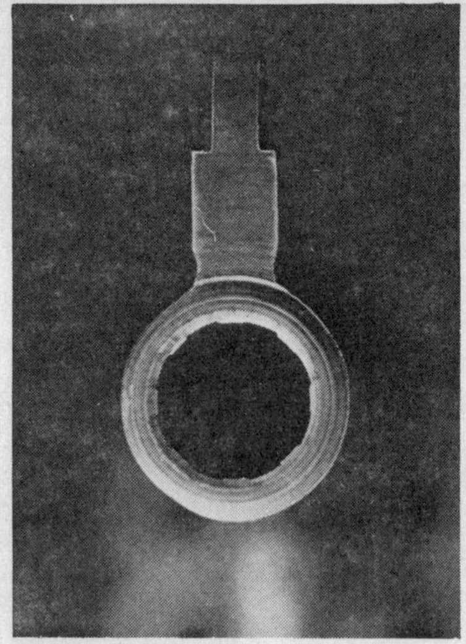

Liner is barely visible at the muzzle of Model 28 converted to 41 Magnum.

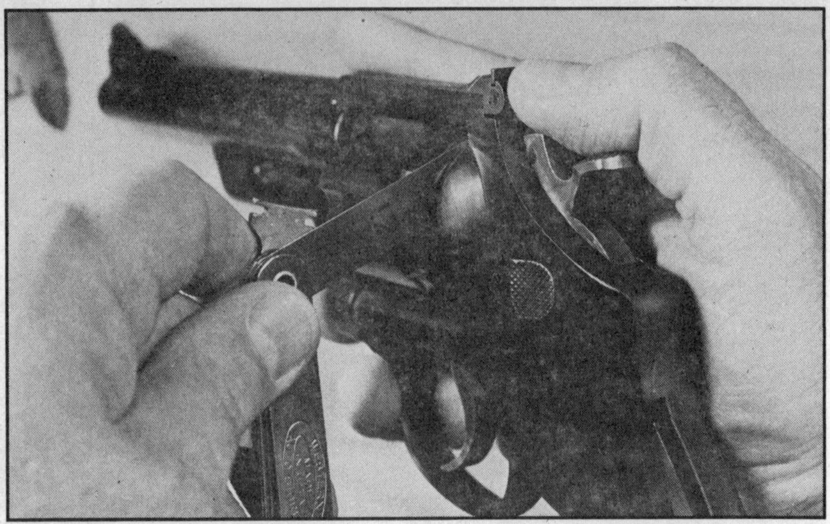

Gauging headspace on the S&W Model 28 before conversion; cylinder/barrel gap was also excessive, causing mediocre accuracy and power.

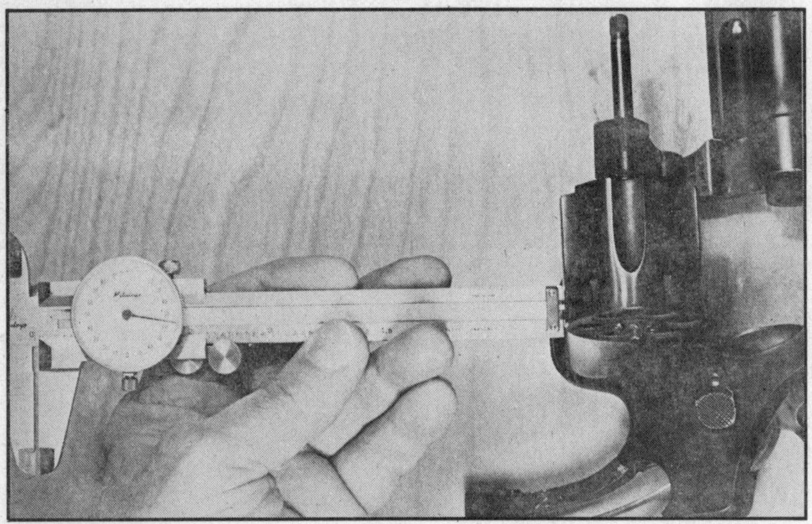

Cylinder notch depth of Model 28 was .055-in., about average and okay for conversion to 41 Magnum, but doubtful for 44 and 45.

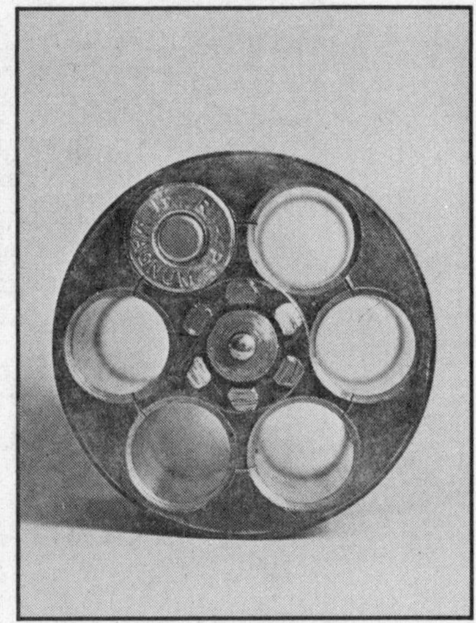

Model 28 cylinder rechambered to 41 Magnum, "in the white." Counterbores were cut shallow to correct headspace.

Measuring a Model 28 for Conversion

When considering any big-bore conversion of a S&W Model 28, the owner should determine the thickness of the cylinder locking notches. These are the thinnest areas and the most likely to bulge or blow out with heavy loads. I have not heard of blown guns, but a number have bulged in 44 and 45 calibers, I have been told.

The problem is that notch depth on individual cylinders varies from about .050-in. to .065-in. This leaves plenty of steel over 357 Magnum chambers, but a large caliber leaves thinner metal, or even none at all. I have heard of 45 Colt conversions with visible brass at the bottom of the notches.

My cylinder has notches .055-in. deep, about average. This was measured with a filler made from a primer cup (anvil removed), thinned with a hand grinder, and fitted to the bottom of the notch. The micrometer caliper gave a total measurement from which the filler diameter was subtracted. The original remaining steel was .063-in. thick at the notch bottoms.

That seems plenty. For comparison, the thickness under my Model 57 notches was .050-in. and my M29 44 Magnum had .043-in. The notches are shallower in these cylinders than in the M28.

To calculate how much metal will be left after conversion, we need the case or chamber diameters. The 357 case mikes .379-in. and a 41 Magnum is .434-in., a difference of 0.55-in. Half of that or .028-in., will be removed from the radius of each chamber, leaving a thickness to be exactly .035-in.

A 45 Colt conversion (diameter, .477-in.) of my gun would leave barely .014-in. at the notch bottoms. Possibly OK for factory ammo, but certainly not for "magnumized" handloads.

These calculations show why some pistolsmiths who used to offer conversion services have either severely restricted their list of acceptable jobs or, in several cases, discontinued conversion entirely.

R.G.

Lee aligning fixture recoils as a heavy load is grouped and chronographed on the Oehler Chronotach.

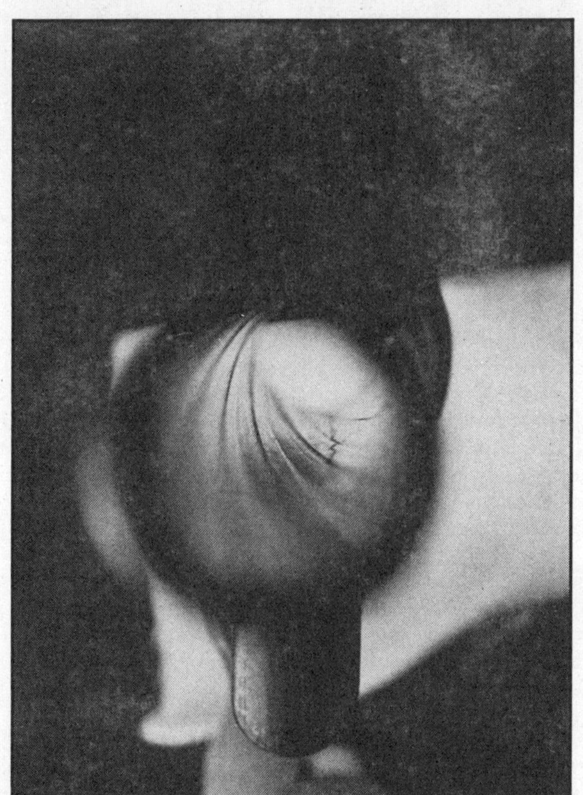

Liner in the author's Model 28 41 Magnum developed a crack after firing heavy loads.

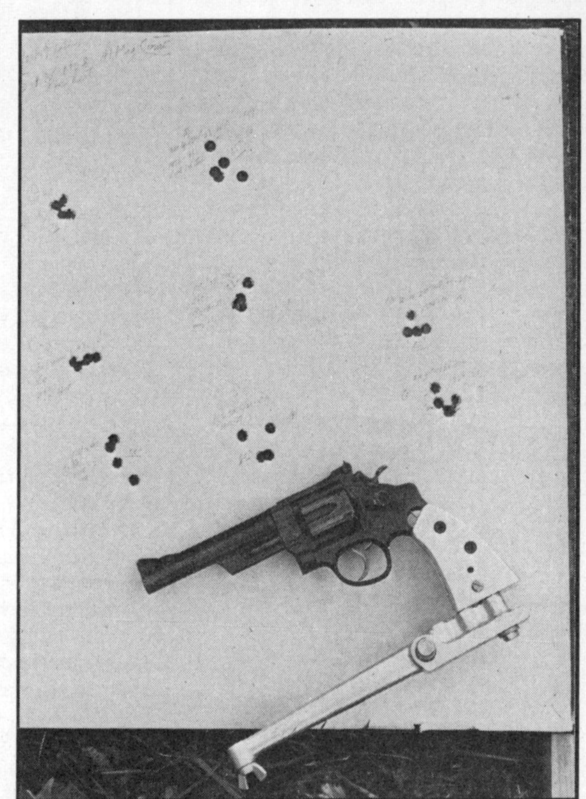

Eight heavy 41 Magnum jacketed loads grouped from Lee rest with converted Model 28. Five of these groups measured exceptionally tight.

thritic could handle the caliber, then any normal adult should be able to learn it.

The idea of a converted 41 Magnum revolver came from the Ruger and the Smith M57. One could not ask for a better single-action than a smoothed-up Blackhawk. For a working, general-purpose field gun, though, I prefer a smooth double-action revolver. That describes the Smith Model 57, a premium, beautifully finished outfit with target features. It also bears a premium price, however, and carrying it in a holster scratches the finish badly. I thought the M57 just too valuable and too pretty to be knocked around. The M57 is also heavy, over 3 pounds loaded, and I hoped to make a 41 at least a half-pound lighter.

Several possibilities occurred to me, but only one make and model was really suitable in strength and size for this conversion—the Smith & Wesson Model 28. The M28 is a big N-frame gun with proper dimensions and steel heat-treated for magnum pressure in 357 Magnum. It scales 44 ounces with 6-inch barrel and the conversion removes an ounce or two of metal. It has good adjustable sights and its somewhat dull black finish and sandblasted frame edges qualify it as tough. The M28 is a working gun.

The 41 Magnum conversion of an M28 was not new, but it is not popular. As far as I can learn, very few had been made and I could not find a description of the converted gun or its performance in print. I had a used M28 on hand, so I looked for someone to do the work.

The mechanics of conversion seem simple, but it's deceptive. The chambers are reamed to the larger caliber and lapped. The rifled bore is drilled and reamed to hold a rifled liner. The liner is sweated into the barrel shell, turned off at the barrel breech, reamed with a tapered forcing cone reamer and crowned at the muzzle.

Good tooling is important. Piloted reamers must be used, for instance. It is not a job for a garage mechanic with a loose drill press.

The author lines up a shot with his new 41 Magnum Model 28.

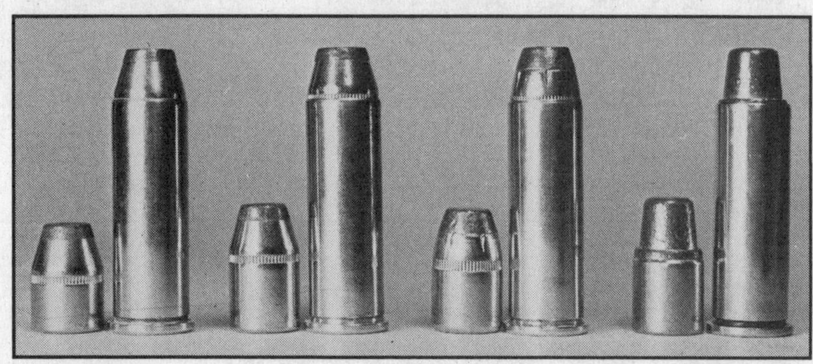

Fine jacketed bullets for heavy 41 Magnum loads in converted Model 28: Sierra 170- and 210-grain JHCs; Winchester-Western 210-grain JHP; Speer 220-grain JSP.

Editor's Note

Russ Gaertner wrote this several years ago, after he had begun to deal with rheumatoid arthritis and to work out ways to keep shooting hard-hitting revolvers. It worked, because at press-time for this issue he was still shooting his big 41s, full-loaded. His life has not been without continuing medical problems, but it has not been without shooting, either.

K.W.

I chose a converter who does no repairs or general pistolsmithing, just conversions at moderate cost. He prefers that the owner or a local gunsmith remove the cylinder with extractor, and the barrel and send them to him. When the machine work has been completed, the owner or his local gunsmith reinstalls and touches up the "white" areas.

I am not going to name the expert who did my conversion. I had worked with him before, but as it turned out, a problem cropped up and it would not be fair to blame him for it.

My Model 28 was a good sound gun. Timing and alignment were correct, and I had smoothed and lightened the action. I also like a smooth trigger face, and I ground off the serrations to give the best double-action feel. It averaged 2.5-3-in. groups with cast bullets and over 2-in. with jacketed slugs from my Lee pistol rest at 25 yards. I hoped to improve the conversion by tightening up both headspace and barrel-cylinder gap during the conversion operations.

After my third session with the converted M28, firing both factory ammo and handloads with excellent accuracy from the Lee rest, I cleaned the gun and checked the bore and got a hell of a shock. A lengthwise crack was clearly visible in the liner, along the lowest groove, extending from about an inch ahead of the barrel breech out to within an inch of the muzzle. I had never heard of this kind of failure before.

None of my loads were heavier than the Remington full-power ammo, and every round was chronographed, so I am not guessing. All of the loads had been developed in my Blackhawk and Smith M57 and seemed to generate very reasonable brass expansion.

Model 28 barrel in homemade wooden vise; liner was finished longer than old breech to correct cylinder/barrel gap.

Model 28 frame being turned up tight on relined barrel: before replacing the barrel pin, the sights must be perfectly aligned.

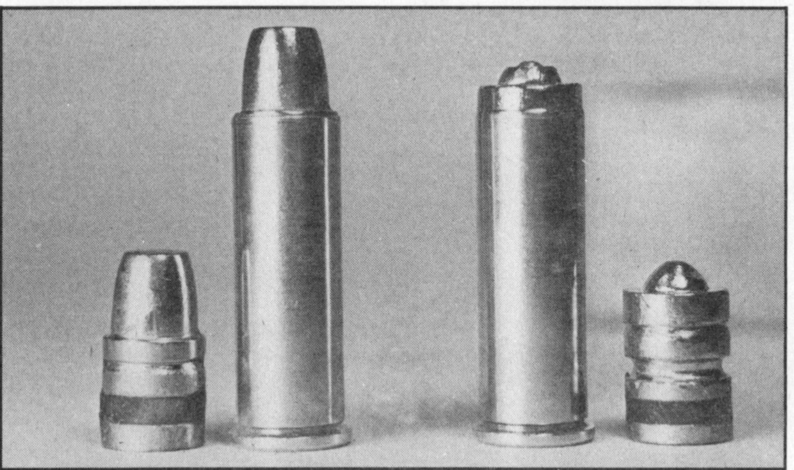

Cast bullets and loads for 41 Magnum: 215-grain SWC, seated deeper than crimping groove to clear short cylinder; 210-grain WC also may need short seating to chamber.

None stuck fired brass in the chambers, of course, and I would swear that the gun was not overpressured.

The converter assured me that this problem was caused by a faulty liner. Another pistolsmith said that the liner had not been soldered full-length, that it was solidly supported only at the ends, and that it was not strong enough to take full magnum pressures without the backing of the barrel shell. This view was reinforced by the fact that the liner had bulged outward along most of the length of the crack. Though small, the bulge was clearly seen by the eye.

This cracked liner could have been dangerous if the original barrel shell had not held the pressures. Other converted guns may have cracked liners which have not been noticed by the owners. *Every relined barrel should be checked periodically, especially before and after full magnum loads are fired.*

My man fully guaranteed his work and he installed another liner at no charge. Apparently a different liner was used and I also insisted on full-length silver-soldering. Having put hundreds of loads through it, from light cast loads to handloads equivalent to full-power factory ammunition, I consider it thoroughly proven.

The converted Model 28 differs from factory 41 Magnums in one key respect. The cylinder is shorter, only 1.62-in. long. This means that long bullets cannot be seated to be crimped into the first, or crimping groove. I seat a long SWC to be crimped just over the full-diameter shoulder. Deeper seating calls for slightly reduced powder charges; do not use standard manuals or maximum charges.

Experts have laid down a gospel to the effect that anyone who can manage a 41 Magnum can also handle a fullhouse 44 Magnum. Thus, they say, the 41 has no useful function. My experience with 41s, including the converted M28, proves that to be pure hogwash!

Most of my 41 load development and shooting was done while recovering from rheumatoid arthritis. After eight years since my original "flare" of RA, I am not as good as I used to be, but I shoot full 41 loads pleasurably. Even the lighter 41 Magnum Model 28 does not bother me in that way.

Recoil energies for magnum calibers, curiously enough, show why this is reasonable. For the full factory loads, these are: 357 Magnum, 6 ft. lbs.; 41 Magnum, 12 ft. lbs.; 44 Magnum, 16-18 ft. lbs. Although 41 recoil is double 357 kick, the 44 adds another third on top of that. It seems to spell the difference between pleasure and pain for me, and maybe there's a dividing line here for many people.

The converted M28 kicks a bit harder than heavier guns with the same loads, but I found some ways to minimize felt recoil with even this handy field gun. The most important for me have been good grips. Several fancy wood grips on the market are excellent, and I have used them on other guns, or I make my own. But for rough field use and carrying in a holster, I chose Pachmayr's rubber stocks. They are not beautiful (dull black) but they will take abuse better than any wood and they fit well in my average hands. They fit in a holster such as the S&W swivel design I use, and they draw easily. They do not slip, even in sweaty hands, and are equally good for one- or two-handed shooting. I have a set on my Ruger Blackhawk 41 also, where they work as well. The design is not bulky but it fits the hand so well that recoil is distributed and absorbed effectively.

I have Mag-na-ports on several 44 Magnums. It is not necessary for me on 41s but it should be worthwhile just for the added control in rapid shooting, whether single- or double-action.

The complete assessment of any gun is a matter of individual preference and opinion, which in turn depend on cost, appearance, utility, and simply how well the shooter handles it. A friend who is a silhouette match winner, hunter, and owner of two much-fired long-barreled Model 29 44 Magnum revolvers watched me put the 41 Magnum conversion through its paces one day. After he had fired it, without a sales talk from me, he said quietly, "I'm going to get one of those." ●

Shotgun Review

by RALPH T. WALKER

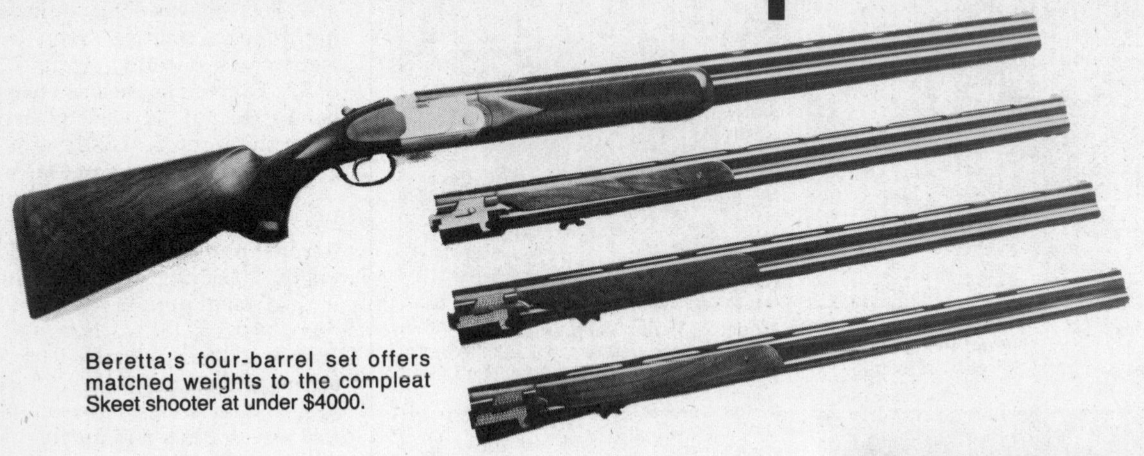

Beretta's four-barrel set offers matched weights to the compleat Skeet shooter at under $4000.

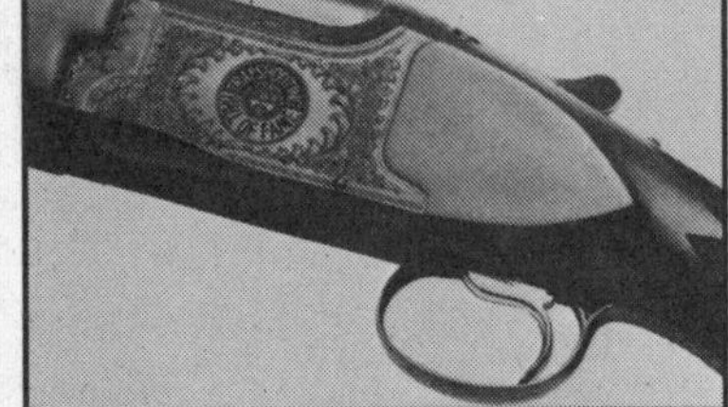

Receiver of Winchester's 101 combination trap set commemorates ATA's Hall of Fame.

Valmet's gun for all trap seasons has choice of barrels, screw-in chokes, and a variable buttstock.

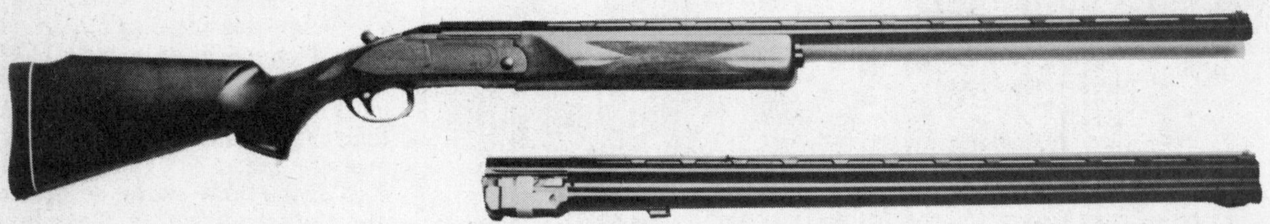

WHAT MOST OF us directly involved in firearms, from those who occasionally visit a gun show or read a gun magazine to the custom gun buyer, fail to realize is we represent only a small fraction of the gun buying public—about 20 percent, in fact. That other 80 percent is the group manufacturers and dealers really go after.

It is not hard to understand, therefore, why most of the shotgun manufacturers have put so much emphasis on the plain-jane versions of their most popular models during these past few years. They are quite simply trying to make their products more affordable to the big market.

It's slow-down time on new models, though there are a certain number of special variations this year. And there is overseas news. Whenever things become tight economically throughout the world, foreign gun makers turn to the market in the United States for more guns are sold here annually than the rest of the world combined. In other words, they want a piece of the biggest pie.

Kassnar in Pennsylvania knows the game. They adopted the well-known name **"Churchill"** for a complete line of shotguns. This ranges from a well-made competition grade over-under down through various equally well-made side-by-sides of European make, to the pumps and semi-autos from the Land of the Rising Sun. Nope, these are not the English Churchill shotguns; they scale price-wise from over a thousand bucks down to a couple of hundred. There are Churchill shotshells nad virtually every accessory that one could desire for shotguns. I was very impressed.

Kendall International of Kentucky imports two excellent Italian shotguns, **di Maroccini Luciano** and **Angelo Zoli**. Both are over-unders in virtually every gauge, barrel length and choke desirable. They offer good quality both mechanically and cosmetically and the prices are extremely attractive. At one time, it was difficult to find European shotgun paraphernalia but no longer, as this and other firms offer just about anything desirable from shell belts to folding-seat shooting sticks. Kendall imports hard to find shotshells and cartridges in addition to odd-ball European rifle barrels.

Valmet last year added to shotgun technology with the best factory method of buttstock adjustment I have seen so far. This year they fulfilled a desire to create a world-class trap gun. It's available as a 32-in. single barrel or a 30-in. over-under. There's a screw-in choke version, too. The stock has a unique release mechanism for stock change to match needs encountered with various trap games and a pre-drilled hole for a re-

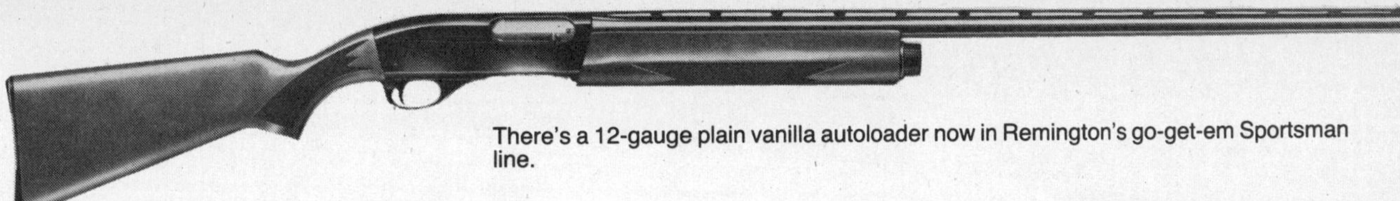

There's a 12-gauge plain vanilla autoloader now in Remington's go-get-em Sportsman line.

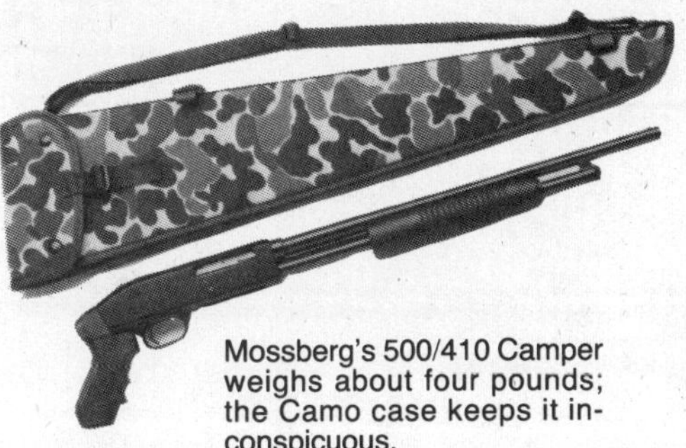

Mossberg's 500/410 Camper weighs about four pounds; the Camo case keeps it inconspicuous.

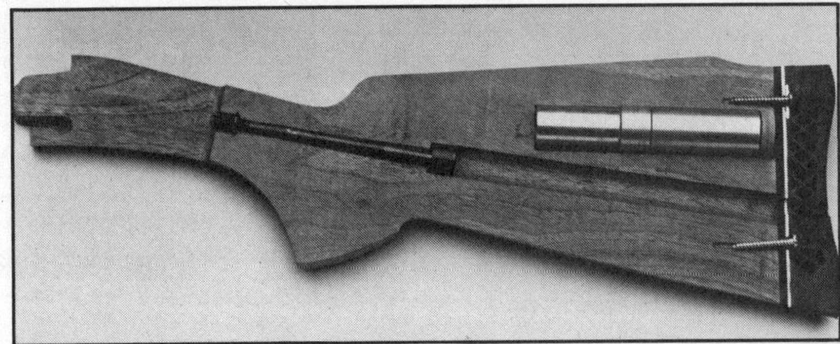

This is the guts of the Valmet variable buttstock system. It's pre-drilled for the recoil reducer.

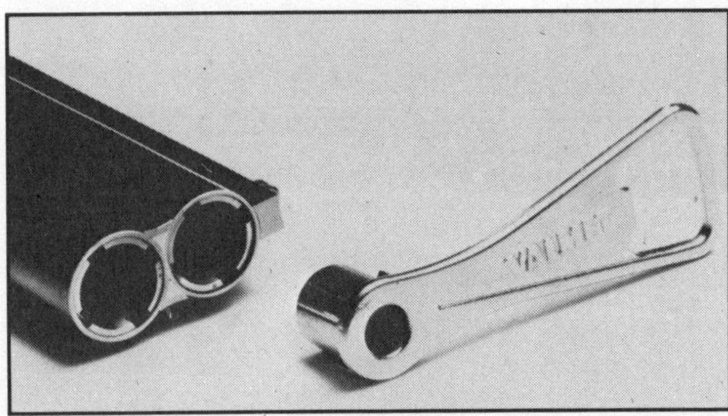

Front end of Valmet's no-nonsense screw-in choke system.

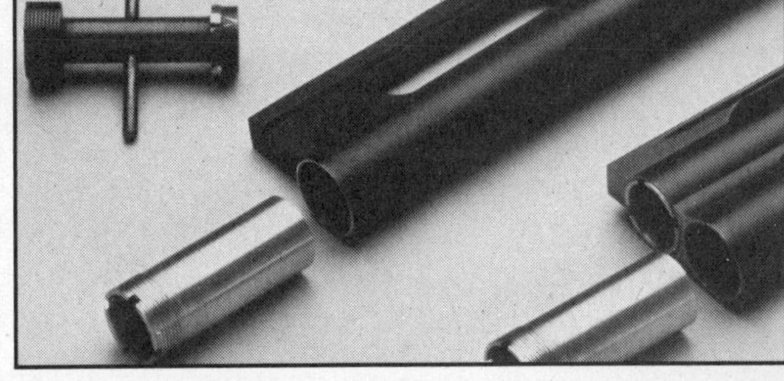

Beretta provides four choke tubes in selected over-under shotguns—no bulge this time.

coil reducer. It all fits onto the time-proven Valmet 412S receiver.

Beretta dropped their choke system that required enlarged barrels and this year came out with a neat completely recessed slim tube arrangement. Beretta dropped their previous club of a side-by-side shotgun and this year offers a beautiful slim receiver and an equally elegant rendition of the entire shotgun.

Navy Arms, best known as one of the early leaders of reproduction black powder arms, is now in the over-under, side-by-side and single barrel shotgun import game. They are a good dollar value with suggested retail below the $500.00 mark. **Sportsman's Emporium** is another recent importer of similar shotguns aimed at the low-end market with a lot of gun per buck spent. Their import is termed **Dan/Arms**. There's a screw-in choke tube version of their over-under.

Exel Arms of America added a jewel this year, a sleek 28-gauge side-by-side that will pluck the heart-strings of any upland game hunter. The 28-gauge shotshell is, in my opinion, about the smallest gauge practical and in the hands of a good shot will push an upland 20-gauge shotgun and this newest addition fills the bill.

Smith & Wesson last year introduced another good firm step in shotgun technology in the form of a semi-auto of gas-operated design that would handle any 12-gauge shotshell made from the light one-ounce to the three-inch shoulder benders interchangeably and without any form of switch. That was a first. Unfortunately, S&W is this year closing out their long gun line. The most persistent rumor, highly placed, states that the Japanese firm that made the gun will enter the market next year under their own name.

Tom Skeus, an avid **Parker** shotgun collector, brought forth a rebirth of this fine old shotgun last year by way of the Winchester Olin-Kodensha plant in Japan and fulfilled a lot of shooters' desire to own a true Parker. The first offering was in the 20 gauge in both 2¾-in. and 3-in. chambers. Latest poop is that we will see the 12-gauge version this year, along with a nut-for-nut and bolt-for-bolt new version of the rare 28-gauge Parker. Incidentally, these parts that make up the new Parker are totally interchangeable with the original and older parts. That's quite an accomplishment.

Remington is unquestionably the pack leader in the U.S. arms manufacturers and this year added a semi-auto gas-operated version to their "budget conscious" economy line. It's a Remington 1100 inside with a hardwood stock walnut-stained outside. The Sportsman 12 is available in 12-gauge only but with a choice of a 30-in. Full or 28-in. Modified barrel with factory rib. Another new pair are the

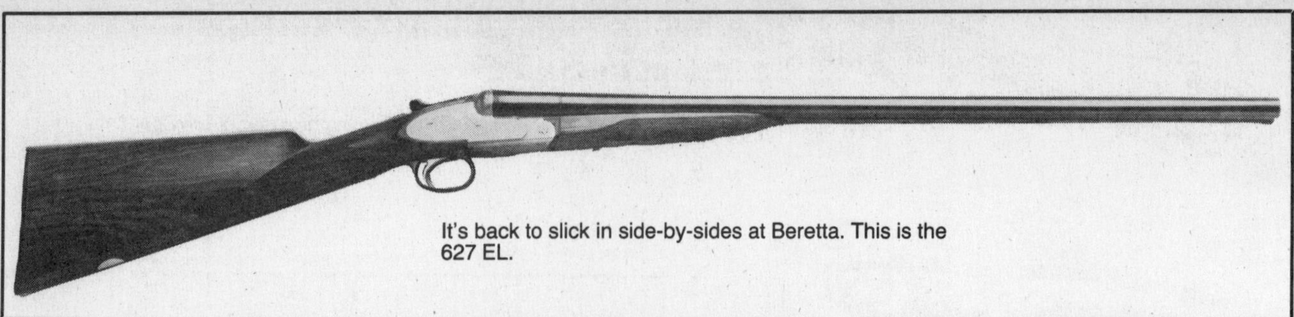

It's back to slick in side-by-sides at Beretta. This is the 627 EL.

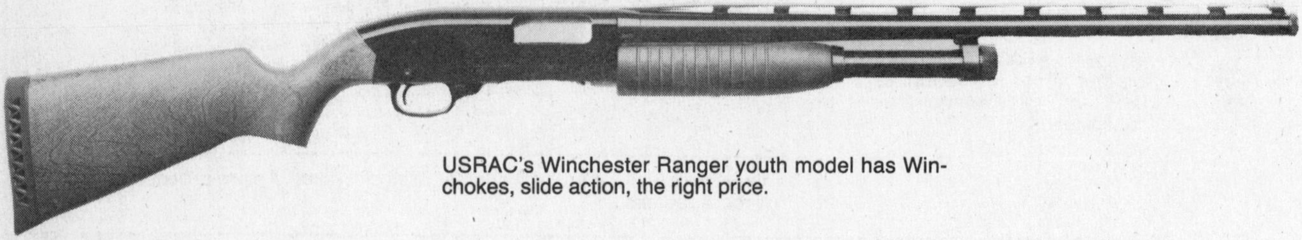

USRAC's Winchester Ranger youth model has Winchokes, slide action, the right price.

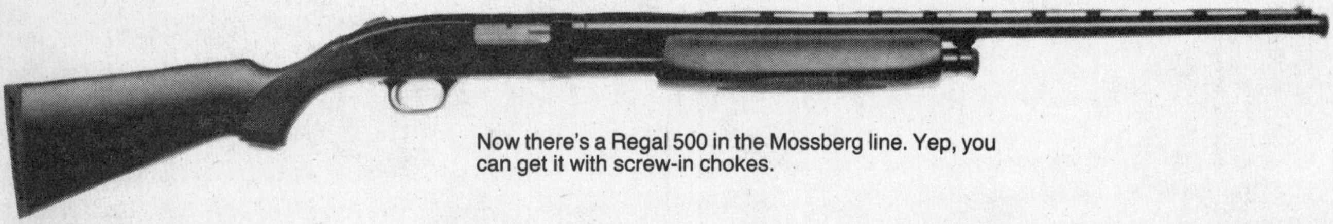

Now there's a Regal 500 in the Mossberg line. Yep, you can get it with screw-in chokes.

Not for turkey hunters, but on behalf of turkeys, Winchester produced 300 special 101s to help the National Wild Turkey Federation raise money.

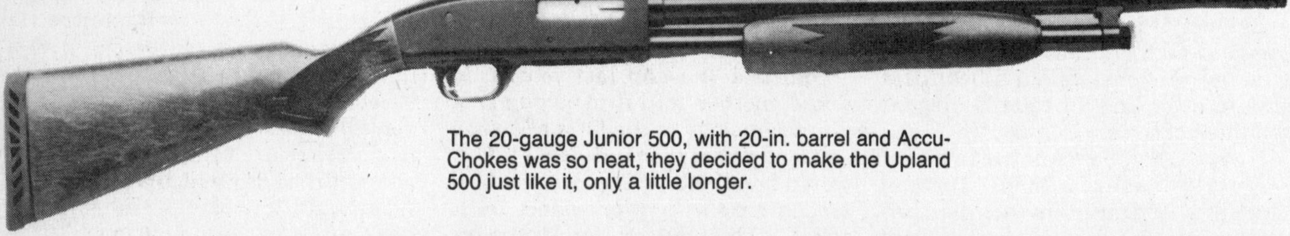

The 20-gauge Junior 500, with 20-in. barrel and Accu-Chokes was so neat, they decided to make the Upland 500 just like it, only a little longer.

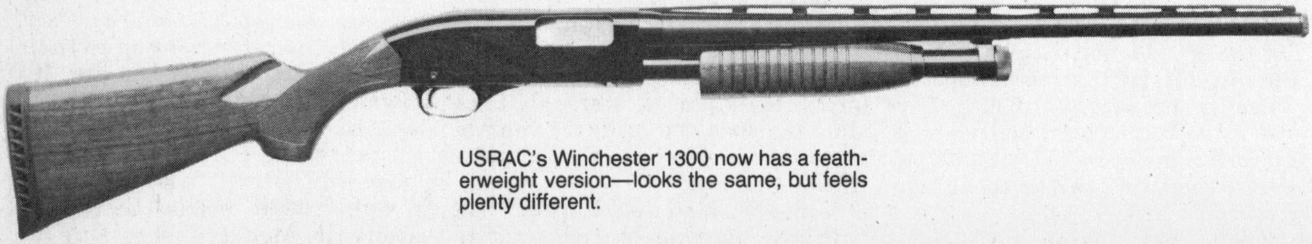

USRAC's Winchester 1300 now has a featherweight version—looks the same, but feels plenty different.

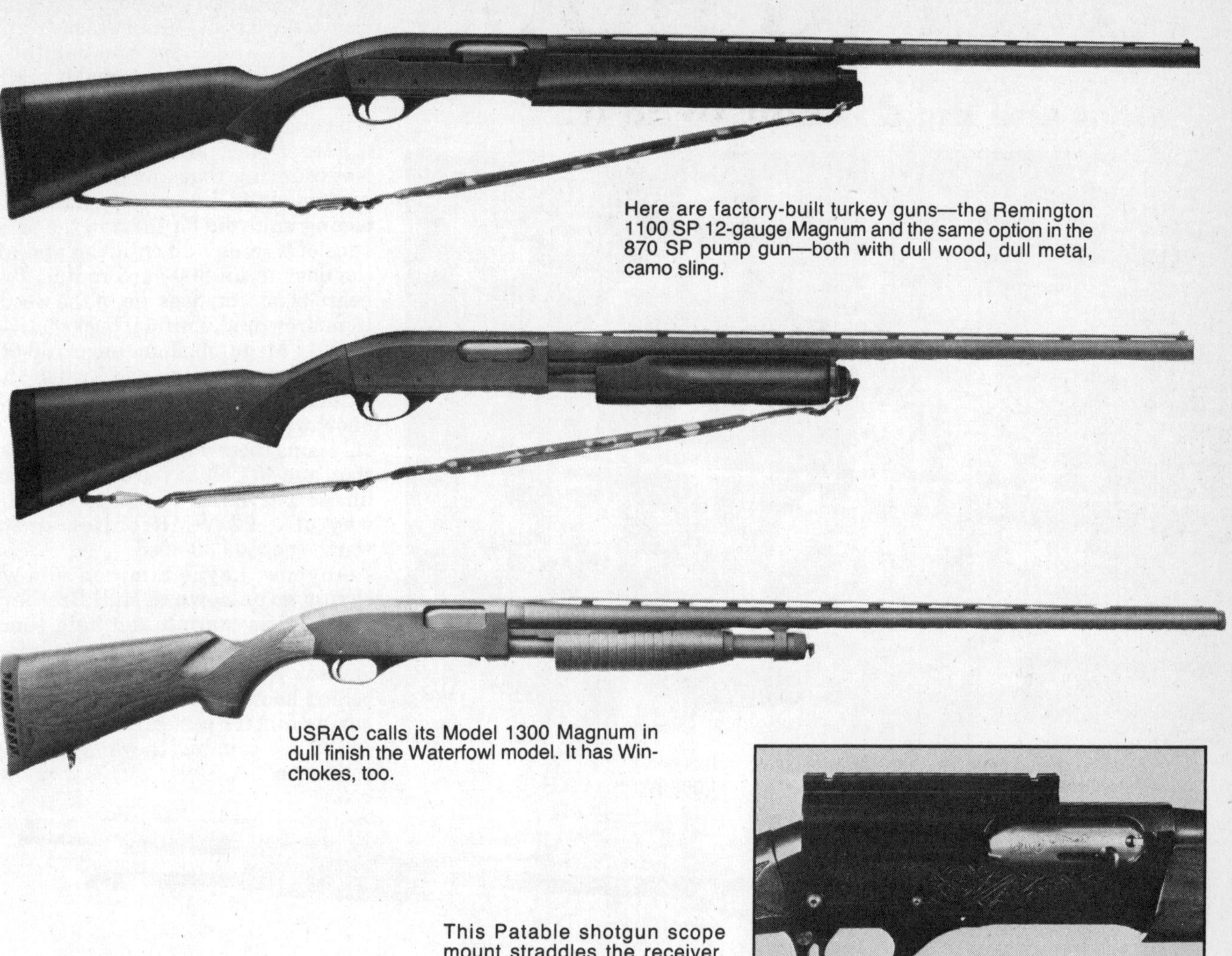

Here are factory-built turkey guns—the Remington 1100 SP 12-gauge Magnum and the same option in the 870 SP pump gun—both with dull wood, dull metal, camo sling.

USRAC calls its Model 1300 Magnum in dull finish the Waterfowl model. It has Winchokes, too.

This Patable shotgun scope mount straddles the receiver, accepts Weaver rings.

1100 Magnum and the 870 Magnum pump in camouflage right out of the factory box. Such treatment has long been practiced by turkey shooters. Remington's new Special Purpose versions make sense with dull Parkerized metal and a padded sling with quick-detachable mounts.

Ithaca has true camouflage-type finish from muzzle to rear of the receiver available on just about every model from the Mag-10 down to the light version of the reliable M37 pump termed the English Lightweight. This latter model, incidentally, will be available with screw-in choke tubes this year in both 12 and 20 gauge.

Both **Winchester** and **U.S. Repeating Arms** are in essence expanding their current lines to fill every available market. **Winchester (Olin)** has made quite a few special edition shotguns for special groups, somewhat like they did in the old days with the commemoratives. **USRAC** this year also added a special turkey/waterfowler to their 1300 pump series. This includes Winchoke, plus a nonglare metal and wood finish.

At the SHOT show, I learned something new. There is another Beretta, Dr. **Franco Beretta**, whose products do pride to the other Beretta. He offers an over-under plus a side-by-side and a single barrel through **Double M Shooting Sports**. My Italian is just past ordering a cup of coffee and I never did find out if the two Berettas were now linked in any way. Anyway, the guns spoke for themselves and at good prices in the $650-$400 bracket.

Mossberg has gone a long way to what is obviously their goal: having the bulk of the inexpensive pump shotgun business. I thought they had brought out every possible version of their Model 500 pump, but this was premature. They have added a 410 in both a regular version and a pistol-grip camper model. Next, there's a Junior line which provides a shorter stock and such for the young hunter. The top of the line is their Regal rendition of the familiar Model 500 with a walnut stock and top-grade bluing of the metal parts terminating in a gold implant of the familiar Mossberg crown on the receiver's right side. Mossberg, incidentally, has been mentioned in the rumor factory as a possible home for the Smith & Wesson pump and shotguns. Recent press releases state that Mossberg will assume responsibility for the sale of these shotguns for Smith & Wesson.

Now enters **Ken Patable Enterprises** with a detachable shotgun scope mount. It is made from extruded aluminum and fits onto both sides of the receiver, instead of one side a la Weaver, and accepts standard Weaver type scope rings. It mounts in the standard cross-pin holes with Allen-head bolts provided; it's solid. ●

KILLING HOGS

Down and dead is how to do it.

Ugly (the dog) suffered from heartworm, but no lack of heart. The fat fellow got there for the fun part with the right gun.

EVERYBODY tries it, sooner or later. I have listened to hog-killings in skyscraper offices and saloons and airplanes and Jeeps and banquets and suburban family rooms. It really catches hold of folks, too—some take it on about full-time.

Part of the charm is the weaponry. Not counting that number I've been around when a 22 Short and an old boning knife did for them in the presence of women and children and all the dogs in an 800-yard radius, I've heard of or seen hogs die in the woods from drowning, knifing, buckshot, 45 Colt, 44 Magnum, 9mm Luger, 30-06, 30-30, strange metric and British and wildcat calibers, arrows and I don't know what all. Up 'til here lately, I'd only done them with a 280 rifle, buckshot, and 45 Colt, if you don't count an innocent javelina who stepped in the way of a 22 WMR bullet and a warthog or so I 30-30ed.

Anyhow, Layne Simpson said we should go on down to Hall Brothers south of Savannah and help some dogs kill some hogs. That, you know, is what you're doing when you hunt behind hounds. The dogs are the ones having fun; it's perfectly obvious they don't need you, but they're generally polite about it.

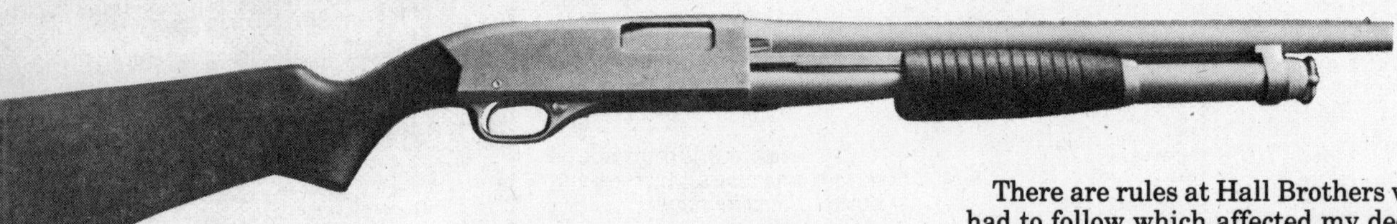

The right gun this time was a Winchester 1300 Police from USRAC. It was fired a successful once.

Everybody traveled in the boats—hunters, dead hogs, live dogs all a-tangle.

The saw grass (or whatever) wasn't much fun dry at low tide; waist high at high tide was ridiculous.

There are rules at Hall Brothers we had to follow which affected my decisions—no scopes and no buckshot allowed being primary. Layne told me he had to shoot a string gun this time and we were joining a dedicated handgunner, name of Gene Tynes.

The last hog I fooled around with with a handgun did a 200-yard run-and-fight number between the first hit and the second. So I skipped much handgun consideration—took one along, of course—and decided to take a Winchester 1300 Police 12-gauge shotgun. My choice of ammo finally settled on BRI sabot slugs. I regretted neither choice.

Highlights of the trip included my first step after the dogs took off. It was just the turn of high tide at dawn and I went to somewhat above my navel in salt water and saw grass. Several thousand such steps later I got out of there. Layne used up the entire contents of a bow quiver; Gene, he told me, did not quite empty the cylinder of his Model 29; and I fired one shot.

The dogs put on a great show. They were 30-to-50-pound dogs, mixed

Bossman Jack Douglas is a dog man clean through; his dogs are hog dogs sure enough.

(Left) Two days of salty mud came off the 1300 easily—I just hosed it down and set it in the sun.

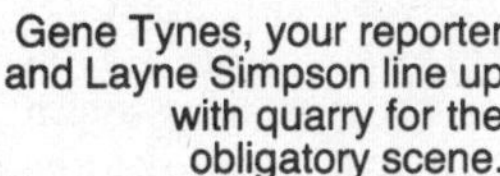

Gene Tynes, your reporter and Layne Simpson line up with quarry for the obligatory scene.

Sort of historic, this hunt: It was the last from this old headquarters, but not the last by Hall Bros.

hounds, and really fierce about hogs. When they bayed the hog I was to shoot they did it amongst a whole lot of thorns. We all have our views of sport, but mine do not include wading about waist-high in serious flagellation, so I really wanted this shot to work.

In preparation I had practiced, of course. No standard 8½×11 manila envelope was safe from my BRI slugs as far out as 35 yards. That turned out to be somewhere between four and six times as far as the actual hog shot, which was most satisfactory. Mindful of those thorns, I put the slug right through his shoulders and he went right down on his nose and that was that. There was, happily, no reason to chase him. Right through the shoulders, incidentally, means just that—all the way through.

So I learned once again the old lesson: When ranges are short, reach for a shotgun. Works fine.

Ken Warner

Reach Jack Douglas about hog hunts at: 912-925-4459

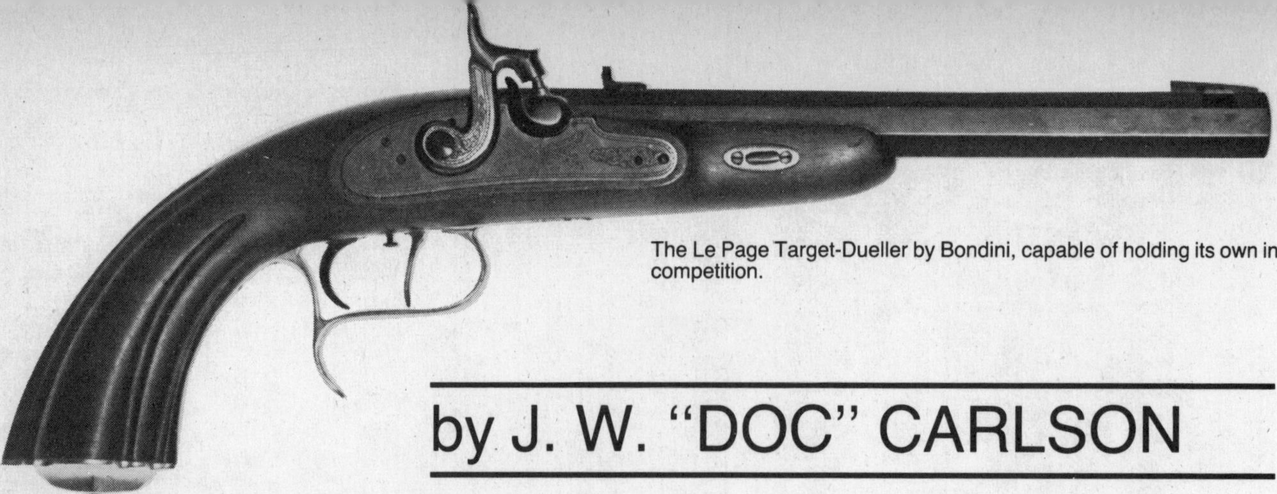

The Le Page Target-Dueller by Bondini, capable of holding its own in competition.

by J. W. "DOC" CARLSON

Modern muzzle-loading has taken another step, this one to . . .

EXTRA-QUALITY GUNS

HISTORY repeats itself, and never more plainly than in the rebirth or rediscovery of muzzle-loading shooting. Firearms began as rather crude, poorly made muzzleloaders and progressed to better and better quality and design. The final products, just before they were rendered obsolete by the breechloader, were efficient firearms and some were works of art. The knowhow and skill carried over, and gave breechloaders a flying start.

We have lately seen a similar sequence of events. Originals in varying stages of repair and completeness were our first latter-day shooters. As

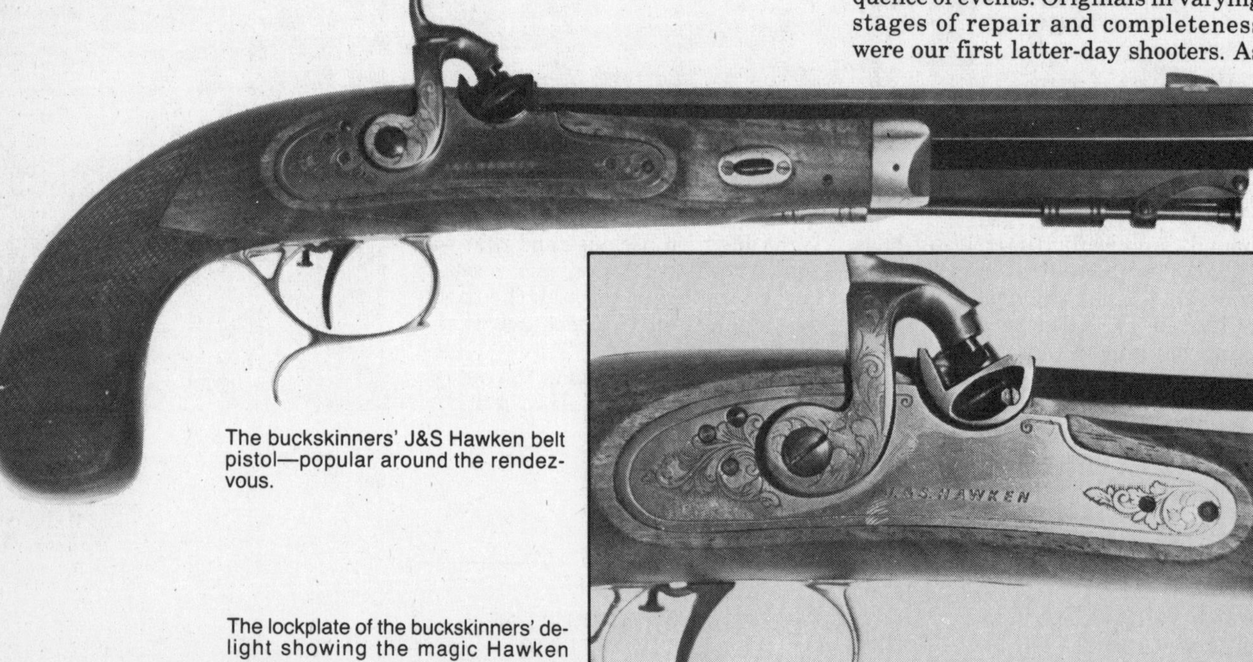

The buckskinners' J&S Hawken belt pistol—popular around the rendezvous.

The lockplate of the buckskinners' delight showing the magic Hawken name.

more folks got into the game and prices rose for original guns, there was a demand for reproductions that could be shot. These very early reproductions tended to be exact copies of original guns, or very close. They were, for the most part, well-made and designed. As the fledgling market expanded, the flow of guns from overseas grew and more and more manufacturers and importers got into the act. Many of these manufacturers and importers knew a great deal more about marketing than they did about muzzle-loading firearms. Many of that new crop of reproductions were very poor copies of original guns. There were design weaknesses that made many of these guns esthetically less than pleasing and some of the faults were downright dangerous. We went—quite quickly—through the "Dark Ages" of modern muzzleloading.

Eventually the makers of poor quality guns went the way of most of their kind in a free enterprise society. Customers became more sophisticated in their buying habits and wanted better quality for their hard earned bucks. The "Enlightened Age" was born.

Now, most all of the guns on the market are good. There are, of course, guns one man doesn't want while another might think them just right. Even the lower end of the market is made up of good, solid, well-designed guns. Beginners can start out with a very adequate gun that looks good and shoots well for about the same money that he can get started shooting breechloaders.

Once started, the neophyte begins to look for guns with better line and nicer finish. If he is of a historical bent, and many of us in the muzzleloading game are, he is always looking for guns that are just a bit more historically correct. The top of this marketing heap is the custom-built gun—the rifle, pistol or shotgun that is hand crafted on a one-at-a-time basis by individual artisans. If built to exacting standards and lovingly hand finished, many of these easily qualify as works of art, to be admired alongside fine paintings and sculpture. The fly in the ointment is the price. The time it takes to make one of these hand-built arms dictates that the price gets up maybe into a range that might buy a pretty good car.

So, on one hand we have the reasonably-priced utility gun and on the other we have the ultra-nice custom. Luckily, for most of us, there is a middle ground. There is a growing class of better quality production guns. These arms, though usually more expensive than the utility grade, are priced within reach of most anyone who is serious about the muzzle-loading hobby. They are priced in the ball-park with modern guns of similar quality and accuracy. Most of these have come along in the last five to ten years.

So, let's take a look at some of the latest to appear:

Not only in America has the muzzle-loading rebirth taken hold, Europeans have been shooting muzzleloading matches for 50 years or more, with time out for wars. Over there, originals or exact replicas of original firearms are generally required for match shooting. One source for these has been Paolo Bondini of Italy. He has built extremely nice quality pistols for some years and has just recently entered the U.S. market. These guns shoot well and are made with an eye to fit and finish that makes them a good buy.

The most common Bondini pistol is the Le Page Dueller. This target-duelling gun is made on the typical French style with a fluted grip. The lockplate shows light, tasteful engraving and the name "LePage." "Le Page a Paris" is also engraved on the barrel flat. The 10-inch, 45-caliber barrel is rifled with 12 lands and grooves as are all Bondini guns I have examined. The twist is one turn in 18 inches which, when combined with a tight patch/ball combination and light charges, gives extremely good accuracy. The ⅞-in. barrel and lockplate are finished bright with no browning or bluing and the barrel key escutcheons, trigger guard, and butt cap are silver-plated. Triggers are conventional adjustable double set—double action, that is, the front trigger can be used to fire the lock either set or unset, although the unset pull is heavy. Sights are either Patridge type—a square notch rear with a squared off blade front—or on some guns a brass blade front sight. Wood to metal fit and finish is good throughout. The lock and triggers are smooth and lock time is reasonably fast, allowing good accuracy.

Two-inch groups at 25 yards and under four inches at 50 yards are not hard to achieve with this little pistol using a 440 round ball combined with a .015-in. Ox Yoke Wonder patch and 20 and 30 grains FFFg respectively. The extra 10 grains lets the gun shoot to the same sight picture at 50 yards with no hold-over, a definite advantage in match shooting. The sights are adjustable for windage by tapping them to one side or the other, but not for elevation. This pistol is priced in the $175 range—a good value for the money. Navy Arms and Dixie Gun Works both import this gun. Navy Arms also has a higher finished version that sells for $275.

Another pistol in the Bondini line, this one popular with buckskinners, is a Hawken percussion pistol. This one has the same rifling as the Le Page, but the barrel is $^{15}/_{16}$-in. across the flats. It's shorter than the Le Page barrel by a full inch, but provides a heavy feel. I'm sure this is the feel the manufacturer was trying to capture—it's a short, heavy buffalo pistol. There is an English-type bag grip, nicely checkered. The European walnut wood stock fits the metal well and is set off by the polished lockplate and silver-plated nose cap, escutcheons, ramrod entry pipe and trigger guard. The blued barrel has a hook breech and just one barrel key; there's an underrib and a swivel ramrod. The trigger is single-set and the lockplate has light engraving on both ends, an engraved border and the name "J & S Hawken." The hammer also has some light engraving.

The single-set trigger will work set or unset. I personally preferred the unset pull of a tad over four pounds to the lighter, crisper set pull. I don't care for a single-set trigger that jumps away from the finger as the gun fires. It's just a quirk of mine and I know many good shooters that get along fine with a single set. The internal parts of the lock show the same polish and hardening that the Le Page does and, if anything, I think the lock on this gun is a bit faster than the Frenchman, though I don't shoot this pistol quite as well as the longer-barreled Le Page. Partly this can be traced to the sights which are a barleycorn front and a V rear—not the clearest sighting set up for eyes over 40. The price on this one is $200; Navy Arms has it in 50 and 54 calibers.

The last of the Bondini pistols—certainly not least—is the William Parker flintlock dueller. This is an extremely graceful, well-balanced pistol. Of 45 caliber with the 12 land and groove rifling, the ⅞-in. barrel is bit over 11 inches, browned, with dovetailed sights—a V-notch rear and a squared front. The trigger is double-set, double acting and can be set very light. The trigger guard and escutcheons are plated silver. The stock is walnut of English style with a flared butt, nicely checkered grip and a schnabel tip. The gun has an extremely nice line to it and points very naturally.

A very graceful addition to the target shooter's battery—the Bondini William Parker dueller.

The lock is nicely finished, well hardened and polished inside, with a roller-style frizzen spring. The geometry and design of the lock is good with the hammer ending its travel with the point of the flint pointing directly at the bottom center of the pan. This throws sparks directly into the pan for fast, reliable ignition. The lock is surefire and reasonably fast. I had no trouble keeping shots in the black using the same loadings that proved successful in the Le Page. Those triggers are adjustable for both let-off and over-travel of the rear trigger. This allows for the rear trigger to be adjusted so that it stays clear of the sear when unset, a safety feature.

Fit and finish are very good and the gun holds and shoots very well. Ignition is quick and accuracy is on a par with the other two guns. Lines of the stock are especially crisp and clean. The lockplate is nicely engraved, as is the hammer. The word "London" appears on the lockplate and "W. Parker" is applied to the top flat of the barrel in semi-script. This gun is imported by Dixie Gun Works and sells for $265. Navy Arms imports the same gun in a percussion version at $250.

Stepping up to the best available of the semi-custom pistols, Beeman Precision Arms, Inc. is bringing in a pistol that is intended for World Class competition. Again, we go back to the match rules followed in Europe. All guns used in competition must either be originals or a reproduction of an existing original gun. The recent relaxing of rules for international competition to allow reproduction guns, as long as they follow the European rule for authenticity, has also opened up a market for this type of gun that was not there before. At any rate, this Beeman import may well be the first of a new wave of ultra-fine guns, both pistols and rifles.

The story of this quality pistol goes back a way. In 1981, the authentic reproduction class was added to the international championship matches. Due to this development, the West German gunmaking firm of Hege began researching available original target grade pistols, looking for one that would be of the quality and accuracy required for today's competitions. Many collections in museums and private hands were scanned. Finally a pistol made by Jean Siber was found that answered all the criteria.

Jean Frederick Siber was a well-known gunmaker of Lausanne, Switzerland, and made fine target guns in the mid-1800s. He was from a Swiss watchmaking family and brought precision to his gunmaking. He was also well known as an engraver. Many of the well-known match

The Hege-Siber target pistol intended for international competition is shown here with some of the available accessories.

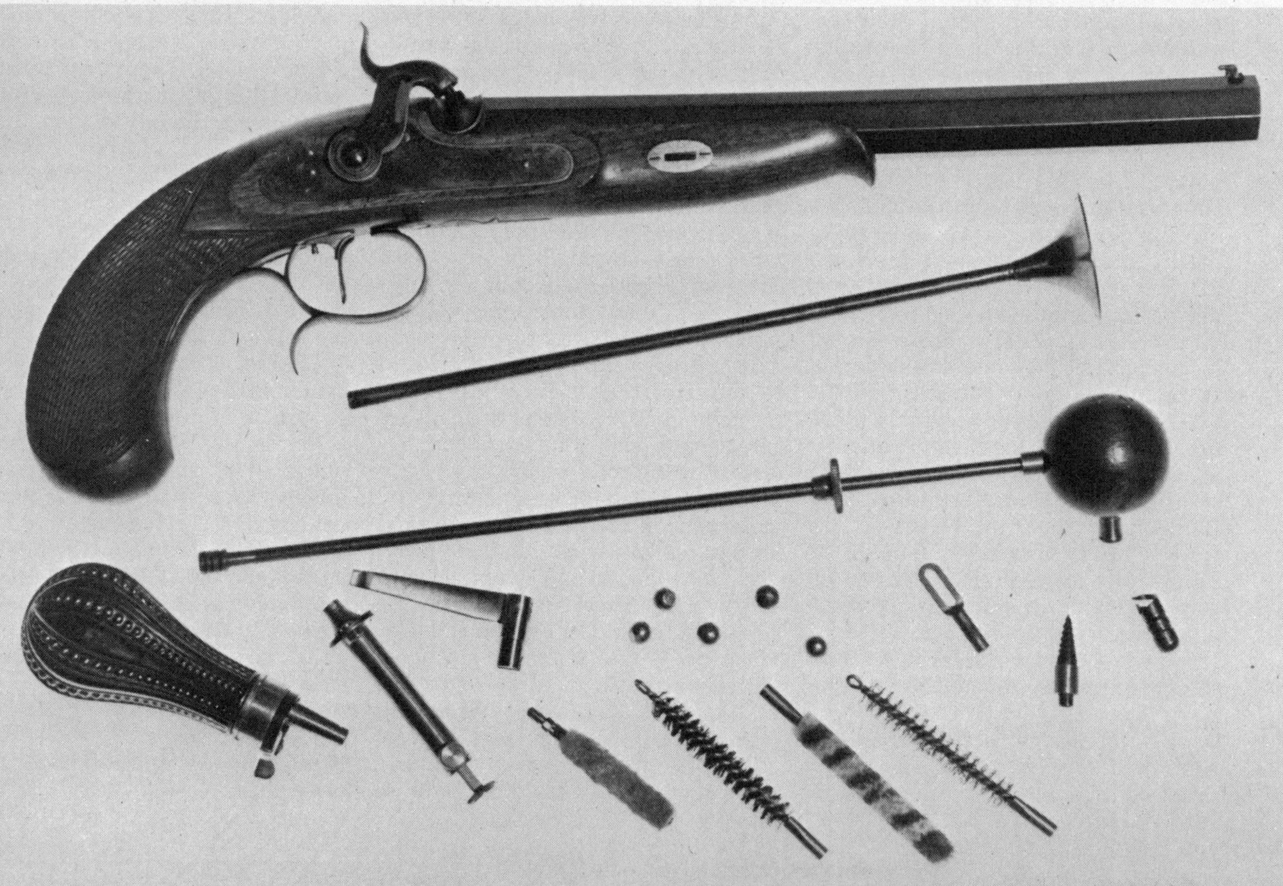

marksmen of the time came, eventually, to his shop door. The pistol found by Hege-Jagd-u. Sporthandels of Überlingen/Bodensee, West Germany, shows some English influence in the stock style.

The reproduction is an exact copy. It is 33-caliber with a right-hand rifling twist of 1 turn in approximately 13 inches. The grooves are .012-in. deep with lands wider at the bottom than at the top for a trapezoidal shape. Coupled with the elimination of sharp corners from the grooves and land tops, this makes fouling build-up very negligible and cleaning easy. The small caliber nearly eliminates recoil, an important consideration in a target gun. The barrel is 10 inches long, and is .850-in. across the flats. The top flat is engraved "Siber*A-*Lausanne" and the barrel is finished in a very attractive brown. It has that purplish-brown color that is so appealing to the eye and very hard to achieve.

The breech plug and tang are finished with color case-hardening, as is the lockplate and hammer. All screw heads are heat blued. The tang holds the rear sight which is adjustable for elevation by means of a screw located behind the sight. The rear sight has a U-notch which matches the gold-colored bead of the front sight. Some might prefer the Patridge type sights, but I found that the bead and U worked well for me.

The browned trigger guard has a finger rest and a tang along the inside curve of the butt. The trigger is a single set—that is, it can be used unset or it can be pushed ahead until the trip sear engages, an event easily noticed by the click of engagement. The trigger will then trip under a very light pressure, firing the gun. The trigger on the test gun tripped the lock at a bit over four pounds unset and right at 4 ounces in the set mode. All trigger parts are highly polished and hardened as are the internal lock parts.

The hammer fall is about .860-in., very short by current standards. The lock time has been measured at 5 milliseconds, figured from the time the hammer starts to move until the bullet exits the barrel, they tell me. Part of this speed of ignition can be traced to the design of the breech. The breech plug has a cylindrical powder chamber .216-in. in diameter designed to hold eight grains of FFFg powder. This charge will fill the chamber with just enough overflow to allow the patch/ball combination to compress the charge slightly. Compression is very uniform due to the design of the chamber. The flash channel enters the chamber in the middle, igniting the powder charge at its center and, according to Jean Siber 100 years ago, gives more uniform ignition and velocities. It does seem to work—my velocities, measured over an Oehler 33 chronograph, varied very little and averaged 879 fps. Groups fired using the 323 soft lead ball cast by the Lee mould supplied with the gun, and patched with a .015-in. Ox Yoke Wonder patch, ran under an inch at 25 yards fired from a rest. Recovered patches showed good obturation and no cutting or burning.

The fit and finish of the gun are extraordinary. The wood to metal fit looks as if the wood grew around the parts. All metal is well finished and polished; there is no "slop" or play in any of the metal to metal fits. The lock and triggers show hand-fitting and polishing, contributing to the secret of fast lock time. The butt of the European walnut stock is checkered with an original and rather coarse pattern that gives a good grip. The checkering has a border around it and the only flaw I could find in the pistol is some runover of the checkering lines into the border. The trigger plate, trigger guard and lockplate show very nice, tasteful engraving and the hammer is of the classic dolphin design.

You can get this Siber gun in two grades—the standard grade, as described, priced at $735, or a hand-engraved version with 24-carat gold inlays around the barrel muzzle and breech, and profuse engraving on all metal parts that closely matches the original gun, which is called the French version and is priced at $1,120. The French version is also available cased in pairs with all accessories, listing at $2,260. I suspect that very few of the French style guns will be shot—most of them will go into collections as prized possessions. They are that good.

The plain or shooting version of the gun comes in an English-style case of composition material with good latches. It won't stand the abuse that a wooden case will, but it is a nice touch, well-made. It makes a good display or carrying case for the pistol, much nicer than if the gun was supplied in a standard cardboard carton. With care, the case or box will last a long time. An accessory set consisting of measure, powder flask, ramrod, loading tube with long drop tube, worm, cleaning swabs and jag is supplied at an extra cost of $149.50.

Because of the small charge and the powder chamber breech plug, the long tubed funnel that is supplied as part of the accessory package should always be used. Just a very few grains of powder lost clinging to the barrel walls or soaked with lube or otherwise changed, will vary the load to a significant amount and this will definitely show up on the target. The powder funnel with drop tube was a very common accessory for target pistols and rifles of days gone by. They put the charge right in the chamber area with no contamination to insure more uniformity.

Custom-quality rifles showed up rather quickly after the rebirth of interest in muzzleloader shooting. In reality, the production of hand-made, one-at-a-time, custom Pennsylvania-Kentuckies and such had never died out. The activity died down during the late 1800s and early 1900s but the building and shooting of these guns never really stopped. Many of the finer rifles on the market today can trace their beginnings back to this craft continuation that never died out entirely.

One company with roots back to the original gunsmiths of old is Hatfield Rifle Works. Ted Hatfield had a great-grandfather who made muzzle-loading rifles in Missouri, not far from the present home of Hatfield Rifle Works in St. Joseph, Missouri. Ted can also trace some of his ancestors back to the Hatfields of the McCoy-Hatfield feud. He is firmly rooted in the firearms industry.

The Hatfield people are building a nicely finished light Pennsylvania-Kentucky style rifle in 32, 36, 45 or 50 caliber. The gun is a full-stock rifle, stocked in select American maple with brass trigger guard and buttplate. The style is typical of the graceful, full-stocked squirrel rifles that were common to the 1760 to 1840 period—a time often called the "Golden Age of the Kentucky Rifle." That was when this uniquely American firearm and art form reached its artistic zenith. The Hatfield rifle has the gracefully drooping buttstock typical of many guns of this era.

Hatfields are made on machinery for most of the initial work, but a great deal of the finishing is done by hand. The barrel is 39½-in. long, octagon $^{13}/_{16}$-in. across the flats, rifled with 8 lands and grooves .012-in. deep. The twist is 1 turn in 40-in. for the 32 and 36 calibers; 1 in 50-in. for 45 caliber; and 1 in 60-in. for 50 caliber. The 50-caliber rifle has a ⅞-in. barrel, measured across the flats.

The weights run from 8 pounds for the 32s down to 7¼ pounds in the 50-caliber, and the balance is nice. They

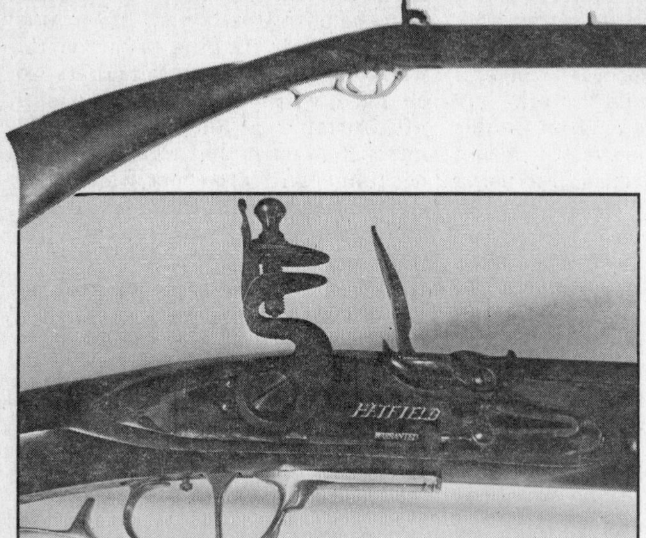

The very gracefully designed Hatfield full-stock Kentucky squirrel rifle.

The Hatfield lock is well fitted and sure fire.

A Hatfield lock with gold inlay and engraving from their Custom Shop.

Example of the delicate carving available on the custom versions of the Hatfield rifles.

"hang" very well and hold solid even without the muzzle heaviness that is common to lesser guns of this style. The lock is a typical Ketland style from 1780. It is narrow and slim to suit the slim lines of the rifle finished with traditional color case-hardening. Inside it's polished and hardened and there is, of course, a fly in the tumbler. The rifle is available in either flint or percussion ignition; both lock types are fast and sure in action. The flintlock has good geometry for spark placement right in the pan.

The Hatfield rifles are supplied with a full buckhorn rear sight and a silver blade front. Both can be drifted in their dovetails. The front sight, as it should be, is too tall, so it may be filed down to zero at whatever range the new owner picks, after he gets his best load.

The triggers are adjustable double-set and double acting. The pull is too heavy unset; set, it is clean and breaks like a piece of glass, like it is supposed to.

The Hatfield I own is a 36-caliber flintlock. I have used it through a couple of squirrel seasons and have really given it a good workout. The accuracy is good. With a 350 Hornady round ball, .015-in. Ox Yoke Wonder patching and 30 grains FFFg Gerhart-Owens powder, I'm getting squirrel head-size groups at 25 yards. It rarely misses in the hunting field, if I do my part. Velocities run around 1600 fps with the 30-grain loading; if I go up to 40 grains, the velocity only raises around 100 fps and accuracy seems to fall off just a bit.

The price on the basic rifle, what the Hatfield folks call their Grade 2 rifle, generally with figured wood with good curl, is $395. A few come out with pretty plain wood. They're exactly the same rifle as the Grade 2 but are just not as fancy, wood-wise. These are called Grade 1 and are sold for $295. Out of every batch of wood there are a very few stocks that class as exceptional. These will run few in number, and are sold as Grade 3 and retail for $550 or so, depending upon the figure of the wood.

The latest wrinkle is carving and engraving on the standard rifle, all done in the Hatfield custom shop. It works like this—the customer writes Hatfield and expresses an interest in a custom-type gun; the custom shop sends a blueprint for a fee of $25 which is deducted from the cost of the rifle, when ordered. The customer then sketches in the type of engraving and/or carving he would like. The blueprint returns to Hatfield, and they draw an original using the customer's ideas and adding what is required to make the designs artistically balanced; then the customer gets another shot at it and returns the print. This process goes on until the

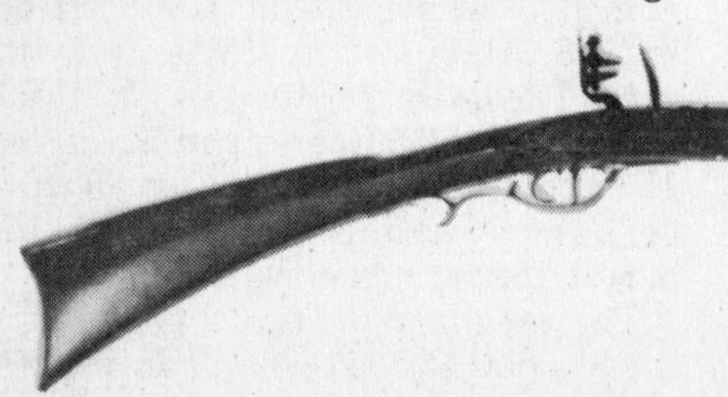

The half-stock Kentucky rifle from Pecos Valley Arms.

customer is satisfied. The gun is then built according to the blueprint. Cost for this type of gun will *start* at around $1,000.

Another good rifle I have been shooting lately is from Pecos Valley Armory. This little half-stock Kentucky rifle is available in 36 and 45 calibers. Many such half-stock rifles were made in the 19th century. This is the "squirrel rifle" so often referred to in accounts of that time.

Pecos Valley stocks their guns in select maple with good curl—grading out a 4 or 5 on a scale of 1 to 7—so all their rifles have eye-catching wood. The 34-inch barrel is browned, rifled with eight lands and grooves, with 1 in 48-in. twist for the 36 and 1 in 72-in. for the 45, and is 13/16 inches across the octagon flats. The rifle has a slim, light feel; the perceived weight is less than the 6½ pounds or so actual weight.

The lock is nicely browned, a Durs Egg-style lock made by the L & R Lock Company. The hammer fall is a short ¾-in. which makes for a very fast lock time. Triggers are double set-double acting. Furniture is polished brass. The ramrod is tipped with a threaded end, riveted in place; it's stained with a candy stripe spiral—a nice touch.

With the 440-caliber Speer round ball, .015-in. Ox Yoke Wonder patching and 60 grains FFFg Gerhart-Owen powder, muzzle velocity averaged 1675 fps and accuracy was good for my eyes and open sights. Groups of 1½-in. at 25 yards and a touch over 3 inches at 50 yards showed that the little rifle will shoot as well as it looks. I had thought that I would experience recoil problems with such a light rifle and the short-for-me pull of 13½ inches. I tend to have that problem with today's rifles in calibers over 40. The angle of buttplate to bore line here doesn't raise the comb into your cheekbone as many will do. This is a very pleasant surprise and something to think about when selecting a rifle for a youngster, wife, girlfriend or other impressionable shooter that is starting down the muzzle-loading path. The retail price is $399.

There's another Bondini gun around; this one is sure different from those pistols. It's a copy of a Germanic Schuetzen rifle made by Sanftl in Munich around 1850. The original is in a private collection in Erlingen, Germany.

The barrel has the poly-groove rifling that has been used so well and made famous by generations of Italian and German world champion shooters. It's 29 inches long and ⅞-in. across the flats, rifled with a 1 in 47-in. twist. The stock is an all-out schuetzen style in oil finished walnut. The cheekpiece is scooped out so deep for a comfortable rest there is a cut-out for the shooter's nose and the head can be held very naturally. The oil finish makes it relatively easy to change things and not look like it has been butchered.

The barrel, lock and sights are in the white and highly polished. The percussion lock is installed backwards on the rifle—that is, the hammer strikes back towards the shooter. The German maker of the original guns believed this arrangement disturbed the sight alignment less than the conventional set-up. There is a brass "blinder" on the left side of the breech plug to block vision with the left non-shooting eye, and there is a high fence behind the drum and nipple that effectively isolates the shooter's face from the cap flash. The aim is to put the shooter in a comfortable position with a stock and rifle that fits the human form and then to isolate him, as much as possible, from the mechanics of firing the shot. This allows the marksman to concentrate on his sight picture, probably one reason for this rifle's winning ways.

The three-lever set triggers can be set very light, to the point where you can't feel your finger touch the trigger when it trips. This loss of the sense of touch on the trigger is not generally liked by American shooters, but is favored by many European shooters. It depends on what you are used to, I guess. At any rate the trigger can be set for a definite "feel" if you wish; it's a very clean-breaking design. It works set only; and there is no half-cock notch. The intent here is to cut down on the friction of the sear riding over the fly. Everything has been done with an eye to fast, sure ignition. This is definitely not a hunting gun; it is every inch a target rifle.

Shooting went very well. I noticed the hammer blew back to full cock with most shots, I thought because the nipple had a large hole all the way through; it didn't squeeze down to prevent powder gas from coming back. This blow-by was enough to cock the hammer. The high fences between the nipple and the shooter's face worked, but I replaced the nipple with one of Uncle Mike's anyway. The most accurate load was 45 grains of FFFg Gerhart-Owens powder behind a 440 Hornady round ball and a .015-in. Ox Yoke Wonder patch. At 25 yards the rifle cut the 10 ring every shot on the standard NMLRA 25-yard target, if I did my part. The holes in the 9 ring were all called as I let the sights wobble off at ignition.

This rifle from Dixie Gun Works seems to have real promise as a target rifle. It is not legal in primitive shoots, of course, but will certainly hold its own in any match allowing schuetzen-type rifles. It looks pretty darn good hanging on the wall when it's not being shot, also. Priced at $595, it is good value for the money.

This was just a quick look at a few of the better quality guns that are in the marketplace. There are others; there will be more as time goes on. It looks like we are on the upswing toward higher grades of guns in muzzle-loading firearms. It's time. ●

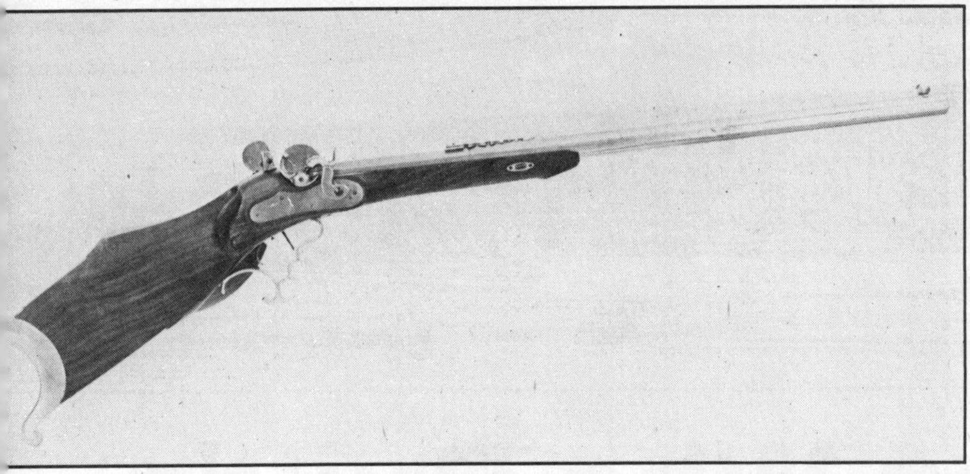

Dixie's Schuetzen target rifle. Note the shielding around the lock and nipple area—the shooter just concentrates on sights and target.

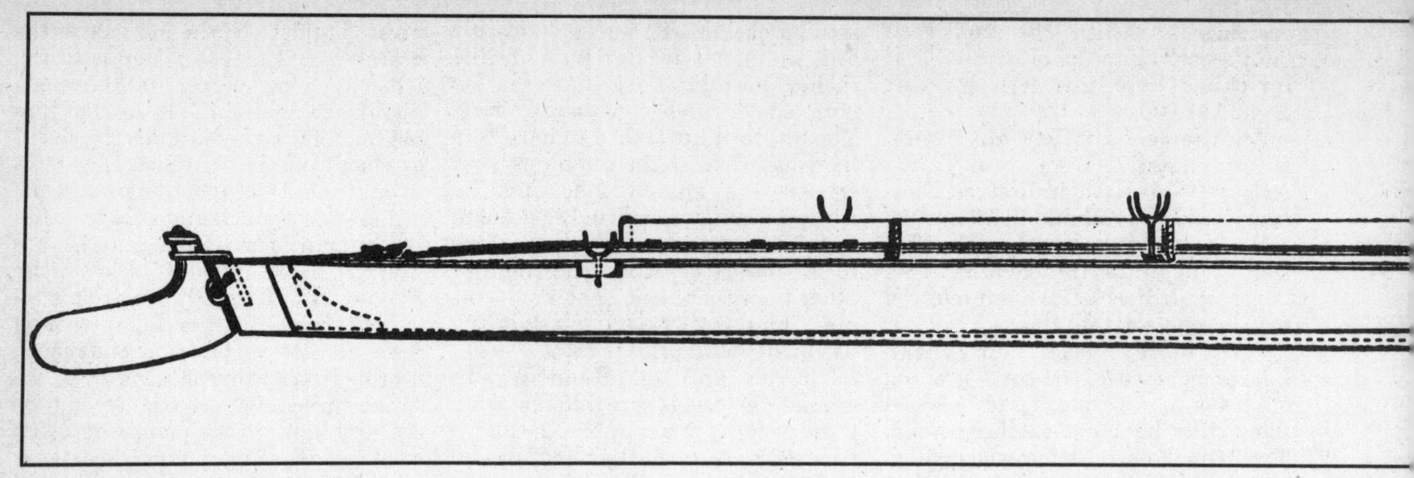

The Man Who Builds

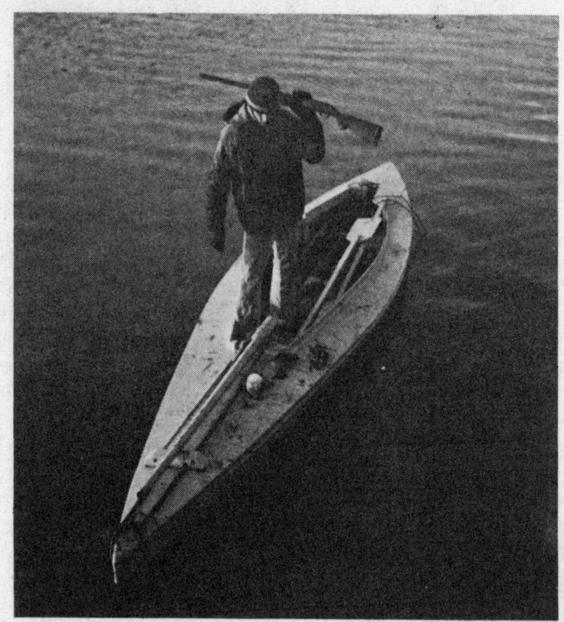

The gunner is looking at his main battery; the gun he holds is just for cripples.

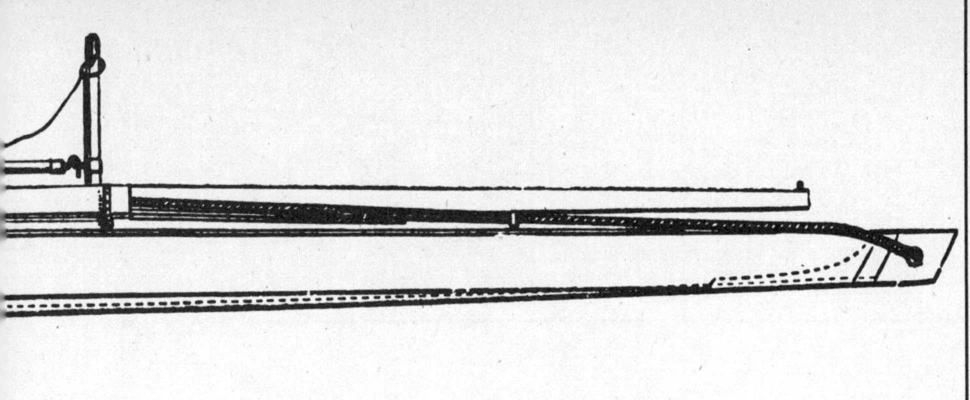

The engraver cautions that the figures shown here are somewhat higher than correct. No doubt.

Two men in a punt like this would scull and paddle hours and miles for one big boom.

Punt Guns

The big guns that once roared on our East Coast still speak to waterfowl in England

by DAVID J. BAKER

THERE ARE fewer than 100, and probably as few as 50, active punt gunners left in the British Isles. Each fires on average no more than 10 shots in anger per season. That must make punt gunning, the stalking of wildfowl with a large caliber shotgun mounted on a punt and shooting them either sitting or as they rise, one of the most specialized sports in the world. It follows, therefore, that a punt gun maker is something of a *rara avis* and probably an individualist in the bargain.

By training, David Adams is a wind tunnel engineer, trained by British

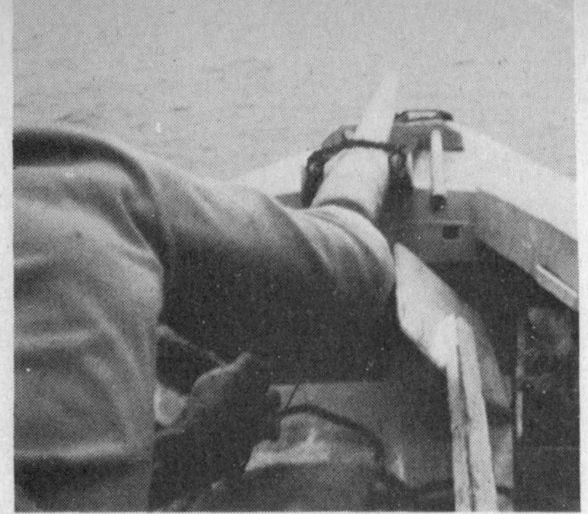

Here's the view as a stalk commences. They may punt in for 1000 yards.

The thrill is the stalk; the satisfaction is the bag resulting from one well-timed shot.

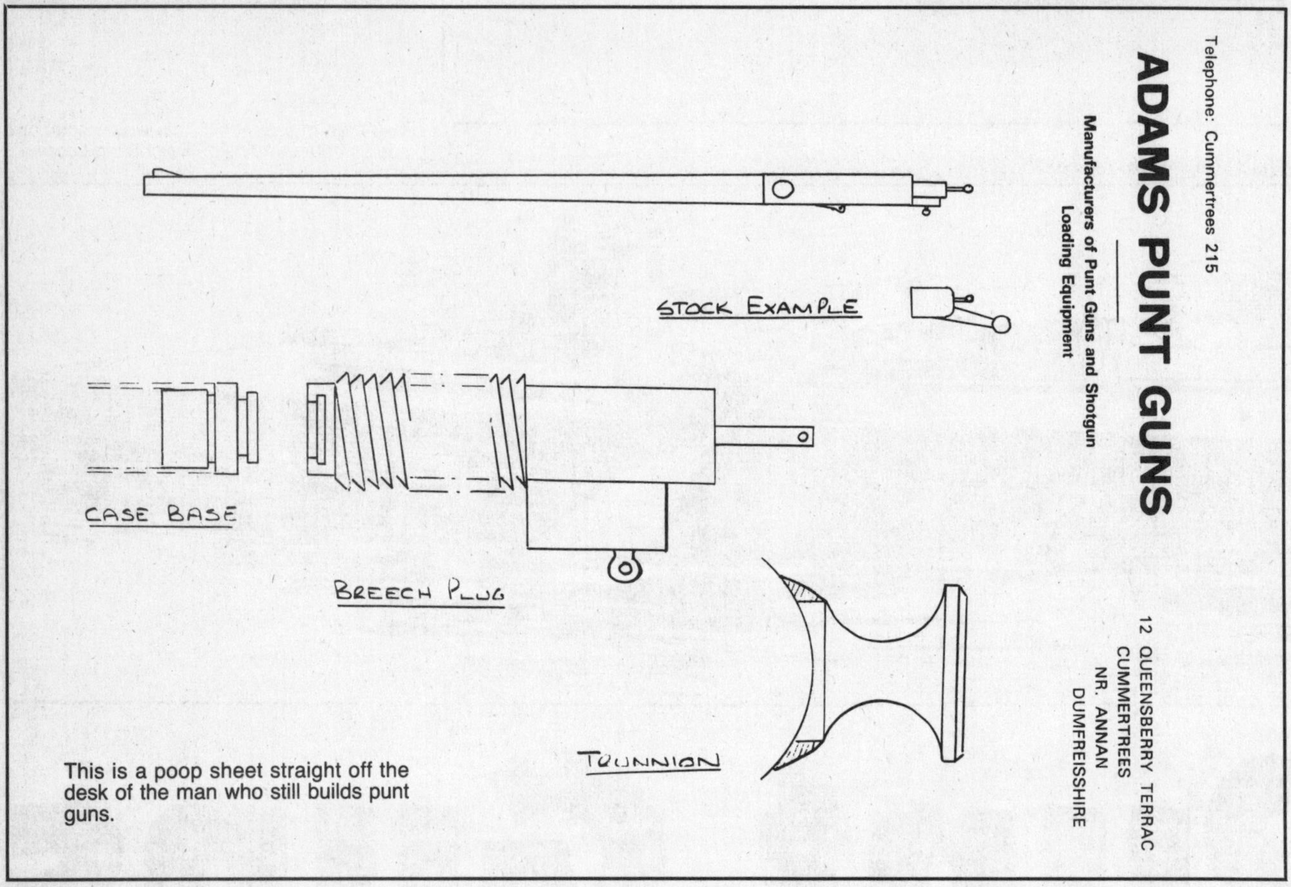

ADAMS PUNT GUNS

Manufacturers of Punt Guns and Shotgun Loading Equipment

Telephone: Cummertrees 215

12 QUEENSBERRY TERRAC
CUMMERTREES
NR. ANNAN
DUMFREISSHIRE

STOCK EXAMPLE

CASE BASE

BREECH PLUG

TRUNNION

This is a poop sheet straight off the desk of the man who still builds punt guns.

Aerospace, who decided to opt out of the rat race and follow his yen to punt and build guns for fellow enthusiasts. To date he has built about 12 guns in all, in a whole gamut of bore sizes from a "little" one-inch gun to the legal maximum size of one and three-quarter inch bore. It speaks again of the individuality of punters that there is no favorite size.

From the days of Col. Hawker in the 1820s there has been a generally accepted bore to barrel length ratio of 60 calibers. An inch and three-quarter gun has a barrel 105 inches long.

Adams' barrels are made by a specialist firm; David Adams' part is to build and fit the breech. Historically there have been many styles of breech mechanism, some quite like shoulder guns. There is obviously no need at all for rapid fire, so in modern times the buttress thread screw-in breechplug has become the most usual. This is the style Adams adopts and it has the advantage that it also acts as an extractor because the breech block and the special cartridge are locked together.

The cartridges for such a gun are as specialized as the gun itself. Those that modern gunners favor consist of turned brass bases which use 38-cal. revolver blanks for a "primer." The actual tube of the case is homemade from rolled paper, which only survives one shot. It is the brass head that is recycled. In addition to these heads, David Adams makes a range of large bore shoulder gun cases and tools to load them.

Perhaps because punt gunning is so specialized it is one of the most widely misunderstood sports. The pound of shot out of a big gun has to obey the same rules as the ounce of shot from your 20-gauge shoulder gun. So the quarry has to be stalked to within 80 yards and the most effective shot, the one that requires the greatest skill and judgment, is at the birds as they jump. One of the claims of those who do not understand punt gunning is that it is "murder."

"Yes," David says, "For the gunner!"

He goes on to relate how hard the toil of managing a punt is and how on one trip, after being afloat for more than 12 hours, he and his companion were caught by a squall and sank. Pressed as to his most memorable shot he tells how he stalked and bagged a group of just 3 widgeon. That, I believe, says a lot about the man who builds punt guns. ●

RIFLE REVIEW

by **LAYNE SIMPSON**

Variety, economy, versatility . . .

VARIETY. I can think of no other single word more appropriate about rifles today. Probably the most exciting news for '85 is a turn-bolt centerfile rifle with its barreled action and all other metal parts made of stainless steel. Such a rifle is especially welcomed by those of us who hunt big game come rain or shine.

Lightweight is another good word this year. The six-pound barrier has finally been broken and I'm not talking about a naked, snub-nosed rifle but rather, one with full-length barrel, outfitted with scope, sling and cartridges.

The phrases free enterprise and competitive industry fit right into this year's report because one of our major rifle makers has literally shrunk the price tag on fiberglass-stocked rifles. At long last, anybody can walk into their local gun shop and buy one off the shelf without first floating a loan on the old home place.

We have to use the word versatility in this report, too. More rifles with interchangeable barrels are here and one bolt-action centerfire even has interchangeable bolt heads so the same receiver will accept a variety of case head diameters. Also, two firearms that used to be thought of as strictly for handgunners have become rifles by the availability of buttstocks, fore-ends and long barrels for attaching to their frames.

The word unique (today, if not historically) aptly describes a new bolt action with a one-piece barrel and receiver, while I'm puzzled by an old 44 Magnum autoloading carbine being discontinued in the same year an old 44 Magnum slide-action carbine is reintroduced.

Wildcat cartridges seem to be enjoying a mild increase in popularity and a couple of rifle makers have met the demand with once-familiar names like 17 Hornet, 22 K-Hornet, 218 Mashburn Bee, 338-284, 338-06 and 35 Whelen. There is also a new wildcat called the 416 Express for short actions and for the first time ever, a factory rifle is available in both Robert Chatfield Taylor's 416 and Frank Barnes' 458 American. As the less popular but nontheless excellent factory cartridges go, we now have one rifle in 6.5 Remington Magnum and two in 350 Magnum.

Now youngsters have another choice in 22 rifles and for those who

The Alpha Alaskan in all stainless steel comes with a lot of options and a lot of chamberings, including wildcats like the 25-284, 338-284, 416 Express and 458 American.

Brown Precision's Professional Hunter weighs 6½ pounds in 375 H&H and 458 Magnum and you'll probably want the optional Mag-na-port muzzle brake.

Weatherby Fiberguard is 1985's VGL carbine with a very nice looking fiberglass stock. It's in 223, 243, 308, 270, 30-06 and 7mm Remington Magnum at $499.95.

The new TCR '83 is called the Hunter. It has a single trigger and finger grooves in the forearm and a $40 smaller price tag.

Beneath the conservative dress lies the heart of the mighty Model 700 in a short-actioned Sportsman 78 and two new chamberings—243 and 308.

Remove the shine and rosewood caps from the Medallion and you've got Browning's new Hunter grade rifle, an A-Bolt in a variety of calibers.

Kids with less money can have a Model 70 carbine, too. This Ranger Mini-Carbine, in 223 and 243, is sized to suit smaller people.

The Model 94AE Big Bore has lost its cut checkering and scope mounts and costs less money. The Standard Big Bore will probably kill a deer about as well as the discontinued XTR.

Is the Standard Big Bore too much for the budget? Try this Ranger Angle-Eject carbine on for size. It's the same gun in plainer garb.

tag along with dad on varmint shoots and big game hunts there's a rifle in 223 and 243 made just for them. In fact, two grades are available; fancy for the city kids and plain for the country kids.

With appetite whetted, let's now move on to the main course:

Alpha Arms

Last year Alpha offered the Alpha Custom, a short-action rifle; and now they've stretched its action a bit for the 25-06, 270, 280, 30-06 and wildcats 338-06, 35 Whelen, and 416 Taylor. The short Custom is still available in various short chamberings plus 222, 223, 22-250, 257 Roberts, 6.5x57mm, 6.5 Remington Magnum, 7x57mm and 350 Remington Magnum. The short action has wildcats too: 338-284, 416 Express and 458 American. And Alpha rifles now have a Model 70-type, 3-position safety lever on the bolt shroud.

Then there's the Grand Slam, an Alpha-barreled action with laminated wood stock, except this is not your ordinary laminated stock. It's made up of about 40 thin pressure-impregnated laminations and is said to be as stable as fiberglass and yet it has a warmth and feel found only with wood.

Last but certainly far from least, Alpha has a bolt-action big game rifle with its barreled action and all other metal parts made of stainless steel. Alpha Arms calls it the Alaskan and I'll bet quite a number of them will end up there.

Anschutz

The fact that American gunmakers are ignoring the rapidly growing sport of 22 rimfire metallic silhouette shooting has long puzzled me. Now it's even more so. For 1985 Anschutz offers a total of five different rifles designed exclusively for this demanding sport. Last year they had three models: 64 MS, 54.18 MS and 54.18 MSL, the latter with its bolt handle over on the side of left-hand shooters. New for '85 are two more models: 54.18 MS-ED and 64 MS-FWT. The former is on the famed Model 54 action and has a 23½-in. barrel with a detachable, 14¼-in. extension tube and three muzzle weights. It weighs 8 pounds, 6 ounces without the tube and weights. The Model 64 Featherweight weighs 6¼ pounds and comes with 21¼-in. barrel.

Bishop

Last year I mentioned three grades of custom rifles offered by this firm, all on the Mark X Mauser action. A higher grade yet is in the offing but I have no idea what it will be called. I really should know since I instigated the new grade and, in fact, will receive the first one out of Bishop's custom shop. Butch Searcy did all the metal work; square bridge action, custom bolt handle, Model 70 safety, etc. He also added a quarter rib and custom sights to the barrel. It looks like delivery of this rifle will be about two weeks late for a Testfire report. It's a 35 Whelen and I'll tell you all about it next year. Perhaps they ought to call it the Whelen Grade rifle.

Blaser Jagdwaffenfabrik

Rifles with interchangeable barrels aren't exactly new on the American hunting scene, nor are bolt-action rifles that take down for easy stowage. But what about a rifle that does all that plus has interchangeable bolt heads and magazine components? It's here and called the Ultimate Rifle. With this rifle you can use, say, a 223 setup on summer groundhogs; convert to 270 for deer-size game and then go after bigger stuff with a 300 Winchester Magnum or maybe a 9.3x64mm. The Ultimate comes with either left-hand or right-hand action in three grades: standard, deluxe and sheep hunter, the latter weighing 6½ pounds. Various chamberings are available, both American and metric.

Brown Precision

The Professional Hunter, as Chet Brown calls it, starts out in life as a Model 700 ADL action and ends up as a 6-pound, 7-ounce rifle for those who'd rather spend time hunting than maintaining. All metal can be had

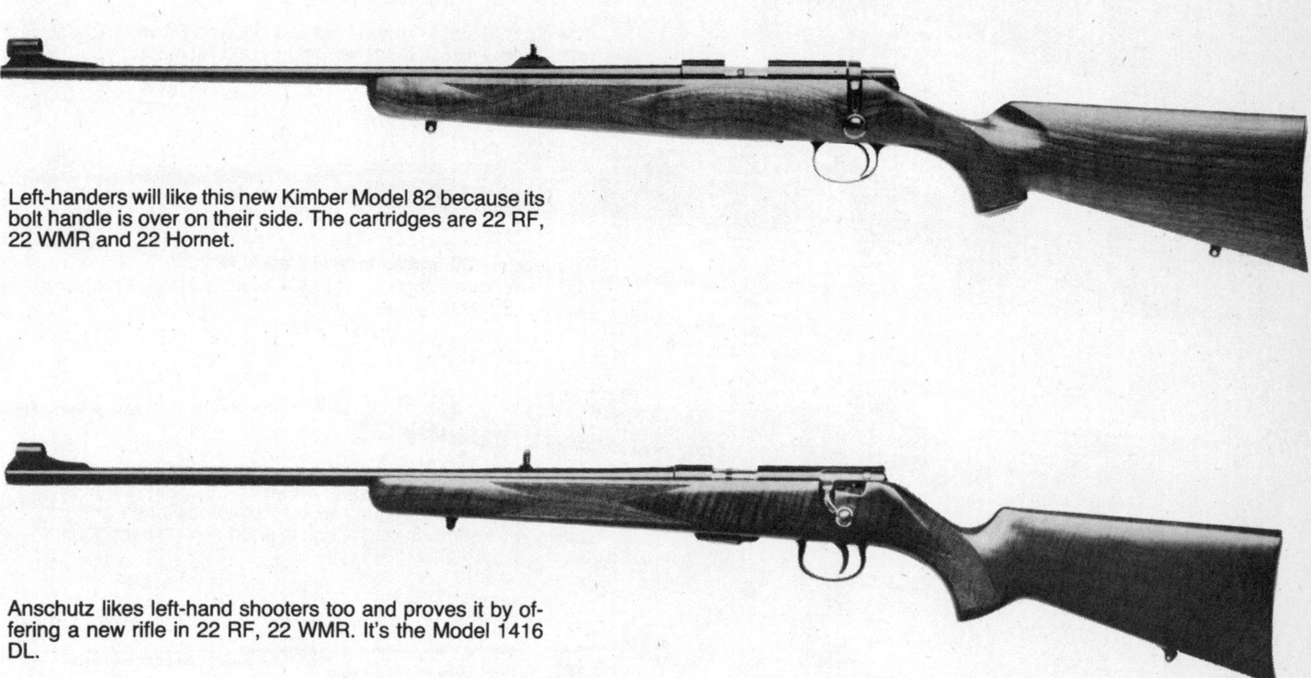

Left-handers will like this new Kimber Model 82 because its bolt handle is over on their side. The cartridges are 22 RF, 22 WMR and 22 Hornet.

Anschutz likes left-hand shooters too and proves it by offering a new rifle in 22 RF, 22 WMR. It's the Model 1416 DL.

with electroless nickel, dull blue or Teflon finish and, of course, the stock is fiberglass in a variety of colors. The bolt is modified for controlled feed with a Mauser-type extractor. The rear sight is a dual leaf, zeroed at 50 and 100 yards. Barrel length is 20 in. in 375 H&H or 458 Magnum. The optional Mag-na-port brake is probably the thing to have on this rifle, as are the Kimber quick-detach scope rings. The Professional Hunter is a rifle for tiptoeing through the alders and thornbush to finish what you started.

Browning

The big Model 1895 lever action in 30-40 Krag sold out so fast, Browning doesn't even show it in their '85 catalog and yet, there will be no more 95s made—or so say they. Strange. Those collectors who managed to latch onto rifles in both 30-06 and 30-40 Krag think they're something, don't they? Since cases are available from B.E.L.L., I'd surely like to see one more batch in 35 Winchester.

Remember the B78 single shot? Now, it's back for another try, this time called the Model 1885 and with a straight buttstock only. The octagon barrel is 28 inches long in 22-250, 270, 45-70 and 7mm Remington Magnum. It will be interesting to see what a lengthy barrel will do for three of those cartridges.

The BBR has been replaced with the A-Bolt. Two styles are available, Medallion with rosewood grip and fore-end caps and Hunter with no rosewood and no shine on its wood and metal. The feeding system is BAR; the bolt lifts 60 degrees and a variety of short and long chamberings are offered.

The old B78 single shot is back but this time Browning calls it the Model 1885. It has an octagon barrel in 270, 45-70, 22-250 and 7mm Remington Magnum.

The Model 700 limited edition classic Classic for '85 is in 350 Remington Magnum. It has a solid butt pad, short action and 22-inch barrel.

Browning calls it the A-Bolt, meaning the BBR has been superceded. It has shiny wood, rosewood caps and is available in short or long action in short or long cartridges.

Kids can have a full-price Model 70, too. This Mini-Carbine has a 20-inch barrel, cut checkering, and 12½ inches pull. It's in 243, so it won't bruise young shoulders.

Custom Gun Guild

Frank Wood and Ken Lindquist are at it again. Last year they came up with a takedown modification to various bolt-action rifles and now they offer a Model 700 so modified. It's called the Pak Master, has a 'glass stock and is available in 22-250, 243, 270, 7mm-08, 308 and 30-06.

This year there is also the Deer Master, a unique bolt-action rifle with receiver and barrel made from a single bar of steel. As you probably already know, the most common way to attach a barrel to a turn bolt receiver is by cutting mating threads into the ends of both. Not so with the Deer Master. Its barreled action is a solid chunk of steel from receiver bridge to muzzle. I've Testfired one of these rifles and will tell you all about it on page 216.

Heckler & Koch

Nothing new but a promise from H&K this year—a new bolt-action centerfire, possibly before we meet again next year.

Iver Johnson

Iver Johnson has several interesting projects going, all designed by Jerry Haskins of Champlin-Haskins rifle fame. Two fit into this report on long guns. Jerry showed me one prototype, a 5-pound single shot with interchangeable barrels. From a distance it looked like a tiny, scaled-down Browning Auto-5 shotgun but close examination proved it to be a unique, tip-up design. There's some very interesting history behind this firearm, going all the way back to the 1960s. If the rifle goes into production I'll tell you all about it next year. Another I.J./Haskins project to watch for is a new bolt-action rifle in centerfire persuasion.

Remember the old Universal slide action carbine in 44 Magnum? I.J. acquired Universal in 1983 and in mid-

1984 all production equipment was moved to the Arkansas plant. Anyhow, I.J. is reintroducing the 44 Magnum carbine and is now making the Universal M1 carbine. It's available in 22 RF, 5.6mm Johnson, 256 Winchester Magnum, 30 M1 and 9mm Parabellum. Also available are 22 RF lever-action, pump and autoloader rifles in civilian dress.

Kimber

According to those who compile information on such things, about 15 percent of the riflemen in our country are left-handers. Even so, until 1985 one could count all the bolt-action rifles made just for them on one hand and have a finger or two left over for other purposes. Times are rapidly changing for the better and the new Kimber South Paw (as they chose to call it) is an excellent example of this new trend. It is a mirror image of the Model 82 right-hand, in 22 LR, 22 WMR and 22 Hornet. New Model 82 chamberings for '85 are the 17 Kimber R2 and 22 K-Hornet. Also, owners of Kimber Hornets can send them back to the factory for rechambering to K-Hornet for a nominal fee.

Varmint shooters who appreciate more mass and weight in a rifle barrel will like the new Model 82 with medium-heavy barrel. The length is 24 inches. One is a repeater in 22 RF and 22 Hornet. The other is made for those of us who prefer the greater rigidity of a single shot bolt gun. That's just what it is; a Model 82 with solid bottom receiver and no magazine cutout. It is available in 22 RF, 22 Hornet and get this—the 218 Bee, 218 Mashburn Bee and 25-20 WCF, the latter with a standard weight barrel. The 25-20 is for turkey hunters and paper punchers while the Bee and Mashburn Bee are for varmint shooting.

Krico

While electric triggers have been around for awhile, to my knowledge, Krico is the first to offer a factory-made rifle with electronic ignition. The rifle is called KRICOtronic 340 Silhouette rifle. It's a 22 RF and, as the name implies, a cartridge in the chamber is fired by heat generated by electrical current. Basically, the trigger is a switch and what appears to be a spring-loaded firing pin protruding through the bolt face is actually an electrode. Simply described, when the trigger is pulled, batteries in the buttstock instantly heat the electrode to over 3,000 degrees F, causing the priming compound in the rim of the case to ignite. It's a bit more complex than that but to describe the system in detail would be to use up about half of my allotted space so I'll leave the rest to the brochure. You can get one from Beeman Precision Arms, Inc.

Marlin

Marlin has dropped the 307 Winchester from the Model 336-ER but the 356 is still there. The new Model 9 Camp Carbine is a clip-fed autoloader in 9mm Parabellum. It weighs a nominal 6¾ pounds and measures 35½-in. long with 16½-in. of Micro-Groove barrel. The safety is in the front of the trigger guard, a la Garand and both 12- and 20-shot clips are available. Other features include manual bolt hold-open; last shot, automatic bolt hold-open and a loaded chamber indicator. The receiver is drilled and tapped in case you need more precision than the open sights offer.

Mossberg

Mossberg has a rifle built for kids, too. It's a clip-fed bolt action with 16½-in. barrel and called the Tadpole. The little critter doesn't demand a great deal of care, only that dad take it out weekends and let the tykes feed it 22 Shorts, Longs and Long Rifles. Grownup 22 RF competitors might be interested in knowing that Mossberg is now importing Tenex ammunition.

M.O.A.

The M.O.A. single shot, described last year by Hal Swiggett, is now available in carbine form, replete with buttstock. I haven't shot it yet but I have examined one and it really looks good. A number of chamberings are available, from 222 to 358 Winchester as well as a number of wildcats.

Remington

Gone from the neat little Model Seven is the 222, no doubt crowded from the trough by the 223. The 308 chambering has been dropped from the Model Six and the 6mm Remington and 25-06 are no more in the Model 700 Varmint Special. That's the bad news, but there's a good bit of the other kind.

Remington polled a number of gunwriters as well as several normal people about what chamberings ought to be offered in their limited edition series of Classic rifles. High on my list was the 350 Magnum for two reasons. I like the cartridge because I've killed a truckload of deer with it in an old Model 600 and I figured there was a small, pent-up demand from woods hunters who missed the boat back in the 1960s. Now they can have a factory loaded, belted 35 Whelen too. But they'd better not tarry; the 350 will come and go during 1985. This classic Classic has a recoil pad, short action and 22-in. barrel with 1-16-in. twist. In this barrel length Remington's 200-grain factory load should exceed 2,600 fps.

A new short action Sportsman 78 joins the long action version with two additional chamberings: 243 and 308. Beneath the no-frills styling beats the heart of the mighty Model 700. Now if they'll just add the 223, varmint shooters can enjoy the luxury of the 78's low price same as big game hunters are doing.

Ruger

Did you buy one of Ruger's 44 Magnum, autoloading carbines yet? If not, you may be too late—it has been dropped from production. Latest to be announced is the XGI, a 308 version of the Mini-14.

Savage

One of the features responsible for the Model 99's smooth, bobble-free feeding of cartridges, the same one that allowed the old classic to stay ahead of other lever-action rifles with pointed bullets is no more. The one surviving model, 99C, is clip loaded. Gone is the famous rotary magazine. Also gone are the fine 250-3000 and 300 Savage chamberings. Sad.

Remaining in the Savage line are the 110-C, 110-CL (left hand), 110-E, 110 Varmint, 110 Silhouette and Model 340. That's a lot of bolt-action rifles.

Searcy Guns

Master gunsmith Butch Searcy has several new and interesting projects in the mill for '85. For one, he adds a Mauser-type, claw extractor and pre-64 Model 70 ejector to the Remington Model 700 and post-64 Model 70. Then he modifies the bolt face for controlled feeding to prevent the possibility of double-loading. Simply described, when the bolt is pushed forward to strip a cartridge from the magazine, the cartridge rim is engaged between the bolt face and extractor hook while on its way to the chamber. Fellows who hunt dangerous game especially like these modifications. Searcy also modifies the Ruger 77 to true, controlled feed and it's a bit less expensive since the claw extractor is already there. Other neat things are a Model 70 safety and bolt release on the Model 700.

Six Enterprises

Lee Six, the fiberglass stock man, tells me that he can now furnish stocks for about any rifle including the Ruger Number One and Remington Model Seven. Lee also makes several styles of stocks for the Remington XP-100, all quite popular with hunters and metallic silhouette shooters. I've been using Lee's stocks for years and they are top-notch.

Smith & Wesson

After making a big rush at the centerfire rifle and shotgun market, S&W has discontinued all long guns. Warranty and repair work on existing guns is to be handled by another company but as this is written no further information is available.

Marlin's Model 9 in 9mm Luger is a well-thought out plinker and general-purpose short rifle in the tradition of the M1 Carbine.

SSK Industries

While T/C offers eight different barrels for their TCR '83 rifle, there are those who yearn for other chamberings. Enter SSK Industries with Shilen blanks and reamers for about five dozen domestic and wildcat chambers. Just to name a few; 17 Remington, 222 Remington, 220 Swift, 6mm Remington, 6.5 JDJ, 25-06, 280 Remington, 45-70 and 375 JDJ. Barrel lengths run from short to long.

Ditto for converting the Contender to a rifle—if T/C doesn't offer the cartridge, SSK will fill the slot. SSK is also offering barrel extensions for permanent attachment to T/C 10-in. and 14-in. barrels to make them legal when using the buttstock.

Thompson/Center

Barrel makers and gunsmiths have been doing it for quite some time now so it was just a matter of time before T/C started doing it too. Of course, I'm talking about converting the Contender to a handy little rifle with a buttstock and longer barrel. T/C now offers such a conversion; buttstock, forearm and 22-in. barrels, all fitting the Contender frame without modification. For now you can get the 22 RF, 22 Hornet, 223, 7mm TCU, 7-30 Waters and 30-30. No doubt, the 410 gauge, 44 Magnum and 35 Remington are next. A nice little rig for shooting whitetails from a treestand, this conversion. Scope mounts made for the other barrels fit these too. And by the way, don't use a barrel less than 16-in. long with the buttstock—it's illegal.

There are now two models of the TCR '83 rifle. The original rifle with double set trigger and checkered forearm is now called the Aristocrat. The Hunter model is new and differs by its single trigger, fore-end with finger grooves in lieu of checkering and $40 smaller price tag. New cartridges for the '83 are 22 Hornet, 270 and 308 Winchester with barrels in 22RF and 20 gauge about ready to leave the drawing board.

Ultra Light Arms, Inc.

Looking for the ultimate in lightweight big game rifles? Well look no more, the Model 20 is here. It's a bolt action with 22″ barrel and it weighs less than 6 pounds with scope, sling and a magazine full of cartridges. Yep, you read it right. The design is basically scaled-down Remington. If all this is music to your ears, you won't want to miss the rest of the song on page 221.

USRAC

Announced as a new chambering in the Model 94 last year, the 444 Marlin appears to have been shelved. On the other hand, the 45 Colt must be working for USRAC; it has been added to the little Trapper carbine.

The Model 9422 and Model 94 are now available in no-frills versions. Even so, the new 9422 Classic with its curved grip has to be one of the most handsome 22s around. The Model 94 Ranger differs from its XTR mate by its hardwood stock and front sight dovetailed to the barrel. You'll not find a more practical lever-action carbine for easing through the kudzu and surprising whitetails.

Take the Model 70 carbine, shorten its length of pull to 12½ in. and you have a neat rifle for some ladies and the younger set. Or, you can let the factory do all the work. It's called the Mini-carbine, weighs 5¾ pounds and measures 39-in. long. The caliber is 243 so it won't bruise tender shoulders. Can't afford it? Then take a look at the Ranger version with hardwood stock, no checkering, no sling swivels and no jeweled bolt. Unlike its more expensive mate, the Ranger Mini-carbine is also available in 223 Remington. Add a standard length stock to that one and you've got the new Ranger carbine. Still with me?

The 1985 Model 94AE in 307, 356 and 375 is called standard grade because it lacks a few refinements of its predecessor. Gone are its checkering and scope mounts. It costs less than the discontinued version but it'll kill whitetails just as dead.

Weatherby

Fiberguard is the name; accuracy, stability, handiness and lightness are its game. Split pea green is its color. Actually, it's nothing more than last year's Vanguard VGL carbine with a very nice-looking fiberglass stock, which is saying a lot to woods hunters and mountain hunters. This is a very nice little rifle. Its no-slip, krinkle finish is nice, as is its price. I liked the idea when I hunted whitetails with a pilot model during the '84 season and I'll like it even better when Fiberguards in 223 and 270 are resting in my gun rack. It's guaranteed to put three shots into 1½ in., just like all the other Weatherbys. Other cartridges are 243, 308, 30-06 and 7mm Remington Magnum (A Big Seven at 20 inches?).

I'm absolutely amazed at the price of the Fiberguard: $499.95, or, only $111 more than the wood-stocked VGL. Wow! How do they do that? What it boils down to is this: Weatherby has literally knocked the bottom out of the 'glass-stocked rifle market and will ship trainloads out to eager hunters before next hunting season. They'll be a long time catching up with the demand for this one out in South Gate. The regular Vanguard with fiberglass stock next year?

As you may have surmised by now, the VGL carbine is now available with both short and long actions, same calibers as the Fiberguard. And, after being out of production for some two years, the Mark XXII autoloader is back.

Roy Weatherby has built rifles for a long time and just to prove it will offer a limited edition Mark V during 1985. It commemorates his 40th year of gun making. Only a few will be made and they are for serious Weatherby collectors only. Forty years from now I expect the Weatherby firm will still be leading the fleet when it comes to sailing uncharted waters. ●

BLACK POWDER REVIEW

by RICK HACKER

SPECIALIZATION seems to be the key word among muzzle-loading manufacturers this year, with a decided slant towards the black powder hunter and the new shooter. A good example of this trend can be found in **Euroarms of America's** introduction of a handsome, yet economically priced, halfstock percussion caplock for the hunter they call the St. Louis Hawken Rifle. Although it looks nothing like a traditional Hawken, it does look like the halfstock sporting rifles of the 1850s. Available in 50-caliber, the 28-in. octagon barrel is well-polished and deeply blued, while the hammer features the light luster of the old-time charcoal bluing, a clear indication that this gun is being manufactured for EOA by one of Italy's premiere black powder gunmakers, Aldo Uberti.

R.V.I. and Olde Pennsylvania are two new sources for hard to find high-quality sure-fire flints.

The rifle's wood-to-metal fit reflects its economical pricing, while the double-set triggers and easy-to-see adjustable buckhorn rear sight (which would look more at home on a Winchester '73) give it shootability. The hammer spring is sufficiently strong to pop the most stubborn cap. For under $200, the muzzle-loading hunter can obtain a very rugged and nicely styled hunting rifle with EOA's St. Louis Hawken.

Navy Arms has created three different LeMats, those Civil War pistols that fired nine 44s and then could finish with one shot from the 20-gauge smoothbore tube.

Connecticut Valley Arms, which recently moved its operations from Haddam, Connecticut to Norcross, Georgia (no, they're *not* changing their name to Georgia Valley Arms) has added two dramatically new products to the line. The first is the CVA Express Rifle, a 50-caliber double rifle that fills a need for hunters in quest of dangerous or fast-moving game; at least, the double rifle was the 19th Century's answer to that problem. The side-by-side percussion is built on the same stock design (or so it seems) as CVA's best-selling 12-gauge shotgun. The twin locks are stamp-engraved and color case-hardened. The twin barrels are deeply blued and held to the stock with a single steel wedge, which removes for easy takedown from the hooked breech. The front sight is a high blade with bead, and the rear sight is fully adjustable for windage and elevation. The 28-in. barrels are rifled one turn in 48 inches, which makes them ideal for conical bullets, my first choice when going after any animal that could quickly transform the hunter into the hunted.

According to CVA, the barrels are regulated to converge at 90 yards, a practical range for a muzzle-loading hunting rifle. However, I am anxiously awaiting a test gun to determine if this is true, for if it is, the economically priced Express Rifle could very well command a large chunk of the big game black powder hunting market. The CVA Express Rifle is available ready-to-shoot, or as a kit.

The weekend shooter who just wants to burn black powder occasionally now has a CVA entry called the Blazer, the most economically priced frontloading percussion rifle on today's market. Available in either kit or built-up, the Blazer is untraditional. Only the ramrod under the barrel and the curl of the percussion hammer directly *behind* the barrel

Both Euroarms of America and Allen Fire Arms import this economical but serviceable St. Louis Rifle, ideally suited for the hunter.

Dixie's Delux Cub is a short and handy 40-caliber, perfect for a first muzzleloader and as a light and accurate rifle for shooters of small stature.

Iver Johnson's over and under 50-caliber caplock rifle has one-piece stock and a lot of modern shotgun styling.

Traditions, Inc. has introduced their Hunter Rifle in 50 and 54 caliber. The caplock halfstock has adjustable sights and a black chromed finish to reduce glare.

Thompson/Center has acquiesced to the needs of southpaws this year by producing their popular Renegade in a left-hand version.

give this straight-line caplock away. Available only in 50-caliber with a slow twist 1 in 66-in. rifling for patched round ball, the Blazer has an easy-to-file brass blade front sight and a fixed rear sight which must be drifted and filed to get it on target. The nipple of the straight-line action goes directly into the powder charge in the breech, adding to the potential sure-firing of this basic, if not traditional, rifle. Due to its centrally-located hammer, the Blazer can be easily shot left-handed.

Pistoleros also have something new; CVA's brass-framed Wells Fargo, an economical copy of the 1849 Colt. This little 31-caliber five-shot revolver comes with an extra cylinder, as did many originals. Like its Colt prototype, the Wells Fargo has no loading lever. Frontier travelers used to carry a second cylinder with them, loaded and ready.

Another economically priced first-time rifle, and one especially suited to women and teenagers is the new Delux Cub from **Dixie Gun Works.** This slim, 28-in. barrel Kentucky is available in either flintlock or caplock and marks the return of caliber 40 to Dixie's line. The Cub is ideal for all small game hunting, including squirrel, rabbit and turkey; it is not powerful enough for deer, but the rifle itself has the accuracy to find some use on the target range as well as the hunting fields. An out-of-the-box test gun fired a ¾ in. group at 25 yards, using 40 grains of FFFg and one of the new 395 swaged balls from Hornady. The Delux Cub has double-set triggers which are unusually crisp, a crowned muzzle and a nicely contoured and fitted brass patchbox. Trigger guard, buttplate and thimbles are all of highly polished brass. The rifle only measures 45 inches over-all and weighs a scant 6¾ pounds.

Mowrey Gun Works has been sold to a new group of owners in Saginaw, Texas. The product line will be basically the same as in past years (including the re-introduction of the 12-gauge shotgun), and all of these Ethan Allen-styled longarms have been reduced by about $100 in price. An extensive dealer program is under way, which means you should be able to find these unique 1835-designed rifles and shotguns at your local gun store.

Mowrey is introducing their Maverick Magnum "for the modern hunter," as they put it. It's their Great Plains 50 or 54-caliber rifle fitted with a modern style pistol grip stock with recoil pad, a half octagon-half tapered round barrel, and scope mounts. Check your local legalities before taking this black powder blend of old and new afield.

Navy Arms has created an aura of excitement with the announcement of their new replica LeMat Revolver. The original LeMat achieved quite a level of notoriety during the War Between the States as a nine-shot 44-caliber revolver that also sported a 20-gauge shotgun barrel underneath the 7⅝-in. pistol barrel. The LeMat was the official officer's sidearm of the 18th Georgia Regiment and the Confederate States Navy. Now this 3½-pound percussion powerhouse has been re-created by Navy Arms in a Cavalry Model (with trigger spur and lanyard loop) as well as the Army and Navy versions, which sport variations in the design of their hammer hoses and takedown assemblies.

Also new from Navy is a Turkey and Trap side-by-side shotgun. This welcomed variation of their popular Classic 12-gauge caplock is fully choked to throw an 80 to 90-percent pattern (depending on load) at 30 yards, one of the few muzzle-loading shotguns capable of performing this feat since most are cylinder choked.

The historic firm of **Iver Johnson** has recognized the growing muzzle-loading hunter market and is introducing a 50-caliber caplock over-under double rifle. Regulated to shoot within a three-inch circle at 50 yards, the Over & Under has a single adjustable rear sight and a gold bead front sight. Its twin back-action locks are nicely case-hardened and the breech plugs can be removed with an Allen wrench. The one-piece checkered walnut stock features a recoil pad and the thick forearm is finished off in a schnabel tip reminiscent of a shotgun styling. The Iver Johnson Over & Under double rifle is accurate for hunting purposes and could prove popular with those who prefer non-traditional styling in a practical muzzleloader.

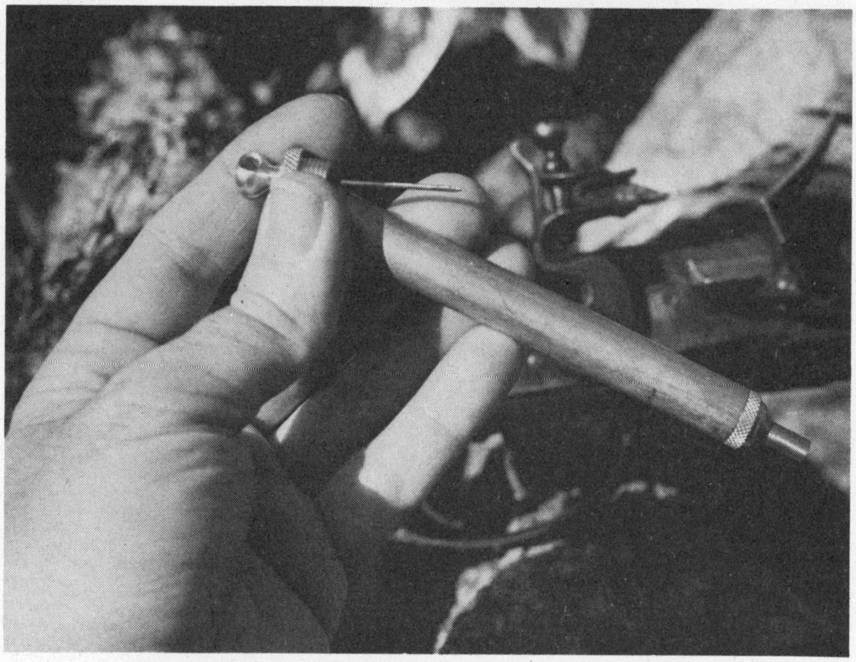

Olde Pennsylvania produces a unique combination pan charger and nipple pick, one of the few such tools on the market today.

Paolo Bondini is an Italian armsmaker best known for his superbly-crafted reproductions of the early English and French duelling pistols. Now he has come out with a classic deluxe Hawken caplock pistol with engraved and polished lockplate (which is stamped J & S Hawken) and silverplated furniture. The octagon barrel is blued and sports a hinged steel ramrod that cannot be separated from the gun and lost. The excellent trigger mechanism is a single set and is adjustable. The walnut stock is hand-checkered along the pistol grip and a single wedge holds in the hooked breech barrel. This highly finished belt pistol is available in 45, 50 or 54 caliber and is currently being imported by **The House of Muskets** and by **Allen Fire Arms,** who also offer a plain version of the Hawken pistol with no engraving or checkering. (See article, page 146, for more on this.)

Hornady has increased its line of ready-to-shoot balls by adding the 315, 395, 495 and 520 sizes. **Ox-Yoke Originals** has perfected Wonder Lube, a new non-chemical lubricant for both patches and conicals that, by my tests, enables shooters to get at least 30 shots without having to swab the bore. And **Olde Pennsylvania** has produced a line of muzzle-loading accessories that include custom-shaped high-quality flints and a unique pan charger with combination vent pick, one of the few such versions on the market. From Vancouver, British Columbia comes a relatively new firm called **R.V.I.,** which supplies a very high quality line of gun flints and handcrafted European muzzle-loading accessories which are better fitted to a cased set of pistols than in a possibles bag.

For the hunter using Mini-bullets, a unique method of loading, without getting grease on your hands, has been devised by **Kenneth Leding.** Called (appropriately enough) the Leding Speed Loader, this elongated plastic device appears somewhat like a loading block for conicals, except that it has a screw that forces a self-contained supply of grease around each conical before it is loaded. It definitely has a practical application for the hunter out in the field. And speaking of hunters, as we have been all through this review, a new magazine called *The Muzzleloading Hunter* (not to be confused with my own Winchester Press book of that same name) has appeared on newstands. ●

BIG NEWS IN

by J. I. GALAN

The Beeman P1—only dual-power spring-piston air pistol in the world.

This cocking position develops 600 fps-plus MV.

The 8.4-inch barrel of the P1 is securely surrounded by the cocking lever "slide."

Galan particularly likes the P1 when shoulder-stocked.

REALLY significant developments in the world of airguns were rather scarce until four or five years ago; however, times have changed drastically. Not only have we witnessed a virtual avalanche of new airgun models in traditional concepts, but *new* concepts are appearing with increasing frequency.

Of the new developments in 1985, two are really important. One is the introduction of the world's only dual-powered spring-piston air pistol and the second is the appearance in America of the air-soft gun from Japan.

The concept of multiple power settings has been explored before, briefly. In the late '40s the Targ-Aire Pistol Co. of Chicago launched an air pistol that had *three* different cocking positions, each for a different muzzle velocity. The quality Targ-Aire pistol was a commercial failure in those long-gone days and it is virtually unknown except in serious airgun collector circles.

Enter the Beeman P1 Magnum. Definitely in tune with the realities of the adult airgun market of the '80s, the 177-caliber Beeman P1 might become the most popular sporting-type spring-air pistol in history, followed closely by such classics as the various Webley models and the elegant Walther LP-53. Like the latter (which imitated closely the looks and firing behavior of a cartridge pistol), the P1 also follows very closely the looks and, to some degree, the "feel" of a famous firearm, none other than the legendary Colt 45 Automatic.

The outward resemblance to the venerable Colt alone is sure to endear the P1 to legions of fans of the big auto. The P1 was specifically designed to duplicate as much as possible the feel of the Colt so that it could be used as a substitute for economical practice at home or in places where the big boomer would be out of place. To that effect, the Beeman P1 has a grip like that of the Colt, so close, in fact, that the grip plates of the Colt (as well as after-market grips) will fit the P1. As sold, the P1 comes with real walnut grips having genuine cut checkering.

Overall, the P1 weighs 2½ pounds and measures just eleven inches. This is remarkable, not to say outstanding, in a spring-air pistol capable of producing 600 fps muzzle velocity. The P1 places the finely-rifled 8.4-in. barrel above the powerplant unit, like the Webley air pistols. The barrel is enclosed by the cocking arm.

Pulling on the "hammer" of the P1 releases the cocking arm. The low-power setting is at right angle to the frame, and produces between 350 and 400 fps, depending on the pellet. Pulling the cocking arm all the way forward (about 130° to the frame) engages the high-power cocking position, which can produce 600 fps-plus with some pellets.

The frame is made of high-strength aircraft aluminum with a semi-matte blue finish. All major working components are steel. The two-stage trigger system is fully adjustable and one of the finest I've seen outside the lofty realm of world-class air pistols costing hundreds of dollars more than the P1. There is an ambidextrous, manual trigger safety in addition to an automatic safety that goes on as soon

AIRGUNS

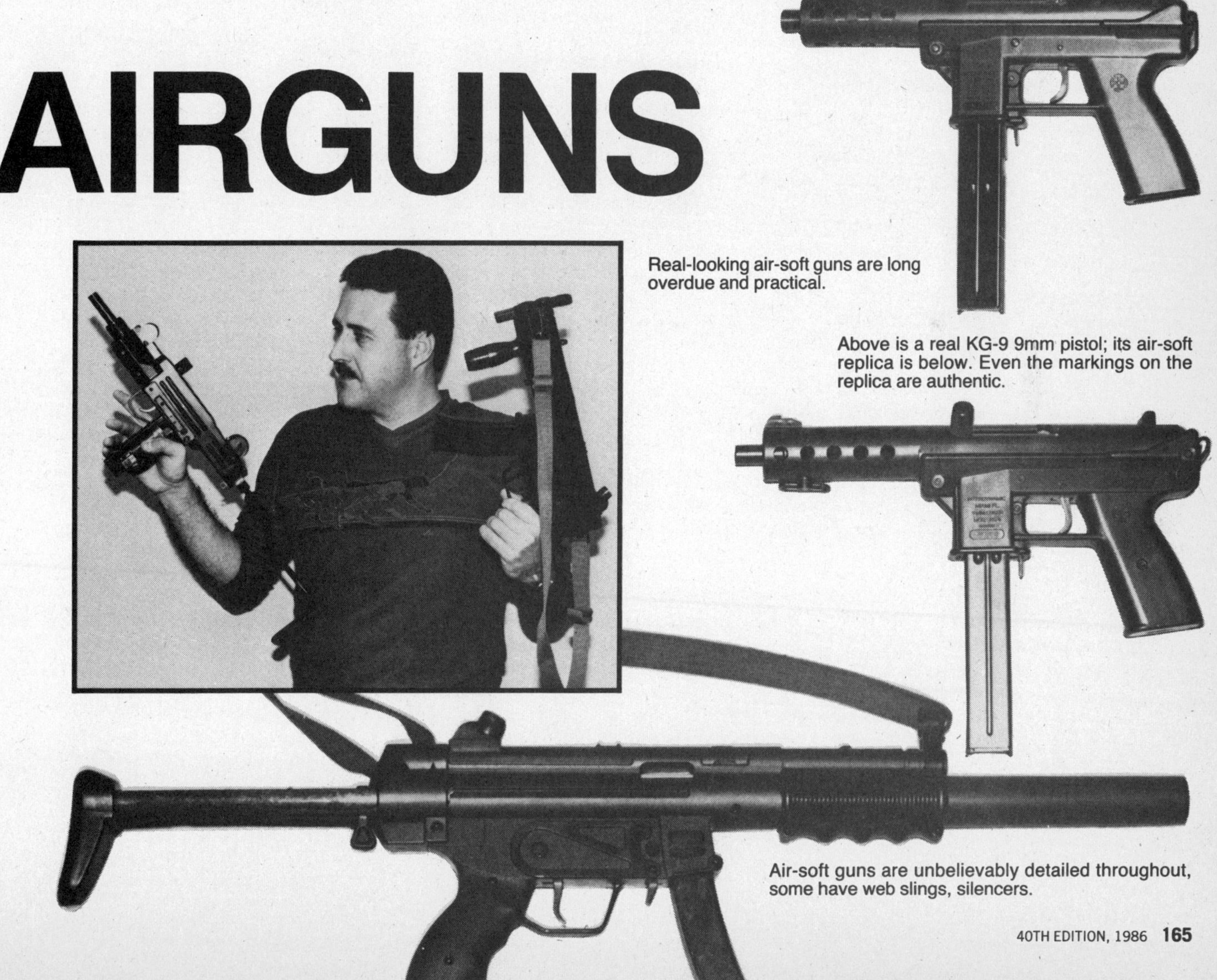

Real-looking air-soft guns are long overdue and practical.

Above is a real KG-9 9mm pistol; its air-soft replica is below. Even the markings on the replica are authentic.

Air-soft guns are unbelievably detailed throughout, some have web slings, silencers.

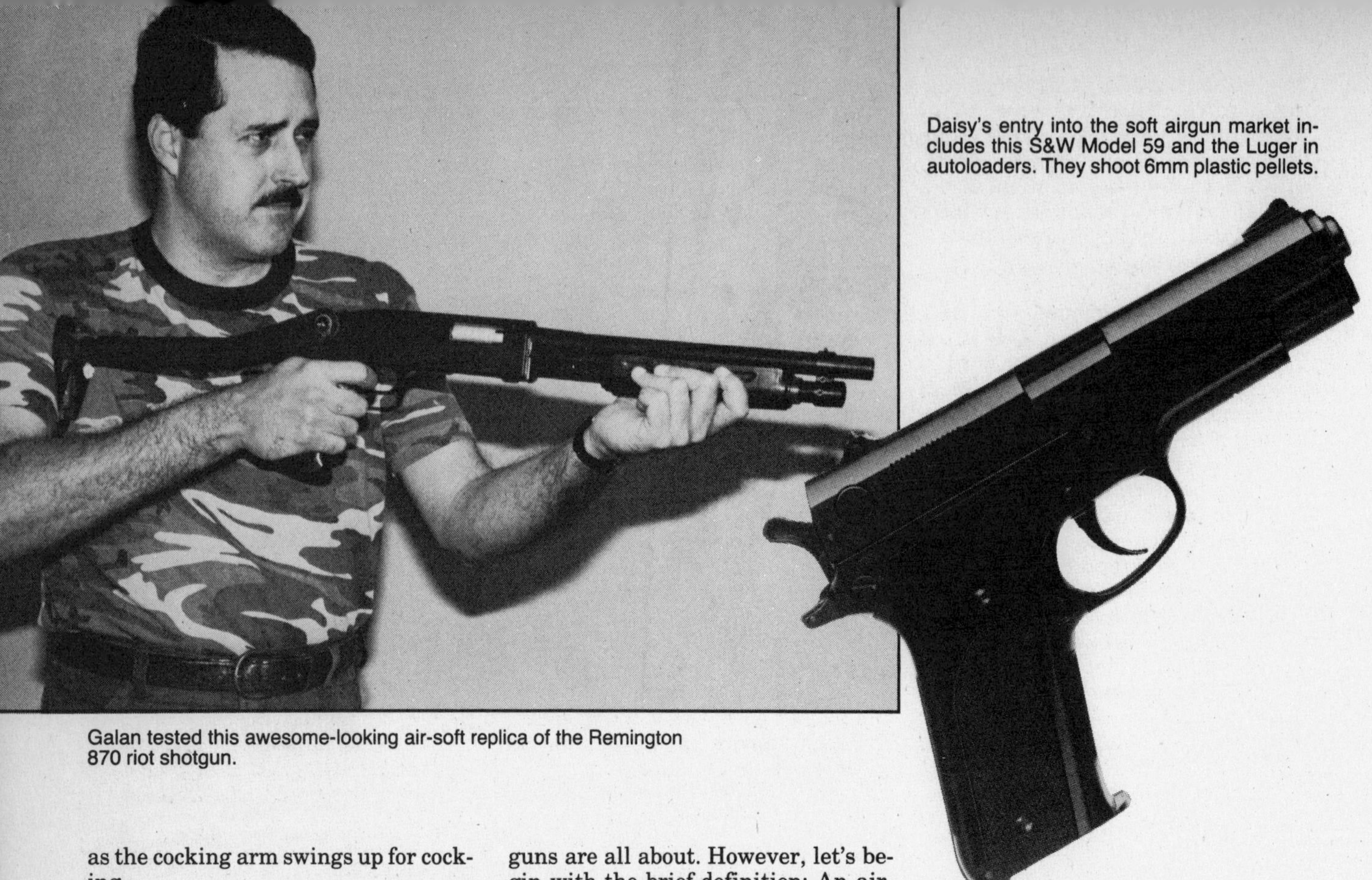

Daisy's entry into the soft airgun market includes this S&W Model 59 and the Luger in autoloaders. They shoot 6mm plastic pellets.

Galan tested this awesome-looking air-soft replica of the Remington 870 riot shotgun.

as the cocking arm swings up for cocking.

The PI has an all-steel Patridge rear sight adjustable for windage and elevation with click micrometer screws, and the top of the cocking arm is grooved for a scope mount. My test sample came with a Beeman Blue Ribbon Model 25 pistol scope that enabled me to print dime-sized groups at 60 feet using the optional shoulder stock.

(The latter is a must accessory. The Beeman shoulder stock will also fit the 1911 Colt, although that would be illegal with standard barrels.)

Cocked for high-power, the Beeman P1 shoots as hard as medium-powered air rifles, so it is entirely capable of bowling over some critters that were previously fair game only for rifles. Excellent precision and penetration were obtained with RWS Super Point pellets at up to 30 yards, while RWS Super Hollow Point pellets performed very well at shorter range. Beeman Silver Jet and Laser pellets also gave impressive results in the P1.

The rearward moving piston of the P1 generates a mild recoil that simulates to an extent the recoil of a firearm. Even in the low-power setting (suitable for informal target shooting and plinking in a reduced area), there is enough recoil for realistic training with this pistol.

Training and plinking in a reduced area is also what the new air-soft guns are all about. However, let's begin with the brief definition: An air-soft gun is a spring-piston-powered replica (in most cases) of a famous firearm that shoots reusable plastic pellets at relatively low velocities. Thus, on the one hand, we have the quest for more powerful airguns (the P1 is a glowing example) while at the same time the concept of the very low-power airgun embodied in air-soft guns emerges. Two other major features of air-soft guns are their intrinsically high quality and incredibly detailed construction.

Air-soft guns originated in Japan, a country where the private ownership of firearms and even regular "hard" airguns is severely restricted. The Japanese already had a thriving industry manufacturing excellent non-shooting replicas of firearms, and it was but a logical step to incorporate a low-energy airgun powerplant into some specially-designed replicas. This enables these guns to be sold and used without harsh restrictions in Japan. As non-shooting replicas managed to do years ago when introduced to the American market, the air-soft guns are virtually certain to catch on big here. They look and feel just like their real firearm counterparts, *and they shoot.*

Besides looking genuine enough to fool even seasoned gun buffs, air-soft guns are remarkable in that they duplicate rather closely the actual function of the firearms they represent. Take the air-soft replica of the Heckler & Koch MP5K submachine gun, for example. The air-soft MP5K replica is slightly larger than the real thing (14.5-in. long as opposed to 12.8-in.), but it is painstakingly faithful in almost every detail, including the finish on the different areas of the gun. Air-soft guns, by the way, are made out of molded ABS for the most part, although zinc alloy and other metals are also used for some components. Anyway, like the real things, the air-soft MP5K also shoots from a closed bolt, ejecting the empty plastic casing once the 6mm plastic BB or pellet leaves it. The gun is then manually recocked for the next shot by cycling the forward handle. This strips a fresh "cartridge" from the 12-round magazine and chambers it.

The muzzle velocities of air-soft guns vary somewhat; however, most of the popular models fall in the 150-200 fps range. Considering that the 6mm plastic BB weighs only about 2.6 grains, the muzzle energy generated seldom tops a quarter of a foot pound. Hardly lethal, even to a small mouse at point-blank range. Some plastic pellets available weigh about 2 grains each. Nonetheless, either stings a lot on an exposed part of the body at short

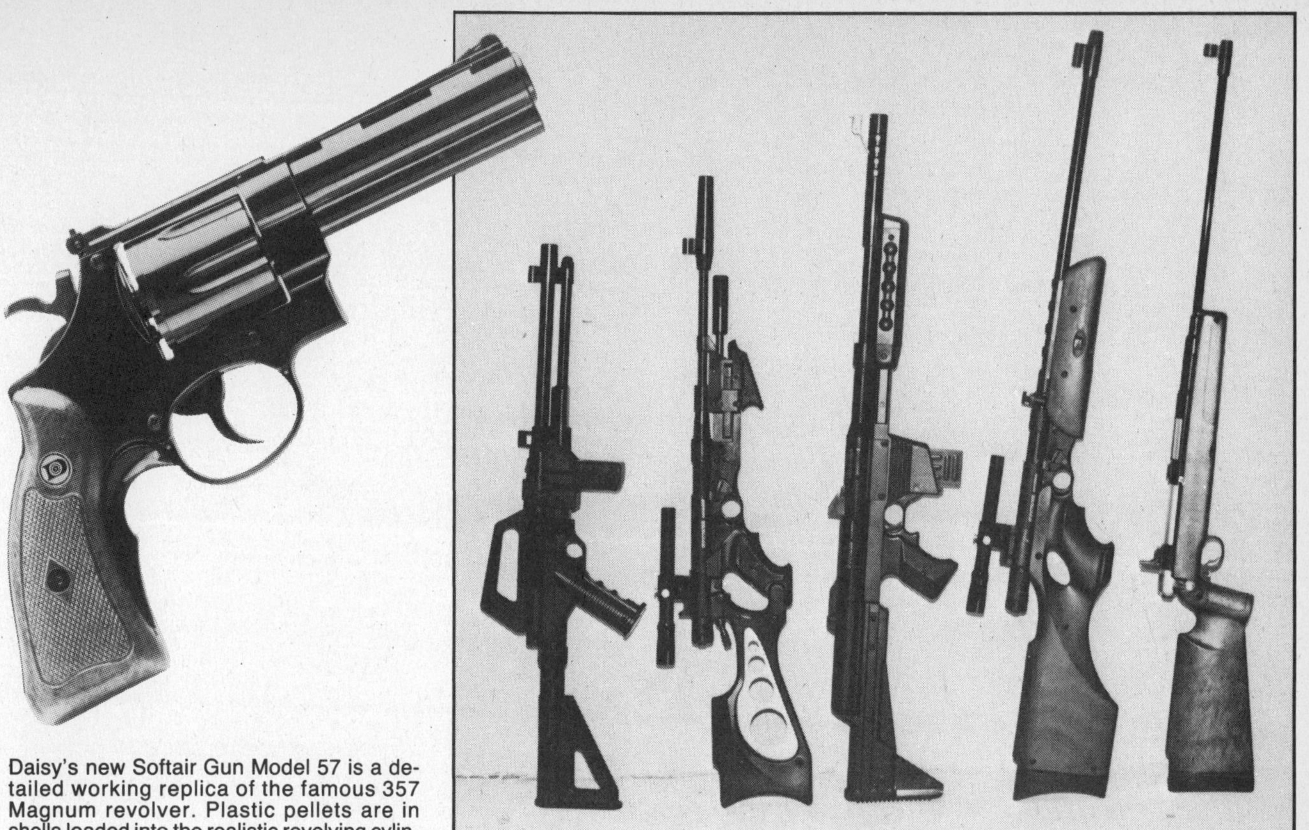

Daisy's new Softair Gun Model 57 is a detailed working replica of the famous 357 Magnum revolver. Plastic pellets are in shells loaded into the realistic revolving cylinder.

Other models Galan tested include these futuristic-looking long guns that shoot 7mm plastic pellets.

range; furthermore, they have the potential to generate a serious injury if an eye is struck.

Other air-soft models currently available include a replica of the Mini-UZI and a copy of the H & K MP5SD3 "silenced" SMG with collapsible stock. The mini-UZI sports a folding skeleton stock; however, unlike the MP5 replicas, it will not eject the empty plastic casing automatically. All of these "submachine guns" take 12 fake cartridges in their respective magazines. Collector's Armoury Inc. sells these air-soft SMGs. In addition, they also sell an air-soft copy of the ubiquitous M1 Carbine that'll blow your socks off. It also takes several fake plastic cartridges loaded with plastic pellets into its magazine.

The Daisy Mfg. Co. has jumped into the air-soft act with both feet. Daisy distributes *four* superb air-soft handgun models made by the same Japanese company that produces the H-K and Uzi replicas. They include the legendary Luger, the P.08; Walther's famous P-38; Smith & Wesson's Model 59; and a modern double-action 357 magnum revolver. Of the semi-autos, the Luger and the Model 59 both shoot 6mm plastic BBs from plastic casings loaded into their respective magazines. Both models eject their empties in a very realistic manner.

The P-38 replica dispenses with the plastic casings and magazine. Instead, it shoots the 6mm BBs from a special pop-up chamber, loaded one at a time for each shot. All three semi-autos shoot about as hard as the much larger models discussed earlier, despite their reduced powerplants.

The revolver is a mixture between a Colt Python and a large-frame S&W. It sports the barrel style and rib of the former mated to the frame and grip style of the latter. This air-soft revolver also has a unique firing system. The plastic pellets load in genuine-looking plastic casings which contain the actual spring-piston powerplant. The gun, like a real revolver, has a plastic pin which strikes the dummy primer, releasing a tiny spring-powered piston inside the casing. The velocity is reduced compared to the semi-autos, but still enough for meaningful short-range plinking.

Air-soft guns do not have rifled bores; they are fun guns intended primarily for safe and highly-realistic plinking action indoors or out. For this purpose, they are certainly accurate enough, even at relatively long range. In fact, some of these may soon replace paint-ball CO^2 powered guns in the increasingly popular weekend war games being played around the nation. Collector's Armoury is also selling hollow 6mm plastic BBs which can be injected with water-soluble ink. These spheres break up upon striking a person or a solid object, leaving a small splash of color. Imagine the realism that can be achieved in these war games by using genuine-looking guns that also mark the "enemy" when he's shot.

Are air-soft guns just a passing fad in the shooting sports in general and in the world of airguns in particular? I don't think so at all. They offer high quality, genuine looks and function, not to mention loads of practically harmless shooting fun for a very modest price. Their ammo is reusable, too. Air-soft guns are perhaps the ultimate toy for grown-ups who love and appreciate guns. Even persons who are ostensibly anti-gun can have a real ball shooting these puny plinkers, as I have personally witnessed on more than one occasion. As the number and variety of air-soft guns increases, we will see that this is but a logical development in the scheme of airgun things. As they say, paraphrasing the ancient cliché: There's more than one way to scare off the cat . . . harmlessly. ●

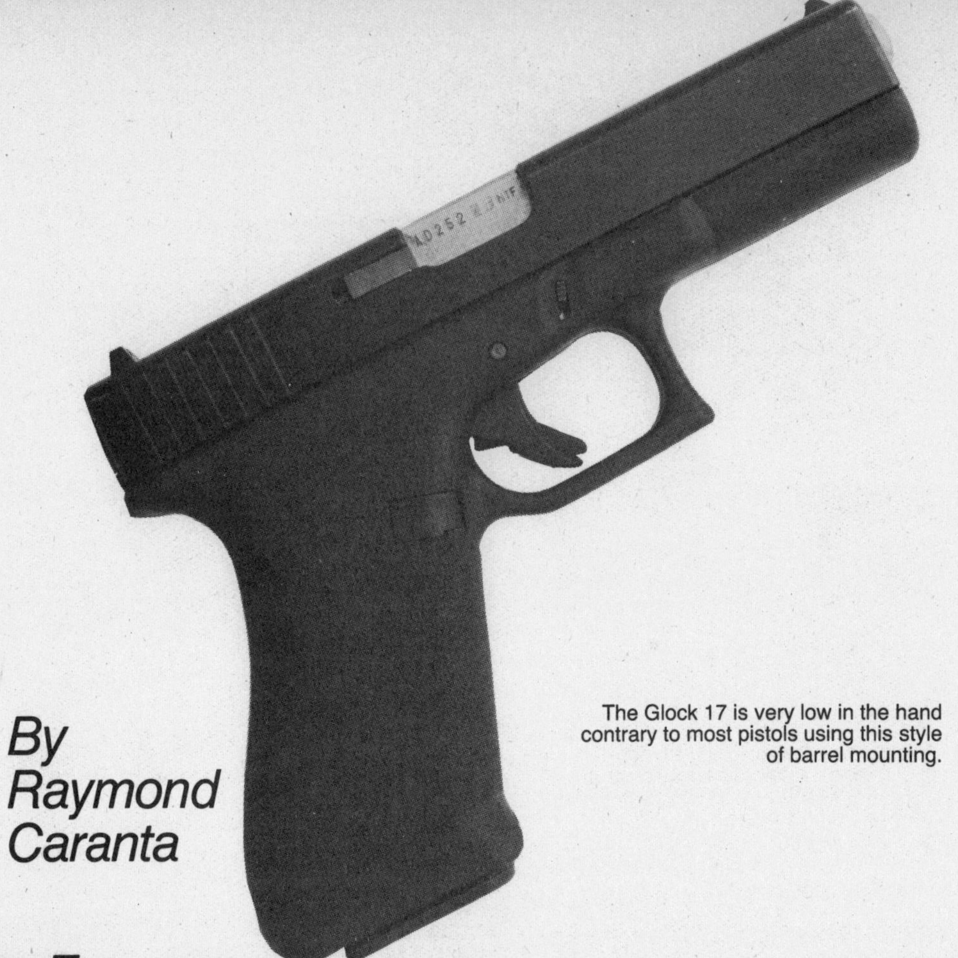

The Glock 17 is very low in the hand contrary to most pistols using this style of barrel mounting.

By Raymond Caranta

the extraordinary

The steel slide-barrel-recoil spring assembly represents 40 percent of the total weight of the pistol.

The trigger mechanism is entirely made of stampings; gun is striker-fired.

Note the slender grip of the Glock 17 in spite of the unusual 17-shot magazine capacity; design allows variation in pitch.

GLOCK

From no idea to radical prototype to selected service pistol in under four years? Where was the bureaucracy?

(Photos by Jean Jordanoglou)

IN OCTOBER, 1982, a Belgian magazine, over the signature of a German gun writer, reported a certain Austrian Glock 17 pistol, chambered in 9mm Luger, mostly made of plastics and stampings. The Glock 17, it was said, was considered for adoption by the Austrian army.

The gun was displayed nowhere at European shows, and was not taken very seriously until this year, when it was learnt that the Glock 17 had been officially approved as the Austrian Army service pistol. It replaces the German P-1, the light alloy descendant of World War II's P38.

In the gun business, only a few people knew the Glock Company, which was until recently mostly involved in cutlery. Headed by Gaston Glock, an independent engineer specializing in advanced plastics and metal technology for more than a quarter of a century, the firm has only 45 employees. It is located in Deutsches-Wagram in Austria.

The first significant commercial success of the Glock Company occurred in 1978 when its Field Knife 78 was adopted by the Austrian army, which placed orders for 150,000 pieces since then. About the same quantity was sold on the sporting market. Then, Gaston Glock designed, in connection with Dynamit Nobel, the German giant of chemical products, powders and ammunition, an extraordinary hand grenade made of plastics and bursting into 5,000 fragments.

In 1980, when Gaston Glock learned that the Austrian army contemplated replacing their old service pistols with a double-action model featuring a large magazine capacity, he immediately realized that the Steyr pistol could not be alone. He soon toured the competitors, asking for subcontracts as an industrial compensation, should a foreign product be selected.

Then, back in his facilities, he was amazed at the conventional technology on which most competitors relied and was soon analyzing the patents and consulting German-speaking experts about the requirements for a new design. He was not, himself, a firearms enthusiast, but five months later, still in 1980, he had developed a first prototype of the Glock 17 which was selected, late in 1983, as the service pistol of Austria. The Army's order is 25,000 units, 5,000 of them to be delivered in 1984.

The Glock 17 is a 9mm Luger short recoil-operated pistol on the Browning "High Power" principle as improved by SIG in their P-220, P-225 and P-226 models. Its capacity is 17 rounds. It is, regardless of operating principle, a most unusual gun.

The slide is a square-section extrusion accommodating a welded machined bolt which carries the striker and pivoted Walther-style extractor. The one-piece hammered barrel is of the linkless cam style, but the breech end is square and matches the inner slide square contour, which offers the centering function necessary for ensuring a high level of accuracy. This slide is 7 inches long and guided over an interrupted length of 5.19 inches by rails. The recoil spring unit is conventionally located under the barrel and the slide-barrel-recoil spring assembly weighs 16.8 ounces so as to dampen the recoil.

The receiver is an extremely light high-resistance casting of plastic material weighing only *5 ounces,* including the trigger mechanism. The receiver slide guides, insuring the sturdiness of the pistol over an expected 15,000-shot service life with NATO ammunition, are made of sheet-metal imbedded in the plastic.

The solid trigger guard is square for two-hand shooting and, as the pistol is striker fired, the trigger mechanism is entirely enclosed in the upper section of the receiver. Therefore, the grip, which only accommodates the magazine, is provided with an important hollow section at the rear and can be pitched as required, according to the customer's wishes.

The two-column staggered magazine is also a new design as it is entirely made of high resistance plastic material, with the exception of the spring and lips which are metalic. Thus it weighs only 1.43 ounces, empty, while accommodating nearly a half-pound load of service ammunition. The magazine catch is fitted at the rear of the lower branch of the trigger guard. The empty magazine lags a little and must sometimes be withdrawn by the weak hand, but this trait disappears when the gun has been broken in.

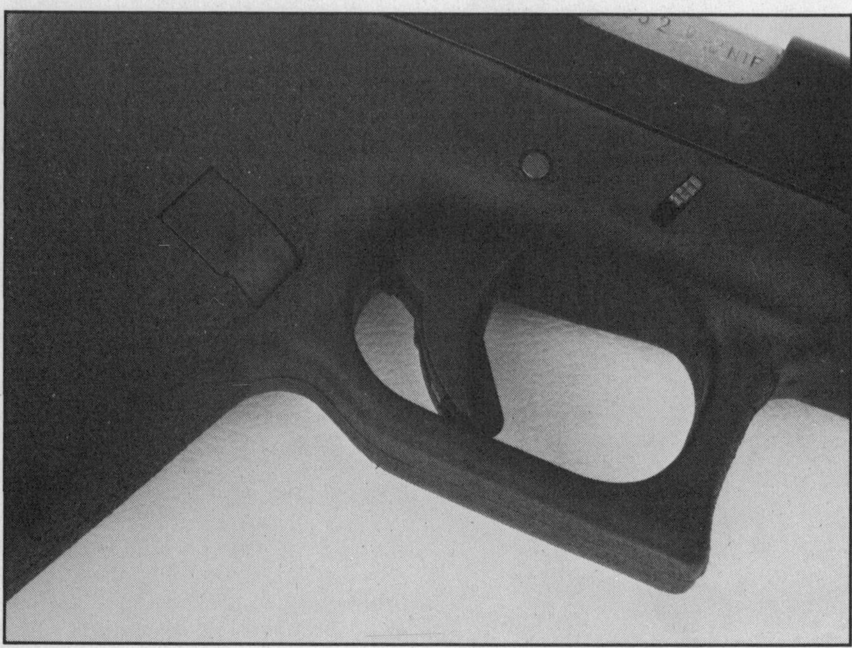

The automatic trigger safety of the Glock 17 is most efficient; it is also very simple.

While not new at all, as its principle was already used in the Austrian cavalry pistol model of 1907 (popularly known as the 8mm Roth-Steyr), the Glock's firing mechanism is the only "pre-cocked" design made today. Single-action pistols must be hand cocked for the first shot; those shooting only double-action require a long pull each shot; and those fitted with selective lockwork require two trigger-finger positions between the first and following shots. The Glock 17 firing mechanism requires a single trigger-finger position as all the shots are fired in a "semi-double-action" mode; the trigger pull equals that of a good service pistol. The trigger travel, while shorter than that of a typical double-action gun, is longer than that of a single-action pistol.

With the Glock 17, when chambering the first round, the striker is "precocked", i.e. it is retained at about half travel and the firing pin is partially compressed. The effort necessary for firing the chambered round is set at about five pounds instead of ten, as usually required in a genuine double action mechanism. The trigger travel is limited to .40-inch.

This facilitates the basic training, avoids the "breaking the glass" climax of single-action handguns and makes the pistol with a chambered round instantly available for action. In case of misfire, the slide must be withdrawn with the weak hand only .40-inch to get another striker blow.

Beside the "semi-double-action" firing mode for all shots, the Glock 17 pistol is fitted with a very clever automatic trigger safety lever consisting of a spring-loaded thin metal plate fitted along the vertical center line of the .27-inch thick plastic trigger. At rest, the safety lever protrudes in front and behind the trigger, its heel preventing any trigger motion until it is depressed. This is automatic when the finger pulls the trigger. Under this action, the front end of the safety lever swings backwards, retracting the upper rear section which normally bears against the receiver, jamming the trigger. The pressure required is very low and the operation seems highly reliable.

With its low and square slide fitted over its slim plastic receiver, the Glock 17 looks quite strange at first glance. The highly pitched grip is attractive. At first handling, one is astonished at its unusually low weight of 23.2 ounces. However, when the gun is loaded with 17 service rounds, its 31-oz. weight, while still very low, enables an excellent control in practical shooting.

The grip of the Glock 17 is perhaps the best of the market as it is suitable for every size of male or female hand, which is an exception to usual large capacity double-action pistols chambered for such a powerful ammunition. Moreover, the high pitch of this grip, combined with the "semi-double-action" feature, is excellent for instinctive shooting.

This grip is exceptionally flat despite the 17-shot magazine capacity (1.18-inch thick) and its sanded temperature-proof plastic surfaces afford a very pleasant contact to the shooting hand and are not slippery. Empty, the Glock is balanced above the front area of the trigger, but this point moves about half an inch backward when loaded with 17 rounds.

The gun has Patridge-type sights

and they are just 1.34-inch above the shooting hand. The rear sight notch contour is underlined in white while the ramp front sight features a $^1/_{10}$-inch white dot. They are better than the average for combat shooting and still good for slow fire.

A seasoned shooter using the Glock 17 for the first time will need some dry-firing to get used to the peculiar trigger pull. Nevertheless, the shooting technique is very simple; while raising the pistol and controlling your breathing, *briskly pull* the trigger over the first ⅞-in. until you feel a definitely stronger resistance and, then, carefully aim while pressing the last ⅛-in. of pull. Tyros will find this quite natural, as will double-action revolver shooters, but people used to conventional automatics may suffer at the beginning.

Computation shows a respectable recoil velocity (defining the pressure on the hand) of 10.55 feet per second, but the recoil actually felt seems lower and just a little more than that of a conventional 9mm Luger service pistol such as our old Beretta Brigadier.

In 25-meter slow fire, offhand, our scores were in the 250 out of 300 range at the I.S.U. big bore target featuring a 2-inch ten, which is standard performance for a service pistol, the best scoring slightly above 260 of 300 and the worst under 240 of 300. On a combat shooting course involving a long run over the 17-shot magazine string with stopping, turning and shooting on command, the Glock 17 was rated by this writer as very good, but his two partners, who normally shoot Star and Colt automatics, missed several times and were slower than usual.

In our sample, bearing a serial number in the 200's, we shot 364 rounds without cleaning that included 100 rounds of French service ammunition made in 1982; 64 very old French submachine gun rounds with hard primers; 50 new German Geco half-jacketed rounds; 50 commercial full jacketed Geco rounds; 50 commercial full jacketed Remington rounds; 50 reloads with jacketed bullets and French powder. The only malfunction was a misfire with the old submachine gun ammunition and some slide hesitation when chambering the first half-jacketed truncated Geco round from the magazine.

The Glock 17 is an original, inexpensive, compact, accurate and reliable service pistol featuring a clever but controversial construction leading one to think of it as the "Tokarev" of this turn of century. ●

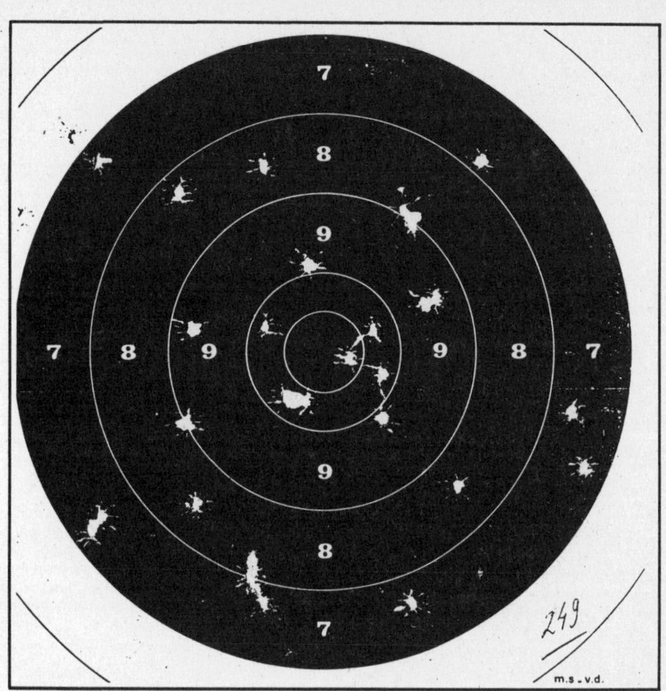

Thirty rounds offhand at 25 meters under I.S.U. slow fire conditions scored 249 out of 300; the 10-ring is two inches (5cm) wide.

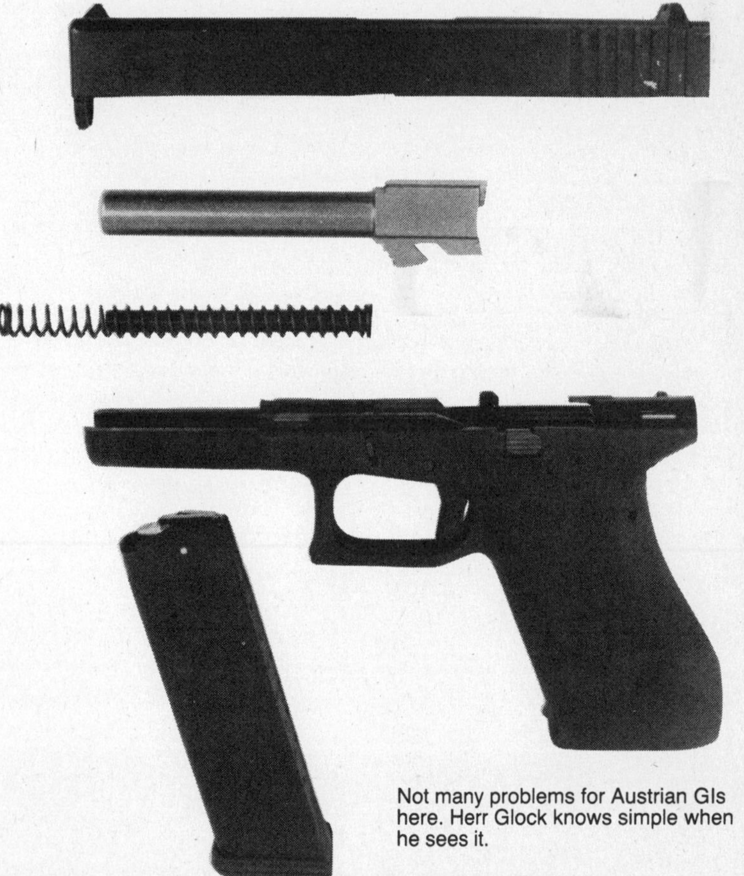

Not many problems for Austrian GIs here. Herr Glock knows simple when he sees it.

In white finish, the Korriphila shows Budischowsky's clean lines, original sighting. Grip frame—fore and aft—and trigger guard are grooved. Many details to order at $2000.00, delivered here.

Now you can get an all-new ALL-OUT

The black gun Cooper shot has controls differently situated, with one lever on the right side, but that doesn't cost extra—it's still $2000.00.

Photos: JEFF COOPER

AUTOLOADER

IN A simpler time, an armorer with an order for personal weapons measured his man and his man's pocketbook and straightforwardly hammered and clanged out the requisites. Everything was just about one-at-a-time anyway. Even the complication of gunpowder didn't change that for centuries. Indeed, 150 short years ago, that was how it was and therefore all those splendid cased pistols, Pennsyltucky rifles and long fowlers.

Here lately, however, anything really personal in a handgun—if it was to be up-to-date—meant the conversion, alteration and/or embellishment of some factory arm. That may be changing, and colleague Jeff Cooper rather likes the idea.

He certainly likes the Korriphila pistol, otherwise called HSP-701, as gotten up by Edgar Budischowsky in Heidelberg, West Germany. The Korriphila is a made-to-measure self-loading handgun built without regard to cost to be, to the limits of its maker's talents, as good as it can be.

According to Cooper's report of the two samples he tried—unfortunately neither made to Cooper measurements or requirements—the Korriphila is pretty good.

But first the options thus far known:

1. Choice of eight calibers, 45 ACP and 10mm down to 9mm Ultra.
2. Four- or six-in. barrel length.
3. Single-action only; double-action only; or selective for both.
4. Finish of choice—black or white.
5. Control levers, trigger, and the like sized to order, and placed (in the case of slide-stop and magazine release) where wished.
6. A normal list of sight and shape (square trigger guard? hook trigger guard?) options.

All except 38 Special and 9mm Ultra have Budischowsky's single-roller-delay blowback action. The barrel is rigid; the sights adjustable; the magazine a single-column affair.

"These pistols were each a pleasure," Cooper said. "The pulls were clean and sharp, the feel fine, the sights just right. In a 35-ounce gun, of course, the recoil was light."

Cooper has long felt eight shots upon command, as in the Model 1911 Colt, are enough and has no problem with the Korriphila's magazine capacity. (His exact words were: "If one cannot solve his immediate problem with six or eight well-placed shots, it is doubtful he can solve it with 10 or 12.") But he does think the gun a tad bulky. Cooper thinks nearly all the service pistols in the world are a little bulky, matter of fact, but has hopes that this design effort may one day provide all the gun he wants and less—that is, if enough cash customers bespeak Korriphilas, and enough of those want slimness with their quality, perhaps it will happen.

Yes, the HSP-701 is expensive. It is not anything like a shotgun one might order in London, which is a comparable undertaking. To get right to it: At this writing, a customer in the U.S. will pay $2000.00 for his Korriphila pistol. (He will talk, we're told, to International Gun Co., P. O. Box 35551, Tucson, AZ 85740.)

Among the Budischowsky design's real—if invisible—charms is the *idea* of it. There is no way Korriphila was meant for the military or for the police—it's for individuals. That's refreshing.

-Ken Warner

Are You Ready

Out of range, the range finder indicated 95 yards, but still some 10-gauge Magnum sky-scrapers shot at them. Their confidence was unjustified.

Ithaca's 10 Mag autoloader is one of the best Big 10s available. Ranging superiority, compared to the smaller bores, is actually about 10 yards, though.

It's more gun than most shooters can handle, and perhaps not as much gun as they need.

by FRANCIS E. SELL

For The BIG 10?

Before you answer that question, let's consider all the merits and limitations of this Big Bertha. Limitations it has, much beyond the limitations of the 12 or 20 gauge. Specialized it is, much beyond these smaller bores. The 10-gauge Magnum is not a gun for the average gunner, looking for a change from his 12-gauge wildfowling gun. There are grave gunning doubts about the practicability of the 11-pound 10-gauge Magnum, chambered for the 3½-inch shells, using 2 or 2¼ oz. shot charges, even for an expert wildfowling gunner.

To get all the gunning implications of the 10-gauge Magnum in perspective, let's go back to that golden age of wildfowling, when duck and geese reportedly darkened the skies. At that time, a lot of wildfowling guns were 10 gauges. Even the upland gunner might be found prowling the ruffed grouse cover with a 10-gauge side-by-side double in hand. These 10 gauges were chambered for 2⅞-inch shells, and threw upland shot charges of 1⅛ ounces.

William Bruce Leffingwell, in his 1888, reports on his favorite wildfowling gun—a side-by-side double, 10 gauge, 30-in. barrels choked full and full. The loading he reports shooting from this ten-pound double was 1 oz. Number 2 chilled shot. He said, *"It is a loading used by myself and companions while goose shooting for years, and there has never been any occasion to complain of the results, when geese are in distance, and the shooter holds right."*

One gunning factor stands out in Leffingwell's 10-gauge loading, a factor often forgotten when the average wildfowler is considering a 10-gauge Magnum as a cure-all for his missing on those high passes, Canada Honkers making the grey December skies alive with the haunting music of their calling. Recoil in a 10-pound gun, using 1 oz. of shot, is practically non-existent. There is no disruption of the swing as the second barrel is whipped in. To some extent this compensates for the slower handing qualities of a big gun, but not fully.

Ten to eleven-pound gun weight makes for deliberation. Nash Buckingham, with whom I used to have considerable correspondence, our mutual love of wildfowling triggering our discussion, used a fairly heavy gun—a 12-gauge Magnum double, chambered for the first Super-X loadings. The shot charge was $1\frac{3}{16}$ oz. of copper plated 4s—here again, a very light loading and consequent recoil, even though a quite heavy gun. But in his salad days, the great Nash Buckingham fought in the ring as a heavyweight, or light heavy, tipping the scales at 196 lbs. So . . .

In the modern 10-gauge Magnum, shooting a maximum charge of 2 oz. of shot, the recoil is rubbing 60 foot-pounds. It is well established that the average gunner cannot stand a recoil of more than 28 pounds in prolonged shooting. Accuracy suffers. After coaching any number of gunners, I would up this figure to around a recoil of 32-35 pounds, if a properly fitted gun is used, but no more. Sure, a gunner may go out on a pass, fire a half-dozen shots with a gun having a recoil of 45-60 pounds and have fair success, if he is an expert wing shot, but he'll never get used to that second barrel.

The 10-gauge Ithaca Magnum autoloader tames the recoil somewhat. Despite all the advertising purple prose, this gun still has plenty of kick. No one has repealed Newton's dynamic law that says there is an equal reaction for every action. This autoloader spreads the recoil over a slightly longer time period, but it still has plenty of kick.

All this doesn't do away with the slowness of the 11-lb. gun. I recall one member of the local Bandtail Pigeon Shooting Club who decided that he needed the extra reach of a 10-gauge Magnum for those high flying bandtails. He showed up with a 10-gauge Magnum Ithaca autoloader. He shot it a few days, then I noticed he was back toeing the line with his 12-gauge Ithaca, a standard pump gun.

About the only superiority the 10-gauge Magnum can claim is that of extra ranging. I have developed 80-

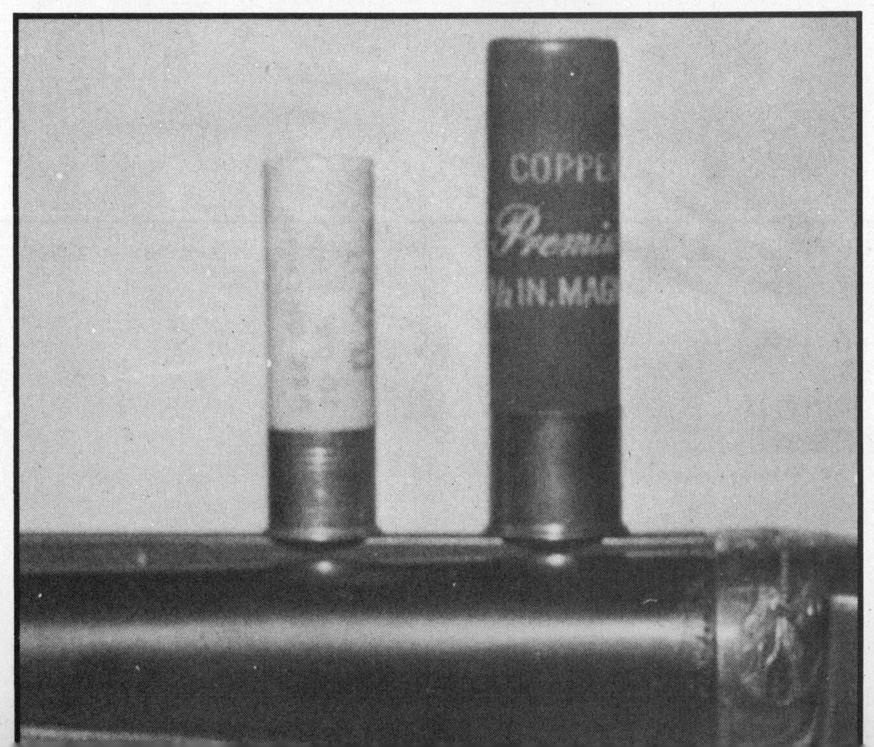

Two shells: 20-gauge 3-inch Magnum loaded with 1¼ oz. of shot, and a factory 10-gauge Magnum loaded with 2 oz. of shot—size 2. The difference downrange is not as big as it looks here.

yard loads, using 2 oz. of 2s, copper plated shot. But it is not an easy gauge to reload.

I found that it responded best to my own interior barrel work, and it was very sensitive to the matter of choke constriction. This is, of course, another way of saying to actual shot charge velocity. I found that size 2 shot, the best choice from the standpoint of pattern density and individual pellet energy, required a muzzle velocity of around 1150 ft. second.

All this complemented long 1½-inch forcing cones, and choke cones of the same length, with choke parallels long enough to contain the entire length of the shot charge, once it passed the choke cones. I gave the barrel a high polish and reduced the choke constriction from the usual .045-in. to .040-in. The Richland 10-gauge Magnum double carried my design work.

I had no problem in getting 90 percent 40-yard patterns, nor in putting 50-55 size 2 pellets in a 30-inch circle at 80 yards. By the same token, I found it no problem to develop a long range handload for the 20-gauge Magnum, chambered for 3-inch shells and carrying my barrel specification. I managed 95% with 1¼ oz. of shot at 40 yards. This loading averaged 50 size 2 shot in a 30-inch circle at 80 yards. With these loads, I never found more than a 5 pellet difference in favor of the 10-gauge Magnum at this extreme range. With regular handloads, the difference is greater, especially compared with the lighter shot charges in the smaller bores.

The actual difference in ranging between one and two ounces of shot is 29%, disregarding a very small fraction. If you have two ounces reaching 80 yards, the same patterning ability from a smaller gauge would take one ounce to disregard the individual pellet energy. Using regular 1¼-oz. factory loads in a 12 or 20 gauge, and the two-ounce 10-gauge Magnum loads, you have only about 17 yards difference in ranging. There is no trouble in reaching 63 yards with top grade factory loads, such as Federal Premiums in 12- and 20-gauge Magnum.

Reduce gun weight and gun pointing accuracy increases, provided recoil is kept within acceptable limits—which is another way of saying that you must reduce shot charges. With just about any ballistic yardstick of measurement, the only possible effective 10-gauge Magnum yardage increase is from 70 to 80 yards—and you have to be mighty charitable to concede even this yardage—30 feet, no more!

What I have said of the 20-gauge Magnum in comparison with the 10-gauge Magnum can, with a few qualifications, be said of the 12 gauge chambered for 2¾-inch shells. I have gotten over 90% patterns with the 12 gauge. Tom Roster, whom I consider a very knowledgeable shotgun ballistician, reported 95%+ patterns with his 12-gauge Remington Model 1100—a gun for which I worked out the barrel interior dimensions, forcing cone and choke constriction with sizes 2 and 4 shot in mind.

Lord Walsingham, an English gunning great of another age, who killed 1000 birds in a day's shooting on driven birds, was asked about his lead on game. He explained in just two words, "Don't check."

The 10-gauge Magnum, due to its weight, has a built-in check. You have to use the so-called sustained lead, which has two impossible requirements. You must hold for the *exact range*, and for the *exact speed*.

Afield the 10-gauge Magnum confirmed this in detail. I used it as an experiment gunning mudhen, where I could see the resulting pattern on the water when I shot at these low flying birds, usually well behind the bird I shot at. Pulling this Big Bertha down out of recoil made for an extremely slow second shot.

Jack Morgan's experience when he took over the 10-gauge Magnum paralleled mine. I put a flock of bluebills across in front of him—one of the few times when actual speed and apparent speed is the same. He managed to

With his beloved Big 20s and a lifetime of acquired skill and judgment, Sell does OK in the real world of real geese on pass.

dump with the first barrel at about 65 yards range—no second barrel due to the heavy recoil. When I congratulated Jack on an excellent shot, he told me the bird he dropped was two birds behind the one he shot at.

On another occasion, while gunning on Lower Klamath Lake in California, a gunner walking along a dike rushed into my blind—an appreciated gesture as about 200 pintails were coming over. I looked at them, but didn't pick up my gun—too high. He asked if he might shoot? I nodded. He brought up his 10-gauge Magnum double Neuman, tracked them and touched off the shot. Not even a feather. I guessed the range around 95 yards.

It seems 10-gauge Magnum gunners are more often "skyscrapers" than gunners using lesser gauges. This, I feel, is because they have exaggerated ideas about the actual reach of those 2-2¼-oz. shot charges.

Les Bowman once told me about trying to gun geese on a lake in Colorado. They were coming out of the game reserve 100-150 yards high. He said the 10-gauge Magnum, loaded with buckshot, was standard for the gunning. He devoted his time to counting the number of shots fired and the number of geese brought down. It checked out at 100 shots for each goose downed. No flocks came over that didn't get a salute from some of these 10-gauge Magnum gunners. With those shells retailing at about $20 a box then, a goose dinner ran into money.

These are, from left: nickel-plated, copper-plated, black shot, steel shot, all size 2. These, and 3s and 2s, are the only sizes a Big 10 should shoot. Number 2 steel shot, due to its poor ballistic performance, cuts the range to 40-45 yards, regardless of the gauge or load.

You can get long range performance in a gun weight compatible with (from left) 1⅛ oz., size 7½ shot and 1¼ oz. size 6, a good load over decoys; the 1½-oz. charges of 4s or 2s can take you way out there.

The 10-gauge Magnum was on the way out of the gunning picture before the advent of steel shot which is supposed to have given it a new lease on life. I think the new lease is not a definite ballistic reprieve.

When steel shot was first required for gunning on some of the flightways, I had an assignment to test it afield. Mossberg supplied one of their splendid Model 500 pump guns in 12 gauge, with four barrels. Federal Cartridge Corporation supplied me with a mixed case of steel shotshells. Bruce Hodgdon supplied me with ten pounds of size 2 steel shot.

To make a short report even shorter, I found steel shot giving less than 50% clean kills at ranges over 40-45 yards. Shooting over the same set of decoys and using Federal lead shot loads, I got better than 95% kills at these ranges and on out to 60 yards.

Steel shot cancelled out the range bracket where the 10-gauge Magnum turned in its best performance. Matter of fact, the use of steel shot in any shotgun reduces the range to about that of all shotguns before the discovery of choke boring.

So I doubt if steel shot, or anything else will make the 10-gauge Magnum a commonly used shotgun in the marshes and on the passes. It bucks a 100-year trend toward lighter guns and smaller gauges.

To answer the question with which I started this perambulation—You ready for a 10-gauge Magnum? The answer is a resounding "No." ●

Sell's personal Big 10 is a double at 11 pounds. It reaches 80 yards on geese, but not a bit more.

HANDGUNS TODAY: AUTOLOADERS

by J. B. WOOD

ON JANUARY 14th, 1985, the U.S. Army gave us the answer to the Big Question: The new 9mm sidearm for all U.S. Military Services will be a Beretta. The original Beretta entry was called the Model 92S-1, and the same design became, commercially, the Model 92SB. The new military pistol is the Model 92SB-F, a modification of the Model 92SB that has a matte finish, a concave-front trigger guard with checkering, and a flared magazine entry, among other good features.

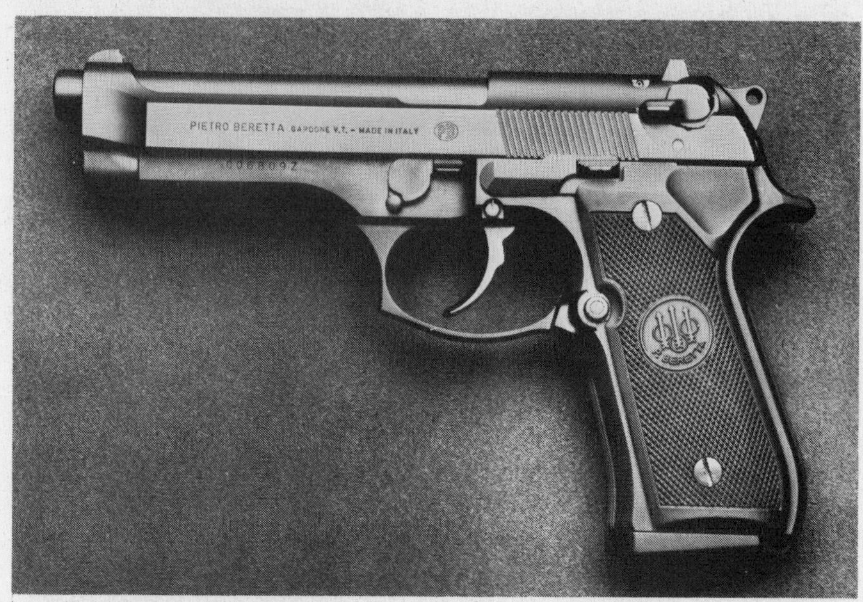

(Above) The Army picked this 9mm from all the rest. Beretta 92SB-F has 15-round magazine, all the trimmings.

According to the terms of the five-year contract, production for the first year will be in Italy. During the second year, parts from Italy will be assembled at the Beretta facility in Accokeek, Maryland. In the final three years, the entire pistols will be made in Maryland. There were several fine pistols in the competition, but the Army chose well. The Model 92SB-F is also available to civilian shooters.

Meanwhile, in the year past, other makers have introduced new models, and variations of current models. In the "new" category, **Sturm, Ruger & Co.** finalized the design of their long-awaited 9mm double action pistol, their first centerfire automatic. A photo of the new Ruger P-85 was initially supplied to firearms editors, but significant changes in the final design made the original photo obsolete. It's safe to say, though, the pistol will have an ambidextrous firing pin blocking safety and a double-column large-capacity magazine, among other features.

This is how the newest GI pistol looks undressed for cleaning. Yep, that's 16 rounds standing there.

Close on the heels of their Series 80 and Combat Grade versions of the Government Model, **Colt** introduced two more new items—a standard Mark IV Series 80 pistol in stainless steel, and a reduced-size pistol in matte blue or satin nickel, the Officer's ACP. Both new guns have high-profile front and rear sights in blue finish, and the Officer's ACP has a quick-pickup three-dot sighting system. The neat little Government Model 380, previously available in blue or satin nickel, is now offered in bright nickel as well.

This is the new 9mm auto pistol by Korth of West Germany. This is serial number 005, in fact.

At **Smith & Wesson,** the beginning of regular production of the new 45

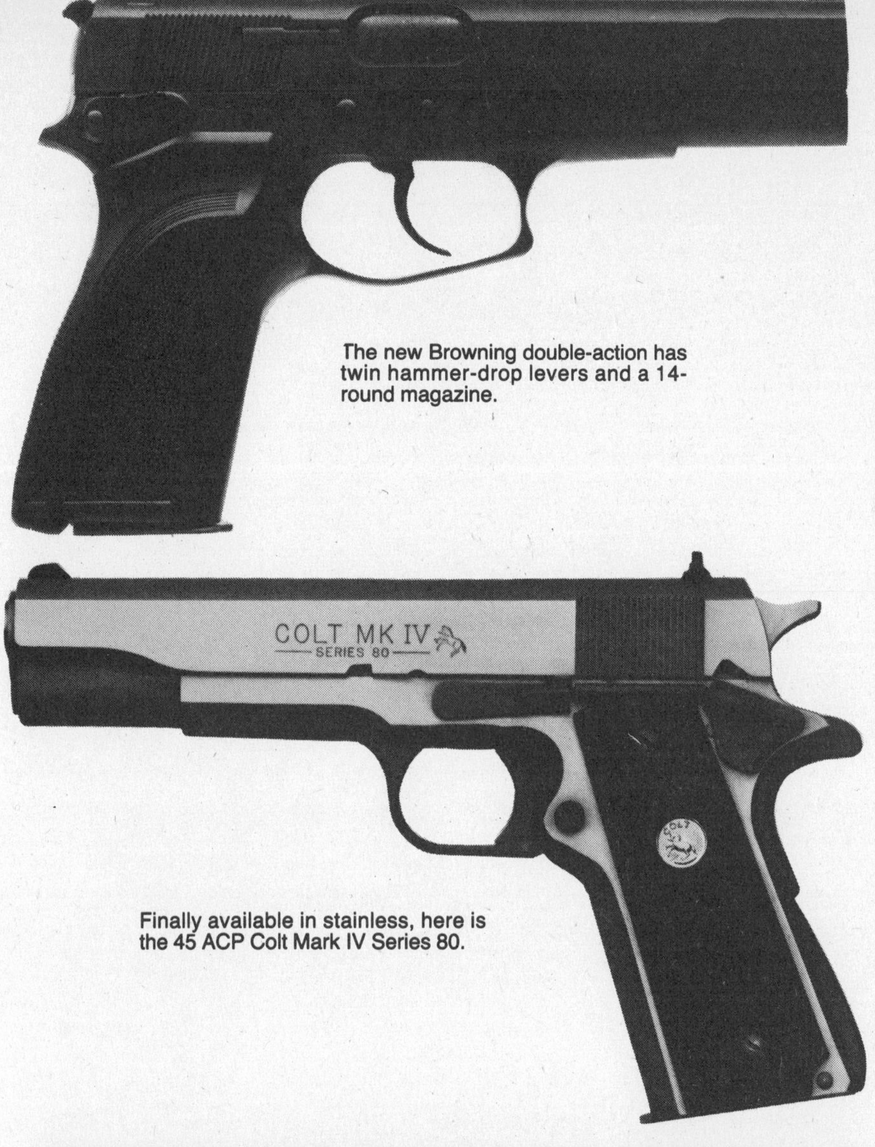

The new Browning double-action has twin hammer-drop levers and a 14-round magazine.

Finally available in stainless, here is the 45 ACP Colt Mark IV Series 80.

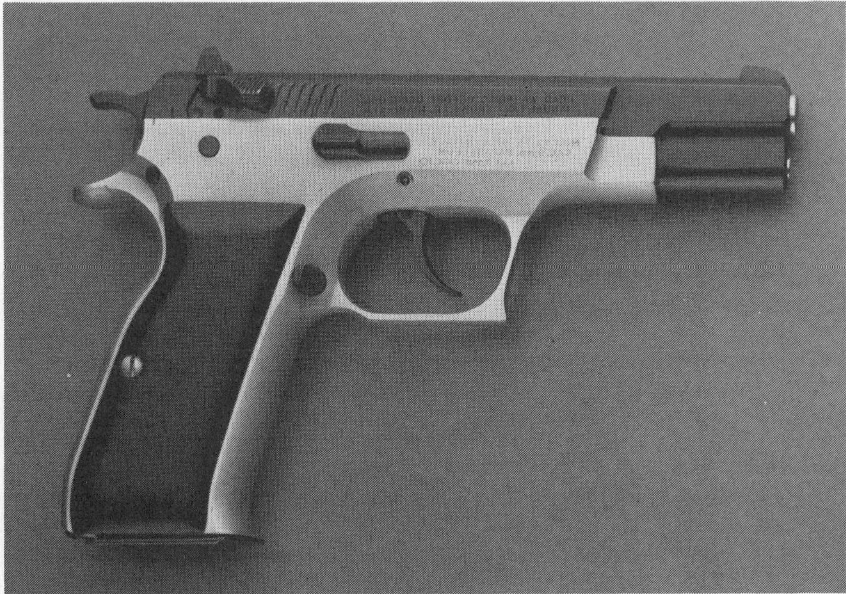

The new two-tone version of the TZ-75 from F.I.E. has the frame finished in satin hard chrome.

Auto, the Model 645, has taken a little longer than originally expected. Assuming that you're reading this in late 1985, the handsome stainless-steel double action 45 should now be generally available. For those who joined us late, the Model 645 has an external resemblance to the original Model 59. It is 8.7 inches long, with a 5-in. barrel, and weighs 36 ounces. The magazine capacity is 8 rounds.

Of the three new **Charter Arms** pistols from Erma Werke in West Germany, the first to be available in quantity was the fine little stainless steel 380 double action, the Model 79K. A blued-steel 22 LR version of the same pistol, the Model 40, was expected by late summer of 1985, and toward the end of the year the 22 LR target pistol, the Model 42, was coming. I haven't fired the 380 yet, but I've examined a sample gun, and it's nicely made. Among its good features is an automatic firing pin block safety that is cleared with the last fraction of trigger movement.

Now that **Arminex, Ltd.** has the Trifire pistol in full production, the company is concentrating on making the gun live up to its name. By the time you're reading this, the conversion units will be available, and Trifire owners can change their pistols to fire 38 Super or 9mm Parabellum by switching a few internal parts. And the Research and Development department has not been idle. Another Arminex pistol is coming, and it will resemble Trifire only in its high quality. It will be a small personal protection piece, and the name is already selected: Sleeping Beauty.

At **Heckler & Koch,** the renowned P7 has developed into a growing "family" of pistols. The P7M8, sidearm of the New Jersey State Police, is now available commercially. It differs from the standard P7 in having an ambidextrous magazine release, a heat-shielded trigger, and improved combat-style sights. The P7M13 has the same features, with a double-column 13-round magazine. There has been speculation about a P7 in 45 Auto chambering, but so far there's no official word on this. Prototypes have been made, but at this point a big-bore P7 is still in the experimental stages.

One of my favorite 9mm pistols, the **Star** Model 28, has been made obsolete by a new offering from **Interarms,** the Star Model 30PK. This is the basic Model 28 shortened, with an alloy frame, modified safety levers, and a few other small differences. It weighs just 30 ounces. If you want the new features along with the size and weight of the Model 28, there's the Model 30M, which has a steel frame. For those who want similar features in a larger caliber, Interarms has the Astra A-80 in 45 Auto, with a nine-round magazine. Also available in 38 Super and 9mm Parabellum (with 15-round magazines), the A-80 is now offered in blue or satin chrome.

The big news from **Browning** is the introduction of the new 9mm double action pistol. In weight and dimensions, it is exactly the same as the venerable Hi-Power, but there the resemblance ends. The new DA has an automatic firing pin block safety and twin decocking levers that will safely lower the hammer from full cock. The wrap-around nylon grips have extensive moulded checkering, and the magazine holds 14 rounds. The finish is a dark Parkerizing non-reflective, and the front of the trigger guard has a concave surface.

Last year, there was some speculation that the classic single action Hi-Power would be discontinued when the new DA pistol arrived. This didn't happen. Not only is the standard Hi-Power still available, but a new version is being offered. Priced around $55 less than the standard blued pistol, it has the same tough Parkerized finish as the DA, and the grip panels are of black nylon.

Another new offering from Browning is the Buck Mark 22. It has grips of the same material as the centerfire pistols described above, Polyamide, a glass-impregnated nylon, and they feature moulded skip-line checkering. The new Buck Mark 22 has the bull barrel of the Challenger III, and a similar shape, but there are mechanical differences—a push-button magazine release, for example. And it sells for around $45 less than the Challenger III.

The **SIG/Sauer** line of fine Swiss/German pistols, formerly handled by Interarms, is now imported exclusively by **Sigarms, Incorporated.** The most recent addition to the SIG/Sauer group is an all-stainless version of the Model P230, designated the Model P230SL. With its stainless frame, it is very slightly heavier than the standard alloy-frame P230, and it has different slide serrations. Otherwise, it is the same as the standard blued/alloy pistol. The P230 is a gun that I carry and use often, and I'm pleased that it's now available in stainless.

After making a certain number of their original 357 Magnum pistols as a "test run," **Coonan Arms** has now settled on a design for regular produc-

J. B. Wood firing the Grizzly 45 Winchester Magnum pistol. This photo was made just after the last round went downrange.

The stainless steel Smith & Wesson Model 645, their first pistol in 45 Auto chambering.

The Star Model 30PK is a lighter and shorter version of the famed Model 28, with an alloy frame and a redesigned safety lever.

Finally in full production, the tiny 22 LR stainless steel DA from Pittsburgh will also have a counterpart in 25 Auto.

The nicely-made Bersa Model 223 in 22 LR, imported from Argentina by Outdoor Sports Headquarters. It's all-steel.

Erma design, Charter quality: The 380 Model 79K in stainless steel and double action.

The new Coonan Model B in 357 Magnum is somewhat different from the early guns.

tion, and they call it the Model B. It has more grip safety extension at upper rear than the earlier guns, and the safety lever and slide latch are both extended over the top of the left grip panel. The main components, with the exception of the barrel, are stainless steel. There will be two options—an adjustable rear sight, and a conversion unit that will allow the use of 38 Special cartridges.

Meanwhile, there's another 357 Magnum pistol that is already available in good quantity, the Israel-made **Desert Eagle,** imported by **Magnum Research, Incorporated.** While the Coonan uses the classic Browning falling-barrel locking system, the Desert Eagle system is closer to the type used in semi-auto rifles. It has a four-lug rotating bolt in the slide, a gas-powered unlocking arrangement, and a fixed barrel. I recently test-fired a Desert Eagle, and it was reliable and accurate. A 44 Magnum version is in the works, they say.

While we're in the magnum category, we shouldn't overlook the **Grizzly,** in current production and chambered for the 45 Winchester Magnum cartridge. I have one of these, and it's the most accurate 45-caliber automatic I have ever fired. I've also used it frequently with a conversion unit installed, firing the 9mm Winchester Magnum, a round that is now to be commercially available. Speaking of the 45 Winchester Magnum round, **Wildey Moore** is working on a new pistol design in this chambering that is entirely unlike his earlier gun. It has an external resemblance to the old Auto Mag, but is not like it internally. I have fired one of the two prototypes, and it works beautifully.

There is a new class of semi-auto handguns that has come to be known as "Assault Pistols," a category that includes such large-frame and large-capacity guns as the **Wilkinson Linda** and the **Interdynamic KG-99** (the latter is now the Intratec TEC-9). There are two new assault pistols that I have seen and examined, and one of these I have been trying over the past few weeks on my own range. It is the **Holmes MP-83,** and my sample gun is in 9mm Parabellum. It is also available in 45 Auto, and can be converted by just changing the barrel, breech block, and magazine.

The MP-83 weighs 56 ounces, is 14½ inches long, and has a six-inch barrel. The magazine capacity is 16 or 32 rounds in 9mm, and 10 or 20 rounds in 45 Auto. The construction is all steel, with grip piece and barrel sleeve in walnut. A 22 Long Rifle ver-

Pachmayr's single shot Dominator works on top of a M1911 frame in 223, 44 Magnum, 308 Winchester and 7mm Remington BR.

The Göncz is offered in choice of 45 Auto, 9mm Parabellum, and 30 Mauser.

The Holmes MP-83 in 9mm Parabellum is one of the new assault pistols.

This is the MP-22, a lightweight version of the Holmes MP-83 in 22 LR chambering.

sion, the MP-22, has an aluminum alloy frame, and it is 16 ounces lighter. The 9mm MP-83 that I fired performed flawlessly. It should be noted that the pistol shown is a very early production piece, and there are a few small differences in the current guns. The trigger, for example, has been redesigned to enclose the trigger bar and spring.

The other new assault pistol is the **Göncz,** and it is offered in four chamberings—9mm Parabellum, 45 Auto, 38 Super, and 30 Mauser. It has a through-the-grip magazine arrangement, with capacities of 18 or 32 rounds in the smaller calibers, and 10 or 20 rounds in 45 Auto. Barrel lengths are 5, 10, and 16 inches, and with the ten-inch barrel the weight of the pistol is 3.8 pounds. I haven't fired the Göncz yet, but it is a well-made and nicely-balanced gun.

While Interarms is the importer of the fine medium-frame and target pistols of **Vincenzo Bernardelli,** the new large-frame 9mm Parabellum pistol will be handled in the U.S. by **Armes de Chasse.** There are now three versions of the Bernardelli P018: A full-sized gun in blue with walnut grips, a full-sized Parkerized gun with plastic grips, and a reduced-size Compact version with walnut grips. The P018 is made entirely of milled steel. It has a double-action firing system, an automatic firing pin block safety, and a manual safety that blocks the hammer, slide, and trigger system. The rear sight is horizontally adjustable. The magazine of the standard pistol holds 15 rounds, and the Compact holds one round less. The P018 is supplied in a special formed case with a combination lock and handle, and comes with a spare magazine.

The well-made **Bersa** automatic from Argentina is now being handled in the U.S. by **Outdoor Sports Headquarters,** and the pistol has been slightly re-designed. A different and fully-enclosed takedown system is being used, and the front of the frame and slide now have cleaner lines. In the original single-action gun, a 380 and three 22 versions are offered. Just before writing this report, I had an opportunity to fire the new double-action Model 223 in 22 Long Rifle, and the impressions were all very favorable. This all-steel gun has every modern feature, and the price is amazingly low.

F. I. E. Corporation has announced two new versions of their excellent TZ-75, the Italian-made copy of the legendary CZ75: A "two-tone" gun in blue and satin chrome, and a pistol done entirely in satin hard-chrome. I've been shooting a standard blued version of the TZ-75 for quite a while, and actually, I prefer it to the expensive and hard-to-get Czech pistol. One feature that I especially like is the slide-mounted firing pin block safety.

At the 1985 SHOT Show, **Iver Johnson** displayed a double-action 9mm Parabellum pistol that is barely larger than their diminutive 380 Pony. The new gun is 6¼ inches long, 4.6 inches in height, and just ⅞ of an inch in width. It weighs about 30 ounces, and the magazine capacity is six rounds. It will initially be offered in blue only, and availability was projected for late 1985. The first small double-action 9mm, the all-stainless **Detonics** Pocket Nine, has been so well-received that the company has had to concentrate on its production, and this has pushed their new large-frame double-action pistol into late 1986.

The **Manurhin** company of France made 22, 32, and 380-cal. pistols for Walther for nearly forty years, and now they are marketing the same guns in the U.S. under their own name. Their version of the PPK/S is now available in Durgarde finish, a satin hard-chrome. I have a 22 Manurhin Model PP, and while the gun has the Manurhin "wheel" instead of the Walther "banner" on the slide, its quality and performance are the same in every way.

Since changing from an "airgun only" company to one handling all types of guns, **Beeman Precision Arms** has become the principal importer of serious target pistols. These include the elegant Agner M-80 from Denmark, the FAS in several models from Italy, and the French Unique Model 823-U. Of these pistols, the Agner M-80 is the one I have fired, and this stainless steel pistol is superb. The FAS Model 603 is a new centerfire, chambered for the 32 S&W Long wadcutter round. The Unique 823-U is designed for 22 Short rapid-fire competition, and the trigger pull can be adjusted as light as eight ounces.

Among the small 22 and 25 pocket pistols, there are two items of good news: At **Steel City Arms,** Chuck Bailey's little stainless 22LR "Double Deuce" finally rolled into full production, and **Precision Small Parts** announced their PSP-25/22, convertible to fire either 25 Auto or 22 Short. The Double Deuce looks very much like a stainless steel Walther TPH, and has similar features, but it is mechanically different. It has, for example, an ambidextrous firing pin block safety system. Originally designed for the 22 Long Rifle cartridge, the pistol will also be offered in 25 Auto. By the end of 1985, Steel City Arms will have an even more ambitious project under way—their War Eagle, a pistol very similar to the little gun, but about one-third larger, and chambered for the 9mm Parabellum round.

The new Seecamp 32 Auto is the size of the 25. One difference: there's a stop pad on the trigger.

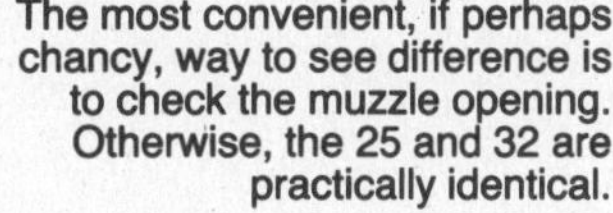

The most convenient, if perhaps chancy, way to see difference is to check the muzzle opening. Otherwise, the 25 and 32 are practically identical.

The PSP-25/22 will have a familiar look, because it is essentially the old Browning/FN Baby, the same pistol currently made in stainless steel and 25 Auto chambering by Fraser Firearms. The PSP version is in regular blued steel, and the thing that makes it special is its easy conversion to either 25 Auto or 22 Short. This is accomplished by changing only the barrel, firing pin, and magazine. The magazine capacity is six rounds in 25 Auto, and seven in 22 Short. The overall length is four inches, and the weight is 9½ ounces.

The last new-gun item in this report is one that I'm particularly pleased to announce: **Larry Seecamp's** tiny double-action 32 Auto has arrived. In a side view, at a glance, it's difficult to distinguish it from the 25 Auto version, as they are practically identical, and they're exactly the same size! I can see only two mechanical differences: The larger recoil spring has no separate guide, and there is a stop stud on the back of the trigger. The gun was specifically designed to use the 32 Winchester Silvertip cartridge, and the magazine holds six rounds. This pistol has caused me to put away my regular carrying-piece—which was, of course, a Seecamp 25 Auto.

The year past saw the end of the High Standard company, and their dependable line of 22 handguns will be missed. Lone Star Arms of Texas had planned to make a copy of the Browning/FN Model 1910 pistol, but in recent months I have been unable to contact the company. On the other hand, there are several pistols so new that right now we know them only from descriptions and photographs. One of these is the Korriphila HSP701, made in West Germany. (See article, p. 172) Another from West Germany is by a maker previously known for an outstanding revolver, Korth. In self-loaders, there's always something new. ●

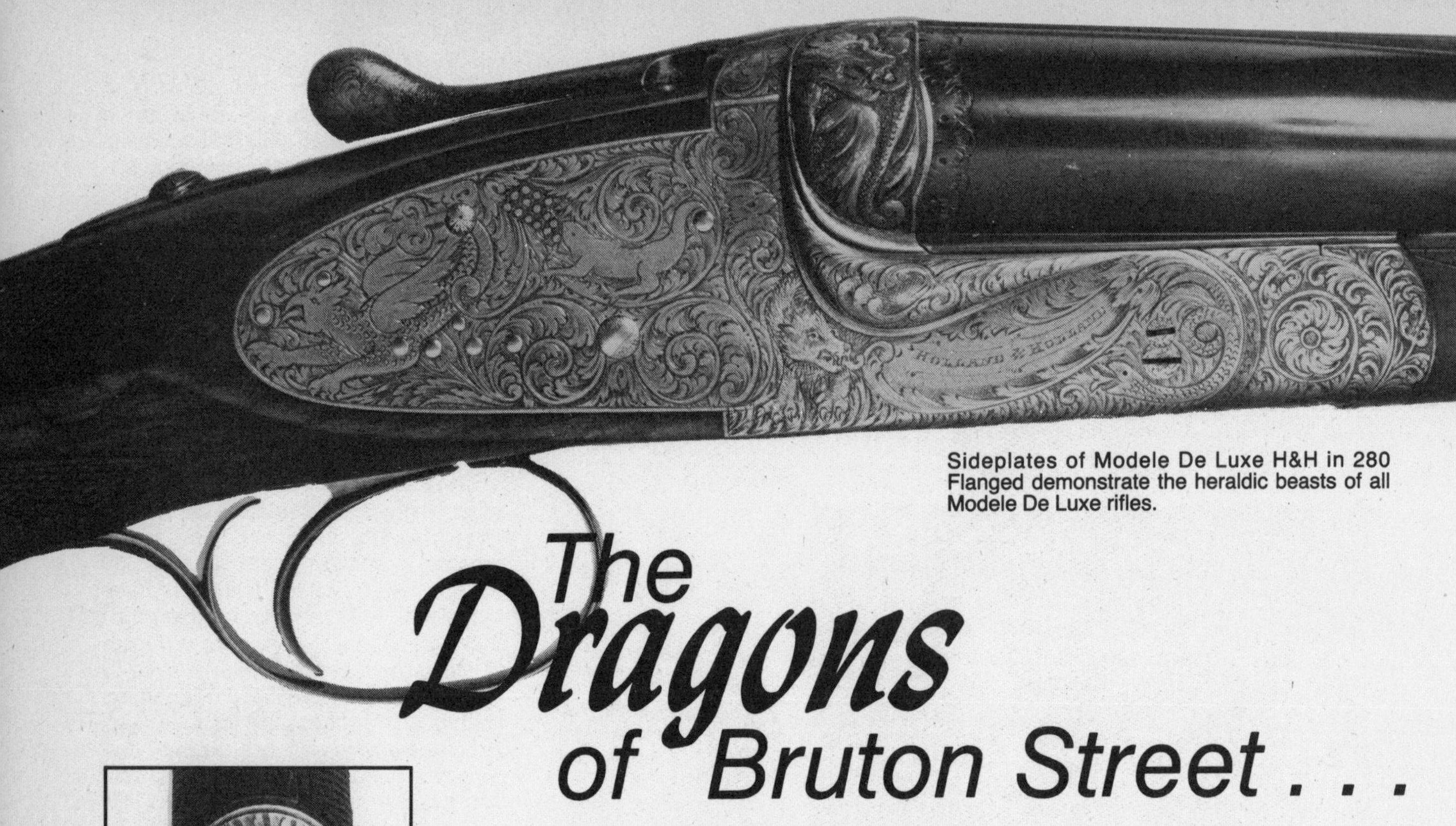

Sideplates of Modele De Luxe H&H in 280 Flanged demonstrate the heraldic beasts of all Modele De Luxe rifles.

The Dragons of Bruton Street . . .

the special stuff of Holland & Holland

Grip cap creature lugubriously surveys an apparently unkind world.

by James W. Williams

DRAGONS, gargoyles, imps and demons—have you ever seen this kind of engraving on a gun? It is the least known and the most interesting form I have found in years of gun collecting. Quite a few years ago I purchased a 375 Holland Modele DeLuxe double rifle and found dragons and griffons on the sidelocks and the action. They were certainly startling after the usual scrolls and rosettes. Peculiarly, this style of engraving was standard on all Holland & Holland Modele DeLuxe double rifles.

I discovered this was traditional when in 1961 I ordered a Modele DeLuxe 577 Nitro double rifle—which finally arrived from England in 1964. The wait was well worth it, and, fondling my new treasure, I saw my old friends the dragons and griffons cavorting on their fields of honor. *Dramatic* is the only way to describe their appearance. Though basically the same as that on the 375, this engraving was a tad different than other specimens of Holland's special rifles. It was more delicate and artistic and the case hardening on the action showed much finer colors.

I vowed I would set out at once to investigate the history of these mythological figures and discover why Holland had this type of work done on their guns, but as happens with good resolutions, I was too busy. Then in 1972, we paid a visit to England, and there I was on the spot with plenty of time to find answers to my questions.

First things first. I paid a visit to Holland & Holland's showroom at 13 Bruton Street in London. Their Mr. C. Keates very courteously gave me all the data they had. It seems that only one workman at Holland's ever did this type of engraving. The gentleman was almost 90 and no longer cut this intricate engraving. He was still engraving for them, but not the mythological themes. Nor was anyone interested in apprenticing to learn his skills. One of his last jobs of this type was done in 1965. Mr. Keates mentioned that the figures depicted in this engraving were peculiar to British heraldry.

This opened up a new avenue of research. I proceeded to study heraldry, discovering the number of sources were staggering. One book lead to another and another, but the most fascinating was John Vinycomb's *Fictitious and Symbolic Creatures in Art with Special Reference to Their Use in British Heraldry*. The author's data was as comprehensive as his title.

The material read like science fiction. The dragon is the number one creature in all forms of heraldry, not just the British. Before the dawn of civilization in Europe, in the legendary lands of Marco Polo, China and Japan, the dragon appeared and, surprisingly, in much the same form as that in British heraldry. Looking at the widespread belief in dragons, there may be some truth that the myth of today is a traditional successor of a once-existent animal. Men like to be frightened as long as they

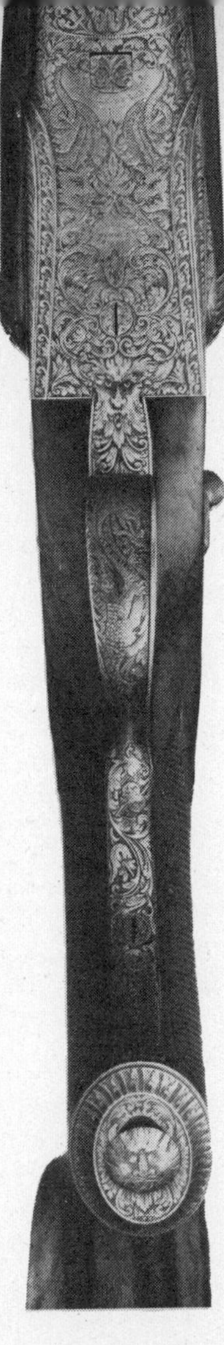

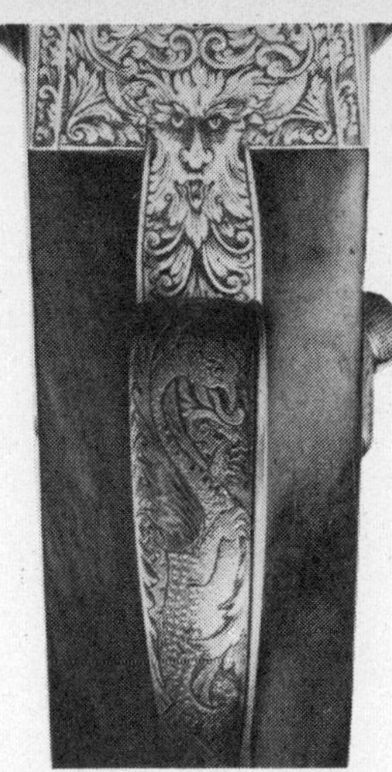

This is the special dragon of the trigger guard of the 280 Flanged shown opposite.

The captioner sees three faces on this action bottom. Perhaps there are more.

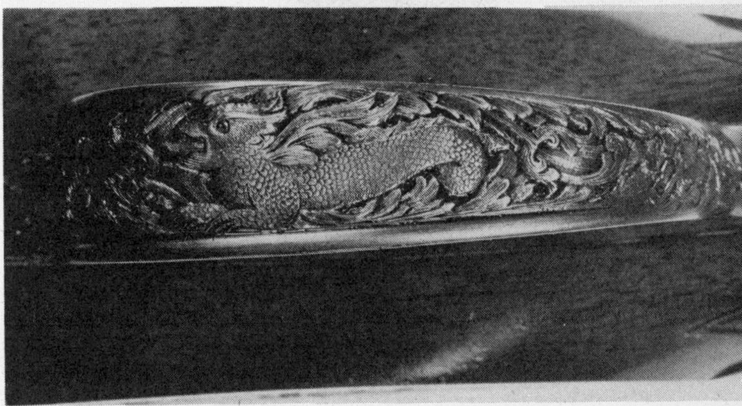

Another Modele De Luxe trigger guard has a deeply chiseled scaled dragon.

are safe and the dragon fills a real need in this respect. King Arthur's father was the great Pendragon of legend, and as we all know, was famous for his strength, courage, and wisdom. The Loch Ness monster in story or unfocussed picture takes the form of a dragon. St. George, patron saint of England, is a subject occurring frequently in both literature and art. The folklore of the dragon is endless.

How does this relate to guns? The British Dragoons and the American Dragoons owe their names to the fearsome dragon. I found that our Colt Dragoon pistols were also named for this beast. I wondered what the connection was. Apparently, with the introduction of firearms, a blunderbuss was issued to the troops. Because the weapon spouted fire like that fabulous beast, the troops were called "Dragoniers." These weapons also carried the mark of the beast: the head of a dragon was engraved on each musket.

The griffon, a chimerical monster, is not as fearsome as the dragon but was very important in British heraldry. It is one of the principal images in heraldry, either charged upon the knight's shield, or emblazoned as the crest upon the helm. It is also embossed on the supporters to the shield of arms of many noble and eminent families. The griffon combines the bodily attributes of the eagle and the lion. Old heralds gravely relate that when he attains his full growth he will never be taken; hence, he is a fit emblem of the valiant hero who, rather than yield himself to his enemy, exposes himself to the worst of dangers. As a symbol of heraldry, the griffon expresses both strength and vigilance to its bearers.

The mythical serpent is less seen in British heraldry and engraving than in that of other countries. Contrary to popular belief, the serpent is a symbol of wisdom, not evil. Aesculapius, son of Apollo, god of medicine, assumed the form of a serpent when he appeared in Rome during a seige of pestilence. Therefore, he is always shown with his staff entwined by a serpent, symbol of healing. Hippocrates, father of medicine, delivered Athens from a dreadful plague at the beginning of the Peloponnesian War and was publically rewarded with a golden crown. Hippocrates, too, is shown with the symbol of healing, the caduceus. Serpents were engraved on a gun attributed to Holland & Holland, a Modele De Luxe 318 Westley Richards caliber rifle made for the Maharaja of Bharwani. Both action and sidelocks were engraved with serpents.

It seemed strange to me that Holland & Holland, one of the most conservative of British gunmakers, would commission such exotic engraving. However, this very uniqueness and high quality of workmanship won for them a special award at Liege, Belgium, during the arms exposition, Grand Prix Paris 1900. Grotesque, baroque, medieval engraving earned them international recognition. This engraving is one hallmark of these gunmakers to a succession of princes and kings. ●

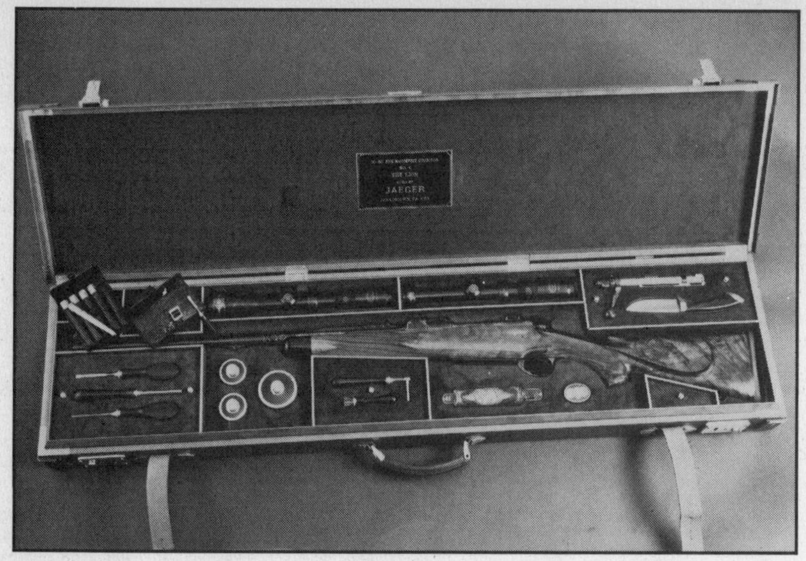

The Safari Club's Jaeger-built 375 H&H, Number 4 in a series, brought $140,000 at auction. Engraver: Willig. Knife: Imel. Case: Huey.

The GUNS of '85

Beyond the opulence of its surfaces, the Jaeger effort is classic in every line.

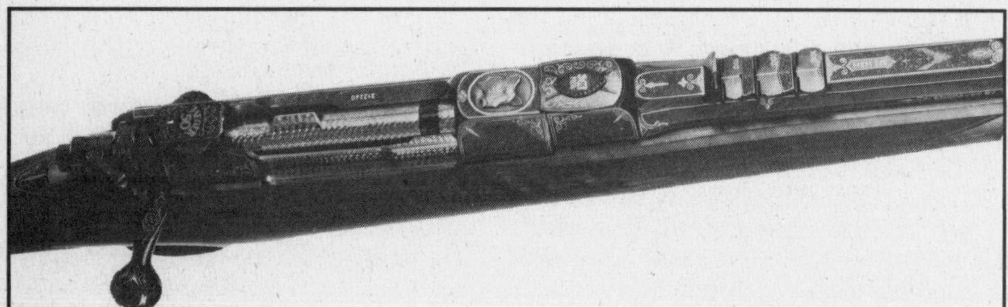

In the Big Five Series, this is the Lion. The Jaeger people say "It all came together," and it certainly looks like it.

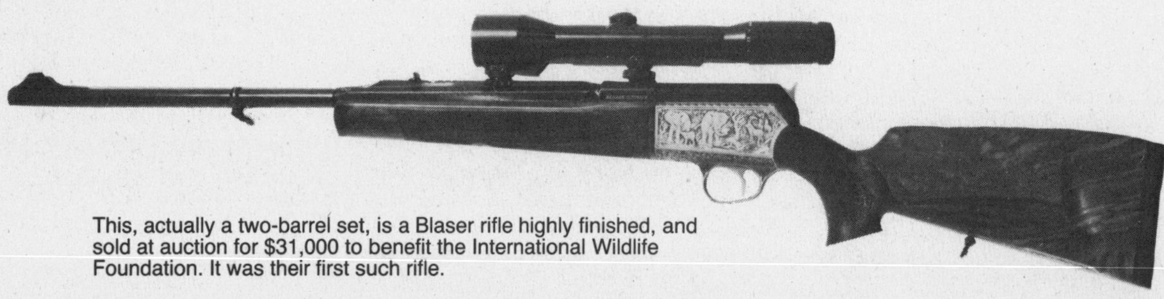

This, actually a two-barrel set, is a Blaser rifle highly finished, and sold at auction for $31,000 to benefit the International Wildlife Foundation. It was their first such rifle.

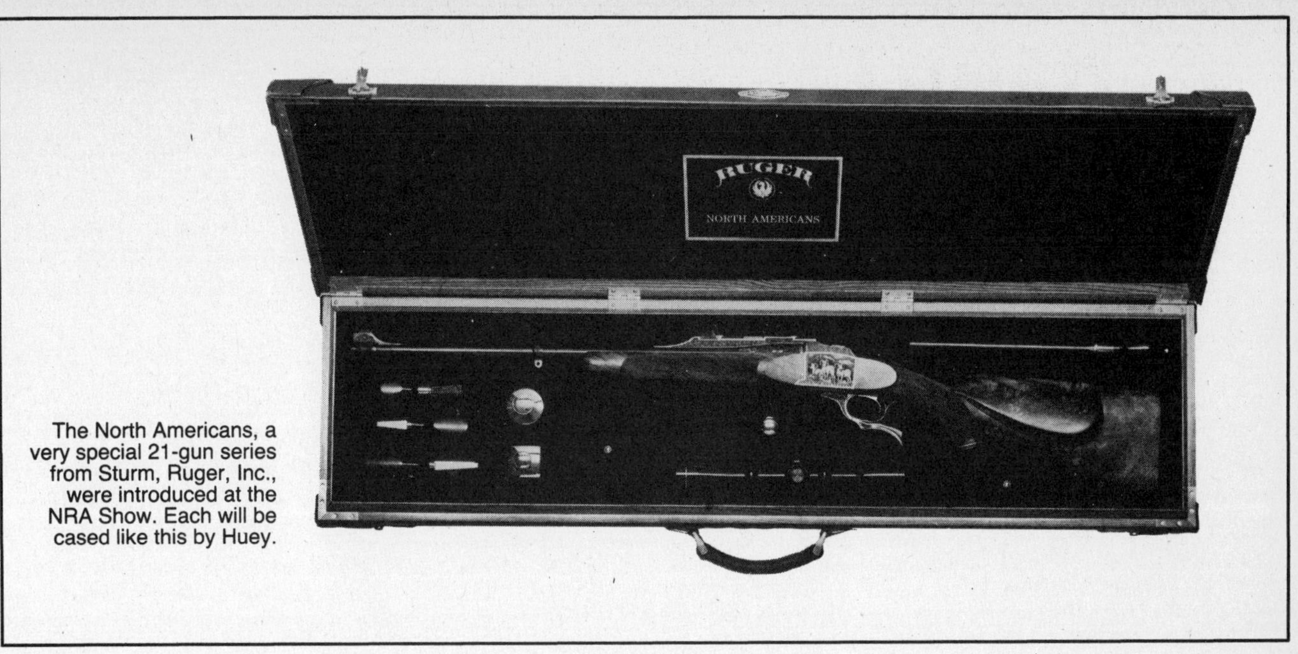

The North Americans, a very special 21-gun series from Sturm, Ruger, Inc., were introduced at the NRA Show. Each will be cased like this by Huey.

Notable guns come along every year, but 1985 gave us a bumper crop.

Rebarreled and fine-tuned by Tim Bolinger and Mark Penrod, and stocked by Bill Dowtin, the North Americans will sell for $45,000 each.

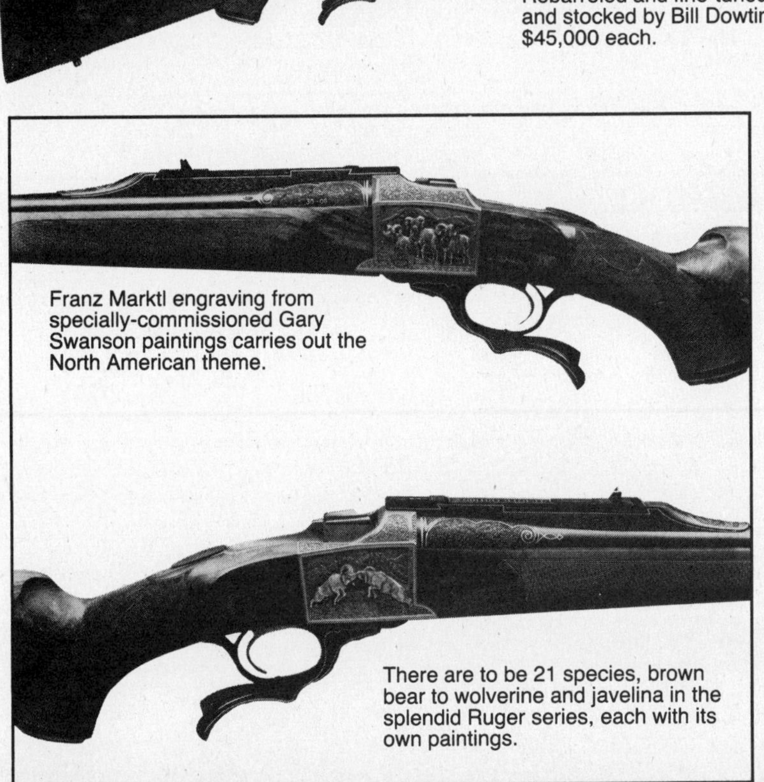

Franz Marktl engraving from specially-commissioned Gary Swanson paintings carries out the North American theme.

There are to be 21 species, brown bear to wolverine and javelina in the splendid Ruger series, each with its own paintings.

There'll be just ten of these Alaska 25th Anniversary S&W Model 29s, each complete as shown at $10,000.

HAND LOADING UPDATE

by **DEAN A. GRENNELL**

THE PAST twelve months were not overly notable for vast breakthrough strides in the field of handloading or reloading. That is to say, it was a year that resembled most other years quite closely. With general economic conditions wallowing through a trough, one still might expect handloading less affected than the traffic in new guns and factory ammunition and, in many examples, that seems to have been the case.

As usual, we will be dealing with the equipment and incidental needfuls, with handloading components being covered in another section. We'll be covering some new things from several manufacturers in alphabetical order.

Forster Products

Newly improved and redesigned is an outside neck-turning accessory for the Forster case trimmer. Unlike the inside neck reamers, also available from Forster and quite handy in their own right, the outside reamer produces neck walls of uniform thickness and concentricity. The outside neck diameter can be controlled to a high degree of precision. Inside neck reaming is done before the case is resized, while outside turning is done after the case has been resized and the neck expanded.

Forster is now handling the various items of the well-known and highly-regarded Bonanza line, including their Bench Rest rifle cartridge reloading dies. Another new Forster item is their decapping tool. It positions a spring-loaded, tool steel pin in an induction-hardened body and comes in the three common thread sizes to replace the decapping rod assemblies in dies from all the major makers. Replacement pins are available.

Hollywood Loading Tools, Inc.

A name once legendary in the field, this one fell upon trying times, but may be making a comeback. They offer parts and accessories for existing machines, as well as complete units. For example, the Hollywood senior turret reloading tool is quoted at $550, complete with one turret indexing handle, one ½-inch die shell holder bushing and one ⅝-inch tie-down rod for swaging. Not having seen, let alone used, the current output, I can but report.

Lee Precision

Not in the least content with developing first the Lee turret press and its semi-automated version, Lee brought forth the Model 2001 press, a single-station O-frame design adapted to an ingenious primer feed system. It is a neat, lightweight and highly capable little press, readily able to handle the larger rifle cartridges as well as those for handguns. It uses universal shell holders and standard loading dies with the ⅞-14 thread size. It has a compound-leverage toggle system and the operating handle is not only reversible left-to-right but the length of the handle can be adjusted to the taste of the given operator. The Lee Ram Prime approach lets you seat primers with the full press leverage, but with the maximum amount of touch and feel for the operation. As we have come to expect from this innovative firm, the asking price is remarkably modest. Sixty bucks and applicable sales tax sets you up with everything for one cartridge and, after that, all you need is another die set. Kits with carbide sizing dies cost an additional ten dollars; still a noteworthy bargain.

Forster has the Bonanza bench rest dies still in production.

On top of that, we have the Lee Progressive 1000 loader, based upon a modified Lee turret press and automated to the point where the operator merely needs to place a bullet on the mouth of the charged case and work the handle. Completed cartridges are kicked out of the shell plate to slide down a ramp into an empty tomato sauce can or such other receptacle as you may employ.

On the Progressive 1000, the shell plate is advanced automatically as the operating handle is stroked, while the dies remain in place, topside. The case is fed into station one and full-length resized on the upstroke, moving to station two and being primed on the downstroke. You can use a case feeder or put the cases into place by hand, at your option. As the case goes up at station two, its mouth is expanded and the measure is cycled to drop a charge of powder into it. As the shell holder comes back down, repeating all prior operations, the primed and charged case moves to station three and you put a bullet in its mouth before it goes back up again.

It sounds simple and it is simple, provided the operator keeps intent track of all the operations being performed simultaneously. It is important to use only full and complete strokes of the operating handle. Hesitation and backtracking can leave you with two dumps of powder in one case and that, in turn, can cause problems. This is not the ideal press for the inexperienced beginner.

Lyman Products Corp.

The Models 600 and 1200 Turbo Tumblers, introduced earlier, have been joined by the new, high-volume Model 3200. A new Turbo Sifter speeds the process of separating cleaned cases from the medium and the Turbo Accessory Bowl converts the 600 to a 1200, with a grid top that also serves to separate cases from media.

For those who favor cast bullets, there's the all-new Lyman Mag 20 electric furnace, with a capacity of 20 pounds and a heat-up time of about 20 minutes from a cold start. Well adapted to the bottom-pour approach, it's also convenient for use of a ladle, should the operator prefer. The adjustable thermostat is graduated up to 825°F nominal temperature and a pilot light indicates when the thermostat is drawing wattage.

The mould chart in the current Lyman catalog does not seem to show any new designs and several of the good, old designs have survived the chopper's blade for yet another year. I scanned the 44 pistol listings and thought for a moment we'd lost the good old #429434 gas-checker, but was relieved to see it shown under the rifle designs for the 44-40 size. Reloaders of the world: It's still a great performer out of wheel-guns, when sized to .430-inch. Buy some blocks and perhaps we can keep it in the 1987 Lyman catalog!

Rounding out a busy year, Lyman reports they've improved their #450 bullet lube/sizer with a better ram and leverage system. It now comes with a patented gas check seater and a stick of Alox/beeswax lubricant at no added cost. The gas check seater is available at $6.50 as an add-on accessory for earlier Lyman #450 lube/sizers, as well as for the Lachmiller/RCBS Lube-A-Matic lube/sizer. The third edition of the *Lyman Shotshell Handbook* is an exhaustive and definitive production, and a trifle altruistic, mindful that Lyman's offering of shotshell reloading equipment has become rather limited, these latter days.

Magma Engineering Co.

For the past several yers, Magma has marketed automated casting machines to commercial producers of cast bullets. In the past year, they developed what they term the Master Caster, a machine that employs the same wing-actuated mould blocks, but in a smaller, considerably less expensive, manually-operated version

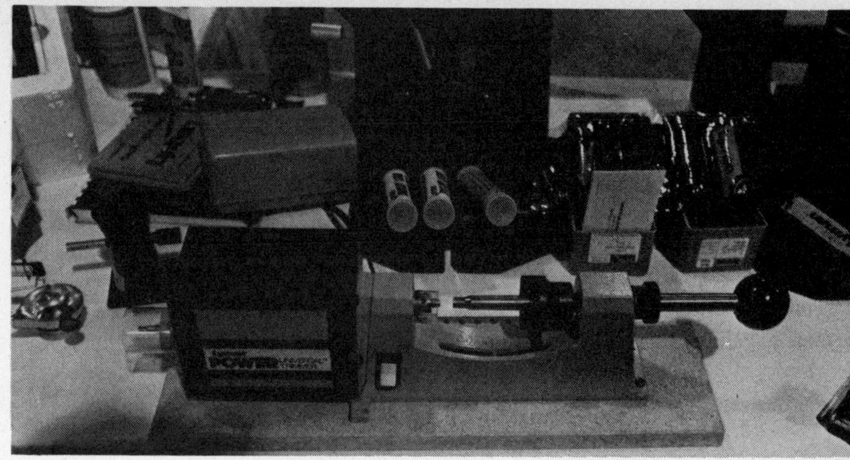

New Lyman power trimmer has universal chuckhead.

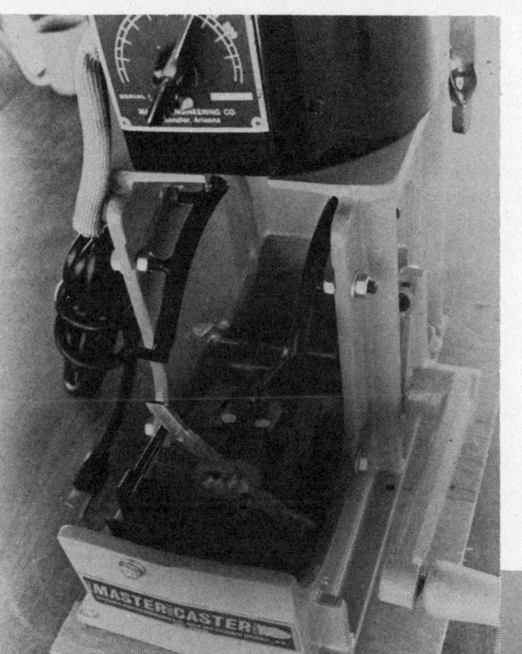

Magma Master Caster ain't cheap but can make 500 bullets an hour.

Grennell's Lee 1000 Progressive cannot be set up without a tomato sauce can; it would be a protocol violation.

Omark's Sidewinder case tumbler will process 300 38 Special cases at once.

of the same basic concept.

In essence, the MasterCaster is an electrically heated furnace, operated by moving a crank-type lever back and forth. You rotate it upward to fill the twin-cavity block by means of a thumb-actuated delivery lever, pause briefly until the exposed sprues are seen to cool and solidify, then bring it down to swing the sprue cutter over. At the end of the stroke, the block segments are wedged apart and the cast bullets are ejected down one delivery chute, while the sprues are sent down another to a container for recycling. Typical production rate is reported at 400 to 500 bullets per hour, possibly a bit higher if a power blower assists in the cooling cycle.

Although less costly than the full-power models, the Master Caster is by no means cheap. It goes for $495, with additional two-cavity mould blocks at $50 the set. Several designs are available. Robert L. Clausen can supply further details, being the owner-manager of Magma.

Mayville Engineering Co. (MEC)

The latest refinement of the MEC-600 Jr. is termed the Mark 5 and it incorporates several features found on the more expensive MEC models, but without a substantial increase in price. Among these are the new Spindex crimp starter, a long-stroke resize and deprime tool and the helpful Pro-Check that prevents spilled powder or shot.

The Spindex crimp starter is moulded of durable Celcon and rotates automatically to realign perfectly on the original crimp fold of the shell mouth. It can be changed from a six-point to an eight-point crimp in a matter of seconds, or vice versa.

The Pro-Check feature keeps the charge bar in the proper sequence and helps to keep the user from losing track of the suitable cycling order. The long-stroke primer punch and resizing tool now is standard on the Mark 5 and needs no adjustment, regardless of base wad or height of the brass shell head. What's more, it requires but a simple adjustment to shift from 2¾-inch to 3-inch shells and no additional parts are required.

MEC has been working in close conjunction with Non-Toxic Components (NTC) to develop and refine the equipment and procedures that enable the experienced and careful reloader to make up steel shot loads at state-of-the-art capability, meanwhile at a substantial saving in cost.

Omark Industries

The corporate heading covers several familiar names: RCBS, CCI, Speer, Outers and, more recently, the scope mount activities of Weaver. Several of the operations have new products of interest to the reloader.

The most recent offering from RCBS is their Model A-5 reloading press, also known as the 4×4. It is what we might term a manually-operated progressive design, of sturdy O-frame construction, with four die stations in the top of the press. The empty cases are carried through the four sequences on a shell plate, advanced by the operator. Rotation of the plate is counter-clockwise, commencing from about 8 o'clock, as viewed by the operator. The first station full-length resizes the case and knocks out the spent primer, which goes down through a dog-leg length of tubing to be captured in a screw-top plastic receptacle. At station two, the case mouth is expanded and flared on the upstroke, then the primer is seated at the conclusion of the downstroke.

The third station carries a powder measure, such as the RCBS Little Dandy or Uniflow, with a movable bushing within the support tube to guide the powder charge neatly into the case neck. Some discretion is indicated here. For example, if you try to load 4831 powder in a 22-250 case, the granules are apt to bridge and cause problems. Three bushings are supplied with the A-5 press to handle the various sizes and types of cases, when using powders of suitable granulations.

The fourth station carries the bullet seating die. It is easy and simple to remove the case from any of the stations for inspection and equally effortless to put it back in place. Broad conical buttons under light spring tension serve to keep the cases positioned in the shell plate.

Once you've gone through the initial start-up routine, the cycle consists of removing the loaded round and replacing it with a raw case; then place a bullet atop the charged case at station three; bring the handle down to run the ram to the top of its stroke; actuate both the powder measure and the lever of the primer feed; raise the handle to lower the ram, paying special attention to the tactile sensation as the primer is seated; advance the shell plate a quarter-turn and repeat the operations.

The shell plates for the A-5 are keyed to the same numbers as the usual RCBS shell holders and the current retail cost is $25 per plate. Six of the shell holders are not available as A-5 plates: #5 for the 348 Winchester; #8 for the 45 Auto Rim; #13 for the 7.62mm Russian; #14 for the 45-70 Government; #29 for the 25 ACP and #31 for the 50-70 Government. The retail price is $289, without plate, dies or measure.

Also new from RCBS is their Sidewinder case cleaner in a choice of 120-volt or 240-volt for international use only. The cleaning chamber is big at the bottom, small at the top and liquid-tight, permitting the use of either dry or fluid cleaners. It rotates on an inclined base and there is an adjustable timer that can be set for operation from five minutes to twelve hours. An eight-ounce bottle of liquid cleaning concentrate is supplied with the unit. A perforated cap doubles as a screen to separate either liquid or dry cleaning medium from the cleaned cases.

The RCBS liquid concentrate appears to be a fairly urgent detergent,

Paco Hammerhead bullets—homemade for heavy-duty use. Cores are cast into formed jackets in special mould blocks.

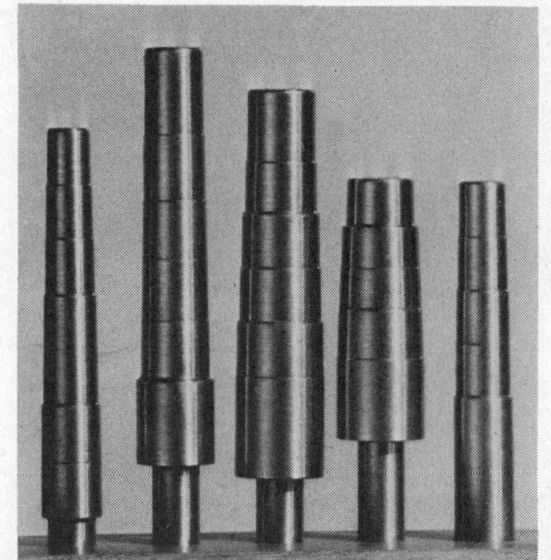

Paco K-Spinners will work with any case—just slip 'em on and spin 'em to a shine.

The RCBS A-5 does everything, including catching spent primers in that little bottle at the bottom.

but not a metal solvent. As a usual procedure, I full-length resize the cases before cleaning, so as to let the liquid remove not only the sizing lube but quite a bit of the residue from the primer pockets. The Sidewinder is rated for a capacity of 300 38 Special or 150 30-06 cases and I find it's better to run a batch near that quantity, since the cases help to clean the other cases.

Also new is the RCBS trim gauge, intended for speedy setup of any case trimmer with a half-inch diameter shaft, such as the #1 or #2 RCBS trimmer. It goes between the crank and the rear of the bushing and can be locked for length adjustment. Between uses, it can be stored with the loading dies for the given cartridge. Six sizes cover the range of standard cartridge case lengths.

RCBS also has a new hand-held priming tool that comes with large and small seating punches and accepts the full range of universal shell holders. A companion to the *Speer Manual* is in the works, in the shape of the *RCBS Cast Bullet Manual*, with 130 pages of information and load data for use with rifles or handguns. These last two items are so new, in fact, that I've yet to see either of them.

Speaking of casting bullets, after my moulds cool, I prefer to give them a light spray of Break Free or a similar rust-preventitive compound to preserve them for future sessions. The spray can degreaser from Omark/Outers is the best stuff I've found to date for getting the preserver off the blocks when setting up for the next run. With the pithy terminology not uncommon among the Good Ol' Boys, they call it Crud Cutter.

Paco

In last year's edition, I wrote up an innovative tool from this firm for producing gas checks to use on cast bullets, using cut-up and flattened-out beverage can metal as the raw material. I referred to the proprietor as Paco Kelly; his correct nickname and surname. Due to an undetected typo, it came out in the discussion as "Pack" Kelly and the listing in the directory was headed simply, "Paco." I can but assume that caused some confusion and I apologize for it. In the year since then, Paco has been busily developing several other new products to beguile handloaders of the world, meanwhile keeping on with the gas check-making tools described last year.

There is, for example, the Hammerhead bullet. Upon initial introduction, it's produced in .458-inch diameter, but other calibers will be added as time goes on. The basic intent is to enable economical production of tough and effective bullets, suitable for use on the largest, most dangerous game species, in Africa or on other continents.

Paco supplies copper tubing for cutting into suitable lengths to serve as the jackets. The test samples had a wall thickness of .040-inch, but lighter tubing will be offered in the same outside diameter (OD). Here's how it works:

Mark the tubing for length and cut it with a tubing cutter. Apply lubricant and use the supplied forming die and punches to shape the jacket nose on a conventional reloading press. Paco suggests STP as the lube, but I used Huntington Die Lube with good results. A word of caution: Do not have the knockout punch in place when forcing the cut section of jacket tubing up into the die, or it can cause vexing problems, as I found to my chagrin.

After forming the jackets, degrease them thoroughly. The Omark/Outers Crud Cutter spray works quite well for the purpose. The core is cast into the jacket by means of a special mould supplied with the Hammerhead kit. Degrease that, as well, and it's best to pre-warm it to some point not far below the melting point of the core alloy in use.

Before doing that, however, disassemble the mould and arrange the series of spacer collars so the base of the jacket comes close to the lower surface of the sprue cutter, carefully retaining the unused spacer collars.

When actually pouring the molten core alloy into the heated mould, the ejection punch can be held down on a flat surface to bring the rear face of the jacket up against the sprue cutter to prevent unwanted full-diameter core at the bullet base. This is a simple operation when using a bottom-delivery electric melting pot and I'd assume it would work just as well when pouring in the core metal from a ladle.

After the core solidifies, knock the sprue cutter over with a mallet and press the punch to eject the completed bullet. Pure lead can be used for the core, but hardened alloys work just as well and no further sizing is performed on the bullet as it emerges from the mould. Since penetration, rather than expansion, is the usual goal for such bullets, a harder alloy would seem indicated.

The distance the cut section of tubing is pushed up into the jacket-forming die controls the amount of exposed core metal at the bullet tip, as well as the diameter at the bullet point. The weight of the finished bullet can be varied across a broad range by controlling the length of the jacket, the size of the bullet nose and the composition of the alloy used in pouring the core. Discounting the operator's time, the cost of producing such bullets is quite modest, particularly when compared to similar bullets from commercial sources.

Another new Paco product is the K-Spinner. Essentially, that's a small mandrel that can be chucked into a drill press, electric hand drill or similar tool. The business end has a series of steps, each slightly tapered, to engage a snug friction fit against the necks of resized cartridge cases. In use, you start the mandrel to spinning and press the mouth of the case to the slightly tapered area, engaging it by clutch action to spin the case, in turn. With that going on, you can remove resizing lube with a piece of paper towel, clean the residue from the primer pocket with a tuft of steel wool on the end of a short piece of wooden dowel, use a larger piece of fine-grade steel wool to remove corrosion and powder residue from the outside of the case. Or, if you like, the case can be polished to the luster of a newly minted coin by application of a metal polish such as Flitz or Happich's Simichrome on another scrap of paper towel, followed by a wipe-down with Kleenex or paper towel. In any example, it's an operation requiring no more than a few seconds, following which you just pluck the processed case off the spinning K-Spinner and replace it with another one in need of cleaning; no need to shut off the motor in the process.

Sierra Manual is now two manuals, plus supplements.

Radix Research & Marketing

According to supplied information, this firm offers products primarily of interest to commercial reloaders and producers of lead bullets. Regarding their Magnum Brass Cleaner, they note it's a two-step process, consisting of a stripper and a polisher. They also market a product called Magnum Dri-Lube, which is a molybdenum-based formula employing methylene chloride as its volatile solvent.

Comprehensive instructions and descriptive discussions are available to qualified and interested parties. Even a casual study of them makes it clear it's not suited for the casual hobbist. As I'd assume this will reach a number of potentially interested readers, I'll cut the discussion here and recommend that they request further particulars from Hank and Lana Chapman at Radix.

Redding Reloading Equipment

Their Ultramag loading press remains the top-of-the-line offering, with its entirely logical pair of full-length links between compound toggle and press head. It appears to represent the ultimate refinement of the basic C-press design, bringing press-spring to the irreducible minimum.

Since last year Redding's honcho, Richard Beebe, has refined their No. 3 powder measure to produce what he calls their Model No. 3BR version, said to take every last bit of play out of the micrometer threads for precise repeatability of charge weights for the given setting through years of use, even compensating for the effects of wear.

Redding has a new Pro-Series of titanium carbide die sets. A request to Beebe will get you complete details.

Sierra Bullets

This noted bulletmaker has made a major revision of its original manual, splitting it up into a rifle manual and a separate handgun manual. Supplements are supplied, with pages to replace previous pages in the loose-leaf binder systems. In addition, there are several discussions produced by noted gunwriters to provide useful educational material for reloaders at all of the various levels of experience. Supplements and/or complete packages are available from your local dealer in Sierra bullets. Other offerings include programs compatible with several makes and models of personal computers, enabling the shooter to set up and generate tables of ballistic data to individual specifications. ●

Presenting the

RUGER®

21 North Americans

A Series of Superb Presentation Engraved No. 1 Rifles Inspired by a Group of America's Leading Wildlife Artists

For the first time in its 37-year history, Sturm, Ruger & Company is offering a unique series of presentation engraved and custom cased Ruger No. 1 single-shot rifles of a magnitude and quality reminiscent of the finest leather cased English guns of a century ago. No effort or expense has been spared to make these rifles truly museum-grade pieces which are unsurpassed in modern firearms manufacture.

Inspired by the works of a group of leading American wildlife artists, the Ruger *North Americans* will consist of a series of 21 Ruger No. 1 rifles, each depicting in fine engraving and deeply sculptured inlaid gold a major North American big-game animal, and will be chambered in a caliber appropriate to the game shown.

The first No. 1 rifle in the Ruger *North Americans* series will depict the Rocky Mountain bighorn sheep as rendered by Arizona artist Gary R. Swanson. One of the most popular wildlife artists today, Swanson's award-winning art is recognized throughout the world for the richness with which he portrays his subjects and surroundings.

The dramatic bighorn sheep painted by Gary Swanson have served as the models for the outstanding sculpture in steel and gold inlays by master engraver Franz Marktl of Phoenix, Arizona. Trained in engraving and serving his apprenticeship at Franz Sodia in Ferlach, Austria, Marktl has become one of America's foremost firearms engravers, and has executed commissions from the White House, Prince Charles of England, King Karl Gustav of Sweden, King Hussein of Jordan, Prince Abdorreza of Iran, the King of Morocco, and other notables.

Each rifle in the series will be accompanied by a one-of-a-kind full color print of both paintings commissioned, each print to be signed by the artist and remarqued in full color. The purchaser of each rifle will receive an Owner's Certificate of Provenance and Authenticity signed by William B. Ruger, President and Chairman of Sturm, Ruger & Company, Inc.

the RUGER *North Americans*

A Unique Limited Edition of 21 Presentation Ruger No. 1 Single-Shot Rifles Created by America's Finest Firearms Craftsmen

Sturm, Ruger & Company has brought together the finest firearms craftsmen in the United States to produce this first offering in the Ruger *North Americans* series. The classic Ruger No. 1 single-shot rifle has served as the subject for the gifted craftsmen selected to execute the project.

The Ruger No. 1 action has been fine-tuned and customized by Mark Penrod of Penrod Precision, North Manchester, Indiana, and rebarreled and chambered for the .30-06 cartridge by Tim Bolinger of MATCO, North Manchester, Indiana. The custom stock is by Bill Dowtin of Flagstaff, Arizona. Marvin Huey of Kansas City, Missouri has built the leather covered fitted case, with accessories hand-made by Mike Marsh in Sheffield, England.

The classic artistry and sculptured gold inlays of master engraver Franz Marktl depict the "Battling Bighorns" of Gary Swanson's painting.

In addition to Franz Marktl's sculptured treatment of the Rocky Mountain bighorn sheep on each side of the French grey finished receiver, the rifle is fully engraved with a typically American scroll pattern, with liberal gold inlay lining. The words "RUGER NORTH AMERICANS" and "LIMITED EDITION" are gold inlayed on the top of the barrel. The Ruger eagle trademark is inlayed in gold on the underside of the lever, and the grip cap bears a remarkable 3-dimensional rendering in gold inlay of the bighorn sheep head.

The trunk style Huey case is covered in heavy cowhide in a rich russet finish, with double locks, trunk studs, and leather grip. The interior of the case is custom French-fitted and is lined in plush burgundy ultrasuede, and includes two teak handled screwdrivers, dust brush, jointed cleaning rod, two brass oil bottles, and striker box. Two lidded compartments with brass knobs are included. In addition, a Leupold M86/6X Compact Scope with engraved scope mounts and rings is fitted in the case. All metal hardware in the case and accessories are gold plated. A brass nameplate is affixed to the top of the case, and a gold-imprinted black leather Ruger *North Americans* label is centered inside the lid.

The beautifully figured wood used in this presentation is costly Northern California English Walnut, a special hybrid of Circassian, and Claro walnut strains. The pistol grip and

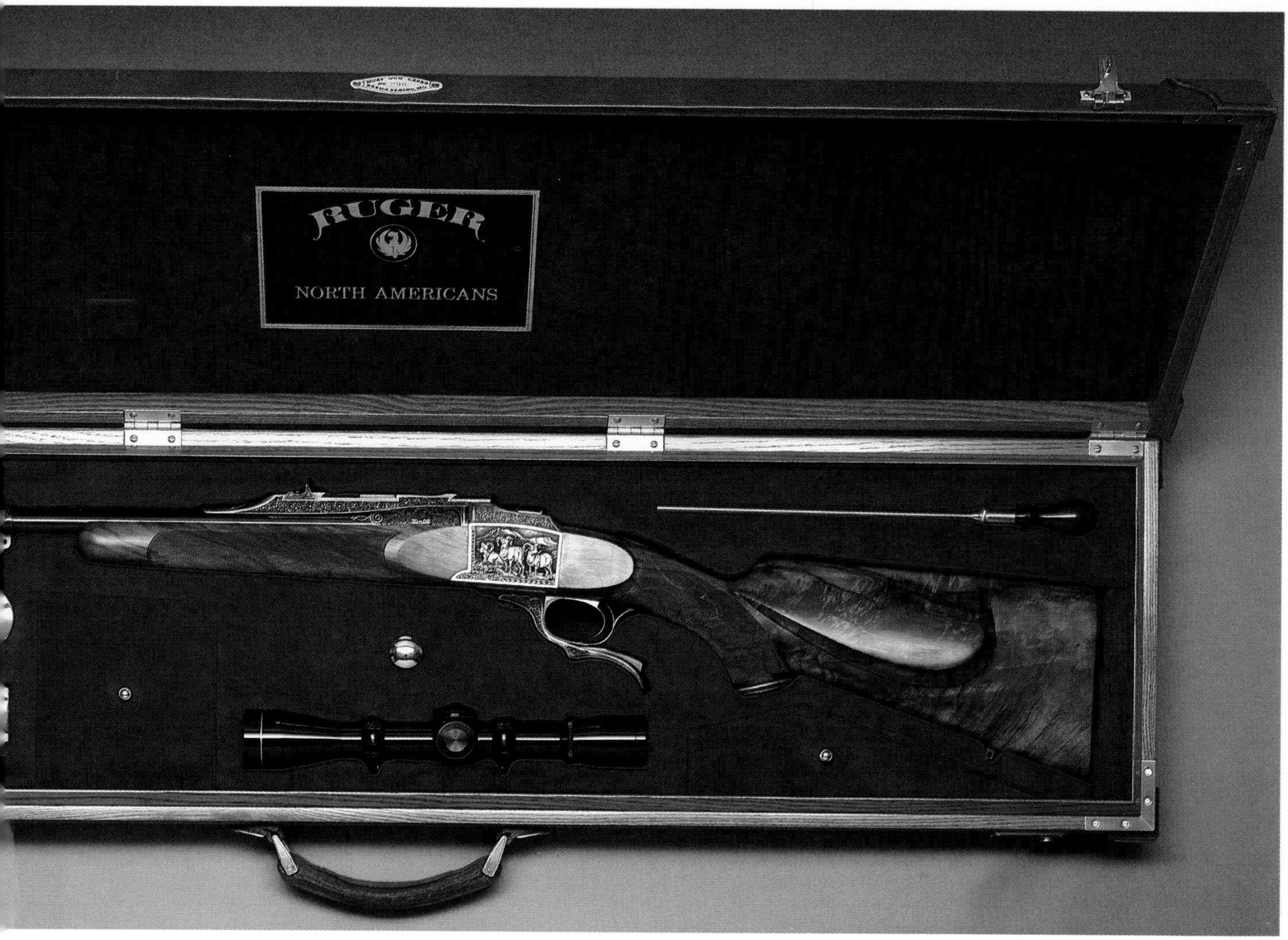

The custom leather covered, French-fitted presentation case by Marvin Huey is a one-of-a-kind work of art.

forend are finely checkered 28 lines to the inch, and the butt is checkered in the European fashion and provided with a gracefully carved cheek-piece of classic pattern. All wood is carefully oil-finished by hand.

Every detail of this first offering in the Ruger *North Americans* series contributes to the overall impression of classic style and outstanding quality of workmanship and artistry that characterize this outstanding Ruger presentation. The collector or investor who purchases this rare offering will clearly own one of the finest Ruger rifles ever made. Price for the Ruger *North Americans* bighorn sheep presentation rifle is $45,000.00 (all Federal excise tax included). Interested parties should contact J. Thompson Ruger, Vice President, Marketing, Sturm, Ruger & Company, Inc.

A Collection of 21 Limited Edition Big-Game Animal Prints

Twenty-one North American big-game animals will be depicted, both in fine paintings and sculptured in metal as a part of this superb offering of presentation engraved Ruger No. 1 rifles. A group of famous wildlife artists, including Greg Beecham, Tom Beecham, Lee Cable, Bob Kuhn, Leon Parson, and Gary Swanson will capture on canvas the excitement and appeal of the animals in their natural settings. The paintings will be reproduced as a series of 21 Limited Edition prints, and re-created by master engraver Franz Marktl on each No. 1 rifle in the series.

Gary Swanson's painting, "Rocky Mountain Bighorns" serves as the inspiration for the first offering in the Ruger North Americans series.

The prints will be lithographed in full color on the finest quality acid-free paper. They are offered at $95.00 each, which includes shipping, handling, and tax. Prints will be shipped in a protective jacket and specially designed shipping container, ready for framing. The first print in the series, *Rocky Mountain Bighorns* by Gary Swanson, measures 18 1/2" X 24" overall (image size is 14" X 20").

For information on this Limited Edition Print Offer, write to: M/W Enterprises, Inc., 12629 No. Tatum Blvd., Suite 164, Phoenix, Arizona 85032.

These are the big-game animals that will be depicted:

- *Bighorn Sheep*
- *Black Bear*
- *Brown Bear (Alaskan)*
- *Bison*
- *Caribou*
- *Elk*
- *Dall Sheep*
- *Desert Sheep*
- *Grizzly Bear*
- *Jaguar*
- *Javelina*
- *Moose (Alaskan)*
- *Mule Deer*
- *Mountain Goat*
- *Mountain Lion*
- *Polar Bear*
- *Pronghorn Antelope*
- *Stone Sheep*
- *Whitetail Deer*
- *Wolf*
- *Wolverine*

Each reproduction of the 21 North American big-game animals in the series will be offered in a Limited Edition of 950 prints, serially numbered and signed by the artist. Matching numbered prints are offered to early subscribers.

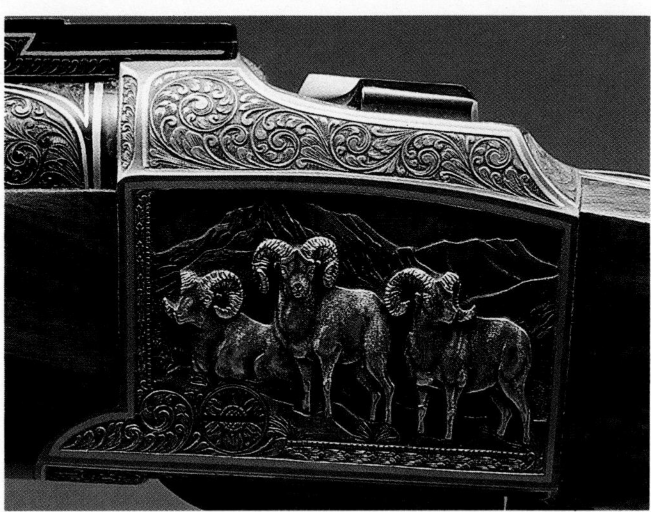

STURM, RUGER & Company, Inc.
Lacey Place
Southport, Connecticut 06490 U.S.A.

ALL RUGER FIREARMS ARE DESIGNED AND MANUFACTURED IN RUGER FACTORIES IN THE UNITED STATES OF AMERICA

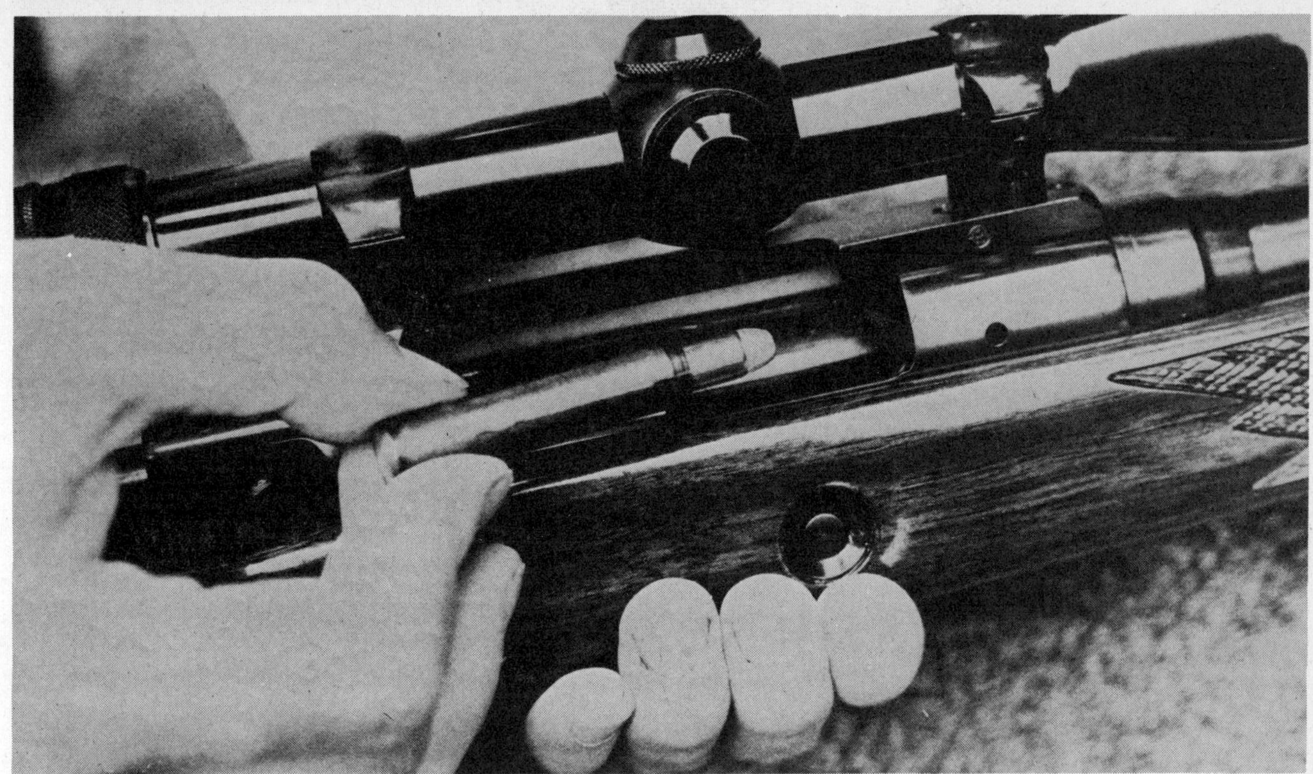

This is an Alex auxiliary cartridge designed to fire a 32 ACP cartridge in a rifle chambered for 30-06.

Things are simple no longer in the new world of . . .

AUXILIARY CARTRIDGES AND OTHER SUCH STUFF

by ELMER KURRUS

YOUR FAVORITE firearm can be easily converted to a sub-caliber. This special "magic" involves the use of an adapter or auxiliary cartridge, an insert barrel, or a conversion unit. Such conversions are simple, efficient, economical.

The *simple* part of any conversion is that the procedure can be accomplished without special tools. In about the time it takes you to read this sentence, you can convert (or unconvert) a magnum or a shotgun to a rimfire, a hunting rifle or handgun to a 22-caliber for target practice, or a wide range of other options. *Efficiency* corresponds to one-inch accuracy at 25 yards and two-inch groups or better out to 50 yards. The *economy* is in the use of lower-cost ammunition.

Assume that you're deer hunting with your 30-06 rifle, and where you hunt smaller game such as grouse or rabbit can be taken along with deer. You are over-matched for the lesser stuff and don't want to carry a second gun. The solution: open the breech of your rifle; replace your 30-06 cartridge with a 32 ACP/30-06 adapter; use the 30-06 rifle to collect camp meat. The 32 ACP in a long barrel is very quiet compared to the 30-06, won't cause excessive damage to small game, and costs about one-third the price of the big game load. A pleased hunter once told me, "That 32 ACP/30-06 adapter is a real grouse-getter."

There are probably a dozen ways to thus get into the fascinating world of adapters, insert barrels, and conversion units. Which you want depends

This auxiliary allows you to fire the 22 Long Rifle in any 22 WMR rifle or handgun.

Savage Model 412, known worldwide as the Four-Tenner, converts a 12-gauge shotgun to use the 410 shotshell.

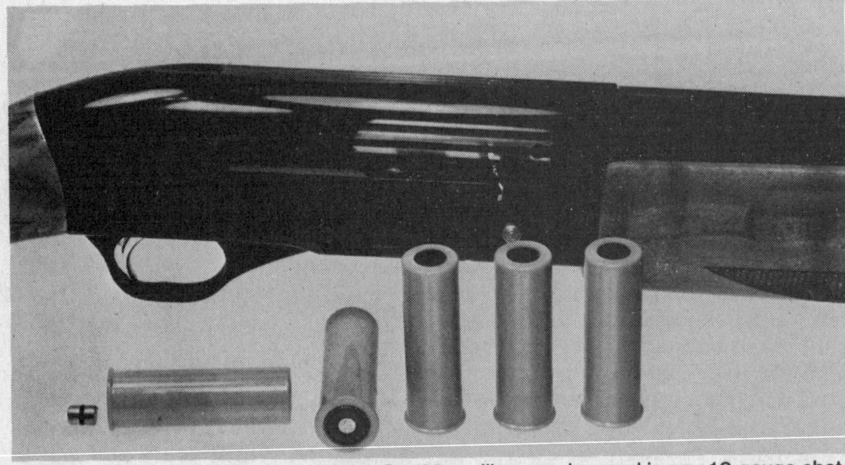
The 2½-inch 12 Ga./22 auxiliary can be used in any 12-gauge shotgun. You could thus have a Winchester Model 12 slide-action 22.

on whether you need to convert a rifle, shotgun, or handgun.

Three retail dealers specialize in firearm conversions. They include:

Alex, Inc., P. O. Box 3034K, Bozeman, MT 59715/406-282-7396; Neil Jermunson.

Gremmel Enterprises, 271 Sterling Dr., Eugene, OR 97404/503-688-3319; Doug Gremmel.

Sport Specialties, P. O. Box 5377DK, Hacienda Heights, CA 91745/818-968-5806; Harry Owen.

Each dealer offers methods to convert firearms. They vary, so it's important to understand the wide variety and difference in cost associated with a change to sub-calibers. Speaking in general terms, a cartridge adapter can be purchased for less than $20.00. Insert barrels vary in price depending on the dealer, the type of conversion, and the length of the insert barrel. An average price for an insert barrel is approximately $35.00 to $50.00. If you wish to convert a centerfire magnum revolver to 22 LR, you're in the price range between $80.00 to $100.00.

Since the variety and options cover a wide range of possibilities, a closer review of adapters, insert barrels, and conversion units is useful:

The Adapter

An adapter—auxiliary cartridge—is machined to the same exterior dimensions as the rifle or pistol cartridge. It is designed to accept the sub-caliber cartridge as a sort of sleeve for your gun's chamber. Some models require a device to transmit the firing-pin blow, most often to rimfire cartridges. The adapter is usually made of soft, durable steel.

With the proper adapter, the same firearm can fire any bullet having the same diameter as its barrel. The 30-06 cartridge can use one adapter to fire the 32 ACP, another to shoot the 30 Carbine, since both are 30-caliber. A rifle or handgun in 223 Remington can use adapters to shoot 22 LR. The combinations are virtually unlimited.

Alex, Inc. and Gremmel Enterprises both offer good selections of adapters. Alex, Inc. manufactures three basic series of adapters, accommodating 22 LR, 25 ACP, and 32 ACP cartridges. Adapters for the 22 LR cover a spread of cartridges from the 221 Remington to the 220 Swift. Adapters that use the 25 ACP cartridge are made for firearms ranging from the 250 Savage through the 25-06 Remington. A 32 ACP adapter is offered to fit cartridges between the 30-30 Winchester and the 300 Winchester Magnum. All Alex, Inc.

Author's 357 Smith & Wesson took this snowshoe with 22 LR with a sub-caliber unit.

Unusual conditions resulted in an exceptional handgun trophy taken with a S&W Model 28 revolver the same day the gun was used on small game as a 22.

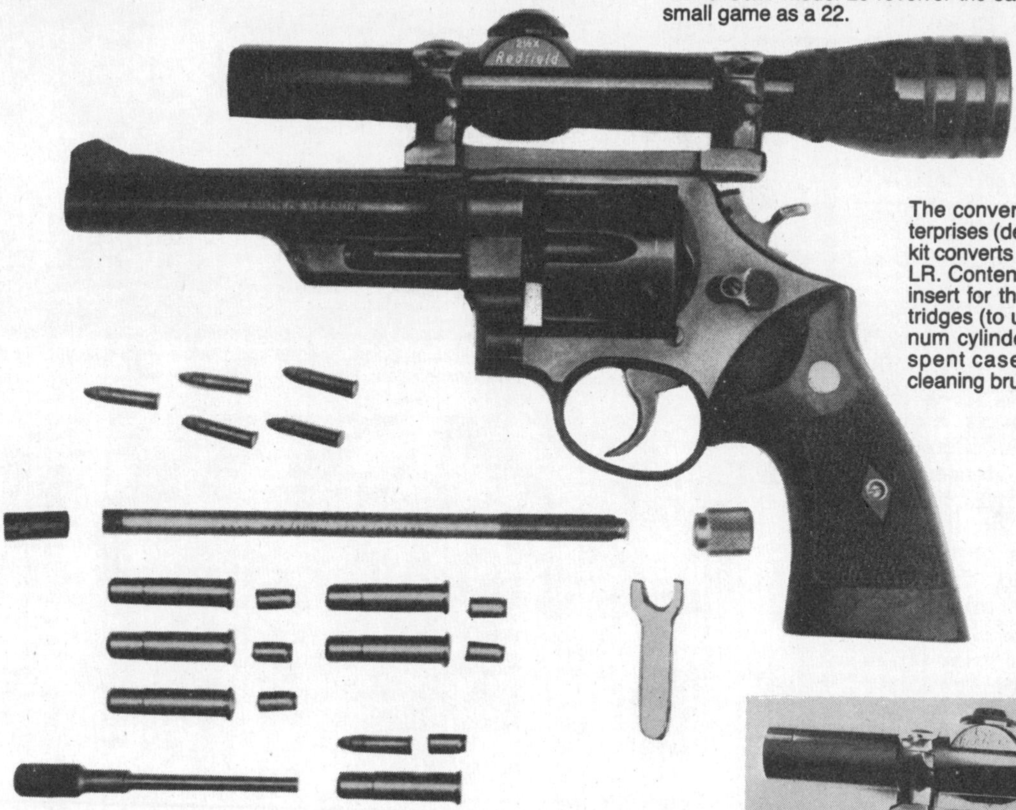

The conversion unit from Gremmel Enterprises (dealer for Lothar Walther). This kit converts a 357 Magnum revolver to 22 LR. Contents of the kit include: A barrel insert for the 6-in. S&W, 6 auxiliary cartridges (to use 22 LR through 357 Magnum cylinder), knockout rod to remove spent cases, and a general purpose cleaning brush.

The rear end of the insert barrel screws into a forcing cone.

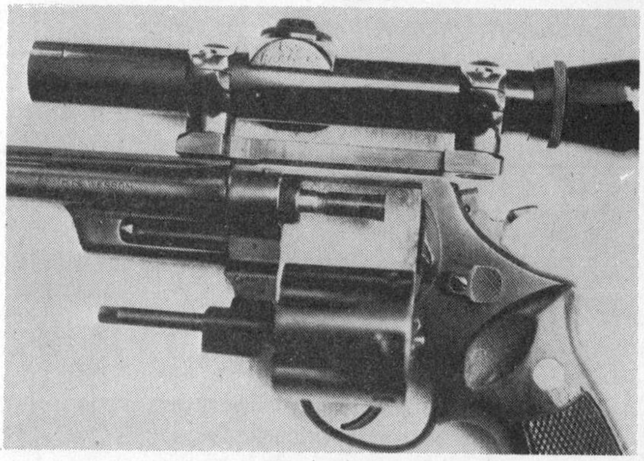

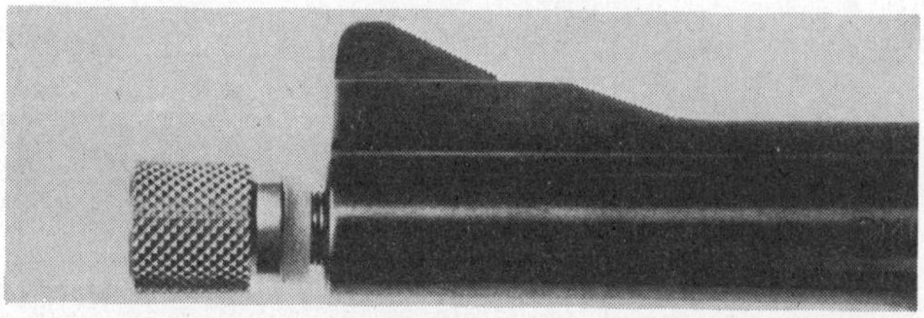

After the forcing cone is tightened, the muzzle of the 22 insert is secured with a threaded friction nut.

adapters, regardless of chamber size, sell for $14.50. Alex calls them "Auxiliary Cartridges."

One of the newest adapter innovations was brought to my attention by Neil Jermunson, owner of Alex, Inc. He's recently developed the capability to use 22 LR cartridges in either the 243 Winchester, or the 6mm. According to his extensive tests, both offer surprising accuracy when used with standard velocity 22 ammunition. Neil has also modified his newest creations to use a low-carbon, alloy material as a firing pin. This softer material offers added protection to the firing pin of the rifle.

Gremmel Enterprises is the primary U.S. agent for Lothar Walther. This company offers a wider range of "Adapter Cartridges"—they add 22 WMR and 22 Hornet to the 22 range. Gremmel also specializes in adapters for European cartridges, plus 32 ACP adapters for the 30 Carbine. Sold as Article No. 99, Gremmel adapters for rifles have a different design and finish, and retail for $30.00 each.

Harry Owen, chief engineer for Sport Specialties, is a different breed of cat! Over a period of 12 years, Harry has developed an inventory of over 400 different adapters, insert barrels, and conversion units, and so Sport Specialties boasts "the most complete line of adapters of any producer in the world."

Their basic price for a blue-steel adapter is $18.95. A stainless steel version is $26.95. In their 1985-86 catalog, at least 48 different models are listed for rifle adapters. A complete series of adapters are offered for the Thompson/Center Contender plus a new innovation for permitting 22 WMR chambers to shoot 22 LR shells.

Sport Specialties has 24 different adapters for the T/C pistol. The 22 LR adapters (and insert barrels we discuss elsewhere) take advantage of the fact that the Contender firing pin is easily switched to rimfire. At a cost of $18.95, any T/C barrel can be converted to a sub-caliber. The most popular is the 22 LR/223 TC, which converts the 223 Remington to use rimfires.

I've frequently used the 22 LR/22 WMR adapter with my Savage Model 24 and with my Ruger Single Six when I preferred not to change revolver cylinders. Other than minor zero changes, I haven't noticed anything unfavorable. I just slip the 22 LR into the sleeve-like adapter, load it, and fire in the normal manner. A small slit in the adapter allows easy removal of the spent case. Then I do it again.

At least three additional companies offer adapters that convert standard

The Thompson/Center Contender, chambered for 44 Magnum and topped with a T/C 4RP pistol scope. Different T/C barrels, such as the 357 Maximum (or 357 Magnum) or 30-30 can be easily converted to 22 LR.

Harry Owen, owner of Sport Specialties, bench-testing a variety of adapters and insert barrels. His catalog lists over 400.

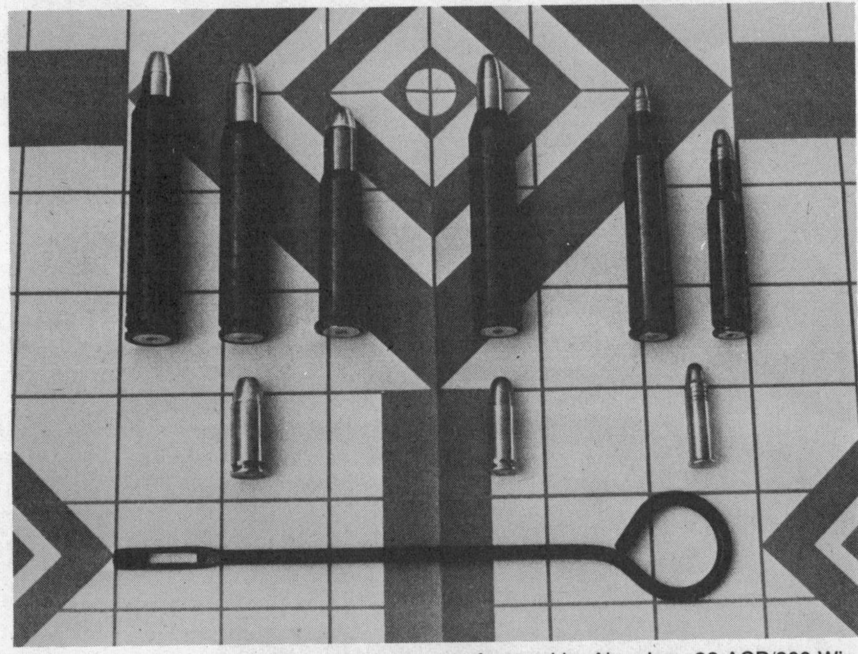

Auxiliary cartridges manufactured by Alex, Inc.: 32 ACP/300 Win. Mag.; 32 ACP/30-06; 32 ACP/30-30; 25 ACP/25-06; 22 LR/220 Swift; and 22 LR/222 Rem. The knock-out rod is used to remove spent cartridges and as a short cleaning rod.

Insert barrels are available to convert derringers. Depicted are Sport Specialties insert barrels that convert the 357 Magnum derringer to 22 LR—great for practice.

With the Cherry Converter by Amimex you can have a double-barreled 38 Special—it's easy. This precision-built adapter is crafted from 2024 aluminum, T-6 hardness, and anodized to its distinctive "cherry" color. Available in 12 and 20 gauge, designed to fire 38 Special only.

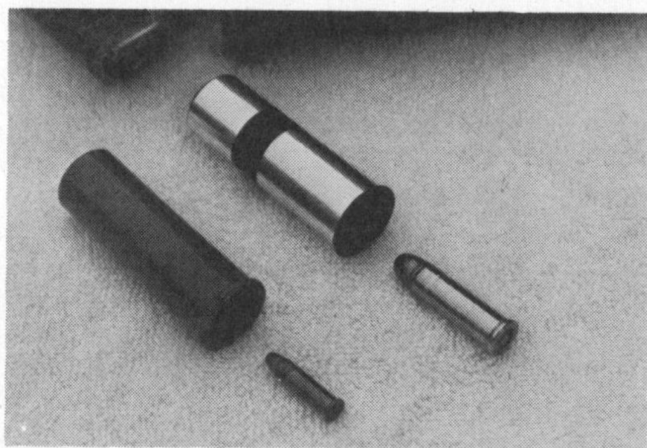

You can turn a double to a 22/38 with a 22 LR/12 gauge adapter from GTM Co. and a 38 Special/12 gauge adapter from Kestmati, Inc. GTM offers 22 LR adapters; Kestmati offers five calibers.

Using different inserts from Sport Specialties, the Savage 24 CS over/under can be converted to a double 22 rifle.

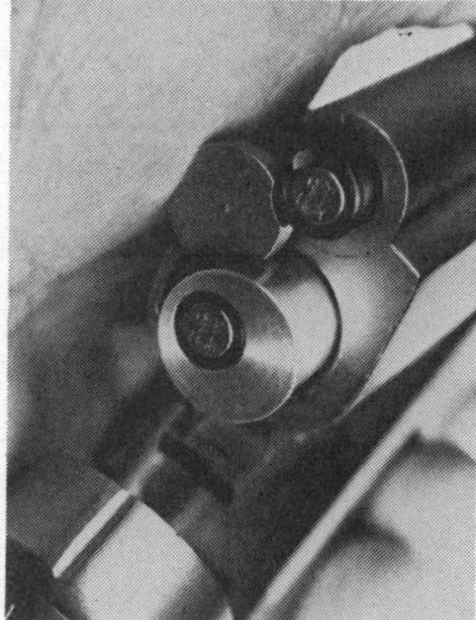

shotgun calibers to a sub-caliber. Each uses a similar design, a shotshell-shaped adapter that chambers pistol or rifle ammunition. Sizes are 12, 16 and 20-gauge, of course. The three companies are:

Amimex, Inc., 2660 John Montgomery Dr., San Jose, CA 95148/408-923-1720; Russ and Janis Meek.

Kestmati, Inc., 23011 Moulton Pkwy., Suite G-6, Laguna Hills, CA 92653/714-855-6452; J. K. Ditty.

GTM Co., 15915B E. Main St., La-Puente, CA 91744/818-968-5806; George T. Mahaney.

Russ Meek developed Amimex's "Cherry Converter" after several prototypes had been designed, evaluated and tested. The original idea is attributed to Lewis Tripp, who gives similar credit to Tony Court. The first production model, the CE-12-38, was patented in January of 1983.

This is a precision product. It's made from 2024 aluminum stock at a T-6 hardness, and anodized. It's chambered for the 38 Special cartridge, and won't accept the 357 Magnum, and is made for 12 and 20 gauge. The adapter has its own rifling—1½ inches of lands and grooves—and boasts 3-inch groups at 25 yards. It's simple, efficient and very economical. It sells for $19.95 each.

A firm called Kestmati, Inc. also sells a "Metallic Ammo Converter" for 12 or 20-gauge shotguns. This adapter is made from hardened aluminum alloy, anodized. The Kestmati Converters offer a choice of 38 Special, 357 Magnum, 44 Magnum, 45 Colt and 223 Remington chamberings at $19.95. Kestmati estimates about 400-500 rounds before their adapter begins to show appreciable wear.

The GTM Co. is named for George T. Mahaney. This company has a new ripple—the 22 rimfire. Their converter allows the use of 22 LR in 12, 16, or 20-gauge shotguns. Capitalizing on the popularity of the 22 rimfire, GTM has designed a lightweight adapter, made from "space-age" aluminum alloy. The adapter houses a steel 22-caliber tube, off-set to allow the firing pin of the shotgun to strike the rim of the 22 cartridge. The device is convenient and simple to use. It allows rapid change-over from shotshell to 22 sub-caliber, and retails for $35.00.

Sports Specialties offers an adapter that will accurately shoot 22-caliber air rifle pellets in a variety of rifles or handguns, using only a rifle primer for propellant. The most popular pellet adapter is for the 223 Remington, but adapters are available for any centerfire 22 at $24.50.

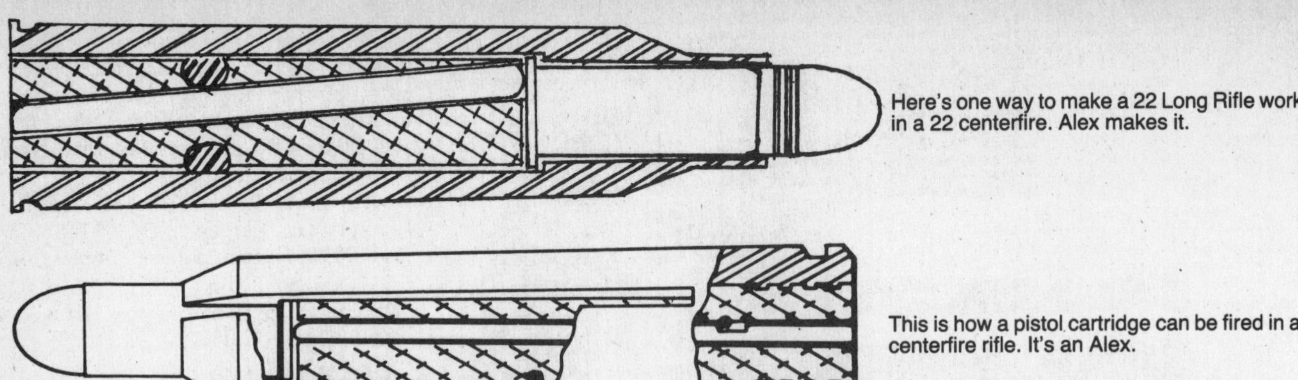

Here's one way to make a 22 Long Rifle work in a 22 centerfire. Alex makes it.

This is how a pistol cartridge can be fired in a centerfire rifle. It's an Alex.

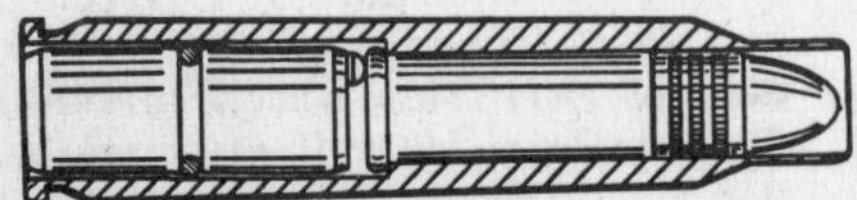

Here's a different way to get a centerfire firing pin blow to shoot a rimfire. From Sport Specialties.

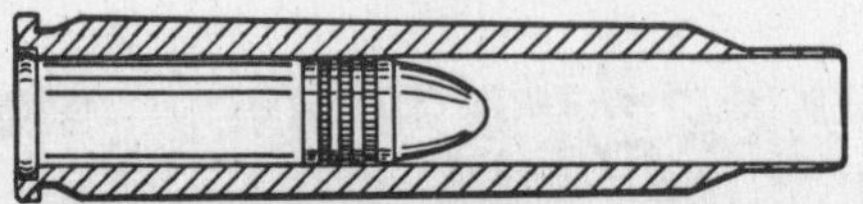

You can switch a T/C Contender to hit a rimfire correctly, so this adapter will shoot a 22 rimfire down a 223 T/C barrel.

And this gadget will fire an air gun pellet down a 223 barrel, powered by a primer.

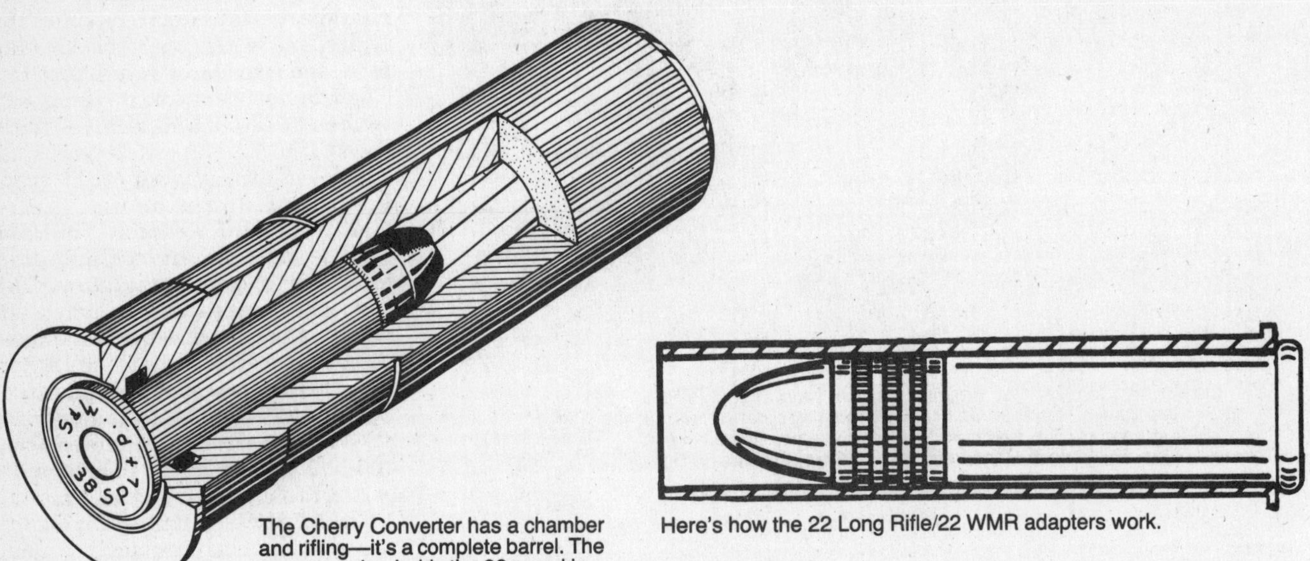

The Cherry Converter has a chamber and rifling—it's a complete barrel. The neoprene ring holds the 38 round in.

Here's how the 22 Long Rifle/22 WMR adapters work.

This style of insert develops more horsepower than short ones. This is a 30-30 barrel for a 20-gauge shotgun.

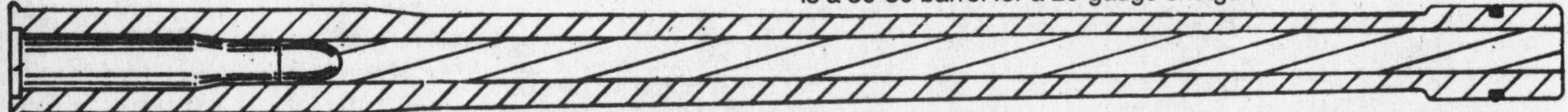

Insert Barrels

Insert barrels offer great flexibility. They are designed to fit into your rifle, shotgun, or handgun to quickly convert it to a different caliber. Of all the options offered by Sport Specialties, 22 LR insert barrels are the most popular. One of the newer innovations has been insert barrels to fire rimfire or centerfire cartridges in 410, 20, 16, 12, and 10-gauge shotguns. These insert barrels work in any type of shotgun, and in 20 different subcalibers. In break-open shotguns, the insert barrel is placed directly into the barrel; in a pump or autoloader it's more complicated, but once you get it into the shotgun barrel, you've converted your scattergun to a single-shot rifle. Most pump and autoloader shotguns have been designed with easy barrel removal in mind, so the modification is simple and can be accomplished in a matter of minutes.

Insert barrels, especially those for break-open guns, have been around for many years. The grand-daddy of insert barrels in the United States here lately is made by Savage Arms. It's called the "Four-Tenner" and is designed to convert either 12 or 20-gauge shotguns to fire 410-gauge shells. It simply slips into the breech of most single, side-by-side, or over-under barrels offering an extremely efficient modification, and weighs only five ounces. They sell for about $34.00 each.

Gremmel Enterprises carries at least three shotshell inserts. One is a rifled insert, similar in size to the standard shotgun shell. The insert is designed to fire either the 25 ACP or 22 LR cartridge. A second shotgun insert uses European sub-caliber shotshells, such as the 6mm with shot, the 22 Long with shot, and the 9mm with shot. The third shotgun insert is tailored to short range indoor practice. It fires a 4mm M20 centerfire cartridge, another European size and is available in 12, 16, and 20 gauge.

Harry Owen seems to have taken the concept a step further. He offers a special insert just for pump and autoloader shotguns that can be used without barrel removal. The insert is identical to a loaded shotgun shell, but is chambered and rifled to use a sub-caliber cartridge. An illustration of the 12-gauge/38 Special model is shown in this article, but these useful inserts are also available from Sport Specialties in 10, 12, 16 and 20 gauge. Sub-caliber selections include: 9mm Luger, 380 ACP, 38 Special, 357 Magnum, 44 Magnum, 44 Special, 45 ACP, 45 Colt, 32 ACP, 25 ACP, 22 WMR, and the world-famous 22 LR. Regardless of gauge or sub-caliber selected, each is priced at $35.00. (Yes, these are like the Amimex and Kestmati offerings in design.)

Before World War II, Ludwig Krieghoff Sr. operated an arms factory in Suhl. As adjuncts to their excellent combination guns, a 22 LR insert barrel was designed for shotgun barrels. These inserts are expensive (about $188.00), but represent the "top-of-the line" if you're looking for the ultimate in insert barrels.

The Krieghoff insert barrel is 10 inches in length and can be purchased for either 22 LR or 22 Magnum. Properly fitted, they say, the "standard" model produces two-inch groups at 50 meters. An "extra" model, carefully selected during factory test-firings, guarantees one-inch accuracy at 50 meters. Krieghoff insert barrels are available through Gremmel Enterprises, Sport Specialties or GTM.

Insert barrels work especially well with combination guns. My favorite Savage combination is the Model 24-V, chambered for 30-30 and 20 gauge. I've added a Weaver V4.5 scope using detachable, see-thru mounts. The scope can be removed, or attached, in a matter of seconds. In my jacket pocket, I carry two insert barrels. One is a 22 LR/30-30, while the second is a 30-30/20 gauge. The first converts the 30-30 rifle to fire a 22 LR cartridge; the 30-30 insert barrel converts my over-under to a double rifle. I've thus modified the 30-30 rifle to 22 LR for $35.00 with a 6-inch insert barrel; the 10-inch barrel which makes my "double rifle" costs $65.00. Such conversions for the many Savage combinations are almost uncountable.

The Thompson/Center Contender is well suited to the use of adapters or insert barrels, as well, and Sport Specialties offers an unusual variety of insert barrels for the T/C. They come in 6-inch, 10-inch and 14-inch lengths. In field tests, I've learned that in spite of weight and packaging advantages of the short ones, the longer barrels are more accurate.

Any of the big-bore Contender barrels, from the 30 Herrett to the 45 Colt can be thus converted to 22 rimfire. (*One could also, of course, simply get a 22 rimfire barrel from T/C. Editor.*) The 6-inch barrels are $35.00; the 10-inch $45.00; the 14-inch versions $55.00.

One of the most innovative of conversions is the ability to modify 357 Magnum or 44 Magnum revolvers to 22 caliber. For the serious hunter, this allows the use of the same handgun for *either* big game or smaller animals such as grouse or rabbit.

In the fall of 1981, I was hunting in remote Alaska, using a Smith & Wesson Model 28, chambered for 357 Magnum. The revolver was fitted with a Redfield 2½ power scope, anticipating its use on medium-sized game. My original plan was to use the Magnum for larger game, and selectively convert to 22 LR for grouse or snowshoe hare.

We were hunting an area west of Mount McKinley, in the foothills along the Kuskokwim Mountains. This area offers excellent habitat for moose, bear and caribou. As soon as you leave the open tundra, you see an abundant variety of lesser game—spruce grouse, the occasional ptarmigan, snowshoe hare, marten, and wolf. Conditions were so favorable, I had been taking grouse and snowshoe for two days with the revolver converted to 22 LR.

Then I saw the black bear. I thought the 357 Magnum light for bear, but I also knew carefully placed shots would produce acceptable results. My handloads were 146-grain jacketed hollow points, with a muzzle velocity over 1400 fps. The bear was 100 yards away, seriously engaged in cleaning up the remains of a moose. It was at least three miles back to camp, so getting a heavier handgun or a rifle was impractical; and a black bear with the handgun is a most respectable trophy.

It boiled down to two possibilities: either use the 357 Magnum at close range or pass up what appeared to be an exceptional trophy. I knew my scope-sighted revolver was super-accurate under 50 yards, so I decided to try for the black *only* if a clear shot was possible and at close range.

In under five minutes, I removed the 22 LR conversion unit returning the revolver to 357 Magnum. Thereafter, the pieces to my unusual puzzle fit together like magic: I got a stationary shot at 35 yards. As I squeezed for the shot, the bear decided to stand up and he took the bullet three inches above his left eye. I've taken larger bear, but few have offered that much excitement and satisfaction.

Gremmel Enterprises and Sport Specialties both offer 22 LR conversion kits for revolvers. Prices are comparable, primarily depending on the barrel length of the revolver to be converted. The "standard" seems to be a conversion kit for 6-inch revolvers that retails for $87.00. Revolver conversion kits consist of a 22 LR barrel insert, 6 auxiliary cartridges, and an ejector rod. Although the conversion kit seems a bit complicated, overall, the modifications are very simple.

All the adapters, insert barrels and conversion units mentioned here can be mailed. There are no Federal controls of any sort on adapters, inserts or conversions. Similarly, no Federal Firearms License is required by any buyer or seller.

Historical data is a bit vague, but gunsmiths have been trying to convert basic firearms for close to a hundred years. About 60 years ago, Marble Arms Company manufactured adapters. And also years ago, Winchester made chrome-plated adapters to fire the 32 S&W Short through 32-40 barrels. Sears sold centerfire rifle insert barrels for 12-gauge shotguns at the turn of the century. So we're not talking about a new idea, but a good idea.

I think the advantages of converting your rifle, shotgun or handgun to a sub-caliber are just too good to ignore. At a minimal price, you can add the benefits of a second cartridge along with a completely different set of ballistics. You can change calibers but still use the same familiar gun. Especially important, the use of adapters, insert barrels, or conversion units is just plain fun. ●

One Good Gun

Plowman looks grumpily pleased with himself here, but he likes the rifle as well.

What John Plowman's 30-06 proves is simple:

A GOOD GUN IS A GOOD GUN

by BOB BELL

A CAR HORN blaring in my driveway took me outside. It was John Plowman, grinning like the cat with a belly full of canary.

"I haven't even been home yet," he yelled. "I wanted you to see my buck."

"Got lucky, huh?" I said. "Guess anyone can kill deer in South Carolina."

A big 6-point with a high wide rack was tied to his Blazer, along with a good-size doe.

"That's really what I wanted to see you about," he said. "I want you to sight in my gun for me."

"You gotta be kidding. How many shots did it take you to get these?"

"Two. One each."

"What you complainin' about then? You got one last December here in Pennsylvania, didn't you? Also with one shot, as I recall."

"Yeah, but there's something wrong just the same. They were all short range shots, 50 or 60 yards at most, standing, and I hit them six or eight inches from where I should have. I don't think my gun's really sighted in."

"When's the last time you checked it?"

"We fooled around with it some down at Santee-Cooper. Couple of guys tried to help me, but we were running out of shells and it still wasn't right. They said there weren't any more clicks left on the scope, to get it in the middle. Said I should just hold some to the left of where I wanted to hit, but it's hard to remember that stuff when you're shooting at a deer."

I couldn't help chuckling. I remembered a similar incident from 40 years ago when a few of us were checking zeroes on our M1's in Germany. One dogface's rifle was hitting a foot and a half to the right at a hundred yards, but he refused to make a correction. Half the time they ran that way, he said, so he had a built-in lead. Maybe that's how John was making his kills.

Truth is, John and that GI have a lot in common. No matter how hard it is for regular GUN DIGEST buyers to believe, few hunters are guncranks. Most buy a rifle, put a scope on it, casually sight it in and maybe check things every couple of years. Mostly what they do is hunt. And kill stuff. Only when something calls their attention to the rifle—a miss or two, say—do they consider verifying things.

I don't know how many deer John Plowman has killed. We've hunted together, one place or another, for 15 or 18 years, and he has a habit of connecting. Not only in Pennsylvania, where we're almost neighbors, but also in South Carolina, Alabama and elsewhere.

It's the same with pheasants. He's so convinced Winchester's weird glass-barreled Model 59 is a shotgun that he's got two of the darn things—and he leaves a Browning Superposed in the cabinet to hunt with them. And he does get pheasants with them.

And turkeys. When it's gobbler time, you're likely to find Ol' John anywhere from Pennsylvania south to Alabama and out to Missouri, blowin' and squeakin' and whatever else it is that turkey callers do—and killing those big old birds. I seriously doubt he knows what kind of shells he's stuffing in his old autoloaders, or maybe even what gauge he's using, but he brings turkeys home. Again, I don't know the total, but it wouldn't surprise me if he's killed more turkeys than I've ever seen in the woods. But back to his deer gun.

"Where is it, John," I asked.

"Right here somewhere." He commenced plowing through piles of well-worn equipment in the back of the Blazer, eventually producing a ragged canvas case from which protruded an even more decrepit rifle. It was a 721 Remington 30-06 with an old Weaver 3-9x in Redfield Jr. mount.

"Your windage is the problem?"

"Yeah. Charley said there were no more clicks. And I hit those deer at least six inches to the right of where I held."

"When you were trying to zero in, did you ever consider doing anything with these?"

I pointed to the windage adjustment screws of the Redfield mount.

"What are they?"

"Never mind. What you got for ammo?"

Some more digging produced a small handful of cartridges. All were '06s, but no two—really—were alike. The make or bullet weight or style of each was distinct from all the rest.

"Listen, there's no sense trying to zero in with this conglomeration. The first thing you have to do is get a couple of boxes of ammo. It doesn't matter much what make you get—Remington, Federal, Winchester—they're all good. But make certain they're all alike. For your hunting, which is mostly deer, get 150-gr. spitzers.

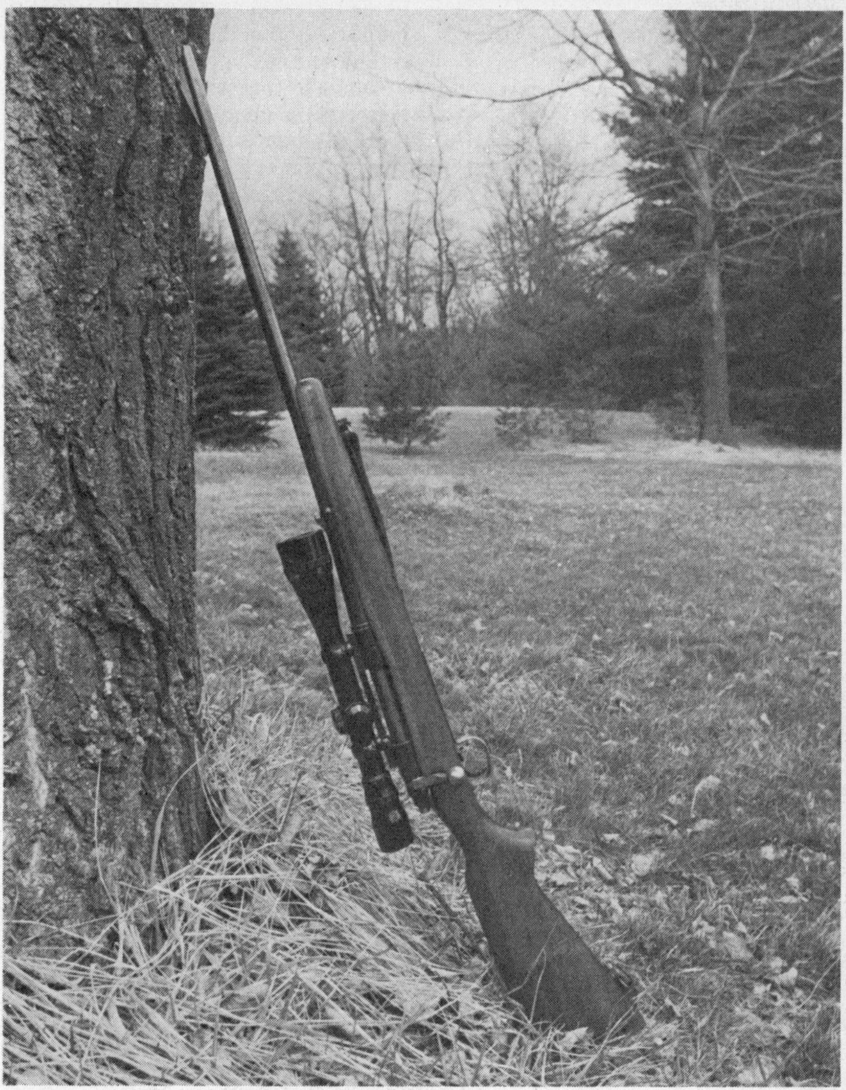

Plowman's old 721 has leaned against a lot of trees in a very long, very busy hunting career.

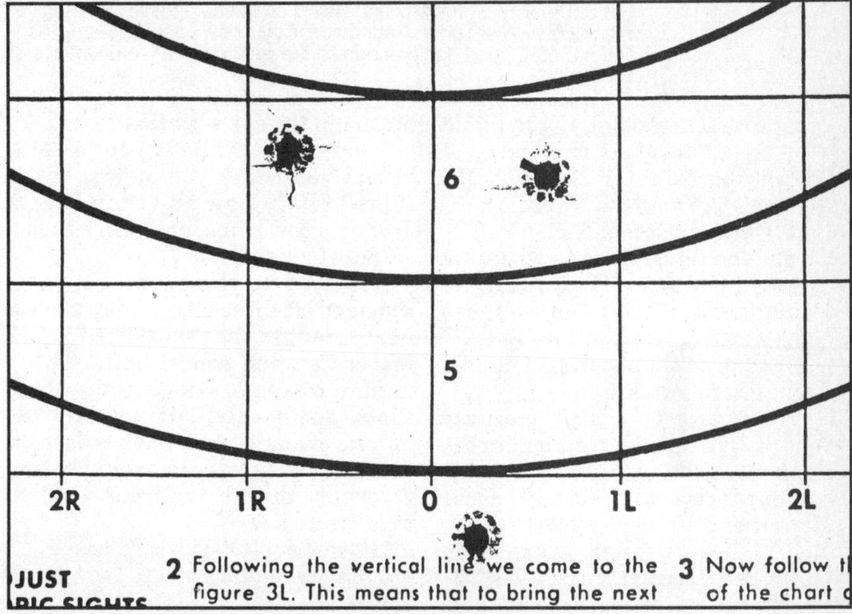

Many would be happy with this three-shot group if they fired it at 100 yards. The one good gun we're talking about produced this one at 300 yards.

Then we'll go up to the range Saturday and get things perking right before our season opens, okay?"

And so, a few days later, we were at the Carlisle Fish & Game Club's rifle range, three spanking new boxes of Federal 150-gr. spitzer ammo on the bench by John's old 721. I knew we weren't going to shoot them all, but I liked looking at them.

"We'd better try this at 25 yards first," I said, and was glad I remembered his windage problem because the first shot was almost off the paper.

I ran the windage dial the other way as far as it would go, counting clicks, then brought it back halfway to center it. Then using the Redfield mount screws to adjust for windage, I carefully boresighted the rifle. My next shot at 25 yards was at zero horizontally and about a half-inch low.

"That should be close to where we want it," I told John. "Put up targets at 100, 200 and 300, and we'll see what's what."

If I had to do the shooting, I figured he could do the walking.

The only targets he had were crazy things with a 6-inch green bull in the center with a white X-ring, surrounded by one-inch scoring rings. The four outer corners of the paper were cutely filled by smaller alternating green and white concentric rings, the whole caboodle being neatly divided by one-inch squares and sprinkled with numbers in two colors and false bullet holes that somehow are supposed to help you zero in. I dunno why it is that so few sources understand that when it comes to targets, simpler is always better. All a shooter wants to see on a piece of paper is a conspicuous aiming point of known size and his bullet holes. Anything else is a distraction.

Anyway, Plowman got his goofy targets on the backboards and I dug into those shiny Federal 150s. My first shot in the 100-yard target was just two inches high, center for windage. Two more made a group that measured 2⅜ inches and centered just 2½ inches high.

"Not bad at all," I said. "You oughta hit 'em in the ear with this."

"How about at 200?" John said. "Don't you think you oughta try it there? Every now and then I see a deer on a powerline, or out in a field."

"Sure 'nough."

I shifted to the second target, squeezed off three more. They made a neat triangle that measured just 2 inches between widest holes. That's minute of angle, friend—only three shots, admittedly, but nevertheless minute of angle. And who needs more accuracy from his old deer shooter? Strangely, though, the group centered four inches low.

"How about 300 yards," I asked.

John gazed downrange. Way downrange.

"I don't think I want to shoot at a deer that far away."

John P. and his pet deer slayer and a nice buck taken in Alabama or South Carolina or somehewre. Beard on left belongs to Rob Keck of the National Wild Turkey Federation. Coy fellow peeping around sapling is Bob Clark. I don't recognize the rest, but they're doubtless of similar ilk.

"You might not want to," I said, "but what if you see one out yonder that far? Don't you want to have some idea of where to hold?" I shoved another shiny cartridge into the chamber, looked up at him, waiting.

"It's your ammo," I said.

That's the kind I like to shoot.

"Okay. I guess I should know these things."

"I'm gonna hold on the top edge of the target. Otherwise they might go off the bottom, judging from that 200-yard group. It was two minutes lower than it should have been."

I couldn't see a bullet hole through the Weaver, even at 9x, so I shot the three of them. Then we walked down to the target. The group was centered for windage but 13 inches under point of aim, which is considerably more drop than published tables suggest. The three holes made a neat triangle measuring 2¼ inches center to center.

"That's pretty good, isn't it," John said.

"Not bad atall."

Lord almighty, I thought. Take a gun that's a third of a century old and been cleaned maybe twice in that time, stick on a scope that's almost as old, stuff it with factory hunting ammo and get a group that'll stay on the woodchuck's head at 300 yards—and decide it's pretty good. Sure nuff, that's a hunter's conclusion. Non-gun-cranks expect such groups. The guys who shoot know that results like this aren't the norm.

"Listen," I said. "This gun and ammo is shooting like crazy. But it's giving more drop than expected. I don't know why. Maybe the velocity is just lower than it should be, maybe it's something else. It won't matter for anything like a normal shot. Just hold in the middle of the shoulder up to 200 yards, okay? And if you should happen to get a shot at 300 or so, use the top of the bottom post as your aiming point. Got that?"

"Sure. I'm not going to shoot that far anyway. And now that we got it right on the button so I don't have to hold off the left side, I'm gonna drill 'em right in."

"Great. Anyone who can kill three deer with three shots with a gun that isn't zeroed won't have any trouble with one that's shooting like yours."

He probably wouldn't have had, either, if he'd seen a legal Pennsylvania deer. But he didn't.

But so far as John Plowman is concerned, his old 721 Remington 30-06 is still one good gun. And he's right. As he'll doubtless prove again next year. ●

To get his this writer had to make an . . .

S&W TRAIL MASTER-PIECE

by TERRY MURBACH

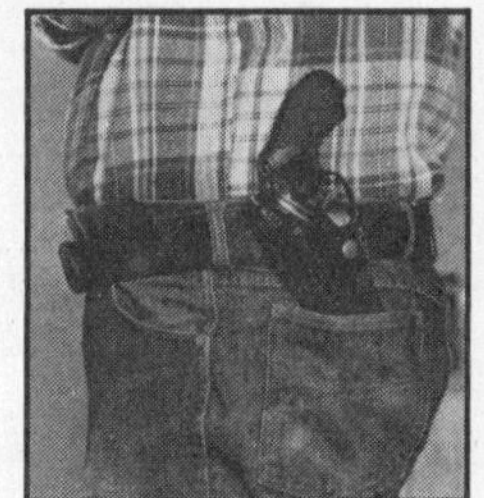

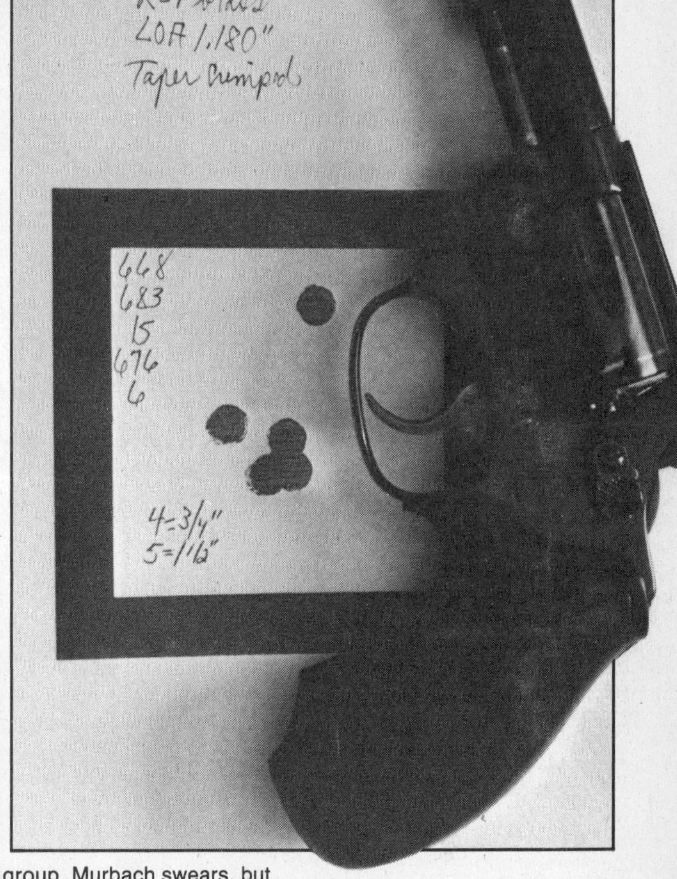

This is a typical 25-yard group, Murbach swears, but you have to shoot a lot to get such results. (Above left) Carries slick in Don Hume's Threepersons holster, a big part of being a Trail Masterpiece.

I LIKE Smith & Wesson revolvers. I like the way they look, the way they feel, and the way they shoot, but the things I liked first, way back when I was knee-high, were their names: Model 3 "American," Model 3 "Russian," 32 "Hand Ejector," "Highway Patrolman," "Chiefs Special," 38/44 "Outsdoorsman," "Combat Magnum." Even someone who knows next to nothing about firearms understands the words "Combat Magnum."

S&W never made a gun called the "Trail Masterpiece," but that's what I call a favorite S&W of mine. It's actually a remodeled Chief's Special.

Several years back, I darn near lost a big fox squirrel I'd hit pretty solid with a hollow point from a four-in. 22 handgun, and decided I needed a light sidearm with some short range punch; a centerfire "Kit Gun" if you will. I wanted a revolver with good to excellent accuracy, good single-action trigger pull, relatively light carrying weight—chambered for a cartridge easy and cheap to reload—and with adjustable sights. I needed a good 32 S&W Long revolver, and looked hard for one for a couple of years.

In January of 1982, Cleland's Gun Shop had the first Model 36-1 S&W I'd ever seen in the ferrous flesh. My mind went into high gear; it sure wasn't a 32, but that heavy barrel points so nice. The 32 idea was shelved; my centerfire Kit Gun would be a 38 Special. I got Gary Cleland to fit J-frame adjustable rear sights to the top strap and a new front sight. I'm happy to say this gun easily outshoots any 22 Kit Gun I've ever seen. Groups measuring 1-1.5 inches at 25 yards are not uncommon with proper loads. Groups at 50 feet will stay in the ten ring of a 50-foot slow-fire target.

I once installed a Bullseye spring kit, both hammer spring and rebound slide spring. That dropped the single-action pull from 40 ounces to 24 ounces and the double-action pull to about six pounds. The gun functioned perfectly through several hundred rounds; then I ran out of the old lot of primers, bought a new pack of 5000, and got a misfire rate of near 50 percent. Putting the original S&W springs back solved that problem; the odd part is I shot the gun better with the 40-ounce trigger pull than I did with the 24-ounce pull. That light pull gave me the "willies"—it was touchy!

Some loads shot with brilliant accuracy; but I noticed these groups moving around the target. The factory round butt configuration and stocks feel great, but I installed a set of Pachmayr rubber grips and solved that problem.

On page 226 of Roy G. Jinks' wonderful book *History of Smith and Wesson* there is a picture of what S&W called the "Chiefs Special Target" revolver. The three-inch gun pictured is almost identical to mine except it has a square butt and a slightly different front sight. Jinks notes that S&W manufactured a total of 2244 "Chief Special Targets" with 213 having the three-inch barrel. At Camp Perry, I asked him why this three-inch gun wasn't being manufactured now.

His answer was "They didn't sell; we could hardly give them away!"

I was surprised, and I didn't see the problem until later. S&W had given those guns a goofy name. Nobody target-shoots with a "Chiefs Special." If they had had a name like Trail Masterpiece, everybody—not just me—would have one. ●

This mountain reedbuck fell to one shot from the 280 at about 350 yards; see text for details of shot.

LIFE WITH MY ULTRA-FEATHERWEIGHTS

The rules seem to have changed, even at long and longer range.

by CLARENCE E. ELLIS

WE WERE creeping through the shoulder-high bushes on the nose of a ridge in the high, arid Cape country of South Africa when John Coleman, my professional hunter, froze and put his glasses on something above. I was crouched behind and only saw John's back.

"There're two of them," he said softly. "Move into that opening on our right and take a sitting position. The one you want is on the left, facing right. Hold on the top of the shoulder."

This was my first day on the Black Eagle concession, and of the four species I was hunting, only the springbok wouldn't be up on the ridge. I already knew how hard it was for me to tell mountain reedbuck from vaal rhebok.

I slithered out and sat down, sling already wound around my arm. I put the crosswire of the Leupold 4x on the top line of whatever was up there and nearly flinched the round into the ground 50 ft. in front of me. Resisting the desire to flinch seemed to take two or three minutes. Finally I stilled my beating heart and touched off the round properly. It probably took about 10 seconds to sit and fire.

"Good shot!" says John as the 154-gr. Hornady dumped the heartless beastie on the rocks.

"What was it?" says I. "Couldn't see horns."

"Mountain reedbuck. Nice one, may go seven inches."

The range was about 275 yards horizontally or 350 yards line of sight.

Sounds sort of like the tale I read in one of the hunting magazines, only the writer was shooting a trophy deer instead of a 60-lb. mountain reedbuck. Also that writer used his story to extoll the virtue of a heavy rifle.

Mine weighed, with the scope, just 6 lb., 4 oz.

The three principal light rifle offerings from the major U.S. makers are the Winchester M70 Featherweight with a 22-in. barrel at 6¾ lb.; the Remington Model 7 at 6½ lb. with 18-in. barrel (short cartridges only); and the Ruger 77 Ultra Light at 6 lb. with a 20-in. barrel. Add scope, mounts, and sling and you add another pound. Smith & Wesson had an entry in this field as well; there are plenty of others on a semi-custom basis.

My 280 has a 22-in. barrel and a synthetic stock. It compares favorably with rifles by Brown Precision (5½-7 lb. scoped), H-S Precision (6½-7 lb. scoped), and others. I have a 257 with a 6x Burris, 22-in. barrel, and English walnut stock that weighs 5¾ lb. This article will not, however, describe the means of achieving these weights, but will tell you what you can expect from the resulting ultrafeatherweights in use.

We are used to hearing that light whippy barrels will not hold good groups if fired rapidly enough to heat up the barrel. This was fairly true in the '50s and '60s, but improved barrel-making techniques and bedding techniques have changed that. My 257 and 280 are both essentially M70 Featherweight contour, and are pressure bedded. I normally fire 5-shot groups fairly rapidly. Neither barrel walks the shots as it warms. Besides, this argument has little purpose unless you fire 5- or 3-shot groups on game animals.

I shall not regale you with tales of 1 or 1½-in. 5-shot groups, for in truth they are exceedingly rare. I expect 2-2½ MOA from the 280, and 2¼-2¾ MOA from the 257. I suffer from both poor bench technique and honesty—plus, the little beggars are damned hard to hold steady on a bench. On the other hand, when practicing for my first hunt with the 257, I shot an 8-shot group offhand at 100 yards that measured just 6-in. Take away the one I pulled, and the other seven went into 3¼ in. I don't reckon I'll miss too many critters with that accuracy.

Surely, no one will disagree that a lighter rifle is more pleasant to carry afield. If heavy rifle advocates sneer at wimps like me who can't carry a real rifle, they have my blessing—and a snicker or two. When young and ignorant I hunted with 10-lb. rifles because they held steady. It only took a couple of years to trade my 10½-lb. 7mm-06 for a 7½-lb. 7x57mm. I built the 257 seven or eight years later purely to amuse myself by seeing how light I could make it. I took a mouflon sheep, Catalina goat, mule deer, and pronghorn with that rifle and carried it for 12 days sheep hunting. I was sufficiently impressed to replace the

Rifle	Position	Animal	Range (yds)	Distance missed point of aim: inches
7mm-06,	offhand	mule deer	60	0
10½ lb.	offhand	mule deer	40	0
7×57mm,	sitting	elk	125	1
7½ lb.	sitting	elk	150	1
	prone, rest	white tail deer	500	0
	prone, rest	elk	150	18 (moved)
	sitting	elk	150	2
	offhand	fox	175	2
375 H&H,	sitting, sling	Kodiak bear	230	6
11 lb.	offhand	Kodiak bear	50	18 moving
	rest	kudu	100	0
	rest	Cape buffalo	40	0
257,	offhand	Catalina goat	90	3
5¾ lb.	offhand	Catalina goat	90	0
	offhand	mouflon sheep	125	2
	rest	mule deer	300	12
	kneeling	pronghorn	150	4
	prone, sling	pronghorn	230	0
280	offhand	moose	200	8
6¼ lb.	rest	impala	60	0
	rest	waterbuck	100	0
	offhand	bushbuck	100	3
	offhand	gemsbok	100	4
	sitting, sling	mtn. reedbuck	350	0
	prone, sling	blesbok	430	0
	prone, sling	springbok	250	6 (moved)
	sitting, sling	springbok	150	0
	rest	vaal rhebok	250	6
	sitting, sling	vaal rhebok	150	3
	rest	nyala	320	4
	offhand	nyala	80	4
	kneeling, sling	pronghorn	280	12
	prone, sling	coyote	240	2

7×57mm with the 280, giving myself another 50 yards of useful range on elk while lightening my load 1¼-lb.

About this time I took a vow of poverty and pledged to donate my modest wealth to starving guides and outfitters anywhere. I like to hunt, but if you sneeze here in Colorado, you miss one or two seasons. Since then I've used the 280 and an 11-lb. 375 H&H in serious pursuits to the delight of various taxidermists.

Many will claim that you need a heavy (or medium weight) rifle for a fast offhand shot when your heart is pounding from exertion. I shall disagree. I lugged my 375 up a rather nasty mountain on Kodiak Island and shot a bear. The bear didn't die right there, so guide Danny Nicolai trailed it into the slide alders and we argued our case. After a long hard day, even adrenaline wouldn't make that 375 get on target fast. Fortunately, the bear was hurting worse.

When I went to South Africa I wanted kudu, Cape buffalo, impala, and gemsbok. I had collected the first three, plus a waterbuck and bushbuck before I got more than a glimpse of gemsbok disappearing in a cloud of dust. Once we concentrated on the critters with the long, rapier-like horns our frustrations mounted. We finally pulled a heart-pounding stalk right up to a herd only to have them spook before a clear shot was presented. We tracked them and jumped them twice but hardly saw them. John then set off on a run after the herd. We'd catch them and they'd run off till they decided they were safe, and then shuffle along 'til we caught up. Then they were off again through the thorn bush. Our course was parallel, 50 or 100 yards off. The fourth time we caught them John saw them before they saw us, and skidded to a halt, snapping up his binoculars. "Shoot the third one to the right, quick!" he panted.

Thundering to a screeching halt I swung to the right and poked the muzzle in the prescribed direction. Crosshairs hit chest, trigger finger did its thing, herd took off again. All of them.

"Hit him high," said John.

"Yeah, about six inches," I replied.

John muttered about how many miles a lung-shot gemsbok usually ran as we walked over to pick up the tracks. This one, however, only made about 200 yards before piling up. The 175-grain Nosler had hit the main arteries on top of the heart.

Could I have done as well with a 7½-8½-lb. rifle? Possibly. Better? Not much.

O.K., you'll acknowledge the lack of disadvantage of the light rifle in fast moving situations like that, but perhaps not when you are forced by terrain or vegetation to shoot offhand, or not at all, and the critter is out a ways? I've been there, too.

First hunt with the 257 was for mouflon sheep and Catalina goat. This was a spring hunt with Alan Baier out of Colbran, Colorado. After the usual slipping and sliding through the March mud and snow I spotted something black at the edge of some pinions below. We dropped below the ridge and closed the distance, peered over and saw the black object as a good goat. Farther away was a mouflon ram making overtures to a domestic ewe. I knew if I shot the ram the goat would be in the pinions in one jump. If I shot the goat, the ram had farther to go, and might be slowed by lust. The goat was about 90 yards out, and the ram about 125.

My first shot caused the goat to stagger and brace his legs, so I gave him a second. The ram was in the throes of indecision, which I ended with the third shot. Not being rushed I pocketed each fired case rather than eject them into the snow.

The author's hunting battery, left to right: 257, 280, 7×57 and 375 H&H; the latter is on a reducing diet, but weighs 11 pounds here.

Judging from the weight of match rifles you would assume that 10 lb. or more is needed for precise shooting. I shall freely admit that my best shooting has been with a rifle weighing over 15 lb. However, this shooting required a string of at least ten shots which must virtually go through the same hole. A properly heavy rifle and tight sling minimizes the effort needed to accomplish this task. A light rifle may be fired very accurately once or twice before muscle tremors creep in from the effort.

Lying prone, head downhill, scoping a herd of blesbok, my thoughts were not whether I could make the shot, but when and if I could try it. John had declared that this was the day I'd shoot a blesbok. For once it seemed he might eat his words, as we chased a herd back and forth between two mountains all morning. Finally they halted on a bench. We climbed mountain number one for the third time and bellied over the top and down to some bushes. Range was a bit much, and John couldn't pick out the ram (both sexes have horns). Making like large worms we slithered closer till we ran out of any semblance of cover. The herd had us spotted, but didn't know what we were. While I got into the least comfortable prone position I've ever been in, John glassed. After much soul searching he decided he was 90% sure the one lying down was a ram.

Unfortunately two were in front, and three behind. John clapped and whistled to get the suspect to rise and present a better target. He finally succeeded, but in the ensuing milling we lost our target. Eventually he lay down in his old spot. Eventually I had a clear shot at him. It was past noon and we hadn't had breakfast. For once John hadn't told me to shoot, indicating some uncertainty on his part.

"Hell with it," I muttered. "I'm going to kill that one." I held on the top of its shoulders, briefly cranked maximum tension onto the sling, applied maximum concentration, causing breathing, heartbeat, and muscle tremors to pause long enough to touch off the round.

I'd put six critters down in a row with single shots with this rifle, and applying mental management technique, I never considered the possibility of a miss. The sling was so tight that I recovered from recoil before the bullet struck. The ram's legs straightened and his head sagged. Seven straight. We calculated the range at almost 350 yards horizontal, or over 400 on the line of sight.

You can see here a list of all the shots I've made on big game. Misses due to wind and faulty range estimation are excluded because I don't know how far I missed. There have been nine of those. One thing is apparent. If you go to Africa you can accumulate years worth of experience in a few weeks. Also apparent is the fact that I've made some very good shots and some rather bad shots, but have done both with heavy, light, and medium weight rifles.

In all modesty, I am not an average shot. I have pieces of cardboard saying Expert, AA, and Master that verify that. I do a lot of shooting to keep those classifications. Because I shoot a lot, and shoot well, I can use about any weight rifle I desire. I make it a point to put 40 rounds of practice ammo through a rifle before taking it on a hunt. Of that 40 rounds, 10 will be sitting and kneeling, and 30 offhand. I find that I need another 10 rounds offhand with the super lights or the heavy recoiling 375.

I conclude that the hunter who doesn't shoot during the off season should avoid the light rifles, because they are harder to master. The same goes for rifles with heavy recoil.

I'm putting a glass stock on the 375, planning to trim it to about 8½-lb. For my money, heavy rifles have their places—the rifle range and the gun rack. ●

The author packing 90 pounds of bull elk at about 12,000 ft. elevation in Colorado. Rifle is the 7½-lb. 7×57, and Ellis is pleased.

This gemsbok lost a foot race to the author's 280 and a quick offhand shot under stress; see text.

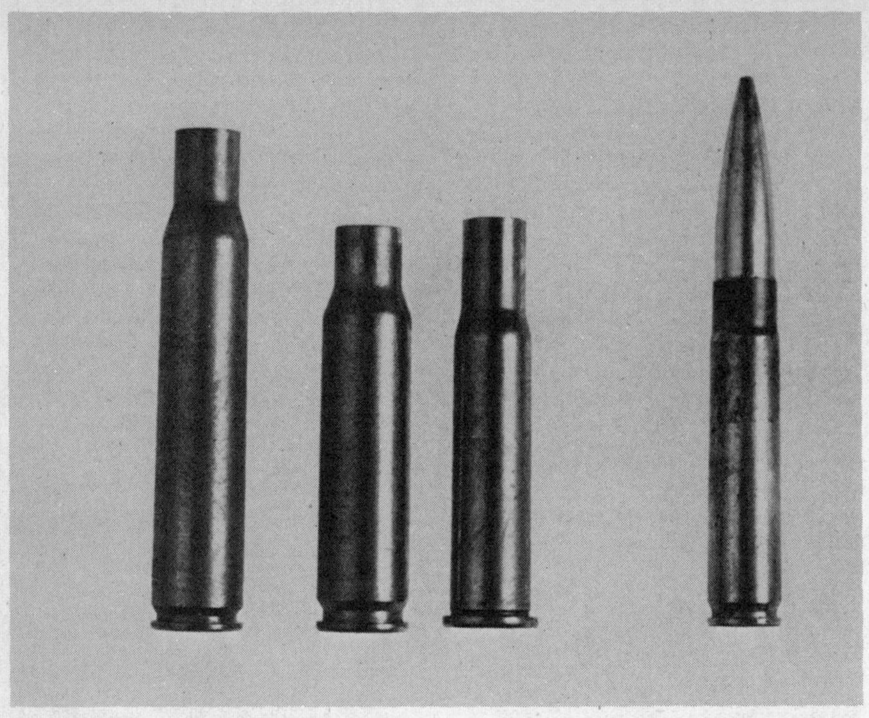

At left are 30-06, 308 and the 30-30 cases; at right, the 30 Apache with 190-gr. Hornady.

So I asked the man about it. Joe looked a little puzzled when I mentioned headspace, and said sometimes a neck split after a case had been loaded and fired twenty or twenty-five times and had to be thrown away. No other problems had turned up that he could remember. The load he used was 28 grains of H-335 powder.

I bought a new Remington Model 788 in 223, dug a discarded 28-inch 308 Douglas heavy match barrel out of scrap, cleaned it up with ammonia and J-B Compound and cut four inches from the breech to get clean rifling. I then turned it down to sporter weight, made a sleeve for the pilot of a 223 reamer and found another of correct size to cut the neck of the chamber and did the barrel. I made loading dies—with neck-expander rod having .224, .240, .260, 270, .280-in. steps. Actually, I eventually made two rods for easier work on cases. Only lost one case, where the neck expanded to uneven length on one side. The finished rifle weighs 8 lbs. 4 oz.

The .30 What?

Small capacity case can surprise with heavy bullets

by ROY F. DUNLAP

SILLY-looking little critter, ain't it? It kept me laughing about five years. That is a 190-grain Hornady boattail match bullet in a 223 Remington case. One shooter soberly stated it was too small to be a wildcat and would have to be called a pussycat. Name it the "30 Pussycat?" Never. "30/223?" Doesn't sound right. Neither does 7.62x45mm—we are getting too many cases with this type of name.

I think maybe we should call it the 30 Apache, in honor of Joe Apache of Raton, NM, who has been using it to knock down heavy high-power rifle metallic silhouettes for years. Yes, including the 500-meter rams, which make a full-sized 308 work pretty hard. The little cartridge seems to have originated along the Border around El Paso, but early became an orphan before adoption by Mr. Apache. Unbelieving competitors (and myself) have watched him methodically knocking down heavy metal in National High Power Rifle Silhouette matches, but no one had guts enough to make up their own rifle.

It finally occurred to me that seeing should be believing and I decided to check it out. While I was making a rifle and talking about things, people told me it couldn't work—the tiny shoulder area would lose headspace, and a case barely bigger than the 30 Carbine, which is nothing but a rimless version of the 100-year-old 32-20, could not possibly do what it was doing. Besides, handgun shooters were already using very similar cases in 30 and 7mm and not setting their world on fire.

I put target-scope bases on for testing, and loaded ammunition. I went with Federal 205M primers, the 28 grains H-335 charge, which is a full case and 190-grain Hornady match, 168-grain Sierra match and the 150-grain Speer bullets, all boattails. Chronographing the 190-grain bullet gave 2079 fps at 15 feet, which means over 2100 at muzzle; call it 2125. The Sierra 168-grain boattail match bullet gave 2190 fps, muzzle; and the Speer 150-grain, 2250 fps, muzzle.

My friend and chronographer, Jim Holden, former NRA Director who was instrumental in getting the NRA interested in silhouette shooting 15 years ago, noticed I had like one-inch

Cont'd.: p. 210

A NEW SNIPER ROUND

by LARRY S. STERETT

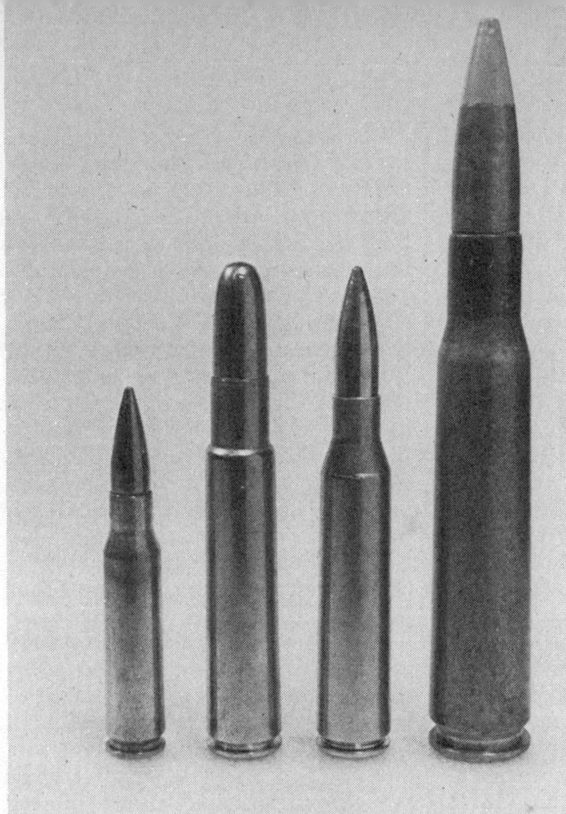

Cartridges, left to right: 7.62 mm NATO, 416 Rigby, the new 8.58x71mm (338/416) Sniper, and the 50 Browning. The 8.58x71mm may represent the sniping cartridge of the future, but none of the cases examined were headstamped.

IN THE PAST, it has often been the custom for military forces to use a modified form of the standard issue rifle as the "sniping" rifle and shoot selected lots of issue ammunition. For example, during World War II the British used the Enfield in various Marks with the No. 4 being the most common; chambered for the 303 British cartridge—for later uses converted to 7.62mm NATO, in fact—this rifle was fitted with a special cheekpiece and a telescopic sight. U.S. snipers of the same era used the scoped M1903A4 Springfield, and also the M1C and M1D Garands, all 30-06s. More recent versions of U.S. sniper rifles have included the M14, HK G3SG1, and the Remington Model 700, all chambered for the 7.62mm NATO cartridge.

On the other side of the fence the Russians have used the M1891/30 Mosin-Nagant rifle, and later the Dragunov rifle, both chambered for the rimmed 7.62x54mm cartridge. These were the "official" sniping rifles, but it is known that both sides have made use of some "unofficial" rifles from time to time for extra-long range sniping, with the two most common being a German anti-tank rifle rebarreled to handle the 50 Browning (12.7x99mm) cartridge for U.S. use, and a Soviet AT rifle chambered for the 12.7x108mm cartridge. As with the regular sniping rifles, the extra-long range models used issue ammunition.

The R.A.I. Model 300 Convertible Long Range Rifle (above) chambered for the 8.58x71mm is a rear-locking bolt-action design with a four-round magazine, fluted 24-inch barrel, fully adjustable stock assembly, and adjustable folding bipod. See exploded view.

Now there is a change underway, at least in U.S. thinking. Although the "official" intended use for the new rifle and cartridge has not been widely advertised, quite a bit of information is available on the cartridge and the rifle for which it is being chambered.

Designated the 8.58x71mm, the new cartridge is based on the 416 Rigby case necked down to handle a 250-grain 338-caliber bullet. Average instrumental velocity at the muzzle, according to the data seen, is just under 3,000 feet per second, with an

Cont'd.: p. 210

Cont'd. from p. 208

groups at 100 meters. He has little bitty frames over his Oehler light screens for their protection, making you shoot through the opening—very carefully! I was using a target during the chronographing. He said, "We gotta shoot this thing at 600 yards."

Off a bench at 600 yards, I fired ten shots for an 8-inch group, which could have been much better had I not screwed up. I found the 10x Unertl Vulture scope was not quite focused and had a little parallax and I tried to correct this during the shooting of the group. This, of course, is just plain stupid. Not only did it keep me changing positions, but I lost the wind reading, and there was a little wind blowing. Incidentally, the 190-grain bullet was still supersonic at the target from 600 yards.

Anyway, both of us are satisfied that the 30 Apache will stay under minute-of-angle at 600 yards. Remember, this test rifle is an 8¼-lb. sporter. The one-pound scope adds nothing to the rifle capability in itself, as a 26-in. heavy match barrel would be expected to do. For a 24-in. standard sporter weight, this test job's performance isn't shabby at all. Recoil with the 190-grain bullet is light, about what might be expected with a factory 100-grain load in a 257 Roberts.

By now, I was no longer laughing and beginning to think of the possibilities of the little cartridge. NRA competition? Several of the 223 bolt actions have five or six-round magazine or clip capacity, so rapid-fire might be achieved with short-loaded rounds. All I had tried were long-loaded and could be used single-loaded only. The 223 military cases such as I had used are readily and cheaply available. A pound of powder will last about 50 percent longer than if used to load 308 or 30-06.

To test the match-rifle capability, I loaded the 125-grain Sierra bullet to same length as the standard 223, using the same powder charge. Our silhouette range being more convenient to use than the high power one, I shot at 200 meters while chronographing. It took more ammunition than expected to get sighted in and I ended up with only nine rounds for the group. I got very light recoil and lower velocity than anticipated. First shot; 2280 fps at 15 feet (add 45 feet to get muzzle velocity); second shot, 2283, lovely. Then increases, but those first five shots averaged 2285 fps, with 18-foot spread, which is quite good. Then I got wide variations in the next four shots—from 2255 low to 2360 high, for a four-shot spread of 105 feet, which is horrible to contemplate. Except that shots kept going into group. The final five shots of group, with widest velocity spread, grouped in $1\frac{5}{16}$-in. This is at 218 yards, remember. The entire nine shots, including one called one inch to right, was $1\frac{5}{16}$-in. high and 3¼-in. wide. The average muzzle velocity for the nine shots was 2347 fps. The group and those large variations in velocities just do not go together, only they did.

The 30 Apache can be rapid-fired fine in short bolt guns when loaded with 125-gr. bullets as shown here.

Quite possibly a somewhat faster-burning powder might do better with the 125-grain bullet, but don't try it with heavier bullets. As it is, the caliber/bullet/weight and X-ring accuracy are OK for our 200 and 300-yard targets, but I'd like a bit more velocity. IMR 4198 won't do; I tried a full case with the 190-grain bullet and got lower velocity than the H-335, but almost no recoil, comparatively speaking.

This possible match-rifle usage is just thrown in for grabs, in case anyone cares to get into competition with the bolt rifle. For a deer-class hunting arm, the 30 Apache has very definite prospects. Rebarrelling any 223 rifle and doing a little magazine alteration can make a lightweight fast-handling outfit for women, boys and old men like me. Will it do the job on game? Look up the factory ballistics of the 30-30, 303 Savage and 32 Winchester Special with heavy bullets and see how the figures compare with those above. You won't laugh. ●

Cont'd. from p. 209

average pressure of just under 55,000 CUP. At 1500 meters, the 250-grain 8.58mm bullet retains slightly less than half its original velocity, or one and one-half times the velocity the 180-grain 7.62mm bullet retains at the same distance. More important, the 8.58mm bullet has nearly 800 foot-pounds of remaining striking energy, while the 7.62mm bullet has just over 250 foot-pounds of remaining energy at 1500 meters. The 338-caliber bullet has one of the best sectional densities and ballistic coefficients of any currently manufactured bullets, although the 300-grain 338 is even better in this regard than the 250-grain.

Manufactured by Research Armament Industries, and distributed by the military arms division of Iver Johnson's Arms as one of the line of "special application" firearms and ammunition, the rifle for which this new cartridge is chambered is labeled the Model 300 Convertible Long Range Rifle. Empty, the rifle weighs 12½ pounds, and features a 24-inch full-fluted, free-floating barrel with rifling twist of 1 turn in 10 inches. (Barrel vibration is dampened by an adjustable tuning rod.)

The rear-locking breech bolt is a bit unusual in having a removable head, a design feature which permits the interchangeability of calibers. The interchangeability is accomplished by replacing the 8.58mm barrel and bolt head with, for instance, a 7.62mm NATO-chambered barrel and corresponding bolt head.

Reportedly capable of ½ minute of angle accuracy in the hands of a skilled marksman, the Model 300s trigger pull is adjustable from 2 to 8 pounds, and the stock assembly adjusts for length of pull, height of comb, and drop at the heel. This degree of stock adjustment allows the shooter perfect alignment with the scope, mounted on a ranging base assembly with increments from 300 meters (zero point) to 1500 meters. This scope base alone weighs 1 pound 5 ounces.

R.A.I. also manufactures a single-shot bolt action rifle chambered for the 50 Browning cartridge. Weighing 30 pounds, empty, this Model 500 has a full-fluted 33-inch free-floating barrel fitted with flash suppressor and accumulator. It has features similar to those of the Model 300, although the two rifles do not share many common parts; receivers, breech bolts, bipods, grip frames, stock assemblies are entirely different. ●

The Burgess of Conyers

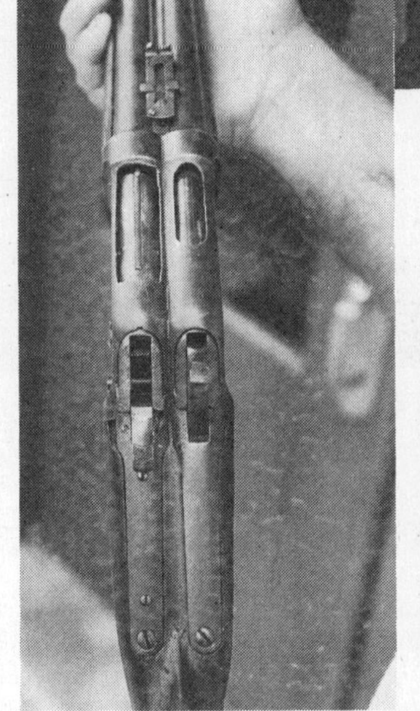

Perhaps 16-gauge on the left and certainly 44-40 on the right, the only mark on the whole thing is the number 770.

(Above) Bill Adams of Conyers, Georgia, with his very special Burgess combination gun.

(Below) The shotgun side got a lever change; some fancy fingerwork was also required for triggering.

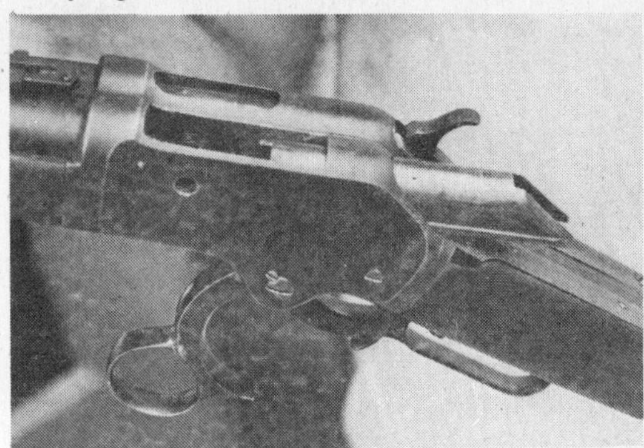

BILL ADAMS has grown to be the kind of fellow who knows a good thing when he sees it and when he saw this peculiar firearm at the Houston Gun Show he knew it was a good thing. So he went for it.

Afterwards, it turned out Colt had a record of one-half of the assembly and that half had been sent to A. Burgess. What is interesting about *that* is that these both were Burgess rifles and A. Burgess is that very Burgess, the one also interested in shotguns. He got the one rifle from the factory in 1885.

Burgess apparently converted a second rifle to shoot shotshells and welded it to this one to get what has to be one of very few twin-actioned lever-operated combination rifle-shotguns in America. Both sides are rigged to act as repeaters, by the bye, which has to be another unusual feature in combination rifle-shotguns. Later, he made a slide-action shotgun Winchester bought and buried.

The rest of the story? There isn't any. This is the gun auctioned by Sotheby in Los Angeles in 1973 and subsequently discussed by Samuel Maxwell, who wrote of Burgess guns in 1976. Adams got it from his good friend Art Schoenfeld, and he cherishes it, very likely to excess.

Ken Warner

Still, it handles very nicely, which is somewhat a surprise.

Norway's Chamber Loader

by NILS KVALE

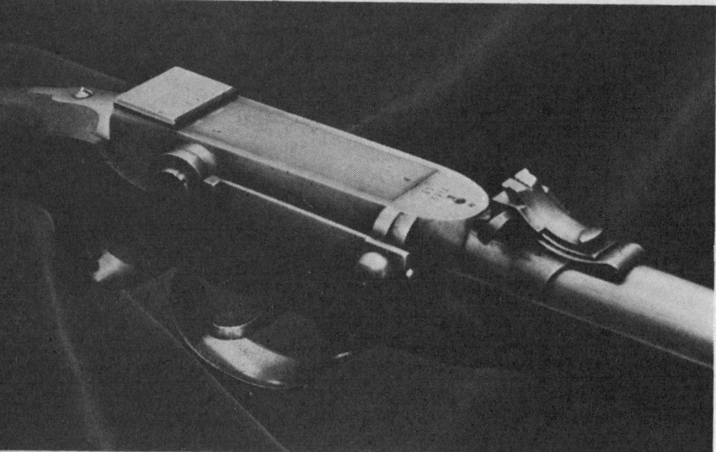

Original Norwegian 1841 chamberloader, action closed. Thumbpiece on right side cocks underhammer when pushed down.

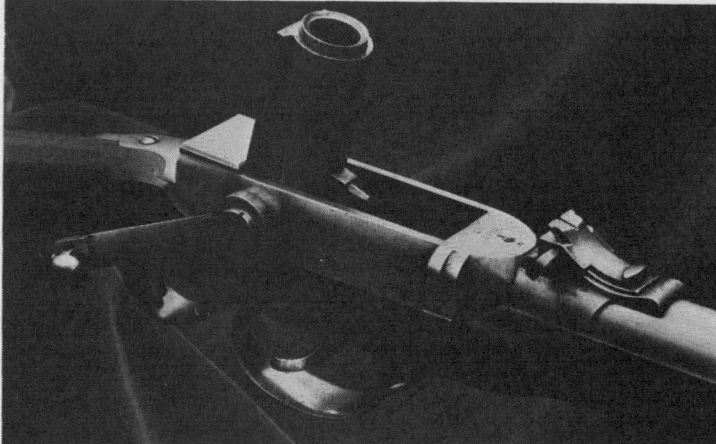

Same with action cranked open. Nipple can be seen; gun was loaded with paper cartridge.

Between muzzleloader and real cartridge gun, these filled the gap for decades.

IN 1867, Norway and Sweden, then a united Kingdom, adopted the American Remington rolling block rifle for their armies. The cartridge was a copper cased, rimfire round of 12.17mm or .47-inch caliber, with a round nose bullet and black powder propellant. Initial quantities of these rifles were bought in the U.S.A., but domestic production soon took over.

While Sweden had gone straight from the percussion lock muzzleloader to the cartridge rifle, Norwegians had for almost 30 years tried to develop a more modern type of infantry rifle, and eventually succeeded. Development and production of a new item like this always takes time in a small country, and the development of small arms advanced at an almost breathtaking clip during the latter half of the 1800s.

Norway had a good muzzleloader, the Model of 1825, but a rifle design commission was organized already in 1837, with the task of designing a more advanced service rifle. The call for a breech-loading system was definite, and the resulting army rifle of 1842 hence became a "chamber loader"—a technically interesting design half way between the muzzleloader and the cartridge gun. It was not an exclusive Norwegian invention—similar designs were worked on in France by Delvignes and Lefaucheux, in Germany by Dreyse and by Loebnitz in Denmark, and the U.S. had its Hall action. The Norwegian commission ran tests involving several of these designs, and then added changes and improvements as they found necessary. The prototype rifles were made at the Army Arse-

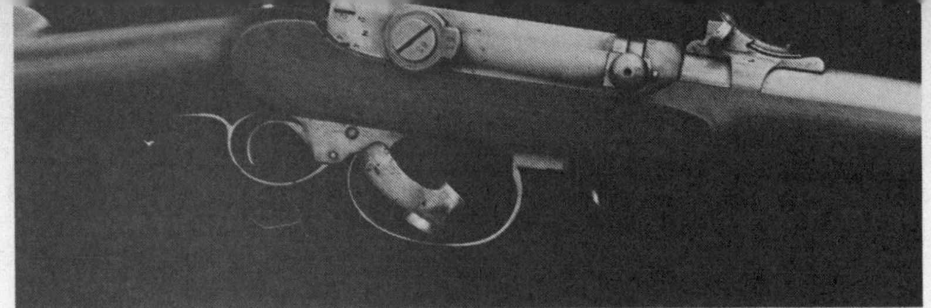

Here's how the Model 1841 looked ready to fire—an elegant layout in many ways.

Here's the Lund conversion, with its leather "safety" inserted between hammer and receiver.

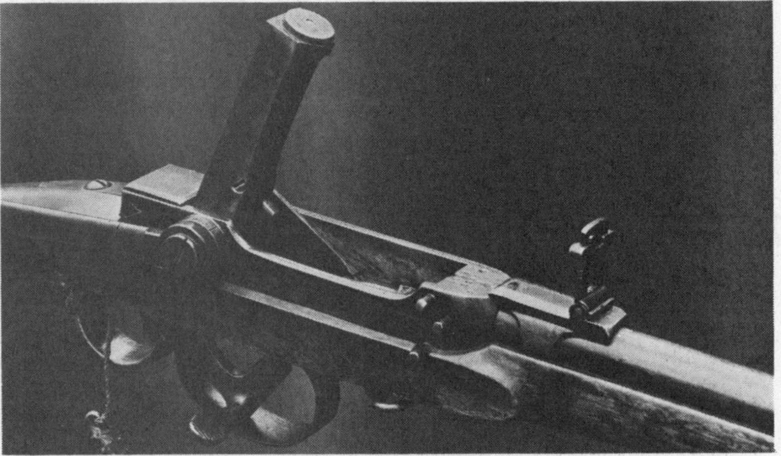

Lund conversion with action open and hammer cocked shows similarity in general plan to Allin Conversion in the U.S. trapdoor rifles.

nal in Kongsberg, and were the combined efforts of Colonel Jens Christian Blich, Captain Frederik Wilhelm Scheel of the Royal Artillery, and the factory gunsmith, Niels Gregersen.

Different from the muzzleloader, the chamber loader has a receiver, initially machined in two halves and soldered to the barrel. One of the test procedures prescribed was to hang the unit by the barrel and sound the receiver like a tuning fork, to check the quality of the soldering operation. The rear end of the receiver consisted of a solid steel block fastened by four screws, and immediately ahead of the block was the cam spindle or center on which the breech block hinged. The breech block, or "chamber," was a smoothbored extension of the barrel, operated by a lever on the right hand side of the receiver. Lifting the lever up and backwards moved the chamber about ⅛ inch to the rear to disengage the receiver and then swung it upwards at the front end. In a way, you were still muzzle-loading, but the muzzle had come much closer, and there was no need for a ramrod to get the bullet in place. The ramrod was still there for the purpose of cleaning the bore, and with the barrel open at both ends, cleaning had become a much easier operation.

The primer nipple was located on the underside of the chamber, well enclosed and protected inside the receiver, and it was struck by an underhammer. This hammer was hinged just in front of the trigger, and is in turn also protected, by a wide steel guard which at closer inspection turns out to be the mainspring! Just one of the little ingenious things in this design. The safety is as simple as it is efficient: A piece of leather that goes between the receiver and the hammer and keeps the latter from reaching up to the primer. There is a small steel peg on the piece of leather that fits into a hole for proper location and an eyelet at the other end for a retaining string. You just cock the hammer, and your safety automatically drops off.

The chamber loader rifle was adopted in the Norwegian Army in 1842. Its caliber was .66 inches. In 1848, the army went to pointed bullets and paper cartridges were developed for the rifle. The paper cartridge contained a lubricated bullet and its black powder charge. Loading procedure as follows: Open breech, prime. Hold bullet end of paper cartridge between teeth, twist off paper and pour powder charge into chamber. Take bullet and thumb seat it onto powder charge, close action and cock hammer, and you're ready for business. Needless to say, this rifle would fire several shots for each one that could be fired with the muzzleloader, and ignition was almost 100%.

Development never ends, but it is interesting to note how quickly and often changes had to be made 130 years ago. Especially considering the fact that the army rifles of the late 1800s remained in service unchanged for 40 or 50 years. There were new model chamber loaders in 1846 and 1849, a special model for the War Academy in 1848, and another new model in 1855—the latter had to have a new sight design for the pointed bullets, as their trajectory was flatter. An interesting detail is that some of the 1842 rifles had an arc-type rear sight like that of the Garand rifle, only it was a sliding type instead of the rack and pinion design.

The pointed bullet was an advantage, but you get nothing for free. It was heavier than the round ball bullet, and the number of rounds the soldier could carry became limited. Here is something that wasn't considered too important during the first half of the 1900s—the modern soldier was to have his ammo brought forward by motorized vehicles. Today, in the 1980s, we are back to the thought that the soldier also must carry his ammo—one good reason for the development of the 223 and similar rounds.

The Norwegian army decided it needed a new rifle to take care of this problem. Besides, a smaller caliber would give higher muzzle velocity with corresponding longer range and flatter trajectory. The new model was adopted in 1860, and while the design remained essentially the same, it was an entirely new rifle, not a conversion. It was lighter, slimmer, handier and had an excellent stock design. The caliber was called four "lines." These lines were something that differed a bit, depending on what you were talking about. Kerosene lamps were designated in lines too, but in the gunmaking business they divided the (Scandinavian) yard into two feet, the foot into ten inches, and the inch into ten lines. This system of caliber measurement was introduced in the Norwegian army in 1843.

The actual caliber of the 1860 model rifle was 3.75 lines, or .46 inches. It, too, was made in different models, some of which had the Whitworth or hexagonal-type rifling. The chamber bore remained round and it seems they initially used round bullets also in the hexagonal bore. Later, the front end of the chamber was cut off and replaced by a piece of hexagonal bore, indicating that the regular Whitworth-type bullet was used.

There is a brass, round-head screw on top of the comb of many of these rifles that has caused grey hairs among collectors. There is no apparent reason for this screw, as the stock does not need reinforcement at that point. If the original sight has been replaced no one could really be expected to find the reason for that screw without inside information. It was placed there to indicate proper eye relief for a range finder sight. The rear sight was a piece of angle iron with one short and one long leg, and it could be flipped into either position. The sighting notch in the short leg was located in the middle of a much larger, square notch—and if the length of an enemy cavalry horse filled the large notch, range was right for that sight, or more correctly vice versa. With the long leg of the angle flipped into position, there were sighting notches on "two floors"—each located in a rectangular hole. If a standing enemy soldier filled the hole, you could hold straight on. Sight setting went up to 700 yards, which is a little over 500 of today's American yards. With the rainbow trajectory of the lead slugs, the range finder sight undoubtedly was of some help.

This 1860 model rifle was an excellent weapon, well made and easy to handle, but it was born a little too late. Only 7 years later, the rolling block rifle was adopted. The ordnance people now had a problem. They had numbers of new 1860-models in the arsenals, and a run of 1600 in the factory not

The Landmark conversion looks more complex, even with the action closed.

This Landmark action has its breech block closed over a cartridge. That rangefinder sight is set for shorter ranges with the "horse" notch up.

Here's the full flavor of the Landmark conversion, open with the breech tilted for loading. A tricky firing-pin arc was demanded.

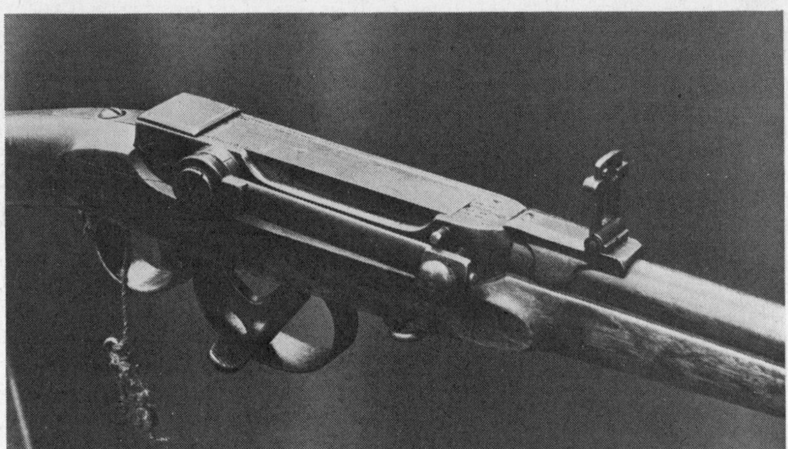

Lund conversion ready to fire—the leather "safety" has dropped away to dangle until needed again.

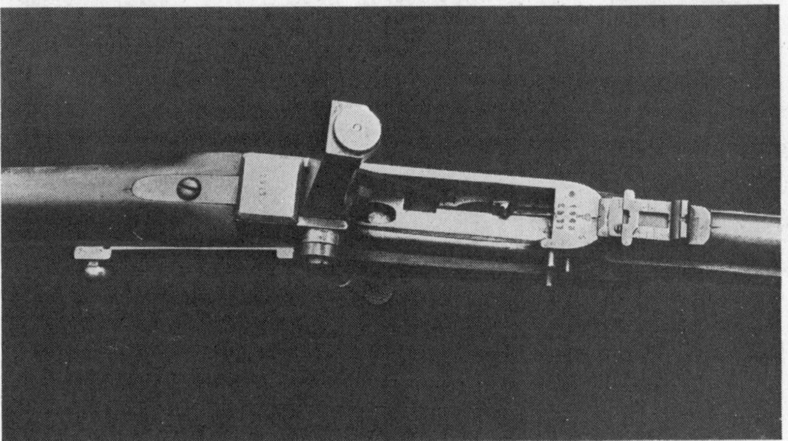

In the Lund conversion, the extractor was emplaced within the left side of the receiver.

even finished. Obviously these rifles could not be junked, so it was decided to convert them for the new 47-caliber rimfire cartridge. Hence were born two interesting designs, that today are better known to Scandinavian collectors than the original. One was developed by the Chief of Ordnance, Col. Alf Lund; the other by the Superintendent of the government arms factory, Col. Jens Landmark. In both cases, the 46-caliber barrel of the 1860 rifle had to be "drawn up" to .47 to fit the new bullet, but that was of course no big problem. The Landmark conversion had a new chamber block with a hinge in the middle. It could be folded backwards after opening, and the cartridge inserted into its front part, with the bullet pointing towards the shooter. The rear part of the block had an arc-shaped firing pin, hit by the old underneath hammer. A case extractor was built into the side of the block. The Landmark conversion was adopted by the Navy and remained in use for several years.

The Lund Conversion went into use with the army, and was perhaps a more modern solution. Here, an actual cartridge chamber was bored into the barrel, and the old chamber piece was replaced by a one piece breech block holding a long firing pin that extended downwards at the rear to meet the hammer. A sliding extractor was built into the lower left-hand side of the chamber.

The rolling block rifle and these two conversions remained in use with the Norwegian forces even after the next service rifle was adopted. This was in 1889, the 40-caliber Jarmann rifle, and the rolling block rifle was still in the reserve after 1894, when the 6.5mm Krag rifle got into production. Both the Jarmann and the Krag were Norwegian designs, and the Krag (in 30 caliber) became the service rifle of the United States in 1898, until it was superseded by the Springfield in 1903.

About 1867, experiments were even carried out to convert the 1840 66-caliber rifles to take a rimfire cartridge, but it became evident that a 66-caliber round would be far too heavy.

If you're tired of reading by now, you might hope that this was the end of the converted Norwegian chamber loaders. If, however, you would like to read more, it wasn't. Towards the end of the century they were sold out of the arsenals to become so-called "house rifles"—farm rifles would be a better word—at about 37 US cents apiece. Lots of them were in excellent condition, but ammunition was getting scarce, and it wasn't cheap. Dyed-in-the-wool reloaders have managed to reload a rimfire cartridge, but farmers at that time did not have the facilities. So this time civilian gunsmiths went to work and came up with a conversion of the conversion, especially with the Lund rifle. They plugged the firing pin hole and moved it to the center of the breech block, opened up the chamber to take a slightly bottle-shaped brass shell. Berdan primed as was common in Europe in those days, but it could be reloaded, and that was the main thing. They also made excellent brass bullet moulds.

This was in the days when German factories offered to make you any brass case you wanted, provided you bought 10,000, and with your own headstamp if you liked. No doubt there are American collectors who have a round or shell marked Lund, and the name of the gunsmith who ordered the batch of brass, Hagen being one of the most active.

About ten years ago I visited a good friend's gun store in Portland, Oregon. In his "collector's rack" he had a $25 relic that nobody knew much about. It was good and rusty and had a very crude stock, or part of one, attached to it. And bore all signs of very extensive use and abuse. I didn't buy it, but that rifle was rarer than most collectors would think. It was the 1860 chamber loader, unconverted. Only a handful of these rifles escaped conversion and were transferred to the army museum, and of this handful all but a couple were destroyed in a fire in 1942. A few similar rifles were made for the Norwegian NRA, and the one in Oregon might have been one of these, brought over by one of the Norwegians who emigrated to work in the Pacific slope forests and lumber yards back in the 1800s. Or maybe he just walked away from the army and on board one of the emigrant ships that docked right outside the main fort of Oslo, taking His Majesty the King's gun with him. You often wish guns could talk. ●

Designed on a cocktail napkin, Frank Woods' Deer Master was shooting 10 days later.

Custom Gun Guild's One-Piece Rifle

TO TEST any firearm with serial number 1 is a bit unusual, but that's what I got when they sent a Deer Master in 257 Roberts. It weighs 6 pounds, 3 ounces and arrived with 4x scope mounted with Kimber rings. The scope and rings plus three cartridges and a nylon sling increased the weight to 7 pounds, 5 ounces. Conventional enough.

The stock is fiberglass with some type of gritty material at the wrist and forearm for a no-slip grip. Sling swivel studs are there too. The stock has a good feel to it and is very well done, including the brown paint job and Pachmayr pad. Black and camoflage are also available. All metal has a dull, matte finish. So far, the Deer Master sounds a lot like several other rifles, right?

For these rifles, the folks at Douglas supply Custom Gun Guild with premium grade, rifled blanks with extra long shanks and here's where it gets different. The bore at the shank end is enlarged and two ports are milled through the wall. After the rear of the newly bored hole is threaded, a sleeve with four integral shoulders inside it is turned in to serve as lug seats. The back end of the barrel blank has now become a receiver while the other 20 inches is the barrel. That's different.

A fire control assembly is attached to what is called the receiver extension or tang. The whole works is held to the receiver bottom by a screw. The trigger, a Timney match grade, is absolutely superb. Just forward of the magazine port, an L-shaped block of steel is welded to the receiver as a recoil lug. Calibers available are 243, 257 Roberts, 270, 7x57mm, 308 and 30-06, and probably others.

The Model 85-B bolt reminds me a little of the Remington 788 except it has four large locking lugs at its rear instead of nine smaller lugs. It also differs in that the front section of the bolt does not rotate. The recessed bolt face is totally enclosed by the breech area; however, the bolt face counterbore wall is interrupted by a Sako-type extractor. The ejector is the familiar spring-loaded pin through the bolt face. Bolt lift is 45 degrees.

An Allen-head screw through the left receiver wall serves as a bolt stop, as a bolt release and also keeps the front section of the bolt from rotating. I'd just as soon see a retracting pin-type bolt release here. The action has four gas relief vents, one on the right side of the receiver ring and three in the bolt body at the ejection port. The bolt handle, with hollow knob, appears to be brazed or silver soldered to the bolt body. The bolt handle also serves as a safety lug since it rests in a recess in the tang.

The cocking piece extends back through the bolt shroud and serves as a cocking indicator. The front of the bolt shroud is the same diameter as the receiver and thus would deflect escaping gases. Atop the bolt shroud sits a 5-position, Model 70-type safety lever. The two extra positions are for left-hand shooters. Yep, the safety is ambidextrous. When the safety tab is pointing straight to the rear, the firing pin is locked but the bolt can be rotated for unloading the chamber. Swinging the lever around about 22 degrees to the right (or to the left) locks the bolt and firing pin. When the lever is pushed to its extreme forward position the safety is disconnect-

This is a handmade lefthander Deer Master with most of the essential elements in view.

ed. Pretty neat.

The receiver is dovetailed on top for most of its length. Kimber rings are furnished with each rifle. Eliminating a scope base and its screws is a good idea but on the test rifle, the grooves terminate up front with a radius. It might be better to have the flat surface of the ring base butt against a flat recoil shoulder. Also, a transverse retaining pin intersecting both grooves for the rear ring would provide a little peace of mind. *(And Custom Gun Guild says they'll do these things: Editor)*

The feeding system consists of a Remington box magazine, the one they make for their pump and autoloading centerfire rifles. Should it be damaged or lost, its replacement is no farther away than the gun dealer in

Simpson had a chance to tote the Deer Master for a bit, found it friendly.

Load	Bullet	Average Accuracy
IMR-4064	Hornady 75 HP	1.14 in. (2)
IMR-4831	Sierra 117 FB	1.26 in. (5)
IMR-4350	Speer 120 FB	1.52 in. (4)
IMR-4350	Speer 100 BT	1.73 in. (4)
Winchester 100 ST	------------	1.53 in. (2)
Remington 117 RN	------------	1.58 in. (3)
Winchester 117 +P	------------	1.83 in. (4)

The numbers in parentheses are the number of 5-shot groups fired with each load.

green. Cartridge feeding is smooth and bobble free. To release the magazine, the end of a spring-loaded latch extends down, just forward of the trigger bow.

I mounted a Burris 4-12x Mini on the rifle, gathered up three factory loads and three handloads known to work in other rifles, and headed for the range. All told, 24 five-shot groups were fired at 100 yards. I charted the results.

Many rifles I've tested didn't settle down and do their best until 75 to 100 rounds had gone through them. Indications are that the test rifle falls in the same category. Group number 22, with the 117 Sierra measures 0.75-inch. The last two groups, fired with the 75 Hornady hollow point, are 1.33 and 0.92-inch.

I'm sure one of the biggest questions in your mind by now is the same one I had when first seeing the rifle. What happens when the barrel is shot out? First of all, you'd be surprised at the relatively small number of barrels on big game rifles that ever get shot out. Few hunters ever put enough rounds through their rifles to wash out the throats. But I still haven't answered the question, have I? It's simple; you send the Deer Master back to CGG, they'll chop off the barrel, cut threads into the receiver and install a new barrel the old timey way. The Deer Master lists for $1,000.

Layne Simpson

Wolf Ears and a 30-30 Derringer

This is no target pistol but it hits derringer targets just fine.

No bones about it—it shoots the real 30-30 factory rifle stuff.

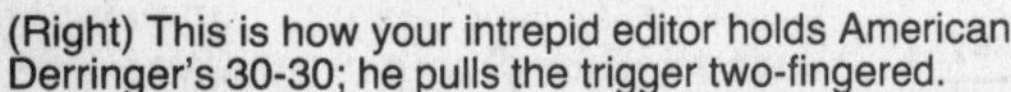

(Right) This is how your intrepid editor holds American Derringer's 30-30; he pulls the trigger two-fingered.

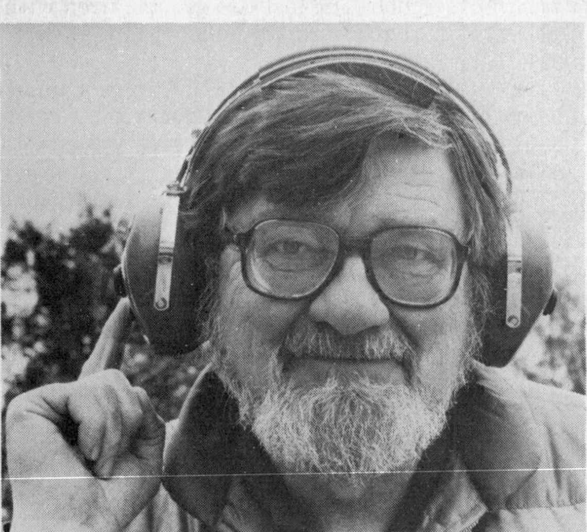

Push this button and Wolf Ears go electronic. Ayoob's address is P. O. Box 122, Concord, NH 03301.

SELDOM do two new shooting products go together as well as the electronic earmuffs Massad Ayoob calls Wolf Ears and American Derringer's preposterous 30-30. The latter is LOUD; the former are, well, *unloud.*

Talking guns first, the 30-30 derringer is an interesting piece of work. It really does chamber and shoot the standard 30-30 rifle cartridge. I have shot it several times and see no reason not to continue. It seems a very sturdy gun and is entirely manageable for the respectful shooter. That is, I wear gloves and hold tight.

Doing that, I would undertake to hit your hat every pop at 30 feet. I suspect from the way it goes I might one day be able to hit your hat—not one of those stingy-brims, mind you—as far as 50 feet. I don't know, however, that all these hats are going to get the full swat of the 30-30 we all know and love. The bore dimensions of the 30-30 derringer seem intelligently generous and the barrel is *very* short.

That's why it's LOUD. With the Wolf Ears on, though, it just seems an ordinary gunshot. The Wolf Ears are more than a bit eerie, but I'm going to be using them just the same. What we have here are microphones and speakers over each ear in a very high quality standard-style earmuff. There's a sensor, and when it detects a loud (over 90 db, they say) noise, it shuts off the microphone until the noise has moderated. The resulting aural sensation is absolutely going to get your attention at first.

Regardless of all that, the Ears are practical. One can converse in normal tones, hear the phone ring, and shoot, all at once. In fact, unloud noises are amplified somewhat, to the point where eating celery is a close encounter of a boisterous kind.

So why a 30-30 derringer? First, I think we're into the Mt. Everest syndrome—because it's there. Then, for the user of a derringer, the 30-30 is as good as anything else except some sort of shotshell (which American Derringer can also handle for you). And it's a great conversation piece and hat-hitter. I like it.

Ken Warner

Pennsylvania's Slug Barrel Shoots Swell

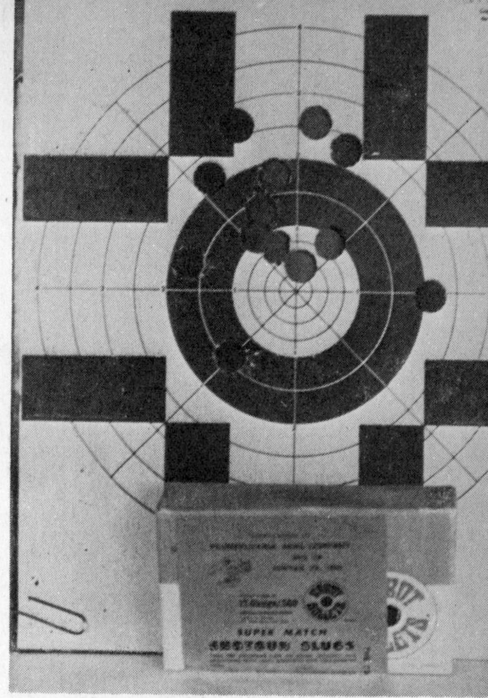

This group was fired at 100 yards with the last 13 BRI slug loads. Extreme spread between the two widest holes is exactly four inches. Remarkable!

THE D in serial number D000001 means the Diana Society, a relatively new organization comprised of those who hunt and compete with shotgun slugs. The rest of the serial number identifies the gun as the first of its kind, and that's the one I shot.

Actually, this firearm probably should be called the Ithaca/Pennsylvania Arms gun since it is the result of a joint venture between the two firms. The reason it isn't is because John Tanis of Pennsylvania Arms loaned me the gun. This shotgun shoots five slugs into 100-yard groups you can cover with your hand. If you've shot many slugs through smoothbore barrels, then you know that is something special.

The receiver is like any other Model 37 pump gun but from there on out it differs a bit. The usual Model 37 barrel is attached to the receiver with interrupted threads so it can be quickly switched. Not so with this gun. The barrel is screwed in tight for increased rigidity and floats since the magazine tube is not attached to it.

The barrel starts out as a long bar of chrome moly or stainless steel, then it's turned and drilled out to the same bore diameter from breech to muzzle. Next, and here's the interesting part, it is button rifled with 6 lands and grooves with a twist rate of 1 in 34 inches. In effect, what we now have is a rifle barrel that fits a shotgun. Considering the simplicity of the idea, plus the thousands of deer hunters who shoot slugs, both by choice and otherwise, it is most surprising that such a much-needed development has been so long in coming.

For testing, I gathered up six slug loads, Winchester, Remington, two from Federal, the Brenneke and the BRI sabot load. The gun came with a Redfield one-piece base attached to the receiver with four screws so I thought it only fitting that I use a Redfield scope—the excellent 3-9x Illuminator. All 5-shot groups were fired from benchrest, the BRI load at 50 and 100 yards, the others at 100 only.

At 50 yards, most groups shot with BRI ammunition ran around two inches and on several occasions four shots would cluster into less space. But there was the occasional flyer to spoil an otherwise impressive group and accuracy would jump to three inches. Not bad, though.

The averages for a minimum of three, 5-shot groups at 100 yards look like this:

BRI	4-in.
Winchester	9-in.
Federal Super Slug (1¼ oz)	12-in.
Federal (1 oz)	14-in.
Remington	14-in.
Brenneke	16-in.

It was easy to see why the BRI load is more accurate. The sabot diameter is the same as the groove diameter in the barrel. Recovered sabot halves had uniform and quite deep rifling marks over their entire lengths. During its trip down the bore, a spin was being imparted to the BRI slug as intended. I don't understand why the Brenneke performed so poorly; an occasional decent group was horribly spoiled by one or two slugs landing sideways, far from the others. This was surprising since the Brenneke slug is 0.005-in. larger than groove diameter and its base wad is 0.018-in. larger. Over stabilization maybe?

Of the four Foster-type slugs tested, the Winchester load was quite the most accurate. This is by no means a mystery. The Winchester slug measured 0.010-in. larger than barrel groove diameter while the Federal and Remington slugs were 0.035-in. SMALLER. In other words, slugs from Federal or Remington shells could freefall through the bore. I checked the muzzle of my Model 1100 slug barrel and its diameter is identical to that of the Pennsylvania barrel.

I am told that it will be quite some time before you can buy one of these special Ithaca slug guns. The first 100, with heavy barrels like the one tested, will go to competitors of the next World Slug Shootng Championship. The first big shoot was held last year with Pennsylvania Arms barrels taking first and second places and a good share of the $10,000 purse. However, you don't have to wait. You can send an Ithaca receiver to Pennsylvania Arms and they'll fit a barrel.

They'll also fit barrels to the Remington 870, Browning Auto-5 and the various Smith & Wesson pump guns, but no other autoloaders as this is written. Barrels are available in 12 or 20 bore. I might also add that the BRI people use one of these barrels for testing loads at the factory. It is screwed into a Mossberg bolt action.

The company will mount iron sights on their barrels, but they like to see hunters use scopes. Recommended are the side mount from B-Square or a Redfield base attached to the top of the receiver.

True enough, $300 is a lot of money for a barrel unless you're a trap shooter. Looking at it another way, it's probably less expensive than buying a new deer rifle. With the BRI load, the gun is said to deliver 1,280 foot pounds of energy at 100 yards, plenty for deer but the slug seems awfully hard and I wonder about expansion. However, a deer with a half-inch hole through the lungs isn't likely to travel very far. We'll see.

It will also be interesting to see how the various state game officials react to such a revolutionary new concept in slug shooting, especially in those states that restrict deer hunters to slugs. I'd say if they are at all wise they'll welcome it with open arms. Four minute-of-angle accuracy with a slug gun can't help but cut down on game wounded and lost.

Layne Simpson

Walker Chokes and the APS

This is an APS—the all-purpose shotgun. Walker likes the 870 Magnum with his chokes in the APS role.

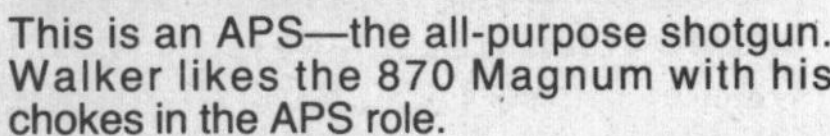

Walker's tool will tell you which choke is in there, used in this fashion.

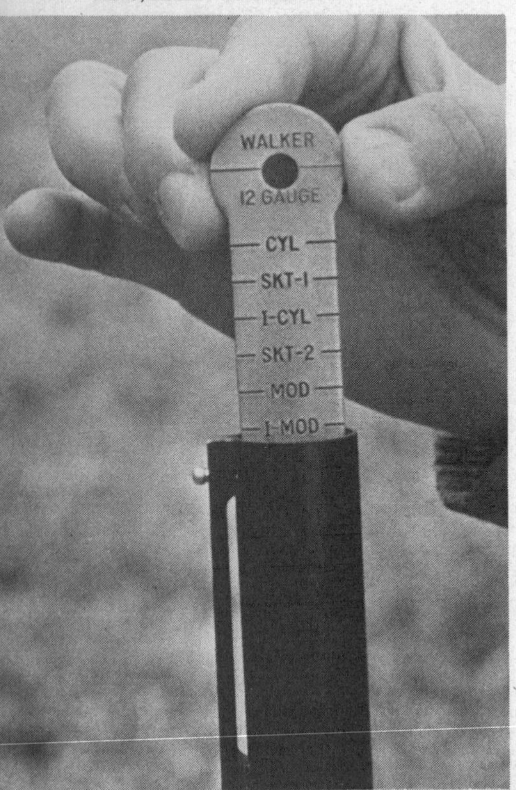

A LONG TIME ago I had a Mossberg shotgun with screw-*on* chokes; I have since had Cutts Comps and Poly-Chokes; then came Win-chokes and suddenly the world is full of screw-*in* choke tubes. Selma, Alabama, is particularly full of choke tubes because Ralph Walker is there and so are Walker Chokes.

OK. Technical stuff: Ralph's chokes are almost as long as your thumb and double-threaded 44 t.p.i. That means they move at a rate of 22 t.p.i., or interminably, into the bore during a tube change. In fact, it takes 35-40 seconds to get one out, and another 35-40 seconds to get one in. Your barrel has to have an outside diameter of .830-in., which eliminates Model 12 Winchesters, but leaves a lot of others available. Unless you look down the muzzle Walker Chokes are invisible. They are slotted for a quarter and for Walker's cute little choke-gauge and tool. And a penny will work unless they're very tight.

Choices abound. Walker will give you any length barrel you want, and there are 10 or 12 choke constrictions. If you want 40 points of choke, Ralph's your guy. Indeed, if you'd rather not mess with an old favorite gun of yours, Ralph Walker will sell you a whole Remington 870 Magnum with a set of his chokes. For Ralph, that's an all-around gun.

As the photos show, I disported with one on a grim afternoon shooting at 3×5 cards. I found out what I knew going in: Walker Chokes work just fine. So do 870s.

Ken Warner

These three tubes and the right threads to take them in your barrel will go about $135.

And you use the quarter-sized other end to do the installing.

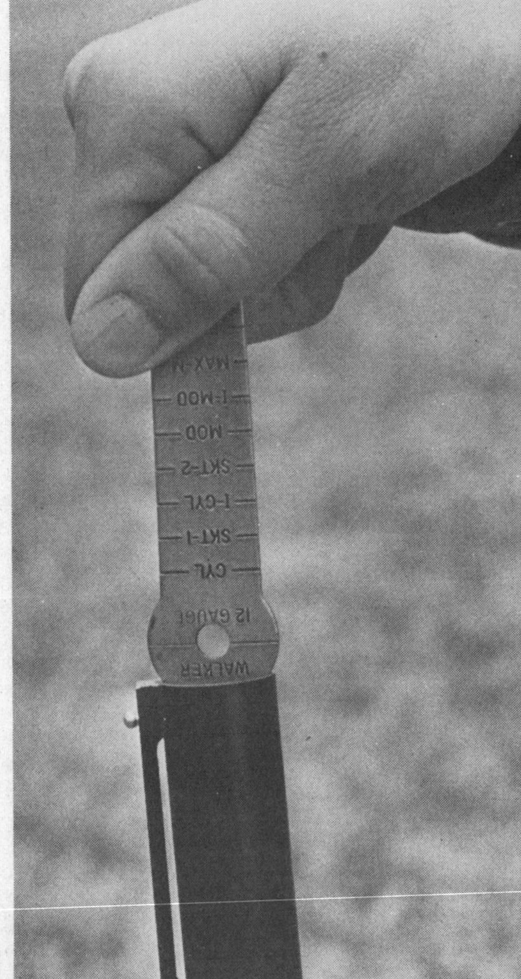

Ultra Light's Model 20 Really Is Ultra Light

THE Model 20 is Melvin Forbes' brainchild. Melvin owns the Ultra Light Arms Company. His action weighs 20 ounces which is why he calls it the Model 20. It is a scaled-down Model 700 Remington with Winchester Model 70 bolt release and Sako extractor.

The Model 20 rifle has a 22-in. Douglas Number 1 contour barrel and weighs 4 pounds 7½ ounces. I installed a Burris 6x Mini in Ultra Light's mounts, attached an Uncle Mike's nylon sling with quick-detach swivels, loaded three 284 Winchester cartridges and the resulting toting weight tallied up to an amazing 5 pounds, 12 ounces.

To put such feathery heft into perspective, the lightest factory bolt action rifle I own weighs six ounces *more* fresh from its box and that rifle has a thinner and shorter barrel. GUN DIGEST Number 40, which you're now holding, weighs almost half as much as my Model 20, even though the Model 20 barrel is full-size and 22 inches long. Weight is not trimmed away at the expense of cartridge performance.

How does the man make such an airweight rifle? It would appear to be quite simple: you build a short-action Model 700, but you squeeze everything down to standard cartridge size and forget magnums. A comparison of the resulting dimensions and weights would look like this:

	Model 700	Model 20
Action weight	40.0 oz.	20.0 oz.
Bolt weight	12.5 oz.	8.0 oz.
Receiver length	8.00 in.	7.50 in.
Receiver ring diameter	1.36 in.	1.225 in.
Magazine length	2.85 in.	3.05 in.
Bolt diameter	0.70 in.	0.60 in.
Bolt throw	4.00 in.	4.00 in.
Bolt length	6.50 in.	6.00 in.

The Model 20 action is both lighter and shorter than the Model 700 short action, but its bolt throw is the same and its magazine box is longer. This latter detail allows bullets to be seated a bit farther out of the powder cavity when handloading the short cartridges.

Excepting the jeweled bolt, all metal is blued over a matte finish and a shiny finish is optional. The bolt handle is trim and neat and sweeps back where it should. The three-shot magazine is blind and I do believe the aluminum trigger bow was made up in Ilion, New York. The Kevlar stock is coated with DuPont Imron, a tough, chip-resistant, polyester-based epoxy paint. In the application it is smooth and run-free, one of the best I've seen. Optional colors are green, black, brown or camouflage pattern. Back at the rear is a Pachmayr Old English pad.

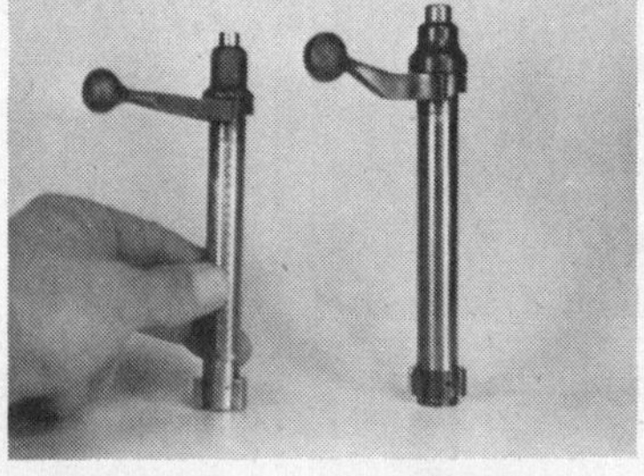

(Above) The Model 20 bolt (left) is almost a dead-ringer for the Model 700 bolt (right) except it's scaled down to smaller dimensions. In fact, the entire rifle is a scaled-down Model 700.

Gun Digest weighs about half as much as the Model 20 Ultra Light. This one is in 284 Winchester.

In case you're not familiar with Kevlar, it's a fabric developed by DuPont for making such things as bulletproof vests, automobile tires and rough duty boats for our Coast Guard. Ultra Light forms it into a shell with amine-based epoxy resins. A Kevlar stock looks the same as one made of fiberglass but it's stronger and a few ounces lighter. It's more expensive too. Graphite is added to make the stock even more rigid.

The Model 20 has a Timney trigger modified by ULAC. The safety lever is pushed forward to "off" and pulled rearward to "on" like any other but there's a difference. Pushing down on the lever allows the bolt to be opened yet the safety is still on. They call it a three-stage safety and, yes, it's patented. They'll sell you one for $20 and fit it to your Model 700 for another $35.

Chamberings as this is written are 22-250, 6mm Remington, 257 Roberts, 7mm-08, 7x57mm, 284 Winchester, 7mm-6.5 Magnum (a wildcat) and 308 Winchester. The 223 Remington should be just around the corner. I tested a 284 and it shot like this with maximum loads of IMR-4350:

Speer 145 flat base	1.07 in.
Nosler 150 solid base	1.16 in.
Speer 130 boattail	1.19 in.
Hornady 139 boattail	1.43 in.
Speer 160 boattail	1.48 in.
Nosler 140 solid base	1.54 in.
Speer 145 boattail	1.73 in.

Those group sizes represent an average of five 5-shot groups fired with each load and they are pretty darned good. Does it kick? Sure it does. Any rifle that pushes the 130-grain Speer to 3,100 fps is bound to, but it's not as bad as you might think. The stock is shaped to handle recoil quite nicely. Anyhow, this is a hunting rifle and hunting rifles are carried much more than they are shot.

The Model 20 is also available with its bolt handle over where left-hand shooters had rather it be. In fact, the southpaw is a true, mirror-image of the right-hand model. Do-it-themselfers can buy these actions, $675 for the right-hand and $100 more for the lefty. ULAC will also fit a 16-ounce stock to your Model 700 for $450, finished and ready to go. A complete Model 20 rifle with its stock built to your specs will cost you $1300.

I like this little rifle for more reasons than its accuracy, quality and airy heft. I like it because it consistently puts the first shot from a cold, clean barrel to the same point of impact as those that follow. I like it because it doesn't walk bullets all over the paper when its barrel gets too hot to touch. I also like it because it puts bullets weighing from 130 to 160 grains into virtually the same group at 100 yards.

There is one thing about the Model 20 I am having a hard time getting used to, though. When it's hanging from my shoulder I tend to forget that it's there.

Layne Simpson

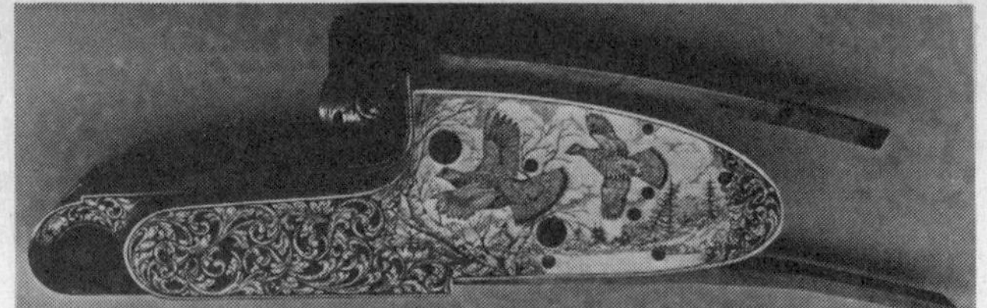

W.P. SINCLAIR

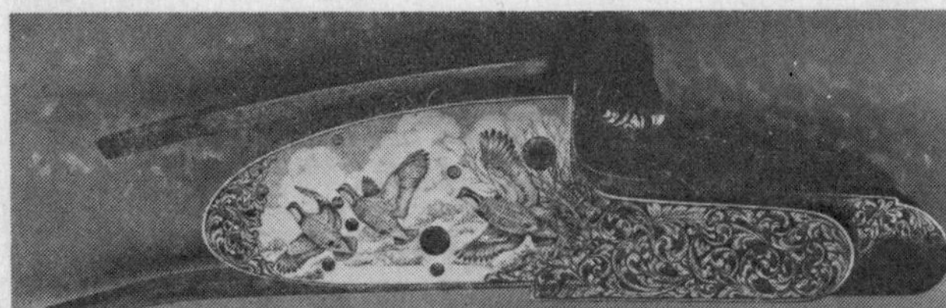

W.P. SINCLAIR

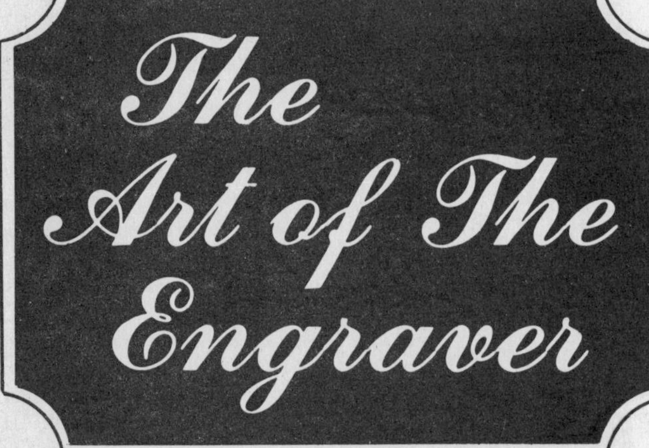

The Art of The Engraver

FRANK MELE

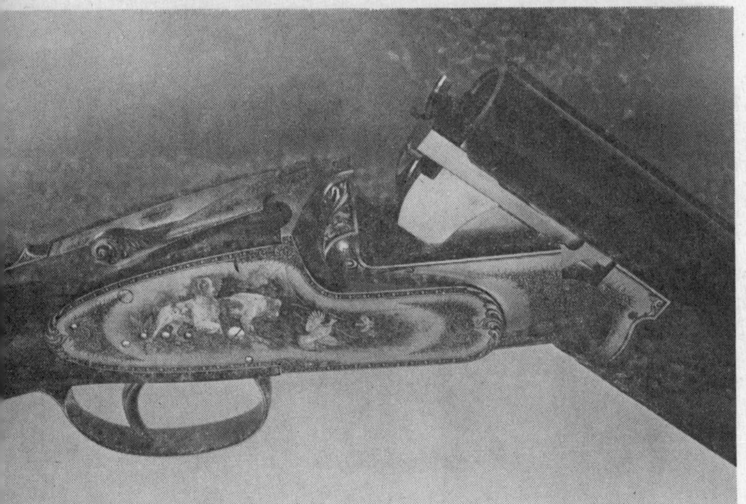

WINSTON CHURCHILL

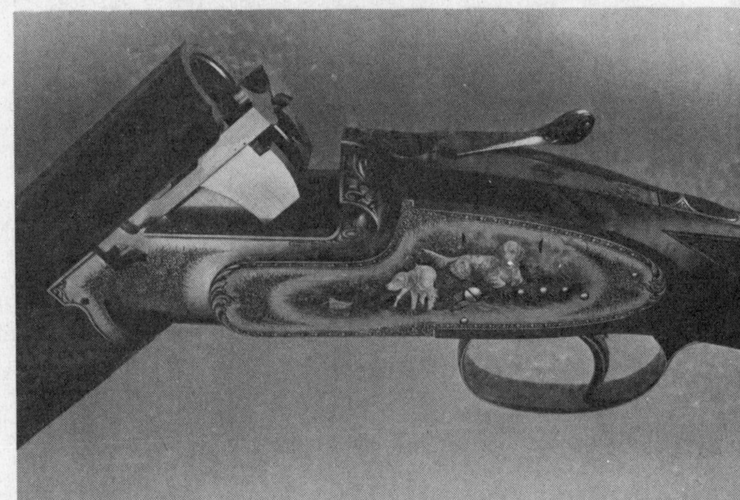

WINSTON CHURCHILL

BYRON BURGESS

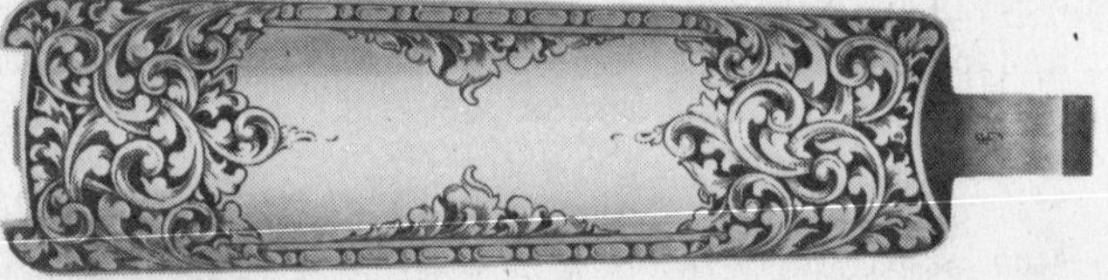

ERIC L. GOLD

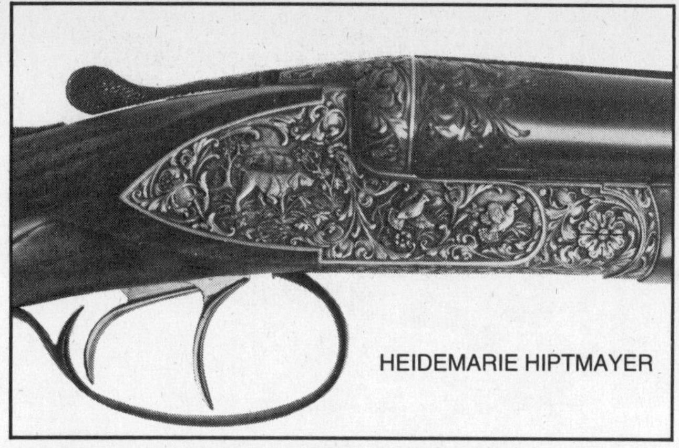

HEIDEMARIE HIPTMAYER

JOHN GWILLIAM

MITCH MOSCHETTI

RACHEL WELLS

H.V. GRANT

JOHN M. KUDLAS

Firearms Engravers Guild

At the fourth annual meeting of the Guild, these three guns were voted the best. Top gun was the Browning Model 92 by Ron Smith, Ft. Worth, TX. The Stevens squirrel rifle by Sam Welch, Kodiak, AK, and the Mauser by Terry Wallace, Vallejo, CA, were runners-up.

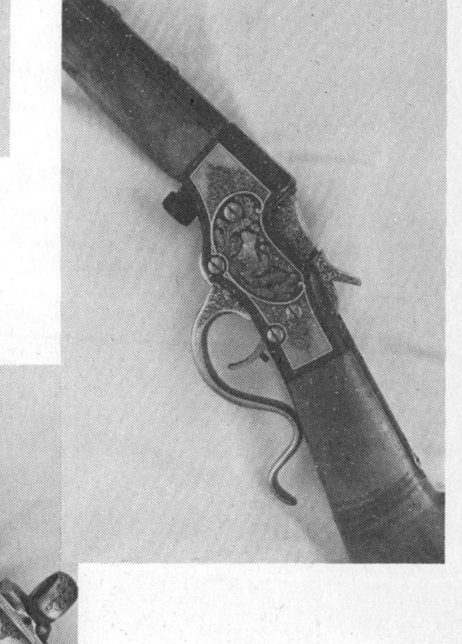

SCHOOL

Robert E. Maki shows Jim Bina scroll on a Sako in Maki's studio course for would-be engravers. He teaches one-on-one in Northbrook, IL.

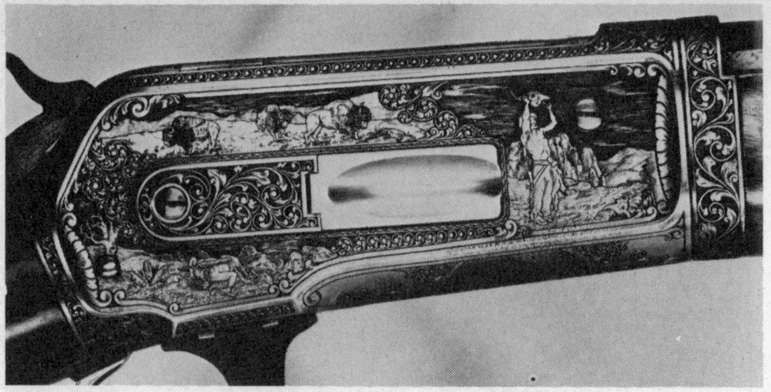

MARCELLO PEDINI

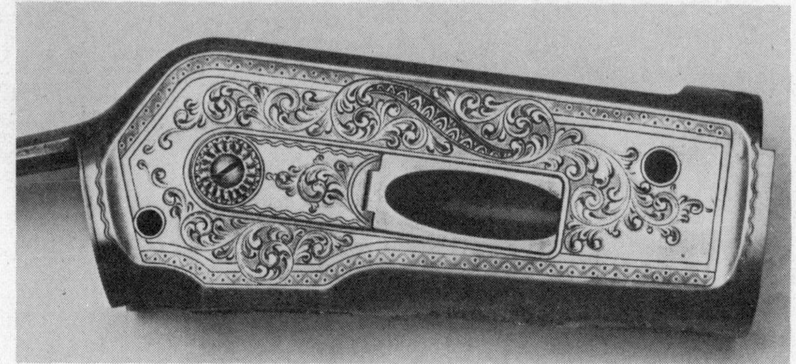

JOHN ADAMS

LANCE KELLY (Weyer photo)

BILLY BATES

JIM RIGGS

RAY VIRAMONTEZ

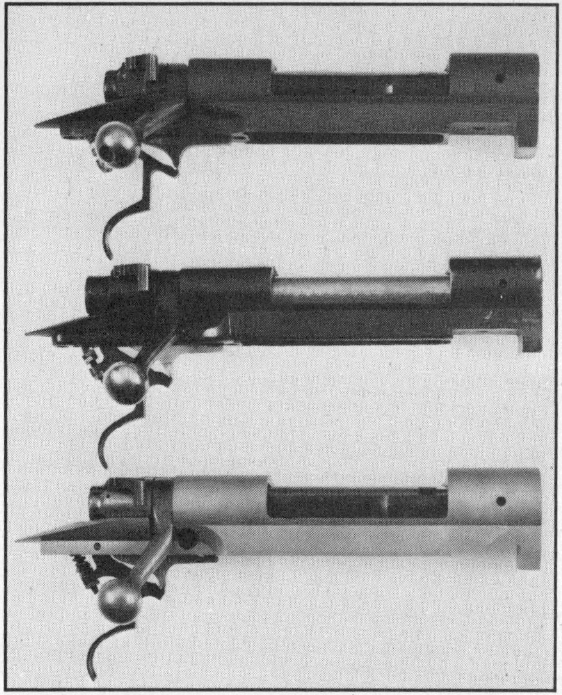

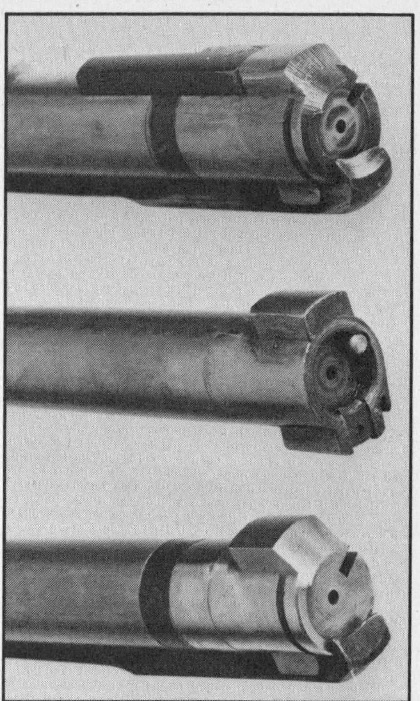

Side view of three classic Model 70 actions. Top: Pre-1964; middle: Post-1964; bottom; USRA/Miller/SCI "G1."

End view of evolutionary Model 70 bolt designs. Top: Pre-1964; middle: Post-1964; bottom: "G1."

A Really Unique Model 70

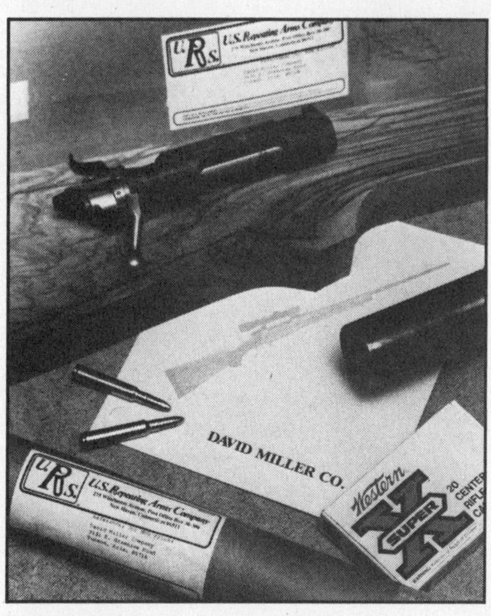

The makings of Big Five No. 5—the special Winchester Model 70 action and the Winchester barrel blank in caliber 338. That's the original shipping carton.

THERE'S ONLY ever going to be one like this one. Coming at the end of a trailblazing and record-setting series of rifles, Number Five—the Leopard—of Safari Club International's Big Five collection figured to be an unusual effort, regardless. David Miller Co. did Number One, reported here then; in the interim, three others have achieved a level of interest SCI could only have hoped they'd get.

It's time for a topper, so a new collaboration came to be—Miller and SCI and Winchester-USRAC. From Connecticut, Miller got number G-1, a once-only special Model 70 action. It has a long extractor, receiver-mounted ejector and controlled feeding along with the benefits of post-64 anti-bind features. The tang-screw hole is hidden and there are no pre-drilled sight holes. USRAC furnished the barrel, too.

On this foundation, David Miller Co. will construct another masterpiece, to be auctioned in 1986 at SCI's Convention. Number Four brought $140,000, providing an interesting goal for Number Five. *K.W.*

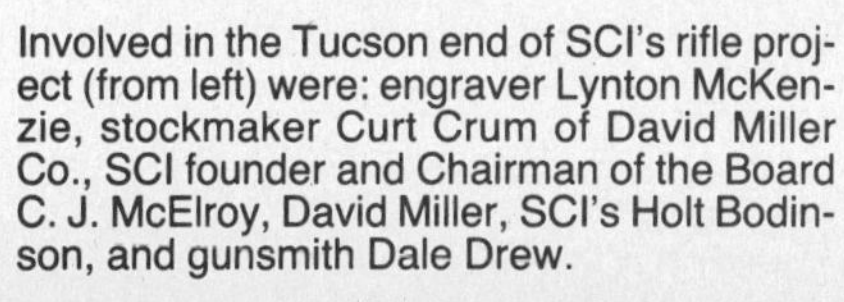

Involved in the Tucson end of SCI's rifle project (from left) were: engraver Lynton McKenzie, stockmaker Curt Crum of David Miller Co., SCI founder and Chairman of the Board C. J. McElroy, David Miller, SCI's Holt Bodinson, and gunsmith Dale Drew.

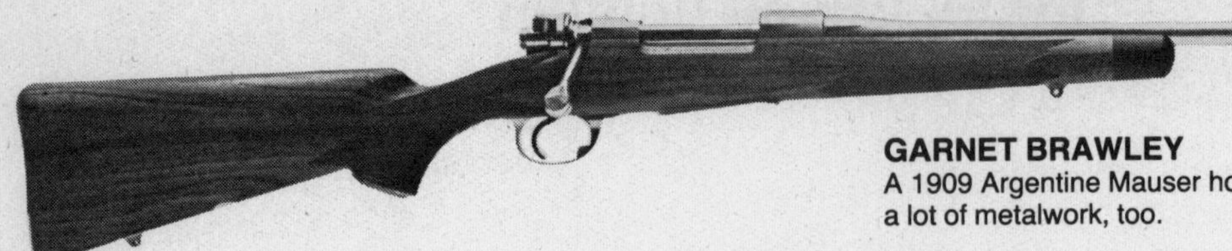

GARNET BRAWLEY
A 1909 Argentine Mauser holds the 257 Improved and a lot of metalwork, too.

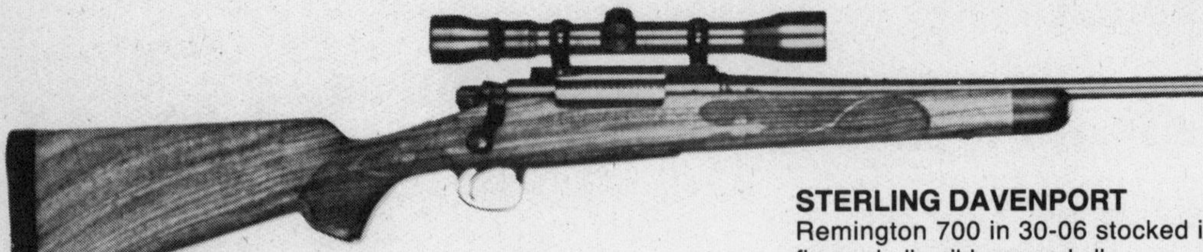

STERLING DAVENPORT
Remington 700 in 30-06 stocked in French walnut, fleurs-de-lis, ribbons and all.

CUSTOM GUNS

JERE EGGLESTON
This Mexican Mauser in 7×57 weighs 7 lb., 6 oz. Eggleston shows it on his letterhead.

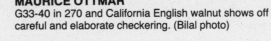

MAURICE OTTMAR
G33-40 in 270 and California English walnut shows off careful and elaborate checkering. (Bilal photo)

PAUL R. NICKELS
Stocked for a southpaw, this Ruger shows special scope bases, nice panels around the action.

DAVE GENTRY
Sako in 222 converted to left-side bolt has glass stock, 21-in. barrel, not a lot of ounces.

JAMES C. TUCKER
FN Mauser in 300 Winchester Magnum has octagonal barrel, integral rib, Zeiss scope.

ROBERT WINTER
Big Remington 700 LH in 458 has Blackburn guard unit, Bastogne walnut, real big gun style.

FRED D. SPEISER
Model 70 in Douglas barrel and Bastogne walnut is a 300 H&H.

FRED WELLS
Lock, stock and barrels made in Prescott—takedown offers one tube in 510 Wells, the other in 400 Wells.

J. J. JENKINS
This is a 416 Rigby as gotten up by the team of Mazur, Fleming and Mains.

GEORGE BEITZINGER
Classic Model 70 in 375 H&H Magnum has 25-in. barrel, G&H side mount, quarter-rib. (Left side facing page)

VIC OLSON
This Model 70 in 280 Remington has, Olson says, a "handmade" French walnut stock, one-piece guard. (Left side on facing page)

STEPHEN L. BILLEB
This 25-06 on a Mauser 98 has Burgess scope mounts, California English walnut stock, point pattern checkering. (Left side on facing page)

R. H. DEVEREAUX
Mesquite and a Sako Magnum action holds a 458 with the help of Mag-na-porting.

PAUL R. NICKELS
This 7×57 in the old Sauer style offers quick offhand shots and a lot of color case hardening. (Left side on facing page)

GANDER MOUNTAIN, INC.
James Tertin put up this Remington 700 308-cal. with 19-in. barrel at 7 pounds and a 13-in. pull. (Left side on facing page)

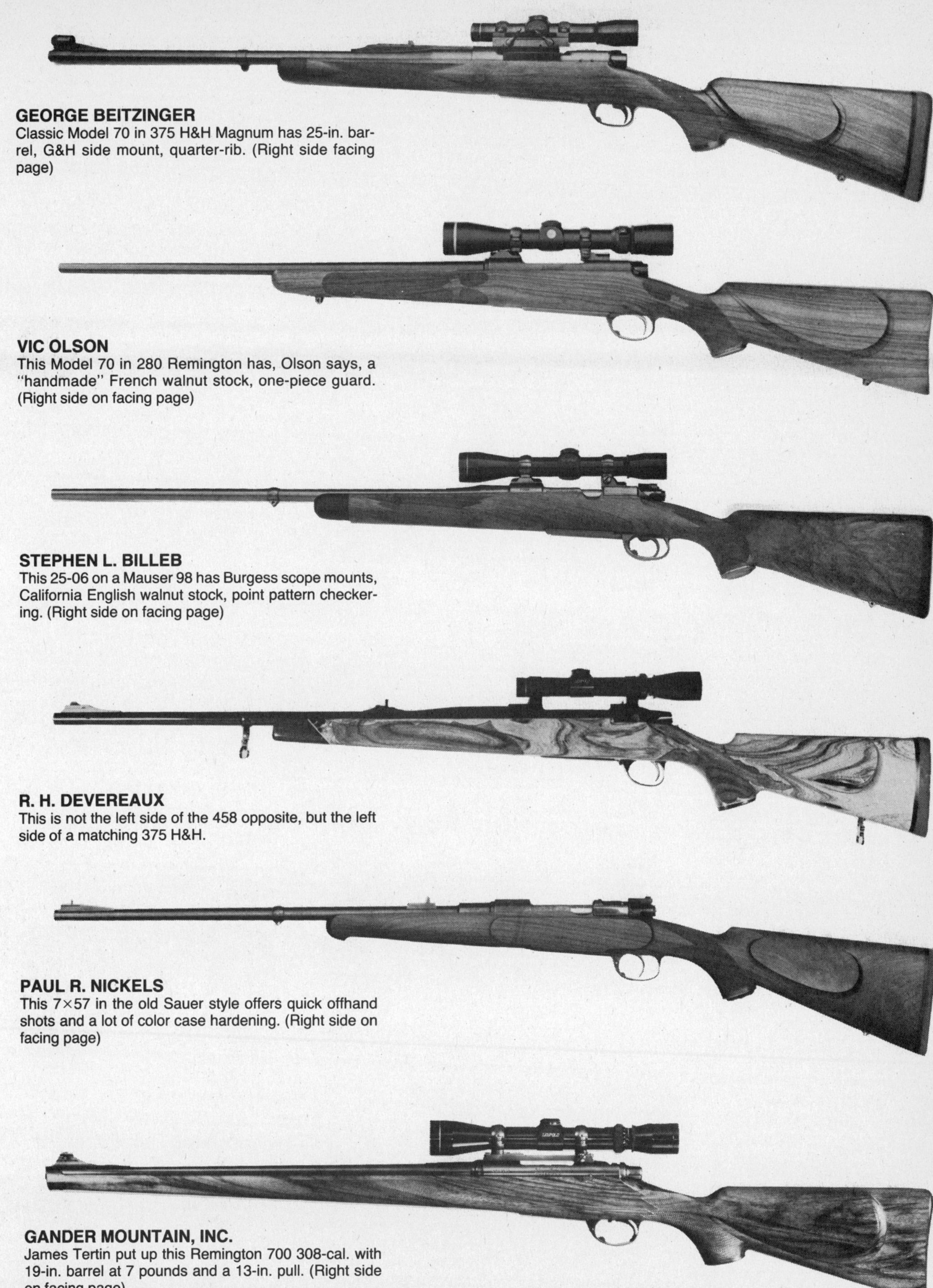

GEORGE BEITZINGER
Classic Model 70 in 375 H&H Magnum has 25-in. barrel, G&H side mount, quarter-rib. (Right side facing page)

VIC OLSON
This Model 70 in 280 Remington has, Olson says, a "handmade" French walnut stock, one-piece guard. (Right side on facing page)

STEPHEN L. BILLEB
This 25-06 on a Mauser 98 has Burgess scope mounts, California English walnut stock, point pattern checkering. (Right side on facing page)

R. H. DEVEREAUX
This is not the left side of the 458 opposite, but the left side of a matching 375 H&H.

PAUL R. NICKELS
This 7×57 in the old Sauer style offers quick offhand shots and a lot of color case hardening. (Right side on facing page)

GANDER MOUNTAIN, INC.
James Tertin put up this Remington 700 308-cal. with 19-in. barrel at 7 pounds and a 13-in. pull. (Right side on facing page)

THE SHOWS OF EUROPE

IWA 1985

by

RAYMOND CARANTA

IWA HAS become by far the most important gun show in Europe, the one where people that count must be seen and where they can meet the genuine bosses of the European gun industry. Last year, there were 399 exhibitors and 114 companies represented; IWA 85 had 446 exhibitors and 108 other firms present.

Of the 550 manufacturers of guns, ammunition and accessories, 223 were German, 77 American, 67 Italian, 40 Austrian, 32 French, 20 Spanish, 19 British, 12 Finnish and 10 Belgian. If, last year, the most fascinating display was Heym's Safari Club rifle, in 1985, we were full of admiration and respect for a Chinese master engraver, Yinshan Chen. He not only wrote poems in ideograms and painted landscapes on small ivory plates, but disclosed a window full of amazing gold- and silver-plated Chinese pistols, lovingly decorated in cloisonné enamels showing gracefully interlaced flowers, birds and dragons. At $8,000 each, plus the taxes, they were all sold the first day.

Among other items worth the trip, we noted a Benelli "Combinato" shotgun which converts from autoloading to pump by rotating a ring; a new compact Bernardelli 14-shot 9mm pistol; an Astra 90, also a 9mm, with a drop-hammer safety instead of the side lever; the new Hungarian FEG

The Diana booth drew its own crowd wherein it was easy to tell the buyers from the sellers.

The new civilian market's development of the French Army assault rifle "FAMAS" by M.A.S. of St. Etienne.

Belgian craftsman Jacquemard displayed a shotgun commemorating the 100th birthday of John M. Browning and, as well, the "smallest shotgun in the world" at SICAT '85.

P9R 14-shot selective double-action pistol also in 9mm, which will be imported by Interarms. Heckler and Koch showed their P7K3 pistol with interchanging barrels chambered in 22 Long Rifle, 32 ACP and 380 ACP.

There was a new variation of the short Uzi assault pistol, burst-firing from a closed bolt and the bullpup Israeli self-loading rifles in 7.62 NATO. The Llama Omni variation adopted by the Spanish army was there, with some smartly decorated Luger pistols by Mauser, shown together with their beautiful replica of the WW I "Artillery" pistol. A new short Tanfoglio "Baby" 12-shot 9mm pistol was seen, as was a gas-operated Voere high-power self-loading sporting rifle (Model 2185) available in ten calibers.

It was a very gun-filled show in Nuremberg, but not the *only* show. In France, there were two we have reported on in the past.

The second Paris modern gun show, called SICAT, received 20,000 visitors, among them 2,300 professionals, which represents a useful progression (8 percent) over last year. More than 300 manufacturers were represented by 154 exhibitors coming from 19 countries and business was slightly improving as a whole.

The most important antique gun show of France was held once more in Saint-Germain-en-Laye from March 23 to March 25. Prices were very high in European currencies but, thanks to the high dollar rate, conversions were less impressive for Amercian buyers. French wheel-lock pistols, the rarest, were priced between $2500 to $6000 and mid-Eighteenth century flintlock pistols from $600 to $8000 according to the quality.

Of course, French guns cost more in their mother country than outside. Among items showing significant price increases since the last show were flintlock and percussion shotguns (about $2500 for the first, and $600 to $1500 range for the second) and American guns. ●

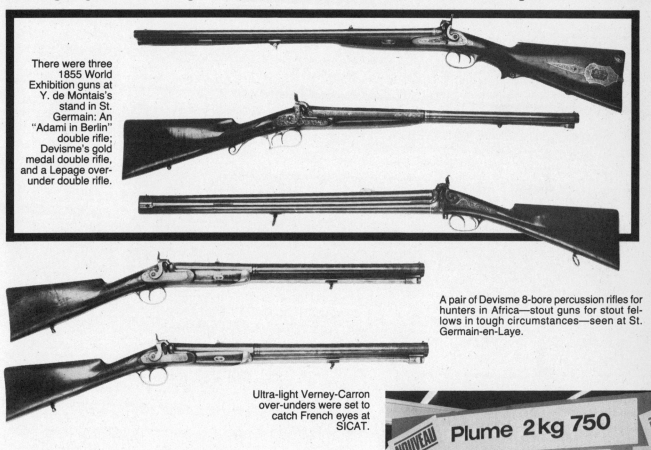

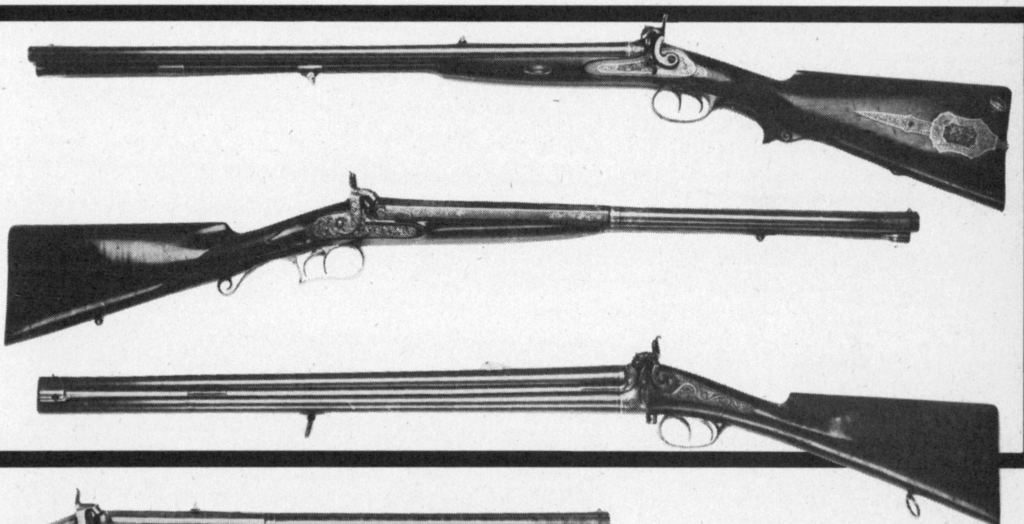

There were three 1855 World Exhibition guns at Y. de Montais's stand in St. Germain: An "Adami in Berlin" double rifle; Devisme's gold medal double rifle, and a Lepage over-under double rifle.

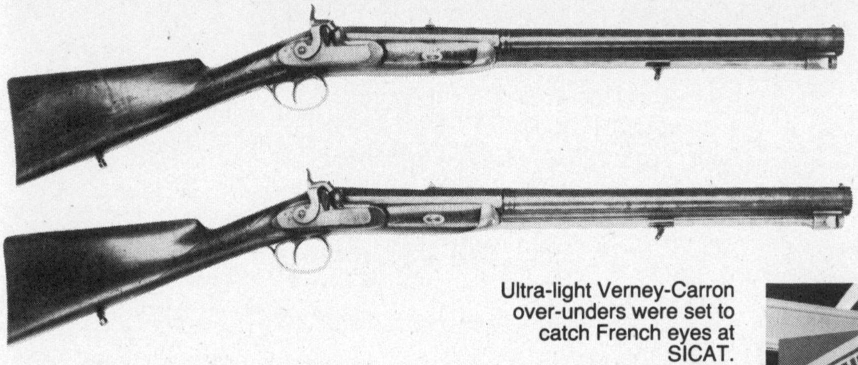

A pair of Devisme 8-bore percussion rifles for hunters in Africa—stout guns for stout fellows in tough circumstances—seen at St. Germain-en-Laye.

Ultra-light Verney-Carron over-unders were set to catch French eyes at SICAT.

The SICAT show in Paris looks like a mini-SHOT Show. (Barraud photo)

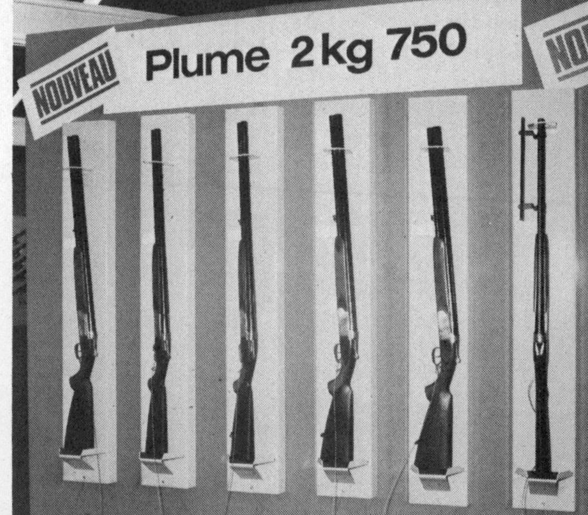

Ammunition, Ballistics and Components

by EDWARD A. MATUNAS

IT'S ALWAYS interesting to review new ammunition and component products. I just have to resist the temptation to editorialize on the worth of the current crop of new items. Some fill real needs; others seem mere razzle-dazzle. It is you, the consumer, who must judge which are worthy.

New packaging of old products is said to be new and exciting. However, I find nothing attractive about hundreds of rounds of 22 rimfire ammo packed in bulk. In fact, I still prefer my rimfire ammo to be packed in the old style, 50-round cartons which fit so easily into my pockets and from which ammo can easily be extracted. And the boxes open and close simply which is more than I can say for some of the current 100-round, plastic challenges-to-cold-fingers. Perhaps I'm just hard to please.

Still, the new Federal Nyclad 38 Special and 357 Magnum loads fill, I believe, a real need. Less pollutants in the air, cleaner (and more accurate) barrels free of difficult-to-remove leading, and good expansion (with hollow points) are always in style and desirable.

My recent trip to PMC's ammunition plants in Korea helped reinforce the idea that quality ammo need not necessarily mean high prices. Price isn't everything, we all know that. But combine it with uniform ballistics and high levels of accuracy and you have something worthwhile to investigate. And while PMC offers no new loads for this year, I found it well worthwhile to discuss my most recent shooting tests with this ammo.

And thus it goes; each year different from the last and yet not really very different at all. So, without further deliberation, allow me to get into those items that are new, or perhaps simply worthy of review.

Remington

Remington's ammo and component line remains relatively unchanged this year, perhaps due to a heavier emphasis on a number of new rifle and shotgun models, the most notable of which will stir up a rebirth of interest in the 350 Remington Magnum cartridge, at least until they have sold out their new limited edition 700 Classic chambered for this round. However, two new loadings have been introduced for the year: a 125-grain semi-jacketed soft point 38 Special +P loading and a new 180-grain semi-

The 357 Remington Maximum with the new 180-grain semi-jacketed hollow point.

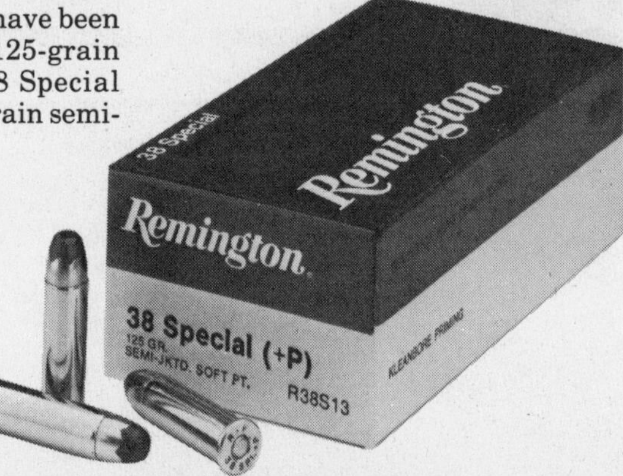

A variation of Remington's 125-grain 38 Special +P is the new semi-jacketed soft point loading, designed for a bit deeper penetration.

Exterior Ballistics Table—Remington

38 Special +P, 125 gr. semi-jacketed SP

	Muzzle	50 yds.	100 yds.
Velocity (ft./sec.)	945	908	875
Energy (ft./lbs.)	248	229	212
Mid-range trajectory	—	1.3″	5.3″

357 Maximum, 180 gr. semi-jacketed HP

	Muzzle	50 yds.	100 yds.
Velocity (ft./sec.)	1,555	1,328	1,154
Energy (ft./lbs.)	966	705	532
Mid-range trajectory	—	0.5″	2.5″

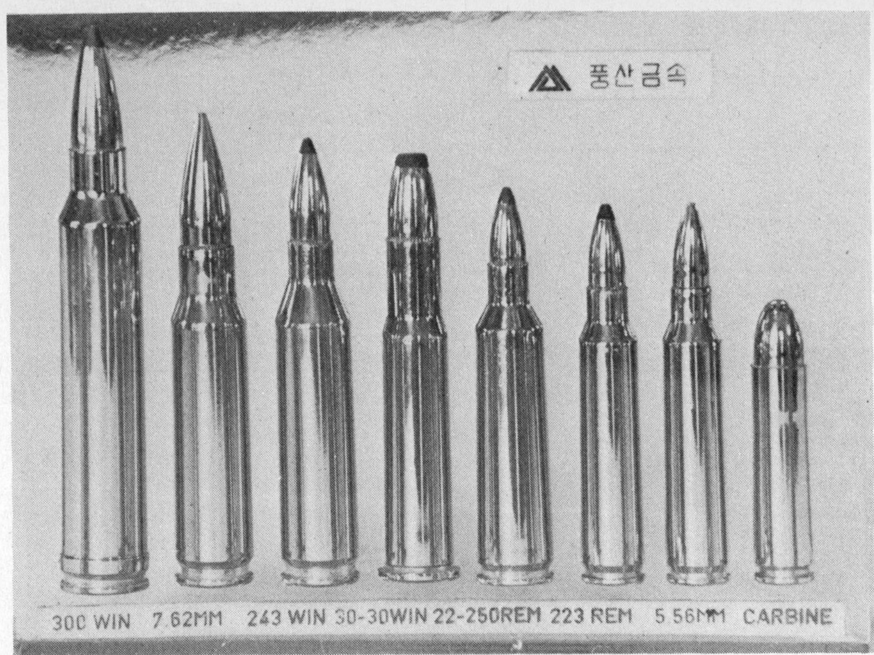

Some of the rifle loads manufactured at the PMC Dongrae plant. Handgun loads are made in PMC's Ankang plant.

jacketed hollow point loading for the 357 Remington Maximum. And they dropped the 10-ga. 1⅝ oz. load in the 2⅞-in. case.

The bullet in the new 38 Special is a positive expanding bullet which would rate a high PIR value, and still offers advantages in penetration. The 125-grain weight is one of the most useful in this cartridge.

The new 357 Remington Maximum loading arouses some ho-hum. The hard-core 357 Maximum fans will like it and it should prove a strong performer for metallic silhouette competition, especially at the longer ranges.

PMC

PMC's arsenal line of Korean-made ammunition has been very popular with survivalists and others who just plain love to shoot up a storm at the range. Using PMC's arsenal ammo can be as cheap as reloading. This company has sold so much such ammo that both Federal and Winchester now offer similar arsenal lines at prices competitive with PMC.

PMC also sells another kind of ammunition—sporting loads with soft point bullets—in such calibers as 38 Special, 357 Magnum, 44 Magnum, 45 ACP, 222 Remington, 223 Remington, 22-250 Remington, 243 Winchester, 30-30 Winchester, 308 Winchester, 30-06 Springfield and 300 Winchester Magnum. Perhaps the most obvious appeal of PMC sporting ammo has been its price. At 15 percent or so below the cost of other similar ammo, the shooter who does not try it is probably either affluent or a small volume consumer. I recently tried 30-06 Springfield, 270 Winchester, 222 Remington, 223 Remington, as well as some 38 Special and 357 Magnum loads. All worked very well indeed, with accuracy and uniformity surprisingly good.

In a Remington Model Seven, the 222 Remington 50-grain SP load produces a standard deviation of 17 feet per second (fps) and a 1⅝-in. group for 10 shots. In a similar rifle, the 223 50-grain soft point produced similar results with a standard deviation of 24 fps. Velocity of both loads was right at the expected level. A Remington 700 Classic was used to check the 270 Winchester 130- and 150-grain loads. Velocity standard deviation for these loads proved to be 26 and 22 respectively, with 1½-in. groups not uncommon. The 30-06 loadings of 150 and 180 grains both shot very well, with the 150-grain load producing an amazingly small velocity standard deviation of 8; 21 for the 180-grain loading. The 38 Special 110-grain load showed a standard deviation of 12 fps while the 357 Magnum load produced a standard deviation of 19 fps with a 158-grain soft point. Accuracy with the 30-06, 38 Special and 357 Magnum loads equalled or exceeded that which I had previously experienced with the test firearms using stateside manufactured ammo.

Federal

Federal ammunition is popular! Just how popular can be understood by considering the fact that at the 1984 Grand American championship trap shoot, over 4,000 shooters consumed almost 2.8 million shotshells, and the largest brand share was Federal shells with more than 1.2 million shells (45.3 percent of the total). The next closest competitor was more than 200,000 shells behind. Federal obviously is doing a number of things right.

One of the right things Federal does so well is to constantly provide the shooter with new products to try. This year is no exception as Federal continues to offer a broad selection of new products; not the least of which is a new 85-grain jacketed hollow point load in the 32 H&R Magnum cartridge. From the short 4⅝-in. Single Six Ruger, this load develops a siz-

Federal has added a jacketed hollow point load to their 32 H&R Magnum cartridges—a fine choice for small game and varmints.

zling 1100 fps and 230 foot pounds (ft. lbs.) of energy at the muzzle. At the 50-yard mark velocity is still above 1000 fps and energy has only dropped 35 ft. lbs. This load complements Federal's original 95-grain lead semiwadcutter loading for the 32 H&R Magnum round and should prove perfect for small varmints and perhaps even personal defense.

Federal has also extended its Premium line of copper-plated buckshot loads to include the 12-gauge Magnum. Buckshot sizes for the new loads will include 00 and #4 Buck. Extra hard copper-plated pellets nested in a granulated polyethelene buffer provide state-of-the-art maximum pattern density. There are 15 pellets in the 00 Buck load and 41 in the #4 Buck; they're packaged in 10-round boxes.

Federal's 223 Blitz Ballistics

	Range in yards					
	-0-	50	100	150	200	250
Velocity (1)	3650	3320	3010	2720	2450	2190
Energy (2)	1185	980	805	660	535	425
Trajectory (3)	-0-	.1	.4	1.0	1.9	3.4
Drift (4)	-0-	.4	1.5	3.5	6.5	10.6

(1) = feet per second; (2) = foot pounds; (3) = mid-range (in inches); (4) = 10 mph crosswind (in inches)

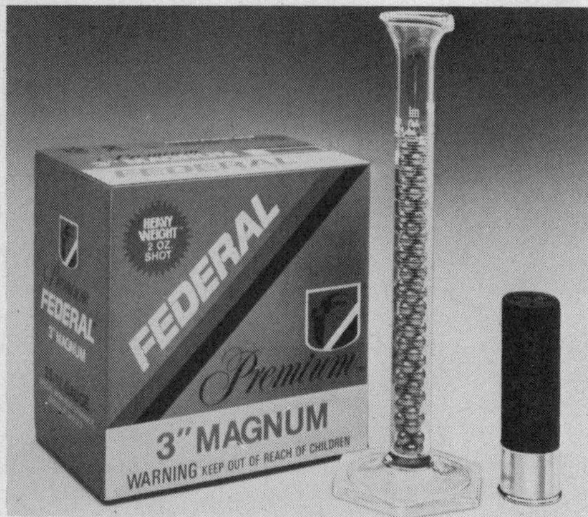

For those who like to "blow up" their varmint targets, Federal has a 40-grain Blitz loading for the 223 Remington.

(Left) Federal's 12-gauge 3" magnum with a full 2 ounces of shot is a real stomper. With No. 6 shot, it will make head-shooting turkeys just a tad easier.

For those whose shotguns pattern well with the Heavyweight™ Premium Federal shotshell loads using 2 ounces of shot, in the 3-in. case with the No. 2 and No. 4 shot sizes, Federal has now broadened this offering to include BB and No. 6 size shot. At 1175 fps, recoil is a bit on the hefty side, but the load is a real stomper on geese and turkey when the appropriate pellet size is used.

Last year Federal introduced their "Blitz" load for the 22-250 Remington cartridge. Now we have a Blitz load for the 223 Remington. The 40-grain Blitz bullet churns up a muzzle velocity of 3650 fps and helps flatten trajectory notably. This load should prove devastating on light varmints. I'll bet a nickel we will soon be treated to still another Blitz round from Federal.

The new Federal ammo that most catches my eye are five new Nyclad revolver loadings for the 38 Special and 357 Magnum, bringing the current total to nine different loadings. The new Nyclad loads include: 38 Special 158-gr. SWC; 38 Special +P 158-gr. SWC; 38 Special +P 125-gr. SWC hollow point; 357 Magnum 158-gr. SWC; and a 357 Magnum 158-gr. SWC hollow point.

Nyclad ammo features lead bullets with a nylon coating. This coating reduces airborne lead contaminant by approximately 80 percent. In addition, barrel leading is virtually eliminated. Impressive bullet expansion on all of the hollow point loads is part of the Nyclad ammo's standard performance. I have always preferred lead hollow point bullets for my revolver shooting but have been greatly disappointed with the bore leading of most of the +P and 357 Magnum loads. Federal's Nyclad line is a real favorite with me.

The new 7-30 Waters lever action cartridge is now in the Federal lineup. I don't see much of a future for this cartridge, as its light 120-grain bullets will not prove equal to the 30-30 for penetration or game-getting ability. However, light recoil will make the cartridge a good selection for youngsters or any shooter who prefers to keep shoulder abuse to a minimum. And the 41 Remington Magnum caliber cartridge case has been added to Federal's component line. And the

Federal's New Nyclad Load Ballistics

	Bullet weight	Bullet type	Muzzle(1) Velocity ft./sec.	Muzzle Energy ft./lbs.
38 Special	158-gr.	L, SWC	755	200
38 Special +P	158-gr.	L, SWC	890	278
38 Special +P	125-gr.	L, HP	945	248
357 Magnum	158-gr.	L, SWC	1235	535
357 Magnum	158-gr.	L, HP	1235	535

(1) = 4-in. barrel

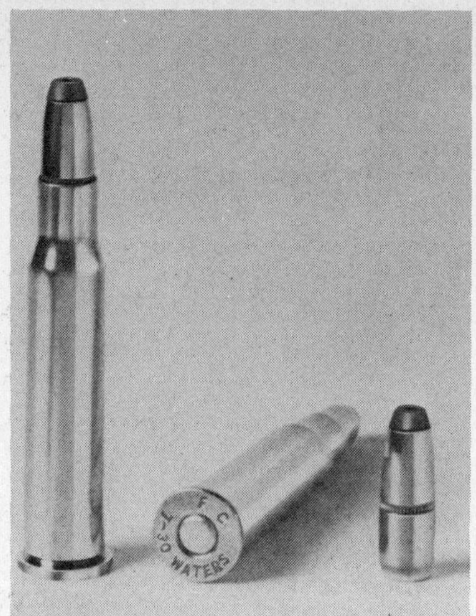

The 7mm-30 Waters is now a factory loading by Federal, of course—has a 120-grain bullet.

Winchester 41 Remington Magnum 175-Grain Silvertip Hollow Point Ballistics (4-in. barrel)

	Muzzle	50 yds.	100 yds.
Velocity	1250	1120	1029
Energy	607	488	412
Mid-range trajectory	—	0.8	3.4

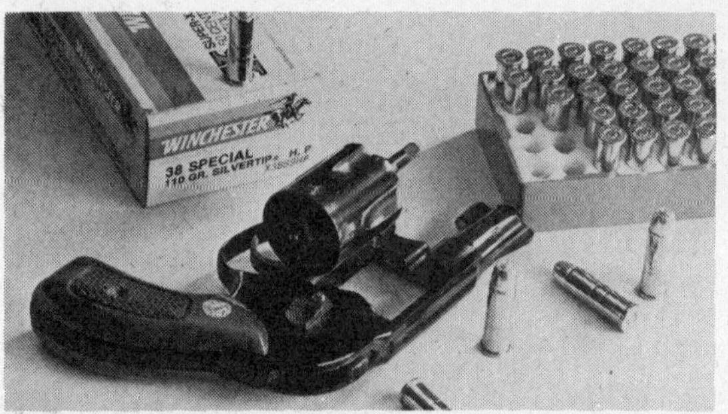

Light frame 38 Special owners have a Silvertip hollow point loading. Winchester's new non-+P load has a 110-grain Silvertip hollow point offering superb expansion even from short snubbies.

(Right) What can you do to further improve expansion in the 41 Remington Magnum? Load it with a 175-grain Silvertip hollow point bullet.

Federal line now also includes a 220-grain Hi-Skor SP bullet for the 30-06 Springfield. It's been another busy year at the Federal research and development facilities.

Winchester

The Winchester ammunition and components line-up continues to grow each year. True to form, the annual expansion of the fabulous Silvertip handgun load line has occurred again. New loads include a 38 Special 110-grain bullet and a 41 Remington Magnum 175-grain bullet. As expected, both loads showed rapid expansion to a very large diameter. In my opinion, the Silvertips are among the best defensive handgun bullets ever designed. Pity they are not available for handloading.

The most attractive aspect of the new 110-grain 38 Special load is that it is not a +P loading and, therefore, can be used in all 38 Special handguns, including the alloy-frame models. Expansion from my S&W Airweight Bodyguard is quite impressive even at 25 yards, with accuracy for five shots at about 3½ inches. The 41 Magnum Silvertip load pushes its 175-grain bullet at over 1200 fps. Muzzle energy is over 600 ft. lbs. with average penetration in gelatin of over 7 inches. That is quite a handful.

In the area of reintroduction, the 9mm Winchester Magnum round has been brought back. The hot 9mm's return is based on the availability of para-military weapons chambered for it. Ballistics are notably increased compared to the 9mm Luger. For those who have taken a fancy to the 357 Remington Maximum cartridge, Winchester is now offering brass. Packaging is the usual 50-round plastic tray with styrofoam insert. This brass was listed in the 1984 catalog, but I have just received my first samples. Also new in brass are the 9mm and 45 Winchester Magnum calibers.

A 250-round bulk pack of the hyper velocity 22 Long Rifle Super-Max rounds is now available. I have shot a goodly number of these and other hyper velocity rounds and with but one exception, accuracy is less than the usual variety of standard and high velocity Long Rifle ammunition. In a Ruger 77/22 with a 20-in. barrel I obtained a muzzle velocity of 1416 fps with my sample Super-Max ammo. Average 50-yard accuracy was 1¾-in. compared to 1½-in. for Winchester Super X 22 Long Rifle hollow point loads.

Also new from Winchester are three new steel shot loads. These incorporate a shot charge of 1⅛ ounces of steel shot in sizes 2, 4 and 6, and all are in the 2¾-in. 12-gauge case. Until now, Winchester has had the heaviest 2¾-in. 12-gauge steel shot load with their 1¼-oz. loading. The introduction of the new 1⅛-oz. leaves me speculating on the future of the 1¼-oz. steel shot loading.

Winchester's 785 Ball Powder has passed into oblivion. Considering the necessary constraints attached to it by the Ball Powder data supplied by Winchester, I am surprised it lasted for the 12 years or so it has been with us. Some may miss it, but for the most part it was a low volume item due to limited applications.

Improved buckshot loads are also being introduced by Winchester. Available in both 12-gauge lengths, the new Super Double X Magnum loads feature copper-plated higher antimony pellets, buffered with granulated polyethelene. Tighter patterns

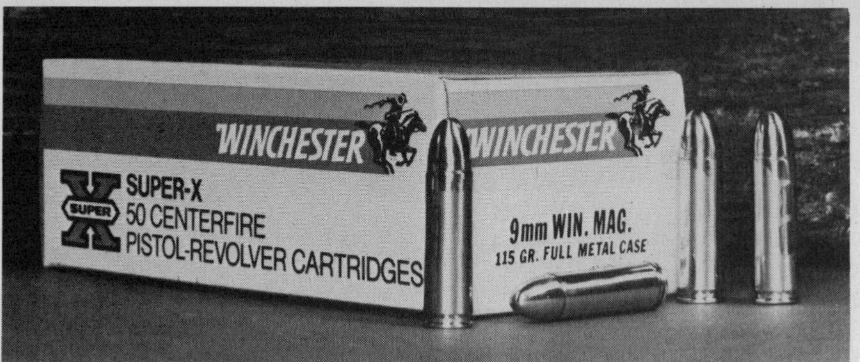

The hottest 9mm: Currently being reintroduced, the 9mm Winchester Magnum will see use in a number of para-military type carbines, where it will provide flatter trajectories than such are used to.

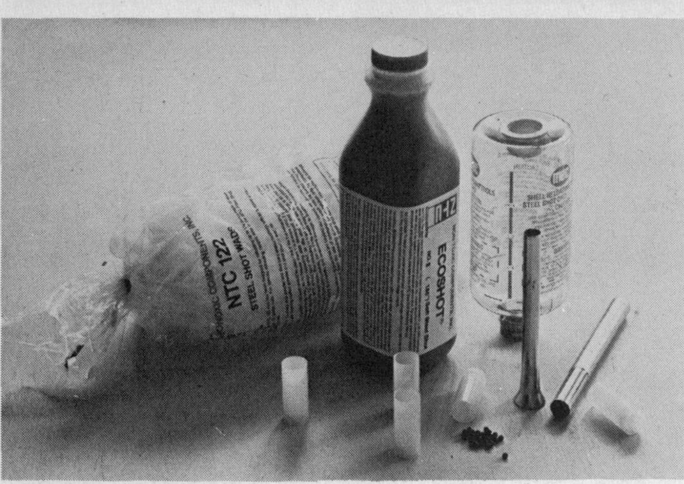

(Below left) Steel shot reloaders have a source of soft steel pellets and suitable steel shot wads from NTC of Oregon. Wad petals are formed by slitting the plastic cups as part of the reloading process.

If you gotta use it, steel shot is being offered in more and more loadings. Shown are 1⅛-oz. Winchester loads size 2, 4, or 6 shot.

are assured compared to standard non-buffered, non-plated, softer shot loadings.

And finally there is a new ¾-oz. steel shot load for 2¾-in. 20-gauge guns. Shot sizes include 4 and 6. I'm betting on 35 yards maximum for positive performance of all 20-gauge ¾-oz. steel shot loads when used on waterfowl.

The metallic rifle line has seen the following loads dropped from the Winchester price list: 125-gr. 7mm Rem. Mag.; 110-gr. 30-06 Springfield; 220-gr. 30-06 Springfield Power Point (the 220-gr. Silvertip continues); 180-gr. 30-40 Krag Silvertip; 180-gr. 300 Savage Silvertip; 110-gr. 308 Win.; 200-gr. 308 Win.; 200-gr. 38 Special; 150-gr. 38 Special +P; 95-gr. 9mm Luger; 158-gr. 38 Special Match. Perhaps the only ones that will be missed are the 110-gr. 30-06 and 308 varmint loads, though the continued 125-gr. load in these calibers should be the preferred choice for varminting.

Non-Toxic Components Inc.

Readers who have followed my ravings on steel shot reloading are well aware of the frequent warnings I have made regarding the loading of steel shot. Times do change, however, and I can now state that it is possible to reload shotshells with steel shot, although not everyone will feel that it is highly practical to do so at this point in time.

Until now the problem has been complex. Steel shot with a Diamond Pyramid Hardness (DPH) of 90 or less has been very difficult to obtain. Steel balls with a higher DPH can cause extensive barrel damage even when fully contained in a heavy-duty steel shot wad. And the wads needed have been equally difficult to locate. Less than suitable shot and wads have been sold to reloaders who did not fully appreciate the problems with steel shot reloading. It is not my intention here to go into all the difficulties, but rather to advise you that a solution to the problem is now being offered by an outfit called Non-Toxic Components, Inc. (P.O. Box 4202, Portland, OR 97208).

NTC is offering steel shot kits which contain 10 pounds of "soft" steel shot (DPH no harder than 90) and 160 wads, along with a complete instruction booklet. Larger kits are also available. The cost of these kits will not allow for the large savings possible when reloading lead shot. Nevertheless, you will be able to save about half of the suggested retail of factory steel shot loads.

NTC's instruction manual, which covers the problems of steel shot loading very nicely and in simple terms, contains only a total of seven loads. And a number of these will, in my opinion, prove less than desirable to waterfowl hunters. One such load is a ⅞-oz. charge for use in the Federal Gold Medal case. Then there are three loads for 1-oz. charges in the Gold Medal case, Winchester's steel shot case and Federal's paper case. Such light payloads will be less than appealing to waterfowlers who, for the most part, are accustomed to using 1½-oz. or even heavier charges. There is but one 1⅛-oz. charge for a 2¾-in. case—this being the Federal steel shot one-piece plastic hull; not exactly the most common reloading case. Not a single load for the very popular Winchester or Remington target cases. Two loads for 3-in. cases are shown, both for 1⅛-oz. loads.

The reason for such oddball listings are based on sound ballistic needs when assembling steel shot loads, as explained in NTC's manual. True enough, but it doesn't offset the reloaders equally justifiable desire to use what he has on hand. But for now that is the state-of-the-art. Steel shot loading is extremely critical, make no mistake about it. Stick to the listed

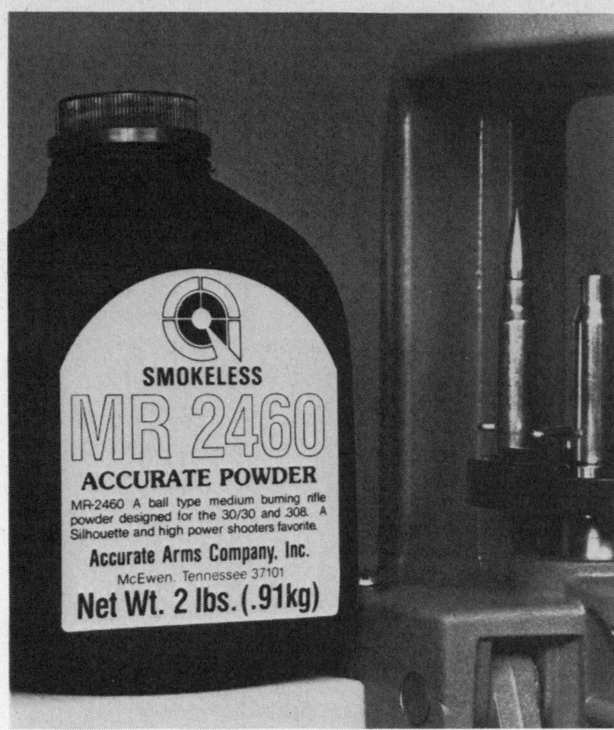

Accurate Powders—a line of newly manufactured spherical type powders produced in Israel—include selections for almost every caliber.

RWS R-50 22 Long Rifle continues to be the most accurate 22 rimfire ammunition that I have ever used. Lot after lot, this ammo is uniformly accurate, producing an average group size of about ¾-in. for ten shots at 50 yards from my favorite squirrel rifle, a Kimber M82 sporter. Both of my 77/22s do their very best (under an inch) with the Dynamit Nobel German import ammo. And my Remington 541-S hangs in there with about ½-in. groups using this fine ammo. Expensive? Yes, but well worth the price for the serious rimfire shooter.

Dynamit Nobel is now offering RWS shotshells in 12 and 20 gauge. Retriever Field loads and Retriever Long Range loads are the new brand identification nomenclature. In addition, the rimfire line now includes two new items, the 22 LR Subsonic and the 22 LR R100 Silhouette. Regrettably, Dynamit Nobel's marketing efforts have never been aggressive enough to cause widespread distribution of their fine ammunition and components.

recipes exactly or a ruined gun could be the least of your problems.

Accurate Arms Co. Inc.

Sometime back, Accurate Arms began selling a line of propellants they called Data Powders. These were surplus powders which were offered with limited reloading data. Quite frankly, I just wasn't impressed with there being one more source of surplus powder. However, this outfit has come of age and is now marketing a line of newly produced spherical powders. These propellants are manufactured in Israel by IMI. Two powders in the Accurate line are extruded types; these being MR-3100, originally produced by DuPont, and MR-5744, originally manufactured by Hercules. The only surplus powder now being sold is MR-8700.

Accurate Arms powders also include #7 for handgun; #9 for magnum handgun; MR-223, primarily used in 223 Remington; MR-2460, which is a tad slower than MR-223; and MR-2520 for rifle. Other powders are planned and at this writing Accurate is also talking about the availability of a new handgun powder said to have characteristics similar to Olin's 231.

While data has been meager in the past, Accurate Arms is now printing a 24-page booklet on their powders; 12 pages of which are devoted to data listings. Some of the data is, indeed, for oddballs, i.e. 290-grain 44 Magnum, but most are of the type that will be put to widespread usage. A copy of the new data booklet ($1.00) can be obtained by writing to Mr. Marty Liggins, Accurate Arms Co. Inc., Box 167, McEwen, TN 37101.

Accurate powders are normally packaged in two-pound plastic containers. The labels feature color coding that helps in easy product identification.

U.S. Ammunition Company

The promised plastic-cased ammo from U.S. just hasn't happened. They have problems and are working their way around them with a change in case material. Rumor has it that the problem has been solved, but that the solution negated the price advantage U.S. had hoped to bring to the market. I think we'll just have to wait and see what happens here. I suspect that the proposed FMJ bullets will present some problems via consumer resistance. Most shooters well appreciate the virtues of expanding bullets.

Dynamit Nobel

Dynamit Nobel's fine line of RWS centerfire rifle cartridges are, unfortunately, not standard gun shop items. However, these difficult to find cartridges can be purchased by your favorite dealer in lots of as few as one box of shells from Paul Jaeger, Inc., Box 449, 1 Madison Ave., Grand Junction, TN 38039.

Sierra

Sierra's reputation as the "Bulletsmiths" is, of course, strong among reloaders of jacketed bullets. Currently there are more than 90 different rifle bullets and 30 handgun bullets being offered by Sierra. New for this year are two rifle offerings and one handgun bullet.

The new 100-grain soft point spitzer boattail Gameking bullet will give 257 Roberts and 25-06 users who favor a 100-grain bullet a choice between a flat base or a tapered heel bullet. And for the 270 Winchester fans who can't decide between the 130- or 150-grain weights, Sierra has added another 140-grain bullet for this year. A boattail base is standard, as it was on the earlier 140-grain hollow point. This new bullet offers the preferred, I believe, spitzer soft point nose.

Handgunners who use the diminutive 25 ACP can now get a Sierra bullet to fit this tiny case. As you might expect, the new projectile is a 50-grain FMC bullet measuring .251-in. Sierra's 90-grain 270 hollow point, and .308-in. diameter 110-grain hollow point, and 125-grain spitzer continue to be my favored varmint type bullets for big game rifles. In the 270 Winchester or the various 30-caliber rifles in my rack these bullets will all shoot approximately 1 MOA and offer violent expansion on targets as small as a tiny 5-pound woodchuck. Big game hunters who participate in off-

Hornady's 85-grain jacketed hollow point for the 32 H&R Mag. and the 71-grain FMC for PPK fans.

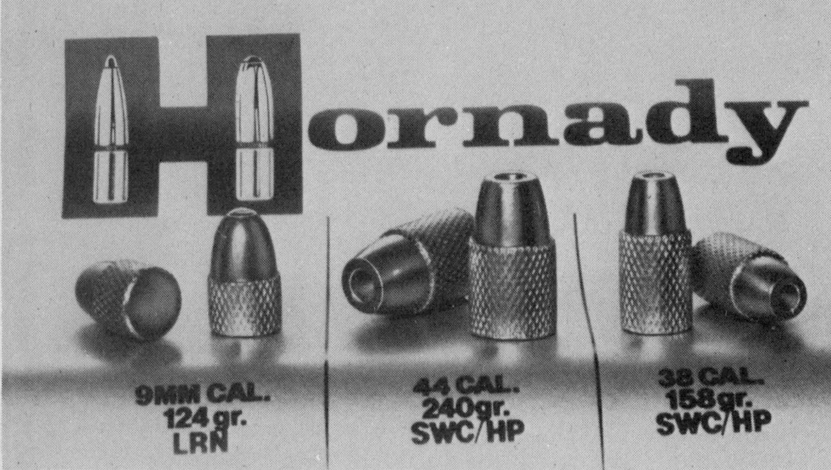

New lead bullets from Hornady. The 158-grain SWC/HP for 38s is sure to be a real favorite.

If you like your 30-caliber 150-grain bullets with boattails, Hornady can help.

season varminting would do well to load up some of these bullets. Don't forget to readjust your sights as required.

Handgunners who want positive expansion from jacketed handgun bullets should give the Sierra 110-grain HP Blitz bullet and the various Sierra "Power-Jacket" bullets a try. These continue to be among the better expanding handgun bullets. The notches at the nose jacket start expansion early and positively. I have been more than satisfied with expansion when using these bullets. The 38-caliber 110-grain Blitz bullet with its extra jacket notches expands well even when fired from a two-inch revolver.

Hornady

Some new loads are available in the Hornady-loaded cartridge line. These include a 139-grain 7mm Remington Magnum and a 190-grain 300 Winchester Magnum. And I have been having exceptional results with two comparatively new Hornady bullets. These are the 150-grain boattail soft point 30 caliber bullet and the 158-grain lead semi-wadcutter hollow point 357 bullet. They are proving very accurate in a wide range of applications. Other new lead bullets include a 9mm 125-grain round nose and a 44-caliber 240-grain hollow point. Hornady's jacketed hollow point 32-caliber, an 85-grain bullet, should prove just perfect in the Ruger Single six 32 H&R Magnum.

Another new 32-caliber Hornady bullet sure to please PPK owners and others is a FMJ 71-grain round nose. At about $8.00 per hundred suggested retail, it's sure to see a lot of use. For those of you who picked up on the earlier mention of Hornady shot, please keep in mind that this shot, produced in Carson City, Nevada, is generally available in the West only.

Nosler

The Nosler Ballistic Tip bullets, reported last year in these pages, are proving to be very rapidly expanding bullets, more so than the Nosler solid base bullets. The polycarbonate nose tip sitting over a hollow cavity seems to initiate expansion somewhat quicker than the conventional soft point spitzer. This kind of expansion is ideal for light to medium, thin-skinned big game; say from 90 to 400 pounds. That covers most deer and antelope on up to a good-sized caribou. For heavy game I still recommend the Nosler Partition bullets above all other types. Deep penetration and positive expansion are typical of the Partition bullet. But, if you want to use one bullet for heavy and light game, the Partition is up to such broad usage application. On light game, these bullets will usually exit the animal thus leaving a good blood trail should it be needed.

Omark

Omark diversification during recent years has been very broad and has included things like Weaver mounts, gun care products, firearm safety storage vaults and new RCBS reloading items. It's a wonder they have any time left to broaden the ammo and component line at all. But despite their busy profile, a few changes have crept into the Omark line-up. New is the 200-round bulk pack of 22 Long Rifle high speed ammunition. This packaging allows the purchase of Long Rifle ammo at a slight cost savings over standard 50 and 100-round packaging. Too, the reusable blue plastic container makes a handy and easy to tote lure box if you happen to also be a fisherman.

If you own a 9.3mm rifle, a bullet supply is now easy; Speer's got a 270-grain semi-spitzer, available now.

(Left) CCI now packages 22 LR high velocity cartridges in a bulk box of 200 rounds. It saves you a few pennies.

Also new, or perhaps better described as a reissue, is the Speer 35-caliber 220-grain flat nose soft point rifle bullet. Discontinued about 11 years ago due to declining sales, this bullet should see a renewed market especially among users of the comparatively new 356 Winchester cartridge. Of course, the current limited production Remington 700 Classic in 350 Remington Magnum will also help create a demand for this bullet. Users of the 357 Remington Maximum may even find application for such a relatively heavy projectile. Owners of rifles chambered for the 35 Remington and the 358 Winchester cartridges will, I believe, still be the major consumers of this oldie-but-goodie, returned to the Speer line.

Other news from Omark will gladden the hearts of owners of 9.3×62 and 9.3×74R rifles. A new .366-in. diameter bullet is being included in the Speer line of Hot-Core hunting bullets. This is a 270-grain semi-spitzer design, packed 50 to a box. This projectile should enable a lot of guns to be put back into service if their owners can come up with the necessary cases and data.

CCI's new cartridge board is a bit of the past in modern dress. The old ammo boards are now collector's items worth thousands of dollars. Perhaps someday the CCI ammo board will also be a collector's item. But for now it sells for $95, including all 53 CCI cartridges and a hardwood frame.

The low cost line of Blazer ammunition now includes a 115-grain jacketed hollow point 9mm Luger round and it's packaged either 50 or 100 rounds to a box. Shooters interested in the 100-round boxes can also select Blazer ammo in 115-grain FMJ 9mm Luger, 148 grain 38 Special (wadcutter) and 158-grain 38 Special (lead round nose). The 45 Auto with a 230-grain bullet is also now available in the aluminum, non-reloadable, but inexpensive, Blazer ammunition.

Cast bullet users may want to obtain a copy of the new *RCBS Cast Bullet Manual*. It contains 130 pages of how-to and loading data; especially useful to the shooter with a keen interest in making his own low cost lead bullets.

All this, and 22 rimfire blanks too.

Dan/Arms

This is a made-in-Denmark 12-gauge line of shotshells that is attractively priced. I tried four loads: the Skeet/World Class; the Trap/World Class; the Max Jagt/World Class; and a load simply identified as "28,5."

The Skeet load uses a white plastic case with a separate plastic inner base wad and a comparatively high brass cup. The shot was well formed and the cases were solidly crimped. The wad petals, on some of the unfired loads I examined, were connected to one another by a tiny tab of plastic. All of the fired wads showed proper petal separation. The wad legs are built up in multiple layers with there being four steps on the 1-oz. load wad. The Skeet load uses No. 9 shot loaded into an easy to identify black box.

The trap loads were similar except they use a red case and brown box, and, of course, they were loaded with 7½ or 8 size shot. Both the Skeet and trap loads were of the heavy (3 dram) type, meaning a velocity of 1200 fps for their 1⅛-oz. shot charges. I fired several hundred rounds of these without a problem through an 870 Remington trap gun and a 1100 Remington Skeet gun. Patterns are presumed excellent as no deviation from my normal scores was noted.

The Max Jagt load is a Danish way of saying high velocity load. These are loaded to a 3¾ dram equivalent (1330 fps) with 1¼ ounces of shot. I used my 100-round sampling of No. 6 size shot to bag a fair number of New England grouse as well as about three dozen crows. I can report perfect functioning and obviously satisfactory patterns. My Max Jagt loads used a red case which will soon be changed to a blue one, clearly marked with the shot size and incorporating an unusually long brass cup. The 1-oz. load (28.5 grams) is available in 6, 7½ and 8 size shot. Cases are a brown color, also with a relatively long brass cup.

Despite the too-fragile packaging (the boxes quickly fell apart) the very attractive price and high level of performance of these shells will make them quite salable to everyone, except perhaps reloaders who will find no data listings for this case in the usual sources of information. This ammo is good and has been used by Olympic medal-winning competitors;

DanArms shotshells pattern superbly and sell for notably less bucks than most in a wide range of shot weights and sizes in 12 gauge now; 20 gauge soon.

a gold medal in 1980 and a silver in 1984.

Hercules

By the time you read this Hercules will be distributing a new version of their data booklet. Data, of course, is the single most important component to a handloader. There never seems to be enough to cover all the available component combinations. Hercules continuously tries to upgrade the amount of data they supply, free of charge, to the consumer.

This year the data booklet has been expanded in eight different categories. These include ⅞-oz. 12-gauge target loads, the Activ shotshell case, Remington Unibody shells, Remington 209 primers, Remington RTL wads, 20-gauge slugs, 20-gauge buckshot, and 12-gauge 1½-oz. loadings (with Blue Dot powder). For those unfamiliar with ballistic testing, I can assure you that the additions to the Hercules data represent a great deal of time and effort.

About the specific additions: The ⅞-oz. loads all generate less than 8,500 LUP's. As such, these loads should always be used with cases that are in good condition to insure a firm crimp. Tightening up on the crimp bevel adjustment will help. Too, such loads are not ideally suited to cold weather use as pressures could drop still further. If you have an autoloader, best pass on the ⅞-oz. loads and instead use 1-oz. loads if you want to insure positive functioning. Select loads that produce a minimum average pressure of 8,500 LUP for any autoloader or for cold temperature use.

The data for the Activ shell is rather extensive and includes loadings for 1, 1⅛, 1¼, 1⅜ and 1½ oz. shot charge weights with Red Dot, Green Dot, Unique, Herco and Blue Dot, depending upon the specific load. Wads used for the Activ case loads include the Activ T-28, T-32, T-35, T-42, as well as the Federal 12S0, 12S3, 12C1, 12S4 and Remington RTL, RXP-12, SP12 and RP12. Also shown are Winchester and PC wads.

The data for the Remington Unibody shells will be welcomed by a great many shooters who have found data for these new one-piece cases just a bit hard to come by. I'm not sure just how many folks will use the new 20-gauge buckshot and slug loads, but they're there for those who must, for one reason or another, use a 20-gauge gun for deer hunting.

The increase in 12-gauge 1½-oz. loads is sure to be welcomed by waterfowlers who may have found that over the past few decades the number of listings for the baby magnum shot charge weight has notably decreased. I, for one, will be burning a great deal more Blue Dot powder during my less than totally effective efforts to control the New England sea ducks.

I was happy to hear of Hercules' position on not supplying data for polyethelene buffered shotshell loads. The use of filler material results in unpredictable increases in pressure. Variations in the filler loading techniques used by individual reloaders as well as variations in the actual filler material, can contribute to significant and possibly dangerous variations in shotshell pressure and performance. With so many "ifs" involved, the reloader is best advised not to attempt the loading of buffered shotshells. ●

CENTERFIRE RIFLE CARTRIDGES—BALLISTICS AND PRICES

(R) = REMINGTON; (W) = WINCHESTER-WESTERN); (F) = FEDERAL; (H) = HORNADY-FRONTIER; (PMC) = Patton & Morgan Corp.

Cartridge	— BULLET — Wt. Grs.	Type	Bbl. (in.)	— VELOCITY (fps) — Muzzle	100 yds.	200 yds.	300 yds.	— ENERGY (ft. lbs.) — Muzzle	100 yds.	200 yds.	300 yds.	— BULLET PATH† — 100 yds.	200 yds.	300 yds.	Price Per Box
17 Remington (R)	25	HPPL	24	4040	3284	2644	2086	906	599	388	242	+0.5	−1.5	−8.5	**N.A.**
22 Hornet (R) (W)	45	PSP,HP, OPE	24	2690	2042	1502	1128	723	417	225	127	0.0	−7.7	−31.3	***25.60**
218 Bee (W)	46	OPE	24	2760	2102	1550	1155	778	451	245	136	0.0	−7.2	−29.4	***38.60**
222 Remington (R) (W) (F) (H)	50	PSP, SX	24	3140	2602	2123	1700	1094	752	500	321	+2.2	0.0	−10.0	**10.95**
222 Remington (R)	50	HPPL	24	3140	2635	2182	1777	1094	771	529	351	+2.1	0.0	−9.5	**N.A.**
222 Remington (W) (R) (PMC)	55	FMC	24	3020	2675	2355	2057	1114	874	677	517	+2.0	0.0	−8.3	**10.95**
222 Remington (F)	55	MC BT	24	3020	2740	2480	2230	1115	915	750	610	+1.9	0.0	−7.7	**10.95**
222 Remington Magnum (R)	55	PSP	24	3240	2748	2305	1906	1282	922	649	444	+1.9	0.0	−8.5	**N.A.**
222 Remington Magnum (R)	55	HPPL	24	3240	2773	2352	1969	1282	939	675	473	+1.8	0.0	−8.5	**N.A.**
223 Remington (R) (W) (F) (H) (PMC)	55	PSP	24	3240	2747	2304	1905	1282	921	648	443	+1.9	0.0	−8.5	**11.95**
223 Remington (R)	55	HPPL	24	3240	2773	2352	1969	1282	939	675	473	+1.8	0.0	−8.2	**10.95**
223 Remington (R) (H)	55	MC	24	3240	2759	2326	1933	1282	929	660	456	+1.9	0.0	−8.4	**11.95**
223 Remington (W) (F) (PMC)	55	FMC, MC BT	24	3240	2877	2543	2232	1282	1011	790	608	+1.7	0.0	−7.1	**11.95**
225 Winchester (W)	55	PSP	24	3570	3066	2616	2208	1556	1148	836	595	+1.2	0.0	−6.2	**13.30**
22-250 Remington (R) (W) (F) (H) (PMC)	55	PSP	24	3730	3180	2695	2257	1699	1235	887	622	+1.0	0.0	−5.7	**11.95**
22-250 Remington (R)	55	HPPL	24	3730	3253	2826	2436	1699	1292	975	725	+0.9	0.0	−5.2	**N.A.**
22-250 Remington (F) — Premium	55	BTHP	24	3730	3330	2960	2630	1700	1350	1070	840	+0.8	0.0	−4.8	**12.95**
220 Swift (H)	55	SP	24	3630	3176	2755	2370	1609	1229	927	686	+1.0	0.0	−5.6	**15.35**
220 Swift (H)	60	HP	24	3530	3134	2763	2420	1657	1305	1016	780	+1.1	0.0	−5.7	**15.35**
243 (W) (R) (F) (H) (PMC)	80	PSP, HPPL, FMJ	24	3350	2955	2593	2259	1993	1551	1194	906	+1.6	0.0	−7.0	**15.35**
243 Winchester (F) — Premium	85	BTHP	24	3320	3070	2830	2600	2080	1770	1510	1280	+1.5	0.0	−6.8	**15.95**
243 Winchester (W) (R) (F) (H) (PMC)	100	PPSP, PSPCL, SP	24	2960	2697	2449	2215	1945	1615	1332	1089	+1.9	0.0	−7.8	**14.95**
243 Winchester (F) — Premium	100	BTSP	24	2960	2760	2570	2380	1950	1690	1460	1260	+1.4	0.0	−5.8	**15.95**
6mm Remington (R) (W) (Also, 244 Rem.)	80	PSP, HPPL	24	3470	3064	2694	2352	2139	1667	1289	982	+1.2	0.0	−6.0	**14.95**
6mm Remington (R) (W) (F)	100	PSPCL, PPSP	24	3130	2857	2600	2357	2175	1812	1501	1233	+1.7	0.0	−6.8	**14.95**
25-20 Winchester (W) (R)	86	SP	24	1460	1194	1030	931	407	272	203	165	0.0	−23.5	−79.6	***24.25**
256 Winchester (W)	60	OPE	24	2760	2097	1542	1149	1015	586	317	176	0.0	−7.3	−29.6	***31.20**
25-35 Winchester (W)	117	SP	24	2230	1866	1545	1282	1292	904	620	427	0.0	−9.2	−33.1	**16.95**
250 Savage (W)	87	PSP	24	3030	2673	2342	2036	1773	1380	1059	801	+2.0	0.0	−8.4	**15.15**
250 Savage (W)	100	ST	24	2820	2467	2140	1839	1765	1351	1017	751	+2.4	0.0	−10.1	**15.15**
250 Savage (R)	100	PSP	24	2820	2504	2210	1936	1765	1392	1084	832	+2.3	0.0	−9.5	**N.A.**
257 Roberts (W)	100	ST	24	2900	2541	2210	1904	1867	1433	1084	805	+2.3	0.0	−9.4	**16.75**
257 Roberts (W) (R)	117	PPSP, SPCL	24	2650	2291	1961	1663	1824	1363	999	718	+2.9	0.0	−12.0	**16.75**
25-06 Remington (R)	87	HPPL	24	3440	2995	2591	2222	2286	1733	1297	954	+1.2	0.0	−6.3	**N.A.**
25-06 Remington (W) (F)	90	PEP, HP	24	3440	3043	2680	2344	2364	1850	1435	1098	+1.2	0.0	−6.1	**16.25**
25-06 Remington (R)	100	PSPCL	24	3230	2893	2580	2287	2316	1858	1478	1161	+1.6	0.0	−6.9	**N.A.**
25-06 Remington (F)	117	SP	24	3060	2790	2530	2280	2430	2020	1660	1360	+1.8	0.0	−7.3	**16.25**
25-06 Remington (R) (W)	120	PSPCL, PEP	24	3010	2749	2502	2269	2414	2013	1668	1372	+1.9	0.0	−7.4	**16.25**
6.5mm Remington Magnum (R)	120	PSPCL	24	3210	2905	2621	2353	2745	2248	1830	1475	+1.3	0.0	−6.6	**N.A.**
264 Winchester Magnum (W)	100	PSP, PSPCL	24	3320	2926	2565	2231	2447	1901	1461	1105	+1.3	0.0	−6.7	**20.95**
264 Winchester Magnum (W) (R)	140	PPSP, PSPCL	24	3030	2782	2548	2326	2854	2406	2018	1682	+1.8	0.0	−7.2	**20.95**
270 Winchester (W) (R)	100	PSP	24	3480	3067	2690	2343	2689	2088	1606	1219	+1.2	0.0	−6.2	**16.25**
270 Winchester (W) (R) (F)	130	PPSP, BP, SP	24	3110	2849	2604	2371	2791	2343	1957	1622	+1.7	0.0	−6.8	**16.25**
270 Winchester (W) (R) (H) (PMC)	130	ST, PSPCL	24	3110	2823	2554	2300	2791	2300	1883	1527	+1.7	0.0	−7.1	**16.25**
270 Winchester (F) — Premium	130	BTSP	24	3110	2880	2670	2460	2790	2400	2050	1740	+1.6	0.0	−6.5	**17.35**
270 Winchester (W) (H)	150	PPSP	24	2900	2632	2380	2142	2801	2307	1886	1528	+2.1	0.0	−8.2	**16.25**
270 Winchester (F) — Premium	150	BTSP	24	2900	2710	2520	2350	2800	2440	2120	1830	+1.6	0.0	−7.0	**17.35**
270 Winchester (R) (F)	150	SPCL, SP	24	2900	2550	2225	1926	2801	2165	1649	1235	+2.2	0.0	−9.3	**16.25**
270 Winchester (F) — Premium	150	NP	24	2900	2630	2380	2140	2800	2310	1890	1530	+2.1	0.0	−8.2	**21.25**
7mm Mauser (W)	175	SP	24	2440	2137	1857	1603	2313	1774	1340	998	0.0	−6.8	−23.7	**16.55**
7mm Mauser (F) (R)	140	SP	24	2660	2450	2260	2070	2200	1865	1585	1330	+2.4	0.0	−3.2	**16.55**
7mm-08 Remington (R)	140	PSPCL	24	2860	2625	2402	2189	2542	2142	1793	1490	+2.1	0.0	−8.1	**N.A.**
280 Remington (R)	150	SPCL	24	2970	2699	2444	2203	2937	2426	1989	1616	+1.9	0.0	−7.8	**N.A.**
280 Remington (R)	165	SPCL	24	2820	2510	2220	1950	2913	2308	1805	1393	+2.3	0.0	−9.4	**N.A.**
284 Winchester (W)	150	PPSP	24	2860	2595	2344	2108	2724	2243	1830	1480	+2.1	0.0	−8.5	**19.15**
7mm Remington Magnum (R) (W) (F)	150	PSPCL, PPSP, SP	24	3110	2830	2568	2320	3221	2667	2196	1792	+1.7	0.0	−7.0	**20.10**
7mm Remington Magnum (F)—Premium	150	BTSP	24	3110	2920	2750	2580	3220	2850	2510	2210	+1.6	0.0	−6.2	**21.25**
7mm Remington Magnum (F)—Premium	165	BTSP	24	2860	2710	2560	2420	3000	2690	2410	2150	+1.6	0.0	−6.9	**21.25**
7mm Remington Magnum (R) (W) (F) (H)	175	PSPCL, PPSP	24	2860	2645	2440	2244	3178	2718	2313	1956	+2.0	0.0	−7.9	**20.10**
7mm Remington Magnum (F)—Premium	160	NP	24	2950	2730	2520	2320	3090	2650	2250	1910	+1.8	0.0	−7.7	**25.70**
30 Carbine (R) (W) (F) (H)	110	SP, HSP, SP, RN	**20**	1990	1567	1236	1035	967	600	373	262	0.0	−13.5	−49.9	***26.05**
30 Carbine (W) (F) (H) (PMC)	110	FMC, MC, FMJ, FMC	**20**	1990	1596	1278	1070	967	622	399	280	0.0	−13.0	−47.4	***26.05**
30 Remington (R)	170	SPCL, ST	24	2120	1822	1555	1328	1696	1253	913	666	0.0	−9.7	−33.8	**N.A.**
30-30 Accelerator (R)	55	SP	24	3400	2693	2085	1570	1412	886	521	301	+2.0	0.0	−10.2	**N.A.**
30-30 Winchester (F)	125	HP	24	2570	2090	1660	1320	1830	1210	770	480	0.0	−7.3	−28.1	**12.75**
30-30 Winchester (W) (F) (PMC)	150	OPE, PPSP, ST, SP	24	2390	2018	1684	1398	1902	1356	944	651	0.0	−7.7	−27.9	**12.75**
30-30 Winchester (R) (H)	150	SPCL	24	2390	1973	1605	1303	1902	1296	858	565	0.0	−8.2	−30.0	**11.65**
30-30 Winchester (W) (R) (F) (PMC)	170	PPSP, ST, SPCL, SP, HPCL	24	2200	1895	1619	1381	1827	1355	989	720	0.0	−8.9	−31.1	**12.75**
300 Savage (W)	150	PPSP	24	2630	2311	2015	1743	2303	1779	1352	1012	+2.8	0.0	−11.5	**16.40**
300 Savage (W) (F) (R)	150	ST, SP, PSPCL	24	2630	2354	2095	1853	2303	1845	1462	1143	+2.7	0.0	−10.7	**16.40**
300 Savage (R) (W) (F)	180	SPCL, PPSP	24	2350	2025	1728	1467	2207	1639	1193	860	0.0	−7.7	−27.1	**16.40**
30-40 Krag (R) (W)	180	SPCL, PPSP	24	2430	2098	1795	1525	2360	1761	1288	929	0.0	−7.1	−25.0	**17.20**
303 Savage (W)	190	ST	24	1940	1657	1410	1211	1588	1158	839	619	0.0	−11.9	−41.4	**18.70**
308 Accelerator (R)	55	PSP	24	3770	3215	2726	2286	1735	1262	907	638	+1.0	0.0	−5.6	**N.A.**
308 Winchester (W)	125	PSP	24	3050	2697	2370	2067	2582	2019	1559	1186	+2.0	0.0	−8.2	**16.25**
308 Winchester (W)	150	PPSP	24	2820	2488	2179	1893	2648	2061	1581	1193	+2.4	0.0	−9.8	**16.25**
308 Winchester (W) (R) (F) (H) (PMC)	150	ST, PSPCL, SP	24	2820	2533	2263	2009	2648	2137	1705	1344	+2.3	0.0	−9.1	**16.25**
308 Winchester (PMC)	147	FMC-BT	24	2750	2473	2257	2052	2428	2037	1697	1403	+2.3	0.0	−9.1	**N.A.**
308 Winchester (H)	165	BTSP	24	2700	2520	2330	2160	2670	2310	1990	1700	+2.0	0.0	−8.4	**15.35**
308 Winchester (W) (R)	180	PPSP, SPCL	24	2620	2274	1955	1666	2743	2086	1527	1109	+2.9	0.0	−12.1	**16.25**
308 Winchester (W) (R) (F) (PMC)	180	ST, PSPCL, SP	24	2620	2393	2178	1974	2743	2288	1896	1557	+2.6	0.0	−9.9	**16.25**
30-06 Springfield (W) (R) (F)	125	PSP, PSP, SP	24	3140	2780	2447	2138	2736	2145	1662	1269	+1.8	0.0	−7.7	**16.25**
30-06 Springfield (W)	150	PPSP	24	2920	2580	2265	1972	2839	2217	1708	1295	+2.2	0.0	−9.0	**16.25**
30-06 Springfield (W) (R) (F) (H) (PMC)	150	ST, PSPCL, SP, SP	24	2910	2617	2342	2083	2820	2281	1827	1445	+2.1	0.0	−8.5	**16.25**
30-06 Springfield (R)	150	BP	24	2910	2656	2416	2189	2820	2349	1944	1596	+2.0	0.0	−8.0	**N.A.**
30-06 Springfield (PMC)	150	FMC (M-2)	24	2810	2555	2310	2080	2630	2170	1780	1440	+2.2	0.0	−8.8	**N.A.**
30-06 Accelerator (R)	55	PSP	24	4080	3485	2965	2502	2033	1483	1074	764	+1.0	0.0	−5.0	**N.A.**
30-06 Springfield (R) (W)	165	PSPCL	24	2800	2534	2283	2047	2872	2352	1909	1534	+2.3	0.0	−9.0	**16.25**
30-06 Springfield (F) (H)	165	BTSP	24	2800	2610	2420	2240	2870	2490	2150	1840	+2.1	0.0	−8.0	**16.25**
30-06 Springfield (R) (W) (PMC)	180	SPCL, PPSP	24	2700	2348	2023	1727	2913	2203	1635	1192	+2.7	0.0	−11.3	**16.25**
30-06 Springfield (R) (W) (F) (H) (PMC)	180	PSPCL, ST	24	2700	2469	2250	2042	2913	2436	2023	1666	+2.4	0.0	−9.3	**16.25**
30-06 Springfield (R)	180	BP	24	2700	2485	2280	2084	2913	2468	2077	1736	+2.4	0.0	−9.1	**N.A.**
30-06 Springfield (W) (R) (F)	220	PPSP, SPCL	24	2410	2130	1870	1632	2837	2216	1708	1301	0.0	−6.8	−23.6	**16.25**
30-06 Springfield (W)	220	ST	24	2410	2192	1985	1791	2837	2347	1924	1567	0.0	−6.4	−21.6	**16.25**
300 H & H Magnum (W) (R)	180	ST, PSPCL	24	2880	2640	2412	2196	3315	2785	2325	1927	+2.1	0.0	−8.0	**20.70**
300 Winchester Magnum (W) (R)	150	PPSP, PSPCL	24	3290	2951	2636	2342	3605	2900	2314	1827	+1.3	0.0	−6.6	**21.35**
300 Winchester Magnum (W) (R) (F) (H)	180	PPSP, PSPCL, SP	24	2960	2745	2540	2344	3501	3011	2578	2196	+1.9	0.0	−7.3	**21.35**
300 Winchester Magnum (F) Premium	200	BTSP	24	2830	2680	2530	2380	3560	3180	2830	2520	+1.7	0.0	−7.1	**22.35**
303 British (R)	180	SPCL	24	2460	2124	1817	1542	2418	1803	1319	950	0.0	−6.9	−24.4	**N.A.**
303 British (W)	180	PPSP	24	2460	2233	2018	1816	2418	1993	1627	1318	0.0	−6.1	−20.8	**16.70**
32-20 Winchester (W) (R)	100	SP	24	1210	1021	913	834	325	231	185	154	0.0	−32.3	−106.3	***24.75**
32-20 Winchester (W) (R)	100	L	24	1210	1021	913	834	325	231	185	154	0.0	−32.3	−106.3	***19.75**

CAUTION: PRICES CHANGE. CHECK AT GUNSHOP.

CENTERFIRE RIFLE CARTRIDGES—BALLISTICS AND PRICES (continued)

Cartridge	— BULLET — Wt. Grs.	Type	Bbl. (in.)	— VELOCITY (fps) — Muzzle	100 yds.	200 yds.	300 yds.	— ENERGY (ft. lbs.) — Muzzle	100 yds.	200 yds.	300 yds.	— BULLET PATH† — 100 yds.	200 yds.	300 yds.	Price Per Box
32 Winchester Special (F) (R)	170	SP	24	2250	1920	1630	1370	1911	1390	1000	710	0.0	− 8.6	− 30.5	**13.60**
8mm Mauser (R) (W)	170	SPCL, PPSP	24	2360	1969	1622	1333	2102	1463	993	671	0.0	− 8.2	− 29.8	**16.75**
8mm Mauser (F)	170	SP	24	2510	2110	1740	1430	2380	1670	1140	770	0.0	− 7.0	− 25.7	**16.75**
8mm Remington Magnum (R)	185	PSPCL	24	3080	2761	2464	2186	3896	3131	2494	1963	+1.8	0.0	− 7.6	**N.A.**
8mm Remington Magum (R)	220	PSPCL	24	2830	2581	2346	2123	3912	3254	2688	2201	+2.2	0.0	− 8.5	**N.A.**
338 Winchester Magnum (W)	200	PPSP	24	2960	2658	2375	2110	3890	3137	2505	1977	+2.0	0.0	− 8.2	**25.35**
338 Winchester Magnum (W)	250	ST	24	2660	2395	2145	1910	3927	3184	2554	2025	+2.6	0.0	− 10.2	**25.35**
348 Winchester (W)	200	ST	24	2520	2215	1931	1672	2820	2178	1656	1241	0.0	− 6.2	− 21.9	**29.85**
351 Winchester S.L. (W)	180	SP	**20**	1850	1556	1310	1128	1368	968	686	508	0.0	−13.6	− 47.5	***42.35**
35 Remington (R)	150	PSPCL	24	2300	1874	1506	1218	1762	1169	755	494	0.0	− 9.2	− 33.0	**N.A.**
35 Remington (R) (F)	200	SPCL, SP	24	2080	1698	1376	1140	1921	1280	841	577	0.0	−11.3	− 41.2	**15.00**
35 Remington (W)	200	PPSP, ST	24	2020	1646	1335	1114	1812	1203	791	551	0.0	−12.1	− 43.9	**15.00**
358 Winchester (W)	200	ST	24	2490	2171	1876	1610	2753	2093	1563	1151	0.0	− 6.5	− 23.0	**22.90**
350 Remington Magnum (R)	200	PSPCL	**20**	2710	2410	2130	1870	3261	2579	2014	1553	+2.6	0.0	− 10.3	**N.A.**
375 Winchester (W)	200	PPSP	24	2200	1841	1526	1268	2150	1506	1034	714	0.0	− 9.5	− 33.8	**19.75**
375 Winchester (W)	250	PPSP	24	1900	1647	1424	1239	2005	1506	1126	852	0.0	−12.0	− 40.9	**19.75**
38-55 Winchester (W)	255	SP	24	1320	1190	1091	1018	987	802	674	587	0.0	−23.4	− 75.2	**18.35**
375 H & H Magnum (R) (W)	270	SP, PPSP	24	2690	2420	2166	1928	4337	3510	2812	2228	+2.5	0.0	− 10.0	**25.20**
375 H & H Magnum (W)	300	ST	24	2530	2268	2022	1793	4263	3426	2723	2141	+2.9	0.0	− 11.5	**25.20**
375 H & H Magnum (W) (R)	300	FMC, MC	24	2530	2171	1843	1551	4263	3139	2262	1602	0.0	− 6.5	− 23.4	**25.20**
38-40 Winchester (W)	180	SP	24	1160	999	901	827	538	399	324	273	0.0	−33.9	−110.6	***31.60**
44-40 Winchester (W) (R)	200	SP, SP	24	1190	1006	900	822	629	449	360	300	0.0	−33.3	−109.5	***32.70**
44 Remington Magnum (R)	240	SP, SJHP	**20**	1760	1380	1114	970	1650	1015	661	501	0.0	−17.6	− 63.1	**N.A.**
44 Remington Magnum (F) (W)	240	HSP	**20**	1760	1380	1090	950	1650	1015	640	485	0.0	−18.1	− 65.1	**12.45**
444 Marlin (R)	240	SP	24	2350	1815	1377	1087	2942	1755	1010	630	0.0	− 9.9	− 38.5	**N.A.**
444 Marlin (R)	265	SP	24	2120	1733	1405	1160	2644	1768	1162	791	0.0	−10.8	− 39.5	**N.A.**
45-70 Government (F)	300	HSP	24	1810	1410	1120	970	2180	1320	840	630	0.0	−17.0	− 61.4	**18.50**
45-70 Government (W)	300	JHP	24	1880	1559	1294	1105	2355	1619	1116	814	0.0	−13.5	− 47.1	**18.50**
45-70 Government (R)	405	SP	24	1330	1168	1055	977	1590	1227	1001	858	0.0	−24.6	− 80.3	**N.A.**
458 Winchester Magnum (W) (R)	500	FMC, MC	24	2040	1823	1623	1442	4620	3689	2924	2308	0.0	− 9.6	− 32.5	**34.05**
458 Winchester Magnum (W) (R)	510	SP, SP	24	2040	1770	1527	1319	4712	3547	2640	1970	0.0	−10.3	− 35.6	**34.05**

*Price for 50. †Bullet Path based on line-of-sight 0.9″ above center of bore. Bullet type abbreviations: BP—Bronze Point; BT—Boat Tail; CL—Core Lokt; FN—Flat Nose; FMC—Full Metal Case; FMJ—Full Metal Jacket; HP—Hollow Point; HSP—Hollow Soft Point; JHP—Jacketed Hollow Point; L—Lead; Lu—Lubaloy; MAT—Match; MC—Metal Case; NP—Nosler Partition; OPE—Open Point Expanding; PCL—Pointed Core Lokt; PEP—Pointed Expanding Point; PL—Power-Lokt; PP—Power Point; Prem.—Premium; PSP—Pointed Soft Point; SJHP—Semi-Jacketed Hollow Point; SJMP—Semi-Jacketed Metal Point; SP—Soft Point; ST—Silvertip; SX—Super Explosive. PMC prices slightly less.

CENTERFIRE HANDGUN CARTRIDGES—BALLISTICS AND PRICES

Win.-Western, Rem.-Peters, Norma, PMC, and Federal

Most loads are available from W-W and R-P. All available Norma loads are listed. Federal cartridges are marked with an asterisk. Other loads supplied by only one source are indicated by a letter, thus: Norma (a); R-P (b); W-W (c); PMC (d); CCI (e). Prices are approximate.

Cartridge	Bullet Gr.	Style	Muzzle Velocity	Muzzle Energy	Barrel Inches	Price Per Box
22 Jet (b)	40	SP	2100	390	8⅜	**$ NA**
221 Fireball (b)	50	SP	2650	780	10½	**NA**
25 (6.35mm) Auto*	50	MC	810	73	2	**15.85**
25 ACP (c)	45	Exp. Pt.	835	70	2	**16.95**
256 Winchester Magnum (c)	60	HP	2350	735	8½	**31.20**
30 (7.65mm) Luger Auto	93	MC	1220	307	4½	**25.95**
32 S&W Blank (b, c)	No bullet		—	—	—	**15.10**
32 S&W Blank, BP (c)	No bullet		—	—	—	**15.10**
32 Short Colt	80	Lead	745	100	4	**15.20**
32 Long Colt IL (c)	82	Lub.	755	104	4	**15.85**
32 Auto (c)	60	STHP	970	125	4	**19.60**
32 (7.65mm) Auto*	71	MC	905	129	4	**18.15**
32 (7.65mm) Auto Pistol (a)	77	MC	900	162	4	**18.15**
32 S&W	88	Lead	680	90	3	**15.30**
32 S&W Long	98	Lead	705	115	4	**16.15**
32-20 Winchester	100	Lead	1030	271	6	**19.75**
32-20 Winchester	100	SP	1030	271	6	**24.45**
357 Magnum	110	JHP	1295	410	4	**23.80**
357 Magnum	110	SJHP	1295	410	4	**23.80**
357 Magnum	125	JHP	1450	583	4	**23.80**
357 Magnum (d)	125	JHC	1450	583	4	**23.80**
357 Magnum (e)	125	JSP	1900	1001	—	**23.80**
357 Magnum (e)	140	JHP	1775	979	—	**23.80**
357 Magnum (e)	150	FMJ	1600	852	—	**23.80**
357 Magnum*	158	SWC	1235	535	4	**20.15**
357 Magnum (b) (e)	158	JSP	1550	845	8⅜	**23.80**
357 Magnum	158	MP	1410	695	8⅜	**23.80**
357 Magnum	158	Lead	1410	696	8⅜	**20.15**
357 Magnum	158	JHP	1450	735	8⅜	**23.80**
9mm Luger (c)	115	FMC	1155	341	4	**22.50**
9mm Luger (c)	115	STHP	1255	383	4	**23.65**
9mm Luger*	115	JHP	1165	349	4	**22.50**
9mm Luger*	125	MC	1120	345	4	**22.50**
9mm Luger (e)	125	JSP	1100	335	—	**22.50**
38 S&W Blank	No bullet		—	—	—	**18.30**
38 Smith & Wesson	145	Lead	685	150	4	**17.05**
38 Special Blank	No bullet		—	—	—	**18.40**
38 Special (e)	110	JHP	1200	351	—	**NA**
38 Special	158	Lead	855	256	6	**17.10**
38 Special	158	MP	855	256	6	**21.70**
38 Special (b)	125	SJHP	Not available			**NA**
38 Special Match, IL	148	Lead	770	195	6	**17.85**
38 Special Match, IL (b)	158	Lead	855	256	6	**NA**
38 Special*	158	LRN	755	200	4	**17.10**
38 Special	158	SWC	755	200	4	**18.40**
38 Special Match*	148	WC	710	166	4	**17.10**
38 Special +P (c)	95	STHP	1100	255	4	**22.80**
38 Special +P (b)	110	SJHP	1020	254	4	**NA**
38 Special +P	125	JSP	945	248	4	**21.70**
38 Special +P*	158	SWCHP	915	294	4	**18.60**
38 Special +P*	158	LSWC	915	294	4	**17.45**
38 Special +P (e)	140	JHP	1275	504	—	**NA**
38 Special +P*	110	JHP	1020	254	4	**21.70**
38 Special +P*	125	JHP	945	248	4	**21.70**
38 Special Norma +P (a)	110	JHP	1542	580	6	**NA**
38 Short Colt	125	Lead	730	150	6	**16.70**
38 Long Colt	150	Lead	730	175	6	**25.60**
38 Super Auto +P (b)	130	MC	1280	475	5	**NA**
38 Super Auto +P (b)	115	JHP	1300	431	5	**NA**
38 Auto	130	MC	1040	312	4½	**20.20**
380 Auto (c)	85	STHP	1000	189	3¾	**19.40**
380 Auto*	95	MC	955	190	3¾	**18.55**
380 Auto (g)	88	JHP	990	191	4	**NA**
380 Auto*	90	JHP	1000	200	3¾	**18.55**
38-40 Winchester	180	SP	975	380	5	**31.60**
41 Remington Magnum	210	Lead	1050	515	8¾	**26.75**
41 Remington Magnum	210	SP	1500	1050	8¾	**31.30**
44 S&W Spec.*	200	LSW	960	410	7½	**23.95**
44 S&W Special	246	Lead	755	311	6½	**23.95**
44 Remington Magnum*	180	JHP	1610	1045	4	**28.35**
44 Remington Magnum (e)	200	JHP	1650	1208	—	**NA**
44 Remington Magnum (e)	240	JSP	1625	1406	—	**NA**
44 Remington Magnum (b)	240	SP	1470	1150	6½	**NA**
44 Remington Magnum	240	Lead	1470	1150	6½	**30.40**
44 Remington Magnum (g)	240	SJHP	1180	741	4	**NA**
44 Remington Magnum (a)	240	JPC	1533	1253	8½	**NA**
44-40 Winchester	200	SP	975	420	7½	**32.70**
45 Colt*	225	SWCHP	900	405	5½	**22.90**
45 Colt	250	Lead	860	410	5½	**NA**
45 Colt, IL (c)	255	Lub., L	860	410	5½	**24.35**
45 Auto (c)[1]	185	STHP	1000	411	5	**10.45**
45 Auto (e)	200	JHP	1025	466	—	**13.02**
45 Auto	230	MC	850	369	5	**NA**
45 Auto WC*	185	MC	775	245	5	**24.80**
45 Auto*	185	JHP	950	370	5	**26.05**
45 Winchester Magnum (c)	230	FMC	1400	1001	5	**27.05**
45 Auto Rim (b)	230	Lead	810	335	5½	**27.05**

[1]20 rounds per box. IL—Inside Lub. JSP—Jacketed Soft Point WC—Wad Cutter RN—Round Nose HP—Hollow Point Lub—Lubricated MC—Metal Case SP—Soft Point MP—Metal Point LGC—Lead, Gas Check JHP—Jacketed Hollow Point SWC—Semi Wad Cutter SJHP—Semi Jacketed Hollow Point PC—Power Cavity

CAUTION: PRICES CHANGE. CHECK AT GUNSHOP.

NORMA C.F. RIFLE CARTRIDGES—BALLISTICS AND PRICES

Cartridge	— Bullet — Wt. Grs.	Type	— Velocity (fps) — Muzzle	100 Yds.	200 Yds.	300 Yds.	— Energy(ft. lbs.) — Muzzle	100 Yds.	200 Yds.	300 Yds.	— Bullet Path† — 100 Yds.	200 Yds.	300 Yds.	Price Per Box
22 Hornet	45	HP	2430	1895	1355	985	590	360	185	95	0.0	−7.7	−31.3	*$26.21
222 Remington	50	SP	3200	2650	2180	1760	1135	780	475	310	+2.2	0.0	−10.0	11.15
222 Remington	50	FMJ	3200	2610	2130	1710	1135	755	454	292	+2.2	0.0	− 9.6	11.15
222 Remington	53	SP	3115	2670	2190	1770	1140	840	480	313	+2.1	0.0	− 9.4	11.15
22-250 Remington	53	SP	3710	3190	2740	2250	1615	1200	751	506	+1.0	0.0	− 5.7	12.32
220 Swift	50	SP	4110	3610	3135	2680	1875	1450	1090	800	+0.6	0.0	− 4.1	17.90
22 Savage Hi-Power	71	SP, FMJ	2790	2295	1885	1560	1225	830	560	385	+2.4	0.0	−11.4	18.85
243 Winchester	100	SP, FMJ	3070	2790	2540	2320	2090	1730	1430	1190	+1.4	0.0	− 6.3	15.31
6.5 × 50 Jap.	139	SBT	2360	2185	2035	1900	1720	1475	1243	1083	+2.8	0.0	−11.1	18.85
6.5 × 50 Jap.	156	SP	2065	1870	1690	1530	1480	1215	990	810	+4.3	0.0	−16.4	18.85
6.5 × 52 Carcano	156	SP	2430	2210	2000	1800	2045	1690	1385	1125	+2.9	0.0	−11.7	18.85
6.5 × 55 Swedish	139	PPC	2855	2660	2500	2350	2512	2181	1875	1657	+1.7	0.0	− 7.6	18.85
6.5 × 55 Swedish	140	Nosler	2855	2665	2500	2350	2530	2210	1930	1677	+1.7	0.0	− 7.6	20.30
6.5 × 55 Swedish	156	SP	2645	2415	2205	2010	2425	2015	1701	1414	+2.5	0.0	−10.6	18.85
270 Winchester	130	SP	3140	2885	2640	2405	2845	2400	2010	1670	+1.4	0.0	− 6.6	16.57
270 Winchester	150	SP	2800	2615	2435	2260	2615	2280	1975	1705	+1.8	0.0	− 7.7	16.57
7 × 57 R	150	SP, FMJ	2690	2475	2285	2080	2410	2040	1830	1515	+2.0	0.0	− 8.4	19.66
7 × 57 Mauser	150	SP	2755	2540	2330	2135	2530	2150	1810	1515	+2.0	0.0	− 8.4	16.90
280 Remington	150	SP	2870	2640	2400	2200	2740	2320	2015	1695	+1.9	0.0	− 7.9	16.57
280 Remington	170	PPC	2710	2460	2220	1945	2765	2280	1910	1510	+2.3	0.0	− 9.2	16.57
7 × 64 Brenneke	150	SP	2890	2600	2330	2115	2780	2250	1810	1490	+1.7	0.0	− 7.5	19.66
7 × 64 Brenneke	170	PPC	2500	2455	2200	1915	2865	2365	1694	1466	+2.8	0.0	−10.0	19.66
7mm Remington Magnum	150	SP	3250	2960	2640	2440	3520	2920	2320	1985	+1.2	0.0	− 5.8	20.51
7mm Remington Magnum	150	FMJ	2995	2780	2460	2260	2985	2575	2118	1788	+1.4	0.0	− 6.0	*46.14
7mm Remington Magnum	170	PPC	3020	2750	2510	2410	3440	2860	2520	2323	+2.0	0.0	− 8.7	20.51
30 Carbine	110	SP	1970	1595	1260	1055	950	620	400	280	0.0	−4.0	−12.5	10.58
7.62 × 39 Soviet	125	SP	2340	1860	1430	1100	1470	1037	614	363	+2.5	0.0	− 8.6	20.11
30-30 Winchester	150	SP	2330	2000	1660	1380	1805	1330	966	666	0.0	−7.7	−27.9	12.98
30-30 Winchester	170	SP	2135	1810	1530	1180	1715	1235	936	557	0.0	−8.9	−31.1	12.98
308 Winchester	130	SP	2900	2590	2270	2060	2430	1935	1545	1273	+1.8	0.0	− 7.9	16.57
308 Winchester	146	FMJBT	2810	2595	2390	2180	2560	2180	1713	1426	+1.8	0.0	− 7.4	*37.25
308 Winchester	150	SP	2860	2570	2300	2050	2725	2200	1760	1400	+1.9	0.0	− 8.5	16.57
308 Winchester	168	HPBT	2550	2370	2180	2010	2276	1966	1663	1414	+2.3	0.0	− 8.7	21.25
308 Winchester	180	DC	2610	2400	2210	2020	2725	2305	1954	1632	+2.4	0.0	− 9.3	16.57
308 Winchester	180	Nosler	2610	2400	2210	2020	2725	2305	1954	1632	+2.4	0.0	− 9.3	21.25
308 Winchester	180	A	2610	2395	2170	1850	2725	2285	1884	1369	+2.4	0.0	− 9.6	16.57
308 Winchester	180	PPC	2610	2400	2180	1870	2725	2305	1901	1399	+2.4	0.0	− 9.3	16.57
308 Winchester	200	PPC	2460	2220	2000	1690	2690	2185	1800	1285	+2.7	0.0	−10.3	16.57
30-06 Springfield	130	SP	3205	2875	2560	2263	2965	2390	1895	1480	+1.4	0.0	− 6.7	16.57
30-06 Springfield	146	FMJBT	2770	2555	2340	2110	2490	2115	1640	1335	+1.7	0.0	− 7.3	*37.25
30-06 Springfield	150	SP	2970	2680	2400	2140	2945	2395	1920	1525	+1.7	0.0	− 7.8	16.57
30-06 Springfield	180	DC	2700	2495	2295	2110	2915	2485	2105	1775	+2.0	0.0	− 8.6	16.57
30-06 Springfield	180	Nosler	2700	2495	2295	2110	2915	2485	2105	1775	+2.0	0.0	− 8.6	21.25
30-06 Springfield	180	A	2700	2490	2270	1940	2915	2480	2061	1505	+2.0	0.0	− 8.5	16.57
30-06 Springfield	180	PPC	2700	2490	2280	1950	2915	2480	2079	1521	+2.0	0.0	− 8.5	16.57
30-06 Springfield	200	PPC	2640	2390	2220	1860	3095	2535	2218	1384	+2.6	0.0	−10.0	16.57
7.5 × 55 Swiss	180	SBT	2650	2460	2250	2060	2800	2380	2020	1690	+2.1	0.0	− 8.9	19.66
7.62 × 54R Russian	180	SBT	2575	2360	2165	1975	2650	2270	1875	1560	+2.3	0.0	− 9.5	20.11
7.65 × 53 Argentine	150	SP	2660	2390	2120	1870	2355	1895	1573	1224	+2.1	0.0	− 8.8	18.86
300 Winchester Magnum	180	SBT	3020	2780	2590	2400	3645	3095	2683	2304	+1.4	0.0	− 7.4	21.63
308 Norma Magnum	180	DC	3020	2780	2580	2385	3645	3095	2670	2270	+1.3	0.0	− 8.0	23.30
303 British	150	SP	2720	2440	2170	1930	2465	1985	1570	1240	+2.2	0.0	− 9.7	17.22
7.7 × 58 Jap.	130	SP	2950	2635	2340	2065	2513	2005	1581	1230	+1.8	0.0	− 8.2	20.10
7.7 × 58 Jap.	180	SBT	2495	2290	2100	1920	2485	2100	1765	1475	+2.6	0.0	−10.4	20.10
8 × 57 Mauser JS	165	PPC	2855	2525	2225	1955	2985	2335	1733	1338	+2.0	0.0	− 8.0	17.22
8 × 57 Mauser JS	196	A	2525	2195	1895	1625	2780	2100	1560	1150	+2.9	0.0	−12.7	17.22
9.3 × 57 Mauser	286	A	2065	1820	1580	1400	2715	2100	1622	1274	+3.4	0.0	−21.7	21.63
9.3 × 62 Mauser	286	A	2360	2090	1830	1580	3545	2770	2177	1622	+3.0	0.0	−20.2	21.63

†Bullet Path based on line of sight 1.5" above center of bore. Bullet type abbreviations: HP—Hollow Point; SP—Soft Point; FMJ—Full Metal Jacket; PPC—Protected Power Cavity; Nosler—Nosler Partition; FMJBT—Full Metal Jacket Boat Tail; SBT—Spitzer Boat Tail; A—Alaska (Round Nose Soft Point); DC—Dual Core. *50 Rounds Per Box

WEATHERBY MAGNUM CARTRIDGES—BALLISTICS AND PRICES

Cartridge	— Bullet — Wt. Grs.	Type	Bbl. (in.)	— Velocity (fps) — Muzzle	100 Yds.	200 Yds.	300 Yds.	— Energy (ft. lbs.) — Muzzle	100 Yds.	200 Yds.	300 Yds.	— Bullet Path† — 100 Yds.	200 Yds.	300 Yds.	Price Per Box
224 Weatherby Magnum	55	PE	26	3650	3214	2808	2433	1627	1262	963	723	+2.8	+3.6	0.0	$22.95
240 Weatherby Magnum	87	PE	26	3500	3165	2848	2550	2367	1935	1567	1256	+2.8	+3.6	0.0	22.95
240 Weatherby Magnum	100	PE	26	3395	3115	2848	2594	2560	2155	1802	1495	+2.8	+3.5	0.0	22.95
240 Weatherby Magnum	100	NP	26	3395	3068	2758	2468	2560	2090	1690	1353	+1.1	0.0	− 5.7	30.95
257 Weatherby Magnum	87	PE	26	3825	3470	3135	2818	2827	2327	1900	1535	+2.1	+2.9	0.0	23.95
257 Weatherby Magnum	100	PE	26	3555	3256	2971	2700	2807	2355	1960	1619	+2.5	+3.2	0.0	23.95
257 Weatherby Magnum	100	NP	26	3555	3242	2945	2663	2807	2335	1926	1575	+0.9	0.0	− 4.7	32.95
257 Weatherby Magnum	117	SPE	26	3300	2853	2443	2074	2830	2115	1551	1118	+3.8	+4.9	0.0	23.95
257 Weatherby Magnum	117	NP	26	3300	3027	2767	2520	2830	2381	1990	1650	+1.2	0.0	− 5.9	32.95
270 Weatherby Magnum	100	PE	26	3760	3341	2949	2585	3140	2479	1932	1484	+2.4	+3.2	0.0	23.95
270 Weatherby Magnum	130	PE	26	3375	3110	2856	2615	3289	2793	2355	1974	+2.8	+3.5	0.0	23.95
270 Weatherby Magnum	130	NP	26	3375	3113	2862	2624	3289	2798	2365	1988	+1.0	0.0	− 5.2	32.95
270 Weatherby Magnum	150	PE	26	3245	3012	2789	2575	3508	3022	2592	2209	+3.1	+3.8	0.0	23.95
270 Weatherby Magnum	150	NP	26	3245	3022	2809	2604	3508	3043	2629	2259	+1.2	0.0	− 5.4	32.95
7mm Weatherby Magnum	139	PE	26	3300	3037	2786	2546	3362	2848	2396	2001	+3.0	+3.7	0.0	23.95
7mm Weatherby Magnum	140	NP	26	3300	3047	2806	2575	3386	2887	2448	2062	+1.1	0.0	− 5.4	32.95
7mm Weatherby Magnum	154	PE	26	3160	2928	2706	2494	3415	2932	2504	2127	+3.3	+4.1	0.0	23.95
7mm Weatherby Magnum	160	NP	26	3150	2935	2727	2528	3526	3061	2643	2271	+1.3	0.0	− 5.8	32.95
7mm Weatherby Magnum	175	RN	26	3070	2714	2383	2082	3663	2863	2207	1685	+1.6	0.0	− 7.5	23.95
300 Weatherby Magnum	110	PE	26	3900	3465	3057	2677	3716	2933	2283	1750	+2.2	+3.0	0.0	23.95
300 Weatherby Magnum	150	PE	26	3545	3248	2965	2696	4187	3515	2929	2422	+2.5	+3.2	0.0	23.95
300 Weatherby Magnum	150	NP	26	3545	3191	2857	2544	4187	3392	2719	2156	+1.0	0.0	− 5.3	33.95
300 Weatherby Magnum	180	PE	26	3245	3010	2785	2569	4210	3622	3100	2639	+3.1	+3.8	0.0	23.95
300 Weatherby Magnum	180	NP	26	3245	2964	2696	2444	4210	3512	2906	2388	+1.3	0.0	− 6.0	33.95
300 Weatherby Magnum	220	SPE	26	2905	2578	2276	2000	4123	3248	2531	1955	+1.9	0.0	− 8.6	23.95
340 Weatherby Magnum	200	PE	26	3210	2947	2696	2458	4577	3857	3228	2683	+3.2	+4.0	0.0	25.95
340 Weatherby Magnum	210	NP	26	3180	2927	2686	2457	4717	3996	3365	2816	+1.3	0.0	− 6.2	40.65
340 Weatherby Magnum	250	SPE	26	2850	2516	2209	1929	4510	3515	2710	2066	+2.0	0.0	− 9.2	25.95
340 Weatherby Magnum	250	NP	26	2850	2563	2296	2049	4510	3648	2927	2331	+1.8	0.0	− 8.2	40.65
378 Weatherby Magnum	270	SPE	26	3180	2796	2440	2117	6064	4688	3570	2688	+1.5	0.0	− 7.3	40.95
378 Weatherby Magnum	300	SPE	26	2925	2564	2234	1935	5700	4380	3325	2495	+1.9	0.0	− 9.0	40.95
378 Weatherby Magnum	300	FMJ	26	2925	2620	2340	2080	5700	4574	3649	2883	+4.9	+6.0	0.0	46.95
460 Weatherby Magnum	500	RN	26	2700	2395	2115	1858	8095	6370	4968	3834	+2.3	0.0	−10.3	44.95
460 Weatherby Magnum	500	FMJ	26	2700	2416	2154	1912	8095	6482	5153	4060	+2.2	0.0	− 9.8	51.95

†Bullet Path based on line of sight 1.5" above center of bore. Bullet type abbreviations: FMJ—Full Metal Jacket; NP—Nosler Partition; PE—Pointed Expanding; RN—Round Nose; SPE—Semi-Pointed Expanding.

CAUTION: PRICES CHANGE. CHECK AT GUNSHOP.

RIMFIRE CARTRIDGES—BALLISTICS AND PRICES

Cartridge Type	Bullet Wt. Grs.	Bullet Type	Velocity (fps) 22½" Barrel Muzzle	Velocity (fps) 22½" Barrel 50 Yds.	Velocity (fps) 22½" Barrel 100 Yds.	Energy (ft. lbs.) 22½" Barrel Muzzle	Energy (ft. lbs.) 22½" Barrel 50 Yds.	Energy (ft. lbs.) 22½" Barrel 100 Yds.	Velocity (fps) 6" Barrel Muzzle	Velocity (fps) 6" Barrel 50 Yds.	Energy (ft. lbs.) 6" Barrel Muzzle	Energy (ft. lbs.) 6" Barrel 50 Yds.	Price Per Box 50 Rds.	Price Per Box 100 Rds.
22 CB Short (CCI & Win. only)	29	Solid	727	667	610	34	29	24	706	—	32	—	$N.A.	$12.55(2)
22 CB Long (CCI only)	29	Solid	727	667	610	34	29	24	706	—	32	—	N.A.	4.86
22 Short Standard Velocity	29	Solid	1045	—	810	70	—	42	865	—	48	—	2.38	N.A.
22 Short High Velocity (Fed., Rem., Win.)	29	Solid	1095	—	903	77	—	53	—	—	—	—	2.38	N.A.
22 Short High Velocity (CCI only)	29	Solid	1132	1004	920	83	65	55	1065	—	73	—	N.A.	4.76
22 Short High Velocity HP (Fed., Rem., Win.)	27	Hollow Point	1120	—	904	75	—	49	—	—	—	—	2.53	N.A.
22 Short High Vel. HP (CCI only)	27	Hollow Point	1164	1013	920	81	62	51	1077	—	69	—	N.A.	5.06
22 Long Standard Vel. (CCI only)	29	Solid	1180	1038	946	90	69	58	1031	—	68	—	N.A.	5.06
22 Long High Velocity (Fed., Rem.)	29	Solid	1240	—	962	99	—	60	—	—	—	—	2.53	N.A.
22 Long Rifle Stand. Velocity (CCI only)	40	Solid	1138	1046	975	115	97	84	1027	925	93	76	N.A.	5.42(3)
22 Long Rifle Stand. Velocity & Sil. (Fed., Rem., Win.)	40	Solid	1150	—	976	117	—	85	—	—	—	—	2.71	5.42
22 Long Rifle High Vel. (CCI only)	40	Solid	1341	1150	1045	160	117	97	1150	1010	117	90	N.A.	5.42
22 Long Rifle High Velocity (Fed., Rem., Win.)	40	Solid	1255	—	1017	140	—	92	—	—	—	—	2.71	5.42
22 Long Rifle High Velocity HP (CCI only)	37	Hollow Point	1370	1165	1040	154	111	89	1190	1040	116	88	N.A.	5.42
22 Long Rifle High Velocity HP (Fed., Rem., Win.)	36-38	Hollow Point	1280	1105	1010	131	100	82	—	—	—	—	3.04	6.08
22 Long Rifle Hyper Velocity (Fed., Rem., Win.(4))	33-34	Hollow Point	1500	1240	1075	165	110	85	—	—	—	—	3.04	14.35(2)
22 Long Rifle Viper (Rem. only)	36	Solid	1410	1187	1056	159	113	89	—	—	—	—	2.73	N.A.
22 Stinger (CCI only)	32	Hollow Point	1687	1300	1158	202	120	95	1430	1100	145	86	3.41	N.A.
22 Winchester Magnum Rimfire (Win., Fed.)	40	FMC or HP	1910	—	1326	324	—	156	—	—	—	—	7.31	N.A.
22 Winchester Magnum Rimfire (CCI only)	40	FMC or HP	2025	1688	1407	364	253	176	1339	1110	159	109	7.31	N.A.
22 Long Rifle Pistol Match (Win., Fed.)	40	Solid	—	—	—	—	—	—	1060	950	100	80	11.00	N.A.
22 Long Rifle Match (Rifle) (CCI only)	40	Solid	1138	1047	975	116	97	84	1027	925	93	76	N.A.	8.32
22 Long Rifle Shot (CCI, Fed., Win.)	—	#11 or #12 shot	1047	—	—	—	—	—	950	—	—	—	5.52	N.A.
22 Winchester Magnum Rimfire Shot (CCI only)	—	#11 shot	1126	—	—	—	—	—	1000	—	—	—	4.14(1)	N.A.
22 Short Match (CCI only)	29	Solid	830	752	695	44	36	31	786	—	39	—	N.A.	5.02
22 Long Rifle Super Silhouette (Win. only)	42	Solid	1220	—	1003	139	—	85	—	—	—	—	N.A.	6.23

Please note that the actual ballistics obtained in your gun can vary considerably from the advertised ballistics. Also, ballistics can vary from lot to lot, even within the same brand. All prices were correct at the time this table was prepared. All prices are subject to change without notice.
(1) 20 to a box. (2) per 250 rounds. (3) Also packaged 200 rounds per box. (4) Also packaged 250 rounds per box.

SHOTSHELL LOADS AND PRICES

Winchester-Western, Remington-Peters, Federal

Dram Equivalent	Shot Ozs.	Load Style	Shot Sizes	Brands	Average Price Per Box	Nominal Velocity (fps)
10 Gauge 3½" Magnum						
4½	2¼	Premium(1)	BB, 2, 4	Fed., Win.	$31.10	1205
4¼	2	H.V.	BB, 2, 4, 5, 6	Fed., Rem.	29.00	1210
Max.	1¾	Slug, rifled	Slug	Fed.	7.10	1280
Max.	Variable	Buck, Premium(1)	00, 4 (Buck)	Fed., Win.	6.00	Variable
Max.	1¾	Steel	BB, 2	Win.	27.00	1280
4¼	1⅝	Steel	BB, 2	Fed.	26.30	1285
10 Gauge 2⅞" Magnum						
4¾	1⅝	H.V.	4	Win.	27.00	1330
12 Gauge 3" Magnum						
4	1⅞	Premium(1)	BB, 2, 4, 6	Fed., Rem., Win.	20.80	1210
4	1⅝	Premium(1)	2, 4, 5, 6	Fed., Rem., Win.	19.45	1280
4	1⅞	H.V.	BB, 2, 4	Fed., Rem.	19.40	1210
4	1⅝	H.V.	2, 4, 6	Fed., Rem.	17.95	1280
4	Variable	Buck, Premium(1)	000, 00, 1, 4	Fed., Rem., Win.	4.55 (10.95)	Variable
3½	1⅜	Steel	BB, 1, 2, 4	Fed.	20.95	1245
3½	1¼	Steel	BB, 1, 2, 4	Rem., Win.	N.A.	1275
4	2	Premium	BB, 2, 4, 6	Fed.	22.10	1175
12 Gauge 2¾" Hunting & Target						
3¾	1½	Premium(1), Mag.	BB, 2, 4, 5, 6	Fed., Rem., Win.	18.45	1260
3¾	1½	H.V., Mag.	BB, 2, 4, 5, 6	Fed., Rem.	16.25	—
3¾	1¼	H.V., Premium(1)	2, 4, 6, 7½	Fed., Rem.	13.45	1330
3¾	1¼	H.V., Promo.	BB, 2, 4, 5, 6, 7½, 9	Fed., Rem., Win.	12.50	1330
3¼	1¼	Std. Vel., Premium	7½, 8	Fed., Rem.	12.00	1220
3¼	1⅛	Std. Vel., Premium	7½, 8	Fed., Rem.	11.55	1255
3¼	1¼	Std. Vel.	7½, 8, 9	Fed., Rem.	11.00	1220
3¼	1⅛	Std. Vel.	4, 5, 6, 7½, 8, 9	Fed., Rem., Win.	10.65	1255
3¼	1	Std. Vel., Promo.	6, 7½, 8	Fed., Rem., Win.	10.00	1290
Max.	1¼	Slug, rifled, Mag.	Slug	Fed.	5.10	1490
Max.	1	Slug, rifled	Slug	Fed., Rem., Win.	4.10	1580
4	Variable	Buck, Mag. (Premium)	00, 1, 4 (Buck)	Fed., Rem., Win.	3.95 (9.40)	Variable
3¾	Variable	Buck (Premium)	000, 00, 0, 1, 4 (Buck)	Fed., Rem., Win.	3.55 (8.45)	Variable
3¾	1⅜	H.V.	2, 4, 6	Fed.	13.50	1295
3¼	1¼	Pigeon	7½, 8	Fed., Win.	14.00	1220
3	1⅛	Trap & Skeet	7½, 8, 9	Fed., Rem. Win.	7.00	1200
2¾	1⅛	Trap & Skeet	7½, 8, 8½, 9	Fed., Rem., Win.	7.00	1145
2¾	1	Trap & Skeet	8, 8½	Fed., Rem., Win.	7.00	1180
3¾	1¼	Steel	BB, 1, 2, 4, 6	Fed., Win.	17.10	1330
3¾	1⅛	Steel	1, 2, 4, 6	Fed., Rem., Win.	15.65	1365
16 Gauge 2¾"						
3¼	1¼	H.V., Mag.	2, 4, 6	Fed., Rem., Win.	15.95	1260
3¼	1⅛	H.V., Promo.	4, 5, 6, 7½, 9	Fed., Rem., Win.	12.00	1295
2¾	1⅛	Std. Vel.	4, 6, 7½, 8, 9	Fed., Rem., Win.	10.60	1185
2½	1	Std. Vel., Promo.	6, 7½, 8	Fed.	N.A.	1165
Max.	⅘	Slug, rifled	Slug	Fed., Rem., Win.	4.10	1600
Max.	12 pellets	Buck	1 (Buck)	Fed., Rem., Win.	3.55	1225
3¼	1¼	Premium	2, 4, 6	Win.	16.05	1260
20 Gauge 3" Magnum						
3	1¼	Premium(1)	2, 4, 6	Fed., Rem., Win.	16.50	1185
3	1¼	H.V.	2, 4, 6, 7½	Fed., Rem.	16.06	1185
Max.	18 pellets	Buck	2 (Buck)	Fed.	3.95	—
Max.	1	Steel	4, 6	Fed., Win.	15.00	—
20 Gauge 2¾" Hunting & Target						
2¾	1⅛	Premium(1), Mag.	4, 6	Fed., Rem., Win.	14.60	1175
2¾	1⅛	H.V., Mag.	4, 6, 7½	Fed., Rem.	13.30	1175
2¾	1	H.V., Premium(1)	4, 6	Fed., Rem.	11.80	1220
2¾	1	H.V., Promo.	4, 5, 6, 7½, 8, 9	Fed., Rem., Win.	11.00	1220
2½	1	Std. Vel., Premium	7½, 8	Fed., Rem.	10.45	1165
2½	1	Std. Vel.	4, 5, 6, 7½, 8, 9	Fed., Rem., Win.	9.65	1165
2¼	⅞	Std. Vel., Promo.	6, 7½, 8	Fed., Rem.	N.A.	1155
Max.	¾	Slug, rifled	Slug	Fed., Rem., Win.	3.75	1600
Max.	20 pellets	Buck	3 (Buck)	Fed., Rem., Win.	3.55	1200
2½	⅞	Skeet	8, 9	Fed., Rem., Win.	5.86	1200
2¾	¾	Steel	4, 6	Fed., Win.	14.05	N.A.
28 Gauge 2¾" Hunting & Target						
2¼	¾	H.V.	6, 7½	Rem., Win.	11.05	1295
2	¾	Skeet	9	Fed., Rem., Win.	6.93	1200
410 Bore Hunting & Target						
Max.	11/16	3" H.V.	4, 5, 6, 7½, 8	Rem., Win.	10.30	1135
Max.	½	2½" H.V.	4, 6, 7½	Fed., Rem., Win.	8.75	1135
Max.	½	2½" Target	9	Fed., Rem., Win.	5.73	1200
Max.	⅕	Slug, rifled	Slug	Fed., Rem., Win.	3.55	1830

(1) Premium Shells usually incorporate high antimony extra-hard shot and a granulated polyethylene buffer to increase pattern density at long ranges. In general, prices are per 25-round box. Rifled slugs and buckshot prices are per 5-round pack. Premium buckshot prices per 10-round pack. Not every brand is available in every shot size. Price of Skeet and trap loads may vary widely.

CAUTION: PRICES CHANGE. CHECK AT GUNSHOP.

BULLET CASTING FLUX

Marvelux® is far and away the most popular—and successful—bullet casting flux on the market.

Marvelux® is non-corrosive to iron and steel and does not produce corrosive fumes as does salammoniac. Reduces dross formation dramatically while increasing fluidity of bullet alloys, making it easier to obtain well filled-out bullets.

Marvelux® is well suited to any lead-alloy melt intended for casting bullets or swaging cores. Nonsmoking, flameless and odorless. Superior to beeswax, tallow, paraffin and other fluxes.

Available in ½-lb. can, $3.56; 1-lb. can $5.85; and 4-lb. can $14.90. From your Dealer or Brownells, Inc., who recently acquired the Marvelux® Company.

BROWNELLS, INC.

POWER TRIMMER

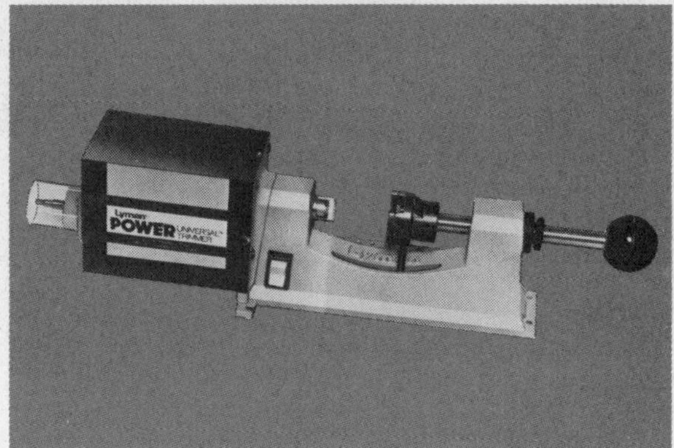

Lyman's new Power Trimmer, with Universal Chuckhead, permits you to trim hundreds of cartridge cases with speed and unprecedented ease.

Lyman's proven and patented Universal Chuckhead eliminates the need to purchase additional caliberized collets while the changeable cutterhead (two furnished) accepts all standard Lyman pilots. A powerful air-cooled electric motor delivers low rpm and high torque for optimum brass-cutting.

The Power Trimmer is available in either 110 or 220 volt versions. Two cutterheads and a set of large and small wire end brushes (for primer pocket cleaning) are included, as are safety covers for the two operating ends.

Suggested retail price: $159.95 (110 volt).

LYMAN PRODUCTS CORP.

DAMASCUS KNIFE BLANKS

Charlton, Ltd., America's largest supplier of Damascus cutlery steel, offers finished forged-to-shape Damascus knife blanks as shown above. Just assemble the handle material of your choice.

These Damascus blades come to you fully finished. Charlton's Damascus blades are 100% hand forged from 512 Layered Steel. By hand-forging the Damascus blade to proper shape, the resulting product presents more and finer layers of steel at the cutting edge.

From top to bottom: The Hunter/Camper, Medium Bowie, and the Tanto. Suggested retail prices, respectively, are $135, $189 and $199. 100% fully-finished knives are also available. (Send $2 for a 24-page illustrated brochure.)

CHARLTON, LTD.

30-ROUND 10-22 MAGAZINE

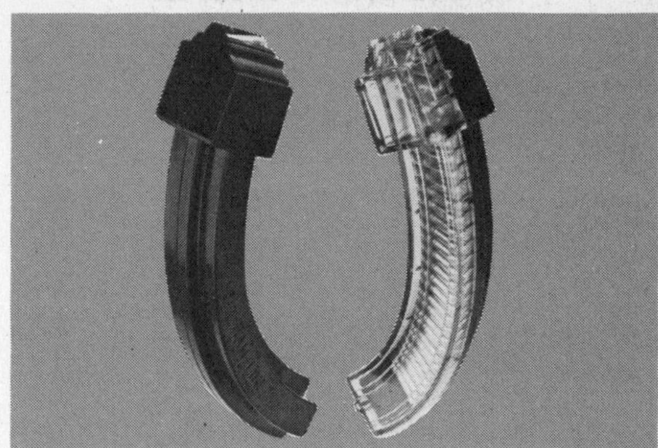

Ram-Line now offers a 30-round magazine for Ruger's 10-22 semiauto, rimfire rifle. This large-capacity magazine is well suited for both small game hunting and plinking. Testing (over 30,000 rounds) has verified anti-jam functioning even at 20° below zero. A full factory replacement warranty comes with each magazine.

Made from specially engineered resin, these magazines are durable and wear resistant. No modification to the gun is required. The basic magazine is black; however, a clear version, which allows the cartridge level to be seen, is also available from Ram-Line, Inc.

Manufacturer's suggested retail price: Black magazine, $16.75; Clear magazine, $17.95.

RAM-LINE, INC.

See manufacturers' addresses following this section.

GUN SAFE

Treadlok's Deluxe Super Safes are available with a choice of interior fitting. For example, the Deluxe Super Safe 26 has wood gun racks that will hold up to 26 guns. The full 63″ height, unique to Tread chests, means that it's now possible to store even Kentucky-Pennsylvania long rifles. If storing guns plus other valuables is on your mind, you may prefer the Super Deluxe Safe 13 (shown) which is fitted with additional shelving and a rack that holds up to 13 guns. Only high quality locking systems can assure you of security—Deluxe Super Safes from Tread put 10 live bolts to work for your peace of mind.

Super Safes are available with combination locks or electronic locking systems. Retail price: Super Safe 26, $1398; Super Safe 13 $1492.

TREAD CORPORATION

BORE CLEANER

J-B Non-Embedding Bore Cleaner was developed for the removal of lead, metal and powder fouling from rifle, pistol and shotgun bores. It is especially suited to small caliber, high pressure, high velocity calibers (such as those used in bench rest competition) which have a tendency to foul quickly.

J-B Non-Embedding Bore Cleaner will quickly and safely remove fouling without injuring the finest bore and restore a barrel to its full potential.

J-B Non-Embedding Bore Cleaner is a proven product having been used for more than 30 years by many top competitive shooters, as well as military organizations worldwide.

Manufacturer's suggested retail price: $3.75 per 2 oz. jar.

J-B BORE CLEANER

NEW HYDRAULIC SWAGING PRESS

MsS Industries' "HYDRO-MAX" is uniquely designed to make swaging and case forming effortless; it also doubles as a manual 3-station reloading press.

A modified 4-ton industrial hydraulic jack is set-screwed to the shell holder bar and the jack's ram is manually drawn up toward the die along with the nose punch and core. A few pumps on the jack's handle does the rest.

The press is designed to use only "HYDRO-MAX" swaging dies and accepts standard T-slot shell holders and ⅞-14 reloading dies.

Expected availability is fall 1985. The suggested retail prices that follow are approximate: Press (less dies) $329.95; Swaging Dies $69.95. For more detailed information, contact MsS directly.

MsS INDUSTRIES, INC.

77mm SPOTTING SCOPES

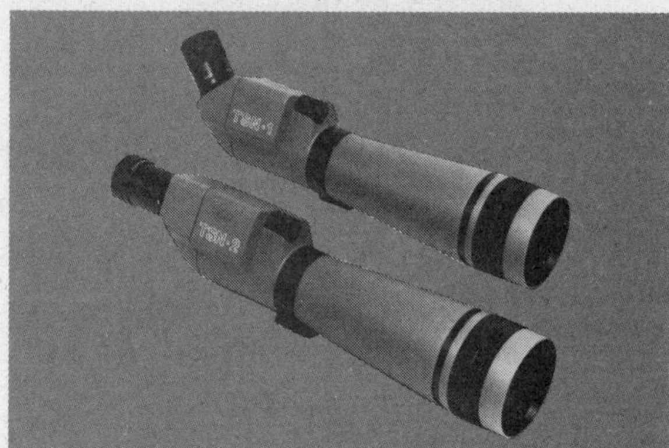

The new Kowa TSN Scopes introduce the world's first high optical quality 77mm objective lens. The expansion from previous Kowa scopes of 60mm to 77mm results in 60% increased light-gathering.

Two Kowa High-Performance eye-piece models are available, TSN-1 (45° offset type) and TSN-2 (straight eye-piece type); both feature a built-in sun shade, bayonet mounted interchangeable eyepieces for water resistance, knob focusing, and a secure tripod mount with rotating ring on TSN-1 model. Options: 800mm f/10 photo attachment and a case.

Suggested retail price: TSN-1 without eyepiece $424.95; TSN-2 without eyepiece $374.95. 20x-60x zoom eyepiece $124.95; 40x eyepiece $74.95; 25x eyepiece $74.95; 20x wide angle $99.95.

KOWA OPTIMED

See manufacturers' addresses following this section.

TUMBLERS

Lyman's family of patented Turbo Tumblers clean and polish cartridge cases quickly and quietly. Their unique design allows the media to swirl around totally immersed cases in a high-speed, agitated motion that cleans and polishes all surfaces simultaneously. This unique Lyman turbo design also permits inspection of the cartridge cases without stopping the polishing operation.

Three different models are offered in both 110 and 220 volt versions: The Turbo 3200 handles up to 1,000 38 Special cases; the Turbo 1200 polishes up to 350 38 Specials and the Turbo 600 handles up to 175 38 Special cases. All clean in 2 hours!

Manufacturer's suggested retail price: from $104.95 to $199.95 (110 volt).

LYMAN PRODUCTS CORP.

DRILL & TAP KIT

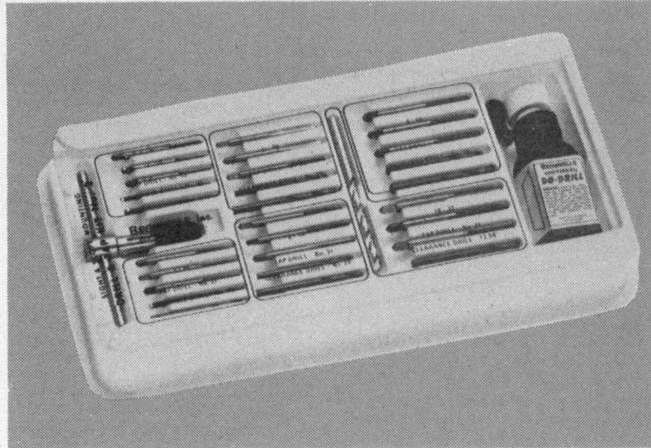

The most frequently used drills and taps in *any* gunshop—large or small—are the ones used by gunsmiths and serious hobbyists to mount sights and scopes. Brownells No. 2 Drill & Tap Kit includes tap-hole and clearance drills, plus the tapper, plug and bottom taps needed for these jobs. Included is a professional-type T-handled tap wrench, a reference chart giving tap-hole drill and clearance drill size for each tap, and a 2-oz. bottle of Do-Drill.

Taps that are included in the Brownells No. 2 Drill & Tap Kit are carbon steel (so when you break one in the hole, you can shatter the stub with a punch and remove the pieces). Drills are made of standard, replaceable, high-speed steel. Suggested retail price: $36.16.

BROWNELLS, INC.

FIREARM REST

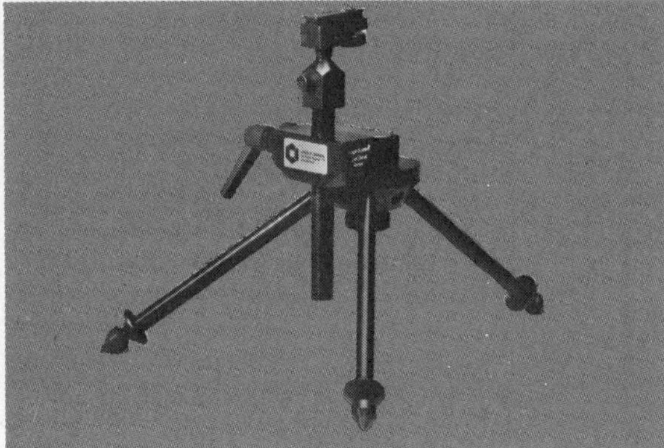

Take your aim—steady, relaxed, accurate and fast. And be sure of a hit with the universally adaptable, combined LOGA, PRECISION 3-2, TRI-BI-POD.

The Loga Rest has been tested by shooting experts who have proven it to be the optimum rest for your favorite scope-sighted sporting rifles. It's also well suited for law enforcement use.

The Loga Rest enables the accurate, continuous maintenance of an optical line of sight. The rest also provides for continuous height adjustment travel up to 4.33". It's small in size, lightweight, and capable of being transported in your favorite gun case. Various models. Trade Mark and U.S. Patents.

Contact manufacturer for availablility and price.

GARBINI LOGA SYSTEM® SWITZERLAND

SHOOTING ACCESSORIES

Parker-Hale's famous quality shooting accessories are once again available in the U.S., imported from England by Precision Sports, a Division of Cortland Line Company.

British-made throughout, the following Parker-Hale accessories provide the knowledgeable shooter with a standard of excellence equal to his choice of fine guns.

- Presentation Cleaning Sets
- Snap Caps
- Rosewood Shotgun Rods
- Steel Rifle Rods
- Phosphor Bronze Brushes
- Jags, Loops, and Mops
- Youngs "303" Cleaner
- Express Oil
- Rangoon Oil
- 009 Nitro Solvent
- Black Powder Solvent
- Comet Super Blue

PARKER-HALE/PRECISION SPORTS

See manufacturers' addresses following this section.

REPLACEMENT MAGAZINES

D&E Magazines, Mfg. is internationally acclaimed for their steel fabricated pistol and rifle clips, featuring standard and extended sizes for new and "hard to find" models.

Throughout the years, D&E has manufactured hundreds of different magazines for both modern and obsolete firearms.

Their magazines are even recommended by law enforcement agencies due to the durable *steel construction*. They last and last!

For answers to your needs, please send a self-addressed stamped envelope. For the pro or serious amateur, D&E has an up-dated production price list of all of their products for which there is a $3 charge. Anyone can order direct.

D&E MAGAZINES, MFG.

CHECKERING TOOLS

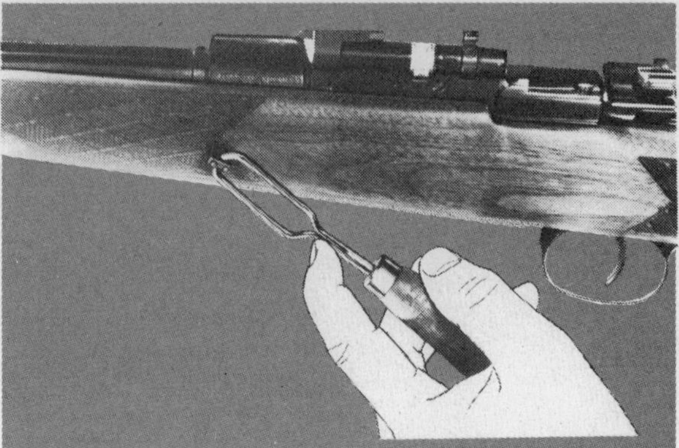

FULL-VIEW checkering tools have been on the market since 1949. The tool features a split shank (which allows the gunsmith to fully view his work at all times), and an adjustable head which lets him checker at any desired angle.

FULL-VIEW cutters are made of the highest quality tool steel and come in all popular sizes. The teeth are self-cleaning and cut equally well backwards or forwards.

FULL-VIEW checkering tools include holders; spacing, single line, superfine, skip-line, border cutters, and short corner tools. A special checkering kit sells for a suggested retail price of $17.50 (plus $1.50 shipping).

Send for free folder and complete price list.

W.E. BROWNELL CHECKERING TOOLS

ELECTRONIC SIGHT

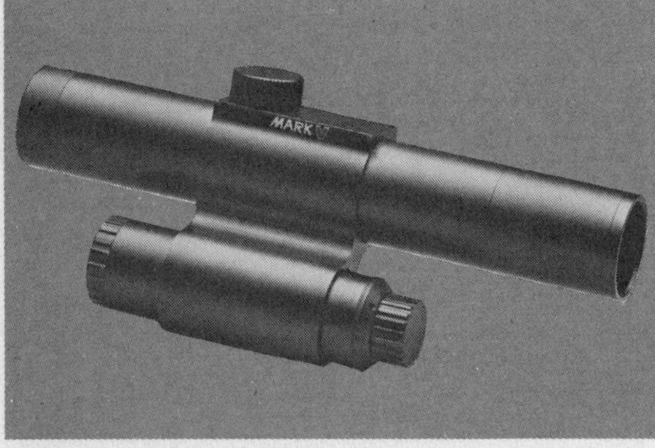

Action Arms Ltd., importers of UZI Firearms and SAMSON Ammunition, recently introduced the fully adjustable Mark V Electronic Sight. The Mark V offers the shooter an advantage over conventional iron sights because it uses an illuminated red dot as its focal point and is parallax-free.

The Mark V is small (5⅛″) and light (5½ oz.) and performs perfectly, especially in low-light conditions. The Mark V also has a light-intensity feature that is fully adjustable.

Best of all, the Mark V features a 1″ diameter tube, making it ideal for most standard 1″ mounts. It comes packaged with batteries and an extension for mounting on rifles and shotguns.

Manufacturer's suggested retail price: $183.50.

ACTION ARMS LTD.

WALKING STICK

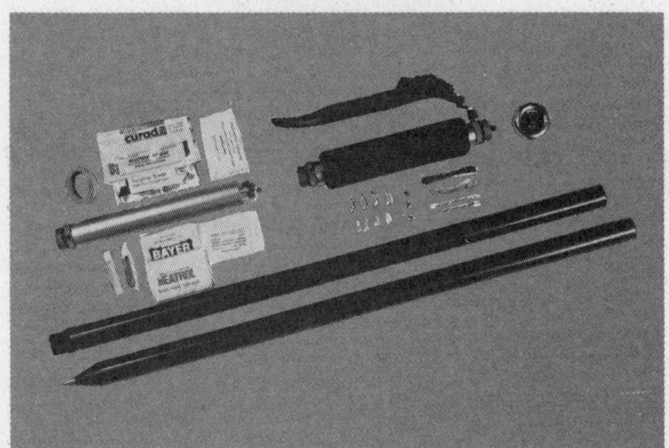

Trailbreaker — the complete walking system! Perfect for any outdoorsman, the Trailbreaker separates into four precision-machined aircraft aluminum sections. The Trailbreaker weighs 19 oz. and is 56 in. long. It features hollow compartments that are O-ring sealed to provide watertight storage for survival gear, food and liquids. Also, a precision compass is built into the top piece for route finding. The fully adjustable wrist loop also allows the staff to be used as either a pistol or rifle brace.

The Trailbreaker comes complete with awl/section wrench, rubber tip, water purification tablets, surgical blade, needle, thread, fish hooks, line, sinkers, matches, snare wire, and more! Suggested retail price: $49.95.

LIFELINE INDUSTRIES

See manufacturers' addresses following this section.

STOCK BEDDING COMPOUND

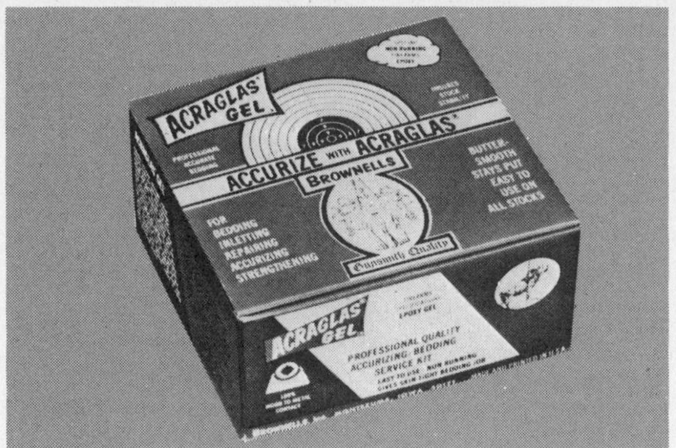

Introduced by Brownells as an update of their well known Acraglas® Stock Bedding Compound, Acraglas Gel® Stock Bedding Compound has a smooth consistency that will not drip, run or leach out from between wood and metal after being put into the gunstock. Acraglas Gel® is formulated with nylon derivatives for greater "thin strength," shock resistance and stability over normal temperature extremes. Shrinkage is less than 1/10th of 1%. Readily blends with atomized metals. Easy to use, 1-to-1 mix.

Acraglas Gel® 2-Gun 4-oz. Kit sells for $8.25. Larger 16-oz. Shop Kit is $24.10. Kits contain two-part epoxy, stock-matching dye, mixing sticks and dish, release agent and detailed instructions.

BROWNELLS, INC.

RELOADING KIT

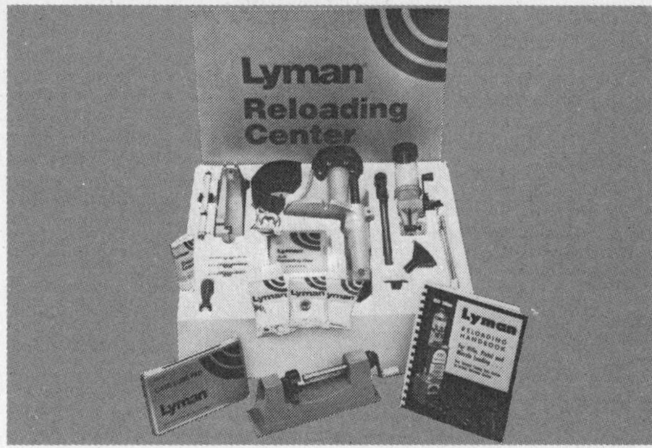

Lyman's Expert Kit, a complete set of all needed reloading implements, eliminates the uncertainty and confusion sometimes experienced by novice reloaders trying to assemble the necessary tools from a variety of manufacturers.

The Expert Kit is ideal for both beginner and the advanced reloader. There is nothing else to buy except components.

The Expert Kit includes a proven turret press made of precision-machined steel and iron. It doesn't require re-learning at every session and easily produces several hundred reloads per hour.

Become an "Expert" with one buy—look at the Lyman Expert Kit before buying any equipment.

Manufacturer's suggested retail price: $299.95.

LYMAN PRODUCTS CORP.

CONVERSION KIT

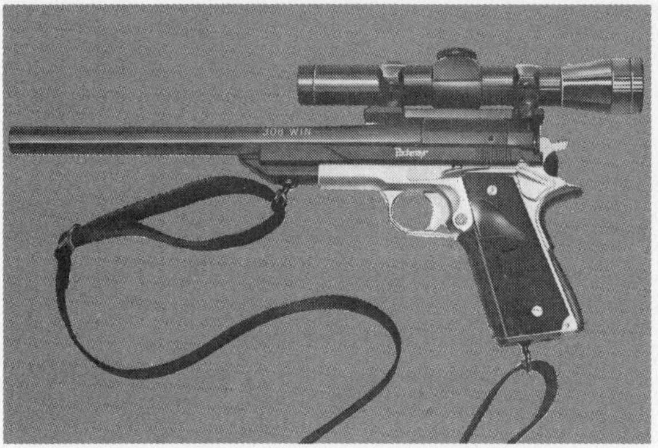

The Pachmayr Dominator Conversion Kit is available in four powerful chamberings, 223 Remington, 7mm-08 Remington, 308 Winchester and 44 Mag.

Virtually any 1911 Colt-type autoloading pistol can be quickly and easily converted to accept this unique, bolt-action type mechanism. No special gunsmithing is required.

Available in two configurations, the micro-adjustable "iron" sight version sells for a suggested retail of $320, while "scope" models (which are predrilled and tapped for a scope mount) sell for a suggested retail of $295.50. No FFL is required to order factory-direct from Pachmayr. A special 56-page Dominator reloading manual is also available from Pachmayr at $5.95.

PACHMAYR GUN WORKS

COMPACT SPOTTING SCOPES

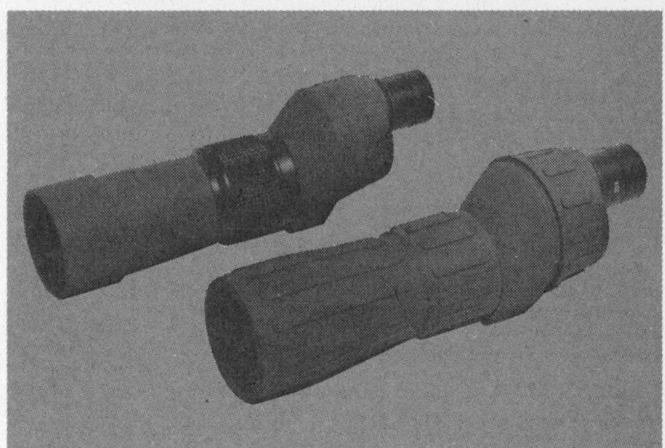

The new Kowa TS-9 Compact Spotting Scope features outstanding performance, at an affordable price. A 50mm objective lens allows exceptional brightness, clarity and sharpness.

Two special lightweight models are available, one in standard gray-crackel finish (TS-9C), the other in green armored (TS-9R), for field protection.

A 20x eyepiece is standard with a 15x and 11-33x Zoom as options. TS-9 Scopes can also use interchangeable eyepieces from Kowa's High Quality Traditional Line. Eyepieces available are 9x, 12x Wide Angle, 15x, 24x, 36x and 15x-30x Zoom.

Manufacturer's suggested retail price: TS-9C $115.95, TS-9R (Rubber Armored) $134.95. Optional 15x Eyepiece $24.95.

KOWA OPTIMED

See manufacturers' addresses following this section.

SHOOTER'S MARKETPLACE

SCREWDRIVER SET

Throw away that ill-fitting screwdriver. The Magna-Tip® Super-Set gives you 39 custom, true hollow-ground, graduated screwdriver bits that fit 99.9% of all gun screw slots.

This unique system has nine different blade *widths* ranging from .120″ to .360″, each with three to six blade *thicknesses* from .020″ through .050″ in .005″ increments spread from narrowest/thinnest through widest/thickest.

The *Master Super-Set* includes 39 Custom Gunsmith bits *and* 10 Allen *and* three Phillips bits *plus* two Handles, Tray and Case. Suggested retail price: $63.75. A *Basic Set* of 39 Custom Gunsmith Bits, one Handle, Tray and Case sells for a suggested retail price of $51.62.

BROWNELLS, INC.

ELECTRIC CASTING FURNACE

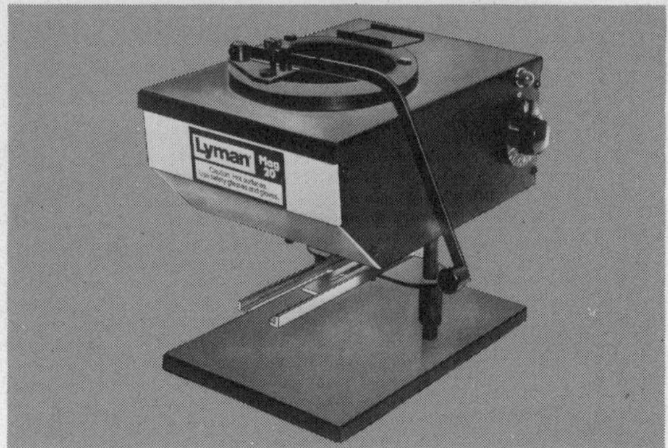

Lyman's new Mag 20 Electric Casting Furnace is the best 20-pound furnace buy on the market today.

It features a steel crucible of 20-pound capacity, incorporates the proven Lyman bottom-pour valve system and comes complete with the best, and only, fully adjustable mould guide on the market.

The Mag 20 features a powerful 800-watt heating system which minimizes "spout freeze," melts cold metal in 20 minutes and brings replenished metal up to temperature (825°F max.) quickly.

The durability and sustained accuracy of the Mag 20's thermostat is enhanced by silver contacts and heavy-duty terminals. Made of heavy-duty material for extra-long life, the Mag 20 comes in 110 or 220 volt versions. Suggested retail price: $159.95.

LYMAN PRODUCTS CORP.

MANUFACTURERS ADDRESSES

ACTION ARMS LTD.
P.O. Box 9573
Philadelphia, PA 19124

W.E. BROWNELL CHECKERING TOOLS
3356 Moraga Pl.
San Diego, CA 92117

BROWNELLS, INC.
222 West Liberty
Montezuma, IA 50171

CHARLTON, LTD.
P.O. Box 448
Edenton, NC 27932

D&E MAGAZINES MFG.
P.O. Box 4876
Sylmar, CA 91342

GARBINI LOGA SYSTEM® SWITZERLAND
St. Galler Strasse 72
CH-9325 Roggwil TG
SWITZERLAND

J-B BORE CLEANER
299 Poplar St.
Hamburg, PA 19526

KOWA OPTIMED, INC.
20001 S. Vermont Avenue
Torrance, CA 90502

LIFELINE INDUSTRIES
P.O. Box 771
Santa Monica, CA 90406

LYMAN PRODUCTS CORP.
Dept. GD-40
Rt. 147
Middlefield, CT 06455

MsS INDUSTRIES, INC.
P.O. Box 6
River Grove, IL 60171

PACHMAYR GUN WORKS
1220 South Grand Ave.
Los Angeles, CA 90015

PARKER-HALE/PRECISION SPORTS
Dept. GD-40
P.O. Box 708-5588
Cortland, NY 13045-5588

RAM-LINE, INC.
406 Violet St.
Golden, CO 80401

TREAD CORPORATION
P.O. Box 13207
Roanoke, VA 24032

THE COMPLETE COMPACT CATALOG

GUNDEX®

A listing of all the guns in the catalog, by name and model, alphabetically and numerically.

This feature of our catalog speeds up the chore of finding the basic facts on a given firearm for the experienced. And it may make the contents of the catalog far more available to the inexperienced.

That is our intention.

To use it, you need the manufacturer's name and model designation. That designation might be a number, as in Winchester Model 94, or it might be a name, as in Colt Python. And you need to know the alphabet.

The manufacturers are listed alphabetically and the entry under each manufacturer is arranged in the quickest way—numbers are in numerical order, names are alphabetical.

It's all very straightforward. It is all pretty voluminous, as well. There are over 1400 entries and at about 230 lines per page, what with headings and all, the GUNDEX® is nine pages long.

We have tried to make it easy to find, too—just look for the black GUNDEX® label along the edge of the page, flip to there, and get your page number in short order.

A

B

C

D

E

F

G

H

I

J

K

L

M

N

O

P

R

S

T

U

V

W

Y

Z

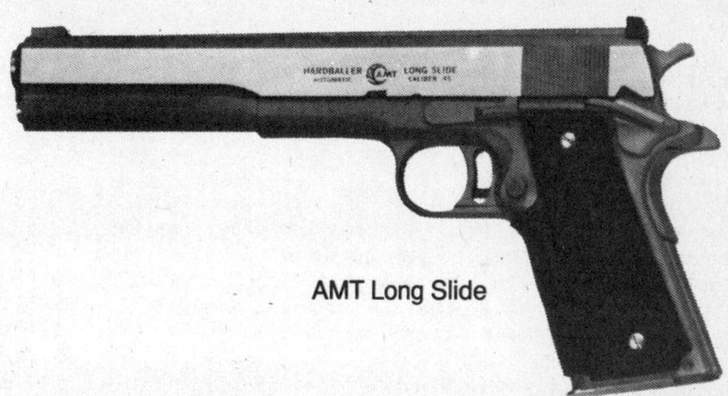

AMT Long Slide

AMT 45 ACP HARDBALLER LONG SLIDE

Caliber: 45 ACP.
Barrel: 7″.
Length: 10½″ over-all.
Stocks: Wrap-around rubber.
Sights: Fully adjustable rear sight.
Features: Slide and barrel are 2″ longer than the standard 45, giving less recoil, added velocity, longer sight radius. Has extended combat safety, serrated matte rib, loaded chamber indicator, wide adjustable trigger. From AMT.
Price: **$500.00**

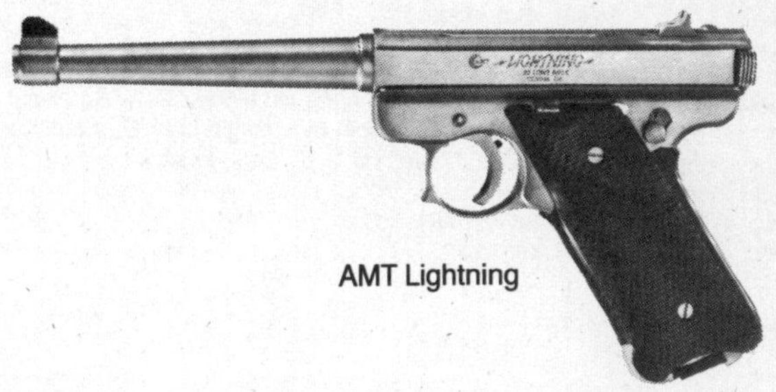

AMT Lightning

AMT LIGHTNING AUTO PISTOL

Caliber: 22 LR, 10-shot magazine.
Barrel: Tapered — 6½″, 8½″, 10½″, 12½″; Bull — 5″, 6½″, 8½″, 10½″, 12½″.
Weight: 45 oz. (6½″ barrel). **Length:** 10¾″ over-all (6½″ barrel).
Stocks: Checkered wrap-around rubber.
Sights: Blade front, fixed rear; adjustable rear available at extra cost.
Features: Made of stainless steel. Uses Clark trigger with adjustable stops; receiver grooved for scope mounting; trigger guard spur for two-hand hold; interchangeable barrels. Introduced 1984. From AMT.
Price: 5″ bull, 6½″ tapered or bull, fixed sight **$230.00**
Price: 8½″, tapered or bull, fixed sight **$240.00**
Price: 12½″, tapered or bull, fixed sight **$250.00**
Price: For adjustable rear sight add **$21.00**

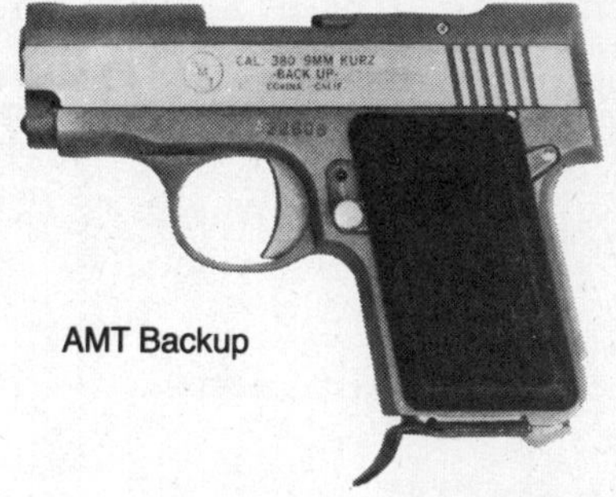

AMT Backup

AMT "BACKUP" AUTO PISTOL

Caliber: 22 LR, 8-shot magazine; 380 ACP, 5-shot magazine
Barrel: 2½″
Weight: 18 oz. **Length:** 4.25″ over-all.
Stocks: Checkered Lexon.
Sights: Fixed, open, recessed.
Features: Concealed hammer, blowback operation; manual and grip safeties. All stainless steel construction. Smallest domestically-produced pistol in 380. From AMT.
Price: 22 LR or 380 ACP **$230.00**

AMT 45 ACP HARDBALLER

Caliber: 45 ACP.
Barrel: 5″
Weight: 39 oz. **Length:** 8½″ over-all.
Stocks: Wrap-around rubber.
Sights: Adjustable.
Features: Extended combat safety, serrated matte slide rib, loaded chamber indicator, long grip safety, beveled magazine well, adjustable target trigger. All stainless steel. From AMT.
Price: **$450.00**
Price: Government model (as above except no rib, fixed sights) **$395.00**

American Arms Eagle

AMERICAN ARMS EAGLE 380

Caliber: 380 ACP, 6-shot magazine.
Barrel: 2½″.
Weight: 20 oz. **Length:** 6¼″ over-all.
Stocks: Checkered walnut.
Sights: Fixed.
Features: Double action, stainless steel construction, firing pin lock safety. Comes with fitted carrying case, belt buckle and one magazine. Introduced 1984. From Wilkerson Firearms Corp.
Price: **$298.00**
Price: As above, except with black rubber grips **$289.00**
Price: With black rubber grips, black Teflon finish **$335.00**

American Derringer 25 Auto

AMERICAN DERRINGER 25 AUTO

Caliber: 25 ACP or 250 Magnum; 7-shot magazine.
Barrel: 2.1".
Weight: 15½ oz. **Length:** 4.4" over-all.
Stocks: Smooth rosewood.
Sights: Fixed.
Features: Stainless or ordnance steel. Magazines have finger extension. Introduced 1980. From American Derringer Corp.
Price: Stainless, 25 ACP **$212.00**
Price: Blue, matte finish, 25 ACP **$200.00**
Price: 250 Mag., stainless **$212.00**
Price: 250 Mag., blued **$200.00**

Arminex Trifire

ARMINEX TRIFIRE AUTO PISTOL

Caliber: 9mm. Para. (9-shot), 38 Super. (9-shot), 45 ACP (7-shot).
Barrel: 5", 6", 7".
Weight: 38 oz. **Length:** 8" over-all.
Stocks: Contoured smooth walnut.
Sights: Interchangeable post front, rear adjustable for windage and elevation.
Features: Single action. Slide mounted firing pin block safety. Specially contoured one-piece backstrap. Convertible by changing barrel, magazine, recoil spring. Introduced 1982. Made in U.S. by Arminex Ltd.
Price: Blue.......... **$396.00**
Price: With wood presentation case **$444.00**
Price: Target model, 6" barrel **$448.00**

Astra A-80 Pistol

ASTRA A-80 DOUBLE-ACTION AUTO PISTOL

Caliber: 9mm Para., 38 Super (15-shot), 45 ACP (9-shot).
Barrel: 3.75".
Weight: 40 oz. **Length:** 7" over-all.
Stocks: Checkered black plastic.
Sights: Square blade front, square notch rear drift-adjustable for windage.
Features: Double or single action; loaded chamber indicator; combat-style trigger guard; optional right-side slide release (for left-handed shooters); automatic internal safety; decocking lever. Introduced 1982. Imported from Spain by Interarms.
Price: Blue.......... **$390.00**
Price: Chrome **$425.00**

ASTRA CONSTABLE AUTO PISTOL

Caliber: 22 LR, 10-shot, 380 ACP, 7-shot.
Barrel: 3½"
Weight: 26 oz.
Stocks: Moulded plastic
Sights: Adj. rear.
Features: Double action, quick no-tool takedown, non-glare rib on slide. 380 available in blue or chrome finish. Engraved guns also available—contact the importer. Imported from Spain by Interarms.
Price: Blue, 22 .... **$275.00**
Price: Chrome, 22 .... **$295.00**
Price: Blue, 380 .... **$255.00**
Price: Chrome, 380 .... **$275.00**

Auto-Nine Pocket Partner

AUTO-NINE POCKET PARTNER PISTOL

Caliber: 22 LR, 8-shot magazine.
Barrel: 2¼", 6-groove rifling.
Weight: 10 oz. **Length:** 4¾" over-all.
Stocks: Checkered plastic.
Sights: Fixed.
Features: New design internal hammer. All ordnance steel construction with brushed blue finish. Made in U.S. by Auto-Nine Corp. Available from FTL Marketing.
Price: About **$199.95**

AUTO-ORDNANCE 1911A1 AUTOMATIC PISTOL

Caliber: 9mm Para., 38 Super, 9-shot, 45 ACP, 7-shot magazine.
Barrel: 5".
Weight: 39 oz. **Length:** 8½" over-all.
Stocks: Checkered plastic with medallion.
Sights: Blade front, rear adj. for windage.
Features: Same specs as 1911A1 military guns—parts interchangeable. Frame and slide blued; each radius has non-glare finish. Made in U.S. by Auto-Ordnance Corp.
Price: Approximately **$324.95**

Auto-Ordnance 1911A1

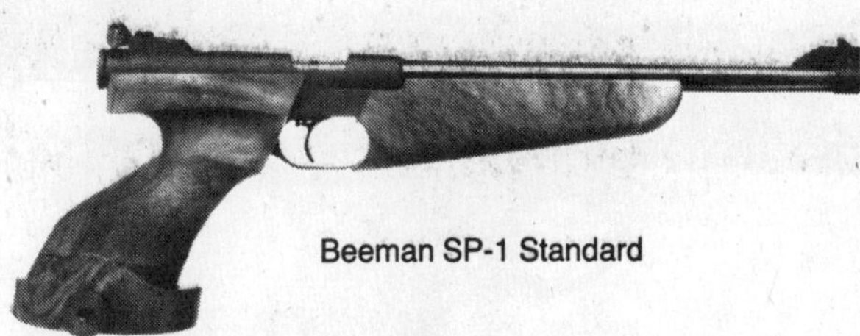
Beeman SP-1 Standard

BEEMAN SP DELUXE PISTOL

Caliber: 22 LR, single shot.
Barrel: 8", 10", 11.2", 15".
Weight: 50 oz. **Length:** 18" over-all.
Stocks: European walnut, anatomically-shaped with adjustable palm rest.
Sights: Blade front, notch rear adjustable for windage and elevation.
Features: Two-stage trigger; loaded chamber indicator; grooved for scope mount. Detachable fore-end and barrel weight. Standard version available without fore-end and barrel weight. Imported by Beeman. Introduced 1984.
Price: Standard, right or left-hand **$249.50**
Price: Deluxe (with fore-end), illus. **$299.50**

BERETTA MODEL 950 BS AUTO PISTOL

Caliber: 22 Short, 25 ACP
Barrel: 2½", 4" (22 Short only).
Weight: 8 oz. (22 Short, 10 oz.). **Length:** 4½" over-all.
Stocks: Checkered black plastic.
Sights: Fixed.
Features: Thumb safety and half-cock safety; barrel hinged at front to pop up for single loading or cleaning. From Beretta U.S.A.
Price: Blue, 25 .... **$190.00**
Price: Blue, 22, 4" **$200.00**
Price: Blue, 25 ACP **$190.00**
Price: Nickel, 22 or 25 .... **$208.00**
Price: EL model (gold etching) **$220.00**

Beretta Model 950 BS

Beretta Models 20, 21 Pistols

Similar to the Model 950 BS except M20 is 25 ACP with 4.9" over-all length, double-action, plastic or walnut stocks, weight is 10.9 ozs. M21 is 22 LR, 2.5" barrel, 4.9" over-all length, double-action, 7-round magazine, walnut grips. Introduced 1985.
Price: Model 20 .... **$214.00**
Price: Model 21 .... **$220.00**

BERETTA MODEL 84/85 DA PISTOLS

Caliber: 380 ACP (13-shot magazine).
Barrel: 3¾"
Weight: About 23 oz. **Length:** 6½" over-all.
Stocks: Smooth black plastic (wood optional at extra cost).
Sights: Fixed front and rear.
Features: Double action, quick take-down, convenient magazine release. Introduced 1977. Imported from Italy by Beretta USA.
Price: M-84 (380 ACP) **$475.00**
Price: With wood grips **$495.00**
Price: M-84, nickel, wood grips **$535.00**
Price: M-85W, 380 ACP, wood grips, 9-shot mag **$475.00**
Price: M-85, nickel, wood grips **$520.00**

Beretta Model 20

BERETTA MODEL 92 SB, 92 SB COMPACT

Caliber: 9mm Parabellum (15-shot magazine, 14-shot on Compact).
Barrel: 4.92"
Weight: 33½ oz. **Length:** 8.54" over-all.
Stocks: Smooth black plastic; wood optional at extra cost.
Sights: Blade front, rear adj. for w.
Features: Double-action. Extractor acts as chamber loaded indicator, inertia firing pin. Finished in blue-black. Introduced 1977. Imported from Italy by Beretta USA.
Price: With plastic grips **$600.00**
Price: With wood grips **$620.00**
Price: Compact, plastic grips **$620.00**
Price: Compact, wood grips **$635.00**
Price: Compact, nickel, wood grips **$680.00**

Beretta Model 92 SB Compact

Beretta Model 92SB-F Pistol

Similar to the Model 92 SB except has squared-off trigger guard, matte blue finish, different grips to allow easier access to the safety. Adopted by U.S. armed forces in 1985.

Price: With plastic grips **$600.00**
Price: With wood grips **$620.00**

BERETTA MODEL 70S PISTOL

Caliber: 22 LR, 380 ACP.
Barrel: 3.5".
Weight: 23 oz. (Steel) **Length:** 6.5" over-all.
Stocks: Checkered black plastic.
Sights: Fixed front and rear.
Features: Polished blue finish. Safety lever blocks hammer. Slide lever indicates empty magazine. Magazine capacity is 8 rounds for both calibers. Introduced 1977. Imported from Italy by Beretta USA.
Price: **$295.00**

BERNARDELLI MODEL 80 AUTO PISTOL

Caliber: 22 LR (10-shot); 380 ACP (7-shot).
Barrel: 3½".
Weight: 26½ oz. **Length:** 6½" over-all.
Stocks: Checkered plastic with thumbrest.
Sights: Ramp front, white outline rear adj. for w. & e
Features: Hammer block slide safety; loaded chamber indicator; dual recoil buffer springs; serrated trigger; inertia type firing pin. Imported from Italy by Interarms.
Price: Model 80, 22 or 380 .... **$215.00**
Price: Model 90 (22 or 32, 6" bbl.) **$245.00**

BERSA MODEL 225 AUTO PISTOL

Caliber: 22 LR, 11-shot.
Barrel: 5".
Weight: 26 oz.
Stocks: Target-type checkered nylon with thumbrest.
Sights: Blade front, square notch rear adjustable for windage.
Features: Blow-back action; combat-type trigger guard; magazine safety; blue finish. Imported from Argentina by Outdoor Sports Headquarters. Introduced 1984.
Price: Model 225 .... **$169.95**
Price: Model 226 (6" barrel) **$169.95**

BERSA MODEL 383 AUTO PISTOL

Caliber: 380 ACP, 9-shot.
Barrel: 3½".
Weight: 25 oz.
Stocks: Target-type checkered black nylon.
Sights: Blade front, square notch rear adjustable for windage.
Features: Blow-back action; magazine safety; combat-type trigger guard; blue finish. Imported from Argentina by Outdoor Sports Headquarters. Introduced 1984.
Price: Model 383 .... **$205.00**
Price: Model 223 (as above except 22 LR) **$165.00**

Beretta Model 92SB-F

Beretta Model 70S Pistol

Bernardelli Model 80

Bersa 225

Bren Ten Standard

BREN TEN STANDARD MODEL

Caliber: 10mm Auto, 11-shot capacity.
Barrel: 5".
Weight: 39 oz. **Length:** 8.37" over-all.
Stocks: Textured black nylon (Hogue Combat).
Sights: Adjustable; replaceable, 3-dot combat-type.
Features: Full-size combat pistol, with selective double or single action. Has reversible thumb safety and firing pin block. Blued slide, natural stainless frame. Introduced 1983. From Dornaus & Dixon Enterprises, Inc.
Price: Standard model **$500.00**
Price: Military & Police (matte black finish) **$550.00**
Price: Dual-Master (same as Standard except comes with extra 45 ACP slide and barrel, better finish, engraving, wood grips, wood case) **$800.00**
Price: Jeff Cooper Commemorative (same as Standard except has extra fine finish, 22K gold-filled engraving, details, cartridges, laser engraved Herrett's grips and wood case) **$2,000.00**
Price: 45 ACP conversion kit (5" bbl.) **$150.00**

CAUTION: PRICES CHANGE. CHECK AT GUNSHOP.

Bren Ten Special Forces

Bren Ten Pocket Model

Similar to the Standard Bren Ten except smaller. Has 4″ barrel giving 7.37″ over-all length, and weighs 28 oz. Fires full load 10mm Auto cartridge with 9 round capacity. Has hard chrome slide, stainless frame.

Price: **$600.00**

Bren Ten Special Forces Model

Similar to the Pocket Model except has standard size grip frame with 11-shot capacity; weight is 33 oz. with 4″ barrel. Available in either all black or natural light finish. Introduced 1984.

Price: Black finish **$600.00**
Price: Light finish **$650.00**

Browning BDA-380 Pistol

BROWNING BDA-380 D/A AUTO PISTOL

Caliber: 380 ACP, 13-shot magazine.
Barrel: $3\frac{13}{16}$″.
Weight: 23 oz. **Length:** $6\frac{3}{4}$″ over-all.
Stocks: Smooth walnut with inset Browning medallion.
Sights: Blade front, rear drift-adj. for w.
Features: Combination safety and de-cocking lever will automatically lower a cocked hammer to half-cock and can be operated by right or left-hand shooters. Inertia firing pin. Introduced 1978. Imported from Italy by Browning.
Price: Blue. **$332.95**
Price: Nickel **$349.95**

Browning Hi-Power Auto

BROWNING HI-POWER 9mm AUTOMATIC PISTOL

Caliber: 9mm Parabellum (Luger), 13-shot magazine.
Barrel: $4\frac{21}{32}$″.
Weight: 32 oz. **Length:** $7\frac{3}{4}$″ over-all.
Stocks: Walnut, hand checkered, or black Polyamide.
Sights: $\frac{1}{8}$″ blade front; rear screw-adj. for w. and e. Also available with fixed rear (drift-adj for w.).
Features: External hammer with half-cock and thumb safeties. A blow on the hammer cannot discharge a cartridge; cannot be fired with magazine removed. Fixed rear sight model available. Imported from Belgium by Browning.
Price: Fixed sight model **$449.95**
Price: 9mm with rear sight adj. for w. and e. **$494.95**
Price: Nickel, fixed sight **$534.95**
Price: Nickel, adj. sight **$584.95**
Price: Standard matte black finish, fixed sight, S/A **$394.95**

Browning Hi-Power Classic & Gold Classic

Same as standard fixed sight Hi-Power except both editions have game scenes of a bald eagle protecting her young from a lynx on satin grey slide and frame, as well as a profile of John M. Browning. The Gold Classic has the main subjects in contrasting gold inlay. Grips are finely checkered walnut with double border and floral designs. Classic series limited to 5,000, Gold Classic to 500, each with its unique serial number, "1 of 500," and so on. Each gun comes in a velvet lined walnut case.

Price: Hi-Power Classic. **$1,000.00**
Price: Hi-Power Gold Classic **$2,000.00**

Browning Double Action

Browning Double Action 9mm

Not a modified Hi-Power, but a new design. Double-action with a firing pin safety block, twin ambidextrous decocking levers that lower the hammer from full cock; squared trigger guard; wrap-around moulded grips; 15-shot capacity; black "Parkerized" finish; rear sight drift adjustable for windage. Introduced 1985.

Price: **$408.95**

Hi-Power 88 Auto Pistol II

Similar to the standard Browning Hi-Power except available only with fixed rear sight, military parkerized finish, black checkered polyamid grips, single-action only. Comes with extra magazine. Introduced 1982. Imported from Belgium by Howco Distributors, Inc.

Price: With extra magazine **$499.50**

Browning Challenger III Sporter

BROWNING CHALLENGER III SPORTER

Caliber: 22 LR, 10-shot magazine.
Barrel: 6¾".
Weight: 29 oz. **Length:** 10⅞" over-all.
Stocks: Smooth impregnated hardwood.
Sights: ⅛" blade front on ramp, rear screw adj. for e., drift adj. for w.
Features: All steel, blue finish. Wedge locking system prevents action from loosening. Wide gold-plated trigger; action hold-open. Standard grade only. Made in U.S. From Browning.
Price: **$239.95**

Browning Challenger III Auto Pistol

Similar to the Challenger III except has a 5½" heavy bull barrel, new lightweight alloy frame and new sights. Over-all length is 9½", weight is 35 oz. Introduced 1982.
Price: **$239.95**

Browning Buck Mark 22 Pistol

Similar to the Challenger III except has black moulded composite grips with skip-line checkering, thumb magazine button, sides of barrel are high-polish blue, rest satin finish. New rear sight screw-adjustable for elevation, drift-adjustable for windage. Introduced 1985.
Price: **$194.95**

Browning Buck Mark

Bushmaster Auto Pistol

BUSHMASTER AUTO PISTOL

Caliber: 223; 30-shot magazine.
Barrel: 11½" (1-10" twist).
Weight: 5¼ lbs. **Length:** 20½" over-all.
Stocks: Synthetic rotating grip swivel assembly.
Sights: Post front, adjustable open "y" rear
Features: Steel alloy upper receiver with welded barrel assembly, AK-47-type gas system, aluminum lower receiver, one-piece welded steel alloy bolt carrier assembly. From Bushmaster Firearms.
Price: **$339.95**
Price: With matte electroless nickel finish **$379.95**

Charter Model 79K

Charter Model 40

CHARTER ARMS MODEL 79K DA AUTO PISTOL

Caliber: 32 ACP, 380 ACP, 7-shot magazine.
Barrel: 3.6".
Weight: 24½ oz. **Length:** 6.5" over-all.
Stocks: Checkered walnut.
Sights: Fixed.
Features: Double action with hammer block, firing pin and magazine safeties. Stainless steel finish. Introduced 1984. Imported from West Germany by Charter Arms.
Price: 32 or 380 ACP **$390.00**

Charter Arms Model 40 DA Auto Pistol

Similar to the Model 79K except chambered for 22 Long Rifle, 3.3" barrel, 6.3" over-all length, and 21½-oz. weight. Stainless steel finish. Introduced 1984. Imported from West Germany by Charter Arms.
Price: **$319.00**

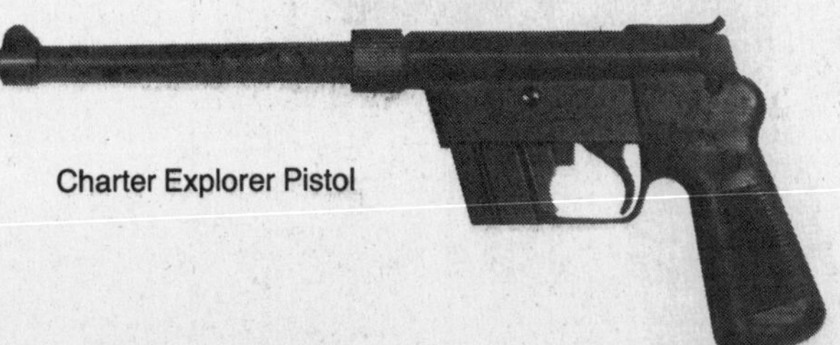
Charter Explorer Pistol

CHARTER EXPLORER II & SII PISTOL

Caliber: 22 LR, 8-shot magazine.
Barrel: 8".
Weight: 28 oz. **Length:** 15½" over-all.
Stocks: Serrated simulated walnut.
Sights: Blade front, open rear adj. for elevation.
Features: Action adapted from the semi-auto Explorer carbine. Introduced 1980. From Charter Arms.
Price: Black or satin finish **$109.00**
Price: Extra 6", 8" or 10" barrel **$27.00**

COLT GOV'T MODEL MK IV/SERIES 80

Caliber: 9mm, 38 Super, 45 ACP, 7-shot.
Barrel: 5".
Weight: 38 oz. **Length:** 8⅜" over-all.
Stocks: Checkered walnut.
Sights: Ramp front, fixed square notch rear.
Features: Grip and thumb safeties, and internal firing pin safety, grooved trigger. Accurizor barrel and bushing. Blue finish or nickel in 45 only.
Price: Blue, 45 cal. **$491.95**
Price: Nickel, 45 cal. **$525.50**
Price: 45, Satin nickel w/blue, Pachmayr grips **$519.95**
Price: 9mm, blue only **$499.95**
Price: 38 Super, blue only **$499.95**
Price: Stainless steel, 45 only, high profile sights **$532.50**

Colt Stainless MK IV/Series 80

Colt Combat Government Model Series 80

Same as the standard Government Model except has a higher undercut front sight, white outline rear, Colt/Pachmayr wrap-around grips, flat mainspring housing, longer trigger, beveled magazine well, and an angled ejection port. Has internal firing pin safety. Introduced 1983.
Price: **$590.95**

COLT 380 GOVERNMENT MODEL

Caliber: 380 ACP, 7-shot magazine.
Barrel: 3.29".
Weight: 21.8 oz. **Length:** 6.15" over-all.
Stocks: Checkered composition.
Sights: Ramp front, square notch rear, fixed.
Features: Scaled down version of the 1911A1 Colt G.M. Has thumb and internal firing pin safeties. Introduced 1983.
Price: Blue **$317.95**
Price: Nickel **$349.95**
Price: Satin nickel **$334.95**

Colt 380 Government

COLT OFFICERS ACP MK IV SERIES 80

Caliber: 45 ACP, 6-shot magazine.
Barrel: 3.63".
Weight: 34 oz. **Length:** 7¼" over-all.
Stocks: Checkered walnut.
Sights: Ramp blade front with white dot, square notch rear with two white dots.
Features: Trigger safety lock (thumb safety), grip safety, firing pin safety; grooved trigger; flat mainspring housing. Also available with lightweight alloy frame and in stainless steel. Introduced 1985.
Price: Matte finish **$482.50**
Price: Satin nickel **$512.95**

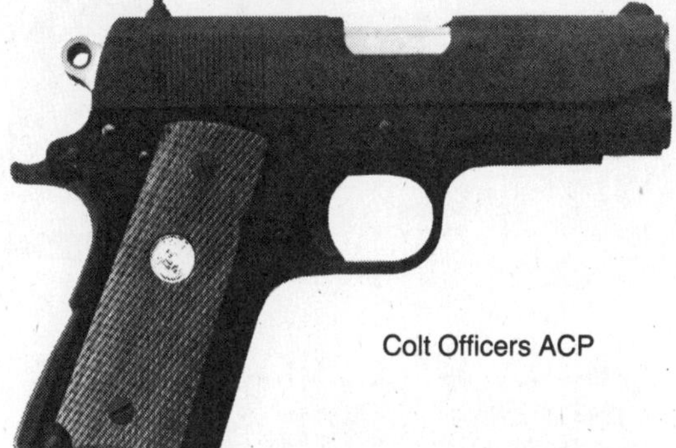
Colt Officers ACP

Consult our Directory pages for the location of firms mentioned.

COLT SERVICE MODEL ACE

Caliber: 22 LR, 10-shot magazine.
Barrel: 5"
Weight: 42 oz. **Length:** 8⅜" over-all.
Stocks: Checkered walnut.
Sights: Blade front, fully adjustable rear.
Features: The 22-cal. version of the Government Model auto. Based on the Service Model Ace last produced in 1945. Patented floating chamber. Original Ace Markings rolled on left side of slide. Introduced 1978.
Price: Blue only **$531.95**

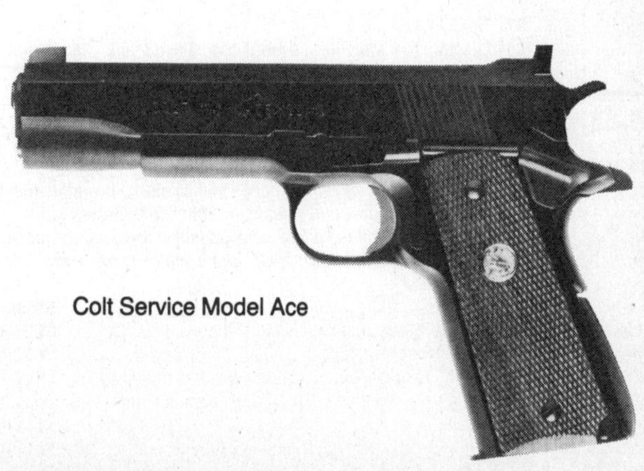
Colt Service Model Ace

Colt Conversion Unit

Permits the 45 and 38 Super Automatic pistols to use the economical 22 LR cartridge. No tools needed. Adjustable rear sight; 10-shot magazine. Designed to give recoil effect of the larger calibers. Not adaptable to Commander models. Blue finish.
Price: **$284.50**
Price: Fixed sight version **$261.50**
Price: 9mm Series 80 Conversion Unit **$284.50**

COLT COMBAT COMMANDER AUTO PISTOL
Caliber: 45 ACP, 7-shot; 38 Super Auto, 9-shot; 9mm Luger, 9-shot.
Barrel: 4¼″.
Weight: 36 oz. **Length:** 8″ over-all.
Stocks: Sandblasted walnut.
Sights: Fixed, glare-proofed blade front, square notch rear.
Features: Grooved trigger and hammer spur; arched housing; grip and thumb safeties.
Price: Blue, 9mm **$499.95**
Price: Blue, 45, Series 80.......... **$491.95**
Price: Blue, 38 super.......... **$499.95**
Price: Satin nickel, 45, Series 80 .... **$519.95**

Colt Combat Commander

Colt Lightweight Commander Mark IV Series 80
Same as Commander except high strength aluminum alloy frame, wood panel grips, weight 27 oz. 45 ACP only.
Price: Blue.......... **$491.95**

CONCORDE PMK 380 AUTO PISTOL
Caliber: 380 ACP.
Barrel: 3.8″.
Weight: 23 oz. **Length:** 6.7″ over-all.
Sights: Fixed.
Features: Blue finish; anodized alloy frame. Introduced 1985. Imported by Kassnar.
Price:.......... **$293.00**

Concorde PMK 380

Coonan 357 Magnum

COONAN 357 MAGNUM PISTOL
Caliber: 357 Mag., 7-shot magazine.
Barrel: 5″.
Weight: 42 oz. **Length:** 8.3″ over-all.
Stocks: Smooth walnut.
Sights: Open, adjustable.
Features: Unique barrel hood improves accuracy and reliability. Many parts interchange with Colt autos. Has grip, hammer, half-cock safeties. From Coonan Arms.
Price: Model A **$595.00**
Price: Model B (linkless barrel, interchangeable ramp front sight, new rear sight).......... **$625.00**

Detonics Auto Pistol

DETONICS 45 PISTOL
Caliber: 45 ACP, 451 Detonics Magnum, 6-shot clip; 9mm Para., 38 Super, 7-shot clip.
Barrel: 3¼″.
Weight: 29 oz. (empty); MK VII is 26 oz. **Length:** 6¾″ over-all, 4½″ high.
Stocks: Checkered walnut.
Sights: Combat type, fixed; adj. sights avail.
Features: Has a self-adjusting cone barrel centering system, beveled magazine inlet, "full clip" indicator in base of magazine; standard 7-shot (or more) clip can be used in the 45. Throated barrel and polished feed ramp. Mark V, VI, VII available in 9mm and 38 Super; MC1 available in 9mm Para. Introduced 1977. From Detonics.
Price: MK. V, matte stainless, fixed sights.......... **$626.00**
Price: MK. VI, polished stainless, adj sights **$635.00**
Price: MK. VII, matte stainless, no sights **$635.00**
Price: Combat Master MC1, non-glare combat stainless, fixed sights **$560.00**
Price: MC2, as above with fixed sights, wallet, Pachmayr grips, cleaning kit, extra magazine.......... **$621.50**
Price: OM-3, non-glare finish, fixed sights, polished slide flats **$575.00**

DETONICS POCKET 9 DOUBLE ACTION AUTO
Caliber: 9mm Para., 6-shot clip.
Barrel: 3″.
Weight: 26 oz. **Length:** 5.7″ over-all, 4″ high.
Stocks: Black micarta.
Sights: Fixed.
Features: Stainless steel construction; ambidextrous firing pin safety; trigger guard hook for two-hand shooting; double and single action trigger mechanism; snag-free hammer; captive recoil spring; "Chamber Lok" breech system.
Price: About **$425.00**

Desert Eagle 357

ERMA KGP22 AUTO PISTOL

Caliber: 22 LR, 8-shot magazine.
Barrel: 4″.
Weight: 29 oz. **Length:** 7¾″ over-all.
Stocks: Checkered plastic.
Sights: Fixed.
Features: Has toggle action similar to original "Luger" pistol. Slide stays open after last shot. Imported from West Germany by Excam. Introduced 1978.
Price: **$216.00**

ERMA KGP38 AUTO PISTOL

Caliber: 380 ACP (5-shot).
Barrel: 4″.
Weight: 22½ oz. **Length:** 7⅜″ over-all.
Stocks: Checkered plastic. Wood optional.
Sights: Rear adjustable for windage.
Features: Toggle action similar to original "Luger" pistol. Slide stays open after last shot. Has magazine and sear disconnect safety systems. Imported from West Germany by Excam. Introduced 1978.
Price: Plastic grips **$216.00**

F.I.E. TZ-75 DA AUTO PISTOL

Caliber: 9mm Parabellum, 15-shot magazine.
Barrel: 4.72″.
Weight: 35.33 oz. **Length:** 8.25″ over-all.
Stocks: Smooth European walnut.
Sights: Undercut blade front, open rear adjustable for windage.
Features: Double action trigger system; squared-off trigger guard; rotating slide-mounted safety. Introduced 1983. Imported from Italy by F.I.E.
Price: **$349.95**
Price: With satin chrome frame **$399.95**
Price: Silver chrome with red outline sights **$449.95**

F.I.E. "THE BEST" A27B PISTOL

Caliber: 25 ACP, 6-shot magazine.
Barrel: 2½″.
Weight: 13 oz. **Length:** 4⅜″ over-all.
Stocks: Checkered walnut.
Sights: Fixed.
Features: All steel construction. Has thumb and magazine safeties, exposed hammer. Blue finish only. Introduced 1978. Made in U.S. by F.I.E. Corp.
Price: **$154.95**

F.I.E. TITAN II PISTOLS

Caliber: 32 ACP, 380 ACP, 6-shot magazine; 22 LR, 10-shot magazine.
Barrel: 3⅞″.
Weight: 25¾ oz. **Length:** 6¾″ over-all.
Stocks: Checkered nylon, thumbrest-type; checkered walnut optional.
Sights: Adjustable.
Features: Magazine disconnector, firing pin block. Standard slide safety. Available in blue or chrome. Introduced 1978. Imported from Italy by F.I.E. Corp.
Price: 32, blue **$136.95**
Price: 32, chrome **$144.95**
Price: 380, blue **$169.95**
Price: 380, chrome **$179.95**
Price: 22 LR, blue **$129.95**

DESERT EAGLE 357 MAGNUM PISTOL

Caliber: 357 Magnum, 9-shot clip.
Barrel: 6″, 8″, 10″, 14″ interchangeable.
Weight: 52 oz. **Length:** 10¼″ over-all (6″ bbl.).
Stocks: Wrap-around soft rubber.
Sights: Blade on ramp front, combat-style rear.
Features: Rotating three lug bolt, ambidextrous safety, combat-style trigger guard, adjustable trigger (optional). Military epoxy finish. Contact importer for extra barrel prices. Announced 1982. Imported from Israel by Magnum Research Inc.
Price: 6″ barrel, standard pistol **$749.00**

Erma KGP22 Pistol

ERMA-EXCAM RX 22 AUTO PISTOL

Caliber: 22 LR, 8-shot magazine.
Barrel: 3¼″.
Weight: 21 oz. **Length:** 5.58″ over-all.
Stocks: Plastic wrap-around.
Sights: Fixed
Features: Polished blue finish. Double action. Patented ignition safety system. Thumb safety. Assembled in U.S. Introduced 1980. From Excam.
Price: **$159.00**

F.I.E. TZ-75

F.I.E. Titan II Pistol

F.I.E. "TITAN 25" PISTOL
Caliber: 25 ACP,6-shot magazine.
Barrel: 2⅞".
Weight: 12 oz. **Length:** 4⅝" over-all.
Stocks: Smooth nylon.
Sights: Fixed.
Features: External hammer; fast simple takedown. Made in U.S.A. by F.I.E. Corp.
Price: Blue **$64.95**
Price: Dyna-Chrome **$74.95**
Price: Blue, walnut grips **$79.95**
Price: Dyna-Chrome, walnut grips **$89.95**
Price: 24K gold with bright blue frame, smooth walnut grips **$124.95**

F.I.E. "SUPER TITAN II" PISTOLS
Caliber: 32 ACP, 380 ACP.
Barrel: 3⅞".
Weight: 28 oz. **Length:** 6¾" over-all.
Stocks: Smooth, polished walnut.
Sights: Adjustable.
Features: Blue finish only. 12 shot (32 ACP), 11 shot (380 ACP). Introduced 1981. Imported from Italy by F.I.E. Corp.
Price: 32 ACP **$189.95**
Price: 380 ACP **$219.95**

Fraser Auto

FRASER AUTOMATIC PISTOL
Caliber: 25 ACP, 6-shot.
Barrel: 2¼".
Weight: 10 oz. **Length:** 4" over-all.
Stocks: Plastic pearl or checkered walnut.
Sights: Recessed, fixed.
Features: Stainless steel construction. Has positive manual safety as well as magazine safety. From Fraser Firearms Corp.
Price: Satin stainless steel, 25 ACP **$129.50**
Price: Gold plated, with book-type case **$247.50**
Price: With black Q.P.Q. finish **$149.50**

Goncz High-Tech Pistol

GONCZ HIGH-TECH LONG PISTOL
Caliber: 9mm Para., 30 Mauser, 38 Super, 18- and 32-shot magazine; 45 ACP, 10- and 20-shot magazine.
Barrel: 4", 9.5".
Weight: 3 lbs., 10 oz. (with 4" barrel). **Length:** 10½" over-all (with 4" barrel).
Stock: Alloy grooved pistol grip.
Sights: Front adjustable for elevation, rear adjustable for windage.
Features: Fires from closed bolt; floating firing pin; safety locks the firing pin. All metal construction. Barrel threaded for accessories. Matte black oxide and anodized finish. Designed by Lajos J. Goncz. Introduced 1985. From Goncz Co.
Price: With 9½" barrel **$350.00**
Price: With 4" barrel **$340.00**

Hammerli 212

HAMMERLI MODEL 212 HUNTER'S PISTOL
Caliber: 22 LR.
Barrel: 4.9".
Weight: 31 oz. **Length:** 8.5" over-all.
Stocks: Checkered walnut.
Sights: White dot front adjustable for elevation, rear adjustable for elevation.
Features: Semi-automatic based on the Model 208, intended for field use. Uses target trigger system which is fully adjustable. Comes with tool kit. Imported from Switzerland by Osborne's Supplies. Introduced 1984.
Price: **$995.00**

HECKLER & KOCH P7-M8 AUTO PISTOL
Caliber: 9mm Parabellum, 8-shot magazine.
Barrel: 4.13".
Weight: 29 oz. **Length:** 6.73" over-all.
Stocks: Stippled black plastic.
Sights: Fixed, combat-type.
Features: Unique "squeeze cocker" in front strap cocks the action. Gas-retarded action. Squared combat-type trigger guard. Blue finish. Compact size. Imported from West Germany by Heckler & Koch, Inc.
Price: P7-M8 .... **$599.00**
Price: Extra magazine (8-shot) **$22.00**
Price: P7-M13 (13-shot capacity, matte black finish, ambidextrous magazine release, forged steel frame) **$669.00**
Price: Extra 13-shot magazine **$55.00**

Heckler & Koch P7-M8

HECKLER & KOCH P9S DOUBLE ACTION AUTO
Caliber: 9mm Para., 9-shot magazine; 45 ACP, 7-shot magazine.
Barrel: 4″.
Weight: 31 oz. **Length:** 7.6″ over-all.
Stocks: Checkered black plastic.
Sights: Open combat type.
Features: Double action; polygonal rifling; delayed roller-locked action with stationary barrel. Loaded chamber and cocking indicators; cocking/decocking lever. Imported from West Germany by Heckler & Koch, Inc.
Price: P-9S Combat Model **$586.00**
Price: P-9S Target Model **$699.00**
Price: Walnut wrap-around competition grips **$104.00**
Price: Sports competition model with 4″ and 5½″ barrels, 2 slides . **$1,189.00**

Heckler & Koch P9S

IVER JOHNSON MODEL PO380 PONY
Caliber: 380 ACP, 6-shot magazine.
Barrel: 3″.
Weight: 20 oz. **Length:** 6″ over-all.
Stocks: Checkered walnut.
Sights: Blade front, rear adj. for w.
Features: All steel construction. Inertia firing pin. Thumb safety locks hammer. No magazine safety. Lanyard ring. Made in U.S., available from Iver Johnson's.
Price: Blue **$260.00**
Price: Nickel **$291.00**
Price: Military (matte finish) **$260.00**

Iver Johnson PO 300

IVER JOHNSON TRAILSMAN PISTOL
Caliber: 22 LR, 10-shot magazine.
Barrel: 4½″ or 6″.
Weight: 46 oz. (4½″ bbl.) **Length:** 8¾″ (4½″ bbl.).
Stocks: Checkered composition.
Sights: Fixed, tagret type.
Features: Slide hold-open latch, positive sear block safety, push button magazine release. Introduced 1984.
Price: Blue only **$170.00**

Iver Johnson Trailsman

IVER JOHNSON TP22B, TP25B AUTO PISTOL
Caliber: 22 LR, 25 ACP, 7-shot magazine.
Barrel: 2.85″.
Weight: 14½ oz. **Length:** 5.39″ over-all.
Stocks: Black checkered plastic.
Sights: Fixed.
Features: Double action; 7-shot magazine. Introduced 1981. From Iver Johnson's.
Price: Either caliber, blue **$140.00**
Price: TP22N (22 cal., nickel) **$170.00**

Iver Johnson TP22B

IVER JOHNSON PP30 "SUPER ENFORCER" PISTOL
Caliber: 30 U.S. Carbine.
Barrel: 9½″.
Weight: 4 lbs. **Length:** 17″ over-all.
Stocks: American walnut.
Sights: Blade front; click adjustable peep rear.
Features: Shortened version of the M1 Carbine. Uses 15 or 30-shot magazines. From Iver Johnson's.
Price: Blue finish **$250.00**

JENNINGS J-22 AUTO PISTOL
Caliber: 22 LR, 6-shot magazine.
Barrel: 2½″.
Weight: 13 oz. **Length:** 4 15/16″ over-all.
Stocks: Walnut on chrome or nickel models; checkered black Cycolac on Teflon model.
Sights: Fixed.
Features: Choice of bright chrome, satin nickel or black Teflon finish. Introduced 1981. From Jennings Firearms.
Price: About **$69.95**

Jennings J-22 Pistol

CAUTION: PRICES CHANGE. CHECK AT GUNSHOP.

Korth Auto Pistol

KORTH SEMI-AUTOMATIC PISTOL

Caliber: 9mm Parabellum, 13-shot magazine.
Barrel: 4½".
Weight: 35 oz. **Length:** 10½" over-all.
Stocks: Checkered walnut.
Sights: Combat-adjustable
Features: Double action; 13-shot staggered magazine; forged machined frame and slide. Matte and polished finish. Introduced 1985. Imported from West Germany by Osbonre's.
Price: **$2,475.00**

L.A.R. GRIZZLY WIN MAG PISTOL

Caliber: 45 Win. Mag., 7-shot magazine.
Barrel: 6½".
Weight: 51 oz. **Length:** 10½" over-all.
Stocks: Checkered rubber, non-slip combat-type.
Sights: Ramped blade front, fully adjustable rear.
Features: Uses basic Browning/Colt 1911-A1 design; interchangeable calibers; beveled magazine well; combat-type flat, checkered rubber mainspring housing; lowered and back-chamfered ejection port; polished feed ramp; throated barrel; solid barrel bushings. Announced 1983. From L.A.R. Mfg. Co.
Price: **$675.00**
Price: Conversion units (9mm Win. Mag., 45 ACP, 357 Mag., 30 Mauser, 38 Super, 38 Spec., 9mm Steyr, 9mm Browning Long, 9mm Luger)..... **$149.00**

L.A.R. Grizzly

Llama Large Frame Auto

LLAMA LARGE FRAME AUTO PISTOL

Caliber: 45 ACP.
Barrel: 5".
Weight: 40 oz. **Length:** 8½" over-all.
Stocks: Checkered walnut.
Sights: Fixed.
Features: Grip and manual safeties, ventilated rib. Imported from Spain by Stoeger Industries.
Price: Blue.. **$263.95**
Price: Satin chrome.. **$334.95**

LLAMA MEDIUM FRAME AUTO PISTOL

Caliber: 9mm Para., 9 shot.
Barrel: 4⁵⁄₁₆".
Weight: 37 oz.
Stocks: Smooth walnut.
Sights: Blade front, rear adjustable for windage.
Features: Scaled-down version of the Large Frame gun. Locked breech mechanism; manual and grip safeties. Introduced 1985. Imported from Spain by Stoeger Industries.
Price: Blue only **$263.95**

Llama Medium Frame

Llama Small Frame Auto

LLAMA SMALL FRAME AUTO PISTOLS

Caliber: 22 LR, 380.
Barrel: 3¹¹⁄₁₆".
Weight: 23 oz. **Length:** 6½" over-all.
Stocks: Checkered plastic, thumb rest.
Sights: Fixed front, adj. notch rear.
Features: Ventilated rib, manual and grip safeties. Model XV is 22 LR, Model IIIA is 380. Both models have loaded indicator; IIIA is locked breech. Imported from Spain by Stoeger Industries.
Price: Blue, 380 .... **$228.95**
Price: Blue, 22 LR **$209.95**
Price: Satin chrome, 22 LR or 380 .... **$263.95**

CAUTION: PRICES CHANGE. CHECK AT GUNSHOP.

LLAMA OMNI DOUBLE-ACTION AUTO

Caliber: 9mm (13-shot), 45 ACP (7-shot).
Barrel: 4¼″.
Weight: 40 oz. **Length:** 9mm—8″, 45–7¾″ over-all.
Stocks: Checkered plastic.
Sights: Ramped blade front, rear adjustable for windage and elevation (45), drift-adjustable for windage (9mm).
Features: New DA pistol has ball-bearing action, double sear bars, articulated firing pin, buttressed locking lug and low-friction rifling. Introduced 1982. Imported from Spain by Stoeger Industries.
Price: 45 ACP **$466.95**
Price: 9mm **$434.95**

Turkish MKE Pistol

MANURHIN-WALTHER PP AUTO PISTOL

Caliber: 22 LR, 10-shot; 32 ACP, 8-shot; 380 ACP, 7-shot.
Barrel: 3.87″.
Weight: 23 oz. (22 LR). **Length:** 6.7″ over-all.
Stocks: Checkered composition.
Sights: White outline front and rear.
Features: Double action; hammer drop safety; all steel construction; high-polish blue finish. Each gun supplied with two magazines. Imported from France by Manurhin International.
Price: 22 LR **$376.50**
Price: 32 and 380.......... **$367.00**

Manurhin-Walther PPK/S Auto Pistol

Similar to the Model PP except has 3.25″ barrel and over-all length of 6.12″.
Price: 22 LR **$376.50**
Price: 32 and 380.......... **$367.00**

O.D.I. Viking D.A. Pistol

Llama Omni D.A. Pistol

MKE AUTO PISTOL

Caliber: 380 ACP; 7-shot magazine.
Barrel: 4″.
Weight: 23 oz. **Length:** 6½″ over-all.
Stocks: Hard rubber.
Sights: Fixed front, rear adjustable for windage.
Features: Double action with exposed hammer; chamber loaded indicator. Imported from Turkey by Mandall Shooting Supplies.
Price: **$350.00**

Manurhin PPK/S

O.D.I. VIKING COMBAT D.A. AUTO PISTOL

Caliber: 9mm, 45 ACP.
Barrel: 5″.
Weight: 39 oz.
Stocks: Smooth teakwood standard; other materials available.
Sights: Fixed. Blade front, notched rear.
Features: Made entirely of stainless steel, brushed satin, natural finish. Features the Seecamp double action system. Spur-type hammer. Magazine holds 7 rounds in 45 ACP, 9 in 9mm. Made in U.S.A. From O.D.I.
Price: **$579.95**

O.D.I. Viking Combat D.A. Auto Pistols

Similar to the standard Viking pistol except 4¼″ barrel, weight of 36 ozs. The Viking II Combat has a slide-mounted thumb-activated firing pin safety.
Price: Combat I, 9mm only.......... **$579.00**
Price: Combat II, 45 ACP only.......... **$639.00**

RG 26 AUTO PISTOL

Caliber: 25 ACP, 6-shot magazine.
Barrel: 2½″.
Weight: 12 oz. **Length:** 4¾″ over-all.
Stocks: Checkered plastic.
Sights: Fixed.
Features: Blue finish. Thumb safety. Imported by RG Industries.
Price: Blue or nickel.......... **$88.00**

RANDALL SERVICE MODEL AUTO PISTOL

Caliber: 9mm, 38 Super, 45 ACP.
Barrel: 5″.
Weight: 38 ozs. **Length:** 8½″ over-all.
Stocks: Checkered walnut.
Sights: Blade front, fixed or adjustable rear.
Features: All stainless steel construction, including springs and pins. Standard with ten grooved barrel, patented long recoil spring guide rod, long trigger, extended slide stop and thumb safety, ported slide, beveled magazine well, checkered walnut grips. Available with round-top slide and fixed sights or ribbed-top slide with adjustable sights. Also available left-handed. Made in U.S.A. by Randall Firearms.
Price: With fixed sights, about **$455.00**
Price: Left-handed, with fixed sights, about **$485.00**
Price: Combat version (9mm, 38 Super, 45 ACP), about **$540.00**
Price: Left-handed Combat version, about **$570.00**
Price: With adjustable sights, about **$540.00**
Price: Left-handed, with adjustable sights, about **$570.00**

Randall Service Model

Randall Raider

Randall Raider Auto Pistol

Same as the Service Model except has a 4½″ barrel, 7¾″ over-all length, and weighs 36 oz. Same standard features and options. Introduced 1984.
Price: With fixed sights, about **$455.00**
Price: Left-handed, with fixed sights, about **$485.00**
Price: Right-handed, with adjustable sights, about **$540.00**
Price: Left-handed, with adjustable sights, about **$570.00**

Randall Curtis E. LeMay Four Star

Similar to the Service Model except has a 4½″ barrel, 7¾″ over-all length, 6-shot magazine capacity, and weighs 35 oz. Squared trigger guard, extended magazine baseplate. Same standard features and options. Introduced 1984.
Price: With fixed sights, about **$520.00**
Price: With adjustable sights, about **$610.00**
Price: Left-handed, fixed sights, about **$555.00**
Price: Left-handed, adjustable sights, about **$645.00**

RAVEN P-25 AUTO PISTOL

Caliber: 25 ACP, 6-shot magazine.
Barrel: 2⁷⁄₁₆″.
Weight: 15 oz. **Length:** 4¾″ over-all.
Stocks: Smooth walnut.
Sights: Ramped front, fixed rear.
Features: Available in blue, nickel or chrome finish. Made in U.S., available from EMF Co.
Price: **$59.95**

Raven P-25 Pistol

Ruger Mark II Stainless

RUGER MARK II STANDARD AUTO PISTOL

Caliber: 22 LR, 10-shot magazine.
Barrel: 4¾″ or 6″.
Weight: 36 oz. (4¾″ bbl.). **Length:** 8⁵⁄₁₆″ (4¾″ bbl.).
Stocks: Checkered hard rubber.
Sights: Fixed, wide blade front, square notch rear adj. for w.
Features: Updated design of the original Standard Auto. Has new bolt hold-open device, 10-shot magazine, magazine catch, safety, trigger and new receiver contours. Introduced 1982.
Price: Blued (MK 4, MK 6) **$168.00**
Price: In stainless steel (KMK 4, KMK 6) **$225.00**

SEECAMP II STAINLESS DA AUTO

Caliber: 25 ACP,8-shot magazine.
Barrel: 2″, integral with frame.
Weight: About 10 oz. **Length:** 4⅛″ over-all.
Stocks: Black plastic.
Sights: Smooth, no-snag, contoured slide and barrel top.
Features: Aircraft quality 17-4 PH stainless steel. Inertia operated firing pin. Hammer fired double action only. Hammer automatically follows slide down to safety rest position after each shot—no manual safety needed. Magazine safety disconnector. Introduced 1980. From L.W. Seecamp.
Price: **$199.95**

Seecamp II Stainless

CAUTION: PRICES CHANGE. CHECK AT GUNSHOP.

SIG P-210-1

SIG P-210-1 AUTO PISTOL
Caliber: 7.65mm or 9mm Para., 8-shot magazine.
Barrel: 4¾".
Weight: 31¾ oz. (9mm) **Length:** 8½" over-all.
Stocks: Checkered walnut, with lacquer finish.
Sights: Blade front, rear adjustable for windage.
Features: Lanyard loop; polished finish. Conversion unit for 22 LR available. Imported from Switzerland by Osborne's and Mandall Shooting Supplies.
Price: P-210-1 about (Mandall) **$1,500.00**
Price: P-210-2 Service Pistol (Mandall) **$1,600.00**
Price: 22 Cal. Conversion unit (Osborne's)...................... **$675.00**
Price: P-210-1 (Osborne's).................................. **$1,450.00**
Price: P-210-2 (Osborne's).................................. **$1,095.00**

SIG P-210-6

SIG P-210-6 AUTO PISTOL
Caliber: 9mm Para., 8-shot magazine.
Barrel: 4¾".
Weight: 36.2 oz. **Length:** 8½" over-all.
Stocks: Checkered black plastic. Walnut optional.
Sights: Blade front, micro. adj. rear for w. & e.
Features: Adjustable trigger stop; target trigger; ribbed front stap; sandblasted finish. Conversion unit for 22 LR consists of barrel, recoil spring, slide and magazine. Imported from Switzerland by Osborne's and SIGARMS, Inc.
Price: P-210-6.. **$1,635.00**
Price: 22 Cal. Conversion unit (Osborne's)...................... **$781.00**
Price: P-210-6 (Osborne's).................................. **$1,295.00**

SIG-Sauer P-220 Pistol

SIG-SAUER P-220 D.A. AUTO PISTOL
Caliber: 9mm, 38 Super; 45 ACP. (9-shot in 9mm and 38 Super, 7 in 45).
Barrel: 4⅜".
Weight: 28¼ oz. (9mm). **Length:** 7¾" over-all.
Stocks: Checkered black plastic.
Sights: Blade front, drift adj. rear for w.
Features: Double action. De-cocking lever permits lowering hammer onto locked firing pin. Squared combat-type trigger guard. Slide stays open after last shot. Imported from West Germany by SIGARMS, Inc.
Price: **$527.00**

Consult our Directory pages for the location of firms mentioned.

SIG-Sauer P-230 D.A. Pistol

SIG-SAUER P-225 D.A. AUTO PISTOL
Caliber: 9mm Parabellum, 8-shot magazine.
Barrel: 3.8".
Weight: 26 oz. **Length:** 7³⁄₃₂" over-all.
Stocks: Checkered black plastic.
Sights: Blade front, rear adjustable for windage.
Features: Double action. De-cocking lever permits lowering hammer onto locked firing pin. Squared combat-type trigger guard. Shortened, lightened version of P-220. Imported from West Germany by SIGARMS, Inc.
Price: **$561.00**

SILE-BENELLI B-76 DA AUTO PISTOL
Caliber: 9mm Para., 8-shot magazine.
Barrel: 4¼", 6-groove. Chrome-lined bore.
Weight: 34 oz. (empty). **Length:** 8¹⁄₁₆" over-all.
Stocks: Walnut with cut checkering and high gloss finish.
Sights: Blade front with white face, rear adjustable for windage with white bars for increased visibility.
Features: Fixed barrel, locked breech. Exposed hammer can be locked in non-firing mode in either single or double action. Stainless steel inertia firing pin and loaded chamber indicator. All external parts blued, internal parts hard-chrome plated. All steel construction. Introduced 1979. From Sile Dist.
Price: About **$349.95**

SIG-SAUER P-230 D.A. AUTO PISTOL
Caliber: 32 ACP (8 shot), 380 ACP (7 shot).
Barrel: 3¾".
Weight: 16 oz. **Length:** 6½" over-all.
Stocks: Checkered black plastic.
Sights: Blade front, rear adj. for w.
Features: Double action. Same basic action design as P-220. Blowback operation, stationary barrel. Introduced 1977. Imported from West Germany by SIGARMS, Inc.
Price: **$397.00**
Price: In stainless steel (P-230 SL)............................ **$453.00**

SMITH & WESSON MODEL 645 DOUBLE ACTION
Caliber: 45 ACP, 8-shot magazine.
Barrel: 5".
Weight: 37.6 ozs. **Length:** 8.7" over-all.
Stocks: Checkered high-impact nylon.
Sights: Red ramp front, rear drift-adjustable for windage.
Features: Double action. Made of stainless steel. Has manual hammer-drop, magazine disconnect and firing pin safeties. Cross-hatch knurling on the recurved front trigger guard and backstrap; bevelled magazine well. Introduced 1985.
Price: .... **NA**

Smith & Wesson Model 645

SMITH & WESSON MODEL 439 DOUBLE ACTION
Caliber: 9mm Luger, 8-shot clip.
Barrel: 4".
Weight: 27 oz. **Length:** 7⁷⁄₁₆" over-all.
Stocks: Checkered walnut.
Sights: ⅛" square serrated ramp front, square notch rear is fully adj. for w. & e. Also available with fixed sights.
Features: Rear sight has protective shields on both sides of the sight blade. Frame is alloy. New trigger actuated firing pin lock in addition to the regular rotating safety. Magazine disconnector. New extractor design. Comes with two magazines. Ambidextrous safety an extra-cost option. Introduced 1980.
Price: Blue, from **$378.50**
Price: Nickel, from **$410.00**
Price: Model 639 (stainless), from **$432.50**

Smith & Wesson Model 659

SMITH & WESSON MODEL 459 DOUBLE ACTION
Caliber: 9mm Luger, 14-shot clip.
Barrel: 4".
Weight: 28 oz. **Length:** 7⁷⁄₁₆" over-all.
Stocks: Checkered high-impact nylon.
Sights: ⅛" square serrated ramp front, square notch rear is fully adj. for w. & e. Also available with fixed sights.
Features: Alloy frame. Rear sight has protective shields on both sides of blade. New trigger actuated firing pin lock in addition to the regular safety. Magazine disconnector; new extractor design. Comes with two magazines. Ambidextrous safety an extra-cost option. Introduced 1980.
Price: Blue, from **$424.50**
Price: Nickel, from **$457.00**
Price: Model 659 (stainless), from **$449.50**

Smith & Wesson Model 469 Mini-Gun
Basically a cut-down version of the Model 459 pistol. Gun has a 3½" barrel, 12-round magazine, over-all length of 6⅞", and weighs 26 oz. Also accepts the 14-shot Model 459 magazine. Cross-hatch knurling on the recurved-front trigger guard and backstrap; magazine has a curved finger extension; bobbed hammer; sandblast blue finish with pebble-grain grips. Ambidextrous safety an extra cost option. Introduced 1983.
Price: **$399.00**
Price: Stainless Model 669 (alloy frame) **$439.00**

Smith & Wesson Model 469

SPRINGFIELD ARMORY 1911-A1 AUTO PISTOL
Caliber: 9mm or 45 ACP, 8-round magazine.
Barrel: 5".
Weight: 2¼ lbs. **Length:** 8½" over-all.
Stocks: NA.
Sights: Blade front, rear drift-adjustable for windage.
Features: All forged parts, including frame, barrel, slide. All new production. Introduced 1985. From Springfield Armory.
Price: Complete pistol **$255.00**
Price: Kit, unassembled **$215.00**
Price: Frame and slide kit **$129.00**
Price: Frame only **$68.00**
Price: Slide only **$75.00**

STAR BM, BKM AUTO PISTOLS
Caliber: 9mm Para., 8-shot magazine.
Barrel: 3.9".
Weight: 25 oz.
Stocks: Checkered walnut.
Sights: Fixed.
Features: Blue or chrome finish. Magazine and manual safeties, external hammer. Imported from Spain by Interarms.
Price: Blue, BM and BKM **$295.00**
Price: Chrome, BM only **$305.00**

Star Model BM, BKM Pistol

CAUTION: PRICES CHANGE. CHECK AT GUNSHOP.

STAR MODEL 30M & 30 PK DOUBLE-ACTION PISTOLS

Caliber: 9mm Para., 15-shot magazine.
Barrel: 4.33″ (Model M); 3.86″ (Model PK).
Weight: 40 oz. (M); 30 oz. (PK). **Length:** 8″ over-all (M); 7.6″ (PK).
Stocks: Checkered black plastic.
Sights: Square blade front, square notch rear click-adjustable for windage and elevation.
Features: Double or single action; grooved front and backstraps and trigger guard face; ambidextrous safety cams firing pin forward; removable backstrap houses the firing mechanism. Model M has steel frame; Model PK is alloy. Introduced 1984. Imported from Spain by Interarms.
Price: Model M or PK **$455.00**

Star Model 30 PK

STAR MODEL PD AUTO PISTOL

Caliber: 45 ACP, 6-shot magazine.
Barrel: 3.94″.
Weight: 28 oz. **Length:** 7 7/16″ over-all.
Stocks: Checkered walnut.
Sights: Ramp front, fully adjustable rear.
Features: Rear sight milled into slide; thumb safety; grooved non-slip front strap; nylon recoil buffer; inertia firing pin; no grip or magazine safeties. Imported from Spain by Interarms.
Price: Blue.. **$295.00**

Star Model PD Pistol

STEEL CITY "DOUBLE DEUCE" PISTOL

Caliber: 22 LR (7-shot), 25 ACP (6-shot).
Barrel: 2½″.
Weight: 18 oz. **Length:** 5½″ over-all.
Stocks: Rosewood.
Sights: Fixed groove.
Features: Double-action; stainless steel construction with matte finish; ambidextrous slide-mounted safety. From Steel City Arms, Inc.
Price: 22 or 25 cal... **$289.95**

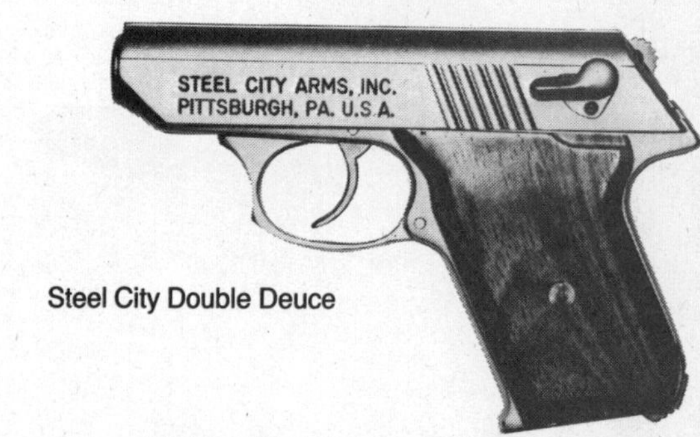

Steel City Double Deuce

STERLING MK-7 PARA PISTOL

Caliber: 9mm Parabellum, 10-shot magazine.
Barrel: 4″ standard, 8″ available.
Weight: 3.6 lbs. **Length:** 14″ over-all.
Stocks: Checkered black plastic.
Sights: Post front, peep rear.
Features: Helical, self-cleaning bolt; two-stage recoil assembly allows wide range of ammunition to be used. Comes with 10-shot magazine (34-shot optional), sling and manual. Five year warranty. Imported from England by Lanchester U.S.A. Introduced 1984.
Price: About **$525.00**

Steyr GB

STEYR GB DOUBLE ACTION AUTO PISTOL

Caliber: 9mm Parabellum; 18-shot magazine.
Barrel: 5.39″.
Weight: 33 oz. **Length:** 8.4″ over-all.
Stocks: Checkered walnut.
Sights: Post front, fixed rear.
Features: Gas-operated, delayed blowback action. Measures 5.7″ high, 1.3″ wide. Introduced 1981. Imported by Gun South, Inc.
Price: About **$595.00**

Stoeger Luger 22 Auto

STOEGER LUGER 22 AUTO PISTOL

Caliber: 22 LR, 10-shot.
Barrel: 4½″.
Weight: 30 oz. **Length:** 8⅞″ over-all.
Stocks: Checkered walnut.
Sights: Fixed.
Features: All steel construction. Action remains open after last shot and as magazine is removed. Grip and balance identical to P-08.
Price: **$199.95**
Price: Kit includes extra clip, charger, holster..................... **$241.95**
Price: Combo (includes extra clip, holster, charger and carrying case) **$249.95**

CAUTION: PRICES CHANGE. CHECK AT GUNSHOP.

TARGA MODELS GT32, GT380 AUTO PISTOLS

Caliber: 32 ACP or 380 ACP, 6-shot magazine.
Barrel: 4⅞".
Weight: 26 oz. **Length:** 7⅜" over-all.
Stocks: Checkered nylon with thumb rest. Walnut optional.
Sights: Fixed blade front; rear drift-adj. for w.
Features: Chrome or blue finish; magazine, thumb, and firing pin safeties; external hammer; safety lever take-down. Imported from Italy by Excam, Inc.
Price: 32 cal., blue **$133.00**
Price: 32 cal., chrome **$143.00**
Price: 380 cal., blue **$159.00**
Price: 380 cal., chrome **$167.00**
Price: 380 cal., chrome, engraved, wooden grips **$214.00**
Price: 380 cal., blue, engraved, wooden grips **$205.00**

TARGA GT380XE GT32XE PISTOLS

Caliber: 32 ACP or 380 ACP, 12-shot magazine.
Barrel: 3.88".
Weight: 28 oz. **Length:** 7.38" over-all.
Stocks: Smooth hardwood.
Sights: Adj. for windage.
Features: Blue or satin nickel. Ordnance steel. Magazine disconnector, firing pin and thumb safeties. Introduced 1980. Imported by Excam.
Price: 32 cal., blue **$189.00**
Price: 380 cal., blue **$205.00**

Taurus PT-99 Auto Pistol

Similar to the PT-92 except has fully adjustable rear sight, smooth Brazilian walnut stocks and is available in polished blue or satin nickel. Introduced 1983.
Price: Polished blue, about **$341.00**
Price: Satin nickel, about **$353.00**

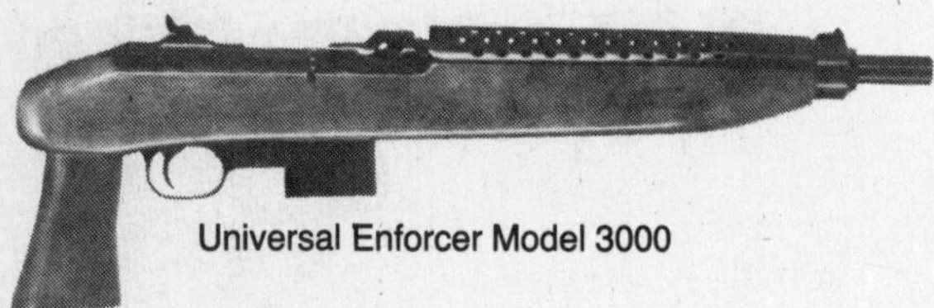

Universal Enforcer Model 3000

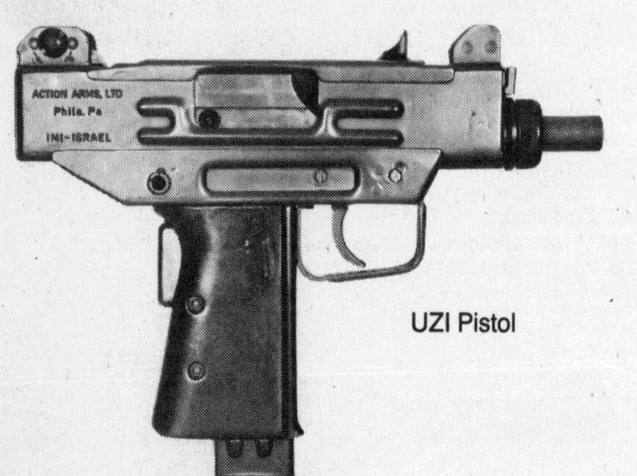

UZI Pistol

WALTHER PP AUTO PISTOL

Caliber: 22 LR, 8-shot; 32 ACP, 380 ACP, 7-shot.
Barrel: 3.86".
Weight: 23½ oz. **Length:** 6.7" over-all.
Stocks: Checkered plastic.
Sights: Fixed, white markings.
Features: Double action, manual safety blocks firing pin and drops hammer, chamber loaded indicator on 32 and 380, extra finger rest magazine provided. Imported from Germany by Interarms.
Price: 22 LR **$520.00**
Price: 32 and 380 .... **$500.00**
Price: Engraved models .... **On Request**

TARGA MODEL GT27 AUTO PISTOL

Caliber: 25 ACP, 6-shot magazine.
Barrel: 2 7/16".
Weight: 12 oz. **Length:** 4⅝" over-all.
Stocks: Checkered nylon.
Sights: Fixed.
Features: Safety lever take-down; external hammer with half-cock. Assembled in U.S. by Excam, Inc.
Price: Blue **$58.50**
Price: Chrome **$64.00**

TAURUS MODEL PT-92 AUTO PISTOL

Caliber: 9mm P., 15-shot magazine.
Barrel: 4.92".
Weight: 34 oz. **Length:** 8.54" over-all.
Stocks: Brazilian walnut.
Sights: Fixed notch rear.
Features: Double action, exposed hammer, chamber loaded indicator. Inertia firing pin. Blue finish. Imported by Taurus International.
Price: About **$317.00**

Taurus PT-99 Pistol

UNIVERSAL ENFORCER MODEL 3000 AUTO

Caliber: 30 M1 Carbine, 5-shot magazine.
Barrel: 11¼" with 12-groove rifling.
Weight: 4 lbs. **Length:** 19" over-all.
Stocks: American walnut with handguard.
Sights: Gold bead ramp front. Peep rear.
Features: Accepts 15 or 30-shot magazines. 4½-6 lb. trigger pull. From Iver Johnson.
Price: Blue finish **$249.95**

UZI PISTOL

Caliber: 9mm Parabellum.
Barrel: 4.5".
Weight: 3.8 lbs. **Length:** 9.45" over-all.
Stocks: Black plastic.
Sights: Post front, open rear adjustable for windage and elevation.
Features: Semi-auto blow-back action; fires from closed bolt; floating firing pin. Comes in a molded plastic case with 20-round magazine; 25 and 32-round magazines available. Imported from Israel by Action Arms. Introduced 1984.
Price: **$550.00**

Walther PP Auto Pistol

Walther American PPK/S Auto Pistol

Similar to Walther PP except made entirely in the United States. Has 3.27" barrel with 6.1" length over-all. Introduced 1980.

Price: 380 ACP only **$459.00**
Price: As above, stainless **$499.00**

Walther PPK/S American

WALTHER P-38 AUTO PISTOL

Caliber: 22 LR, 30 Luger or 9mm Luger, 8-shot.
Barrel: 4$^{15}/_{16}$" (9mm and 30), 5$^{1}/_{16}$" (22 LR).
Weight: 28 oz. **Length:** 8½" over-all.
Stocks: Checkered plastic.
Sights: Fixed.
Features: Double action, safety blocks firing pin and drops hammer, chamber loaded indicator. Matte finish standard, polished blue, engraving and/or plating available. Imported from Germany by Interarms.

Price: 22 LR **$665.00**
Price: 9mm or 30 Luger **$635.00**
Price: Engraved models .... **On Request**

Walther P-38IV Auto Pistol

Same as P-38 except has longer barrel (4½"); over-all length is 8", weight is 29 oz. Sights are non-adjustable. Introduced 1977. Imported by Interarms.

Price: **$625.00**

Walther P-38 Auto Pistol

Walther P-5 Auto Pistol

Latest Walther design that uses the basic P-38 double-action mechanism. Caliber 9mm Luger, barrel length 3½"; weight 28 oz., over-all length 7".

Price: **$650.00**

Consult our Directory pages for the location of firms mentioned.

Walther P-5 Pistol

WILDEY PISTOL

Caliber: 475, 44, 41 Wildey Magnum, 45 Win. Mag., 357 Peterbuilt, 44 Auto Mag.; 7-shot.
Barrel: 6", 7", 8", 10".
Weight: About 58 oz. (6" barrel).
Stocks: Black rubber or walnut.
Sights: Interchangeable blade front, Eliason-type rear.
Features: Right or left-hand ejection (bolts), safety and slide lock stop; ambidextrous magazine catch; interchangeable barrels; drilled and tapped for scope mounting; dual cam-up tilt bolt lock; patented auto. gas system; adjustable trigger. Announced 1985. From Wildey, Inc.

Price: **$799.00**

Wilkinson "Linda" Auto Pistol

WILKINSON "LINDA" PISTOL

Caliber: 9mm Para., 31-shot magazine.
Barrel: 8$^{5}/_{16}$".
Weight: 4 lbs., 13 oz. **Length:** 12¼" over-all.
Stocks: Checkered black plastic pistol grip, maple fore-end.
Sights: Protected blade front, Williams adjustable rear.
Features: Fires from closed bolt. Semi-auto only. Straight blowback action. Cross-bolt safety. Removable barrel. From Wilkinson Arms.

Price: **$463.00**

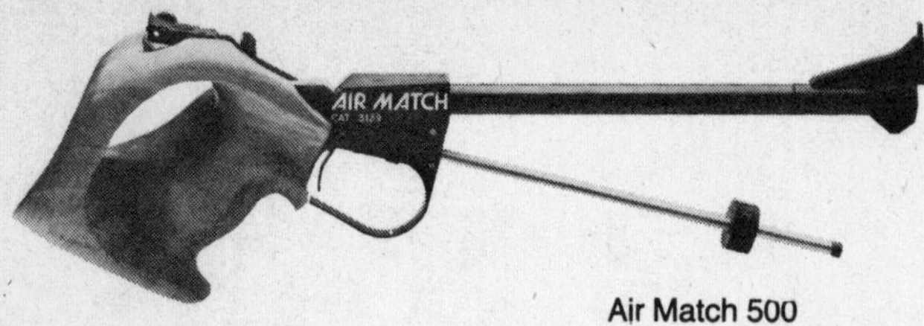

Air Match 500

AIR MATCH 500 TARGET PISTOL

Caliber: 22 LR, single shot.
Barrel: 10.4".
Weight: 28 oz.
Stocks: Anatomically shaped match grip of stippled hardwood. Right or left hand.
Sights: Match post front, fully adjustable match rear.
Features: Sight radius adjustable from 14.1" to 16.1"; easy disassembly for cleaning or adjustment. Comes with case, tools, spare front and rear sight blades. Imported from Italy by Kendall International Arms. Introduced 1984.
Price: **$718.75**

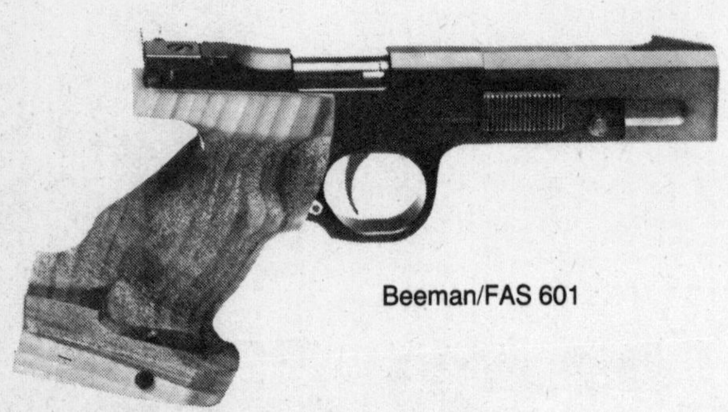
Beeman/FAS 601

BEEMAN/FAS 602 MATCH PISTOL

Caliber: 22 LR, 5-shot.
Barrel: 5.6".
Weight: 37 oz. **Length:** 11" over-all.
Stocks: Walnut wrap-around; sizes small, medium or large, or adjustable.
Sights: Match. Blade front, open notch rear fully adj. for w. and e. Sight radius is 8.66".
Features: Line of sight is only 11/32" above centerline of bore; magazine is inserted from top; adjustable and removable trigger mechanism; single lever takedown. Full 5 year warranty. Imported from Italy by Beeman Inc.
Price: .... **$1,100.00** to **$1,140.00**

Beeman/FAS 601 Match Pistol

Similar to SP 602 except has different match stocks with adj. palm, shelf, 22 Short only for rapid fire shooting; weighs 40 oz., 5.6" bbl., has gas ports through top of barrel and slide to reduce recoil, slightly different trigger and sear mechanisms.
Price: .... **$995.00** to **$1,045.00**

BEEMAN/AGNER MODEL 80 TARGET PISTOL

Caliber: 22 LR, 5-shot magazine.
Barrel: 5.9".
Weight: 36 oz. **Length:** 9½" overall.
Stocks: French walnut briar; anatomically shaped, adjustable.
Sights: Fixed blade front, rear adjustable for windage and elevation; 8¾" radius.
Features: Security "key" locks trigger, magazine and slide. Design minimizes gun movement; dry-fire button allows trigger practice. Imported from Denmark by Beeman. Introduced 1984.
Price: Right-hand **$1,295.00**
Price: Left-hand **$1,395.00**

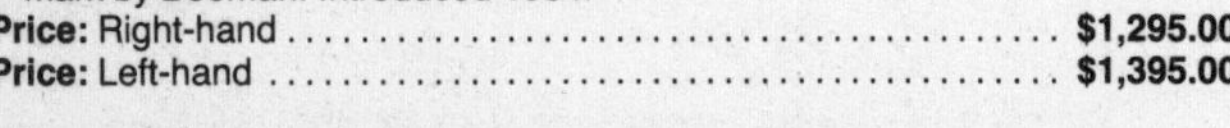

Beeman/Agner 80

Beeman/Unique 69

BEEMAN/UNIQUE D.E.S. 69 TARGET PISTOL

Caliber: 22 LR, 5-shot magazine.
Barrel: 5.91".
Weight: 35.3 oz. **Length:** 10.5" over-all.
Stocks: French walnut target style with thumbrest and adjustable shelf; hand checkered panels.
Sights: Ramp front, micro. adj. rear mounted on frame; 8.66" sight radius.
Features: Meets U.I.T. standards. Comes with 260 gram barrel weight; 100, 150, 350 gram weights available. Fully adjustable match trigger; dry firing safety device. Imported from France by Beeman.
Price: Right-hand **$799.00**
Price: Left-hand **$849.00**

Beeman/Unique 2000-U

BEEMAN/UNIQUE MODEL 2000-U MATCH PISTOL

Caliber: 22 Short, 5-shot magazine.
Barrel: 5.9".
Weight: 43 oz. **Length:** 11.3" over-all.
Stocks: Anatomically shaped, adjustable, stippled French walnut.
Sights: Blade front, fully adjustable rear; 9.7" sight radius.
Features: Light alloy frame, steel slide and shock absorber; five barrel vents reduce recoil, three of which can be blocked; trigger adjustable for position and pull weight. Comes with 340 gram weight housing, 160 gram available. Imported from France by Beeman. Introduced 1984.
Price: Right-hand **$1,095.00**
Price: Left-hand **$1,150.00**

Bernardelli Model 100

BERNARDELLI MODEL 100 PISTOL
Caliber: 22 LR only, 10-shot magazine.
Barrel: 5.9".
Weight: 37¾ oz. **Length:** 9" over-all.
Stocks: Checkered walnut with thumbrest.
Sights: Fixed front, rear adj. for w. and e.
Features: Target barrel weight included. Heavy sighting rib with interchangeable front sight. Accessories include cleaning equipment and assembly tools, case. Imported from Italy by Interarms.
Price: With case **$360.00**

Beretta Model 76

BERETTA MODEL 76 PISTOL
Caliber: 22 LR, 10-shot magazine.
Barrel: 6".
Weight: 33 ozs. (empty). **Length:** 8.8" over-all.
Stocks: Checkered plastic.
Sights: Interchangeable blade front (3 widths), rear is fully adj. for w. and e.
Features: Built-in, fixed counterweight, raised, matted slide rib, factory adjusted trigger pull from 3 lbs. 5 ozs. to 3 lbs. 12 ozs. Thumb safety. Blue-black finish. Wood grips available at extra cost. Introduced 1977. Imported from Italy by Beretta Arms Co.
Price: With plastic grips **$395.00**
Price: With wood grips (right or left hand) **$445.00**

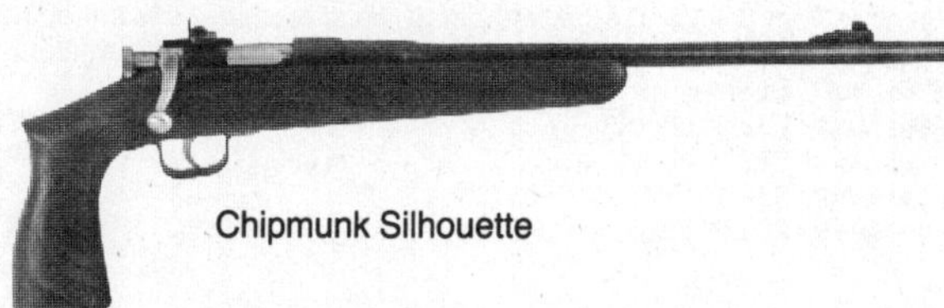

Chipmunk Silhouette

CHIPMUNK SILHOUETTE PISTOL
Caliber: 22 LR.
Barrel: 14⅞".
Weight: About 2 lbs. **Length:** 20" over-all.
Stock: American walnut rear grip.
Sights: Post on ramp front, peep rear.
Features: Meets IHMSA 22-cal. unlimited category for competition. Introduced 1985.
Price: **$149.95**

COLT GOLD CUP NAT'L MATCH MK IV Series 80
Caliber: 45 ACP, 7-shot magazine.
Barrel: 5", with new design bushing.
Weight: 38½ oz. **Length:** 8⅜"
Stocks: Checkered walnut, gold plated medallion.
Sights: Ramp-style front, Colt-Elliason rear adj. for w. and e., sight radius 6¾".
Features: Arched or flat housing; wide, grooved trigger with adj. stop; ribbed-top slide, hand fitted, with improved ejection port.
Price: Colt Royal Blue **$642.50**

Colt Gold Cup Series 80

DETONICS SCOREMASTER TARGET PISTOL
Caliber: 45 ACP, 451 Detonics Magnum, 7-shot clip.
Barrel: 5" heavy match barrel with recessed muzzle; 6" optional.
Weight: 41 oz. **Length:** 8¾" over-all.
Stocks: Pachmayr checkered with matching mainspring housing.
Sights: Blade front, Low-Base Bomar rear.
Features: Stainless steel; self-centering barrel system; patented Detonics recoil system; combat tuned, ambidextrous safety; extended grip safety; National Match tolerances; extended magazine release. Comes with two spare magazines, three interchangeable front sights, and carrying case. Introduced 1983. From Detonics.
Price: 45 ACP or 451 Mag., 6" barrel **$995.00**
Price: As above, 5" barrel **$985.00**

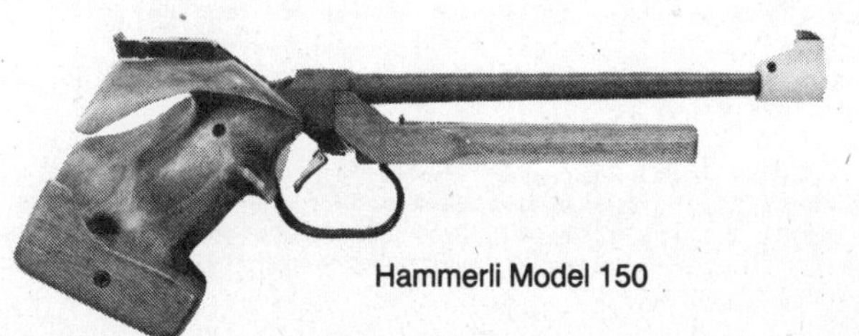

Hammerli Model 150

HAMMERLI MODEL 150 FREE PISTOL
Caliber: 22 LR. Single shot.
Barrel: 11.3"
Weight: 43 ozs. **Length:** 15.35" over-all.
Stocks: Walnut with adjustable palm shelf.
Sights: Sight radius of 14.6". Micro rear sight adj. for w. and e.
Features: Single shot Martini action. Cocking lever on left side of action with vertical operation. Set trigger adjustable for length and angle. Trigger pull weight adjustable between 5 and 100 grams. Guaranteed accuracy of .78", 10 shots from machine rest. Imported from Switzerland by Osborne's, Mandall Shooting Supplies and Beeman.
Price: About (Mandall) **$1,500.00**
Price: With electric trigger (Model 152), about (Mandall) **$1,650.00**
Price: Model 150 (Osborne's) **$1,375.00**
Price: Model 152 (Osborne's) **$1,445.00**
Price: Model 150 (Beeman) **$1,725.00**
Price: Model 152 (Beeman) **$1,830.00**

Hammerli 208

HAMMERLI STANDARD, MODELS 208 & 211

Caliber: 22 LR.
Barrel: 5.9", 6-groove.
Weight: 37.6 oz. (45 oz. with extra heavy barrel weight). **Length:** 10".
Stocks: Walnut. Adj. palm rest (208), 211 has thumbrest grip.
Sights: Match sights, fully adj. for w. and e. (click adj.). Interchangeable front and rear blades.
Features: Semi-automatic, recoil operated. 8-shot clip. Slide stop. Fully adj. trigger (2¼ lbs. and 3 lbs.). Extra barrel weight available. Imported from Switzerland by Osborne's, Mandall Shooting Supplies, Beeman.
Price: Model 208, approx. (Mandall) **$1,295.00**
Price: Model 211, approx. (Mandall) **$1,195.00**
Price: Model 215, approx. (Mandall) **$1,195.00**
Price: Model 208 (Osborne's) **$1,029.00**
Price: Model 211 (Osborne's) **$1,005.00**
Price: Model 215 (Osborne's) **$835.00**
Price: Model 208 (Beeman) **$1,300.00**
Price: Model 211 (Beeman) **$1,250.00**
Price: Model 215 (Beeman) **$1,060.00**

Hammerli 232

HAMMERLI MODEL 232 RAPID FIRE PISTOL

Caliber: 22 Short, 6-shot.
Barrel: 5", with six exhaust ports.
Weight: 44 oz. **Length:** 10.4" over-all.
Stocks: Stippled walnut; wraparound on Model 232-2, adjustable on 232-1.
Sights: Interchangeable front and rear blades, fully adjustable micrometer rear.
Features: Recoil operated semi-automatic; nearly recoilless design; trigger adjustable from 8.4 to 10.6 oz. with three lengths offered. Wraparound grips available in small, medium and large sizes. Imported from Switzerland by Osborne's, Beeman. Introduced 1984.
Price: Model 232-1, about **$902.00**
Price: Model 232-2, about **$954.00**
Price: Model 232-1 (Beeman) **$1,150.00**
Price: Model 232-2 (Beeman) **$1,225.00**

HECKLER & KOCH P9S COMPETITION PISTOL

Caliber: 9mm Para.
Barrel: 5.5".
Weight: 32 oz. **Length:** 9.1" over-all.
Stocks: Stippled walnut, target-type.
Sights: Blade front, fully adjustable rear.
Features: Comes with extra standard 4" barrel, slide and grips, as well as the target gun parts and tools and is fully convertible. Imported from West Germany by Heckler & Koch, Inc.
Price: **$1,189.00**

H&K P9S Competition

M-S Safari Arms Matchmaster Pistol

M-S SAFARI ARMS MATCHMASTER PISTOL

Caliber: 45 ACP, 7-shot magazine.
Barrel: 5".
Weight: 45 oz. **Length:** 8.7" overall.
Stocks: Combat rubber or checkered walnut.
Sights: Combat adjustable.
Features: Beavertail grip safety, ambidextrous extended safety, extended slide release, combat hammer, threaded barrel bushing; throated, ported, tuned. Finishes: blue, Armaloy, Parkerize, electroless nickel. Also available in a lightweight version (30 oz.) and stainless steel. Made by M-S Safari Arms.
Price: **$681.80**

M-S Safari Arms Enforcer Pistol

Shortened version of the Matchmaster. Has 3.8" barrel, over-all length of 7.7", and weighs 40 oz. (standard weight), 27 oz. in lightweight version. Other features are the same. From M-S Safari Arms.
Price: **$681.80**

M-S Safari Arms Model 81 Pistol

Similar to Matchmaster except chambered for 45 or 38 Spec. mid-range wadcutter; available with fixed or adjustable walnut target match grips; Aristocrat rib with extended front sight is optional. Other features are the same. From M-S Safari Arms.
Price: **$868.00**
Price: Model 81L long slide **$995.00**

M-S Safari Arms Model 81BP

Similar to the Matchmaster except designed for shooting the bowling pin matches. Extended slide gives 6″ sight radius but also fast slide cycle time. Combat adjustable sights, magazine chute, plus same features as Matchmaster.

Price: **$956.00**

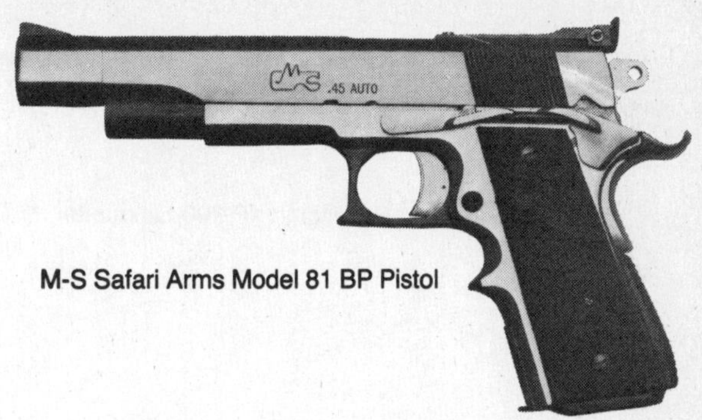

M-S Safari Arms Model 81 BP Pistol

M-S Safari Arms Model 81NM Pistol

Similar to the Matchmaster except weighs 28 oz., is 8.2″ over-all, has Ron Power match sights. Meets all requirements for National Match Service Pistols. Throated, ported, tuned and has threaded barrel bushing. Available in blue, Armaloy, Parkerize, stainless steel and electroless nickel. From M-S Safari Arms.

Price: **$868.00**

M-S SAFARI ARMS UNLIMITED SILHOUETTE PISTOL

Caliber: Any caliber with 308 head size or smaller.
Barrel: 14 15/16″ tapered
Weight: 72 oz. **Length:** 21½″ over-all.
Stocks: Fiberglass, custom painted to customer specs.
Sights: Open iron.
Features: Electronic trigger, bolt action single shot. Made by M-S Safari Arms.
Price: **$945.00**
Price: Ultimate model, heavy fluted barrel, shorter action **$945.00**

Manurhin MR.32

MANURHIN MR. 32 MATCH REVOLVER

Caliber: 32 S&W Long, 6-shot.
Barrel: 6″.
Weight: 42 oz. **Length:** 11¾″ over-all.
Stocks: Anatomically shaped grip for target shooting; supplied shaped but not finished; small, medium and large sizes.
Sights: Interchangeable blade front, adjustable underlying micrometer rear.
Features: Target/match 6-shot revolver. Trigger is externally adjustable for weight of pull, and comes with shoe. Imported from France by Manurhin International, Inc. Introduced 1984.
Price: **$665.00**
Price: Model MR. 38—same as MR. 32 except chambered for 38 Special, 5¾″ barrel. **$665.00**

Consult our Directory pages for the location of firms mentioned.

MANURHIN MR 73 LONG RANGE/SILHOUETTE REVOLVER

Caliber: 357 Magnum; 6-shot.
Barrel: 9″ (Long Range), 10¾″ (Silhouette).
Weight: 45 oz. (9″ bbl.); 50 oz. (10¾″ bbl.) **Length:** 14″ over-all (9″); 16¾″ (10¾″).
Stocks: Checkered walnut.
Sights: Interchangeable blade front, adjustable micrometer rear.
Features: Trigger externally adjustable for backlash and weight of pull. Single action only. Trigger shoe available. Imported from France by Manurhin International, Inc. Introduced 1984.
Price: **$700.00**

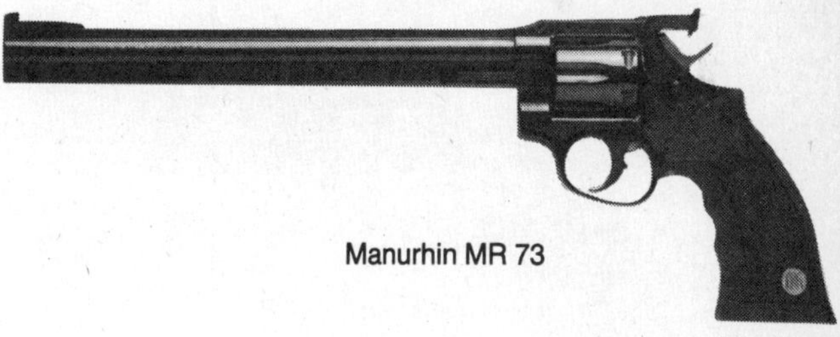
Manurhin MR 73

Morini Model CM-80

MORINI MODEL CM-80 SUPER COMPETITION

Caliber: 22 Long Rifle; single shot.
Barrel: 10″, free floating.
Weight: 30 oz., with weights. **Length:** 21.25″ over-all.
Stocks: Walnut, adjustable or wrap-around in three sizes.
Sights: Match; square notch rear adjustable for w. and e.; up to 15.6″ radius.
Features: Adjustable grip/frame angle, adjustable barrel alignment, adjustable trigger weight (5 to 120 grams), adjustable sight radius. Comes with 20-shot test target (50 meters) and case. Introduced 1985. Imported from Italy by Osborne's.
Price: Standard **$810.00**
Price: Deluxe **$955.00**

OLYMPIC RAPID FIRE PISTOL

Caliber: 22 Short.
Barrel: 5″, with exhaust ports.
Weight: 43 oz. **Length:** 10.4″ over-all.
Stocks: Wrap-around walnut; three sizes.
Sights: Fully adjustable micrometer rear.
Features: Recoil-operated semi-automatic. Trigger adjustable for weight of pull. I.S.U. legal for international competition. Introduced 1985. Imported from Spain by Osborne's.
Price: **$895.00**

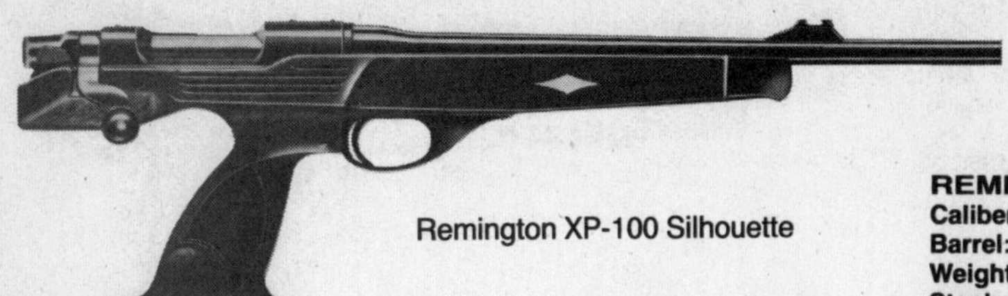
Remington XP-100 Silhouette

REMINGTON XP-100 SILHOUETTE PISTOL
Caliber: 7mm BR Remington, single-shot.
Barrel: 14¾″.
Weight: 4⅛ lbs. **Length:** 21¼″ over-all.
Stocks: Brown nylon, one piece, checkered grip.
Sights: None furnished. Drilled and tapped for scope mounts.
Features: Universal grip fits right or left hand; match-type grooved trigger, two-position thumb safety.
Price: About **$375.00**

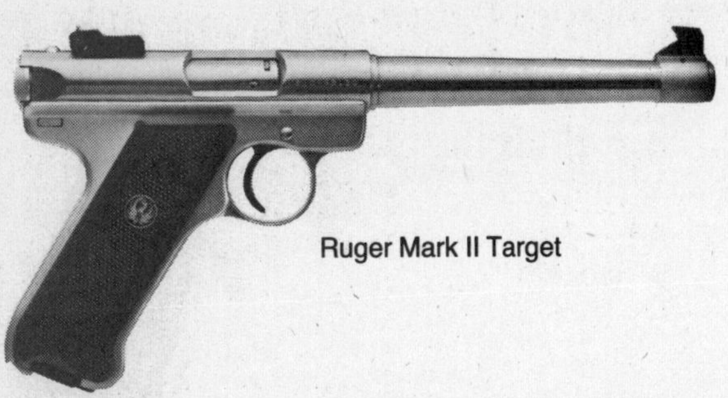
Ruger Mark II Target

RUGER MARK II TARGET MODEL AUTO PISTOL
Caliber: 22 LR only, 10-shot magazine.
Barrel: 6⅞″.
Weight: 42 oz. with 6⅞″ bbl. **Length:** 11⅛″ over-all.
Stocks: Checkered hard rubber.
Sights: .125″ blade front, micro click rear, adjustable for w. and e. Sight radius 9⅜″. Introduced 1982.
Price: Blued (MK 678) **$196.00**
Price: Stainless, (KMK 678) **$255.00**

Ruger Mark II Bull Barrel
Same gun as the Target Model except has 5½″ or 10″ heavy barrel (10″ meets all IHMSA regulations). Weight with 5½″ barrel is 42 oz., with 10″ barrel, 52 oz.
Price: Blued (MK-512, MK-10) **$196.00**
Price: Stainless (KMK-512, KMK-10) **$255.00**

Ruger Mark II Bull Barrel

SEVILLE "SILHOUETTE" SINGLE ACTION
Caliber: 357, 41, 44, 45 Win. Mag.
Barrel: 10½″.
Weight: About 55 oz.
Stocks: Smooth walnut thumbrest, or Pachmayr.
Sights: Undercut Patridge-style front, adjustable rear.
Features: Available in stainless steel or blue. Six-shot cylinder. From United Sporting Arms.
Price: Stainless **$400.00**
Price: Blue **$325.00**

SIG/Hammerli P-240

SIG/HAMMERLI P-240 TARGET PISTOL
Caliber: 32 S&W Long wadcutter, 5-shot.
Barrel: 5.9″.
Weight: 49 oz. **Length:** 10″ over-all.
Stocks: Walnut, target style with thumbrest. Adjustable palm rest optional.
Sights: Match sights; ⅛″ undercut front, ⅛″ notch micro rear click adj. for w. and e.
Features: Semi-automatic, recoil operated; meets I.S.U. and N.R.A. specs for Center Fire Pistol competition; double pull trigger adj. from 2 lbs., 15 ozs. to 3 lbs., 9 ozs.; trigger stop. Comes with cleaning kit, test targets. Imported from Switzerland by Osborne's Supplies and Mandall Shooting Supplies.
Price: About (Mandall) **$1,500.00**
Price: 22 cal. conversion unit (Osborne's) **$700.00**
Price: With standard grips (Osborne's) **$1,195.00**
Price: With adjustable grips (Osborne's) **$1,250.00**

SMITH & WESSON MODEL 29 SILHOUETTE
Caliber: 44 Magnum, 6-shot.
Barrel: 10⅝″.
Weight: 58 oz. **Length:** 16⅛″ over-all.
Stocks: Over-size target-type, checkered Goncalo Alves.
Sights: Four-position front to match the four distances of silhouette targets; micro-click rear adjustable for windage and elevation.
Features: Designed specifically for silhouette shooting. Front sight has click stops for the four pre-set ranges. Introduced 1983.
Price: Without presentation case **$455.50**

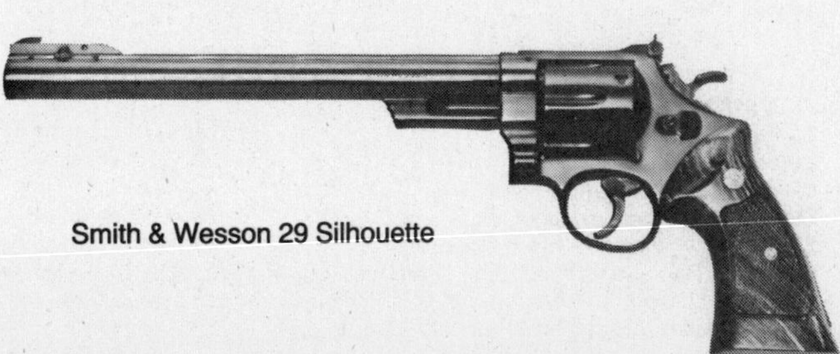
Smith & Wesson 29 Silhouette

CAUTION: PRICES CHANGE. CHECK AT GUNSHOP.

Smith & Wesson Model 41

SMITH & WESSON 22 AUTO PISTOL Model 41
Caliber: 22 LR, 10-shot clip.
Barrel: 7⅜", sight radius 9$\frac{5}{16}$".
Weight: 43½ oz. **Length:** 12" over-all.
Stocks: Checkered walnut with thumbrest, usable with either hand.
Sights: Front, ⅛" Patridge undercut; micro click rear adj. for w. and e.
Features: ⅜" wide, grooved trigger with adj. stop.
Price: S&W Bright Blue, satin matted bbl. **$417.00**

SMITH & WESSON 22 MATCH HEAVY BARREL M-41
Caliber: 22 LR, 10-shot clip.
Barrel: 5½" heavy. Sight radius, 8".
Weight: 44½ oz. **Length:** 9".
Stocks: Checkered walnut with modified thumbrest, usable with either hand.
Sights: ⅛" Patridge on ramp base. S&W micro click rear adj. for w. and e.
Features: ⅜" wide, grooved trigger; adj. trigger stop.
Price: S&W Bright Blue, satin matted top area **$417.00**

Smith & Wesson Model 52

SMITH & WESSON 38 MASTER Model 52 AUTO
Caliber: 38 Special (for Mid-range W.C. with flush-seated bullet only). 5-shot magazine.
Barrel: 5".
Weight: 41 oz. with empty magazine. **Length:** 8⅝"
Stocks: Checkered walnut.
Sights: ⅛" Patridge front, S&W micro click rear adj. for w. and e.
Features: Top sighting surfaces matte finished. Locked breech, moving barrel system; checked for 10-ring groups at 50 yards. Coin-adj. sight screws. Dry firing permissible if manual safety on.
Price: S&W Bright Blue **$591.00**

Sokolovsky Automaster

SOKOLOVSKY 45 AUTOMASTER
Caliber: 45 ACP, 6-shot magazine.
Barrel: 6".
Weight: 3.6 lbs. **Length:** 9½" over-all.
Stocks: Smooth walnut.
Sights: Ramp front, Millett fully adjustable rear.
Features: Intended for target shooting, not combat. Semi-custom built with precise tolerances. Has special "safety trigger" next to regular trigger. Most parts made of stainless steel. Introduced 1985. From Sokolovsky Corp.
Price: **$3,000.00**

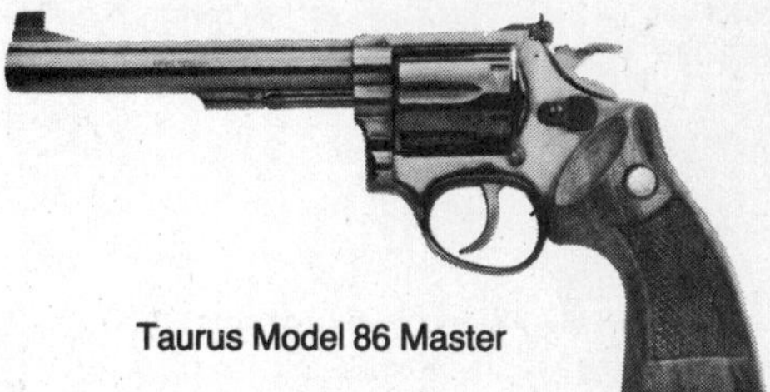
Taurus Model 86 Master

TAURUS MODEL 86 MASTER REVOLVER
Caliber: 38 Spec., 6-shot.
Barrel: 6" only.
Weight: 34 oz. **Length:** 11¼" over-all.
Stocks: Over size target-type, checkered Brazilian walnut.
Sights: Patridge front, micro. click rear adj. for w. and e.
Features: Blue finish with non-reflective finish on barrel. Imported from Brazil by Taurus International.
Price: About **$233.99**
Price: Model 96 Scout Master, same except in 22 cal., about **$233.99**

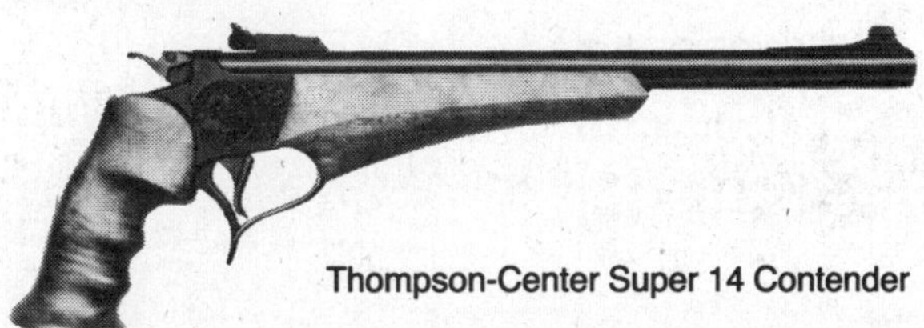
Thompson-Center Super 14 Contender

THOMPSON-CENTER SUPER 14 CONTENDER
Caliber: 22 LR, 222 Rem., 223 Rem., 6.5 TCU, 7mm TCU, 30 Herrett, 357 Herrett, 30-30 Win., 35 Rem., 357 Rem. Maximum, 44 Mag. Single shot.
Barrel: 14".
Weight: 45 oz. **Length:** 17¼" over-all.
Stocks: Select walnut grip and fore-end.
Sights: Fully adjustable target-type.
Features: Break-open action with auto safety. Interchangeable barrels for both rimfire and centerfire calibers. Introduced 1978.
Price: **$295.00**
Price: Extra barrels **$130.00**

VIRGINIAN DRAGOON STAINLESS SILHOUETTE
Caliber: 357 Mag., 44 Mag.
Barrel: 7½", 8⅜", 10½", heavy.
Weight: 51 oz. (7½" bbl.) **Length:** 11½" over-all (7½" bbl.).
Stocks: Smooth walnut; also comes with Pachmayr rubber grips.
Sights: Undercut blade front, special fully adjustable square notch rear.
Features: Designed to comply with IHMSA rules. Made of stainless steel; comes with two sets of stocks. Introduced 1982. Made in the U.S. by Interarms.
Price: Either barrel, caliber **$425.00**

Walther Free Pistol

WALTHER FREE PISTOL
Caliber: 22 LR, single shot.
Barrel: 11.7″.
Weight: 48 ozs. **Length:** 17.2″ over-all.
Stocks: Walnut, special hand-fitting design.
Sights: Fully adjustable match sights.
Features: Special electronic trigger. Matte finish blue. Introduced 1980. Imported from Germany by Interarms.
Price: **$1,195.00**

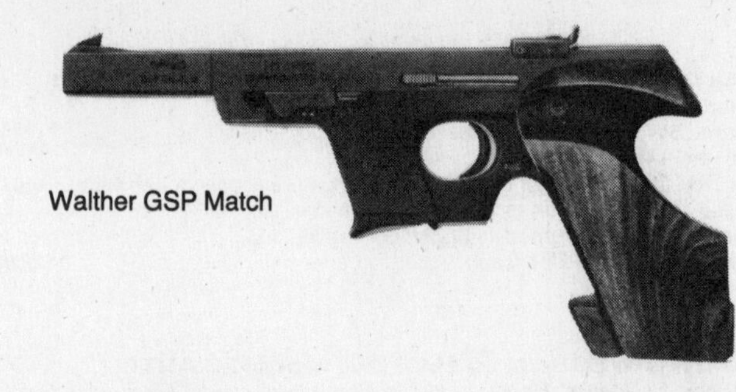
Walther GSP Match

WALTHER GSP MATCH PISTOL
Caliber: 22 LR, 32 S&W wadcutter (GSP-C), 5-shot.
Barrel: 5¾″.
Weight: 44.8 oz. (22 LR), 49.4 oz. (32). **Length:** 11.8″ over-all.
Stocks: Walnut, special hand-fitting design.
Sights: Fixed front, rear adj. for w. & e.
Features: Available with either 2.2 lb. (1000 gm) or 3 lb. (1360 gm) trigger. Spare mag., bbl. weight, tools supplied in Match Pistol Kit. Imported from Germany by Interarms.
Price: GSP **$895.00**
Price: GSP-C **$995.00**
Price: 22 LR conversion unit for GSP-C **$575.00**
Price: 22 Short conversion unit for GSP-C **$625.00**

Walther OSP Rapid-Fire Pistol
Similar to Model GSP except 22 Short only, stock has adj. free-style hand rest.
Price: **$895.00**

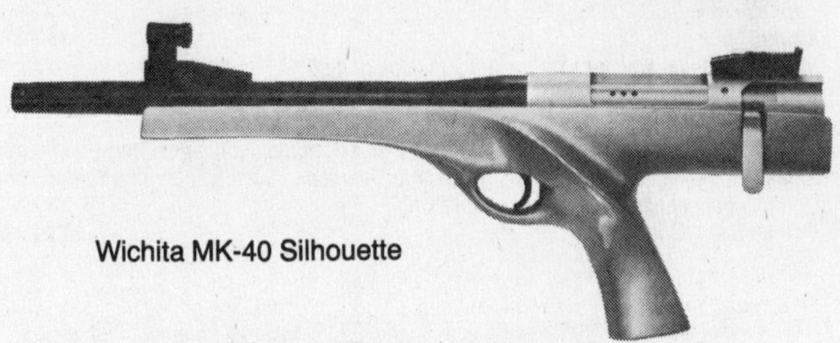
Wichita MK-40 Silhouette

WICHITA MK-40 SILHOUETTE PISTOL
Caliber: 7mm IHMSA, 308 Win. F.L. Other calibers available on special order. Single shot.
Barrel: 13″, non-glare blue; .700″ dia. muzzle.
Weight: 4½ lbs. **Length:** 19⅜″ over-all.
Stocks: Metallic gray fiberthane glass.
Sights: Wichita Multi-Range sighting system.
Features: Aluminum receiver with steel insert locking lugs, measures 1.360″ O.D.; 3 locking lug bolts, 3 gas ports; flat bolt handle; completely adjustable Wichita trigger. Introduced 1981. From Wichita Arms.
Price: **$640.00**

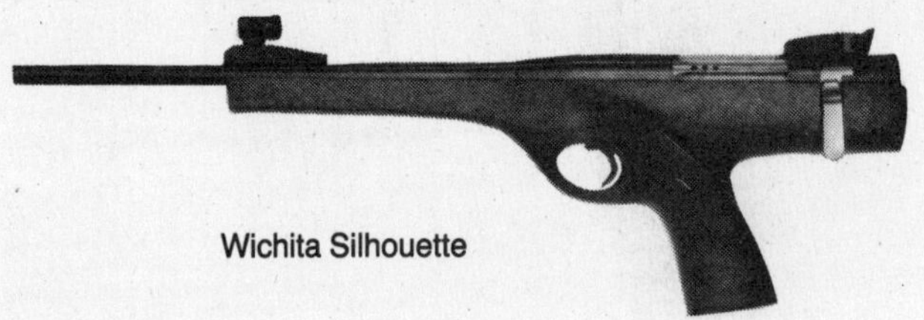
Wichita Silhouette

WICHITA SILHOUETTE PISTOL
Caliber: 7mm IHMSA, 308, 7mm x 308. Other calibers available on special order. Single shot.
Barrel: 14$\frac{15}{16}$″ or 10¾″.
Weight: 4½ lbs. **Length:** 21⅜″ over-all.
Stocks: American walnut with oil finish, or gray fiberglass. Glass bedded.
Sights: Wichita Multi-Range sight system.
Features: Comes with either right- or left-hand action with right-hand grip. Fluted bolt, flat bolt handle. Action drilled and tapped for Burris scope mounts. Non-glare satin blue finish. Wichita adjustable trigger. Introduced 1979. From Wichita Arms.
Price: Center grip stock **$750.00**
Price: As above except with Rear Position Stock and target-type Lightpull trigger. (Not illus.) **$820.00**

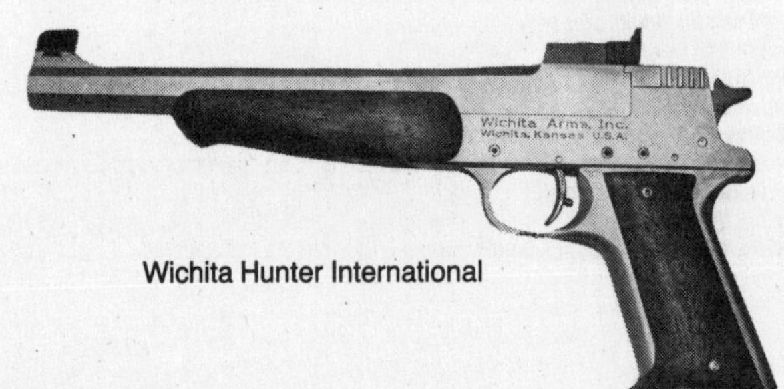

Wichita Hunter International

WICHITA CLASSIC PISTOL
Caliber: Any, up to and including 308 Win.
Barrel: 11¼″, octagon.
Weight: About 5 lbs.
Stock: Exhibition grade American black walnut. Checkered 20 lpi. Other woods available on special order.
Sights: Micro open sights standard. Receiver drilled and tapped for scope mount.
Features: Receiver and barrel octagonally shaped, finished in non-glare blue. Bolt has three locking lugs and three gas escape ports. Completely adjustable Wichita trigger. Introduced 1980. From Wichita Arms.
Price: **$1,615.00**
Price: Engraved, in walnut presentation case **$3,500.00**

WICHITA HUNTER, INTERNATIONAL PISTOL
Caliber: 7mm INT-R, 30-30 Win., 357 Mag., 357 Super Mag., single shot.
Barrel: 10½″.
Weight: International — 3 lbs., 13 oz.; Hunter — 3 lbs., 14 oz.
Stock: Walnut grip and fore-end.
Sights: International — target front, adjustable rear; Hunter has scope mount only.
Features: Made of 17-4PH stainless steel. Break-open action. Grip dimensions same as Colt 45 auto. Safety supplied only on Hunter model. Extra barrels are factory fitted. Introduced 1983. Available from Wichita Arms.
Price: International **$595.00**
Price: Hunter **$595.00**
Price: Extra barrels **$235.00**

 CAUTION: PRICES CHANGE. CHECK AT GUNSHOP.

ARMINIUS REVOLVERS
Caliber: 38 Special, 357 Magnum, 32 S&W, 22 Magnum, 22 LR.
Barrel: 2", 4", 6".
Weight: 35 oz. (6" bbl.). **Length:** 11" (6" bbl. 38).
Stocks: Checkered plastic; walnut optional for $14.95.
Sights: Ramp front, fixed rear on standard models, w. & e. adj. on target models.
Features: Thumb-release, swing-out cylinder. Ventilated rib, solid frame, swing-out cylinder. Interchangeable 22 Mag. cylinder available with 22 cal. versions. Imported from West Germany by F.I.E. Corp.
Price: .... **$112.95** to **$214.95**

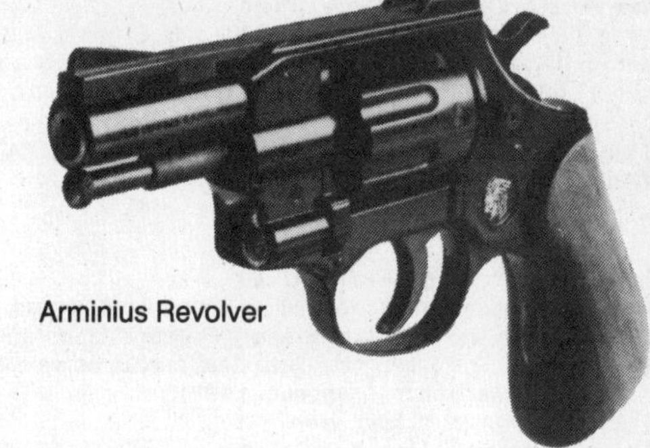
Arminius Revolver

ASTRA 357 MAGNUM REVOLVER
Caliber: 357 Magnum, 6-shot.
Barrel: 3", 4", 6", 8½".
Weight: 40 oz. (6" bbl.). **Length:** 11¼" (6" bbl.).
Stocks: Checkered walnut.
Sights: Fixed front, rear adj. for w. and e.
Features: Swing-out cylinder with countersunk chambers, floating firing pin. Target-type hammer and trigger. Imported from Spain by Interarms.
Price: 3", 4", 6" **$255.00**
Price: 8½" **$265.00**
Price: 4", stainless **$285.00**

Astra Model 41, 44, 45 Double Action Revolver
Similar to the 357 Mag. except chambered for the 41 Mag., 44 Mag. or 45 Colt. Barrel length of 6" only, giving over-all length of 11⅜". Weight is 2¾ lbs. Introduced 1980.
Price: **$275.00**
Price: 8½" bbl. (44 Mag. only) **$285.00**
Price: 6", stainless, 44 Mag. **$295.00**

CHARTER ARMS BULLDOG
Caliber: 44 Special, 5-shot.
Barrel: 2½", 3".
Weight: 19 oz. **Length:** 7¾" over-all.
Stocks: Checkered walnut, Bulldog.
Sights: Patridge-type front, square-notch rear.
Features: Wide trigger and hammer; beryllium copper firing pin.
Price: Service Blue 3" **$208.00**
Price: Stainless steel **$267.00**
Price: Service blue, 2½" **$211.00**
Price: Stainless steel, 3", neoprene grips **$271.00**

Charter Arms Stainless Bulldog

Charter Arms Bulldog Tracker
Similar to the standard Bulldog except has adjustable rear sight, 2½", 4" or 6" bull barrel, ramp front sight, square butt checkered walnut grips on 4" and 6"; Bulldog-style grips on 2½". Available in blue finish only.
Price: **$214.00**

CHARTER ARMS POLICE BULLDOG
Caliber: 32 H&R Mag., 38 Special, 6-shot.
Barrel: 4", 4" straight taper bull.
Weight: 21 oz. **Length:** 9" over-all.
Stocks: Hand checkered American walnut; square butt.
Sights: Patridge-type ramp front, notched rear (adjustable on 32 Mag.).
Features: Spring loaded unbreakable beryllium copper firing pin; steel frame; accepts +P ammunition; enclosed ejector rod; full length ejection of fired cases.
Price: Blue, 32 Mag. **$208.00**
Price: Blue, 38 Spec. **$201.00**
Price: Stainless steel, 38 Spec. only **$263.00**

Charter Arms Police Bulldog

CHARTER ARMS UNDERCOVER REVOLVER
Caliber: 38 Special, 5 shot; 32 S & W Long, 6 shot.
Barrel: 2", 3".
Weight: 16 oz. (2"). **Length:** 6¼" (2").
Stocks: Smooth walnut or checkered square butt.
Sights: Patridge-type ramp front, notched rear.
Features: Wide trigger and hammer spur. Steel frame. Police Undercover, 2" bbl. (for 38 Spec. + P loads) carry same prices as regular 38 Spec. guns.
Price: Polished Blue **$195.00**
Price: 32 S & W Long, blue, 2" **$195.00**
Price: Stainless, 38 Spec., 2" **$252.00**
Price: "P" model, blue **$198.00**
Price: "P" model, stainless **$256.00**

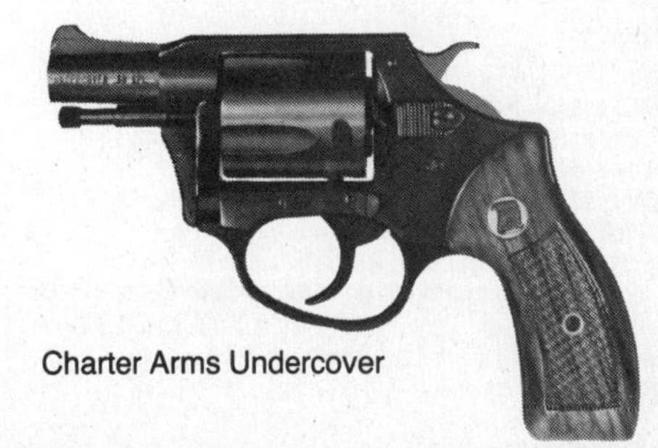
Charter Arms Undercover

Charter Stainless Off-Duty

Charter Arms Off-Duty Revolver
Similar to the Undercover except 38 Special only, 2″ barrel, Mat-Black non-glare finish. This all-steel gun comes with Red-Dot front sight and choice of smooth or checkered walnut or neoprene grips. Also available in stainless steel. Introduced 1984.
Price: Mat-Black finish **$164.00**
Price: Stainless steel **$219.00**

Charter Arms Police Undercover
Similar to the standard Undercover except 2″ barrel only, chambered for the 32 H&R Magnum and 38 Spec. (6-shot). Patridge-type front with fixed square notch rear. Blue finish or stainless steel; checkered walnut grips. Also available with Pocket Hammer. Introduced 1984.
Price: Standard hammer, 32 Mag., blue **$198.00**
Price: Pocket hammer, 32 Mag., blue **$202.00**
Price: Standard hammer, 38 Spec., blue **$195.00**
Price: Pocket hammer, 38 Spec., blue **$198.00**
Price: Standard hammer, 38 Spec., stainless **$252.00**
Price: Pocket hammer, 38 Spec., stainless **$256.00**

Charter Arms Pathfinder
Same as Undercover but in 22 LR or 22 Mag., and has 2″, 3″ or 6″ bbl. Fitted with adjustable rear sight, ramp front. Weight 18½ oz.
Price: 22 LR, blue, 3″ **$204.00**
Price: 22 LR, square butt, 6″ **$237.00**
Price: Stainless, 22 LR, 3″ **$257.00**
Price: 2″, either caliber, blue only **$204.00**

COLT DETECTIVE SPECIAL
Caliber: 38 Special, 6 shot.
Barrel: 2″.
Weight: 22 oz. **Length:** 6⅝″ over-all (2″ bbl.).
Stocks: Full, checkered walnut, round butt.
Sights: Fixed, ramp front, square notch rear.
Features: Glare-proofed sights, smooth trigger. Nickel finish, hammer shroud available as options.
Price: Blue, 2″ **$399.95**
Price: Nickel, 2″ **$449.95**

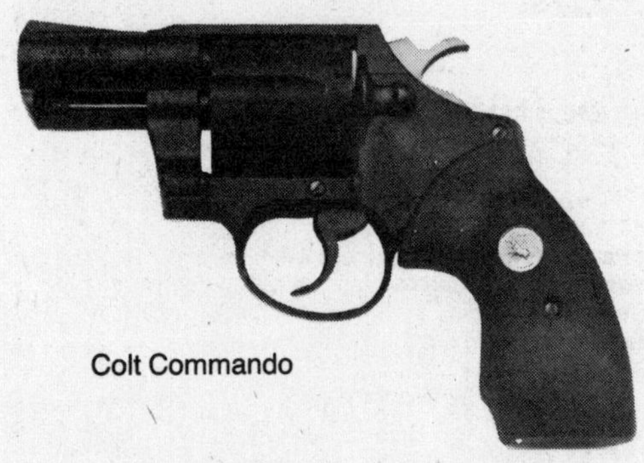
Colt Commando

Colt Commando Special
Same gun as the Detective Special except comes with rubber grips and combat-grade finish. Introduced 1984.
Price: **$254.95**

COLT AGENT
Caliber: 38 Special, 6-shot.
Barrel: 2″.
Weight: 16¾ ozs. **Length:** 6⅞″ over-all.
Stocks: Checkered walnut.
Sights: Fixed.
Features: A no-frills, lightweight version of the Detective Special. Parkerized-type finish. Name re-introduced 1982.
Price: **$220.50**

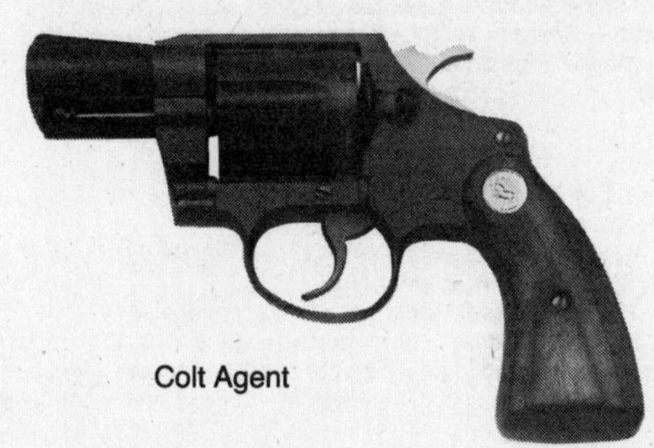
Colt Agent

COLT DIAMONDBACK REVOLVER
Caliber: 22 LR or 38 Special, 6 shot.
Barrel: 4″ or 6″ with ventilated rib.
Weight: 24 oz. (2½″ bbl.), 28½ oz. (4″ bbl.). **Length:** 9″ (4″ bbl.)
Stocks: Checkered walnut, target type, square butt.
Sights: Ramp front, adj. notch rear.
Features: Ventilated rib; grooved, crisp trigger; swing-out cylinder; wide hammer spur.
Price: Blue, 4″ or 6″, 22 or 38 .... **$429.95**
Price: Nickel, 4″ or 6″, 22 LR **$479.95**

COLT PYTHON REVOLVER
Caliber: 357 Magnum (handles all 38 Spec.), 6 shot.
Barrel: 2½″, 4″, 6″ or 8″, with ventilated rib.
Weight: 38 oz. (4″ bbl.). **Length:** 9¼″ (4″ bbl.).
Stocks: Checkered walnut, target type.
Sights: ⅛″ ramp front, adj. notch rear.
Features: Ventilated rib; grooved, crisp trigger; swing-out cylinder; target hammer.
Price: Blue, 2½″, 4″, 6″, 8″ **$642.50**
Price: Nickel, 4″, 6″, 8″ **$692.50**
Price: Stainless, 4″, 6″ **$724.95**
Price: Bright stainless, 2½″, 4″, 6″ **$734.95**

Colt Python 357

CAUTION: PRICES CHANGE. CHECK AT GUNSHOP.

COLT TROOPER MK V REVOLVER
Caliber: 357 Magnum, 6-shot.
Barrel: 4", 6".
Weight: 38 oz. (4"). **Length:** 9⅛" over-all (4").
Stocks: Checkered walnut target-style.
Sights: Orange insert ramp front, adjustable white outline rear.
Features: Vent. rib and shrouded ejector rod. Re-designed action results in short hammer throw, lightened trigger pull and faster lock time. Also has re-designed grip frame. Introduced 1982.
Price: 4" blue **$318.95**
Price: 4" nickel **$349.50**
Price: 6", blue **$318.95**
Price: 6", nickel **$349.50**

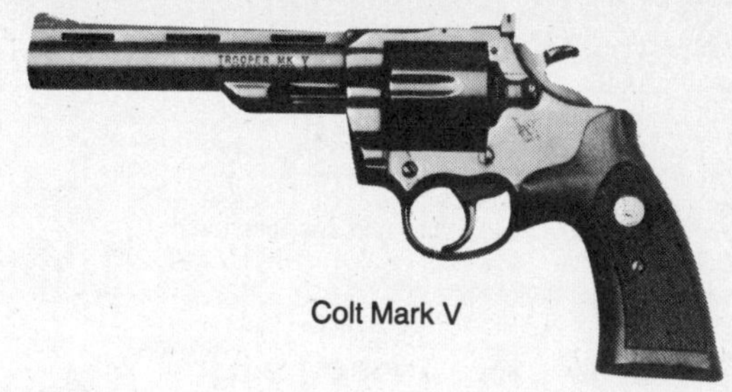

Colt Mark V

Colt Peacekeeper Revolver
Similar to the Trooper MK V. Available with 4" or 6" barrel. Weighs 42 oz. with 4" barrel; has red insert ramp front sight, white outline fully adjustable rear; rubber "gripper" round bottom combat grips; matte blue finish. Introduced 1985.
Price: 4" or 6" **$282.95**

Colt Lawman MK V Revolver
Same as the Trooper MK V except has plain bull barrel, fixed sights and is available only with 2" or 4" barrel. Blue or nickel finish. Introduced 1982.
Price: 2", 4", blue **$308.50**
Price: 2", nickel **$327.95**

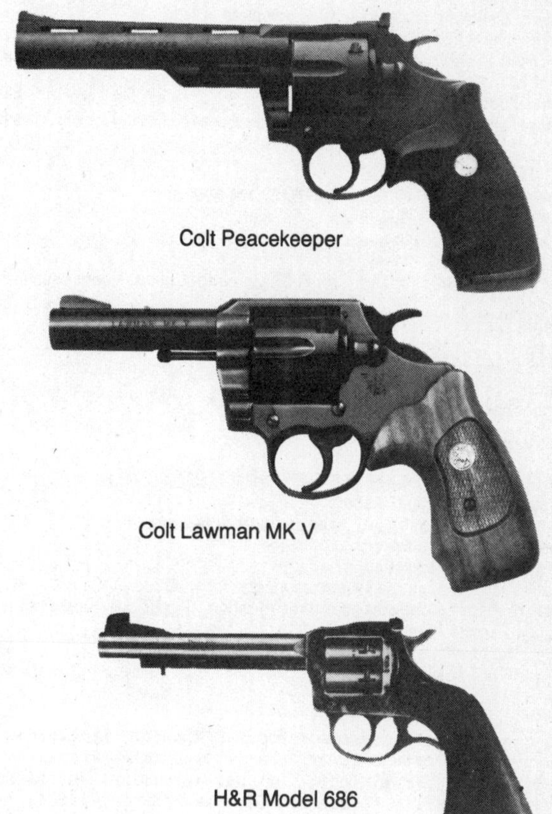
Colt Peacekeeper

Colt Lawman MK V

F.I.E. MODEL N38 "Titan Tiger" REVOLVER
Caliber: 38 Special.
Barrel: 2" or 4".
Weight: 27 oz. **Length:** 6¼" over-all. (2" bbl.)
Stocks: Checkered plastic, Bulldog style. Walnut optional ($15.95).
Sights: Fixed.
Features: Thumb-release swing-out cylinder, one stroke ejection. Made in U.S.A. by F.I.E. Corp.
Price: Blue **$129.95**
Price: Chrome **$144.95**

HARRINGTON & RICHARDSON M686 REVOLVER
Caliber: 22 LR/22 WMRF, 6-shot.
Barrel: 4½", 5½", 7½", 10" or 12".
Weight: 31 oz. (4½"), 41 oz. (12").
Stocks: Two piece, smooth walnut-finished hardwood.
Sights: Western type blade front, adj. rear.
Features: Blue barrel and cylinder, "antique" color case-hardened frame, ejector tube and trigger. Comes with extra cylinder.
Price: 4½", 5½", 7½", 10" bbl. **$176.50**
Price: 12" bbl. **$195.50**

H&R Model 686

Harrington & Richardson Model 586 H&R Magnum
Similar to the Model 686 except chambered for 32 H&R Magnum. Redesigned action, 5-shot cylinder, available with 4½", 5½", 7½" and 10" barrel. Color case-hardened frame. Introduced 1984.
Price: **$195.00**

Harrington & Richardson Model 649 Revolver
Similar to model 686 except has 5½" or 7½" barrel, two piece walnut-finished hardwood grips, western-type blade front sight, adjustable rear. Loads and ejects from side. Weighs 32 oz.
Price: **$152.50**
Price: Model 650—as above except nickel finish, 5½" only **$162.50**

HARRINGTON & RICHARDSON M622 REVOLVER
Caliber: 22 S, L or LR, 6 shot.
Barrel: 2½", 4", round bbl.
Weight: 20 oz. (2½" bbl.).
Stocks: Checkered black Cycolac.
Sights: Fixed, blade front, square notch rear.
Features: Solid steel, Bantamweight frame; patented safety rim cylinder; non-glare finish on frame; coil springs.
Price: Blued, 2½", 4" bbl. **$103.50**
Price: Model 632 (32 cal.), 2½" bbl. only **$103.50**

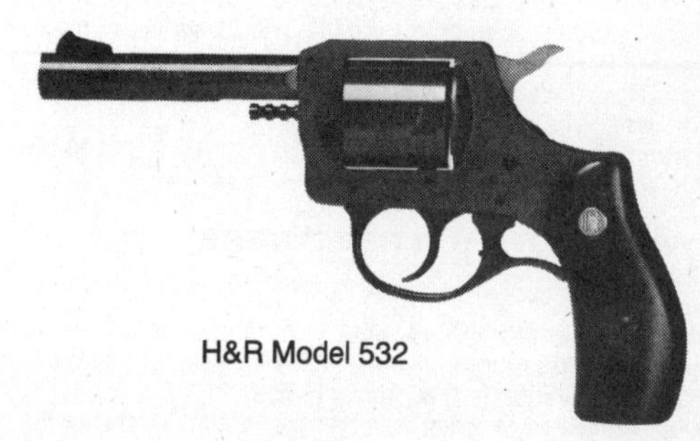
H&R Model 532

Harrington & Richardson Model 532 H&R Magnum
Similar to the Model 622/632 except redesigned to accept the 32 H&R Magnum cartridge with 5-shot cylinder. Solid frame design. Available with 2½" barrel (round butt), 4" barrel (round butt); blue finish, wood grips. Introduced 1984.
Price: **$115.00**

HARRINGTON & RICHARDSON M732
Caliber: 32 S&W or 32 S&W Long, 6 shot.
Barrel: 2½" or 4" round barrel.
Weight: 23½ oz. (2½" bbl.), 26 oz. (4" bbl.).
Stocks: Checkered, black Cycolac or walnut.
Sights: Blade front; fixed notch rear.
Features: Swing-out cylinder with auto. extractor return.
Price: Blued, 2½" or 4" bbl. **$126.50**
Price: Nickel, 2½" bbl. (Model 733) **$136.50**

H&R Model 732

HARRINGTON & RICHARDSON M929
Caliber: 22 S, L or LR, 9 shot.
Barrel: 2½", 4" or 6".
Weight: 26 oz. (4" bbl.).
Stocks: Checkered, black Cycolac or walnut.
Sights: Blade front; adjustable rear on 4" and 6" models.
Features: Swing-out cylinder with auto. extractor return. Round-grip frame on 2½" only.
Price: Blued, 2½", 4" or 6" bbl. **$126.50**
Price: Nickel (Model 930), 2½" or 4" bbl. **$136.50**

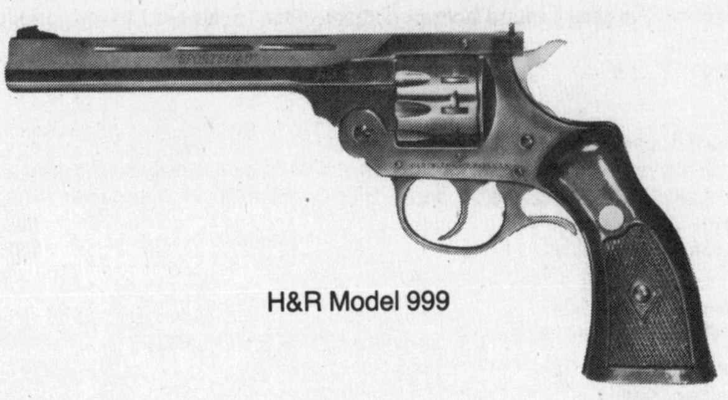
H&R Model 999

HARRINGTON & RICHARDSON M949
Caliber: 22 S, L or LR, 9 shot.
Barrel: 5½" round with ejector rod.
Weight: 31 oz.
Stocks: Two-piece, smooth frontier style wrap-around, walnut-finished hardwood.
Sights: Western-type blade front, rear adj. for w.
Features: Contoured loading gate; wide hammer spur; single and double action. Western type ejector-housing.
Price: H&R Crown Luster Blue **$126.50**
Price: Nickel (Model 950) **$136.50**

H&R SPORTSMAN MODEL 999 REVOLVER
Caliber: 22 S, L or LR, 9 shot.
Barrel: 4", 6" top-break (16" twist), integral fluted vent. rib.
Weight: 34 oz. (6"). **Length:** 10½".
Stocks: Checkered walnut.
Sights: Front adjustable for elevation, rear for windage.
Features: Simultaneous automatic ejection, trigger guard extension. H&R Crown Lustre Blue.
Price: Blued, 4" **$215.00**
Price: Blued, 6" engraved **$525.00**

Harrington & Richardson Model 504 H&R Magnum
Similar to the Model 904 swing-out except has redesigned action for the 32 H&R Magnum; 5-shot cylinder, wood grips. Available in 3" with round butt, 4" round or square butt, 6" square butt. Blue finish. Introduced 1984.
Price: **$185.00**

KORTH REVOLVER
Caliber: 22 LR, 22 Mag., 357 Mag., 9mm Parabellum.
Barrel: 3", 4", 6".
Weight: 33 to 38 oz. **Length:** 8" to 11" over-all.
Stocks: Checkered walnut, sport or combat.
Sights: Blade front, rear adjustable for windage and elevation.
Features: Four interchangeable cylinders available. Major parts machined from hammer-forged steel; cylinder gap of .002". High polish blue finish. Presentation models have gold trim. Imported from Germany by Osborne's, Beeman.
Price: Polished (Osborne's) **$1,095.00**
Price: Matte finish (Osborne's) **$995.00**
Price: From Beeman .... **$1,100.00** to **$2,995.00**

LLAMA COMANCHE II REVOLVERS
Caliber: 357 Mag.
Barrel: 6", 4".
Weight: 28 oz. **Length:** 9¼" (4" bbl.).
Stocks: Checkered walnut.
Sights: Fixed blade front, rear adj. for w. & e.
Features: Ventilated rib, wide spur hammer. Satin chrome finish available. Imported from Spain by Stoeger Industries.
Price: Blue finish **$244.95**
Price: Satin chrome **$324.95**

HARRINGTON & RICHARDSON MODELS 904, 905
Caliber: 22 LR, 9-shot (M904, 905).
Barrel: 4" (M904 only), 6" target bull.
Weight: 32 oz.
Stocks: Smooth walnut.
Sights: Blade front, fully adjustable "Wind-Elv" rear.
Features: Swing-out cylinder design with coil spring construction. Single stroke ejection. Target-style bull barrel has raised solid rib giving a 7¼" sight radius.
Price: 904 .... **$167.50**
Price: M905, 4", H&R "Hard-Guard" nickel finish **$179.50**

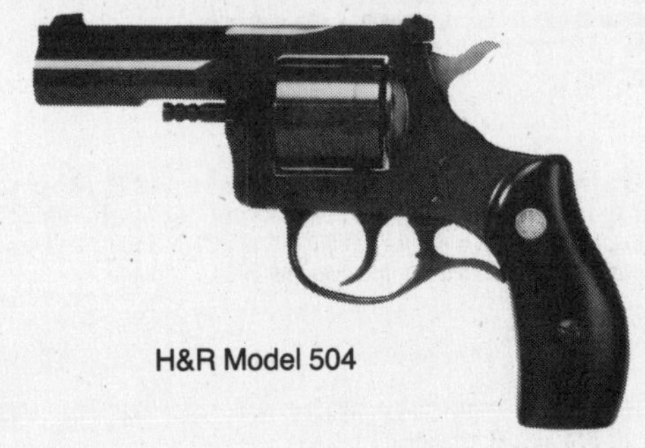
H&R Model 504

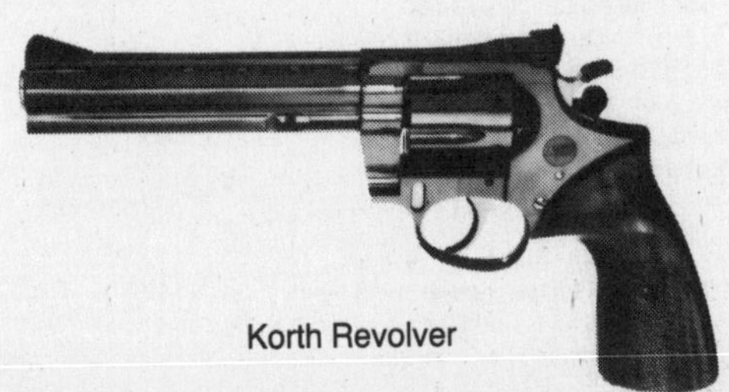
Korth Revolver

CAUTION: PRICES CHANGE. CHECK AT GUNSHOP.

Llama Super Comanche V Revolver
Similar to the Comanche except; large frame, 357 or 44 Mag., 4″, 6″ or 8½″ barrel only; 6-shot cylinder; smooth, extra wide trigger; wide spur hammer; over-size walnut, target-style grips. Weight is 3 lbs., 2 ozs. Blue finish only.
Price: 44 Mag. **$334.95**
Price: 357 Mag. **$314.95**

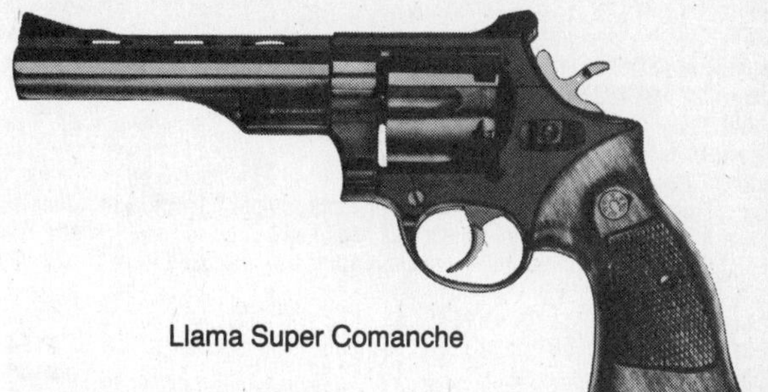
Llama Super Comanche

MANURHIN MR 73 SPORT REVOLVER
Caliber: 357 Magnum, 6-shot.
Barrel: 5.25″.
Weight: 37 oz. **Length:** 10.4″ over-all.
Stocks: Checkered walnut.
Sights: Blade front, fully adjustable rear.
Features: Double action with adjustable trigger. High-polish blue finish, "Straw' colored hammer and trigger. Comes with sight adjusting tool. Imported from France by Manurhin International, Inc. Introduced 1984.
Price: **$665.00**

RG MODEL 23 REVOLVER
Caliber: 22 LR, 6 shot.
Barrel: 1¾″ or 3⅜″.
Weight: 16 oz. **Length:** 5⅛″ over-all.
Stocks: Checkered plastic.
Sights: Fixed.
Features: Swing out cylinder with central ejector. From RG Industries.
Price: Blue, either barrel **$76.00**
Price: Nickel, 1¾″ barrel **$88.00**
Price: Nickel, 3⅜″ barrel **$66.15**

Consult our Directory pages for the location of firms mentioned.

RG MODEL 38S REVOLVER
Caliber: 38 Special, 6-shot.
Barrel: 3″ or 4″.
Weight: 32 oz. (3″ bbl.). **Length:** 8¼″ over-all.
Stocks: Checkered walnut or plastic.
Sights: Blade front, rear adjustable for windage.
Features: Swing out cylinder with spring ejector. From RG Industries.
Price: With plastic grips **$125.55**
Price: With wood grips **$135.00**

RG MODEL 39 REVOLVER
Caliber: 32 S&W (6-shot) or 38 Special (5-shot).
Barrel: 2″.
Weight: 21 oz. **Length:** 7″ over-all.
Stocks: Checkered walnut.
Sights: Fixed.
Features: Swing out cylinder with ejector spring. Blue finish. From RG Industries.
Price: 32 S&W **$125.00**
Price: 38 Special **$130.00**
Price: As above, nickel **$147.00**
Price: Model 39P (bobbed hammer) **$134.00**

ROSSI MODELS 68, 69 & 70 DA REVOLVERS
Caliber: 22 LR (M 70), 32 S & W (M 69), 38 Spec. (M 68).
Barrel: 2″, 3″.
Weight: 22 oz.
Stocks: Checkered wood.
Sights: Ramp front, low profile adj. rear.
Features: All-steel frame. Thumb latch operated swing-out cylinder. Introduced 1978. Imported from Brazil by Interarms.
Price: 22, 32, or 38, blue **$139.00**
Price: As above, 38 Spec. only with 4″ bbl. as M 31 .... **$139.00**
Price: Model 51 (6″ bbl., 22 cal.) **$149.00**
Price: M68, M69, M70 in nickel **$144.00**
Price: M68/2 (2″ barrel) **$149.00**

RG MODEL 14S REVOLVER
Caliber: 22 LR, 6-shot.
Barrel: 1¾″ or 3″.
Weight: 15 oz. **Length:** 5½″ over-all.
Stocks: Checkered plastic.
Sights: Fixed.
Features: Pull-pin swing out cylinder. From RG Industries.
Price: **$61.25**

RG 38S

RG 39

Rossi Model 68

Rossi Model 88 Stainless

ROSSI MODEL 88, 89 STAINLESS REVOLVERS

Caliber: 32 S&W, 38 Spec., 5-shot.
Barrel: 2″, 3″.
Weight: 22 oz. **Length:** 7.5″ over-all.
Stocks: Checkered wood, service-style.
Sights: Ramp front, square notch rear drift adjustable for windage.
Features: All metal parts except springs are of 440 stainless steel; matte finish; small frame for concealability. Introduced 1983. Imported from Brazil by Interarms.
Price: 3″ barrel **$164.00**
Price: M88/2 (2″ barrel).......... **$174.00**
Price: M89 (32 cal.).......... **$149.00**

Rossi Model 85 Stainless

ROSSI MODEL 951 REVOLVER

Caliber: 38 Special, 6 shot.
Barrel: 4″, vent. rib.
Weight: 30 oz. **Length:** 9″ over-all.
Stocks: Checkered hardwood, combat-style.
Sights: Colored insert front, fully adjustable rear.
Features: Polished blue finish, shrouded ejector rod. Medium-size frame. Introduced 1985. Imported from Brazil by Interarms.
Price: M951.......... **$184.00**
Price: M851 (as above, stainless).......... **$204.00**
Price: M85 (as above, 3″ barrel).......... **$204.00**
Price: M941 (as above, solid rib).......... **$169.00**
Price: M841 (as above, stainless steel).......... **$189.00**
Price: M94 (3″ barrel, solid rib) **$169.00**

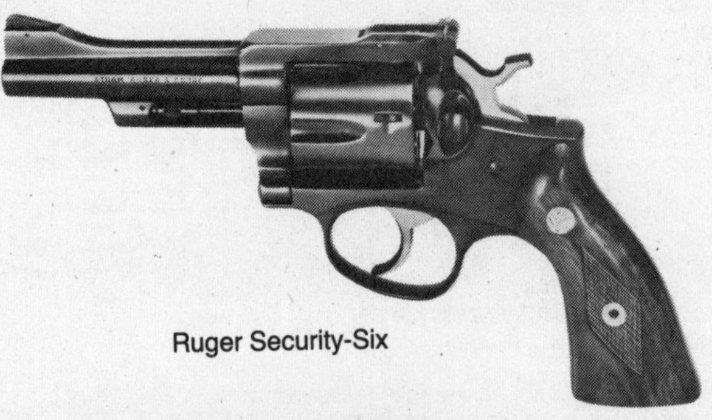
Ruger Security-Six

RUGER SECURITY-SIX Model 117

Caliber: 357 Mag. (also fires 38 Spec.), 6-shot.
Barrel: 2¾″, 6″, or 4″ heavy barrel.
Weight: 33½ oz. (4″ bbl.) **Length:** 9¼″ (4″ bbl.) over-all.
Stocks: Goncalo Alves semi-target style, oversized target, or checkered rubber.
Sights: Patridge-type front on ramp, white outline rear adj. for w. and e.
Features: Music wire coil springs throughout. Hardened steel construction. Integral ejector rod shroud and sighting rib. Can be disassembled using only a coin.
Price: 2¾″, 6″ and 4″ heavy barrel **$309.00**
Price: 4″ HB, 6″ with target grips, white outline rear sight, red ramp front.......... **$324.00**

Ruger Police Service-Six

RUGER POLICE SERVICE-SIX 107, 108, 707, 708

Caliber: 357 (Model 107, 707), 38 Spec. (Model 108, 708), 6-shot.
Barrel: 2¾″ or 4″.
Weight: 33½ oz. (4″ bbl.). **Length:** 9¼″ (4 bbl.) over-all.
Stocks: Checkered rubber or Goncalo Alves.
Sights: Fixed, non-adjustable.
Features: Solid frame; barrel, rib and ejector rod housing combined in one unit. All steel construction Field strips without tools.
Price: Model 107 (357) 2¾″ and 4″.......... **$287.50**
Price: Model 108 (38) 4″.......... **$287.50**
Price: Mod. 707 (357), Stainless, 4″, Goncalo Alves or rubber grips. **$310.00**
Price: Mod. 708 (38), Stainless, 4″, Goncalo Alves or rubber grips... **$310.00**

Ruger Speed-Six

RUGER SPEED-SIX Models 207, 208, 737, 738

Caliber: 357 (Model 207), 38 Spec. (Model 208), 6-shot.
Barrel: 2¾″ or 4″.
Weight: 31 oz. (2¾″ bbl.). **Length:** 7¾″ over-all (2¾″ bbl.).
Stocks: Goncalo Alves or checkered rubber with finger grooves.
Sights: Fixed, non-adjustable.
Features: Same basic mechanism as Security-Six. Hammer without spur available on special order. All steel construction. Music wire coil springs used throughout.
Price: Model 207 (357 Mag., 2¾″, 4″, Goncalo Alves or checkered rubber grips).......... **$292.00**
Price: Model 208 (38 Spec. only, 2¾″, Goncalo Alves or checkered grips).......... **$292.00**
Price: Mod. 737 (357 Mag., stainless, 2¾″, 4″, Goncalo Alves or checkered rubber grips) **$320.00**
Price: Mod. 738 (38 Spec. only, stainless, 2¾″, Goncalo Alves grips) **$320.00**

CAUTION: PRICES CHANGE. CHECK AT GUNSHOP.

RUGER STAINLESS SECURITY-SIX Model 717
Caliber: 357 Mag. (also fires 38 Spec.), 6-shot.
Barrel: 2¾", 4" or 6".
Weight: 33 oz. (4 bbl.). **Length:** 9¼" (4" bbl.) over-all.
Stocks: Goncalo Alves or checkered rubber.
Sights: Patridge-type front, fully adj. rear.
Features: All metal parts except sights made of stainless steel. Sights are black alloy for maximum visibility. Same mechanism and features found in regular Security-Six.
Price: 2¾", 6" and 4" heavy barrel **$338.00**
Price: 4" HB, 6" with checkered rubber grips, red ramp front, white outline rear sight **$353.00**

Ruger Security-Six 717

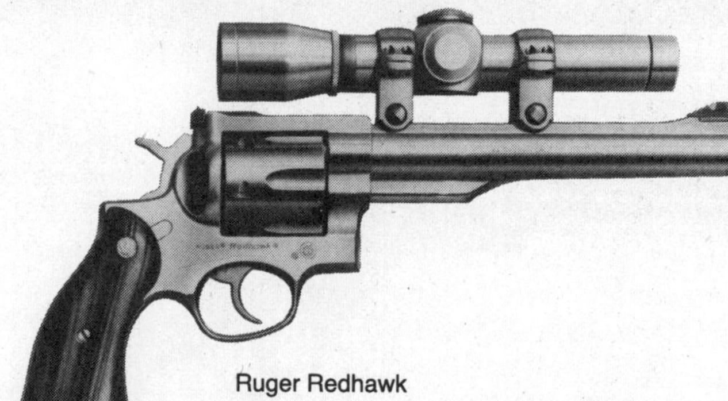
Ruger Redhawk

RUGER REDHAWK
Caliber: 357 Mag., 41 Mag., 44 Rem. Mag., 6-shot.
Barrel: 5½", 7½".
Weight: About 54 oz. (7½" bbl.). **Length:** 13" over-all (7½" barrel).
Stocks: Square butt Goncalo Alves.
Sights: Interchangeable Patridge-type front, rear adj. for w. & e.
Features: Stainless steel, brushed satin finish. Has a 9½" sight radius. Introduced 1979.
Price: **$397.00**
Price: With Ruger stainless scope rings (44 Mag. only) **$436.00**

SMITH & WESSON M&P Model 10 REVOLVER
Caliber: 38 Special, 6 shot.
Barrel: 2", 4", 5" or 6".
Weight: 30½ oz. (4" bbl.). **Length:** 9¼" (4" bbl.).
Stocks: Checkered walnut, Magna. Round or square butt.
Sights: Fixed, ⅛" ramp front, square notch rear.
Price: Blued **$247.00**
Price: Nickeled **$265.50**

Smith & Wesson 38 M&P Heavy Barrel Model 10
Same as regular M&P except: 3" or 4" ribbed bbl. with ⅛" ramp front sight, square rear, square butt, wgt. 34 oz.
Price: Blued **$247.00**
Price: Nickeled **$265.50**

S&W Model 10-H.B.

SMITH & WESSON 38 M&P AIRWEIGHT Model 12
Caliber: 38 Special, 6 shot.
Barrel: 2" or 4".
Weight: 18 oz. (2" bbl.). **Length:** 6⅞" over-all.
Stocks: Checkered walnut, Magna. Round or square butt.
Sights: Fixed, ⅛" serrated ramp front, square notch rear.
Price: Blued **$320.50**
Price: Nickeled **$360.50**

S&W Model 13

SMITH & WESSON Model 13 H.B. M&P
Caliber: 357 and 38 Special, 6 shot.
Barrel: 3" or 4".
Weight: 34 oz. **Length:** 9¼" over-all (4" bbl.).
Stocks: Checkered walnut, service.
Sights: ⅛" serrated ramp front, fixed square notch rear.
Features: Heavy barrel, K-frame, square butt.
Price: Blue, M-13 .... **$247.00**
Price: Nickel **$268.00**
Price: Model 65, as above in stainless steel **$268.50**

SMITH & WESSON COMBAT MASTERPIECE
Caliber: 38 Special (M15) or 22 LR (M18), 6 shot.
Barrel: 2" or 4" (M15) 4" (M18).
Weight: Loaded, 22 36½ oz., 38 34 oz. **Length:** 9⅛" (4" bbl.).
Stocks: Checkered walnut, Magna. Grooved tangs and trigger.
Sights: Front, ⅛" Baughman Quick Draw on ramp, micro click rear, adjustable for w. and e.
Price: Blued, M-15, 2" or 4" **$290.50**
Price: Nickel M-15, 2" or 4" **$311.00**
Price: Blued, M-18, 4" (sq. butt, adj. sights) **$352.00**

SMITH & WESSON MODEL 17 K-22 MASTERPIECE
Caliber: 22 LR, 6-shot.
Barrel: 6", 8⅜".
Weight: 38½ oz. (6" bbl). **Length:** 11⅛" over-all.
Stocks: Checkered walnut, service.
Sights: Patridge front, S&W micro. click rear adjustable for windage and elevation.
Features: Grooved tang and trigger. Polished blue finish.
Price: 6" **$357.00**
Price: 8¾" bbl. **$371.00**
Price: Model 48, as above in 22 Mag., 4" or 6" **$364.00**
Price: 8⅜" bbl. **$380.50**

SMITH & WESSON 357 COMBAT MAGNUM Model 19
Caliber: 357 Magnum and 38 Special, 6 shot.
Barrel: 2½", 4", 6".
Weight: 35 oz. **Length:** 9½" (4" bbl.).
Stocks: Checkered Goncalo Alves, target. Grooved tangs and trigger.
Sights: Front, ⅛" Baughman Quick Draw on 2½" or 4" bbl., Patridge on 6" bbl., micro click rear adjustable for w. and e.
Price: S&W Bright Blue or Nickel, adj. sights, from **$285.50**

S&W Model 19

SMITH & WESSON MODEL 25 REVOLVER
Caliber: 45 Colt, 6-shot.
Barrel: 4", 6", 8⅜".
Weight: About 45 oz. **Length:** 11⅞" over-all (6" bbl.).
Stocks: Checkered Goncalo Alves, target-type.
Sights: ⅛" S&W red ramp front, S&W micrometer click rear with white outline.
Features: Available in Bright Blue or nickel finish; target trigger, target hammer. Contact S&W for complete price list.
Price: 4", 6", blue or nickel **$347.00**
Price: 8⅜", blue or nickel **$359.50**

S&W Model 25

SMITH & WESSON 357 MAGNUM M-27 REVOLVER
Caliber: 357 Magnum and 38 Special, 6 shot.
Barrel: 4", 6", 8⅜".
Weight: 44 oz. (6" bbl.). **Length:** 11¼" (6" bbl.).
Stocks: Checkered walnut, Magna. Grooved tangs and trigger.
Sights: Any S&W target front, micro click rear, adjustable for w. and e.
Price: S&W Bright Blue or Nickel, 4", 6" **$327.00**
Price: 8⅜" bbl., sq. butt, target hammer, trigger, stocks **$351.00**

SMITH & WESSON HIGHWAY PATROLMAN Model 28
Caliber: 357 Magnum and 38 Special, 6 shot.
Barrel: 4", 6".
Weight: 44 oz. (6" bbl.). **Length:** 11¼" (6" bbl.).
Stocks: Checkered walnut, Magna. Grooved tangs and trigger.
Sights: Front, ⅛" Baughman Quick Draw, on plain ramp, micro click rear, adjustable for w. and e.
Price: S&W Satin Blue, sandblasted frame edging and barrel top ... **$305.50**
Price: With target stocks.................................... **$327.00**

S&W Model 29

SMITH & WESSON 44 MAGNUM Model 29 REVOLVER
Caliber: 44 Magnum, 44 Special or 44 Russian, 6 shot.
Barrel: 4", 6", 8⅜", 10⅝".
Weight: 47 oz. (6" bbl.), 43 oz. (4" bbl.). **Length:** 11⅞" (6½" bbl.).
Stocks: Oversize target type, checkered Goncalo Alves. Tangs and target trigger grooved, checkered target hammer.
Sights: ⅛" red ramp front, micro click rear, adjustable for w. and e.
Features: Includes presentation case.
Price: S&W Bright Blue or Nickel 4", 6" **$409.00**
Price: 8⅜" bbl., blue or nickel **$423.50**
Price: 10⅝", blue only.. **$423.50**
Price: Model 629 (stainless steel), 4", 6" **$472.50**
Price: Model 629, 8⅜" barrel.................................. **$488.50**

S&W Model 31

SMITH & WESSON 32 REGULATION POLICE Model 31
Caliber: 32 S&W Long, 6 shot.
Barrel: 2", 3".
Weight: 18¾ oz. (3" bbl.). **Length:** 7½" (3" bbl.).
Stocks: Checkered walnut, Magna.
Sights: Fixed, ⅒" serrated ramp front, square notch rear.
Features: Blued
Price:.. **$290.00**

SMITH & WESSON 1953 Model 34, 22/32 KIT GUN
Caliber: 22 LR, 6 shot.
Barrel: 2", 4".
Weight: 22½ oz. (4" bbl.). **Length:** 8" (4" bbl. and round butt).
Stocks: Checkered walnut, round or square butt.
Sights: Front, ⅒" serrated ramp, micro. click rear, adjustable for w. & e.
Price: Blued **$284.50**
Price: Nickeled... **$308.00**
Price: Model 63, as above in stainless, 4"....................... **$331.50**

Smith & Wesson Model 650/651 Magnum Kit Gun
Similar to the Models 34 and 63 except chambered for the 22 WMR. Model 650 has 3" barrel, round butt and fixed sights; Model 651 has 4" barrel, square butt and adjustable sights. Both guns made of stainless steel. Introduced 1983.
Price: Model 650 .... **$288.00**
Price: Model 651 .... **$316.00**

SMITH & WESSON 38 CHIEFS SPECIAL & AIRWEIGHT
Caliber: 38 Special, 5 shot.
Barrel: 2″, 3″.
Weight: 19 oz. (2″ bbl.); 14 oz. (AIRWEIGHT). **Length:** 6½″ (2″ bbl. and round butt).
Stocks: Checkered walnut, Magna. Round or square butt.
Sights: Fixed, 1/10″ serrated ramp front, square notch rear.
Price: Price: Blued, standard Model 36 .... **$254.00**
Price: As above, nickel **$274.00**
Price: Blued, Airweight Model 37 .... **$285.50**
Price: As above, nickel **$321.50**

S&W Model 38

Smith & Wesson 60 Chiefs Special Stainless
Same as Model 36 except: 2″ bbl. and round butt only.
Price: Stainless steel **$316.00**

SMITH & WESSON BODYGUARD MODEL 38
Caliber: 38 Special; 5 shot, double action revolver.
Barrel: 2″.
Weight: 14½ oz. **Length:** 6⅜″.
Stocks: Checkered walnut, Magna.
Sights: Fixed 1/10″ serrated ramp front, square notch rear.
Features: Alloy frame; integral hammer shroud.
Price: Blued **$303.00**
Price: Nickeled **$340.50**

S&W Model 649

Smith & Wesson Bodyguard Model 49, 649 Revolvers
Same as Model 38 except steel construction, weight 20½ oz.
Price: Blued, Model 49 .... **$270.00**
Price: Nickeled, Model 49 .... **$293.00**
Price: Stainless Model 649 .... **$323.00**

SMITH & WESSON 41 MAGNUM Model 57 REVOLVER
Caliber: 41 Magnum, 6 shot.
Barrel: 4″, 6″ or 8⅜″.
Weight: 48 oz. (6″ bbl.). **Length:** 11⅜″ (6″ bbl.).
Stocks: Oversize target type checkered Goncalo Alves.
Sights: ⅛″ red ramp front, micro. click rear, adj. for w. and e.
Features: Includes presentation case.
Price: S&W Bright Blue or Nickel 4″, 6″ **$347.00**
Price: 8⅜″ bbl. **$359.50**

S&W Model 57

SMITH & WESSON MODEL 64 STAINLESS M&P
Caliber: 38 Special, 6-shot.
Barrel: 4″.
Weight: 30½ oz. **Length:** 9½″ over-all.
Stocks: Checkered walnut, service style.
Sights: Fixed, ⅛″ serrated ramp front, square notch rear.
Features: Satin finished stainless steel, square butt.
Price: **$268.50**

SMITH & WESSON MODEL 66 STAINLESS COMBAT MAGNUM
Caliber: 357 Magnum and 38 Special, 6-shot.
Barrel: 2½″, 4″, 6″.
Weight: 35 oz. **Length:** 9½″ over-all.
Stocks: Checkered Goncalo Alves target.
Sights: Front, ⅛″ Baughman Quick Draw on plain ramp, micro clock rear adj. for w. and e.
Features: Satin finish stainless steel, combat trigger with adj. stop.
Price: **$319.50**

S&W Model 64-H.B.

SMITH & WESSON MODEL 67 K-38 STAINLESS COMBAT MASTERPIECE
Caliber: 38 Special, 6-shot.
Barrel: 4″.
Weight: 34 oz. (loaded). **Length:** 9⅛″ over-all.
Stocks: Checkered walnut, service style.
Sights: Front, ⅛″ Baughman Quick Draw on ramp, micro click rear adj. for w. and e.
Features: Stainless steel. Square butt frame with grooved tangs, grooved trigger with adj. stop.
Price: **$325.50**

SMITH & WESSON MODEL 547
Caliber: 9mm Parabellum
Barrel: 3″ or 4″ heavy.
Weight: 34 oz. (4″ barrel). **Length:** 9⅛″ over-all (4″ barrel).
Stocks: Checkered square butt Magna Service (4″), checkered walnut target, round butt (3″).
Sights: ⅛″ Serrated ramp front, fixed ⅛″ square notch rear.
Features: K-frame revolver uses special extractor system—no clips required. Has ¼″ half-spur hammer. Introduced 1981.
Price: Blue only **$317.00**

SMITH & WESSON MODEL 586 Distinguished Combat Magnum
Caliber: 357 Magnum.
Barrel: 4", 6", both heavy.
Weight: 46 oz. (6"), 42 oz. (4").
Stocks: Goncalo Alves target-type with speed loader cutaway.
Sights: Baughman red ramp front, S&W micrometer click rear (or fixed).
Features: Uses new L-frame, but takes all K-frame grips. Full length ejector rod shroud. Smooth combat-type trigger, semi-target type hammer. Trigger stop on 6" models; 4" models factory fitted with target hammer and trigger will have trigger stop. Also available in stainless as Model 686. Introduced 1981.
Price: Model 586 (blue only) **$310.00**
Price: Model 586, nickel **$310.00**
Price: Model 686 (stainless) **$340.00**
Price: Model 581 (fixed sight, blue), 4" **$256.00**
Price: Model 581, nickel **$279.00**
Price: Model 681 (fixed sight, stainless) **$279.00**

S&W Model 586

SMITH & WESSON MODEL 624 REVOLVER
Caliber: 44 Special, 6 shot.
Barrel: 4" or 6".
Weight: 41½ oz. (4" bbl.). **Length:** 9½" over-all (4" bbl.)
Stocks: Checkered Goncalo Alves, target-type.
Sights: Black ramp front, fully adjustable micrometer click rear.
Features: Limited production of 10,000 guns. Stainless version of the Model 24. The 6" version has target hammer and trigger. Introduced 1985.
Price: 4" barrel **$449.50**
Price: 6" barrel **$463.50**

S&W Model 624

Smith & Wesson Accessories
Target hammers with low, broad, deeply-checkered spur, and wide-swaged, grooved target trigger. For all frame sizes, **$14.20** (target hammers not available for small frames). Target stocks: **$17.75** to **$21.30.** These prices applicable only when specified on original order. Combat stocks J, K or L frame, **$14.20** to **$23.05.**

TAURUS MODEL 66 REVOLVER
Caliber: 357 Magnum, 6-shot.
Barrel: 3", 4", 6".
Weight: 35 ozs.
Stocks: Checkered walnut, target-type. Standard stocks on 3".
Sights: Serrated ramp front, micro click rear adjustable for w. and e.
Features: Wide target-type hammer spur, floating firing pin, heavy barrel with shrouded ejector rod. Introduced 1978. From Taurus International.
Price: Blue, about **$204.00**
Price: Satin nickel, about **$213.00**
Price: Model 65 (similar to M66 except has a fixed rear sight and ramp front), blue, about **$190.00**
Price: Model 65, satin nickel, about **$200.00**

Taurus Model 66

TAURUS MODEL 73 SPORT REVOLVER
Caliber: 32 S&W Long, 6-shot.
Barrel: 3", heavy.
Weight: 22 oz. **Length:** 8¼" over-all.
Stocks: Oversize target-type, checkered Brazilian walnut.
Sights: Ramp front, notch rear.
Features: Imported from Brazil by Taurus International.
Price: Blue, about **$178.00**
Price: Satin nickel, about **$191.00**

Taurus Model 82

TAURUS MODEL 80 STANDARD REVOLVER
Caliber: 38 Spec., 6-shot.
Barrel: 3" or 4".
Weight: 31 oz. (4" bbl.). **Length:** 9¼" over-all (4" bbl.).
Stocks: Checkered Brazilian walnut.
Sights: Serrated ramp front, square notch rear.
Features: Imported from Brazil by Taurus International.
Price: Blue, about **$170.00**
Price: Satin nickel, about **$180.00**

TAURUS MODEL 82 HEAVY BARREL REVOLVER
Caliber: 38 Spec., 6-shot.
Barrel: 3" or 4", heavy.
Weight: 33 oz. (4" bbl.). **Length:** 9¼" over-all (4" bbl.).
Stocks: Checkered Brazilian walnut.
Sights: Serrated ramp front, square notch rear.
Features: Imported from Brazil by Taurus International.
Price: Blue, about **$170.00**
Price: Satin nickel, about **$180.00**

 CAUTION: PRICES CHANGE. CHECK AT GUNSHOP.

TAURUS MODEL 83 REVOLVER
Caliber: 38 Spec., 6-shot.
Barrel: 4″ only, heavy.
Weight: 34½ oz.
Stocks: Over-size checkered walnut.
Sights: Ramp front, micro. click rear adj. for w. & e.
Features: Blue or nickel finish. Introduced 1977. Imported from Brazil by Taurus International.
Price: Blue, about **$181.00**
Price: Satin nickel, about **$196.00**

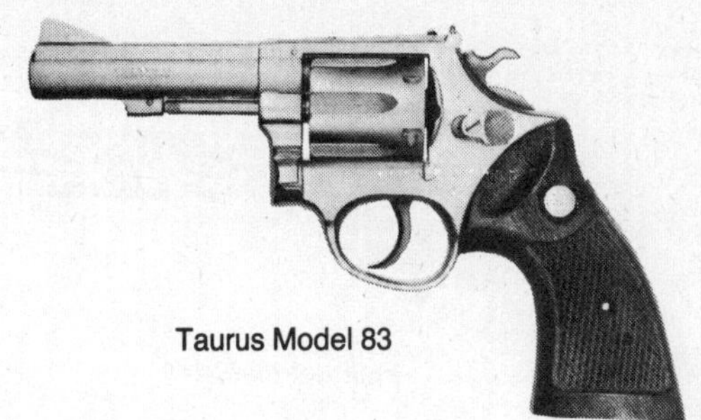
Taurus Model 83

Consult our Directory pages for the location of firms mentioned.

TAURUS MODEL 85 REVOLVER
Caliber: 38 Spec., 5-shot.
Barrel: 2″, 3″.
Weight: 21 oz.
Stocks: Checkered walnut.
Sights: Ramp front, square notch rear.
Features: Blue or satin nickel finish. Introduced 1980. Imported from Brazil by Taurus International.
Price: Blue, about **$178.00**
Price: Satin nickel, about **$192.00**
Price: Stainless steel, about.......... **$226.00**

DAN WESSON MODEL 41V & MODEL 44V
Caliber: 41 Mag., 44 Mag., six-shot.
Barrel: 4″, 6″, 8″, 10″; interchangeable.
Weight: 48 oz. (4″). **Length:** 12″ over-all (6″ bbl.).
Stocks: Smooth.
Sights: ⅛″ serrated front, white outline rear adjustable for windage and elevation.
Features: Available in blue or stainless steel. Smooth, wide trigger with adjustable over-travel; wide hammer spur. Available in Pistol Pac set also.
Price: 41 Mag., 4″, blue.......... **$373.40**
Price: As above except in stainless **$416.05**
Price: 44 Mag., 4″, blue.......... **$373.40**
Price: As above except in stainless **$416.05**

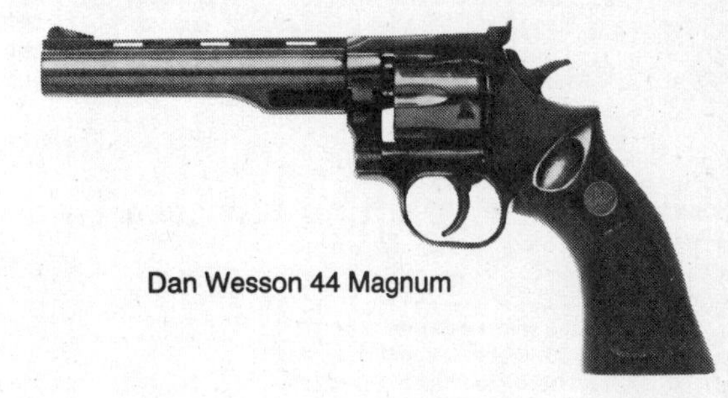
Dan Wesson 44 Magnum

DAN WESSON MODEL 8-2 & MODEL 14-2
Caliber: 38 Special (Model 8-2); 357 (14-2), both 6-shot.
Barrel: 2½″, 4″, 6″, 8″; interchangeable.
Weight: 30 oz. (2½″). **Length:** 9¼″ over-all (4″ bbl.).
Stocks: Checkered, interchangeable.
Sights: ⅛″ serrated front, fixed rear.
Features: Interchangeable barrels and grips; smooth, wide trigger; wide hammer spur with short double action travel. Available in stainless or brite blue. Contact Dan Wesson for complete price list.
Price: Model 8-2, 2½″, blue **$220.75**
Price: As above except in stainless **$253.65**
Price: Model 14-2, 4″, blue.......... **$227.15**
Price: As above except in stainless **$259.20**
Price: Model 714-2 Pistol Pac, stainless **$430.65**

Dan Wesson 9-2 & 15-2 Revolvers
Same as Models 8-2 and 14-2 except they have adjustable sight. Model 9-2 chambered for 38 Special, Model 15-2 for 357 Magnum. Available in blue or stainless. Contact Dan Wesson for complete price list.
Price: Model 9-2 or 15-2, 2½″, blue **$272.50**
Price: As above except in stainless **$306.55**
Price: Model 15-2, 8″, blue.......... **$297.90**
Price: As above, with 15″ barrel, blue.......... **$365.25**

Dan Wesson Model 15-2

DAN WESSON MODEL 22 REVOLVER
Caliber: 22 LR, 22 Mag., six-shot.
Barrel: 2½″, 4″, 6″, 8″, 10″; interchangeable.
Weight: 36 oz. (2½″), 44 oz. (6″). **Length:** 9¼″ over-all (4″ barrel).
Stocks: Checkered; undercover, service or over-size target.
Sights: ⅛″ serrated, interchangeable front, white outline rear adjustable for windage and elevation.
Features: Built on the same frame as the Dan Wesson 357; smooth, wide trigger with over-travel adjustment, wide spur hammer, with short double-action travel. Available in brite blue or stainless steel. Contact Dan Wesson for complete price list.
Price: 2½″ bbl., blue **$272.50**
Price: As above, stainless **$306.55**
Price: With 4″, vent. rib, blue **$300.85**
Price: As above, stainless **$335.15**
Price: Stainless Pistol Pac, 22 LR.......... **$525.95**

Dan Wesson 22

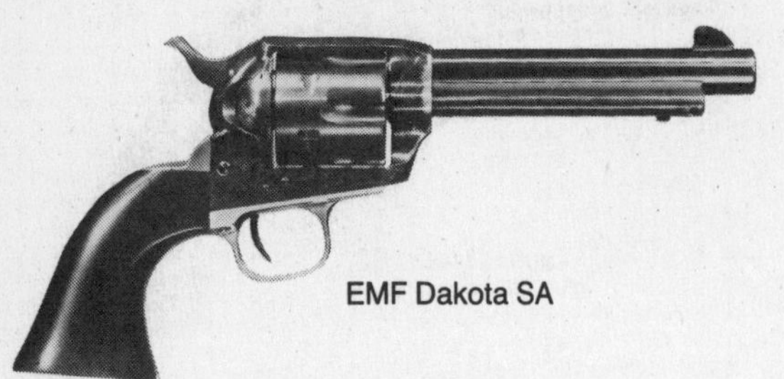
EMF Dakota SA

F.I.E. TEXAS RANGER REVOLVER
Caliber: 22 LR, 22 Mag.
Barrel: 4¾", 6½", 9",.
Weight: 31 oz. (4¾" bbl.). **Length:** 10" over-all.
Stocks: American hardwood.
Sights: Blade front, notch rear.
Features: Single-action, blue/black finish. Introduced 1983. Made in the U.S. by F.I.E.
Price: 22 LR, 4¾" **$69.95**
Price: As above, combo (22 LR/22 Mag.) **$84.95**
Price: 22 LR, 6½" **$77.95**
Price: As above, combo (22 LR/22 Mag.) **$92.95**
Price: 22 LR, 9" **$84.95**
Price: As above, combo (22 LR/22 Mag.) **$99.95**

F.I.E. "HOMBRE" SINGLE ACTION REVOLVER
Caliber: 357 Mag., 44 Mag., 45 LC.
Barrel: 6" or 7½".
Weight: 45 oz. (6" bbl.).
Stocks: Smooth walnut with medallion.
Sights: Blade front, grooved topstrap (fixed) rear.
Features: Color case hardened frame. Bright blue finish. Super-smooth action. Introduced 1979. Imported from West Germany by F.I.E. Corp.
Price: 357, 45 Colt **$179.95**
Price: 44 Mag. **$199.95**
Price: 357, 45 Colt, brass backstrap and trigger guard **$199.95**
Price: As above, 44 Magnum **$219.95**
Price: 357, 45 Colt, 24K gold plated **$219.95**
Price: As above, 44 Magnum **$239.95**

F.I.E. E15 BUFFALO SCOUT REVOLVER
Caliber: 22 LR/22 Mag., 6-shot.
Barrel: 4¾".
Weight: 32 oz. **Length:** 10" over-all.
Stocks: Black checkered nylon, walnut optional.
Sights: Blade front, fixed rear.
Features: Slide spring ejector. Blue, chrome, gold or blue with gold backstrap and trigger guard models available.
Price: Blued, 22 LR, 4¾" **$59.95**
Price: Blue, 22 combo, 4¾" **$74.95**
Price: Chrome or blue/gold, 22 LR, 4¾" **$74.95**
Price: Chrome or blue/gold, combo, 4¾" **$89.95**
Price: Gold, 22 combo, 4¾" **$134.95**

FREEDOM ARMS 454 CASULL
Caliber: 454 Casull, 5-shot.
Barrel: 4¾", 7½", 10", 12".
Weight: 50 oz. **Length:** 14" over-all (7½" bbl.).
Stocks: Impregnated hardwood.
Sights: Blade front, notch or adjustable rear.
Features: All stainless steel construction; sliding bar safety system. Made in U.S.A.
Price: Fixed sight **$795.00**
Price: Adjustable sight **$895.00**

COLT NEW FRONTIER 22
Caliber: 22 LR, 6-shot.
Barrel: 4¾", 6", 7½".
Weight: 29½ oz. (4¾" bbl.). **Length:** 9⅝" over-all.
Stocks: Black composite rubber.
Sights: Ramp-style front, fully adjustable rear.
Features: Cross-bolt safety. Color case-hardened frame. Available in blue only. Re-introduced 1982.
Price: 4¾", 6", 7½", blue **$169.00**

DAKOTA SINGLE ACTION REVOLVERS
Caliber: 22 LR, 22 Mag., 357 Mag., 30 Carbine, 44-40, 45 Colt.
Barrel: 3½", 4⅝", 5½", 7½", 12", 16¼".
Weight: 45 oz. **Length:** 13" over-all (7½" bbl.).
Stocks: Smooth walnut.
Sights: Blade front, fixed rear.
Features: Colt-type hammer with firing pin, color case-hardened frame, blue barrel and cylinder, brass grip frame and trigger guard. Available in blue or nickel plated, plain or engraved. Imported by E.M.F.
Price: 22 LR, 30 Car., 357, 44-40, 45 L.C., 4⅝", 5½", 7½" **$295.00**
Price: 22 LR/22 Mag. Combo, 5½", 7½" **$330.00**
Price: 357, 44-40, 45, 12" **$330.00**
Price: 357, 44-40, 45, 3½" **$325.00**

F.I.E. Texas Ranger

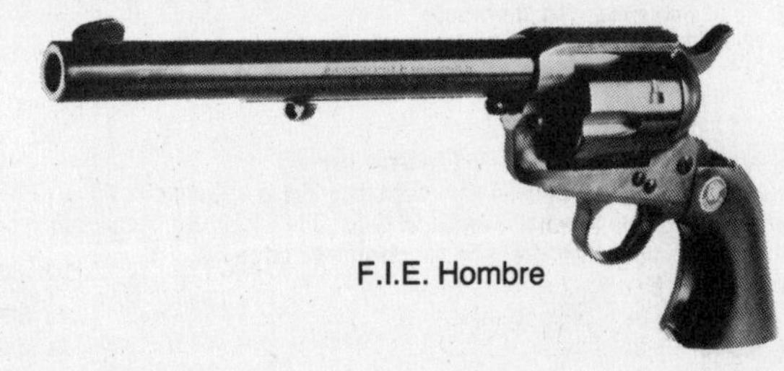
F.I.E. Hombre

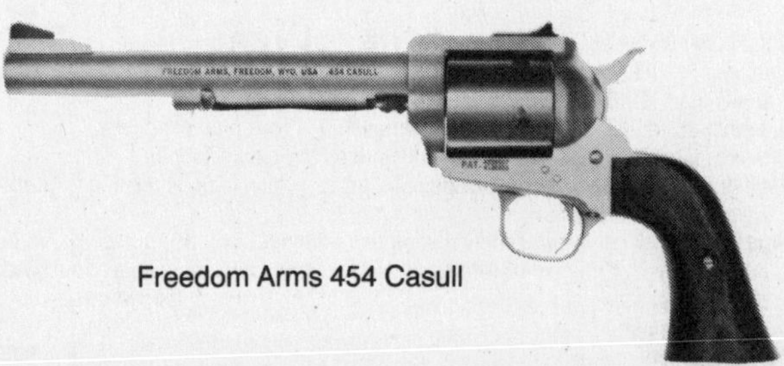

Freedom Arms 454 Casull

CAUTION: PRICES CHANGE. CHECK AT GUNSHOP.

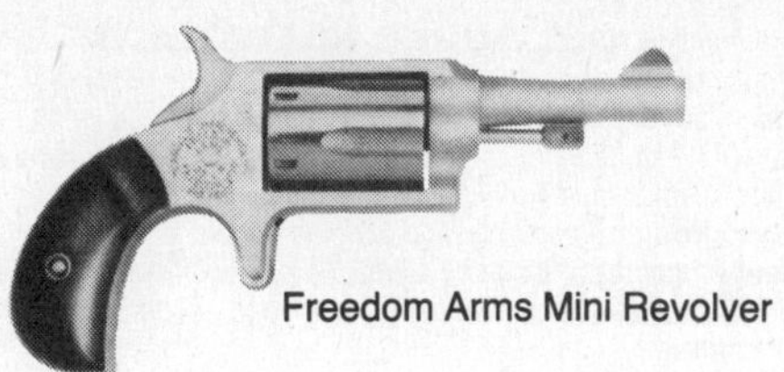
Freedom Arms Mini Revolver

FREEDOM ARMS MINI REVOLVER

Caliber: 22 Short, Long, Long Rifle, 5-shot, 22 Mag., 4-shot.
Barrel: 1",1¾", 3".
Weight: 4 oz. **Length:** 4" over-all.
Stocks: Black ebonite.
Sights: Blade front, notch rear.
Features: Made of stainless steel, simple take down; half-cock safety; floating firing pin; cartridge rims recessed in cylinder. Comes in gun rug. Lifetime warranty. Also available in percussion — see black powder section. From Freedom Arms.
Price: 22 LR, 1" barrel **$105.35**
Price: 22 LR, 1¾" barrel **$105.35**
Price: 22 LR, 3" barrel **$118.70**
Price: 22 Mag., 1" barrel **$124.00**
Price: 22 Mag., 1¾" barrel **$124.00**
Price: 22 Mag., 3" barrel **$137.35**

Freedom Arms Boot Gun

Similar to the Mini Revolver except has 3" barrel, weighs 5 oz. and is 5⅞" over-all. Has over-size grips, floating firing pin. Made of stainless steel. Lifetime warranty. Comes in rectangular gun rug. Introduced 1982. From Freedom Arms.
Price: 22 LR **$118.70**
Price: 22 Mag. **$137.35**

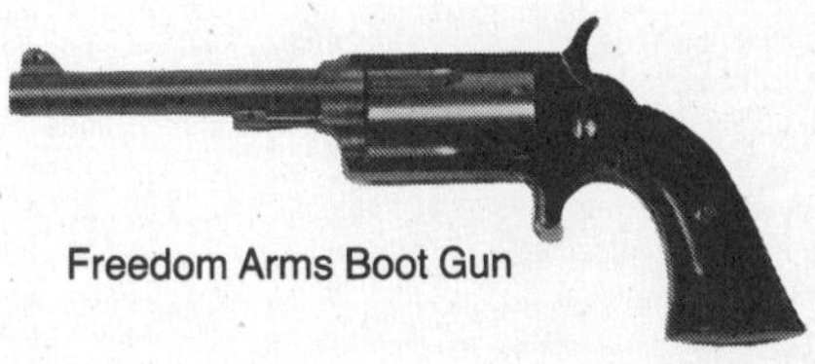
Freedom Arms Boot Gun

Ruger Super Single-Six

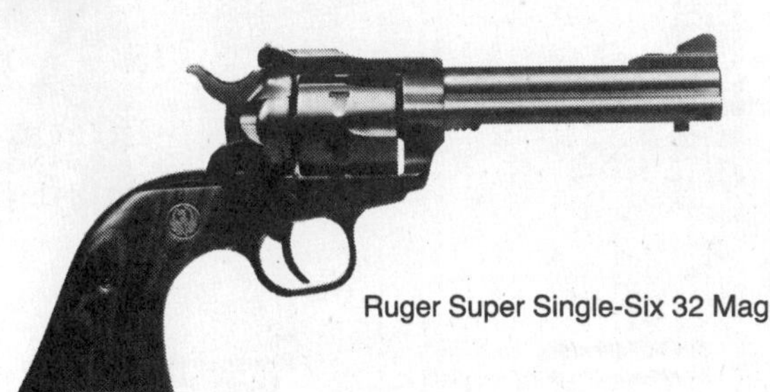
Ruger Super Single-Six 32 Mag.

RUGER NEW MODEL SUPER SINGLE-SIX CONVERTIBLE REVOLVER

Caliber: 22 S, L, LR, 6-shot. 22 Mag. in extra cylinder.
Barrel: 4⅝", 5½", 6½" or 9½" (6-groove).
Weight: 34½ oz. (6½" bbl.). **Length:** 11¹³⁄₁₆" over-all (6½" bbl.).
Stocks: Smooth American walnut.
Sights: Improved Patridge front on ramp, fully adj. rear protected by integral frame ribs.
Features: New Ruger "interlocked" mechanism, transfer bar ignition, gate-controlled loading, hardened chrome-moly steel frame, wide trigger, music wire springs throughout, independent firing pin.
Price: 4⅝", 5½", 6½", 9½" barrel **$195.00**
Price: 5½", 6½" bbl., stainless steel **$265.00**

Ruger New Model Single-Six Revolver

Similar to the Super Single-Six revolver except chambered for 32 H&R Magnum (also handles 32 S&W and 32 S&W Long). Weight is about 34 oz. with 6½" barrel. Same barrel lengths as Super Single-Six. Introduced 1985.
Price: **$205.00**

Ruger New Model Bisley Single-Six

Similar to the New Model Single-Six except frame is styled after the classic Bisley "flat-top." Most mechanical parts are unchanged. Hammer is lower and smoothly curved with a deeply checkered spur. Trigger is strongly curved with a wide smooth surface. Longer grip frame designed with a hand-filling shape, and the trigger guard is a large oval. Dovetail rear sight drift-adjustable for windage; front sight base accepts interchangeable square blades of various heights and styles. Weight about 41 oz. Chambered for 22 LR and 32 H&R Mag., 6½" barrel only. Introduced 1985.
Price: **$258.00**

RUGER NEW MODEL BLACKHAWK REVOLVER

Caliber: 30 Carbine, 357 or 41 Mag., 6-shot.
Barrel: 4⅝" or 6½", either caliber, 7½" (30 Carbine only).
Weight: 42 oz. (6½" bbl.). **Length:** 12¼" over-all (6½" bbl.).
Stocks: American walnut.
Sights: ⅛" ramp front, micro click rear adj. for w. and e.
Features: New Ruger interlocked mechanism, independent firing pin, hardened chrome-moly steel frame, music wire springs throughout.
Price: 30 Carbine **$237.00**
Price: Blue, 357, 41 .... **$237.50**
Price: Stainless steel (357) **$307.50**
Price: Convertible (with extra 9mm Para. cyl.) blue only **$260.00**

Ruger New Model Blackhawk

Ruger New Model Bisley Blackhawk

Similar to standard New Model Blackhawk except the hammer is lower with a smoothly curved, deeply checkered wide spur, the trigger is strongly curved with a wide smooth surface. Longer grip frame has a hand-filling shape. Adjustable rear sight, ramp-style front. Cylinder is unfluted and is roll-marked with a classic foliate engraving pattern and depiction of the old time Bisley marksman and a Bisley trophy. Chambered for 357, 41, 44 Mags. and 45 Colt; 7½" barrel; over-all length of 13". Introduced 1985.
Price: **$307.00**

Ruger N.M. Super Blackhawk

RUGER NEW MODEL SUPER BLACKHAWK
Caliber: 44 Magnum, 6-shot. Also fires 44 Spec.
Barrel: 7½" (6-groove, 20" twist), 10½".
Weight: 48 oz. (7½" bbl.) 51 oz. (10½" bbl.). **Length:** 13⅜" over-all (7½" bbl.).
Stocks: Genuine American walnut.
Sights: ⅛" ramp front, micro click rear adj. for w. and e.
Features: New Ruger interlocked mechanism, non-fluted cylinder, steel grip and cylinder frame, square back trigger guard, wide serrated trigger and wide spur hammer.
Price: Blue (S-47N, S-411N) $276.00
Price: Stainless (KS-47N, KS-411N) $325.00

SEVILLE SINGLE ACTION REVOLVER
Caliber: 357 Mag., 357 Max./Super Mag., 375 USA Super Mag., 41 Mag., 44 Mag., 45 Colt, 454 Mag.
Barrel: 2½", 3½", 4⅝", 5½", 6½", 7½", 10½".
Weight: 52 oz. (4⅝", loaded)
Stocks: Smooth walnut, thumbrest, or Pachmayr.
Sights: Ramp front with red insert, fully adj. rear.
Features: Available in blue or stainless steel. Six-shot cylinder. From United Sporting Arms Inc.
Price: Blue.. $325.00
Price: Blue with brass backstrap.............................. $320.00
Price: Stainless, all cals.................................... $375.00

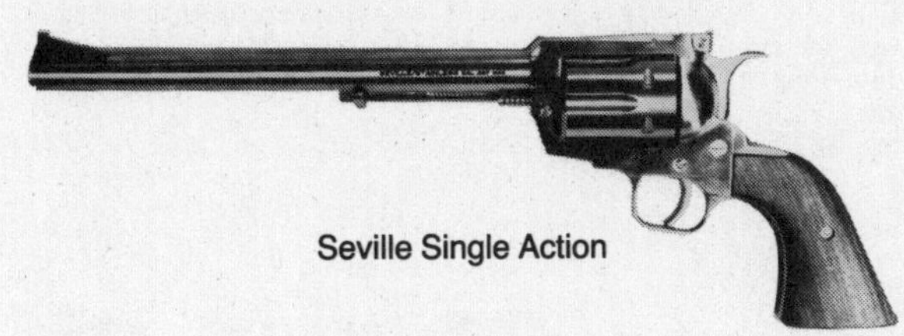
Seville Single Action

Seville Stainless Super Mag
Similar to the standard Seville revolver except chambered for 357 Rem. Maximum, or 454 Magnum; 5½" or 7½" barrel only; grips of smooth walnut or Pachmayr rubber. Available only in stainless steel. Super Mag. and 454 Mag. in 7½" barrel only. Introduced 1983.
Price: 357 Maximum $400.00
Price: 454 Magnum $500.00

Texas Longhorn South Texas Army

TANARMI S.A. REVOLVER MODEL TA22S LM
Caliber: 22 LR, 22 Mag., 6-shot.
Barrel: 4¾".
Weight: 32 oz. **Length:** 10" over-all.
Stocks: Walnut.
Sights: Blade front, rear adj. for w. & e.
Features: Manual hammer block safety; color hardened steel frame; brass backstrap and trigger guard. Imported from Italy by Excam.
Price: 22 LR/22 Mag. $103.00

TANARMI SINGLE ACTION MODEL TA76
Same as TA22 models except blue backstrap and trigger guard.
Price: 22 LR, blue $59.00
Price: Combo, blue $75.50
Price: 22 LR, chrome... $75.00
Price: Combo, chrome $89.00

Texas Longhorn Texas Border

TEXAS LONGHORN RIGHT-HAND SINGLE ACTION
Caliber: All centerfire pistol calibers.
Barrel: 4¾".
Weight: NA. **Length:** NA.
Stocks: One-piece fancy walnut, or any fancy AAA wood.
Sights: Blade front, grooved top-strap rear.
Features: Loading gate and ejector housing on left side of gun. Cylinder rotates to the left. All steel construction; color case-hardened frame; high polish blue; music wire coil springs. Lifetime guarantee to original owner. Introduced 1984. From Texas Longhorn Arms.
Price: South Texas Army Limited Edition — hand-made, only 1,000 to be produced; "One of One Thousand" engraved on barrel; comes with glass-covered display case $1,500.00

Texas Longhorn Arms Texas Border Special
Similar to the South Texas Army Limited Edition except has 3½" barrel, birds-head style grip. Same special features, display case. Introduced 1984.
Price: $1,500.00

Texas Longhorn Arms West Texas Flat Top Target
Similar to the South Texas Army Limited Edition except choice of barrel length from 7½" through 15"; flat-top style frame; ⅛" contoured ramp front sight, old model steel micro-click rear adjustable for w. and e. Same special features, display case. Introduced 1984.
Price: $1,500.00

Texas Longhorn Arms Cased Set
Set contains one each of the Texas Longhorn Right-Hand Single Actions, all in the same caliber, same serial numbers (100, 200, 300, 400, 500, 600, 700, 800, 900). Ten sets to be made (#1000 donated to NRA museum). Comes in hand-tooled leather case. All other specs same as Limited Edition guns. Introduced 1984.
Price: $5,750.00
Price: With ¾-coverage "C-style" engraving.................... $7,650.00

THE VIRGINIAN DRAGOON REVOLVER
Caliber: 44 Mag.
Barrel: 6″, 7½″, 8⅜″.
Weight: 50 oz. (6″ barrel). **Length:** 10″ over-all (6″ barrel).
Stocks: Smooth walnut.
Sights: Ramp-type Patridge front blade, micro. adj. target rear.
Features: Color case-hardened frame, spring-loaded floating firing pin, coil main spring. Firing pin is lock-fitted with a steel bushing. Introduced 1977. Made in the U.S. by Interarms Industries, Inc.
Price: 6″, 7½″, 8⅜″, blue **$295.00**
Price: 44 Mag., 6″, 7½″, 8⅜″, stainless **$295.00**
Price: 44 Mag., 7½″, 8⅜″, 10½″ Sil. model **$425.00**

Virginian Dragoon

Virginian Dragoon Engraved Models
Same gun as the standard Dragoon except offered only in 44 Mag. 6″ or 7½″ barrel; choice of fluted or unfluted cylinder, stainless or blued. Hand-engraved frame, cylinder and barrel. Each gun comes in a felt-lined walnut presentation case. Introduced 1983.
Price: **$625.00**

Virginian Dragoon "Deputy" Model
Similar to the standard Dragoon except comes with traditional fixed sights, blue or stainless, in 357 (5″ barrel), 44 Mag. (6″ barrel). Introduced 1983.
Price: **$285.00**

VIRGINIAN 22 CONVERTIBLE REVOLVERS
Caliber: 22 LR, 22 Mag.
Barrel: 5½″.
Weight: 38 oz. **Length:** 10¾″ over-all.
Stocks: Smooth walnut.
Sights: Ramp-type Patridge front, open fully adjustable rear.
Features: Smaller version of the big-bore Dragoon revolvers; comes with both Long Rifle and Magnum cylinders, the latter unfluted; color case-hardened frame, rest blued. Introduced 1983. Made by Uberti; imported from Italy by Interarms.
Price: Blue, with two cylinders **$209.00**
Price: Stainless with two cylinders **$229.00**

Virginian 22 Convertible

HANDGUNS—MISCELLANEOUS

ADVANTAGE ARMS 422 DERRINGER
Caliber: 22 LR, 22 Mag., 4-shot.
Barrel: 2½″.
Weight: 15 oz. **Length:** 4½″ over-all.
Stocks: Smooth walnut.
Sights: Fixed.
Features: Top break design with four barrels, double action trigger and rotating firing pin, spring loaded extractors. Nickel, blue or Q.P.Q. black finish. Introduced 1983. From Advantage Arms USA, Inc.
Price: 22 LR **$149.95**
Price: 22 Mag. **$159.95**

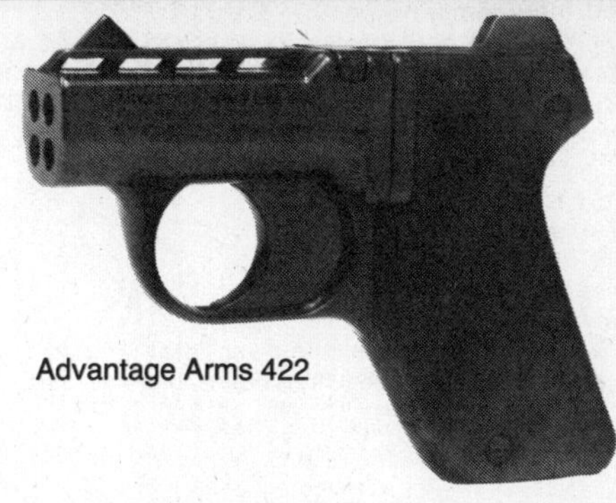
Advantage Arms 422

American Derringer Model 1

AMERICAN DERRINGER MODEL 1
Caliber: 22 LR, 22 Mag., 22 Hornet, 223 Rem., 30 Luger, 30-30 Win., 32 ACP, 38 Super, 380 ACP, 38 Spec., 9 × 18, 9mm Para., 357 Mag., 41 Mag., 44-40 Win., 44 Spec., 44 Mag., 45 Colt, 45 ACP, 410-ga. (2½″).
Barrel: 3″.
Weight: 15½ oz. (38 Spec.). **Length:** 4.82″ over-all.
Stocks: Rosewood, Zebra wood.
Sights: Blade front.
Features: Made of stainless steel with high-polish or satin finish. Two shot capacity. Manual hammer block safety. Introduced 1980. Contact the factory for complete list of available calibers and prices. From American Derringer Corp.
Price: 22 LR or Mag. **$212.00**
Price: 223 Rem. **$369.00**
Price: 38 Spec. **$199.00**
Price: 357 Mag. **$225.00**
Price: 9mm, 380, 38 Super **$199.95**
Price: 44 Spec. **$275.00**
Price: 44-40 Win., 45 ACP, 45 Colt **$275.00**
Price: 41, 44 Mags. **$369.00**
Price: Lightweight (7½ oz.) Model 7, 38 Spec., 38 S&W, 380, 22 LR only **$199.00**
Price: 45-70 (as above), single shot **$369.00**

AMERICAN DERRINGER MODEL 3
Caliber: 38 Special.
Barrel: 2.5″.
Weight: 8.5 oz. **Length:** 4.9″ over-all.
Stocks: Rosewood.
Sights: Blade front.
Features: Made of stainless steel. Single shot with manual hammer block safety. Introduced 1985. From American Derringer Corp.
Price: **$115.00**

C. O. P. 357 MAGNUM
Caliber: 38/357 Mag., 4 shots.
Barrel: 3¼″.
Weight: 28 oz. **Length:** 5.5″ over-all.
Stocks: Checkered composition.
Sights: Open, fixed.
Features: Double-action, 4 barrels, made of stainless steel. Width is only one inch, height 4.1″. From M & N Distributors.
Price: About **$250.00**
Price: In 22 Mag. **$250.00**
Price: In 22 LR (blued, aluminum frame) **$229.95**

F.I.E. MODEL D-38 DERRINGER
Caliber: 38 Special.
Barrel: 3″.
Weight: 14 oz.
Stocks: Checkered white nylon, walnut optional.
Sights: Fixed.
Features: Dyna-Chrome finish. Spur trigger. Tip-up barrel, extractors. Made in U.S. by F.I.E. Corp.
Price: With nylon grips **$81.95**
Price: With walnut grips **$98.95**

GUNWORKS MODEL 9 DERRINGER
Caliber: 38/357 Mag., 9mm/9mm Mag.
Barrel: 3″; button rifled, bottom hinged.
Weight: 15 oz.
Stocks: Smooth wood.
Sights: Millett blaze orange bar front, fixed rear.
Features: All steel; half-cock, through-frame safety; dual extraction; electroless nickel finish; comes with in-pant holster. Made in U.S. by Gunworks, Ltd.
Price: **$148.50**

LJUTIC LJ II PISTOL
Caliber: 22 Magnum.
Barrel: 2¾″.
Stocks: Checkered walnut.
Sights: Fixed.
Features: Stainless steel; double action; ventilated rib; side-by-side barrels; positive on/off safety. Introduced 1981. From Ljutic Industries.
Price: **$799.00**

Ljutic Space Pistol

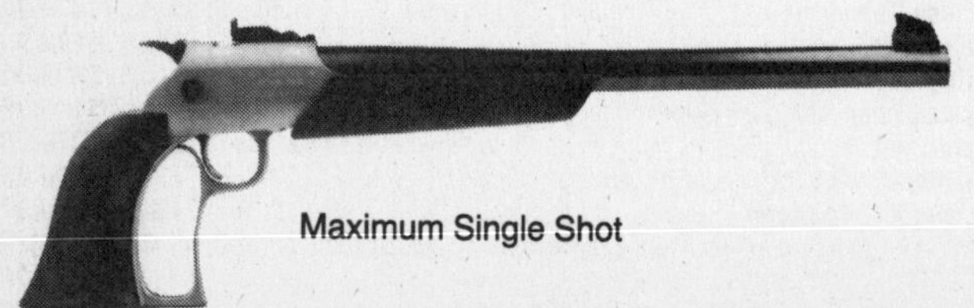

Maximum Single Shot

American Derringer Model 4
Similar to the Model 1 except has 4.1″ barrel, over-all length of 6″, and weighs 16½ oz.; chambered for 3″ 410-ga. shotshells or 45 Colt. Can be had with 45-70 upper barrel and 3″ 410-ga. or 45 Colt bottom barrel. Made of stainless steel. Manual hammer block safety. Introduced 1985.
Price: 3″ 410/45 Colt (either barrel) **$359.00**
Price: 3″ 410/45 Colt or 45-70 (Alaskan Survival model) **$369.00**

ARM TECH. DERRINGER
Caliber: 22 LR, 22 Mag., 4-shot.
Barrel: 2.6″.
Weight: 19 ozs. **Length:** 4.6″ over-all.
Stocks: Hard rubber or walnut, checkered or smooth.
Sights: Fixed, non-snagging.
Features: Four barrels with 90° rotating-indexing firing pin system. All stainless steel parts. Double-action only. Blued model available. Introduced 1983. From Armament Technologies Inc.
Price: Stainless, 22 LR, rubber grips **$184.50**
Price: As above, 22 Mag. **$189.00**
Price: Blued, 22 LR, walnut grips **$174.50**
Price: As above, 22 Mag. **$179.00**

Gunworks Model 9

Ljutic LJ II Pistol

LJUTIC RECOILESS SPACE PISTOL
Caliber: 22 Mag., 357 Mag., 44 Mag., 308 Win.; single shot.
Barrel: 13½″.
Weight: 5 lbs. (with scope).
Stocks: Walnut grip and fore-end.
Sights: Scope mounts extra.
Features: Twist-bolt action; button trigger. From Ljutic Industries.
Price: **$995.00**

MAXIMUM SINGLE SHOT PISTOL
Caliber: 22 Hornet, 223 Rem., 22-250, 6mm BR, 6mm-223, 243, 250 Savage, 6.5mm-35, 7mm TCU, 7mm BR, 7mm-35, 7mm INT-R, 7mm-08, 30 Herrett, 308 Win., 357 Mag., 358 Win., 44 Mag.
Barrel: 10½″, 14″.
Weight: 61 oz. (10½″ bbl.), 78 oz. (14″ bbl.). **Length:** 15″, 18½″ over-all (with 10½″ and 14″ bbl., respectively).
Stocks: Smooth walnut stocks and fore-end.
Sights: Ramp front, fully adjustable open rear.
Features: Falling block action; drilled and tapped for most popular scope mounts; integral grip frame/receiver; adjustable trigger; Douglas barrel (interchangeable); Armoloy finish. Introduced 1983. Made in U.S. by M.O.A. Corp.
Price: Either barrel length **$499.00**
Price: Extra barrel **$129.00**
Price: Scope mount **$39.00**

CAUTION: PRICES CHANGE. CHECK AT GUNSHOP.

MERRILL SPORTSMAN'S SINGLE SHOT PISTOL

Caliber: 22 LR, 22 Mag., 22 Hornet, 225 Win., 256 Win. Mag., 25-35 Win., 32-20, 32 H&R Mag., 357 Max., 357 Mag., 357/44 B & D, 30-30 Win., 30 Herrett, 357 Herrett, 41 Mag., 44 Mag., 45 Colt, 30-40 Krag, 375 Win., 7mm Merrill, 30 Merrill, 7mm Rocket, 270 Rocket, 7mm Laser Jr., 45-70.
Barrel: 9″ or 10¾″, semi-octagonal; .450″ wide vent. rib, matted to prevent glare; 14″ barrel in all except 22 cals.
Weight: About 54 oz. **Length:** 10½″ over-all (9″ bbl.)
Stocks: Smooth walnut with thumb and heel rest.
Sights: Front .125″ blade (.080″ blade optional); rear adj. for w. and e.
Features: Polished blue finish, hard chrome optional. Barrel is drilled and tapped for scope mounting. Cocking indicator visible from rear of gun. Has spring-loaded barrel lock, positive thumb safety. Trigger adjustable for weight of pull and over-travel. For complete price list contact Rock Pistol Mfg.
Price: Regular ¾″ frame, right hand action **$405.00**
Price: As above, left hand action................................ **$430.00**
Price: Wide ⅞″ frame, right hand action only **$455.00**
Price: Extra barrel, 8″-10¾″..................................... **$180.00**
Price: Extra barrel, 12″-14″..................................... **$250.00**

Merrill Sportsman's Single Shot

REMINGTON MODEL XP-100 Bolt Action Pistol

Caliber: 221 Fireball, single shot.
Barrel: 10½″, ventilated rib.
Weight: 60 oz. **Length:** 16¾″.
Stock: Brown nylon one-piece, checkered grip with white spacers.
Sights: Fixed front, rear adj. for w. and e. Tapped for scope mount.
Features: Fits left or right hand, is shaped to fit fingers and heel of hand. Grooved trigger. Rotating thumb safety, cavity in fore-end permits insertion of up to five 38 cal., 130-gr. metal jacketed bullets to adjust weight and balance. Included is a black vinyl, zippered case.
Price: Including case, about...................................... **$335.00**

Remington XP-100

SEMMERLING LM-4 PISTOL

Caliber: 45 ACP.
Barrel: 3½″.
Weight: 24 oz. **Length:** 5.2″ over-all.
Stocks: Checkered black plastic.
Sights: Ramp front, fixed rear.
Features: Manually operated repeater. Over-all dimensions are 5.2″ x 3.7″ x 1″. Has a four-shot magazine capacity. Comes with manual, leather carrying case, spare stock screw and wrench. From Semmerling Corp.
Price: Complete.. **$894.00**
Price: Thin Version (blue sideplate instead of grips) **$894.00**

Consult our Directory pages for the location of firms mentioned.

TANARMI O/U DERRINGER

Caliber: 38 Special.
Barrel: 3″.
Weight: 14 oz. **Length:** 4¾″ over-all.
Stocks: Checkered white nylon.
Sights: Fixed.
Features: Blue finish; tip-up barrel. Assembled in U.S. by Excam, Inc.
Price: **$75.00**

THOMPSON-CENTER ARMS CONTENDER

Caliber: 7mm T.C.U., 30-30 Win., 22 S, L, LR, 22 Mag., 22 Hornet, 6.5 T.C.U., 223 Rem., 30 & 357 Herrett, 357 Mag., 357 Rem. Max., also 222 Rem., 41 Mag., 44 Mag., 45 Colt, single shot.
Barrel: 10″, tapered octagon, bull barrel and vent. rib.
Weight: 43 oz. (10″ bbl.). **Length:** 13¼″ (10″ bbl.).
Stocks: Select walnut grip and fore-end, with thumb rest. Right or left hand.
Sights: Under cut blade ramp front, rear adj. for w. & e.
Features: Break open action with auto-safety. Single action only. Interchangeable bbls., both caliber (rim & centerfire), and length. Drilled and tapped for scope. Engraved frame. See T/C catalog for exact barrel/caliber availability.
Price: Blued (rimfire cals.) **$285.00**
Price: Blued (centerfire cals.)..................................... **$285.00**
Price: Extra bbls. (standard octagon)............................... **$120.00**
Price: Bushnell Phantom scope base.................................. **$8.75**
Price: 357 and 44 Mag. vent. rib, internal choke bbl................ **$130.00**

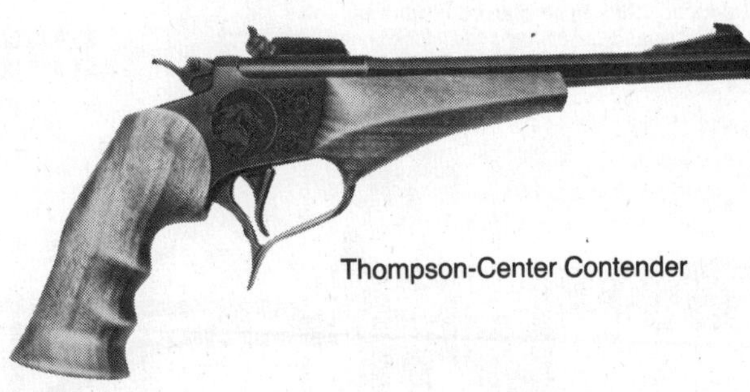
Thompson-Center Contender

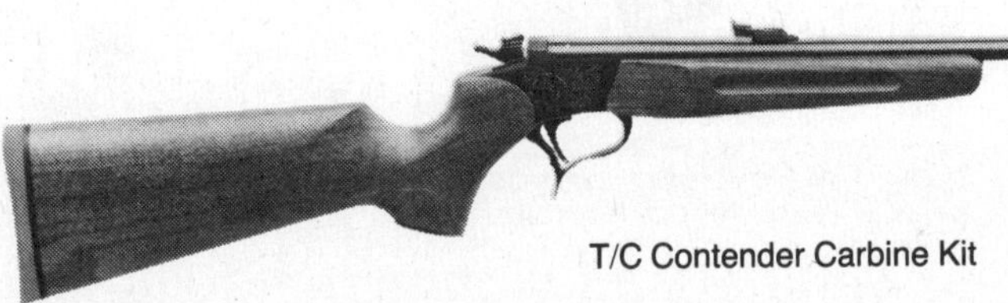
T/C Contender Carbine Kit

T/C Contender Carbine Kit

Converts the Contender pistol into a carbine. Kit includes 21″ barrel with fully adjustable sights and is drilled and tapped for scope mounting. Wood is American black walnut with checkered pistol grip, grooved fore-end. Available in 22 LR, 22 Hornet, 223, 7mm T.C.U., 7x30 Waters, 30-30. Introduced 1985.
Price: **$240.00**
Price: Barrel only **$135.00**

AKM Auto Rifle

AKM AUTO RIFLE
Caliber: 7.62x39, 30-shot magazine.
Barrel: 16.33".
Weight: 6.4lbs. **Length:** 34.65" over-all.
Stock: Laminated hardwood. Checkered composition pistol grip.
Sights: Protected post front, U-notch rear adjustable for elevation.
Features: Semi-auto only. Detachable box magazine. Cleaning kit, bayonet and scabbard, and sling available. Introduced to U.S. market 1982. Imported from Egypt by Gun South, Inc.
Price: Standard rifle **$995.00**

Auto Ordnance 27 A-1

AUTO ORDNANCE MODEL 27 A-1 THOMPSON
Caliber: 45 ACP, 30-shot magazine.
Barrel: 16".
Weight: 11½ lbs. **Length:** About 42" over-all (Deluxe).
Stock: Walnut stock and vertical fore-end.
Sights: Blade front, open rear adj. for w.
Features: Re-creation of Thompson Model 1927. Semi-auto only. Deluxe model has finned barrel, adj. rear sight and compensator; Standard model has plain barrel and military sight. From Auto-Ordnance Corp.
Price: Deluxe **$595.00**
Price: Standard (horizontal fore-end) **$575.00**
Price: 1927A5 Pistol (M27A1 without stock; wgt. 7 lbs.) **$556.00**
Price: Lightweight model **$469.95**

Auto Ordnance Thompson M1
Similar to the Model 27 A-1 except is in the M-1 configuration with side cocking knob, horizontal fore-end, smooth un-finned barrel, sling swivels on butt and fore-end. Matte black finish. Introduced 1985.
Price: **$565.00**

Barrett Light-Fifty

BARRETT LIGHT-FIFTY MODEL 82
Caliber: 50 BMG; 11-shot detachable box magazine.
Barrel: 33".
Weight: 35 lbs. **Length:** 63" over-all.
Stock: Uni-body construction.
Sights: None furnished. Comes with Weaver-type base.
Features: Semi-automatic, recoil operated with recoiling barrel. Three-lug locking bolt; six-port harmonica-type muzzle brake. Bipod legs and M-60 mount standard. Fires same 50-cal. ammunition as the M2HB machine gun. Introduced 1985. From Barrett Firearms.
Price: Parkerized **$2,995.00**
Price: Dry Film Lubricant finish **$3,320.00**

BERETTA AR70 RIFLE
Caliber: 223, 30-shot magazine.
Barrel: 17¾".
Weight: 8¼ lbs. **Length:** 38" over-all.
Stock: Black high-impact plastic.
Sights: Blade front, diopter rear adjustable for windage and elevation.
Features: Matte black epoxy finish; easy take-down. Imported from Italy by Beretta U.S.A. Corp. Introduced 1984.
Price: **$820.00**

Bushmaster Auto Rifle

BUSHMASTER AUTO RIFLE
Caliber: 223; 30-shot magazine
Barrel: 18½".
Weight: 6¼ lbs. **Length:** 37.5" over-all.
Stock: Rock maple
Sights: Protected post front adj. for elevation, protected quick-flip rear peep adj. for windage; short and long range.
Features: Steel alloy upper receiver with welded barrel assembly, AK-47-type gas system, aluminum lower receiver; silent sling and swivels; bayonet lug; one-piece welded steel alloy bolt carrier assembly. From Bushmaster Firearms.
Price: With maple stock **$384.95**
Price: With nylon-coated folding stock **$394.95**
Price: Matte electroless finish, maple stock **$394.95**
Price: As above, folding stock **$394.95**

CAUTION: PRICES CHANGE. CHECK AT GUNSHOP.

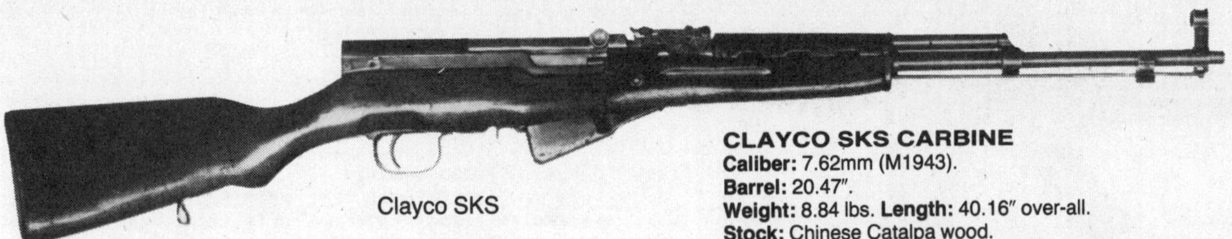

Clayco SKS

CLAYCO SKS CARBINE
Caliber: 7.62mm (M1943).
Barrel: 20.47″.
Weight: 8.84 lbs. **Length:** 40.16″ over-all.
Stock: Chinese Catalpa wood.
Sights: Hooded post front, tangent leaf rear.
Features: Chinese-made version of the Soviet SKS carbine. Has fixed, 10-round, double-row magazine. Comes with cleaning kit. Imported from China by Clayco Sports.
Price: **$399.00**

Colt AR-15A2

COLT AR-15A2 SPORTER II
Caliber: 223 Rem.
Barrel: 20″.
Weight: 7½ lbs. **Length:** 39″ over-all.
Stock: High-strength nylon.
Sights: Post front, adjustable for elevation, flip-type rear for short, long range, windage.
Features: 5-round detachable box magazine, recoil pad, flash suppressor, sling swivels. Forward bolt assist included. Introduced 1985.
Price: **$659.95**

Colt AR-15A2 Carbine
Same as standard AR-15A2 except has telescoping nylon-coated aluminum buttstock and redesigned fore-end. Over-all length collapsed is 32″, extended 35″. Barrel length is 16″, weight is 5.8 lbs. Has 14½″ sight radius. Introduced 1985.
Price: **$699.95**

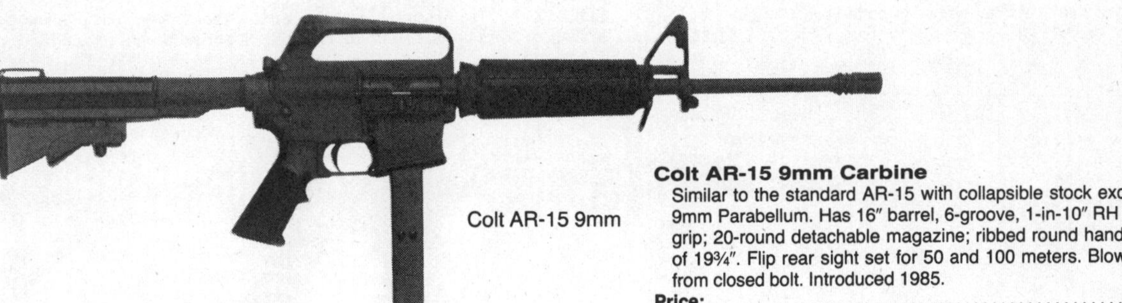

Colt AR-15 9mm

Colt AR-15 9mm Carbine
Similar to the standard AR-15 with collapsible stock except chambered for 9mm Parabellum. Has 16″ barrel, 6-groove, 1-in-10″ RH twist; M16A2 pistol grip; 20-round detachable magazine; ribbed round handguard; sight radius of 19¾″. Flip rear sight set for 50 and 100 meters. Blow-back system fires from closed bolt. Introduced 1985.
Price: . . . . **NA**

COMMANDO ARMS CARBINE
Caliber: 45 ACP.
Barrel: 16½″.
Weight: 8 lbs. **Length:** 37″ over-all.
Stock: Walnut buttstock.
Sights: Blade front, peep rear.
Features: Semi-auto only. Cocking handle on left side. Choice of magazines—5, 20, 30 or 90 shot. From Commando Arms.
Price: Mark 9 or Mark 45, blue **$219.00**
Price: Nickel plated **$254.00**

Consult our Directory pages for the location of firms mentioned.

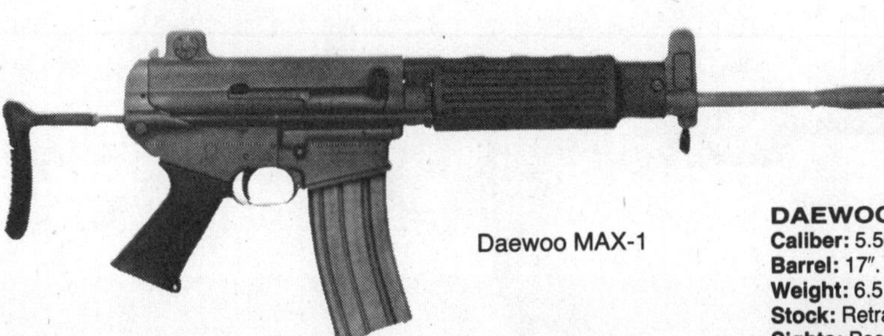

Daewoo MAX-1

DAEWOO MAX-1 AUTO RIFLE
Caliber: 5.56mm (223), 30-round magazine.
Barrel: 17″.
Weight: 6.5 lbs. **Length:** 38.4″ over-all (butt extended).
Stock: Retractable.
Sights: Post front, adjustable peep rear.
Features: Machine-forged receiver; gas-operated action; uses AR-15/M-16 magazines. Introduced 1985. Imported from Korea by Stoeger Industries.
Price: **$591.95**

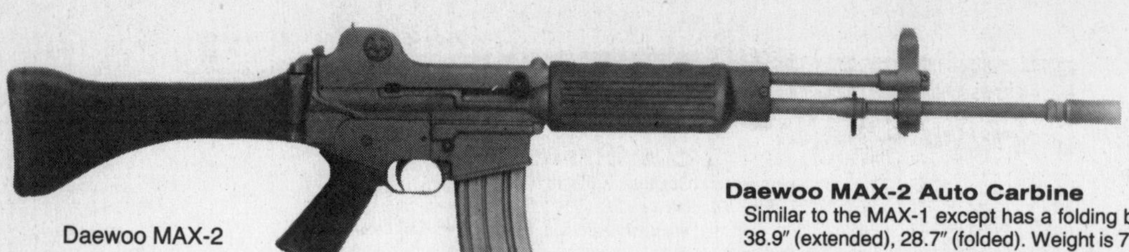

Daewoo MAX-2

Daewoo MAX-2 Auto Carbine
Similar to the MAX-1 except has a folding buttstock giving over-all length of 38.9″ (extended), 28.7″ (folded). Weight is 7.5 lbs.; barrel length is 18.3″. Has hooded post front sight, adjustable peep rear. Uses AR-15/M-16 magazines. Introduced 1985. Imported from Korea by Stoeger Industries.
Price: **$608.95**

DEMRO TAC-1M CARBINE
Caliber: 9mm (32-shot magazine), 45 ACP (30-shot magazine).
Barrel: 16⅞″.
Weight: 7¾ lbs. **Length:** 35¾″ over-all.
Stock: American walnut, removable.
Sights: Removable blade front, open rear adjustable for w. & e.
Features: Fires from open bolt. Thumb safety, integral muzzle brake. From Demro Products.
Price: **$523.25**
Price: With fitted attache case **$575.40**

Demro XF-7 Wasp Carbine
Similar to the TAC-1 Carbine except has collapsible buttstock, high impact synthetic fore-end and pistol grip. Has 5, 15 or 30-shot magazine (45 ACP) or 32-shot magazine (9mm).
Price: **$619.20**
Price: With fitted attache case **$685.60**

FN-LAR Competition

FN-LAR COMPETITION AUTO
Caliber: 308 Win., 20-shot magazine.
Barrel: 21″ (24″ with flash hider).
Weight: 9 lbs., 7 oz. **Length:** 44½″ over-all.
Stock: Black composition butt, fore-end and pistol grip.
Sights: Post front, aperture rear adj. for elevation, 200 to 600 meters.
Features: Has sling swivels, carrying handle, rubber recoil pad. Consecutively numbered pairs available at additional cost. Imported by Gun South, Inc.
Price: **$1,744.31**

FN 308 Model 50-63
Similar to the FN-LAR except has 18″ barrel, skeleton-type folding buttstock, folding cocking handle. Introduced 1982. Imported from Belgium by Gun South, Inc. Distr., Inc.
Price: **$2,016.79**

FNC Auto Rifle

FNC AUTO RIFLE
Caliber: 223 Rem.
Barrel: 18″.
Weight: 9.61 lbs.
Stock: Synthetic stock.
Sights: Post front; flip-over aperture rear adj. for elevation.
Features: Updated version of FN-FAL in shortened carbine form. Has 30-shot box magazine, synthetic pistol grip, fore-end. Introduced 1981. Imported by Gun South, Inc.
Price: Standard model **$1,243.75**
Price: Paratrooper, with folding stock **$1,438.50**

FN-LAR Paratrooper 308 Match 50-64
Similar to FN-LAR competition except with folding skeleton stock, shorter barrel, modified rear sight. Imported by Gun South, Inc.
Price: **$1,822.27**

FN-LAR Heavy Barrel 308 Match
Similar to FN-LAR competition except has wooden stock and fore-end, heavy barrel, folding metal bipod. Imported by Gun South, Inc.
Price: With wooden, stock **$2,310.77**
Price: With synthetic stock **$2,132.65**

GALIL 308 ARM SEMI-AUTO RIFLE
Caliber: 308 Win., 20-shot magazine.
Barrel: 21″.
Weight: 8.7 lbs. **Length:** 41.3″ over-all (stock extended).
Stock: Tube-type metal folding stock.
Sights: Post-type front, flip-type "L" rear.
Features: Gas operated, rotating bolt. Cocking handle, safety and magazine catch can be operated from either side. Folding bipod, carrying handle. Introduced 1982. Imported from Israel by Magnum Research Inc.
Price: **$1,099.00**
Price: As above in 223 (18.1″ bbl., 38.6″ o.a.l.) **$999.00**

Galil Auto Rifle

Goncz Carbine

GONCZ HIGH-TECH CARBINE

Caliber: 9mm Para., 30 Mauser, 38 Super, 18- and 32-shot magazine; 45 ACP, 10- and 20-shot magazine.
Barrel: 16.1″.
Weight: 4 lbs., 2 oz. **Length:** 31″ over-all.
Stock: Grooved alloy pistol grip, black high-impact plastic butt. Walnut optional at extra cost.
Sights: Front adjustable for e., rear adjustable for w.
Features: Fires from closed bolt; floating firing pin; safety locks the firing pin; all metal construction; barrel threaded for accessories. Matte black oxide and anodized finish. Designed by Lajos J. Goncz. Introduced 1985. From Goncz Co.
Price: **$375.00**
Price: With laser sight system **$1,495.00**

Heckler & Koch HK-91

HECKLER & KOCH HK-91 AUTO RIFLE

Caliber: 308 Win., 5- or 20-shot magazine.
Barrel: 17.71″.
Weight: 9½ lbs. **Length:** 40¼″ over-all.
Stock: Black high-impact plastic.
Sights: Post front, aperture rear adj. for w. and e.
Features: Delayed roller lock action. Sporting version of West German service rifle. Takes special H&K clamp scope mount. Imported from West Germany by Heckler & Koch, Inc.
Price: HK-91 A-2 with plastic stock.......... **$599.00**
Price: HK-91 A-3 with retractable metal stock **$665.00**
Price: HK-91 scope mount.......... **$226.00**

Heckler & Koch HK-93 Auto Rifle

Similar to HK-93 except in 223 cal., 16.13″ barrel, over-all length of 35½″, weighs 7¾ lbs. Same stock, fore-end.
Price: HK-93 A-2 with plastic stock.......... **$599.00**
Price: HK-93 A-3 with retractable metal stock **$665.00**

HECKLER & KOCH HK-94 AUTO CARBINE

Caliber: 9mm Parabellum, 15-shot magazine.
Barrel: 16″.
Weight: 6½ lbs. (fixed stock). **Length:** 34¾″ over-all.
Stock: High-impact plastic butt and fore-end or retractable metal stock.
Sights: Hooded post front, aperture rear adjustable for windage and elevation.
Features: Delayed roller-locked action; accepts H&K quick-detachable scope mount. Introduced 1983. Imported from West Germany by Heckler & Koch, Inc..
Price: HK94-A2 (fixed stock) **$505.00**
Price: HK94-A3 (retractable metal stock) **$572.00**
Price: 30-shot magazine.......... **$23.00**
Price: Clamp to hold two magazines **$17.00**

Iver Johnson PM 30HB

IVER JOHNSON PM30HB CARBINE

Caliber: 30 U.S. Carbine, 5.7 MMJ.
Barrel: 18″ four-groove.
Weight: 6½ lbs. **Length:** 35½″ over-all.
Stock: Glossy-finished hardwood or walnut.
Sights: Click adj. peep rear.
Features: Gas operated semi-auto carbine. 15-shot detachable magazine.
Price: Blue finish, hardwood stock **$219.00**
Price: Stainless steel, walnut stock.......... **$250.00**
Price: Blue finish, walnut stock **$234.00**

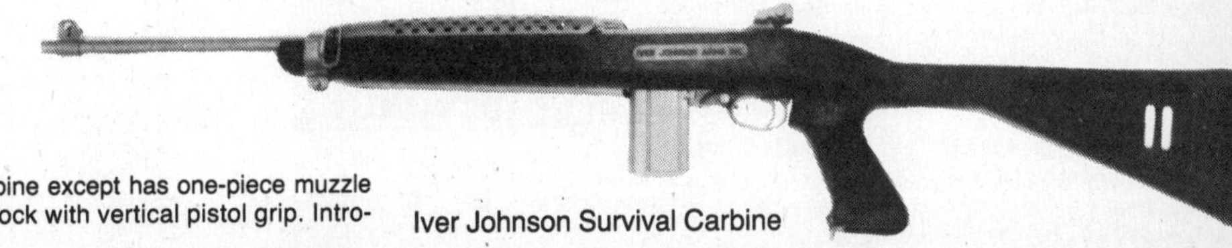

Iver Johnson Survival Carbine

Iver Johnson Survival Carbine

Similar to the stainless steel military carbine except has one-piece muzzle brake/flash hider, black DuPont Zytel stock with vertical pistol grip. Introduced 1983.
Price: **$250.00**
Price: With folding stock.......... **$297.00**
Price: In blue steel.......... **$227.00**
Price: As above with folding stock **$258.00**

CENTERFIRE RIFLES—MILITARY STYLE AUTOLOADERS

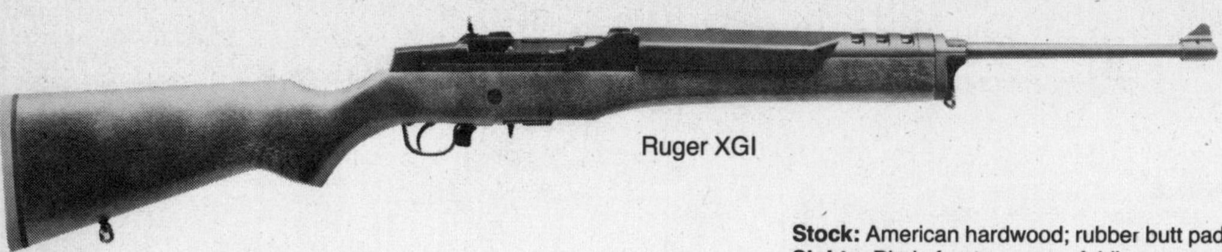

Ruger XGI

RUGER XGI AUTO RIFLE
Caliber: 308 Win., 5-shot detachable box magazine.
Barrel: 20″.
Weight: 7.9 lbs. **Length:** 39⅞″ over-all.
Stock: American hardwood; rubber butt pad.
Sights: Blade front on ramp, folding peep rear adjustable for w. and e.
Features: Uses a Garand-type gas system with fixed cylinder and moving piston with a simplified Garand-type rotating bolt. Ruger integral scope mounting system. Patented recoil buffer system; bolt lock mechanism. Introduced 1985.
Price: **$425.00**

Ruger Mini-14

RUGER MINI-14/5R RANCH RIFLE
Caliber: 223 Rem., 7.62 x 39, 5-shot detachable box magazine.
Barrel: 18½″.
Weight: 6.4 lbs. **Length:** 37¼″ over-all.
Stock: American hardwood, steel reinforced.
Sights: Ramp front, fully adj. rear.
Features: Fixed piston gas-operated, positive primary extraction. New buffer system, redesigned ejector system. Ruger S100R scope rings included. 20-shot magazines available from Ruger dealers, 30-shot magazine available only to police departments and government agencies.
Price: **$380.50**

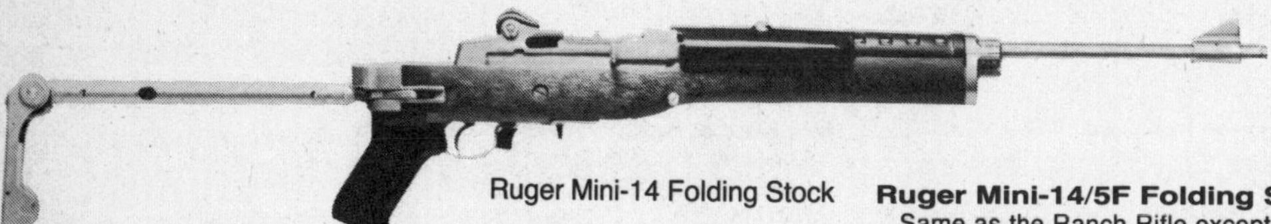

Ruger Mini-14 Folding Stock

Ruger Mini-14/5F Folding Stock
Same as the Ranch Rifle except available only in 223 and has a folding stock, checkered high impact plastic verticle pistol grip. Over-all length with stock open is 37¾″, length closed is 27½″. Weight is about 7¾ lbs.
Price: Blued ordnance steel, standard stock.................. **$351.75**
Price: Stainless **$393.75**
Price: Blued, folding stock **$430.00**
Price: Stainless, folding stock **$476.75**

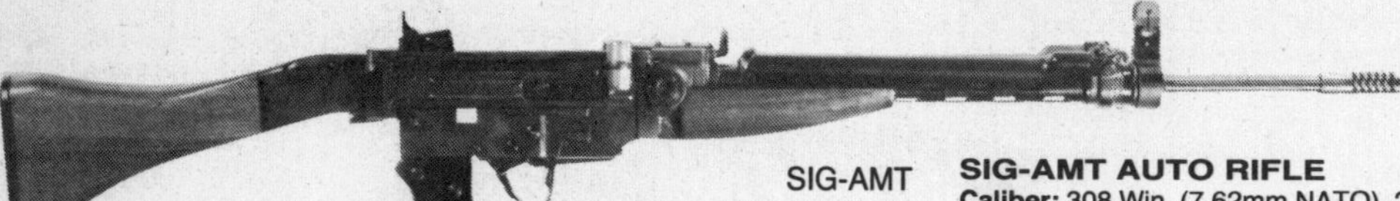

SIG-AMT

SIG PE-57 AUTO RIFLE
Caliber: 7.5mm Swiss, 24-round box magazine.
Barrel: 23.8″, with flash suppressor.
Weight: 12.6 lbs. **Length:** 43.6″ over-all.
Stock: Black high-impact synthetic butt and pistol grip.
Sights: Folding hooded post front, folding click-adjustable aperture rear.
Features: Semi-automatic, gas-assisted delayed roller-lock action; bayonet lug, bipod, winter trigger, leather sling, maintenance kit, and 6-round magazine included; quick detachable scope mount optional. Imported from Switzerland by Osborne's. Introduced 1984.
Price: About.. **$2,195.00**

SIG-AMT AUTO RIFLE
Caliber: 308 Win. (7.62mm NATO), 20-shot magazine.
Barrel: 18¾″.
Weight: 9½ lbs. **Length:** 39″ over-all.
Stock: Walnut butt and fore-end, black grooved synthetic pistol grip.
Sights: Adjustable post front, adjustable aperture rear.
Features: Roller-locked breech system with gas-assisted action; right-side cocking lever; loaded chamber indicator. No tools needed for take-down. Comes with bipod and winter trigger. Spare 5- and 10-shot magazines available. Imported from Switzerland by Osborne's. Introduced 1984.
Price: About.. **$2,195.00**

SPRINGFIELD ARMORY SAR-48 RIFLE
Caliber: 7.62mm NATO (308 Win.); 20-round magazine.
Barrel: 21″.
Weight: 9.9 lbs. **Length:** 43.3″ over-all.
Stock: Fiberglass or walnut.
Sights: Adjustable front, adjustable peep rear.
Features: New production. Introduced 1985. From Springfield Armory.
Price: **$905.00**

Springfield Armory SAR-48

CAUTION: PRICES CHANGE. CHECK AT GUNSHOP.

Springfield Armory M1A

SPRINGFIELD ARMORY M1A RIFLE

Caliber: 7.62mm Nato (308), 5-, 10- or 20-round box magazine.
Barrel: 25$\frac{1}{16}$" with flash suppressor, 22" without suppressor.
Weight: 8¾ lbs. **Length:** 44¼" over-all.
Stock: American walnut or birch with walnut colored heat-resistant fiberglass handguard. Matching walnut handguard available.
Sights: Military, square blade front, full click-adjustable aperture rear.
Features: Commercial equivalent of the U.S. M-14 service rifle with no provision for automatic firing. From Springfield Armory. Military accessories available including 3x-9x2 ART scope and mount.
Price: Standard M1A Rifle, about **$782.00**
Price: Match Grade, about **$998.00**
Price: Super Match (heavy Premium barrel), about **$1,125.00**
Price: M1A-A1 Assault Rifle, about **$936.00**

Springfield Armory BM-59

SPRINGFIELD ARMORY BM-59

Caliber: 7.62mm NATO (308 Win.); 20-round box magazine.
Barrel: 17.5".
Weight: 9¼ lbs. **Length:** 38.5" over-all.
Stock: Walnut, with trapped rubber butt pad.
Sights: Military square blade front, click adj. peep rear.
Features: Full military-dress Italian service rifle. Available in selective fire or semi-auto only. Refined version of the M-1 Garand. Accessories available include: folding alpine stock, muzzle brake/flash suppressor/grenade launcher combo, bipod, winter trigger, grenade launcher sights, bayonet, oiler. Extremely limited quantities. Introduced 1981.
Price: Standard Italian model, about **$1,326.00**
Price: Ital-Alpine model, about **$1,526.00**
Price: Alpine Paratrooper model, about **$1,727.00**
Price: Nigerian Mark IV model, about **$1,453.00**

SPRINGFIELD ARMORY M1 GARAND RIFLE

Caliber: 30-06, 8-shot clip.
Barrel: 24".
Weight: 9½ lbs. **Length:** 43½" over-all.
Stock: Walnut, military.
Sights: Military square blade front, click adjustable peep rear.
Features: Commercially-made M-1 Garand duplicates the original service rifle. Introduced 1979. From Springfield Armory.
Price: Standard, about **$696.00**
Price: National Match, about **$837.00**
Price: Ultra Match, about **$944.00**
Price: M1-T26 "Tanker", about **$797.00**

STERLING MARK 6 CARBINE

Caliber: 9mm Parabellum, 34-shot magazine.
Barrel: 16.1".
Weight: 7½ lbs. **Length:** 35" over-all (stock extended), 27" folded.
Stock: Folding, metal skeleton.
Sights: Post front, flip-type peep rear.
Features: Semi-auto version of Sterling submachine gun. Comes with extra 8" display barrel. Black wrinkle finish paint on exterior. Blowback operation with floating firing pin. Imported from England by Lanchester U.S.A. Introduced 1983.
Price: About **$595.00**

Sterling Mark 6 Carbine

STEYR A.U.G. AUTOLOADING RIFLE

Caliber: 223 Rem.
Barrel: 20".
Weight: 8½ lbs. **Length:** 31" over-all.
Stock: Synthetic, green. One-piece moulding houses receiver group, hammer mechanism and magazine.
Sights: 1.5x scope only; scope and mount form the carrying handle.
Features: Semi-automatic, gas-operated action; can be converted to suit right or left-handed shooters, including ejection port. Transparent 30- or 40-shot magazines. Folding vertical front grip. Introduced 1983. Imported from Austria by Interarms.
Price: Right or left-hand model **$895.00**

Steyr A.U.G. Rifle

Universal 1006 Carbine

UNIVERSAL 1003 AUTOLOADING CARBINE
Caliber: 30 M1, 5-shot magazine.
Barrel: 16″, 18″.
Weight: 5½ lbs. **Length:** 35½″ over-all.
Stock: American hardwood stock inletted for "issue" sling and oiler, blued metal handguard.
Sights: Blade front with protective wings, adj. rear.
Features: Gas operated, cross lock safety. Receiver tapped for scope mounts. From Iver Johnson.
Price: **$203.00**
Price: Model 1256 "Ferret" in 256 Win. **$219.00**

Universal Model 1006 Stainless Steel Carbine
Similar to the Model 1003 Carbine except made of stainless steel. Barrel length 18″. Weighs 6 lbs., birch stock with satin finish. Introduced 1982.
Price: **$235.00**

Universal 5000 Carbine

Universal Model 5000PT Carbine
Same as standard Model 1003 except comes with "Schmeisser-type paratrooper" folding stock. Barrel length 18″. Over-all length open 36″; folded 27″.
Price: Blue. **$235.00**
Price: As above with 16″ bbl. (Model 5000-16) **$235.00**
Price: As above, stainless steel (Model 5006) **$281.00**

UZI CARBINE
Caliber: 9mm Parabellum, 25-round magazine.
Barrel: 16.1″.
Weight: 8.4 lbs. **Length:** 24.4″ (stock folded).
Stock: Folding metal stock. Wood stock available as an accessory.
Sights: Post-type front, "L" flip-type rear adj. for 100 meters and 200 meters. Both click-adjustable for w. and e.
Features: Adapted by Col. Uzi Gal to meet BATF regulations, this semi-auto has the same qualities as the famous submachine gun. Made by Israel Military Industries. Comes in moulded carrying case with sling, magazine, sight adjustment key, and a short "display only" barrel. Exclusively imported from Israel by Action Arms Ltd. Introduced 1980.
Price: **$627.00**

UZI Carbine

Valmet M82

VALMET M82 BULLPUP CARBINE
Caliber: 223, 15- or 30-shot magazine.
Barrel: 17″.
Weight: 7¾ lbs. **Length:** 27″ over-all.
Stock: High-impact resin composition.
Sights: Post front, peep rear; both sights off-set to the left.
Features: Semi-automatic only. Uses Kalashnikov AK action. Introduced 1985. Imported by Bumble Bee Wholesale.
Price: **$549.95**

Valmet M76

VALMET M76 STANDARD RIFLE
Caliber: 223, 15-round magazine.
Barrel: 24″.
Weight: 8 lbs. **Length:** 37¼″ over-all.
Stock: Birch buttstock or folding metal, composition fore-end and pistol grip.
Sights: Hooded post front, open fully adj. rear with "night-sight" blade.
Features: Semi-automatic only. Uses basic Kalashnikov action. Introduced 1985. Imported by Bumble Bee Wholesale.
Price: **$599.95**
Price: Folding stock model **$649.95**

VALMET M-76 CARBINE
Caliber: 223, 15 or 30-shot magazine.
Barrel: 18″.
Weight: About 8½ lbs. **Length:** 37¾″ over-all.
Stock: Wood or folding metal type; composition fore-end.
Sights: Hooded adjustable post front, peep rear with luminous night sight.
Features: Semi-automatic only. Has sling swivels, flash supressor. Bayonet, cleaning kit, 30-shot magazine, scope adaptor cover optional. Imported from Finland by Valmet, Inc.
Price: Wood stock **$686.00**
Price: Folding stock **$873.00**

Valmet M78/A2 Semi-Auto
Similar to M76 Standard rifle except is chambered for 7.62 x 51 NATO (308 Win.). Weight is 12 lbs.; over-all length 44¼″; barrel length 24″. Has straight 20-round box magazine, rubber recoil pad, folding carrying handle. Introduced 1981. Imported by Bumble Bee Wholesale.
Price: **$799.95**

CENTERFIRE RIFLES—MILITARY STYLE AUTOLOADERS

Weaver Nighthawk

WEAVER ARMS NIGHTHAWK

Caliber: 9mm Para., 25-shot magazine.
Barrel: 16.1".
Weight: 7 lbs. **Length:** 26½" (stock retracted).
Stock: Retractable metal frame.
Sights: Hooded blade front, adjustable peep V rear.
Features: Semi-auto fire only; fires from a closed bolt. Has 21" sight radius. Black nylon pistol grip and finger-groove front grip. Matte black finish. Introduced 1983. From Weaver Arms Corp.
Price: With black web sling **$525.00**

Wilkinson "Terry"

WILKINSON "TERRY" CARBINE

Caliber: 9mm Para., 30-shot magazine.
Barrel: 16³⁄₁₆".
Weight: 7 lbs. 2 oz. **Length:** 28½" over-all.
Stock: Maple stock and fore-end, grip is PVC plastic.
Sights: Williams adjustable.
Features: Closed breech, blow-back action. Bolt-type safety and magazine catch. Ejection port has spring operated cover. Receiver dovetailed for scope mount. Semi-auto only. Introduced 1977. From Wilkinson Arms.
Price: **$488.00**

CENTERFIRE RIFLES—SPORTING AUTOLOADERS

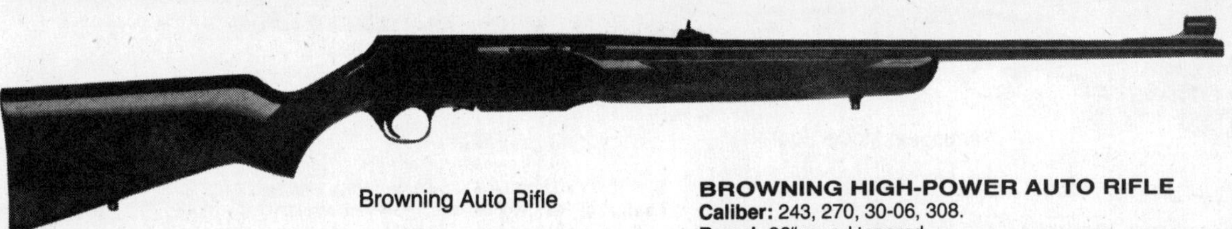
Browning Auto Rifle

BROWNING HIGH-POWER AUTO RIFLE

Caliber: 243, 270, 30-06, 308.
Barrel: 22" round tapered.
Weight: 7⅜ lbs. **Length:** 43" over-all.
Stock: French walnut p.g. stock (13⅝"x2"x1⅝") and fore-end, hand checkered.
Sights: Adj. folding-leaf rear, gold bead on hooded ramp front.
Features: Detachable 4-round magazine. Receiver tapped for scope mounts. Trigger pull 3½ lbs. Gold plated trigger on Grade IV. Imported from Belgium by Browning.
Price: Grade I **$524.95**
Price: Grade III **$880.00**
Price: Grade IV **$1,670.00**

Browning Commemorative BAR

Similar to the standard BAR except has silver grey receiver with engraved and gold inlaid whitetail deer on the right side, a mule deer on the left; a gold-edged scroll banner frames "One of Six Hundred" on the left side, the numerical edition number replaces "One" on the right. Chambered only in 30-06. Fancy, highly figured walnut stock and fore-end. Introduced 1983.
Price: **$3,550.00**

Browning Magnum Auto Rifle

Same as the standard caliber model, except weighs 8⅜ lbs., 45" over-all, 24" bbl., 3-round mag. Cals. 7mm Mag., 300 Win. Mag.
Price: Grade I **$574.95**
Price: Grade III **$928.00**
Price: Grade IV **$1,720.00**

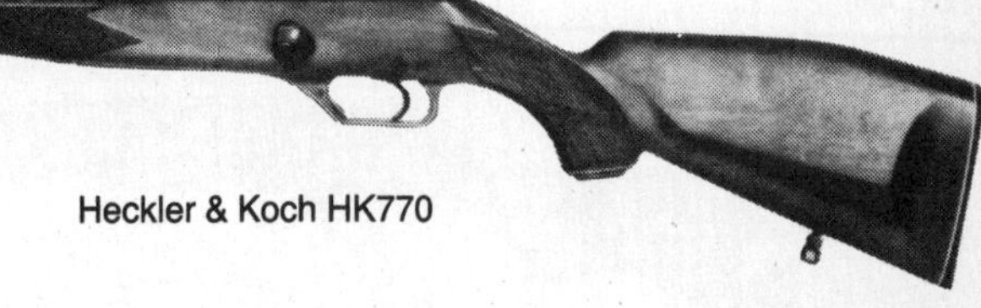
Heckler & Koch HK770

HECKLER & KOCH HK770 AUTO RIFLE

Caliber: 308 Win., 3-shot magazine.
Barrel: 19.6".
Weight: 7½ lbs. **Length:** 42.8" over-all.
Stock: European walnut. Checkered p.g. and fore-end.
Sights: Vertically adjustable blade front, open, fold-down rear adj. for w.
Features: Has the delayed roller-locked system and polygonal rifling. Magazine catch located at front of trigger guard. Receiver top is dovetailed to accept clamp-type scope mount. Imported from West Germany by Heckler & Koch, Inc.
Price: **$532.00**
Price: HK630, 223 Rem. **$599.00**
Price: HK940, 30-06 .... **$618.00**
Price: Scope mount with 1" rings **$152.00**

Heckler & Koch SL7

HECKLER & KOCH SL7 AUTO RIFLE

Caliber: 308 Win., 3-shot magazine.
Barrel: 17".
Weight: 8 lbs. **Length:** 39¾" over-all.
Stock: European walnut, oil finished.
Sights: Hooded post front, adjustable aperture rear.
Features: Delayed roller-locked action; polygon rifling; receiver is dovetailed for H&K quick-detachable scope mount. Introduced 1983. Imported from West Germany by Heckler & Koch, Inc.
Price: **$532.00**
Price: Model SL6 (as above except in 223 Rem.) **$532.00**
Price: Quick-detachable scope mount **$152.00**
Price: 10-shot magazine **$26.00**

Marlin Model 9

MARLIN MODEL 9 CAMP CARBINE

Caliber: 9mm Parabellum, 12-shot magazine (20-shot available).
Barrel: 16½", Micro-Groove® rifling.
Weight: 6¾ lbs. **Length:** 35½" over-all.
Stock: Walnut-finished hardwood; rubber butt pad; Mar-Shield® finish.
Sights: Ramp front with bead with Wide-Scan™ hood, adjustable open rear.
Features: Manual bolt hold-open; Garand-type safety, magazine safety; loaded chamber indicator; receiver drilled, tapped for scope mounting. Introduced 1985.
Price: **$247.00**

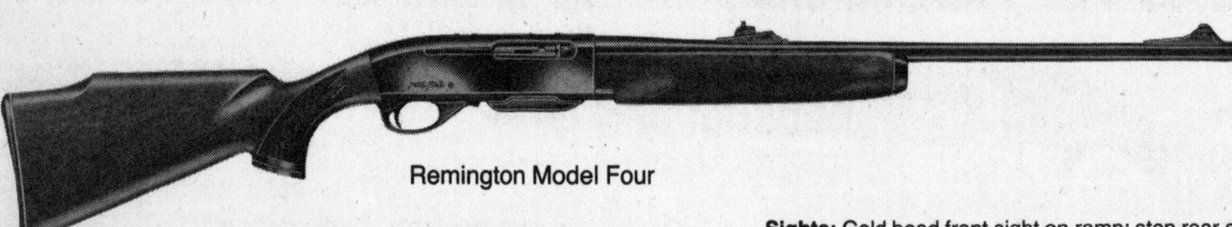

Remington Model Four

REMINGTON MODEL FOUR AUTO RIFLE

Caliber: 243 Win., 6mm Rem., 270 Win., 7mm Exp. Rem., 308 Win. and 30-06.
Barrel: 22" round tapered.
Weight: 7½ lbs. **Length:** 42" over-all.
Stock: Walnut, deluxe cut checkered p.g. and fore-end. Full cheekpiece, Monte Carlo.
Sights: Gold bead front sight on ramp; step rear sight with windage adj.
Features: Redesigned and improved version of the Model 742. Positive cross-bolt safety. Receiver tapped for scope mount. 4-shot clip mag. Has cartridge head medallion denoting caliber on bottom of receiver. Introduced 1981.
Price: About **$495.00**
Price: Peerless Grade, about **$2,245.00**
Price: Premier Grade, about **$4,627.00**
Price: Premier Grade with gold inlays, about **$6,939.00**

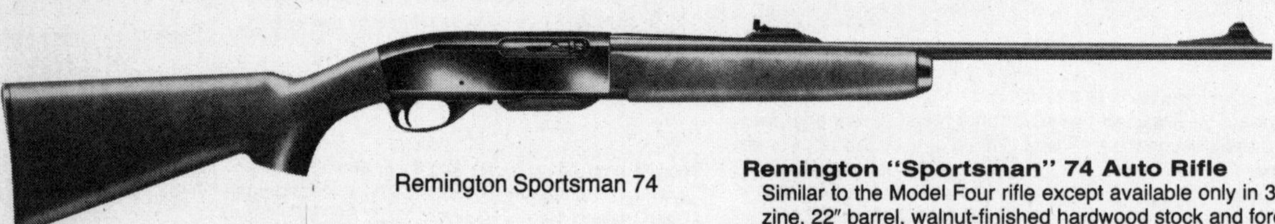

Remington Sportsman 74

Remington Model 7400 Auto Rifle

Similar to Model Four except does not have full cheekpiece Monte Carlo stock, has slightly different fore-end design, impressed checkering, no cartridge head medallion. Introduced 1981.
Price: About **$440.00**

Remington "Sportsman" 74 Auto Rifle

Similar to the Model Four rifle except available only in 30-06, 4-shot magazine, 22" barrel, walnut-finished hardwood stock and fore-end, open adjustable sights. Introduced 1984.
Price: About **$370.00**

Ruger 44 Carbine

RUGER 44 AUTOLOADING CARBINE YR-25

Caliber: 44 Magnum, 4-shot tubular magazine.
Barrel: 18½" round tapered.
Weight: 5¾ lbs. **Length:** 36¾" over-all.
Stock: One-piece walnut p.g. stock (13⅜"x1⅝"x2¼").
Sights: $\frac{1}{16}$" front, folding leaf rear sight adj. for e.
Features: Wide, curved trigger. Sliding cross-bolt safety. Receiver tapped for scope mount; unloading button. 25th Anniversary Model, last year of manufacture.
Price: **$495.00**

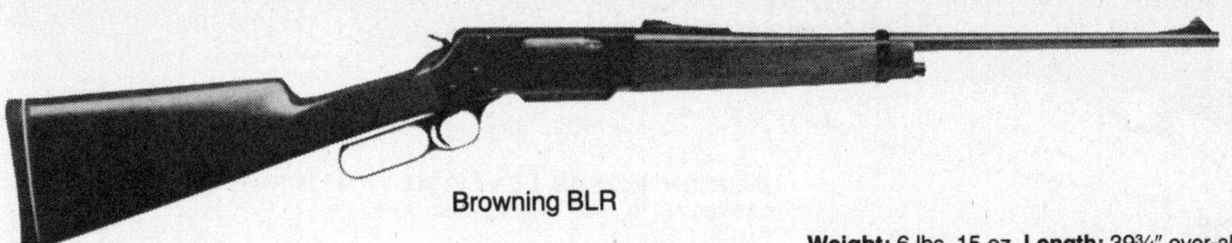
Browning BLR

BROWNING BLR LEVER ACTION RIFLE

Caliber: 222, 223, 22-250, 243, 257 Roberts, 7mm-08, 308 Win. or 358 Win. 4-shot detachable mag.
Barrel: 20″ round tapered.
Weight: 6 lbs. 15 oz. **Length:** 39¾″ over-all.
Stock: Checkered straight grip and fore-end, oil finished walnut.
Sights: Gold bead on hooded ramp front; low profile square notch adj. rear.
Features: Wide, grooved trigger; half-cock hammer safety. Receiver tapped for scope mount. Recoil pad installed. Imported from Japan by Browning.
Price: **$394.95**

Browning B-92

BROWNING B-92 LEVER ACTION

Caliber: 357 Mag., 44 Rem. Mag., 11-shot magazine.
Barrel: 20″ round.
Weight: 5 lbs., 8 oz. **Length:** 37½″ over-all.
Stock: Straight grip stock and classic fore-end in French walnut with high gloss finish. Steel, modified crescent buttplate. (12¾″ x 2″ x 2⅞″).
Sights: Post front, classic cloverleaf rear with notched elevation ramp. Sight radius 16⅝″.
Features: Tubular magazine. Follows design of original Model 92 lever-action. Introduced 1979. Imported from Japan by Browning.
Price: **$324.95**

BROWNING MODEL 1895 LEVER ACTION RIFLE

Caliber: 30-40 Krag, 4-shot magazine.
Barrel: 24″, round.
Weight: 8 lbs. **Length:** 42″ over-all.
Stock: Straight grip walnut stock and fore-end with matte finish. High Grade has Grade III French walnut, fine checkering, high gloss finish.
Sights: Gold bead on elevated ramp front, buckhorn rear with elevator.
Features: Exact replica of John M. Browning's first successful box-magazine lever-action repeater. Top loading magazine, half-cock hammer safety. High Grade model has gold plated moose and grizzly on engraved and grey receiver. Introduced 1984.
Price: Grade I **$499.95**
Price: High Grade **$750.00**

Dixie Model 1873

DIXIE ENGRAVED MODEL 1873 RIFLE

Caliber: 44-40, 11-shot magazine.
Barrel: 20″, round.
Weight: 7¾ lbs. **Length:** 39″ over-all.
Stock: Walnut.
Sights: Blade front, adj. rear.
Features: Engraved and case hardened frame. Duplicate of Winchester 1873. Made in Italy. From Dixie Gun Works.
Price: **$550.00**
Price: Plain, blued carbine **$495.00**

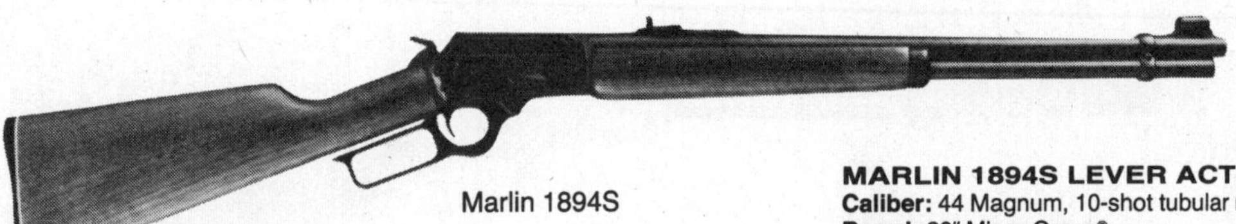
Marlin 1894S

MARLIN 1894S LEVER ACTION CARBINE

Caliber: 44 Magnum, 10-shot tubular magazine
Barrel: 20″ Micro-Grove®.
Weight: 6 lbs. **Length:** 37½″.
Stock: American black walnut, straight grip and fore-end. Mar-Shield® finish.
Sights: Wide-Scan™ hooded ramp front, semi-buckhorn folding rear adj. for w. & e.
Features: Hammer block safety. Receiver tapped for scope mount, offset hammer spur, solid top receiver sand blasted to prevent glare.
Price: **$300.95**

Marlin Model 1894CS Carbine

Similar to the standard Model 1894S except chambered for 38 Special/357 Magnum with 9-shot magazine, 18½″ barrel, hammer block safety, brass bead front sight. Introduced 1983.
Price: **$300.95**

Marlin 1895SS

MARLIN 1895SS LEVER ACTION RIFLE
Caliber: 45-70, 4-shot tubular magazine.
Barrel: 22″ round.
Weight: 7½ lbs. **Length:** 40½″.
Stock: American black walnut, full pistol grip. Mar-Shield® finish; rubber buttpad; q-d. swivels; leather carrying strap.
Sights: Bead front with Wide-Scan hood, semi-buckhorn folding rear adj. for w. and e.
Features: Hammer block safety. Solid receiver tapped for scope mounts or receiver sights, offset hammer spur.
Price: **$323.95**

Marlin 30AS Lever Action Carbine
Same as the Marlin 336CS except: checkered walnut-finished hardwood p.g. stock, 30-30 only, 6-shot. Hammer block safety.
Price: **$287.95**

Marlin Model 336 Extra-Range Carbine
Similar to the standard Model 336CS except chambered for 356 Win.; has new hammer block safety, rubber butt pad, 5-shot magazine. Comes with detachable sling swivels and branded leather sling. Introduced 1983.
Price: **$323.95**

Marlin 336TS Lever Action Carbine
Same as the 336CS except: straight stock; cal. 30-30 only. Squared finger lever, 18½″ barrel, weight 6¾ lbs. Hammer block safety.
Price: **$281.95**

MARLIN 336CS LEVER ACTION CARBINE
Caliber: 30-30 or 35 Rem., 6-shot tubular magazine
Barrel: 20″ Micro-Grove®.
Weight: 7 lbs. **Length:** 38½″.
Stock: Select American black walnut, capped p.g. with white line spacers. Mar-Shield® finish.
Sights: Ramp front with Wide-Scan™ hood, semi-buckhorn folding rear adj. for w. & e.
Features: Hammer block safety. Receiver tapped for scope mount, offset hammer spur; top of receiver sand blasted to prevent glare.
Price: Less scope **$281.95**

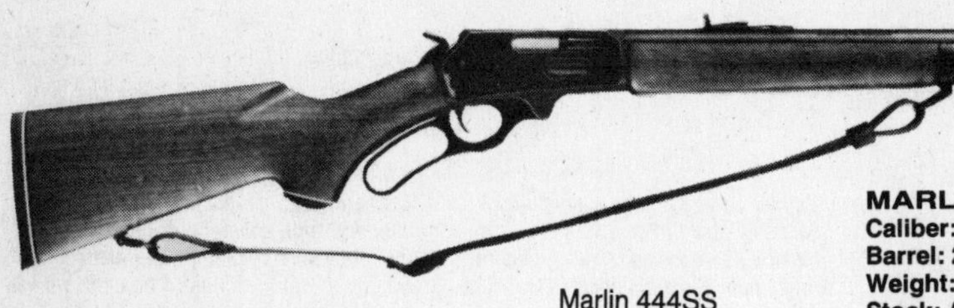
Marlin 444SS

MARLIN 444SS LEVER ACTION SPORTER
Caliber: 444 Marlin, 5-shot tubular magazine
Barrel: 22″ Micro-Grove®.
Weight: 7½ lbs. **Length:** 40½″.
Stock: American black walnut, capped p.g. with white line spacers, rubber rifle butt pad. Mar-Shield® finish; q.d. swivels, leather carrying strap.
Sights: Hooded ramp front, folding semi-buckhorn rear adj. for w. & e.
Features: Hammer block safety. Receiver tapped for scope mount, offset hammer spur, leather sling with detachable swivels.
Price: **$323.95**

Mossberg 479 PCA

MOSSBERG 479 PCA LEVER ACTION RIFLE
Caliber: 30-30, 6-shot.
Barrel: 20″.
Weight: About 7 lbs. **Length:** 38½″ over-all.
Stock: Walnut-finish hardwood; straight or pistol-grip style.
Sights: Bead on ramp front, adjustable open rear.
Features: Blue finish; hammer block safety and rebounding hammer. Trigger built into the cocking lever. Ejection port on right side of receiver. Re-introduced 1983.
Price: About **$231.95**

Navy Arms Henry

NAVY ARMS HENRY CARBINE
Caliber: 44-40 or 44 rimfire.
Barrel: 21″.
Weight: About 9 lbs. **Length:** About 39″ over-all.
Stock: Oil stained American walnut.
Sights: Blade front, rear adj. for e.
Features: Reproduction of the original Henry carbine with brass frame and buttplate, rest blued. Will be produced in limited edition of 1,000 standard models, plus 50 engraved guns. Made in U.S. by Navy Arms.
Price: Standard **$500.00**
Price: Engraved **$1,500.00**

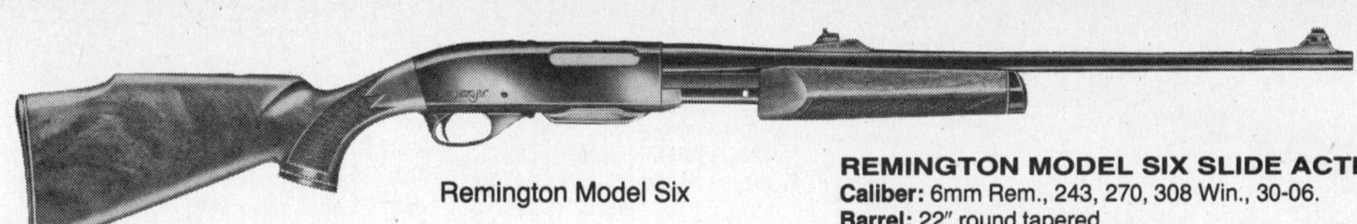
Remington Model Six

REMINGTON MODEL SIX SLIDE ACTION
Caliber: 6mm Rem., 243, 270, 308 Win., 30-06.
Barrel: 22" round tapered.
Weight: 7½ lbs. **Length:** 42" over-all.
Stock: Cut-checkered walnut p.g. and fore-end, Monte Carlo with full cheekpiece.
Sights: Gold bead front sight on matted ramp, open step adj. sporting rear.
Features: Redesigned and improved version of the Model 760. Has cartridge head medallion denoting caliber on bottom of receiver. Detachable 4-shot clip. Cross-bolt safety. Receiver tapped for scope mount. Also available in high grade versions. Introduced 1981.
Price: About ... **$450.00**

Remington Model 7600 Slide Action Rifle
Similar to Model Six except does not have Monte Carlo stock or cheekpiece no cartridge head medallion. Slightly different fore-end design. Impressed checkering. Introduced 1981.
Price: About ... **$398.00**

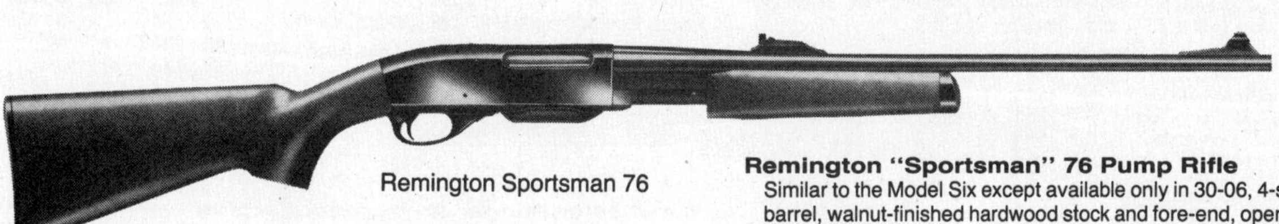
Remington Sportsman 76

Remington "Sportsman" 76 Pump Rifle
Similar to the Model Six except available only in 30-06, 4-shot magazine, 22" barrel, walnut-finished hardwood stock and fore-end, open adjustable sights. Introduced 1984.
Price: About ... **$330.00**

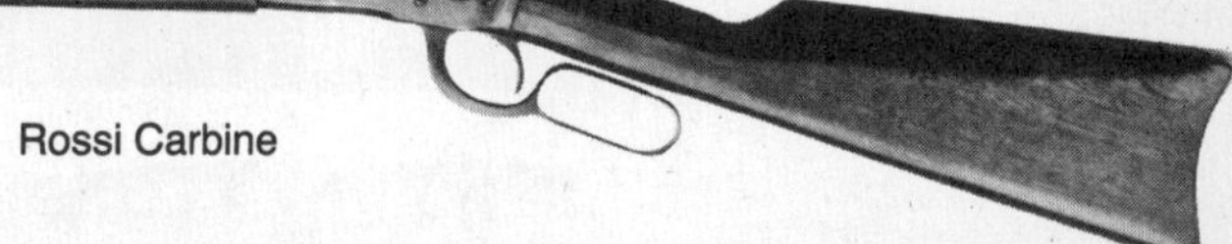
Rossi Carbine

ROSSI SADDLE-RING CARBINE M92 SRC
Caliber: 38 Spec., 357 Mag., 44-40, 44 Mag., 10-shot magazine.
Barrel: 20".
Weight: 5¾ lbs. **Length:** 37" over-all.
Stock: Walnut.
Sights: Blade front, buckhorn rear.
Features: Re-creation of the famous lever-action carbine. Handles 38 and 357 interchangeably. Introduced 1978. Imported by Interarms.
Price: ... **$224.00**
Price: Blue, engraved ... **$279.00**
Price: 44-40 ... **$234.00**
Price: 44 Spec./44 Mag. ... **$239.00**

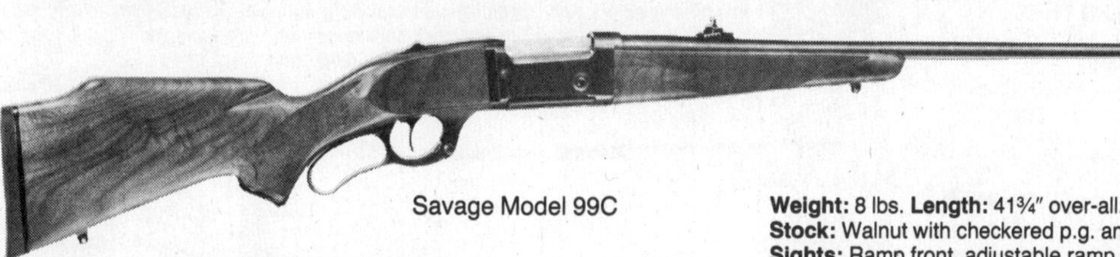
Savage Model 99C

SAVAGE 99C LEVER ACTION RIFLE
Caliber: 243 or 308 Win., detachable 4-shot rotary magazine.
Barrel: 22", chrome-moly steel.
Weight: 8 lbs. **Length:** 41¾" over-all.
Stock: Walnut with checkered p.g. and fore-end.
Sights: Ramp front, adjustable ramp rear sight. Tapped for scope mounts.
Features: Grooved trigger, top tang slide safety locks trigger and lever. Black rubber butt pad.
Price: ... **$428.00**

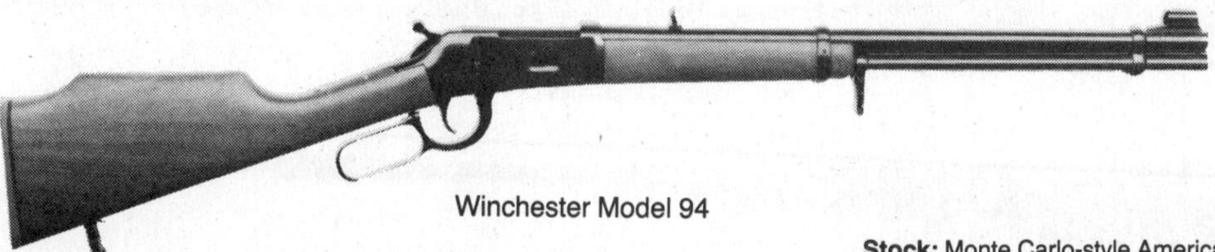
Winchester Model 94

WINCHESTER MODEL 94 ANGLE EJECT
Caliber: 307 Win., 356 Win., 375 Win., 6-shot magazine.
Barrel: 20".
Weight: 7 lbs. **Length:** 38⅝" over-all.
Stock: Monte Carlo-style American walnut. Satin finish.
Sights: Hooded ramp front, semi-buckhorn rear adjustable for w. & e.
Features: All external metal parts have Winchester's deep blue high polish finish. Rifling twist 1 in 12". Rubber recoil pad fitted to buttstock. Introduced 1983. Made under license by U.S. Repeating Arms Co.
Price: With scope rings and bases, about ... **$278.00**

Winchester Model 94XTR Angle Eject Carbine
Same as standard Model 94 except has high-grade finish on stock and fore-end with cut checkering on both. Metal has highly polished deep blue finish.
Price: About ... **$259.00**

Winchester Model 94XTR Angle Eject, 7x30 Waters
Same as Model 94 Angle Eject except has 24" barrel, 7-shot magazine, over-all length of 41¾" and weight is 7 lbs. Barrel twist is 1-12". Rubber butt pad instead of plastic. Introduced 1984.
Price: About ... **$282.00**
Price: Carbine (20" barrel), about ... **$259.00**

Winchester 94 Angle Eject

WINCHESTER MODEL 94 ANGLE EJECT CARBINE

Caliber: 30-30, (12″ twist), 38-55 Win., 6-shot tubular magazine; 44 Rem. Mag./S&W Special, 45 Colt (38″ twist), 11-shot magazine.
Barrel: 16″, 20″.
Weight: 6½ lbs. (30-30) **Length:** 37¾″ over-all.
Stock: Straight grip walnut stock and fore-end.
Sights: Hooded blade front, semi-buckhorn rear. Drilled and tapped for receiver sight and scope mount.
Features: Solid frame, forged steel receiver; angle ejection, exposed rebounding hammer with automatic trigger-activated safety transfer bar. Introduced 1984.
Price: 30-30, about **$239.00**
Price: 38-55 Win., about **$263.00**
Price: 44 Rem. Mag./44 Spec., about **$258.00**
Price: Trapper model (16″ bbl., 30-30), about **$239.00**
Price: As above, 45 Colt, about **$258.00**

Winchester Model 94 Wrangler II Angle Eject

Similar to the standard Model 94 except has a 16″ barrel, hoop-type finger lever, roll-engraved Western scenes on receiver. Chambered for 38-55 Win. only. Weighs 6⅛ lbs. and is 33¾″ o.a.l. Introduced 1983.
Price: About **$263.00**

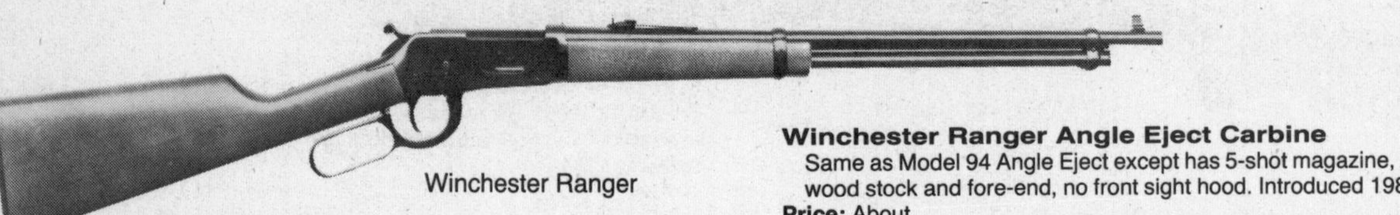

Winchester Ranger

Winchester Ranger Angle Eject Carbine

Same as Model 94 Angle Eject except has 5-shot magazine, American hardwood stock and fore-end, no front sight hood. Introduced 1985.
Price: About **$217.00**

CENTERFIRE RIFLES—BOLT ACTIONS

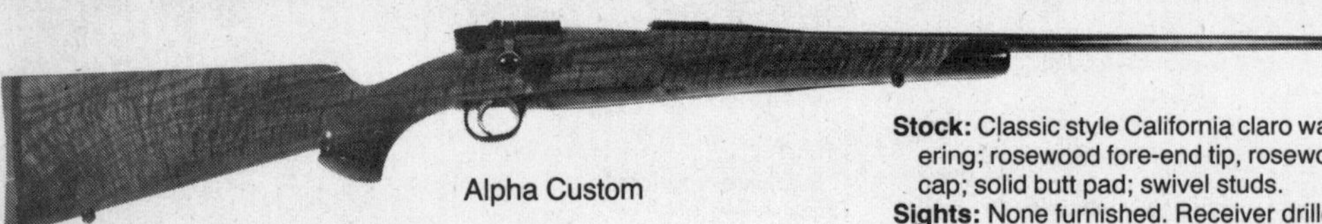

Alpha Custom

ALPHA CUSTOM BOLT ACTION RIFLE

Caliber: 243, 7mm-08, 308, 284, 25-284, 3-shot magazine.
Barrel: 21″ (284 and 25-284), 20″ all others.
Weight: About 6¼ lbs. **Length:** 39½″ over-all (20″ barrel).
Stock: Classic style California claro walnut, hand rubbed oil finish, hand checkering; rosewood fore-end tip, rosewood or Niedner-type checkered steel grip cap; solid butt pad; swivel studs.
Sights: None furnished. Receiver drilled and tapped for scope mounting.
Features: Medium-length action with three-lug locking system and 60° bolt rotation; side safety; cocking indicator; aluminum bedding block system; steel or aluminum trigger guard/floorplate assembly; medium luster or dull matte bluing. Introduced 1984. From Alpha Arms, Inc.
Price: With hard case **$1,275.00**

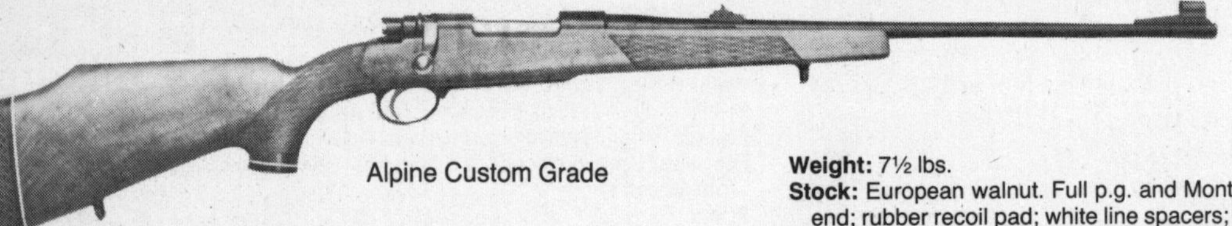

Alpine Custom Grade

ALPINE BOLT ACTION RIFLE

Caliber: 22-250, 243 Win., 264 Win., 270, 30-06, 308, 308 Norma Mag., 7mm Rem Mag., 8mm, 300 Win. Mag., 5-shot magazine (3 for magnum).
Barrel: 23″ (std. cals.), 24″ (mag.).
Weight: 7½ lbs.
Stock: European walnut. Full p.g. and Monte Carlo; checkered p.g. and fore-end; rubber recoil pad; white line spacers; sling swivels.
Sights: Ramp front, open rear adj. for w. and e.
Features: Made by Firearms Co. Ltd. in England. Imported by Mandall Shooting Supplies.
Price: Standard Grade **$375.00**
Price: Custom Grade (illus.) **$395.00**

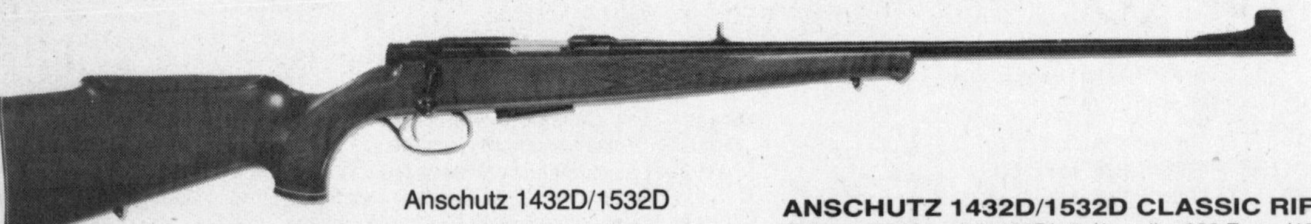

Anschutz 1432D/1532D

ANSCHUTZ 1432D/1532D CLASSIC RIFLES

Caliber: 22 Hornet (1432D), 5-shot clip, 222 Rem. (1532D), 2-shot clip.
Barrel: 23½″; 13/16″ dia. heavy.
Weight: 7¾ lbs. **Length:** 42½″ over-all.
Stock: Select European walnut with checkered pistol grip and fore-end.
Sights: None furnished, drilled and tapped for scope mounting.
Features: Adjustable single stage trigger. Receiver drilled and tapped for scope mounting. Introduced 1982. Imported from Germany by PSI.
Price: 1432D (22 Hornet) **$607.00**
Price: 1532D (222 Rem.) **$607.00**

ANSCHUTZ 1432D/1532D Custom Rifles

Similar to the Classic models except have roll-over Monte Carlo cheekpiece, slim fore-end with Schnabel tip, Wundhammer palm swell on pistol grip, rosewood grip cap with white diamond insert. Skip-line checkering on grip and fore-end. Introduced 1982. Imported from Germany by PSI.
Price: 1432D (22 Hornet) **$650.00**
Price: 1532D (222 Rem.) **$650.00**

CAUTION: PRICES CHANGE. CHECK AT GUNSHOP.

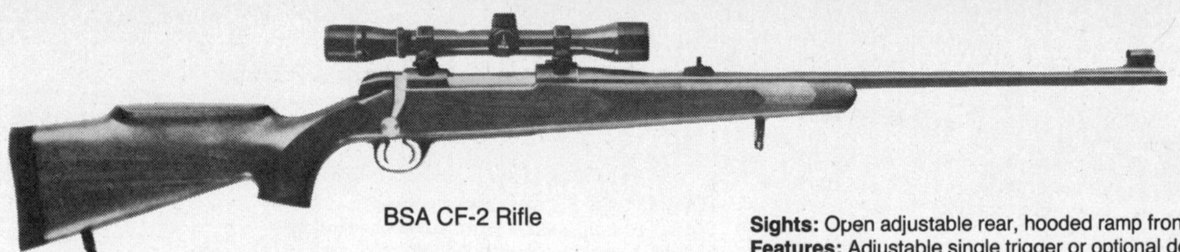
BSA CF-2 Rifle

BSA CF-2 BOLT ACTION RIFLE

Caliber: 222 Rem., 22-250, 243, 6.5x55, 7mm Mauser, 7x64, 270, 308, 30-06, 7mm Rem. Mag., 300 Win. Mag.
Barrel: 24".
Weight: 7¾ lbs. **Length:** 45" over-all.
Stock: European walnut with roll-over Monte Carlo, palm swell on right side of pistol grip, skip-line checkering. High gloss finish.
Sights: Open adjustable rear, hooded ramp front. Removable.
Features: Adjustable single trigger or optional double-set triggers, side safety, visible cocking indicator. Ventilated rubber recoil pad. North American-style stock has high gloss finish, European has oil. Introduced 1980. From Precision Sports.
Price: Standard calibers, North American style **$479.95**
Price: Magnum calibers, North American style.................... **$479.95**
Price: Double-set triggers, extra **$59.95**
Price: Heavy barrel model **$529.95**
Price: Standard calibers, European style **$479.95**
Price: Magnum calibers, European style......................... **$479.95**

BSA CF-2 Stutzen

BSA CF-2 Stutzen Stock Rifle

Similar to the standard CF-2 except has improved bolt guide rib circlip and precision-ground striker; 20.5" barrel; full-length Stutzen-style stock with constrasting Schnabel fore-end tip and grip cap. Available in 222, 6.5 x 55, 308 Win., 30-06, 270, 7 x 64. Measures 41.3" over-all, weighs 7½ lbs. Introduced 1982. From Precision Sports.
Price: **$529.95**
Price: Double set triggers, add **$59.95**

Beeman/Krico Model 420

BEEMAN/KRICO MODEL 600/700L DELUXE BOLT ACTION

Caliber: 17 Rem., 222, 223, 22-250, 243, 308, 7x57, 7x64, 270, 30-06, 9.3x62, 8x68S, 7mm Rem. Mag., 300 Win. Mag., 9.3x64.
Barrel: 24" (26" in magnum calibers).
Weight: 7.5 lbs. **Length:** 44" over-all (24" barrel).
Stock: Traditional European style, select fancy walnut with rosewood Schnable fore-end, Bavarian cheekpiece, 28 lpi checkering.
Sights: Hooded front ramp, rear adjustable for windage.
Features: Butterknife bolt handle; gold plated single-set trigger; front sling swivel attached to barrel with ring; silent safety. Introduced 1983. Made in West Germany. Imported by Beeman.
Price: Model 600, varmint calibers **$1,049.00**
Price: Model 600, standard calibers **$1,049.00**
Price: Model 700, magnum calibers **$1,049.00**

BEEMAN/KRICO MODEL 400 BOLT ACTION RIFLE

Caliber: 22 Hornet, 5-shot magazine.
Barrel: 23.5".
Weight: 6.8 lbs. **Length:** 43" over-all.
Stock: Select European walnut, curved European comb with cheekpiece; solid rubber butt pad; cut checkered grip and fore-end.
Sights: Blade front on ramp, open rear adjustable for windage.
Features: Detachable box magazine; action has rear locking lugs, twin extractors. Available with single or optional match and double set trigger. Receiver grooved for scope mounts. Made in West Germany. Imported by Beeman.
Price: **$649.00**
Price: Model 420 (as above except 19.5" bbl., full-length Mannlicher-style stock, double set trigger)..................................... **$749.50**

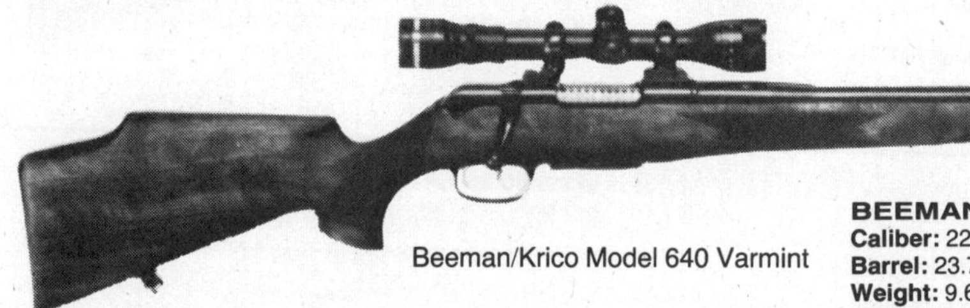
Beeman/Krico Model 640 Varmint

Beeman/Krico Model 620/720 Bolt Action Rifle

Similar to the Model 600/700 except has 20.75" barrel,. weighs 6.8 lbs., and has full-length Mannlicher-style stock with metal Schnabel fore-end tip; doubel set trigger with optional match trigger available. Receiver drilled and tapped for scope mounting. Imported from West Germany by Beeman.
Price: Model 620 (308 Win.) **$992.00**
Price: Model 720 (270 Win.) **$899.00**
Price: Model 720 (30-06) **$995.00**

BEEMAN/KRICO MODEL 640 VARMINT RIFLE

Caliber: 222 Rem., 4-shot magazine.
Barrel: 23.75".
Weight: 9.6 lbs. **Length:** 43½" over-all.
Stock: Select European walnut with high Monte Carlo comb, Wundhammer palm swell, rosewood fore-end tip; cut checkered grip and fore-end.
Sights: None furnished. Drilled and tapped for scope mounting.
Features: Free floating heavy bull barrel; double set trigger with optional match trigger available. Imported from West Germany by Beeman.
Price: **$995.00**

Beretta 500 Series

BERETTA 500 SERIES BOLT ACTION RIFLE

Caliber: 222, 223 (M500); 243, 308 (M501DL); 6.5x55, 270, 7x64, 7mm Rem. Mag., 30-06, 300 Win. Mag., 375 H&H (M502).
Barrel: 23.62″ to 24.41″.
Weight: 6.4 to 8.4 lbs. **Length:** NA
Stock: Walnut, with oil finish, hand checkering.
Sights: None furnished; drilled and tapped for scope mounting.
Features: Model 500 — short action; 501 — medium action; 502 — long action. All models have rubber butt pad. Imported from Italy by Beretta U.S.A. Corp. Introduced 1984.
Price: Model 500, 501 .... **$610.00** to **$1,500.00**
Price: Model 502, from .... **$650.00** to **$1,545.00**

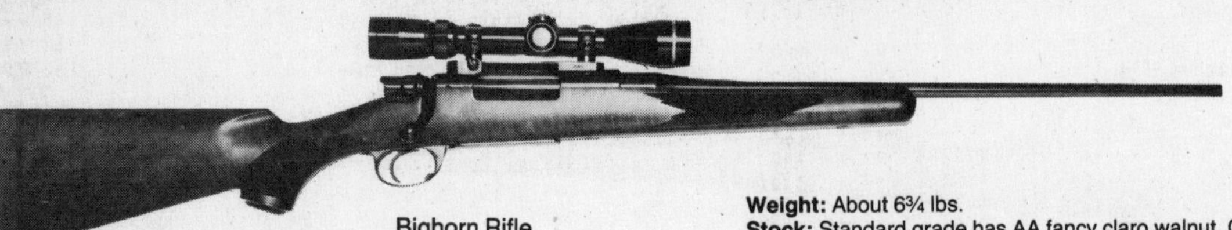

Bighorn Rifle

BIGHORN BOLT ACTION RIFLE

Caliber: To customer specs — 22-250 through all standard magnums.
Barrel: Two barrels supplied with rifle. Length and contour to customer specs.
Weight: About 6¾ lbs.
Stock: Standard grade has AA fancy claro walnut. Classic style.
Sights: None furnished. Drilled and tapped for scope mounting.
Features: Commercial Mauser action. Rifle comes with two easily interchangeable barrels, flush Pachmayr swivel sockets, black recoil pad. Available in several grades with many options. Introduced 1983. From Bighorn Rifles.
Price: With two barrels **$2,495.00**

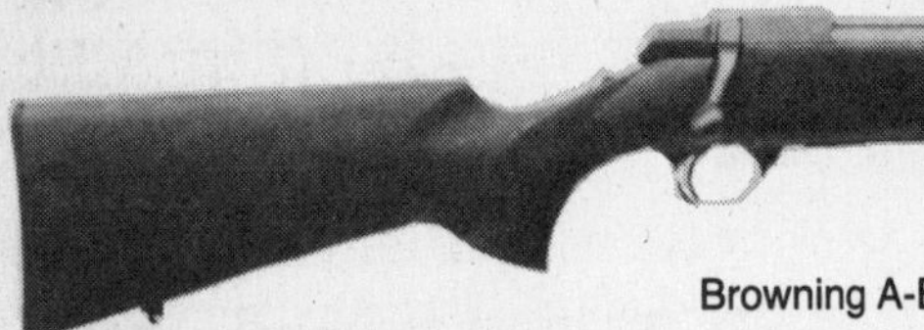

Browning A-Bolt

BROWNING A-BOLT RIFLE

Caliber: 25-06, 270, 30-06, 7mm Rem. Mag., 300 Win. Mag., 338 Win. Mag.
Barrel: 22″ medium sporter weight with recessed muzzle.
Weight: 6½ to 7½ lbs. **Length:** 44¾″ over-all. (Magnum and standard), 41¾″ (short action).
Stock: Classic style American walnut; recoil pad standard on magnum calibers.
Features: Short-throw (60°) fluted bolt, 9 locking lugs, plunger-type ejector; adjustable trigger is grooved and gold plated. Hinged floorplate, detachable box magazine (4 rounds std. cals., 3 for magnums). Slide tang safety. Medallion has glossy stock finish, rosewood grip and fore-end caps, high polish blue; Hunter has oil finish stock, matte blue. Introduced 1985. Imported from Japan by Browning.
Price: Medallion, no sights **$424.95**
Price: Hunter, no sights **$379.95**
Price: Hunter, with sights **$424.95**

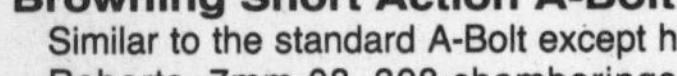

Browning Short Action A-Bolt

Similar to the standard A-Bolt except has short action for 22-250, 243, 257 Roberts, 7mm-08, 308 chamberings. Available in Hunter or Medallion grades. Weighs 6½ lbs. Other specs essentially the same. Introduced 1985.
Price: Medallion, no sights **$424.95**
Price: Hunter, no sights **$379.95**
Price: Hunter, with sights **$424.95**

Champlin

CHAMPLIN RIFLE

Caliber: All std. chamberings, including 458 Win. and 460 Wea. Many wildcats on request.
Barrel: Any length up to 26″ for octagon. Choice of round, straight taper octagon, or octagon with integral quarter rib, front sight ramp and sling swivel stud.
Weight: About 8 lbs. **Length:** 45″ over-all.
Stock: Hand inletted, shaped and finished. Checkered to customer specs. Select French, Circassian or claro walnut. Steel p.g. cap, trap buttplate or recoil pad.
Sights: Bead on ramp front, 3-leaf folding rear.
Features: Right or left hand Champlin action, tang safety or optional shroud safety, Canjar adj. trigger, hinged floorplate.
Price: From **$5,400.00**

Consult our Directory pages for the location of firms mentioned.

Colt Sauer Short Action Rifle

Same as standard rifle except chambered only for 243 Win.; 24″ bbl., 43″ over-all. Weighs 7½ lbs. 3-shot magazine
Price: **$1,256.95**

COLT SAUER GRAND AFRICAN

Caliber: 458 Win. Mag.
Barrel: 24″, round tapered.
Weight: 10½ lbs. **Length:** 44½″ over-all.
Stock: Solid African bubinga wood, cast-off M.C. with cheekpiece, contrasting rosewood fore-end and p.g. caps with white spacers. Checkered fore-end and p.g.
Sights: Ivory bead hooded ramp front, adj. sliding rear.
Price: **$1,398.50**

 CAUTION: PRICES CHANGE. CHECK AT GUNSHOP.

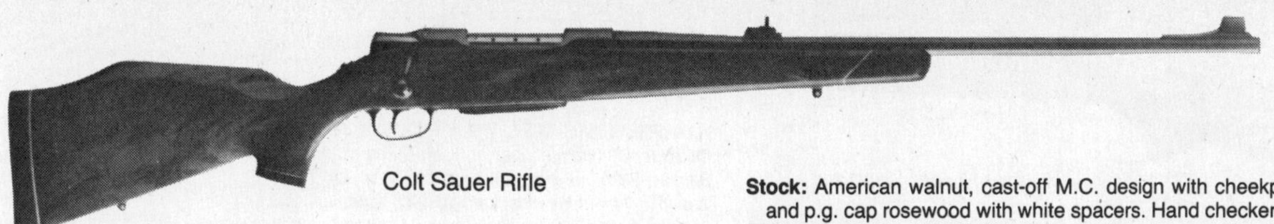

Colt Sauer Rifle

COLT SAUER RIFLE

Caliber: 25-06, 270, 30-06, (std.), 7mm Rem. Mag., 300 Wea. Mag., 300 Win. Mag. (Magnum).
Barrel: 24", round tapered.
Weight: 8 lbs. (std.). **Length:** 43¾" over-all.
Stock: American walnut, cast-off M.C. design with cheekpiece. Fore-end tip and p.g. cap rosewood with white spacers. Hand checkering.
Sights: None furnished. Specially designed scope mounts for any popular make scope furnished.
Features: Unique barrel/receiver union, non-rotating bolt with cam-actuated locking lugs, tang-type safety locks sear. Detachable 3- and 4-shot magazines.
Price: Standard calibers **$1,256.95**
Price: Magnum calibers.................................... **$1,299.50**

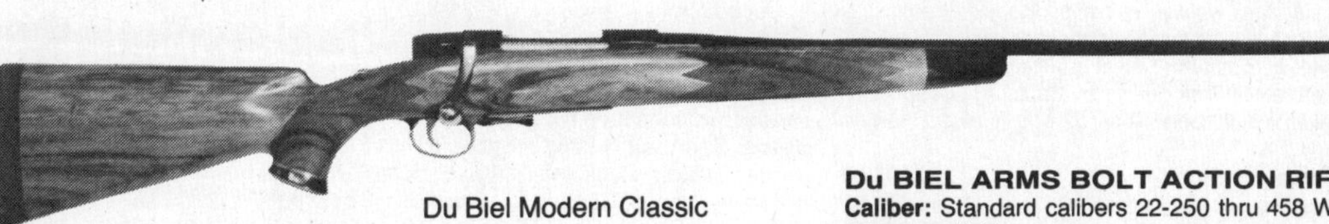

Du Biel Modern Classic

Du BIEL ARMS BOLT ACTION RIFLES

Caliber: Standard calibers 22-250 thru 458 Win. Mag. Selected wildcat calibers available.
Barrel: Selected weights and lengths. Douglas Premium
Weight: About 7½ lbs.
Stock: Five styles. Walnut, maple, laminates. Hand checkered.
Sights: None furnished. Receiver has integral milled bases.
Features: Basically a custom-made rifle. Left or right-hand models available. Five-lug locking mechanism; 36 degree bolt rotation; adjustable Canjar trigger; oil or epoxy stock finish; Presentation recoil pad; jeweled and chromed bolt body; sling swivel studs; lever latch or button floorplate release. All steel action and parts. Introduced 1978. From Du Biel Arms.
Price: Rollover Model, left or right-hand....................... **$2,500.00**
Price: Thumbhole, left or right hand **$2,500.00**
Price: Classic, left or right hand............................. **$2,500.00**
Price: Modern Classic, left or right hand....................... **$2,500.00**
Price: Thumbhole Mannlicher, left or right hand **$2,500.00**

Heym Model SR-20L

HEYM MODEL SR-20 BOLT ACTION RIFLES

Caliber: 5.6x57, 243, 6.5x55, 6.5x57, 270, 7x57, 7x64, 308, 30-06 (SR-20L); 9.3x62 (SR-20N) plus SR-20L cals.; SR-20G—6.5x68, 7mm Rem. Mag., 300 Win. Mag., 8x68S, 375H&H.
Barrel: 20½" (SR-20L), 24" (SR-20N), 26" (SR-20G).
Weight: 7-8 lbs. depending upon model.
Stock: Dark European walnut, hand-checkered p.g. and fore-end. Oil finish. Recoil pad, rosewood grip cap. Monte Carlo-style. SR-20L has full Mannlicher-style stock, others have sporter-style with schnabel tip.
Sights: Silver bead ramp front, adj. folding leaf rear.
Features: Hinged floorplate, 3-position safety,. Receiver drilled and tapped for scope mounts. Adjustable trigger. Options available include double-set triggers, left-hand action and stock, Suhler claw mounts, deluxe engraving and stock carving. Imported from West Germany by Paul Jaeger, Inc.
Price: SR-20L.. **$895.00**
Price: SR-20N **$795.00**
Price: SR-20-G.. **$835.00**
Price: Single set trigger...................................... **$60.00**

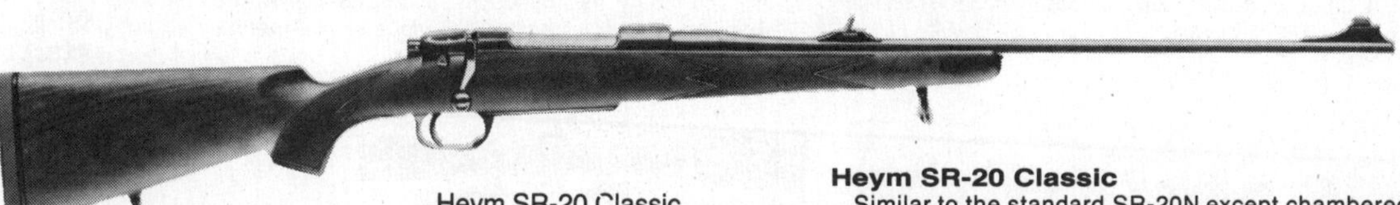

Heym SR-20 Classic

Heym SR-40 Bolt Action Rifle

Same as the SR-20 except has short action, chambered for 222 Rem., 223 Rem., 5.6x50 Mag. Over-all length of 44", weight about 6¼ lbs., 24" barrel. Carbine Mannlicher-style stock. Introduced 1984.
Price: **$725.00**
Price: Single set trigger, add **$60.00**

Heym SR-20, SR-40 Left Hand Rifles

All Heym bolt action rifles are available with true left-hand action and stock, in all calibers listed for the right-hand version, for an additional ..... **$150.00.**

Heym SR-20 Classic

Similar to the standard SR-20N except chambered for 5.6x57, 6.5x57, 6.5x55 SM, 7x57, 7x64, 9.3x62, 243, 270, 308, 30-06 (standard cals.); 6.5x68, 8x68 S, 7mm Rem. Mag., 300 Win. Mag., 375 H&H (magnum cals.). Has 24" barrel (std. cals.), 25" (mag. cals.). Classic-style French walnut stock with cheekpiece, hand checkering, Pachmayr Old English pad, q.d. swivels, oil finish, steel grip cap. Open sights on request. Choice of adjustable, single-set or double-set trigger. Introduced 1985.
Price: SR-20 Classic, right-hand............................... **$835.00**
Price: SR-20 Classic, left-hand................................ **$985.00**
Price: Magnum calibers, right or left-hand add **$40.00**
Price: Single set trigger, add **$60.00**
Price: Open sights, from **$95.00**

Kimber Hornet Sporter

Kimber Model 82,84 Super America

Super-grade version of the Model 82. Has a Classic stock only of specially selected, high-grade, California claro walnut, with Continental cheekpiece and ebony fore-end tip; borderless, full-coverage 20 lpi checkering; Niedner-type checkered steel buttplate; comes with barrel quarter-rib which has a folding leaf sight. Receiver on the 1985 model is dovetailed to accept Kimber's own scope mounts. Available in 22 Long Rifle, 22 Magnum, 22 Hornet, 223 Rem.

Price: Model 82, 22 Long Rifle, less 4x scope **$995.00**
Price: Model 82, 22 Mag., less scope **$1,023.00**
Price: Model 82, 22 Hornet, less scope **$1,073.00**
Price: Model 84, 223 Rem. **$1,105.00**

KIMBER MODEL 82 SPORTER

Caliber: 22 Hornet; 3-shot flush-fitting magazine; 218 Bee, 25-20, single shot.
Barrel: 22½", 6 grooves; 1-in-14" twist; 24" heavy.
Weight: About 6¼ lbs. **Length:** 42" over-all.
Stock: Three styles available. "Classic" is Claro walnut with plain, straight comb; "Cascade" has Monte Carlo comb with cheekpiece. "Custom Classic" is of fancy select grade Claro walnut, ebony fore-end tip, Niedner-style buttplate. All have 18 lpi hand cut, borderless checkering, steel grip cap, checkered steel buttplate.
Sights: Hooded ramp front with bead, folding leaf rear (optional).
Features: All steel construction; twin rear horizontally opposed locking lugs; fully adjustable trigger; rocker-type safety. Receiver grooved for Kimber scope mounts. Available in true left-hand version in selected models. Introduced 1982.
Price: Classic stock, no sights **$618.00**
Price: Cascade stock, no sights **$668.00**
Price: Custom Classic, no sights.................................. **$748.00**
Price: Kimber scope mounts, from **$48.00**
Price: Open sights fitted (optional) **$55.00**
Price: Custom stock, left-hand, 22 Hornet.......................... **$638.00**
Price: As above, Custom Classic stock, 22 Hornet **$768.00**
Price: 218 Bee, Custom Classic, plain or heavy barrel **$695.00**
Price: 25-20, Custom Classic, plain barrel **$695.00**

Kimber Model 84

KIMBER MODEL 84 223 SPORTER

Caliber: 223 Rem.; 5-shot magazine.
Barrel: 22½", 6 grooves; 1-in-12" twist.
Weight: About 6¼ lbs. **Length:** 42" over-all.
Stock: Three styles available. "Classic" is Claro walnut with plain, straight comb; "Cascade" has Monte Carlo comb with cheekpiece. "Custom Classic" is of fancy select grade Claro walnut, ebony fore-end tip, Niedner-style buttplate. All have 18 lpi hand cut, borderless checkering, steel grip cap, checkered steel buttplate.
Sights: Hooded ramp front with bead, folding leaf rear (optional).
Features: All new Mauser-type head locking bolt action; steel trigger guard and hinged floorplate; Mauser-type extractor; fully adjustable trigger; chrome-moly barrel. Receiver grooved for scope mounting. Introduced 1984.
Price: Classic stock, no sights.................................. **$650.00**
Price: Cascade stock, no sights **$700.00**
Price: Custom Classic stock, no sights **$780.00**
Price: Kimber scope mounts, from **$48.00**
Price: Open sights fitted (optional) **$55.00**

Kleinguenther K-15 Insta-Fire

KLEINGUENTHER K-15 INSTA-FIRE RIFLE

Caliber: 243, 25-06, 270, 30-06, 308 Win., 7x57, 308 Norma Mag., 7mm Rem. Mag., 375 H&H, 257-270-300 Weath. Mag.
Barrel: 24" (Std.), 26" (Mag.).
Weight: 7 lbs., 12 oz. **Length:** 43½" over-all.
Stock: European walnut M.C. with 1" recoil pad. Left or right hand. Rosewood grip cap. Hand checkered. High luster or satin finish.
Sights: None furnished. Drilled and tapped for scope mounts. Iron sights optional.
Features: Ultra-fast lock/ignition time. Clip or feed from top of receiver. Guaranteed ½" 100 yd. groups. Many optional stock features available. Imported from Germany, assembled and accurized by Kleinguenther's.
Price: All calibers, choice of European or American walnut with oil finish.. **$1,044.00**

M-S Safari Varmint

M-S SAFARI ARMS VARMINT RIFLE

Caliber: Any standard centerfire; single shot.
Barrel: 24", stainless
Weight: To customer specs.
Stock: Fiberglass, custom painted. Thumbhole or pistol grip style.
Sights: None furnished. Drilled and tapped for scope mounting.
Features: Electronic trigger; high-speed lock time; stainless steel action. Custom built to customer specs. From M-S Safari Arms.
Price: From **$1,145.00**

 CAUTION: PRICES CHANGE. CHECK AT GUNSHOP.

Marathon Sportsman

MARATHON SPORTSMAN BUSH & FIELD RIFLE

Caliber: 243, 308, 7x57, 30-06, 270, 7mm Rem. Mag., 300 Win. Mag.
Barrel: 24″.
Weight: 7.9 lbs. **Length:** 45″ over-all.
Stock: Select walnut with Monte Carlo and rubber recoil pad.
Sights: Bead front on ramp, open adjustable rear.
Features: Uses the Santa Barbara Mauser action. Triple thumb locking safety blocks trigger, firing pin and bolt. Blue finish. Also available as a kit requiring assembly, wood and metal finishing. Introduced 1984. Imported from Spain by Marathon Products.
Price: Finished **$339.99**
Price: Kit **$209.99**

Mossberg Model 1500

MOSSBERG M1500 MOUNTAINEER RIFLE

Caliber: 222, 223, 22-250, 243, 25-06, 270, 30-06, 308, 7mm Rem. Mag., 300 Win. Mag., 338 Win. Mag.
Barrel: 22″ (24″ in magnum calibers.).
Weight: 7½-7¾ lbs. **Length:** 42″ over-all (42½″ for 270, 30-06, 7mm).
Stock: American walnut with Monte Carlo comb and cheekpiece; 18-line-per-inch checkering on p.g. and fore-end.
Sights: Hooded ramp gold bead front, open round-notch rear adj. for w. & e. Drilled and tapped for scope mounts.
Features: Trigger guard and magazine box are a single unit with a hinged floorplate. Comes with q.d. swivel studs. Composition non-slip buttplate with white spacer. Magnum models have rubber recoil pad. Introduced 1979.
Price: Standard cals., no sights .... **NA**
Price: Magnum cals., no sights .... **NA**
Price: Standard cals., with sights .... **NA**
Price: Magnum cals., with sights .... **NA**

Mossberg Model 1500 Deluxe Rifle

Similar to Standard model except comes without sights, has engine-turned bolt; floorplate has decorative scroll. Stock has skip-line checkering, pistol grip cap with inset S&W seal, white spacers. Sling, swivels and swivel posts are included. Magnum models have vent, recoil pad.
Price: Deluxe, std. cals. .... **NA**
Price: Deluxe, magnum cals. .... **NA**

Mossberg Varmint

Mossberg Model 1500 Varmint Deluxe Rifle

Similar to the standard 1500 except has a 22″ heavy barrel and fully adjustable trigger. Chambered for 222, 22-250 and 223. Weighs 9 lbs. 5 oz. Skip-line checkering, q.d. swivels. Introduced 1982.
Price: Blue .... **NA**
Price: Parkerized, oil finished stock .... **NA**

Mossberg Classic Hunter

Mossberg Model 1700LS "Classic Hunter"

Similar to the standard Model 1500 except has classic-style stock with tapered fore-end and Schnabel tip, ribbon hand checkering, black rubber butt pad with black spacer; flush mounted sling swivels; removeable 5-shot magazine; jeweled bolt body with knurled bolt knob. Chambered only for 243, 270, 30-06. Introduced 1983.
Price: .... **NA**

Parker-Hale 2100

PARKER-HALE MODEL 2100 MIDLAND RIFLE

Caliber: 22-250, 243, 6mm, 270, 6.5x55, 7x57, 7x64, 308, 30-06.
Barrel: 22″.
Weight: About 7 lbs. **Length:** 43″ over-all.
Stock: European walnut, cut-checkered pistol grip and fore-end; sling swivels.
Sights: Hooded post front, flip-up open rear.
Features: Mauser-type action has twin front locking lugs, rear safety lug, and claw extractor; hinged floorplate; adjustable single stage trigger; silent side safety. Imported from England by Precision Sports, Inc. Introduced 1984.
Price: **$299.00**

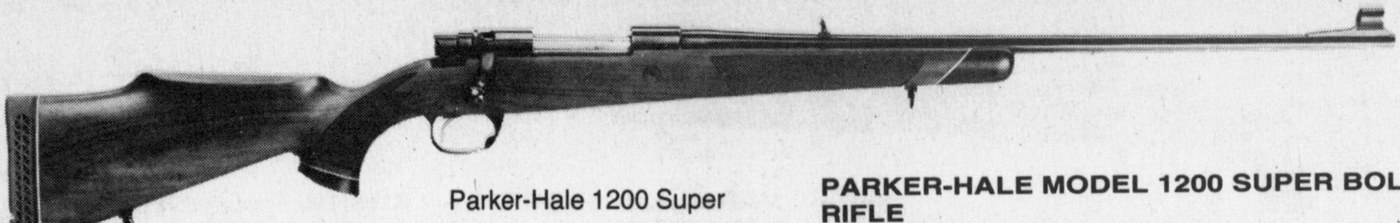
Parker-Hale 1200 Super

PARKER-HALE MODEL 1200 SUPER BOLT ACTION RIFLE
Caliber: 22-250, 243, 6mm, 270, 6.5x55, 7x57, 7x64, 308, 30-06.
Barrel: 24″.
Weight: About 7½ lbs. **Length:** 44½″ over-all.
Stock: European walnut, rosewood grip and fore-end tips, hand-cut checkering; roll-over cheekpiece; palm swell pistol grip; ventilated recoil pad; skip-line checkering.
Sights: Hooded post front, open rear.
Features: Uses Mauser-style action with claw extractor; gold plated adjustable trigger; silent side safety locks trigger, sear and bolt; aluminum trigger guard. Imported from England by Precision Sports, Inc. Introduced 1984.
Price: $479.95
Price: Optional set trigger $69.95

Parker-Hale Model 1200 Super Clip Rifle
Same as the Model 1200 Super except has a detachable steel box magazine and steel trigger guard. Imported from England by Precision Sports, Inc. Introduced 1984.
Price: $529.95
Price: Optional set trigger $69.95

Parker-Hale Model 1000 Standard Rifle
Similar to the Model 1200 Super except has standard walnut Monte Carlo stock with satin varnish finish, no rosewood grip/fore-end caps; fitted with checkered buttplate, standard sling swivels. Imported from England by Precision Sports, Inc. Introduced 1984.
Price: $379.95
Price: Optional set trigger $69.95

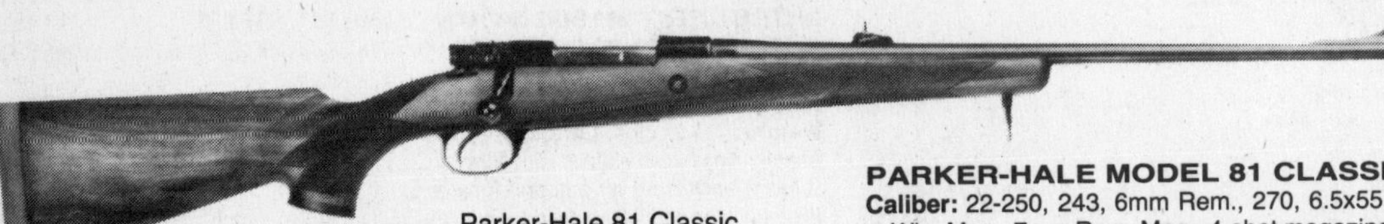
Parker-Hale 81 Classic

PARKER-HALE MODEL 81 CLASSIC RIFLE
Caliber: 22-250, 243, 6mm Rem., 270, 6.5x55, 7x57, 7x64, 308, 30-06, 300 Win. Mag., 7mm Rem. Mag., 4-shot magazine.
Barrel: 24″.
Weight: About 7¾ lbs. **Length:** 44½″ over-all.
Stock: European walnut in classic style with oil finish, hand-cut checkering; palm swell pistol grip, rosewood grip cap.
Sights: None furnished. Drilled and tapped for open sights and scope mounting.
Features: Uses Mauser-style action; one-piece steel, Oberndorf-style trigger guard with hinged floorplate; rubber butt pad; quick-detachable sling swivels. Imported from England by Precision Sports, Inc. Introduced 1984.
Price: $574.95
Price: Optional set trigger $69.95

Parker-Hale Model 1100M African Magnum
Similar to the Model 1000 Standard except has 24″ barrel, 46″ over-all length, weighs 9½ lbs., and is chambered for 375 H&H Magnum and 458 Win. Magnum. Has hooded post front sight, shallow V-notch rear, 180° flag safety (low 45° scope safety available). Specially lengthened steel magazine has hinged floorplate; heavily reinforced, glass bedded and weighted stock has a ventilated rubber recoil pad. Imported from England by Precision Sports, Inc. Introduced 1984.
Price: $769.95
Price: Optional set trigger $69.95

Parker-Hale Model 1100

Parker-Hale Model 1100 Lightweight Rifle
Similar to the Model 81 Classic except has slim barrel profile, hollow bolt handle, alloy trigger guard/floorplate. The Monte Carlo stock has a Schnabel fore-end hand-cut checkering, swivel studs, palm swell pistol grip. Comes with hooded ramp front sight, open Williams rear adjustable for windage and elevation. Same calibers as Model 81. Over-all length is 43″, weight 6½ lbs., with 22″ barrel. Imported from England by Precision Sports, Inc. Introduced 1984.
Price: $479.95
Price: Optional set trigger $69.95

Remington 700 Classic

REMINGTON 700 ADL BOLT ACTION RIFLE
Caliber: 222, 22-250, 6mm Rem., 243, 25-06, 270, 308 and 30-06.
Barrel: 22″ or 24″ round tapered.
Weight: 7 lbs. **Length:** 41½″ to 43½″.
Stock: Walnut, RKW finished p.g. stock with impressed checkering, Monte Carlo (13⅜″x1⅝″x2⅜″).
Sights: Gold bead ramp front; removable, step-adj. rear with windage screw.
Features: Side safety, receiver tapped for scope mounts.
Price: About $380.00
Price: 7mm Rem. Mag., about $395.00

REMINGTON 700 "CLASSIC" RIFLE
Caliber: 22-250, 243, 270, 30-06, 7mm Rem. Mag., 350 Rem. Mag.
Barrel: 22″ (243, 270, 30-06), 24″ (22-250, 7mm Rem. Mag., 350 Rem. Mag.).
Weight: About 7 lbs. **Length:** 43½″ over-all (24″ bbl.).
Stock: American walnut, 20 l.p.i. checkering on p.g. and fore-end. Classic styling. Satin finish.
Sights: No sights furnished. Receiver drilled and tapped for scope mounting.
Features: A "classic" version of the M700ADL with straight comb stock. Fitted with rubber butt pad on all but magnum caliber, which has a full recoil pad. Sling swivel studs installed.
Price: All cals. except 7mm Rem. Mag., about $400.00
Price: 7mm Rem. Mag., about $420.00
Price: 350 Rem. Mag., about $430.00

CAUTION: PRICES CHANGE. CHECK AT GUNSHOP.

Remington 700 BDL

Remington 700 BDL Bolt Action Rifle

Same as 700-ADL, except: also available in 222, 223, 6mm, 7mm-08 Rem.; skip-line checkering; black fore-end tip and p.g. cap, white line spacers. Matted receiver top, quick release floorplate. Hooded ramp front sight. Q.D. swivels and 1″ sling.

Price: About **$445.00**

Available also in 17 Rem., 7mm Rem. Mag. and 300 Win. Mag. calibers. 44½″ over-all, weight 7½ lbs.

Price: About **$460.00**
Price: Custom Grade I, about.... **$1,100.00**
Price: Custom Grade II, about **$2,015.00**
Price: Custom Grade III, about.... **$3,120.00**
Price: Custom Grade IV, about **$4,284.00**

Remington 700 BDL Varmint Special

Same as 700 BDL, except: 24″ heavy bbl., 43½″ over-all, wgt. 9 lbs. Cals. 222, 223, 22-250, 243, 25-06, 7mm-08 Rem. and 308. No sights.

Price: About **$465.00**

Remington 700 Safari

Same as the 700 BDL except 375 H&H or 458 Win. Magnum calibers only. Hand checkered, oil finished stock with recoil pad installed. Delivery time is about five months.

Price: About **$760.00**

Remington 700BDL Left Hand

Same as 700 BDL except: mirror-image left-hand action, stock. Available in 270, 30-06 only.

Price: About **$485.00**
Price: 7mm Rem. Mag., about.... **$500.00**

Remington Sportsman 78

Remington "Sportsman" 78 Bolt Action Rifle

Similar to the Model 700 except available only in 243, 308, 270 Win. or 30-06, 4-shot magazine, 22″ barrel, straight comb walnut-finished hardwood stock. Open adjustable sights; weight about 7 lbs. Introduced 1984.

Price: About **$315.00**

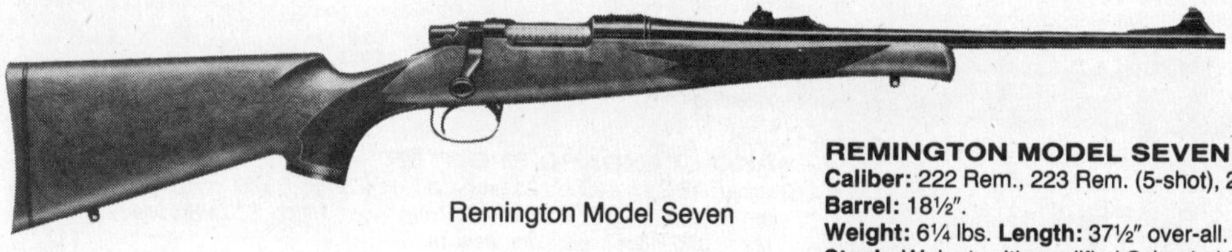

Remington Model Seven

REMINGTON MODEL SEVEN BOLT ACTION RIFLE

Caliber: 222 Rem., 223 Rem. (5-shot), 243, 7mm-08, 6mm, 308 (4-shot).
Barrel: 18½″.
Weight: 6¼ lbs. **Length:** 37½″ over-all.
Stock: Walnut, with modified Schnabel fore-end. Cut checkering.
Sights: Ramp front, adjustable open rear.
Features: New short action design; silent side safety; free-floated barrel except for single pressure point at fore-end tip. Introduced 1983.
Price: About **$440.00**

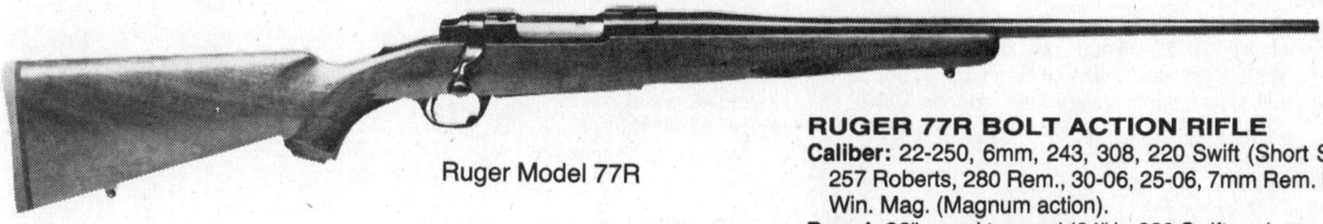

Ruger Model 77R

RUGER 77R BOLT ACTION RIFLE

Caliber: 22-250, 6mm, 243, 308, 220 Swift (Short Stroke action); 270, 7x57, 257 Roberts, 280 Rem., 30-06, 25-06, 7mm Rem. Mag., 300 Win. Mag., 338 Win. Mag. (Magnum action).
Barrel: 22″ round tapered (24″ in 220 Swift and magnum action calibers).
Weight: 6¾ lbs. **Length:** 42″ over-all (22″ barrel).
Stock: Hand checkered American walnut (13¾″x1⅝″x2⅛″), p.g. cap, sling swivel studs and recoil pad.
Sights: None supplied; comes with scope rings.
Features: Integral scope mount bases, diagonal bedding system, hinged floor plate, adj. trigger, tang safety.
Price: With Ruger steel scope rings, no sights (77R) **$440.00**

Ruger Model 77RS Tropical Rifle

Similar to the Model 77RS Magnum except chambered only for 458 Win. Mag., 24″ barrel, steel trigger guard and floorplate. Weight about 8¾ lbs. Comes with open sights and Ruger 1″ scope rings.

Price: **$600.00**

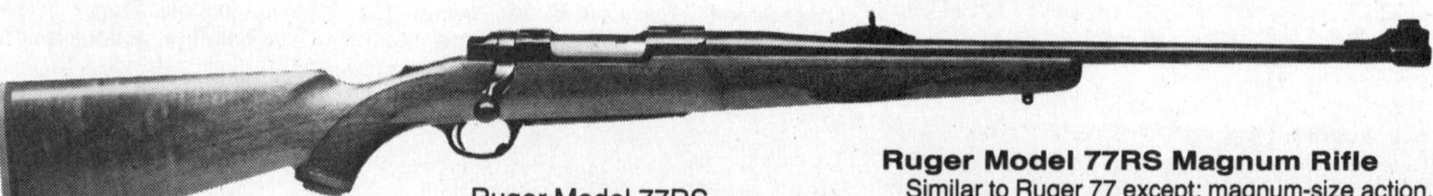

Ruger Model 77RS

Ruger Model 77RS Magnum Rifle

Similar to Ruger 77 except: magnum-size action. Calibers 270, 7x57, 30-06, 243, 308 have 22″ barrel, 25-06, 7mm Rem. Mag., 300 Win., Mag., 338 Win. Mag., with 24″ barrel. Weight about 7 lbs. Integral-base receiver, Ruger 1″ rings and open sights.

Price: Model 77 RS **$474.00**

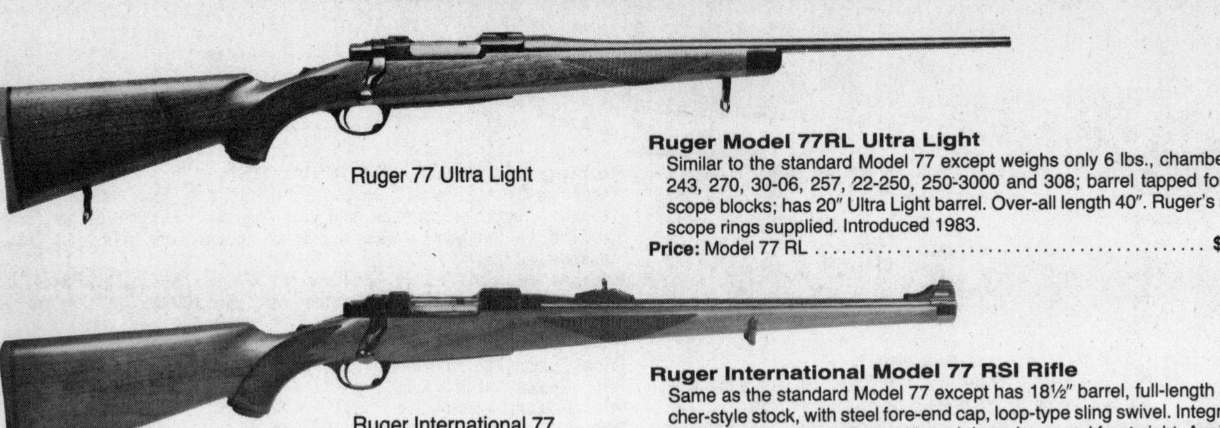

Ruger 77 Ultra Light

Ruger International 77

Ruger Model 77RL Ultra Light

Similar to the standard Model 77 except weighs only 6 lbs., chambered for 243, 270, 30-06, 257, 22-250, 250-3000 and 308; barrel tapped for target scope blocks; has 20″ Ultra Light barrel. Over-all length 40″. Ruger's steel 1″ scope rings supplied. Introduced 1983.

Price: Model 77 RL **$455.00**

Ruger International Model 77 RSI Rifle

Same as the standard Model 77 except has 18½″ barrel, full-length Mannlicher-style stock, with steel fore-end cap, loop-type sling swivel. Integral base receiver, open sights, Ruger 1″ steel rings. Improved front sight. Available in 22-250, 250-3000, 243 or 308. Weighs 6 lbs., 4 oz. and uses the Ruger short action. Length over-all is 38⅜″.

Price: **$480.00**

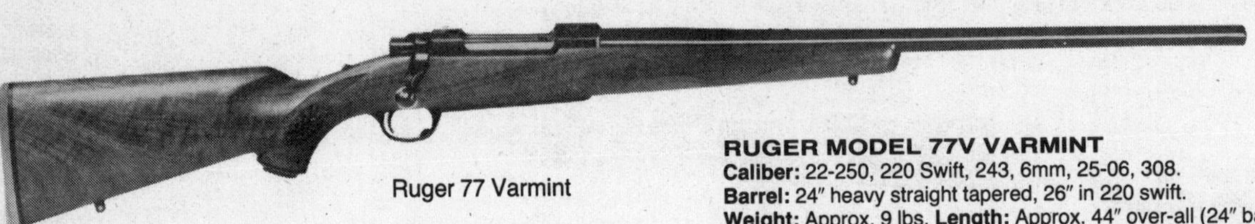

Ruger 77 Varmint

RUGER MODEL 77V VARMINT

Caliber: 22-250, 220 Swift, 243, 6mm, 25-06, 308.

Barrel: 24″ heavy straight tapered, 26″ in 220 swift.

Weight: Approx. 9 lbs. **Length:** Approx. 44″ over-all (24″ barrel).

Stock: American walnut, similar in style to Magnum Rifle.

Sights: Barrel drilled and tapped for target scope blocks. Integral scope mount bases in receiver.

Features: Ruger diagonal bedding system, Ruger steel 1″ scope rings supplied. Fully adj. trigger. Barreled actions available in any of the standard calibers and barrel lengths.

Price: (Model 77V) **$440.00**

Sako Classic Sporter

SAKO STANDARD SPORTER

Caliber: 17 Rem., 222, 223 (short action); 22-250, 220 Swift, 243, 308 (medium action); 25-06, 270, 30-06, 7mm Rem. Mag., 300 Win. Mag., 338 Win. Mag., 375 H&H Mag. (long action).

Barrel: 23″ (222, 223, 243), 24″ (other cals.).

Weight: 6¾ lbs. (short); 6¾ lbs. (med.); 8 lbs. (long).

Stock: Hand-checkered European walnut.

Sights: None furnished. Scope mounts included.

Features: Adj. trigger, hinged floorplate. 222 and 223 have short action, 243 and 22-250 have medium action, others are long action. Imported from Finland by Stoeger.

Price: Short and medium action **$763.95**
Price: Long action **$779.95**
Price: Magnum cals. **$796.95**
Price: 375 H&H **$813.95**

Sako Classic Sporter

Similar to the Standard Sporter except: available in 17 Rem., 222, 223 (short action), 243, 308 (medium action), 270, 30-06 and 7mm Rem. Mag. (long action) only; straight-comb "classic-style" stock with oil finish; solid rubber recoil pad; recoil lug. No sights. Scope mounts included. Introduced 1980.

Price: 17 Rem., 222, 223 .... **$953.95**
Price: 243, 308 .... **$953.95**
Price: 270, 30-06, 7mm Rem. Mag. **$1,006.95**

Sako Deluxe Sporter

Same action as Standard Sporter except has select wood, rosewood p.g. cap and fore-end tip. Fine checkering on top surfaces of integral dovetail bases, bolt sleeve, bolt handle root and bolt knob. Vent. recoil pad, skip-line checkering, mirror finish bluing.

Price: 222 or 223 cals. **$1,041.95**
Price: 22-250, 243, 308 .... **$1,041.95**
Price: 25-06, 270, 30-06 .... **$1,041.95**
Price: 7mm Rem. Mag., 300 Win. Mag., 338 Mag., 375 H&H...... **$1,066.95**

Sako Safari Grade Bolt Action

Similar to the Standard Grade Sporter except available in long action, calibers 300 Win. Mag., 338 Win. Mag. or 375 H&H Mag. only. Stocked in French walnut, checkered 20 l.p.i., solid rubber butt pad; grip cap and fore-end tip; quarter-rib "express" rear sight, hooded ramp front. Front sling swivel band-mounted on barrel.

Price: **$2,095.00**

Sako Heavy Barrel

Same as std. Super Sporter except has beavertail fore-end; available in 222, 223 (short action), 220 Swift, 22-250, 243, 308 (medium action). Weight from 8¼ to 8½ lbs. 5-shot magazine capacity.

Price: 222, 223 (short action) **$919.95**
Price: 22-250, 243, 308 (medium action) **$919.95**

Sako Finnsport 2700 Sporter

Similar to the Standard Sporter except has Monte Carlo stock design, different checkering, comes with scope mounts. Same calibers, actions as on Standard model. Weight, 6½ to 8 lbs. Introduced 1983.

Price: **$909.95**

Sako Super Deluxe Sporter

Similar to Deluxe Sporter except has select European Walnut with high gloss finish and deep cut oak leaf carving. Metal has super high polish, deep blue finish.

Price: **$2,095.00**

CAUTION: PRICES CHANGE. CHECK AT GUNSHOP.

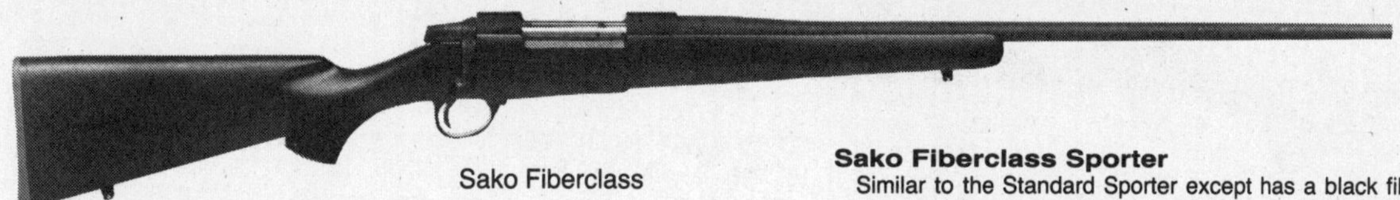

Sako Fiberclass

Sako Carbine

Same action as the Standard Sporter except has full "Mannlicher" style stock, 20" barrel, weighs 7½ lbs., chambered for 222 Rem., 243, 270, 308 and 30-06. Introduced 1977. From Stoeger.

Price: **$866.95**
Price: 338, 375 H&H **$919.95**

Sako Fiberclass Sporter

Similar to the Standard Sporter except has a black fiberglass stock in the classic style, with wrinkle finish, rubber butt pad. Barrel length is 23", weight 7 lbs., 2 oz. Long action only. Comes with scope mounts. Introduced 1985.

Price: 25-06, 270, 30-06 .... **$1,110.00**
Price: 7mm Rem. Mag., 300, 338 Win. Mag., 375 H&H **$1,140.00**

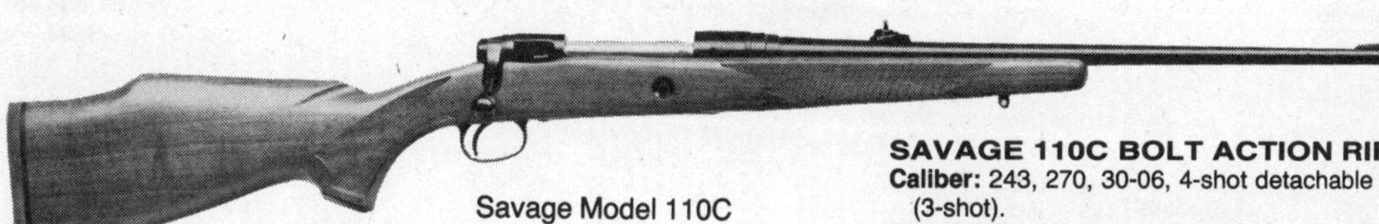

Savage Model 110C

SAVAGE 110C BOLT ACTION RIFLE

Caliber: 243, 270, 30-06, 4-shot detachable box magazine, 7mm Rem. Mag. (3-shot).
Barrel: 22"; 24" in magnum calibers.
Weight: 7lbs. **Length:** 43" over-all.
Stock: Select walnut with Monte Carlo, skip-line cut checkered p.g. and fore-end. Swivel studs.
Sights: Removable ramp front, open rear adj. for w. & e.
Features: Tapped for scope mounting, free floating barrel, top tang safety, detachable clip magazine, rubber recoil pad on all calibers. Model 110CL (left-hand) in calibers 243, 270, 30-06, 308, 7mm Rem. Mag. only.
Price: Right hand 110C **$428.00**
Price: Left hand 110CL **$468.00**

Savage Model 110-V Varmint Rifle

Same as the Model 110C except chambered only for 22-250, with heavy 26" barrel, special "varmint" stock. Introduced 1983.

Price: **$385.00**

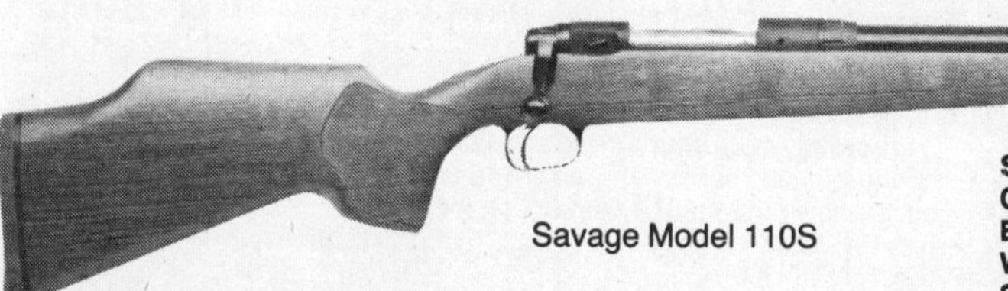

Savage Model 110S

SAVAGE 110S, SILHOUETTE RIFLE

Caliber: 308 Win., 5-shot.
Barrel: 22", heavy tapered.
Weight: 8 lbs., 10 oz. **Length:** 43" over-all.
Stock: Special Silhouette stock of select walnut. High fluted comb, Wundhammer swell, stippled p.g. and fore-end. Rubber recoil pad.
Sights: None. Receiver drilled and tapped for scope mounting.
Features: Receiver has satin blue finish to reduce glare. Barrel is free-floating. Top tang safety, internal magazine. Available in right-hand only. Introduced 1978.
Price: **$385.00**

SAVAGE 110E BOLT ACTION RIFLE

Caliber: 270, 308, 30-06, 243, 7mm Rem. Mag., 4-shot.
Barrel: 22" round tapered, 24" for magnum.
Weight: 6¾ lbs. **Length:** 43" (22"barrel).
Stock: Walnut finished hardwood with Monte Carlo; hard rubber buttplate.
Sights: Gold bead removable ramp front, removeable step adj. rear.
Features: Top tang safety, receiver tapped for scope mount.
Price: **$271.00**
Price: Without sights **$263.10**

Savage Model 340

SAVAGE 340 CLIP REPEATER

Caliber: 22 Hornet, 222 Rem., 223 (4-shot) and 30-30 (3-shot).
Barrel: 24", 22" for 30-30.
Weight: About 7½ lbs. **Length:** 40"-42".
Stock: Walnut, Monte Carlo.
Sights: Hooded ramp front, folding-leaf rear.
Features: Detachable clip magazine, sliding thumb safety. Comes with scope mount and rings.
Price: **$256.90**

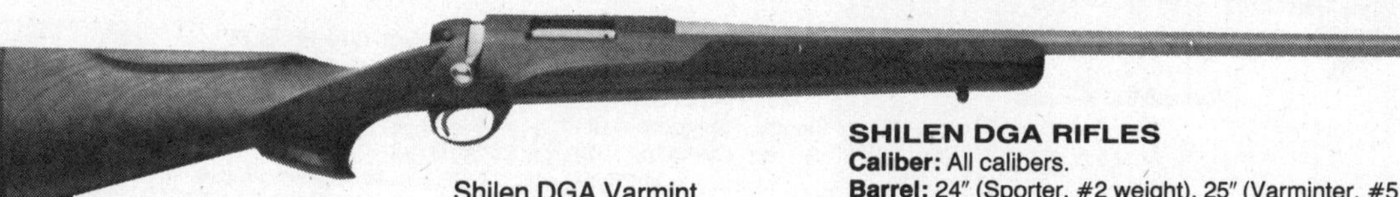

Shilen DGA Varmint

SHILEN DGA RIFLES

Caliber: All calibers.
Barrel: 24" (Sporter, #2 weight), 25" (Varminter, #5 weight).
Weight: 7½ lbs. (Sporter), 9 lbs., (Varminter).
Stock: Selected Claro walnut. Barrel and action hand bedded to stock with free-floated barrel, bedded action. Swivel studs installed.
Sights: None furnished. Drilled and tapped for scope mounting.
Features: Shilen Model DGA action, fully adjustable trigger with side safety. Stock finish is satin sheen epoxy. Barrel and action non-glare blue-black. From Shilen Rifles, Inc.
Price: Sporter or Varminter rifle, from **$1,600.00**

Steyr-Mannlicher L

STEYR-MANNLICHER MODELS SL & L

Caliber: SL—222, 222 Rem. Mag., 223; SL Varmint—222; L—22-250, 6mm, 243, 308 Win.; L Varmint—22-250, 243, 308 Win.; L optional cal.—5.6x57.
Barrel: 20″ (full stock); 23.6″ (half stock).
Weight: 6 lbs. (full stock). **Length:** 38¼″ (full stock).
Stock: Hand checkered walnut. Full Mannlicher or standard half-stock with Monte Carlo.
Sights: Ramp front, open U-notch rear.
Features: Choice of interchangeable single or double set triggers. Five-shot detachable "Makrolon" rotary magazine, 6 rear locking lugs. Drilled and tapped for scope mounts. Imported by Gun South, Inc.
Price: Full Stock **$1,056.10**
Price: Half-stock **$998.94**
Price: Optional caliber, add **$73.56**

Steyr-Mannlicher Varmint, Models SL and L

Similar to standard SL and L except chambered only for: 222 Rem. (SL), 22-250, 243, 308 and optional 5.6x57 (L). Has 26″ heavy barrel, no sights (drilled and tapped for scope mounts). Choice of single or double-set triggers. Five-shot detachable magazine.
Price: **$1,056.10**
Price: Optional caliber, add **$73.56**
Price: Spare magazine **$25.00**

Steyr-Mannlicher Professional

STEYR-MANNLICHER MODEL M

Caliber: 7x64, 7x57, 25-06, 270, 30-06. Left-hand action cals.—7x64, 25-06, 270, 30-06. Optional cals.—6.5x57, 8x57JS, 9.3x62, 6.5x55, 7.5x55.
Barrel: 20″ (full stock); 23.6″ (half stock).
Weight: 6.8 lbs. to 7.5 lbs. **Length:** 39″ (full stock); 43″ (half stock).
Stock: Hand checkered walnut. Full Mannlicher or std. half stock with M.C. and rubber recoil pad.
Sights: Ramp front, open U-notch rear.
Features: Choice of interchangeable single or double set triggers. Detachable 5-shot rotary magazine. Drilled and tapped for scope mounting. Available as "Professional" model with parkerized finish and synthetic stock (right hand action only). Imported by Gun South, Inc.
Price: Full stock (carbine) **$1,056.10**
Price: Half stock (rifle) **$998.94**
Price: For left hand action add **$200.00**
Price: Professional model with iron sights **$897.82**

Steyr-Mannlicher ML79 "Luxus"

Similar to Steyr-Mannlicher models L and M except has single-set trigger and detachable 3-shot steel magazine; 6-shot magazine optional. Same calibers as L and M. Oil finish or high gloss lacquer on stock.
Price: Full stock **$1,372.49**
Price: Half stock **$1,298.41**
Price: Optional cals., add **$68.77**
Price: Extra 3-shot magazine **$52.39**

STEYR-MANNLICHER MODELS S & S/T

Caliber: Model S—300 Win. Mag., 338 Win. Mag., 7mm Rem. Mag., 300 H&H Mag., 375 H&H Mag. (6.5x68, 8x68S, 9.3x64 optional); S/T—375 H&H Mag., 458 Win. Mag. (9.3x64 optional).
Barrel: 25.6″.
Weight: 8.4 lbs. (Model S). **Length:** 45″ over-all.
Stock: Half stock with M.C. and rubber recoil pad. Hand checkered walnut. Available with optional spare magazine inletted in butt.
Sights: Ramp front, U-notch rear.
Features: Choice of interchangeable single or double set triggers., detachable 4-shot magazine. Drilled and tapped for scope mounts. Imported by Gun South, Inc.
Price: Model S **$1,258.20**
Price: Model ST 375 H&H, 458 Win. Mag **$1,332.27**

TIKKA MODEL 55 DELUXE RIFLE

Caliber: 17 Rem., 222, 22-250, 6mm Rem., 243, 308
Barrel: 23″.
Weight: About 6½ lbs. **Length:** 41½″ over-all.
Stock: Hand checkered walnut with rosewood fore-end tip and grip cap.
Sights: Bead on ramp front, rear adjustable for windage and elevation.
Features: Detachable 3-shot magazine with 5- or 10-shot magazines available. Roll-over cheekpiece, palm swell in pistol grip. Adjustable trigger. Receiver dovetailed for scope mounting. Imported from Finland by Mandall and Armsport.
Price: **$650.00**
Price: QD scope mounts **$89.95**

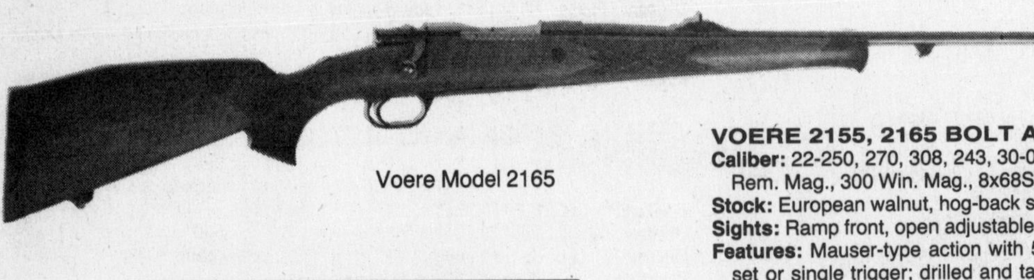

Voere Model 2165

VOERE 2155, 2165 BOLT ACTION RIFLE

Caliber: 22-250, 270, 308, 243, 30-06, 7x64, 5.6x57, 6.5x55, 8x57 JRS, 7mm Rem. Mag., 300 Win. Mag., 8x68S, 9.3x62, 9.3x64, 6.5x68.
Stock: European walnut, hog-back style; checkered pistol grip and fore-end.
Sights: Ramp front, open adjustable rear.
Features: Mauser-type action with 5-shot detachable box magazine; double set or single trigger; drilled and tapped for scope mounting. Imported from Austria by L. Joseph Rahn. Introduced 1984.
Price: Standard calibers, single trigger **$423.00**
Price: As above, double set triggers **$445.00**
Price: Magnum calibers, single trigger **$456.00**
Price: As above, double set triggers **$475.00**
Price: Full-stock, single trigger **$551.00**
Price: As above, double set triggers **$570.00**

Consult our Directory pages for the location of firms mentioned.

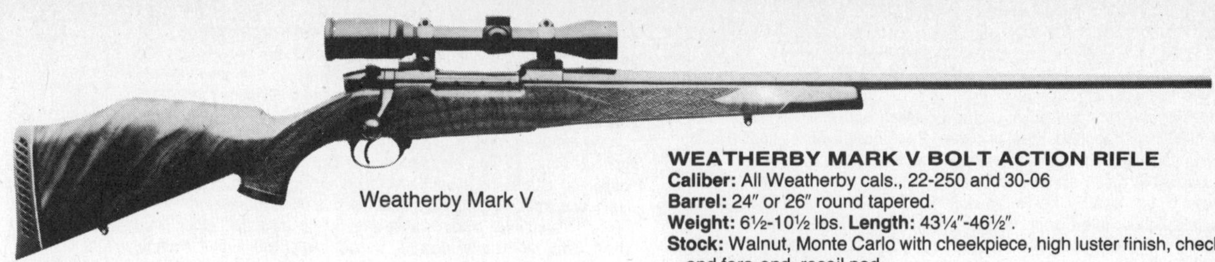
Weatherby Mark V

WEATHERBY MARK V BOLT ACTION RIFLE
Caliber: All Weatherby cals., 22-250 and 30-06
Barrel: 24″ or 26″ round tapered.
Weight: 6½-10½ lbs. **Length:** 43¼″-46½″.
Stock: Walnut, Monte Carlo with cheekpiece, high luster finish, checkered p.g. and fore-end, recoil pad.
Sights: Optional (extra).
Features: Cocking indicator, adj. trigger, hinged floorplate, thumb safety, quick detachable sling swivels.
Price: Cals. 224 and 22-250, std. bbl. **$764.95**
Price: With 26″ semi-target bbl. **$779.95**
Price: Cals. 240, 257, 270, 7mm, 30-06 and 300 (24″ bbl.) **$784.95**
Price: With 26″ No. 2 contour bbl. **$804.95**
Price: Cal. 340 (26″ bbl.). **$804.95**
Price: Cal. 378 (26″ bbl.). **$959.95**
Price: Cal. 460 (26″ bbl.) **$1,099.95**

Weatherby Mark V Rifle Left Hand
Available in all Weatherby calibers except 224 and 22-250 (and 26″ No. 2 contour 300WM). Complete left handed action; stock with cheekpiece on right side. Prices are $20 higher than right hand models except the 378 and 460WM are unchanged.

Weatherby Fibermark Rifle

Weatherby Fibermark Rifle
Same as the standard Mark V except the stock is of fiberglass; finished with a non-glare black wrinkle finish and black recoil pad; receiver and floorplate have low luster blue finish; fluted bolt has a satin finish. Currently available in right-hand model only, 24″ or 26″ barrel, 240 Weatherby Mag. through 340 Weatherby Mag. calibers. Introduced 1983.
Price: 240 W.M. through 300 W.M., 24″ bbl. **$889.95**
Price: 240 W.M. through 340 W.M., 26″ bbl. **$909.95**

Weatherby Vanguard VGL Rifle
Similar to the standard Vanguard except has a short action, chambered for 223, 243, 270, 30-06, 7mm Rem. Mag. with 20″ barrel. Barrel and action have a non-glare blue finish. Guaranteed to shoot a 1½″ 3-shot group at 100 yards. Stock has a non-glare satin finish, hand checkering and a black butt pad with black spacer. Introduced 1984.
Price: **$389.00**

Weatherby Lazer Mark V Rifle
Same as standard Mark V except stock has extensive laser carving under cheekpiece, on butt, p.g. and fore-end. Introduced 1981.
Price: 22-250, 224 Wea., 24″ bbl. **$879.95**
Price: As above, 26″ bbl. **$894.95**
Price: 240 Wea. thru 300 Wea., 24″ bbl. **$899.95**
Price: As above, 26″ bbl. **$919.95**
Price: 340 Wea. **$919.95**
Price: 378 Wea. **$1,074.95**
Price: 460 Wea. **$1,214.95**

WEATHERBY VANGUARD VGX, VGS RIFLES
Caliber: 22-250, 25-06, 243, 270, and 30-06 (5-shot), 7mm Rem. and 300 Win. Mag. (3-shot).
Barrel: 24″ hammer forged.
Weight: 7⅞ lbs. **Length:** 44½″ over-all.
Stock: American walnut, p.g. cap and fore-end tip, hand inletted and checkered. 13½″ pull.
Sights: Optional, available at extra cost.
Features: Side safety, adj. trigger, hinged floorplate, receiver tapped for scope mounts. Imported from Japan by Weatherby.
Price: VGS **$389.95**
Price: VGX—deluxe wood, different checkering, ventilated recoil pad **$479.95**

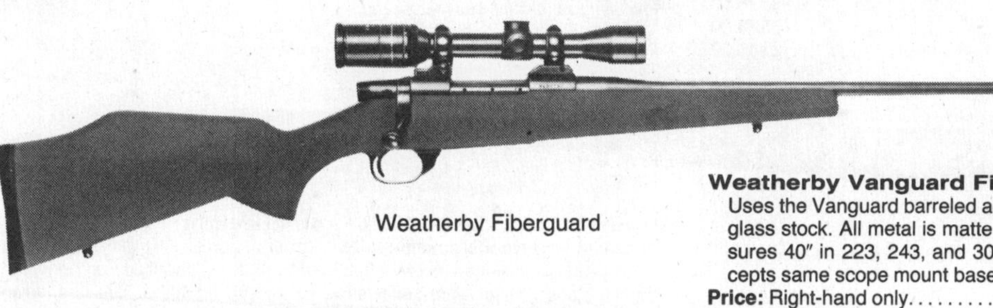
Weatherby Fiberguard

Weatherby Vanguard Fiberguard Rifle
Uses the Vanguard barreled action and a forest green wrinkle-finished fiberglass stock. All metal is matte blue. Has a 20″ barrel, weighs 6½ lbs., measures 40″ in 223, 243, and 308; 40½″ in 270, 7mm Rem. Mag., 30-06. Accepts same scope mount bases as Mark V action. Introduced 1985.
Price: Right-hand only. **$499.95**

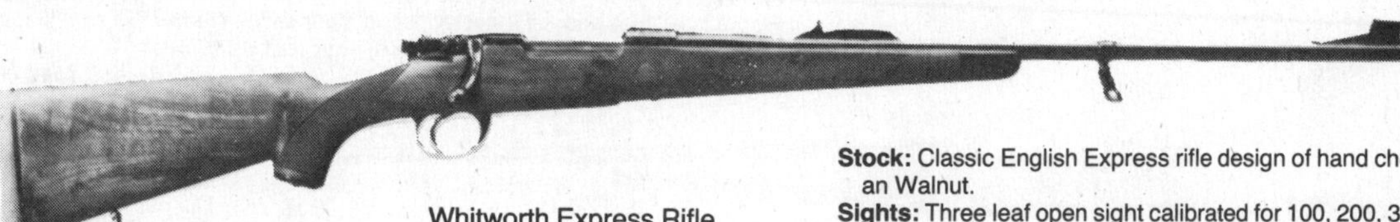
Whitworth Express Rifle

WHITWORTH EXPRESS RIFLE
Caliber: 22-250, 243, 25-06, 270, 7x57, 308, 30-06, 300 Win. Mag., 7mm Rem. Mag., 375 H&H, 458 Win. Mag.
Barrel: 24″.
Weight: 7½-8 lbs. **Length:** 44″.
Stock: Classic English Express rifle design of hand checkered, select European Walnut.
Sights: Three leaf open sight calibrated for 100, 200, 300 yards on ¼-rib, ramp front with removable hood (375, 458 only); other calibers have standard open sights.
Features: Solid rubber recoil pad, barrel mounted sling swivel, adjustable trigger, hinged floor plate, solid steel recoil cross bolt. Imported by Interarms.
Price: **$499.00**
Price: 375, 458, with express sights **$614.00**
Price: Mannlicher-style carbine, cals. 243, 270, 308, 7x57, 30-06 only, 20″ bbl. **$644.00**

WICHITA CLASSIC RIFLE
Caliber: 17 Rem. thru 308 Win., including 22 and 6mm PPC.
Barrel: 21⅛".
Weight: 8 lbs. **Length:** 41" over-all.
Stock: AAA Fancy American walnut. Hand-rubbed and checkered (20 l.p.i). Hand-inletter, glass bedded, steel grip cap. Pachmayr rubber recoil pad.
Sights: None. Drilled and tapped for scope mounting.
Features: Available as single shot or repeater. Octagonal barrel and Wichita action, right or left-hand. Checkered bolt handle. Bolt is hand-fitted, lapped and jewelled. Adjustable Canjar trigger is set at 2 lbs. Side thumb safety. Firing pin fall is 3/16". Non-glare blue finish. Shipped in hard case. From Wichita Arms.
Price: Single shot **$1,725.00**
Price: With blind box magazine **$1,855.00**

WICHITA MAGNUM STAINLESS RIFLE
Caliber: From 270 Win. through 458 Win. Mag.
Barrel: 22" or 24".
Weight: 8½ lbs. **Length:** 44¾" over-all (24" barrel).
Stock: AAA fancy walnut; hand inletted; glass bedded; steel grip cap; Pachmayr rubber recoil pad.
Sights: None. Drilled and tapped for Burris scope mounts.
Features: Stainless steel barrel and action, round contour. Target grade barrel. Available as a single shot or with a blind magazine. Fully adj. trigger. Bolt is ⅞" in diameter with recessed face. Hand rubbed stock finish, checkered 20 l.p.i. Shipped in a hard case. Introduced 1980. From Wichita Arms.
Price: Single shot **$2,155.00**
Price: With blind box magazine **$2,285.00**

Wichita Varmint Rifle

WICHITA VARMINT RIFLE
Caliber: 17 Rem. thru 308 Win., including 22 and 6mm PPC.
Barrel: 20⅛".
Weight: 9 lbs. **Length:** 40⅛" over-all.
Stock: AAA Fancy American walnut. Hand-rubbed finish, hand-checkered, 20 l.p.i. pattern. Hand-inletted, glass bedded steel grip cap, Pachmayr rubber recoil pad.
Sights: None. Drilled and tapped for scope mounts.
Features: Right or left-hand Wichita action with three locking lugs. Available as a single shot or repeater with 3-shot magazine. Checkered bolt handle. Bolt is hand fitted, lapped and jeweled. Side thumb safety. Firing pin fall is 3/16". Non-glare blue finish. Shipped in hard case. From Wichita Arms.
Price: Single shot **$1,075.00**
Price: With blind box magazine **$1,205.00**

Winchester 70 Lightweight

WINCHESTER MODEL 70 LIGHTWEIGHT CARBINE
Caliber: 270, 30-06 (standard action); 22-250, 223, 243, 308 (short action), both 5-shot magazine, except 6-shot in 223.
Barrel: 20".
Weight: 6¼ lbs. (std.), 6 lbs. (short). **Length:** 40½" over-all (std.), 40" (short).
Stock: American walnut with satin finish, deep-cut checkering.
Sights: None furnished. Drilled and tapped for scope mounting.
Features: Three position safety; stainless steel magazine follower; hinged floorplate; sling swivel studs. Introduced 1984.
Price: With sights, about **$376.00**
Price: Without sights, about **$358.00**
Price: As Mini-Carbine, 243 only, 12½" stock pull, about **$388.00**

WINCHESTER 70 XTR SPORTER MAGNUM
Caliber: 264 Win. Mag., 7mm Rem. Mag., 300 Win. Mag., 338 Win. Mag., 3-shot magazine.
Barrel: 24".
Weight: 7¾ lbs. **Length:** 44½" over-all.
Stock: American walnut with Monte Carlo cheekpiece. XTR checkering and satin finish.
Sights: None furnished; optional hooded ramp front, adjustable folding leaf rear.
Features: Three-position safety, detachable sling swivels, stainless steel magazine follower, rubber butt pad, epoxy bedded receiver recoil lug. Made under license by U.S. Repeating Arms Co.
Price: With sights, about **$440.00**
Price: Without sights, about **$422.00**

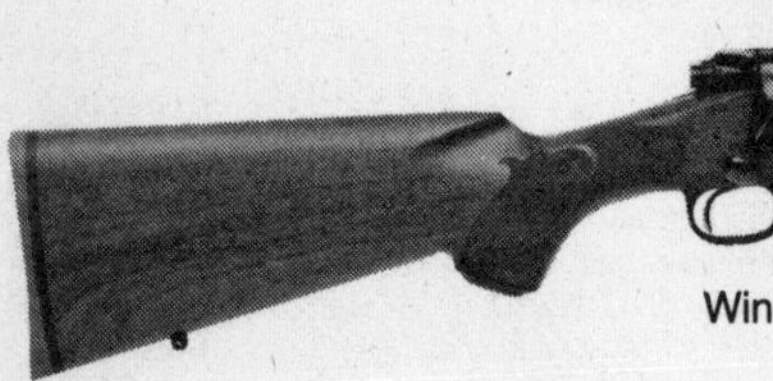
Winchester 70 Featherweight

Winchester Model 70 XTR Featherweight
Available with standard action in 257 Roberts, 25-06, 270 Win., 7mm Mauser, 30-06, short action in 22-250, 223, 243, 308; 22" tapered Featherweight barrel; classic-style American walnut stock with Schnabel fore-end, wrap-around XTR checkering fashioned after early Model 70 custom rifle patterns. Red rubber butt pad with black spacer; sling swivel studs. Weighs 6¾ lbs. (standard action), 6½ lbs. (short action). Introduced 1984.
Price: About **$440.00**

Wincnester Ranger

Winchester Ranger Rifle
Similar to Model 70 XTR Sporter except chambered only for 270, 30-06, with 22" barrel. 7mm Rem. Mag. has 24" barrel; American hardwood stock, no checkering, composition butt plate. Metal has matte blue finish. Introduced 1985.
Price: About **$293.00**
Price: Ranger Youth, 223, 243 only, scaled-down stock **$302.00**

 CAUTION: PRICES CHANGE. CHECK AT GUNSHOP.

CENTERFIRE RIFLES—BOLT ACTIONS

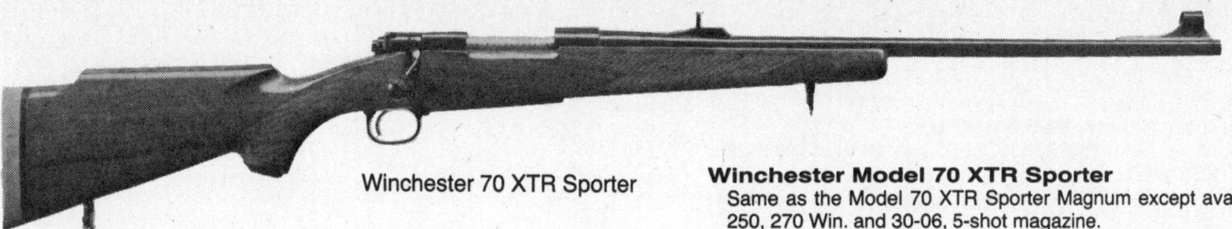

Winchester 70 XTR Sporter

Winchester Model 70 XTR Sporter
Same as the Model 70 XTR Sporter Magnum except available only in 22-250, 270 Win. and 30-06, 5-shot magazine.
Price: With sights, about $430.00
Price: Without sights, about $413.00

Winchester 70 XTR Sporter Varmint Rifle
Same as 70 XTR Sporter Magnum except: 223, 22-250 and 243 only, no sights, 24" heavy bbl., 44½" over-all, 7¾ lbs. American walnut Monte Carlo stock with cheekpiece, high luster finish.
Price: About $422.00

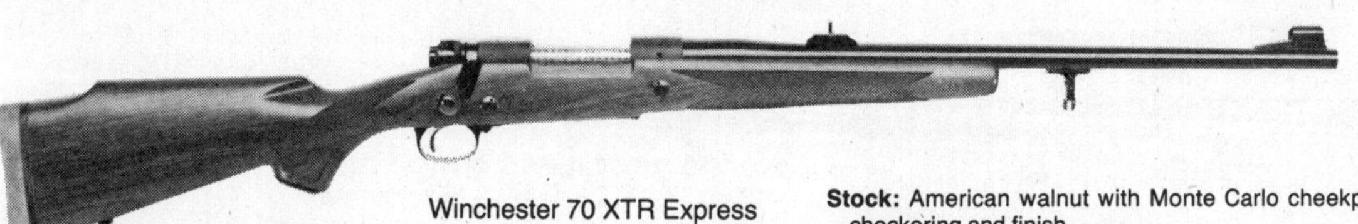

Winchester 70 XTR Express

WINCHESTER 70 XTR SUPER EXPRESS MAGNUM
Caliber: 375 H&H Mag., 458 Win. Mag., 3-shot magazine.
Barrel: 24" (375), 22" (458).
Weight: 8½ lbs.
Stock: American walnut with Monte Carlo cheekpiece. XTR wrap-around checkering and finish.
Sights: Hooded ramp front, open rear.
Features: Two steel crossbolts in stock for added strength. Front sling swivel mounted on barrel. Contoured rubber butt pad. Made under license by U.S. Repeating Arms Co.
Price: 375 H&H, about $656.00
Price: 458 Win., about $683.00

CENTERFIRE RIFLES—SINGLE SHOTS

Browning Model 1885

BROWNING MODEL 1885 SINGLE SHOT RIFLE
Caliber: 22-250, 270, 7mm Rem. Mag., 45-70.
Barrel: 28".
Weight: About 8½ lbs. **Length:** 43½" over-all.
Stock: Walnut with straight grip, Schnabel fore-end.
Sights: None furnished; drilled and tapped for scope mounting.
Features: Replica of J.M. Browning's high-wall falling-block rifle. Octagon barrel with recessed muzzle. Imported from Japan by Browning. Introduced 1985.
Price: $499.95

H&R Model 171

HARRINGTON & RICHARDSON Model 171 Deluxe Cavalry Model Carbine
Caliber: 45-70 single shot.
Barrel: 22".
Weight: 7 lbs. **Length:** 41".
Stock: American walnut with saddle ring and bridle.
Sights: Blade front, barrel mounted leaf rear adj. for e.
Features: Replica of the 1873 Springfield Carbine. Blue-black finish. Deluxe version has engraved breech block, side lock & hammer.
Price: $395.00

H&R Model 158

HARRINGTON AND RICHARDSON 158 RIFLE
Caliber: 30-30, 22 Hornet, single shot.
Barrel: 22" round tapered.
Weight: 6 lbs. **Length:** 37".
Stock: Walnut finished hardwood stock and fore-end.
Sights: Blade front; folding adj. rear.
Features: Side lever break-open action with visible hammer. Easy takedown.
Price: $109.50

Harrington & Richardson Model 058 Combo Gun
Same as Model 158, except fitted with accessory 20-ga. barrel (26", Mod.).
Price: 22 Hornet, or 30-30 Win., plus 20-ga. $134.50
Price: Model 258 (as above except nickel finish) 22 Hornet, 30-30, 357 Mag., 357 Max., 44 Mag. (with case) $184.50

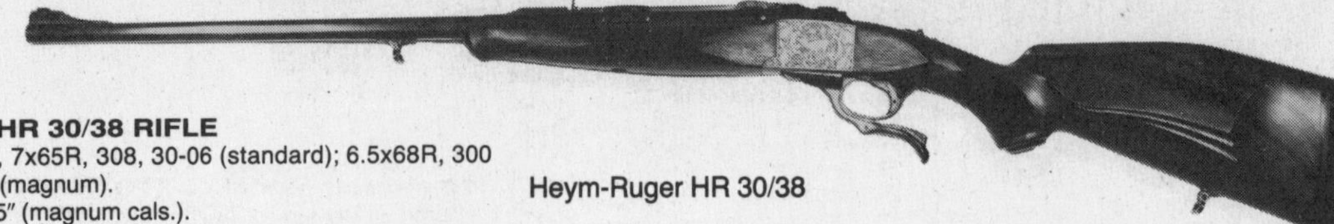
Heym-Ruger HR 30/38

HEYM-RUGER Model HR 30/38 RIFLE
Caliber: 243, 6.5x57R, 7x64, 7x65R, 308, 30-06 (standard); 6.5x68R, 300 Win. Mag., 8x68S, 9.3x74R (magnum).
Barrel: 24″ (standard cals.), 25″ (magnum cals.).
Weight: 6½ to 7 lbs.
Stock: Dark European walnut, hand checkered p.g. and fore-end. Oil finish, recoil pad. Full Mannlicher-type or sporter-style with Schnabel fore-end, Bavarian cheekpiece.
Sights: Bead on ramp front, leaf rear.
Features: Ruger No. 1 action and safety, Canjar single-set trigger, hand-engraved animal motif. Options available include deluxe engraving and stock carving. Imported from West Germany by Paul Jaeger Inc.
Price: HR-30N, round bbl., sporter stock, std. cals **$1,895.00**
Price: HR-30G, as above except in mag. cals **$1,895.00**
Price: HR-30L, round bbl., full stock, std. cals **$1,995.00**
Price: For octagon barrel, add **$235.00**
Price: For sideplates with large hunting scenes, add **$610.00**

Ljutic Space Rifle

LJUTIC RECOILESS SPACE RIFLE
Caliber: 22-250, 30-30, 30-06, 308; single-shot.
Barrel: 24″.
Weight: 8¾ lbs. **Length:** 44″ over-all.
Stock: Walnut stock, fore-end and grip.
Sights: Iron sights or scope mounts.
Features: Revolutionary design has anti-recoil mechanism. Twist-bolt action uses six moving parts. Scope and mounts extra. Introduced 1981. From Ljutic Industries.
Price: **$3,595.00**

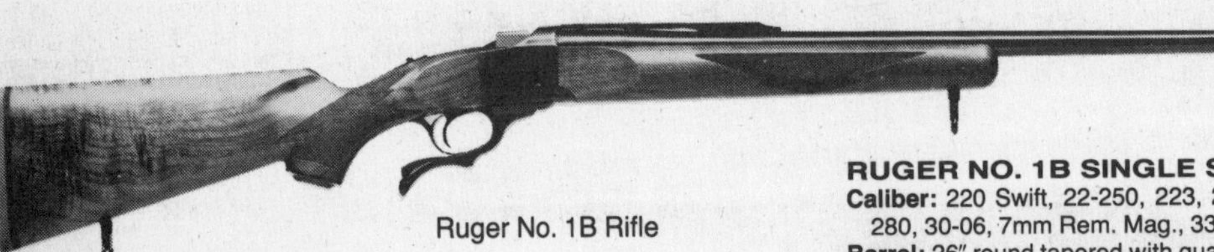
Ruger No. 1B Rifle

RUGER NO. 1B SINGLE SHOT
Caliber: 220 Swift, 22-250, 223, 243, 6mm Rem., 25-06, 257 Roberts, 270, 280, 30-06, 7mm Rem. Mag., 338 Win. Mag.
Barrel: 26″ round tapered with quarter-rib; with Ruger 1″ rings.
Weight: 8 lbs. **Length:** 43⅜″ over-all.
Stock: Walnut, two-piece, checkered p.g. and semi-beavertail fore-end.
Sights: None, 1″ scope rings supplied for integral mounts.
Features: Under lever, hammerless falling block design has auto ejector, top tang safety. Standard Rifle 1B illus.
Price: **$475.00**
Price: Barreled action, blued only **$324.50**

Ruger No. 1A Light Sporter
Similar to the No. 1-B Standard Rifle except has lightweight 22″ barrel, Alexander Henry style fore-end, adjustable folding leaf rear sight on quarter-rib, dovetailed ramp front with gold bead. Calibers 243, 30-06, 270 and 7x57. Weight about 7¼ lbs.
Price: No. 1-A **$475.00**

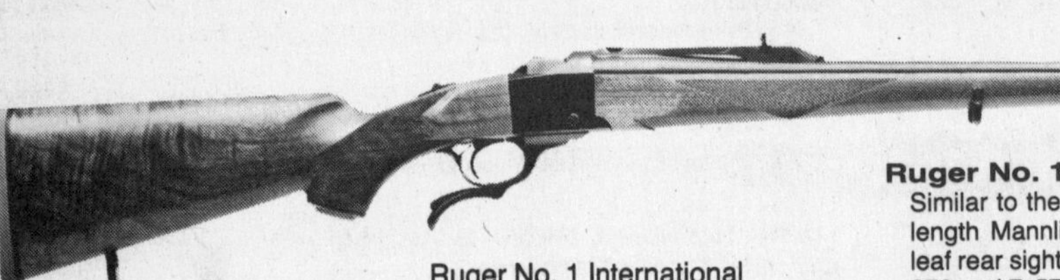
Ruger No. 1 International

Ruger No. 1 RSI International
Similar to the No. 1-B Standard Rifle except has lightweight 20″ barrel, full length Mannlicher-style fore-end with loop sling swivel, adjustable folding leaf rear sight on quarter rib, ramp front with gold bead. Calibers 243, 30-06, 270 and 7x57. Weight is about 7¼ lbs.
Price: No. 1-RSI **$495.00**

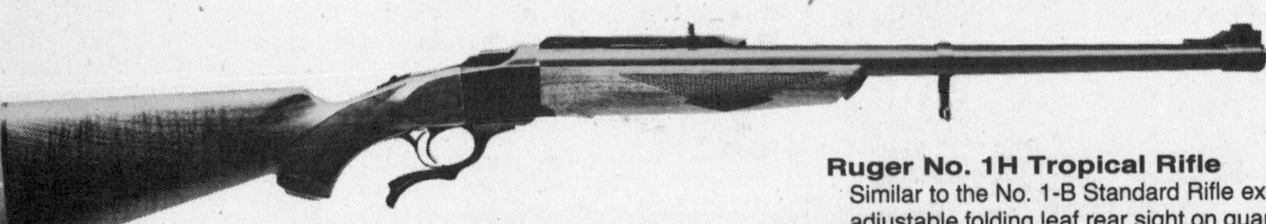
Ruger No. 1H Tropical

Ruger No. 1H Tropical Rifle
Similar to the No. 1-B Standard Rifle except has Alexander Henry fore-end, adjustable folding leaf rear sight on quarter-rib, ramp front with dovetail gold bead front, 24″ heavy barrel. Calibers 375 H&H (weight about 8¼ lbs.) and 458 Win. Mag. (weight about 9 lbs.).
Price: No. 1-H **$475.00**

Ruger No. 1V Special Varminter
Similar to the No. 1-B Standard Rifle except has 24″ heavy barrel. Semi-beavertail fore-end, barrel tapped for target scope block, with 1″ Ruger scope rings. Calibers 22-250, 220 Swift, 223, 25-06, 6mm. Weight about 9 lbs.
Price: No. 1-V **$475.00**

Ruger No. 1S Medium Sporter
Similar to the No. 1B Standard Rifle except has Alexander Henry style fore-end, adjustable folding leaf rear sight on quarter-rib, ramp front sight base and dovetail-type gold bead front sight. Calibers 7mm Rem. Mag., 338 Win. Mag., 300 Win. Mag., and 45-70 with 26″ barrel. Weight about 7½ lbs. in 45-70.
Price: No. 1-S **$475.00**

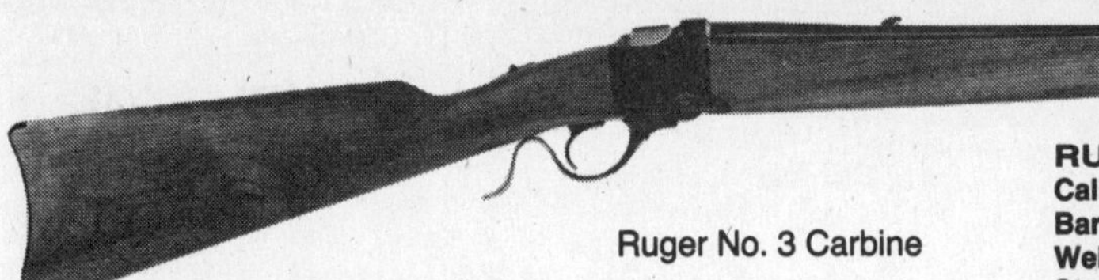

Ruger No. 3 Carbine

RUGER NO. 3 CARBINE SINGLE SHOT
Caliber: 44 Magnum, 45-70.
Barrel: 22" round.
Weight: 7¼ lbs. **Length:** 38½".
Stock: American walnut, carbine-type.
Sights: Gold bead front, adj. folding leaf rear.
Features: Same action as No. 1 Rifle except different lever. Has auto ejector, top tang safety, adj. trigger. Drilled and tapped for Ruger bases and Ruger 1" rings.
Price: **$284.00**

NAVY ARMS ROLLING BLOCK RIFLE
Caliber: 45-70.
Barrel: 26½".
Stock: Walnut finished.
Sights: Fixed front, adj. rear.
Features: Reproduction of classic rolling block action. Available in Buffalo Rifle (octagonal bbl.) and Creedmore (half round, half octagonal bbl.) models. Made in U.S. by Navy Arms.
Price: 18", 26", 30" full octagon barrel **$374.00**
Price: Creedmore Model, 30" full octagon.......... **$399.00**
Price: 30", half-round.......... **$379.00**
Price: 26", half-round.......... **$374.00**
Price: Half-round Creedmore.......... **$399.00**

Consult our directory pages for the location of firms mentioned.

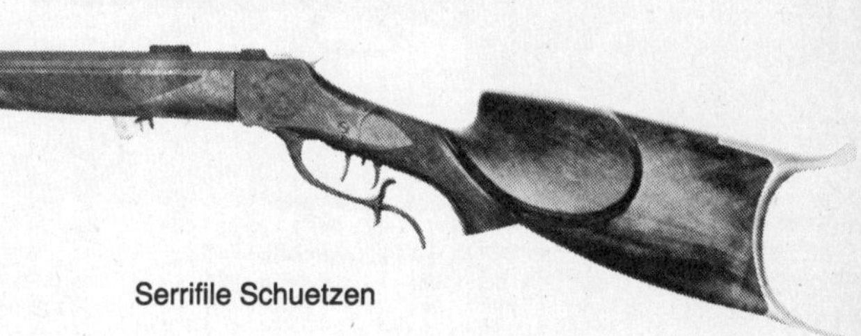

Serrifile Schuetzen

SERRIFILE SCHUETZEN RIFLE
Caliber: 32, 33, 38, 41, 44, 45; single shot.
Barrel: To customer specs up to 32"; octagon, half-octagon, round.
Weight: To customer specs.
Stock: Fancy walnut in early Helm pattern.
Sights: None furnished; comes with scope blocks.
Features: Based on a replica Winchester Hi-Wall action with flat top receiver ring, thick or thin wall design, blue or case hardened. Hammer action uses Niedner-type firing pin; hammerless model uses a coil spring striker. Many options in finger levers, buttplates available. Introduced 1984. From Serrifile, Inc.
Price: Hammer model, from **$1,685.00**

Thompson/Center TCR '83 Hunter

THOMPSON/CENTER TCR '83 SINGLE SHOT RIFLE
Caliber: 22 Hornet, 223 Rem., 22-250, 243 Win., 270, 308, 7mm Rem. Mag., 30-06.
Barrel: 23".
Weight: About 6¾ lbs. **Length:** 39½" over-all.
Stock: American black walnut, checkered p.g. and fore-end.
Sights: Blade on ramp front, open rear adj. for windage only.
Features: Break-open design with interchangeable barrels. Double-set or single-stage trigger function. Cross-bolt safety. Sights removable for scope mounting. Made in U.S. by T/C. Introduced 1983.
Price: Aristocrat **$475.00**
Price: Hunter model (single trigger, grooved fore-end, no cheekpiece) **$435.00**
Price: Extra barrel **$150.00**

DRILLINGS, COMBINATION GUNS, DOUBLE RIFLES

ARMSPORT "EMPEROR" 4000 DOUBLE RIFLE
Caliber: 243, 270, 284, 7.65, 308, 30-06, 7mm Rem. Mag., 9.3, 300 H&H, 375 H&H; Shotgun barrels in 12, 16 or 20-ga.
Barrel: Shotgun barrel length and chokes to customer specs.
Stock: Dimensions to customer specs. Stock and fore-end of root walnut.
Sights: Rifle barrels have blade front with bead, leaf rear adj. for w.
Features: Receiver and sideplates engraved. Gun comes with extra set of barrels fitted to action. Packaged in a hand-made, fitted luggage-type leather case lined with Scotch loden cloth. Introduced 1978. From Armsport.
Price: Complete **$16,300.00**

ARMSPORT "EMPEROR" 4010 DOUBLE RIFLE
Side-by-side version of the Model 4000 over-under rifle. Available in 243, 270, 284, 7.65, 308, 30-06, 7mm Rem. Mag., 9.3, 300 H&H, 338 Win. and 375 H&H. Shotgun barrels in 16 or 20 ga., choice of length and choke. Comes in fitted luggage-type case.
Price: **$12,750.00**

BERETTA EXPRESS S689 DOUBLE RIFLE
Caliber: 30-06, 9.3x74R, 375 H&H, 458 win. Mag.
Barrel: 23".
Weight: 7.7 lbs.
Stock: European walnut, checkered grip and fore-end.
Sights: Blade front on ramp, open V-notch rear.
Features: Boxlock action with silvered, engraved receiver; ejectors; double triggers; solid butt pad. Imported from Italy by Beretta U.S.A. Corp. Introduced 1984.
Price: S689, 30-06, 9.3x74R **$2,300.00**
Price: SSO, 375 H&H, 458 Win. Mag. **$7,500.00**

Browning Continental

BROWNING SUPERPOSED CONTINENTAL

Caliber/Gauge: 20 ga. x 20 ga. with extra 30-06x30-06 o/u barrel set.
Barrel: 20 ga.—26½" (Mod. & Full, 3" chambers), vent. rib, with medium raised German nickel silver sight bead. 30-06—24".
Weight: 6 lbs. 14 oz. (rifle barrels), 5 lbs. 14 oz. (shotgun barrels)
Stock: Select high grade American walnut with oil finish. Straight grip stock and Schnabel fore-end with 26 lpi hand checkering.
Sights: Rifle barrels have flat face gold bead front on matted ramp, folding leaf rear.
Features: Action is based on a specially engineered Superposed 20-ga. frame. Single selective trigger works on inertia; let-off is about 4½ lbs. Automatic selective ejectors. Manual top tang safety incorporated with barrel selector. Furnished with fitted luggage-type case. Introduced 1979. Imported from Belgium by Browning.
Price: **$4,375.00**

BROWNING EXPRESS RIFLE

Caliber: 270 or 30-06.
Barrel: 24".
Weight: About 6 lbs., 14 oz. **Length:** 41" over-all.
Stock: Select walnut with oil finish; straight grip, Schnabel fore-end; hand checkered to 25 lpi.
Sights: Gold bead on ramp front, adjustable folding leaf rear.
Features: Specially engineered Superposed action with reinforced breech face. Receiver hand engraved. Single selective trigger, auto. selective ejectors, manual safety. Comes in fitted luggage case. Imported from Belgium by Browning.
Price: Either caliber **$3,125.00**

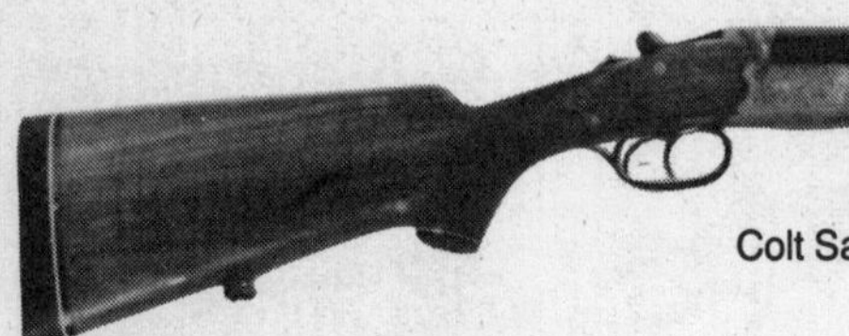

Colt Sauer Drilling

COLT SAUER DRILLING

Caliber/Gauge: 12 ga., over 30-06, 12 ga. over 243.
Action: Top lever, cross bolt, box lock.
Barrel: 25" (Mod. & Full).
Weight: 8 lbs. **Length:** 41¾" over-all.
Stock: American walnut, oil finish. Checkered p.g. and fore-end. Black p.g. cap, recoil pad. 14¼"x2"x1½".
Sights: Blade front with brass bead, folding leaf rear.
Features: Cocking indicators, tang barrel selector, automatic sight positioner, set rifle trigger, side safety. Blue finish with bright receiver engraved with animal motifs and European-style scrollwork. Imported from West Germany by Colt.
Price: **$4,227.95**

H&R 258 Handy Gun II

HARRINGTON & RICHARDSON 258 HANDY GUN II

Caliber/Gauge: 22 Hornet, 30-30 Win., 357 Mag., 357 Maximum, 44 Mag. with interchangeable 20-ga. 3" barrel.
Barrel: 22" (rifle), 22" (Mod.) shotgun.
Weight: About 6½ lbs. **Length:** 37" over-all.
Stock: American hardwood with walnut finish.
Sights: Bead front on shotgun; ramped blade front, adjustable folding leaf rear on rifle barrel.
Features: Interchangeable barrels. All metal parts have H&R Hard-Gard electroless matte nickel finish. Comes with heavy duck case. Introduced 1982.
Price: **$184.50**

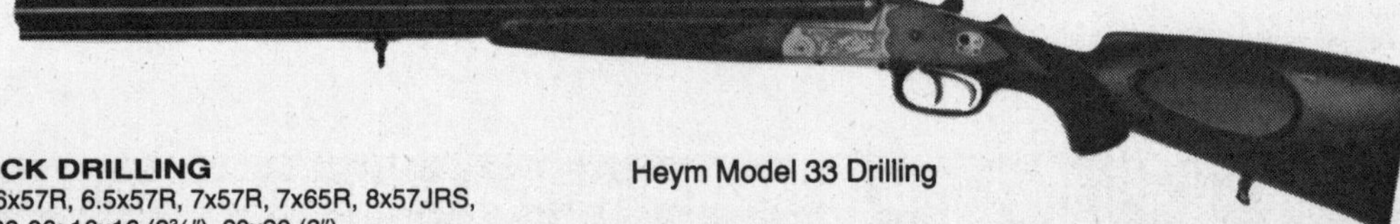

Heym Model 33 Drilling

HEYM MODEL 33 BOXLOCK DRILLING

Caliber/Gauge: 5.6x50R Mag., 5.6x57R, 6.5x57R, 7x57R, 7x65R, 8x57JRS, 9.3x74R, 222, 243, 270, 308, 30-06; 16x16 (2¾"), 20x20 (3").
Barrel: 25" (Full & Mod.).
Weight: About 6½ lbs. **Length:** 42" over-all.
Stock: Dark European walnut, checkered p.g. and fore-end; oil finish.
Sights: Silver bead front, folding leaf rear. Automatic sight positioner. Available with scope and Suhler claw mounts.
Features: Greener-type crossbolt and safety, double under-lugs. Double set triggers. Plastic or steel trigger guard. Engraving coverage varies with model. Imported from West Germany by Paul Jaeger Inc.
Price: Model 33, from.......... **$3,180.00**

Heym Model 37

HEYM MODEL 37B DOUBLE RIFLE DRILLING

Caliber/Gauge: 7x65R, 30-06, 8x57JRS, 9.3x74R; 20 ga. (3").
Barrel: 25" (shotgun barrel choked Full or Mod.).
Weight: About 8½ lbs. **Length:** 42" over-all.
Stock: Dark European walnut, hand-checkered p.g. and fore-end. Oil finish.
Sights: Silver bead front, folding leaf rear. Available with scope and Suhler claw mounts.
Features: Full side-lock construction. Greener-type crossbolt, double under lugs, cocking indicators. Imported from West Germany by Paul Jaeger, Inc.
Price: Model 37 double rifle drilling **$6,520.00**
Price: Model 37 Deluxe (hunting scene engraving) from, ... **$7,450.00**

 CAUTION: PRICES CHANGE. CHECK AT GUNSHOP.

Consult our Directory pages for the location of firms mentioned.

Heym Model 37 Sidelock Drilling

Similar to Model 37 Double Rifle Drilling except has 12x12, 16x16 or 20x20 over 5.6x50R Mag., 5.6x57R, 6.5x57R, 7x57R, 7x65R, 8x57JRS, 9.3x74R, 222, 243, 270, 308 or 30-06. Rifle barrel is manually cocked and uncocked.

Price: Model 37 with border engraving **$4,930.00**
Price: As above with engraved hunting scenes **$5,860.00**

Heym 22S Combo

HEYM MODEL 22S SAFETY COMBO GUN

Caliber/Gauge: 16 or 20 ga. (2¾", 3"), 12 ga. (2¾") over 22 Hornet, 22 WMR, 222 Rem., 222 Rem. Mag., 223, 243 Win., 5.6x50R, 6.5x57R, 7x57R, 8x57 JRS.
Barrel: 24", solid rib.
Weight: About 5½ lbs.
Stock: Dark European walnut, hand-checkered p.g. and fore-end. Oil finish.
Sights: Silver bead ramp front, folding leaf rear.
Features: Tang mounted cocking slide, separate barrel selector, single set trigger. Base supplied for quick-detachable scope mounts. Patented rocker-weight system automatically uncocks gun if accidentally dropped or bumped hard. Imported from West Germany. Contact Heym for more data.

Price: Model 22S **$1,320.00**
Price: Model 22SZ takedown **$1,500.00**
Price: Scope mounts, add **$120.00**

HEYM MODEL 55B/55SS O/U DOUBLE RIFLE

Caliber: 7x65R, 308, 30-06, 8x57JRS, 9.3x74R; 375 H&H.
Barrel: 25"
Weight: About 8 lbs., depending upon caliber. **Length:** 42" over-all.
Stock: Dark European walnut, hand-checkered p.g. and fore-end. Oil finish.
Sights: Silver bead ramp front, open V-type rear.
Features: Boxlock or full sidelock; Kersten double crossbolt, cocking indicators; hand-engraved hunting scenes. Options available include interchangeable barrels, Zeiss scopes in claw mounts, deluxe engravings and stock carving, etc. Imported from West Germany by Paul Jaeger, Inc.

Price: Model 55B boxlock **$3,490.00**
Price: Model 55SS sidelock **$5,540.00**
Price: Interchangeable shotgun barrels **$1,630.00**
Price: Interchangeable rifle barrels **$2,310.00**

Heym Model 55BF/55BFSS O/U Combo Gun

Similar to Model 55B/77B o/u rifle except chambered for 12, 16 or 20 ga. (2¾" or 3") over 5.6x50R, 222 Rem., 5.6x57R, 243, 6.5x57R, 270, 7x57R, 7x65R, 308, 30-06, 8x57JRS, 9.3x74R, or 375 H&H. Has solid rib barrel. Available as boxlock or sidelock, with interchangeable shotgun and rifle barrels.

Price: Model 55BF boxlock **$2,920.00**
Price: Model 55BFSS sidelock **$4,970.00**

Heym Model 88B

HEYM MODEL 88B SIDE-BY-SIDE DOUBLE RIFLE

Caliber: 7x57, 270, 30-06, 8x57JRS, 300 Win. Mag., 9.3x74R, 375 H&H.
Barrel: 25".
Weight: 7½ lbs. (std. cals), 8½ lbs. (mag.) **Length:** 42" over-all.
Stock: Fancy French walnut, classic North American design.
Sights: Silver bead post on ramp front, fixed or 3-leaf express rear.
Features: Action has complete coverage hunting scene engraving. Available as boxlock or with q.d. sidelocks. Imported from West Germany by Paul Jaeger, Inc.

Price: Boxlock, from **$4,700.00**
Price: Sidelock, Model 88B-SS, from **$6,590.00**
Price: Disengageable ejectors, add **$180.00**
Price: Interchangeable barrels, add **$2,580.00**

Heym 88B Safari

HEYM MODEL 88B SAFARI DOUBLE RIFLE

Caliber: 375 H&H, 458 Win. Mag., 470 Nitro Express.
Action: Boxlock with interceptor sear. Automatic ejectors with disengagement sear.
Barrel: 25".
Weight: About 10 lbs.
Stock: Best quality Circassian walnut; classic design with cheekpiece; oil finish, hand-checkering; Presentation butt pad; steel grip cap.
Sights: Large silver bead on ramp front, quarter-rib with three-leaf express rear.
Features: Double triggers; engraved, silvered frame. Introduced 1985. Imported from West Germany by Paul Jaeger, Inc.

Price: 375 and 458 .... **$6,000.00**
Price: 470 Nitro Express **$6,700.00**
Price: Trap door grip cap **$210.00**
Price: Best quality leather case **$550.00**

LEBEAU-COURALLY SIDELOCK DOUBLE RIFLE

Caliber: 8x57 JRS, 9.3x74R, 375 H&H, 458 Win.
Barrel: 23½" to 26".
Weight: 7 lbs., 8 oz. to 9 lbs., 8 oz.
Stock: Dimensions to customer specs. Best quality French walnut selected for maximum strength, pistol grip with cheekpiece, splinter or beavertail fore-end; steel grip cap.
Sights: Bead on ramp front, express rear on ¼-rib.
Features: Holland & Holland pattern sidelock with ejectors, chopper lump barrels; reinforced action with classic pattern; choice of numerous engraving patterns; can be furnished with scope in fitted claw mounts. Imported from Belgium by Wm. Larkin Moore.

Price: From **$16,300.00**

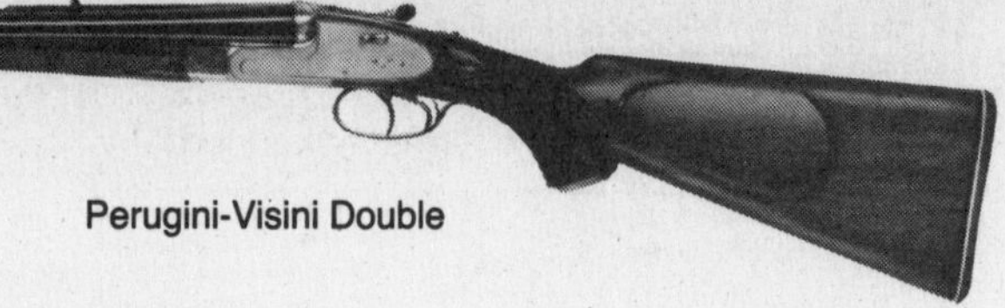

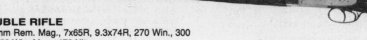

Perugini-Visini Double

PERUGINI-VISINI DOUBLE RIFLE

Caliber: 22 Hornet, 30-06, 7mm Rem. Mag., 7x65R, 9.3x74R, 270 Win., 300 H&H, 338 Win., 375 H&H, 458 Win. Mag., 470 Nitro.
Barrel: 22"-26".
Weight: 7¼ to 8½ lbs., depending upon caliber. **Length:** 39½" over-all (22" bbl.).
Stock: Oil-finished walnut; checkered grip and fore-end; cheekpiece.
Sights: Bead on ramp front, express rear on ¼-rib.
Features: True sidelock action with ejectors; sideplates are hand detachable; comes with leather trunk case. Introduced 1983. Imported from Italy by Wm. Larkin Moore.
Price: $10,000.00

LEBEAU-COURALLY BOXLOCK DOUBLE RIFLE

Caliber: 8x57 JRS, 9.3x74R, 375 H&H, 458 Win.
Barrel: 23½" to 26".
Weight: 7 lbs., 8 oz. to 9 lbs., 8 oz.
Stock: Dimension to customer specs. Select French walnut, hand rubbed oil finish, pistol grip stock with cheekpiece, splinter or beavertail fore-end.
Sights: Bead on ramp front, express rear on ¼-rib.
Features: Anson & Deeley boxlock with ejectors and Purdey-type third fastener; choice of classic or rounded action; choice of numerous engraving patterns; can be furnished with scope in fitted claw mounts. Imported from Belgium by Wm. Larkin Moore.
Price: From $8,300.00

Perugini-Visini O/U Double

PERUGINI-VISINI O/U DOUBLE RIFLE

Caliber: 7mm Rem. Mag., 7x65R, 9.3x74R, 270 Win., 338 Win. Mag., 375 H&H, 458 Win. Mag.
Barrel: 24".
Weight: 8 lbs. **Length:** 40½" over-all.
Stock: Oil-finished walnut; checkered grip and fore-end; cheekpiece, rubber recoil pad.
Sights: Bead on ramp front, express rear on ¼-rib; Swarovski scope and claw mounts optional.
Features: Boxlock action with ejectors; silvered receiver, rest blued; double triggers. Comes with trunk case. Deluxe engraving, better wood, etc. available. Introduced 1983. Imported from Italy by Wm. Larkin Moore.
Price: $3,950.00

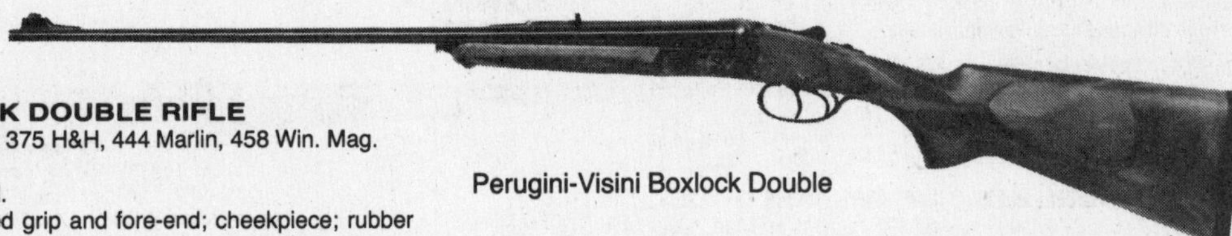

Perugini-Visini Boxlock Double

PERUGINI-VISINI BOXLOCK DOUBLE RIFLE

Caliber: 7x65R, 7x57, 308, 9.3x74R, 375 H&H, 444 Marlin, 458 Win. Mag.
Barrel: 25".
Weight: 8 lbs. **Length:** 41½" over-all.
Stock: Oil-finished walnut; checkered grip and fore-end; cheekpiece; rubber recoil pad.
Sights: Bead on ramp front, express rear on ¼-rib.
Features: Boxlock action with ejectors; color case-hardened receiver; double triggers. Comes with trunk case. Introduced 1983. Imported from Italy by Wm. Larkin Moore.
Price: From $3,450.00

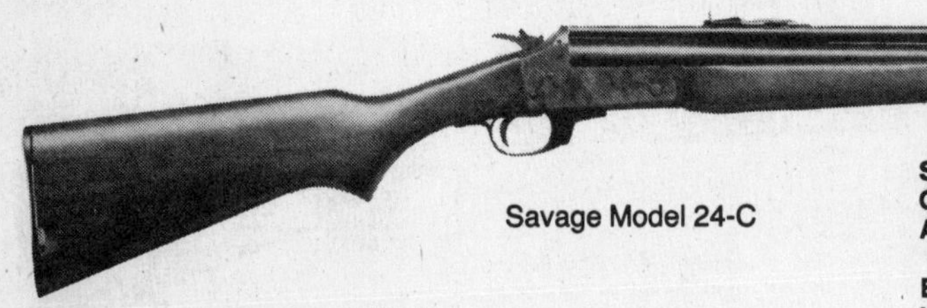

Savage Model 24-C

SAVAGE MODEL 24 O/U

Caliber/Gauge: 22LR over 20 ga. or 410; 22 Mag. over 20 ga.
Action: Bottom opening lever, low rebounding visible hammer, single trigger, barrel selector spur on hammer, separate extractors.
Barrel: 24", separated barrels.
Weight: 6½ lbs. **Length:** 40".
Stock: Walnut-finished hardwood.
Sights: Ramp front, rear open adj. for e.
Features: Receiver grooved for scope mounting.
Price: $180.00

Savage Model 24-F.G. O/U

Same as Model 24 except: color case hardened frame, stock is walnut finished hardwood, no checkering or M.C.
Price: $180.00

SAVAGE MODEL 24-C O/U

Caliber/Gauge: Top bbl. 22 S, L, LR; bottom bbl. 20 gauge cyl. bore.
Action: Take-down, low rebounding visible hammer. Single trigger, barrel selector spur on hammer.
Barrel: 20" separated barrels.
Weight: 5¾ lbs. **Length:** 35" (taken down 20").
Stock: Walnut finished hardwood.
Sights: Ramp front, rear open adj. for e.
Features: Trap door butt holds one shotshell and ten 22 cartridges, comes with special carrying case. Measures 7"x22" when in case.
Price: $199.95

Savage Model 24-V

Similar to Model 24 except: 22 Hornet, 222 Rem, or 30-30 and 20 ga., 223 or 357 Rem. Max. and 20 ga.; stronger receiver; color case-hardened frame; folding leaf rear sight; receiver tapped for scope.
Price: $256.50

CAUTION: PRICES CHANGE. CHECK AT GUNSHOP.

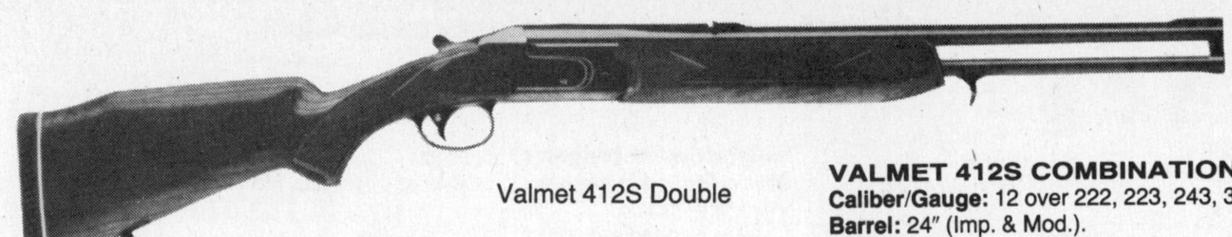

Valmet 412S Double

VALMET 412S DOUBLE RIFLE
Caliber: 243, 308, 30-06, 375 Win., 9.3x74R.
Barrel: 24"
Weight: 8⅝ lbs.
Stock: American walnut with Monte Carlo style.
Sights: Ramp front, adjustable open rear.
Features: Barrel selector mounted in trigger. Cocking indicators in tang. Recoil pad. Valmet scope mounts available. Interchangeable barrels. Introduced 1980. Imported from Finland by Valmet.
Price: Extractors, 243, 308, 30-06 .... **$999.00**
Price: With ejectors, 375 Win., 9.3x74R **$1,099.00**
Price: Extra barrels, from **$599.00**

VALMET 412S COMBINATION GUN
Caliber/Gauge: 12 over 222, 223, 243, 308, 30-06.
Barrel: 24" (Imp. & Mod.).
Weight: 7⅝ lbs.
Stock: American walnut, with recoil pad. Monte Carlo style. Standard measurements 14"x1⅗"x2"x2⅗".
Sights: Blade front, flip-up-type open rear.
Features: Barrel selector on trigger. Hand checkered stock and fore-end. Barrels are screw-adjustable to change bullet point of impact. Barrels are interchangeable. Introduced 1980. Imported from Finland by Valmet.
Price: **$899.00**
Price: Extra barrels, from **$499.00**

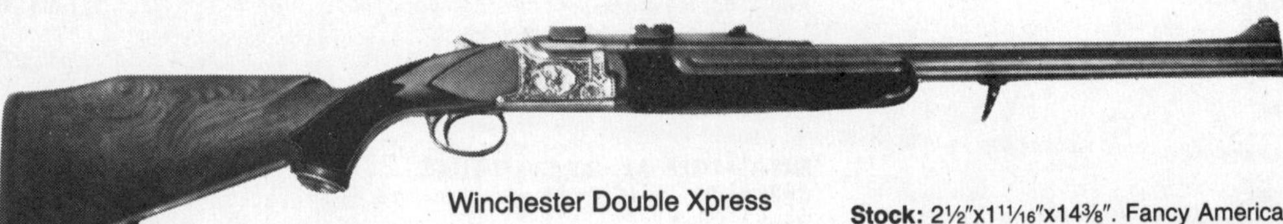

Winchester Double Xpress

WINCHESTER DOUBLE XPRESS O/U RIFLE
Caliber: 270/270, 257 Roberts/257 Roberts, 7.65R/7.65 R.
Barrel: 23½".
Weight: 8½ lbs. **Length:** 39⅝" over-all.
Stock: 2½"x1¹¹⁄₁₆"x14⅜". Fancy American walnut with hand checkered pistol grip and fore-end, solid rubber butt pad.
Sights: Bead on ramp front, folding leaf rear on quarter-rib.
Features: Integral scope bases; q.d. sling swivels. Uses Model 101 action; receiver silvered and engraved, barrels blued. Comes with hard case. Introduced 1982. Manufactured in and imported from Japan by Winchester Group, Olin Corp.
Price: **$2,995.00**

WINCHESTER SUPER GRADE O/U COMBO
Caliber/Gauge: 12 ga. over 30-06.
Barrel: 25". Shot barrel uses Winchoke system.
Weight: 8½ lbs. **Length:** 41¼" over-all.
Stock: 2½"x1¾"x14". Fancy American walnut with hand checkered pistol grip and fore-end; ventilated rubber recoil pad.
Sights: Bead front, folding leaf rear.
Features: Single selective mechanical trigger, combination barrel selector. Full length top barrel rib with integral scope bases. Uses Model 101 frame. Silvered and engraved receiver, blued barrels. Manufactured in and imported from Japan by Winchester Group, Olin Corp.
Price: **$2,550.00**

A. ZOLI RIFLE-SHOTGUN O/U COMBO
Caliber/Gauge: 12 ga./308 Win., 12 ga./222, 12 ga./30-06.
Barrel: Combo—24"; shotgun—28" (Mod. & Full).
Weight: About 8 lbs. **Length:** 41" over-all (24" bbl.).
Stock: European walnut.
Sights: Blade front, flip-up rear.
Features: Available with German claw scope mounts on rifle/shotgun barrels. Comes with set of 12/12 (Mod. & Full) barrels. Imported from Italy by Mandall Shooting Supplies.
Price: With two barrel sets, without claw mounts **$1,495.00**
Price: With two barrel sets, scope and claw mounts **$1,895.00**

RIMFIRE RIFLES—AUTOLOADERS

AMT Lightning 25/22

AP-74 AUTO RIFLE
Caliber: 22 LR, 32 ACP, 15 shot magazine.
Barrel: 20" including flash reducer.
Weight: 6½ lbs. **Length:** 38½" over-all.
Stock: Black plastic.
Sights: Ramp front, adj. peep rear.
Features: Pivotal take-down, easy disassembly. AR-15 look-alike. Sling and sling swivels included. Imported by EMF.
Price: **$250.00**
Price: With walnut stock and fore-end **$275.00**
Price: 32 ACP **$265.00**
Price: With wood stock and fore-end **$290.00**

AMT LIGHTNING 25/22 RIFLE
Caliber: 22 LR, 25-shot magazine.
Barrel: NA.
Weight: 6 lbs. **Length:** 26½" (folded).
Stock: Folding stainless steel; finger-grooved vertical pistol grip.
Sights: Ramp front, rear adjustable for windage.
Features: Made of stainless steel with matte finish. Receiver dovetailed for scope mounting. Extended magazine release. Standard or "bull" barrel. Introduced 1984. From AMT.
Price: **$260.00**

Anschutz Model 520/61

ANSCHUTZ DELUXE MODEL 520/61 AUTO
Caliber: 22 LR, 10-shot clip.
Barrel: 24″.
Weight: 6½ lbs. **Length:** 43″ over-all.
Stock: European hardwood; checkered pistol grip, Monte Carlo comb, beavertail fore-end.
Sights: Hooded ramp front, folding leaf rear.
Features: Rotary safety, empty shell deflector, single stage trigger. Receiver grooved for scope mounting. Introduced 1982. Imported from Germany by PSI.
Price: **$234.00**

Auto-Ordnance 1927A-3

AUTO ORDNANCE MODEL 1927A-3
Caliber: 22 LR, 10, 30 or 50-shot magazine.
Barrel: 16″, finned.
Weight: About 7 lbs.
Stock: Walnut stock and fore-end.
Sights: Blade front, open rear adjustable for windage and elevation.
Features: Re-creation of the Thompson Model 1927, only in 22 Long Rifle. Alloy receiver, finned barrel.
Price: **$424.75**

BINGHAM PPS-50 CARBINE
Caliber: 22 LR, 50-shot drum.
Barrel: 16.1″.
Weight: 6½ lbs. **Length:** 33¾″ over-all.
Stock: Beechwood (standard), walnut optional.
Sights: Blade front, folding leaf rear.
Features: Semi-auto carbine with perforated barrel jacket. Standard model has blue finish with oil-finish wood. From Bingham Ltd.
Price: Standard **$229.95**
Price: Deluxe (blue with walnut stock) **$249.95**
Price: Duramil (chrome with walnut stock) **$259.95**

BINGHAM AK-22 CARBINE
Caliber: 22 LR, 15-shot magazine.
Barrel: 17¾″.
Weight: 6 lbs., 1 oz. **Length:** 35½″ over-all.
Stock: Beechwood (standard), walnut optional.
Sights: Hooded post front, open adjustable rear.
Features: Semi-auto rimfire version of the Soviet assault rifle. A 28-shot "Military Look-Alike" magazine optional. From Bingham Ltd.
Price: Standard **$229.95**
Price: Deluxe (walnut stock) **$249.95**

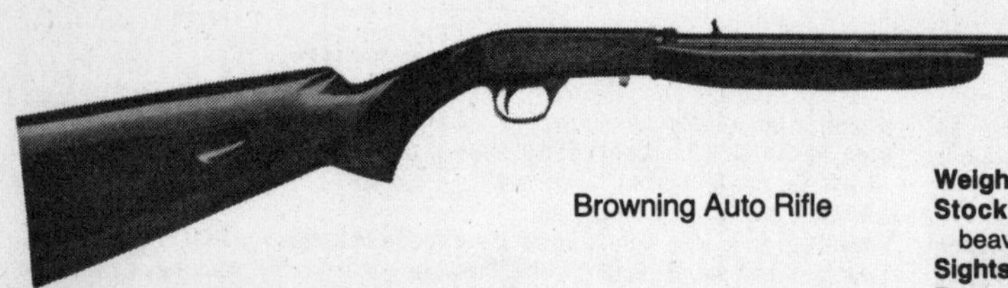
Browning Auto Rifle

BROWNING AUTOLOADING RIFLE
Caliber: 22 LR, 11-shot.
Barrel: 19¼″.
Weight: 4¾ lbs. **Length:** 37″ over-all.
Stock: Checkered select walnut (13¾″x1$^{13}/_{16}$″x2⅝″) with p.g. and semi-beavertail fore-end.
Sights: Gold bead front, folding leaf rear.
Features: Engraved receiver is grooved for tip-off scope mount; cross-bolt safety; tubular magazine in buttstock; easy take down for carrying or storage. Imported from Japan by Browning.
Price: Grade I **$267.95**

Browning BAR-22

BROWNING BAR-22 AUTO RIFLE
Caliber: 22 LR only, 15-shot tube magazine.
Barrel: 20¼″.
Weight: About 5¾ lbs. **Length:** 38¼″ over-all.
Stock: French walnut. Cut checkering at p.g. and fore-end.
Sights: Gold bead front, folding leaf rear. Receiver grooved for scope mounting.
Features: Magazine tube latch locks closed from any position. Cross bolt safety in rear of trigger guard. Trigger pull about 5 lbs. Introduced 1977. Imported from Japan by Browning.
Price: Grade I **$244.95**
Price: Grade II **$349.95**

Charter AR-7 Explorer

CHARTER AR-7 EXPLORER CARBINE
Caliber: 22 LR, 8-shot clip.
Barrel: 16″ alloy (steel-lined).
Weight: 2½ lbs. **Length:** 34½″/16½″ stowed.
Stock: Moulded grey Cycloac, snap-on rubber butt pad.
Sights: Square blade front, aperture rear adj. for e.
Features: Take-down design stores bbl. and action in hollow stock. Light enough to float.
Price: Black or Silvertone finish **$115.00**

CAUTION: PRICES CHANGE. CHECK AT GUNSHOP.

Concorde Model 20 P/S

CONCORDE MODEL 20 P/S RIFLE

Caliber: 22 Long Rifle, 15-shot magazine.
Barrel: 20″.
Weight: 6 lbs. **Length:** 41″ over-all.
Stock: Philippine mahogany with walnut finish.
Sights: Blade on ramp front, V-notch rear adjustable for elevation.
Features: Receiver grooved for scope mounting. Gun comes with 4x scope installed. Imported from the Philippines by Kassnar.
Price: $126.00
Price: Model 20P without scope $116.00
Price: Model 2000 (checkered stock, adj. rear sight)............... $129.00

CONCORDE MODEL M-16

Caliber: 22 LR, 15-shot magazine.
Barrel: 19½″, including flash hider/muzzle brake.
Weight: 6 lbs. **Length:** 38″ over-all.
Stock: Mahogany, painted black.
Sights: Post front adjustable for elevation, peep rear adjustable for windage.
Features: Replica of AR-15 rifle. Comes with carrying sling. Imported from the Philippines by Kassnar.
Price: $164.00
Price: With collapsible buttstock as M-16R........................ $176.00

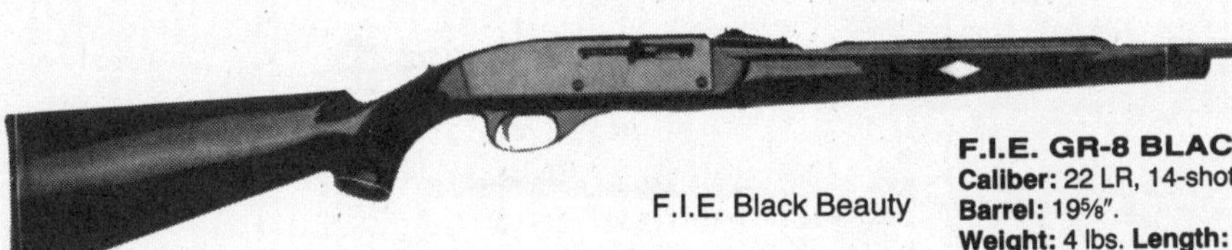

F.I.E. Black Beauty

F.I.E. GR-8 BLACK BEAUTY AUTO RIFLE

Caliber: 22 LR, 14-shot tubular magazine.
Barrel: 19⅝″.
Weight: 4 lbs. **Length:** 38½″ over-all.
Stock: Moulded black nylon, checkered pistol grip and fore-end.
Sights: Blade on ramp front, adjustable open rear.
Features: Made mostly of moulded nylon; tube magazine housed in buttstock; top tang safety; receiver grooved for tip-off scope mounts. Imported from Brazil by F.I.E. Introduced 1984.
Price: $99.95

FEDERAL XC-220 AUTO

Caliber: 22 Long Rifle, 28-shot magazine.
Barrel: 16½″.
Weight: 7½ lbs. **Length:** 34½″ over-all.
Stock: Tubular steel.
Sights: Globe front, peep rear.
Features: Semi-automatic only; fires from closed bolt. All machined steel; Parkerized finish; quick take-down. Introduced 1984. From Wilkerson Firearms.
Price: $349.95

Federal XC-220

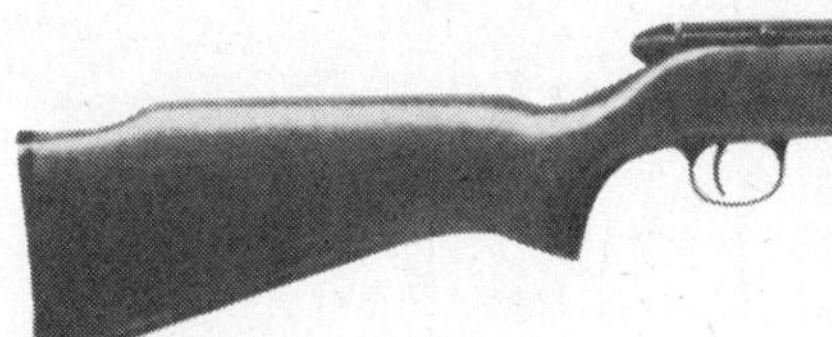

H&R Model 700 Auto

HARRINGTON & RICHARDSON Model 700 Auto Rifle

Caliber: 22 Mag., 5-shot clip.
Barrel: 22″.
Weight: 6½ lbs. **Length:** 43¼″ over-all.
Stock: Walnut, Monte Carlo, full p.g., composition buttplate.
Sights: Blade front, folding leaf rear.
Features: Drilled and tapped for scope mounting. 10-shot clip available. Made in U.S. by H&R.
Price: $199.50

H&R Model 700 Deluxe Rifle

Same as Model 700 except has select walnut stock with cheekpiece, checkered grip and fore-end, rubber rifle recoil pad. No iron sights; comes with H&R Model 432 4x, 1″ tube scope, with base and rings.
Price: $325.00

H&K Model 270 Auto

HECKLER & KOCH HK270 AUTO RIFLE

Caliber: 22 LR, 5-shot magazine.
Barrel: 19¾″.
Weight: 5.5 lbs. **Length:** 38.2″ over-all.
Stock: European walnut.
Sights: Post front, diopter rear adjustable for windage and elevation.
Features: Straight blow-back action; 3½ lb. trigger pull. Extra 20-shot magazine available. Receiver grooved for scope mount. Introduced 1978. Imported from West Germany by Heckler & Koch, Inc.
Price: $199.00
Price: Scope mount, rings $75.00
Price: 20-shot magazine... $26.00

HECKLER & KOCH MODEL 300 AUTO RIFLE

Caliber: 22 Mag., 5-shot box mag.
Barrel: 19¾".
Weight: 5¾ lbs. **Length:** 39½" over-all.
Stock: European walnut, Monte Carlo with cheek rest; checkered p.g. and Schnabel fore-end.
Sights: Post front adj. for elevation, V-notch rear adj. for windage.
Features: Polygonal rifling, comes with sling swivels; straight blow-back inertia bolt action; single-stage trigger (3½-lb. pull). Clamp scope mount with 1" rings available at extra cost. Imported from West Germany by Heckler & Koch, Inc.
Price: HK300 .... **$310.00**
Price: Scope mount with 1" rings **$152.00**
Price: 15-shot magazine **$26.00**

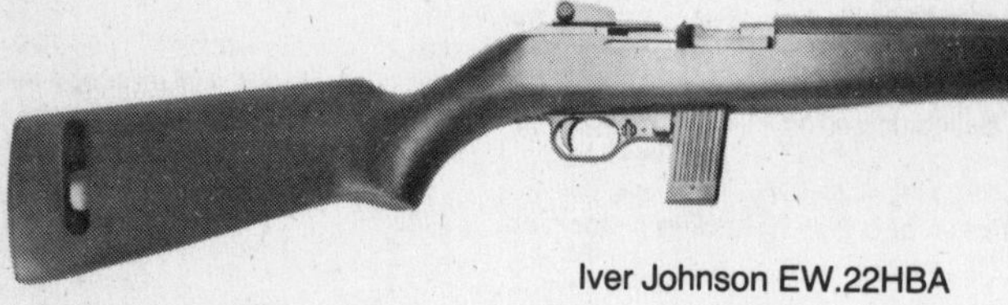

Iver Johnson EW.22HBA

IVER JOHNSON MODEL EW.22HBA RIFLE

Caliber: 22 Long Rifle (15-shot magazine).
Barrel: 18½".
Weight: 5.8 lbs. **Length:** 38" over-all.
Stock: Walnut-finished hardwood.
Sights: Blade front, peep rear adjustable for w. and e.
Features: Resembles the U.S. 30-cal. M-1 Carbine. Introduced 1985. From Iver Johnson.
Price: **$180.00**

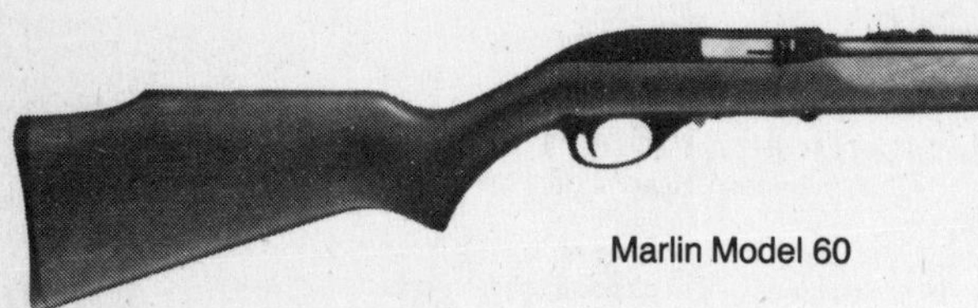

Marlin Model 60

MARLIN 60 SEMI-AUTO RIFLE

Caliber: 22 LR, 18-shot tubular mag.
Barrel: 22" round tapered.
Weight: About 5½ lbs. **Length:** 41" over-all.
Stock: Walnut finished Monte Carlo, full pistol grip; Mar-Shield® finish.
Sights: Ramp front, open adj. rear.
Features: Matted receiver is grooved for tip-off mounts. Manual bolt hold-open; automatic last-shot bolt hold-open.
Price: Less scope **$104.95**

Marlin Model 70

MARLIN 70 AUTO

Caliber: 22 LR, 7-shot clip magazine.
Barrel: 18" (16-groove rifling).
Weight: 4½ lbs. **Length:** 36½" over-all.
Stock: Walnut-finished hardwood with Monte Carlo, full p.g.
Sights: Ramp front, adj. open rear. Receiver grooved for scope mount.
Features: Receiver top has serrated, non-glare finish; chrome plated trigger; cross-bolt safety; manual bolt hold-open; automatic last-shot bolt hold-open; chrome plated magazine.
Price: Less scope **$104.95**

MARLIN MODEL 75C SEMI-AUTO RIFLE

Caliber: 22 LR, 14-shot tubular magazine.
Barrel: 18".
Weight: 5 lbs. **Length:** 36¾" over-all.
Stock: Walnut-finished hardwood; Monte Carlo with full p.g.
Sights: Ramp front, adj. open rear.
Features: Manual bolt hold-open; automatic last-shot bolt hold-open; cross-bolt safety; receiver grooved for scope mounting.
Price: **$104.95**

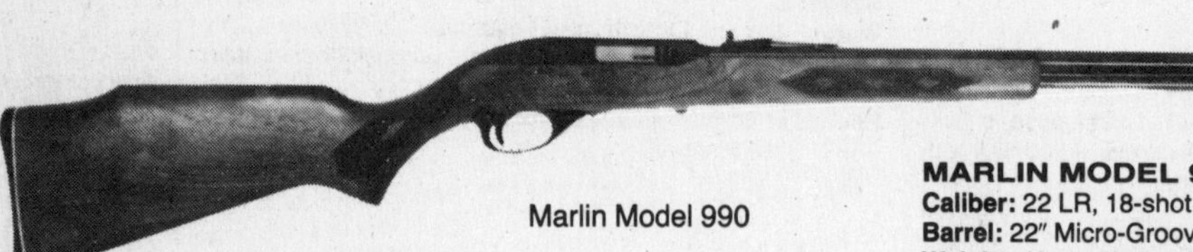

Marlin Model 990

MARLIN MODEL 990 SEMI-AUTO RIFLE

Caliber: 22 LR, 18-shot tubular magazine.
Barrel: 22" Micro-Groove®.
Weight: About 5½ lbs. **Length:** 40¾" over-all.
Stock: American black walnut, Monte Carlo style with fluted comb and full pistol grip; checkered p.g. and fore-end; white buttplate spacer; Mar-Shield® finish.
Sights: Ramp bead front with Wide-Scan™ hood, adjustable folding semi-buckhorn rear.
Features: Receiver grooved for tip-off mount; bolt hold-open device; cross-bolt safety. Introduced 1979.
Price: **$140.95**

MARLIN MODEL 995 SEMI-AUTO RIFLE

Caliber: 22 LR, 7-shot clip magazine
Barrel: 18" Micro-Grove®.
Weight: 5 lbs. **Length:** 36¾" over-all.
Stock: American black walnut, Monte Carlo-style, with full pistol grip. Checkered p.g. and fore-end; white buttplate spacer; Mar-Shield® finish.
Sights: Ramp bead front with Wide-Scan hood; adjustable folding semi-buckhorn rear.
Features: Receiver grooved for tip-off scope mount; bolt hold-open device; cross-bolt safety. Introduced 1979.
Price: **$131.95**

CAUTION: PRICES CHANGE. CHECK AT GUNSHOP.

Mossberg Model 480S

MOSSBERG MODEL 354 AUTO LOADING RIFLE
Caliber: 22 LR, 7-shot clip.
Barrel: 18" AC-KRO-GRUV.
Weight: 5 lbs. **Length:** 38" over-all.
Stock: Walnut, checkered at p.g. and fore-end. Black Tenite two-position fold-down fore-end.
Sights: Open step adj. U-notch rear, bead front on ramp.
Features: Sling swivels and web strap on left of stock, extension fore-end folds down for steady firing from prone position. Receiver grooved for scope mounting.
Price: About **$110.95**

MOSSBERG MODEL 480S AUTO RIFLE
Caliber: 22 LR, 15-shot tube magazine.
Barrel: 20", tapered, with AC-KRO-GRUV.
Weight: About 5½ lbs. with scope.
Stock: Walnut-finished hardwood, with black non-slip buttplate.
Sights: Bead front, adj. open rear.
Features: Receiver grooved for scope mounting. Available with optional 4x scope, mount. Magazine feeds through buttstock. Introduced 1981.
Price: With open sights, about **$110.00**
Price: With 4x scope, about **$115.95**

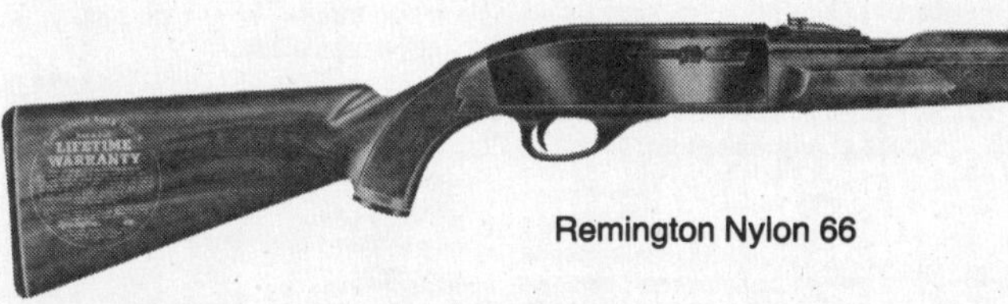

Remington Nylon 66

Remington Nylon 66BD Auto Rifle
Same as the Model 66MB except has black stock, barrel, and receiver cover. Black diamond-shape inlay in fore-end. Introduced 1978.
Price: About **$130.00**

REMINGTON NYLON 66MB AUTO RIFLE
Caliber: 22 LR, 14-shot tubular mag.
Barrel: 19⅝" round tapered.
Weight: 4 lbs. **Length:** 38½" over-all.
Stock: Moulded Mohawk Brown Nylon, checkered p.g. and fore-end.
Sights: Blade ramp front, adj. open rear.
Features: Top tang safety, double extractors, receiver grooved for tip-off mounts.
Price: About **$130.00**

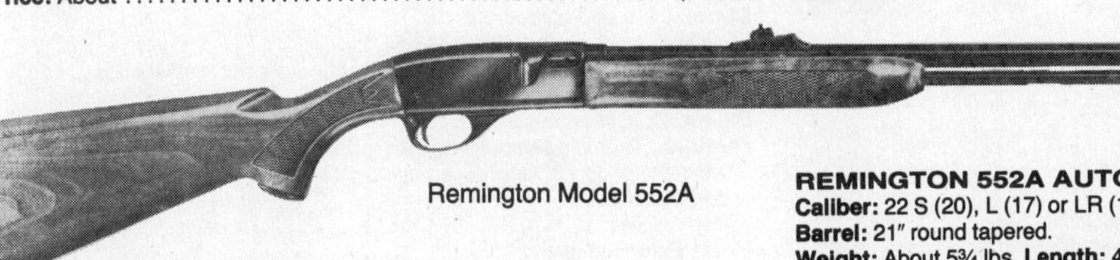
Remington Model 552A

Remington Model 552BDL Deluxe Auto Rifle
Same as Model 552A except: Du Pont RKW finished walnut stock, checkered fore-end and capped p.g. stock. Blade ramp front and fully adj. rear sights.
Price: About **$200.00**

REMINGTON 552A AUTOLOADING RIFLE
Caliber: 22 S (20), L (17) or LR (15) tubular mag.
Barrel: 21" round tapered.
Weight: About 5¾ lbs. **Length:** 40" over-all.
Stock: Full-size, walnut-finished hardwood.
Sights: Bead front, step open rear adj. for w. & e.
Features: Positive cross-bolt safety, receiver grooved for tip-off mount.
Price: About **$170.00**

Ruger 10/22 Sporter

Ruger 10/22 Auto Sporter
Same as 10/22 Carbine except: Walnut stock with hand checkered p.g. and fore-end with straight buttplate, no bbl. band, has sling swivels.
Price: Model 10/22 DSP **$222.00**

RUGER 10/22 AUTOLOADING CARBINE
Caliber: 22 LR, 10-shot rotary mag.
Barrel: 18½" round tapered.
Weight: 5 lbs. **Length:** 37¼" over-all.
Stock: American hardwood with p.g. and bbl. band.
Sights: Gold bead front, folding leaf rear adj. for e.
Features: Detachable rotary magazine fits flush into stock, cross-bolt safety, receiver tapped and grooved for scope blocks or tip-off mount. Scope base adapter furnished with each rifle.
Price: Model 10/22 RB **$152.00**

Stevens Model 987T

STEVENS MODEL 987T AUTO RIFLE
Caliber: 22 LR, 15-shot magazine.
Barrel: 20".
Weight: About 6 lbs. **Length:** 40½" over-all.
Stock: Walnut finish with Monte Carlo; checkered pistol grip and fore-end.
Sights: Bead front, open adjustable rear.
Features: Top tang safety; metal parts blued. Comes with 4x scope and mount.
Price: Model 987T, with scope **$106.50**

CAUTION: PRICES CHANGE. CHECK AT GUNSHOP.

Tradewinds Model 260-A

TRADEWINDS MODEL 260-A AUTO RIFLE

Caliber: 22 LR, 5-shot (10-shot mag. avail.).
Barrel: 22½".
Weight: 5¾ lbs. **Length:** 41½".
Stock: Walnut, with hand checkered p.g. and fore-end.
Sights: Ramp front with hood, 3-leaf folding rear, receiver grooved for scope mount.
Features: Double extractors, sliding safety. Imported by Tradewinds.
Price: **$250.00**

Voere 2115

VOERE MODEL 2115 AUTO RIFLE

Caliber: 22 LR, 8 or 15-shot magazine.
Barrel: 18.1".
Weight: 5.75 lbs. **Length:** 37.7" over-all.
Stock: Walnut-finished beechwood with cheekpiece; checkered pistol grip and fore-end.
Sights: Post front with hooded ramp, leaf rear.
Features: Clip-fed autoloader with single stage trigger, wing-type safety. Imported from Austria by L. Joseph Rahn. Introduced 1984.
Price: Model 2115 .... **$234.00**
Price: Model 2114S (as above except no cheekpiece, checkering or white line spacers at grip, buttplate) **$218.00**

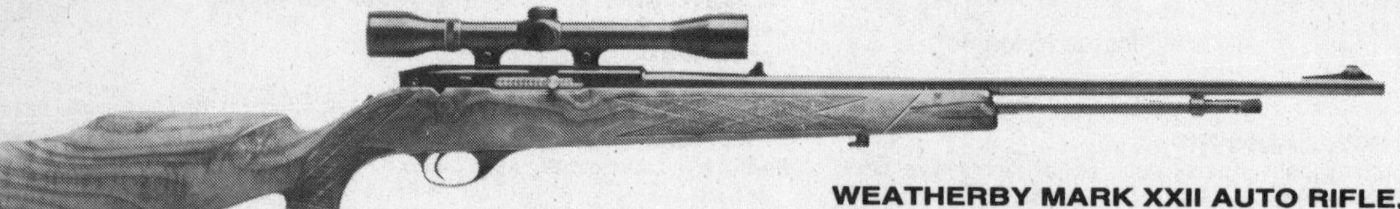
Weatherby Mark XXII

WEATHERBY MARK XXII AUTO RIFLE, CLIP MODEL

Caliber: 22 LR only, 5- or 10-shot clip.
Barrel: 24" round contoured.
Weight: 6 lbs. **Length:** 42¼" over-all.
Stock: Walnut, Monte Carlo comb and cheekpiece, rosewood p.g. cap and fore-end tip. Skip-line checkering.
Sights: Gold bead ramp front, 3-leaf folding rear.
Features: Thumb operated tang safety. Single shot or semi-automatic side lever selector. Receiver grooved for tip-off scope mount. Single pin release for quick takedown.
Price: **$339.95**
Price: Extra 5-shot clip **$8.00**
Price: Extra 10-shot clip **$10.00**

Weatherby Mark XXII Tubular Model

Same as Mark XXII Clip Model except: 15-shot tubular magazine.
Price: **$349.95**

RIMFIRE RIFLES—LEVER & SLIDE ACTIONS

Browning BL-22

BROWNING BL-22 LEVER ACTION RIFLE

Caliber: 22 S(22), L(17) or LR(15). Tubular mag.
Barrel: 20" round tapered.
Weight: 5 lbs. **Length:** 36¾" over-all.
Stock: Walnut, 2-piece straight grip Western style.
Sights: Bead post front, folding-leaf rear.
Features: Short throw lever, ½-cock safety, receiver grooved for tip-off scope mounts. Imported from Japan by Browning.
Price: Grade I **$239.95**
Price: Grade II, engraved receiver, checkered grip and fore-end **$274.95**

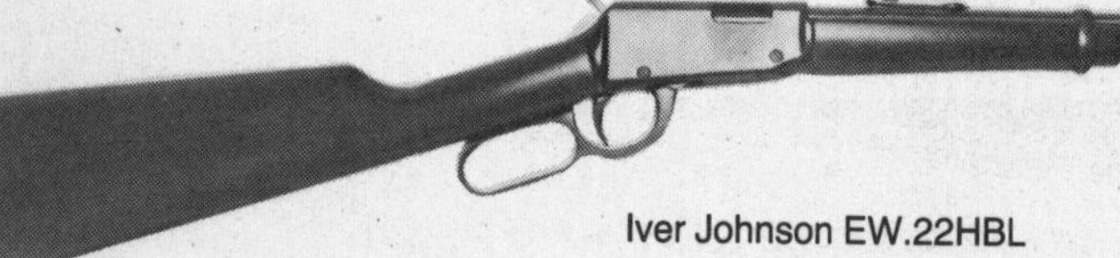
Iver Johnson EW.22HBL

IVER JOHNSON EW.22HBL RIFLE

Caliber: 22 Long Rifle (21 Short, 17 Long, 15 Long Rifle), 22 Mag. (12-shot magazine).
Barrel: 18½".
Weight: 5¾" lbs. **Length:** 36½" over-all.
Stock: Walnut-finished hardwood.
Sights: Hooded ramp front, open adjustable rear.
Features: Polished blue finish. Receiver grooved for scope mounting. Introduced 1985. From Iver Johnson.
Price: 22 Long Rifle **$210.00**
Price: 22 Magnum **$225.00**
Price: Junior Model (16¼" barrel, stock is 1¼" shorter, 22 LR only) . **$210.00**

CAUTION: PRICES CHANGE. CHECK AT GUNSHOP.

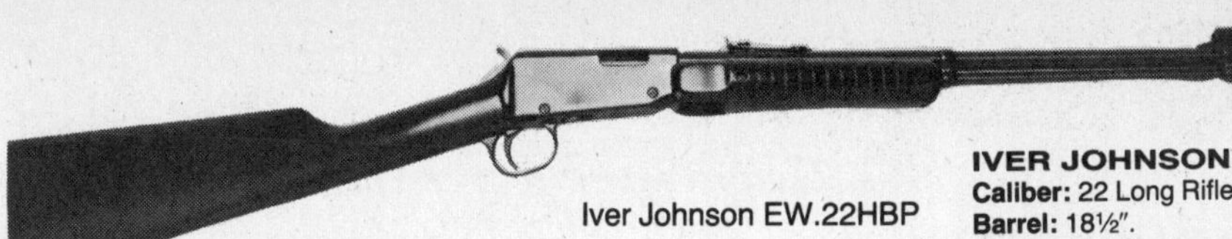

Iver Johnson EW.22HBP

IVER JOHNSON MODEL EW.22HBP RIFLE
Caliber: 22 Long Rifle (19 Short, 15 Long, 12 Long Rifle).
Barrel: 18½".
Weight: 5¾ lbs. **Length:** 36½" over-all.
Stock: Walnut-finished hardwood.
Sights: Hooded ramp front, open adjustable rear.
Features: Polished blue finish. Receiver grooved for scope mounting. Introduced 1985. From Iver Johnson.
Price: Standard or Youth Model **$210.00**

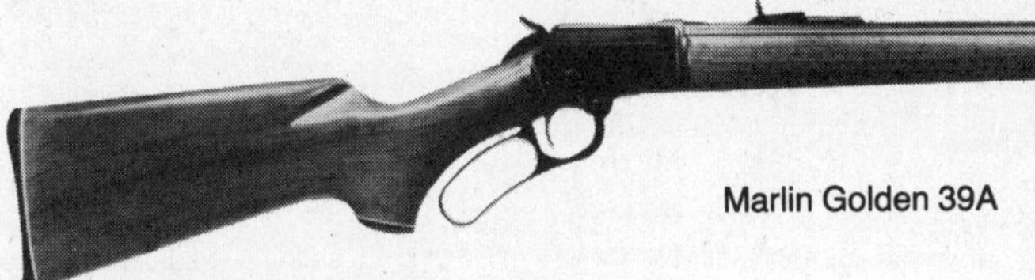

Marlin Golden 39A

MARLIN GOLDEN 39A LEVER ACTION RIFLE
Caliber: 22 S(26), L(21), LR(19), tubular magazine.
Barrel: 24" Micro-Groove®.
Weight: 6½ lbs. **Length:** 40" over-all.
Stock: American black walnut with white line spacers at p.g. cap and buttplate; Mar-Shield® finish.
Sights: Bead ramp front with detachable "Wide-Scan"™ hood, folding rear semi-buckhorn adj. for w. and e.
Features: Take-down action, receiver tapped for scope mount (supplied), offset hammer spur; gold plated steel trigger.
Price: **$267.95**

MARLIN GOLDEN 39M CARBINE
Caliber: 22 S(21), L(16), LR(15), tubular magazine.
Barrel: 20" Micro-Grove®.
Weight: 6 lbs. **Length:** 36" over-all.
Stock: American black walnut, straight grip, white line buttplate spacer. Mar-Shield® finish.
Sights: "Wide-Scan"™ ramp front with hood, folding rear semi-buckhorn adj. for w. and e.
Features: Squared finger lever. Receiver tapped for scope mount (supplied) or receiver sight, offset hammer spur, take-down action; gold plated steel trigger.
Price: **$267.95**

Marlin 1894M

MARLIN MODEL 1894M CARBINE
Caliber: 22 Mag., 11-shot magazine.
Barrel: 20" Micro-Groove®.
Weight: 6¼ lbs. **Length:** 37½" over-all.
Stock: Straight grip stock of American black walnut, Mar-Shield® finish.
Sights: Ramp front with brass bead, adjustable semi-buckhorn folding rear.
Features: Has new hammer block safety. Side-ejecting solid-top receiver tapped for scope mount or receiver sight; squared finger lever, reversible offset hammer spur for scope use. Scope shown is optional. Introduced 1983.
Price: **$300.95**

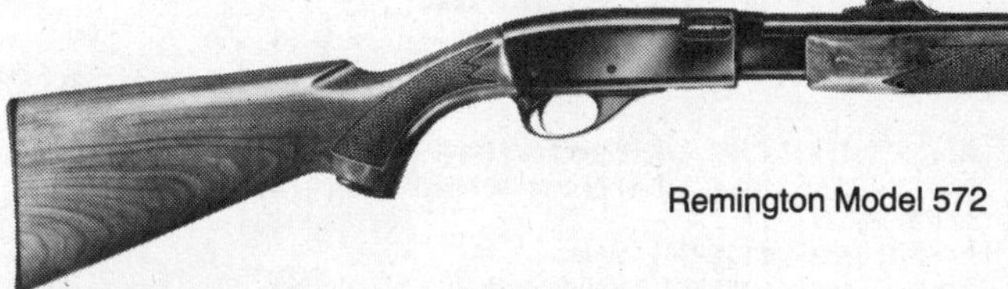

Remington Model 572

REMINGTON 572 FIELDMASTER PUMP RIFLE
Caliber: 22 S(20), L(17) or LR(14). Tubular mag.
Barrel: 21" round tapered.
Weight: 5½ lbs. **Length:** 42" over-all.
Stock: Walnut-finished hardwood with p.g. and grooved slide handle.
Sights: Blade ramp front; sliding ramp rear adj. for w. & e.
Features: Cross-bolt safety, removing inner mag. tube converts rifle to single shot, receiver grooved for tip-off scope mount.
Price: About **$180.00**

Remington Model 572 BDL Deluxe
Same as the 572 except: p.g. cap, walnut stock with RKW finish, checkered grip and fore-end, ramp front and fully adj. rear sights.
Price: About **$205.00**

Rossi 62 SA

ROSSI 62 SA PUMP RIFLE
Caliber: 22 S, L or LR, 22 Mag.
Barrel: 23", round or octagon.
Weight: 5¾ lbs. **Length:** 39¼" over-all.
Stock: Walnut, straight grip, grooved fore-end.
Sights: Fixed front, adj. rear.
Features: Capacity 20 Short, 16 Long or 14 Long Rifle. Quick takedown. Imported from Brazil by Interarms.
Price: Blue **$149.00**
Price: Nickel **$164.00**
Price: Blue, with octagon barrel **$174.00**
Price: 22 Mag., as Model 59 .... **$184.00**

Rossi 62 SAC Carbine
Same as standard model except has 16¼" barrel. Magazine holds slightly fewer cartridges.
Price: Blue **$149.00**
Price: Nickel **$164.00**

Winchester 9422

WINCHESTER 9422 XTR LEVER ACTION RIFLE
Caliber: 22 S(21), L(17), LR(15). Tubular mag.
Barrel: 20½". (16" twist).
Weight: 6¼ lbs. **Length:** 37⅛" over-all.
Stock: American walnut, 2-piece, straight grip (no p.g.).
Sights: Hooded ramp front, adj. semi-buckhorn rear.
Features: Side ejection, receiver grooved for scope mounting, takedown action. Has XTR wood and metal finish. Made under license by U.S. Repeating Arms Co.
Price: About **$272.00**

Winchester 9422M XTR Lever Action Rifle
Same as the 9422 except chambered for 22 Mag. cartridge, has 11-round mag. capacity.
Price: About **$272.00**

Winchester 9422 Classic

Winchester 9422 XTR Classic
Similar to 9422 XTR except has uncheckered, satin-finished walnut stock with fluted comb, crescent steel buttplate, curved finger lever, and capped pistol grip. Over-all length is 39⅛", barrel length 22½", weight is 6½ lbs. In 22 Short, Long, Long Rifle and 22 Magnum. Introduced 1985.
Price: About **$301.00**

Winchester 9422 Boy Scout

Winchester 9422 Eagle Scout Commemorative
Similar to 9422 XTR except receiver is deep etched in triple levels and plated in antique gold; left side has Boy Scout law, right side has Boy Scout oath. Frame has "1910-1985" anniversary inscription. Stock and fore-end have spade-pattern checkering, high luster finish. Stock has an Eagle Scout commemorative medallion embedded in right side, crescent steel buttplate. Jeweled bolt, antique gold-plated fore-end cap, brass magazine tube. Comes with oak presentation case, crystal commemorative disc. Only 1,000 will be made. Introduced 1985.
Price: About.. **$2,052.00**

Winchester 9422 Boy Scouts of America Commemorative
Similar to the 9422 XTR except receiver is roll-engraved and plated in antique pewter, illustrating the Boy Scout oath and law. Frame carries the 75th anniversary inscription "1910-1985." Finger lever has an engraved decorative frieze of scouting knots. "Boy Scouts of America" is inscribed on the barrel. Antique pewter-plated medallion embedded in the stock. Only 15,000 will be made. Introduced 1985.
Price: About **$589.00**

RIMFIRE RIFLES—BOLT ACTIONS & SINGLE SHOTS

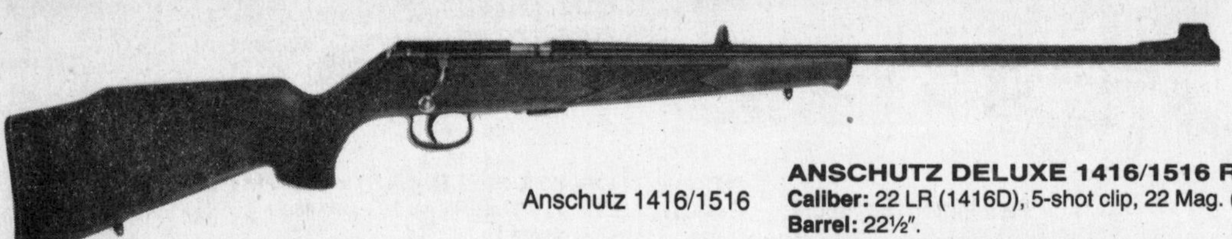
Anschutz 1416/1516

ANSCHUTZ DELUXE 1416/1516 RIFLES
Caliber: 22 LR (1416D), 5-shot clip, 22 Mag. (1516D), 4-shot clip.
Barrel: 22½".
Weight: 6 lbs. **Length:** 41" over-all.
Stock: European walnut; Monte Carlo with cheekpiece, Schnabel fore-end, checkered pistol grip and fore-end.
Sights: Hooded ramp front, folding leaf rear.
Features: Uses Model 1403 target rifle action. Adjustable single stage trigger. Receiver grooved for scope mounting. Imported from Germany by PSI.
Price: 1416D, 22 LR **$350.00**
Price: 1516D, 22 Mag. **$353.00**

Anschutz 1418D/1518D Deluxe Rifles
Similar to the 1416D/1516D rifles except has full length Mannlicher-style stock, shorter 19¾" barrel. Weighs 5½ lbs. Stock has buffalo horn Schnabel tip. Double set trigger available on special order. Model 1418D chambered for 22 LR, 1518D for 22 Mag. Imported from Germany by PSI.
Price: 1418D.. **$490.00**
Price: 1518D.. **$499.00**

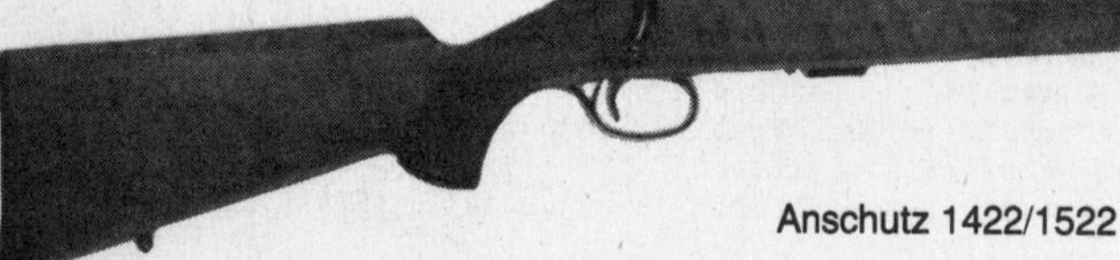
Anschutz 1422/1522

ANSCHUTZ 1422D/1522D CLASSIC RIFLES
Caliber: 22 LR (1422D), 5-shot clip, 22 Mag. (1522D), 4-shot clip.
Barrel: 24".
Weight: 7¼ lbs. **Length:** 43" over-all.
Stock: Select European walnut; checkered pistol grip and fore-end.
Sights: Hooded ramp front, folding leaf rear.
Features: Uses Match 54 action. Adjustable single stage trigger. Receiver drilled and tapped for scope mounting. Introduced 1982. Imported from Germany by PSI.
Price: 1422D (22 LR) **$564.00**
Price: 1522D (22 Mag.).. **$564.00**

Anschutz 1422D/1522D Custom Rifles
Similar to the Classic models except have roll-over Monte Carlo cheekpiece, slim fore-end with Schnabel tip, Wundhammer palm swell on pistol grip, rosewood grip cap with white diamond insert. Skip-line checkering on grip and fore-end. Introduced 1982. Imported from Germany by PSI.
Price: 1422D **$598.00**
Price: 1522D **$598.00**

Krico 120M

BEEMAN/KRICO MODEL 320 BOLT ACTION RIFLE
Caliber: 22 LR, 5-shot magazine.
Barrel: 19.5″.
Weight: 6 lbs. **Length:** 38½″ over-all.
Stock: Select European walnut; full length Mannlicher-style with curved European comb and cheekpiece; cut checkered grip and fore-end.
Sights: Blade front on ramp, open rear adjustable for windage.
Features: Single or double set trigger; blued steel fore-end cap; detachable box magazine. Imported from West Germany by Beeman.
Price: **$549.50**

Cabanas Master

Cabanas Espronceda IV Bolt Action Rifle
Similar to the Leyre model except has full sporter stock, 18¾″ barrel, 40″ over-all length, weighs 5½ lbs.
Price: **$119.95**

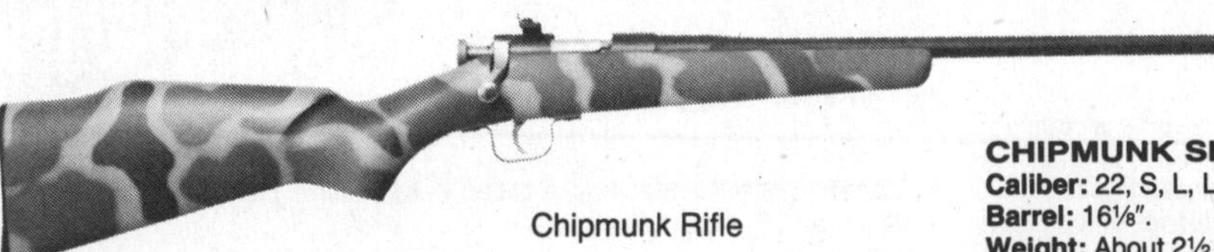
Chipmunk Rifle

CLAYCO MODEL 4 BOLT ACTION RIFLE
Caliber: 22 LR, 5-shot clip.
Barrel: 24″.
Weight: 5¾″ lbs. **Length:** 42″ over-all.
Stock: Hardwood with walnut finish.
Sights: Ramp front with bead, open rear adjustable for windage and elevation.
Features: Wing-type safety on rear of bolt. Receiver grooved for tip-off scope mount. Black composition buttplate and pistol grip cap. Introduced 1983. Imported from China by Clayco Sports Ltd.
Price: **$150.00**

BEEMAN/KRICO MODEL 300 BOLT ACTION RIFLE
Caliber: 22 LR, 5-shot magazine.
Barrel: 23.5″.
Weight: 6.5 lbs. **Length:** 43″ over-all.
Stock: European walnut with straight American-style comb; cut checkered grip and fore-end.
Sights: Hooded blade front on ramp, open rear adjustable for windage.
Features: Dual extractors; single, match or double set triggers available; detachable box magazine. Imported from West Germany by Beeman.
Price: **$495.50**

BEEMAN/KRICO MODEL 120M MILITARY TRAINER
Caliber: 22 LR, 5-shot magazine.
Barrel: 19½″.
Weight: 6 lbs. **Length:** 36″ over-all.
Stock: European hardwood.
Sights: Hooded blade front, tangent rear adjustable for elevation.
Features: Receiver grooved for scope mounting; adjustable trigger; polished blued metal, oil finish wood. Imported from West Germany by Beeman. Introduced 1984.
Price: **$249.00**

BINGHAM "BANTAM" BOLT ACTION
Caliber: 22 LR or 22 Mag., single shot.
Barrel: 18½″.
Weight: 3¼ lbs. **Length:** 34″ over-all.
Stock: Walnut finished hardwood.
Sights: Hooded ramp front, open adjustable rear.
Features: Classic-style stock, visual safe/fire indicator, manually cocked action. From Bingham Ltd.
Price: 22 LR or 22 Mag. **$119.95**

CABANAS MASTER BOLT ACTION RIFLE
Caliber: 177, round ball or pellet; single shot.
Barrel: 19½″.
Weight: 8 lbs. **Length:** 45½″ over-all.
Stock: Walnut target-type with Monte Carlo.
Sights: Blade front, fully adjustable rear.
Features: Fires round ball or pellet with 22-cal. blank cartridge. Bolt action. Imported from Mexico by Mandall Shooting Supplies. Introduced 1984.
Price: **$149.95**
Price: Varmint model (21½″ barrel, 4½ lbs., 41″ o.a.l., varmint-type stock) **$109.95**

Cabanas Leyre Bolt Action Rifle
Similar to Master model except 44″ over-all, has sport/target stock.
Price: **$134.95**
Price: Model R83 (17″ barrel, hardwood stock, 40″ o.a.l.) **$79.95**
Price: Mini 82 Youth (16½″ barrel, 33″ o.a.l., 3½ lbs.) **$69.95**

CHIPMUNK SINGLE SHOT RIFLE
Caliber: 22, S, L, LR, or 22 Mag., single shot.
Barrel: 16⅛″.
Weight: About 2½ lbs. **Length:** 30″ over-all.
Stock: American walnut, or camouflage.
Sights: Post on ramp front, peep rear adj. for windage and elevation.
Features: Drilled and tapped for scope mounting using special Chipmunk base ($9.95). Made in U.S.A. Introduced 1982. From Chipmunk Mfg.
Price: **$119.95**
Price: Fully engraved Presentation Model with hand checkered fancy stock **$500.00**

RIMFIRE RIFLES—BOLT ACTIONS & SINGLE SHOTS

Concorde Model 1500

CONCORDE M-1500 RIFLE
Caliber: 22 Mag., 5-shot magazine.
Barrel: 23″.
Weight: 7 lbs. **Length:** 41¼″ over-all.
Stock: Philippine mahogany, hand checkered.
Sights: Blade on ramp front, open rear adjustable for windage and elevation.
Features: Blued metal; twin locking locks. Imported by Kassnar.
Price: $180.00
Price: Model 14 P/S (22 LR, no checkering, 4x scope installed) $132.00
Price: Model 14P (22 LR, no scope) $123.00

HARRINGTON & RICHARDSON MODEL 750
Caliber: 22 S, L or LR, single shot.
Barrel: 22″ round tapered.
Weight: 5 lbs. **Length:** 39″ over-all.
Stock: Walnut finished hardwood with Monte Carlo comb and p.g.
Sights: Blade front, step adj. open rear.
Features: Double extractors, feed platform, cocking indicator, sliding side safety, receiver grooved for tip-off scope mount.
Price: **$89.50**

H&R Model 865

HARRINGTON & RICHARDSON MODEL 865 RIFLE
Caliber: 22 S, L or LR. 5-shot clip mag.
Barrel: 22″ round tapered.
Weight: 5 lbs. **Length:** 39″ over-all.
Stock: Walnut finished hardwood with Monte Carlo and p.g.
Sights: Blade front, step adj. open rear.
Features: Cocking indicator, sliding side safety, receiver grooved for tip-off scope mounts.
Price: **$99.50**

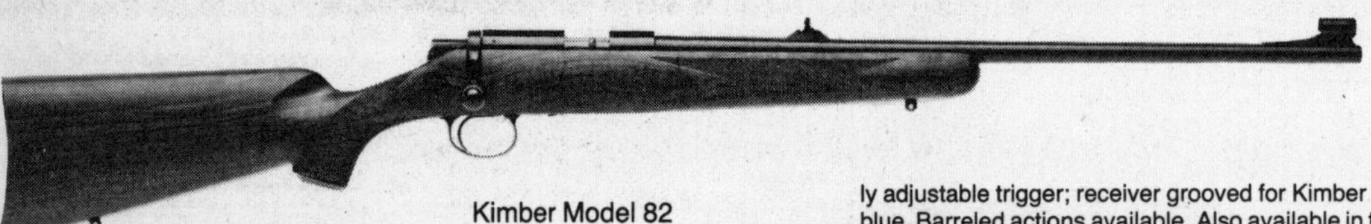

Kimber Model 82

KIMBER MODEL 82 BOLT ACTION RIFLE
Caliber: 22 LR, 22 Mag.; 5-shot detachable magazine (LR), 4-shot (Mag.).
Barrel: 22½″; 6-grooves; 1-in 16″ twist; 24″ heavy (22 LR only).
Weight: About 6¼ lbs. **Length:** 42″ over-all.
Stock: Three styles available. "Classic" is Claro walnut with plain, straight comb; "Cascade" has Monte Carlo comb with cheekpiece; "Custom Classic" is of fancy select grade Claro walnut, ebony fore-end tip, Niedner-style buttplate. All have 18 lpi hand cut, borderless checkering, steel grip cap, checkered steel buttplate.
Sights: Hooded ramp front with bead, folding leaf rear (optional).
Features: High quality, adult-sized, bolt action rifle. Barrel screwed into receiver; rocker-type silent safety; twin rear locking lugs. All steel construction. Fully adjustable trigger; receiver grooved for Kimber scope mounts. High polish blue. Barreled actions available. Also available in true left-hand version in selected models. Made in U.S.A. Introduced 1979.
Price: 22 LR Classic stock, no sights, plain or heavy bbl. **$545.00**
Price: As above, Cascade stock **$595.00**
Price: As above, Custom Classic, plain or heavy bbl. **$675.00**
Price: 22 Mag Classic stock, no sights **$568.00**
Price: As above, Cascade stock **$618.00**
Price: As above, Custom Classic stock **$698.00**
Price: Classic stock, left-hand action, plain barrel **$565.00**
Price: As above, Custom Classic stock **$695.00**
Price: Extra 22 LR 5-shot clip **$12.00**
Price: Extra 22 LR 10-shot clip **$16.50**
Price: Extra 22 Mag. 4-shot clip **$15.00**
Price: Kimber scope mounts, from **$48.00**
Price: Optional open sights fitted **$55.00**

Kimber Super America

Kimber Model 82, 84 Super America
Super-grade version of the Model 82. Has the Classic stock only of specially selected, high-grade, California claro walnut, with Continental cheekpiece and ebony fore-end tip; borderless, full-coverage 20 lpi checkering; Niedner-type checkered steel buttplate; comes with barrel quarter-rib which has a folding leaf sight. Receiver of the 1985 model is dovetailed to accept Kimber's own scope mounts. Available in 22 Long Rifle, 22 Magnum, 22 Hornet, 223 Rem.
Price: Model 82 22 Long Rifle, less 4x scope **$955.00**
Price: Model 82 22 Mag., less scope **$1,023.00**
Price: Model 82 22 Hornet, less scope **$1,073.00**
Price: Model 84, 223 .... **$1,105.00**

KLEINGUENTHER K-22 BOLT ACTION RIFLE
Caliber: 22 LR, 5-shot magazine.
Barrel: 21½″.
Weight: 6½ lbs. **Length:** 40″ over-all.
Stock: Walnut-stained beechwood; Monte Carlo; hand-cut checkering; sling swivels.
Sights: None furnished, drilled and tapped for scope mounting. Iron sights optional.
Features: Action has two forward locking lugs, 60° bolt lift; adjustable trigger (optional double set); silent safety locks sear, trigger and trigger lever. Will shoot into ½″ or less at 50 yds. Imported from West Germany and accurized by Kleinguenther. Introduced 1984.
Price: **$366.00**
Price: For 22 Mag. add **$99.00**
Price: Double set trigger **$125.00**

 CAUTION: PRICES CHANGE. CHECK AT GUNSHOP.

Marathon Super Shot

MARATHON SUPER SHOT 22 BOLT ACTION

Caliber: 22 LR, single shot.
Barrel: 24″.
Weight: 4.9 lbs. **Length:** 41½″ over-all.
Stock: Select hardwood.
Sights: Bead front, step-adjustable open rear.
Features: Blued metal parts; receiver grooved for scope mounting. Also available as a kit, requiring assembly and metal and wood finishing. Introduced 1984. Imported from Spain by Marathon.
Price: Finished **$74.99**
Price: Kit **$55.99**
Price: First Shot (youth model of above with 16½″ barrel, 3.8 lbs., 31″ o.a.l.), assembled **$74.99**
Price: As above, kit **$55.99**

MARLIN MODEL 15 BOLT ACTION RIFLE

Caliber: 22, S, L, LR, single shot.
Barrel: 22″.
Weight: 5½ lbs. **Length:** 41″ over-all.
Stock: Walnut-finished hardwood with Monte Carlo and full p.g.; Mar-Shield® finish.
Sights: Ramp front, adjustable open rear.
Features: Receiver grooved for tip-off scope mount; thumb safety; red cocking indicator.
Price: **$99.95**

Marlin Model 780

MARLIN 780 BOLT ACTION RIFLE

Caliber: 22 S, L, or LR; 7-shot clip magazine.
Barrel: 22″ Micro-Groove.
Weight: 5½ lbs. **Length:** 41″.
Stock: Monte Carlo American black walnut with checkered p.g. and fore-end. White line spacer at buttplate. Mar-Shield® finish.
Sights: "Wide-Scan"™ ramp front, folding semi-buckhorn rear adj. for w. & e.
Features: Receiver anti-glare serrated and grooved for tip-off scope mount.
Price: **$134.95**

Marlin 781 Bolt Action Rifle

Same as the Marlin 780 except: tubular magazine holds 25 Shorts, 19 Longs or 17 Long Rifle cartridges. Weight 6 lbs.
Price: **$140.95**

Marlin Model 783

Marlin 783 Bolt Action Rifle

Same as Marlin 782 except: Tubular magazine holds 12 rounds of 22 Rimfire Magnum ammunition.
Price: **$153.95**

Marlin 782 Bolt Action Rifle

Same as the Marlin 780 except: 22 Rimfire Magnum cal. only, weight about 6 lbs. Sling and swivels attached
Price: **$148.95**

Marlin Model 25M Bolt Action Rifle

Similar to the Model 25 except chambered for 22 Mag. Has 7-shot clip magazine, 22″ Micro-Groove® barrel, walnut-finished hardwood stock. Introduced 1983.
Price: **$117.95**

Marlin 25 Bolt Action Repeater

Similar to Marlin 780, except: walnut finished p.g. stock, adjustable open rear sight, ramp front.
Price: **$103.95**

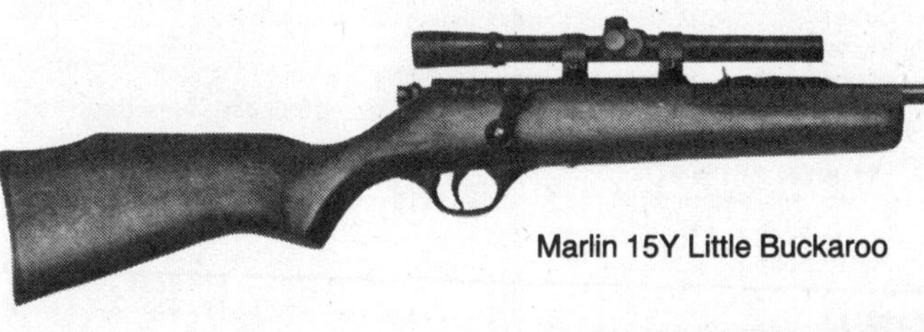

Marlin 15Y Little Buckaroo

Marlin Model 15Y "Little Buckaroo" Rifle

Similar to the standard Model 15 rifle except is shorter and lighter. Buttstock, fore-end and barrel have been scaled down for young shooters. Barrel length is 16¼″, over-all length is 33¼″, and weight is 4¼ lbs. Comes with 4x15 scope and mount. Introduced 1984.
Price: With scope and mount **$99.95**

Mossberg Model 344

MOSSBERG MODEL 344 RIFLE

Caliber: 22 S, L, LR, 7-shot clip.
Barrel: 20″, tapered, AC-KRO-GRUV.
Weight: 6½ lbs. **Length:** 39½″ over-all.
Stock: Walnut, checkered p.g. and fore-end, Monte Carlo and cheekpiece. Buttplate with white line spacer.
Sights: Bead front, U-notch rear adj. for w. and e.
Features: Sliding side safety, 8 groove rifling.
Price: About **$115.95**

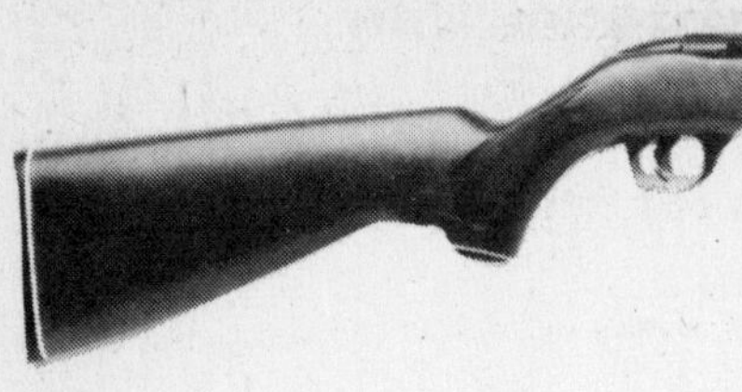

Mossberg Model 640K

MOSSBERG MODEL 640K CHUCKSTER
Caliber: 22 Mag. 5-shot clip mag.
Barrel: 24″ AC-KRO-GRUV.
Weight: 6¼ lbs. **Length:** 44¾″ over-all.
Stock: Walnut, checkered p.g. and fore-end, Monte Carlo comb and cheekpiece.
Sights: Ramp front with bead, fully adj. leaf rear.
Features: Grooved trigger, sliding side safety, double extractors, receiver grooved for tip-off scope mounts and tapped for aperture rear sight.
Price: About **$125.95**

Ruger 77/22

RUGER 77/22 RIMFIRE BOLT ACTION RIFLE
Caliber: 22 Long Rifle, 10-shot magazine.
Barrel: 20″.
Weight: About 5¾ lbs. **Length:** 39¾″ over-all.
Stock: Straight-grained American walnut.
Sights: Gold bead front, adjustable folding leaf rear, or no sights.
Features: Mauser-type action uses Ruger's 10-shot rotary magazine; 3-position safety; simplified bolt stop; patented bolt locking system. Uses the dual-screw barrel attachment system of the 10/22 rifle. Integral scope mounting system with 1″ Ruger rings. Announced 1983.
Price: 77/22 R (plain barrel, no sights, with Ruger 1″ rings) **$326.00**
Price: 77/22 S (gold bead front sight, folding leaf rear) **$326.00**
Price: 77/22 RS (scope rings and open sights) **$346.00**

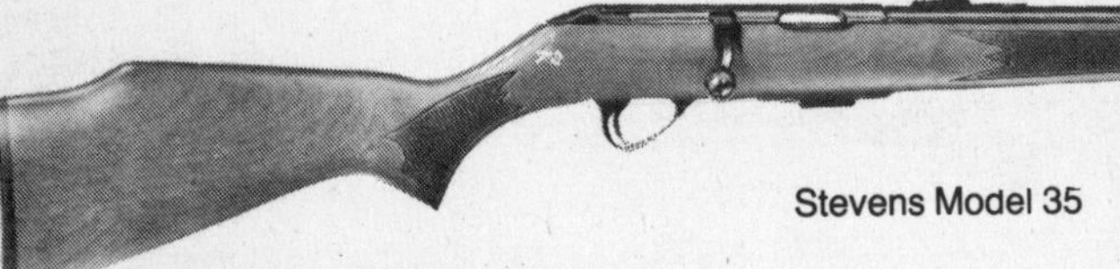

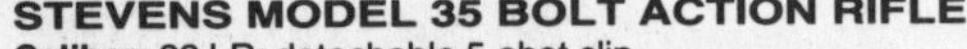

Stevens Model 35

STEVENS MODEL 35 BOLT ACTION RIFLE
Caliber: 22 LR; detachable 5-shot clip.
Barrel: 22″.
Weight: 4¾ lbs. **Length:** 41″ over-all.
Stock: Walnut-finished hardwood.
Sights: Ramp front, step-adjustable open rear.
Features: Checkered pistol grip and fore-end. Receiver grooved for scope mounting. Introduced 1982. From Savage Arms.
Price: Model 35 .... **$99.95**

SAVAGE-STEVENS MODEL 72 CRACKSHOT
Caliber: 22 S, L, LR, single shot.
Barrel: 22″ octagonal.
Weight: 4½ lbs. **Length:** 37″ over-all.
Stock: Walnut, straight grip stock and fore-end.
Sights: Blade front, step adj. rear.
Features: Falling block action, color case hardened frame.
Price: **$138.75**

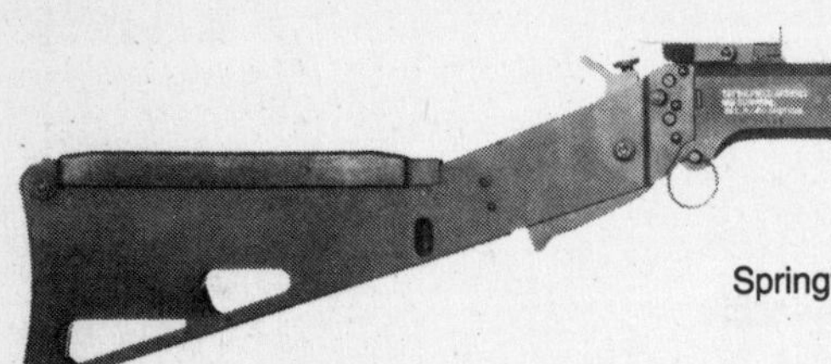

Springfield Armory M6

SPRINGFIELD ARMORY M6 SURVIVAL RIFLE
Caliber: 22 LR, 22 Mag., 22 Hornet over 410 shotgun.
Barrel: 18″.
Weight: 4 lbs. **Length:** 31½″ over-all.
Stock: Steel, folding, with magazine for 15 22 LR, four 410 cartridges.
Sights: Blade front, military aperture for 22; V-notch for 410.
Features: All metal construction. Designed for quick disassembly and minimum maintenance. Folds for compact storage. Introduced 1982. Made in U.S. by Springfield Armory.
Price: About **$154.00**

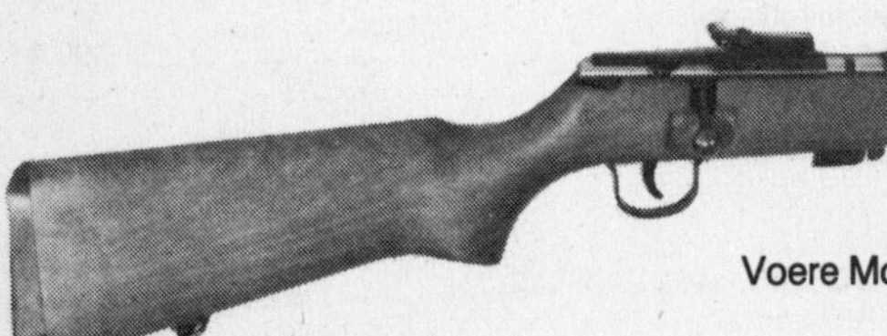

Voere Model 1007/1013

VOERE MODEL 1007/1013 BOLT ACTION RIFLE
Caliber: 22 LR (M1007 Biathlon), 22 Mag. (M1013).
Barrel: 18″.
Weight: About 5½ lbs. (M1007)
Stock: Oil-finished beechwood.
Sights: Hooded front, open adjustable rear.
Features: Single-stage trigger (M1013 available with double set). Military-look stock; sling swivels. Convertible to single shot. Imported from Austria by L. Joseph Rahn. Introduced 1984.
Price: 1007 Biathlon **$203.00**
Price: 1013 22 Mag. **$301.00**

CAUTION: PRICES CHANGE. CHECK AT GUNSHOP.

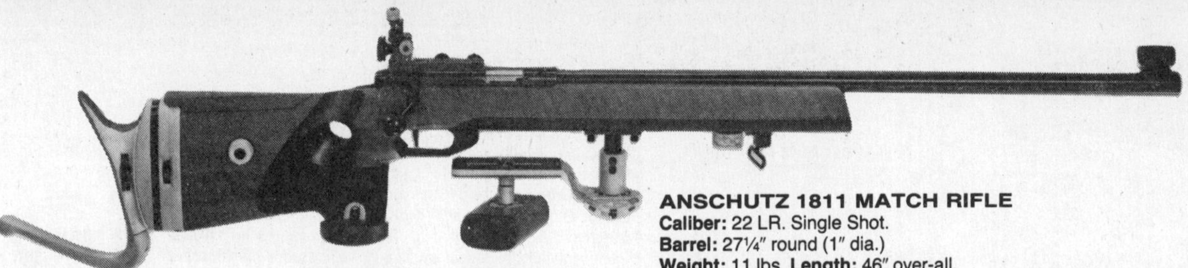

Anschutz 1813 Super Match

ANSCHUTZ 1811 MATCH RIFLE
Caliber: 22 LR. Single Shot.
Barrel: 27¼″ round (1″ dia.)
Weight: 11 lbs. **Length:** 46″ over-all.
Stock: French walnut, American prone style with Monte Carlo, cast-off cheekpiece, checkered p.g., beavertail fore-end with swivel rail and adj. swivel, adj. rubber buttplate.
Sights: None. Receiver grooved for Anschutz sights (extra). Scope blocks.
Features: Single stage adj. trigger, wing safety, short firing pin travel. Imported from West Germany by PSI.
Price: Right hand, no sights **$792.00**
Price: M1811-L (true left-hand action and stock) **$872.00**
Price: Anschutz Int'l. sight set **$149.75**

Anschutz 1813 Super Match Rifle
Same as the model 1811 except: International-type stock with adj. cheekpiece, adj. aluminum hook buttplate, weight 15½ lbs., 46″ over-all. Imported from West Germany by PSI.
Price: Right hand, no sights **$1,165.00**
Price: M1813-L (left-hand action and stock) **$1,218.00**

Anschutz 1807 Match Rifle
Same as the model 1811 except: 26″ bbl. (⅞″ dia.), weight 10 lbs. 44½″ over-all to conform to ISU requirements and also suitable for NRA matches.
Price: Right hand, no sights **$693.00**
Price: M1807-L (true left-hand action and stock) **$762.00**
Price: Int'l sight set **$149.75**
Price: Match sight set **$107.50**

Anschutz Model 1810 Super Match II
Similar to the Super Match 1813 rifle except has a stock of European hardwood with tapered fore-end and deep receiver area. Hand and palm rests not included. Uses Match 54 action. Adjustable hook buttplate and cheekpiece. Sights not included. Introduced 1982. Imported from Germany by PSI.
Price: Right-hand **$987.00**
Price: Left-hand **$1,086.00**
Price: International sight set **$149.75**
Price: Match sight set **$107.50**

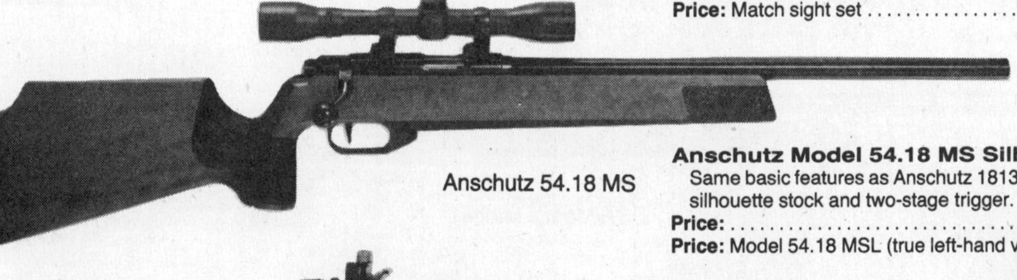

Anschutz 54.18 MS

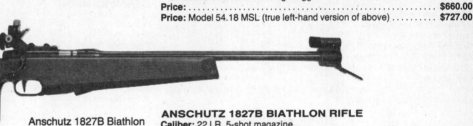

Anschutz Model 54.18 MS Silhouette Rifle
Same basic features as Anschutz 1813 Super Match but with special metallic silhouette stock and two-stage trigger.
Price: **$660.00**
Price: Model 54.18 MSL (true left-hand version of above) **$727.00**

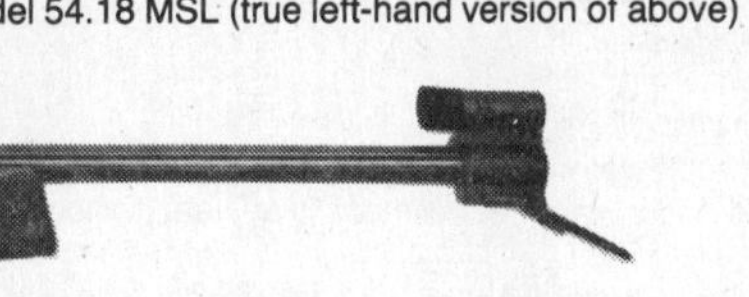

Anschutz 1827B Biathlon

ANSCHUTZ 1827B BIATHLON RIFLE
Caliber: 22 LR, 5-shot magazine.
Barrel: 21½″.
Weight: 9 lbs. with sights. **Length:** 42½″ over-all.
Stock: Walnut-finished hardwood; cheekpiece, stippled pistol grip and fore-end.
Sights: Globe front specially designed for Biathlon shooting, micrometer rear with hinged snow cap.
Features: Uses Match 54 action and adjustable trigger; adjustable wooden buttplate, Biathlon butt hook, adjustable hand-stop rail. **Special Order Only.** Introduced 1982. Imported from Germany by PSI.
Price: Right-hand **$913.40**
Price: Left-hand **$1,041.70**

ANSCHUTZ 1808ED SUPER RUNNING TARGET
Caliber: 22 LR, single shot.
Barrel: 23½″; ⅞″ diameter.
Weight: 9¼ lbs. **Length:** 42″ over-all.
Stock: European hardwood. Heavy beavertail fore-end, adjustable cheekpiece, buttplate, stippled pistol grip and fore-end.
Sights: None furnished. Receiver grooved for scope mounting.
Features: Uses Super Match 54 action. Adjustable trigger from 14 oz. to 3.5 lbs. Removable sectioned barrel weights. **Special Order Only.** Introduced 1982. Imported from Germany by PSI.
Price: Right-hand **$777.00**
Price: Left-hand, 1808EDL **$864.00**

ANSCHUTZ MODEL 64-MS
Caliber: 22 LR, single shot.
Barrel: 21¾″, medium heavy, ⅞″ diameter.
Weight: 8 lbs. 1 oz. **Length:** 39½″ over-all.
Stock: Walnut-finished hardwood, silhouette-type.
Sights: None furnished. Receiver drilled and tapped for scope mounting.
Features: Designed for metallic silhouette competition. Stock has stippled checkering, contoured thumb groove with Wundhammer swell. Two-stage trigger is adj. for weight of pull, take-up, and over-travel. Slide safety locks sear and bolt. Introducted 1980. Imported from West Germany by PSI.
Price: **$351.00**

ANSCHUTZ MODEL 1403D MATCH RIFLE
Caliber: 22 LR only. Single shot.
Barrel: 26″ round (1¹⁄₁₆″ dia.)
Weight: 7¾ lbs. **Length:** 44″ over-all.
Stock: Walnut finished hardwood, cheekpiece, checkered p.g., beavertail fore-end, adj. buttplate.
Sights: None furnished.
Features: Sliding side safety, adj. single stage trigger, receiver grooved for Anschutz sights. Imported from West Germany by PSI.
Price: Without sights **$379.00**
Price: 1403DL (left hand) **$401.00**
Price: Match sight set **$107.50**

Anschutz Mark 2000

ANSCHUTZ MARK 2000 TARGET RIFLE

Caliber: 22 LR, single-shot.
Barrel: 26", heavy. 7/8" diameter.
Weight: 8 lbs. **Length:** 43" over-all.
Stock: Walnut finished hardwood.
Sights: Globe front (insert-type), micro-click peep rear.
Features: Action similar to the Anschutz Model 1403D. Stock has thumb groove, Wundhammer swell p.g., adjustable hand stop and sling swivel. Imported from West Germany by PSI.
Price: Without sights **$195.00**
Price: Sight set **$30.00**

BSA CFT Target

BSA CFT TARGET RIFLE

Caliber: 308 Win. (7.62mm), single shot.
Barrel: 26.5".
Weight: 11 lbs. **Length:** 47.6" over-all.
Stock: Beechwood. Full target style with adjustable rubber buttplate, broad fore-end with full length hand-stop rail, rotating front sling swivel, palm swell pistol grip, and high cheekpiece.
Sights: Removable tunnel front with five elements; Parker aperture rear with choice of three base locations, fully adjustable for windage and elevation.
Features: Receiver bottom is flat for perfect bedding; top surface has a machined 19mm dovetail rail for scope mounting; fully adjustable trigger; full length guide rib on bolt, two locking lugs, recessed bolt face. Imported from England by Precision Sports, Inc. Introduced 1984.
Price: **$999.95**

BSA Martini Match

BSA MARTINI ISU MATCH RIFLE

Caliber: 22 LR, single shot.
Barrel: 28".
Weight: 10¾ lbs. **Length:** 43-44" over-all.
Stock: Match type French walnut butt and fore-end; flat cheekpiece, full p.g.; spacers are fitted to allow length adjustment to suit each shooting position; adj. buttplate.
Sights: Modified PH-1 Parker-Hale tunnel front, PH-25 aperture rear with aperture variations from .080" to .030".
Features: Fastest lock time of any commercial target rifle; designed to meet I.S.U. specs. for the Standard Rifle. Fully adjustable trigger (less than ½ lb. to 3½ lbs.). Mark V has heavier barrel, weighs 12¼ lbs. Imported from England by Freelands Scope Stands.
Price: I.S.U., Standard weight **$950.00**
Price: Mark V heavy bbl. **$1,000.00**

Beeman/FWB 2000 M.S.

BEEMAN/FEINWERKBAU 2000 TARGET RIFLE

Caliber: 22 LR.
Barrel: 26¼"; 22" for Mini-Match.
Weight: 9 lbs. 12 oz. **Length:** 43¾" over-all (26¼" bbl.).
Stock: Standard match. Walnut with stippled p.g. and fore-end; walnut-stained birch for the Mini-Match.
Sights: Globe front with interchangeable inserts; micrometer match aperture rear.
Features: Meets ISU standard rifle specifications. Shortest lock time of any small bore rifle. Electronic or mechanical trigger, fully adjustable for weight, release point, length, lateral position, etc. Available in Standard and Mini-Match models. Introduced 1979. Imported from West Germany by Beeman.
Price: Model 2000 .... **$795.00** to **$925.00**
Price: Mini-Match .... **$765.00** to **$868.00**

BEEMAN/FWB 2000 METALLIC SILHOUETTE RIFLE

Caliber: 22 LR, single shot.
Barrel: 21.8".
Weight: 6.8 lbs. **Length:** 39" over-all.
Stock: Walnut, anatomical grip and fore-end are stippled.
Sights: None furnished; grooved for standard mounts.
Features: Fully adjustable match trigger from 3.5 to 8.5 ozs. Heavy bull barrel. Introduced 1985. Imported by Beeman.
Price: **$795.00**

Consult our Directory pages for the location of firms mentioned.

CAUTION: PRICES CHANGE. CHECK AT GUNSHOP.

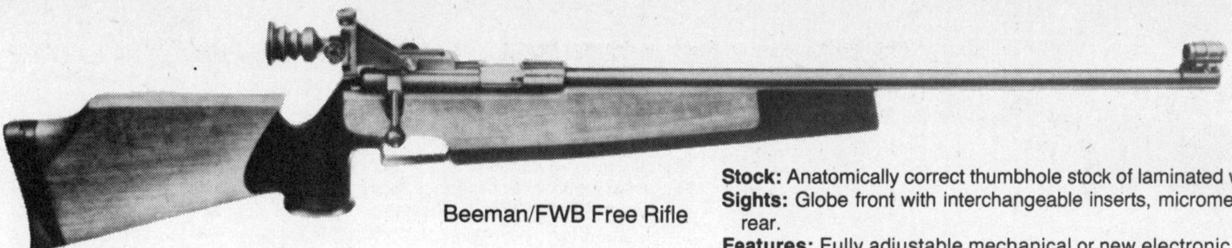
Beeman/FWB Free Rifle

BEEMAN/FEINWERKBAU ULTRA MATCH 22 FREE RIFLE
Caliber: 22 LR, single shot.
Barrel: 26.4″.
Weight: 17 lbs. (with accessories).
Stock: Anatomically correct thumbhole stock of laminated wood.
Sights: Globe front with interchangeable inserts, micrometer match aperture rear.
Features: Fully adjustable mechanical or new electronic trigger; accessory rails for moveable weights and adjustable palm rest; adjustable cheekpiece and hooked buttplate. Right or left hand. Introduced 1983. Imported by Beeman.
Price: Right hand, electronic trigger **$1,595.00**
Price: As above, mechanical trigger **$1,400.00**
Price: Left hand, electronic trigger.......... **$1,695.00**
Price: As above, mechanical trigger **$1,400.00**

Beeman/KRICOtronic 340

Beeman/KRICOtronic 340 Silhouette Rifle
Same basic specs as standard 340 Silhouette rifle except has KRICOtronic electronic ignition system for conventional ammunition. System replaces the firing pin with an electrical mechanism that ignites the primer electrically. Lock time is so fast it is not measureable by present technology. Introduced 1985.
Price: **$795.00**

BEEMAN/KRICO 340 SILHOUETTE RIFLE
Caliber: 22 Long Rifle, 5-shot clip.
Barrel: 21″, match quality.
Weight: 7.5 lbs. **Length:** 39.5″ over-all.
Stock: European walnut match-style designed for off-hand shooting. Suitable for right- or left-hand shooters. Stippled grip and fore-end.
Sights: None furnished. Receiver grooved for tip-off mounts.
Features: Free-floated heavy barrel; fully adjustable two-stage match trigger or double-set trigger. Meets NRA official MS rules. Introduced 1983. Imported by Beeman.
Price: **$649.00**

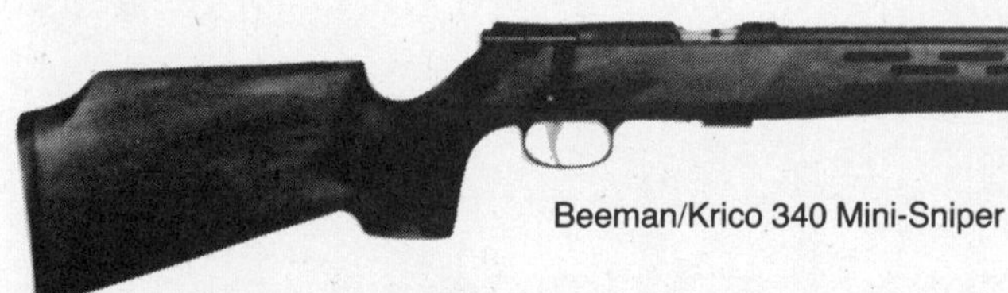
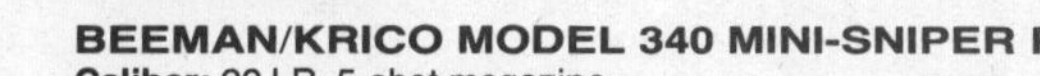
Beeman/Krico 340 Mini-Sniper

BEEMAN/KRICO 650 STANDARD SNIPER
Caliber: 308 Win.
Barrel: 20″, semi-bull.
Weight: 7.5 lbs.
Stock: French walnut with ventilated fore-end.
Sights: None furnished.
Features: Five-shot repeater with detachable box magazine. Available with single or double-set trigger. Imported from West Germany by Beeman.
Price: 308 Win. **$1,049.00**
Price: Model 440S, 22 Hornet **$795.00**

BEEMAN/KRICO MODEL 340 MINI-SNIPER RIFLE
Caliber: 22 LR, 5-shot magazine.
Barrel: 21″.
Weight: 8 lbs. **Length:** 40″ over-all.
Stock: Select European walnut with high comb; stippled grip with palm swell, stippled ventilated fore-end.
Sights: None furnished. Receiver grooved for scope mounting.
Features: Free floating bull barrel with muzzle brake; large bolt knob; match quality single trigger; barrel and receiver have sandblast finish. Scaled down version of big-bore 640/650 rifles. Imported from West Germany by Beeman.
Price: **$795.00**

Beeman/Krico 650 Super Sniper

BEEMAN/WEIHRAUCH HW60 TARGET RIFLE
Caliber: 22 LR, single shot.
Barrel: 26.8″.
Weight: 10.8 lbs. **Length:** 45.7″ over-all.
Stock: Walnut with adjustable buttplate. Stippled p.g. and fore-end. Rail with adjustable swivel.
Sights: Hooded ramp front, match-type aperture rear.
Features: Adj. match trigger with push-button safety. Left-hand version also available. Introduced 1981. Imported from West Germany by Beeman.
Price: Right-hand **$495.00**
Price: Left-hand **$545.00**

BEEMAN/KRICO 650 SUPER SNIPER
Caliber: 223, 308.
Barrel: 26″. Specially designed match bull barrel, matte blue finish, with muzzle brake/flash hider.
Weight: 9.6 lbs. **Length:** 44¾″ over-all.
Stock: Select walnut with oil finish. Spring-loaded, adj. cheekpiece, adjustable recoil pad. Standard model (640S) is without adjustable stock.
Sights: None furnished. Drilled and tapped for scope mounts.
Features: Match trigger with 10mm wide shoe; single standard or double set trigger available. All metal has matte blue finish. Bolt knob has 1¼″ diameter. Scope mounts available for special night-sight devices. Imported from West Germany by Beeman.
Price: Without scope, mount.......... **$1,298.50**
Price: Model 640S, as above but without moveable cheekpiece ... **$1,049.50**

Finnish Lion Standard

FINNISH LION STANDARD TARGET RIFLE
Caliber: 22 LR, single-shot.
Barrel: 27⅝".
Weight: 10½ lbs. **Length:** 44 9/16" over-all.
Stock: French walnut, target style.
Sights: None furnished. Globe front, International micrometer rear available.
Features: Optional accessories: palm rest, hook buttplate, fore-end stop and swivel assembly, buttplate extension, 5 front sight aperture inserts, 3 rear sight apertures, Allen wrench. Adjustable trigger. Imported from Finland by Mandall Shooting Supplies.
Price: **$500.00**
Price: Thumbhole stock model **$695.00**
Price: Heavy barrel model (either stock) **$535.00**
Price: Sight set (front and rear) **$100.00**

HARRINGTON & RICHARDSON MODEL 5200 RIFLE
Caliber: 22 LR, single shot.
Barrel: 28" target-weight with recessed muzzle.
Weight: 11 lbs. **Length:** 46" over-all.
Stock: American walnut; target-style with full length accessory rail, rubber butt pad. Comes with hand-stop.
Sights: None supplied. Receiver drilled and tapped for receiver sight, barrel for front sight.
Features: Fully adj. trigger (1.1 to 3.5 lbs.), heavy free-floating target weight barrel, "Fluid-Feed" loading platform, dual extractors. Polished blue-black metal finish. Introduced 1981. From Harrington & Richardson.
Price: **$350.00**

M-S SAFARI ARMS SILHOUETTE RIFLE
Caliber: 22 LR or any standard centerfire cartridge; single shot.
Barrel: 23" (rimfire); 24" (centerfire). Fluted or smooth.
Weight: 10 lbs., 2 oz. (with scope).
Stock: Fiberglass, silhouette-design; custom painted.
Sights: None furnished. Drilled and tapped for scope mounting.
Features: Electronic trigger, stainless steel action, high-speed lock time. Custom built to customer specs. From M-S Safari Arms.
Price: 22 LR.. **$1,145.00**
Price: Centerfire, from **$1,145.00**

M-S SAFARI ARMS 1000 YARD MATCH RIFLE
Caliber: 30-338, 300 Win. Mag.; single shot.
Barrel: 28", heavy.
Weight: 18½ lbs. with scope.
Stock: Fiberglass, custom painted to customer specs.
Sights: None furnished. Drilled and tapped for scope mounting.
Features: Sleeved stainless steel action, high-speed lock time. Fully adjustable prone stock. Electronic trigger. From M-S Safari Arms.
Price: **$2,045.00**

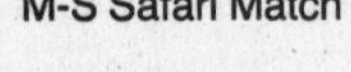
M-S Safari Match

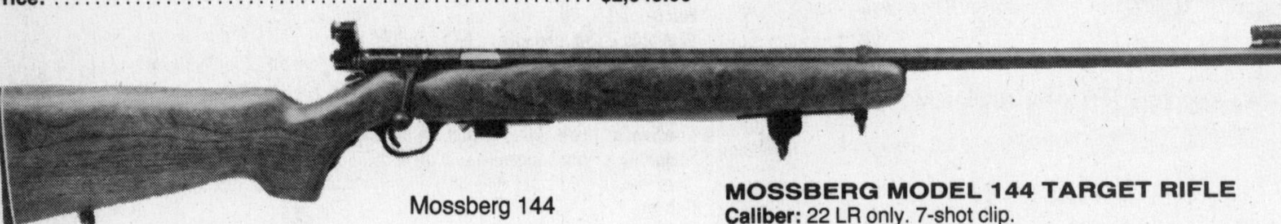
Mossberg 144

MOSSBERG MODEL 144 TARGET RIFLE
Caliber: 22 LR only. 7-shot clip.
Barrel: 27" round (15/16" dia.)
Weight: About 8 lbs. **Length:** 43" over-all.
Stock: Target-style walnut with high thick comb, cheekpiece, p.g., beavertail fore-end, adj. handstop and sling swivels.
Sights: Lyman 17A hooded front with inserts, Mossberg S331 receiver peep with ¼-minute clicks.
Features: Wide grooved trigger adj. for wgt. of pull, thumb safety, receiver grooved for scope mounting.
Price: About **$209.95**

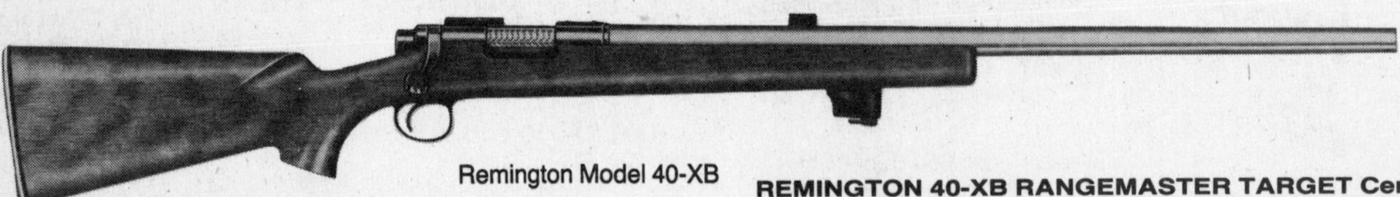
Remington Model 40-XB

REMINGTON 40-XR RIMFIRE POSITION RIFLE
Caliber: 22 LR, single-shot.
Barrel: 24", heavy target.
Weight: 10 lbs. **Length:** 43" over-all.
Stock: Position-style with front swivel block on fore-end guide rail.
Sights: Drilled and tapped. Furnished with scope blocks.
Features: Meets all I.S.U. specifications. Deep fore-end, buttplate vertically adjustable, wide adjustable trigger.
Price: About **$725.00**

REMINGTON 40-XB RANGEMASTER TARGET Centerfire
Caliber: 222 Rem., 22-250, 6mm Rem., 243, 25-06, 7mm Rem. Mag., 30-338 (30-7mm Rem. Mag.), 300 Win. Mag., 7.62 NATO (308 Win.), 30-06. Single shot.
Barrel: 27¼" round (Stand. dia.—¾", Hvy. dia.—⅞")
Weight: Std.—9¼ lbs., Hvy.—11¼ lbs. **Length:** 47".
Stock: American walnut with high comb and beavertail fore-end stop. Rubber non-slip buttplate.
Sights: None. Scope blocks installed.
Features: Adjustable trigger pull. Receiver drilled and tapped for sights.
Price: Standard s.s., stainless steel barrel, about **$920.00**
Price: Repeating model, about **$985.00**
Price: Extra for 2 oz. trigger, about............................ **$110.00**

CAUTION: PRICES CHANGE. CHECK AT GUNSHOP.

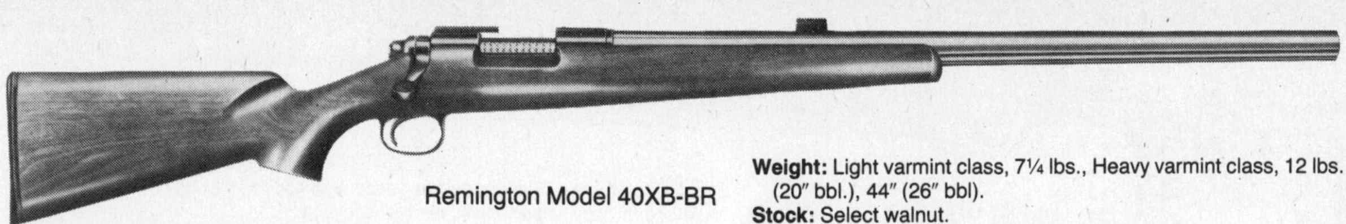

Remington Model 40XB-BR

REMINGTON MODEL 40XB-BR

Caliber: 22 BR Rem., 222 Rem., 223, 6mm x47, 6mm BR Rem., 7.62 NATO (308 Win.).

Barrel: 20″ (light varmint class), 26″ (heavy varmint class).

Weight: Light varmint class, 7¼ lbs., Heavy varmint class, 12 lbs. **Length:** 38″ (20″ bbl.), 44″ (26″ bbl).

Stock: Select walnut.

Sights: None. Supplied with scope blocks.

Features: Unblued stainless steel barrel, trigger adj. from 1½ lbs. to 3½ lbs. Special 2 oz. trigger at extra cost. Scope and mounts extra.

Price: About **$975.00**

Price: Extra for 2-oz. trigger, about **$110.00**

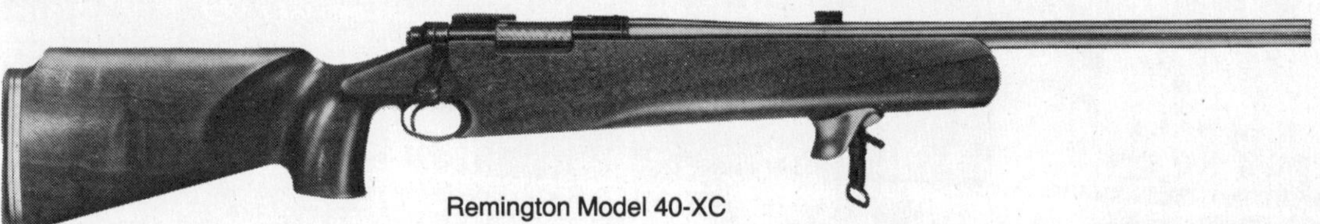

Remington Model 40-XC

REMINGTON 40-XC NAT'L MATCH COURSE RIFLE

Caliber: 7.62 NATO, 5-shot.

Barrel: 23¼″, stainless steel.

Weight: 10 lbs. without sights. **Length:** 42½″ over-all.

Stock: Walnut, position-style, with palm swell.

Sights: None furnished.

Features: Designed to meet the needs of competitive shooters firing the national match courses. Position-style stock, top loading clip slot magazine, anti-bind bolt and receiver, bright stainless steel barrel. Meets all I.S.U. Army Rifle specifications. Adjustable buttplate, adjustable trigger.

Price: About **$1,000.00**

SIG SAUER SSG 2000 RIFLE

Caliber: 223, 308, 7.5 Swiss, 300 Weatherby Magnum; 4-shot detachable box magazine.

Barrel: 24″ (25.9″ in 300 W.M.).

Weight: 13.2 lbs. (without scope). **Length:** 47.6″ (24″ barrel).

Stock: Walnut; thumbhole-type with adjustable comb and buttplate; adjustable fore-end rail; stippled grip and fore-end.

Sights: None furnished. Comes with scope mounts.

Features: Uses the Sauer 80/90 rifle action. Available in right- or left-hand models; flash hider/muzzle brake; double-set triggers; push-button sliding safety; EAW scope mount. Introduced 1985. Imported by SIGARMS, Inc.

Price: **$2,733.00**

Price: Zeiss ZA 8x56 scope **$681.00**

Price: Schmidt & Bender 1½-6x42 scope **$830.00**

SHILEN DGA BENCHREST SINGLE SHOT RIFLE

Caliber: 22, 22-250, 6x47, 308.

Barrel: Select/Match grade stainless. Choice of caliber, twist, chambering, contour or length shown in Shilen's catalog.

Weight: To customer specs.

Stock: Fiberglass. Choice of Classic or thumbhole pattern.

Sights: None furnished. Specify intended scope and mount.

Features: Fiberglass stocks are spray painted with acrylic enamel in choice of basic color. Comes with Benchrest trigger. Basically a custom-made rifle. From Shilen Rifles, Inc.

Price: From **$1,600.00**

Steyr SSG Marksman

STEYR-MANNLICHER SSG MARKSMAN

Caliber: 308 Win.

Barrel: 25.6″.

Weight: 8.6 lbs. **Length:** 44.5″ over-all.

Stock: Choice of ABS "Cycolac" synthetic half stock or walnut. Removable spacers in butt adjusts length of pull from 12¾″ to 14″.

Sights: Hooded blade front, folding leaf rear.

Features: Parkerized finish. Choice of interchangeable single or double set triggers. Detachable 5-shot rotary magazine (10-shot optional). Drilled and tapped for scope mounts. Imported from Austria by Gun South, Inc.

Price: Synthetic half stock **$873.17**

Price: Walnut half stock **$1,058.59**

Price: Optional 10-shot magazine **$74.46**

Steyr-Mannlicher SSG Match

Same as Model SSG Marksman except has heavy barrel, match bolt, Walther target peep sights and adj. rail in fore-end to adj. sling travel. Weight is 11 lbs.

Price: Synthetic half stock **$1,334.00**

Price: Walnut half stock **$1,495.00**

STEYR-MANNLICHER MATCH UIT RIFLE

Caliber: 243 Win. or 308 Win., 10-shot magazine.

Barrel: 25.5″.

Weight: 10.9 lbs. **Length:** 44.48″ over-all.

Stock: Walnut with stippled grip and fore-end. Special UIT Match design.

Sights: Walther globe front, Walther peep rear.

Features: Double-pull trigger adjustable for let-off point, slack, weight of first-stage pull, release force and length; buttplate adjustable for height and length. Meets UIT specifications. Introduced 1984. Imported from Austria by Gun South, Inc.

Price: **$2,100.00**

SWISS K-31 TARGET RIFLE

Caliber: 308 Win., 6-shot magazine.

Barrel: 26″.

Weight: 9½ lbs. **Length:** 44″ over-all.

Stock: Walnut.

Sights: Protected blade front, ladder-type adjustable rear.

Features: Refined version of the Schmidt-Rubin straight-pull rifle. Comes with sling and muzzle cap. Imported from Switzerland by Mandall Shooting Supplies.

Price: **$1,000.00**

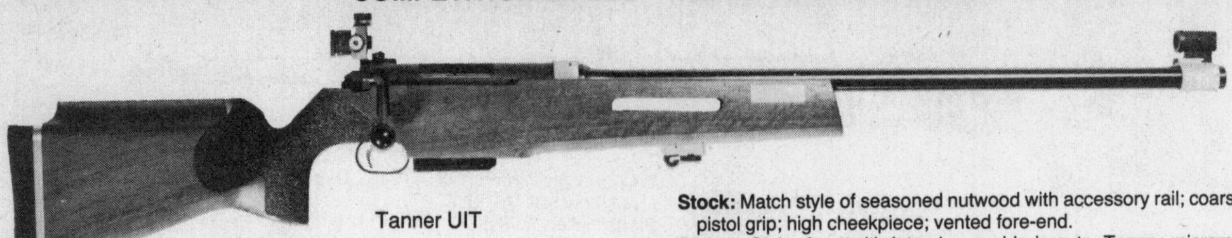

Tanner UIT

TANNER STANDARD UIT RIFLE
Caliber: 308, 7.5mm Swiss, 10-shot.
Barrel: 25.8".
Weight: 10.5 lbs. **Length:** 40.6" over-all.
Stock: Match style of seasoned nutwood with accessory rail; coarsely stippled pistol grip; high cheekpiece; vented fore-end.
Sights: Globe front with interchangeable inserts, Tanner micrometer-diopter rear with adjustable aperture.
Features: Two locking lug revolving bolt encloses case head. Trigger adjustable from ½ to 6½ lbs.; match trigger optional. Comes with 300-meter test target. Imported from Switzerland by Osborne's. Introduced 1984.
Price: About. **$2,295.00**

Tanner Free Rifle

TANNER 50 METER FREE RIFLE
Caliber: 22 LR; single shot.
Barrel: 27.7".
Weight: 13.9 lbs. **Length:** 43.4" over-all.
Stock: Seasoned nutwood with palm rest, accessory rail, adjustable hook buttplate.
Sights: Globe front with interchangeable inserts, Tanner micrometer-diopter rear with adjustable aperture.
Features: Bolt action with externally adjustable set trigger. Supplied with 50-meter test target. Imported from Switzerland by Osborne's Supplies. Introduced 1984.
Price: About. **$1,995.00**

TANNER 300 METER FREE RIFLE
Caliber: 308 Win., 7.5 Swiss; single shot.
Barrel: 28.7".
Weight: 15 lbs. **Length:** 45.3" over-all.
Stock: Seasoned walnut, thumb-hole style, with accessory rail, palm rest, adjustable hook butt.
Sights: Globe front with interchangeable inserts, Tanner-design micrometer-diopter rear with adjustable aperture.
Features: Three-lug revolving-lock bolt design; adjustable set trigger; short firing pin travel; supplied with 300-meter test target. Imported from Switzerland by Osborne's Supplies. Introduced 1984.
Price: About. **$2,395.00**

TIKKA MODEL 65 WILD BOAR RIFLE
Caliber: 7x64, 308, 30-06, 7mm Rem. Mag., 300 Win. Mag.; 5-shot detachable clip.
Barrel: 20½".
Weight: About 7½ lbs. **Length:** 41" over-all.
Stock: Hand checkered walnut; vent. rubber recoil pad.
Sights: Bead on post front, special ramp-type open rear.
Features: Adjustable trigger; palm swell in pistol grip. Sight system developed for low-light conditions. Imported from Finland by Mandall Shooting Supplies.
Price: **$595.00**

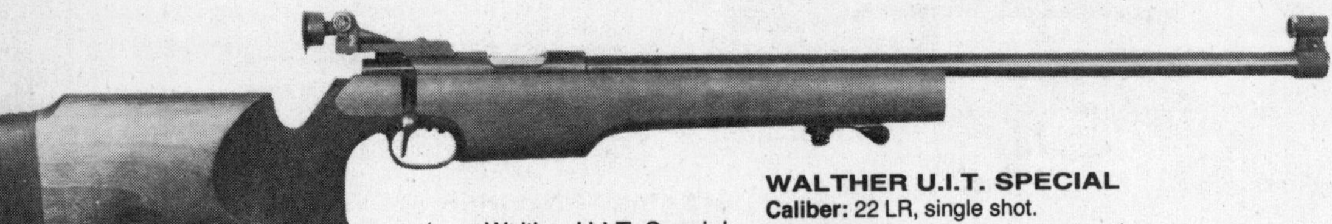

Walther U.I.T. Special

WALTHER U.I.T. SPECIAL
Caliber: 22 LR, single shot.
Barrel: 25½".
Weight: 10 lbs., 3 oz. **Length:** 44¾".
Stock: Walnut, adj. for length and drop; fore-end guide rail for sling or palm rest.
Sights: Globe-type front, fully adj. aperture rear.
Features: Conforms to both NRA and U.I.T. requirements. Fully adj. trigger. Left hand stock available on special order. Imported from Germany by Interarms.
Price: **$745.00**

Walther Model U.I.T.-E Match Rifle
Similar to the U.I.T. Special model except has state-of-the-art electronic trigger. Introduced 1984.
Price: **$1,095.00**

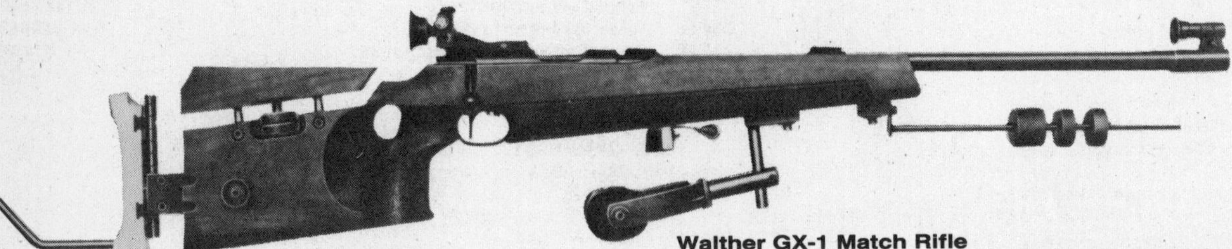

Walther GX-1 Match

Walther GX-1 Match Rifle
Same general specs as U.I.T. except has 25½" barrel, over-all length of 44½", weight of 15½ lbs. Stock is designed to provide every conceivable adjustment for individual preference and anatomical compatibility. Left-hand stock available on special order. Imported from Germany by Interarms.
Price: **$1,095.00**

CAUTION: PRICES CHANGE. CHECK AT GUNSHOP.

Walther U.I.T. Match

Walther U.I.T. Match

Same specifications and features as standard U.I.T. Super rifle but has scope mount bases. Fore-end had new tapered profile, fully stippled. Imported from Germany by Interarms.

Price: **$815.00**

WALTHER RUNNING BOAR MATCH RIFLE

Caliber: 22 LR, single shot.
Barrel: 23.6".
Weight: 8 lbs. 5 oz. **Length:** 42" over-all.
Stock: Walnut thumb-hole type. Fore-end and p.g. stippled.
Features: Especially designed for running boar competition. Receiver grooved to accept dovetail scope mounts. Adjustable cheekpiece and butt plate. 1.1 lb. trigger pull. Left hand stock available on special order. Imported from Germany by Interarms.
Price: **$715.00**

Wichita Silhouette

WICHITA SILHOUETTE RIFLE

Caliber: All standard calibers with maximum over-all cartridge length of 2.800".
Barrel: 24" free-floated Matchgrade.
Weight: About 9 lbs.
Stock: Metallic gray fiberthane with ventilated rubber recoil pad.
Sights: None furnished. Drilled and tapped for scope mounts.
Features: Legal for all NRA competitions. Single shot action. Fluted bolt, 2-oz. Canjar trigger; glass-bedded stock. Comes with hard case. Introduced 1983. From Wichita Arms.
Price: **$1,185.00**
Price: Left-hand **$1,285.00**

SHOTGUNS—AUTOLOADERS

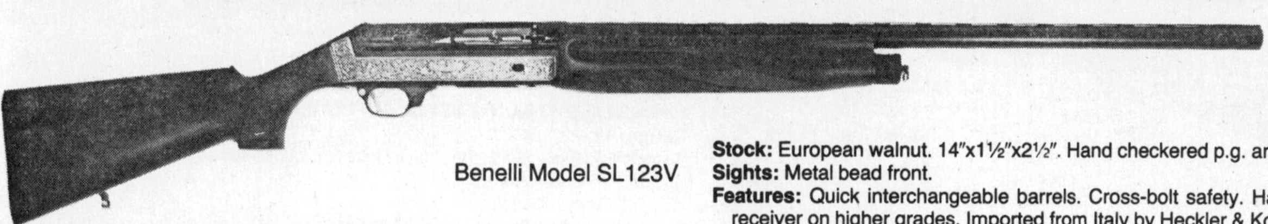

Benelli Model SL123V

BENELLI AUTOLOADING SHOTGUN

Gauge: 12 ga. (5-shot, 3-shot plug furnished).
Barrel: 26" (Skeet, Imp. Cyl., Mod.); 28" (Full, Imp. Mod., Mod.). Vent. rib.
Weight: 6¾ lbs.
Stock: European walnut. 14"x1½"x2½". Hand checkered p.g. and fore-end.
Sights: Metal bead front.
Features: Quick interchangeable barrels. Cross-bolt safety. Hand engraved receiver on higher grades. Imported from Italy by Heckler & Koch, Inc.
Price: Standard model, SL 121V **$397.00**
Price: Engraved, SL 123V **$464.00**
Price: Slug gun, 121V **$434.00**
Price: Model SL 201, 20 ga. **$399.00**
Price: Extra barrels **$237.00**

Beretta Model A-302

BERETTA A-302 AUTO SHOTGUN

Gauge: 12 or 20, 2¾" or 3".
Barrel: 12 ga. — 22" (Slug); 26" (Imp. Cyl., Skeet); 28" (Mod., Full, Multi-choke); 30" (Full, Full Trap); 20 ga. — 26" (Imp. Cyl., Skeet); 28" (Mod., Full).
Weight: About 6½ lbs. (20 ga.).
Stock: European walnut; hand checkered grip and fore-end.
Features: Gas-operated action, alloy receiver with scroll engraving; magazine cut-off, push-button safety. Multi-choke models come with four interchangeable screw-in choke tubes. Introduced 1983. Imported from Italy by Beretta U.S.A.
Price: 12 or 20 ga., standard chokes **$595.00**
Price: Multi-choke, 12 ga. or 20 ga. **$690.00**
Price: 12 ga. trap with Monte Carlo stock **$625.00**
Price: 12 or 20 ga. Skeet **$620.00**
Price: Slug, 12 or 20 ga. **$620.00**
Price: Super Lusso (custom gun), 12 or 20 ga. **$2,500.00**

Browning Auto-5 Classic & Gold Classic

Same as the standard Auto-5 Light 12 with 28" (Mod.) barrel. Classic edition has hunting and wildlife scenes engraved on the satin grey receiver, including a portrait of John M. Browning, and is limited to 5,000 guns. Also engraved is "Browning Classic. One of Five Thousand." The Gold Classic has a variation of the engraved scenes but with gold animals and portrait. Only 500 will be made, each numbered "1 of Five Hundred," etc. with "Browning Gold Classic."

Both editions have select, figured walnut, special checkering with carved border, and the semi-pistol grip stock. Scheduled for 1984 delivery. Introduced 1984.

Price: Auto-5 Classic **$1,200.00**
Price: Auto-5 Gold Classic **$6,500.00**

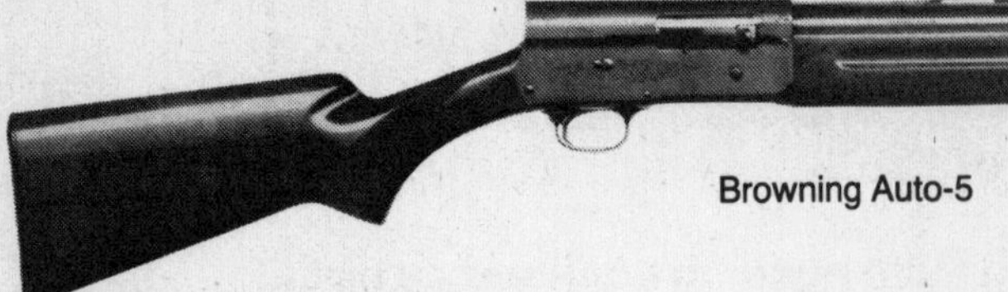
Browning Auto-5

Browning Auto-5 Magnum 12

Same as Std. Auto-5 except: chambered for 3″ magnum shells (also handles 2¾″ magnum and 2¾″ HV loads). 28″ Mod., Full; 30″ and 32″ (Full) bbls. Also available with Invector choke tubes. 14″x1⅝″x2½″ stock. Recoil pad. Wgt. 8¾ lbs.

Price: Vent. rib only **$569.95**
Price: Invector model **$599.95**

Browning Auto-5 Magnum 20

Same as Magnum 12 except barrels 28″ Full or Mod., or 26″ Full, Mod., Imp. Cyl. or Invector. With ventilated rib, 7½ lbs.

Price: **$569.95**
Price: Invector model **$599.95**

BROWNING AUTO-5 LIGHT 12 and 20

Gauge: 12, 20; 5-shot; 3-shot plug furnished; 2¾″ chamber.
Action: Recoil operated autoloader; takedown.
Barrel: 26″ (Skeet boring in 12 & 20 ga., Cyl., Imp. Cyl., Mod in 20 ga.); 28″ (Skeet in 12 ga., Mod., Full); 30″ (Full in 12 ga.); also available with 26″, 28″, 30″ and 32″ Invector (choke tube) barrel.
Weight: 12 ga. 7¼ lbs., 20 ga. 6⅜ lbs.
Stock: French walnut, hand checkered half-p.g. and fore-end. 14¼″ x 1⅝″ x 2½″.
Features: Receiver hand engraved with scroll designs and border. Double extractors, extra bbls. interchangeable without factory fitting; mag. cut-off; cross-bolt safety. Buck Special no longer inventoried, but can be ordered as a Buck Special extra barrel, plus an action only. Imported from Japan by Browning.
Price: Vent. rib only **$559.95**
Price: Extra barrels, vent. rib only **$175.00**
Price: Invector model **$589.95**

Browning B-80 Auto

BROWNING B-80 AUTO SHOTGUN

Gauge: 12 (2¾″ & 3″), 20 (2¾″ & 3″)
Barrel: 22″ (Slug), 26″ (Imp. Cyl., Cyl., Skeet, Full, Mod.), 28″ (Full, Mod.), 30″ (Full), 32″ (Full). Invector barrels in 26″, 28″, 30″, 12 or 20 ga.
Weight: About 6½ lbs.
Stock: 14¼″ x 1⅝″ x 2½″. Hand checkered French walnut. Solid black recoil pad.
Features: Vent. rib barrels have non-reflective rib; alloy receiver with high-polish; cross-bolt safety; interchangeable barrels. Buck Special no longer inventoried, but can be ordered as a Buck Special extra barrel and action only. Introduced 1981. Imported from Belgium by Browning.
Price: Invector, vent. rib, 12 or 20 ga. **$508.95**
Price: Extra Invector barrels **$179.95**
Price: Extra fixed-choke barrels **$149.95**
Price: Extra Buck Special barrel **$179.95**

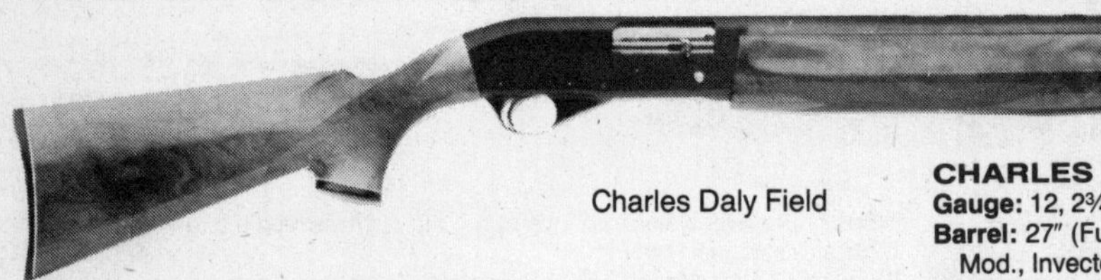
Charles Daly Field

CHARLES DALY FIELD AUTO SHOTGUN

Gauge: 12, 2¾″ or 3″.
Barrel: 27″ (Full, Mod., Imp. Cyl., Invector choke tubes), 30″ (Extra Full, Full, Mod., Invector choke tubes).
Weight: About 7¼ lbs.
Stock: Walnut, with checkered pistol grip and fore-end, high gloss finish.
Features: Alloy receiver with bright chromed bolt; cross-bolt safety; stainless steel gas piston. Imported from Japan by Outdoor Sports Headquarters. Introduced 1984.
Price: **$374.95**

COSMI AUTOMATIC SHOTGUN

Gauge: 12 or 20, 2¾″ or 3″ chamber.
Barrel: 22″ to 35″. Choke and length to customer specs.
Weight: 6¼ lbs. (20 ga.)
Stock: Length and style to customer specs. Exhibition grade walnut.
Features: Hand-made, essentially a custom gun. Recoil-operated auto with tip-up barrel. Made completely of stainless steel (lower receiver polished); magazine tube in buttstock holds 7 rounds. Comes with fitted leather case. Imported from Italy by Incor Inc.
Price: From **$6,200.00**

Churchill Windsor

CHURCHILL GAS AUTO SHOTGUNS

Gauge: 12, 2¾″ or 3″.
Barrel: 20″ (Slug); 26″ (Imp. Cyl., Skeet); 28″ (Mod., Full); 30″ (Full); or with ICT choke tubes in 26″, 27″, 28″, 30″.
Weight: About 7½ lbs.
Stock: Select claro walnut with high gloss or matte finish, checkered pistol grip and fore-end; rosewood grip cap with white inlay.
Features: Stainless steel gas piston; cross-bolt safety; Windsor model has anodized alloy receiver, Regent has etched and polished receiver. Imported from Japan by Kassnar. Introduced 1984.
Price: Windsor, fixed chokes **$479.00**
Price: Regent, fixed chokes **$548.00**
Price: Windsor, ICT choke tubes **$509.00**
Price: Regent, ICT choke tubes **$539.00**
Price: Deerfield slug gun **$509.00**
Price: Windsor Flyweight, 23″, ICT **$509.00**
Price: Regent Flyweight, 23″, ICT **$539.00**

Consult our Directory pages for the location of firms mentioned.

CAUTION: PRICES CHANGE. CHECK AT GUNSHOP.

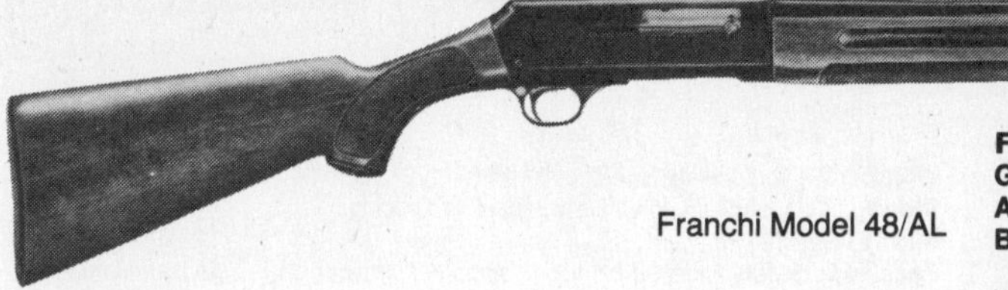

Franchi Model 48/AL

FRANCHI 48/AL AUTO SHOTGUN

Gauge: 12 or 20, 5-shot. 2¾" or 3" chamber.
Action: Recoil-operated automatic.
Barrel: 24" (Imp. Cyl. or Cyl.); 26" (Imp. Cyl. or Mod); 28" (Skeet, Mod. or Full); 30", 32" (Full). Interchangeable barrels.
Weight: 12 ga. 6¼ lbs., 20 ga. 5 lbs. 2 oz.
Stock: Epoxy-finished walnut, with cut-checkered pistol grip and fore-end.
Features: Chrome-lined bbl., easy takedown, 3-round plug provided. Ventilated rib barrel. Imported from Italy by F.I.E.
Price: Vent. rib 12, 20 .... **$394.95**
Price: Hunter model (engraved) **$419.95**
Price: 12 ga. Magnum **$419.95**
Price: Extra barrel **$154.95**

Franchi Slug Gun

Same as Standard automatic except 22" Cylinder bored plain barrel, adj. rifle-type sights, sling swivels.
Price: 12 or 20 ga., standard **$394.95**
Price: As above, Hunter grade **$419.95**
Price: Extra barrel **$154.95**

Ithaca Model 51A

ITHACA MODEL 51A AUTOMATIC

Gauge: 12 or 20 ga., 2¾" chamber.
Action: Gas-operated, rotary bolt has three locking lugs. Takedown. Self-compensating for high or low base loads.
Barrel: Roto-Forged, 28" (Mod.). Extra barrels available. Raybar front sight.
Weight: About 7½ lbs.
Stock: 14"x1⅝"x2½". Hand checkered walnut, white spacers on p.g. and under recoil pad.
Features: Hand fitted, engraved receiver, 3 shot capacity, safety is reversible for left hand shooter.
Price: With vent, rib **$477.00**

Ithaca Model 51A Waterfowler 12 Ga. Magnum

Same Standard Model 51 except has 3" chamber, 30" barrel, matte finish, sling and swivels.
Price: With vent rib **$477.00**
Price: As Turkey Gun, 26" barrel **$477.00**
Price: Camouflage Waterfowler **$556.00**
Price: Camouflage Turkey **$556.00**

Ithaca Model 51A Supreme Skeet

Same gun as Model 51 Skeet with fancy American walnut stock, 26" (Skeet) barrel, 12 or 20 ga..
Price: **$604.00**

Ithaca Model 51A Supreme Trap

Same gun as standard Model 51 with fancy American walnut trap stock, 30" (Full).
Price: **$614.00**
Price: With Monte Carlo stock **$650.00**

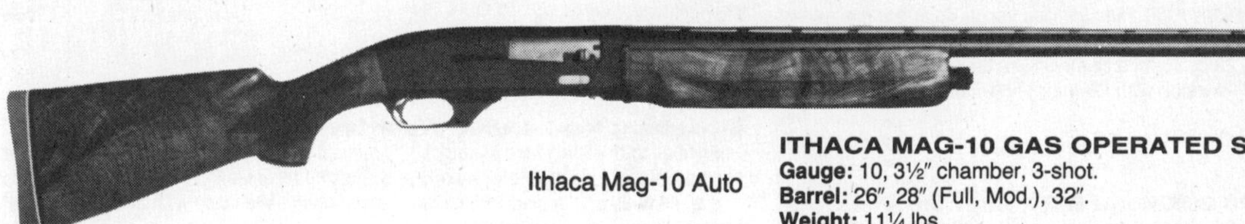

Ithaca Mag-10 Auto

ITHACA MAG-10 GAS OPERATED SHOTGUN

Gauge: 10, 3½" chamber, 3-shot.
Barrel: 26", 28" (Full, Mod.), 32".
Weight: 11¼ lbs.
Stock: American walnut, checkered p.g. and fore-end (14⅛"x2⅜"x1½"), p.g. cap, rubber recoil pad.
Sights: White Bradley.
Features: "Countercoil" gas system. Piston, cylinder, bolt, charging lever, action release and carrier made of stainless steel. ⅜" vent. rib. Vapor Blast matte finish. Reversible cross-bolt safety. Low recoil force. Supreme has full fancy claro American black walnut.
Price: Standard, plain barrel, 32" (Full) only **$683.00**
Price: Deluxe, vent. rib **$877.00**
Price: Standard, vent. rib **$745.00**
Price: Supreme, vent. rib **$1,014.00**
Price: Camouflage, 26" and 32" (Full), standard vent **$809.00**

Ithaca Mag-10 Deerslayer

Similar to the standard Mag-10 except has 22" barrel, rifle sights.
Price: Std., vent. rib, Vapor Blast finish **$745.00**
Price: Deluxe, blue finsih **$877.00**
Price: Supreme grade **$1,014.00**

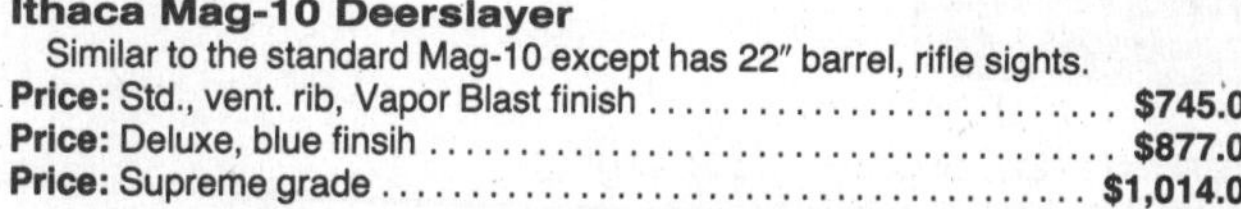

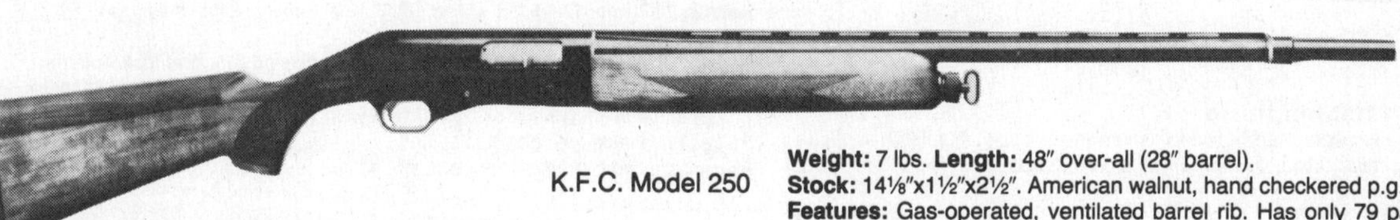

K.F.C. Model 250

KAWAGUCHIYA K.F.C. M-250 AUTO SHOTGUN

Gauge: 12, 2¾".
Barrel: 26" (Imp. Cyl.), 28" (Mod.), 30" (Full); or with Tru-Choke interchangeable choke tube system.
Weight: 7 lbs. **Length:** 48" over-all (28" barrel).
Stock: 14⅛"x1½"x2½". American walnut, hand checkered p.g. and fore-end.
Features: Gas-operated, ventilated barrel rib. Has only 79 parts. Cross-bolt safety is reversible for left-handed shooters. Available with fixed or Tru-Choke interchangeable choke tube system. Introduced 1980. Imported from Japan by La Paloma Marketing.
Price: Standard Grade **$485.00**
Price: Deluxe Grade (silvered, etched receiver) **$520.00**
Price: With Tru-Choke, Standard Grade **$565.00**
Price: As above, Deluxe Grade **$599.00**

Mossberg Model 5500

MOSSBERG 5500 AUTO SHOTGUN

Gauge: 12 only, 2¾" or 3" chamber.
Barrel: 18½" (Cyl.), 24" (Slugster), 26" (Imp. Cyl.), 28" (Mod.), 30" (Full, 2¾" or 3").
Weight: 7½ lbs. **Length:** 48" over-all (with 28" barrel).
Stock: 14"x1½"x2½". Walnut-finished hardwood.
Sights: Bead front.
Features: Safety located on top of receiver. Interchangeable barrels and AC-CU-CHOKE choke tubes. Introduced 1983.
Price: About $344.95
Price: Slug gun, about.......... $326.95

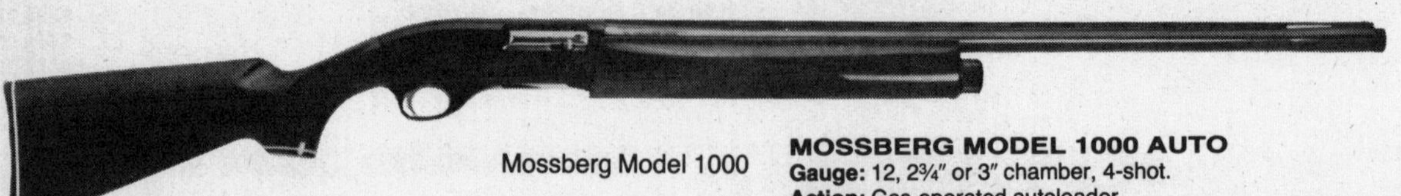
Mossberg Model 1000

MOSSBERG MODEL 1000 AUTO

Gauge: 12, 2¾" or 3" chamber, 4-shot.
Action: Gas-operated autoloader.
Barrel: 26" (Skeet, Imp. Cyl.), 28" (Mod. Full). Also available with screw-in Multi-Choke tubes.
Weight: 7½ lbs. (28" bbl.). **Length:** 48" over-all (28" bbl.).
Stock: 14"x1½"x2⅜", American walnut.
Features: Interchangeable cross-bolt safety, vent. rib with front and middle beads, engraved alloy receiver, pressure compensator and floating piston for light recoil.
Price: .... NA

Mossberg Model 1000 Trap Shotgun

Similar to the standard Model 1000 except has Monte Carlo trap stock, medium width stepped rib with white middle bead, Bradley front; integral wire shell catcher; specially tuned trigger; 30" Multi-Choke barrel with Full, Mod. and Imp. Mod. tubes. Steel receiver. Introduced 1983.
Price: .... NA

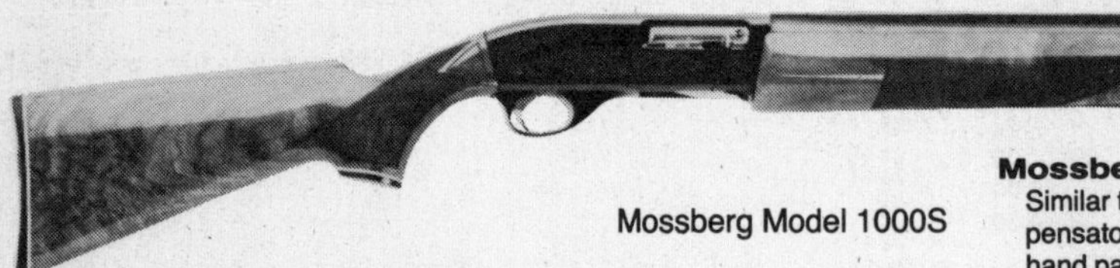
Mossberg Model 1000S

Mossberg Model 1000 Super 12 Shotgun

Similar to the standard Model 1000 auto shotgun except has a new gas metering system to allow the gun to handle any shell from 3-inch mags to 1-oz. 2¾-inch field loads without changing the barrel. Super 12 barrels are not interchangeable with other Model 1000 guns, or vice versa. A longer magazine tube gives four-shot capability. In 12-gauge only, the Super 12 has a 3-inch chamber with choice of 26, 28 or 30-inch Multi-Choke barrel; also available in a Parkerized "Waterfowler" version with 28-inch Multi-Choke barrel.
Price: Super 12.......... NA
Price: Waterfowler .... NA

Mossberg Model 1000 20 Gauge & 20 Magnum

Similar to 12 ga. model except scaled down to weigh only 6½ lbs. Has self-cleaning gas system. Choice of four interchangeable barrels (26", Imp. Cyl. or Skeet, 28" Mod., Full) or Multi-Choke system which includes tubes for Imp. Cyl., Mod., Full.
Price: .... NA

Mossberg Model 1000S Super Skeet, 12 & 20

Similar to Model 1000 except has "recessed-type" Skeet choke with a compensator system to soften recoil and reduce muzzle jump. Stock has right-hand palm swell. Trigger is contoured (rounded) on right side; pull is 2½ to 3 lbs. Vent. rib has double sighting beads with a "Bright Point" fluorescent red front bead. Fore-end cap weights (included) of 1 and 2 oz. can be used to change balance. Select-grade walnut with oil finish. Barrel length is 25", weight 8¼ lbs., over-all length 45.7". Stock measures 14"x1½"x2½" with .08" cast-off at butt, .16" at toe.
Price: .... NA

Mossberg Model 1000 Waterfowler Auto

Similar to the standard Model 1000 except all exterior metal is Parkerized to reduce glare, bolt is black oxidized, stock has a dull oil finish. Comes with q.d. swivels and a padded, camouflaged sling. Available with 30" (Full) barrel with 3" chamber. Introduced 1982.
Price: .... NA
Price: Super 12 Waterfowler.......... NA

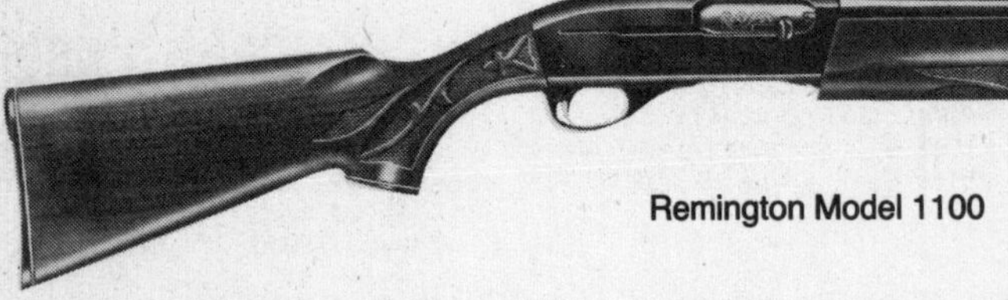
Remington Model 1100

REMINGTON MODEL 1100 AUTO

Gauge: 12, 3-shot plug furnished.
Action: Gas-operated autoloader.
Barrel: 26" (Imp. Cyl.), 28" (Mod., Full), 30" Full in 12 ga. only.
Weight: 12 ga. 7½ lbs.
Stock: 14"x1½"x2½" American Walnut, checkered p.g. and fore-end.
Features: Quickly interchangeable barrels within gauge. Matted receiver top with scroll work on both sides of receiver. Cross-bolt safety.
Price: With vent. rib, about.......... $480.00
Price: Left hand model with vent. rib, about $550.00

Remington 1100 Magnum

Same as 1100 except: chambered for 3" magnum loads. Available in 12 ga. (30") or 20 ga. (28") Mod. or Full, 14"x1½"x2½" stock with recoil pad, Wgt. 7¾ lbs.
Price: With vent rib, about $525.00
Price: Left hand model with vent. rib, about $600.00

Remington 1100D Tournament Auto

Same as 1100 Standard except: vent, rib, better wood, more extensive engraving.
Price: About.......... $2,245.00

Remington 1100 Small Gauge

Same as 1100 except: 28 ga. 2¾" (5-shot) or 410, 3" (except Skeet, 2½" 4-shot). 45½" over-all. Available in 25" bbl. (Full, Mod., or Imp. Cyl.) only.
Price: With vent. rib, about.......... $525.00
Price: SA Skeet, about $550.00
Price: Tournament Skeet, about.......... $650.00

CAUTION: PRICES CHANGE. CHECK AT GUNSHOP.

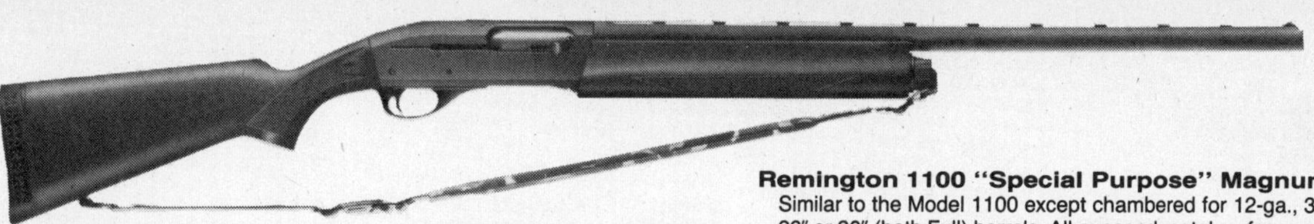

Remington Special Purpose

Remington 1100F Premier Auto

Same as 1100D except: select wood, better engraving

Price: About $4,630.00
Price: With gold inlay, about $7,000.00

Remington 1100 "Special Purpose" Magnum

Similar to the Model 1100 except chambered for 12-ga., 3″ shells, vent. rib, 26″ or 30″ (both Full) barrels. All exposed metal surfaces are finished in dull, non-reflective black. Wood has an oil finish. Comes with padded Cordura, 2″ wide sling, quick-detachable swivels. Chrome-lined bores. Dark recoil pad. Introduced 1985.

Price: About $525.00

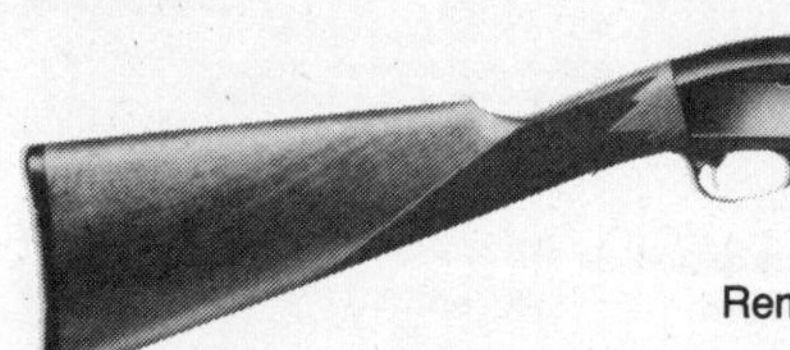

Remington 1100 Special Field

Remington 1100 "Special Field"

Similar to standard Model 1100 except comes with 21″ barrel only, choked Imp. Cyl., Mod., Full; 12 ga. weighs 7¼ lbs., LT-20 version 6½ lbs.; has straight-grip stock, shorter fore-end, both with cut checkering. Comes with vent rib only; matte finish receiver without engraving. Introduced 1983.

Price: About $505.00

Remington 1100 LT-20

Basically the same design as Model 1100, but with special weight-saving features that retain strength and dependability of the standard Model 1100.

Barrel: 28″ (Full, Mod.), 26″ (Imp. Cyl.).
Weight: 6½ lbs.
Price: About $480.00
Price: LT-20 Deer Gun (20″ bbl.), about $480.00

Remington 1100 SA Skeet

Same as the 1100 except: 26″ bbl., special Skeet boring, vent. rib (high rib on LT-20), ivory bead front and metal bead middle sights. 14″x1½″x2½″ stock. 12, 20, 28, 410 ga. Wgt. 7½ lbs., cut checkering, walnut, new receiver scroll.

Price: 12 ga., Skeet SA, about $540.00
Price: 12 ga. Left hand model with vent. rib, about $570.00
Price: 28 & 410 ga., 25″ bbl., about $550.00
Price: Tournament Skeet (28, 410), about $650.00
Price: Tournament Skeet (12 or 20), about $640.00

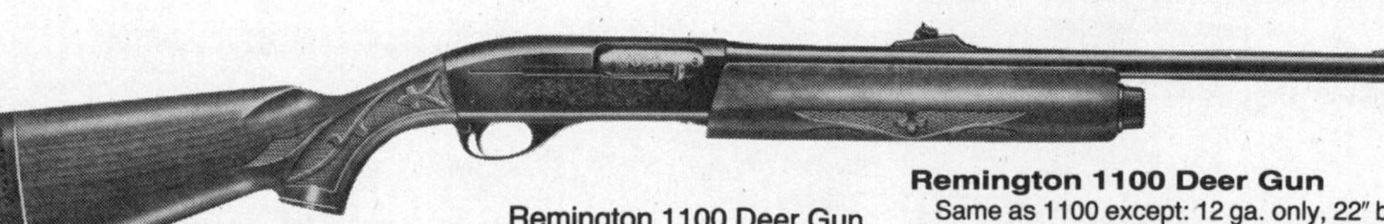

Remington 1100 Deer Gun

Remington 1100 Deer Gun

Same as 1100 except: 12 ga. only, 22″ bbl. (Imp. Cyl.), rifle sights adjustable for w. and e.; recoil pad with white spacer. Weight 7¼ lbs.

Price: About $480.00
Price: Left-hand Deer Gun, about $550.00

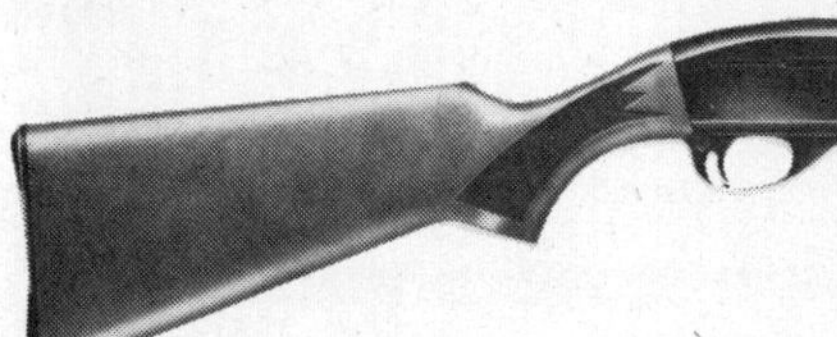

Remington Sportsman

Remington "Sportsman" 12 Auto Shotgun

Similar to the Model 1100 except in 12 ga. only with 2¾″ chamber, 28″ (Mod.), 30″ (Full) barrels. Stock and fore-end are checkered, walnut-stained hardwood with satin finish. Weight about 7¾ lbs. Introduced 1985.

Price: About $390.00

Remington 1100 TA Trap

Remington 1100 TA Trap

Same as the standard 1100 except: recoil pad. 14⅜″x1⅜″x1¾″ stock. Right- or left-hand models. Wgt. 8¼ lbs. 12 ga. only. 30″ (Mod. Trap, Full) vent. rib bbl. Ivory bead front and white metal middle sight.

Price: About $550.00
Price: With Monte Carlo stock, about $560.00
Price: 1100TA Trap, left hand, about $580.00
Price: With Monte Carlo stock, about $590.00
Price: Tournament Trap, about $650.00
Price: Tournament Trap with M.C. stock, better grade wood, different checkering, cut checkering, about $660.00

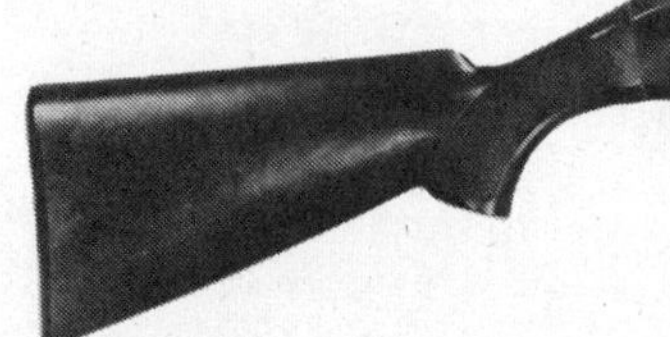

Tradewinds Model H-170

TRADEWINDS H-170 AUTO SHOTGUN

Gauge: 12 only, 2¾″ chamber.
Action: Recoil-operated automatic.
Barrel: 26″, 28″ (Mod.) and 28″ (Full), chrome lined.
Weight: 7 lbs.
Stock: Select European walnut stock, p.g. and fore-end hand checkered.
Features: Light alloy receiver, 5-shot tubular magazine, ventilated rib. Imported from Italy by Tradewinds.
Price: $395.00

CAUTION: PRICES CHANGE. CHECK AT GUNSHOP.

SHOTGUNS—AUTOLOADERS

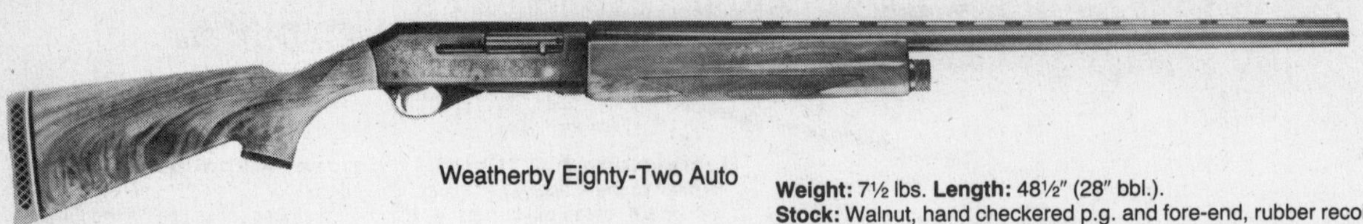

Weatherby Eighty-Two Auto

WEATHERBY EIGHTY-TWO AUTO

Gauge: 12 only, 2¾" and 3" chamber.

Barrel: 22" Slug (with sights), 26", 28", 30" with IMC (Integral Multi-Choke) tubes; 26" available with Mod., Imp. Cyl., Skeet, others with Full, Mod., Imp. Cyl.

Weight: 7½ lbs. **Length:** 48½" (28" bbl.).

Stock: Walnut, hand checkered p.g. and fore-end, rubber recoil pad.

Features: Gas operated autoloader with "Floating Piston." Cross-bolt safety, fluted bolt, gold plated trigger. Each gun comes with three flush fitting IMC choke tubes. Imported from Japan by Weatherby. Introduced 1982.

Price: **$445.00**

Price: Extra interchangeable barrel **$193.00**

Price: Extra IMC choke tubes **$12.50**

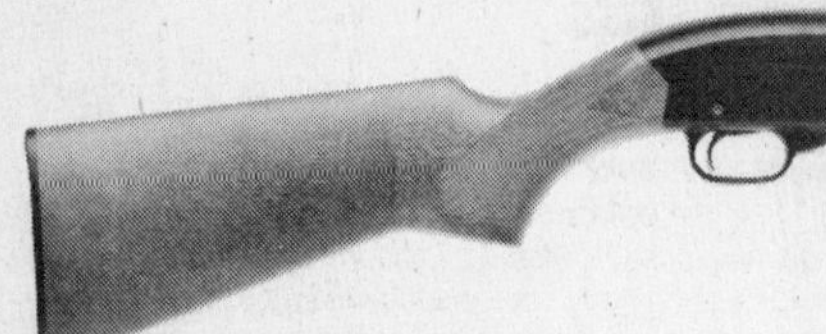

Winchester Ranger

WINCHESTER RANGER AUTO SHOTGUN

Gauge: 12 and 20, 2¾" chamber.

Barrel: 28" vent. rib with Winchoke tubes (Imp. Cyl., Mod., Full), or 28" plain barrel (Mod.).

Weight: 7 to 7¼ lbs. **Length:** 48⅝" over-all.

Stock: Walnut-finished hardwood, finger-grooved fore-end with deep cut checkering.

Sights: Metal bead front.

Features: Cross-bolt safety, front-locking rotating bolt, black serrated butt-plate, gas-operated action. Made under license by U.S. Repeating Arms. Co.

Price: Vent. rib with Winchoke, about.......... **$281.00**

Price: Deer barrel combo, about.......... **$313.00**

Price: Deer gun, about **$281.00**

SHOTGUNS—SLIDE ACTIONS

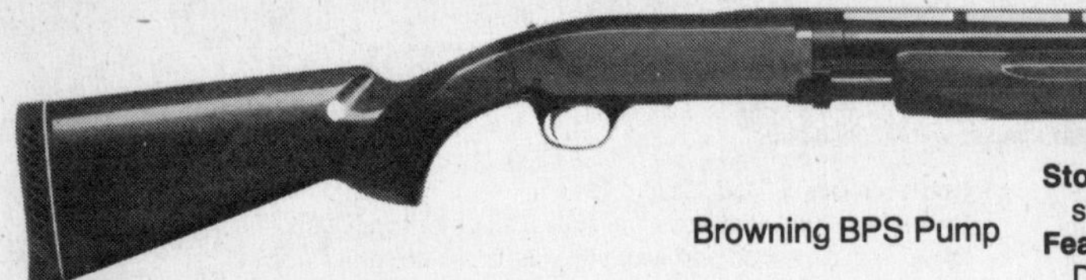

Browning BPS Pump

BROWNING BPS PUMP SHOTGUN

Gauge: 12 or 20 gauge, 3" chamber (2¾" in target guns), 5-shot magazine.

Barrel: 22", 24", 26", 28", 30", 32" (Imp. Cyl., Mod. or Full). Also available with Invector choke tubes, 12 or 20 ga.; Upland Special has 22" barrel with Invector tubes.

Weight: 7 lbs. 8 oz. (28" barrel). **Length:** 48¾" over-all (28" barrel).

Stock: 14¼"x1½"x2½". Select walnut, semi-beavertail fore-end, full p.g. stock.

Features: Bottom feeding and ejection, receiver top safety, high post vent. rib. Double action bars eliminate binding. Vent. rib barrels only. Introduced 1977. Imported from Japan by Browning.

Price: Grade I Hunting, Upland Special, Invector.......... **$349.95**

Price: Extra Invector barrel.......... **$159.95**

Price: Extra fixed-choke barrel **$119.95**

Price: Invector trap barrel.......... **$159.95**

Price: Non-Invector trap barrel **$139.95**

Price: Buck Special barrel with rifle sights.......... **$144.95**

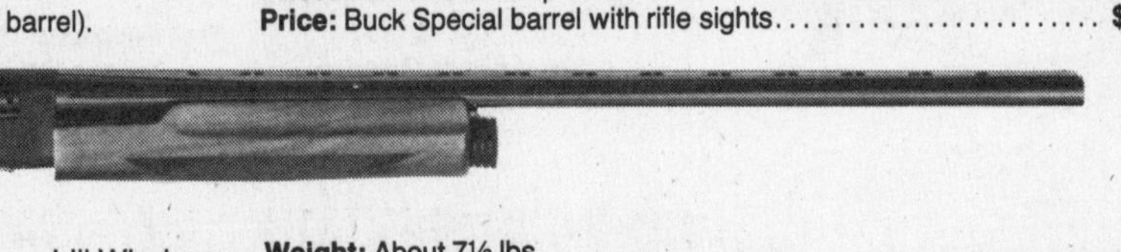

Churchill Windsor

CHURCHILL PUMP SHOTGUNS

Gauge: 12, 2¾" or 3" chamber.

Barrel: 20" (Slug), 26" (Imp. Cyl., Skeet), 28" (Mod.), 30" (Full), fixed chokes; 26", 27", 28", 30" for ICT choke tubes.

Weight: About 7½ lbs.

Stock: Select claro walnut with matte or high gloss finish, checkered pistol grip and fore-end, rosewood grip cap with inlay.

Features: Short stroke action with twin action bars; anodized aluminum receiver. Imported from Japan by Kassnar.

Price: With fixed chokes.......... **$473.00**

Price: Deerfield slug gun **$494.00**

Price: With ICT choke tubes **$494.00**

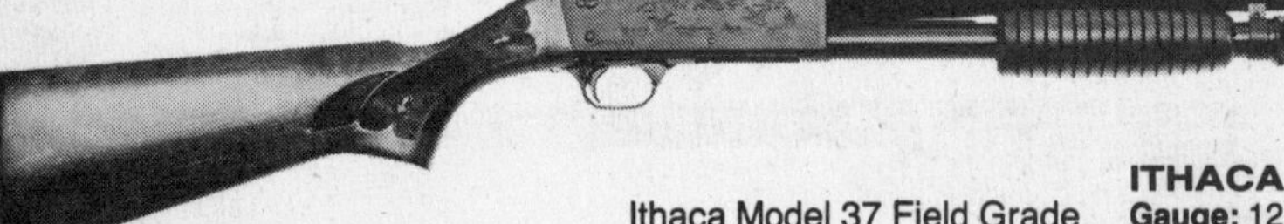

Ithaca Model 37 Field Grade

ITHACA MODEL 37 FIELD GRADE

Gauge: 12, 20 (5-shot; 3-shot plug furnished).

Action: Slide; takedown; bottom ejection.

Barrel: 26", 28", 30" in 12 ga.; 26" or 28" in 20 ga. (Full, Mod. or Imp. Cyl.)

Weight: 12 ga. 6½ lbs., 20 ga. 5¾ lbs.

Stock: 14"x1⅝"x2⅝". Checkered hardwood p.g. stock and ring-tail fore-end.

Features: Ithaca Raybar front sight; decorated receiver, cross-bolt safety; action release for removing shells.

Price: Standard **$298.00**

Price: Standard Vent Rib **$340.00**

Ithaca Model 37 Ultralite

Weighs five pounds. Same as standard Model 37 except 20 ga. comes only with 25" vent. rib barrel choked Full, Mod. or Imp. Cyl.; 12 ga., 26" barrel with same chokes as 20 ga. Has recoil pad, gold plated trigger, Sid Bell-designed grip cap. Also available as Ultra-Deerslayer with 20" barrel, 20 ga. only.

Price: **$447.00**

Price: Deerslayer model **$425.00**

Price: With choke tubes (Full, Mod., Imp. Cyl.), 25" only **$480.00**

CAUTION: PRICES CHANGE. CHECK AT GUNSHOP.

Ithaca Model 37

Ithaca Model 37 Field Grade Magnum
Similar to the standard Model 37 Field Grade pump except has American hardwood stock, traditional "ring-tail" fore-end. Plain or vent. rib, 12 or 20 gauge, 3" chamber only, interchangeable choke tubes. Raybar front sight. Introduced 1984.
Price: Vent. rib, 25" and 28" **$374.00**

Ithaca 37 English Ultra

Ithaca Model 37 Deerslayer
Same as Model 37 except: 26" or 20" bbl. designed for rifled slugs; sporting rear sight, Raybar front sight: rear sight ramp grooved for Redfield long eye relief scope mount. 12, or 20 gauge. With checkered stock, beavertail fore-end and recoil pad.
Price: **$396.00**
Price: Super Deluxe model **$447.00**

Ithaca Model 37 Magnum D/X
Same as standard Model 37 except chambered for 3" shells with resulting longer receiver. Stock dimensions are 14"x1⅞"x1½". Grip cap has a Sid Bell-designed flying mallard on it. Has a recoil pad, vent. rib barrel with Raybar front sight. Available in 12 or 20 ga. with 30" (Full), 28" (Mod.) and 26" (Imp. Cyl.) barrel. Weight about 7¼ lbs. Introduced 1978.
Price: **$425.00**
Price: Camouflage model, 12 ga., 26" (Full) only **$500.00**

Ithaca Model 37 English Ultralite
Similar to the standard Model 37 Ultralite except vent. rib barrel has straight-grip stock with better wood, cut-checkered pump handle, grip area and butt, oil finished wood. Introduced 1981.
Price: **$450.00**
Price: With choke tubes (Full, Mod., Imp. Cyl.) **$484.00**

Ithaca Model 37 Supreme
Same as Model 37 except: hand checkered fore-end and p.g. stock, Ithaca recoil pad and vent, rib. Model 37 Supreme also with Skeet (14"x1½"x2¼") or Trap (14½"x1½"x1⅞") stocks available at no extra charge. Other options available at extra charge.
Price: **$668.00**

Mossberg Model 500ASG Slugster
Same as standard Mossberg Model 500 except has Slugster barrel with ramp front sight, open adj. folding-leaf rear, running deer scene etched on receiver. 12 ga.—18½", 24", 20-ga.—24" bbl.
Price: **$236.95**

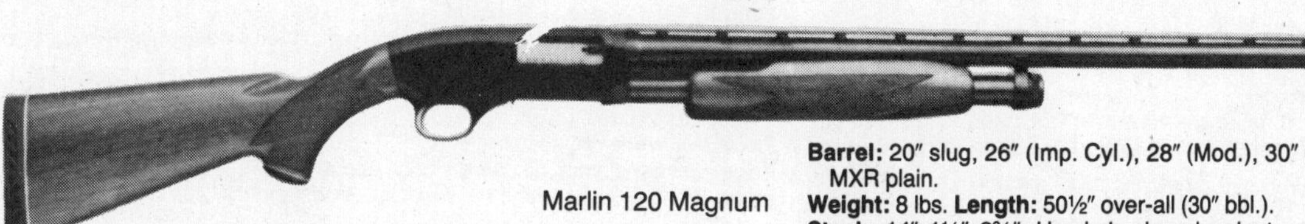
Marlin 120 Magnum

MARLIN 120 MAGNUM PUMP GUN
Gauge: 12 ga. (2¾" or 3" chamber) 5-shot; 3-shot plug furnished.
Action: Hammerless, side ejecting, slide action.
Barrel: 20" slug, 26" (Imp. Cyl.), 28" (Mod.), 30" (Full), with vent. rib. or 38" MXR plain.
Weight: 8 lbs. **Length:** 50½" over-all (30" bbl.).
Stock: 14"x1½"x2⅜". Hand-checkered walnut, capped p.g., semi-beavertail fore-end. Mar-Shield® finish.
Features: Interchangeable bbls., slide lock release; large button cross-bolt safety.
Price: **$335.95**
Price: Extra barrels, about **$107.95**

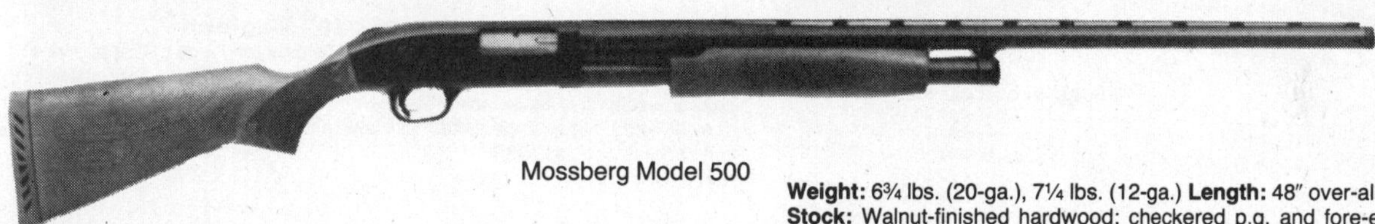
Mossberg Model 500

MOSSBERG MODEL 500
Gauge: 12, 20, 410, 3".
Action: Takedown.
Barrel: 28" ACCU-CHOKE (interchangeable tubes for Imp. Cyl., Mod., Full). Vent. rib only.
Weight: 6¾ lbs. (20-ga.), 7¼ lbs. (12-ga.) **Length:** 48" over-all.
Stock: Walnut-finished hardwood; checkered p.g. and fore-end; recoil pad. (14"x1½"x2½").
Features: Side ejection; top tang safety; trigger disconnector prevents doubles. Easily interchangeable barrels within gauge.
Price: Vent rib, ACCU-CHOKE, either gauge, about **$315.00**
Price: Extra barrels, from **$31.50**
Price: Youth model, 20 ga., 13" buttstock, 20" (ACCU-CHOKE), about **$257.95**

Mossberg 500 AHT/AHTD

Mossberg Model 500 410 Ga.
Similar to Mossberg Model 500 except: 410 bore only, 26" bbl. (Full); 2½", 3" shells; holds six 2¾" or five 3" shells. Walnut-finished stock with checkered p.g. and fore-end, fluted comb and recoil pad (14"x1¼"x2½"). Weight about 6 lbs., length over-all 45¾".
Price: With vent. rib barrel **$221.00**

Mossberg Model 500AHT/AHTD
Same as Model 500 except 12 ga. only with extra-high Simmons Olympic-style free floating rib and built-up Monte Carlo trap-style stock. 30" barrel (Full), 28" ACCU-CHOKE with 3 interchangeable choke tubes (Mod., Imp. Mod., Full).
Price: With 30" barrel, fixed choke **$326.95**
Price: With ACCU-CHOKE barrel, 28" or 30" **$346.95**

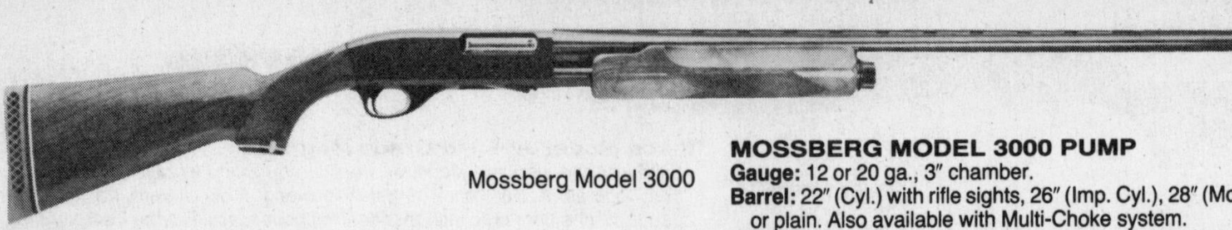

Mossberg Model 3000

MOSSBERG MODEL 3000 PUMP

Gauge: 12 or 20 ga., 3″ chamber.
Barrel: 22″ (Cyl.) with rifle sights, 26″ (Imp. Cyl.), 28″ (Mod.), 30″ (Full), vent. rib or plain. Also available with Multi-Choke system.
Weight: About 7½ lbs. **Length:** 48½″ over-all (28″ bbl.).
Stock: 14″x1⅜″x2¼″. American walnut
Features: Dual action bars for smooth functioning. Rubber recoil pad, steel receiver, chrome plated bolt. Cross-bolt safety reversible for left-handed shooters. Introduced 1980.
Price: .... **NA**

Mossbers Model 3000 Waterfowler Pump

Similar to the standard Model 3000 except all exterior metal is Parkerized to reduce glare, bolt is black oxidized, stock has a dull oil finish. Comes with q.d. swivels and a padded, camouflaged sling. Available with 30″ (Full) barrel with 3″ chamber. Introduced 1982.
Price: .... **NA**

OMEGA PUMP SHOTGUNS

Gauge: 12, 2¾″ chamber.
Barrel: 20″, 26″ (Imp. Cyl.); 28″ (Mod.); 30″ (Full).
Weight: 6¾ lbs. (Slug) to 7½ lbs.
Stock: Stained hardwood.
Sights: Bead front; rifle-type on Deerfield Slug.
Features: Blued receiver; Damascened bolt; cross-bolt safety. Imported from the Philippines by Kassnar. Introduced 1984.
Price: Field **$189.00**
Price: Deerfield Slug **$199.00**

Consult our Directory pages for the location of firms mentioned.

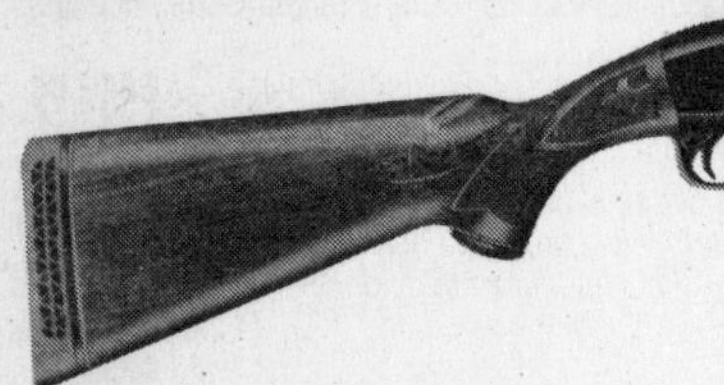

Remington Model 870

REMINGTON 870 WINGMASTER PUMP GUN

Gauge: 12, 20, (5-shot; 3-shot wood plug).
Action: Takedown, slide action
Barrel: 12, 20, ga., 26″ (Imp. Cyl.); 28″ (Mod. or Full); 12 ga., 30″ (Full).
Weight: 7 lbs., 12 ga. (7¾ lbs. with Vari-Weight plug); 6½ lbs., 20 ga.
Length: 48½″ over-all (28″ bbl.).
Stock: 14″x1⅝″x2½″. Checkered walnut, p.g.; fluted extension fore-end; fitted rubber recoil pad.
Features: Double action bars, crossbolt safety. Receiver machined from solid steel. Hand fitted action.
Price: With vent. rib, about **$380.00**
Price: Left hand, vent. rib., 12 ga. only, about **$430.00**
Price: Youth Gun, 21″ vent. rib, Imp. Cyl., Mod., about **$380.00**

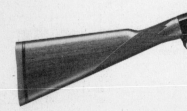

Remington 870 Magnum

Same as the M870 except 3″ chamber, 12 ga. 30″ bbl. (Mod. or Full), 20 ga. 28″ bbl. (Mod. or Full). Recoil pad installed. Wgt., 12 ga. 8 lbs., 20 ga. 7½ lbs.
Price: With vent. rib, about **$380.00**
Price: Left hand model, vent rib. bbl, about **$430.00**

Remington 870 Special Purpose

Remington 870 "Special Purpose" Magnum

Similar to the Model 870 except chambered only for 12-ga., 3″ shells, vent. rib. 26″ or 30″ (both Full) barrels. All exposed metal surfaces are finished in dull, non-reflective black. Wood has an oil finish. Comes with padded Cordura, 2″ wide sling, quick-detachable swivels. Chrome-lined bores. Dark recoil pad. Introduced 1985.
Price: About **$380.00**

Remington 870 Small Gauges

Exact copies of the large ga. Model 870, except that guns are offered in 28 and 410 ga. 25″ barrel (Full, Mod., Imp. Cyl.). D and F grade prices same as large ga. M870 prices.
Price: With vent. rib barrel, about **$410.00**

Remington 870D Tournament

Same as 870 except: better walnut, hand checkering. Engraved receiver and bbl. Vent. rib. Stock dimensions to order.
Price: About **$2,245.00**

Remington 870F Premier

Same as M870, except select walnut, better engraving
Price: About **$4,630.00**
Price: With gold inlay, about **$7,000.00**

Remington Model 870 20 Ga. Lt. Wt.

Same as standard Model 870 except weighs 6 lbs.; 26″ (Imp. Cyl.), 28″ (Full, Mod.), 30″ (Full).
Price: Vent. rib barrel, about **$380.00**

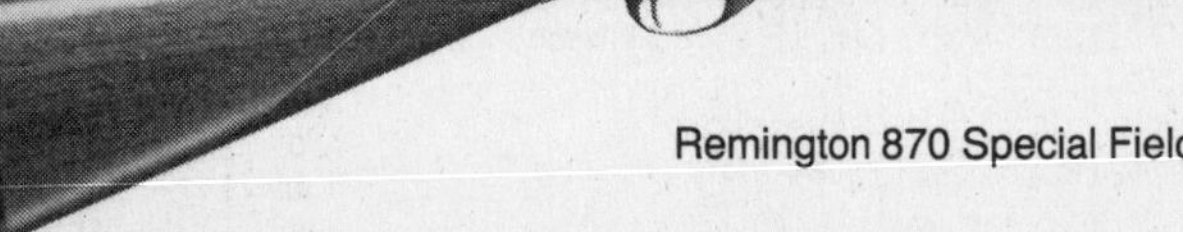

Remington 870 Special Field

Remington Model 870 "Special Field"

Similar to the standard Model 870 except comes with 21″ barrel only, 3″ chamber, choked Imp. Cyl., Mod., Full; 12 ga. weighs 6¾ lbs., Ltwt. 20 weighs 6 lbs.; has straight-grip stock, shorter fore-end, both with cut checkering. Vent. rib barrel only. Introduced 1984.
Price: About **$410.00**

CAUTION: PRICES CHANGE. CHECK AT GUNSHOP.

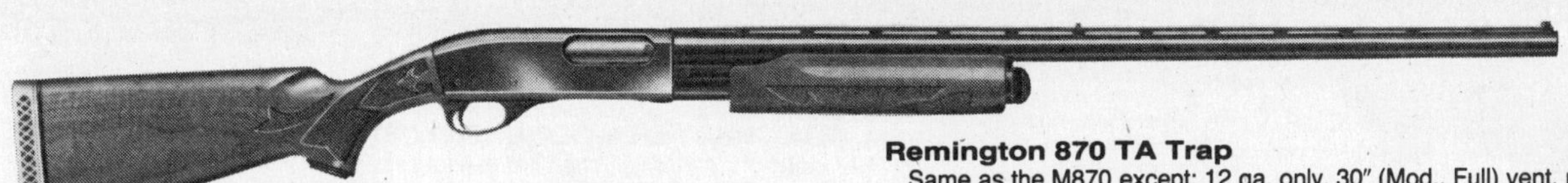

Remington 870 TA Trap

Remington 870 TA Trap
Same as the M870 except: 12 ga. only, 30″ (Mod., Full) vent. rib. bbl., ivory front and white metal middle beads. Special sear, hammer and trigger assy. 14⅜″x1½″x1⅞″ stock with recoil pad. Hand fitted action and parts. Wgt. 8 lbs.
Price: Model 870TA Trap, about **$415.00**
Price: TA Trap with Monte Carlo stock, about **$425.00**

Remington Model 870 Brushmaster Deluxe
Carbine version of the M870 with 20″ bbl. (Imp. Cyl.) for rifled slugs. 40½″ over-all, wgt. 6½ lbs. Recoil pad. Adj. rear, ramp front sights, 12 or 20 ga. Deluxe.
Price: About **$360.00**
Price: Left-hand model, about **$410.00**

Remington Model 870 Competition Trap
Same as standard 870 except single shot, gas reduction system, select wood. Has 30″ (Full choke) vent. rib barrel
Price: About **$650.00**

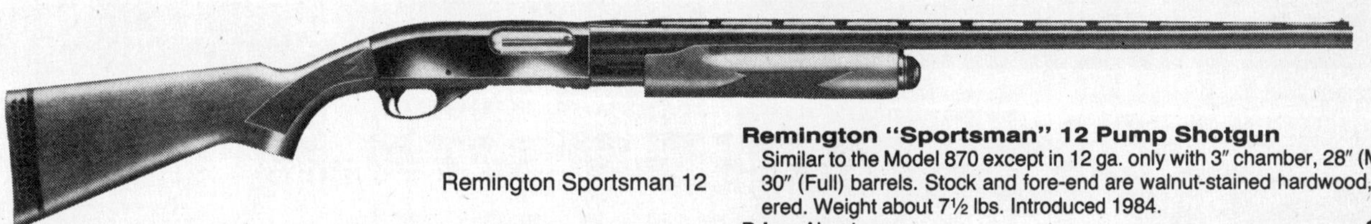

Remington Sportsman 12

Remington "Sportsman" 12 Pump Shotgun
Similar to the Model 870 except in 12 ga. only with 3″ chamber, 28″ (Mod.) or 30″ (Full) barrels. Stock and fore-end are walnut-stained hardwood, checkered. Weight about 7½ lbs. Introduced 1984.
Price: About **$260.00**

Stevens 67VR

STEVENS MODEL 67 PUMP SHOTGUN
Gauge: 12, 20 (2¾″ & 3″), 410 (2½″ & 3″).
Barrel: 26″ (Full, 410 ga.), 28″ (Mod., Full), 30″ (Full, 12 ga.), or interchangeable choke tubes.
Weight: 7 lbs. **Length:** 49½″ over-all (30″ bbl.).
Stock: Walnut-finished hardwood; checkered p.g. and slide handle. 14″x1½″x2½″.
Sights: Metal bead front.
Features: Grooved slide handle, top tang safety, steel receiver. From Savage Arms. Introduced 1981.
Price: Model 67 .... **$194.00**
Price: Model 67VR (vent. rib)................................... **$205.00**
Price: Model 67 Slug Gun (21″ barrel, rifle sights) **$196.50**
Price: Model 67-T (with 3 choke tubes) **$210.00**
Price: Model 67-VRT (as above with vent. rib) **$226.00**
Price: Model 67-TY (youth gun, 20 ga.) **$213.00**

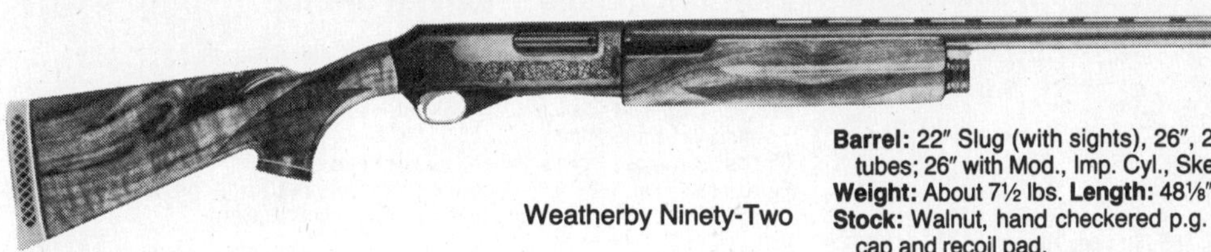

Weatherby Ninety-Two

WEATHERBY NINETY-TWO PUMP
Gauge: 12 only, 3″ chamber.
Action: Short stroke slide action.
Barrel: 22″ Slug (with sights), 26″, 28″, 30″ with IMC (Integral Multi-Choke) tubes; 26″ with Mod., Imp. Cyl., Skeet, others with Full, Mod., Imp. Cyl.
Weight: About 7½ lbs. **Length:** 48⅛″ (28″ bbl.)
Stock: Walnut, hand checkered p.g. and fore-end, white line spacers at p.g. cap and recoil pad.
Features: Short stroke action, cross-bolt safety. Comes with three flush-fitting IMC choke tubes. Introduced 1982. Imported from Japan by Weatherby.
Price: **$359.95**
Price: Extra interchangeable bbls. **$158.00**
Price: Extra IMC choke tubes **$12.50**

Winchester Ranger

WINCHESTER RANGER PUMP GUN
Gauge: 12 or 20, 3″ chamber, 4-shot magazine.
Barrel: 2[illegible] rib or plain with Full, Mod., Imp. Cyl. Winchoke tubes, or 30″ plain.
Weight: 7 to 7¼ lbs. **Length:** 48⅝″ to 50⅝″ over-all.
Stock: Walnut finished hardwood with ribbed fore-end.
Sights: Metal bead front.
Features: Cross-bolt safety, black rubber butt pad, twin action slide bars, front-locking rotating bolt. Made under license by U.S. Repeating Arms Co.
Price: Plain barrel, about **$189.95**
Price: Vent. rib barrel, Winchoke, about **$219.95**
Price: Vent. rib. Mod. choke, about.............................. **$206.00**

Winchester Ranger Youth Pump Gun
Similar to the standard Ranger except chambered only for 3″ 20 ga., 22″ plain barrel with Winchoke tubes (Full, Mod., Imp. Cyl.) or 22″ plain barrel with fixed Mod. choke. Weighs 6½ lbs., measures 41⅝″ o.a.l. Stock has 13″ pull length and gun comes with discount certificate for full-size stock. Introduced 1983. Made under license by U.S. Repeating Arms Co.
Price: Plain barrel, Winchoke, about **$225.00**
Price: Plain barrel, Mod. choke, about............................ **$196.00**

Winchester Ranger Pump Gun Combination
Similar to the standard Ranger except comes with two barrels: 24⅛″ (Cyl.) deer barrel with rifle-type sights and an interchangeable 28″ vent. rib Winchoke barrel with Full, Mod. and Imp. Cyl. choke tubes. Available in 12 and 20 gauge 3″ only, with recoil pad. Introduced 1983.
Price: With two barrels, about **$255.00**

SHOTGUNS—SLIDE ACTIONS

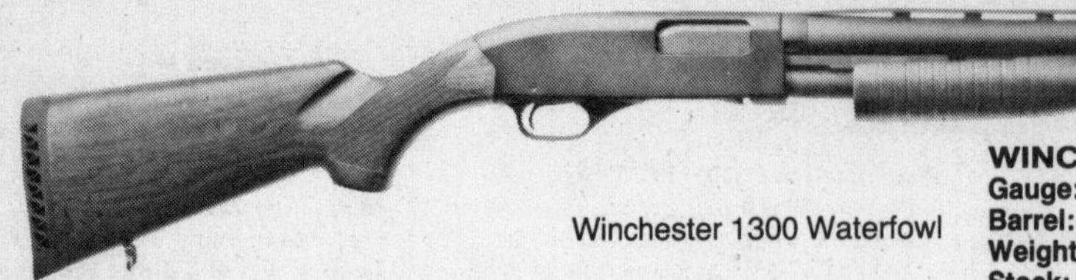

Winchester 1300 Waterfowl

Winchester 1300 Waterfowl Pump

Similar to the 1300 Featherweight except in 3" 12 ga. only, 30" vent. rib barrel with Winchoke system; stock and fore-end of walnut with low-luster finish. All metal surfaces have special non-glare matte finish. Introduced 1985.

Price: About **$298.00**

WINCHESTER MODEL 1300 FEATHERWEIGHT PUMP

Gauge: 12 and 20, 3" chamber, 5-shot capacity.
Barrel: 22", vent. rib, with Full, Mod., Imp. Cyl. Winchoke tubes.
Weight: 6⅜ lbs. **Length:** 42⅝" over-all.
Stock: American walnut, with deep cut checkering on pistol grip, traditional ribbed fore-end; high luster finish.
Sights: Metal bead front.
Features: Twin action slide bars; front-locking rotating bolt; roll-engraved receiver; blued, highly polished metal; cross-bolt safety with red indicator. Introduced 1984.
Price: About **$283.00**

SHOTGUNS—OVER-UNDERS

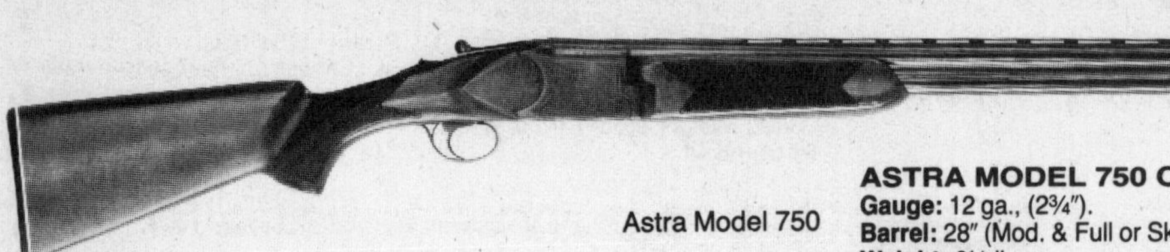

Astra Model 750

Astra Model 650 O/U Shotgun

Same as Model 750 except has double triggers.

Price: With extractors **$495.00**
Price: With ejectors **$630.00**

ASTRA MODEL 750 O/U SHOTGUN

Gauge: 12 ga., (2¾").
Barrel: 28" (Mod. & Full or Skeet & Skeet), 30" Trap (Mod. & Full).
Weight: 6½ lbs.
Stock: European walnut, hand-checkered p.g. and fore-end.
Features: Single selective trigger, scroll-engraved receiver, selective auto ejectors, vent. rib. Introduced 1980. From L. Joseph Rahn, Inc.
Price: **$735.00**
Price: With extractors only **$600.00**
Price: Trap or Skeet (M.C. stock and recoil pad.)................ **$850.00**

Beretta Model 686

ARMSPORT MODEL 2500 O/U

Gauge: 12 or 20 ga.
Barrel: 26" (Imp. Cyl. & Mod.); 28" (Mod. & Full); vent. rib.
Weight: 8 lbs.
Stock: European walnut, hand checkered p.g. and fore-end.
Features: Single selective trigger, automatic ejectors, engraved receiver. Imported by Armsport.
Price: **$695.00**
Price: With extractors only **$595.00**

BERETTA SERIES 680 OVER-UNDER

Gauge: 12 (2¾").
Barrel: 29½" (Imp. Mod. & Full, Trap), 28" (Skeet & Skeet).
Weight: About 8 lbs.
Stock: Trap—14⅜"x1¼"x2⅛"; Skeet—14⅜"x1⅜"x2 7/16". European walnut with hand checkering.
Sights: Luminous front sight and center bead.
Features: Trap Monte Carlo stock has deluxe trap recoil pad, Skeet has smooth pad. Imported from Italy by Beretta U.S.A. Corp.
Price: M682, Trap or Skeet, from................................ **$1,875.00**
Price: M682X, Trap or Skeet, from **$1,875.00**
Price: M682 Field **$1,875.00**
Price: M685 Field................................ **$900.00**
Price: M686 Field, from **$1,100.00**
Price: M687 Field, from **$1,150.00**

Beretta Model SO-4

Beretta SO-4 Target Shotguns

Target guns derived from Model SO-3EL. Light engraving coverage. Single trigger. Skeet gun has 28" (Skeet & Skeet) barrels, 10mm rib, p.g. stock (14⅛"x2 9/16"x1⅜"), fluted beavertail fore-end. "Skeet" is inlaid in gold into trigger guard. Weight is about 7 lbs. 10 ozs. Trap guns have 30" (Imp. Mod. & Full or Mod. & Full) barrels, trap stock dimensions, fitted recoil pad, fluted beavertail fore-end. Weight is about 7 lbs. 12 ozs. "Trap" is inlaid in gold into trigger guard. Special dimensions and features, within limits, may be ordered. Introduced 1977.

Price: Skeet or trap **$7,200.00**
Price: Trap Combo................................ **$9,500.00**

BERETTA SO-3 O/U SHOTGUN

Gauge: 12 ga. (2¾" chambers).
Action: Back-action sidelock.
Barrel: 26", 27", 28", 29" or 30", chokes to customer specs.
Stock: Standard measurements—14⅛"x1 7/16"x2⅜". Straight "English" or p.g.-style. Hand checkered European walnut.
Features: SO-3—"English scroll" floral engraving on action body, sideplates and trigger guard. Stocked in select walnut. SO-3EL—as above, with full engraving coverage. Hand-detachable sideplates. SO-3EELL—as above with deluxe finish and finest full coverage engraving. Internal parts gold plated. Top lever is pierced and carved in relief with gold inlaid crown. Introduced 1977. Imported from Italy by Beretta U.S.A. Corp.
Price: SO-3 .... **$6,500.00**
Price: SO-3EL................................ **$8,100.00**
Price: SO-3EELL **$10,000.00**

CAUTION: PRICES CHANGE. CHECK AT GUNSHOP.

Baby Bretton

BABY BRETTON OVER-UNDER SHOTGUN

Gauge: 12 or 20, 2¾" chambers.
Barrel: 27½" (Cyl.,Imp. Cyl., Mod., Full choke tubes).
Weight: About 5 lbs.
Stock: Walnut, checkered pistol grip and fore-end, oil finish.
Features: Receiver slides open on two guide rods, is locked by a large thumb lever on the right side. Extractors only. Light alloy barrels. Imported from France by Mandall Shooting Supplies.
Price: **$695.00**

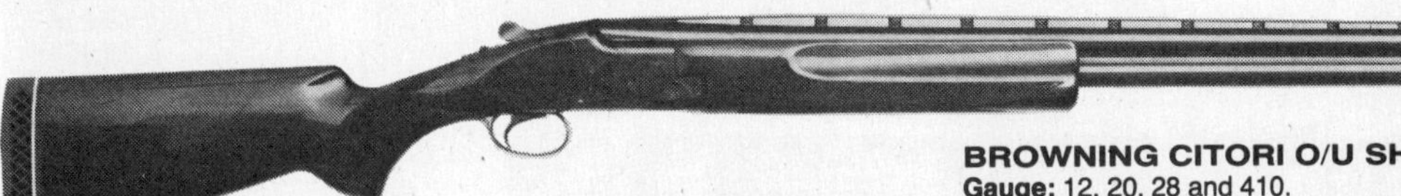

Browning Citori Field

BROWNING CITORI O/U SHOTGUN

Gauge: 12, 20, 28 and 410.
Barrel: 26", 28" (Mod. & Full, Imp. Cyl. & Mod.), in all gauges, 30" (Mod. & Full, Full & Full) in 12 ga. only. Also offered with Invector choke tubes.
Weight: 6 lbs. 8 oz. (26" 410) to 7 lbs. 13 oz. (30" 12-ga.).
Length: 43" over-all (26" bbl.).
Stock: Dense walnut, hand checkered, full p.g., beavertail fore-end. Field-type recoil pad on 12 ga. field guns and trap and Skeet models.
Sights: Medium raised beads, German nickel silver.
Features: Barrel selector integral with safety, auto ejectors, three-piece takedown. Imported from Japan by Browning.
Price: Grade I, Invector **$810.00**
Price: Grade I, 12 and 20, fixed chokes **$775.00**
Price: Grade III, Invector, 12 and 20 .... **$1,100.00**
Price: Grade VI, Invector, 12 and 20 .... **$1,600.00**
Price: Grade I, 28 and 410, fixed chokes **$800.00**
Price: Grade III, 28 and 410, fixed chokes **$1,200.00**
Price: Grade VI, 28 and 410, high post rib, fixed chokes **$1,700.00**

Browning Citori O/U Skeet Models

Similar to standard Citori except: 26", 28" (Skeet & Skeet) only; stock dimensions of 14⅜"x1½"x2", fitted with Skeet-style recoil pad; conventional target rib and high post target rib.
Price: Grade I Invector (high post rib) **$895.00**
Price: Grade I, 12 & 20 (high post rib) **$865.00**
Price: Grade I, 28 & 410 (high post rib) **$900.00**
Price: Grade III, all gauges (high post rib) **$1,200.00**
Price: Grade VI, all gauges, (high post rib) **$1,700.00**
Price: Four barrel Skeet set — 12, 20, 28, 410 barrels, with case, Grade I only **$2,900.00**
Price: Grade III, four-barrel set (high post rib) **$3,200.00**
Price: Grade VI, four-barrel set (high post rib) **$3,600.00**

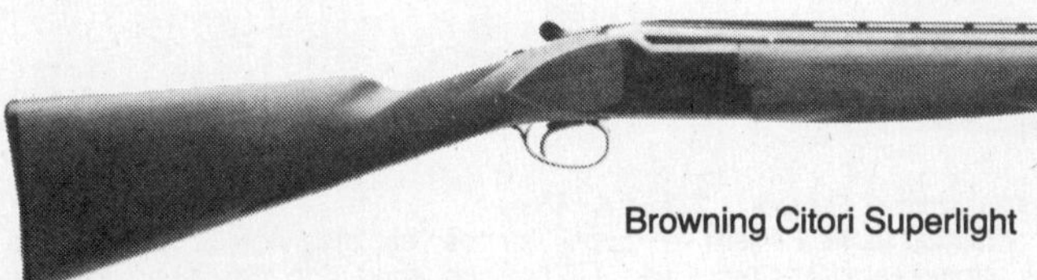

Browning Citori Superlight

Browning Superlight Citori Over-Under

Similar to the standard Citori except availiable in 12, 20, 28 or 410 with 24", 26" barrels choked Imp. Cyl. & Mod. or 28" choked Mod. & Full. Has straight grip stock, Schnabel fore-end tip. Superlight 12 weighs 6 lbs., 9 oz. (26" barrels); Superlight 20, 5 lbs., 12 oz. (26" barrels). Introduced 1982.
Price: Grade I only, 12, 20, 28 or 410 .... **$800.00**
Price: Grade III, Invector **$1,100.00**
Price: Grade VI, Invector **$1,600.00**
Price: Grade I Invector **$835.00**
Price: Grade I Invector, Upland Special (24" bbls.) **$835.00**

Browning Citori O/U Trap Models

Similar to standard Citori except: 12 gauge only; 30", 32" (Full & Full, Imp. Mod. & Full, Mod. & Full), 34" single barrel in Combo Set (Full, Imp. Mod., Mod.), or Invector model; Monte Carlo cheekpiece (14⅜"x1⅜"x1⅜"x2"); fitted with trap-style recoil pad; conventional target rib and high post target rib.
Price: Grade I, Invector high post target rib **$900.00**
Price: Grade I, fixed chokes, high post target rib **$865.00**
Price: Grade III, Invector, high post target rib **$1,200.00**
Price: Grade VI, Invector, high post target rib **$1,700.00**

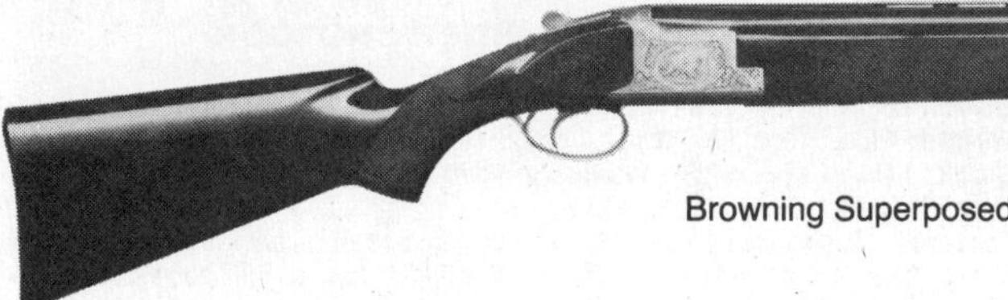

Browning Superposed

BROWNING SUPERPOSED SUPERLIGHT GRADE I

Gauge: 12 & 20, 2¾" chamber.
Action: Boxlock, top lever, single selective trigger. Bbl. selector combined with manual tang safety.
Barrel: 26½" (Mod. & Full, or Imp. Cyl. & Mod.)
Weight: 6⅜ lbs., average
Stock: Straight grip (14¼"x1⅝"x2½") hand checkered (fore-end and grip) select walnut.
Features: The Superposed is available in four grades. Pigeon, Pointer, Diana grades have silver grayed receivers with hand-engraved game scenes ascending in artistic design with each successive grade. Midas grade has specially blued steel with deeply hand-carved background and 18 carat gold inlaid pheasants and ducks on the 12 ga., smaller game birds on 20 ga. Lightning has full pistol grip stock, Superlight has straight grip. Basically this gives the buyer a wide choice of engraving styles and designs and mechanical options which would place the gun in a "custom" bracket. Options are too numerous to list here and the reader is urged to obtain a copy of the latest Browning catalog for the complete listing. Imported from Belgium by Browning.
Price: Grade I, Lightning and Superlight **$1,995.00**
Price: Pigeon Grade, Lightning and Superlight **$3,200.00**
Price: Pointer Grade, Lightning and Superlight **$4,000,00**
Price: Diana Grade, Lightning and Superlight **$4,800.00**
Price: Midas Grade, Lightning and Superlight **$6,000.00**

Browning Limited Edition Waterfowl Superposed

Same specs as the Lightning Superposed. Available in 12 ga. only, 28" (Mod. & Full). Limited to 500 guns, the edition number of each gun is inscribed in gold on the bottom of the receiver with "Black Duck" and its scientific name. Sides of receiver have two gold inlayed black ducks, bottom has two, and one on the trigger guard. Receiver is completely engraved and grayed. Stock and fore-end are highly figured dark French walnut with 24 lpi checkering, hand-oiled finish, checkered butt. Comes with form fitted, velvet-lined, black walnut case. Introduced 1983.
Price: **$8,000.00**
Price: Similar treatment as above except for the Pintail Duck Issue **$7,700.00**

Browning Superposed Classic & Gold Classic

Same as the standard Superposed 20-ga. with 26″ (Imp. Cyl. & Mod.) barrels except has an upland setting of bird dogs, pheasant and quail on the satin grey receiver. Gold Classic has the animals in inlaid gold. Straight grip stock and Schnabel fore-end are of select American walnut. Classic has pearl borders around the checkering and high gloss finish; Gold Classic has fine checkering and decorative carving with oil finish. Delivery scheduled for 1986. Introduced 1984.

Price: Superposed Classic **$2,500.00**
Price: Superposed Gold Classic **$8,800.00**

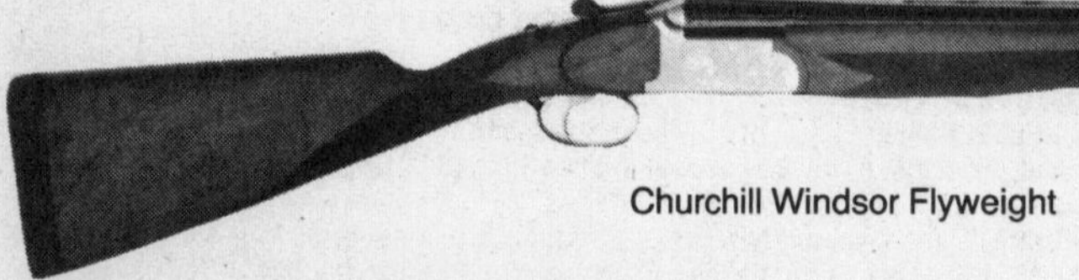

Churchill Windsor Flyweight

Churchill Regent Over-Under Shotguns

Similar to the Windsor Grade except better wood with oil finish, better engraving; available only in 12 or 20 gauge (2¾″ chambers), 27″ barrels, with ICT interchangeable choke tubes (Imp. Cyl., Mod., Full). Regent V has standard boxlock action, Regent VII has dummy sideplates. Introduced 1984.

Price: Regent V, 12 or 20 ga. **$1,073.00**
Price: Regent VII, 12 or 20 ga. **$1,200.00**
Price: Regent V, Flyweight, 23″, 25″, ICT **$1,073.00**
Price: Regent VII Flyweight, 23″, 25″, ICT **$1,200.00**

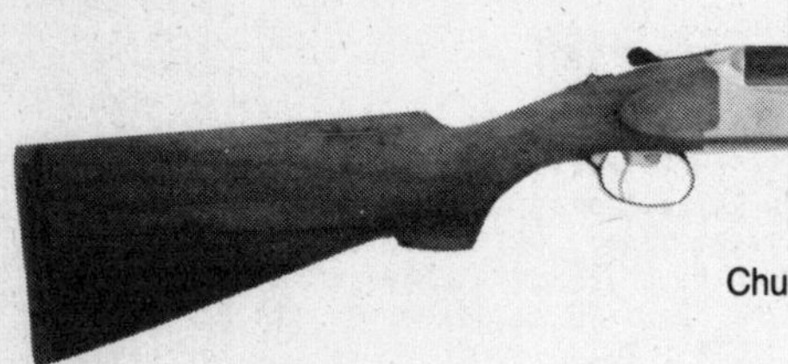

Churchill Regent Skeet

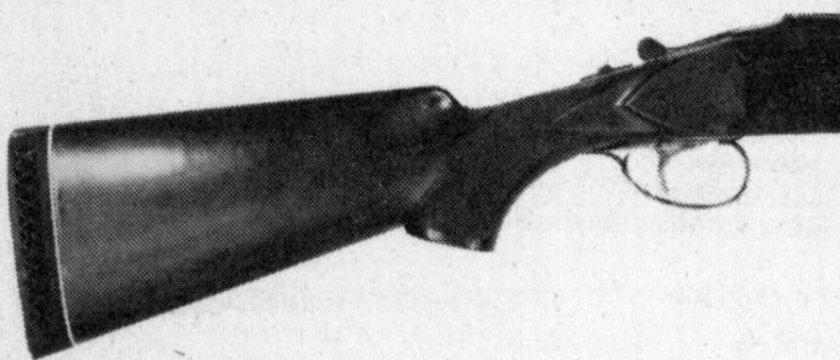

Clayco Model 6

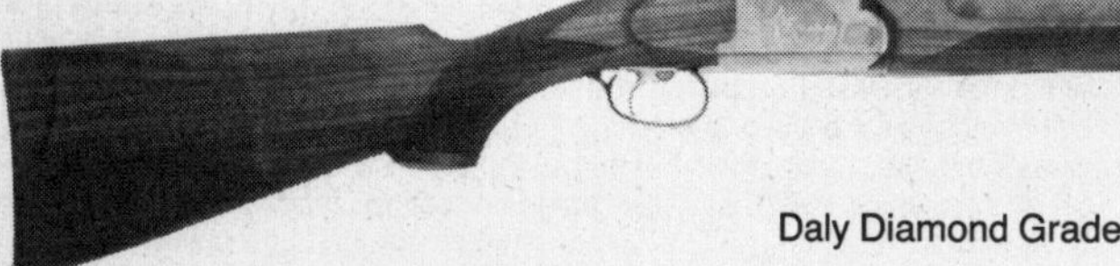

Daly Diamond Grade

Charles Daly Diamond Trap Over-Under

Similar to the Diamond Grade except has competition vent. top and middle ribs, target trigger; oil-finished Monte Carlo stock. Available in 12 gauge, 30″ (Full & Imp. Mod.).

Price: **$1,030.00**

CAPRINUS SWEDEN OVER-UNDER SHOTGUN

Gauge: 12 only, 2¾″ chambers
Barrel: 28″, 30″ (interchangeable choke tubes—Cyl., Skeet, Imp. Cyl., Mod., Imp. Mod. and Full)
Weight: 6.8 lbs. (Game model).
Stock: 14″x1¾″x2⅛″ (Game model). High-grade walnut with rubber pad or checkered butt. Monte Carlo optional. Tru-oil or linseed oil finish.
Features: Made completely of stainless steel. Single selective trigger; barrel selector in front of the trigger; gas pressure activated auto. ejectors; firing pins set by top lever action; double safety system. Six standard choke tubes, plus optional tubes to change point of impact. Imported from Sweden by Caprinus U.S.A. Introduced 1982.

Price: Skeet Special, from **$5,500.00**
Price: Skeet Game, from **$5,800.00**
Price: Game, from **$5,800.00**
Price: Trap, from **$5,840.00**

CHURCHILL WINDSOR OVER-UNDER SHOTGUNS

Gauge: 12, 20, 410, 3″ chambers.
Barrel: 26″ (Skeet & Skeet, Imp. Cyl. & Mod.), 28″ (Mod. & Full), 30″ (Mod. & Full, Full & Full), 12 ga.; 26″ (Skeet & Skeet, Imp. Cyl. & Mod.), 28″ (Mod. & Full) 20 ga.; 24″, 26″ (Full & Full), 410 ga.; or 27″, 30″ ICT choke tubes.
Stock: European walnut, checkered pistol grip, oil finish.
Features: Boxlock action with silvered, engraved finish; single selective trigger; automatic ejectors on Windsor IV, extractors only on Windsor III. Also available in Flyweight version with 23″, 25″ barrels, fixed or ICT chokes, straight-grip stock.Imported from Italy by Kassnar. Introduced 1984.

Price: Windsor III, fixed chokes .... **$689.00** to **$773.00**
Price: 12 or 20 ga. ICT choke tubes **$773.00**
Price: Windsor IV, fixed chokes **$809.00**
Price: 12 or 20 ga., ICT choke tubes **$893.00**

Churchill Regent Trap & Skeet

Similar to the Regent V except Trap has ventilated side rib, Monte Carlo stock, ventilated recoil pad. Oil finished wood, fine checkering, chrome bores. Weight is 8 lbs. Regent Skeet available in 12 or 20 ga., 26″ (Skeet & Skeet); oil finished stock measures 14½″, 1½″ x 2⅜″. Both guns have silvered and engraved receivers. Introduced 1984.

Price: Regent Trap (30″ Imp. Mod. & Full) **$1,178.00**
Price: Regent Skeet, 12 or 20 ga. **$1,139.00**
Price: Regent Trap (30″ ICT) **$1,260.00**

CLAYCO MODEL 6 OVER-UNDER SHOTGUN

Gauge: 12, 2¾″ chambers.
Barrel: 26″ (Imp. Cyl. & Mod.), 28″ (Mod. & Full).
Weight: 7 lbs. 15 oz. (26″ bbls.). **Length:** 43″ over-all (26″ bbls.).
Stock: 14¼″ x 1⅝″ x 2½″. Walnut finished hardwood. Checkered pistol grip and fore-end.
Features: Mechanical single trigger, automatic safety; ventilated rubber recoil pad. Scroll-engraved blued receiver. Ventilated top rib. Introduced 1983. Imported from China by Clayco Sports Ltd.

Price: **$295.00**

CHARLES DALY DIAMOND GRADE OVER-UNDER

Gauge: 12 and 20.
Barrel: 27″ (Full, Mod., Imp. Cyl. choke tubes); three tubes included.
Weight: 7 lbs.
Stock: Select extra-fancy European walnut, oil finish.
Features: Boxlock action with single selective competition trigger; silvered and engraved receiver; selective automatic ejectors; 22 lpi checkering on grip and fore-end. Imported from Italy by Outdoor Sports Headquarters. Introduced 1984.

Price: **$895.00**

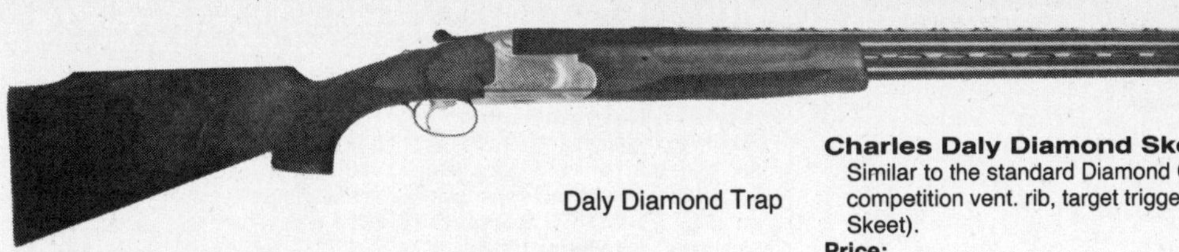
Daly Diamond Trap

Charles Daly Diamond Skeet Over-Under
Similar to the standard Diamond Grade except has oil-finished Skeet stock, competition vent. rib, target trigger. Available in 12 gauge only, 26″ (Skeet & Skeet).
Price: $1,030.00

Charles Daly Presentation Grade Over-Under
Similar to the Diamond Grade except has dummy sideplates, better wood, finish, and extensive game scene engraving on the silvered receiver and sideplates.
Price: $1,165.00

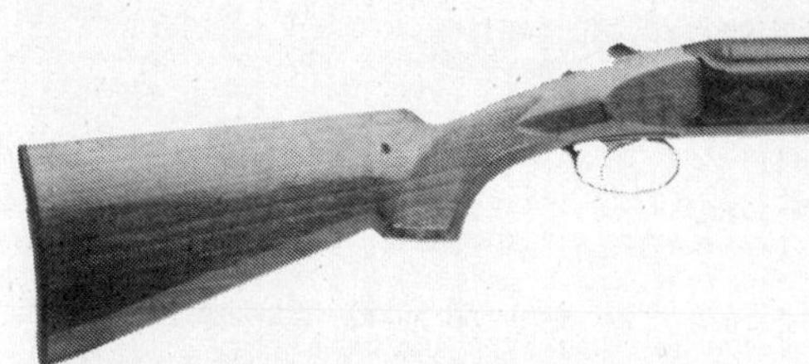
Daly Field III

CHARLES DALY FIELD III OVER-UNDER
Gauge: 12 or 20.
Barrel: 26″ (Imp. Cyl. & Mod.), 28″, 30″ (Full & Mod.); vent. rib.
Weight: About 6¾ lbs.
Stock: Select European walnut, checkered pistol grip and fore-end.
Features: Single selective trigger; extractors only; blued and engraved frame; chrome lined bores. Imported from Italy by Outdoor Sports Headquarters. Introduced 1984.
Price: $569.95

Charles Daly Superior II Over-Under
Similar to the Field II model except better wood, silvered receiver, more and better engraving. Same barrel lengths and chokes.
Price: $674.00

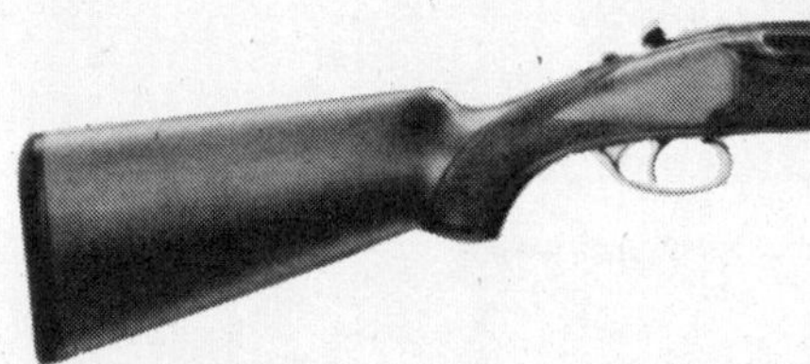
Exel Series 100

EXEL SERIES 100 OVER-UNDER SHOTGUNS
Gauge: 12 only; 2¾″, 3″ chambers.
Barrel: 26″ (Imp. Cyl. & Mod., M101), 27⅝″ (Imp. Cyl. & Mod., Imp. Cyl. & Imp. Mod., or choke tubes, M102, M104, M105, M106), 29½″ (Mod. & Full, choke tubes, M103, M107).
Weight: 6⅞ to 7¾ lbs.
Stock: 14⅜″ × 1½″ × 2½″ (14½″× 1¼″× 1¾″ for Trap M107); checkered European walnut.
Features: Single selective trigger, selective auto. ejectors. Virtually any choke combination on special order. M105, 106 come with five choke tubes; M107 Trap has upper barrel Full choke, lower barrel three choke tubes. Made in Spain by Lanber. Imported by Exel Arms.
Price: Model 101, 102 .... $450.80
Price: Model 103 .... $466.91
Price: Model 104 .... $543.29
Price: Model 105 .... $644.00
Price: Model 106, 107 .... $845.25

Exel Model 305

EXEL SERIES 300 OVER-UNDER SHOTGUNS
Gauge: 12, 20 ga., 2¾″ or 3″ (20 ga. only) chambers.
Barrel: 28″ (Full & Mod.), 29″ (Full & Mod. or Full & Imp. Mod.).
Weight: 6½ to 8 lbs.
Stock: 14⅜″ x 1⅜″ x 2½″ (Field), 14⅜″ x 1½″ x 1⅝″ (Monte Carlo). European walnut with checkered grip and fore-end.
Features: Boxlock action with silvered and engraved finish; ventilated rib; full pistol grip stock; automatic selective ejectors. Made in Spain by Laurona; imported by Exel Arms of America. Introduced 1984.
Price: Model 301, 302 .... $552.92
Price: Model 303, 304 .... $622.71
Price: Model 305, 306, 305A, 306A (choke tubes) $710.71
Price: Model 307, 308 .... $668.31
Price: Model 309, 310 .... $726.49
Price: Model 306T Turkey Gun (matte finish wood, metal, four choke tubes) $710.71

Consult our Directory pages for the location of firms mentioned.

ARMI FAMARS FIELD OVER-UNDER
Gauge: 12 (2¾″), 20 (3″).
Barrel: 26″, 28″, 30″ (Mod. & Full).
Weight: 6½ to 6¾ lbs.
Stock: 14½″ x 1½″ x 2½″. European walnut.
Sights: Gold bead front.
Features: Boxlock action with single selective trigger; automatic selective trigger. Color case-hardened receiver with engraving. Imported from Italy by Mandall Shooting Supplies.
Price: $750.00

FRANCHI DIAMOND GRADE OVER-UNDER
Gauge: 12 ga. only, 2¾″ chambers.
Barrel: 28″ (Mod. & Full).
Weight: 6 lbs. 13 oz.
Stock: French walnut with cut checkered pistol grip and fore-end.
Features: Top tang safety, automatic ejectors, single selective trigger. Chrome plated bores. Decorative scroll on silvered receiver. Introduced 1982. Imported from Italy by F.I.E. Corp.
Price: Diamond Grade $850.00

Franchi Falconet Super

Franchi Falconet Super
Similar to the Diamond Grade except has a lightweight alloy receiver, single selective mechanical trigger with the barrel selector button on the trigger, and a rubber butt pad. Higher quality hand engraved receiver. Available in 12 ga. only, 27″ (Imp. Cyl. & Mod.) or 28″ (Mod. & Full) barrels. Translucent front sight bead. Introduced 1982.
Price: Falconet Super **$1,015.00**

Franchi Alcione SL Super Deluxe
Similar to the Falconet Super except has best quality hand engraved, silvered receiver, 24K gold plated trigger, elephant ivory bead front sight. Comes with luggage-type fitted case. Has 14K gold inlay on receiver. Same barrel and chokes as on Falconet Super. Introduced 1982.
Price: Alcione Super Deluxe **$1,595.00**

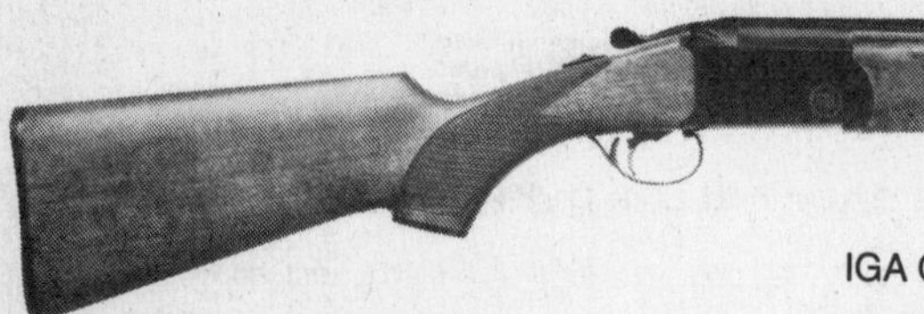

IGA Over-Under

IGA OVER-UNDER SHOTGUN
Gauge: 12, 20, 3″ chambers.
Barrel: 26″ (Full & Full, 410 only, Imp. Cyl. & Mod.), 28″ (Mod. & Full).
Weight: 6¾ to 7 lbs.
Stock: 14½″ x 1½″ x 2½″. Oil finished hardwood with checkered pistol grip and fore-end.
Features: Manual safety, double triggers, extractors only, ventilated top rib. Introduced 1983. Imported from Brazil by Stoeger Industries.
Price: Double triggers **$417.00**
Price: Single trigger **$499.95**

K.F.C. "FG" Standard

K.F.C. "FG" OVER-UNDER SHOTGUN
Gauge: 12 only (2¾″).
Barrel: 26″, 28″ (Imp. Cyl. & Imp. Mod.); vent. rib.
Weight: About 6.8 lbs.
Stock: 14″x1½″x2⅜″. High grade French walnut.
Sights: Sterling silver front bead.
Features: Selective single trigger, selective auto ejectors, non-automatic safety; chrome lined bores, chrome trigger. Introduced 1981. Imported from Japan by La Paloma Marketing.
Price: **$748.00**

K.F.C. OT-Trap-E2 Shotgun
Same as E-1 model except chromed receiver has high grade scroll engraving, super deluxe French walnut stock and fore-end.
Price: **$1,660.00**

K.F.C. OT-Trap-E1 Shotgun
Trap version of FG over-under. Has 30″ (Imp. Mod. & Full) barrels, 13mm vent. rib, bone white middle and front beads, scroll-engraved, blued receiver, wide gold-colored trigger. Stock dimensions are 14″x1¼″x1¼″x2″; high grade French walnut; rubber recoil pad; oil finish. Weight is about 7.9 lbs. Introduced 1981. From La Paloma Marketing.
Price: **$1,070.00**

K.F.C. OT-Skeet Shotguns
Skeet versions of FG model. Model E-1 has 26″ or 28″ (Skeet & Skeet) barrels with 13mm vent. rib, middle and front bead sights, gold colored wide trigger. Stock dimensions are 14″x1½″x2½″. Plastic buttplate, push-button fore-end release. Weight is about 7½ lbs.
Price: E-1 . . . . **$1,070.00**
Price: E-2 . . . . **$1,660.00**

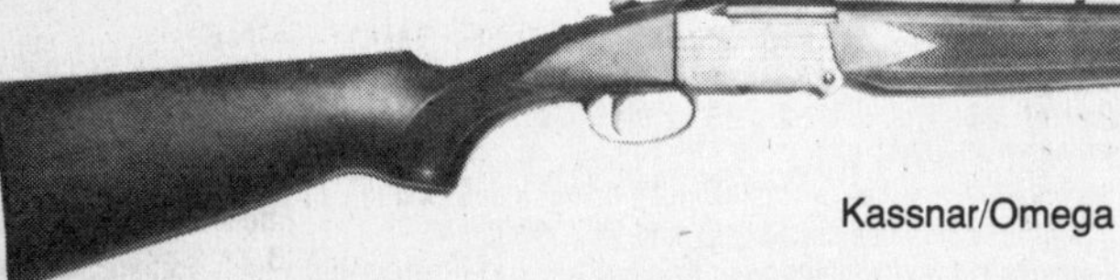

Kassnar/Omega

KASSNAR/OMEGA OVER-UNDER SHOTGUN
Gauge: 410, 3″.
Barrel: 24″ (Full & Full).
Weight: 5½ lbs.
Stock: Checkered European walnut.
Features: Single trigger; automatic safety; ventilated rib. Imported from Italy by Kassnar. Introduced 1984.
Price: **$299.00**

LEBEAU-COURALLY BOSS MODEL O-U SHOTGUN
Gauge: 12 or 20 (std.), 28 (optional).
Barrel: 26″ to 30″; choked to customer specs.
Weight: 5 lbs., 4 oz. (28-ga.) to 8 lbs. 4 oz. (12-ga.).
Stock: Dimensions to customer specs. Finest quality French walnut with very fine checkering with lace borders; straight or pistol grip stock, classic or splinter fore-end.
Features: Boss pattern sidelock ejector with low profile action; classic Boss sculpturing; double or single trigger; barrels normally furnished with ventilated rib. Imported from Belgium by Wm. Larkin Moore.
Price: From **$24,800.00**

Lanber Model 2004 Over-Under
Same basic specifications as Model 844 except fitted with LanberChoke interchangeable choke tube system. Available in trap, Skeet, pigeon and field models; ejectors only; single selective trigger; no middle rib on target guns (2008, 2009). Imported from Spain by Lanber Arms of America and Exel Arms of America.
Price: Model 2004 . . . . **$698.00**
Price: Model 2008 . . . . **$859.00**
Price: Model 2009 (30″ bbl., illus.) **$859.00**

LANBER MODEL 844 OVER-UNDER
Gauge: 12, 2¾″ or 3″.
Barrel: 28″ (Imp. Cyl. & Imp. Mod.), 30″ (Mod. & Full).
Weight: About 7 lbs. **Length:** 44⅜″ (28″ bbl.).
Stock: 14¼″ x 1⅝″ x 2½″. European walnut; checkered grip and fore-end.
Features: Single non-selective or selective trigger, double triggers on magnum model. Available with or without ejectors. Imported from Spain by Lanber Arms of America, and Exel Arms of America. Introduced 1981.
Price: Field, with selective trigger, extractors **$475.00**
Price: As above, 3″ Mag., 844 MST **$499.00**

Ljutic BiGun Super Deluxe

LJUTIC BIGUN O/U SHOTGUN

Gauge: 12 ga only.
Barrel: 28″ to 34″; choked to customer specs for live birds, trap, International Trap.
Weight: To customers specs.
Stock: To customer specs. Oil finish, hand checkered.
Features: Custom-made gun. Hollow-milled rib, pull or release trigger, push-button opener in front of trigger guard. From Ljutic Industries.
Price: **$7,995.00**
Price: BiGun Combo (interchangeable single barrel, two trigger guards, one for single trigger, one for doubles) **$12,995.00**
Price: Super Deluxe LTD TC BiGun **$9,984.00**
Price: Extra barrels with screw-in chokes or O/U barrel sets **$3,500.00**

Ljutic Four Barrel Skeet Set

Similar to BiGun except comes with matched set of four 28″ barrels in 12, 20, 28 and 410. Ljutic Paternator chokes and barrel are integral. Stock is to customer specs, of American or French walnut with fancy checkering.
Price: Four barrel set **$19,995.00**

Manufrance 979 Falcor

MANUFRANCE 979 FALCOR COMPETITION TRAP

Gauge: 12, 2¾″ chambers.
Barrel: 30″ (Imp. Mod. & Full, Special Trap), chrome lined bores.
Weight: About 8¼ lbs. **Length:** 48″ over-all.
Stock: Choice French walnut, hand checkered, hand-rubbed oil finish; smooth beavertail fore-end.
Sights: Ivory front bead in metal sleeve, middle ivory bead.
Features: Boxlock action with inertia-type trigger, top tang safety/barrel selector, special heavy-duty automatic ejectors, coil springs. Light alloy, 9/16″ wide, high-post rib. Each gun adjusted for point of impact. Imported from France by Armsource, Inc. Introduced 1984.
Price: **$1,860.00**

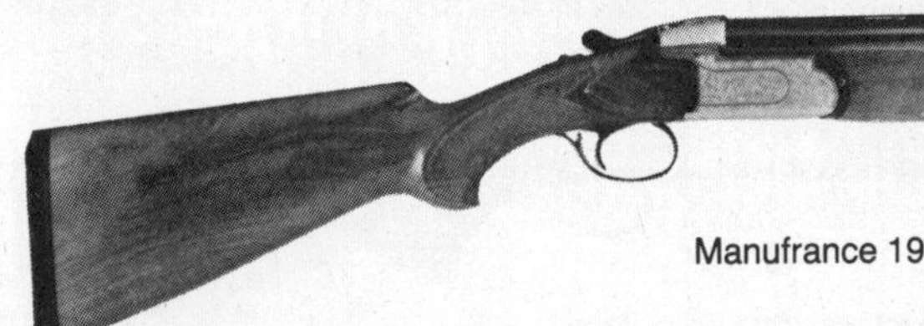

Manufrance 1977 Falcor

MANUFRANCE 1977 FALCOR PHEASANT GUN

Gauge: 12, 2¾″ chambers.
Barrel: 27½″ (Mod. & Full), chrome-lined bores.
Weight: About 7¼ lbs. **Length:** 44¼″ over-all.
Stock: Choice French walnut, hand checkered grip and fore-end.
Sights: Metal bead front.
Features: Boxlock action with single trigger, top tang safety/barrel selector, automatic ejectors. Silver-gray finish and scroll engraving on receiver, top lever, trigger guard. Imported from France by Armsource, Inc. Introduced 1984.
Price: **$940.00**

MAROCCHI CONTRAST TARGET SHOTGUN

Gauge: 12 or 20 ga., 2¾″ chambers.
Barrel: 26″ to 29″ (Skeet), 27″ to 32″ trap.
Weight: 7¼ to 8 lbs.
Stock: Select walnut with hand rubbed wax finish; hand checkered p.g. and fore-end; beavertail or Schnabel fore-end; grip has right or left palm swell.
Features: Lightly engraved frame on standard grade, or can be ordered with custom engraving and inlays in choice of three finishes. Optional different buttstock available. Gun comes with fitted hard shell case. Introduced 1983. Imported from Italy by Marocchi U.S.A.
Price: From **$2,000.00**

MAROCCHI AMERICA TARGET SHOTGUN

Gauge: 12 or 20, 2¾″ chambers.
Barrel: 26″ to 29″ (Skeet), 27″ to 32″ (trap), 32″ (trap mono, choice of top single or high rib under), 30″ (over-under with extra 32″ single).
Weight: 7¼ to 8 lbs.
Stock: Hand checkered select walnut with left or right-hand palm swell; choice of beavertail or Schnabel fore-end.
Features: Designed specifically for American target sports. Frame has medium engraving coverage with choice of three finishes. No extra charge for special stock dimensions or stock finish. Comes with fitted hard shell case. Custom engraving and inlays available. Introduced 1983. Imported from Italy by Marocchi U.S.A.
Price: From **$2,000.00**

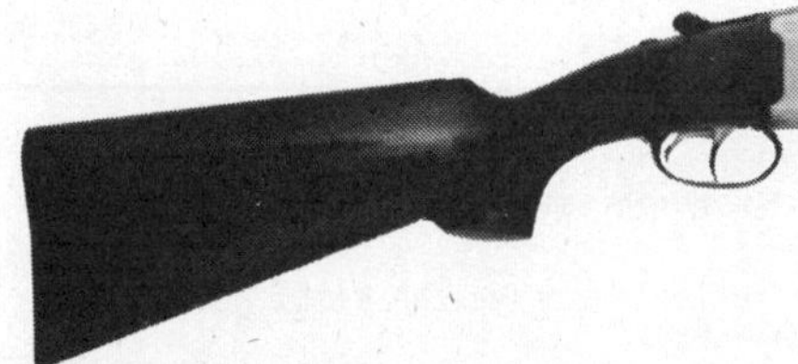

Navy Bird Hunter

MAROCCINI O/U SHOTGUN

Gauge: 12 or 20 ga., 3″.
Barrel: 28″ (Mod. & Full); vent. top and middle ribs.
Weight: 7¾ lbs.
Stock: Walnut, hand checkered.
Features: Auto. safety; extractors; double triggers; engraved antique silver receiver. Imported from Italy by F.I.E.
Price: **$399.95**

NAVY ARMS MODEL 83/93 BIRD HUNTER O-U

Gauge: 12, 20; 3″ chambers.
Barrel: 28″ (Imp. Cyl. & Mod., Mod. & Full).
Weight: About 7½ lbs.
Stock: European walnut, checkered grip and fore-end.
Sights: Metal bead front.
Features: Boxlock action with double triggers; extractors only; silvered, engraved receiver; vented top and middle ribs. Imported from Italy by Navy Arms. Introduced 1984.
Price: Model 83 (extractors) **$289.00**
Price: Model 93 (ejectors) **$349.00**

ROTTWEIL FIELD SUPREME O/U SHOTGUN

Gauge: 12 only.
Action: Boxlock.
Barrel: 28″ (Mod. & Full, Imp. Cyl. & Imp. Mod.), vent. rib.
Weight: 7¼ lbs. **Length:** 47″ over-all.
Stock: Select French walnut, hand checkered and rubbed. Checkered p.g. and fore-end, plastic buttplate. Unfinished stocks available.
Sights: Metal bead front.
Features: Removable single trigger assembly with button selector (same trigger options as on American Trap Combo); retracting spring mounted firing pins; engraved action. Extra barrels available. Imported from West Germany by Dynamit Nobel.
Price: **$2,295.00**
Price: Live Pigeon (28″ Mod. & Full) **$2,295.00**

ROTTWEIL OLYMPIA '72 SKEET SHOTGUN

Gauge: 12 ga. only.
Action: Boxlock.
Barrel: 27″ (special Skeet choke), vent. rib. Chromed lined bores, flared chokes.
Weight: 7¼ lbs. **Length:** 44½″ over-all.
Stock: French walnut, hand checkered, modified beavertail fore-end. Oil finish.
Sights: Metal bead front.
Features: Inertia-type trigger, interchangeable for any system. Frame and lock milled from steel block. Retracting firing pins are spring mounted. All coil springs. Selective single trigger. Action engraved. Extra barrels are available. Introduced 1976. Imported from West Germany by Dynamit Nobel.
Price: **$2,295.00**
Price: Trap model (Montreal) is similar to above except has 30″ (Imp. Mod. & Full) bbl., weighs 8 lbs., 48½″ over-all **$2,295.00**

Rottweil Field Supreme

ROTTWEIL 72 AMERICAN SKEET

Gauge: 12, 2¾″.
Barrel: 26¾″ (Skeet & Skeet).
Weight: About 7½ lbs.
Stock: 14½″ x 1⅜″ x 1⅜″ x ¼″. Select French walnut with satin oil finish; hand checkered grip and fore-end; double ventilated recoil pad.
Sights: Plastic front in metal sleeve, center bead.
Features: Interchangeable trigger groups with coil springs; interchangeable buttstocks; special .433″ ventilated rib; matte finish silvered receiver with light engraving. Introduced 1978. Imported from West Germany by Dynamit Nobel.
Price: **$2,295.00**

ROTTWEIL AAT TRAP GUN

Gauge: 12, 2¾″.
Barrel: 32″ (Imp. Mod. & Full).
Weight: About 8 lbs.
Stock: 14½″x1⅜″x1⅜″x1⅞″. Monte Carlo style of selected French walnut with oil finish. Checkered fore-end and p.g.
Features: Has infinitely variable point of impact via special muzzle collar. Extra single lower barrels available—32″ (Imp. Mod.) or 34″ (Full). Special trigger groups—release/release or release/pull—also available. Introduced 1979. From Dynamit Nobel.
Price: With single lower barrel **$2,295.00**
Price: Combo (single and o/u barrels) **$2,295.00**
Price: Interchangeable trap trigger group **$345.00**

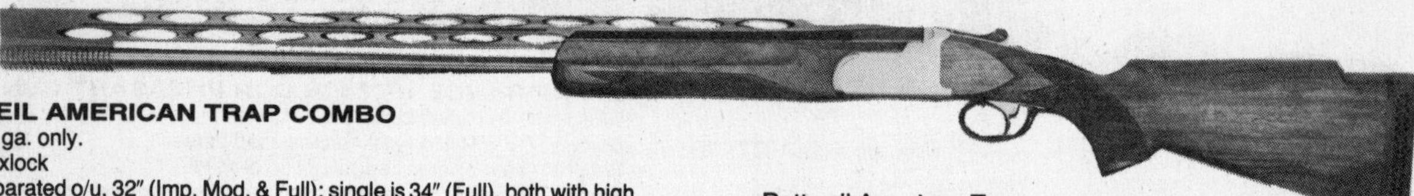

Rottweil American Trap

ROTTWEIL AMERICAN TRAP COMBO

Gauge: 12 ga. only.
Action: Boxlock
Barrel: Separated o/u, 32″ (Imp. Mod. & Full); single is 34″ (Full), both with high vent. rib.
Weight: 8½ lbs. (o/u and single)
Stock: Monte Carlo style, walnut, hand checkered and rubbed. Unfinished stocks available. Double vent. recoil pad. Choice of two dimensions.
Sights: Plastic front in metal sleeve, center bead.
Features: Interchangeable inertia-type trigger groups. Trigger groups available: single selective; double triggers;, release/pull; release/release selective. Receiver milled from block steel. Chokes are hand honed, test fired and reworked for flawless patterns. All coil springs, engraved action. Introduced 1977. Imported from West Germany by Dynamit Nobel.
Price: **$2,850.00**
Price: American Trap O/U (as above except only with o/u bbls.) ... **$2,295.00**

Royal Model 100

ROYAL ARMS MODEL 100 OVER-UNDER

Gauge: 12 or 20 ga., 2¾″ or 3″ chambers.
Action: Boxlock with Greener cross-bolt.
Barrel: 26″ (Imp. & Mod.), 28″, 30″ (Mod. & Full).
Weight: 7 lbs.
Stock: 14″ × 1⅜″ × 2¼″. European walnut, checkered grip and fore-end.
Features: Extractors only; vent. rib; automatic safety; double triggers; silver gray action with arabesque scroll etching. Imported by Royal Arms International. Introduced 1985.
Price: **$389.95**
Price: Model 100AE (3″, 12 ga. only, single trigger, selective auto ejectors) **$429.95**

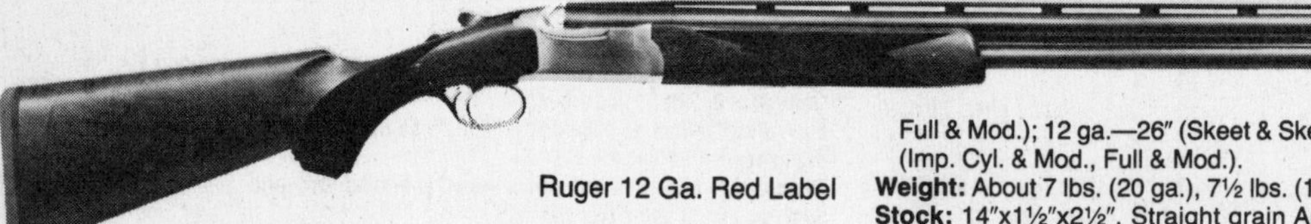

Ruger 12 Ga. Red Label

RUGER "RED LABEL" O/U SHOTGUN

Gauge: 20, 3″ chambers, 12, 2¾″ and 3″ chambers.
Barrel: 20 ga.—26″ (Skeet & Skeet, Imp. Cyl. & Mod.), 28″ (Imp. Cyl. & Mod., Full & Mod.); 12 ga.—26″ (Skeet & Skeet, Imp. Cyl. & Mod., Full & Mod.), 28″ (Imp. Cyl. & Mod., Full & Mod.).
Weight: About 7 lbs. (20 ga.), 7½ lbs. (12 ga.). **Length:** 43″ (26″ barrels).
Stock: 14″x1½″x2½″. Straight grain American walnut. Checkered p.g. and fore-end, rubber recoil pad.
Features: Automatic safety/barrel selector, stainless steel trigger. Patented barrel side spacers may be removed if desired. 20 ga. available in blued steel only, 12 ga. available only with stainless receiver. 20 ga. introduced 1977; 12 ga. introduced 1982.
Price: 20 ga., blued **$798.00**
Price: 12 ga., stainless receiver **$798.00**

CAUTION: PRICES CHANGE. CHECK AT GUNSHOP.

SILE SKY STALKER FOLDING SHOTGUN

Gauge: 410, 3" chambers.
Barrel: 26" (Full & Full or Mod. & Full), with vent. rib.
Weight: About 6 lbs.
Stock: Walnut with cut checkering and Schnabel fore-end.
Features: Gun folds in half for storage or carrying. Chrome lined bores; matte finished hard chrome finish on receiver. Introduced 1984. Imported by Sile.
Price: **$199.95**

TECHNI-MEC MODEL SPL 640 FOLDING O-U

Gauge: 12, 16, 20, 28, (2¾") 410 (3").
Barrel: 26" (Mod. & Full).
Weight: 5½ lbs.
Stock: European walnut.
Features: Gun folds in half for storage, transportation. Chrome lined barrels; ventilated rib; photo-engraved silvered receiver. Imported from Italy by L. Joseph Rahn. Introduced 1984.
Price: Double triggers **$240.00**
Price: Single trigger **$256.00**

TECHNI-MEC MODEL SR 692 EM OVER-UNDER

Gauge: 12, 16, 20, 2¾" or 3".
Barrel: 26", 28", 30" (Mod., Full, Imp. Cyl., Cyl.).
Weight: 6½ lbs.
Stock: 14½" x 1½" x 2½". European walnut with checkered grip and fore-end.
Features: Boxlock action with dummy sideplates, fine game scene engraving; single selective trigger; automatic ejectors available. Imported from Italy by L. Joseph Rahn. Introduced 1984.
Price: **$550.00**

VALMET MODEL 412S OVER-UNDER

Gauge: 12 or 20 ga. (2¾" or 3").
Barrel: 26" (Imp. Cyl. & Mod.), 28" (Mod. & Full), 30" (Mod. & Full); vent. rib.
Weight: About 7½ lbs.
Stock: American walnut. Standard dimensions-13⁹⁄₁₀"x1½"x2⅖". Checkered p.g. and fore-end.
Features: Model 412S is extractor (basic) model. Free interchangeability of barrels, stocks and fore-ends into double rifle model, combination gun, etc. Barrel selector in trigger; auto. top tang safety; barrel cocking indicators. Double triggers optional. Introduced 1980. Imported from Finland by Valmet.
Price: Model 412S (extractors), from **$799.00**
Price: Extra barrels from **$399.00**

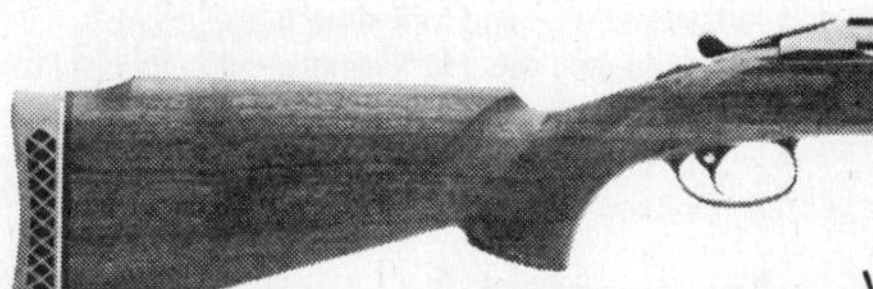

Valmet 412 ST

Valmet 412 ST Target Series

Both trap and Skeet versions of the 412S gun. Stocks are drilled for insertion of a recoil reducer; quick-change butt stocks; beavertail fore-end; Monte Carlo stock has wider comb and double palm swell; trap stock has Pachmayr pad; wide trigger; barrel indicators near the tang. Choice of low- or high-gloss wood finish. High vent rib, stepped and tapered on trap gun. Trap guns have choke tubes, 32", 34" barrel (mono), 30", 32" (o/u); weight 9 lbs. Skeet has 26", 28" barrels (12 and 20 ga.); weight 8 lbs. Introduced 1985.
Price: Trap **$899.00**
Price: Skeet **$849.00**

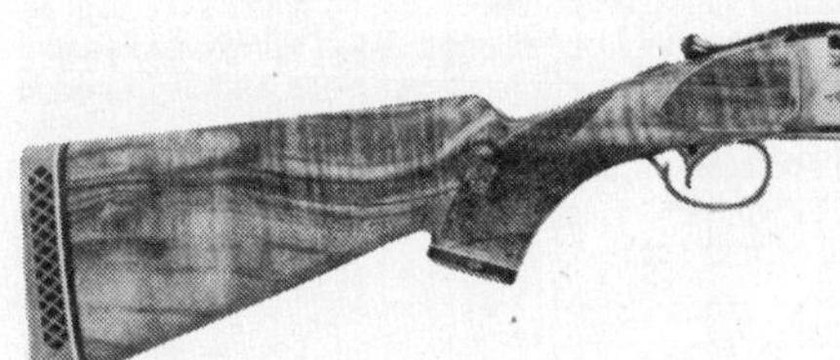

Weatherby Orion

WEATHERBY ORION O/U SHOTGUN

Gauge: 12 or 20 ga. (3" chambers; 2¾" on Trap gun).
Action: Boxlock (simulated side-lock).
Barrel: 12 ga. 30" (Full & Mod.), 28" (Full & Mod., Mod. & Imp. Cyl.), 26" (Mod. & Imp. Cyl., Skeet & Skeet); 20 ga. 28" (Full & Mod., Mod. & Imp. Cyl.), 26" (Mod. & Imp. Cyl., Skeet & Skeet).
Weight: 7 lbs., 8 oz. (12 ga. 26").
Stock: American walnut, checkered p.g. and fore-end. Rubber recoil pad. Dimensions for field and Skeet models, 20 ga. 14"x1½"x2½".
Features: Selective auto ejectors, single selective mechanical trigger. Top tang safety, Greener cross-bolt. Introduced 1982. Imported from Japan by Weatherby.
Price: 12 ga. Field, fixed choke **$799.00**
Price: Skeet, fixed choke **$839.00**
Price: 12 ga. Trap, fixed choke **$849.00**
Price: IMC Multi-Choke Field **$829.00**
Price: IMC Multi-Choke Trap **$879.00**
Price: Extra IMC choke tubes **$12.50**

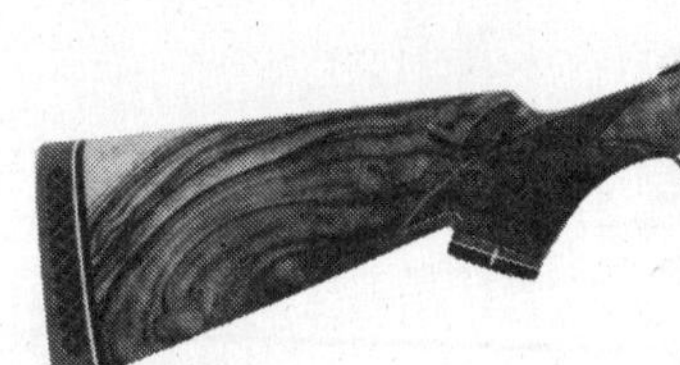

Weatherby Athena

WEATHERBY ATHENA O/U SHOTGUN

Gauge: 12 or 20 ga. (3" chambers; 2¾" on Trap gun).
Action: Boxlock (simulated side-lock) top lever break-open. Selective auto ejectors, single selective trigger (selector inside trigger guard).
Barrel: Fixed choke, 12 or 20 ga. — 26" (Mod. & Imp. Cyl., Skeet & Skeet), 28" (Mod. & Imp. Cyl., Full & Mod.), 30" (Full & Mod., Full & Imp. Mod.), 32" Trap (Full & Imp. Mod.). IMC Multi-Choke, 12 ga. only — 26" (Mod., Imp. Cyl., Skeet), 28" (Full, Mod., Imp. Cyl.), 30" (Full, Mod., Imp. Mod.).
Weight: 12 ga. 7⅜ lbs., 20 ga. 6⅞ lbs.
Stock: American walnut, checkered p.g. and fore-end (14¼"x1½"x2½").
Features: Mechanically operated trigger. Top tang safety, Greener cross-bolt, fully engraved receiver, recoil pad installed. IMC models furnished with three interchangeable flush-fitting choke tubes. Imported from Japan by Weatherby. Introduced 1982.
Price: 12 or 20 ga. Field, fixed choke **$1,229.95**
Price: Skeet **$1,239,00**
Price: 12 ga. Trap Model **$1,249.00**
Price: IMC Multi-Choke Field **$1,259.00**
Price: IMC Multi-Choke Trap **$1,279.00**
Price: Extra IMC Choke tubes **$12.50**

Consult our Directory pages for the location of firms mentioned.

Winchester 501 Grand European

WINCHESTER MODEL 501 GRAND EUROPEAN O-U
Gauge: 12 ga. (Trap), 12 and 20 ga. (Skeet). 2¾" chambers.
Barrel: 27" (Skeet & Skeet), 30" (Imp. Mod. & Full), 32" (Imp. Mod. & Full).
Weight: 7½ lbs. (Skeet), 8½ lbs. (Trap) **Length:** 47⅛" over-all (30" barrel).
Stock: 14⅛"x1½"x2½" (Skeet). Full fancy walnut, hand-rubbed oil finish.
Features: Silvered, engraved receiver; engine-turned breech interior. Slide-button selector/safety, selective auto. ejectors. Chrome bores, tapered vent. rib. Trap gun has Monte Carlo or regular stock, recoil pad; Skeet gun has rosewood buttplate. Introduced 1981. Manufactured in and imported from Japan by Winchester Group, Olin Corp.
Price: Trap or Skeet **$2,060.00**
Price: Grand European Featherweight 20 ga., 25½" (Imp. Cyl. & Mod.) **$2,060.00**

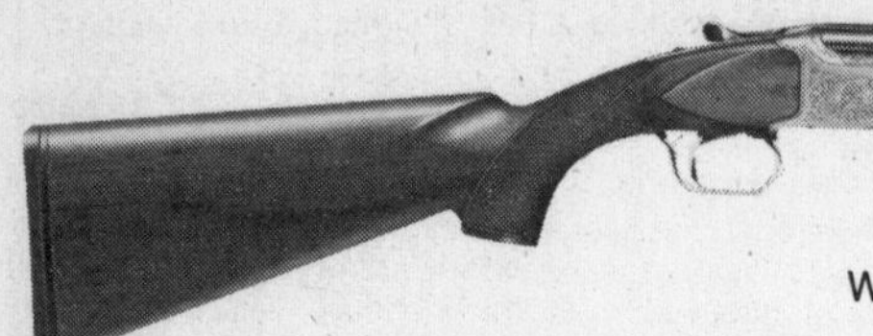

Winchester 101 Field

Winchester Model 101 Waterfowl Winchoke
Same as Model 101 Field Grade except in 12 ga. only, 3" chambers, 30" or 32" barrels. Comes with four Winchoke tubes: Mod., Imp. Mod., Full, Extra-Full. Blued receiver with hand etching and engraving. Introduced 1981. Manufactured in and imported from Japan by Winchester Group, Olin Corp.
Price: **$1,355.00**

WINCHESTER 101 WINCHOKE O/U FIELD GUN
Gauge: 12, or 20, 3" chambers.
Action: Top lever, break open. Manual safety combined with bbl. selector at top of receiver tang.
Barrel: 27", Winchoke interchangeable choke tubes.
Weight: 12 ga. 7 lbs. Others 6½ lbs. **Length:** 44¾" over-all.
Stock: 14"x1½"x2½". Checkered walnut p.g. and fore-end; fluted comb.
Features: Single selective trigger, auto ejectors. Hand engraved satin gray receiver. Comes with hard gun case. Manufactured in and imported from Japan by Winchester Group, Olin Corp.
Price: **$1,355.00**

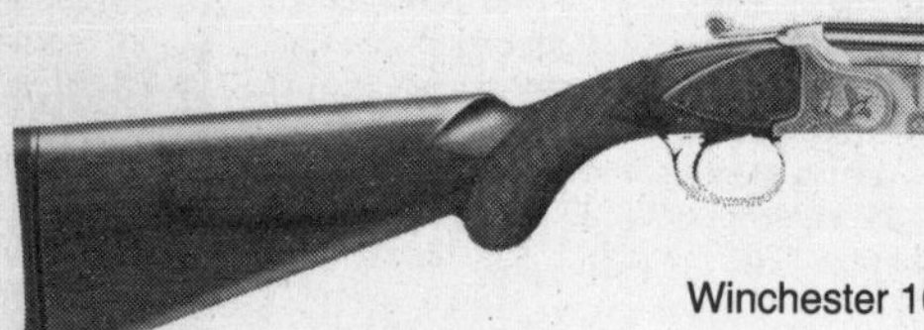

Winchester 101 Pigeon Grade

Winchester Model 101 Pigeon Grade
Similar to the Model 101 Field except comes in three styles: Lightweight (12 or 28 ga., Mod. & Full, Mod. & Imp. Cyl., 28"), Lightweight-Winchoke (12 or 20 ga., six choke tubes for 12 ga., four for 20, 28 ga., 27", 28"), Featherweight (12 or 20 ga., Imp. Cyl. & Mod., 25½"), all with 3" chambers. Vent. rib barrel with middle bead, fancy American walnut. Featherweight has English-style stock. Hard case included. Introduced 1983. Manufactured in and imported from Japan by Winchester Group, Olin Corp.
Price: Lightweight and Featherweight **$1,610.00**
Price: Lightweight-Winchoke **$1,705.00**

Winchester 101 Diamond Grade Target Guns
Similar to the Model 101 except designed for trap and Skeet competition, with tapered and elevated rib, anatomically contoured trigger and internationally-dimensioned stock. Receiver has deep-etched diamond-pattern engraving. Skeet guns available in 12, 20, 28 and 410 with ventilated muzzles to reduce recoil. Trap guns in 12 ga. only; over-under, combination and single-barrel configurations in a variety of barrel lengths with Winchoke system. Straight or Monte Carlo stocks available. Introduced 1982. Manufactured in and imported from Japan by Winchester Group, Olin Corp.
Price: Trap, o/u, standard and Monte Carlo, 30", 32" **$1,730.00**
Price: Trap, single barrel, 32" or 34" **$1,840.00**
Price: Trap, o/u-single bbl. combo sets **$2,800.00**
Price: Skeet, 12 and 20 .... **$1,730.00**
Price: Skeet, 28 and 410 .... **$1,730.00**
Price: Four barrel Skeet set (12, 20, 28, 410) **$4,450.00**

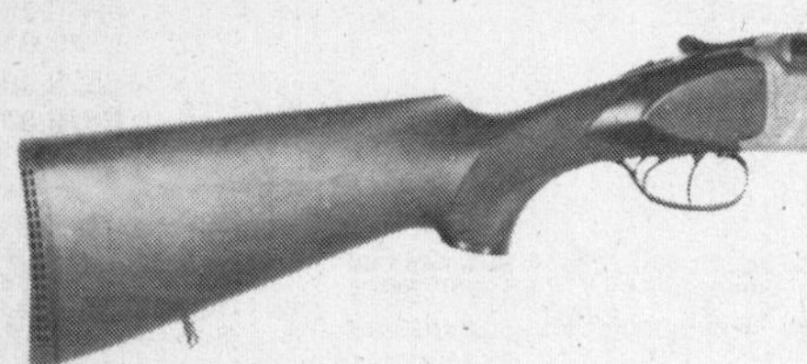

Zanoletti 2000 Field

PIETRO ZANOLETTI MODEL 2000 FIELD O-U
Gauge: 12 only.
Barrel: 28" (Mod. & Full).
Weight: 7 lbs.
Stock: European walnut, checkered grip and fore-end.
Sights: Gold bead front.
Features: Boxlock action with auto ejectors, double triggers; engraved receiver. Imported from Italy by Mandall Shooting Supplies. Introduced 1984.
Price: **$695.00**

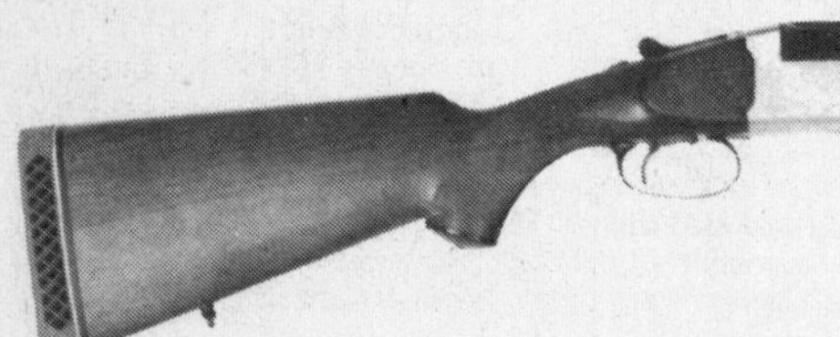

Zoli Angel

A. ZOLI MODEL ANGEL FIELD GRADE O-U
Gauge: 12, 20.
Barrel: 26", 28", 30" (Mod. & Full).
Weight: About 7½ lbs.
Stock: Straight grained walnut with checkered grip and fore-end.
Sights: Gold bead front.
Features: Boxlock action with single selective trigger, auto ejectors; extra-wide vent. top rib. Imported from Italy by Mandall Shooting Supplies.
Price: **$895.00**
Price: Condor model **$895.00**

CAUTION: PRICES CHANGE. CHECK AT GUNSHOP.

Zoli Silver Snipe

ZOLI SILVER SNIPE O/U SHOTGUN

Gauge: 12, 20 (3″ chambers).
Action: Purdey-type double boxlock, crossbolt.
Barrel: 26″ (Imp. Cyl. & Mod.), 28″ (Mod. & Full), 30″, 12 only (Mod. & Full); 26″ Skeet (Skeet & Skeet), 30″ Trap (Full & Full).
Weight: 6½ lbs. (12 ga.).
Stock: Hand checkered p.g. and fore-end, European walnut.
Features: Auto. safety (exc. Trap and Skeet), vent rib, single trigger, chrome bores. Imported from Italy by Mandall Shooting Supplies.
Price: Field $795.00

Zoli Golden Snipe O/U Shotgun

Same as Silver Snipe except selective auto. ejectors.
Price: Field $895.00

A. ZOLI DELFINO S.P. O/U

Gauge: 12 or 20 (3″ chambers).
Barrel: 28″ (Mod. & Full); vent. rib.
Weight: 5½ lbs.
Stock: Walnut. Hand checkered p.g. and fore-end; cheekpiece.
Features: Color case hardened receiver with light engraving; chrome lined barrels; automatic sliding safety; double triggers; ejectors. From Mandall Shooting Supplies.
Price: $795.00

SHOTGUNS—SIDE-BY-SIDES

AyA XXV SL

AYA MODEL XXV BL, SL DOUBLE

Gauge: 12, 20, 28, 410.
Barrel: 25″, chokes as specified.
Weight: 5 lbs., 2 oz. to 6 lbs., 8 oz.
Stock: 14½″x2¼″x1½″. European walnut. Straight grip stock with classic pistol grip, checkered butt.
Features: Boxlock (Model BL), sidelock (Model SL). Churchill rib, auto ejectors, double triggers (single available), color case-hardened action (coin-finish available). Imported from Spain by Precision Sports, Inc.
Price: BL, 12 ga. $1,995.00
Price: BL, 20 ga. $1,995.00
Price: SL, 12 ga. $3,350.00
Price: SL, 20 ga. $3,350.00
Price: SL, 28 or 410 .... $3,450.00

AYA MODEL 117 DOUBLE BARREL SHOTGUN

Gauge: 12 (2¾″), 20 (3″).
Action: Holland & Holland sidelock, Purdey treble bolting.
Barrel: 26″ (Imp. Cyl. & Mod.) 28″ (Mod. & Full).
Stock: 14½″x2⅜″x1½″. Select European walnut, hand checkered p.g. and beavertail fore-end.
Features: Single selective trigger, automatic ejectors, cocking indicators; concave barrel rib; hand-detachable lockplates; hand engraved action. Imported from Spain by Precision Sports, Inc.
Price: $1,675.00

ARMSPORT WESTERN DOUBLE

Gauge: 12 only (3″ chambers).
Barrel: 20″.
Weight: 6½ lbs.
Stock: European walnut, checkered p.g. and beavertail fore-end.
Sights: Metal front bead on matted solid rib.
Features: Exposed hammers. Imported by Armsport.
Price: $375.00

ARMSPORT GOOSEGUN SIDE-BY-SIDE

Gauge: 10 ga. (3½″ chambers).
Barrel: 32″ (Full & Full). Solid matted rib.
Weight: 11 lbs.
Stock: European walnut, checkered p.g. and fore-end.
Features: Double triggers, vent. rubber recoil pad with white spacer. Imported by Armsport.
Price: $450.00

AyA Model No. 2

AYA No. 2 SIDE-BY-SIDE

Gauge: 12, 16, 20, 28, 410.
Barrel: 26″, 27″, 28″, choked to customer specs.
Weight: 5 lbs. 2 oz. to 7½ lbs.
Stock: 14½″x2¼″x1½″. European walnut. Straight grip stock, checkered butt, classic fore-end. Can be made to custom dimensions.
Features: Sidelock action with auto. ejectors, double triggers standard, single trigger optional. Hand-detachable locks. Color case-hardened action. Imported from Spain by Precision Sports, Inc.
Price: 12, 16, 20 ga. $2,235.00
Price: 28 ga. $2,300.00
Price: 410 ga. $2,300.00

AYA No. 1 Side-by-Side

Similar to the No. 2 except barrel lengths to customer specifications. Barrels are of chrome-nickel steel. Imported from Spain by Precision Sports, Inc.
Price: 12, 16, 20 ga., from $5,500.00
Price: 28 ga., from $6,000.00
Price: 410 ga., from $6,000.00

AYA Model 56 Side-By-Side

Similar to the No. 1 except in 12, 16 or 20 ga. only, third fastener and side-clips; heavier weight in 12-ga.; available with raised, level or vent rib. Does not have hand-detachable locks. Imported from Spain by Precision Sports, Inc.
Price: $5,750.00

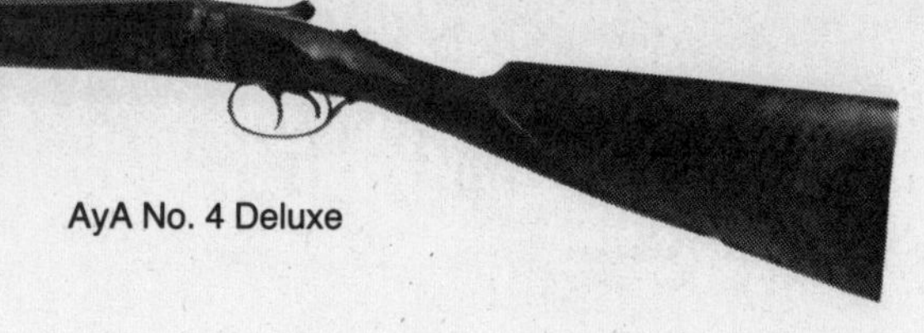
AyA No. 4 Deluxe

AYA No. 4 DELUXE SIDE-BY-SIDE

Gauge: 12, 20, 28 & 410.
Barrel: 26", 27", 28" (Imp. Cyl. & Mod. or Mod. & Full).
Weight: 5 lbs. 2 oz. to 6½ lbs.
Stock: 14½"x2¼"x1½". European walnut. Straight grip with checkered butt, classic fore-end.
Features: Boxlock action, color case-hardened, automatic ejectors, double triggers (single trigger available). Imported from Spain by Precision Sports, Inc.
Price: 12, 16 ga. **$2,250.00**
Price: 20 ga. **$2,250.00**
Price: 28, 410 ga. **$2,325.00**

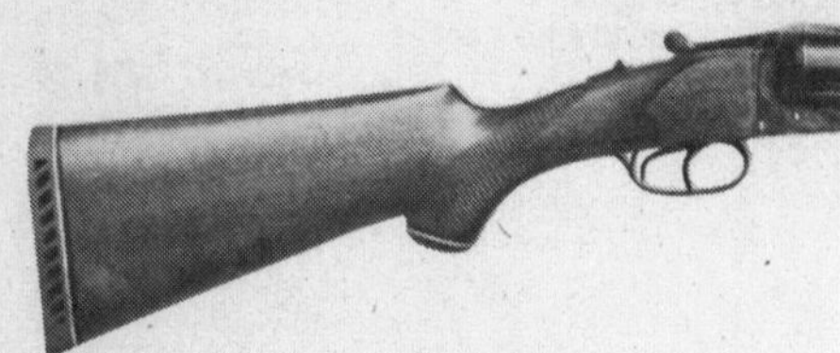
BGJ 10 Gauge

BGJ 10 GAUGE MAGNUM SHOTGUN

Gauge: 10 ga. (3½" chambers).
Action: Boxlock.
Barrel: 32" (Full).
Weight: 11 lbs.
Stock: 14½"x1½"x2⅝". European walnut, checkered at p.g. and fore-end.
Features: Double triggers; color hardened action, rest blued. Front and center metal beads on matted rib; ventilated rubber recoil pad. Fore-end release has positive Purdey-type mechanism. Imported from Spain by Mandall Shooting Supplies.
Price: **$500.00**

BERNARDELLI SERIES S. UBERTO DOUBLES

Gauge: 12, 16, 20, 28; 2½", 2¾", or 3" chambers.
Barrel: 25⅝", 26¾", 28", 29⅛" (Mod. & Full).
Weight: 6 to 6½ lbs.
Stock: 14⅛" x 2⅝" x 1⁹⁄₁₆" standard dimensions. Select walnut with hand checkering.
Features: Anson & Deeley boxlock action with Purdey locks, choice of extractors or ejectors. Uberto 1 has color case hardened receiver, Uberto 2 and F.S. silvered and differ in amount and quality of engraving. Custom options available. Imported from Italy by Armes De Chasse and Quality Arms.
Price: S. Uberto 1 .... **$860.00**
Price: As above with ejectors **$970.00**
Price: S. Uberto 2 .... **$901.00**
Price: As above with ejectors **$1,010.00**
Price: S. Uberto F.S. **$1,054.00**
Price: As above with ejectors **$1,164.00**

Bernardelli Series Roma Shotguns

Similar to the Series S. Uberto models except with dummy sideplates to simulate sidelock action. Same gauges and specifications apply.
Price: Roma 3 .... **$944.00**
Price: As above with ejectors **$1,054.00**
Price: Roma 4 .... **$1,079.00**
Price: As above with ejectors **$1,188.00**
Price: Roma 6 .... **$1,316.00**
Price: As above with ejectors **$1,426.00**

Bernardelli System Holland H. Side-by-Side

Similar to the Las Palomas model with true sidelock action. Available in 12 gauge only, reinforced breech, three round Purdey locks, automatic ejectors, folding right trigger. Model VB Liscio has color case hardened receiver and sideplates with light engraving, VB and VB Tipo Lusso are silvered and engraved.
Price: VB Liscio **$4,743.00**
Price: VB **$5,496.00**
Price: VB Tipo Lusso **$6,432.00**

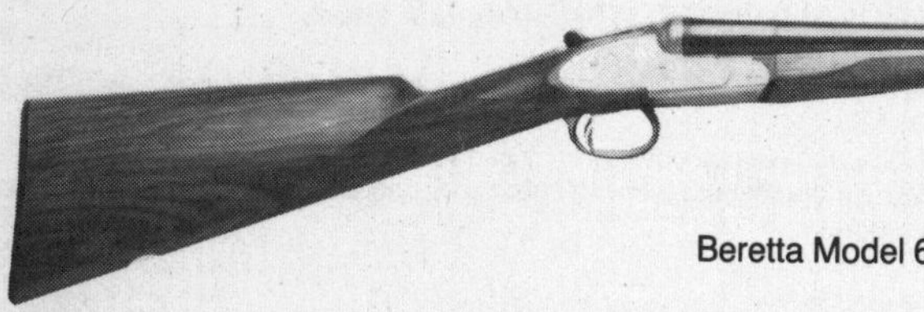
Beretta Model 627 EL

BERETTA 625 SERIES SIDE-BY-SIDES

Gauge: 12 (2¾"), 20 (3").
Action: Beretta patent boxlock; double underlugs and bolts.
Barrel: 12 ga.—26" (Imp. Cyl. & Mod.), 28" (Mod. & Full); 20 ga.—26" (Imp. Cyl. & Mod.), 28" (Mod. & Full).
Weight: 6 lbs. 10 oz. (12 ga.).
Stock: 14⅛"x1⁹⁄₁₆"x2⁹⁄₁₆". "English" straight-type or pistol grip, hand checkered European walnut.
Features: Coil springs throughout action; double triggers (front is hinged); automatic safety; extractors. Concave matted barrel rib. Introduced 1985. Imported by Beretta U.S.A. Corp.
Price: M625, 12 or 20 ga. **$925.00**
Price: M626, 12 or 20 ga. **$1,175.00**
Price: M627, from **$2,100.00**

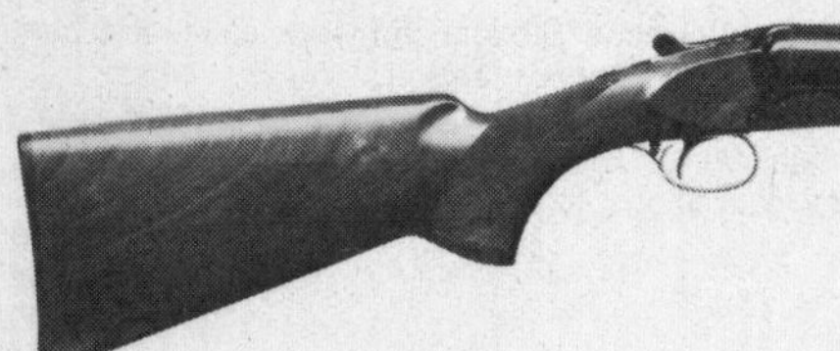
Browning B-SS

BROWNING B-SS

Gauge: 12, 20 (3").
Action: Top lever break-open action, top tang safety, single trigger.
Barrel: 26" (Mod. and Full or Imp. Cyl. and Mod.), 28" (Mod. and Full), 30" (Full & Full or Mod. & Full).
Weight: 6¾ lbs. (26" bbl., 20 ga.); 7½ lbs. (30" bbl., 12 ga.).
Stock: 14¼"x1⅝"x2½". French walnut, hand checkered. Full p.g., full beavertail fore-end.
Features: Automatic safety, automatic ejectors. Hand engraved receiver, mechanical single selective trigger with barrel selector in rear of trigger guard. Imported from Japan by Browning.
Price: Grade I, 12 or 20 ga. **$775.00**

CAUTION: PRICES CHANGE. CHECK AT GUNSHOP.

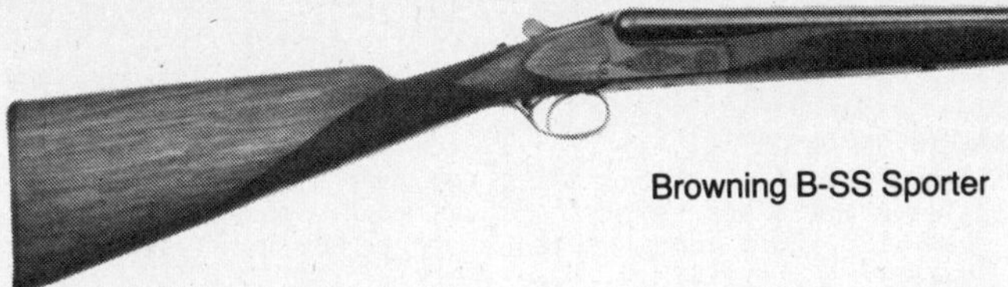

Browning B-SS Sporter

Browning B-SS Sidelock
Similar to the B-SS Sporter except gun is a true sidelock. Receiver, fore-end iron, trigger guard, top lever, and tang are all satin grey with rosettes and scroll work. Straight grip stock with checkered butt of French walnut. Double triggers, automatic safety and cocking indicator. Introduced 1984.
Price: 12 or 20 gauge **$1,500.00**

Browning B-SS Sporter
Similar to standard B-SS except has straight-grip stock and full beavertail fore-end with traditional oil finish. Introduced 1977.
Price: Grade I, 12 or 20 ga. **$775.00**

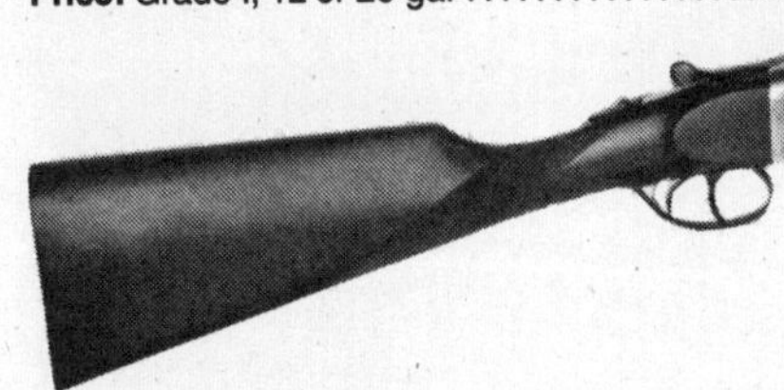

Churchill Windsor I

CHURCHILL WINDSOR SIDE-BY-SIDE SHOTGUNS
Gauge: 10 (3½"), 12, 16, 20, 28, 410 (2¾" 16 ga., 3" others).
Barrel: 24" (Mod. & Full), 410 and 20 ga.; 26" (Imp. Cyl. & Mod., Mod. & Full); 28" (Mod. & Full, Skeet & Skeet — 28 ga.); 30" (Full & Full, Mod. & Full); 32" (Full & Full — 10 ga.).
Weight: About 7½ lbs. (12 ga.).
Stock: Hand checkered European walnut with rubber butt pad.
Features: Anson & Deeley boxlock action with silvered and engraved finish; automatic top tang safety; double triggers; beavertail fore-end. Windsor I with extractors only; Windsor II has selective automatic ejectors. Also available in Flyweight versions, 23", 25", fixed or ICT chokes, straight stock. ICT choke tubes also available on Windsor. Imported from Spain by Kassnar. Introduced 1984.
Price: Windor I, 10 ga. **$569.00**
Price: Windsor I, 12 through 410 ga. .... **$434.00** to **$449.00**
Price: Windsor II, 12 or 20 ga. only **$569.00**
Price: Windsor II, ICT **$698.00**

Churchill Regent

Churchill Regent Side-by-Side Shotguns
Similar to the Windsor Grade except fancy walnut, better checkering and engraving; tapered Churchill rib; 25" (Imp. Cyl. & Mod.) or 28" (Mod. & Full) barrels only; 12 or 20 ga., 2¾" only. Regent IV is boxlock; Regent VI is full sidelock, both with double triggers, automatic selective ejectors, straight English-style stock and splinter fore-end. Introduced 1984.
Price: Regent IV **$653.00**
Price: Regent IV, ICT choke tubes **$773.00**
Price: Regent VI **$938.00**
Price: Regent VI, ICT **$1,109.00**

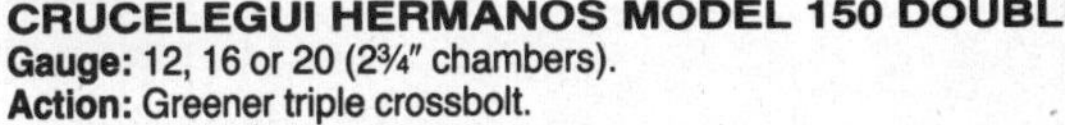

Hermanos Model 150

CRUCELEGUI HERMANOS MODEL 150 DOUBLE
Gauge: 12, 16 or 20 (2¾" chambers).
Action: Greener triple crossbolt.
Barrel: 20", 26", 28", 30", 32" (Cyl. & Cyl., Full & Full, Mod. & Full, Mod. & Imp. Cyl., Imp. Cyl. & Full, Mod. & Mod.).
Weight: 5 to 7¼ lbs.
Stock: Hand checkered walnut, beavertail fore-end.
Features: Exposed hammers; double triggers; color case hardened receiver; sling swivels; chrome lined bores. Imported from Spain by Mandall Shooting Supplies.
Price: **$399.95**
Price: Model 225 (hammerless version) **$399.95**

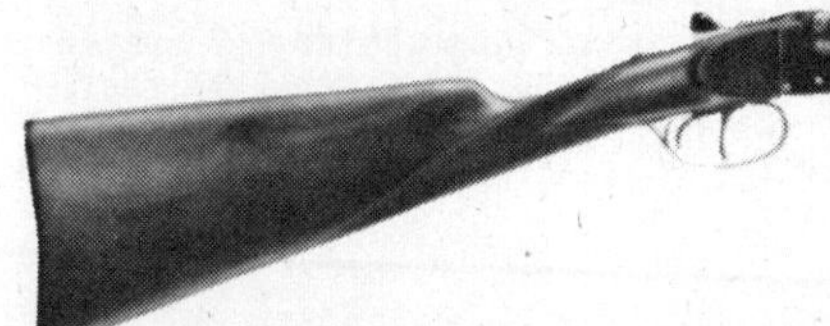

Exel Series 200

EXEL MODELS 201, 202, 203 DOUBLES
Gauge: 12, 2¾" chambers (M201, 202); 20, 3" chambers (M203).
Barrel: Model 201 — 28" (Full & Mod.); Model 202 — 26" (Imp. Cyl. & Mod.); Model 203 — 27" (Full & Mod.).
Weight: 6½-7 lbs.
Stock: 14⅜" x 1½" x 2½". Walnut, straight or full pistol grip.
Sights: Metal bead front.
Features: Boxlock action with color case hardened finish; double triggers; extractors only; high matted rib; hand checkered stock and fore-end. Made in Spain by Ugartechea; imported by Exel Arms of America.
Price: **$428.91**

Exel Models 207, 208, 209, 210 Doubles
Similar to the Models 201, 202, 203 except full sidelock action. Models 207, 208, 209 in 12 ga., 2¾" chambers; 28" (Mod. & Full) for 207 and 208, 26" (Imp. Cyl. & Mod.) for 209, 20 ga., 3", 27" (Mod. & Full) for 210. Selective ejectors, trigger, stock and frame finish to customer specs.
Price: Model 207 .... **$611.83**
Price: Model 208, 209, 210 .... **$671.52**
Price: Models 211, 212, 213 (similar to above but with better wood, engraving) **$3,100.00**
Price: Model 281, 281A (28 ga., 26" Mod. & Full) **$471.79**
Price: Model 240, 240A (410, 26" Full & Mod., Imp. Cyl. & Mod.) **$471.79**

Exel Models 204, 205, 206 Doubles
Similar to Models 201, 202, 203 except with silvered and engraved receiver, automatic selective ejectors, single or double triggers. Others specs are the same.
Price: **$626.76**

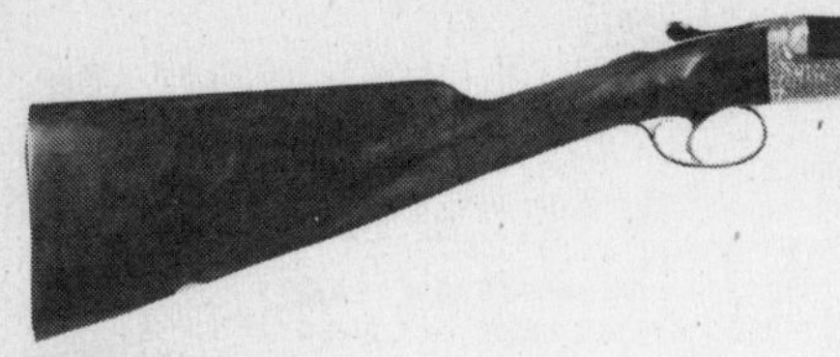

Ferlib Model FVII

FERLIB MODEL F VII DOUBLE SHOTGUN

Gauge: 12, 20, 28, 410.
Barrel: 25" to 28".
Weight: 5½ lbs. (20 ga.).
Stock: Oil-finished walnut, checkered straight grip and fore-end.
Features: Boxlock action with fine scroll engraved, silvered receiver. Double triggers standard. Introduced 1983. Imported from Italy by Wm. Larkin Moore.
Price: 12 or 20 ga. **$3,200.00**
Price: 28 or 410 ga. **$3,550.00**
Price: Extra for single trigger, beavertail fore-end **$250.00**

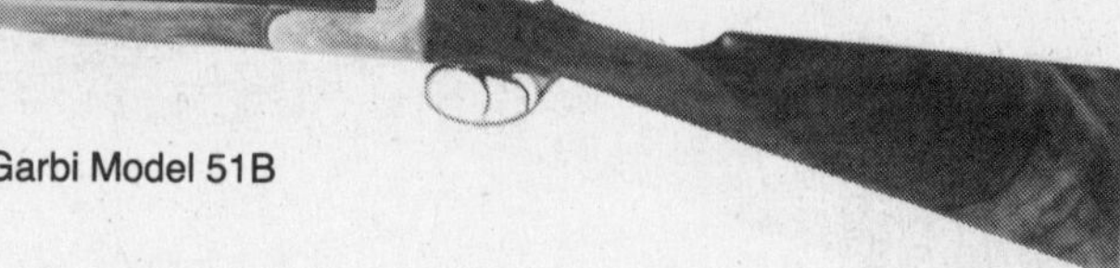

Garbi Model 51B

GARBI MODEL 51 SIDE-BY-SIDE

Gauge: 12, 16, 20 (2¾" chambers).
Barrel: 28" (Mod. & Full).
Weight: 5½ to 6½ lbs.
Stock: Walnut, to customer specs.
Features: Boxlock action; hand-engraved receiver; hand-checkered stock and fore-end; double triggers; extractors. Introduced 1980. Imported from Spain by L. Joseph Rahn, Inc.
Price: Model 51A, 12 ga., extractors **$515.00**
Price: Model 51B, 12, 16, 20 ga., ejectors....................... **$890.00**

Garbi Model 60

GARBI MODEL 60 SIDE-BY-SIDE

Gauge: 12, 16, 20 (2¾" chambers).
Barrel: 26", 28", 30"; choked to customers specs.
Weight: 5½ to 6½ lbs.
Stock: Select walnut. Dimensions to customer specs.
Features: Sidelock action. Scroll engraving on receiver. Hand checkered stock. Double triggers. Extractors. Imported from Spain by L. Joseph Rahn, Inc.
Price: Model 60A, 12 ga. only **$830.00**
Price: With demi-bloc barrels and ejectors, 12, 16, 20 ga. **$1,139.00**

Garbi Model 62

Similar to Model 60 except choked Mod. & Full, plain receiver with engraved border, demi-bloc barrels, gas exhaust valves, jointed triggers, extractors. Imported from Spain by L. Joseph Rahn.
Price: Model 62A, 12 ga., only.................................. **$830.00**
Price: Model 62B, 12, 16, 20 ga., ejectors **$1,115.00**

Garbi Model 71

GARBI MODEL 71 DOUBLE

Gauge: 12, 16, 20.
Barrel: 26", 28", choked to customer specs.
Weight: 5 lbs., 15 oz. (20 ga.).
Stock: 14½x2¼"x1½". European walnut. Straight grip, checkered butt, classic fore-end.
Features: Sidelock action, automatic ejectors, double triggers standard. Color case-hardened action, coin finish optional. Five other models are available. Imported from Spain by L. Joseph Rahn.
Price: Model 71, from.. **$1,528.00**

GARBI MODEL 100 DOUBLE

Gauge: 12, 16, 20.
Barrel: 26", 28", choked to customer specs.
Weight: 5½ to 7½ lbs.
Stock: 14½x2¼"x1½". European walnut. Straight grip, checkered butt, classic fore-end.
Features: Sidelock action, automatic ejectors, double triggers standard. Color case-hardened action, coin finish optional. Single trigger; beavertail fore-end, etc. optional. Five other models are available. Imported from Spain by Wm. Larkin Moore.
Price: From **$1,750.00**

Garbi Model 103A, B Side-by-Side

Similar to the Garbi Model 100 except has Purdey-type fine scroll and rosette engraving. Better over-all quality than the Model 101. Model 103B has nickel-chrome steel barrels, H&H-type easy opening mechanism; other mechanical details remain the same. Imported from Spain by Wm. Larkin Moore.
Price: Model 103A **$2,500.00**
Price: Model 103B **$3,250.00**

Garbi Model 200

Garbi Model 200 Side-by-Side

Similar to the Garbi Model 100 except has barrels of nickel-chrome steel, heavy duty locks, magnum proofed. Very fine continental-style floral and scroll engraving, well figured walnut stock. Other mechanical features remain the same. Imported from Spain by Wm. Larkin Moore.
Price: **$3,600.00**

Garbi Model Special Side-by-Side

Similar to the Garbi Model 100 except has best quality wood and metal work. Special game scene engraving with or without gold inlays, fancy figured walnut stock. Imported from Spain by Wm. Larkin Moore.
Price: From **$3,500.00**

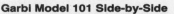

Garbi Model 101 Side-by-Side

Similar to the Garbi Model 100 except is available with optional level, file-cut, Churchill or ventilated top rib, and in a 12-ga. pigeon or wildfowl gun. Has Continental-style floral and scroll engraving, select walnut stock. Better over-all quality than the Model 100. Imported from Spain by Wm. Larkin Moore.
Price: **$2,500.00**

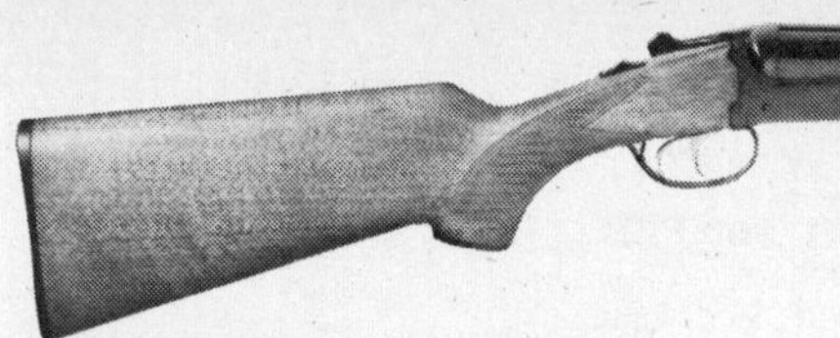

IGA Side-by-Side

GARBI MODEL 102 SHOTGUN

Gauge: 12, 16, 20.
Barrel: 12 ga.-25″ to 30″; 16 & 20 ga.-25″ to 28″. Chokes as specified.
Weight: 20 ga.-5 lbs., 15 oz. to 6 lbs., 4 oz.
Stock: 14½″x2¼x1½″; select walnut.
Features: Holland pattern sidelock ejector with chopper lump barrels, Holland-type large scroll engraving. Double triggers (hinged front) std., non-selective single trigger available. Many options available. Imported from Spain by Wm. Larkin Moore.
Price: From **$2,500.00**

IGA SIDE-BY-SIDE SHOTGUN

Gauge: 12, 20, 28 (2¾″), 410 (3″).
Barrel: 26″ (Full & Full, 410 only, Imp. Cyl. & Mod.), 28″ (Mod. & Full).
Weight: 6¾ to 7 lbs.
Stock: 14½″ x 1½″ x 2½″. Oil-finished hardwood. Checkered pistol grip and fore-end.
Features: Automatic safety, extractors only, solid matted barrel rib. Double triggers only. Introduced 1983. Imported from Brazil by Stoeger Industries.
Price: **$325.00**
Price: Coach Gun, 12 or 20 ga., 20″ bbls. **$283.95**

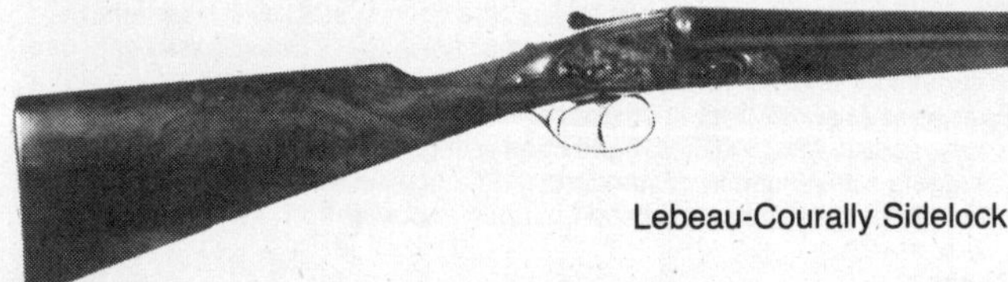

Lebeau-Courally Sidelock

LEBEAU-COURALLY BOXLOCK SHOTGUN

Gauge: 12, 16, 20, 28.
Barrel: 26″ to 30″, choked to customer specs.
Weight: 6 lbs., 6 oz. to 8 lbs., 4 oz. (12 ga.).
Stock: Dimensions to customer specs. Select French walnut with hand rubbed oil finish, straight grip (p.g. optional), splinter fore-end (beavertail optional).
Features: Anson & Deeley boxlock with ejectors, Purdey-type fastener; choice of rounded action, with or without sideplates; choice of level rib, file cut or smooth; choice of numerous engraving patterns. Imported from Belgium by Wm. Larkin Moore.
Price: **$6,900.00**
Price: With sideplates **$7,500.00**

LEBEAU-COURALLY SIDELOCK SHOTGUN

Gauge: 12, 16, 20 (standard), 28 (optional).
Barrel: 26″ to 30″, choked to customer specs.
Weight: 6 lbs., 6 oz. to 8 lbs., 4 oz. (12 ga.)
Stock: Dimensions to customer specs. Best quality French walnut with hand rubbed oil finish, straight grip stock and checkered butt (std.), classic splinter fore-end.
Features: Holland & Holland pattern sidelock ejector double with chopper lump barrels; choice of classic or rounded action; concave or level rib, file cut or smooth; choice of numerous engraving patterns. Can be furnished with H&H type self-opening mechanism. Imported from Belgium by Wm. Larkin Moore.
Price: From **$15,000.00**

Manufrance 264 Robust Elite Double

Same as the Robust Deluxe except has single trigger and flat rather than concave rib. Introduced 1985.
Price: **$1,250.00**

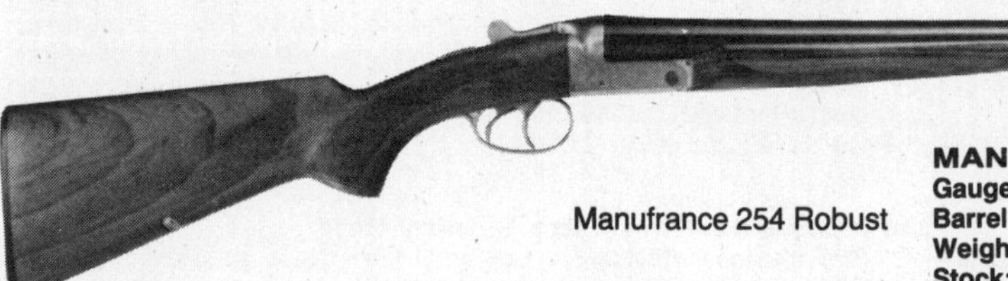

Manufrance 254 Robust

Manufrance 222 Robust Field Side-by-Side

Same as the Robust Deluxe model except has plain color case-hardened receiver. Available with 27½″ (Mod. & Full) or 20½″ (Imp. Cyl. & Imp. Cyl.), extractors only. Introduced 1984.
Price: **$620.00**

MANUFRANCE 254 ROBUST DELUXE DOUBLE

Gauge: 12, 2¾″ chambers.
Barrel: 27½″ (Mod. & Full), chrome-lined bores.
Weight: About 6½ lbs. **Length:** 44¼″ over-all.
Stock: Choice, dense French walnut with 21 lpi checkering; beavertail fore-end.
Features: Boxlock action with double triggers, automatic ejectors, top tang safety. Silver-gray finish and fine scroll engraving on receiver, top lever and trigger guard. Retractable sling in butt optional. Imported from France by Armsource, Inc. Introduced 1984.
Price: **$870.00**

Mercury Magnum

MERCURY MAGNUM DOUBLE BARREL SHOTGUN

Gauge: 10 (3½″).
Action: Triple-lock Anson & Deeley type.
Barrel: 32″ (Full & Full).
Weight: 10⅛ lbs.
Stock: 14″x1⅝″x2¼″ walnut, checkered p.g. stock and beavertail fore-end, recoil pad.
Features: Double triggers, front hinged, auto safety, extractors; safety gas ports, engraved frame. Imported from Spain by Tradewinds.
Price: (10 ga.) **$480.00**

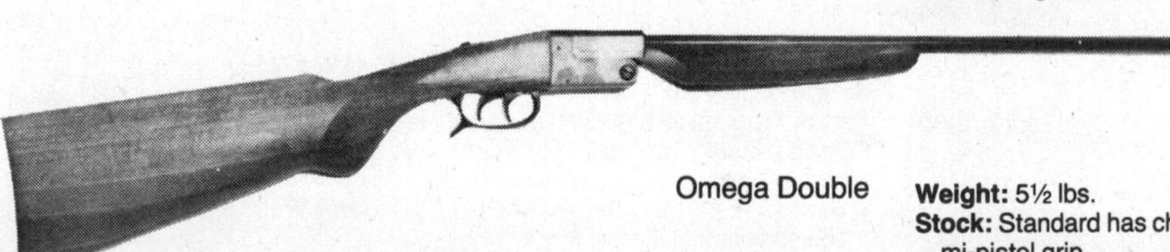

Omega Double

OMEGA SIDE-BY-SIDE SHOTGUNS

Gauge: 410, 3″.
Barrel: 24″ (Full & Full).
Weight: 5½ lbs.
Stock: Standard has checkered beechwood, Deluxe has walnut; both have semi-pistol grip.
Features: Blued barrels and receiver; top tang safety. Imported from Spain by Kassnar. Introduced 1984.
Price: Standard **$239.00**
Price: Deluxe **$269.00**

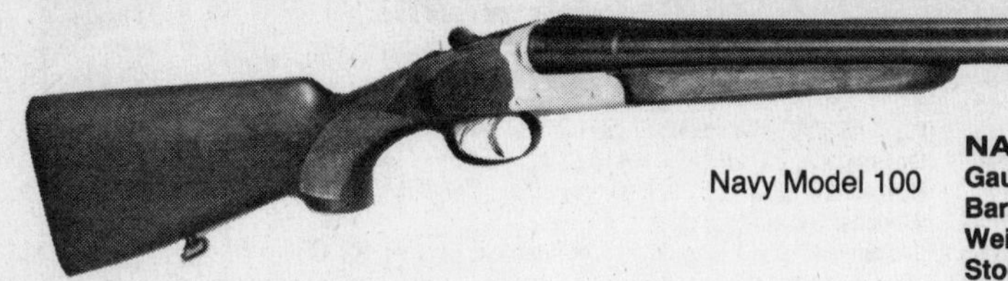

Navy Model 100

PARKER DHE SIDE-BY-SIDE SHOTGUN

Gauge: 20, 28, 2¾" or 3" chambers.
Barrel: 26" (Imp. Cyl. & Mod., 2¾" chambers), Skeet & Skeet available, 28" (Mod. & Full, 3" chambers only).
Weight: About 6½ lbs. (20 ga.), 5½ lbs. (28 ga.).
Stock: Fancy American walnut, checkered grip and fore-end. Straight stock or pistol grip, splinter or beavertail fore-end; 28 l.p.i. checkering.
Features: Reproduction of the original Parker DHE — most parts interchangeable with original. Double or single selective trigger; checkered skeleton buttplate; selective ejectors; bores hard chromed, excluding choke area. Two-barrel sets available. Hand engraved scroll and scenes on case-hardened frame. Fitted leather trunk included. Introduced 1984. Made by Winchester in Japan. Imported by Parker Div. of Reagent Chemical.
Price: **$2,800.00**

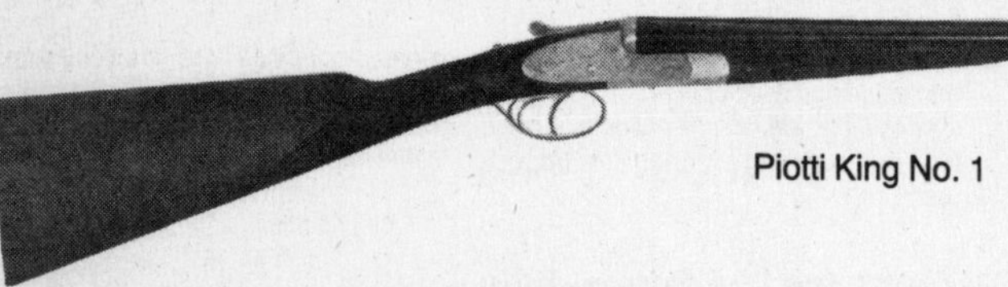

Piotti King No. 1

Piotti Model Monte Carlo Side-by-Side

Similar to the Piotti King No. 1 except has Purdey-style scroll and rosette engraving, no gold inlays, over-all workmanship not as finely detailed. Other mechanical specifications remain the same. Imported from Italy by Wm. Larkin Moore.
Price: **$8,000.00**

Piotti Model Lunik Side-by-Side

Similar to the Piotti King No. 1 except better over-all quality. Has Renaissance-style large scroll engraving in relief, gold crown in top lever, gold name, and gold crest in fore-end. Best quality Holland & Holland-pattern sidelock ejector double with chopper lump (demi-bloc) barrels. Other mechanical specifications remain the same. Imported from Italy by Wm. Larkin Moore.
Price: **$10,600.00**

ROSSI "SQUIRE" DOUBLE BARREL

Gauge: 12, 20, 410 (3" chambers).
Barrel: 12 — 28" (Mod. & Full); 20 ga.—26" (Imp. Cyl. & Mod.), 28" (Mod. & Full); 410—26" (Full & Full).
Weight: About 7½ lbs.
Stock: Walnut finished hardwood.
Features: Double triggers, raised matted rib, beavertail fore-end. Massive twin underlugs mesh with synchronized sliding bolts. Introduced 1978. Imported by Interarms.
Price: 12 or 20 ga. **$274.00**
Price: 410 .... **$281.00**

NAVY ARMS MODEL 100 FIELD HUNTER

Gauge: 12 and 20, 3" chambers.
Barrel: 28" (Imp. Cyl. & Mod., Mod. & Full).
Weight: About 7 lbs.
Stock: Checkered walnut.
Features: Chrome-lined barrels; engraved hard chrome receiver; gold plated double triggers. Introduced 1985. Imported from Italy by Navy Arms.
Price: **$319.00**

PIOTTI MODEL PIUMA SIDE-BY-SIDE

Gauge: 12, 16, 20, 28, 410.
Barrel: 25" to 30" (12 ga.), 25" to 28" (16, 20, 28, 410).
Weight: 5½ to 6¼ lbs. (20 ga.).
Stock: Dimensions to customer specs. Straight grip stock with checkered butt, classic splinter fore-end, hand rubbed oil finish are standard; pistol grip, beavertail fore-end, satin luster finish optional.
Features: Anson & Deeley boxlock ejector double with chopper lump barrels. Level, file-cut rib, light scroll and rosette engraving, scalloped frame. Double triggers with hinged front standard, single non-selective optional. Coin finish standard, color case hardened optional. Imported from Italy by Wm. Larkin Moore.
Price: **$4,000.00**

PIOTTI KING NO. 1 SIDE-BY-SIDE

Gauge: 12, 16, 20, 28, 410.
Barrel: 25" to 30" (12 ga.), 25" to 28" (16, 20, 28, 410). To customer specs. Chokes as specified.
Weight: 6½ lbs. to 8 lbs. (12 ga., to customer specs.)
Stock: Dimensions to customer specs. Finely figured walnut; straight grip with checkered butt with classic splinter fore-end and hand-rubbed oil finish standard. Pistol grip, beavertail fore-end, satin luster finish optional.
Features: Holland & Holland pattern sidelock action, auto, ejectors. Double trigger with front trigger hinged standard; non-selective single trigger optional. Coin finish standard; color case-hardened optional. Top rib: level, file cut standard; concave, ventilated optional. Very fine, full coverage scroll engraving with small floral bouquets, gold crown in top lever, name in gold, and gold crest in fore-end. Imported from Italy by Wm. Larkin Moore.
Price: **$10,000.00**

Piotti Model King Extra Side-by-Side

Similar to the Piotti King No. 1 except highest quality wood and metal work. Choice of either bulino game scene engraving or game scene engraving with gold inlays. Engraved and signed by a master engraver. Exhibition grade wood. Other mechanical specifications remain the same. Imported from Italy by Wm. Larkin Moore.
Price: **$13,200.00**

ROSSI OVERLAND DOUBLE BARREL

Gauge: 12, 20, 410 (3" chambers).
Action: Sidelock with external hammers; Greener crossbolt.
Barrel: 12 ga., 20" (Imp. Cyl., Mod.) 28" (Mod. & Full), 20 ga., 20", 26" (Imp. Cyl. & Mod.), 410 ga., 26" (Full & Full).
Weight: 6½ to 7 lbs.
Stock: Walnut p.g. with beavertail fore-end.
Features: Solid raised matted rib. Exposed hammers. Imported by Interarms.
Price: 12 or 20 .... **$249.00**
Price: 410 .... **$256.00**

Royal Model 600

ROYAL ARMS MODEL 800 SIDE-BY-SIDE

Gauge: 12, 20, 28, 410.
Action: True quick detachable bar spring sidelocks.
Barrel: 24", 26", 28" (Mod. & Full, Imp. Cyl. & Mod., Imp. Cyl. & Full).
Weight: 7 lbs.
Stock: 15" x 2½" x 1½". Fancy select European walnut; straight grip with fine-line checkering, classic fore-end and butt.
Features: Holland & Holland auto. selective ejectors; gated and fully scroll engraved grayed action; cocking indicators; articulated front trigger; Churchill rib; vented firing pins; auto safety. Introduced 1985. Imported from Spain by Royal Arms International.
Price: All gauges **$899.00**

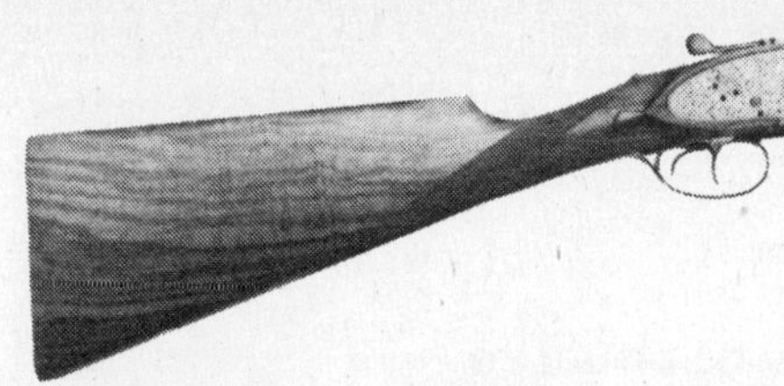

Royal Model 800

ROYAL ARMS MODEL 600 SIDE-BY-SIDE
Gauge: 12, 20, 28, 410.
Action: Boxlock, Purdey double bolting.
Barrel: 25″, 26″, 28″, 30″ (four chokes from Skeet & Skeet through Imp. Cyl. & Full.
Weight: 7 lbs., 12 ozs.
Stock: Oil finished European walnut; checkered grip and fore-end.
Features: Double triggers; vent rib; automatic safety; chrome lined barrels. Introduced 1985. Imported from Spain by Royal Arms International.
Price: **$329.95**
Price: Model 600AE (3″, 12 ga. only, single selective trigger, selective auto ejectors) **$419.95**

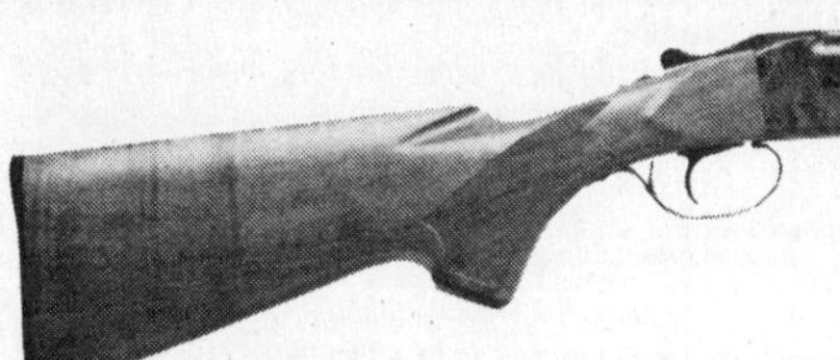

Savage-Fox B-SE

SAVAGE FOX MODEL B-SE DOUBLE
Gauge: 12, 20, 410 (20, 2¾″ and 3″; 410, 2½″ and 3″ shells).
Action: Hammerless, takedown; non-selective single trigger; auto. safety. Automatic ejectors.
Barrel: 12, 20 ga., 26″ (Imp. Cyl., Mod.); 12 ga. (Mod., Full); 410, 26″ (Full, Full). Vent. rib on all.
Weight: 12 ga. 7 lbs., 16 ga. 6¾ lbs., 20 ga. 6½ lbs., 410 ga. 6¼ lbs.
Stock: 14″x1½″x2½″. Walnut, checkered p.g. and beavertail fore-end.
Features: Decorated, blued frame; white bead front and middle sights.
Price: **$427.95**

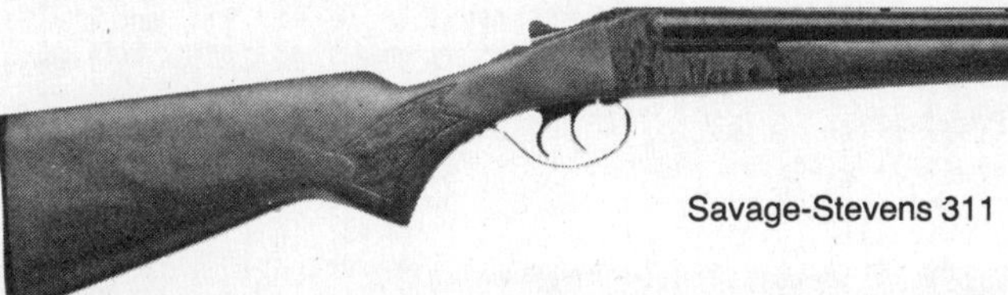

Savage-Stevens 311

SAVAGE-STEVENS MODEL 311 DOUBLE
Gauge: 12, 20, 410 (12, 20 and 410, 3″ chambers).
Action: Top lever, hammerless; double triggers, auto. top tang safety.
Barrel: 12, 20 ga. 26″ (Imp. Cyl., Mod.); 12 ga. 28″ (Mod., Full); 12 ga. 30″ (Mod., Full); 410 ga. 26″ (Full, Full).
Weight: 7-8 lbs. (30″ bbl.). **Length:** 45¾″ over-all.
Stock: 14″x1½″x2½″. Walnut finish, p.g., fluted comb.
Features: Box-type blued frame.
Price: **$274.50**

W&C SCOTT BLENHEIM GAME GUN
Gauge: 12.
Barrel: 25″, 26″, 27″, 28″, 30″ (chokes to order); concave rib standard, flat or Churchill optional.
Weight: 6½ lbs.
Stock: Measurements to order. French walnut with 28 l.p.i. checkering (32 l.p.i. checkering and exhibition grade wood on Deluxe model).
Features: Best quality bar action sidelock ejector, finest rose and scroll engraving; gold name plate. Introduced 1985. Imported from England by British Guns.
Price: Blenheim **$16,500.00**
Price: Blenheim Deluxe **$18,500.00**

W&C Scott Bowood DeLuxe Game Gun
Similar to the Chatsworth Grande Luxe except less ornate metal and wood work; checkered 24 lpi at fore-end and pistol grip. Imported from England by L. Joseph Rahn and British Guns.
Price: 12 or 16 ga. .... **$5,020.00** to **$5,000.00**
Price: 20 ga. .... **$5,700.00** to **$5,755.00**
Price: 28 ga. .... **$6,000.00** to **$6,035.00**

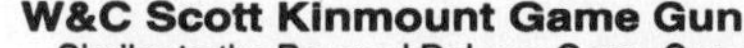

W&C Scott Chatsworth

W&C SCOTT CHATSWORTH GRANDE LUXE DOUBLE
Gauge: 12, 16, 20, 28.
Barrel: 25″, 26″, 27″, 28″, 30″ (chokes to order); concave rib standard, Churchill or flat rib optional.
Weight: About 6½ lbs. (12 ga.).
Stock: 14¾″ x 1½″ x 2¼″, or made to customer specs. French walnut with 32 lpi checkering.
Features: Entirely hand fitted; boxlock action (sideplates optional); English scroll engraving; gold name plate shield in stock. Imported from England by L. Joseph Rahn and British Guns.
Price: 12 or 16 ga. .... **$7,000.00** to **$7,346.00**
Price: 20 ga. .... **$7,800.00** to **$8,431.00**
Price: 28 ga. .... **$8,200.00** to **$8,846.00**

W&C Scott Kinmount Game Gun
Similar to the Bowood DeLuxe Game Gun except less ornate engraving and wood work; checkered 20 lpi; other details essentially the same. Imported from England by L. Joseph Rahn and British Guns.
Price: 12 or 16 ga. .... **$3,602.00** to **$3,900.00**
Price: 20 ga. .... **$4,128.00** to **$4,400.00**
Price: 28 ga. .... **$4,307.00** to **$4,600.00**

Ventura 66/66 XXV-SL

VENTURA 66/66 XXV-SL DOUBLES
Gauge: 12 ga. (2¾″), 20 ga. (3″), 28 ga. (2¾″), 410 (3″)..
Action: H&H sidelock with double underlugs.
Barrel: 25″, 27½″, 30″ (12 ga. only), with chokes according to use.
Weight: 12 ga.—6½ lbs.; 28 ga.—5¾ lbs.
Stock: Select French walnut, hand checkered. Straight English or pistol grip stock, slender beavertail fore-end.
Features: Single selective or double triggers, auto. ejectors, gas escape valves, and intercepting safeties. Extensive hand engraving and finishing. Can be made to customer specs. Accessories, extra barrels also available. Imported by Ventura Imports.
Price: From. .... **$1,100.00** to **$1,396.00**

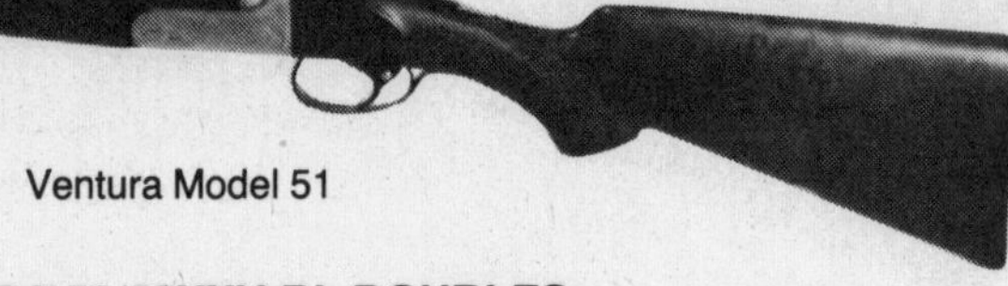

Ventura Model 51

VENTURA MODEL 51 DOUBLE

Gauge: 12 ga. (2¾″), 20 ga. (3″).
Action: Anson & Deeley with double underlugs.
Barrel: 27½″, 30″ (12 ga. only) with chokes according to use.
Weight: 6 to 6½ lbs.
Stock: Select French walnut, hand checkered pistol grip stock with slender beavertail fore-end.
Features: Single selective trigger, auto ejectors, hand-engraved action. Leather trunk cases, wood cleaning rods and brass snap caps available. Imported by Ventura Imports.
Price: From **$696.00**

VENTURA 53/53XXV-BL DOUBLES

Gauge: 12 ga. (2¾″), 20 ga. (3″), 28 ga. (2¾″), 410 ga. (3″).
Action: Anson & Deeley with double underlugs.
Barrel: 25″, 27½″, 30″ (12 ga. only), with chokes according to use.
Weight: 12 ga.—6½ lbs.; 28 ga.—5½ lbs.
Stock: Select French walnut, hand checkered. Straight English or pistol grip stock with slender beavertail fore-end.
Features: Single selective or double triggers, auto ejectors, hand-engraved scalloped frames. Accessories also available. Imported by Ventura Imports.
Price: From .... **$736.00** to **$996.00**

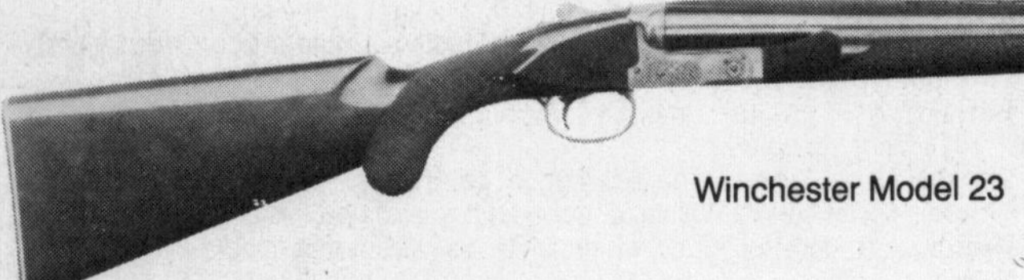

Winchester Model 23

WINCHESTER MODEL 23 PIGEON GRADE DOUBLE

Gauge: 12, 20, 3″ chambers.
Barrel: 26″, (Imp. Cyl. & Mod.), 28″ (Mod. & Full). Vent. rib.
Weight: 7 lbs. (12 ga.); 6½ lbs. (20 ga.). **Length:** 46¾″ over-all (28″ bbls.).
Stock: 14″x1½″x2½″ High grade American walnut, beavertail fore-end. Hand cut checkering.
Features: Mechanical trigger; tapered ventilated rib; selective ejectors. Receiver, top lever and trigger guard have silver gray satin finish and fine line scroll engraving. Introduced 1978. Manufactured in and imported from Japan by Winchester Group, Olin Corp.
Price: **$1,345.00**

Winchester Model 23 XTR Lightweight

Similar to standard Pigeon Grade except has 25½″ barrels, English-style straight grip stock, thinner semi-beavertail fore-end. Available in 12 or 20 gauge (Imp. Cyl. & Mod.). Silver-gray frame has engraved bird scenes. Comes with hard case. Introduced 1981. Manufactured in and imported from Japan by Winchester Group, Olin Corp.
Price: **$1,435.00**

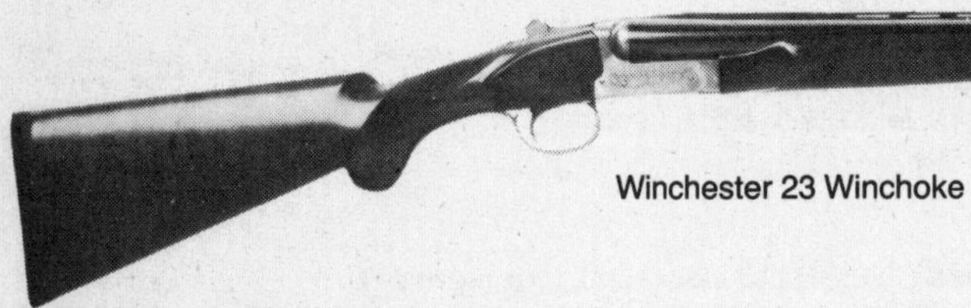

Winchester 23 Winchoke

Winchester Model 23 Pigeon Grade Winchoke

Same features as standard Model 23 Pigeon Grade except has 25½″ barrels with interchangeable Winchoke tubes. Six are supplied with 12 ga. (Skeet, Imp. Cyl., Mod., Imp. Mod., Full, Extra Full), four with 20 ga. (Skeet, Imp. Cyl., Mod., Full). Comes with hard case. Introduced 1983.
Price: **$1,475.00**

Winchester Model 23 Light Duck

Same basic features as the standard Model 23 Pigeon Grade except has plain, blued frame, 28″ barrels choked Full and Full; 20 ga.; 3″ chambers. Comes with hard case. Matching serial numbers to previously issued Heavy Duck. Introduced 1983.
Price: **$1,675.00**

SHOTGUNS—BOLT ACTIONS

Marlin Model 55

MARLIN MODEL 55 GOOSE GUN BOLT ACTION

Gauge: 12 only, (3″ mag. or 2¾″).
Action: Bolt action, thumb safety, detachable 2-shot clip. Red cocking indicator.
Barrel: 36″, Full choke.
Weight: 8 lbs. **Length:** 57″ over-all.
Stock: Walnut-finished hardwood, p.g., ventilated recoil pad, leather strap & swivels. Mar-Shield® finish.
Features: Tapped for receiver sights. Swivels and leather carrying strap. Brass bead front sight, U-groove rear sight.
Price: **$171.95**

MARLIN SUPERGOOSE 10 M5510

Gauge: 10, 3½″ Magnum or 2⅞″ regular, 2-shot clip.
Barrel: 34″ (Full), bead front sight, U-groove rear sight.
Weight: About 10½ lbs. **Length:** 55½″ over-all.
Stock: Extra long walnut-finished hardwood with p.g., Pachmayr vent. pad., white butt spacer; Mar-Shield® finish.
Features: Bolt action, removable 2-shot clip magazine. Positive thumb safety, red cocking indicator. Comes with quick-detachable swivels and leather carrying strap.
Price: **$281.95**

CAUTION: PRICES CHANGE. CHECK AT GUNSHOP.

Mossberg 595/585

MOSSBERG MODEL 183K BOLT ACTION

Gauge: 410, 3-shot (3" chamber).
Action: Bolt; top-loading mag.; thumb safety.
Barrel: 25" with C-Lect-Choke.
Weight: 5¾ lbs. **Length:** 45¼" over-all.
Stock: Walnut finish, p.g., Monte Carlo comb., rubber recoil pad w/spacer.
Features: Moulded trigger guard with finger grooves, gold bead front sight.
Price: About $125.95

MOSSBERG 595/585 BOLT ACTION

Gauge: 12, 2¾" or 3" (M595), 12 or 20 ga., 2¾" or 3" (M585).
Barrel: 28" (C-LECT-CHOKE), 38" (Full, fixed, M595).
Weight: 7½ lbs. (12 ga.).
Stock: Walnut-finished hardwood, vent. recoil pad.
Sights: Bead front.
Features: Rotary safety at rear of bolt blocks trigger; 2-shot magazine. Introduced 1984.
Price: $134.95

SHOTGUNS—SINGLE SHOTS

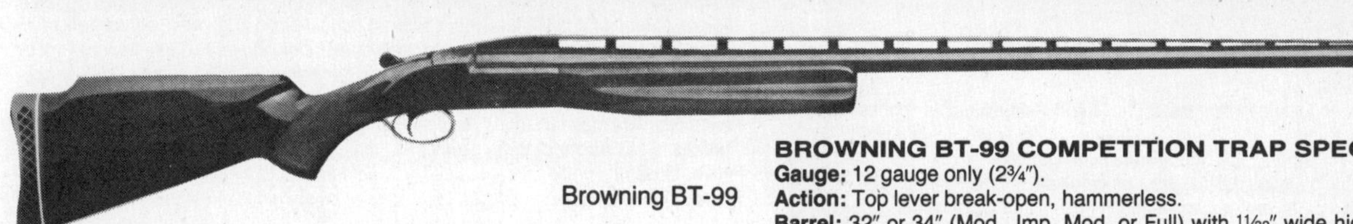
Browning BT-99

EXEL MODEL 51 FOLDING SHOTGUN

Gauge: 410, 3".
Barrel: 26" (Mod. & Full).
Weight: 4 lbs.
Stock: Folding. Splinter fore-end.
Features: Non-ejector; case-hardened frame; exposed hammers. Introduced 1985. Imported from Spain by Exel Arms.
Price: $217.00

BROWNING BT-99 COMPETITION TRAP SPECIAL

Gauge: 12 gauge only (2¾").
Action: Top lever break-open, hammerless.
Barrel: 32" or 34" (Mod., Imp. Mod. or Full) with 11/32" wide high post floating vent. rib. Also comes with Invector choke tubes.
Weight: 8 lbs. (32" bbl.).
Stock: French walnut; hand checkered, full pistol grip, full beavertail fore-end; recoil pad. Trap dimensions with M.C. 14⅜"x1⅜"x1⅜"x2".
Sights: Ivory front and middle beads.
Features: Gold plated trigger with 3½-lb. pull, deluxe trap-style recoil pad, auto ejector, no safety. Available with either Monte Carlo or standard stock. Imported from Japan by Browning.
Price: Grade I Invector $795.00
Price: Grade I Competition, fixed choke $765.00

FIE Hamilton & Hunter

FIE "S.S.S." SINGLE BARREL

Gauge: 12, 20, 410 (3").
Action: Button-break on trigger guard.
Barrel: 18½" (Cyl.).
Weight: 6½ lbs.
Stock: Walnut finished hardwood, full beavertail fore-end.
Features: Exposed hammer. Automatic ejector. Imported from Brazil by F.I.E. Corp.
Price: $99.95

FIE "HAMILTON & HUNTER" SINGLE BARREL

Gauge: 12, 20, 410 (3").
Barrel: 12 ga. & 20 ga. 28" (Full); 410 ga. (Full).
Weight: 6½ lbs.
Stock: Walnut stained hardwood, beavertail fore-end.
Sights: Metal bead front.
Features: Trigger guard button is pushed to open action. Exposed hammer, auto ejector, three-piece takedown. Imported from Brazil by F.I.E. Corp.
Price: $74.95
Price: Youth model $79.95

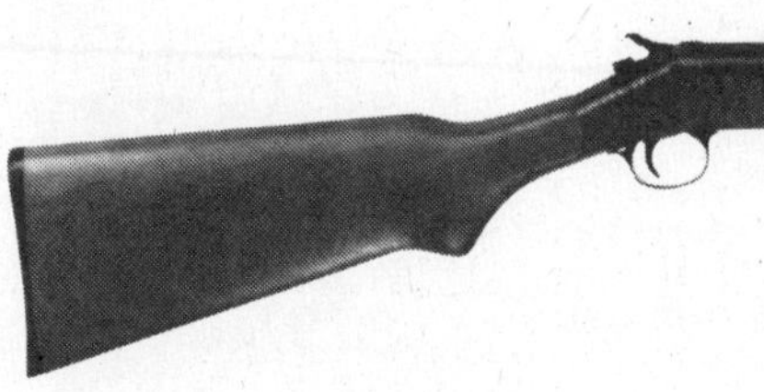
H&R Model 088

H & R Model 162

Same as the 088 except 12 or 20 ga., 24" Cyl. bored bbl., adj. folding leaf rear sight, blade front, 5½ lbs.; over-all 40". Cross bolt safety; push-button action release.
Price: $109.50

HARRINGTON & RICHARDSON MODEL 088 DELUXE

Gauge: 12, 16, 20, 410 (3" chamber); 16 (2¾").
Barrel: 12 ga. 28" (Full, Mod.); 16 ga. 28" (Mod.); 20 ga. 26" (Full, Mod.); 410 ga. 25" (Full).
Weight: About 5½ lbs. **Length:** 43" over-all (28" barrel).
Stock: Semi-pistol grip walnut finished hardwood; semi-beavertail fore-end. 13¾"x1½"x2½".
Sights: Bead front.
Features: Color case-hardened frame, blued barrel.
Price: $88.50
Price: 12 ga., 20", 32" (Full) $89.50
Price: 12 ga., 36" (Full) $92.50

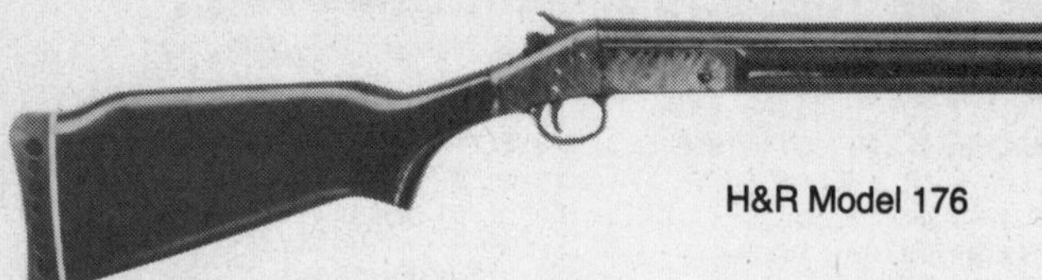
H&R Model 176

H & R Model 176 Magnum
Similar to the Model 088 except in 10 gauge (3½″ chamber) only with 36″ (Full) barrel. Also available with 32″ (Full) barrel. All barrels specially designed for steel shot use. Special long fore-end and recoil pad.
Price: From **$116.50**

H & R Model 176 10 Ga. Slug Gun
Similar to standard Model 176 magnums except chambered for 10 ga. slugs. Ramp front sight, adjustable folding leaf rear sight, recoil pad, sling swivels. Has 28″ barrel (Cyl.), 3½″ chamber. Extra length magnum-type fore-end. Weighs 9¼ lbs. Introduced 1982.
Price: **$134.50**

Ithaca 5E Single

ITHACA 5E GRADE SINGLE BARREL TRAP GUN
Gauge: 12 only.
Action: Top lever break open hammerless, dual locking lugs.
Barrel: 32″ or 34″, rampless vent. rib.
Stock: (14½″x1½″x1⅞″). Select walnut, checkered p.g. and beavertail fore-end, p.g. cap, recoil pad, Monte Carlo comb, cheekpiece. Cast-on, cast-off or extreme deviation from standard stock dimensions $100 extra. Reasonable deviation allowed without extra charge.
Features: Frame, top lever and trigger guard extensively engraved and gold inlaid. Gold name plate in stock.
Price: Custom made **$7,000.00**
Price: Dollar Grade **$9,700.00**

LJUTIC MONO GUN SINGLE BARREL
Gauge: 12 ga. only.
Barrel: 34″, choked to customer specs; hollow-milled rib, 35½″ sight plane.
Weight: Approx. 9 lbs.
Stock: To customer specs. Oil finish, hand checkered.
Features: Totally custom made. Pull or release trigger; removable trigger guard contains trigger and hammer mechanism; Ljutic pushbutton opener on front of trigger guard. From Ljutic Industries.
Price: **$3,595.00**
Price: With Olympic Rib, custom 32″ barrel **$3,795.00**
Price: As above with screw-in chokes **$3,995.00**

Ljutic LTX Mono

Ljutic LTX Super Deluxe Mono Gun
Super Deluxe version of the standard Mono Gun except has exhibition quality wood, extra-fancy checkering pattern in 24 lpi, double recessed choking. Weight is 8¼ lbs., extra light 33″ barrel; medium-height Olympic rib. Introduced 1984.
Price: **$4,995.00**
Price: With three screw-in choke tubes **$5,595.00**

Ljutic Space Gun

LJUTIC RECOILLESS SPACE GUN SHOTGUN
Gauge: 12 only, 2¾″ chamber.
Barrel: 30″ (Full).
Weight: 8½ lbs.
Stock: 14½″ to 15″ pull length; universal comb; medium or large p.g.
Sights: Choice of front sight or vent. rib model.
Features: Choice of pull or release button trigger; anti-recoil mechanism. Revolutionary new design. Introduced 1981. From Ljutic Industries.
Price: From **$3,595.00**

OMEGA FOLDING SHOTGUN
Gauge: 12, 16, 20, 28, 410, 2¾″, 3″ chamber.
Barrel: 410 — 26″ (Full); 12, 16, 20, 28 — 28″ (Full); 12 — 30″ (Full).
Stock: Standard has checkered beechwood, Deluxe has checkered walnut.
Sights: Metal bead front.
Features: Standard model has matte chrome receiver, top opening lever; Deluxe has blued receiver, vent. rib. Both guns fold for storage and transport. Imported from Italy by Kassnar. Introduced 1984.
Price: Standard **$164.00**
Price: Deluxe **$203.00**

Snake Charmer II

SNAKE CHARMER II SHOTGUN
Gauge: 410, 3″ chamber.
Barrel: 18⅛″ (Cyl.).
Weight: 3½ lbs. **Length:** 28⅛″ over-all.
Stock: Moulded high impact plastic, thumbhole type.
Sights: None.
Features: Redesigned positive safety mechanism. Measures 19″ when taken apart. All stainless steel construction. Storage compartment in buttstock holds four spare rounds of 410. Reintroduced 1984. From Sporting Arms, Inc.
Price: About **$115.00**

CAUTION: PRICES CHANGE. CHECK AT GUNSHOP.

SHOTGUNS—SINGLE SHOTS

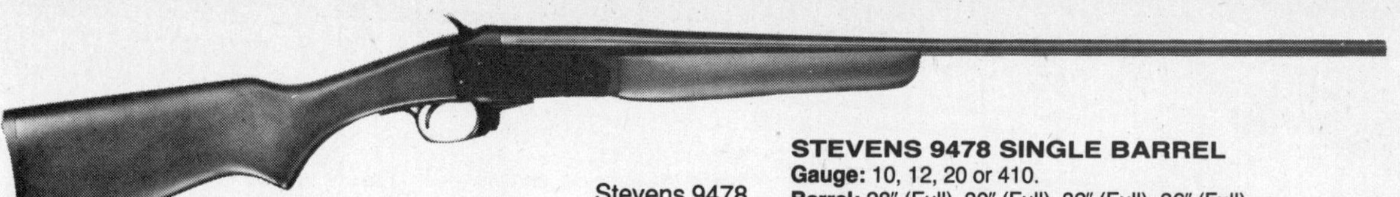

Stevens 9478

STEVENS 9478 SINGLE BARREL

Gauge: 10, 12, 20 or 410.
Barrel: 28″ (Full), 30″ (Full), 32″ (Full), 36″ (Full).
Weight: 6¼ lbs. (9½ lbs. for 10 ga.) **Length:** 42″ to 52″ over-all.
Stock: Walnut finished hardwood. 14″x1½″x2½″.
Features: Bottom opening action "lever", manually cocked hammer, auto. ejection. Blued frame.
Price: 9478, and youth model **$95.00**
Price: 10 ga., 36″ (Full) **$126.00**

SHOTGUNS—MILITARY & POLICE

Benelli Model 121-M1

BENELLI MODEL 121-MI POLICE SHOTGUN

Gauge: 12, 2¾″ chamber.
Barrel: 20″ (Cyl.).
Weight: About 7½ lbs.
Stock: Oil-finished Beech.
Sights: Post front, buckhorn-type rear.
Features: All metal parts black Parkerized, including bolt; smooth, non-checkered stock, swivel stud on butt. Imported by Heckler & Koch, Inc..
Price: **$499.00**

FIE SPAS 12

FIE SPAS 12 PUMP/AUTO ASSAULT SHOTGUN

Gauge: 12, 2¾″.
Barrel: 21½″. Barrel threaded for SPAS choke tubes.
Weight: 9.6 lbs. **Length:** 31¾″ (stock folded).
Stock: Folding, metal.
Sights: Blade front, aperture rear.
Features: Functions as pump or gas-operated auto. Has 9-shot magazine. Parkerized alloy receiver, chrome lined bore, resin pistol grip and pump handle. Made in Italy by Franchi. Introduced 1983. Imported by FIE Corp.
Price: **$599.95**
Price: Mod. or Full choke tube **$24.95**

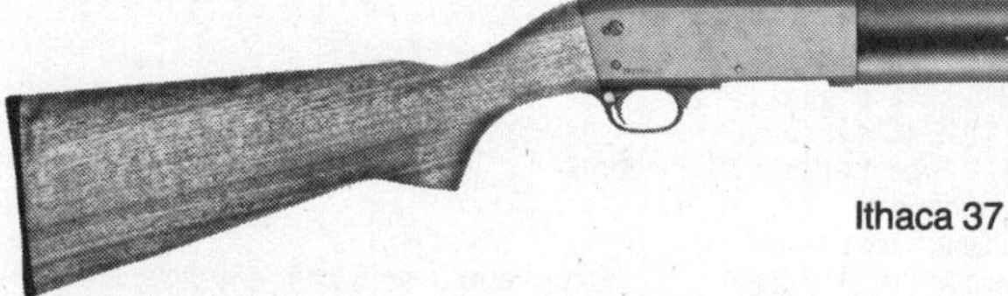

Ithaca 37 M&P

ITHACA MODEL 37 M & P SHOTGUN

Gauge: 12, 2¾″ chamber, 5-shot and 8-shot magazine.
Barrel: 18½″ (Cyl.), 20″ (Cyl. or Full).
Weight: 6½ lbs.
Stock: Oil-finished walnut with grooved walnut pump handle.
Sights: Bead front.
Features: Metal parts are Parkerized. Available with vertical hand grip instead of full butt.
Price: 5-shot, Parkerized, 18½″ or 20″ **$335.00**
Price: 8-shot, Parkerized, 20″ only **$350.00**
Price: Handgrip stock, 5-shot, 18½″ **$359.00**
Price: Handgrip stock, 8-shot, 20″ **$374.00**
Price: M&P II, Handgrip with buttstock **$352.00**

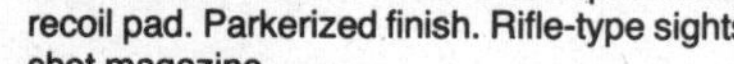

Ithaca Model 37 LAPD

Similar to the Model 37 DSPS except comes with sling, swivels, sling, rubber recoil pad. Parkerized finish. Rifle-type sights, checkered pistol grip stock, 5-shot magazine.
Price: **$405.00**

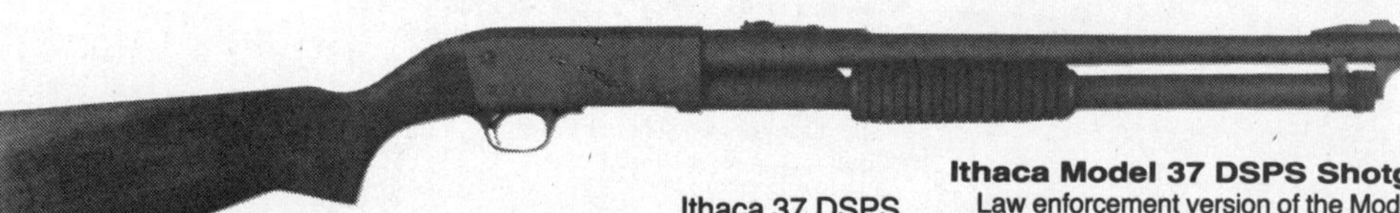

Ithaca 37 DSPS

Ithaca Model 37 DSPS Shotgun

Law enforcement version of the Model 37 Deerslayer. Designed primarily for shooting rifled slugs but equally effective with buckshot. Available in either 5- or 8-shot models in Parkerized finish. Has 20″ barrel, oil-finished stock, adjustable rifle-type sights.
Price: Parkerized, 5-shot **$371.00**
Price: Parkerized 8-shot **$386.00**
Price: With Handgrip and buttstock (DSPS II) **$388.00**

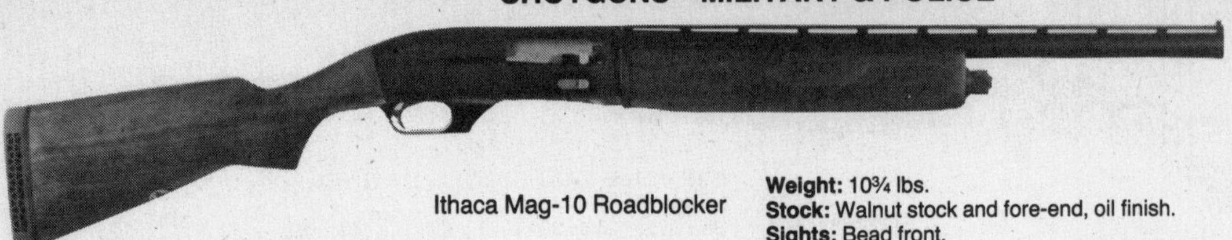
Ithaca Mag-10 Roadblocker

ITHACA MAG-10 ROADBLOCKER

Gauge: 10, 3½" chamber.
Barrel: 22" (Cyl.).
Weight: 10¾ lbs.
Stock: Walnut stock and fore-end, oil finish.
Sights: Bead front.
Features: Non-glare finish on metal parts. Uses Ithaca's Countercoil gas system. Rubber recoil pad. Vent. rib or plain barrel.
Price: Plain barrel **$707.00**
Price: Vent rib barrel **$736.00**

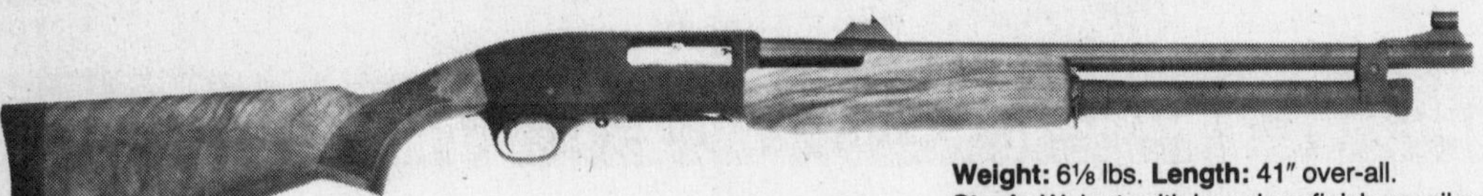
Manufrance RG-860

MANUFRANCE RG-860 SHOTGUN

Gauge: 12, 2¾" chamber.
Barrel: 20" (Cyl.).
Weight: 6⅛ lbs. **Length:** 41" over-all.
Stock: Walnut, with low-gloss finish, recoil pad.
Sights: Hooded ramp front, open rear.
Features: Matte black light alloy receiver; 7-shot magazine; interchangeable 26", 28" barrel; fitted with sling swivels, rubber recoil pad. Imported from France by Armsource, Inc. Introduced 1984.
Price: **$445.00**
Price: Sporting model (Full or Mod. choke, vent. rib) **$410.00**

Mossberg 500

MOSSBERG MODEL 500 SECURITY SHOTGUNS

Gauge: 12, 20 (2¾"), 410 (3").
Barrel: 18½", 20" (Cyl.).
Weight: 5½ lbs. (410), 7 lbs. (12 ga.).
Stock: Walnut-finished hardwood; synthetic on some models, or folding metal.
Sights: Rifle-type front and rear or metal bead front.
Features: Available in 6- or 8-shot models. Top-mounted safety, double action slide bars, sling swivels, rubber recoil pad. Blue, Parkerized or electroless nickel finishes. Price list not complete—contact Mossberg for full list.
Price: 12 ga., 6-shot, 18½", blue, bead sight, about **$178.95**
Price: As above, Parkerized, about **$215.00**
Price: As above, nickel, about **$240.00**
Price: 12 ga., 8-shot, 20" Parkerized, rifle sights, about **$218.00**
Price: 20 ga., 6-shot, 18½", blue, bead sight, about **$202.00**
Price: Model 500 US, Parkerized finish, handguard, about **$220.00**
Price: Model 500 ATP, blued, bayonet lug, sling, about **$245.00**

Mossberg Cruiser Persuader Shotgun

Similar to the Model 500 Security guns except fitted with the "Cruiser" pistol grip. Grip and fore-end are solid black. Available in either blue or electroless nickel; 12 gauge only with 18½" (6-shot) or 20" (8-shot) barrel. Folding stock. Muzzle cut with "Muzzle Brake" slots to reduce recoil. Comes with extra long black web sling. Weight is 5¾ lb. (18½"), 6 lb. (20"). Over-all length is 28" with 18½" barrel.
Price: 6-shot, 18½", blue, about **$200.00**
Price: As above, nickel, about **$240.00**
Price: 8-shot, 20", blue, about **$215.00**
Price: As above, nickel, about **$240.00**

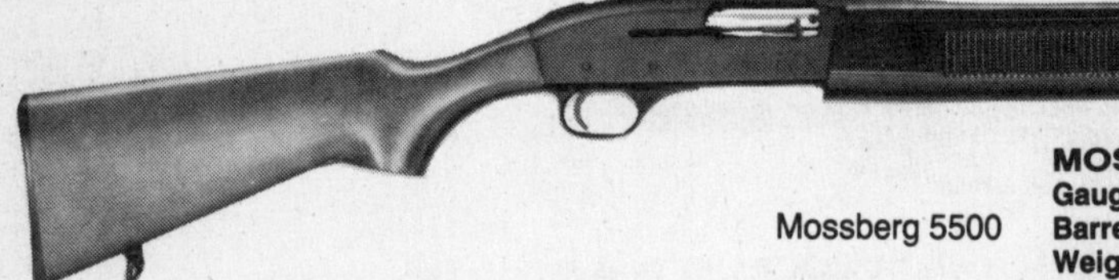
Mossberg 5500

MOSSBERG 5500 GUARDIAN SHOTGUN

Gauge: 12, 2¾" chamber.
Barrel: 18½" (Cyl.).
Weight: 7½ lbs. **Length:** 38½" over-all.
Stock: Hardwood.
Sights: Bead front.
Features: Matte blue finish, grooved fore-end. Also available with Cruiser pistol grip. Introduced 1983.
Price: **$312.95**

Mossberg 595

MOSSBERG 595 BOLT ACTION SHOTGUN

Gauge: 12 ga., 2¾" chamber.
Barrel: 18½".
Weight: 7½ lbs. **Length:** 38½" over-all.
Stock: Hardwood.
Sights: Bead front, open rear.
Features: Detachable 5-shot box magazine, rubber recoil pad, grooved fore-end. Comes with sling swivel studs. Introduced 1983.
Price: **$135.95**

OMEGA RIOT PUMP SHOTGUN

Gauge: 12, 2¾" chamber.
Barrel: 20" (Imp. Cyl.).
Weight: 7½ lbs.
Stock: European hardwood.
Sights: Metal bead front.
Features: Blued receiver, Damascened bolt; cross-bolt safety. Imported from the Philippines by Kassnar. Introduced 1984.
Price: With 5-shot magazine **$255.00**
Price: With 8-shot magazine **$260.00**

CAUTION: PRICES CHANGE. CHECK AT GUNSHOP.

Remington 870 Police

REMINGTON MODEL 870P POLICE SHOTGUN
Gauge: 12, 2¾" chamber.
Barrel: 18", 20" (Police Cyl.), 20" (Imp. Cyl.).
Weight: About 7 lbs.
Stock: Lacquer-finished hardwood or folding stock.
Sights: Metal bead front or rifle sights.
Features: Solid steel receiver, double-action slide bars.
Price: Wood stock, 18" or 20", bead sight, about **$320.00**
Price: Wood stock, 20", rifle sights, about **$340.00**

SILE TP8 POLICE/SURVIVAL SHOTGUN
Gauge: 12, 2¾" chamber, 7-shot magazine.
Barrel: 19¾".
Weight: 6¾ lbs. **Length:** 39½" over-all with stock, 29½" without.
Stock: Hollow, plastic coated, steel tube, plastic fore-end.
Sights: Bead on ramp front, open bar rear.
Features: Dual action bars, non-reflective electroless nickel finish. Stock holds spare ammunition or survival equipment. Rotating sling swivels. Hard chrome lined barrel. Introduced 1982. Imported from Italy by Sile.
Price: **$255.00**

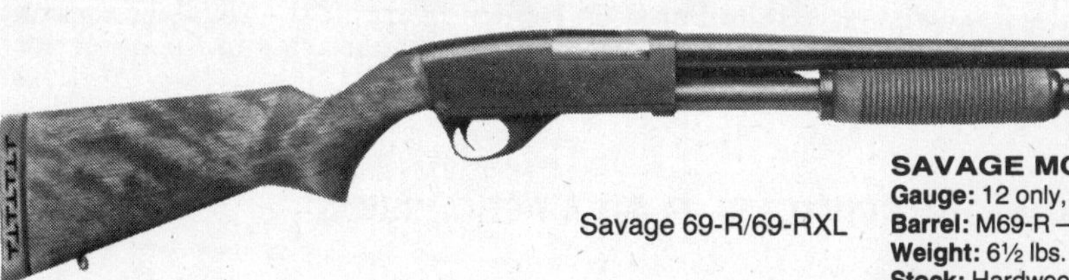

Savage 69-R/69-RXL

SAVAGE MODEL 69-R/69-RXL PUMP SHOTGUN
Gauge: 12 only, 3" chamber.
Barrel: M69-R — 18¼" (Cyl.), M69-RXL — 20" (Cyl.).
Weight: 6½ lbs. **Length:** 38" over-all.
Stock: Hardwood, tung-oil finish.
Sights: Bead front.
Features: Top tang safety, 5-shot (69-R) or 7-shot (69-RXL). Stock has fluted comb and full pistol grip, ventilated rubber pad. QD swivel studs. Introduced 1982.
Price: Either model **$196.50**

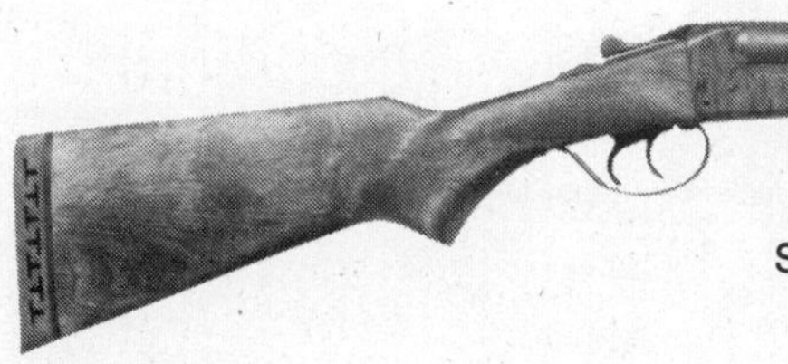

Stevens Model 311-R

STEVENS MODEL 311-R GUARD GUN DOUBLE
Gauge: 12 ga.
Barrel: 18¼" (Cyl. & Cyl.).
Weight: 6¾ lbs. **Length:** 35¼" over-all.
Stock: Hardwood, tung-oil finish.
Sights: Bead front.
Features: Top tang safety, double triggers, color case-hardened frame, blue barrels. Ventilated rubber recoil pad. Introduced 1982.
Price: **$274.50**

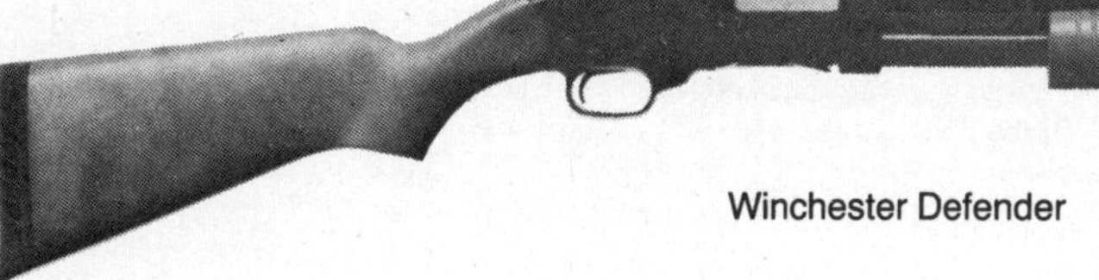

Winchester Defender

WINCHESTER DEFENDER PUMP GUN
Gauge: 12, 20, 3" chamber, 7-shot capacity.
Barrel: 18" (Cyl.).
Weight: 6¾ lbs. **Length:** 38⅝" over-all.
Stock: Walnut finished hardwood stock and ribbed fore-end.
Sights: Metal bead front.
Features: Cross-bolt safety, front-locking rotating bolt, twin action slide bars. Black rubber butt pad. Made under license by U.S. Repeating Arms Co.
Price: About **$198.00**

Winchester "Stainless Marine" Pump Gun
Same as the Defender except has bright chrome finish, stainless-steel barrel, rifle-type sights only. Has special fore-end cap for easy cleaning and inspection.
Price: About **$340.00**

Winchester Stainless Police Pump Gun
Same as the Defender except has satin chrome finish, 7-shot capacity, stainless steel barrel, detachable sling swivels. Metal bead front sight or rifle-type front and rear sights.
Price: With bead front sight, about **$327.00**
Price: With rifle-type sights, about **$340.00**

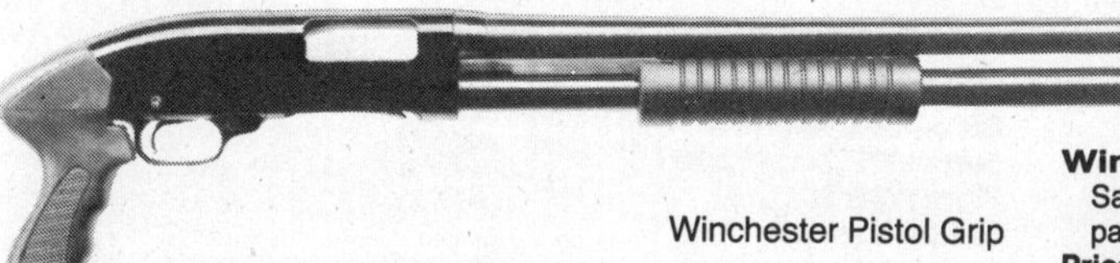

Winchester Pistol Grip

Winchester Pistol Grip Pump Security Shotguns
Same as regular Security Series but with pistol grip and fore-end of high-impact resistant ABS plastic with non-glare black finish. Introduced 1984.
Price: Pistol Grip Defender (12 and 20 ga.), about **$198.00**
Price: Pistol Grip Stainless Police Bead Sight, about **$276.00**
Price: As above with rifle sights, about **$290.00**
Price: Pistol Grip Stainless Marine, about **$299.00**

The following pages catalog the black powder arms currently available to U.S. shooters. These range from quite precise replicas of historically significant arms to totally new designs created expressly to give the black powder shooter the benefits of modern technology.

Most of the replicas are imported, and many are available from more than one source. Thus examples of a given model such as the 1860 Army revolver or Zouave rifle purchased from different importers may vary in price, finish and fitting. Most of them bear proof marks, indicating that they have been test fired in the proof house of their country of origin.

A list of the importers and the retail price range are included with the description for each model. Many local dealers handle more than one importer's products, giving the prospective buyer an opportunity to make his own judgment in selecting a black powder gun. Most importers have catalogs available free or at nominal cost, and some are well worth having for the useful information on black powder shooting they provide in addition to their detailed descriptions and specifications of the guns.

A number of special accessories are also available for the black powder shooter. These include replica powder flasks, bullet moulds, cappers and tools, as well as more modern devices to facilitate black powder cleaning and maintenance. Ornate presentation cases and even detachable shoulder stocks are also available for some black powder pistols from their importers. Again, dealers or the importers will have catalogs.

The black powder guns are arranged in four sections: Single Shot Pistols, Revolvers, Muskets & Rifles, and Shotguns. The guns within each section are arranged roughly by date of the original, with the oldest first. Thus the 1836 Paterson replica leads off the revolver section, and flintlocks precede percussion arms in the other sections.

BLACK POWDER SINGLE SHOT PISTOLS—FLINT & PERCUSSION

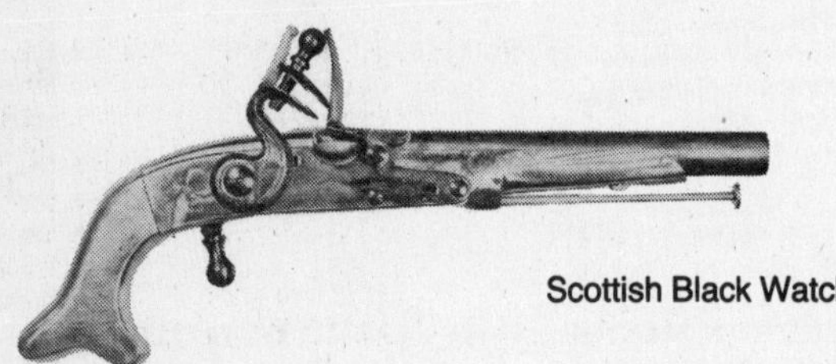
Scottish Black Watch

BLACK WATCH SCOTCH PISTOL

Caliber: 577 (.550″ round ball).
Barrel: 7″, smoothbore.
Weight: 1½ lbs. **Length:** 12″ over-all.
Stock: Brass.
Sights: None.
Features: Faithful reproduction of this military flintlock. From Dixie.
Price: **$135.00**

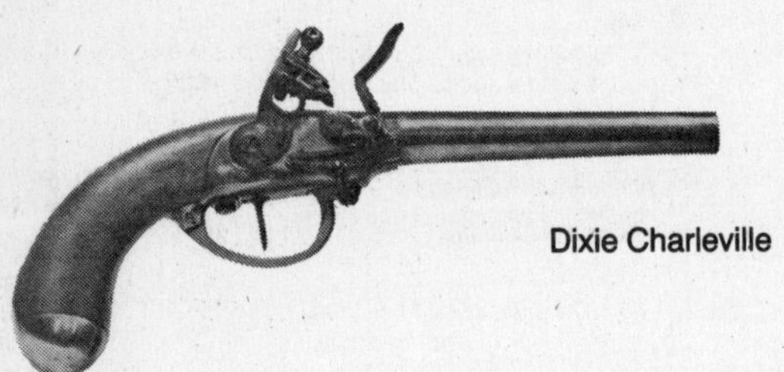
Dixie Charleville

CHARLEVILLE FLINTLOCK PISTOL

Caliber: 69, (.680″ round ball).
Barrel: 7½″.
Weight: 48 oz. **Length:** 13½″ over-all.
Stock: Walnut.
Sights: None.
Features: Brass frame, polished steel barrel, iron belt hook, brass buttcap and backstrap. Replica of original 1777 pistol. Imported by Dixie.
Price: **$135.00**

CVA TOWER PISTOL

Caliber: 45.
Barrel: 9″, octagon at breech, tapering to round at muzzle. Rifled.
Weight: 36 oz. **Length:** 15¼″ over-all.
Stock: Selected hardwood.
Sights: None.
Features: Color case-hardened and engraved lock plate; early-style brass trigger; brass trigger guard, nose cap, thimbles, grip cap; blued barrel and ramrod. Introduced 1981.
Price: Complete, percussion **$104.95**
Price: Kit form, percussion **$73.95**
Price: Kit form, flintlock **$83.95**

HARPER'S FERRY 1806 PISTOL

Caliber: 58 (.570″ round ball).
Barrel: 10″.
Weight: 40 oz. **Length:** 16″ over-all.
Stock: Walnut.
Sights: Fixed.
Features: Case hardened lock, brass mounted browned bbl. Replica of the first U.S. Gov't.-made flintlock pistol. Imported by Navy Arms, Dixie.
Price: .... **$135.00 to $165.00**

Dixie Queen Anne

DIXIE QUEEN ANNE FLINTLOCK PISTOL

Caliber: 50 (.490″ round ball).
Barrel: 7½″, smoothbore.
Stock: Walnut.
Sights: None.
Features: Browned steel barrel, fluted brass trigger guard, brass mask on butt. Lockplate left in the white. Made by Pedersoli in Italy. Introduced 1983. Imported by Dixie Gun Works.
Price: **$99.95**

CAUTION: PRICES CHANGE. CHECK AT GUNSHOP.

BLACK POWDER SINGLE SHOT PISTOLS—FLINT & PERCUSSION

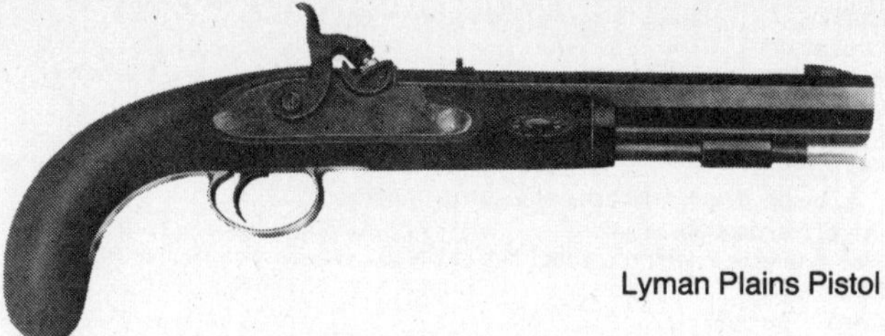

Lyman Plains Pistol

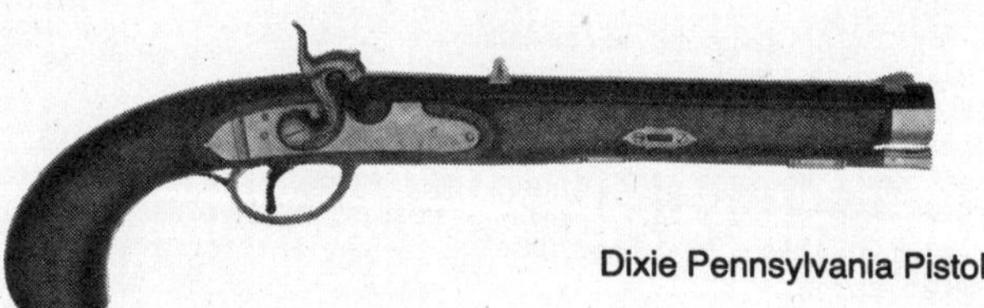

Dixie Pennsylvania Pistol

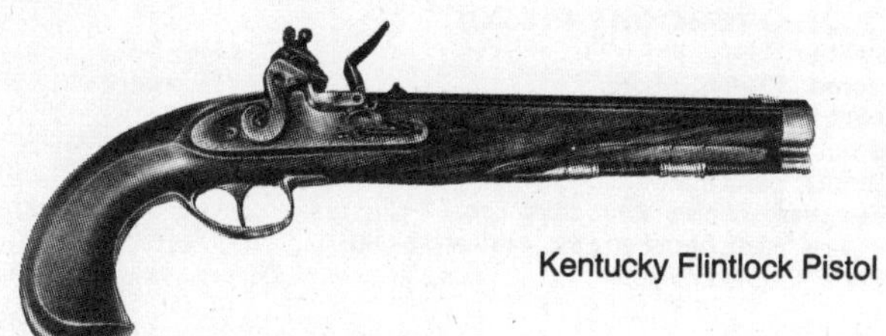

Kentucky Flintlock Pistol

Kentucky Percussion Pistol
Similar to flint version but percussion lock. Imported by The Armoury, Dixie, Navy Arms, CVA, Armsport.
Price: About .... **$97.50** to **$120.00**
Price: Brass barrel (Navy Arms) **$136.75**
Price: In kit form .... **$35.95** to **$102.00**
Price: Single cased set (Navy Arms) **$208.00**
Price: Double cased set (Navy Arms) **$335.00**
Price: Brass bbl. single cased set (Navy Arms) **$225.00**
Price: Brass bbl., double cased set (Navy Arms) **$370.00**

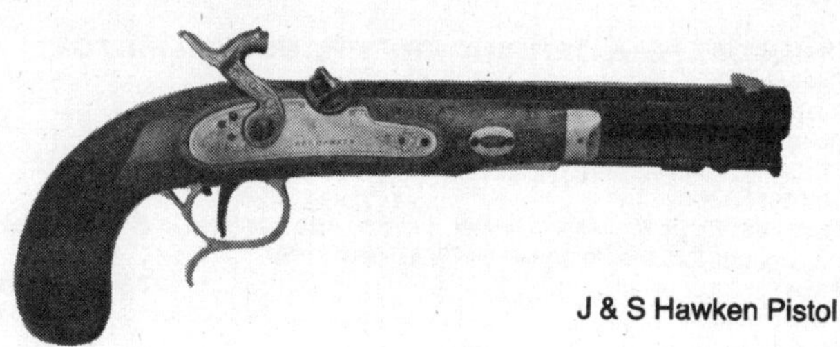

J & S Hawken Pistol

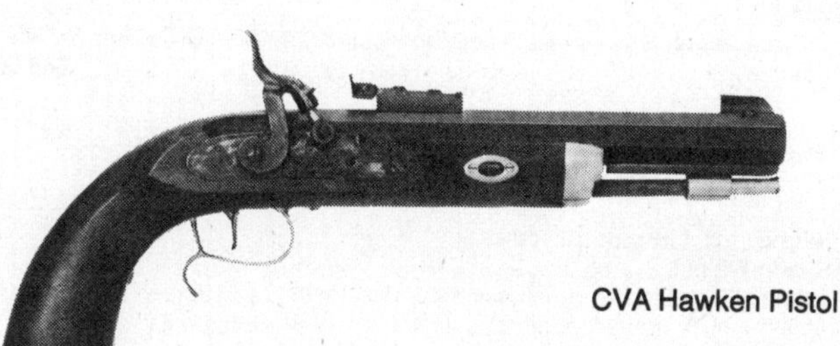

CVA Hawken Pistol

LYMAN PLAINS PISTOL
Caliber: 50 or 54.
Barrel: 8″, 1-in-30″ twist, both calibers.
Weight: 50 oz. **Length:** 15″ over-all.
Stock: Walnut half-stock.
Sights: Blade front, square notch rear adj. for windage.
Features: Polished brass trigger guard and ramrod tip, color case-hardened coil spring lock, spring-loaded trigger, stainless steel nipple, blackened iron furniture. Hooked patent breech, detachable belt hook. Introduced 1981. From Lyman Products.
Price: Finished **$129.95**
Price: Kit **$99.95**

DIXIE PENNSYLVANIA PISTOL
Caliber: 44 (.430″ round ball).
Barrel: 10″ (7/8″ octagon).
Weight: 2½ lbs.
Stock: Walnut-stained hardwood.
Sights: Blade front, open rear drift-adj. for windage; brass.
Features: Available in flint or percussion. Brass trigger guard, thimbles, nose-cap, wedgeplates; high-lustre blue barrel. Imported from Italy by Dixie Gun Works.
Price: Flint, finished **$119.95**
Price: Percussion, finished **$105.00**
Price: Flint, kit **$85.00**
Price: Percussion, kit **$72.50**

KENTUCKY FLINTLOCK PISTOL
Caliber: 44, 45.
Barrel: 10⅛″.
Weight: 32 oz. **Length:** 15½″ over-all.
Stock: Walnut.
Sights: Fixed.
Features: Specifications, including caliber, weight and length may vary with importer. Case hardened lock, blued bbl.; available also as brass bbl. flint Model 1821 ($136.75, Navy). Imported by Navy Arms, The Armoury, Dixie.
Price: .... **$40.95** to **$142.00**
Price: In kit form, from .... **$90.00** to **$112.00**
Price: Brass barrel (Navy Arms) **$153.00**
Price: Single cased set (Navy Arms) **$225.00**
Price: Double cased set (Navy Arms) **$370.00**
Price: Brass bbl., single cased set (Navy Arms) **$240.00**
Price: Brass bbl., double cased set (Navy Arms) **$400.00**

J&S HAWKEN PERCUSSION PISTOL
Caliber: 50, uses 50-cal. mini; 54, uses 54-cal. mini.
Barrel: 9″.
Weight: 41 oz. **Length:** 14″ over-all.
Stock: European walnut with checkered grip.
Sights: Fixed.
Features: Blued steel barrel with swivel-type rammer, three-quarter stocked, adj. single set trigger, German silver furniture, scroll engraved lock. From Allen Fire Arms, Navy Arms.
Price: Finished, either cal. **$200.00**

CVA HAWKEN PISTOL
Caliber: 50.
Barrel: 9¾″, octagonal, 1″ flats; rifled.
Weight: 50 oz. **Length:** 16½″ over-all.
Stock: Select walnut.
Sights: Beaded blade front, fully adjustable rear.
Features: Hooked breech, early-style brass trigger. Color case-hardened lock plate; brass wedge plate, nose cap, ramrod thimbles, trigger guard, grip cap; blue barrel and sights.
Price: Finished, percussion **$111.95**
Price: Finished, flintlock **$121.95**
Price: Kit, percussion **$73.95**
Price: Kit, flintlock **$83.95**

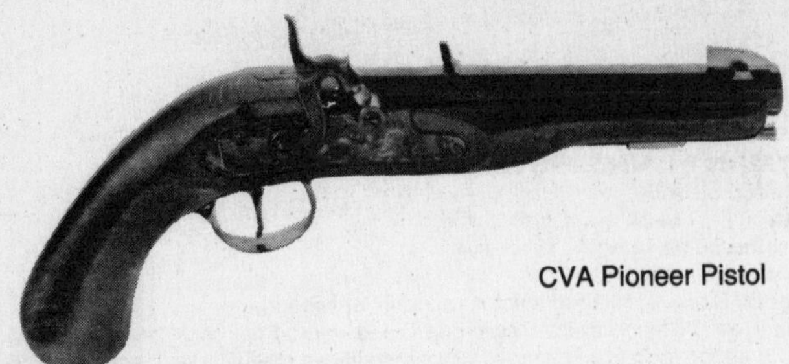

CVA Pioneer Pistol

CVA MOUNTAIN PISTOL

Caliber: 45 or 50 cal.
Barrel: 9″, octagon. 15/16″ across flats.
Weight: 40 oz. **Length:** 14″ over-all.
Stock: Select hardwood.
Sights: German silver blade front, fixed primitive rear.
Features: Engraved color case-hardened lock. Adjustable sear engagement. Fly and bridle. Hooked breech. Browned steel on finished pistol. German silver wedge plates. Stainless steel nipples. Hardwood ramrod. Belt hook optional. Introduced 1978. From CVA.
Price: 50-cal. only in finished form **$131.95**
Price: Kit form, percussion **$115.95**
Price: Kit form, flintlock **$115.95**

Dixie Overcoat Pistol

Dixie Philadelphia

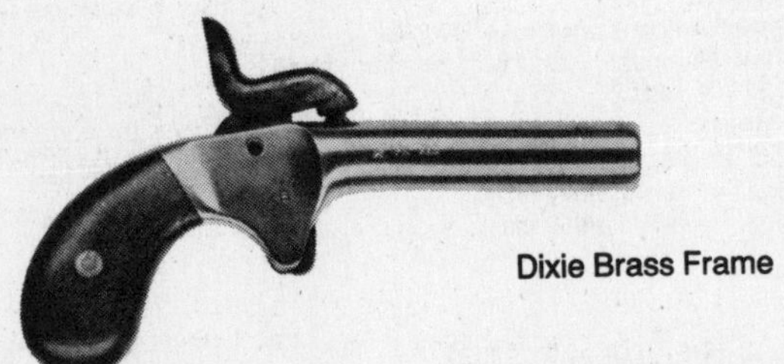

Dixie Brass Frame

DIXIE ABILENE DERRINGER

Caliber: 41.
Barrel: 2½″, 6-groove rifling.
Weight: 8 oz. **Length:** 6½″ over-all.
Stocks: Walnut.
Features: All steel version of Dixie's brass-framed derringers. Blued barrel, color case hardened frame and hammer. Shoots .395″ patched ball. Comes with wood presentation case.
Price: **$54.95**
Price: Kit form **$45.00**

CVA COLONIAL PISTOL

Caliber: 45.
Barrel: 6¾″, octagonal, rifled.
Length: 12¾″ over-all.
Stocks: Selected hardwood.
Features: Case hardened lock, brass furniture, fixed sights. Steel ramrod. Available in either flint or percussion. Imported by CVA.
Price: Percussion **$73.95**
Also available in kit form, either flint or percussion. Stock 95% inletted.
Price: Flint **$62.95**
Price: Percussion **$49.95**

CVA PIONEER PERCUSSION PISTOL

Caliber: 32.
Barrel: 7½″ octagonal, ⅞″ across flats.
Weight: 14 oz. **Length:** 13″ over-all.
Stock: Hardwood.
Sights: Dovetailed brass blade front, fixed open rear.
Features: Color case-hardened and engraved lock plate, screw-adjustable sear engagement, V-type mainspring, brass trigger guard, thimble and ramrod tip, rest blued. Introduced 1984.
Price: Finished **$69.95**
Price: Kit **$59.95**

DIXIE OVERCOAT PISTOL

Caliber: 39.
Barrel: 4″, smoothbore.
Weight: 13 oz. **Length:** 8″ over-all.
Stock: Walnut-finished hardwood. Checkered p.g.
Sights: Bead front.
Features: Shoots .380″ balls. Breech plug and engraved lock are burnished steel finish; barrel and trigger guard blued.
Price: Engraved model **$34.50**

DIXIE LINCOLN DERRINGER

Caliber: 41.
Barrel: 2″, 8 lands, 8 grooves.
Weight: 7 oz. **Length:** 5½″ over-all.
Stock: Walnut finish, checkered.
Sights: Fixed.
Features: Authentic copy of the "Lincoln Derringer." Shoots .400″ patched ball. German silver furniture includes trigger guard with pineapple finial, wedge plates, nose, wrist, side and teardrop inlays. All furniture, lockplate, hammer, and breech plug engraved. Imported from Italy by Dixie Gun Works.
Price: With wooden case **$159.95**
Price: Kit (not engraved) **$59.95**

PHILADELPHIA DERRINGER PERCUSSION PISTOL

Caliber: 45.
Barrel: 3⅛″.
Weight: 14 oz. **Length:** 7″ over-all.
Stock: Walnut, checkered grip.
Sights: Fixed.
Features: Engraved wedge holder and bbl. Also available in flintlock version (Armoury, $29.95). Imported by CVA, Navy Arms.
Price: .... **$29.95** to **$131.00**
Price: Kit form **$98.50**

DIXIE PHILADELPHIA DERRINGER

Caliber: 41.
Barrel: 3½″, octagon.
Weight: 8 oz. **Length:** 5½″ over-all.
Stock: Walnut, checkered p.g.
Sights: Fixed.
Features: Barrel and lock are blued; brass furniture. From Dixie Gun Works.
Price: **$45.00**

DIXIE BRASS FRAME DERRINGER

Caliber: 41.
Barrel: 2½″.
Weight: 7 oz. **Length:** 5½″ over-all.
Stocks: Walnut.
Features: Brass frame, color case hardened hammer and trigger. Shoots .395″ round ball. Engraved model available. From Dixie Gun Works.
Price: Plain model **$49.95**
Price: Engraved model **$59.95**
Price: Kit form, plain model **$37.50**

BLACK POWDER SINGLE SHOT PISTOLS—FLINT & PERCUSSION

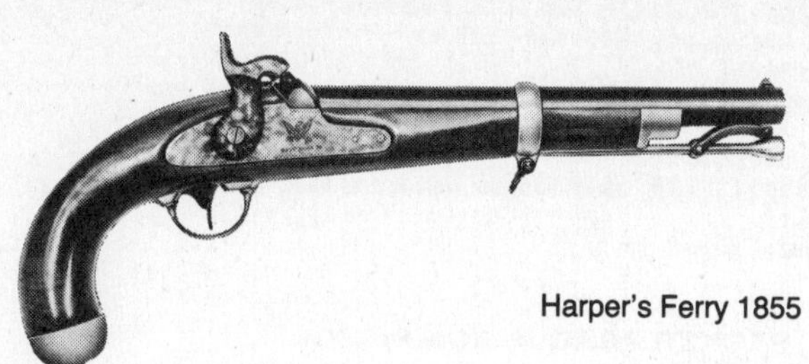

Harper's Ferry 1855

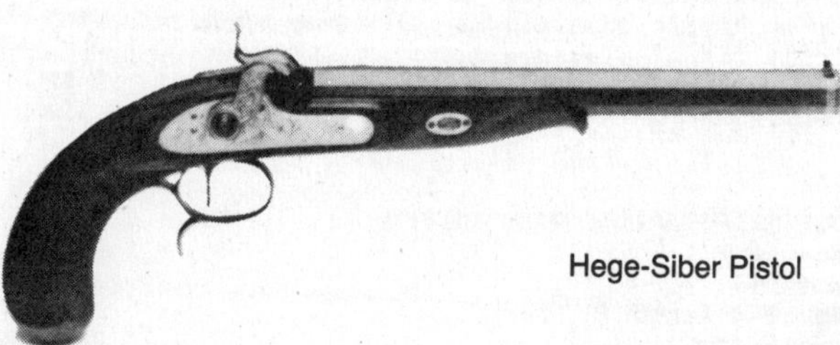

Hege-Siber Pistol

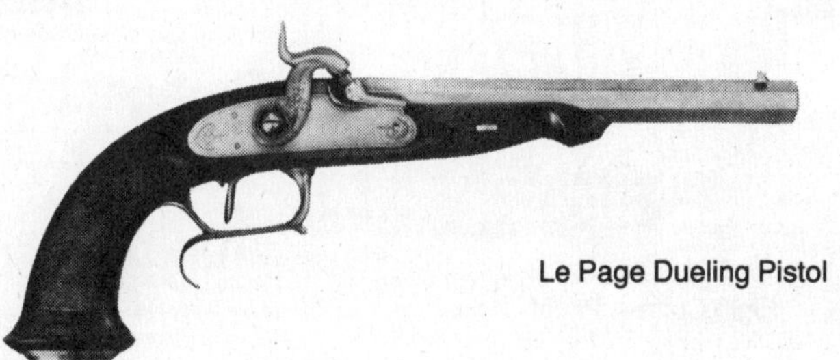

Le Page Dueling Pistol

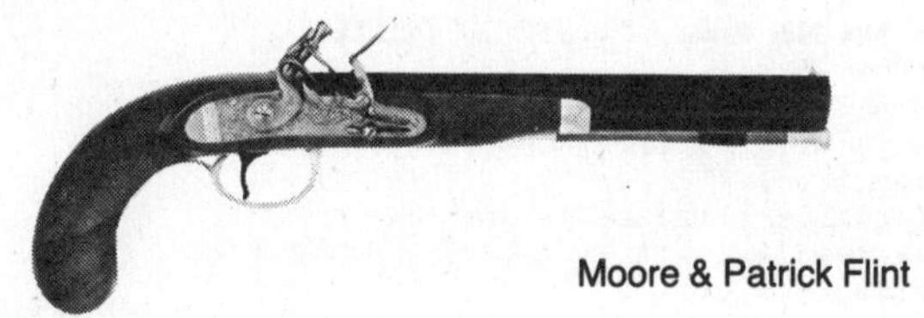

Moore & Patrick Flint

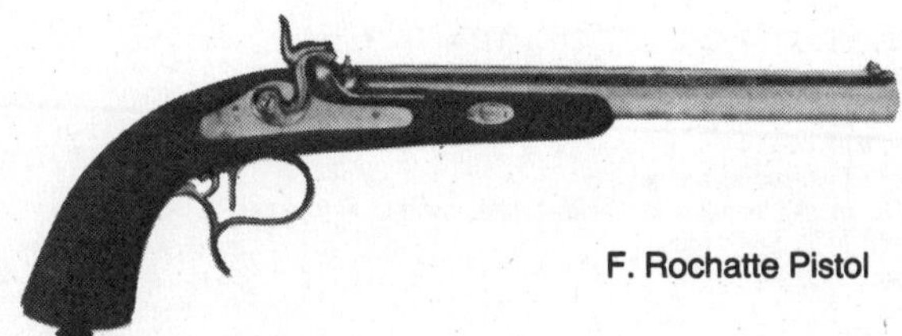

F. Rochatte Pistol

H&A 1810 ENGLISH DUELING PISTOL
Caliber: 45.
Barrel: 11".
Weight: 2 lbs., 5 oz. **Length:** 15" over-all.
Stock: European walnut, checkered, with German silver inlays.
Sights: Fixed.
Features: Double set triggers, precision "match" barrel, silver plated furniture, browned barrel. Percussion lock only. From Hopkins & Allen.
Price: **$265.30**

HARPER'S FERRY MODEL 1855 PERCUSSION PISTOL
Caliber: 58.
Barrel: 11¾", rifled.
Weight: 56 oz. **Length:** 18" over-all.
Stock: Walnut.
Sights: Fixed.
Features: Case hardened lock and hammer; brass furniture; blued bbl. Shoulder stock available, priced at $35.00. Imported by Navy Arms.
Price: **$218.50**
Price: With detachable shoulder stock **$263.50**

HEGE-SIBER PISTOL
Caliber: 33, 44.
Barrel: 10".
Weight: 34 oz. **Length:** 15½" over-all.
Stock: French walnut, cut-checkered grip.
Sights: Barleycorn front, micro adjustable rear.
Features: Reproduction of pistol made by Swiss watchmaker Jean Siber in the 1800s. Precise lock and set trigger give fast lock time. French Deluxe version (illus.) is engraved, has gold trim on blued barrel; English/British version has less ornate engraving, plum browned barrel, trigger guard. Imported by Beeman, 33-cal. only, Navy Arms, 33, 44 cals. Introduced 1984.
Price: French **$1,120.00**
Price: British **$735.00**
Price: French, matched pair **$2,260.00**

NAVY ARMS LE PAGE DUELING PISTOL
Caliber: 44.
Barrel: 9", octagon, rifled.
Weight: 34 oz. **Length:** 15" over-all.
Stock: European walnut.
Sights: Adjustable rear.
Features: Single set trigger. Polished metal finish. From Navy Arms.
Price: **$275.00**
Price: Single cased set **$440.00**
Price: Double cased set **$725.00**

BRITISH DRAGOON FLINT PISTOL
Caliber: .615".
Barrel: 12", polished steel.
Weight: 3 lbs., 2 oz. **Length:** 19" over-all.
Stock: Walnut, with brass furniture.
Features: Lockplate marked "Willets 1761." Brass trigger guard and butt cap. Made in U.S. by Navy Arms.
Price: **$475.00**
Price: Kit **$295.00**

MOORE & PATRICK FLINT DUELING PISTOL
Caliber: 45.
Barrel: 10", rifled.
Weight: 32 oz. **Length:** 14½" over-all.
Stock: European walnut, checkered.
Sights: Fixed.
Features: Engraved, silvered lock plate, blue barrel. German silver furniture. Imported from Italy by Dixie and Navy Arms.
Price: .... **$200.00 to $225.00**

H & A ENGLISH FLINTLOCK TARGET PISTOL
Caliber: 45.
Barrel: 10".
Weight: 2 lbs. 4 oz. **Length:** 15" over-all.
Stock: English walnut with checkered grip.
Sights: Fixed.
Features: Engraved lock in white, browned barrel, German silver furniture. Special roller bearing frizzen spring. Also available in percussion lock. From Hopkins & Allen.
Price: **$254.30**

F. ROCHATTE PERCUSSION PISTOL
Caliber: 45, uses .440" round ball.
Barrel: 10", rifled.
Weight: 32 oz. **Length:** 16½" over-all.
Stock: European walnut.
Sights: Dovetailed front and rear, adj. for windage.
Features: Single adj. trigger, highly polished lock and round barrel with top flat; all steel furniture. French-style finial on butt. From Navy Arms.
Price: Finished gun **$250.00**

BLACK POWDER SINGLE SHOT PISTOLS—FLINT & PERCUSSION

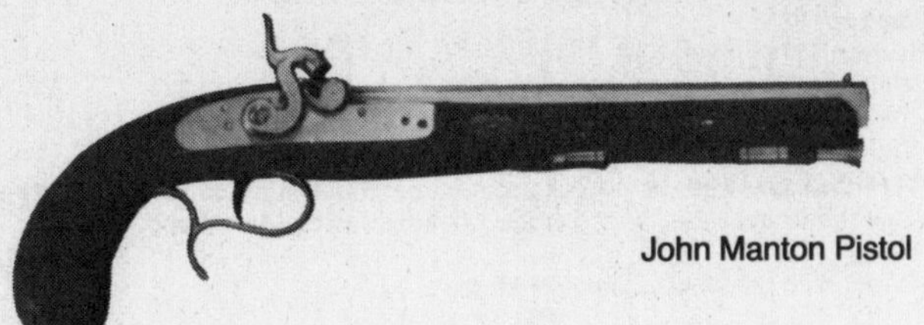

John Manton Pistol

JOHN MANTON MATCH PISTOL
Caliber: 45, uses .440" round ball.
Barrel: 10", rifled.
Weight: 36 oz. **Length:** 15½" over-all.
Stock: European walnut; checkered grip.
Sights: Bead front.
Features: Highly polished steel barrel and lock, brass furniture. From Navy Arms.
Price: Finished gun $225.00

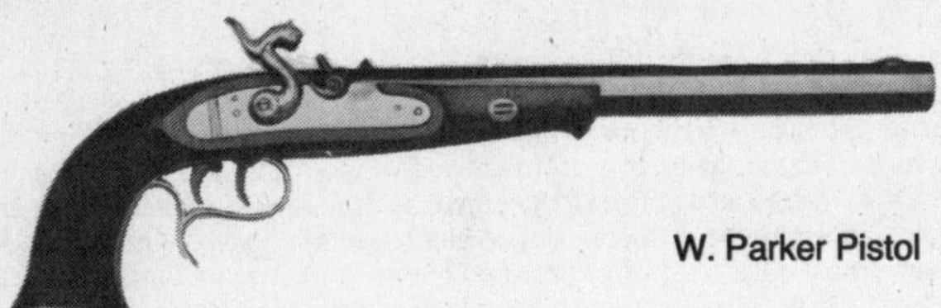

W. Parker Pistol

W. PARKER PERCUSSION PISTOL
Caliber: 45, uses .440" round ball.
Barrel: 10", rifled.
Weight: 40 oz. **Length:** 16" over-all.
Stock: European walnut; checkered grip.
Sights: Dovetailed front and rear, adj.for windage.
Features: Fully adj. double set triggers, German silver furniture; lock engraved "London." From Navy Arms.
Price: Finished gun $250.00
Price: As above from Dixie, 11" bbl. $250.00

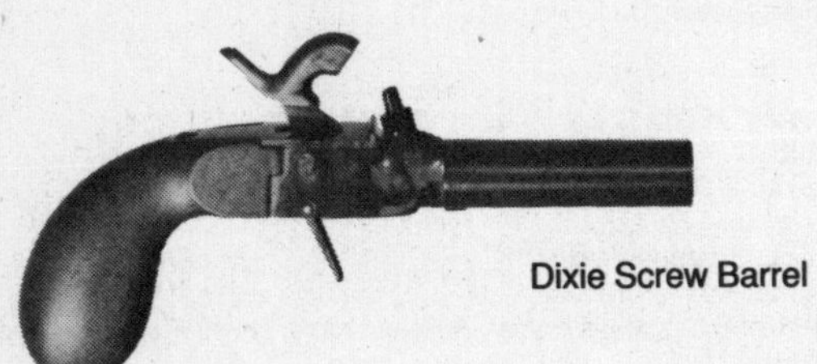

Dixie Screw Barrel

DIXIE SCREW BARREL PISTOL
Caliber: .445".
Barrel: 2½".
Weight: 8 oz. **Length:** 6½" over-all.
Stocks: Walnut.
Features: Trigger folds down when hammer is cocked. Close copy of the originals once made in Belgium. Uses No. 11 percussion caps.
Price: $79.95

ELGIN CUTLASS PISTOL
Caliber: 44 (.440").
Barrel: 4¼".
Weight: 21 oz. **Length:** 12" over-all.
Stock: Walnut.
Sights: None.
Features: Replica of the pistol used by the U.S. Navy as a boarding weapon. Smoothbore barrel. Available as a kit or finished. Made in U.S. by Navy Arms.
Price: Kit $78.50
Price: Finished $104.95

Elgin Cutlass Pistol

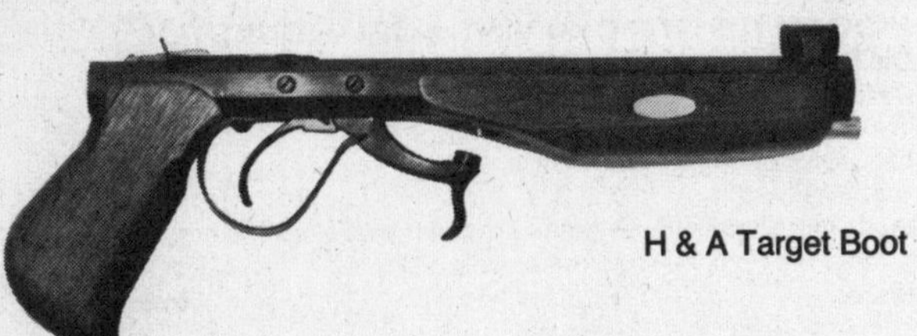

H & A Target Boot

HOPKINS & ALLEN BOOT PISTOL
Caliber: 45.
Barrel: 6".
Weight: 42 oz. **Length:** 13" over-all.
Stock: Walnut.
Sights: Silver blade front; rear adj. for e.
Features: Under-hammer design. From Hopkins & Allen.
Price: $71.50
Price: Kit form $55.20
Price: Target version with wood fore-end, ramrod, hood front sight, elevator rear $89.80

Consult our Directory pages for the location of firms mentioned.

CVA VEST POCKET DERRINGER
Caliber: 44.
Barrel: 2½", brass.
Weight: 7 oz.
Stock: Two-piece walnut.
Features: All brass frame with brass ramrod. A muzzle-loading version of the Colt No. 3 derringer.
Price: Finished $39.95
Price: Kit $34.95

Thompson/Center Patriot

THOMPSON/CENTER PATRIOT PERCUSSION PISTOL
Caliber: 36, 45.
Barrel: 9¼".
Weight: 36 oz. **Length:** 16" over-all.
Stock: Walnut.
Sights: Patridge-type. Rear adj. for w. and e.
Features: Hook breech system; double set triggers; coil mainspring. From Thompson/Center Arms.
Price: $195.00

CAUTION: PRICES CHANGE. CHECK AT GUNSHOP.

BLACK POWDER SINGLE SHOT PISTOLS—FLINT & PERCUSSION

Dixie Tornado Target

DIXIE TORNADO TARGET PISTOL
Caliber: 44 (.430″ round ball).
Barrel: 10″, octagonal, 1-in-22″ twist.
Stock: Walnut, target-style. Left unfinished for custom fitting. Walnut fore-end.
Sights: Blade on ramp front, micro-type open rear adjustable for windage and elevation.
Features: Grip frame style of 1860 Colt revolver. Improved model of the Tingle and B.W. Southgate pistol. Trigger adjustable for pull. Frame, barrel, hammer and sights in the white, brass trigger guard. Comes with solid brass, walnut-handled cleaning rod with jag and nylon muzzle protector. Introduced 1983. From Dixie Gun Works.
Price: **$145.00**

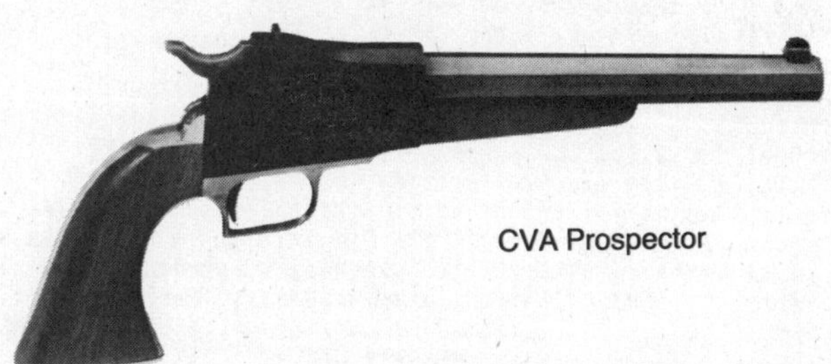
CVA Prospector

CVA PROSPECTOR SINGLE SHOT PERCUSSION PISTOL
Caliber: 44.
Barrel: 8½″, octagonal.
Weight: 42 oz. **Length:** 12¾″ over-all.
Stocks: One-piece walnut.
Sights: Blade front, hammer notch rear.
Features: Brass backstrap and trigger guard, rest blued. Frame engraved with two different scenes. Introduced 1984.
Price: Finished **$81.95**
Price: Kit **$62.95**

BLACK POWDER REVOLVERS

TEXAS PATERSON 1836 REVOLVER
Caliber: 36 (.376″ round ball).
Barrel: 7½″.
Weight: 42 oz.
Stocks: One-piece walnut.
Sights: Fixed.
Features: Copy of Sam Colt's first commercially-made revolving pistol. Has no loading lever but comes with loading tool. From Dixie Gun Works, Navy Arms.
Price: **$225.00**

TEXAS MOUNTED VOLUNTEERS COMMEMORATIVE 1847 WALKER
Caliber: 44, 6 shot.
Barrel: 9″.
Weight: 73 oz.
Stocks: Walnut.
Sights: Fixed.
Features: Case hardened frame, loading lever, hammer; cylinder engraved and in the white as original; brass trigger guard; commemorative markings and book on the history of the Walker pistol. From Whittington Arms.
Price: **$285.00**

WALKER 1847 PERCUSSION REVOLVER
Caliber: 44, 6-shot.
Barrel: 9″.
Weight: 72 oz. **Length:** 15½″ over-all.
Stocks: Walnut.
Sights: Fixed.
Features: Case hardened frame, loading lever and hammer; iron backstrap; brass trigger guard; engraved cylinder. Imported by Navy Arms, Dixie, Armsport, Allen Fire Arms.
Price: .... **$125.00** to **$249.00**
Price: Single cased set (Navy Arms) **$264.00**

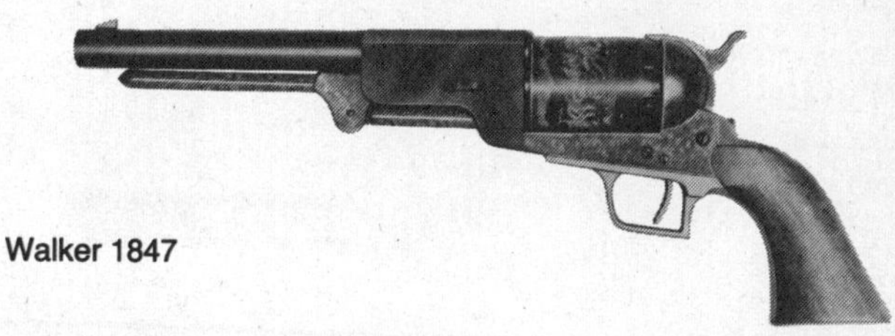
Walker 1847

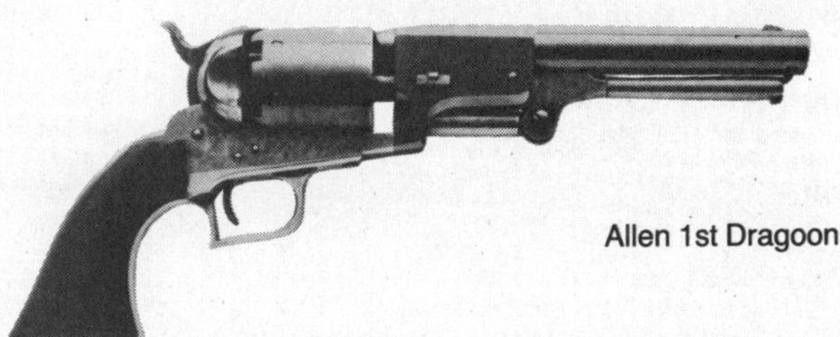
Allen 1st Dragoon

ALLEN 1st MODEL DRAGOON
Caliber: 44.
Barrel: 7½″, part round, part octagon.
Weight: 66 oz.
Stocks: One piece walnut.
Sights: German silver blade front, hammer notch rear.
Features: First model has oval bolt cuts in cylinder, square-back flared trigger guard, V-type mainspring, short trigger. Ranger and Indian scene on cylinder. Color cased frame, loading lever, plunger and hammer; blue barrel, cylinder, trigger and wedge. Available with old-time charcoal blue or standard blue-black finish. Polished brass backstrap and trigger guard. From Allen Fire Arms.
Price: **$229.00**

Allen 2nd Dragoon

Allen 2nd Model Dragoon Revolver
Similar to the 1st Model except this model is distinguished by its rectangular bolt cuts in the cylinder, straight square-back trigger guard, short trigger and flat mainspring with roller in hammer.
Price: **$229.00**
Price: As Confederate Tucker & Sherrard, with 3rd Model loading lever and special cylinder engraving.................................. **$239.00**

Allen 3rd Model Dragoon Revolver
Similar to the 2nd Model except has oval trigger guard, long trigger.
Price: **$225.00**
Price: With silver plated guard and backstrap.................... **$239.00**

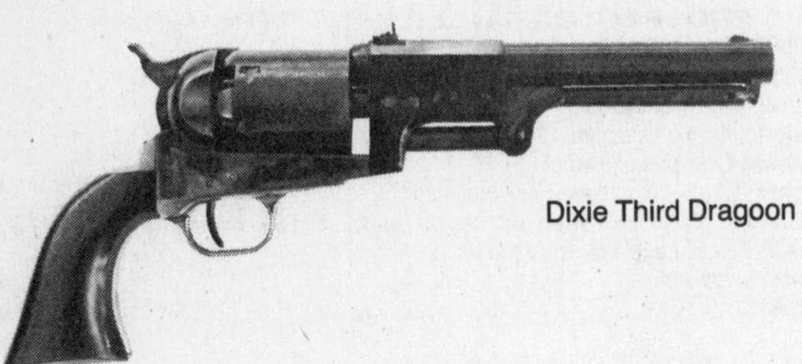
Dixie Third Dragoon

DIXIE THIRD MODEL DRAGOON
Caliber: 44 ((.454″ round ball).
Barrel: 7⅜″.
Weight: 4 lbs., 2½ oz.
Stocks: One-piece walnut.
Sights: Brass pin front, hammer notch rear, or adjustable folding leaf rear.
Features: Cylinder engraved with Indian fight scene. This is the only Dragoon replica with folding leaf sight. Brass backstrap and trigger guard; color case-hardened steel frame, blue-black barrel. Imported by Dixie Gun Works.
Price: **$140.00**

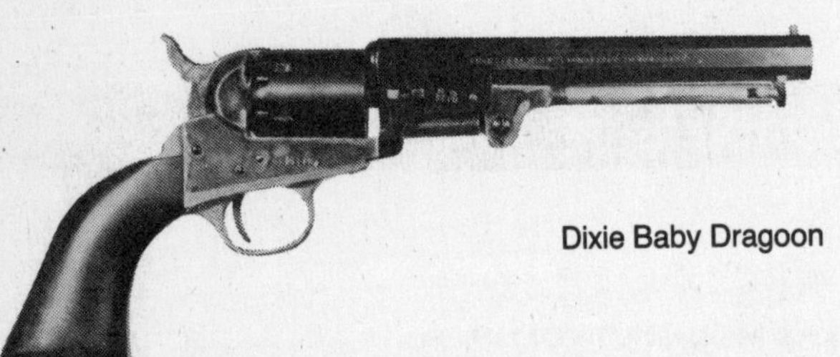
Dixie Baby Dragoon

BABY DRAGOON AND MODEL 1849 REVOLVERS
Caliber: 31.
Barrel: 3″, 4″, 5″; 7 groove, RH twist.
Weight: About 21 oz.
Stocks: Varnished walnut.
Sights: Brass pin front, hammer notch rear.
Features: No loading lever on Allen Baby Dragoon models. Unfluted cylinder with Ranger and Indian scene; cupped cylinder pin; no grease grooves; one safety pin on cylinder and slot in hammer face; straight (flat) mainspring. Silver backstrap and trigger guard. From Allen Fire Arms, Dixie, CVA.
Price: **$199.00**
Price: 6″ barrel, with loading lever (Dixie) **$125.00**
Price: 4″ barrel, brass frame, no loading lever (CVA) **$88.95**
Price: Kit (CVA) **$74.95**

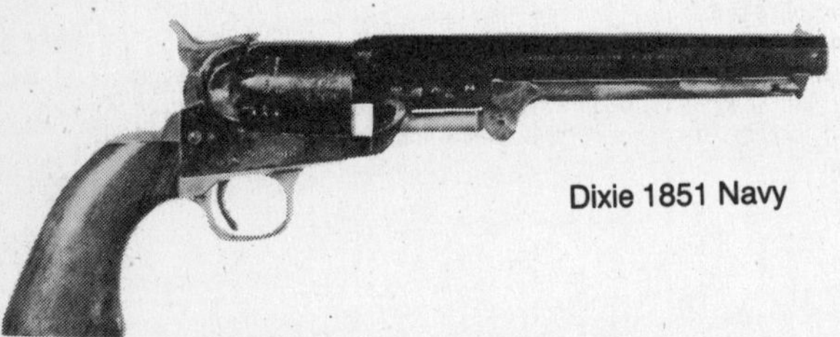
Dixie 1851 Navy

NAVY MODEL 1851 PERCUSSION REVOLVER
Caliber: 36, 6-shot.
Barrel: 7½″.
Weight: 44 oz. **Length:** 13″ over-all.
Stocks: Walnut finish.
Sights: Post front, hammer notch rear.
Features: Brass backstrap and trigger guard; some have 1st model square-back trigger guard, engraved cylinder with navy battle scene; case hardened frame, hammer, loading lever. Imported by The Armoury, Navy Arms, Allen, Dixie, Euroarms of America, Armsport, Hopkins & Allen, CVA.
Price: Brass frame .... **$40.95** to **$140.95**
Price: Steel frame .... **$31.50** to **$209.00**
Price: Stainless Squareback (Allen)............................ **$239.00**
Price: Kit form.................................... **$30.95** to **$119.95**
Price: Engraved model (Dixie)................................. **$97.50**
Price: Also as "Hartford Pistol," Kit (Richard) ...... **$59.95** Complete **$79.95**
Price: Also as "Buntline" (Hopkins & Allen, Dixie)................ **$166.95**
Price: Navy-Civilian model (Navy Arms, Allen)..................... **$124.50**
Price: Single cased set, steel frame (Navy Arms) **$207.00**
Price: Double cased set, steel frame (Navy Arms) **$339.75**
Price: As above, civilian model (Navy Arms) **$212.00**
Price: Double cased set, civilian model (Navy Arms) **$350.00**
Price: Shoulder stock (Navy Arms).............................. **$45.00**
Price: London Model with iron backstrap (Allen) **$219.00**

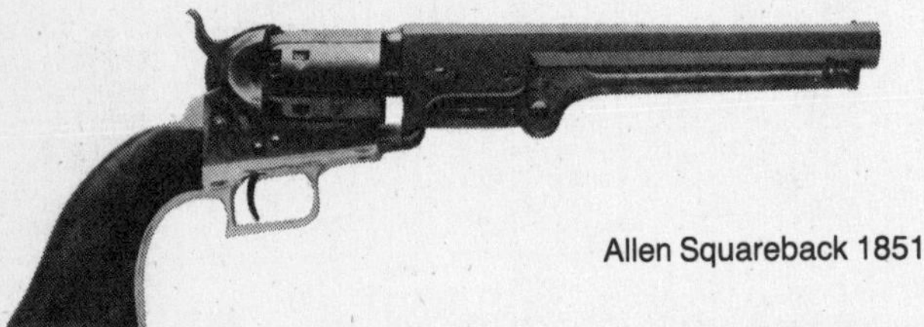
Allen Squareback 1851

ARMY 1851 PERCUSSION REVOLVER
Caliber: 44, 6-shot.
Barrel: 7½″.
Weight: 45 oz. **Length:** 13″ over-all.
Stocks: Walnut finish.
Sights: Fixed.
Features: 44 caliber version of the 1851 Navy. Imported by The Armoury.
Price: **$138.00**

1851 NAVY-SHERIFF
Same as 1851 Sheriff model except has 4″ barrel. Imported by Allen, Euroarms of America.
Price: .... **$50.00** to **$114.95**

Allen 1861 Navy Percussion Revolver
Similar to 1851 Navy except has round 7½″ barrel, rounded trigger guard, German silver blade front sight, "creeping" loading lever.
Price: **$215.00**
Price: Stainless **$219.00**

CAUTION: PRICES CHANGE. CHECK AT GUNSHOP.

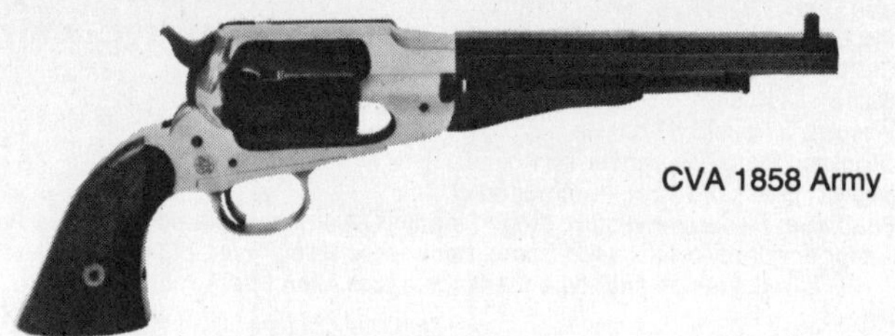
CVA 1858 Army

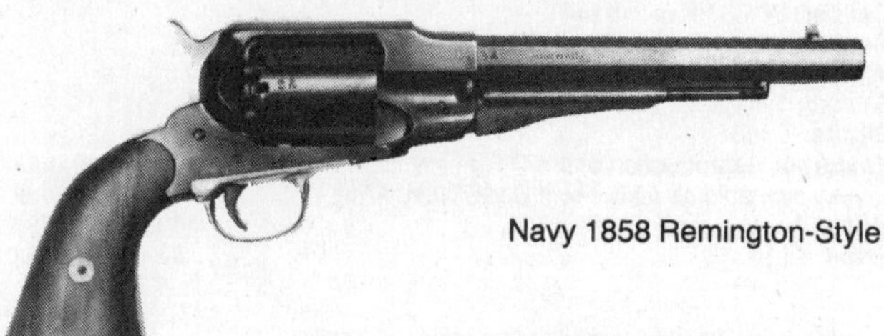
Navy 1858 Remington-Style

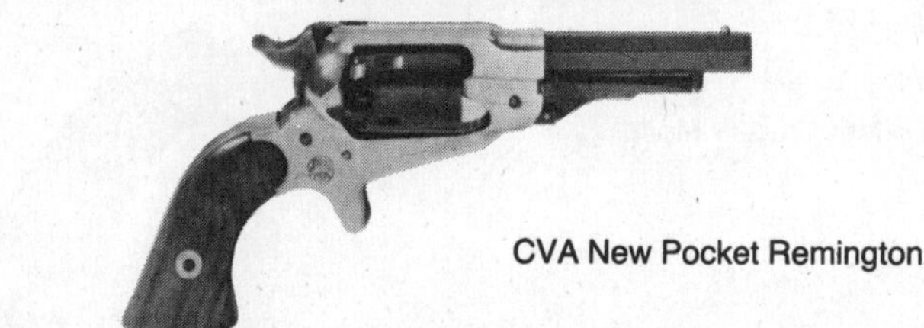
CVA New Pocket Remington

Dixie 1860 Army

ROGERS & SPENCER PERCUSSION REVOLVER

Caliber: 44.
Barrel: 7½″.
Weight: 47 oz. **Length:** 13¾″ over-all.
Stocks: Walnut.
Sights: Cone front, integral groove in frame for rear.
Features: Accurate reproduction of a Civil War design. Solid frame; extra large nipple cut-out on rear of cylinder; loading lever and cylinder easily removed for cleaning. Comes with six spare nipples and wrench/screwdriver. From Euroarms of America (engraved, burnished, target models), Navy Arms, Dixie.
Price: .... **$120.00** to **$169.00**
Price: Nickel plated **$120.00**
Price: Kit version **$95.00**
Price: Target version **$200.00**

1862 POCKET POLICE PERCUSSION REVOLVER

Caliber: 36, 5-shot.
Barrel: 4½″, 5½″, 7½″.
Weight: 26 oz. **Length:** 12″ (6½″ bbl.).
Stocks: Walnut.
Sights: Fixed.
Features: Half-fluted and rebated cylinder; case hardened frame, loading lever and hammer; silver trigger guard and backstrap. Imported by Navy Arms (5½″ only), Euroarms of America (7½″ only) Allen (all lengths).
Price: .... **$198.00** to **$209.00**
Price: Cased with accessories (Navy Arms) **$250.00**
Price: Stainless steel (Allen) **$235.00**

NEW MODEL 1858 ARMY PERCUSSION REVOLVER

Caliber: 36 or 44, 6-shot.
Barrel: 6½″ or 8″.
Weight: 40 oz. **Length:** 13½″ over-all.
Stocks: Walnut.
Sights: Blade front, groove-in-frame rear.
Features: Replica of Remington Model 1858. Also available from some importers as Army Model Belt Revolver in 36 cal., shortened and lightened version of the 44. Target Model (Allen, Navy) has fully adj. target rear sight, target front, 36 or 44 ($74.95-$209.00). Imported by CVA, (as 1858 Remington Army), Dixie, Navy Arms, Hopkins & Allen, The Armoury, Euroarms of America (engraved, stainless and plain), Armsport, Allen.
Price: .... **$49.95** to **$215.00**
Price: Single cased set (Navy Arms) **$225.00**
Price: Double cased set (Navy Arms) **$375.00**
Price: Kit form .... **$66.95** to **$123.95**
Price: Nickel finish (Navy Arms) **$152.75**
Price: Single cased set (Navy Arms) **$240.00**
Price: Double cased set (Navy Arms) **$400.00**
Price: Stainless steel (Euroarms, Navy Arms, Allen) .... **$140.00** to **$259.00**
Price: Target model (Euroarms, Navy Arms, Allen) .... **$95.95** to **$185.00**
Price: Brass frame, finished (CVA) **$119.95**
Price: As above, kit (CVA) **$99.95**

NAVY ARMS 1858 REMINGTON-STYLE REVOLVER

Caliber: 44.
Barrel: 8″.
Weight: 2 lbs., 13 ozs.
Stock: Smooth walnut.
Sights: Dovetailed blade front.
Features: First exact reproduction — correct in size and weight to the original, with progressive rifling; highly polished with charcoal blue finish. From Navy Arms.
Price: **$225.00**

CVA NEW MODEL POCKET REMINGTON

Caliber: 31.
Barrel: 4″, octagonal.
Weight: 15½ oz. **Length:** 7½″ over-all.
Stocks: Two-piece walnut.
Sights: Post front, grooved top-strap rear.
Features: Spur trigger, brass frame with blued barrel and cylinder. Available finished or in kit form. Introduced 1984.
Price: Finished **$80.95**
Price: Kit **$66.95**

1860 ARMY PERCUSSION REVOLVER

Caliber: 44, 6-shot.
Barrel: 8″.
Weight: 40 oz. **Length:** 13⅝″ over-all.
Stocks: Walnut.
Sights: Fixed.
Features: Engraved navy scene on cylinder; brass trigger guard; case hardened frame, loading lever and hammer. Some importers supply pistol cut for detachable shoulder stock, have accessory stock available. Imported by Navy Arms, The Armoury, Dixie (half-fluted cylinder, not roll engraved), Euroarms of America (engraved, stainless steel or burnished steel model), Armsport, Hopkins & Allen, Allen.
Price: .... **$44.95** to **$219.00**
Price: Single cased set (Navy Arms) **$220.00**
Price: Double cased set (Navy Arms) **$365.00**
Price: 1861 Navy: Same as Army except 36 cal., 7½″ bbl., wt. 41 oz., cut for stock; round cylinder (fluted avail.), from Navy, Allen, CVA (brass frame) .... **$99.95** to **$245.00**
Price: Single cased set (Navy Arms) **$230.00**
Price: Double cased set (Navy Arms) **$386.50**
Price: Kit (CVA) **$121.95**
Price: Stainless steel (Euroarms, Allen) .... **$200.00** to **$245.00**

1862 LEECH & RIGDON REVOLVER

Caliber: 36.
Barrel: 7½″.
Weight: 2 lbs., 10 oz. **Length:** 13½″ over-all.
Stocks: Smooth walnut.
Sights: Fixed.
Features: Modern version of the famous Civil War revolver. Brass backstrap and trigger guard. Color case hardened frame. Copy of the Colt Navy but with rounded Dragoon-type barrel. From Navy Arms, Allen Fire Arms.
Price: **$136.50**

BLACK POWDER REVOLVERS

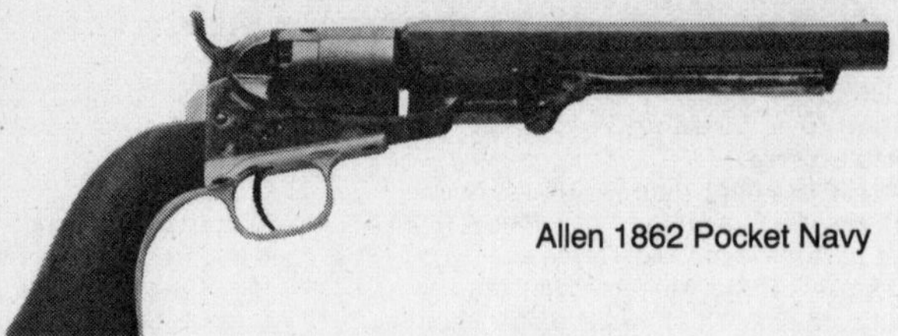

Allen 1862 Pocket Navy

ALLEN 1862 POCKET NAVY PERCUSSION REVOLVER

Caliber: 36.
Barrel: 4½″, 5½″, 6½″, octagonal, 7 groove, LH twist.
Weight: 27 oz. (5½″ barrel)
Stocks: One piece varnished walnut.
Sights: Brass pin front, hammer notch rear.
Features: Rebated cylinder, hinged loading lever, silver plated backstrap and trigger guard, color cased frame, hammer, loading lever, plunger and latch, rest blued. Has original-type markings. From Allen Fire Arms.
Price: **$209.00**

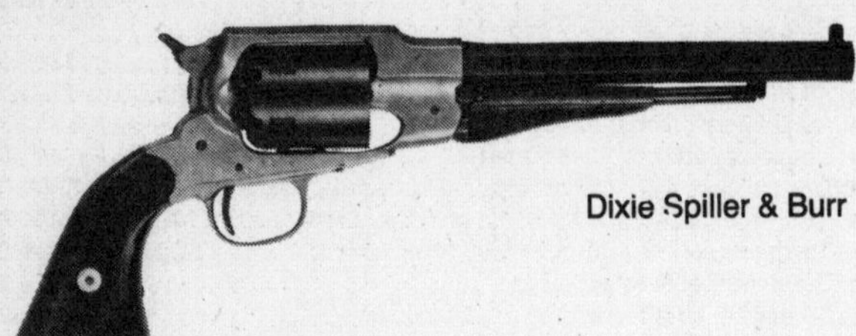

Dixie Spiller & Burr

SPILLER & BURR REVOLVER

Caliber: 36 (.375″ round ball).
Barrel: 7″, octagon.
Weight: 2½ lbs. **Length:** 12½″ over-all.
Stocks: Two-piece walnut.
Sights: Fixed.
Features: Reproduction of the C.S.A. revolver. Brass frame and trigger guard. Also available as a kit. From Dixie, Navy Arms.
Price: .... **$69.95** to **$109.00**
Price: Kit form .... **$39.95** to **$65.00**

LE MAT CAVALRY MODEL REVOLVER

Caliber: 44/65.
Barrel: 6¾″ (revolver); 4⅞″ (single shot).
Weight: NA.
Stocks: Hand-checkered walnut.
Sights: Post front, hammer-notch rear.
Features: Exact reproduction with all-steel construction; 44-cal. 9-shot cylinder, 65-cal. single barrel; color case-hardened hammer with selector; spur trigger guard; ring at butt; lever-type barrel release. From Navy Arms.
Price: **$500.00**
Price: Army model (round trigger guard, pin-type barrel release) **$500.00**
Price: Naval-style (thumb selector or hammer) **$500.00**

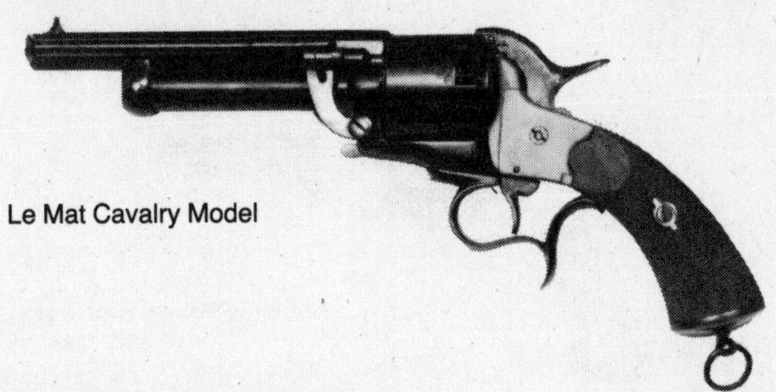

Le Mat Cavalry Model

Consult our Directory pages for the location of firms mentioned.

DIXIE "WYATT EARP" REVOLVER

Caliber: 44.
Barrel: 12″ octagon.
Weight: 46 oz. **Length:** 18″ over-all.
Stocks: Two piece walnut.
Sights: Fixed.
Features: Highly polished brass frame, backstrap and trigger guard; blued barrel and cylinder; case hardened hammer, trigger and loading lever. Navy-size shoulder stock ($45.00) will fit with minor fitting. From Dixie Gun Works.
Price: **$99.95**

GRISWOLD & GUNNISON PERCUSSION REVOLVER

Caliber: 36 or 44, 6-shot.
Barrel: 7½″.
Weight: 44 oz. (36 cal.). **Length:** 13″ over-all.
Stocks: Walnut.
Sights: Fixed.
Features: Replica of famous Confederate pistol. Brass frame, backstrap and trigger guard; case hardened loading lever; rebated cylinder (44 cal. only). Rounded Dragoon-type barrel. Imported by Navy Arms, Allen.
Price: **$169.00**
Price: Kit (Navy Arms) **$76.75**
Price: Single cased set (Navy Arms) **$180.00**
Price: Double cased set (Navy Arms) **$288.00**
Price: Shoulder stock (Navy Arms) **$60.00**

Freedom Mini Percussion

FREEDOM ARMS PERCUSSION MINI REVOLVER

Caliber: 22, 5-shot.
Barrel: 1″, 1¾″, 3″.
Weight: 4¾ oz. (1″ bbl.).
Stocks: Simulated ebony, or rosewood (optional).
Sights: Fixed.
Features: Percussion version of the 22 RF gun. All stainless steel; spur trigger. Gun comes with leather carrying pouch, bullet setting tool, powder measure, 20 29-gr. bullets. Introduced 1983. From Freedom Arms.
Price: 1″ barrel **$130.00**
Price: 1¾″ barrel **$130.00**
Price: 3″ barrel **$142.70**

Ruger Old Army

RUGER 44 OLD ARMY PERCUSSION REVOLVER

Caliber: 44, 6-shot. Uses .457″ dia. lead bullets.
Barrel: 7½″ (6-groove, 16″ twist).
Weight: 46 oz. **Length:** 13¾″ over-all.
Stocks: Smooth walnut.
Sights: Ramp front, rear adj. for w. and e.
Features: Stainless steel standard size nipples, chrome-moly steel cylinder and frame, same lockwork as in original Super Blackhawk. Also available in stainless steel in very limited quantities. Made in USA. From Sturm, Ruger & Co.
Price: Stainless steel (Model KBP-7) **$285.00**
Price: Blued steel (Model BP-7) **$216.50**

CAUTION: PRICES CHANGE. CHECK AT GUNSHOP.

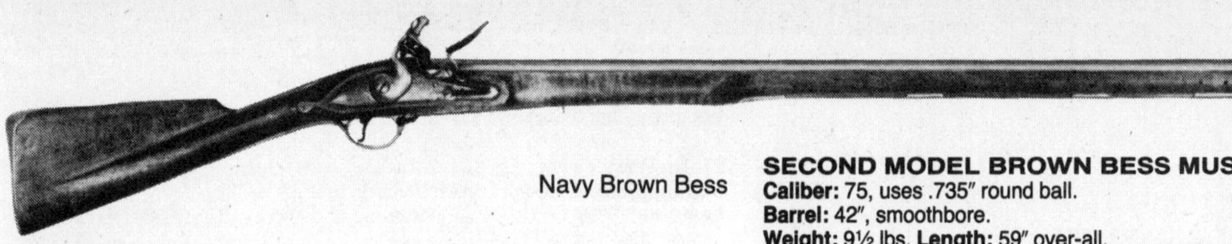

Navy Brown Bess

NAVY ARMS CHARLEVILLE MUSKET
Caliber: 69
Barrel: 44⅝″.
Weight: 8¾ lbs. **Length:** 59⅜″ over-all.
Stock: Walnut.
Sights: Blade front.
Features: Replica of Revolutionary War 1763 musket. Bright metal, walnut stock. From Navy Arms.
Price: Finished **$400.00**
Price: Kit **$310.00**

SECOND MODEL BROWN BESS MUSKET
Caliber: 75, uses .735″ round ball.
Barrel: 42″, smoothbore.
Weight: 9½ lbs. **Length:** 59″ over-all.
Stock: Walnut (Navy); walnut-stained hardwood (Dixie).
Sights: Fixed.
Features: Polished barrel and lock with brass trigger guard and buttplate. Bayonet and scabbard available. From Navy Arms, Dixie.
Price: Finished .... **$290.00 to $450.00**
Price: Kit .... **$265.00 to $342.00**

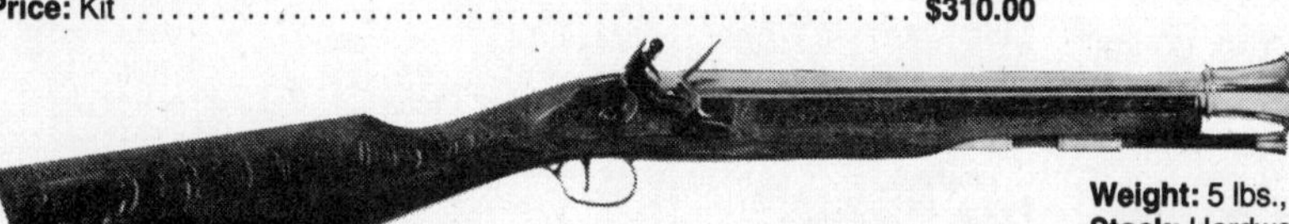

CVA Blunderbuss

CVA BLUNDERBUSS
Caliber: 69.
Barrel: 16″, brass smoothbore, tapered to flared muzzle.
Weight: 5 lbs., 5 oz. **Length:** 31½ oz.
Stock: Hardwood.
Sights: None.
Features: Styled after 1700s British guns. Historically correct oval-shaped barrel. Engraved, color case hardened flintlock with screw-adjustable sear engagement and authentic V-type mainspring. Solid brass buttplate, ramrod thimbles, trigger, trigger guard, barrel and engraved sideplate. Introduced 1984.
Price: Finished **$249.95**
Price: Kit **$209.95**

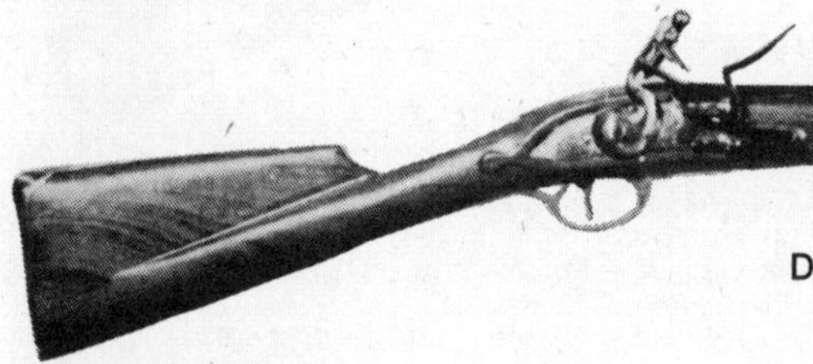

Dixie Indian Gun

DIXIE INDIAN GUN
Caliber: 75.
Barrel: 31″, round tapered.
Weight: About 9 lbs. **Length:** 47″ over-all.
Stock: Hardwood.
Sights: Blade front.
Features: Modified Brown Bess musket; brass furniture, browned lock and barrel. Lock is marked "GRICE 1762" with crown over "GR." Serpent-style sideplate. Introduced 1983.
Price: Complete **$375.00**
Price: As above, in kit form **$360.00**

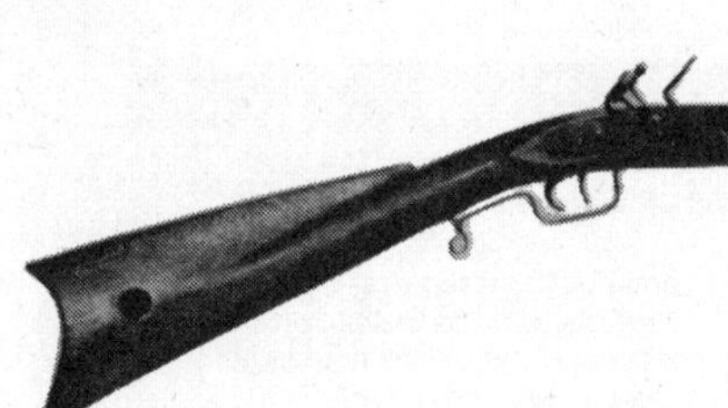

Dixie Tennessee Rifle

DIXIE TENNESSEE MOUNTAIN RIFLE
Caliber: 32 or 50.
Barrel: 41½″, 6-groove rifling, brown finish.
Length: 56″ over-all.
Stock: Walnut, oil finish; Kentucky-style.
Sights: Silver blade front, open buckhorn rear.
Features: Re-creation of the original mountain rifles. Early Schultz lock, interchangeable flint or percussion with vent plug or drum and nipple. Tumbler has fly. Double-set triggers. All metal parts browned. From Dixie.
Price: Flint or Percussion, finished rifle, 50 cal. **$250.00**
Price: Kit, 50 cal. **$195.00**
Price: Left-hand model, flint or perc. **$250.00**
Price: Left-hand kit, flint or perc., 50 cal. **$225.00**
Price: Squirrel Rifle (as above except in 32 cal. with 13/16″ barrel), flint or percussion **$295.00**
Price: Kit, 32 cal., flint or percussion **$255.00**

KENTUCKY FLINTLOCK RIFLE
Caliber: 44 or 45.
Barrel: 35″.
Weight: 7lbs. **Length:** 50″ over-all.
Stock: Walnut stained, brass fittings.
Sights: Fixed.
Features: Available in Carbine model also, 28″ bbl. Some variations in detail, finish. Kits also available from some importers. Imported by Navy Arms, The Armoury, CVA, Armsport, Hopkins & Allen.
Price: .... **$59.95 to $273.75**
Price: Kit form (CVA, Numrich) .... **$72.95 to 189.95**
Price: Deluxe model, flint or percussion (Navy Arms), about **$400.00**
Price: As above, 50-cal. (Navy Arms) **$273.75**

Kentucky Percussion Rifle
Similar to flintlock except percussion lock. Finish and features vary with importer. Imported by Navy Arms, The Armoury, CVA, Hopkins & Allen, Armsport (rifle-shotgun combo).
Price: .... **$54.95 to 250.00**
Price: Armsport combo **$295.00**
Price: Deluxe model (Navy Arms) **$375.00**
Price: 50 cal. (Navy Arms) **$246.00**

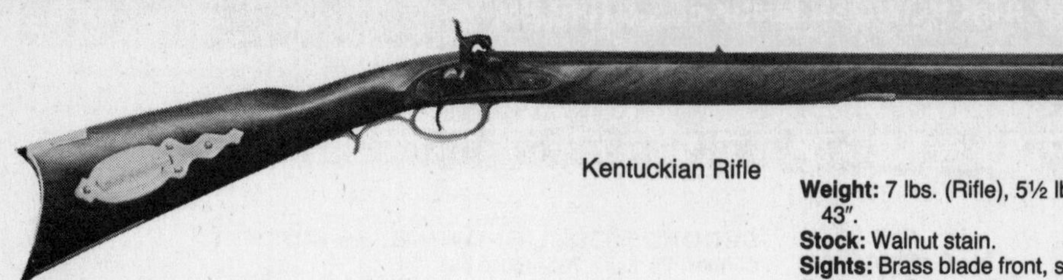

Kentuckian Rifle

KENTUCKIAN RIFLE & CARBINE

Caliber: 44.
Barrel: 35″ (Rifle), 27½″ (Carbine).
Weight: 7 lbs. (Rifle), 5½ lbs. (Carbine). **Length:** 51″ (Rifle) over-all, Carbine 43″.
Stock: Walnut stain.
Sights: Brass blade front, steel V-Ramp rear.
Features: Octagon bbl., case hardened and engraved lock plate. Brass furniture. Imported by Dixie.
Price: Rifle or carbine, flint **$185.00**
Price: As above, percussion **$175.00**

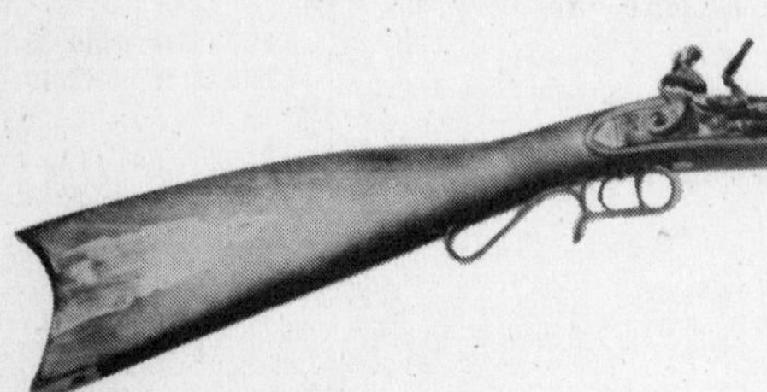

Dixie York County

YORK COUNTY RIFLE

Caliber: 45 (.445″ round ball).
Barrel: 36″, rifled, ⅞″ octagon, blue.
Weight: 7½ lbs. **Length:** 51½″ over-all.
Stock: Maple, one piece.
Sights: Blade front, V-notch rear, brass.
Features: Adjustable double-set triggers. Brass trigger guard, patchbox, buttplate, nosecap and sideplate. Case-hardened lockplate. From Dixie Gun Works.
Price: Percussion........ **$210.00**
Price: Flint........ **$215.00**
Price: Percussion Kit........ **$149.00**
Price: Flint Kit........ **$160.00**

Hatfield Squirrel Rifle

HATFIELD SQUIRREL RIFLE

Caliber: 32, 36, 45, 50
Barrel: 39½″, octagon, 32″ on half-stock.
Weight: 8 lbs. (32 cal.).
Stock: American fancy maple fullstock.
Sights: Silver blade front, buckhorn rear
Features: Recreation of the traditional squirrel rifle. Available in flint or percussion with brass trigger guard and buttplate. From Hatfield Rifle Works. Introduced 1983.
Price: Full-stock, flint or percussion Grade I **$295.00**
Price: As above, Grade II........ **$359.00**
Price: As above, Grade III **$395.00**

PECOS VALLEY HALF STOCK PENNSYLVANIA RIFLE

Caliber: 36, 45.
Barrel: 35½″; 1-in-48″ twist (36-cal.), 1-in-72″ twist (45-cal.).
Weight: About 6½ lbs. **Length:** 50½″ over-all.
Stock: Select grade maple with satin finish, 13½″ length of pull.
Sights: Silver blade, buckhorn rear.
Features: Durrs Egg percussion lock by L&R; Davis double set trigger; brass furniture. Made in U.S. by Pecos Valley Armory. Introduced 1984.
Price:........ **$399.00**

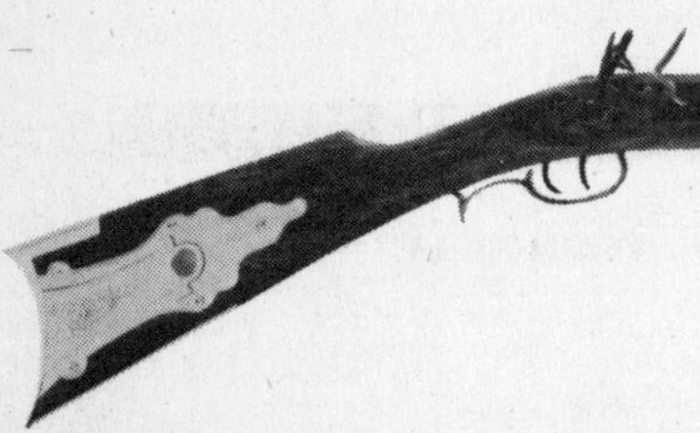

CVA Pennsylvania

CVA PENNSYLVANIA LONG RIFLE

Caliber: 50.
Barrel: 40″, octagonal; ⅞″ flats.
Weight: 8 lbs., 3 ozs. **Length:** 55¾″ over-all.
Stock: Select walnut.
Sights: Brass blade front, fixed semi-buckhorn rear.
Features: Color case-hardened lock plate, brass buttplate, toe plate, patchbox, trigger guard, thimbles, nosecap; blued barrel, double-set triggers; authentic V-type mainspring. Introduced 1983. From CVA.
Price: Finished, percussion **$289.95**
Price: Finished, flintlock **$299.95**
Price: Kit, percussion **$249.95**
Price: Kit, flintlock **$259.95**

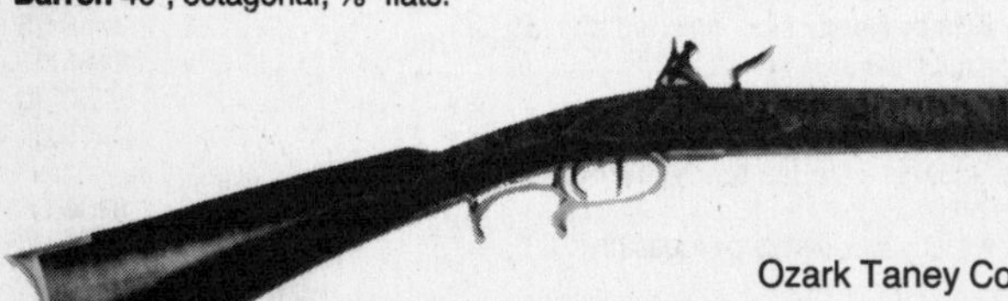

Ozark Taney County

OZARK MOUNTAIN TANEY COUNTY RIFLE

Caliber: 32, 36, 40.
Barrel: 36″.
Weight: 7½ lbs. **Length:** 53″ over-all.
Stock: American maple, fullstock design.
Sights: German silver blade front, full buckhorn rear.
Features: Available in flint or percussion, right or left hand; double set trigger.
Price: From........ **$585.00**

Ozark Mountain Muskrat Rifle

Same as the Taney County rifle except has maple half-stock. Available in right or left hand, flint or percussion.
Price: From........ **$525.00**

CAUTION: PRICES CHANGE. CHECK AT GUNSHOP.

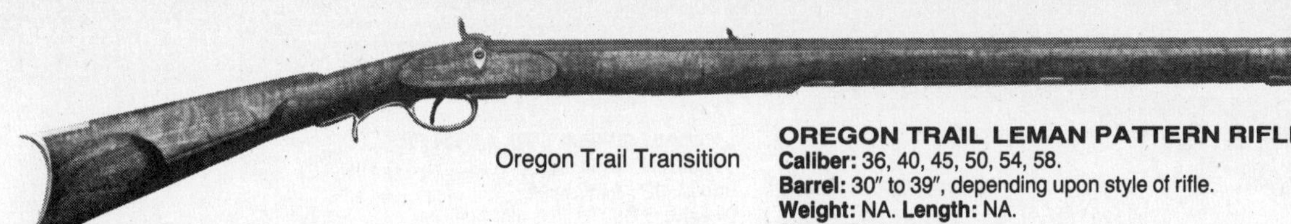
Oregon Trail Transition

CVA MOUNTAIN RIFLE

Caliber: 50.
Barrel: 32", octagon; 15/16" across flats; 1-66" twist.
Weight: 7 lbs., 14 oz. **Length:** 48" over-all.
Stock: Select hardwood with cheekpiece.
Sights: German silver blade front, screw-adj. rear.
Features: Available in percussion or flintlock. Engraved lock with adj. sear engagement; hooked breech with two barrel tenons; rifled 1-in-66"; double set triggers; German silver patch box, tenon plates, pewter-type nosecap; browned iron furniture. From CVA.
Price: Kit, percussion $189.95
Price: Kit, flintlock $199.95
Price: Finished rifle, percussion $299.95
Price: Finished rifle, flintlock $299.95

MOWREY ETHAN ALLEN SQUIRREL RIFLE

Caliber: 32, 36, or 45.
Barrel: 28", 8-groove rifling, octagon, gain-twist rifling optional.
Weight: 7½ lbs. **Length:** 43" over-all.
Stock: Curly maple, standard or premium grade.
Sights: Open, adjustable buckhorn.
Features: Box-lock action, cut-rifled barrel, hand-rubbed oil finish; adjustable trigger. Available with either brass or browned steel furniture, action. Made in U.S. Add $38 for premium wood.
Price: Complete, brass frame $264.00
Price: Complete, steel frame $254.00
Price: Kit, brass frame $184.00
Price: Kit, steel frame $174.00

MOWREY MAVERICK MAGNUM

Caliber: 50, 54.
Barrel: 1" octagon at breech, taper-turned round to muzzle.
Weight: 7½ lbs. **Length:** 48" over-all.
Stock: Walnut sporter-style; oil finish; recoil pad.
Sights: Open; drilled and tapped for scope mounting.
Features: Boxlock action; fully adjustable trigger; cut rifling; steel action and furniture; blue finish. Introduced 1985. Made in U.S.A. by Mowrey.
Price: Complete $299.00

OREGON TRAIL LEMAN PATTERN RIFLES

Caliber: 36, 40, 45, 50, 54, 58.
Barrel: 30" to 39", depending upon style of rifle.
Weight: NA. **Length:** NA.
Stock: Plain maple.
Sights: Steel blade front, semi-buckhorn rear.
Features: Available as various Leman patterns, right- or left-hand—Early Rifle (15/16" or 1" × 39" barrel), Transition Rifle (1" × 34" barrel), Indian Trade Rifle (1" or 1 1/16" × 30" barrel), Light Rifle (7/8" × 38" barrel). Full stock or half stock, single trigger, brass furniture. Many options available. From Oregon Trail Riflesmiths.
Price: Half stock Leman, percussion $685.00
Price: As above, left-hand $710.00
Price: Half stock, flintlock $725.00
Price: Full stock Indian Trade, Transition, percussion, right-hand $745.00
Price: As above, flintlock, right- or left-hand $785.00

CVA Big Bore Mountain Rifle

Similar to the standard Mountain Rifle except comes in 54 or 58 cal. only. Barrel flats measure 1" across. Stock does not have a patch box. Introduced 1980.
Price: 54 cal., percussion, complete rifle $309.95
Price: 54 cal., percussion, kit $220.95
Price: 58 cal. percussion, 1-72" twist, kit only $220.95

Mowrey Ethan Allen Rocky Mountain Hunter

Similar to the Squirrel rifle except 50 or 54 caliber, 28" octagon barrel with 1" flats; weighs 8 lbs.; modern fully adjustable sights. Steel action and furniture only. Add $38 for premium wood.
Price: Complete $264.00
Price: Kit $184.00

Mowrey Ethan Allen Plains Rifle

Similar to Squirrel Rifle except in 50 or 54 caliber, 32" barrel, weighs 10 lbs.; "semi-Schuetzen" buttplate. Add $38 for premium wood.
Price: Complete $279.00
Price: Kit $198.00

Consult our Directory pages for the location of firms mentioned.

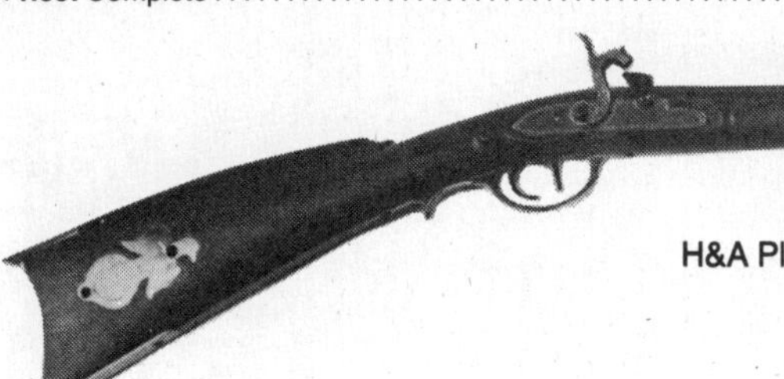

H&A Plainsman Rifle

HOPKINS & ALLEN PLAINSMAN RIFLE

Caliber: 45.
Barrel: 37".
Weight: 7½ lbs. **Length:** 53" over-all.
Stock: Walnut.
Sights: Blade front, rear adjustable for w. & e.
Features: Double set triggers, blued barrel has 13/16" flats, solid brass barrel rib, engraved percussion lockplate. From Hopkins & Allen.
Price: $292.60

CVA Squirrel Rifle

CVA SQUIRREL RIFLE

Caliber: 32.
Barrel: 25", octagonal; 11/16" flats.
Weight: 5 lbs., 12 oz. **Length:** 40¾" over-all.
Stock: Hardwood.
Sights: Beaded blade front, fully adjustable hunting-style rear.
Features: Available in right or left-hand versions. Color case-hardened lock plate, brass buttplate, trigger guard, wedge plates, thimbles; double-set triggers; hooked breech; authentic V-type mainspring. Introduced 1983. From CVA.
Price: Finished, percussion, right hand $189.95
Price: Finished, left hand $199.95
Price: Finished, flintlock $199.95
Price: Kit, percussion, right hand $134.95
Price: Kit, left hand $144.95
Price: Kit, flintlock $144.95

Lyman Great Plains

LYMAN GREAT PLAINS RIFLE
Caliber: 50 or 54 cal.
Barrel: 32″, 1-66″ twist.
Weight: 9 lbs.
Stock: Walnut.
Sights: Steel blade front, buckhorn rear adj. for w. & e. and fixed notch primitive sight included.
Features: Blued steel furniture. Stainless steel nipple. Coil spring lock, Hawken-style trigger guard and double set triggers. Round thimbles recessed and sweated into rib. Steel wedge plates and toe plate. Introduced 1980. From Lyman.
Price: Percussion $284.95
Price: Flintlock $294.95
Price: Percussion Kit $199.95

TRYON RIFLE
Caliber: 50, 54 cal.
Barrel: 34″, octagon; 1-63″ twist.
Weight: 9 lbs. **Length:** 49″ over-all.
Stock: European walnut with steel furniture.
Sights: Blade front, fixed rear.
Features: Reproduction of an American plains rifle with double set triggers and back-action lock. Imported from Italy by Dixie.
Price: $299.00
Price: Kit $249.00

PENNSYLVANIA HALF-STOCK PLAINS RIFLE
Caliber: 45 or 50.
Barrel: 32″ rifled, 15/16″ dia.
Weight: 8½ lbs.
Stock: Walnut.
Sights: Fixed.
Features: Available in flint or percussion. Blued lock and barrel, brass furniture. Offered complete or in kit form. From The Armoury.
Price: Flint $235.00
Price: Percussion $210.00

CVA KENTUCKY RIFLE
Caliber: 45 (.451″ bore).
Barrel: 33½″, rifled, octagon (7/8″ flats).
Length: 48″ over-all.
Stock: Select hardwood.
Sights: Brass Kentucky blade type front, dovetail open rear.
Features: Available in either flint or percussion. Stainless steel nipple included. From CVA.
Price: Percussion $184.95
Price: Flint $194.95
Price: Percussion Kit $109.95
Price: Flint Kit $117.95

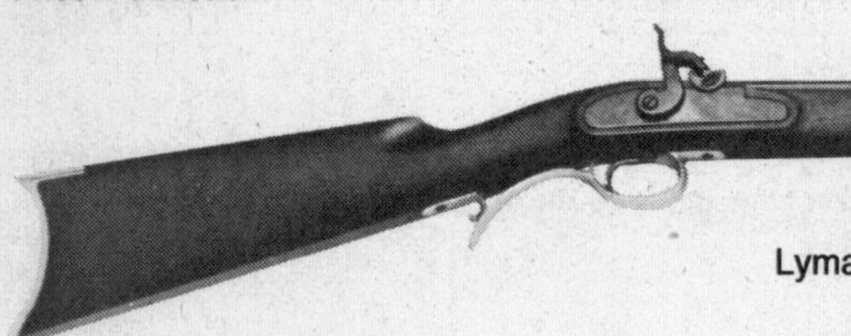

Lyman Trade Rifle

LYMAN TRADE RIFLE
Caliber: 50 or 54.
Barrel: 28″ octagon, 1-48″ twist.
Weight: 8¾ lbs. **Length:** 45″ over-all.
Stock: European walnut.
Sights: Blade front, open rear adj. for w. or optional fixed sights.
Features: Fast twist rifling for conical bullets. Polished brass furniture with blue steel parts, stainless steel nipple. Hook breech, single trigger, coil spring percussion lock. Steel barrel rib and ramrod ferrules. Introduced 1979. From Lyman.
Price: Percussion $199.95
Price: Kit, percussion $149.95
Price: Flintlock $209.95

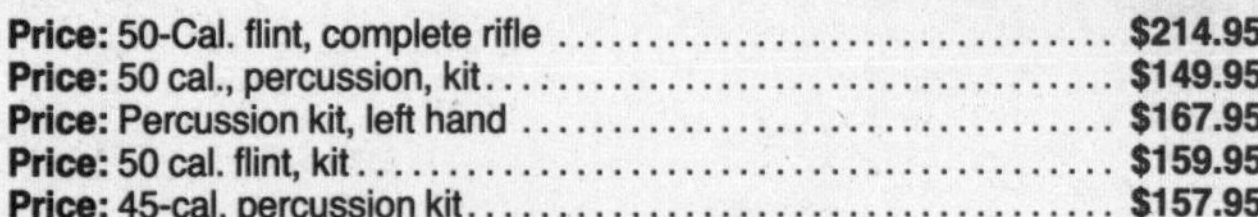

CVA Frontier

CVA FRONTIER RIFLE
Caliber: 45, 50.
Barrel: 28″, octagon; 15/16″ flats, 1-66″ twist.
Weight: 6 lbs., 14 oz. **Length:** 44″ over-all.
Stock: American hardwood.
Sights: Brass blade front, fully adjustable hunting-style rear.
Features: Available in flint or percussion. Solid brass nosecap, trigger guard, buttplate, thimbles and wedge plates; blued barrel; color case-hardened lock and hammer. Double set triggers, patented breech plug bolster, V-type mainspring. Hooked breech. Introduced 1980.
Price: 50 cal., percussion, complete rifle $204.95
Price: Finished, left hand $225.95
Price: 50-Cal. flint, complete rifle $214.95
Price: 50 cal., percussion, kit $149.95
Price: Percussion kit, left hand $167.95
Price: 50 cal. flint, kit $159.95
Price: 45-cal. percussion kit $157.95

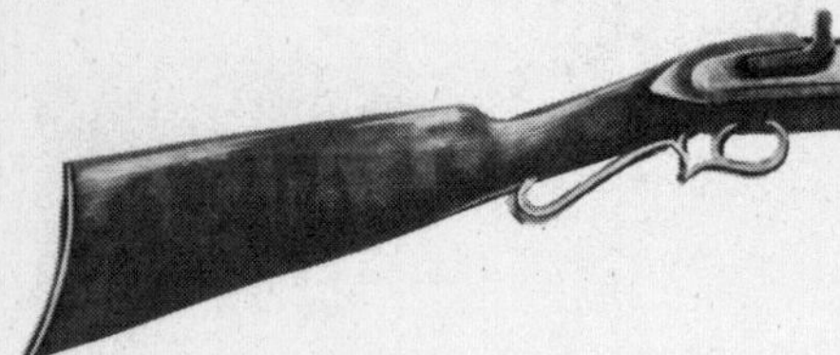

Navy Country Boy

NAVY ARMS COUNTRY BOY RIFLE
Caliber: 50.
Barrel: 26″.
Weight: 6 lbs.
Stock: Walnut.
Sights: Blade front, buckhorn rear.
Features: Octagonal rifled barrel; blue finish; Mule Ear lock for fast ignition. From Navy Arms.
Price: $179.95

 CAUTION: PRICES CHANGE. CHECK AT GUNSHOP.

H&A Pa. Hawken

ST. LOUIS HAWKEN RIFLE
Caliber: 50.
Barrel: 28" octagon.
Weight: 8½ lbs.
Stock: Walnut.
Sights: Adjustable buckhorn.
Features: Double set triggers and percussion lock. Typical halfstock sporting rifle of the 1850s period. Imported by Allen Firearms and Euroarms of America.
Price: **$189.95**

DIXIE DELUX CUB RIFLE
Caliber: 40.
Barrel: 28".
Weight: 6½ lbs.
Stock: Walnut.
Sights: Fixed.
Features: Short rifle for small game and beginning shooters. Brass patchbox and furniture. Flint or percussion.
Price: Finished **$240.00**
Price: Kit **$195.00**

HOPKINS & ALLEN PA. HAWKEN RIFLE
Caliber: 50.
Barrel: 29".
Weight: 7½ lbs. **Length:** 44" over-all.
Stock: Walnut.
Sights: Blade front, open rear adjustable for elevation.
Features: Single trigger, dual barrel wedges. Convertible ignition system. Brass patch box.
Price: With percussion lock **$199.50**
Price: Conversion kit (percussion to flint) **$39.95**

TENNESSEE VALLEY TENNESSEE RIFLE
Caliber: 32, 36, 40, 45, 50, 54, 58
Barrel: 42" standard; shorter lengths available.
Weight: 7½-8 lbs. **Length:** 56" (with 42" barrel).
Stock: Maple, walnut or cherry.
Sights: Silver blade front, buckhorn rear.
Features: Steel mounted, double-set triggers standard. Metal parts browned, oil-finished stock. From Tennessee Valley Mfg.
Price: Percussion **$410.00**
Price: Flintlock **$425.00**
Price: Left hand, flint or percussion **$440.00**
Price: Brass-mounted early Lancaster rifle **$695.00**
Price: Steel-mounted early Virginia rifle **$595.00**

H&A Brush Rifle

HOPKINS & ALLEN BRUSH RIFLE
Caliber: 36 or 45.
Barrel: 25", octagon, 15/16" flats.
Weight: 7 lbs.
Stock: Hardwood.
Sights: Silver blade front, notch rear.
Features: Convertible ignition system. Brass furniture. Introduced 1983.
Price: Percussion **$189.00**
Price: Flint **$200.10**
Price: Pre-assembled kit, percussion **$129.00**
Price: As above, flint **$140.10**
Price: Kit, percussion **$99.50**
Price: Kit, flint **$110.60**

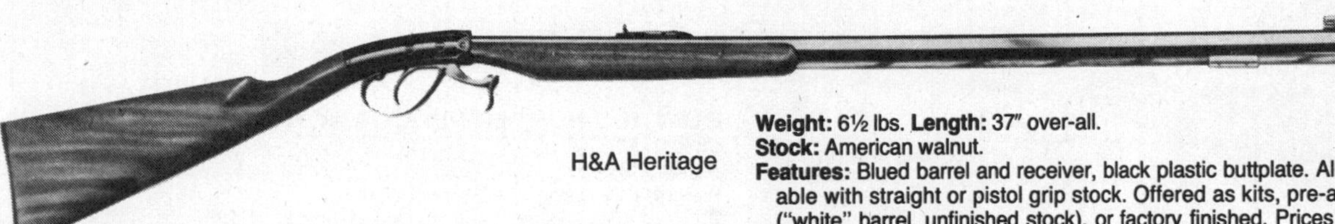
H&A Heritage

HOPKINS & ALLEN UNDERHAMMER RIFLES
Caliber: 31, 36, 45, 50, 58.
Barrel: 20", 25" 32", 42", octagonal.
Weight: 6½ lbs. **Length:** 37" over-all.
Stock: American walnut.
Features: Blued barrel and receiver, black plastic buttplate. All models available with straight or pistol grip stock. Offered as kits, pre-assembled kits ("white" barrel, unfinished stock), or factory finished. Prices shown are for factory finished guns.
Price: 31, 36, 45, 20" or 25" bbl. × 15/16" **$214.50**
Price: Heritage, 36, 45, 50-cal. 32" bbl. × 15/16" **$226.50**
Price: Deerstalker, 58-cal., 28" bbl. × 1⅛" **$233.95**
Price: Target, 45-cal., 42" bbl. × 1⅛" **$245.95**

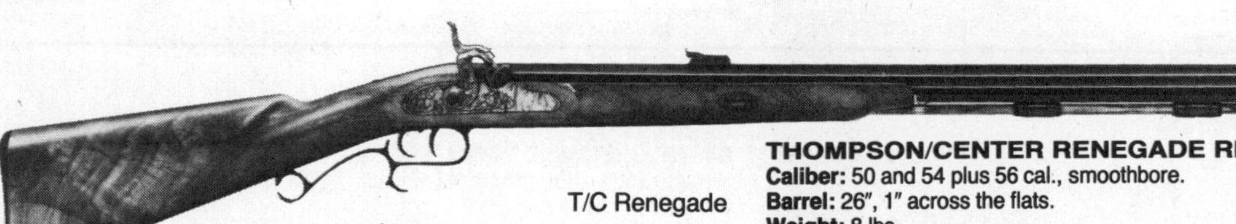
T/C Renegade

THOMPSON/CENTER RENEGADE RIFLE
Caliber: 50 and 54 plus 56 cal., smoothbore.
Barrel: 26", 1" across the flats.
Weight: 8 lbs.
Stock: American walnut.
Sights: Open hunting (Patridge) style, fully adjustable for w. and e.
Features: Coil spring lock, double set triggers, blued steel trim.
Price: Percussion model **$235.00**
Price: Flintlock model, 50 and 54 cal. only **$247.50**
Price: Percussion kit **$185.00**
Price: Flintlock kit **$195.00**
Price: Left-hand precussion, 50 or 54 cal. **$235.00**

Thompson/Center Hawken

THOMPSON/CENTER HAWKEN RIFLE
Caliber: 45, 50 or 54.
Barrel: 28" octagon, hooked breech.
Stock: American walnut.
Sights: Blade front, rear adj. for w. & e.
Features: Solid brass furniture, double set triggers, button rifled barrel, coil-type main spring. From Thompson/Center Arms.
Price: Percussion Model (45, 50 or 54 cal.) **$275.00**
Price: Flintlock model (50 or 54 cal.) **$287.50**
Price: Percussion kit **$205.00**
Price: Flintlock kit **$215.00**

Thompson/Center Hawken Cougar
Similar to the standard T/C Hawken except stock is of highly figured walnut; all furniture—lock plate, hammer, triggers, trigger plate, trigger guard, fore-end cap, thimbles escutcheons, etc. are of stainless steel with matte finish. Replacing the patch box is a stainless steel medallion cast in deep relief depicting a crouching cougar. Internal parts, breech plug, tang, barrel, sights and under rib are ordnance steel. Barrel, sights and under rib are blued. Buttplate is solid brass, hard chromed to match the stainless parts. Limited production. Introduced 1982. From Thompson/Center Arms.
Price: **$350.00**

Thompson/Center Cherokee

THOMPSON/CENTER CHEROKEE RIFLE
Caliber: 32 or 45.
Barrel: 24"; 13/16" across flats.
Weight: About 6 lbs.
Stock: American walnut. Same as Seneca except minus patch box, toe plate, fore-end cap.
Sights: Open hunting style; square notch rear fully adjustable for w. and e.
Features: Interchangeable barrels. Uses T/C Seneca breech, lock, triggers, sights and stock. Brass buttplate, trigger guard, fore-end escutcheons and lock plate screw bushing. Introduced 1984.
Price: 32 or 45 caliber **$235.00**
Price: Interchangeable 32 or 45-cal. barrel **$110.00**
Price: Kit, percussion, 32 or 45 .... **$185.00**
Price: Kit barrels **$75.00**

T/C Seneca

THOMPSON/CENTER SENECA RIFLE
Caliber: 36, 45.
Barrel: 27".
Weight: 6½ lbs.
Stock: American walnut.
Sights: Open hunting style, square notch rear fully adj. for w. and e.
Features: Coil spring lock, octagon bbl. measures 13/16" across flats, brass stock furniture.
Price: **$275.00**

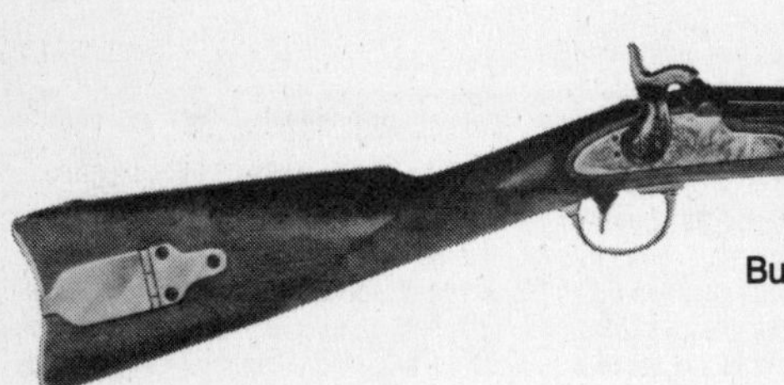

Buffalo Hunter Rifle

BUFFALO HUNTER PERCUSSION RIFLE
Caliber: 58.
Barrel: 25½".
Weight: 8 lbs. **Length:** 41½" over-all.
Stock: Walnut finished, hand checkered, brass furniture.
Sights: Fixed.
Features: Designed for primitive weapons hunting. 20 ga. shotgun bbl. also available $90.00. Imported by Navy Arms, Dixie.
Price: .... **$215.00 to $264.00**

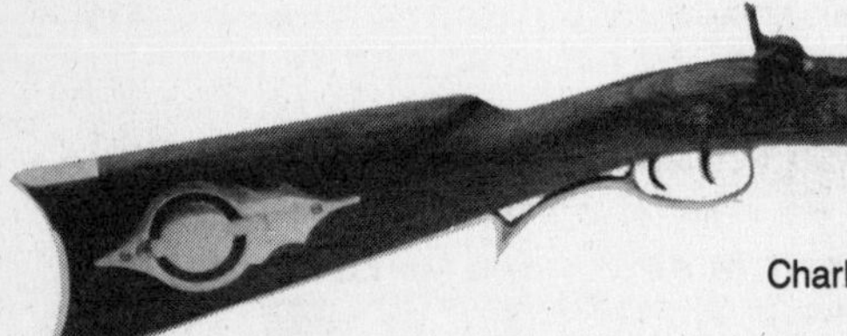

Charles Daly Hawken

CHARLES DALY HAWKEN RIFLE
Caliber: 45, 50.
Barrel: 28" octagonal, ⅞" flats.
Weight: 7½ lbs. **Length:** 45½" over-all.
Stock: European hardwood.
Sights: Blade front, open fully adjustable rear.
Features: Color case-hardened lock uses coil springs; trigger guard, buttplate, fore-end cap, ferrules and ramrod fittings are polished brass. Left-hand model available in 50-cal. only. Imported by Outdoor Sports Headquarters. Introduced 1984.
Price: Right-hand, percussion **$299.95**
Price: Left-hand, percussion (50-cal. only) **$245.00**
Price: Right-hand, flintlock **$239.95**
Price: Left-hand, flintlock (50-cal. only) **$278.95**

 CAUTION: PRICES CHANGE. CHECK AT GUNSHOP.

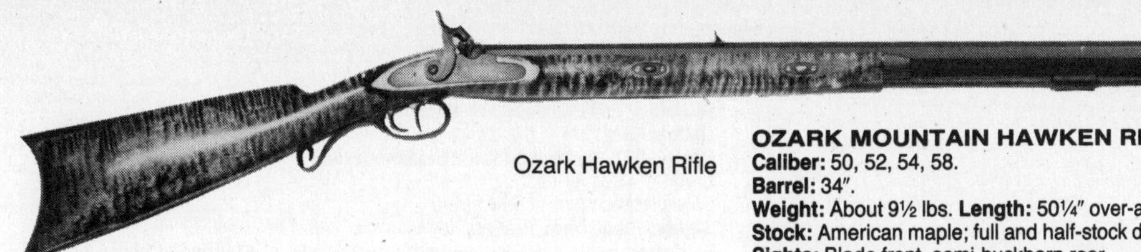
Ozark Hawken Rifle

OZARK MOUNTAIN HAWKEN RIFLE
Caliber: 50, 52, 54, 58.
Barrel: 34″.
Weight: About 9½ lbs. **Length:** 50¼″ over-all.
Stock: American maple; full and half-stock designs available.
Sights: Blade front, semi-buckhorn rear.
Features: Flint or percussion, right or left hand models (except in flintlock — right-hand only); browned steel furniture.
Price: From **$675.00**

Navy Hawken Mark I

NAVY ARMS MARK I HAWKEN RIFLE
Caliber: 50 and 54.
Barrel: 26″.
Weight: 9 lbs. **Length:** 43″ over-all.
Stock: American walnut with cheek rest.
Sights: Blade front, adjustable Williams rear.
Features: Designed specifically for maxi-ball shooting. Double set triggers, blued barrel, polished brass furniture. Stainless steel chamber insert. Flint or percussion. Made in U.S. by Navy Arms.
Price: Finished, percussion, 50 or 54 .... **$263.00**
Price: As above, kit **$175.95**
Price: Finished, flintlock, 50 or 54 .... **$275.00**
Price: As above, kit **$186.00**

ARMOURY R140 HAWKIN RIFLE
Caliber: 45, 50 or 54.
Barrel: 29″.
Weight: 8¾ to 9 lbs. **Length:** 45¾″ over-all.
Stock: Walnut, with cheekpiece.
Sights: Dovetail front, fully adjustable rear.
Features: Octagon barrel, removable breech plug; double set triggers; blued barrel, brass stock fittings, color case hardened percussion lock. From Armsport, The Armoury.
Price: **$282.00**

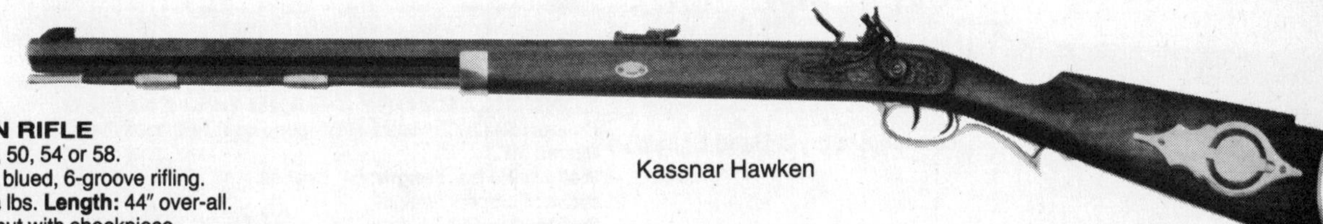
Kassnar Hawken

HAWKEN RIFLE
Caliber: 45, 50, 54 or 58.
Barrel: 28″, blued, 6-groove rifling.
Weight: 8¾ lbs. **Length:** 44″ over-all.
Stock: Walnut with cheekpiece.
Sights: Blade front, fully adj. rear.
Features: Coil mainspring, double set triggers, polished brass furniture. Also available with chrome plated bore or in flintlock model from Sile. Introduced 1977. From Kassnar (flint or percussion, right- or left-hand), Dixie (45 or 50 only, walnut stock), Armsport, Hopkins & Allen, 50-cal. only.
Price: .... **$175.00** to **$278.00**
Price: True left-hand rifle, percussion (Kassnar) **$224.00**

Armsport Hawken Rifle-Shotgun Combo
Similar to Hawken above except 50-cal. only, with 20 gauge shotgun barrel. From Armsport.
Price: **$250.00**

CVA HAWKEN RIFLE
Caliber: 50 or 54.
Barrel: 28″, octagon; 1″ across flats; 1-66″ twist.
Weight: 7 lbs. 15 oz. **Length:** 44″ over-all.
Stock: Select walnut.
Sights: Beaded blade front, fully adj. open rear.
Features: Fully adj. double set triggers; brass patch box, wedge plates, nose cap, thimbles, trigger guard and buttplate; blued barrel; color case-hardened, engraved lockplate. Percussion or flintlock. Hooked breech. Introduced 1981.
Price: Finished rifle, percussion **$262.95**
Price: Finished rifle, flintlock **$272.95**
Price: Kit, percussion **$169.95**
Price: Kit, flintlock **$179.95**

ITHACA-NAVY HAWKEN RIFLE
Caliber: 50 and 54.
Barrel: 32″ octagonal, 1-inch dia.
Weight: About 9 lbs.
Stock: Black walnut.
Sights: Blade front, rear adj. for w.
Features: Completely made in U.S. Hooked breech, 1⅞″ throw percussion lock. Attached twin thimbles and under-rib. German silver barrel key inlays, Hawken-style toe and buttplates, lock bolt inlays, barrel wedges, entry thimble, trigger guard, ramrod and cleaning jag, nipple and nipple wrench. American made. Introduced 1977. Made in U.S. by Navy Arms.
Price: Complete, percussion **$460.00**
Price: Kit, percussion **$320.00**
Price: Complete, flint **$525.00**
Price: Kit, flint **$410.00**

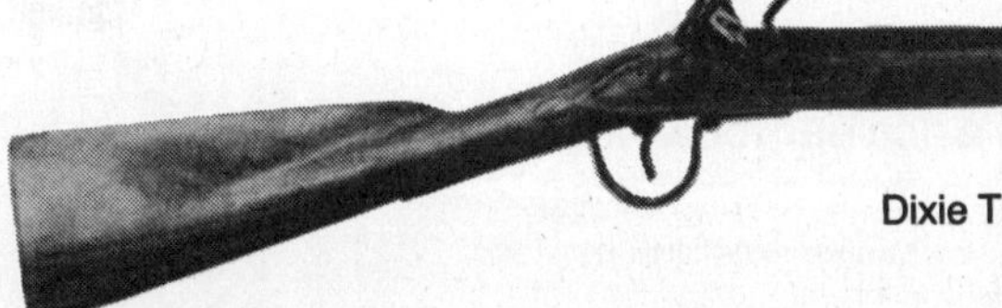
Dixie Trade Gun

DIXIE NORTHWEST TRADE GUN
Caliber/Gauge: 20 (.600″ round ball or 1 oz.#6 shot).
Barrel: 36″, smoothbore.
Weight: 7½ lbs. **Length:** 53½″ over-all.
Stock: Walnut, 13½″ pull.
Sights: Brass blade front only.
Features: Flintlock. Brass buttplate, serpentine sideplate; browned barrel, Wheeler flint lock, triggerguard; hickory ramrod with brass tip. From Dixie Gun Works.
Price: Finished **$495.00**
Price: Kit **$350.00**

Dixie Wesson Rifle

DIXIE PERCUSSION WESSON RIFLE
Caliber: 50.
Barrel: 28"; 1⅛" octagon, with false muzzle.
Length: 45" over-all.
Stock: Hand checkered walnut.
Sights: Blade front, rear adj. for e.
Features: Adjustable double set triggers, color case hardened frame. Comes with loading rod and loading accessories. From Dixie Gun Works.
Price: With false muzzle **$325.00**

Parker-Hale 1853

PARKER-HALE ENFIELD 1853 MUSKET
Caliber: .577".
Barrel: 39", 3-groove cold-forged rifling.
Weight: About 9 lbs. **Length:** 55" over-all.
Stock: Seasoned walnut.
Sights: Fixed front, rear step adj. for elevation.
Features: Three band musket made to original specs from original gauges. Solid brass stock furniture, color hardened lock plate, hammer; blued barrel, trigger. Imported from England by Navy Arms.
Price: **$475.00**

PARKER-HALE ENFIELD PATTERN 1858 NAVAL RIFLE
Caliber: .577".
Barrel: 33".
Weight: 8½ lbs. **Length:** 48½" over-all.
Stock: European walnut.
Sights: Blade front, step adj. rear.
Features: Two-band Enfield percussion rifle with heavy barrel. 5-groove progressive depth rifling, solid brass furniture. All parts made exactly to original patterns. Imported from England by Navy Arms.
Price: **$435.00**

London Armory 3-Band Enfield

LONDON ARMORY 3-BAND 1853 ENFIELD
Caliber: 58 (.577" Minie, .575" round ball, .580" maxi ball).
Barrel: 39".
Weight: 9½ lbs. **Length:** 54" over-all.
Stock: European walnut.
Sights: Inverted "V" front, traditional Enfield folding ladder rear.
Features: Re-creation of the famed London Armory Company Pattern 1862 Enfield Musket. One-piece walnut stock, brass buttplate, trigger guard and nosecap. Lockplate marked "London Armoury Co." and with a British crown. Blued Baddeley barrel bands. From Dixie, Euroarms of America, Navy Arms.
Price: .... **$285.00** to **$385.00**

LONDON ARMORY 2-BAND ENFIELD 1858
Caliber: .577" Minie, .575" round ball.
Barrel: 33".
Weight: 10 lbs. **Length:** 49" over-all.
Stock: Walnut.
Sights: Folding leaf rear adjustable for elevation.
Features: Blued barrel, color case-hardened lock and hammer, polished brass buttplate, trigger guard, nose cap. From Navy Arms, Euroarms of America, Dixie.
Price: **$315.00**

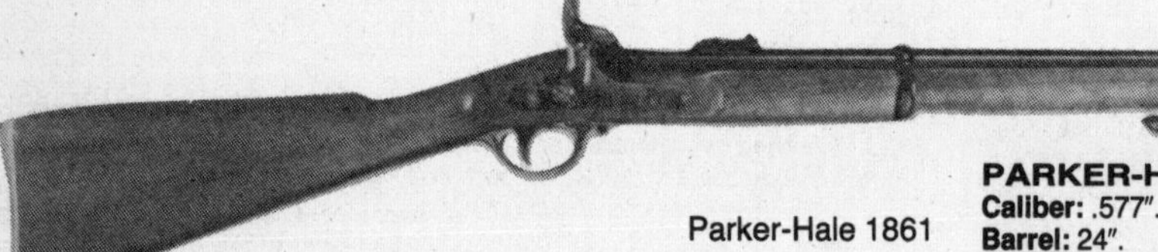

Parker-Hale 1861

PARKER-HALE ENFIELD 1861 CARBINE
Caliber: .577".
Barrel: 24".
Weight: 7½ lbs. **Length:** 40¼" over-all.
Stock: Walnut.
Sights: Fixed front, adj. rear.
Features: Percussion muzzle loader, made to original 1861 English patterns. Imported from England by Navy Arms.
Price: **$335.00**

PARKER-HALE VOLUNTEER RIFLE
Caliber: .451".
Barrel: 32".
Weight: 9½ lbs. **Length:** 49" over-all.
Stock: Walnut, checkered wrist and fore-end.
Sights: Globe front, adjustable ladder-type rear.
Features: Recreation of the type of gun issued to volunteer regiments during the 1860's. Rigby-pattern rifling, patent breech, detented lock. Stock is glass bedded for accuracy. Comes with comprehensive accessory/shooting kit. From Navy Arms.
Price: **$575.00**

COOK & BROTHER CONFEDERATE CARBINE
Caliber: 58.
Barrel: 24".
Weight: 7½ lbs. **Length:** 40½" over-all.
Stock: Select walnut.
Features: Re-creation of the 1861 New Orleans-made artillery carbine. Color case-hardened lock, browned barrel. Buttplate, trigger guard, barrel bands, sling swivels and nosecap of polished brass. From Euroarms of America.
Price: **$190.00**

CAUTION: PRICES CHANGE. CHECK AT GUNSHOP.

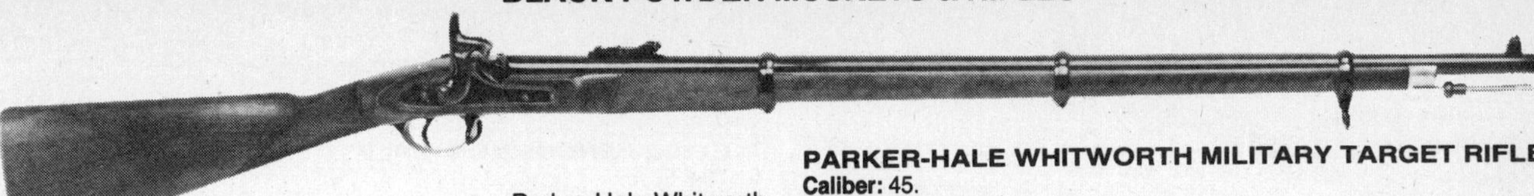

Parker-Hale Whitworth

PARKER-HALE WHITWORTH MILITARY TARGET RIFLE

Caliber: 45.
Barrel: 36″.
Weight: 9¼ lbs. **Length:** 52½″ over-all.
Stock: Walnut. Checkered at wrist and fore-end.
Sights: Hooded post front, open step-adjustable rear.
Features: Faithful reproduction of the Whitworth rifle, only bored for 45-cal. Trigger has a detented lock, capable of being adjusted very finely without risk of the sear nose catching on the half-cock bent and damaging both parts. Introduced 1978. Imported from England by Navy Arms.
Price: **$575.00**

J. P. Murray Carbine

J.P. MURRAY ARTILLERY CARBINE

Caliber: 58 (.577″ Minie).
Barrel: 23½″.
Weight: 7 lbs., 9 oz. **Length:** 39″ over-all.
Stock: Walnut.
Sights: Blade front, rear drift adj. for windage.
Features: Browned barrel, color case-hardened lock, blued swivel and band springs, polished brass buttplate, trigger guard, barrel bands. From Navy Arms.
Price: **$263.00**

U.S. M-1862 REMINGTON CONTRACT RIFLE

Caliber: 58.
Barrel: 33″.
Weight: 9½ lbs. **Length:** 48½″ over-all.
Stock: Walnut, brass furniture.
Sights: Blade front, folding 3-leaf rear.
Features: Re-creation of the 1862 military rifle. Each rifle furnished with two stainless steel nipples. From Euroarms of America.
Price: About **$200.00**

Shiloh New Model 1863 Sharps Carbine

Shortened, carbine version of the 1863 rifle. Caliber 54. Has 22″ barrel, black walnut stock without patch box, single barrel band. Weighs 8 lbs., 12 oz., over-all length is 39⅛″. Made in U.S. by C. Sharps Arms Co.
Price: **$515.00**

SHILOH NEW MODEL 1863 SHARPS RIFLE

Caliber: 54.
Barrel: 30″, 1-in-48″.
Weight: 8¾ lbs. **Length:** 47″ over-all.
Stock: Black walnut, oil finish.
Sights: Blade front, rear leaf adj. tor e.
Features: Duplicate of original percussion rifle. Receiver, sideplate, hammer, buttplate, patch box color hardened; barrel is blue-black. Twelve different models of the Sharps now available in many original chamberings. Made in U.S. by C. Sharps Arms Co.
Price: Sporting Rifle.......... **$630.00**
Price: Military Rifle.......... **$650.00**

Dixie Sharps Rifle

Dixie Sharps Rifle

Similar to the Shiloh Sharps except has 28½″ barrel, checkered half-stock fore-end and stock wrist, flat lockplate. Carbine-style case hardened buttplate. Imported from Italy by Dixie Gun Works.
Price: **$349.95**
Price: Military Carbine (22″ barrel) **$329.95**

Dixie 1863 Musket

DIXIE 1863 SPRINGFIELD MUSKET

Caliber: 58 (.570″ patched ball or .575″ Minie).
Barrel: 50″, rifled.
Stock: Walnut stained.
Sights: Blade front, adjustable ladder-type rear.
Features: Bright-finish lock, barrel, furniture. Reproduction of the last of the regulation muzzle loaders. Imported from Japan by Dixie Gun Works.
Price: Finished **$265.00**
Price: Kit **$225.00**

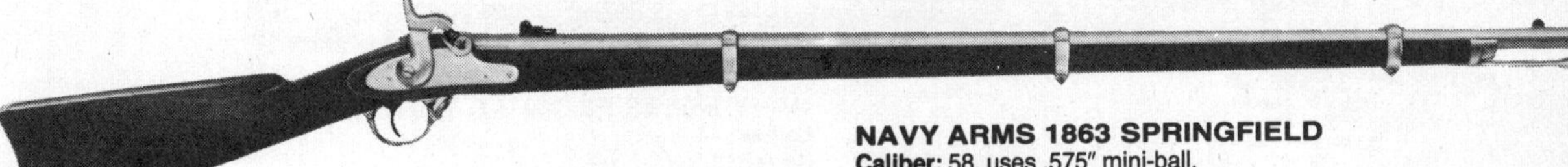

Navy 1863 Springfield

NAVY ARMS 1863 SPRINGFIELD

Caliber: 58, uses .575″ mini-ball.
Barrel: 40″, rifled.
Weight: 9½ lbs. **Length:** 56″ over-all.
Stock: Walnut.
Sights: Open rear adj. for elevation.
Features: Full-size 3-band musket. Polished bright metal, including lock. From Navy Arms.
Price: Finished rifle **$400.00**
Price: Kit **$310.00**

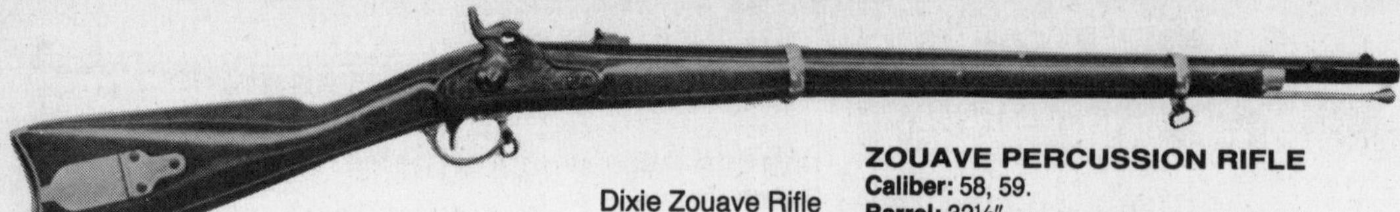
Dixie Zouave Rifle

ZOUAVE PERCUSSION RIFLE
Caliber: 58, 59.
Barrel: 32½″.
Weight: 9½ lbs. **Length:** 48½″ over-all.
Stock: Walnut finish, brass patch box and buttplate.
Sights: Fixed front, rear adj. for e.
Features: Some small details may vary with importers. Also available from Navy Arms as carbine, with 22″ bbl. Extra 20 ga. shotgun bbl. $45.00. Imported by Navy Arms, Dixie.
Price: .... **$87.95** to **$265.00**
Price: Deluxe Model (Navy Arms) **$400.00**

Mississippi Model 1841 Percussion Rifle
Similar to Zouave Rifle but patterned after U.S. Model 1841. Imported by Navy Arms, Dixie.
Price: .... **$225.00** to **$275.00**

SHILOH SHARPS 1874 MILITARY RIFLE
Caliber: 45-70, 50-70.
Barrel: 30″, Round.
Weight: 8¾ lbs.
Stock: American walnut.
Sights: Blade front, Lawrence-style open rear.
Features: Military-style fore-end with three barrel bands and 1¼″ sling swivels. Color case-hardened receiver, buttplate and barrel bands, blued barrel. Recreation of the original Sharps rifles. Five other models in many original chamberings available. From C. Sharps Arms Co.
Price: 1874 Military Rifle **$650.00**
Price: 1874 Carbine **$515.00**
Price: 1874 Business Rifle **$590.00**
Price: 1874 Sporting Rifle No. 1 .... **$735.00**
Price: 1874 Sporting Rifle No. 3 .... **$630.00**
Price: 1874 Long Range Express Sporting Rifle **$790.00**

Consult our Directory pages for the location of firms mentioned.

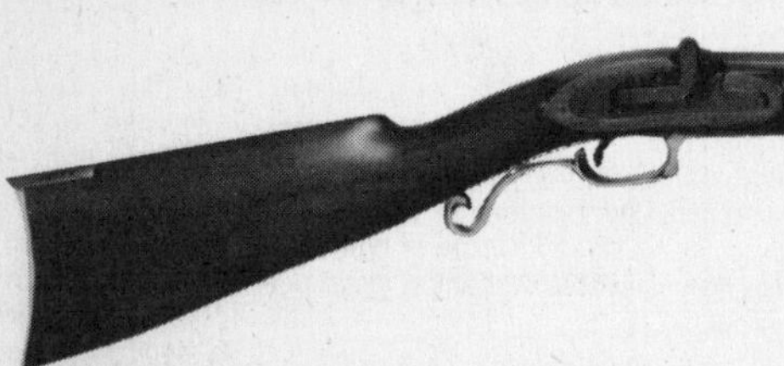
Navy Mule Ear

NAVY ARMS MULE EAR SQUIRREL RIFLE
Caliber: 32, 36, 45.
Barrel: 26″.
Weight: 5½ lbs.
Stock: Pennsylvania black walnut with satin finish.
Sights: Blade front, open adjustable rear.
Features: Mule ear action gives fast ignition; brass buttplate, trigger guard, fore-end cap, ramrod tip; color case-hardened lock. Made in U.S.A. by Navy Arms. Introduced 1984.
Price: Finished **$185.00**
Price: Kit **$134.00**

MAC Silverwolf

MAC WOLVERINE RIFLE
Caliber: 45, 50, 54; 20-ga. shotgun.
Barrel: 26″, octagon, 1″ flats.
Weight: 7¾ lbs.
Stock: Choice of walnut or maple; soft recoil pad.
Sights: Brass-bead front, adjustable folding leaf rear.
Features: New design uses straight-line ignition with #209 shotshell primer. Fires from an open bolt; has positive safety notch. Fully adjustable trigger. Introduced 1980. Made in U.S. by Michigan Arms Corp.
Price: Blue ordnance steel **$398.00**
Price: As above except in stainless steel (Silverwolf) **$595.00**
Price: Friendship Special (select barrel, Lyman globe front, Williams target peep rear, adjustable recoil pad, custom stock, special breech block) **$599.00**

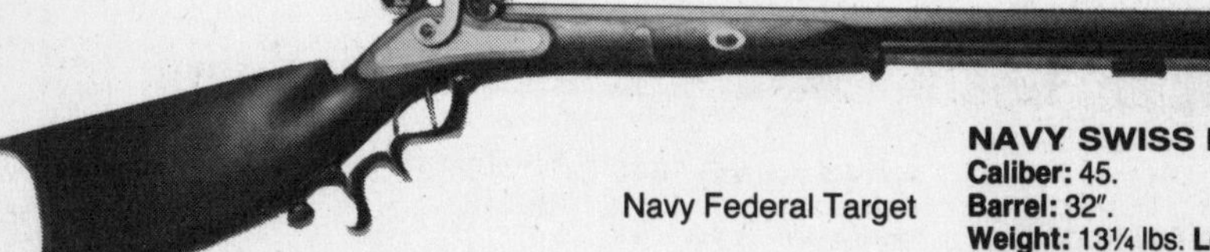
Navy Federal Target

NAVY SWISS FEDERAL TARGET RIFLE
Caliber: 45.
Barrel: 32″.
Weight: 13¼ lbs. **Length:** 49½″ over-all.
Stock: European walnut with hook buttplate, Schuetzen-style trigger guard.
Sights: Tunnel front, aperture rear adjustable for windage and elevation.
Features: Hand-built reproduction of 1800s target rifle; quick detachable, five-lever, double-set trigger, adjustable to 4 oz. Color case-hardened furniture. Imported from Italy by Navy Arms. Introduced 1984.
Price: **$795.00**
Price: Swiss-style palm rest **$35.00**

CAUTION: PRICES CHANGE. CHECK AT GUNSHOP.

Sanftl Schuetzen

SANFTL SCHUETZEN PERCUSSION TARGET RIFLE

Caliber: 45 (.445" round ball).
Barrel: 29", 7/8" octagon.
Weight: 9 lbs. **Length:** 43" over-all.
Stock: Walnut, Schuetzen-style.
Sights: Open tunnel front post, peep rear adjustable for windage & elevation.
Features: True back-action lock with "backward" hammer; screw-in breech plug; buttplate, trigger guard and stock inlays are polished brass. Imported from Italy by Dixie Gun Works, Hopkins & Allen.
Price: $595.00

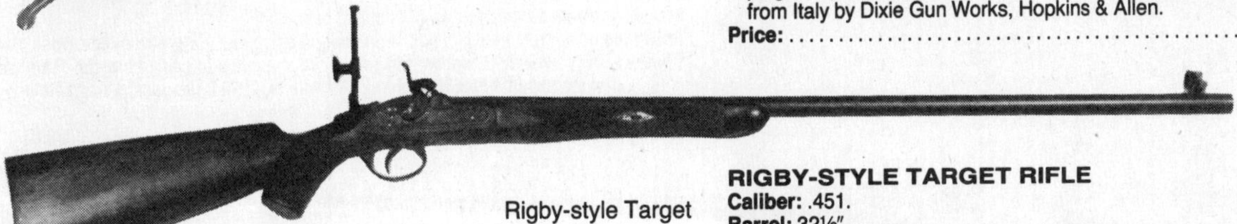

Rigby-style Target

RIGBY-STYLE TARGET RIFLE

Caliber: .451.
Barrel: 32½".
Weight: 7¾ lbs.
Stock: Walnut; hand-checkered pistol grip, fore-end.
Sights: Target front with micrometer adjustment; adjustable vernier peep rear.
Features: Comes cased with loading accessories—bullet starter, bullter sizer, special ramrod. Introduced 1985. From Navy Arms.
Price: $500.00

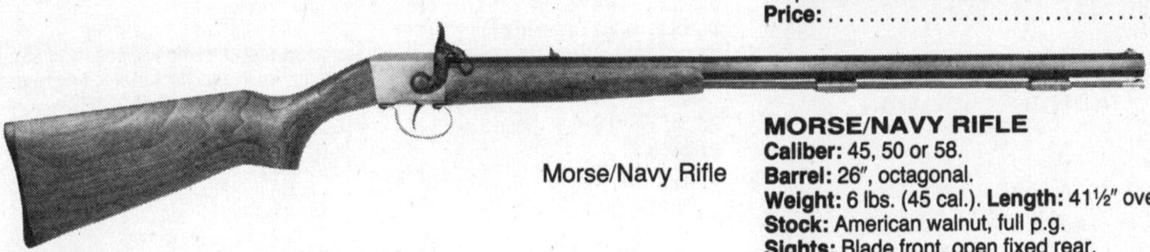

Morse/Navy Rifle

MORSE/NAVY RIFLE

Caliber: 45, 50 or 58.
Barrel: 26", octagonal.
Weight: 6 lbs. (45 cal.). **Length:** 41½" over-all.
Stock: American walnut, full p.g.
Sights: Blade front, open fixed rear.
Features: Brass action, trigger guard, ramrod pipes. Made in U.S. by Navy Arms.
Price: $167.00
Price: Kit $100.00

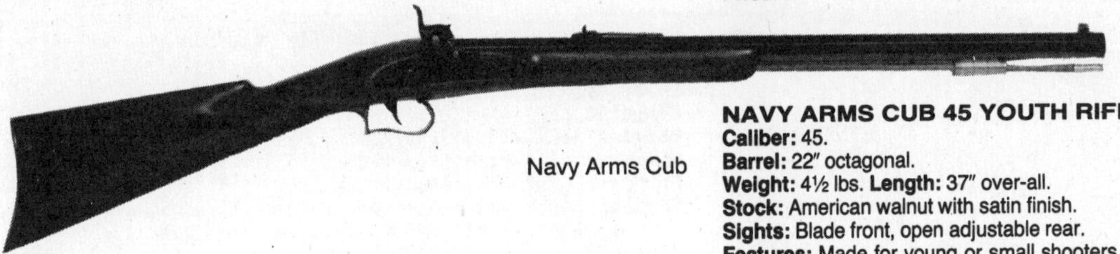

Navy Arms Cub

NAVY ARMS CUB 45 YOUTH RIFLE

Caliber: 45.
Barrel: 22" octagonal.
Weight: 4½ lbs. **Length:** 37" over-all.
Stock: American walnut with satin finish.
Sights: Blade front, open adjustable rear.
Features: Made for young or small shooters. Color case-hardened lock, polished brass furniture. Made in U.S.A. by Navy Arms.
Price: $119.00

CVA BLAZER RIFLE

Caliber: 50 (.490" ball)
Barrel: 28", octagon.
Weight: 6 lbs., 13 oz.
Stock: Hardwood.
Sights: Fixed.
Features: Straight-line percussion with pistol-grip stock of modern design. Introduced 1985. From CVA.
Price: Finished $99.95
Price: Kit $79.95

CVA EXPRESS RIFLE

Caliber: 50 (.490" ball)
Barrels: 28", round.
Weight: 9 lbs.
Stock: Walnut-stained hardwood.
Sights: Bead and post front, adjustable rear.
Features: Double rifle with twin percussion locks and triggers. Hooked breech. Introduced 1985. From CVA.
Price: Finished $299.95
Price: Kit $269.95

Iver Johnson Double Rifle

IVER JOHNSON O-U MODEL BP.50HB RIFLE

Caliber: 50.
Barrel: 26".
Weight: 8½ lbs. **Length:** 41¼" over-all.
Stock: Checkered walnut
Sights: Blade front with gold bead, folding rear adjustable for w. and e.
Features: Two-shot over-under with two hammers, two triggers. Polished blue finish. Removeable breechplugs. Barrels regulated to 50 yards. Introduced 1985. From Iver Johnson.
Price: $351.50

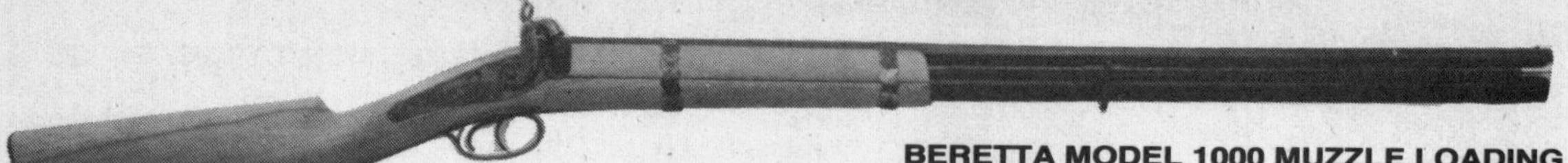

Beretta O-U Shotgun

BERETTA MODEL 1000 MUZZLE LOADING O-U SHOTGUN

Gauge: 12 only.
Barrel: 30″.
Weight: About 7 lbs. **Length:** 46½″ over-all.
Stock: Walnut; English-style with checkpiece.
Features: Special limited production replica of an early Beretta over-under. Silvered, engraved lockplates, trigger guard, hammers, barrel bands. Ramrod fits on right side of blued barrels. Introduced 1981. Imported from Italy by Beretta U.S.A. Corp.
Price: **$840.00**

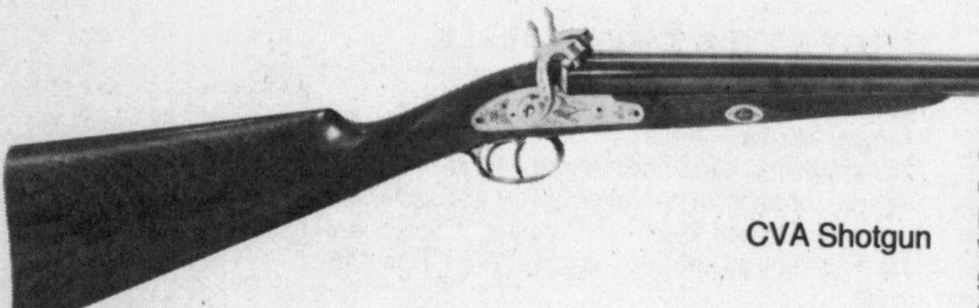

CVA Shotgun

CVA PERCUSSION SHOTGUN

Gauge: 12.
Barrel: 28″.
Weight: 6 lbs., 10 oz. **Length:** 44½″over-all.
Stock: Select hardwood; checkered pistol grip and fore-end.
Sights: Brass bead front.
Features: Hooked breech system. Blued barrels and thimbles, polished steel wedge plates, trigger guard, triggers, tang, lock and hammers; engraved lock, hammers, tang and trigger guard. Introduced 1983. From CVA.
Price: Finished **$259.95**
Price: Kit **$199.95**

EUROARMS OF AMERICA MAGNUM CAPE GUN

Gauge: 12.
Barrel: 32″ (Cyl.).
Weight: 7½ lbs.
Stock: Walnut.
Features: Single barrel percussion with polished steel lock, blued trigger guard and buttplate; hooked breech for easy takedown. From Euroarms of America.
Price: **$215.00**

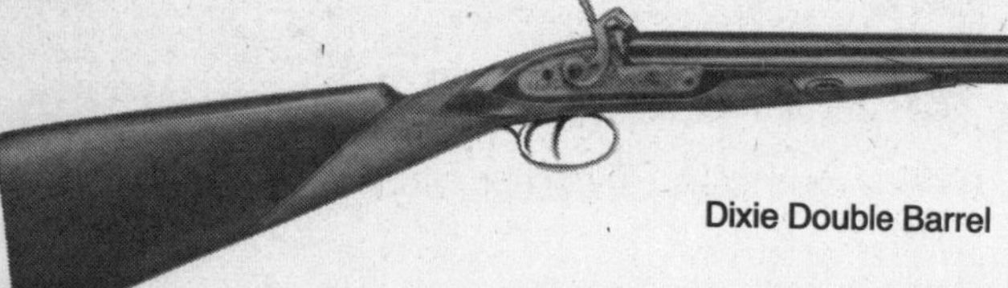

Dixie Double Barrel

DIXIE MAGNUM PERCUSSION SHOTGUN

Gauge: 10, 12.
Barrel: 30″ (I.C.&Mod.) in 10 ga.; 28″ in 12 ga.
Weight: 6¼ lbs. **Length:** 45″ over-all.
Stock: Hand checkered walnut, 14″ pull.
Features: Double triggers, light hand engraving. Case hardened locks in 12 ga.; polished steel in 10 ga. with sling swivels. From Dixie.
Price: Upland **$299.85**
Price: 12 ga. kit **$235.00**
Price: 10 ga. **$335.00**
Price: 10 ga. kit **$285.00**

MAC WOLVERINE FOWLER SHOTGUN

Gauge: 20.
Barrel: 28″.
Weight: 7½ lbs. **Length:** 46″ over-all.
Stock: Choice of walnut or curly maple.
Features: Fires from an open bolt, uses #209 shotshell primer for ignition. Modern rifle trigger; O-ring barrel seal; aluminum ramrod drilled and tapped for shotgun and standard blackpowder cleaning accessories. Left-hand model available at no extra charge. Introduced 1985. Made in U.S. by Michigan Arms Corp.
Price: **$395.00**

Mowrey Ethan Allen

MOWREY ETHAN ALLEN 12 GAUGE SHOTGUN

Gauge: 12 or 28 ga.
Barrel: 32″, octagon (12 ga.); 28″ octagon (28 ga.).
Weight: 8 lbs. **Length:** 48″ over-all.
Stock: Curly maple, oil finish, brass furniture; standard or premium grade.
Sights: Bead front.
Features: Available in percussion only. Steel or brass action and furniture. Box-lock action. Uses standard 12 ga. wadding. Add $38 for premium wood. Made by Mowrey.
Price: Complete, brass or steel frame **$269.00**
Price: Kit, brass or steel frame **$189.00**
Price: 28 ga., brass frame, complete **$264.00**
Price: 28 ga., steel frame, complete **$254.00**
Price: 28 ga., brass frame, kit **$184.00**
Price: 28 ga., steel frame, kit **$174.00**

CAUTION: PRICES CHANGE. CHECK AT GUNSHOP.

BLACK POWDER SHOTGUNS

Morse/Navy Shotgun

MORSE/NAVY SINGLE BARREL SHOTGUN

Gauge: 12 ga.
Barrel: 26″.
Weight: 5 lbs. **Length:** 41½″ over-all.
Stock: American walnut, full p.g.
Sights: Front bead
Features: Brass receiver, black buttplate. Made in U.S. by Navy Arms.
Price: **$167.00**
Price: Kit **$105.00**

Navy T&T Shotgun

NAVY ARMS T&T SHOTGUN

Gauge: 12.
Barrel: 28″ (Full & Full).
Weight: 7½ lbs.
Stock: Walnut.
Sights: Bead front.
Features: Color case-hardened locks, blued steel furniture. From Navy Arms.
Price: **$342.00**

Navy Classic Double

NAVY CLASSIC DOUBLE BARREL SHOTGUN

Gauge: 10, 12.
Barrel: 28″.
Weight: 7 lbs., 12 ozs. **Length:** 45″ over-all.
Stock: Walnut.
Features: Color case-hardened lock plates and hammers; hand checkered stock. Imported by Navy Arms.
Price: 12 ga. **$342.00**
Price: 10 ga. **$360.00**
Price: Kit, 12 ga. **$265.00**
Price: Kit, 10 ga. **$280.00**

AIR GUNS—HANDGUNS

AIR MATCH MODEL 600 PISTOL

Caliber: 177, single shot.
Barrel: 8.8″.
Weight: 32 oz. **Length:** 13.19″ over-all.
Power: Single stroke pneumatic.
Stocks: Match-style with adjustable palm shelf.
Sights: Interchangeable post front, fully adjustable match rear with interchangeable blades.
Features: Velocity of 420 fps. Adjustable trigger with dry-fire option. Comes with fitted case. Available with three different grip styles, barrel weight, sight extension. Add $5.00 for left-hand models. Introduced 1984. Imported from Italy by Kendall International Arms.
Price: With adjustable or fixed grip **$386.25**

Air Match 600

BSA SCORPION AIR PISTOL

Caliber: 177 or 22, single shot.
Barrel: 7⅞″, rifled.
Weight: 3.6 lbs. **Length:** 15¾″ over-all.
Power: Spring-air, barrel cocking.
Stock: Moulded black plastic contoured with thumbrest.
Sights: Interchangeable bead or blade front with hood, open rear adjustable for w. & e.
Features: Muzzle velocity of 510 fps (177) and 380 fps (22). Comes with pellets, oil, targets and steel target holder. Scope and mount optional. Introduced 1980. Imported from England by Precision Sports.
Price: 177 or 22 cal. **$99.95**
Price: 1.5x15 scope and mount **$49.95**

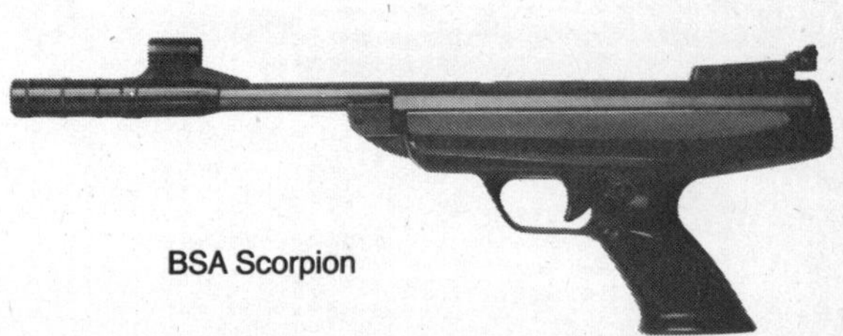

BSA Scorpion

Beeman P1 Magnum

BEEMAN P1 MAGNUM AIR PISTOL
Caliber: 177, single shot.
Barrel: 8.4″.
Weight: 2.5 lbs. **Length:** 11″ over-all.
Power: Top lever cocking; spring piston.
Stocks: Checkered walnut.
Sights: Blade front, square notch rear with click micrometer adjustments for w. and e. Grooved for scope mounting.
Features: Dual power: low setting gives 350-400 fps; high setting 500-600 fps. Rearward expanding mainspring simulates firearm recoil. All Colt 45 auto grips fit gun. Optional wooden shoulder stock. Introduced 1985. Imported by Beeman.
Price: **$189.95**

Beeman/Webley Hurricane

BEEMAN/WEBLEY HURRICANE PISTOL
Caliber: 177 or 22, single shot.
Barrel: 8″, rifled.
Weight: 2.4 lbs. **Length:** 11½″ over-all.
Power: Spring piston.
Stocks: Thumbrest, checkered high-impact synthetic.
Sights: Hooded front, micro-click rear adj. for w. and e.
Features: Velocity of 470 fps (177-cal.). Single stroke cocking, adjustable trigger pull, manual safety. Rearward recoil like a firearm pistol. Steel piston and cylinder. Scope base included; 1.5x scope **$39.95** extra. Shoulder stock available. Introduced 1977. Imported from England by Beeman.
Price: **$139.50**

Beeman/Webley Tempest

BEEMAN/WEBLEY TEMPEST AIR PISTOL
Caliber: 177 or 22, single shot.
Barrel: 6.75″, rifled ordnance steel.
Weight: 32 oz. **Length:** 9″ over-all.
Power: Spring piston.
Stocks: Checkered black epoxy with thumbrest.
Sights: Post front; rear has sliding leaf adjustable for w. and e.
Features: Adjustable trigger pull, manual safety. Velocity 470 fps (177 cal.). Steel piston in steel liner for maximum performance and durability. Unique rearward spring simulates firearm recoil. Shoulder stock available. Introduced 1979. Imported from England by Beeman.
Price: **$109.50**

BEEMAN/FEINWERKBAU MODEL 2 CO^2 PISTOL
Caliber: 177, single shot
Barrel: 10.1″.
Weight: 2.5 lbs. **Length:** 16¼″ over-all.
Power: Special CO^2 cylinder.
Stocks: Stippled walnut with adjustable palm shelf.
Sights: Blade front with interchangeable inserts; open micro. click rear with adjustable notch width.
Features: Power adjustable from 360 fps to 525 fps. Fully adjustable trigger; three weights for balance and weight adjustments. Short-barrel Mini-2 model also available. Introduced 1983. Imported by Beeman.
Price: Right hand **$610.00**
Price: Left hand **$650.00**
Price: Mini-2, right hand **$635.00**
Price: Mini-2, left hand **$675.00**

FWB Mini-2

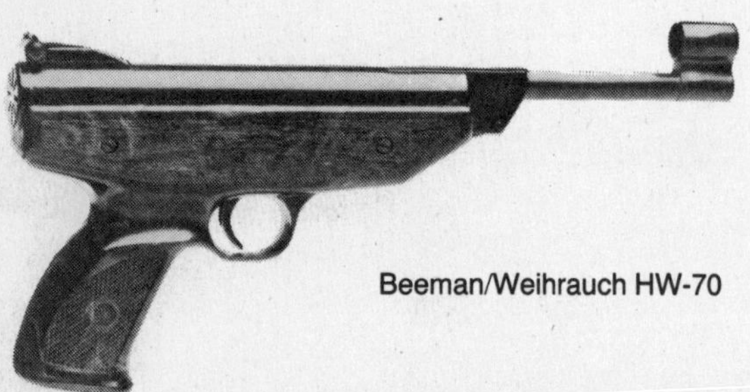
Beeman/Weihrauch HW-70

BEEMAN/WEIHRAUCH HW-70 AIR PISTOL
Caliber: 177, single shot.
Barrel: 6¼″, rifled.
Weight: 38 oz. **Length:** 12¾″ over-all.
Power: Spring, barrel cocking.
Stocks: Plastic, with thumbrest.
Sights: Hooded post front, square notch rear adj. for w. and e.
Features: Adj. trigger. 24-lb. cocking effort, 410 f.p.s. M.V.; automatic barrel safety. Imported by Beeman.
Price: From Beeman **$119.50**

BEEMAN/FEINWERKBAU MODEL 90 PISTOL
Caliber: 177, single shot.
Barrel: 7.5″, 12-groove rifling.
Weight: 3.0 lbs. **Length:** 16.4″ over-all.
Power: Spring piston, single stroke sidelever cocking.
Stocks: Stippled walnut with adjustable palm shelf.
Sights: Interchangeable blade front, fully adjustable open notch rear.
Features: Velocity of 475 to 525 fps. Has new adjustable electronic trigger. Recoilless action, metal piston ring and dual mainsprings. Cocking effort is 12 lbs. Introduced 1983. Imported by Beeman.
Price: .... **$685.00** to **$718.00**

CAUTION: PRICES CHANGE. CHECK AT GUNSHOP.

BEEMAN/FEINWERKBAU FWB-65 MKII AIR PISTOL

Caliber: 177, single shot.
Barrel: 6.1″; fixed bbl. wgt. avail.
Weight: 42 oz. **Length:** 14.1″ over-all.
Power: Spring, sidelever cocking.
Stocks: Walnut, stippled thumbrest; adjustable or fixed.
Sights: Front, interchangeable post element system, open rear, click adj. for w. & e. and for sighting notch width. Scope mount avail.
Features: New shorter barrel for better balance and control. Cocking effort 9 lbs. 2-stage trigger, 4 adjustments. Quiet firing, 525 fps. Programs instantly for recoil or recoilless operation. Permanently lubricated. Steel piston ring. Special switch converts trigger from 17.6 oz. pull to 42 oz. let-off. Imported by Beeman.
Price: Right-hand .... **$525.00** to **$623.00**
Price: Left-hand .... **$560.00** to **$633.00**
Price: Model 65 Mk.I (7.5″ bbl.) .... **$485.00** to **$575.00**

FWB 65 Mk. II

Beeman/FAS 604

BEEMAN/FAS MODEL 604 AIR PISTOL

Caliber: 177, single shot.
Barrel: 7.5″, 10-groove rifled steel.
Weight: 2.3 lbs. **Length:** 11.3″ over-all.
Power: Single stroke pneumatic.
Stocks: Anatomically shaped stippled walnut; small, medium, large sizes.
Sights: Adjustable.
Features: Top of receiver is cocking arm, requires 13 lbs. effort. Adjustable trigger may be dry-fired without fully cocking pistol. Imported from Italy by Beeman. Introduced 1984.
Price: .... **$495.00** to **$525.00**

BENJAMIN SUPER S. S. TARGET PISTOL SERIES 130

Caliber: BB, single shot.
Barrel: 8″; BB smoothbore; 22 and 177, rifled.
Weight: 2 lbs. **Length:** 11″ over-all.
Power: Hand pumped.
Features: Bolt action; fingertip safety; adj. power.
Price: M130, BB **$73.80**

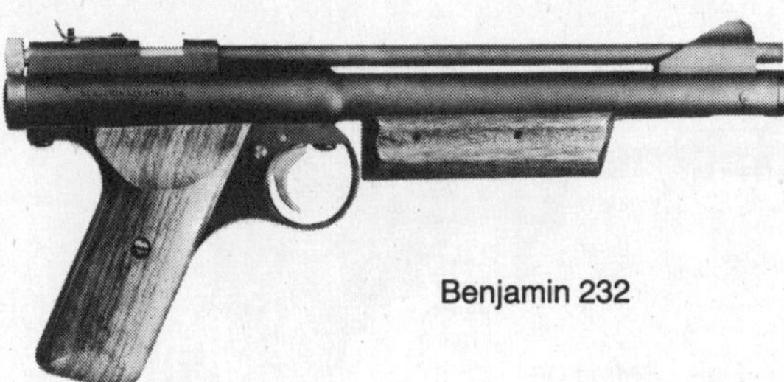

Benjamin 232

BENJAMIN 232/237 SINGLE SHOT PISTOLS

Caliber: 177 and 22.
Weight: 32 oz. **Length:** 11¾″ over-all.
Power: Hand pumped.
Stocks: Walnut, with walnut pump handle.
Sights: Blade front, open adjustable rear.
Features: Bolt action; fingertip safety; adjustable power.
Price: Model 232 (22 cal.) **$82.00**
Price: Model 237 (177 cal.) **$82.00**

Consult our Directory pages for the location of firms mentioned.

Crosman Model 357

CROSMAN MODEL 357 AIR PISTOL

Caliber: 177, 6-shot.
Barrel: 4″ (Model 357 Four), 6″ (Model 357 six), 8″ (Model 357 Eight); rifled steel.
Weight: 32 oz. (6″) **Length:** 11⅜″ over-all.
Power: CO_2 Powerlet.
Stocks: Checkered wood-grain plastic.
Sights: Ramp front, fully adjustable rear.
Features: Average 430 fps (Model 357 Six). Break-open barrel for easy loading. Single or double action. Vent rib barrel. Wide, smooth trigger. Two speed loaders come with each gun. Models Four and Six introduced 1983, Model Eight introduced 1984.
Price: 4″ or 6″, about **$45.00**
Price: 8″, about **$70.00**

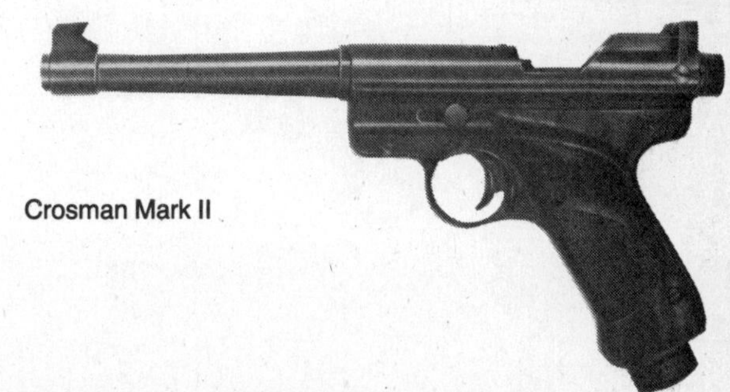

Crosman Mark II

CROSMAN MARK II TARGET PISTOL

Caliber: 177 or BB.
Barrel: 7¼″, button rifled.
Weight: 44 oz. **Length:** 11⅛″ over-all.
Power: Crosman Powerlet CO_2 cylinder.
Features: New system provides same shot-to-shot velocity of 435-485 fps (pellets). Checkered thumbrest grips, right or left. Patridge front sight, rear adj. for w. & e. Adj. trigger.
Price: About **$58.00**

CAUTION: PRICES CHANGE. CHECK AT GUNSHOP.

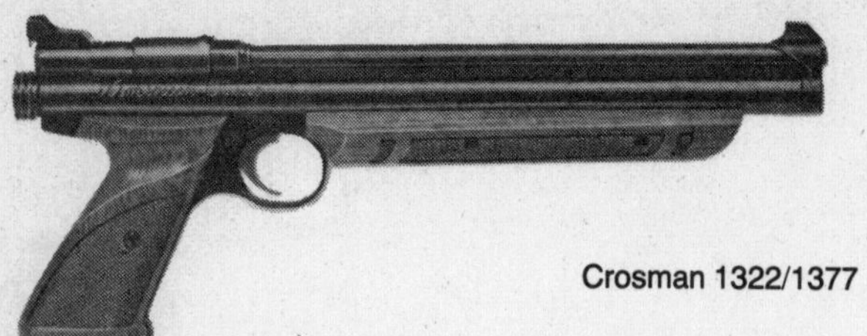

Crosman 1322/1377

DAISY MODEL 188 BB PISTOL

Caliber: BB.
Barrel: 9.9″, steel smoothbore.
Weight: 1.67 lbs. **Length:** 11.7″ over-all.
Stocks: Die-cast metal; checkered with thumbrest.
Sights: Blade and ramp front, open fixed rear.
Features: 24-shot repeater. Spring action with under-barrel cocking lever. Grip and receiver of die-cast metal. Introduced 1979.
Price: About **$20.00**

DAISY MODEL 08 SOFTAIR PISTOL

Caliber: 25 (6mm) plastic pellets; 6-shot clip.
Barrel: Smoothbore.
Weight: NA. **Length:** 9¾″ over-all.
Stocks: Woodtone, molded with checkering.
Sights: Post front, notch rear.
Features: Fires 25-cal. plastic pellets loaded into plastic cartridges; semi-auto action ejects spent shells. Introduced 1985.
Price: About **$25.00**

Daisy Softair 57

Daisy Softair 59

Daisy Softair 38

CROSMAN MODEL 1322 AIR PISTOL

Caliber: 22, single shot.
Barrel: 8″, button rifled.
Weight: 37 oz. **Length:** 13⅝″.
Power: Hand pumped.
Sights: Blade front, rear adj. for w. and e.
Features: Moulded plastic grip, hand size pump forearm. Cross bolt safety. Also available in 177 Cal. as **Model 1377** (same price).
Price: About **$45.00**

CROSMAN 1600 BB PISTOL

Caliber: BB, 17-shot.
Barrel: 7¾″.
Weight: 29 oz. **Length:** 11⅜″ over-all.
Power: Standard CO_2.
Stocks: Contoured with thumbrest.
Sights: Patridge-type front, fully adj. rear.
Features: Gives about 80 shots per powerlet, slide-action safety, steel barrel, die-cast receiver. Introduced 1983.
Price: About **$28.00**

Daisy Model 188

Daisy Softair 08

DAISY MODEL 57 SOFTAIR REVOLVER

Caliber: 25 (6mm) plastic pellets; 6-shot.
Barrel: Smoothbore.
Weight: NA. **Length:** 10½″ over-all.
Stocks: Molded woodgrain with checkering.
Sights: Blade and ramp front, notch rear.
Features: Fires spring-activated 25-cal. plastic pellets loaded into plastic cartridges. Cylinder swings out for loading. Introduced 1985.
Price: About **$25.00**

DAISY MODEL 38 SOFTAIR PISTOL

Caliber: 25 (6mm) plastic pellets; single shot.
Barrel: Smoothbore.
Weight: NA. **Length:** 10″ over-all.
Stocks: Molded, grooved plastic.
Sights: Post front, notch rear.
Features: Fires 25-cal. plastic pellets loaded into a pop-up chamber in barrel. Introduced 1985.
Price: About **$25.00**

DAISY MODEL 59 SOFTAIR PISTOL

Caliber: 25 (6mm) plastic pellets; 10-shot clip.
Barrel: Smoothbore.
Weight: NA. **Length:** 9″ over-all.
Stocks: Molded with checkering.
Sights: Blade and ramp front, notch rear.
Features: Fires 25-cal. plastic pellets loaded into plastic cartridges. Clip fed, semi-auto action ejects spent bullets. Introduced 1985.
Price: About **$25.00**

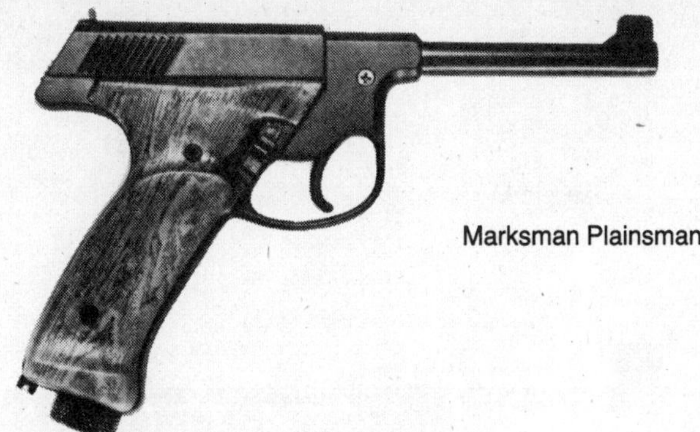
Marksman Plainsman

MARKSMAN PLAINSMAN 1049 CO_2 PISTOL

Caliber: BB, 100-shot repeater.
Barrel: 5⅞", smooth.
Weight: 28 oz. **Length:** 9½" over-all.
Stocks: Simulated walnut with thumbrest.
Power: 8.5 or 12.5 gram CO_2 cylinders.
Features: Velocity of 400 fps. Three-position power switch. Auto. ammunition feed. Positive safety.
Price: **$32.95**

HAMMERLI "MASTER" CO_2 TARGET PISTOL

Caliber: 177, single shot.
Barrel: 6.4", 12-groove.
Weight: 38.4 oz. **Length:** 16" over-all.
Power: 12 gram cylinder.
Stocks: Plastic with thumbrest and checkering.
Sights: Ramp front, micro rear, click adj. Adj. sight radius from 11.1" to 13.0".
Features: Single shot, manual loading. Residual gas vented automatically. 5-way adj. trigger. Available from Mandall Shooting Supplies.
Price: **$495.00**

MARKSMAN #1010 REPEATER PISTOL

Caliber: 177, 20-shot repeater.
Barrel: 2½", smoothbore.
Weight: 24 oz. **Length:** 8¼".
Power: Spring
Features: Thumb safety. Uses BBs, darts or pellets. Repeats with BBs only.
Price: Matte black finish **$15.50**
Price: Model 1020 (as above except fires BBs only) **$15.50**

Marksman 1010

Norica Black Widow

NORICA BLACK WIDOW AIR PISTOL

Caliber: 177, single shot.
Barrel: 7¾".
Weight: 3 lbs. **Length:** 15" over-all.
Power: Spring air, barrel cocking.
Stocks: Target-style of black high-impact plastic.
Sights: Hooded front, open adjustable rear.
Features: Velocity 395 fps. Side mounted automatic safety; receiver grooved for scope mounting. Imported from Spain by Kassnar.
Price: **$74.00**

POWER LINE MATCH 777 PELLET PISTOL

Caliber: 177, single shot.
Barrel: 9.61" rifled steel by Lothar Walther.
Weight: 32 oz. **Length:** 13½" over-all.
Power: Sidelever, single pump pneumatic.
Stocks: Smooth hardwood, fully contoured with palm and thumb rest.
Sights: Blade and ramp front, match-grade open rear with adj. width notch, micro. click adjustments.
Features: Adjustable trigger; manual cross-bolt safety. MV of 385 fps. Comes with cleaning kit, adjustment tool and pellets.
Price: About **$200.00**

Power Line 777

POWER LINE 717 PELLET PISTOL

Caliber: 177, single shot.
Barrel: 9.61".
Weight: 2.8 lbs. **Length:** 13½" over-all.
Stocks: Molded wood-grain plastic, with thumbrest.
Sights: Blade and ramp front, micro. adjustable notch rear.
Features: Single pump pneumatic pistol. Rifled steel barrel. Cross-bolt trigger block. Muzzle velocity 385 fps. From Daisy. Introduced 1979.
Price: About **$40.00**

POWER LINE CO_2 1200 PISTOL

Caliber: BB, 177.
Barrel: 10½", smooth.
Weight: 1.6 lbs. **Length:** 11.1" over-all.
Power: Daisy CO_2 cylinder.
Stocks: Contoured, checkered molded wood-grain plastic.
Sights: Blade ramp front, fully adj. square notch rear.
Features: 60-shot BB reservoir, gravity feed. Cross-bolt safety. Velocity of 420-450 fps for more than 100 shots.
Price: About **$25.00**

Power Line 717

PRECISE/RO-72 BULLSEYE AIR PISTOL

Caliber: 177, single shot.
Barrel: 7¼", rifled.
Weight: 35 oz.
Power: Spring air, barrel cocking.
Stock: Molded plastic with thumbrest.
Sights: Hooded front, micro. adj. open rear for w. and e.
Features: Four interchangeable front sights—triangle, bead, narrow post, wide post. Rear sight rotates to give four distinct sight pictures. Muzzle velocity 325 fps. Precise International, importer.
Price: **$40.00**

Precise RO-72

RWS MODEL 5G AIR PISTOL

Caliber: 177, single shot.
Barrel: 7".
Weight: 2¾ lbs. **Length:** 16" over-all.
Power: Spring air, barrel cocking.
Stocks: Plastic, thumbrest design.
Sights: Tunnel front, micro click open rear.
Features: Velocity of 410 fps. Two-stage trigger with automatic safety. Imported from West Germany by Dynamit Nobel of America, also available from Great Lakes Airguns.
Price: **$125.00**

RWS Model 5G

RWS MODEL 5GS AIR PISTOL

Same as the Model 5G except comes with 1.5×15 pistol scope with ramp-style mount, muzzle brake/weight. No open sights supplied. Introduced 1983.
Price: **$160.00**

RWS Model 6M

RWS MODEL 6M MATCH AIR PISTOL

Caliber: 177, single shot.
Barrel: 7".
Weight: 3 lbs. **Length:** 16" over-all.
Power: Spring air, barrel cocking.
Stocks: Walnut-finished hardwood with thumbrest.
Sights: Adjustable front, micro click open rear.
Features: Velocity of 410 fps. Recoilless double piston system, moveable barrel shroud to protect front sight during cocking. Imported from West Germany by Dynamit Nobel of America.
Price: **$235.00**

RWS Model 10

RWS Model 10 Match Air Pistol

Refined version of the Model 6M. Has special adjustable match trigger, oil finished and stippled match grips, barrel weight. Also available in left-hand version, and with fitted case.
Price: Model 10 .... **$435.00**
Price: Model 10, left hand **$460.00**
Price: Model 10, with case **$455.00**
Price: Model 10, left hand, with case **$475.00**

RECORD "JUMBO" DELUXE AIR PISTOL

Caliber: 177, single shot.
Barrel: 6", rifled.
Weight: 1.9 lbs. **Length:** 7.25" over-all.
Power: Spring air, lever cocking.
Stocks: Smooth walnut.
Sights: Blade front, fully adjustable open rear.
Features: Thumb safety. Grip magazine compartment for extra pellet storage. Introduced 1983. Imported from West Germany by Great Lakes Airguns and Beeman.
Price: From Great Lakes **$68.50**
Price: From Beeman **$65.00**

Record Jumbo

Sheridan Model HB

SHERIDAN MODEL HB PNEUMATIC PISTOL

Caliber: 5mm; single shot.
Barrel: 9⅜", rifled.
Weight: 36 oz. **Length:** 12" over-all.
Power: Underlever pneumatic pump.
Stocks: Checkered simulated walnut; fore-end is walnut.
Sights: Blade front, fully adjustable rear.
Features: "Controller-Power" feature allows velocity and range control by varying the number of pumps—3 to 10. Maximum velocity of 400 fps. Introduced 1982. From Sheridan Products.
Price: **$80.40**

CAUTION: PRICES CHANGE. CHECK AT GUNSHOP.

Sheridan Model EB

SHERIDAN MODEL EB CO_2 PISTOL
Caliber: 20 (5mm).
Barrel: 6½", rifled, rust proof.
Weight: 27 oz. **Length:** 9" over-all.
Power: 12 gram CO_2 cylinder.
Stocks: Checkered simulated walnut. Left- or right-handed.
Sights: Blade front, fully adjustable rear.
Features: Turn-bolt single-shot action. Gives about 40 shots at 400 fps per CO_2 cylinder.
Price: $60.35

WALTHER CP CO_2 AIR PISTOL
Caliber: 177, single shot.
Barrel: 9".
Weight: 40 oz. **Length:** 14¾" over-all.
Power: CO_2.
Stocks: Full target type stippled wood with adjustable hand-shelf.
Sights: Target post front, fully adjustable target rear.
Features: Velocity of 520 fps. CO_2 powered; target-quality trigger; comes with adaptor for charging with standard CO_2 air tanks, case, and accessories. Introduced 1983. Imported from West Germany by Interarms.
Price: $535.00
Price: Junior model (modified grip, shorter gas cylinder) $535.00

WALTHER MODEL LP-3
Caliber: 177, single shot.
Barrel: 9⅜", rifled.
Weight: 45½ oz. **Length:** 13 3/16" over-all.
Power: Compressed air, lever cocking.
Features: Recoilless operation, cocking in grip frame. Micro-click rear sight, adj. for w. & e., 4-way adj. trigger. Plastic thumbrest grips. Imported by Interarms.
Price: $325.00

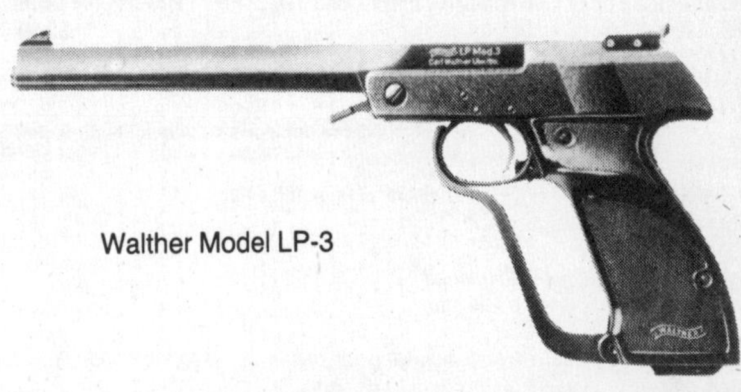
Walther Model LP-3

Walther Model LP-3 Match Pistol
Same specifications as LP-3 except for grips, frame shape and weight. Has adjustable walnut grips to meet international shooting regulations. Imported by Interarms.
Price: $375.00

WISCHO BSF S-20 PISTOL
Caliber: 177, single shot.
Barrel: 7" rifled.
Weight: 45 oz. **Length:** 15.8" over-all.
Power: Spring piston barrel cocking.
Stocks: Walnut with thumbrest.
Sights: Bead front, rear adj. for e.
Features: Cocking effort of 17 lbs.; M.V. 450 f.p.s.; adj. trigger. Optional scope and mount available. Detachable aluminum stock optional. Available from Great Lakes Airguns.
Price: Standard.. $94.50
Price: Match model (adj. sight, thumbrest stocks) $119.95

Wischo BSF S-20

AIR GUNS—LONG GUNS

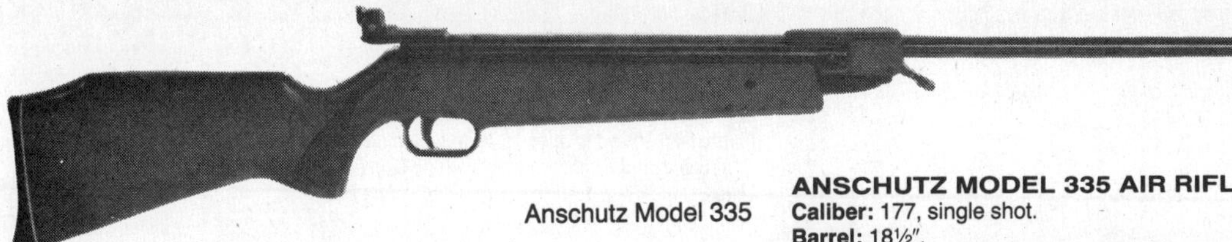
Anschutz Model 335

ANSCHUTZ MODEL 335 AIR RIFLE
Caliber: 177, single shot.
Barrel: 18½".
Weight: 7¼ lbs. **Length:** 43¼" over-all.
Power: Spring piston; barrel cocking.
Stock: European hardwood; checkered pistol grip.
Sights: Williams peep rear, Anschutz globe front.
Features: Specially designed for 10 meter "novice-expert" shooters. Adjustable two-stage trigger. Introduced 1982. Imported from Germany by PSI.
Price: Without sight $172.50
Price: Magnum model, no sights.................................. $174.50
Price: Sight set $28.35

ANSCHUTZ MODEL 380 AIR RIFLE
Caliber: 177, single shot.
Barrel: 20¼".
Weight: 10.8 lbs. (including sights). **Length:** 42⅛" over-all.
Power: Spring piston; sidelever cocking.
Stock: European hardwood with stippled pistol grip and fore-end. Adjustable cheekpiece and rubber buttpad.
Sights: Globe front; match aperture rear.
Features: Recoilless and vibration free. Two-stage adjustable match trigger. Introduced 1982. Imported from Germany by PSI.
Price: With sights... $867.00
Price: Left-hand, with sights.................................. $892.00

BSA Airsporter-S

BSA AIRSPORTER-S AIR RIFLE

Caliber: 177 or 22.
Barrel: 19.5", rifled.
Weight: 8 lbs. **Length:** 44.7" over-all.
Power: Spring air, underlever action.
Stock: Oil-finished walnut, high comb Monte Carlo cheekpiece.
Sights: Ramp front with interchangeable bead and blade, adjustable for height; tangent-type rear adj. for w. & e.
Features: Muzzle velocity of 825 fps (177) and 635 fps (22). Fully adj. trigger. Cylinder is a large diameter, one-piece impact extrusion. Scope and mount optional. Introduced 1980. Imported from England by Precision Sports.
Price: 177 or 22 cal. **$329.95**
Price: Standard Airsporter **$249.95**
Price: 4x20 scope and mount **$49.95**

BSA Mercury-S Air Rifle

Similar to the standard Mercury model except weighs 7¼ lbs., has European walnut stock with oil finish, checkered fore-end and pistol grip. Muzzle velocity of 825 fps (177), 635 fps (22). Introduced 1982. From Precision Sports.
Price: **$249.95**

BSA MERCURY AIR RIFLE

Caliber: 177 or 22, single shot.
Barrel: 18.5", rifled.
Weight: 7 lbs. **Length:** 43.5" over-all.
Power: Spring-air, barrel cocking.
Stock: European hardwood. Monte Carlo cheekpiece, ventilated butt pad.
Sights: Adjustable bead/blade front, tangent rear adj. for w. & e.
Features: Muzzle velocity of 700 fps (177) and 550 fps (22). Reversible "V" and "U" notch rear sight blade. Single stage match-type trigger, adj. for weight of pull and sear engagement. Scope and mount optional. Introduced 1980. Imported from England by Precision Sports.
Price: 177 or 22 cal. **$199.95**
Price: 4x20 scope and mount **$49.95**

BSA Meteor Super

BSA METEOR/METEOR SUPER AIR RIFLES

Caliber: 177 or 22, single shot.
Barrel: 18.5", rifled.
Weight: 6 lbs. **Length:** 42" over-all.
Power: Spring air, barrel cocking.
Stock: European hardwood.
Sights: Adj. bead/blade front, adj. tangent rear with reversible "U" and "V" notch blade.
Features: Muzzle velocity of 650 fps (177) and 500 fps (22). Aperture rear sight element supplied. Cylinder is dovetailed for scope mounting. Adjustable trigger mechanism. Meteor Super has M.C. cheekpiece, vent. rubber recoil pad. Introduced 1980. Imported from England by Precision Sports.
Price: Meteor **$129.95**
Price: Meteor Super **$139.95**

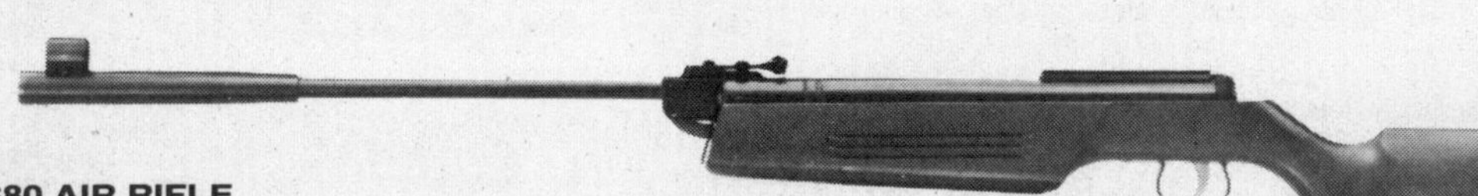
BSF Model S80

BSF MODEL S80 AIR RIFLE

Caliber: 177, single shot.
Barrel: 19½".
Weight: 8.5 lbs. **Length:** 44" over-all.
Power: Spring-air, barrel cocking.
Stock: Walnut-finished hardwood.
Sights: Hooded post front with bead, open fully adjustable rear.
Features: Velocity of 850 fps. Permanently attached barrel weight. Monte Carlo stock with rubber butt pad; adjustable trigger. Scope mount rail installed. Introduced 1984. Imported from West Germany by Great Lakes Airguns.
Price: **$188.50**

BSF MODEL S70 AIR RIFLE

Caliber: 177, single shot.
Barrel: 19", rifled.
Weight: 7 lbs. **Length:** 43¼" over-all.
Power: Spring-air, barrel cocking.
Stock: Walnut-stained hardwood.
Sights: Hooded bead front, open fully adjustable rear.
Features: Velocity about 850 fps. Scope mount base installed; rubber butt pad; blued metal. Imported from West Germany by Great Lakes Airguns.
Price: **$156.80**

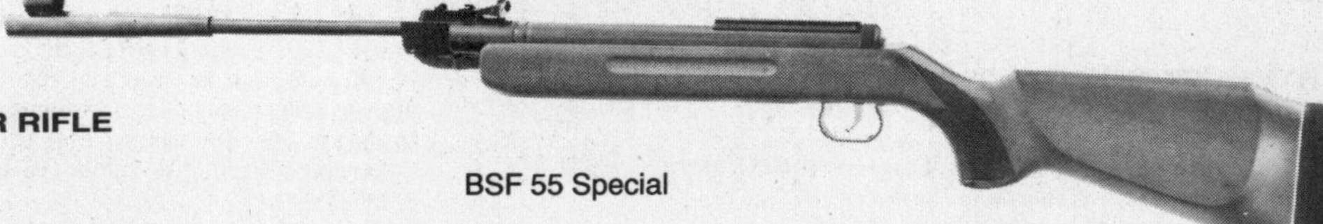
BSF 55 Special

BSF MODEL 55 SPECIAL AIR RIFLE

Caliber: 177, 22, single shot.
Barrel: 16.5", rifled.
Weight: 7.5 lbs. **Length:** 44.5" over-all.
Power: Spring air, barrel cocking.
Stock: Walnut-stained hardwood.
Sights: Hooded bead front, fully adjustable open rear.
Features: Velocity of 870-900 fps. Permanently attached barrel weight, rubber butt pad, blued metal. Introduced 1984. Imported from West Germany by Great Lakes Airguns.
Price: **$174.30**

CAUTION: PRICES CHANGE. CHECK AT GUNSHOP.

Beeman FWB 124/127

BEEMAN/FEINWERKBAU 124/127 MAGNUM
Caliber: 177 (FWB-124); 22 (FWB-127); single shot.
Barrel: 18.3", 12-groove rifling.
Weight: 6.8 lbs. **Length:** 43½" over-all.
Power: Spring piston air; single stroke barrel cocking.
Stock: Walnut finished hardwood.
Sights: Tunnel front; click-adj. rear for w., slide-adj. for e.
Features: Velocity 680-820 fps, cocking effort of 18 lbs. Forged steel receiver; nylon non-drying piston and breech seals. Auto. safety, adj. trigger. Standard model has no checkering, cheekpiece. Deluxe has hand-checkerd p.g. and fore-end, high comb cheekpiece, and buttplate with white spacer. Imported by Beeman.
Price: Standard model **$286.50**
Price: Deluxe model (illus.) **$319.50**

FWB 300-S Universal

BEEMAN/FEINWERKBAU 300-S "UNIVERSAL" MATCH
Caliber: 177, single shot.
Barrel: 19.9".
Weight: 10.2 lbs. (without barrel sleeve). **Length:** 43.3" over-all.
Power: Spring piston, single stroke sidelever.
Stock: Walnut, stippled p.g. and fore-end. Detachable cheekpieces (one std., high for scope use.) Adjustable buttplate, accessory rail. Buttplate and grip cap spacers included.
Sights: Two globe fronts with interchangeable inserts. Rear is match aperture with rubber eyecup and sight viser. Front and rear sights move as a single unit.
Features: Recoilless, vibration free. Grooved for scope mounts. Steel piston ring. Cocking effort about 9½ lbs. Barrel sleeve optional. Left-hand model available. Introduced 1978. Imported by Beeman.
Price: Right-hand **$830.00**
Price: Left-hand **$890.00**

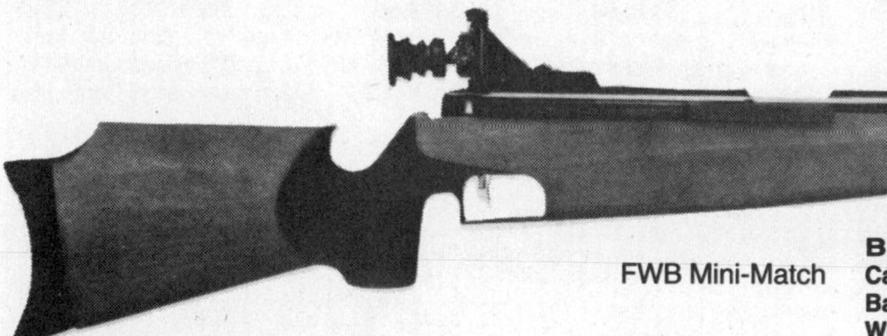

FWB Mini-Match

BEEMAN/FEINWERKBAU 300-S SERIES MATCH RIFLE
Caliber: 177, single shot.
Barrel: 19.9", fixed solid with receiver.
Weight: Approx. 10 lbs. with optional bbl. sleeve. **Length:** 42.8" over-all.
Power: Single stroke sidelever, spring piston.
Stock: Match model—walnut, deep fore-end, adj. buttplate.
Sights: Globe front with interchangeable inserts. Click micro. adj. match aperture rear. Front and rear sights move as a single unit.
Features: Recoilless, vibration free. Five-way adjustable match trigger. Grooved for scope mounts. Permanent lubrication, steel piston ring. Cocking effort 9 lbs. Optional 10 oz. bbl. sleeve. Available from Beeman.
Price: Right hand **$735.00**
Price: Left hand **$785.00**

BEEMAN/FEINWERKBAU 300-S MINI-MATCH
Caliber: 177, single shot.
Barrel: 17⅛".
Weight: 8.8 lbs. **Length:** 40" over-all.
Power: Spring piston, single stroke sidelever cocking.
Stock: Walnut. Stippled grip, adjustable buttplate. Scaled-down for youthful or slightly built shooters.
Sights: Globe front with interchangeable inserts, micro. adjustable rear. Front and rear sights move as a single unit.
Features: Recoilless, vibration free. Grooved for scope mounts. Steel piston ring. Cocking effort about 9½ lbs. Barrel sleeve optional. Left-hand model available. Introduced 1978. Imported by Beeman.
Price: Right-hand **$685.00**
Price: Left-hand **$735.00**

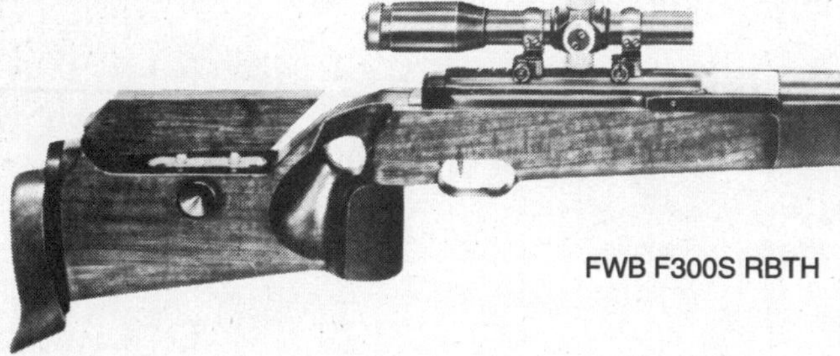

FWB F300S RBTH

BEEMAN/FEINWERKBAU F300-S RUNNING BOAR (TH)
Caliber: 177, single shot.
Barrel: 19.9", rifled.
Weight: 10.9 lbs. **Length:** 43" over-all.
Power: Single stroke sidelever, spring piston.
Stock: Walnut with adjustable buttplate, grip cap and comb. Designed for fixed and moving target use.
Sights: None furnished; grooved for optional scope.
Features: Recoilless, vibration free. Permanent lubrication and seals. Barrel stabilizer weight included. Crisp single-stage trigger. Available from Beeman.
Price: Right-hand **$735.00**
Price: Left-hand **$795.00**

Beeman/Feinwerkbau 600

BEEMAN/FEINWERKBAU MODEL 600 AIR RIFLE

Caliber: 177, single shot.
Barrel: 16.6″.
Weight: 10.8. **Length:** 43″ over-all.
Power: Single stroke pneumatic.
Stock: Special laminated hardwoods and hard rubber for stability.
Sights: Tunnel front with interchangeable inserts, click micrometer match aperture rear.
Features: Recoilless action; double supported barrel; special, short rifled area frees pellet from barrel faster so shooter's motion has minimum effect on accuracy. Fully adjustable match trigger. Trigger and sights blocked when loading latch is open. Imported by Beeman. Introduced 1984.
Price: Right hand **$875.00**
Price: Left hand **$899.50**

Weihrauch Model 35EB

BEEMAN HW 35L/35EB SPORTER RIFLES

Caliber: 177 (35L), 177 or 22 (35EB), single shot.
Barrel: 19½″.
Weight: 8 lbs. **Length:** 43½″ over-all (35L).
Power: Spring, barrel cocking.
Stock: Walnut finish with high comb, full pistol grip.
Sights: Globe front with five inserts, target micrometer rear with rubber eyecup.
Features: Fully adjustable trigger, manual safety. Thumb-release barrel latch. Model 35L has Bavarian cheekpiece stock, 35EB has walnut, American-style stock with cheekpiece, sling swivels, white spacers. Imported by Beeman.
Price: Model 35L **$269.50**
Price: Model 35EB........ **$309.50**

BEEMAN HW 55 TARGET RIFLES

Model:	**55SM**	**55MM**	**55T**
Caliber:	177	177	177
Barrel:	18½″	18½″	18½″
Length:	43½″	43½″	43½″
Wgt. lbs.:	7.8	7.8	7.8
Rear sight:	All aperture		
Front sight:	All with globe and 4 interchangeable inserts.		
Power:	All spring (barrel cocking). 660-700 fps.		
Price:	**$369.50**	**$399.50**	**$469.50**

Features: Trigger fully adj. and removable. Micrometer rear sight adj. for w. and e. on all. Pistol grip high comb stock with beavertail fore-end, walnut finish stock on 55SM. Walnut stock on 55MM, Tyrolean stock on 55T. Imported by Beeman.

Beeman HW77

BEEMAN/HW77 AIR RIFLE & CARBINE

Caliber: 177 or 22, single shot.
Barrel: 18.5″, 12-groove rifling.
Weight: 8.9 lbs. **Length:** 43.7″ over-all.
Power: Spring-piston; underlever cocking.
Stock: Walnut-stained beech; rubber buttplate, cut checkering on grip; cheekpiece.
Sights: Blade front, open adjustable rear.
Features: Velocity 830 fps. Fixed-barrel with fully opening, direct loading breech. Extended underlever gives good cocking leverage. Adjustable trigger. Grooved for scope mounting. Carbine has 14.5″ barrel, weighs 8.7 lbs., and is 39.7″ over-all. Imported by Beeman.
Price: Right-hand, rifle or carbine **$359.50**
Price: Left-hand, rifle or carbine **$389.50**

BEEMAN/WEBLEY OMEGA AIR RIFLE

Caliber: 177.
Barrel: 19¼″, rifled.
Weight: 7.8 lbs. **Length:** 43½″ over-all.
Power: Spring-piston air; barrel cocking.
Stock: Walnut-stained beech with cut-checkered grip; cheekpiece; rubber butt pad.
Features: Special quick-snap barrel latch; self-lubricating piston seal; receiver grooved for scope mounting. Introduced 1985. Imported from England by Beeman.
Price: **$249.50**

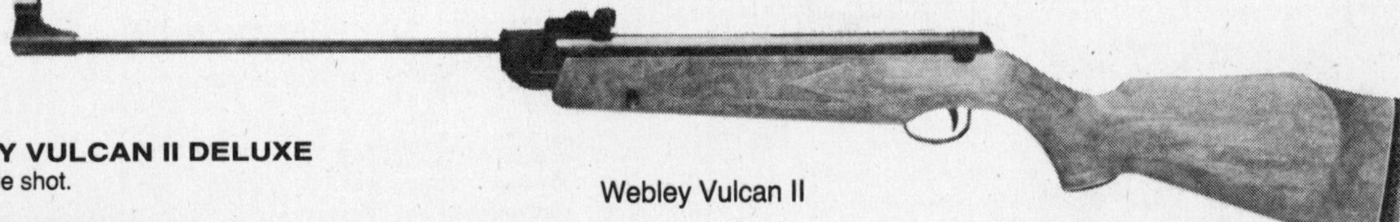

Webley Vulcan II

BEEMAN/WEBLEY VULCAN II DELUXE

Caliber: 177 or 22, single shot.
Barrel: 17″, rifled.
Weight: 7.6 lbs. **Length:** 43.7″ over-all.
Power: Spring piston air, barrel cocking.
Stock: Walnut. Cut checkering, rubber butt pad, checkpiece. Standard version has walnut-stained beech.
Sights: Hooded front, micrometer rear.
Features: Velocity of 830 fps (177), 675 fps (22). Single stage adjustable trigger; receiver grooved for scope mounting. Self-lubricating piston seal. Introduced 1983. Imported by Beeman.
Price: Standard **$198.50**
Price: Deluxe **$245.00**

Consult our Directory pages for the location of firms mentioned.

CAUTION: PRICES CHANGE. CHECK AT GUNSHOP.

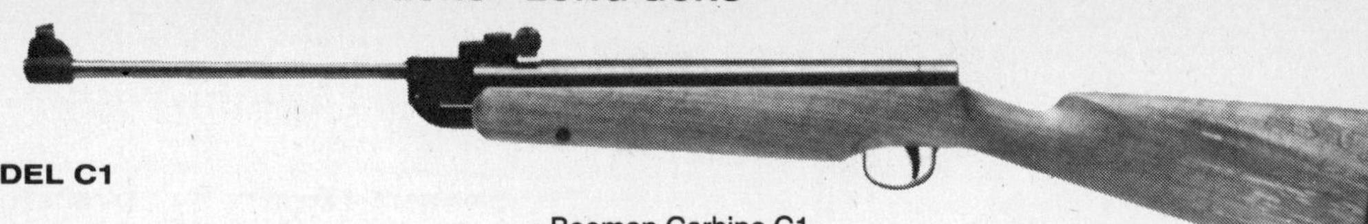

Beeman Carbine C1

BEEMAN CARBINE MODEL C1
Caliber: 177, single shot.
Barrel: 14″, 12-groove rifling.
Weight: 6¼ lbs. **Length:** 38″ over-all.
Power: Spring-piston, barrel cocking.
Stock: Walnut-stained beechwood with rubber butt pad.
Sights: Blade front, rear click-adjustable for windage and elevation.
Features: Velocity 830 fps. Adjustable trigger. Receiver grooved for scope mounting. Imported by Beeman.
Price: **$177.50**

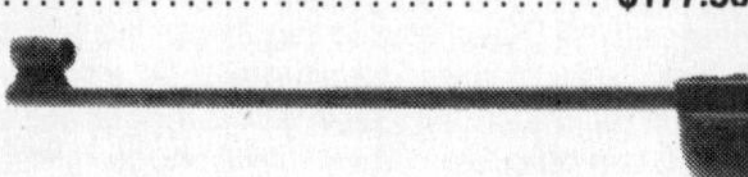

Beeman Model R1

BEEMAN R1 AIR RIFLE
Caliber: 177, 20 or 22, single shot.
Barrel: 19.6″, 12-groove rifling.
Weight: 8.5 lbs. **Length:** 45.2″ over-all.
Power: Spring-piston, barrel cocking.
Stock: Walnut-stained beech; cut checkered pistol grip Monte Carlo comb and cheekpiece; rubber butt pad.
Sights: Tunnel front with interchangeable inserts, open rear click adjustable for windage and elevation. Grooved for scope mounting.
Features: Velocity of 940-1050 fps (177), 860 fps (20), 800 fps (22). Non-drying nylon piston and breech seals. Adjustable metal trigger. Right or left hand stock. Imported by Beeman.
Price: Right hand **$349.50**
Price: Left hand **$379.50**

BEEMAN R8 AIR RIFLE
Caliber: 177, single shot.
Barrel: 18.3″.
Weight: 7.2 lbs. **Length:** 43.1″ over-all.
Power: Barrel cocking, spring-piston.
Stock: Walnut with Monte Carlo cheekpiece; checkered pistol grip.
Sights: Globe front, fully adjustable rear; interchangeable inserts.
Features: Velocity of 735 fps. Similar to the R1. Nylon piston and breech seals. Adjustable match-grade, two-stage, grooved metal trigger. Rubber butt pad. Imported by Beeman.
Price: **$246.50**

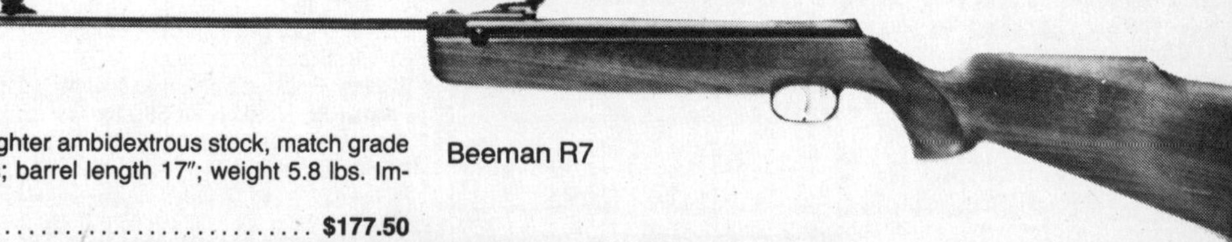

Beeman R7

Beeman R7 Air Rifle
Similar to the R8 model except has lighter ambidextrous stock, match grade trigger block; velocity of 680-700 fps; barrel length 17″; weight 5.8 lbs. Imported by Beeman.
Price: **$177.50**

Beeman FX-1

BEEMAN FX-1 AIR RIFLE
Caliber: 177, single shot.
Barrel: 18″, rifled.
Weight: 6.6 lbs. **Length:** 43″ over-all.
Power: Spring-piston, barrel cocking.
Stock: Walnut-stained hardwood.
Sights: Tunnel front with interchangeable inserts; rear with rotating disc to give four sighting notches.
Features: Velocity 680 fps. Match-type adjustable trigger. Receiver grooved for scope mounting. Imported by Beeman.
Price: **$146.50**

Beeman FX-2 Air Rifle
Similar to the FX-1 except weighs 5.8 lbs., 41″ over-all; front sight is hooded post on ramp, rear sight has two-way click adjustments. Adjustable trigger. Imported by Beeman.
Price: **$116.50**

Benjamin Series 340

BENJAMIN SERIES 340 AIR RIFLE
Caliber: 22 or 177, pellets or BB; single shot.
Barrel: 23″, rifled and smoothbore.
Weight: 6 lbs. **Length:** 35″ over-all.
Power: Hand pumped.
Features: Bolt action, walnut Monte Carlo stock and pump handle. Ramp-type front sight, adj. stepped leaf type rear. Push-pull safety.
Price: M340, BB **$101.00**
Price: M343, 22 .... **$101.00**
Price: M347, 177 .... **$101.00**

BENJAMIN SERIES 3100 SUPER REPEATER RIFLES
Caliber: BB, 100-shot; 22, 85-shot.
Barrel: 23″, rifled or smoothbore.
Weight: 6¼ lbs. **Length:** 35″ over-all.
Power: Hand pumped.
Features: Bolt action. Piggy back full view magazine. Bar V adj. rear sight. Walnut stock and pump handle.
Price: M3100, BB **$101.00**
Price: M3120, 22 rifled **$101.00**

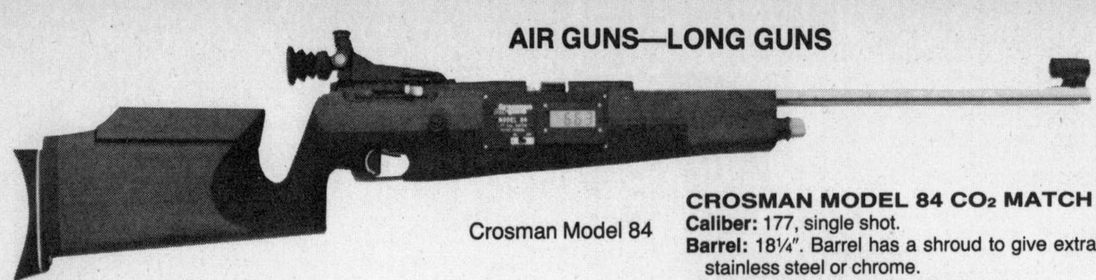

Crosman Model 84

CROSMAN MODEL 1 RIFLE

Caliber: 22, single shot.
Barrel: 19", rifled brass.
Weight: 5 lbs., 1 oz. **Length:** 39" over-all.
Power: Pneumatic, variable power.
Stock: Walnut stained American hardwood.
Sights: Blade front, Williams rear with micrometer click settings.
Features: Precision trigger mechanism for light, clean pull. Metal receiver grooved for scope mounting. Bolt action with cross-bolt safety. Muzzle velocities range from 365 fps (three pumps) to 625 fps (10 pumps). Introduced 1981.
Price: About **$79.00**

CROSMAN MODEL 84 CO_2 MATCH RIFLE

Caliber: 177, single shot.
Barrel: 18¼". Barrel has a shroud to give extra sight radius. Choice of blue, stainless steel or chrome.
Weight: 10.2 lbs. **Length:** 43" over-all.
Power: Refillable CO_2 cylinders.
Stock: Walnut; Olympic match design with stippled pistol grip and fore-end, adjustable buttplate and comb.
Sights: Match sights — globe front micrometer adjustable rear.
Features: A CO_2 pressure regulated rifle with adjustable velocity up to 720 fps. Each CO_2 cylinder has more than enough power to complete a 60-shot Olympic match course. Electric trigger adjustable from ½ oz. to 3 lbs. Each gun can be custom fitted to the shooter. Made in U.S.A. Introduced 1984.
Price: About **$1,500.00**

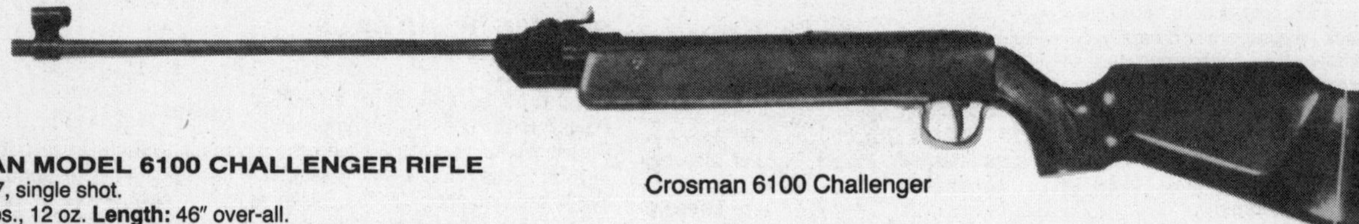

Crosman 6100 Challenger

CROSMAN MODEL 6100 CHALLENGER RIFLE

Caliber: 177, single shot.
Weight: 7 lbs., 12 oz. **Length:** 46" over-all.
Power: Spring air, barrel cocking.
Stock: Stained hardwood with checkered pistol grip, rubber recoil pad.
Sights: Globe front, open fully adjustable rear.
Features: Average velocity 820 fps. Automatic safety, two-stage adjustable trigger. Receiver grooved for scope mounting. Introduced 1982. Imported from West Germany by Crosman Air Guns.
Price: About **$180.00**

CROSMAN MODEL 6300 CHALLENGER AIR RIFLE

Caliber: 177.
Power: Spring-air, barrel-cocking.
Stock: Stained hardwood.
Sights: Hooded front, micrometer adjustable rear.
Features: Velocity of 680 to 710 fps. Adjustable trigger; comes with mount base for peep sight or scope. Introduced 1985.
Price: About **$126.00**

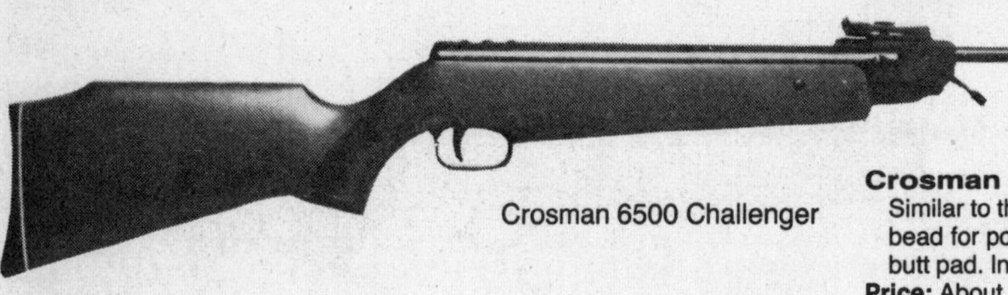

Crosman 6500 Challenger

Crosman Model 6500 Challenger Air Rifle

Similar to the Model 6300 except has tunnel front sight with interchangeable bead for post or aperture inserts; positive barrel locking mechanism; rubber butt pad. Introduced 1985.
Price: About **$140.00**

Crosman Model 66

CROSMAN MODEL 66 POWERMASTER

Caliber: 177 (single shot) or BB
Barrel: 20", rifled, solid steel.
Weight: 3 lbs., 14 oz. **Length:** 38½" over-all.
Stock: Wood-grained plastic; checkered p.g. and fore-end.
Sights: Ramp front, fully adjustable open rear.
Features: Velocity about 675 fps. Bolt action, cross-bolt safety. Introduced 1983.
Price: About **$40.00**

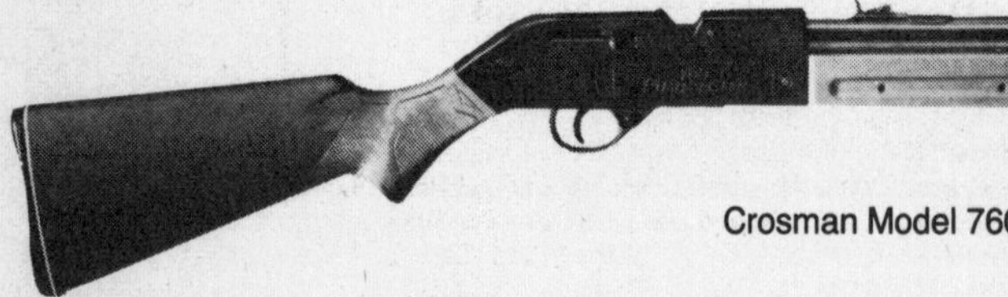

Crosman Model 760

Crosman Model 760 Commemorative

Similar to the standard Model 760 except has a hardwood stock and fore-end with a special medallion inset into the stock, and special receiver graphics. Commemorates 20 years of continuous production and five million guns.
Price: About **$32.00**

CROSMAN MODEL 760 PUMPMASTER

Caliber: 177 pellets or BB, 200 shot.
Barrel: 19½", rifled steel.
Weight: 4 lbs., 3 oz. **Length:** 35" over-all.
Power: Pneumatic, hand pump.
Features: Short stroke, power determined by number of strokes. Walnut finished plastic checkered stock and fore-end. Post front sight and adjustable rear sight. Cross-bolt safety. Introduced 1983.
Price: About **$30.00**

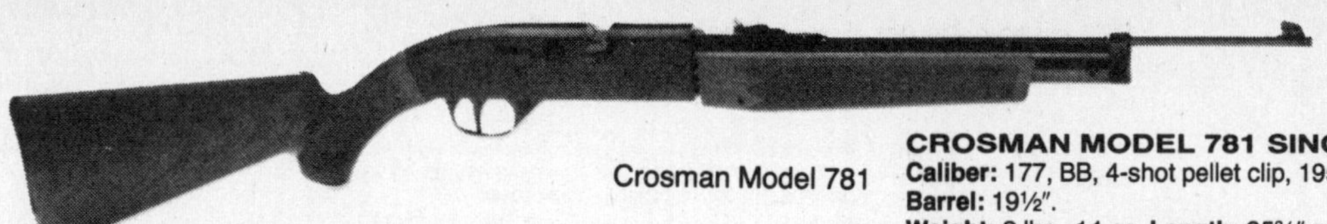

Crosman Model 781

CROSMAN MODEL 788 BB SCOUT RIFLE

Caliber: 177, BB.
Barrel: 14″, steel.
Weight: 2 lbs. 7 oz. **Length:** 31″ over-all.
Stock: Wood-grained ABS plastic.
Sights: Blade on ramp front, open adj. rear.
Features: Variable pump power—3 pumps give MV of 330 fps, 6 pumps 437 fps, 10 pumps 470 fps (BBs, average). Steel barrel, cross-bolt safety. Introduced 1978.
Price: About **$26.00**

CROSMAN MODEL 781 SINGLE PUMP

Caliber: 177, BB, 4-shot pellet clip, 195-shot BB magazine.
Barrel: 19½″.
Weight: 2 lbs., 14 oz. **Length:** 35¾″ over-all.
Power: Pneumatic, single pump.
Stock: Wood-grained plastic; checkered p.g. and fore-end.
Sights: Blade front, open adjustable rear.
Features: Velocity of 350-400 fps (pellets). Uses only one pump. Hidden BB reservoir holds 195 shots; pellets loaded via 4-shot clip. Introduced 1984.
Price: About **$25.00**

Crosman 2100 Classic

CROSMAN MODEL 2100 CLASSIC AIR RIFLE

Caliber: 177 pellets or BBs, 180-shot BB magazine.
Barrel: 21″, rifled.
Weight: 4 lbs., 13 oz. **Length:** 39¾″ over-all.
Power: Pump-up, pneumatic.
Stock: Wood-grained checkered ABS plastic.
Features: Three pumps gives about 450 fps, 10 pumps about 700 fps. Cross-bolt safety; concealed reservoir holds over 180 BBs.
Price: About **$45.00**

Crosman 2200 Magnum

CROSMAN MODEL 2200 MAGNUM AIR RIFLE

Caliber: 22, single-shot.
Barrel: 19″, rifled steel.
Weight: 4 lbs., 13 oz. **Length:** 39¾″ over-all.
Stock: Full-size, wood-grained plastic with checkered p.g. and fore-end.
Sights: Ramp front, open step-adjustable rear.
Features: Variable pump power—3 pumps give 395 fps, 6 pumps 530 fps, 10 pumps 620 fps (average). Full-size adult air rifle. Has white line spacers at pistol grip and buttplate. Introduced 1978.
Price: About **$54.00**

Daisy Model 840

DAISY MODEL 840

Caliber: 177 pellet (single-shot) or BB (350-shot).
Barrel: 19″, smoothbore, steel.
Weight: 2.7 lbs. **Length:** 36.8″ over-all.
Stock: Molded wood-grain stock and fore-end.
Sights: Ramp front, open, adj. rear.
Features: Single pump pneumatic rifle. Muzzle velocity 335 fps (BB), 300 fps (pellet). Steel buttplate; straight pull bolt action; cross-bolt safety. Fore-end forms pump lever. Introduced 1978.
Price: About **$30.00**

Daisy Model 95

DAISY YOUTHLINE RIFLES

Model:	**95**	**111**	**105**
Caliber:	BB	BB	BB
Barrel:	18″	18″	13½″
Length:	35.2″	34.3″	29.8″
Power:	Spring	Spring	Spring
Capacity:	700	650	400
Price: About	**$25.00**	**$20.00**	**$20.00**

Features: Model 95 stock and fore-end are wood; 105 and 111 have plastic stocks.

Daisy Model 1894

DAISY 1894 SPITTIN' IMAGE CARBINE

Caliber: BB, 40-shot.
Barrel: 17½″, smoothbore.
Weight: 3 lbs. **Length:** 38″ over-all.
Power: Spring.
Stock: Molded wood-grain stock and fore-end.
Sights: Blade and ramp front, open adjustable rear.
Features: Cocks halfway on forward stroke of lever, halfway on return.
Price: About **$30.00**

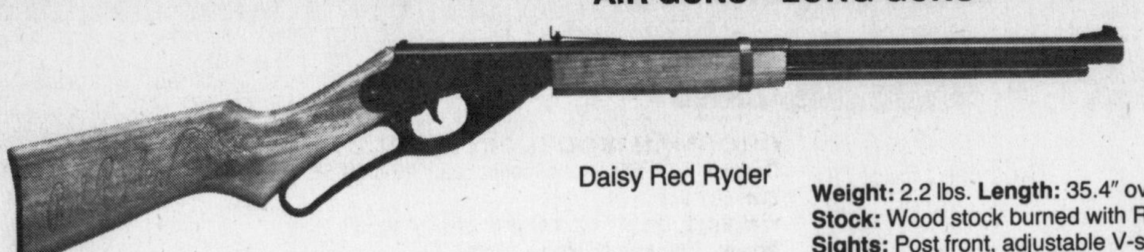

Daisy Red Ryder

DAISY 1938 RED RYDER COMMEMORATIVE

Caliber: BB, 650-shot repeating action.
Barrel: Smoothbore steel with shroud.
Weight: 2.2 lbs. **Length:** 35.4″ over-all.
Stock: Wood stock burned with Red Ryder lariat signature.
Sights: Post front, adjustable V-slot rear.
Features: Wood fore-end. Saddle ring with leather thong. Lever cocking. Gravity feed. Controlled velocity. Commemorates one of Daisy's most popular guns, the Red Ryder of the 1940s and 1950s.
Price: About **$30.00**

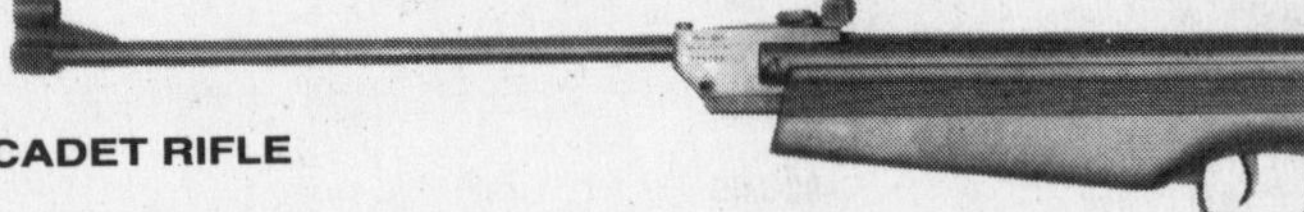

Power Line 120 Cadet

POWER LINE MODEL 120 CADET RIFLE

Caliber: 177, single shot.
Barrel: 15.7″, rifled.
Weight: 5 lbs. **Length:** 36.8″ over-all.
Power: Spring air, barrel cocking.
Stock: Stained hardwood.
Sights: Hooded post front on ramp, open micro-adjustable rear.
Features: Velocity of 500 fps. Lever-type automatic safety, blued steel receiver. Imported from Spain by Daisy. Introduced 1984.
Price: About **$50.00**

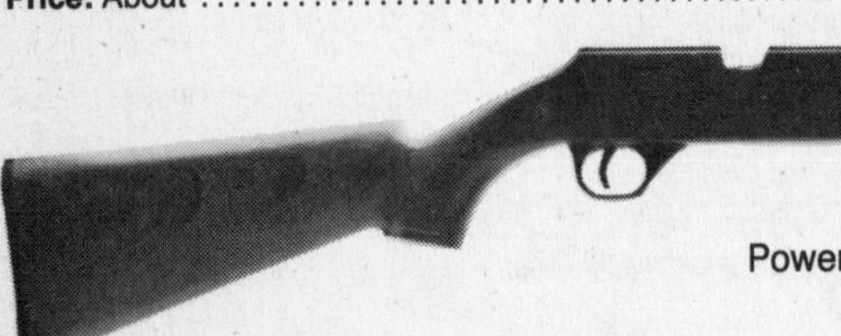

Power Line Model 856

POWER LINE 856 PUMP-UP AIR GUN

Caliber: 177 (pellets), BB, 100-shot BB mgazine.
Barrel: Rifled steel with shroud.
Weight: $2^3/_4$ lbs. **Length:** 37.4″ over-all.
Power: Pneumatic pump-up.
Stock: Molded woodgrain plastic.
Sights: Ramp and blade front, open rear adjustable for e.
Features: Velocity from 315 fps (two pumps) to 650 fps (10 pumps). Finger grooved fore-end. Cross-bolt trigger-block safety. Introduced 1985. From Daisy.
Price: About **$30.00**

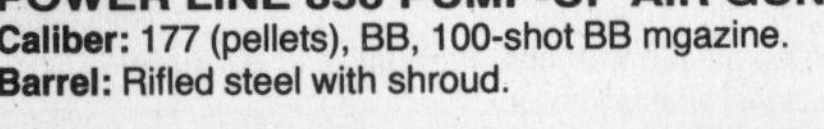

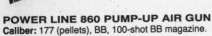

Power Line Model 860

POWER LINE 860 PUMP-UP AIR GUN

Caliber: 177 (pellets), BB, 100-shot BB magazine.
Barrel: Rifled steel with shroud.
Weight: 4.18 lbs. **Length:** 37.4″ over-all.
Power: Pneumatic pump-up.
Stock: Molded woodgrain with Monte Carlo cheekpiece.
Sights: Ramp and blade front, open rear adjustble for e.
Features: Velocity from 315 fps (two pumps) to 650 fps (10 pumps). Shoots BBs or pellets. Heavy die cast metal receiver. Cross-bolt trigger-block safety. Introduced 1984. From Daisy.
Price: About **$30.00**

Power Line Model 880

POWER LINE 880 PUMP-UP AIR GUN

Caliber: 177 pellets, BB.
Barrel: Rifled steel with shroud.
Weight: 4.5 lbs. **Length:** $37^3/_4$″ over-all.
Power: Pneumatic pump-up.
Stock: Wood grain molded plastic with Monte Carlo cheekpiece.
Sights: Ramp front, open rear adj. for e.
Features: Crafted by Daisy. Variable power (velocity and range) increase with pump strokes. 10 strokes for maximum power. 100-shot BB magazine. Cross-bolt trigger safety. Positive cocking valve.
Price: About **$40.00**
Price: Model 980 (as above with hardwood stock and fore-end), about **$50.00**

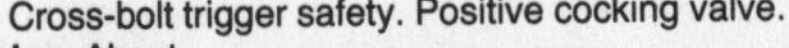

Power Line Model 922

POWER LINE MODEL 922

Caliber: 22, 5-shot clip.
Barrel: Rifled steel with shroud.
Weight: 4.5 lbs. **Length:** $37^3/_4$″ over-all.
Stock: Molded wood-grained plastic with checkered p.g. and fore-end, Monte Carlo cheekpiece.
Sights: Ramp front, full adj. open rear.
Features: Muzzle velocity from 270 fps (two pumps) to 530 fps. (10 pumps). Straight pull bolt action. Separate buttplate and grip cap with white spacers. Introduced 1978.
Price: About **$50.00**
Price: Models 970/920 (as above with hardwood stock and fore-end), about.. **$60.00**

El Gamo 126

EL GAMO 126 SUPER MATCH TARGET RIFLE
Caliber: 177, single shot.
Barrel: Match grade, precision rifled.
Weight: 10.6 lbs. **Length:** 43.8″ over-all.
Power: Single pump pneumatic.
Stock: Match-style, hardwood, with stippled grip and fore-end.
Sights: Hooded front with interchangeable elements, fully adjustable match rear.
Features: Velocity of 590 fps. Adjustable trigger; easy loading pellet port; adjustable butt pad. Introduced 1984. Imported from Spain by Daisy.
Price: About $250.00

Marathon Model 100

MARATHON MODEL 100 AIR RIFLE
Caliber: 177, single shot.
Barrel: 17″, rifled.
Weight: 5.7 lbs. **Length:** 41″ over-all.
Stock: Walnut-stained hardwood with Monte Carlo cheekpiece.
Sights: Hooded post front, micro click open rear.
Features: Velocity of 525 fps. Automatic safety; receiver grooved for scope mounting. Introduced 1984. Imported from Spain by Marathon Products.
Price: $59.95

Marathon Model 50 Youth Air Rifle
Similar to the Model 100 rifle except scaled down for small shooters. Over-all length is 36″, barrel length is 15″, length of pull is 12″, and weight is 4.7 lbs. Available in 177-caliber only. Introduced 1985.
Price: $49.99

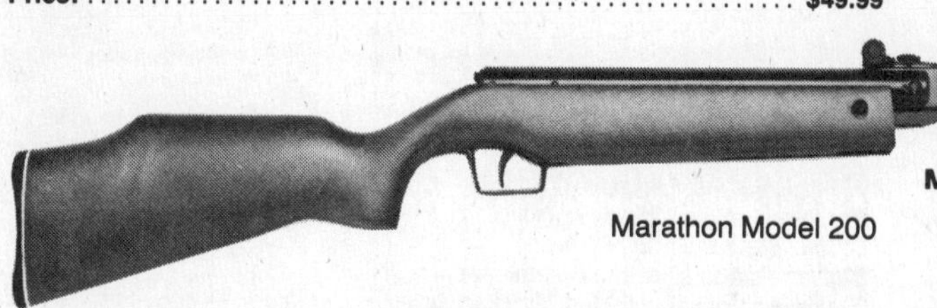

Marathon Model 200

Marathon Model 200 Air Rifle
Similar to the Model 100 except has adjustable trigger, velocity of 640 fps, tunnel front sight with interchangeable inserts, buttplate with white line spacer, and over-all length of 41¾″. Available in 177 or 22 caliber. Introduced 1984.
Price: $74.99

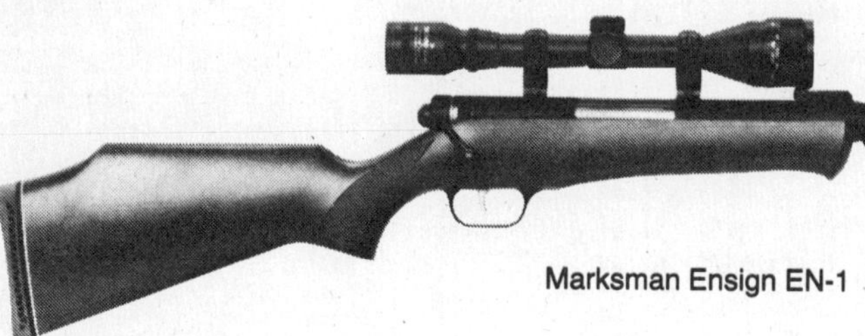

Marksman Ensign EN-1

MARKSMAN ENSIGN MODEL EN-1 AIR RIFLE
Caliber: 177 or 22, 2-shot repeater.
Barrel: 17½″.
Weight: 6½ lbs. **Length:** 41″ over-all.
Power: Compressed air cartridges.
Stock: Walnut on the Royale, walnut-stained beechwood on Elite.
Sights: Open, fully adjustable.
Features: Velocity of 1000 fps (177), 800 fps (22). Bolt action, uses pre-primed centerfire cartridges; recoilless action; fully adjustable 2-stage trigger. Interchangeable barrels available to switch calibers. Comes with a charging unit for the cartridges and 10 cartridges. Introduced 1984. Imported from England.
Price: Royale, about $375.00
Price: Elite, about. $335.00

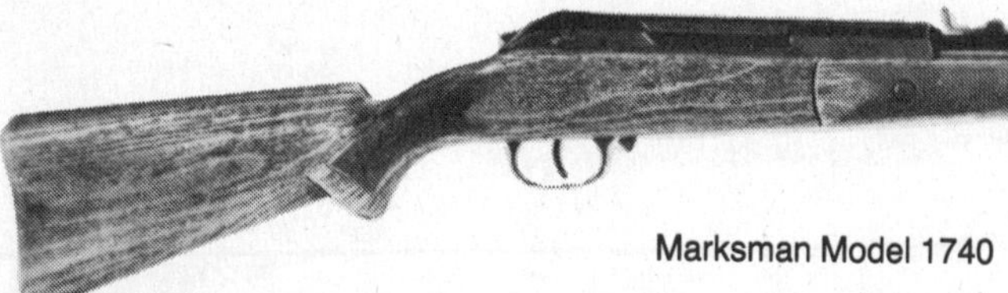

Marksman Model 1740

MARKSMAN 1740 AIR RIFLE
Caliber: 177 or 100-shot BB repeater.
Barrel: 15½″, smoothbore.
Weight: 5 lbs., 1 oz. **Length:** 36½″ over-all.
Power: Spring, barrel cocking.
Stock: Moulded high-impact ABS plastic.
Sights: Ramp front, open rear adj. for e.
Features: Automatic safety; fixed front, adj. rear sight; shoots 177 cal. BB's pellets and darts. Velocity about 475-500 fps.
Price: $29.50
Price: Model 1744 (as above with 4 x 15 scope) $43.50

MARKSMAN MODEL #1770 AIR RIFLE
Caliber: 177, 25-shot repeater.
Barrel: 17″.
Weight: 5¾ lbs. **Length:** 42″ over-all.
Power: Spring air, barrel cocking.
Stock: Walnut-finished beechwood with Monte Carlo.
Sights: Hooded ramp front, micro adjustable rear.
Features: Velocity of 575 fps. Fully adjustable trigger. Magazine tube on top of action. Introduced 1984.
Price: With open sights $120.00
Price: With 3-7 x 20 scope $150.00

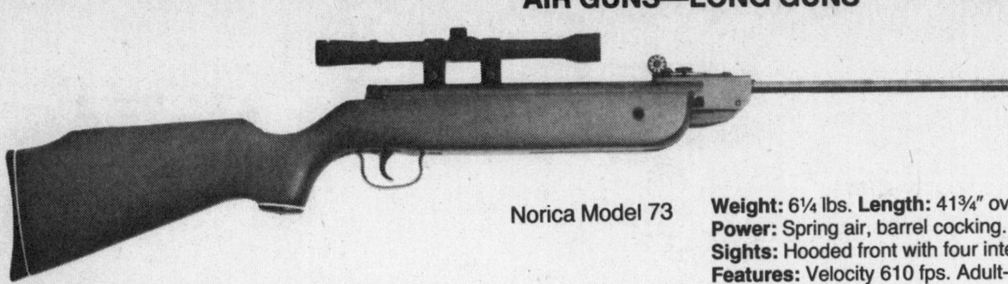

Norica Model 73

NORICA MODEL 73 AIR RIFLE

Caliber: 177 or 22, single shot.
Barrel: 18″.
Weight: 6¼ lbs. **Length:** 41¾″ over-all.
Power: Spring air, barrel cocking.
Sights: Hooded front with four interchangeable blades, open adjustable rear.
Features: Velocity 610 fps. Adult-size stock with full pistol grip; two-stage trigger; receiver grooved for scope mounting. Imported from Spain by Kassnar. Introduced 1984.
Price: **$104.00**

Norica Model 80G

NORICA MODEL 80G AIR RIFLE

Caliber: 177 or 22, single shot.
Barrel: 18″.
Weight: 7¼ lbs. **Length:** 43″ over-all.
Power: Spring air, barrel cocking.
Stock: Monte Carlo competition-style.
Sights: Hooded front with four interchangeable blades, fully adjustable diopter rear on ramp.
Features: Velocity 610 fps. Adjustable trigger; target-type buttplate; blued metal. Imported from Spain by Kassnar. Introduced 1984.
Price: **$134.00**

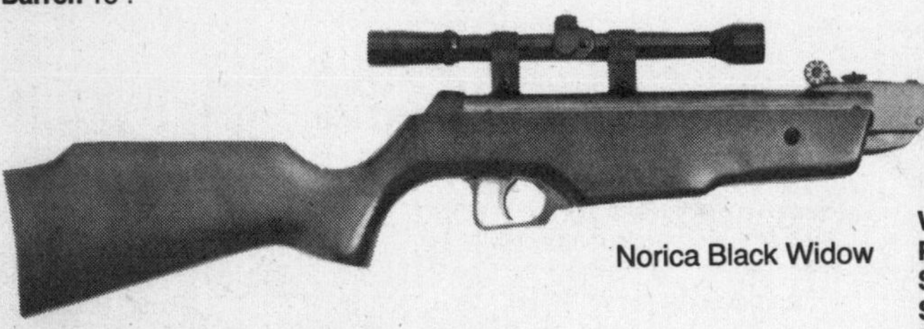

Norica Black Widow

NORICA BLACK WIDOW AIR RIFLE

Caliber: 177 or 22, single shot.
Barrel: 16½″.
Weight: 5¼ lbs. **Length:** 37½″ over-all.
Power: Spring air, barrel cocking.
Stock: Black stained hardwood.
Sights: Hooded front, open adjustable rear.
Features: Velocity 500 fps. Stocked for young shooters. Receiver grooved for scope mounting. Imported from Spain by Kassnar. Introduced 1984.
Price: **$83.00**

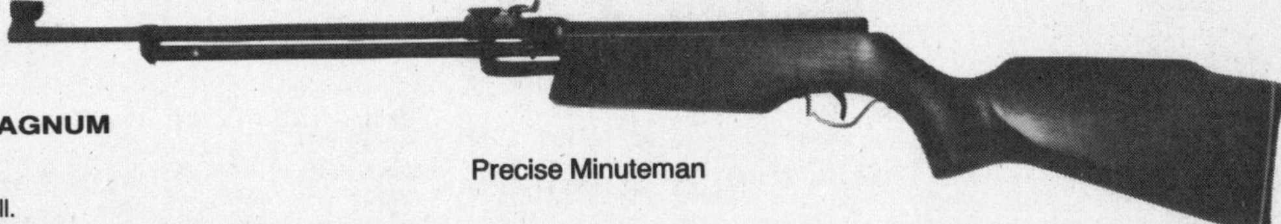

Precise Minuteman

PRECISE MINUTEMAN® MAGNUM

Caliber: 177, single shot.
Barrel: 19.4″, rifled.
Weight: 7¼ lbs. **Length:** 44″ over-all.
Power: Spring, under-lever cocking.
Stock: Stained hardwood, with cheek rest.
Sights: Hooded front, open rear adj. for w. and e.
Features: Velocity of 575 fps. Blued finish. Receiver grooved for scope mounting. Precise International, importer.
Price: **$100.00**

RWS Model 35 Air Rifle

Similar to the Model 27 except slightly heavier and needs less cocking effort. Has hardwood stock with cheekpiece, checkered pistol grip, rubber butt pad. Globe front sight uses optional interchangeable inserts. Available in 177 or 22 caliber. Weighs 6½ lbs.
Price: **$185.00**

RWS Model 27

RWS MODEL 27 AIR RIFLE

Caliber: 177 or 22, single shot.
Weight: 6 lbs. **Length:** 42″ over-all.
Power: Spring air, barrel cocking.
Stock: Walnut-finished hardwood.
Sights: Globe front, micro click rear with four-way blade.
Features: Velocity of 541 fps. Fully adjustable two-stage trigger; dovetail base for peep sight or scope mounting. Small dimensions for young shooters. Imported from West Germany by Dynamit Nobel of America.
Price: **$155.00**

RWS Model 45S Air Rifle

Same as the standard Model 45 except comes without sights and has a 4×20 scope, ramp-type mount, muzzle brake/weight, sling and swivels. Introduced 1983.
Price: **$250.00**
Price: As above, without scope, mount, sling, swivels **$200.00**

RWS MODEL 45 AIR RIFLE

Caliber: 177 or 22, single shot.
Weight: 7¾ lbs. **Length:** 46″ over-all.
Power: Spring air, barrel cocking.
Stock: Walnut-finished hardwood with rubber recoil pad.
Sights: Globe front with interchangeable inserts, micro click open rear with four-way blade.
Features: Velocity of 820 fps (177 cal.), 689 fps (22 cal.). Dovetail base for either micrometer peep sight or scope mounting. Automatic safety. Imported from West Germany by Dynamit Nobel of America.
Price: 177 or 22 .... **$210.00**
Price: With deluxe walnut stock. **$245.00**

CAUTION: PRICES CHANGE. CHECK AT GUNSHOP.

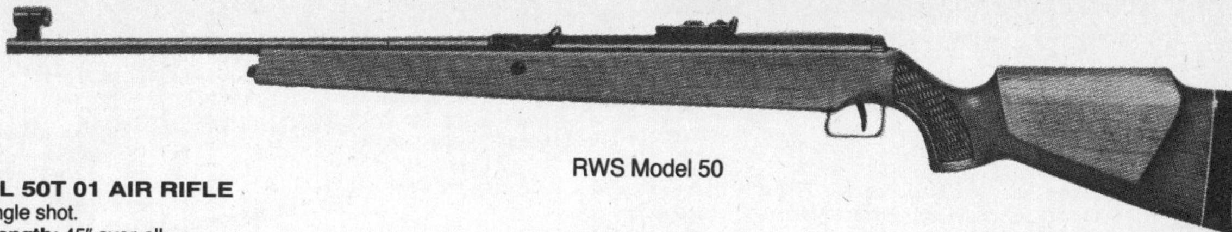
RWS Model 50

RWS MODEL 50T 01 AIR RIFLE
Caliber: 177, single shot.
Weight: 8 lbs. **Length:** 45" over-all.
Power: Spring air, under-lever cocking.
Stock: Walnut-finished hardwood with cheekpiece, checkered grip, rubber butt pad.
Sights: Globe front, micro click open rear.
Features: Velocity of 750 fps. Automatic safety. Dovetail base for scope or peep sight mounting. Imported from West Germany by Dynamit Nobel of America.
Price: **$250.00**

RWS Model 75

RWS MODEL 75T 01 MATCH AIR RIFLE
Caliber: 177, single shot.
Barrel: 19".
Weight: 11 lbs. **Length:** 43.7" over-all.
Power: Spring air, side-lever cocking.
Stock: Oil finished walnut with stippled grip, adjustable buttplate, accessory rail, Conforms to I.S.U. rules.
Sights: Globe front with 5 inserts, fully adjustable match peep rear.
Features: Velocity of 574 fps. Fully adjustable trigger. Model 75 HV has stippled fore-end, adjustable cheekpiece. Uses double opposing piston system for recoilless operation. Imported from West Germany by Dynamit Nobel of America.
Price: Model 75T 01 .... **$600.00**
Price: Model 75 HVT 01 .... **$695.00**
Price: Model 75T 01 left hand **$630.00**
Price: Model 75 HVT 01 left hand **$730.00**
Price: Model 75 UT 01 (adj. cheekpiece, buttplate, M82 sight) **$745.00**

RWS Model 75KT 01 Running Boar Air Rifle
Similar to the Model 75 Match except has adjustable cheekpiece and buttplate, different stock, sandblasted barrel sleeve, detachable barrel weight, elevated-grip cocking lever, and a 240mm scope mount. Introduced 1983.
Price: **$730.00**

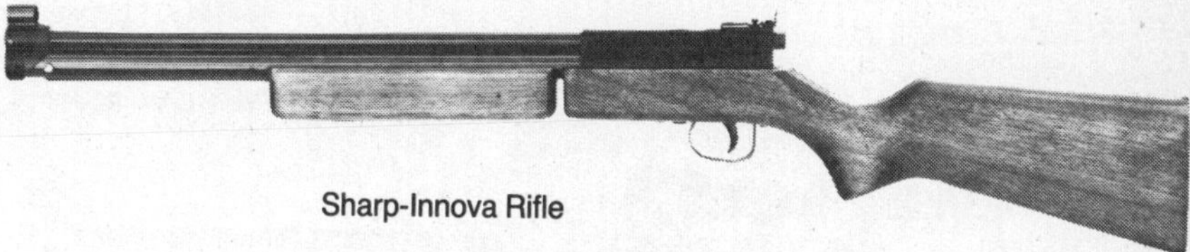
Sharp-Innova Rifle

SHARP-INNOVA AIR RIFLE
Caliber: 177 and 22, single shot.
Barrel: 19.5", rifled.
Weight: 4.4 lbs. **Length:** 34.6" over-all.
Power: Pneumatic, multi-stroke.
Stock: Mahogany.
Sights: Hooded front, adjustable aperture rear.
Features: Velocity of 960 fps with 8 pumps (177). Adjustable trigger. Receiver grooved for scope mount. Introduced 1983. Imported from Japan by Great Lakes Airguns and Beeman.
Price: From Great Lakes **$129.00**
Price: From Beeman **$125.00**

SIG-HAMMERLI MILITARY LOOK 420
Caliber: 177 or 22, single shot.
Barrel: 19", rifled.
Weight: About 7 lbs. **Length:** 44¼" over-all.
Stock: Synthetic stock and handguard.
Sights: Open, fully adj.
Features: Side lever cocking; adjustable trigger; rifled steel barrel. Introduced 1977. Imported by Mandall Shooting Supplies.
Price: **$295.00**

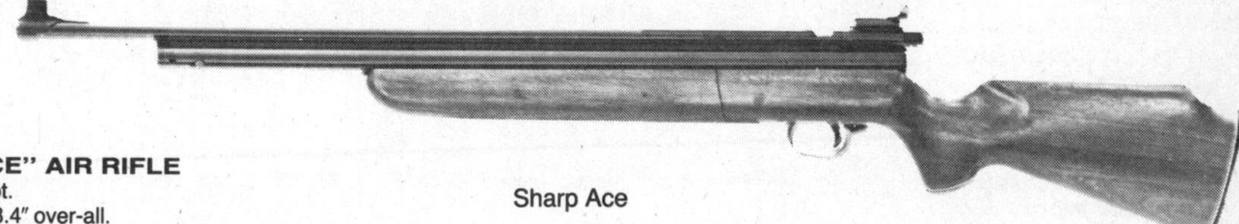
Sharp Ace

SHARP MODEL "ACE" AIR RIFLE
Caliber: 177, 22, single shot.
Weight: 6.3 lbs. **Length:** 38.4" over-all.
Power: Pneumatic, multi-stroke.
Stock: Stained hardwood.
Sights: Hooded ramp front, fully adjustable peep rear.
Features: Velocity of 1019 fps (177-cal.), 892 fps (22-cal.). Receiver grooved for scope mounting. Turn-bolt action for loading. Introduced 1984. Imported from Japan by Great Lakes Airguns and Beeman.
Price: From Great Lakes **$228.00**
Price: From Beeman **$225.00**

Sharp Model Ace Target Standard Air Rifle
Similar to the Model Ace except the under-barrel pump assembly has been rotated about 120° to the side, new one-piece stock, globe front sight takes interchangeable elements, micro. adjustable peep rear. Checkered p.g. and fore-end, adjustable buttplate. Adjustable trigger. Introduced 1985.
Price: **$289.50**

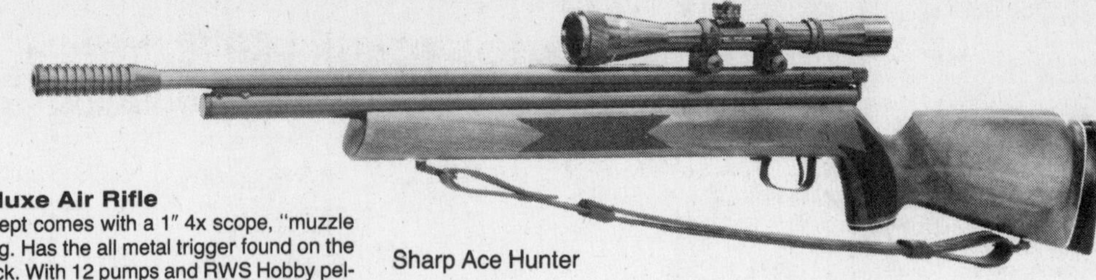

Sharp Ace Hunter

Sharp Model Ace Hunter Deluxe Air Rifle

Similar to the Ace Target model except comes with a 1" 4x scope, "muzzle brake," sling swivels and leather sling. Has the all metal trigger found on the Target model and the checkered stock. With 12 pumps and RWS Hobby pellets velocity is 1006 fps. Introduced 1985.

Price: **$298.50**

Sheridan CO_2

SHERIDAN CO_2 AIR RIFLES

Caliber: 5mm (20 cal.), single shot.
Barrel: 18½", rifled.
Weight: 6 lbs. **Length:** 37" over-all.
Power: Standard 12.5 gram CO_2 cylinder.
Stock: Walnut sporter.
Sights: Open, adj. for w. and e. Optional Sheridan-Williams 5D-SH receiver sight or Weaver D4 scope.
Features: Bolt action single shot, CO_2 powered. Velocity approx. 514 fps., manual thumb safety. Blue or Silver finish. Left-hand models avail. at same prices.
Price: CO_2 Blue Streak **$88.95**
Price: CO_2 Silver Streak **$92.95**
Price: CO_2 Blue Streak with receiver sight **$105.75**
Price: CO_2 Blue Streak with scope **$121.95**

Sheridan Blue Streak

SHERIDAN BLUE AND SILVER STREAK RIFLES

Caliber: 5mm (20 cal.), single shot.
Barrel: 18½", rifled.
Weight: 5 lbs. **Length:** 37" over-all.
Power: Hand pumped (swinging fore-end).
Features: Rustproof barrel and piston tube. Takedown. Thumb safety. Mannlicher type walnut stock. Left-hand models same price.
Price: Blue Streak **$101.55**
Price: Silver Streak **$105.40**

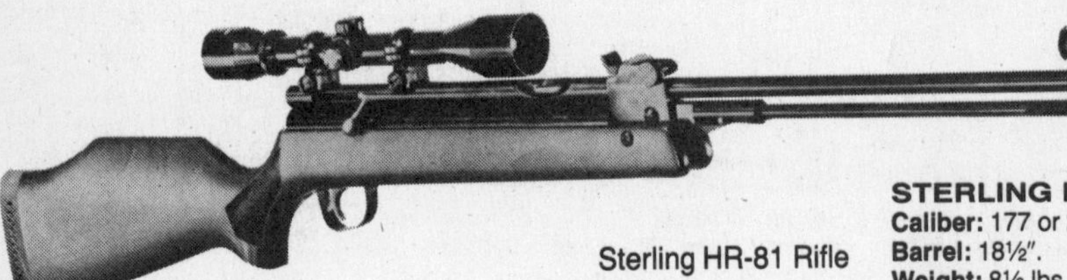

Sterling HR-81 Rifle

STERLING HR-81/HR-83 AIR RIFLE

Caliber: 177 or 22, single-shot.
Barrel: 18½".
Weight: 8½ lbs. **Length:** 42½" over-all.
Power: Spring air, (barrel cocking).
Stock: Stained hardwood, with checkpiece, checkered pistol grip.
Sights: Tunnel-type front with four interchangeable elements, open adjustable V-type rear.
Features: Velocity of 900 fps (177), 660 fps (22). Bolt action with easily accessible loading port; adjustable single-stage match trigger; rubber recoil pad. Integral scope mount rails. Scope and mount optional. Introduced 1983. Made in U.S.A. by Benjamin Air Rifle Co.
Price: HR 81-7 (177 cal., standard walnut stock) **$229.00**
Price: HR 81-2 (as above, 22 cal.) **$238.00**
Price: HR 83-7 (177 cal., deluxe walnut stock) **$325.00**
Price: HR 83-2 (as above, 22 cal.) **$329.00**
Price: For 4x40 wide angle scope, add **$79.95**

WALTHER LGR UNIVERSAL MATCH AIR RIFLE

Caliber: 177, single shot.
Barrel: 25.5".
Weight: 13 lbs. **Length:** 44¾" over-all.
Power: Spring air, barrel cocking.
Stock: Walnut match design with stippled grip and fore-end, adjustable cheekpiece, rubber butt pad.
Features: Has the same weight and contours as the Walther U.I.T. rimfire target rifle. Comes complete with sights, accessories and muzzle weight. Imported from West Germany by Interarms.
Price: **$675.00**

Walther LGR Match Air Rifle

Same basic specifications as standard LGR except has a high comb stock, sights are mounted on riser blocks. Introduced 1977.

Price: **$645.00**

WALTHER LGR RIFLE

Caliber: 177, single-shot.
Barrel: 19½", rifled.
Weight: 10.2 lbs. **Length:** 44¼" over-all.
Power: Side lever cocking, compressed air.
Stock: French walnut.
Sights: Replaceable insert hooded front, Walther micro. adjustable rear.
Features: Recoilless operation. Trigger adj. for weight, pull and position. High comb stock with broad stippled fore-end and p.g. Imported from Germany by Interarms.
Price: **$595.00**

CAUTION: PRICES CHANGE. CHECK AT GUNSHOP.

Chokes & Brakes

Baker Superior Choke Tubes

Stan Baker's Superior choke tubes can be installed only in single-barrel guns. The external diameter of the barrel is enlarged by swaging, allowing enough for reaming and threading to accept the screw-in WinChoke-style tube. Installation on a single-barrel gun without rib is **$85.00**; with vent rib, cost is **$110.00.** Prices are higher for target guns, so contact Baker for specifics. Price includes honing the bore. Extra choke tubes are $15.95 each. One tube and wrench are provided. Baker also installs WinChoke tubes.

Briley Screw-In Chokes

Installation of these choke tubes requires that all traces of the original choking be removed, the barrel threaded internally with square threads and then the tubes are custom fitted to the specific barrel diameter. The tubes are thin and, therefore, made of stainless steel. Cost of installation for single-barrel guns (pumps, autos) runs **$75.00**; un-single target guns run **$150.00**; over-unders and side-by-sides cost **$150.00** per barrel. Prices include one choke tube and a wrench for disassembly. Extra tubes are **$40.00** each.

Briley also makes "Excentrix" choke tubes that allow horizontal or vertical movement of the pattern up to 11″. Add **$35.00** to the prices above. Installation available only from Briley.

Cellini Recoil Reducer

Designed for handgun and rifle applications, the Cellini Reducer is available as a removable factory-installed accessory. Over-all length is 2½″, weight is 3.5 ounces, and the unit must be installed by the maker. It is said to reduce muzzle jump to zero, even for automatic weapons. Cost starts at $150. Contact Cellini for full details.

Cutts Compensator

The Cutts Compensator is one of the oldest variable choke devices available. Manufactured by Lyman Gunsight Corporation, it is available with a steel body. A series of vents allows gas to escape upward and downward. For the 12-ga. Comp body, six fixed-choke tubes are available: the Spreader—popular with Skeet shooters; Improved Cylinder; Modified; Full; Superfull, and Magnum Full. Full, Modified and Spreader tubes are available for 12, or 20, and an Adjustable Tube, giving Full through Improved Cylinder chokes, is offered in 12, or 20 gauges. Cutts Compensator, complete with wrench, adaptor and any single tube **$63.35;** with adjustable tube **$80.80.** All single choke tubes **$17.50** each. No factory installation available.

Emsco Choke

E. M. Schacht of Waseca, Minn., offers the Emsco, a small diameter choke which features a precision curve rather than a taper behind the 1½″ choking area. 9 settings are available in this 5 oz. attachment. Its removable recoil sleeve can be furnished in dural if desired. Choice of three sight heights. For 12, 16 or 20 gauge. Price installed, **$29.95**. Not installed, **$22.00**.

Lyman CHOKE

The Lyman CHOKE is similar to the Cutts Comp in that it comes with fixed-choke tubes or an adjustable tube, with or without recoil chamber. The adjustable tube version sells for **$34.95** with recoil chamber, in 12 or 20 gauge. Lyman also offers Single-Choke tubes at **$17.50**. This device may be used with or without a recoil-reduction chamber; cost of the latter is **$7.95** extra. Available in 12 or 20 gauge only. No factory installation offered.

Mag-Na-Port

Electrical Discharge Machining works on any firearm except those having shrouded barrels. EDM is a metal erosion technique using carbon electrodes that control the area to be processed. The Mag-na-port venting process utilizes small trapezoidal openings to direct powder gases upward and outward to reduce recoil.

No effect is had on bluing or nickeling outside the Mag-na-port area so no refinishing is needed. Cost for the Mag-na-port treatment is **$53.00** for handguns, **$69.00** for rifles, plus transportation both ways, and **$2.50** for handling.

Poly-Choke

Marble Arms Corp., manufacturers of the Poly-Choke adjustable shotgun choke, now offers two models in 12, 16, 20, and 28 gauge—the Ventilated and Standard style chokes. Each provides nine choke settings including Xtra-Full and Slug. The Ventilated model reduces 20% of a shotgun's recoil, the company claims, and is priced at $60.00. The Standard Model is **$54.00**. Postage not included. Contact Marble Arms for more data.

Pro-Choke

Pro-Choke is a system of interchangeable choke tubes that can be installed in any single or double-barreled shotgun, including over-unders. The existing chokes are bored out, the muzzles over-bored and threaded for the tubes. A choice of three Pro-Choke tubes are supplied—Skeet, Imp. Cyl., Mod., Imp. Mod., or Full. Cost of the installation is **$179.95** for single-barrel guns, **$229.95** for doubles. Extra tubes cost **$40** each. Postage and handling charges are **$8.50**.

Pro-Port

A compound ellipsoid muzzle venting process similar to Mag-na-porting, only exclusively applied to shotguns. Like Mag-na-porting, this system reduces felt recoil, muzzle jump, and shooter fatigue. Very helpful for Trap doubles shooters. Pro-Port is a patented process and installation is available in both the U.S. and Canada. Cost for the Pro-Port process is **$110.00** for over-unders (both barrels); **$80.00** for only the bottom barrel; and **$69.00** for single barrel shotguns. Prices do not include shipping and handling.

Walker Choke Tubes

This interchangeable choke tube system uses an adaptor fitted to the barrel without swaging. Therefore, it can be fitted to any single-barreled gun. The choke tubes use the conical-parallel system as used on all factory-choked barrels. These tubes can be used in Winchester, Mossberg, Smith & Wesson, Weatherby, or similar barrels made for the standard screw-in choke system. Available for 10 gauge, 12, 16 and 20. Factory installation (single barrel) with choice of Standard Walker Choke tube is **$105.00, $210.00** for double barrels with two choke tubes. A full range of constriction is available. Contact Walker Arms for more data.

Micrometer Receiver Sights

BEEMAN/WEIHRAUCH MATCH APERTURE SIGHT
Micrometer ¼-minute click adjustment knobs with settings indicated on scales. Price **$69.95**

BEEMAN/FEINWERKBAU MATCH APERTURE SIGHTS
Locks into one of four eye-relief positions. Micrometer ¼-minute click adjustments; may be set to zero at any range. Extra windage scale visible beside eyeshade. Primarily for use at 5 to 20 meters. Price **$99.95**

BEEMAN SPORT APERTURE SIGHT
Positive click micrometer adjustments. Standard units with flush surface screwdriver adjustments. Deluxe version has target knobs.
Price: Standard **$32.98**
Price: Deluxe **$38.98**

BUEHLER
"Little Blue Peep" auxiliary rear sight used with Buehler scope mounts. Price **$4.75**

FREELAND TUBE SIGHT
Uses Unertl 1" micrometer mounts. For 22-cal. target rifles, inc. 52 Win., 37, 40X Rem. and BSA Martini. Price **$123.00**

LYMAN No. 57
¼-min. clicks. Stayset knobs. Quick release slide, adjustable zero scales. Made for almost all modern rifles. Price **$47.95**

LYMAN No. 66
Fits close to the rear of flat-sided receivers, furnished with Stayset knobs. Quick release slide, ¼-min. adj. For most lever or slide action or flat-sided automatic rifles. Price **$47.95**

Lyman No. 66U shotgun sight.

LYMAN No. 66U
Light-weight, designed for most modern shotguns with a flat-sided, round-top receiver. ¼-minute clicks. Requires drilling, taping. Not for Browning A-5, Rem. M11. Price **$47.95**

REDFIELD "PALMA" TARGET SIGHT
Windage and elevation adjustments are ¼-MOA and can be adjusted for "hard" or "soft" feel. Repeatability error limited to .001" per click. Windage latitude 36 MOA, elevation 60 MOA. Mounting arm has three positions, providing ample positioning latitude for other sighting aids such as variable diopter correction, adjustable filters. An insert in the sighting disc block accepts either the standard American sighting disc thread or the European 9.5mm × 1 metric thread. Elevation staff and the sighting disc block have dovetail construction for precise travel. Price **$209.95**

WILLIAMS FP
Internal click adjustments. Positive locks. For virtually all rifles, T/C Contender, Heckler & Koch HK-91, Ruger Mini-14, plus Win., Rem. and Ithaca shotguns. Price **$38.55**
With Twilight Aperture **$39.75**
With Target Knobs **$45.85**
With Target Knobs & Twilight Aperture **$47.05**
With Square Notched Blade **$40.60**
With Target Knobs & Square Notched Blade **$47.90**
FP-GR (for dovetail-grooved receivers, 22s and air guns) **$38.55**

WILLIAMS 5-D SIGHT
Low cost sight for shotguns, 22's and the more popular big game rifles. Adjustment for w. and e. Fits most guns without drilling or tapping. Also for Br. SMLE. Price **$21.90**
With Twilight Aperture **$23.10**
Extra Shotgun Aperture **$5.15**

WILLIAMS GUIDE
Receiver sight for .30 M1 Car., M1903A3 Springfield, Savage 24's, Savage-Anschutz rifles and Wby. XXII. Utilizes military dovetail; no drilling. Double-dovetail W. adj., sliding dovetail adj. for e. Price **$20.75**
With Twilight Aperture **$21.95**
With Open Sight Blade **$19.05**

Sporting Leaf and Open Sights

BINGHAM SPORTING RIFLE SIGHTS
All-steel sights are imported from Europe. Many styles of both front and rear sights available; random sampling listed here.
European express gold bead for European express ramp **$4.25**
European express ramp **$7.50**
Semi-buckhorn rear, with elevator **$6.50**
Rocky Mountain front, blue or bright **$3.95**
European 2-leaf folding express rear (V and U notch) **$12.50**

BINGHAM CLASSIC SIGHTS
All-steel sights for "classic" rifles. Rear sights only. This listing not complete; contact Bingham for full list.
Model 66 folding ladder-type **$19.95**
Model Saddle Ring Carbine (73, 92, 94, etc.) **$14.95**
Elevator, Winchester-type, early series (1876-WW II) **$4.95**

BURRIS SPORTING REAR SIGHT
Made of spring steel, supplied with multi-step elevator for coarse adjustments and notch plate with lock screw for finer adjustments. Price **$13.95**

LYMAN No. 16
Middle sight for barrel dovetail slot mounting. Folds flat when scope or peep sight is used. Sight notch plate adjustable for e. White triangle for quick aiming. 3 heights: A—.400" to .500", B—.345" to .445", C—.500" to .600". Price **$10.50**

MARBLE FALSE BASE #72, #73, #74
New screw-on base for most rifles replaces factory base. ⅜" dovetail slot permits installation of any Marble rear sight. Can be had in sweat-on models also. Price **$4.85**

MARBLE CONTOUR RAMP #14R
For late model Rem. 725, 740, 760, 742 rear sight mounting. 9/16" between mounting screws. Price **$10.75**

MARBLE FOLDING LEAF
Flat-top or semi-buckhorn style. Folds down when scope or peep sights are used. Reversible plate gives choice of "U" or "V" notch. Adjustable for elevation. Price **$9.65**
Also available with both w. and e. adjustment **$11.25**

MARBLE SPORTING REAR
With white enamel diamond, gives choice of two "U" and two "V" notches of different sizes. Adjustment in height by means of double step elev,2a,2t,2o,2r
and sliding notch piece. For all rifles; screw or dovetail installation. Price .... **$6.70-$11.25**

MILLETT RIFLE SIGHT
Open, fully adjustable rear sight fits standard ⅜" dovetail cut in barrel. Choice of white outline or target rear blades, .360". Front with white or orange bar, .343", .400", .430", .460", .500", .540".
Price: Rear sight **$47.29**
Price: Front sight **$10.49**

MILLETT RUGER 10/22 SIGHT COMBO
Replacement sight system for the 10/22 rifle has a fully adjustable open rear with deep notch and white outline or target blade. Combo set includes interchangeable white or orange bar front. Also fits Win. 77, 94, Rem. 740-760, 700 old model dovetail rear.
Price: Combo set **$77.69**
Price: Without quick-change front sight feature **$56.69**

WICHITA MULTI RANGE SIGHT SYSTEM
Designed for silhouette shooting. System allows you to adjust the rear sight to four repeatable range settings, once it is pre-set. Sight clicks to any of the settings by turning a serrated wheel. Front sight is adjustable for weather and light conditions with one adjustment. Specify gun when ordering.
Price: Rear sight **$69.95**
Front sight **$39.95**

WILLIAMS DOVETAIL OPEN SIGHT
Open rear sight with w. and e. adjustment. Furnished with "U" notch or choice of blades. Slips into dovetail and locks with gib lock. Heights from .281" to .531". Price with blade **$11.60**
Less Blade **$7.60**
Extra Blades **$3.70**

WILLIAMS GUIDE OPEN SIGHT
Open rear sight with w. and e. adjustment. Bases to fit most military and commercial barrels. Choice of square "U" or "V" notch blade, 3/16", ¼", 5/16", or ⅜" high. Price with blade **$14.00**
Extra blades, each **$4.00**
Price, less blade **$10.00**

Front Sights

LYMAN HUNTING SIGHTS
Made with gold or white beads 1/16" to 3/32" wide and in varying heights for most military and commercial rifles. Dovetail bases. Price ... **$6.95**

CAUTION: PRICES CHANGE. CHECK AT GUNSHOP.

MARBLE STANDARD
Ivory, red, or gold bead. For all American made rifles, 1/16" wide bead with semi-flat face which does not reflect light. Specify type of rifle when ordering. Price $5.90

MARBLE-SHEARD "GOLD"
Shows up well even in darkest timber. Shows same color on different colored objects; sturdily built. Medium bead. Various models for different makes of rifles so specify type of rifle when ordering. Price $7.35

MARBLE CONTOURED
Same contour and shape as Marble-Sheard but uses standard 1/16" or 3/32" bead, ivory, red or gold. Specify rifle type. Price $6.80

POLY-CHOKE
Rifle front sights available in six heights and two widths. Model A designed to be inserted into the barrel dovetail; Model B is for use with standard .350 ramp; both have standard 3/8" dovetails. Gold or ivory color 1/16" bead. Price $4.95

WILLIAMS GUIDE BEAD SIGHT
Fits all shotguns, 1/8" ivory, red or gold bead. Screws into existing sight hole. Various thread sizes and shank lengths. Price $4.05

Globe Target Front Sights

FREELAND SUPERIOR
Furnished with six 1" plastic apertures. Available in 4½"-6½" lengths. Made for any target rifle. Price $37.00
Price with 6 metal insert apertures $39.00
Price, front base $8.00

FREELAND TWIN SET
Two Freeland Superior or Junior Globe Front Sights, long or short, allow switching from 50 yd. to 100 yd. ranges and back again without changing rear sight adjustment. Sight adjustment compensation is built into the set; just interchange and you're "on" at either range. Set includes 6 plastic apertures. Price with 6 metal apertures $58.00

FREELAND MILITARY
Short model for use with high-powered rifles where sight must not extend beyond muzzle. Screw-on base; six plastic apertures. Price .. $35.00
Price with 6 metal apertures $39.00
Price, front base $8.00

LYMAN No. 17A TARGET
Includes 7 interchangeable inserts; 4 apertures, one transparent amber and two posts .50" and .100" in width. Price $19.95

REDFIELD Nos. 63 and 64
For rifles specially stocked for scopes where metallic sights must be same height as scopes. Instantly detachable to permit use of scope. Two styles and heights of bases. Interchangeable inserts. No. 64 is 1/4" higher.
Price No. 63.......... $39.85
No. 64 .... $39.65

REDFIELD No. 65
1" long, 5/8" diameter. Standard dovetail base with 7 aperture or post inserts which are not reversible. For any rifle having standard barrel slot. 13/32" height from bottom of base to center of aperture. No. 65NB **($29.90)** same as above with narrow base. Price $29.90

REDFIELD No. 66
Replaces entire removable front sight stud, locked in place by screw in front of barrel band. 3/4" from bottom of base to center of aperture. For Spgfld. 1903. Price $33.90

REDFIELD No. 68
For Win. 52, heavy barrel, Sav. 19 and 33, and other rifles requiring high front sight. 17/32" from bottom of base to center of aperture. Standard dovetail size only. Price $29.90

REDFIELD OLYMPIC FRONT
Detachable. 10 inserts—5 steel, sizes .090", .110", .120", .140", .150"; one post insert, size .100"; four celluloid, sizes .090", .110", .120", .140". For practically all rifles and with any type rear sight. Fits all standard Redfield, Lyman, or Fecker scope blocks. Price $59.85

REDFIELD INTERNATIONAL SMALLBORE FRONT
Similar to Olympic. Drop-in insertion of eared inserts. Outer sleeve prevents light leakage. Comes complete with 6 clear inserts and 6 skeleton inserts. Price $59.85

REDFIELD INTERNATIONAL BIG BORE
Same as International Match except tube only 2¼" long. For 30 cal. use. Price $55.80

Ramp Sights

JAEGER CUSTOM FRONT SIGHT RAMP
Banded style machined from bar stock. Front sights are interchangeable and slide into the ramp, lock with a set screw. Sights available are Silver Bead ($7.50), Sourdough Bead ($9.00), Silver Bead with Folding Night Sight ($20.00), and Reflective Bead (Raybar-type, $9.00).
Price: Ramp with set screw, wrenches $45.00
Price: Sight hood $3.90

LYMAN SCREW-ON RAMP
Used with 8-40 screws but may also be brazed on. Heights from .10" to .350". Ramp without sight $12.95

MARBLE FRONT RAMPS
Available in either screw-on or sweat-on style. 5 heights; 3/16", 5/16", 3/8", 7/16", 9/16". Standard 3/8" dovetail slot. Price $11.35
Hoods for above ramps $2.50

WILLIAMS SHORTY RAMP
Companion to "Streamlined" ramp, about ½" shorter. Screw-on or sweat-on. It is furnished in 1/8", 3/16", 9/32", and 3/8" heights without hood only.
Price $10.00

WILLIAMS STREAMLINED RAMP
Hooded style in screw-on or sweat-on models. Furnished in 9/16", 7/16", 3/8", 5/16", 3/16" heights. Price with hood $15.85
Price without hood.......... $13.10

WILLIAMS SHOTGUN RAMP
Designed to elevate the front bead for slug shooting or for guns that shoot high. Diameters to fit most 12, 16, 20 ga. guns. Fastens by screw-clamp, no drilling required. Price, with Williams gold bead $8.95
Price, without bead $6.60
Price, with Guide Bead $10.25

Handgun Sights

BINGHAM PISTOL SIGHTS
All-steel sights of various designs for Colt Government Model and Browning Hi-Power. Low profile "battle sights" (front and rear) for either Colt G.M. or Browning HP. Price $16.95
Combat sight set, low profile, white outline for Colt G.M., front and rear $21.95
National Match front sight, Colt G.M. $3.75
Camp Perry front sight, Colt G.M. $4.95

BO-MAR DE LUXE BMCS
Gives 3/8" w. and e. adjustment at 50 yards on Colt Gov't 45, sight radius under 7". For GM and Commander models only. Uses existing dovetail slot. Has shield-type rear blade. Price $49.50

BO-MAR LOW PROFILE RIB & ACCURACY TUNER
Streamlined rib with front and rear sights; 7⅛" sight radius. Brings sight line closer to the bore than standard or extended sight and ramp. Weighs 5 oz. Made for Colt Gov't 45, Super 38, and Gold Cup 45 and 38. Price $79.00

BO-MAR COMBAT RIB
For S&W Model 19 revolver with 4" barrel. Sight radius 5¾"; weight 5½ oz. Price $69.00

BO-MAR FAST DRAW RIB
Streamlined full length rib with integral Bo-Mar micrometer sight and serrated fast draw sight. For Browning 9mm, S&W 39, Colt Commander 45, Super Auto and 9mm. Price $69.00

BO-MAR WINGED RIB
For S&W 4" and 6" length barrels—K-38, M10, HB 14 and 19. Weight for the 6" model is about 7¼ oz. Price $79.00
For 4", 6" Python $89.00

BO-MAR COVER-UP RIB
Adj. rear sight, winged front guards. Fits right over revolver's original front sight. For S&W 4" M-10HB, M-13, M-58, M-64 & 65, Ruger 4" models SDA-34, SDA-84, SS-34, SS-84, GF-34, GF-84. Price $75.00

C-MORE SIGHTS
Replacement front sight blades offered in two types and five styles. Made of DuPont Acetal, they come in a set of five high-contrast colors: blue, green, pink, red and yellow. Easy to install. Patridge style for Colt Python (all barrels), Ruger Super Blackhawk (7½"), Ruger Blackhawk (4⅝"); Ramp style for Python (all barrels), Blackhawk (4⅝"), Super Blackhawk (7½" and 10½"). From Mag-num Sales Ltd., Inc. Price, per set $14.95

MICRO
Click adjustable w. and e. rear with plain or undercut front sight in 1/8" widths. Standard model available for 45, Super 38 or Commander autos. Low model for above pistols plus Colt Service Ace. Also for Ruger with 4¾" or 6" barrel. Price for sets $35.00
Price with ramp front sight $43.00
Adjustable rear sight only $29.50
Front ramp only, with blade $19.00

MICRO
All-steel replacement for Ruger single-action and double-action revolvers. Two styles: MR-44 for square front end of sight leaf. Price ... $18.00

MMC MODEL 84 SIGHT SYSTEM
Replacement sight system for Colt 1911 autos and Browning Hi-Power. Streamlined 1.94" long base covers the dovetail for a custom look. Ideally suited for PPC, metallic silhouette, bowling pin shooting. Contact MMC for details, full prices.
Complete rear sight $69.00
Serrated ramp front $8.80
Ramp Bar Cross front $14.40

MMC "BAR CROSS" SIGHT SYSTEM
Provides a quick, clear sight picture in a variety of lighting conditions. Black oxide finish is non-reflective. Front sight has a horizontal white bar with vertical white bar, gives illusion of cross hair in poor light. Fixed rear comes with or without white outline. Various front blades available.
White outline rear sight ... **$19.05**
Plain rear ... **$14.85**
Ramp Bar Cross front ... **$13.65**

MMC COMBAT DESIGN
Available specifically for Colt M1911 and descendants, High Standard autos, Ruger standard autos. Adaptable to other pistols. Some gunsmithing required. Not necessary to replace front sight. Contact MMC for complete details.
Price, less leaf ... **$28.75**
Plain leaf ... **$8.55**
White outline leaf ... **$12.55**
With reflector beads, add ... **$2.50**

MILLETT SERIES 100 SIGHTS
Replacement sights for revolvers and auto pistols. Positive click adjustments for windage and elevation. Designed for accuracy and ruggedness. Made to fit S&W, Colt, High Standard, Ruger, Dan Wesson, Browning, AMT Hardballer and Abilene handguns. Rear blades are available in white outline or positive black target. All steel construction and easy to install.
Price ... **$41.95** to **$59.79**

MILLETT MARK SERIES PISTOL SIGHTS
Mark I and Mark II replacement combat sights for government-type auto pistols. Mark I is high profile, Mark II low profile. Both have horizontal light deflectors.
Mark I, front and rear ... **$29.39**
Mark II, front and rear ... **$41.95**

MILLETT FRONT SIGHTS
All-steel replacement front sights with either white or orange bar. Easy to install. For Ruger Redhawk, Security-Six, Police-Six, Speed-Six, Colt Python, Dan Wesson 22 and 15-2. Price ... **$11.55 to $13.59**

MILLETT DUAL-CRIMP/STAKE-ON FRONT SIGHTS
Replacement front sights for automatic pistols. Dual-Crimp uses an all-steel two-point hollow rivet system. Available in eight heights and four styles. Stake-On sights have skirted base that covers the front sight pad. Easily installed with the Millett Installation Tool Set. Available in seven heights and four styles—Blaze Orange Bar, White Bar, Serrated Ramp, Plain Post. Price ... **$13.59**

MILLETT DUAL-CRIMP/STAKE-ON FRONT SIGHT
Replacement front sight for automatic pistols. Dual-Crimp uses an all-steel two-point hollow rivet system. Available in eight heights and four styles. Stake-On sights have a skirted base that covers the front sight pad. Easily installed with the Millett Installation Tool Set. Available in seven heights and four styles—Blaze Orange Bar, White Bar, Serrated Ramp, Plain Post. Price ... **$12.95**

OMEGA OUTLINE SIGHT BLADES
Replacement rear sight blades for Colt and Ruger single action guns and the Interarms Virginian Dragoon. Standard Outline available in gold or white notch outline on blue metal. Price ... **$5.95**

OMEGA MAVERICK SIGHT BLADES
Replacement "peep-sight" blades for Colt, Ruger SAs, Virginian Dragoon. Three models available—No. 1, Plain, No. 2, Single Bar, No. 3 Double Bar Rangefinder. Price, each ... **$ 6.95**

WICHITA SIGHT SYSTEMS
For 45 auto pistols. Target and Combat styles available. Designed by Ron Power. All-steel construction, click adjustable. Each sight has two traverse pins, a large hinge pin and two elevation return springs. Sight blade is serrated and mounted on an angle to deflect light. Patridge front for target, ramp front for combat. Both are legal for ISPC and NRA competitons.
Rear sight, target or combat ... **$49.50**
Front sight, patridge or ramp ... **$8.95**

WICHITA GRAND MASTER DELUXE RIBS
Ventilated rib has wings machined into it for better sight acquisition. Made of stainless steel, sights blued. Uses Wichita Multi-Range rear sight, adjustable front sight. Made for revolvers with 6″ barrel.
Price: Model 301 (adj. sight K-frames with custom bbl. of 1.000″-1.032″ dia., L and N frames with 1.062″-1.100″ bbl.) ... **$129.95**
Price: Model 302 (fixed-sight K-frames; M10, 65, 13 with 1.000″ bbl. N-frame with 1.062″ bbl.) ... **$129.95**
Price: Model 303 (Model 29, 629 with factory bbl., adj. sight K, L, N frames) ... **$129.95**
Price: Extra for white outline rear sight ... **$6.00**

WICHITA COMBAT V RIBS
Designed by Ron Power, the ventilated rib has a lengthwise V-groove that emphasizes the front sight and reduces glare and distortion. Over-size rear sight blade for the click-adjustable sight. Made for Browning Hi-Power, Colt Commander, Govt. and Gold Cup models, Ruger Mark I, 4″ S&W K-frames—models 10HB, 13, 64HB, 65, 58 with 4″ barrel. From Wichita Arms Inc. Price: With sights ... **$89.95**
Price: Extra for white outline rear sight ... **$6.00**

Sight Attachments

FREELAND LENS ADAPTER
Fits 1⅛″ O.D. presciption ground lens to all standard tube and receiver sights for shooting without glasses. Price without lens ... **$44.00**
Clear lens ground to prescription ... **$21.00**
Yellow or green prescription lens ... **$21.00**

MERIT ADAPTER FOR GLOBE FRONT SIGHTS
An Iris Shutter Disc with a special adapter for mounting in Lyman or Redfield globe front sights. Price ... **$46.00**

MERIT IRIS SHUTTER DISC
Eleven clicks gives 12 different apertures. No. 3 and Master, primarily target types, 0.22″ to .125″; No. 4, ½″ dia. hunting type, .025″ to .155″. Available for all popular sights. The Master Disc, with flexible rubber light shield, is particularly adapted to extension, scope height, and tang sights. All Merit Deluxe models have internal click springs; are hand fitted to minimum tolerance.
Master Deluxe ... **$60.00**
No. 4 Hunting Disc ... **$40.00**

MERIT LENS DISC
Similar to Merit Iris Shutter (Model 3 or Master) but incorporates provision for mounting prescription lens integrally. Lens may be obtained locally from your optician. Sight disc is 7/16″ wide (Mod. 3), or ¾″ wide (Master).
Model 3 Deluxe. Price ... **$63.00**
Master Deluxe ... **$74.00**

MERIT OPTICAL ATTACHMENT
For revolver and pistol shooters, instantly attached by rubber suction cup to regular or shooting glasses. Any aperture .020″ to .156″. Price, Deluxe (swings aside) ... **$60.00**

WILLIAMS APERTURES
Standard thread, fits most sights. Regular series ⅜″ to ½″ O.D., .050″ to .125″ hole. "Twilight" series has white reflector ring. .093″ to .125″ inner hole. Price, regular series . . . **$3.20.** Twilight series ... **$4.40**
New wide open 5/16″ aperture for shotguns fits 5-D and Foolproof sights. Price ... **$5.75**

Shotgun Sights

ACCURA-SITE
For shooting shotgun slugs. Three models to fit most shotguns—"A" for vent. rib barrels, "B" for solid ribs, "C" for plain barrels. Rear sight has windage and elevation provisions. Easily removed and replaced. Includes front and rear sights. Price ... **$25.95** to **$27.95**

FOR DOUBLE BARREL SHOTGUNS (PRESS FIT)
Marble 214—Ivory front bead, 11/64″ . . . **$3.25; 215**—same with .080″ rear bead and reamers . . . **$10.75. Marble 220**—Bi-color (gold and ivory) front bead, 11/64″ and .080″ rear bead, with reamers . . . **$12.35; Marble 221**—front bead only . . . **$4.70. Marble 223**—Ivory rear .080″ . . . **$3.00. Marble 224**—Front sight reamer for 214-221 beads . . . **$2.35; Marble 226**—Rear sight reamer for 223. Price ... **$2.35**

FOR SINGLE OR DB SHOTGUNS (SCREW-ON FIT)
Marble 217—Ivory front bead 11/64″ . . . **$3.55; Marble 216 . . . $7.35; Marble 218**—Bi-color front, 11/64″ . . . **$5.15; Marble 219 . . . $9.00; Marble 223T**—Ivory rear .080″ Price ... **$4.85**
Marble Bradley type sights 223BT—⅛″, 5/64″ and 11/64″ long. Gold, Ivory or Red bead ... **$3.35**

MILLETT SHURSHOT SHOTGUN SIGHT
A sight system for shotguns with a ventilated rib. Rear sight attaches to the rib, front sight replaces the front bead. Front has an orange face, rear has two orange bars. For 870, 1100, or other models.
Price: Front and rear ... **$31.49**
Price: Adjustable front and rear ... **$41.95**

POLY-CHOKE
Replacement front sights in four styles—Xpert, Poly Bead, Xpert Mid Rib sights, and Bev-L-Block. Xpert Front available in 3x56, 6x48 thread, 3/32″ or 5/32″ shank length, gold, ivory (**$3.00**); or Sun Spot orange bead (**$4.00**); Poly Bead is standard replacement ⅛″ bead, 3x56 or 6x48, short, medium, long shank (**$2.00**); Xpert Mid Rib in tapered carrier (ivory only) or 3x56 threaded shank (gold only), **$2.00**; Hi and Lo Blok sights with 6x48 thread, gold or ivory (**$3.00**) or Sun Spot Orange (**$4.00**).

SLUG SITE
A combination V-notch rear and bead front sight made of adhesive-backed formed metal approx. 7″ over-all. May be mounted, removed and re-mounted as necessary, using new adhesive from the pack supplied.
Price ... **$10.00**

SCOPES & MOUNTS
HUNTING, TARGET ■ & VARMINT ■ SCOPES

Maker and Model	Magn.	Field at 100 Yds (feet)	Relative Bright-ness	Eye Relief (in.)	Length (in.)	Tube Diam. (in.)	W&E Adjust-ments	Weight (ozs.)	Price	Other Data
Aimpoint										
Mark III	0	—	—	—	6	—	Int.	12	**219.95**	Projects variable intensity aiming dot. Has potentiometer to give fixed dot intensity. Dot covers about 3" @ 100 meters. No parallax. Unlimited eye relief. 3x magnification lens, $94.95, 1.5-4x lens $135.95. Imported by Aimpoint USA, Inc.
American Import Co.										
Dickson 200[1]	4	19	13.7	3.5	11.5	¾	Int.	6	**12.50**	[1]Complete with mount for 22-cal. RF rifles. [2]Standard crosshair reticle, coated lenses. [3]Anodized finish. [4]Wide angle. [5]Complete with bridge mount. [6]Rubber armored. [7]Also wide angle.
Dickson 218 32mm	2½	32	164	3.7	12	1	Int.	9.3	**47.95**	
Dickson 220 32mm[2]	4	29	64	3.6	12	1	Int.	9.1	**49.95**	
Dickson 224 40mm	4	30	100	3.5	12½	1	Int.	10	**54.95**	
Dickson 226 40mm[3]	6	20	44.7	3.7	13	1	Int.	10	**54.95**	
Dickson 228 32mm[4]	4	37	64	3.3	12	1	Int.	10.5	**73.95**	
Dickson 230 40mm[4]	4	37	100	3.8	12.4	1	Int.	12	**78.95**	
Dickson 231 40mm[4]	6	24½	44.5	3.8	12.4	1	Int.	12	**81.00**	
Dickson 232 32mm[4]	3-9	42-14	112.4-13	3.1-2.5	12.9	1	Int.	12	**93.95**	
Dickson 240 32mm	3-9	37-12.3	112-13	3	12.8	1	Int.	13.8	**62.95**	
Dickson 242 40mm	3.9	37-12.3	177-19.4	3	12.8	1	Int.	15.2	**78.95**	
Dickson 244 20mm	1½-4½	46	177	4.3	11.3	1	Int.	10.3	**67.95**	
Dickson Pistol 250[5]	1½	15.3	100	11-16	8½	¾	Int.	6	**19.95**	
2532[6]	2.5	33	—	3.5	11.7	1	Int.	10	**57.95**	
4401[6,7]	4	29	—	3.3	11	1	Int.	11	**63.95**	
6401[6]	6	18.5	—	3.2	13	1	Int.	11	**66.95**	
3932[6,7]	3-9	35.3-13.2	—	3.3-3.0	12.2	1	Int.	13.5	**81.95**	
Apollo										
4x32 Compact	4	29	—	3.3	11.7	1	Int.	10	**132.95**	Rubber armored, water and fog proof. Comes with see through filter caps; ¼-minute click adjustments. Imported from Japan by Senno Corp.
3-9x40 Variable	3-9	35.3-13.2	—	3.3-3	12	1	Int.	14	**159.95**	
Bausch & Lomb										
3x-9x 40mm	3-9	36-12	267	3.2	13	1	Int.	17	**339.95**	Contact Bushnell for details.
4x 40 mm	4	28	150	3.2	12¾	1	Int.	14½	**219.95**	
1.5x-6x	1.5-6	60-15	294-18.4	3.2	11	1	Int.	13.9	**299.95**	
6x-24x	6-24	18-4.5	66.1-4.2	3.1	16.5	1	Int.	21.2	**399.95**	
Beeman										
Blue Ring 20[1]	1.5	14	150	11-16	8.3	¾	Int.	3.6	**49.95**	All scopes have 5-pt. reticle, all glass, fully coated lenses. [1]Pistol scope; cast mounts included. [2]Pistol scope; silhouette knobs. [3]Rubber armor coating; built-in double adj. mount, parallax-free setting. [4]Objective focus, built-in double-adj. mount; matte finish. [5]Objective focus. [6]Has 8 lenses; objective focus; milled mounts included. [7]Includes cast mounts. [8]Objective focus; silhouette knobs; matte finish. [9]Has 9 lenses; objective focus. Imported by Beeman.
Blue Ribbon 25[2]	2	19	150	10-24	9 1/16	1	Int.	7.4	**119.50**	
SS-1[3]	2.5	30	61	3.25	5½	1	Int.	7	**129.95**	
SS-2[4]	3	34.5	74	3.5	6.8	1.38	Int.	13.6	**189.50**	
Blue Ribbon 50R[5]	2.5	33	245	3.5	12	1	Int.	11.8	**94.50**	
Blue Ring 35R[6]	3	25	67	2.5	11¼	¾	Int.	5.1	**44.95**	
30A[7]	4	21	21	2	10.2	¾	Int.	4.5	**29.99**	
Blue Ribbon 66R[8]	2-7	62-16	384-31	3	11.4	1	Int.	14.9	**168.50**	
Blue Ring 45R[9]	3-7	26-12	67-9	2.5	10⅝	¾	Int.	6	**69.95**	
MS-1	4	23	30	3.5	7.5	1	Int.	8	**129.95**	
SS-3[4]	1.5-4	44.6-24.6	172-24	3	5.75	⅞	Int.	8.5	**169.50**	
Blue Ribbon 67R[8]	3-9	435-15	265-29	3	14.4	1	Int.	15.2	**229.50**	
Blue Ribbon 68R[8]	4-12	30.5-11	150-13.5	3	14.4	1	Int.	15.2	**239.50**	
Blue Ribbon 54R[5]	4	29	96	3.5	12	1	Int.	12.3	**94.50**	
SS-2[4]	4	24.6	41	5	7	1.38	Int.	13.7	**189.50**	
29	4	21	21	2	10.2	¾	Int.	4.5	**19.98**	
Burris										
4x Fullfield[1]	3.8	37	49	3¼	11¼	1	Int.	11	**174.95**	½-minute dot $7 extra. LER = Long Eye Relief—ideal for forward mounting on handguns. Plex or cross-hair only. Matte "Satin" finish avail. on 4x, 6x, 2-7x, 3-9x, 4x Mini, 1½-4x LER, 2x LER, 4x LER P.A. at extra cost. [1]3" dot $8 extra. [2]1"-3" dot $6 extra. [3]1"-3" dot $7 extra. [4]With parallax adjustment $149.95. [5]With parallax adjustment $195.95. [6]With parallax adjustment $167.95. [7]With parallax adjustment $177.95. Parallax adjustment adds 5 oz. to weight. [8]Available with Fine Plex crosshair.
2x-7x Fullfield[2] HiLume	2.5-6.8	50-19	81-22	3¼	11⅞	1	Int.	14	**231.95**	
3x-9x Fullfield[3] HiLume	3.3-8.6	40-15	72-17.6	3¼	12¾	1	Int.	15	**245.95**	
2¾ Fullfield	2.7	53	49	3¼	10½	1	Int.	9	**159.95**	
6x Fullfield	5.8	24	36	3¼	13	1	Int.	12	**188.95**	
1¾-5x Fullfield HiLume	2.5-6.8	70-27	121-25	3¼	10¾	1	Int.	13	**204.95**	
4x-12x Fullfield[8]	4.4-11.8	28-10½	—	3-3¼	15	1	Int.	18	**285.95**	
■ 6x-18x Fullfield[8]	6.5-17.6	17-7.5	—	3-3¾	15.8	12	Int.	18.5	**292.95**	
■ 10x Fullfield[8]	9.8	12½	—	3¼	15	1	Int.	15	**231.95**	
■ 12x Fullfield[8]	11.8	11	—	3¼	15	1	Int.	15	**238.95**	
2x LER	1.7	21	—	10-24	8¾	1	Int.	6.8	**131.95**	
3x LER	2.7	17	—	10-20	8⅞	1	Int.	6.8	**142.95**	
4x LER[6]	3.7	11	—	10-22	9⅝	1	Int.	8.5	**149.95**	
5x LER[7]	4.5	8.7	—	12-22	10⅞	1	Int.	9.5	**159.95**	
7x IER[8]	6.5	6.5	—	10-16	11¼	1	Int.	10	**177.95**	
10x IER	9.5	4	—	8-12	13.6	1	Int.	14	**213.95**	
1½x-4x LER	1.6-3.8	16-11	—	11-24	10½	1	Int.	11	**213.95**	
2x-7x Mini	2.5-6.9	32-14	—	3¾	9⅜	1	Int.	10.5	**177.95**	
4x Mini[4,8]	3.6	24	—	3¾	8¼	1	Int.	7.8	**131.95**	
6x Mini	5.5	17	—	3¾	9	1	Int.	7.8	**142.95**	
3x-9x Mini	3.6-8.8	25-11	—	3¾	9⅞	1	Int.	11.5	**183.95**	
4-12x Mini	4.5-11.6	19-8	—	3¾	11.2	1	Int.	15	**249.95**	
Bushnell										
Scope Chief VI	4	29	96	3½	12	1	Int.	9.3	**119.95**	All ScopeChief, Banner and Custom models come with Multi-X reticle, with or without BDC (bullet drop compensator) that eliminates holdover. Prismatic Rangefinder (PRF) on some models. Contact Bushnell for data on full line. Prices include BDC—deduct $5 if not wanted. Add $30 for PRF. BDC feature available in all Banner models, except 2.5x. [1]Equipped with Wind Drift
Scope Chief VI	3-9	35-12.6	267-30	3½-3⅓	12.6	1	Int.	14.3	**191.95**	
Scope Chief VI	3-9	43-14.6	241-26.5	3	12.1	1	Int.	15.4	**239.95**	
Scope Chief VI	2½-8	45-14	247-96	3.7-3.3	11.2	1	Int.	12.1	**169.95**	
Scope Chief VI	1½-4½	73.7-24.5	267-30	3.5-3.5	9.6	1	Int.	9.5	**165.95**	
Scope Chief VI	4-12	29-10	150-17	3.2	13.5	1	Int.	17	**235.95**	

HUNTING, TARGET ■ & VARMINT ■ SCOPES

Maker and Model	Magn.	Field at 100 Yds (feet)	Relative Bright-ness	Eye Relief (in.)	Length (in.)	Tube Diam. (in.)	W&E Adjust-ments	Weight (ozs.)	Price	Other Data
Bushnell (cont'd.)										Compensator and Parallax-free adjustment. [2]Parallax focus adjustment. [3]Wide angle. [4]Wide angle. [5]Parallax focus adjustment. [6]Phantoms intended for handgun use. [7]Mount separate. [8]Has battery-powered, lighted reticle. [9]With mounts.
Centurion Handgun 4x32mm	4	10.2	96	10-20	8¾	1	Int.	9.3	129.95	
Custom 22	4	28.4	—	2½	10 5/16	⅞	Int.	5¼	43.95	
Custom 22	3-7	29-13.6	28-5	2¼-2½	10	⅞	Int.	6½	53.95	
Banner	2½	45	96	3½	10.9	1	Int.	8	87.95	
Banner 32mm	4	29	96	3½	12	1	Int.	10	93.95	
Banner 40mm	4	37⅓	150	3	12⅓	1	Int.	12	123.95	
Banner Lite-Site 4x[9]	4	28	150	3.3	12.9	1	Int.	11½	219.95	
Banner 40mm	6	19.5	67	3	13.5	1	Int.	11.5	109.95	
Banner 22[1]	4	27.5	37.5	3	11⅝	1	Int.	8	49.95	
■ Banner Silhouette[2]	10	12	24	3	14½	1	Int.	14.6	167.95	
Banner[3]	1½-4	63-28	294-41	3½	10½	1	Int.	10.3	123.95	
Banner[4]	1¾-4½	71-27	216-33	3	10.2	1	Int.	11½	143.95	
Banner Lite-Site 3x-9x[9]	3.9	36-12	267	3.5-3.3	13.6	1	Int.	14	259.95	
Banner 32mm	3-9	39-13	171-19	3½	11.5	1	Int.	11	137.95	
Banner 38mm[5]	3-9	43-14.6	241-26½	3	12	1	Int.	14	161.95	
Banner[6]	4-12	29-10	150-17	3.2	13½	1	Int.	15½	163.95	
Magnum Phantom[7]	1.3	17	441	7-21	7.8	15/16	Int.	5½	77.95	
Magnum Phantom[8]	2½	9	100	8-21	9.7	15/16	Int.	6½	85.95	
Sportview	3-9	41.5-13.6	241-26.5	3	12.5	1	Int.	14	93.95	
Sportview	4	34.5	135	3	12.5	1	Int.	11.5	73.95	
Sportview 22	3-7	26-12	67.4-12.6	2.5	11.5	1	Int.	5.5	31.95	
Sportview 4x32mm	4	28	96	4	11.8	1	Int.	11.3	53.95	
Sportview 4x15mm[9]	4	17	21	2.3	10.2	⅞	Int.	6	13.95	
Colt										
AR-15 3x	3	40	—	—	6	—	Int.	—	$192.95	All Colt scopes come complete with mount and allow use of iron sights.
AR-15 4x	4	30	—	—	6	—	Int.	—	212.95	
Davis Optical										
Spot Shot 1½"	10,12 15,20 25,30	10-4	—	2	25	.75	Ext.	—	116.00	Focus by moving non-rotating obj. lens unit. Ext. mounts included. Recoil spring $4.50 extra.
Interarms										
Electro-Point 4x40[1]	4	40	—	3.3	13	1	Int.	16	150.00	Uses 1.4-volt mercury battery with 60-hour life. Horizontal line with dot reticle. Also available in conventional styles. Imported by Interarms.
Electro-Point 3-9x40[1]	3-9	43.5-15	—	3.3-3	13	1	Int.	16.7	220.00	
Jason										
860	4	29	64	3	11.8	1	Int.	9.2	50.00	Constantly centered reticles, ballbearing click stops, nitrogen filled tubes, coated lenses. 4-Post crosshair about $3.50 extra on models 860, 861, 864, 865.
861	3-9	35-13	112-12	3	12.7	1	Int.	10.9	76.00	
862	4	19	14	2	11	¾	Int.	5.5	13.50	
863C	3-7	23-10	43-8	3	11	¾	Int.	8.4	44.00	
865	3-9	35-13	177-19	3	13	1	Int.	12.2	80.00	
869	4	19	25	2	11.4	¾	Int.	6	23.00	
873	4	29	100	3	12.7	1	Int.	11.1	75.00	
875	3-9	35-13	177-19	3	13	1	Int.	12.2	80.00	
877	4	37	100	3	11.6	1	Int.	11.6	85.00	
878	3-9	42.5-13.6	112-12	2.7	12.7	1	Int.	12.7	110.00	
Kahles										
Helia Super 2.5 x 20[1]	2.5	50	64	3.25	9.8	1	Int.	12.6	279.00	[1]Lightweight model weighs 10.1 oz. [2]Lightweight—11.2 oz. [3]Lightweight—13 oz. [4]Lightweight—16 oz. [5]Lightweight—12.6 oz. [6]Lightweight—15.4 oz. [7]Lightweight—15.7 oz. [8]Lightweight—17.8 oz. [9]Calibrated for 7.62 NATO ammo, 100 to 800 meters. All scopes have constantly centered reticles except ZF69; all come with lens caps. 30mm rings available for Redfield, Burris, Leupold bases. Imported from Austria by Kahles of America. (Del-Sports, Inc.).
Helia Super 4 x 32[2]	4	30	60	3.25	11.6	1	Int.	15	319.00	
Helia 6 x 42[3]	6	21.1	49	3.25	12.8	1	Int.	17.5	349.00	
Helia 8 x 56[4]	8	15.6	49	3.25	14.8	1	Int.	23	389.00	
Helia 1.1-4.5 x 20[5]	1.1-4.5	72.2-27	328-18	3.25	10.8	30mm	Int.	15	369.00	
Helia 1.5-6 x 20[6]	1.5-6	55.6-19.5	784-49	3.25	12.8	30mm	Int.	20	399.00	
Helia 2.2-9 x 42[7]	2.2-9	36.1-13.5	364-21	3.25	13.7	30mm	Int.	20.3	449.00	
Helia 3-12 x 56[8]	3-12	27.1-10	347-21	3.25	15.6	30mm	Int.	24.8	499.00	
ZF69 Sniper[9]	6	22.5	49	3.25	12.2	26mm	Int.	16.8	499.00	
Kassnar										
2x-7x Wide Angle	2-7	49-19	258-21	3-2.7	11	1	Int.	12.8	138.00	Other models avail., including ¾" and ⅞" tubes for 22-cal. rifles. Contact Kassnar for details. [1]Also in 3x-9x40. [2]Also in 4x40. [3]Also in 3x-9x40.
3x-9x Wide Angle[1]	3-9	42-15	112-13	3-2.7	12.2	1	Int.	13	149.00	
4x32 Wide Angle[2]	4	36	64	3.5	12	1	Int.	9.2	86.00	
6x40 Wide Angle	6	24	44	3	12.8	1	Int.	12	99.00	
1.5-4x Std.	1.5-4	52-27	177-25	4.4-3	10	1	Int.	9.5	86.00	
2x-7x Std.	2-7	42-16	256-21	3.1-3	11	1	Int.	12.5	91.00	
3x-9x Std.[3]	3-9	36-13	112-13	3.1-3	12.2	1	Int.	13.5	117.00	
4x-12x40 Std.	4-12	27-9.6	100-11	3-2.7	13.5	1	Int.	16	155.00	
2.5x32 Std.	2.5	36	164	3.6	12	1	Int.	9.3	62.00	
Kilham										
Hutson Handgunner II	1.7	8	—	—	5½	⅞	Int.	5.1	119.95	Unlimited eye relief; internal click adjustments; crosshair reticle. Fits Thompson/Center rail mounts, for S&W K, N, Ruger Blackhawk, Super, Super Single-Six, Contender
The Handgunner	3	8	—	10-12	6	⅞	Int.	5.3	119.95	
Leatherwood										
ART II	3.0-8.8	31-12	—	3.5	13.9	1	Int.	42	675.00	
ART/MPC	3.0-8.7	31-12	—	3.7	14.1	1	Int.	33	349.50	
4x	4.1	27	—	4	12.25	1	Int.	12.3	125.00	
Leupold										
M8-2X EER[1]	1.8	22.0	—	12-24	8.1	1	Int.	6.8	156.50	Constantly centered reticles, choice of Duplex, tapered CPC, Leupold Dot, Crosshair and Dot. CPC and Dot reticles extra. [1]2x and 4x scope have from 12"-24" of eye relief and are suitable for handguns, top ejection arms and muzzleloaders. [2]3x9 Compact, 6x Compact, 12x, 3x9, 3.5x10 and 6.5x20 come with Adjustable Objective. [3]Target scopes have 1-min divisions with ¼ min clicks, and Adjustable Objectives. 50-ft. Focus Adaptor available for indoor target ranges, **$39.45.** Sunshade available for all Adjustable Ob-
M8-2X EER Silver[1]	1.8	22.0	—	12-24	8.1	1	Int.	6.8	174.40	
M8-4X EER[1]	3.5	9.5	—	12-24	8.4	1	Int.	7.6	191.05	
M8-4X EER Silver[1]	3.5	9.5	—	12-24	8.4	1	Int.	8.5	208.80	
M8-2.5X Compact	2.3	42	—	4.3	8.5	1	Int.	7.4	172.50	
M8-4X Compact	3.6	26.5	—	4.1	10.3	1	Int.	8.5	196.90	
2-7x Compact	2.5-6.6	41.7-16.5	—	3.8-3.0	9.9	1	Int.	8.5	248.30	
6x Compact & A.O.	5.7	16	—	3.9	10.7	1	Int.	8.5	200.90	

 CAUTION: PRICES CHANGE. CHECK AT GUNSHOP.

HUNTING, TARGET ■ & VARMINT ■ SCOPES

Maker and Model	Magn.	Field at 100 Yds (feet)	Relative Bright-ness	Eye Relief (in.)	Length (in.)	Tube Diam. (in.)	W&E Adjust-ments	Weight (ozs.)	Price	Other Data
Leupold (cont'd.)										
3-9x Compact & A.O.	3.2-8.5	34.5-13.5	—	3.8-3.1	11	1	Int.	9.5	**267.75**	jective scopes, **$11.40.** [4]Also available in matte finish for about **$20.00** extra.
M8-4X[4]	3.6	28	—	4.4	11.4	1	Int.	8.8	**196.90**	
M8-6X	5.9	18.0	—	4.3	11.4	1	Int.	9.9	**209.20**	
M8-8X[2]	7.8	14.5	—	4.0	12.5	1	Int.	13.0	**280.25**	
M8-12X[2]	11.6	9.2	—	4.2	13.0	1	Int.	13.5	**283.90**	
6.5 x 20 Target AO	6.5-19.2	14.8-5.7	—	5.3-3.7	14.2	1	Int.	16	**447.30**	
M8-12X Target[3]	11.6	9.2	—	4.2	13.0	1	Int.	14.5	**336.80**	
M8-24X[3]	24.0	4.7	—	3.2	13.6	1	Int.	14.5	**447.30**	
M8-36X[3]	36.0	3.2	—	3.4	13.9	1	Int.	15.5	**447.30**	
Vari-X-II 2X7	2.5-6.6	44.0-19.0	—	4.1-3.7	10.7	1	Int.	10.4	**263.20**	
Vari-X-II 3X9[4]	3.5-9.0	32.0-13.5	—	4.1-3.7	12.3	1	Int.	13.1	**285.60**	
Vari-X-II 3X9[2]	3.5-9.0	32.0-13.5	—	4.1-3.7	12.3	1	Int.	14.5	**319.90**	
Vari-X-III 1.5X5	1.5-4.6	66.0-24.0	—	4.7-3.5	9.4	1	Int.	9.3	**288.75**	
Vari-X-III 2.5X8[4]	2.7-7.9	38.0-14.0	—	4.2-3.4	11.3	1	Int.	11.0	**343.55**	
Vari-X-III 3.5X10	3.4-9.9	29.5-10.5	—	4.6-3.6	12.4	1	Int.	13.0	**340.70**	
Vari-X-III 3.5X10[2]	3.4-9.9	29.5-10.5	—	4.6-3.6	12.4	1	Int.	14.4	**379.30**	
Vari-X-III 6.5X20[2]	6.5-19.2	14.8- 5.7	—	5.3-3.7	14.2	1	Int.	16	**403.50**	
Nikon										
4x40	4	26	—	3.4	11.6	1	Int.	13.5	**NA**	Multi-coated lenses; 1/4-minute windage and elevation adjustments; nitrogen filled; waterproof. From Nikon Inc.
3-9x40	3-9	34.5-11.5	—	3.5-3.4	12.3	1	Int.	16	**NA**	
RWS										
100 4x32	4	20	—	—	10 7/8	3/4	Int.	6	**33.00**	Air gun scopes. All have Dyna-Plex reticle. Imported from Japan by Dynamit Nobel of America.
200 3-7x-20	3-7	24-17	—	—	11 1/4	3/4	Int.	6	**51.00**	
350 4x32	4	28	—	—	10	1	Int.	10	**85.00**	
400 2-7x32	2-7	56-17	—	—	12 3/4	1	Int.	12	**125.00**	
800 1.5x20	1.5	19	—	—	8 3/4	1	Int.	6 1/2	**85.00**	
Redfield										
Illuminator Trad. 3-9x	2.9-8.7	33-11	—	3 1/2	12 3/4	1	Int.	17	**359.20**	*Accutrac feature avail. on these scopes at extra cost. Traditionals have round lenses. 4-Plex reticle is standard. [1]"Magnum Proof." Specially designed for magnum and auto pistols. Uses "Double Dovetail" mounts. [2]Mounts solidly on receiver. CH or dot. 20x—$308.20, 24x—$317.65.
Illuminator Widefield 3-9x*	2.9-8.7	38-13	—	3 1/2	12 3/4	1	Int.	17	**394.95**	
Tracker 4x	3.9	28.9	—	3 1/2	11.02	1	Int.	9.8	**110.75**	
Tracker 2-7x	2.3-6.9	36.6-12.2	—	3 1/2	12.20	1	Int.	11.6	**148.30**	
Tracker 3-9x	3.0-9.0	34.4-11.3	—	3 1/2	14.96	1	Int.	13.4	**166.15**	
Traditional 4x3/4"	4	24 1/2	27	3 1/2	9 3/8	3/4	Int.	—	**105.40**	
Traditional 2 1/2x	2 1/2	43	64	3 1/2	10 1/4	1	Int.	8 1/2	**146.50**	
Traditional 4x	4	28 1/2	56	3 1/2	11 3/8	1	Int.	9 3/4	**164.40**	
Traditional 6x	6	19	—	3 1/2	12 1/2	1	Int.	11 1/2	**193.00**	
Traditional 3x-9x* Royal	3-9	34-11	—	3 1/2-4 1/4	12 1/2	1	Int.	13	**285.95**	
Traditional 2x-7x*	2-7	42-14	207-23	3 1/2	11 1/4	1	Int.	12	**225.15**	
Traditional 3x-9x*	3-9	34-11	163-18	3 1/2	12 1/2	1	Int.	13	**246.60**	
Traditional 8xMS	8	16.6	—	3-3 3/4	14 1/8	1	Int.	17 1/5	**251.95**	
Traditional 10xMS	10	12.6	—	3-3 3/4	14 1/8	1	Int.	17 1/2	**262.70**	
Traditional 12xMS	12.4	8.1	—	3-3 3/4	14 1/8	1	Int.	17 1/2	**277.00**	
Pistol Scopes										
4xMP	3.6	9	—	12-22	9 11/16	1	Int.	11.1	**175.10**	
Traditional 4x-12x*	4-12	26-9	112-14	3 1/2	13 7/8	1	Int.	14	**343.15**	
Traditional 6x-18x*	6-18	18-6	50-6	3 1/2	13 15/16	1	Int.	18	**382.45**	
Low Profile Scopes										
Widefield 2 3/4xLP	2 3/4	55 1/2	69	3 1/2	10 1/2	1	Int.	8	**184.05**	
Widefield 4xLP	3.6	37 1/2	84	3 1/2	11 1/2	1	Int.	10	**205.05**	
Widefield 6xLP	5.5	23	—	3 1/2	12 3/4	1	Int.	11	**225.15**	
Widefield 1 3/4x5xLP	1 3/4-5	70-27	136-21	3 1/2	10 3/4	1	Int.	11 1/2	**255.54**	
Widefield 2x7xLP*	2-7	49-19	144-21	3 1/2	11 3/4	1	Int.	13	**264.50**	
Widefield 3x-9xLP*	3-9	39-15	112-18	3 1/2	12 1/2	1	Int.	14	**309.15**	
Sanders										
Bisley 2 1/2x20	2 1/2	42	64	3	10 3/4	1	Int.	8 1/4	**48.50**	Alum. alloy tubes, 1/4" adj. coated lenses. Five other scopes are offered; 6x45 at $68.50, 8x45 at $70.50, 2 1/2x7x at $69.50, 3-9x33 at $72.50 and 3-9x40 at $78.50. Rubber lens covers (clear plastic) are $3.50. Write to Sanders for details. Choice of reticles in CH, PCH, 3-post.
Bisley 4x33	4	28	64	3	12	1	Int.	9	**52.50**	
Bisley 6x40	6	19	45	3	12 1/2	1	Int.	9 1/2	**56.50**	
Bisley 8x40	8	18	25	3 1/4	12 1/2	1	Int.	9 1/2	**62.50**	
Bisley 10x40	10	12 1/2	16	2 1/2	12 1/2	1	Int.	10 1/4	**64.50**	
Bisley 5-13x40	5-13	29-10	64-9	3	14	1	Int.	14	**86.50**	
Schmidt & Bender										
Vari-M 1 1/4-4x20[1]	1 1/4-4	96-16	—	3 1/4	10.4	30mm	Int.	12.3	**364.00**	[1]Heavy duty aluminum. [2]Black chrome finish. [3]For silhouette and varmint shooting. Choice of nine reticles. 30-year warranty. All have 1/3-min. click adjustments, centered reticles, nitrogen filling. Most models avail. in aluminum with mounting rail. Imported from West Germany by Paul Jaeger, Inc.
Vari-M 1 1/2-6x42	1 1/2-6	60-19.5	—	3 1/4	12.2	30mm	Int.	17.5	**412.00**	
Vari-M 2 1/2-10x56	2 1/2-10	37.5-12	—	3 1/4	14.6	30mm	Int.	21.9	**478.00**	
All Steel 1 1/2x15[2]	1 1/2	90	—	3 1/4	10	1	Int.	11.8	**271.00**	
All Steel 4x36[2]	4	30	—	3 1/4	11.4	1	Int.	14	**286.00**	
All Steel 6x42[2]	6	21	—	3 1/4	13.2	1	Int.	17.3	**308.00**	
All Steel 8x56[2]	8	16.5	—	3 1/4	14.8	1	Int.	21.9	**350.00**	
■ All Steel 12x42[3]	12	16.5	—	3 1/4	13	1	Int.	17.9	**332.00**	
Shepherd										
3 x 9 40mm	3-9	43.5-15.0	—	3.3	13	1	Int.	13 1/2	**NA**	Instant range finding and bullet drop compensating; choice of plain, range finding or bullet drop reticle by turning cover cap; built-in collimator. From Shepherd Scope Ltd.
Simmons										
1002 Rimfire[1]	4	23	—	3	11.5	3/4	Int.	6	**11.00**	[1]With ring mount. [2]With ring mount. [3]With rings. [4]3-9x32; also avail. 3-9x40. [5]3-9x32; also avail. 3-9x40. [6]4x32; also avail. 4x40 as #1034. [7]3-9x32; also avail. 3-9x40 as #1038. [8]Avail. in brushed aluminum finish as #1052. [9]Avail. with silhouette knobs as #1085, in brushed aluminum as #1088. [10]1/2-min. dot or Truplex; Truplex reticle also avail. with dot. Sunshade, screw-in lens covers. Parallax adj.; Silhouette knobs; graduated drums.
1004 Rimfire[2]	3-7	22.5-9.5	—	3	11	3/4	Int.	8.4	**44.50**	
1007 Rimfire[3]	4	25	—	3	10	1	Int.	9	**77.00**	
1005 Waterproof	2 1/2	46	—	3	11.5	1	Int.	9.3	**71.00**	
1006 Waterproof	4	29	—	—	12	1	Int.	9.1	**55.00**	
1010 Waterproof[4]	3-9	37-12.7	—	3-3 1/4	12.8	1	Int.	12.8	**74.00**	
1014 Waterproof	4-12	30-11	—	3-3 1/4	14	1	Int.	14.9	**120.00**	

HUNTING, TARGET ■ & VARMINT ■ SCOPES

Maker and Model	Magn.	Field at 100 Yds (feet)	Relative Bright-ness	Eye Relief (in.)	Length (in.)	Tube Diam. (in.)	W&E Adjust-ments	Weight (ozs.)	Price	Other Data
Simmons (cont'd.)										[11]Battery powered, roof prism design. [12]Speed focus, parallax adj., matte finish. Max-Ilume Mono Tube models have dull finish, speed focus, rubber shock ring, Truplex reticle in all models. All scopes sealed, fog-proof, with constantly centered reticles. Imported from Japan by Simmons Outdoor Corp. **Prices are approximate.**
1016 Waterproof	6-18	19-6.7	—	3-3¼	15.7	1	Int.	16.2	**153.00**	
1024 W.A.	4	37	—	3	11.8	1	Int.	10.5	**91.50**	
1025 W.A.	6	24.5	—	3	12.4	1	Int.	12	**112.50**	
1026 W.A.	1½-4½	86-28.9	—	3-3¼	10.6	1	Int.	13.2	**121.50**	
1027 W.A.	2-7	54.6-18.3	—	3-3¼	12	1	Int.	12.8	**121.50**	
1028 W.A.[5]	3-9	42-14	—	3-3¼	12.9	1	Int.	12.9	**113.00**	
1032 Mono Tube[6]	4	37	—	3	12.2	1	Int.	11.5	**132.00**	
1036 Mono Tube[7]	3-9	42-14	—	3-3¼	13.3	1	Int.	13	**172.00**	
1040 Mono Tube	2-7	54-18	—	3-3¼	13.1	1	Int.	12.9	**180.00**	
1049 Compact	2½	37	—	3	9.3	1	Int.	9.1	**149.00**	
1050 Compact[8]	4	22	—	3	9	1	Int.	9.1	**149.00**	
1053 Compact	1½-4½	86-28.9	—	3-3¼	10.6	1	Int.	9.1	**200.00**	
1054 Compact	3-9	40-14	—	3-3¼	10.5	1	Int.	10.5	**190.00**	
1063 Armored	4	37	—	3	12.4	1	Int.	16	**151.50**	
1064 Armored	3-9	42-14	—	3-3¼	12.3	1	Int.	17.6	**168.00**	
1074	6½-20	18-6	—	3	15	1	Int.	16	**260.00**	
1075	6½-10	22-12	—	3	15	1	Int.	16	**260.00**	
1076[10]	15	8	—	3	15	1	Int.	16	**220.00**	
1078[10]	24	6	—	3	15	1	Int.	16	**220.00**	
1057 Illum.	4	21	—	3	8	1	Int.	11	**185.00**	
410[11]	4-10	40-15	—	3	12.75	1	Int.	15	**175.00**	
1073 Sil. Airgun	2-7	54.6-18.3	—	3-3¼	12.1	1	Int.	15.7	**160.00**	
1080 Handgun	2	18	—	10-20	7.1	1	Int.	8.1	**102.00**	
1084 Handgun[9]	4	9	—	10-20	8.7	1	Int.	9.5	**156.00**	
Swarovski Habicht										
Nova 1.5x20	1.5	61	—	3⅛	9.6	1	Int.	12.7	**330.00**	All models offered in either steel or lightweight alloy tubes except 1.5x20, ZFM 6x42 and Cobras. Weights shown are for lightweight versions. Choice of nine constantly centered reticles. Eyepiece recoil mechanism and rubber ring shield to protect face. Cobra and ZFM also available in NATO Stanag 2324 mounts. Imported by Swarovski America Ltd.
Nova 4x32	4	33	—	3⅛	11.3	1	Int.	13	**340.00**	
Nova 6x42	6	23	—	3⅛	12.6	1	Int.	14	**380.00**	
Nova 8x56	8	17	—	3⅛	14.4	1	Int.	17	**455.00**	
Nova 1.5 6x42	1.5-6	61-21	—	3⅛	12.6	1	Int.	17	**470.00**	
Nova 2.2-9x42	2.2-9	39.5-15	—	3⅛	13.3	1	Int.	16.5	**580.00**	
Nova 3-12x56	3-12	30-11	—	3⅛	15.25	1	Int.	19	**640.00**	
ZFM 6x42	6	23	—	3⅛	12	1	Int.	18	**535.00**	
Cobra 1.5-14	1.5	50	—	3.9	7.87	1	Int.	10	**325.00**	
Cobra 3x14	3	21	—	3.9	8.75	1	Int.	11	**340.00**	
Swift										
600 4x15	4	16.2	—	2.4	11	¾	Int.	4.7	**19.98**	All Swift Mark I scopes, with the exception of the 4x15, have Quadraplex reticles and are fog-proof and waterproof. The 4x15 has crosshair reticle and is non-waterproof.
650 4x32	4	29	—	3½	12	1	Int.	9	**68.00**	
651 4x32 WA	4	37	—	3½	11¾	1	Int.	10½	**76.50**	
653 4x40 WA	4	35½	—	3¾	12¼	1	Int.	12	**89.50**	
654 3-9x32	3-9	35¾-12¾	—	3	12¾	1	Int.	13¾	**92.50**	
656 3-9x40 WA	3-9	42½-13½	—	2¾	12¾	1	Int.	14	**105.00**	
657 6x40	6	18	—	3¾	13	1	Int.	10	**78.00**	
658 1½-4½x32	1½-4½	55-22	—	3½	12	1	Int.	13	**98.00**	
Tasco										
WA 4x40 Wide Angle[2,9]	4	36	100	3¼	12⅝	1	Int.	12½	**124.95**	[1]MAG-IV gives one-third more power. [2]Supercon®, fully coated lenses; waterproof, shockproof, fogproof; includes haze filter caps, lifetime warranty. [3]Trajectory-Range Finding scopes. [4]30/30 range finding reticle; rubber covered; built-in mounting rings. Also avail. in wide angle models. [5]Waterproof; anodized finish; ¼-min. click stops; R.F. reticle. [6]R.F. reticle, fully coated lenses; ¼-min. clicks; waterproof. [7]Integral mount for 22 RF, airguns with grooved receiver. Also avail. in brushed aluminum finish. [8]Adj., built-in mount; adj. rheostat, polarizer; ½-min. clicks. Avail. to fit Rem. 870, 1100, also with side mounts, in wide angle. [9]World Class Wide Angle®. [10]Target-Silhouette, ⅛-min. adjustments. Contact Tasco for complete list of models offered.
WA 3-9x40 Wide Angle[2,9]	3-9	43½-15	178-20	3¼	12⅝	1	Int.	11½	**129.95**	
WA 2.5x32 Wide Angle[2,9]	2.5	52	44	3¼	12	1	Int.	9½	**149.95**	
WA 2-7x32 Wide Angle[2,9]	2-7	56-17	256-21	3¼	11½	1	Int.	11½	**109.95**	
WA 1¾-5 x 20 Wide Angle[2,9]	1.75-5	72-24	131-16	3¼	10⅝	1	Int.	10¾	**139.95**	
RC 3-9 x 40 WA[2,4,9]	3-9	43½-15	178-20	3¼	—	1	Int.	12⅝	**189.95**	
RC 4 x 40 WA[2,4,9]	4	36	100	3¼	11⅞	1	Int.	11	**169.95**	
TR 3-12 x 32 TRF[3]	3-12	34-9	112-7	3	12¼	1	Int.	13¾	**134.95**	
TR 4-16 x 40 TRF[3]	4-16	25½-7	100-6	3	14¼	1	Int.	16¾	**199.95**	
W 4 x 32[5]	4	28	64	3¼	11¾	1	In.t	9½	**64.95**	
W 3-12 x 4 MAG-IV[1]	3-12	34-9	178-11	3	12¾	1	Int.	13¾	**139.95**	
TS 8-32 x 44[10]	8-32	10¾-3½	30-2	3	16½	1	Int.	19½	**349.95**	
PM 4 x 18[6,7]	4	—	20	3	16¼	⅞	Int.	—	**69.95**	
BDIXCFV Battery Dot[8]	1	—	—	—	7½	—	Int.	10	**199.95**	
Thompson/Center										
Lobo 1½ x[1]	1.5	16	127	11-20	7¾	⅞	Int.	5	**85.00**	[1]May be used on light to medium recoil guns, including muzzleloaders. Coated lenses, nitrogen filled, lifetime warranty. [2]For heavy recoil guns. Nitrogen filled. Duplex reticle only. Target turrets avail. on 1½x, 3x models. Electra Dot illuminated reticle available in RP 2½x ($31 extra) and RP 3x ($36 extra).[3] Rifle scopes have Electra Dot reticle. [4]Rail model for grooved receivers also available—$155.00. With Electra Dot reticle.
Lobo 3x[1]	3	9	49	11-20	9	⅞	Int.	6.3	**90.00**	
RP 1½ x[2]	1.5	28	177	11-20	7½	1	Int.	5.1	**109.00**	
RP 2½x[2]	2.5	15	64	11-20	8½	1	Int.	6.5	**109.00**	
RP 3x[2]	3	13	44	11-20	8¾	1	Int.	5.4	**109.00**	
RP 4x[2]	4	10	71	12-20	9¼	1	Int.	10.4	**130.00**	
TC 4x Rifle[3]	4	29	64	3.3	12⅞	1	Int.	12.3	**135.00**	
TC 3/9V Rifle[3]	3-9	35.3-13.2	177-19	3.3	12⅞	1	Int.	15.5	**205.00**	
Short Tube 8630[4]	4	29	20	3	7¾	1	Int.	10.1	**145.00**	
Unertl										
■ 1″ Target	6,8,10	16-10	17.6-6.25	2	21½	¾	Ext.	21	**154.00**	[1]Dural ¼ MOA click mounts. Hard coated lenses. Non-rotating objective lens focusing. [2]¼ MOA click mounts. [3]With target mounts. [4]With calibrated head. [5]Same as 1″ Target but without objective lens focusing. [6]Price with ¼ MOA click mounts. [7]With new Posa mounts. [8]Range focus until near rear of tube. Price is with Posa mounts. Magnum clamp. With standard mounts and clamp ring **$266.00.**
■ 1¼″ Target[1]	8,10,12,14	12-16	15.2-5	2	25	¾	Ext.	21	**206.00**	
■ 1½″ Target	8,10,12,14 16,18,20	11.5-3.2	—	2¼	25½	¾	Ext.	31	**235.00**	
■ 2″ Target[2]	8,10,12, 14,16,18, 24,30,36	8	22.6-2.5	2¼	26¼	1	Ext.	44	**322.00**	
■ Varmint, 1¼∞[3]	6,8,10,12	1-7	28-7.1	2½	19½	⅞	Ext.	26	**207.00**	
■ Ultra Varmint, 2″[4]	8,10 12,15	12.6-7	39.7-11	2½	24	1	Ext.	34	**301.00**	

CAUTION: PRICES CHANGE. CHECK AT GUNSHOP.

HUNTING, TARGET ■ & VARMINT ■ SCOPES

Maker and Model	Magn.	Field at 100 Yds (feet)	Relative Brightness	Eye Relief (in.)	Length (in.)	Tube Diam. (in.)	W&E Adjustments	Weight (ozs.)	Price	Other Data
Unertl (cont'd.)										
■ Small Game[5]	4,6	25-17	19.4-8.4	2¼	18	¾	Ext.	16	117.00	
■ Vulture[6]	8 10	11.2 10.9	29 18½	3-4 —	15⅝ 16⅛	1	Ext.	15½	231.00	
■ Programmer 200[7]	8,10,12 14,16,18, 20,24,30,36	11.3-4	39-1.9	—	26½	1	Ext.	45	403.00	
■ BV-20[8]	20	8	4.4	4.4	17⅞	1	Ext.	21¼	287.00	
Weatherby										
Mark XXII	4	25	50	2.5-3.5	11¾	⅞	Int.	9.25	85.35	Lumiplex reticle in all models. Blue-black, non-glare finish.
Supreme 1¾-5x20	1.7-5	66.6-21.4	—	3.4	10.7	1	Int.	11	190.00	
Supreme 4x34	4	32	—	3.1	11⅛	1	Int.	9.6	190.00	
Supreme 2-7x34	2.1-6.8	59-16	—	3.4	11¼	1	Int.	10.4	240.00	
Supreme 4x44	3.9	32	—	3	12½	1	Int.	11.6	240.00	
Supreme 3-9x44	3.1-8.9	36-13	—	3.5	12.7	1	Int.	11.6	280.00	
Williams										
Twilight Crosshair	2½	32	64	3¾	11¼	1	Int.	8½	115.75	TNT models
Twilight Crosshair	4	29	64	3½	11¾	1	Int.	9½	124.75	
Twilight Crosshair	2-6	45-17	256-28	3	11½	1	Int.	11½	164.65	
Twilight Crosshair	3-9	36-13	161-18	3	12¾	1	Int.	13½	178.00	
Pistol Scopes										
Twilight 1.5x	1.5	19	177	18-25	8.2	1	Int.	6.4	96.95	
Twilight 2x	2	17.5	100	18-25	8.5	1	Int.	6.4	97.95	
Zeiss										
Diatal C 4x32	4	30	—	3.5	10.6	1	Int.	11.3	305.00	All scopes have ¼-minute click-stop adjustments. Choice of Z-Plex or fine crosshair reticles. Rubber armored objective bell, rubber eyepiece ring. Lenses have T-Star coating for highest light transmission. Imported from West Germany by Carl Zeiss, Inc.
Diatal C 6x32	6	20	—	3.5	10.6	1	Int.	11.3	340.00	
Diatal C 10x36	10	12	—	3.5	12.7	1	Int.	14.1	395.00	
Diavari C 3-9x36	3-9	36-13	—	3.5	11.2	1	Int.	15.2	540.00	

■ Signifies target and/or varmint scope. Hunting scopes in general are furnished with a choice of reticle—crosshairs, post with crosshairs, tapered or blunt post, or dot crosshairs, etc. The great majority of target and varmint scopes have medium or fine crosshairs but post or dot reticles may be ordered. W—Windage E—Elevation MOA—Minute of angle or 1" (approx.) at 100 yards, etc.

New for 1985 is Nikon's entry into the Riflescope field with a 4x (above) and 3-9x variable (below). They're world renowned optics.

Beeman Blue Ribbon Model 68R 4-12x is one of five variables offered.

Beeman SS-3 is a short (5.75"), light (8.5 oz.) 1.5-4x variable ideally suited to carbine-size rifles.

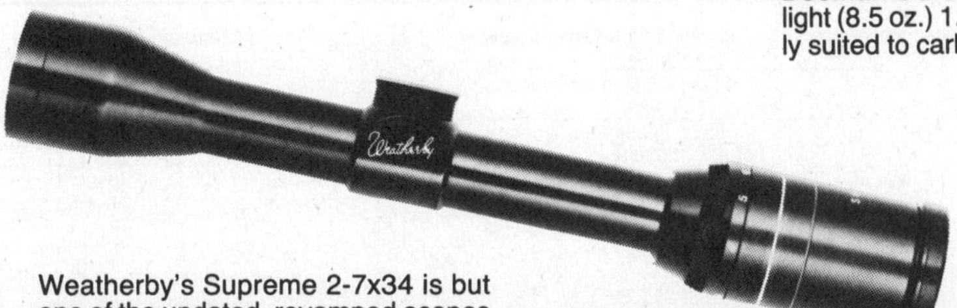

Weatherby's Supreme 2-7x34 is but one of the updated, revamped scopes in their line of six models.

SCOPE MOUNTS

Maker, Model, Type	Adjust.	Scopes	Price	Suitable for
B-Square				
Pistols				
Colt Python[1]	W&E	1″	**$ 49.95**	[1]Clamp-on, blue finish. Stainless finish **$59.95.** [2]For Bushnell Phantom only. [3]Blue finish; stainless finish **$59.95.** [4]For solid rib—requires drilling & tapping. [5]Clamp-on, blue; stainless finish **$49.95.** [6]Clamp-on, for Bushnell Phantom only, blue; stainless finish **$49.95.** [7]Requires drilling & tapping. [8]No gunsmithing, no sight removal; blue; stainless finish **$59.95.** [9]Clamp-on. [10]Also M600, 660. Partial listing of mounts shown here. Contact B-Square for more data. B-Square also has mounts for Aimpoint scopes to fit many popular military rifles, shotguns and handguns. Write them for a complete listing.
Dan Wesson Clamp-On[3]	W&E	1″	**49.95**	
Dan Wesson Integral[4]	W&E	1″	**39.95**	
Hi-Standard Victor	W&E	1″	**49.95**	
Ruger 22 Auto Mono-Mount[6]	No	1″	**39.95**	
Ruger Single-Six[7]	No	1″	**39.95**	
T-C Contender	W&E	1″	**49.95**	
Rifles				
Daisy 717/722 Champion[2]	No	1″	**19.95**	
Mini-14[8]	W&E	1″	**49.95**	
Mini-14[9]	W&E	1″	**49.95**	
M-94 Side Mount	W&E	1″	**49.95**	
Ruger 77[10]	W&E	1″	**49.95**	
SMLE Side Mount	W only	1″	**49.95**	
T-C Single-Shot Rifle	W&E	1″	**49.95**	
Rem. Model Seven[11]	W&E	1″	**39.95**	
Military				
M1-A	W&E	1″	**59.95**	
AR-15/16	W&E	1″	**49.95**	
FN-LAR	W only	1″	**149.95**	
HK-91/93	W only	1″	**69.95**	
Shotguns				
Rem. 870/1100	W&E	1″	**59.95**	
S&W 1000P	W&E	1″	**59.95**	
Beeman				
Double Adjustable	W&E	1″	**24.98**	All grooved receivers and scope bases on all known air rifles and 22-cal. rimfire rifles (½″ to ⅝″—6mm to 15mm). [1]Centerfire rifles. Scope detaches easily, returns to zero.[2] Designed specifically for Krico rifles.
Deluxe Ring Mounts	No	1″	**21.58**	
Professional Mounts	W&E	1″	**82.50**	
Professional Pivot[1]	W	1″	**129.50**	
Buehler[2]	W	1″	**79.00**	
Buehler				
One Piece (T)[1]	W only	1″ split rings, 3 heights. 1″ split rings, 3 heights, engraved 26mm, 30mm, 2 heights	**Complete—62.50** **Rings only—87.00** **Rings only—45.50**	[1]Most popular models. 30mm rings **$55.** [2]Most popular models. [3]Most popular models. [4]Sako dovetail receivers. [5]15 models. [6]No drilling & tapping. [7]Aircraft alloy, dyed blue or to match stainless; for Colt Diamondback, Python, Trooper, Ruger Blackhawk, Single-Six, Security-Six, S&W K-frame, Dan Wesson.
One Piece Micro Dial (T)[2]	W&E	1″ split rings.	**Complete—77.25**	
Two Piece (T)[3]	W only	1″ split rings.	**Complete—62.50**	
Two Piece Dovetail (T)[4]	W only	1″ split rings.	**Complete—77.25**	
One Piece Pistol (T)[5]	W only	1″ split rings.	**Complete—62.50**	
One Piece Pistol Stainless (T)[1]	W only	1″ split rings. Stainless steel	**Complete—81.75**	
One Piece Ruger Mini 14 (T)[6]	W only	1″ split rings.	**Complete—77.25**	
One Piece Pistol Model 83[6,7]	W only	1″ split rings.	**62.50**	
One Piece Pistol Model 83 Stainless[6,7]	W only	1″ split rings.	**81.75**	
Burris				
Supreme One Piece (T)[1]	W only	1″ split rings, 3 heights.	**1 piece-base—20.95**	[1]Most popular rifles. Universal, rings, mounts fit Burris. Universal, Redfield, Leupold and Browning bases. Comparable prices. [2]Browning Standard 22 Auto rifle. [3]Most popular rifles. [4]Grooved receivers. [5]Universal dovetail; accept Burris, Universal, Redfield, Leupold rings. For Dan Wesson, S&W, Virginian, Ruger Blackhawk, Win. 94. [6]Medium standard front, extension rear, per pair. Low standard front, extension rear, per pair. Selected rings and bases available with matte Safari finish.
Trumount Two Piece (T)	W only	1″ split rings, 3 heights.	**2 piece base—18.95**	
Browning Auto Mount[2]	No	¾″, 1″ split rings.	**20.95**	
Sight-Thru Mount[3]	No	1″ Split rings.	**17.95**	
Rings Mounts[4]	No	¾″, 1″ split rings.	**1″ rings—16.95**	
L.E.R. Mount Bases[5]	No	1″ split rings.	**18.95**	
Extension Rings[6]	No	1″ scopes.	**31.95**	
Bushnell				
Detachable (T) mounts only[1]	W only	1″ split rings, uses Weaver base.	**Rings—15.95**	[1]Most popular rifles. Includes windage adj. [2]V-block bottoms lock to chrome-moly studs seated into two 6-48 holes. Rem. XP-100. [3]Heavy loads in Colt, S&W, Ruger revolvers, Ruger Hawkeye. [4]M94 Win., center dovetail.
22 mount	No	1″ only.	**Rings— 7.95**	
All Purpose[2]	No	Phantom.	**19.95**	
Rigid[3]	No	Phantom.	**19.95**	
94 Win.[4]	No	Phantom.	**19.95**	
Clearview				
Universal Rings (T)[1]	No	1″ split rings.	**19.95**	[1]All popular rifles including Sav. 99. Uses Weaver bases. [2]Allows use of open sights. [3]For 22 rimfire rifles, with grooved receivers or bases. [4]Fits 13 models. Broadest view area of the type. [5]Side mount for both M94 and M94-375 Big Bore.
Mod 101, & 336[2]	No	1″ split rings.	**19.95**	
Broad-View[4]	No	1″	**19.95**	
Model 22[3]	No	¾″, ⅞″, 1″	**11.95**	
94 Winchester [5]	No	1″	**19.95**	
Conetrol				
Huntur[1]	W only	1″, 26mm, 26.5mm solid or split rings, 3 heights.	**48.93**	[1]All popular rifles, including metric-drilled foreign guns. Price shown for base, two rings. Matte finish. [2]Gunnur grade has mirror-finished rings, satin-finish base. Price shown for base, two rings. [3]Custum grade has mirror-finished rings and mirror-finished, contoured base. Price shown for base, 2 rings. [4]Win. 94, Krag, older split-bridge Mannlicher-Schoenauer, Mini-14, M-1 Garand, etc. Prices same as above. [5]For all popular guns with integral mounting provision, including Sako, BSA, Ithacagun, Ruger, H&K and many others. Also for grooved-receiver rimfires and air rifles. Prices same as above. [6]For XP-100, T/C Contender, Colt SAA, Ruger Blackhawk, S&W. [7]Sculptured 2-piece bases as found on fine custom rifles. Price shown is for base alone. Also available unfinished—**$49.98.** [8]Replaces Ruger rib, positions scope farther back. [9]Horizontally split screw connections; 2 heights.
Gunnur[2]	W only	1″, 26mm, 26.5mm solid or split rings, 3 heights.	**59.91**	
Custum[3]	W only	1″, 26mm, 26.5mm solid or split rings, 3 heights.	**74.91**	
One Piece Side Mount Base[4]	W only	1″, 26mm, 26.5mm solid or split rings, 3 heights.		
Daptar Bases[5]	W only	1″, 26mm, 26.5mm solid or split rings, 3 heights.		
Pistol Bases, 2 or 3-ring[6]	W only	1″ scopes.		
Fluted Bases[7]	W only	Standard Conetrol rings	**74.97**	
Ruger No. 1 Base[8]	No	1″, 26mm, 26.5mm solid or split rings.	**NA**	
30mm Rings[9]	—	30mm	**74.94**	

CAUTION: PRICES CHANGE. CHECK AT GUNSHOP.

SCOPE MOUNTS

Maker, Model, Type	Adjust.	Scopes	Price	Suitable for
EAW				
Quick Detachable Top Mount	W&E	1"/26mm	150.00	Most popular rifles. Elevation adjusted with variable-height sub-bases for rear ring. Imported by Paul Jaeger, Inc., Kahles of America.
	W&E	1"/26mm with front extension ring.	155.00	
	W&E	30mm	160.00	
	W&E	30mm with front extension ring.	165.00	
Griffin & Howe				
Standard Double Lever (S).	No	1" or 26mm split rings.	145.00	All popular models (Garand $175; Win. 94 $175). All rings $50. Top ejection $75.
Holden				
Wide Ironsighter®	No	1" Split rings.	20.95	[1]Most popular rifles including Ruger Mini-14, H&R M700, and muzzleloaders. Rings have oval holes to permit use of iron sights. [2]For 1" dia. scopes. [3]For 3/4" or 7/8" dia. scopes. [4]For 1" dia. extended eye relief scopes. [5]702—Browning A-Bolt; 709—Marlin 39A. [6]732—Ruger 77/22 R&RS, No. 1 Ranch Rifle; 777 fits Ruger 77R, RS. Both 732, 777 fit Ruger integral bases.
Ironsighter Center Fire[1]	No	1" Split rings.	20.95	
Ironsighter S-94	No	1" split rings	25.95	
Ironsighter 22 cal. rimfire				
Model #500[2]	No	1" Split rings.	11.49	
Model #600[3]	No	7/8" Split rings also fits 3/4".	11.49	
Series #700[5]	No	1", split rings	20.95	
Model 732, 777[6]	No	1", split rings	49.95	
Ironsighter Handguns[4]	No	1" Split rings.	22.95	
Jaeger				
QD, with windage (S)	W only	1", 3 heights.	190.00	All popular models. From Paul Jaeger, Inc.
Kimber				
Standard[1]	No	1", split rings	48.90	[1]High rings; low rings—**$45.00**; both only for Kimber rifles. [2]For Kimber rifles only. Also avail. for Mauser (FN,98) Rem. 700, 721, 722, 725, Win. M70, Mark X. [3]Vertically split rings; for Kimber and other popular CF rifles.
Double Lever[2]	No	1", split rings	69.00	
Non-Detachable[3]	No	1", split rings	48.00	
Kris Mounts				
Side-Saddle[1]	No	1", 26mm split rings.	11.98	[1]One-piece mount for Win. 94. [2]Most popular rifles and Ruger. [3]Blackhawk revolver. Mounts have oval hole to permit use of iron sights.
Two Piece (T)[2]	No	1", 26mm split rings.	7.98	
One Piece (T)[3]	No	1", 26mm split rings.	11.98	
Kwik-Site				
KS-See-Thru[1]	No	1"	19.95	[1]Most rifles. Allows use of iron sights. [2]22-cal. rifles with grooved receivers. Allows use of iron sights. [3]Model 94, 94 Big Bore. No drilling or tapping. [4]Most rifles. One-piece solid construction. Use on Weaver bases. 32mm obj. lens or larger. [5]Non-see-through model; for grooved receivers.
KS-22 See-Thru[2]	No	1"'	17.95	
KS-W94[3]	Yes	1"	39.95	
KSM Bench Rest[4]	No	1"	27.95	
KS-WEV	No	1"	19.95	
KS-WEV-HIGH	No	1"	19.95	
KS-T22 1"[5]	No	1"	17.95	
Leatherwood				
M-1A, M-14	W only	ART II, ART/MPC (Weaver rings)	75.00	[1]Popular bolt actions. [2]With M-16 adaptor. [3]Adaptor base for H&K rail mounts.
AR-15, M-16	No	As above	17.95	
FN-FAL	No	As above	175.00	
SSG	No	As above	50.00	
One-piece Bridge[1]	No	As above	9.95	
Night Vision Adaptor[2]	No	Night vision scopes	37.50	
H&K Adaptor[3]	No	ART II, ART/MPC (Weaver rings)	59.95	
Leupold				
STD Bases (T)[1]	W only	One piece base (dovetail front, windage rear)	Base—19.70	[1]Most popular rifles. Also available in 2-piece version, same price. [2]Ruger revolvers, Thompson/Center Contender, S&W K&N Frame revolvers and Colt .45 "Gold Cup" N.M. Available with silver or blue finish. [3]Reversible extended front; regular rear rings, in two heights.
STD Handgun mounts[2] Base and two rings[2]	No	1"	50.70	
STD Rings		1", 3 ring heights interchangeable with other mounts of similar design.	1" rings—28.40	
Extension-Ring Sets[3]		1"	39.30	
Marlin				
One Piece QD (T)	No	1" split rings.	12.10	Most Marlin and Glenfield lever actions.
Millett				
Black Onyx Smooth		1" Low, medium, high	26.95	Rem. 40X, 700, 722, 725, Ruger 77 (round top) Weatherby, etc. FN Mauser, FN Brownings, Colt 57, Interarms MkX, Parker-Hale, Sako (round receiver). many others.
Chaparral Engraved		Engraved	39.95	
Universal Two Piece Bases				
700 Series	W only	Two-piece bases	20.95	
FN Series	W only	Two-piece bases	20.95	
Numrich				
Side Mount	No	1" split rings.	7.95	M-1 carbine.
Pachmayr				
Lo-Swing (S)[1]	Yes	3/4", 7/8", 1", 26mm solid or split loops.	65.00	[1]All popular rifles, including Ruger Mini-14, Browning BBR, Scope swings aside for instant use of iron sights. [2]Adjustable base. Win. 70, 88; Rem. 721, 722, 725, 740, 760; Mar. 336; Sav. 99, New Model for Colt Sauer.
Lo-Swing (T)[2]	Yes	3/4", 7/8", 1", 26mm split rings.	65.00	
Redfield				
JR-SR(T)[1]	W only	3/4", 1", 26mm.	JR—19.80-26.95 SR—23.95-51.85	[1]Low, med. & high, split rings. Reversible extension front rings for 1". 2-piece bases for Sako. Colt Sauer bases $63.90. [2]Split rings for grooved 22's. See-thru mounts $23.30. [3]Used with MP scopes for: S&W K or N frame. XP-100, Colt J or I frame. T/C Contender, Colt autos, black powder rifles.
Ring (T)[2]	No	3/4" and 1".		
Double Dovetail MP[3]	No	1", split rings.	52.90	
S&K				
Insta-Mount (T) base only[1]	W only	Use S&K rings only.	18.00-81.00	[1]1903, A3, M1 Carbine, Lee Enfield #1, MK. III, #4, #5, M1917, M98 Mauser, FN Auto, AR-15, AR-180, M-14, M-1, Ger. K-43, Mini-14, M1-A, Krag, AKM, AK-47. [2]Most popular rifles already drilled and tapped. For "see through underneath" risers, add $10.00.
Conventional rings and bases[2]	W only	1" split rings.	40.00	
Sako				
QD Dovetail	W only	1" only.	96.95	Sako, or any rifle using Sako action, 3 heights available, Stoeger, importer.

CAUTION: PRICES CHANGE. CHECK AT GUNSHOP.

SCOPE MOUNTS

Maker, Model, Type	Adjust.	Scopes	Price	Suitable for
Simmons				
1401	No	1″	9.00	Weaver-type bases. #1401 (low) also in high style (#1403). #1406, 1408 for grooved receiver 22s. Bases avail. for most popular rifles; one- and two-piece styles. Most popular rifles; 1-piece bridge mount. Ring sets—$39.00. [1]For 22 RF rifles.
1406	No	1″	9.00	
1408	No	1″	20.00	
All Steel 1800 Series	No	1″, 26mm	31.50	
All Steel Tip-Off[1]	No	1″	39.00	
Tasco				
791 and 793 series[1]	No	1″, regular or high.	9.95	[1]Many popular rifles. [2]For 22s with grooved receivers. [3]Most popular rifles. [4]Most popular rifles. [5]"Quick Peep" 1″ ring mount; fits all 22-cal. rifles with grooved receivers. [6]For Ruger Mini-14; also in brushed aluminum. [7]Side mount for Win. 94. [8]Side mount rings and base for Win. 94 in 30-30, 375 Win.
797[2]	No	Split rings.	9.95	
798 Quick Peep[3]	No	1″ only.	9.95	
799[5]	No	1″ only	9.95	
885 BK[8]	No	1″ only	23.95	
895[7]	No	1″ only	5.95	
896[6]	No	1″ only	39.95	
800L Series (with base)[4]	No	1″ only. Rings and base.	13.95	
Thompson/Center				
Contender 9746[1]	No	T/C Lobo	8.75	[1]All Contenders except vent. rib. [2]T/C rail mount scopes; all Contenders except vent. rib. [3]All S&W K and Combat Masterpiece, Hi-Way Patrolman, Outdoorsman, 22 Jet, 45 Target 1955. Requires drilling, tapping. [4]Blackhawk, Super Blackhawk, Super Single-Six. Requires drilling, tapping. [5]45 or 50 cal.; replaces rear sight. [6]Rail mount scopes; 54-cal. Hawken, 50, 54, 56-cal. Renegade. Replaces rear sight. [7]Cherokee 32 or 45 cal., Seneca 36 or 45 cal. Replaces rear sight.
Contender 9741[2]	No	2½, 4 RP	8.75	
Contender 7410	No	Bushnell Phantom 1.3, 2.5x	8.75	
S&W 9747[3]	No	Lobo or RP	8.75	
Ruger 9748[4]	No	Lobo or RP	8.75	
Hawken 9749[5]	No	Lobo or RP	8.75	
Hawken/Renegade 9754[6]	No	Lobo or RP	8.75	
Cherokee/Seneca[7]	No	Lobo or RP	8.75	
Unertl				
Posa (T)[1]	Yes	¾″, 1″ scopes.	Per set 70.00	[1]Unertl target or varmint scopes. [2]Any with regular dovetail scope bases.
¼ Click (T)[2]	Yes	¾″, 1″ target scopes.	Per set 66.00	
Weaver				
Detachable Mount (T & S)[1]	No	¾″, ⅞″, 1″ 26mm	20.00	[1]Nearly all modern rifles. Extension rings, 1″ $23.45. [2]Most modern big bore rifles. [3]22s with grooved receivers. [4]Same. Adapter for Lee Enfield—$9.65. [5]⅞″—$13.45. 1″ See-Thru extension—$23.45. [6]Colt Officer's Model, Python, Ruger B'hawk, Super B'hawk, Security Six, 22 Autos, Mini-14, Ruger Redhawk, S&W N frames. No drilling or tapping. Also in stainless steel—$58.95.
Pivot Mount (T)[2]	No	1″	25.75	
Tip-Off (T)[3]	No	¾″, ⅞″.	11.15	
Tip-Off (T)[4]	No	1″, two-piece.	20.00	
See-Thru Mount[5]	No	1″ Split rings and ⅞″-tip-off. Fits all top mounts.	20.00	
Mount Base System[6]	No	1″	44.95	
Williams				
Offset (S)[1]	No	⅞″, 1″, 26mm solid, split or extension rings.	52.95	[1]Most rifles, Br. S.M.L.E. (round rec) $3.85 extra. [2]Same. [3]Most rifles including Win. 94 Big Bore. [4]Most rifles. [5]Many modern rifles. [6]Most popular rifles.
QC (T)[2]	No	Same.	41.60	
QC (S)[3]	No	Same.	41.60	
Low Sight-Thru[4]	No	1″, ⅞″, sleeves $1.80.	17.75	
Sight-Thru[5]	No	1″, ⅞″, sleeves $1.80.	17.75	
Streamline[6]	No	1″ (bases form rings).	18.70	

(S)—Side Mount (T)Top Mount 22mm—.866″ 25.4mm = 1″1.024″ 26.5mm = 1.045″ 30mm = 1.81″

B-Square offers an extensive line of scope mounts, to include those for Aimpoint sights (above, on Ruger's 22 pistol), and for standard scopes as on the Ruger Mini-14 (below).

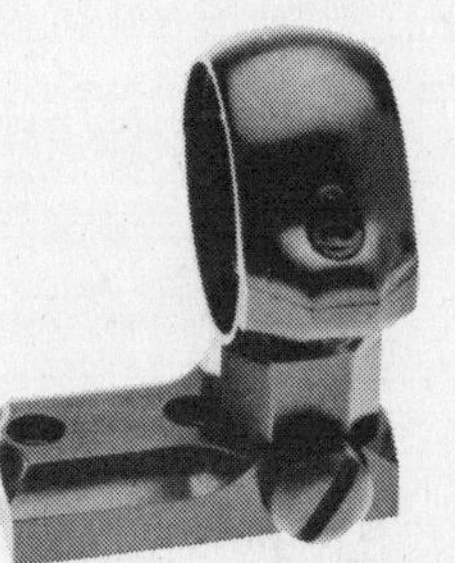

In addition to metallic sights, Millett offers their smooth Black Onyx rings with 700 Series bases (above), and Chaparral Engraved rings and sculptured bases (below).

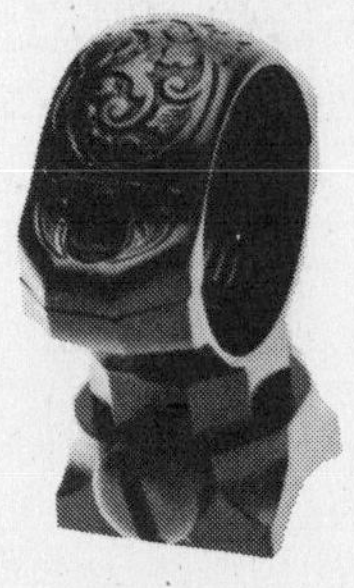

CAUTION: PRICES CHANGE. CHECK AT GUNSHOP.

SPOTTING SCOPES

APOLLO 20 X 50 BOBCAT—50mm objective lens. Field of view at 1000 yds. is about 100 ft. Length 9.4", weight 17.5 oz. Tripod socket.
Price: $154.95
Compact tripod, about $20.00

BAUSCH & LOMB DISCOVERER—15X to 60X zoom, 60mm objective. Constant focus throughout range. Field at 1000 yds. 40 ft (60X), 156 ft. (15X). Comes with lens caps. Length 17½", wgt. 48½ oz.
Price: $449.95

BUSHNELL SPACEMASTER—60MM objective. Field at 1000 yds., 158′ to 37′. Relative brightness, 5.76. Wgt., 36 oz. Length closed, 11⅝". prism focusing, without eyepiece.
Price: $269.95
15X, 20X, 40X and 60X eyepieces, each $49.95
22X wide angle eyepiece $59.95

BUSHNELL SPACEMASTER 45°—Same as above except: Wgt., 43 oz., length closed 13". Eyepiece at 45°, without eyepiece.
Price: $339.95

BUSHNELL ZOOM SPACEMASTER—15X-45X zoom. 60mm objective. Field at 1000 yards 130′-65′. Relative brightness 9-1.7. Wgt. 36 oz., length 11⅝". Shooter's Stand tripod, carrying case.
Price: $439.95

BUSHNELL SENTRY®—50mm objective. Field at 1000 yards 120′-45′. Relative brightness 6.25. Wgt., 25½ oz., length 12⅝", without eyepiece.
Price: $139.95
20X, 32X and 48X eyepieces, each $49.95

BUSHNELL ZOOM SPOTTER—40mm objective. 9X-30X var. power.
Price: $99.95

BUSHNELL COMPETITOR—40mm objective. Prismatic. Field at 1000 yards 140′. Minimum focus 33′. Length 9.5", weight 14.5 oz.
Price: With tripod $99.95

BUSHNELL TROPHY—12X-36X zoom. Rubber armored, prismatic. 50mm objective. Field at 1000 yards 150′ to 80′. Minimum focus 20′. Length with caps 13⅝", weight 38 oz.
Price: With tripod and carrying case $379.95
With interchangeable eyepieces—20x, 32x, 48x $259.95

BUSHNELL—10x30mm hand telescope. Field 183 ft. at 1000 yards. Weight 11 ozs.; 10" long. Tripod mount
Price: $39.95

DICKSON 270—20x to 60x variable, 60mm objective, achromatic coated objective lens, complete with metal table tripod with 5 vertical and horizontal adjustments. Turret type, 20x, 30x, 40x 60x
Price: $249.95

DICKSON 274A—20x to 60x variable zoom. 60mm achromatic coated objective lens, complete with adjustable metal table tripod.
Price: $150.00

DICKSON 274B—As above but with addition of 4 × 16 Finder Scope.
Price: $161.95

KOWA TS-1-45—Off-set-type. 60mm objective, 25X, fixed and zoom interchangeable eyepieces; field at 1000 yds. 93′; relative brightness 5.8; length 16.5"; wgt. 47.8 oz. Lens shade and caps. Straight-type also available; similar specs **($284.98).**
Price: $349.95
Price: 25X eyepiece $49.95
Price: 20X eyepiece (wide angle) $64.95
Price: 15X eyepiece $59.95
Price: 105X eyepiece $69.95

KOWA TSN-1-45°—Off-set-type. 77mm objective, 25X, fixed and zoom eyepieces; field at 1000 yds. 94′; relative brightness 9.6; length 15.4"; wgt. 48.8 oz. Lens shade and caps. Straight-type also available with similar specs and prices.
Price: $499.95
Price: 20X-60X zoom eyepiece $124.95
Price: 20X eyepiece (wide angle) $99.95
Price: 25X, 40X eyepiece $74.95

KOWA TS-3—Straight-type. 50mm objective, 20X, standard size, fixed and zoom eyepieces; field at 1000 yds. 120′; relative brightness 6.3; length 13.4"; wgt. 29.4 oz. Lens shade and caps.
Price: $179.95
Price: 20X-40X zoom eyepiece $119.95
Price: 20X eyepiece $49.95
Price: 16X eyepiece (wide angle) $64.95
Price: 12X eyepiece $59.95
Price: 32X, 48X eyepiece $54.95
Price: 84X eyepiece $69.95

KOWA TS-4-45—Off-set-type. 50mm objective, 20X, compact size (measures 12.6", wgt. 37 oz.). Other specs are same as Model TS-3. Uses TS-3 eyepieces.
Price: $279.95

KOWA TS-8—Straight-type. 50mm objective, 20X, compact model; fixed power eyepieces; field at 1000 yds. 157′; relative brightness 6.3; length 9.25"; wgt. 23.3 oz. Lens caps.
Price: $139.95
Price: 10X, 15X eyepieces, each $34.95

KOWA TS-9C—Straight-type. 50mm objective, 20X compact model; fixed power eyepieces; objective focusing down to 17 ft.; field at 1000 yds. 157′; relative brightness 6.3; length 9.65"; wgt. 22.9 oz. Lens caps.
Price: $115.95
Price: 15X, 20X eyepieces, each $24.95
Price: As above, rubber armored (TS-9R) $129.95

OPTEX MODEL 420—15x-60x-60 Zoom; 18" overall; weighs 4 lbs. with folding tripod (included). From Southern Precision Instrument
Price: $135.00

Optex Model 420

OPTEX MODEL 421—15x-45x-50 Zoom; 18" over-all; weighs 4 lbs. with folding tripod (included). From Southern Precision Instrument
Price: $110.00

OPTEX MODEL 422—8x-25x-30 Zoom. Armour coated; 18" over-all; weighs 3 lbs. with tripod (included). From Southern Precision Instrument
Price: $100.00

OPTEX MODEL 423—Same as Model 422 except 12x-40x-40
Price: $120.00

REDFIELD 30x SPOTTER—60mm objective, 30x. Field of view 9.5 ft. at 100 yds. Uses catadioptric lens system. Length over-all is 7.5", weight is 11.5 oz. Eye relief 0.5".
Price: $411.05

SIMMONS 1210—50mm objective, 25x standard, 16, 20, 40, 48, 16-36x zoom eyepieces available. Field at 1000 yds. 22 ft. Length 12.2", weight 32 oz. Comes with tripod, 3x finder scope with crosshair.
Price: About $183.50
Price: Fixed eyepieces $56.00
Price: Zoom eyepiece $154.00

SIMMONS 1215—50mm objective, 25x standard, 16, 20, 40, 48, 16-36x zoom eyepieces available. Field at 1000 yds. 22 ft. Length 12.2", weight 48 oz. Comes with tripod, 3x finder scope with crosshair.
Price: About $289.00
Price: Fixed eyepieces $56.00
Price: Zoom eyepiece $154.00

SIMMONS 1220—60mm objective, 25x standard, 16, 20, 40, 48, 16-36x zoom eyepieces available. Field at 1000 yds. 22 ft. Length 13.8", weight 44 oz. with tripod (included). Has 3x finder scope with crosshairs.
Price: About $344.00
Price: Fixed eyepieces $56.00
Price: Zoom eyepiece $154.00

SWAROVSKI HABICHT HAWK 30x75S TELESCOPE—75mm objective, 30X. Field at 1,000 yds. 90ft. Minimum, focusing distance 90 ft. Length: closed 13 in., extended 20½". Weight: 47 oz. Precise recognition of smallest details even at dusk. Leather or rubber covered, with caps and carrying case.
Price: $895.00
Same as above with short range supplement. Minimum focusing distance 24 to 30 ft. $935.00

SWAROVSKI 25-40X75 TELESCOPE—75mm objective, variable power from 25x to 40x with a field of 98 ft. (25x) and 72 ft. (40x). Minimum focusing distance 66 ft. (26 ft. with close focus model). Length closed is 11", extended 15.5"; weight 46 oz. Rubber covered.
Price: Standard $880.00
Price: Close focus model 910.00

SWIFT TELEMASTER M841—60mm objective. 15X to 60X variable power. Field at 1000 yards 160 feet (15X) to 40 feet (60X). Wgt. 3.4 lbs. 17.6" over-all.
Price: $399.95
Tripod for above $79.95
Photo adapter $16.00
Case for above $57.00

SWIFT M844A COMMANDO PRISMATIC SPOTTING SCOPE/ TELEPHOTO LENS, MK.II—60mm objective. Comes with 20X eyepiece; 15X, 30X, 40X, 50X, 60X available. Built-in sunshade. Field at 1000 yds. with 20X, 120 ft. Length 13.7", wgt. 2.1 lbs.

Price: **$260.00**

SWIFT M847 SCANNER—50mm objective. Comes with 25x eyepiece; 20x, 30x, 35x eyepieces available. Field of view at 1000 yds. is 112 ft. (25x). Length 13.6", weight 23 oz.

Price: **$139.50**
Each additional eyepiece **$27.50**
Tubular case **$25.00**
Tripod **$79.95**

SWIFT M700 SCOUT—9X-30X, 30mm spotting scope. Length 15½", weighs 2.1 lbs. Field of 204 ft. (9X), 60 ft. (30X).

Price: **$87.00**

TASCO 25T/25P RUBBER COVERED SPOTTING SCOPE—60mm objective. 25X. Field at 1000 yds. 94 ft. Prismatic. With Tasco 25P deluxe tripod, olive green to match rubber covering. Weight 38.3 oz. Length 11½".

Price: **$499.95**

TASCO 34TZ RUBBER COVERED—50mm objective. 18-36X zoom. Comes with tripod and built-in tripod adapter. Weight 29.9 oz., length 13¾".

Price: **$239.95**

UNERTL "FORTY-FIVE"—54mm objective. 20X (single fixed power). Field at 100 yds. 10'10"; eye relief 1"; focusing range infinity to 33 ft. Wgt. about 32 oz.; over-all length 15¾". With lens covers.

Price: With multi-layer lens coating **$295.00**
Price: With mono-layer magnesium coating **$225.00**

UNERTL RIGHT ANGLE—63.5mm objective, 24X. Field at 100 yds., 7 ft. Relative brightness, 6.96. Eye relief, ½". Wgt., 41 oz. Length closed, 19". Push-pull and screw-focus eyepiece. 16X and 32X eyepieces **$38.00** each.

Price: **$265.00**

Swift 847 Scanner

Swift 844A Commando

Tasco Model 25TPC

Tasco Model 39T

TASCO 19T ZOOM SPOTTING SCOPE—40mm objective, 15X and 45X. Wgt. 3½ lbs. With tripod and 45° swivel turret. Panhead lever, built-in tripod adaptor.

Price: **$119.95**
Price: Model 18E (60mm, 20X and 60X) **$179.95**
Price: Model 20 (50mm, 15X and 45X) **$89.95**

TASCO 39T COMPACT SPOTTING SCOPE—50mm objective, 20X. With BAK-4 prism. Wgt. 3 lbs. With tripod.

Price: **$179.95**

TASCO 33T ZOOM SQUARE SPOTTING SCOPE—60mm objective. Prismatic. 20X to 45X. Field at 1000 yds. 104 ft. (20X) to 70 ft. (45X). With tripod and 45° angle swivel turret. Weight 52 oz. Length 15".

Price: **$299.95**

TASCO 34T RUBBER COVERED SPOTTING SCOPE—50mm objective. 25X. Field at 1000 yds. 136 ft. With tripod and built-in tripod adapter. Weight 29.9 oz. Length 13¾".

Price: **$199.95**

TASCO 21T SPOTTING SCOPE—40mm objective. 20X. Field at 1000 yds. 136 ft. With Tasco 8P tripod. Weight 18.2 oz. Length 12⅜".

Price: **$109.95**

UNERTL STRAIGHT PRISMATIC—Same as Unertl Right Angle except: straight eyepiece and wgt. of 40 oz.

Price: **$225.00**

UNERTL 20X STRAIGHT PRISMATIC—54mm objective. 20X. Field at 100 yds., 8.5 ft. Relative brightness, 6.1. Eye relief, ½". Wgt. 36 oz. Length closed, 13½". Complete with lens covers.

Price: **$190.00**

UNERTL TEAM SCOPE—100mm objective. 15X, 24X, 32X eyepieces. Field at 100 yds. 13 to 7.5 ft. Relative brightness, 39.06 to 9.79. Eye relief, 2" to 1½". Weight 13 lbs. 29⅞" overall. Metal tripod, yoke and wood carrying case furnished (total weight, 67 lbs.)

Price: **$975.00**

WEATHERBY—60mm objective, 20X-60X zoom

Price: Scope only **$323.95**
Price: Scope and tripod **$379.95**
Price: Tripod for above **$69.95**

CAUTION: PRICES CHANGE. CHECK AT GUNSHOP.

PERIODICAL PUBLICATIONS

Airgun World
10 Sheet St., Windsor, Berks., SL4 1BG, England.£11.50 for 12 issues. Monthly magazine catering exclusively to the airgun enthusiast.

Alaska Magazine
Alaska Northwest Pub. Co., Box 4-EEE, Anchorage, AK 99509. $21.00 yr. Hunting, fishing and Life on the Last Frontier articles of Alaska and western Canada.

American Field†
222 W. Adams St., Chicago, IL. 60606. $18.00 yr. Field dogs and trials, occasional gun and hunting articles.

American Firearms Industry
Nat'l. Assn. of Federally Licensed Firearms Dealers, 2801 E. Oakland Park Blvd., Ft. Lauderdale, FL 33306. $20 yr. For firearms dealers & distributors.

American Handgunner*
591 Camino de la Reina, San Diego, CA 92108. $11.95 yr. Articles for handgun enthusiasts, collectors and hunters.

American Hunter (M)
Natl. Rifle Assn., 1600 Rhode Island Ave. N.W., Washington, DC 20036. $15.00 yr. Wide scope of hunting articles.

American Rifleman (M)
National Rifle Assn., 1600 Rhode Island Ave., N.W., Wash., DC 20036. $15.00 yr. Firearms articles of all kinds.

The American Shotgunner
P.O. Box 3351, Reno, NV 89505. $24.00 yr. Official publ. of the American Assn. of Shotgunning. Shooting, reloading, hunting, investment collecting, new used gun classifieds.

American Survival Guide
McMullen Publishing, Inc., 2145 West La Palma Ave., Anaheim, CA 92801. 12 issues $20.98.

American West*
Amer. West Publ. Co., 3033 No. Campbell, Tucson, AZ 85719. $15.00 yr.

AMI
New Fashion Media, Avenue Louise 60, B1050 Brussels, Belgium. Belg. Franc 325, 11 issues. Arms, shooting militaria information; French text.

Angler & Hunter
Ontario's Wildlife Magazine, P.O. Box 1541, Peterborough, Ont. K9J 7H7, Canada.

Antique Arms and Militaria
Gauntlet Publications Ltd., P.O. Box 389, Windsor, Berkshire SL46RG, England

Arms Collecting (Q)
Museum Restoration Service P.O. Drawer 390, Bloomfield, Ont., Canada K0K IG0 and P.O. Box 70, Alexandria Bay, NY 13607. $10.00 yr. $27.50 3 yrs.

Austrialian Shooters' Journal
Sporting Shooter's Assn. of Australia, Box 1064 G.P.O., Adelaide, SA 5001, Australia. $25.00 yr. locally; $30.00 yr. overseas surface mail only. Hunting and shooting articles.

The Backwoodsman Magazine
Rte. 8, Box 579, Livingston, TX 77351. $11.00 for 6 issues pr. yr.; sample copy $2. Subject incl. muzzle-loading, woodslore, trapping, homesteading, et al.

The Black Powder Report
The Buckskin Press, Inc., P.O. Box 789, Big Timber, MT 59011. $18.00 yr. Shooting, hunting, gun-building and restoration articles; entire section for BP cartridge rifles.

The Blade Magazine*
P.O. Box 22007, Chattanooga, TN 37422. $15.99 yr. Add $13 f. foreign subscription. A magazine for all enthusiasts of the edged blade.

Combat Handguns*
Harris Publications, Inc., 1115 Broadway, New York, NY 10010. Single copy $2.75 U.S.A.; $2.95 Canada.

Competitor USA
SAM Publications Inc., P.O. Box 74515, Dallas, TX 75374. $12.00 yr. Magazine of handgun shooting and competition.

Deer Unlimited*
P.O. Box 509, Clemson, SC 29631. $12.00 yr.

Deutsches Waffen Journal
Journal-Verlag Schwend GmbH, Postfach 100340, D7170 Schwäbisch Hall, Germany. DM76.00 yr. plus DM16.80 for postage. Antique and modern arms. German text.

Ducks Unlimited, Inc. (M)
1 Waterfowl Way at Gilmer, Long Grove, IL 60047

FFL Business News
Nat'l. Assn. of Federally Licensed Firearms Dealers, 2801 E. Oakland Pk. Blvd., Ft. Lauderdale, FL 33306. $6.00 yr. For firearms dealers & distributors.

The Field†
The Harmsworth Press Ltd., Carmelite House, London EC4Y OJA, England. $88.00 yr. Hunting and shooting articles, and all country sports.

Field & Stream
CBS Magazines, 1515 Broadway, New York, NY 10036. $11.94 yr. Articles on firearms plus hunting and fishing.

Fur-Fish-Game
A.R. Harding Pub. Co., 2878 E. Main St., Columbus, OH 43209. $10.00 yr. "Gun Rack" column by Don Zutz.

Gray's Sporting Journal
Gray's Sporting Journal Co., 205 Willow St., So. Hamilton, MA 01982. $24.95 per yr. f. 4 consecutive issues. Hunting and fishing journals.

Gun Owner(Q)
Gun Owners Inc., 1025 Front St., Suite 300, Sacramento, CA 95814. With membership $20 yr.; single copy $3. An outdoors magazine for sportsmen everywhere.

The Gun Report
World Wide Gun Report, Inc., Box 111, Aledo, IL 61231. $25.00 yr. For the antique gun collector.

The Gunrunner
Div. of Kexco Publ. Co. Ltd., Box 565, Lethbridge, Alb., Canada T1J 3Z4. $15.00 yr. Monthly newspaper, listing everything from antiques to artillery.

The Gun Gazette
P.O. Box 2685, Warner Robins, GA 31099. $12.00 yr. Extensive gun show listings, with articles on guns, knives and hunting.

Gun Week†
Second Amendment Foundation, P.O. Box 488, Station C, Buffalo NY 14209. $20.00 yr. U.S. and possessions; $24.00 yr. other countries. Tabloid paper on guns, hunting, shooting and collecting.

Gun World
Gallant Publishing Co., 34249 Camino Capistrano, Capistrano Beach, CA 92624. $17.00 yr. For the hunting, reloading and shooting enthusiast.

Guns & Action
P.O. Box 349, Mt. Morris, IL 61054. $12.00 yr. Defense, adventure, survival articles.

Guns & Ammo
Petersen Pub. Co., 8490 Sunset Blvd., Los Angeles, CA 90069. $13.94 yr. Guns, shooting, and technical articles.

Guns
Guns Magazine, 591 Camino de la Reina, San Diego, CA 92108. $14.95 yr. Articles for gun collectors, hunters and shooters.

Guns Review
Ravenhill Pub. Co. Ltd., Box 35, Standard House, Bonhill St., London E.C. 2A 4DA, England. £12.50 sterling (approx. U.S. $16) USA & Canada yr. For collectors and shooters.

Handloader*
Wolfe Pub. Co. Inc., Box 3030, Prescott, AZ 86302 $16.00 yr. The journal of ammunition reloading.

The IMAS Journal (M)
International Military Arms Society, P.O. Box 122, Williamstown, WV 26187. Military gun collecting articles.

INSIGHTS*
NRA, 1600 Rhode Island Ave. N.W., Washington, DC 20036. Editor Mary E. Shelsby. $5.00 yr. (12 issues). Plenty of details for the young hunter and target shooter.

International Shooting Sport*
International Shooting Union (UIT), Bavariaring 21, D-8000 Munich 2, Fed. Rep. of Germany. Europe: (Deutsche Mark) DM39.00 yr., p.p.; outside Europe: DM45.00. For the International target shooter.

The Journal of the Arms & Armour Society (M)
A.R.E. North (Secy.), Dept. of Metalwork, Victoria and Albert Museum, London, England. $16.00 yr. Articles for the historian and collector.

Journal of the Historical Breechloading Smallarms Assn.
Publ. annually, Imperial War Museum, Lambeth Road, London SE1 6HZ, England. $8.00 yr. Articles for the collector plus mailings of lecture transcripts, short articles on specific arms, reprints, newsletter, etc.; a surcharge is made f. airmail.

Kaliber
Uitgeverij Magnum, Marktstraat 237, 6431 LR Hoensbroek, Netherlands. 6 issues f20.00/Bfr.400. Magazine for the sportshooter.

Knife World
Knife World Publications, P.O. Box 3395, Knoxville, TN 37917. $10.00 yr., $17.00 2 yrs. Published monthly f. knife enthusiasts and collectors. Articles on custom and factory knives; other knife related interests.

Law and Order
Law and Order Magazine, 1000 Skokie Blvd., Wilmette, IL 60091. $15.00 yr. Articles on weapons for law enforcement, etc.

The List/Guns for Sale
P.O. Box 7387, Columbia, MO 65205. $8.00 yr. (12 issues); $15.00 2 yrs.

Man At Arms*
Box 460, Lincoln, RI 02865. $18.00 yr. The magazine of arms collecting-investing, with excellent brief articles for the collector of antique arms and militaria.

MAN/MAGNUM
S.A. Man (1982) (Pty) Ltd., P.O. Box 35204, Northway, Durban 4065, Rep. of South Africa. R20 f. 12 issues. Africa's only publication on hunting, shooting, firearms, bushcraft, knives, etc.

The Marlin Collector (M)
R.W. Paterson, 407 Lincoln Bldg., 44 Main St., Champaign, IL 61820.

Muzzle Blasts (M)
National Muzzle Loading Rifle Assn., P.O. Box 67, Friendship, IN 47021. $16.00 yr. For the black powder shooter.

Muzzleloader Magazine*
Rebel Publishing Co., Inc., Route 5, Box 347-M, Texarkana, TX 75501. $10.00 U.S., $12.00 foreign yr. The publication for black powder shooters.

National Defense (M)*
American Defense Preparedness Assn., Rosslyn Center, Suite 900, 1700 North Moore St., Arlington, VA 22209. $25.00 yr. Articles on military-related topics, including weapons, materials technology, management.

National Knife Collector (M)
Natl. Knife Coll. Assn., P.O. Box 21070, Chattanooga, TN 37421. Membership $15 yr, $40.00 International yr.

National Rifle Assn. Journal (British) (Q)
Natl. Rifle Assn. (BR.), Bisley Camp, Brookwood, Woking, Surrey, England. GU24, OPB. $14.00 inc. air postage.

National Wildlife*
Natl. Wildlife Fed., 1412 16th St. N.W., Washington, DC 20036. $12.00 yr. (6 issues); *International Wildlife*, 6 issues, $12.00 yr. Both, $19.00 yr., plus membership benefits. Write to this addr., attn.: Promotion Dept., for the proper information.

New Zealand Wildlife (Q)
New Zealand Deerstalkers Assoc. Inc., P.O. Box 6514, Wellington, N.Z. $13.00 (N.Z.). Hunting, shooting and firearms/game research articles.

North American Hunter* (M)
7901 Flying Cloud Dr., P.O. Box 35557, Minneapolis, MN 55435. $18.00 yr. (6 issues). Articles on North American game hunting.

Outdoor Life
Times Mirror Magazines, Inc., 380 Madison Ave., New York, NY 10017. $11.94 yr. Shooting columns by Jim Carmichel, and others.

Point Blank
Citizens Committee for the Right to Keep and Bear Arms (sent to contributors) Liberty Park, 12500 NE 10th Pl., Bellevue, WA 98005

The Police Marksman*
6000 E. Shirley Lane, Montgomery, AL 36117. $15.00 yr.

Police Times/Command (M)
1100 N.E. 125th St., No. Miami, FL 33161

Popular Mechanics
Hearst Corp., 224 W. 57th St., New York, NY 10019. $11.97 yr. Hunting, shooting and camping articles.

Precision Shooting
Precision Shooting, Inc., 37 Burnham St., East Hartford, CT 06108. $15.00 yr. Journal of the International Benchrest Shooters, National Benchrest Shooting Assn., and target shooting in general.

Rendezvous & Longrifles (M)
Canadian Black Powder Federation Newsletter, P.O. Box 2876, Postal Sta. "A", Moncton, N.B. E1C, 8T8, Canada. 6 issues per yr. w. $15.00 membership.

Rifle*
Wolfe Publishing Co. Inc., Box 3030, Prescott, AZ 86302. $16.00 yr. The magazine for shooters.

Rod & Rifle Magazine
Lithographic Serv. Ltd., P.O. Box 38-138, Petone, New Zealand. $30.00 yr. (6 issues) Hunting and shooting articles.

Safari* (M)
Safari Magazine, 5151 E. Broadway, Suite 1680, Tucson, AZ 85711. $20 (6 times). Official journal of Safari Club International; the journal of big game hunting.

Saga
Lexington Library, Inc., 355 Lexington Ave., New York, NY 10017. Currently annual. No subscription. $1.75 p. issue U.S.

Schweizer Waffen Magazin
Orell Füssli Zeitschriften, Postfach CH-8036 Zürich, Switzerland. SF 105.00 (approx. U.S. $46.70 air mail) f. 10 issues. Modern and antique arms. German text.

Second Amendment Reporter
Second Amendment Fdn., James Madison Bldg., 12500 NE 10th Pl., Bellevue, WA 98005. $15.00 yr. (non-contributors).

Shooting Industry
Publisher's Dev. Corp., 591 Camino de la Reina, Suite 200, San Diego, CA 92108. $25.00 yr. To the trade $12.50

Shooting Magazine
10 Sheet St., Windsor, Berks. SL4 1BG England. £11.50 for 12 issues. Monthly journal catering mainly to claypigeon shooters.

The Shooting Times & Country Magazine (England)†
10 Sheet St., Windsor, Berkshire SL4 1BG, England. £38 (approx. $48.75) yr. (52 issues). Game shooting, wild fowling, hunting, game fishing and firearms articles.

Shooting Times
PJS Publications, News Plaza. P.O. Box 1790, Peoria, IL 61656. $15.00 yr. Guns, shooting, reloading; articles on every gun activity.

The Shotgun News‡
Snell Publishing Co., Box 669, Hastings, NE 68901. $15.00 yr.; all other countries $100.00 yr. Sample copy $3.00. Gun ads of all kinds.

Shotgun Sports
P.O. Box 340, Lake Havasu City, AZ 86403. $20. yr.

Shotgun West
2052 Broadway, Santa Monica, CA 90404. $8.50 yr. Trap, Skeet and international shooting, scores; articles, schedules.

The Sixgunner (M)
Handgun Hunters International, P.O. Box 357, MAG. Bloomingdale, OH 43910

The Skeet Shooting Review
National Skeet Shooting Assn., P.O. Box 28188, San Antonio, TX 78228. $15.00 yr. (Assn. membership of $20.00 includes mag.) Competition results, personality profiles of top Skeet shooters, how-to articles, technical, reloading information.

Soldier of Fortune
Subscription Dept., P.O. Box 348, Mt. Morris, IL 61054. $26.00 yr. U.S., Can., Mex.; $33.00 all other countries surface mail.

SOF's Combat Weapons (Q)
P.O. Box 693, Boulder, CO 80306. $3.50 p. issue. Guide to international military firepower.

Sporting Goods Business
Gralla Publications, 1515 Broadway, New York, NY 10036. Trade journal.

The Sporting Goods Dealer
1212 No. Lindbergh Blvd., St. Louis, Mo. 63132. $30.00 yr. The sporting goods trade journal.

Sporting Gun
Bretton Court, Bretton, Peterborough PE3 8DZ, England £16.00 (approx. U.S. $28.00) (airmail £24.00) yr. For the game and clay enthusiasts.

Sports Afield
The Hearst Corp., 250 W. 55th St., New York, NY 10019. $13.97 yr. Grits Gresham on firearms, ammunition and Thomas McIntyre, Lionel Atwill, Gerald Almy on hunting.

Sports Merchandiser
A W.R.C. Smith Publication, 1760 Peachtree Rd. NW, Atlanta, GA 30357. Trade Journal.

TACARMI
Via E. De Amicis, 25;20123 Milano, Italy. $30.00 yr. approx. Antique and modern guns. (Italian text.).

Then And Now*
P.O. Box 842, Mount Vernon, WA 98273. $15.00 for 6 issues. Magazine for black powder activities; test reports.

Trap & Field
1000 Waterway Blvd., Indianapolis, IN 46202. $18.00 yr. Official publ. Amateur Trapshooting Assn. Scores, averages, trapshooting articles.

Turkey Call* (M)
Natl. Wild Turkey Federation, Inc., P.O. Box 530, Edgefield, SC 29824. $15.00 w. membership (6 issues p. yr.)

The U.S. Handgunner* (M)
U.S. Revolver Assn., 96 West Union St., Ashland, MA 01721. $6.00 yr. General handgun and competition articles. Bi-monthly sent to members.

Waterfowler's World*
P.O. Box 38306, Germantown, TN 38183. $12.00 yr.

The Weekly Bullet
Second Amendment Fdn., James Madison Bldg., 12500 NE 10th Pl., Bellevue, WA 98005. $35.00 yr.

Wisconsin Sportsman*
Wisconsin Sportsman, Inc., P.O. Box 2266, Oshkosh, WI 54903. $9.95. Hunting, hiking, outdoors articles.

---

*Published bi-monthly † Published weekly ‡ Published three times per month. All others are published monthly.
M = Membership requirements; write for details. Q = Published Quarterly.

The Arms Library *for*

COLLECTOR • HUNTER • SHOOTER • OUTDOORSMAN

A selection of books—old, new and forthcoming—for everyone in the arms field, with a brief description by . . . JOE RILING

IMPORTANT NOTICE TO BOOK BUYERS

Books listed here may be bought from Ray Riling Arms Books Co., 6844 Gorsten St., Philadelphia, PA 19119, phone 215/438-2456. Joe Riling, the proprietor, is the researcher and compiler of "The Arms Library" and a seller of gun books for over 30 years.

The Riling stock includes books classic and modern, many hard-to-find items, and many not obtainable elsewhere. These pages list a portion of the current stock. They offer prompt, complete service, with delayed shipments occurring only on out-of-print or out-of-stock books.

NOTICE FOR ALL CUSTOMERS: Remittance in U.S. funds must accompany all orders. For U.S. add $1.50 per book for postage and insurance. Minimum order $10.00. For U.P.S. add 50% to mailing costs.

All foreign countries add $2.00 per book for postage and handling, plus $3.30 per 10-lb. package or under for safe delivery by registered mail. Parcels not registered are sent at the "buyers risk."

Payments in excess of order or for "Backorders" are credited or fully refunded at request. Books "As-Ordered" are not returnable except by permission and a handling charge on these of $2.00 per book is deducted from refund or credit. Only Pennsylvania customers must include current sales tax.

A full variety of arms books are also available from Rutgers Book Center, 127 Raritan Ave., Highland Park, NJ 08904.

NEW BOOKS

(Alphabetically, no categories)

ABC's of Reloading, 3rd Edition, by Dean A. Grennell, DBI Books, Inc., Northfield, IL, 1985. 288 pp., illus. Paper covers. $11.95.

An all-new book with everything from discussion of the basics up through and including advanced techniques and procedures.

African Section Special Field Edition SCI 4th Edition Record Book of Trophy Animals, edited by C.J. McElroy, Safari Club International, Tucson, AZ, 1984. 302 pp., illus. Paper covers. $20.00.

Tabulations of outstanding big game trophies.

The Airgun Book, 3rd Edition, by John D. Walter, Stackpole Books, Harrisburg, PA, 1984. 176 pp., illus. $19.95.

A fully revised assessment of the most recent developments on the airgun scene.

American Big-Game Hunting, The Book of the Boone and Crockett Club, edited by Theodore Roosevelt and George Bird Grinnell, a limited edition reprint by the Boone and Crockett Club, Alexandria, VA, 1983. 345 pp., illus. $35.00.

A collection of unique hunting adventures in America by members of the Boone and Crockett Club.

American Percussion Revolvers, by Frank M. Sellers and Samuel E. Smith, Museum Restoration Service, Ottawa, Canada, 1971. 231 pp., illus. $29.95.

The ultimate reference book on American percussion revolvers.

Alaska Bear Trails, by Larry Kaniut, Alaska Northwest Publishing Co., Anchorage, AK, 1984. 310 pp. Paper covers. $9.95.

Factual stories on the Alaskan bears.

Alaska Game Trails with a Master Guide, by Charles J. Keim, Alaska Northwest Publishing Co., Anchorage, AK, 1984. 310 pp., illus. Paper covers. $6.95.

High adventure tales of fair chase with Alaska's first master guide—Hal Waugh.

The Ames Sword Co., 1829-1935, by John D. Hamilton, Mowbray Co., Providence, RI, 1983. 255 pp., illus. $45.00.

The story of the most prolific American sword makers over the longest period of time.

The Bayonet, an Evolution and History, by R.D.C. Evans and Frederick J. Stephens, Militaria Collector Inc., Northridge, CA, 1985. 200 pp., illus. Paper covers. $19.95.

Traces the story of the bayonet through the centuries from its simple beginnings in 17th century France right up to the present age.

Be an Expert Shot with Rifle, Handgun, or Shotgun, by Clair Rees, Winchester Press, Piscataway, NJ, 1984. 192 pp., illus. $19.95.

The illustrated self-coaching method that turns shooters into fine marksmen.

Bear Attacks, their Causes and Deterrence, by Stephen Herrero, Winchester Press, Piscataway, NJ, 1985. 288 pp., illus. $14.95.

For everyone who camps, hikes or tours the wilderness and wants to know more about a mighty and formidable creature.

Benchrest Actions and Triggers, by Suart Otteson, Wolfe Publishing Co., Inc., Prescott, AZ, 1983. 61 pp., illus. Paper covers. $9.50.

A combined reprinting of the author's articles "Custom Benchrest Actions" which appeared in the Rifle magazine.

Beretta Automatic Pistols: A Comprehensive Collector's and Shooter's Guide, by J.B. Wood, Stackpole Books, Inc., Harrisburg, PA, 1985. 192 pp., illus. $19.95.

The only English-language book devoted entirely to the Beretta line. From an internationally-recognized authority on automatic pistols.

The Best Shotguns Ever Made in America, by Michael McIntosh, Charles Scribner's Sons, New York, 1981. 185 pp., illus. $17.95.

Seven vintage doubles to shoot and treasure.

Big Game Records of British Columbia, compiled by The Trophy Wildlife Records Club of British Columbia, Nanoose, British Columbia, 1983. 216 pp., illus. $35.00.

The official record book for native big game trophies taken in British Columbia.

Big Game Rifles and Cartridges, by Elmer Keith, reprint edition by The Gunroom Press, Highland Park, NJ, 1984. 161 pp., illus. $19.95.

Reprint of Elmer Keith's first book, a most original and accurate work on big game rifles and cartridges.

Blue Book of Gun Values, 5th edition, by S.P. Fjestad, Investment Rarities, Inc., Minn., MN, 1984. 502 pp. Paper covers. $13.95.

Uses the percentage grading system to accurately determine each gun's value based on its unique condition.

Bolt Action Rifles, revised edition, by Frank de Haas, DBI Books, Inc., Northfield, IL, 1984. 448 pp., illus. Paper covers. $14.95.

Detailed coverage of over 110 turnbolt actions, including how they function, take-down and assembly, strengths and weaknesses, dimensional specifications.

The Book of the Black Bear, by Richard P. Smith, Winchester Press, Piscataway, NJ, 1985. 224 pp., illus. $18.95.

A comprehensive guide for the wildlife photographer, naturalist, wilderness hiker—and anyone who ventures into bear country.

The British Shotgun, Volume 1, 1850-1870, by I.M. Crudgington and D.J. Baker, Barrie & Jenkins, London, England, 1979. 256 pp., illus. $29.95.

An attempt to trace, as accurately as is now possible, the evolution of the shotgun during its formative years in Great Britain.

The British Sniper, by Ian Skennerton, Margate, Australia, 1984. 266 pp., illus. $32.50.

British and Commonwealth sniping and equipments, 1915-1983.

The Broomhandle Pistol 1896-1936, by Wayne R. Erickson and Charles E. Pate, E & P Enterprises, San Antonio, TX, 1985. 300 pp., illus. $49.95.

A new updated publication on the Mauser "Broomhandle" pistol. Detailed historical and text information, plus a collector's value guide.

The Browning Connection, by Richard Rattenbury, Buffalo Bill Historical Center, Cody, WY, 1982. 71 pp., illus. Paper covers. $10.00.

Patent prototypes in the Winchester Museum.

The Browning High Power Automatic Pistol, by R. Blake Stevens, Collector Grade Publications, Toronto, Canada, 1984. 271 pp., illus. $39.95.

Exhaustive new treatise on this famous automatic pistol.

Bugling for Elk, by Dwight Schuh, Stoneydale Press Publishing Co., Stevensville, MT, 1983. 162 pp., illus. $13.95.

A complete guide to early-season elk hunting.

Cartridges of the World, 5th Edition, by Frank Barnes, DBI Books, Inc., Northbrook, IL, 1985. 416 pp., illus. Paper covers. $15.95.

Completely updated encyclopedic work on cartridges.

A Catalog Collection of 20th Century Winchester Repeating Arms Co., compiled by Roger Rule, Alliance Books, Inc., Northridge, CA, 1985. 396 pp., illus. $29.95.

Reflects the full line of Winchester products from 1901-1931 with emphasis on Winchester firearms.

Churchill's Game Shooting, edited by Macdonald Hastings, Arms and Armour Press, London, England, 1979. 252 pp., illus. Paper covers. $15.00.
The standard textbook on the successful use of the shotgun.

A Collector's Guide to Tokarev Pistols, by John Remling, Collector's Services, Buchanan, NY, 1984. 81 pp., illus. Paper covers. $9.95.
A brief history of the development and production of Tokarev's pistol and provides the means by which many of the variations may be identified.

Colt Rimfire Automatic Pistols, by E.A. Brink, The Colt Connection, Fairborn, OH, 1984. 103 pp., illus. Limited, numbered, deluxe edition. $100.00
A collectors guide to Colt rimfire automatic pistols.

The Colt Whitneyville-Walker Pistol, by Lt. Col. Robert D. Whittington, Brownlee Books, Hooks, TX, 1984. 96 pp., illus. Limited edition. $20.00.
A study of the pistol and associated characters 1846-1851.

Colt's Dates of Manufacture 1837-1978, by R.L. Wilson, published by Maurie Albert, Coburg, Australia; N.A. distributor, I.D.S.A. Books, Hamilton, OH, 1983. 61 pp. $10.00.
An invaluable pocket guide to the dates of manufacture of Colt firearms up to 1978.

Combat Shotgun Training, by Charles R. Skillen, Charles C. Thomas, Publisher, Springfield, IL, 1982. 201 pp., illus. $40.00.
Complete, authoritative information on the use of the shotgun in law enforcement.

Commando Dagger, by Leroy Thompson, Paladin Press, Boulder, CO, 1984. 176 pp., illus. $25.00.
The complete illustrated history of the Fairbairn-Sykes fighting knife.

The Complete Shooter, by Sam Fadala, DBI Books, Inc., Northfield, IL, 1985. 448 pp., illus. Paper covers. $17.95.
A guide for the experienced shooter going beyond the basics.

Deer & Deer Hunting: The Serious Hunter's Guide, by Dr. Rob Wegner, Stackpole Books, Harrisburg, PA, 1984. 384 pp., illus. $29.95.
In-depth information from the editor of "Deer & Deer Hunting" magazine. Major bibliography of English language books on deer and deer hunting from 1838-1984.

Development of the Henry Cartridge and Self-Contained Cartridges for the Toggle-Link Winchesters, by R. Bruce McDowell, A.M.B., Metuchen, NJ, 1984. 69 pp., illus. Paper covers. $10.00.
From powder and ball to the self-contained metallic cartridge.

Discover Swaging, by David R. Corbin, Stackpole Books, Harrisburg, PA, 1979. 283 pp., illus. $18.95.
A guide to custom bullet design and performance.

The Double Shotgun, by Don Zutz, Winchester Press, Piscataway, NJ, 1985. 304 pp., illus. $19.95.
Revised, updated, expanded edition of the history and development of the world's classic sporting firearms.

Elk Hunting in the Northern Rockies, by Ed. Wolff, Stoneydale Press, Stevensville, MT, 1984. 162 pp., illus. $13.95.
Helpful information about hunting the premier elk country of the northern Rocky Mountain states—Wyoming, Montana and Idaho.

English Gunmakers, by DeWitt Bailey and Douglas A. Nie, ARCO Publishing Co., New York, NY, 1978. 127 pp., illus. $24.95.
The Birmingham and Provincial gun trade in the 18th and 19th centuries.

Fair Chase, by Jim Rikhoff, Amwell Press, Clinton, NJ, 1984. 323 pp., illus. $25.00.
A collection of hunting experiences from the Arctic to Africa, Mongolia to Montana, taken from over 25 years of writing.

Fast and Fancy Revolver Shooting, by Ed. McGivern, Anniversary Edition, Winchester Press, Piscataway, NJ, 1984. 484 pp., illus. $15.95.
A fascinating volume, packed with handgun lore and solid information by the acknowledged dean of revolver shooters.

First Wheel, by Bunny Allen, Amwell Press, Clinton, NJ, 1984, limited, signed and numbered edition in the NSFL "African Hunting Heritage Series." 292 pp., illus. $75.00.
A white hunter's diary 1927-47.

The Formidable Game, by John H. Batten, Amwell Press, Clinton, NJ, 1983. 264 pp., illus. $175.00.
Deluxe, limited, signed and numbered edition. Big game hunting in India, Africa and North America by a world famous hunter.

French Military Weapons, 1717-1938, by Major James E. Hicks, N. Flayderman & Co., Publishers, New Milford, CT, 1973. 281 pp., illus. $14.50.
Firearms, swords, bayonets, ammunition, artillery, ordnance equipment of the French army.

Fur Trapping in North America, by Steven Geary, Winchester Press, Piscataway, NJ, 1985. 160 pp., illus. Paper covers. $10.95.
A comprehensive guide to techniques and equipment, together with fascinating facts about fur bearers.

The Grand Spring Hunt for America's Wild Turkey Gobbler, by Bart Jacob with Ben Conger, Winchester Press, Piscataway, NJ, 1985. 176 pp., illus. $15.95.
Describes and pictures all varieties of turkey. Offers complete coverage on calls, calling techniques, appropriate guns, bows, cameras and other equipment.

The Great Rifle Controversy, by Edward Ezell, Stackpole Books, Harrisburg, PA, 1984. 352 pp., illus. $29.95.
Search for the ultimate infantry weapon from WWII through Vietnam and beyond.

Gun Collector's Digest, 4th Edition, edited by Joseph J. Schroeder, Jr., DBI Books, Inc., Northbrook, IL, 1985. 224 pp., illus. Paper covers. $12.95.
The latest edition of this sought-after series.

Gun Digest 1986, 40th Edition, edited by Ken Warner, DBI Books, Inc., Northbrook, IL, 1985. 488 pp., illus. Paper covers. $15.95.
All-new articles in this most famous of gun annuals.

Gun Digest Book of Gun Care, Cleaning and Refinishing, Book One: Handguns, by J.B. Wood, DBI Books, Inc., Northfield, IL, 1984. 160 pp., illus. Paper covers. $8.95.
The how, when and why of proper maintenance: revolvers, autoloaders, blackpowder handguns.

Gun Digest Book of Gun Care, Cleaning and Refinishing, Book Two: Long Guns, by J.B. Wood, DBI Books, Inc., Northfield, IL, 1984. 160 pp., illus. Paper covers. $8.95.
The care and maintenance of long guns with meticulous detail and step-by-step, illustrated, clearly written text.

Gun Digest Book of Modern Gun Values, 5th Edition, by Jack Lewis, ed. by Harold A. Murtz, DBI Books, Inc., Northfield, IL, 1985. 432 pp., illus. Paper covers. $14.95.
All-new expanded edition covers the current values of all non-military guns in production from 1900-1983.

Gun Digest Book of Popular Sporting Rifle Cartridges, by Clay Harvey, DBI Books, Inc., Northfield, IL, 1984. 320 pp., illus. Paper covers. $13.95.
Provides the hunter/shooter with extensive information on the most popular cartridges introduced during this century.

Gun Digest Book of Sporting Dogs, by Carl P. Wood, DBI Books, Inc., Northbrook, IL, 1985. 256 pp., illus. Paper covers. $11.95.
Investigates various training philosophies, problem dogs, training for versatility, kenneling, etc. Covers most all hunting/sporting dogs.

Gun Digest 1986 Hunting Annual, 3rd Edition, edited by Robert S.L. Anderson, DBI Books, Inc., Northbrook, IL, 1985. 256 pp., illus. Paper covers. $12.95.
Well-rounded, fully-illustrated collection of expert hunting tips and techniques.

Gun Traders Guide, 11th edition, by Paul Wahl, Stoeger Industries, So. Hackensack, NJ, 1984. 415 pp., illus. Paper covers. $12.95.
Complete fully illustrated guide to the identification of modern firearms with current market values.

Guns of the American West, by Joseph G. Rosa, Crown Publishers, New York, NY, 1985. 192 pp., illus. $24.95.
More than 300 photos, line drawings and engravings complement this lively account of the taming of the West.

Guns Illustrated, 1986, 18th Edition, edited by Harold A. Murtz, DBI Books, Northbrook, IL, 1985. 344 pp., illus. Paper covers. $13.95.
Packed with timely interesting articles and solid field testing on a wide variety of firearms.

Gunsmithing at Home, by John E. Traister, Stoeger Publishing Co., So. Hackensack, NJ, 1985. 256 pp., illus. Paper covers. $11.95.
Over 25 chapters of explicit information on every aspect of gunsmithing.

The Handbook of Shotshell Reloading, by Kenneth W. Couger, SKR Industries, San Angelo, TX, 1984. 248 pp., illus. Paper covers. $17.95.
All the present-day methods and techniques and up-to-date advice on reloading equipment and components.

Handloader's Digest, 10th edition, edited by Ken Warner, DBI Books, Inc., 1985. 320 pp., illus. Paper covers. $12.95.
The big book on handloading with dozens of "how to" features, covering everything from tools and materials to techniques and tips.

Handloader's Guide, by Stanley W. Trzoniec, Stoeger Publishing Co., So. Hackensack, NJ, 1985. 256 pp., illus. Paper covers. $11.95.
The complete step-by-step fully illustrated guide to handloading ammunition. All up-to-date information.

Hartman on Skeet, by Barney Hartman, Stackpole Books, Harrisburg, PA, 1973. 143 pp., illus. $10.00.
A definitive book on Skeet shooting by a pro.

"Hell, I Was There!", by Elmer Keith, Peterson Publishing Co., Los Angeles, CA, 1979. 308 pp., illus. $19.50.
Adventures of a Montana cowboy who gained world fame as a big game hunter.

Henry Wilkinson's Observations on Muskets, Rifles and Projectiles, a facsimile reprint of the scarce 1852 London edition. Reprinted by W.S. Curtis, Bucks, England, 1983. 68 pp., illus. Paper covers. $12.95.
Includes the author's scarce work "Treatise on the Elastic Concave Wadding."

The History and Development of Small Arms Ammunition, Volume 3, by George A. Hoyem, Armory Publications, Tacoma, WA, 1985. 238 pp., illus. $39.50.
Covering 19th and 20th century British rifle cartridges.

History of Winchester Firearms 1866-1980, by Duncan Barnes, et al, Winchester Press, Piscataway, NJ, 1985. 256 pp., illus. $16.95.
A most complete and authoritative account of Winchester firearms.

Home Gunsmithing Digest, 3rd Edition, by Tommy L. Bish, DBI Books, Inc., Northfield, IL, 1984. 256 pp., illus. Paper covers. $11.95.
The know-how supplied by an expert.

How to Buy and Sell Used Guns, by John Traister, Stoeger Publishing Co., So. Hackensack, NJ, 1984. 192 pp., illus. Paper covers. $9.95.
A new guide to buying and selling guns.

A Hunter's Wanderings in Africa, by F.C. Selous, Books of Zimbabwe, Bulawayo, So. Africa, 1981. 455 pp., illus. $85.00.
Facsimile reprint of the scarce 1881 classic on African hunting.

Hunting the African Buffalo, edited by Jim Rikhoff, Amwell Press, Clinton, NJ, 1985. 575 pp., illus. $175.00.
Deluxe, limited, signed and numbered edition of the most definitive work on hunting the African Cape buffalo that has ever been compiled.

Hunting Ducks and Geese, by Steve Smith, Stackpole Books, Harrisburg, PA, 1984. 160 pp., illus. $14.95.
Hard facts, good bets, and serious advice from a duck hunter you can trust.

The Illustrated Encyclopedia of Pistols and Revolvers, by Major Frederick Myatt, Crescent Books, New York, NY, 1980. 208 pp., illus. $14.95.
An illustrated history of hand guns from the 16th century to the present day.

The Japanese Sword, by Kanzan Sato, Kodansha International Ltd. and Shibundo, Tokyo, Japan, 1983. 210 pp., illus. $19.95.
The history and appreciation of the Japanese sword, with a detailed examination of over a dozen of Japan's most revered blades.

Japanese Swordsmanship, by Gordon Warner and Don F. Draeger, Weatherhill, New York, NY, 1984. 296 pp., illus. $29.95.
Technique and practice of Japanese swordsmanship.

Karamojo Safari, by W.D.M. Bell, Neville Spearman, Suffolk, England, 1984. 288 pp. $35.00.
The true story of Bell's life in Karamojo.

Knives '86, 6th Edition, edited by Ken Warner, DBI Books, Inc., Northbrook, IL, 1985. 256 pp., illus. Paper covers. $11.95.
Covers trends and technology for both custom and factory knives.

Levine's Guide to Knife Values, by Bernard R. Levine, DBI Books, Inc., Northbrook, IL, 1985. 480 pp., illus. Paper covers. $19.95.
An important guide to today's knife values.

A Listening Walk . . . and Other Stories, by Gene Hill, Winchester Press, Piscataway, NJ, 1985. 208 pp., illus. $15.95.
Vintage Hill. Over 60 stories.

Lyman Shotshell Handbook, 3rd edition, edited by C. Kenneth Ramage, Lyman Publications, Middlefield, CT, 1984. 312 pp., illus. Paper covers. $16.95.
2,000 loads including slugs and buckshot, plus feature articles and a full-color I.D. section.

The Manufacture of Gunflints, by Sydney B.J. Skertchly, facsimile reprint with new introduction by Seymour de Lotbiniere, Museum Restoration Service, Ontario, Canada, 1984. 90 pp., illus. $24.50.
Limited edition reprinting of the very scarce London edition of 1879.

Military Small Arms of the 20th Century, 5th Edition, by Ian V. Hogg & John Weeks, DBI Books, Inc., Northfield, IL, 1985. 304 pp., illus. Paper covers. $14.95.
Fully revised and updated edition of the standard reference in its field.

M1 Carbine Owner's Manual, M1, M2 & M3 .30 Caliber Carbines, Firepower Publications, Cornville, AZ, 1984. 102 pp., illus. Paper covers. $9.95.
The complete book for the owner of an M1 carbine.

Modern Guns Identification and Values, revised 5th edition, edited by Russell Quertermous and Steve Quetermous, Collector Books, Paducah, KY, 1984. 446 pp., illus. Paper covers. $11.95.
A guide to the current values of modern revolvers, pistols, rifles and shotguns.

Modern Military Bullpup Rifles, by T.B. Dugelby, Collector Grade Publications, Toronto, Canada, 1984. 97 pp., illus. $20.00.
The EM-2 concept comes to age.

Modern Small Arms, by Ian V. Hogg, Presidio Press, Novato, CA, 1984. 200 pp., illus. $20.00.
Covers 171 weapons test fired by expert Ian V. Hogg.

Modern Small Arms, by Major Frederick Myatt, Crescent Books, New York, NY, 1978. 240 pp., illus. $12.98.
An illustrated encyclopedia of famous military firearms from 1873 to the present day.

Olson's Encyclopedia of Small Arms, by John Olson, Winchester Press, Piscataway, NJ, 1985. 336 pp., illus. $22.95.
The most complete, authoritative, and up-to-date reference available for shooters, ballisticians, gun collectors, and everyone interested in firearms.

Outdoor Yarns & Outright Lies, by Gene Hill and Steve Smith, Stackpole Books, Harrisburg, PA, 1984. 168 pp., illus. $12.95.
Fifty or so stories by two good sports.

The P-38 Pistol: The Contract Pistols 1940-45, Volume Two, by Warren H. Buxton, Ucross Books, Los Alamos, NM, 1984. 247 pp., illus. $45.50.
The production of the pistol in Germany and its occupied areas during the war by firms other than Walther.

Police Handgun Manual, by Bill Clede, Stackpole Books, Inc., Harrisburg, PA, 1985. 128 pp., illus. $11.95.
How to get street-smart survival habits.

The Practical Hunter's Dog Book, updated and expanded, by John R. Falk, Winchester Press, Piscataway, NJ, 1984. 336 pp., illus. Paper covers. $11.95.
Everything you need to know from selecting a puppy to basic and advanced training, health care and breeding.

Purdey's, the Guns and the Family, by Richard Beaumont, David and Charles, Pomfret, VT, 1984. 248 pp., illus. $28.00.
Records the history of the Purdey family from 1814 to today. How the guns were and are built and daily functioning of the factory. Numbering of Purdey guns from 1814-1984.

Rediscover Swaging, by David R. Corbin, Corbin Manufacturing and Supply, Inc., Phoenix, OR, 1983. 240 pp., illus. $18.50.
A new textbook on the subject of bullet swaging.

Records of Alaska Big Game, edited by Norman B. Grant, Alaska Big Game Trophy Club, Anchorage, Alaska, 1971. 111 pp., illus. $95.00.
Contains the recorded and tabulated trophies of Alaskan big game including the name of the hunter, date and place of hunt, and measurement.

Reloader's Guide, 3rd Edition, by R.A. Steindler, Stoeger Publishing Co., So. Hackensack, NJ, 1984. 224 pp., illus. Paper covers. $8.95.
Complete, fully illustrated step-by-step guide to handloading ammunition.

Reloading for Shotgunners, 2nd Edition, edited by Robert S.L. Anderson, DBI Books, Inc., Northbrook, IL, 1985. 256 pp., illus. Paper covers. $11.95.
The very latest in reloading information for the shotgunner.

Revolvers, by Ian V. Hogg, Arms & Armour Press, London, England, 1984. 72 pp., illus. $12.95.
An illustrated guide with prices based on recent auction records.

The Ross Rifle Story, by R. Phillips, F. Dupuis, J. Chadwick, John A. Chadwick, Nova Scotia, Canada, 1984. 475 pp., illus. $49.50.
This book explores the myths and folklore surrounding Ross and his rifle and tries to set the record straight.

Rowland Ward's African Records of Big Game, XIX Edition, edited by Edward R. Bryant, Rowland Ward Publications, a division of Game Conservation International, San Antonio, TX, 1984. 640 pp., illus. Trade edition, $100.00; Deluxe, limited, signed, and numbered edition, $300.00.
The premier source book for African trophy hunters.

Safari: The Last Adventure, by Peter Capstick, St. Martin's Press, New York, NY, 1984. 291 pp., illus. $15.95.
A modern comprehensive guide to African safari.

The Samurai Sword: An American Perspective, by Gary Murtha, H.S.M. Publications, Independence, MO, 1980. 126 pp., illus. $30.00.
The origin and development of the sword and its historical background.

The Samurai Sword: An American Perspective, Vol. 2, Sword Fittings, by Gary Murtha, R&M Enterprises, Kansas City, MO, 1984. 156 pp., illus. $30.00.
Identification of signatures, family crests, and designs that are encountered on Japanese sword fittings.

Secrets of the Samurai, by Oscar Ratti and Adele Westbrook, Charles E. Tuttle Co., Rutland, VT, 1983. 483 pp., illus. $35.00.
A survey of the martial arts of feudal Japan.

Serial Numbers on U.S. Martial Arms, by Franklin B. Mallory, Springfield Research Service, Silver Spring, MD, 1983. 103 pp. Paper covers. $10.00.
A valuable aid to collectors of U.S. martial arms.

Shoot Better with Centerfire Rifle Cartridges, by Charles W. Matthews, Bill Matthews, Inc., Lakewood, CO, 1985. 560 pp., illus. Paper covers. $16.95.
Exciting new data shows how your bullet flies. Gives information for over 450 centerfire rifle cartridges.

Shoot a Handgun, by Dave Arnold, PVA Books, Canyon County, CA, 1983. 144 pp., illus. Paper covers. $8.95.
A complete manual of simplified handgun instruction.

Shooter's Bible, 1986, No.77, edited by William Jerrett, Stoeger Publishing Co., So. Hackensack, NJ, 1985. 576 pp., illus. Paper covers. $12.95.
A standard firearms reference book for decades.

Sierra Bullets Updated Supplement Reloading Manual, by Robert Hayden et al, The Leisure Group, Inc., Santa Fe Springs, CA, 1985. Loose-leaf pages. $16.50.
An updated supplement of loose-leaf pages to be the 2nd edition manual for the most comprehensive reloading material ever assembled.

Sixgun Cartridges and Loads, by Elmer Keith, reprint edition by The Gun Room Press, Highland Park, NJ, 1984. 151 pp., illus. $19.95.
A manual covering the selection, use and loading of the most suitable and popular revolver cartridges.

Small Arms Today, by Edward Ezell, Stackpole Books, Harrisburg, PA, 1984. 224 pp., illus. Paper covers. $16.95.
Latest reports on the world's weapons and ammunition.

The Springfield 1903 Rifles, by Lt. Col. William S. Brophy, USAR, Ret., Stackpole Books, Inc., Harrisburg, PA, 1985. 608 pp., illus. $49.95.
The illustrated, documented story of the design, development, and production of all the models, appendages, and accessories.

Stress Fire, Vol. 1: Stress Fighting for Police, by Massad Ayoob, Police Bookshelf, Concord, NH, 1984. 149 pp., illus. Paper covers. $9.95.
Gunfighting for police, advanced tactics and techniques.

Swords and Daggers, by Frederick Wilkinson, Stackpole Books, Inc., Harrisburg, PA, 1985. 80 pp., illus. $10.95.
Included are European weapons, scabbards, Japanese swords, Indian, African, and Asian weapons, and Third Reich daggers, with a guide to their value.

Thoughts on the Kentucky Rifle in its Golden Age, by Joe Kindig, George Shumway, Publisher, York, PA, 1984. 561 pp., illus. $75.00.
A new printing of the classic work on Kentucky rifles.

Track of the Kodiak, by Marvin H. Clark, Great Northwest Publishing and Distributing Co., Anchorage, AK, 1984. 224 pp., illus. $20.00.
A full perspective on Kodiak Island bear hunting.

Trade Muskets or Northwest Guns, by Pryor Mt. Bill Newton, Bill Newton, Beaver, WY, 34 pp., illus. Paper covers. $7.50.
The history, patterns and methods of the Whately 1770s and the Barnett, 1830. Work shop manual.

A Treatise on the British Military Martini: The Martini-Henry 1869-c1900, by B.A. Temple and I.D. Skennerton, B.A. Temple, Burbank, Australia, 1983. 246 pp., illus. $39.95.
The development of the Martini-Henry rifle.

Uganda Safaris, by Brian Herne, Winchester Press, Piscataway, NJ, 1979. 236 pp., illus. $12.95.
The chronicle of a professional hunter's adventures in Africa.

The Voice and Vocabulary of the Wild Turkey, by Lovett E. Williams, "Real Turkeys", Gainesville, FL, 1984. 85 pp., illus. $13.95.
First serious treatment of the 28 calls of the wild turkey.

A White Hunters Life, by Angus MacLagan, an African Hunting Heritage Book, published by Amwell Press, Clinton, NJ, 1983. 283 pp., illus. Limited, signed, and numbered deluxe edition, in slipcase. $75.00.
True to life, a sometimes harsh yet intriguing story.

White-Tailed Deer: Ecology and Management, by Lowell K. Halls, Stackpole Books, Harrisburg, PA, 1984. 864 pp., illus. $39.95.
The definitive work on the world's most popular big-game animal.

Wild Ivory, by Horace S. Mazet, Nautilus Books, No. Plainfield, NJ, 1971. 280 pp., illus. $30.00.
The true story of the last of the old elephant hunters.

Wild Sheep and Wild Sheep Hunters of the Old World, by Raul Valdez, Wild Sheep & Goat International, Mesilla, NM, 1983. 207 pp., illus. Limited, signed and numbered edition. $65.00.
A definitive work on Old World sheep hunting.

Winchester Dates of Manufacture 1849-1984, by George Madis, Art and Reference House, Brownsboro, TX, 1984. 59 pp. $5.95.
A most useful work, compiled from records of the Winchester factory.

Winchester: The Golden Age of American Gunmaking and the Winchester 1 of 1000, by R.L. Wilson, Winchester Arms Museum, Cody, WY, 1983. 144 pp., illus. $45.00.
The author traces the evolution of the firm; against this background he then examines the Winchester Model 1873 and 1876, 1 of 100 and 1000 series rifles.

The Winchester Model Twelve, by George Madis, David Madis, Dallas, TX, 1984. 176 pp., illus. $19.95.
A definitive work on this famous American shotgun.

World Bayonets, 1800-Present, by Anthony Carter, Arms & Armour Press, London, England, 1984. 72 pp., illus. $12.95.
Lavishly illustrated guide to the bayonets of the world.

ABC's of Reloading, 3rd Edition, by Dean A. Grennell, DBI Books, Inc., Northfield, IL, 1985. 288 pp., illus. Paper covers. $11.95.
An all-new book with everything from discussion of the basics up through and including advanced techniques and procedures.
American Ammunition and Ballistics, by Edward A. Matunas, Winchester Press, Piscataway, NJ, 1979. 288 pp., illus. $18.95.
A complete reference book covering all presently made and much discontinued American rimfire, centerfire, and shotshell ammunition.
The Art of Bullet Casting from Handloader & Rifle Magazines 1966-1981, compiled by Dave Wolfe, Wolfe Publishing Co., Prescott, AZ, 1981. 258 pp., illus. Paper covers. $12.95. Deluxe hardbound. $19.50.
Articles from "Handloader" and "Rifle" magazines by authors such as Jim Carmichel, John Wootters, and the late George Nonte.
Ballistic Science for the Law Enforcement Officer, by Charles G. Wilber, Ph.D., Charles C. Thomas, Springfield, IL, 1977. 309 pp., illus. $45.00.
A scientific study of the ballistics of civilian firearms.
Basic Handloading, by George C. Nonte, Jr., Outdoor Life Books, New York, NY, 1982. 192 pp., illus. Paper covers. $4.50.
How to produce high-quality ammunition using the safest, most efficient methods known.
The Bullet's Flight, by Franklin Mann, Wolfe Publishing Co., Inc., Prescott, AZ, 1980. 391 pp., illus. $22.00.
The ballistics of small arms. A reproduction of Harry Pope's personal copy of this classic with his marginal notes.
Cartridges of the World 5th Edition, by Frank Barnes, DBI Books, Inc., Northbrook, IL, 1985. 416 pp., illus. Paper covers. $15.95.
Completely updated encyclopedic work on cartridges.
Cast Bullets, by Col. E. H. Harrison, A publication of the National Rifle Association of America, Washington, DC, 1979. 144 pp., illus. Paper covers. $12.95.
An authoritative guide to bullet casting techniques and ballistics.
Computer for Handloaders, by Homer Powley. A Slide rule plus 12 page instruction book for use in finding charge, most efficient powder and velocity for any modern centerfire rifle. $6.95.
Discover Swaging, by David Corbin, Stackpole Books, Harrisburg, PA, 1980. 288 pp., illus., $18.95.
A book for the serious rifle and handgun reloading enthusiast.
Firearms Identification, by Dr. J. H. Mathews, Charles C. Thomas, Springfield, IL, 1973. 3 vol. set. A massive, carefully researched, authoritative work published as:
Vol. I **The Laboratory Examination of Small Arms** 400 pp., illus. $56.75.
Vol. II **Original Photographs and Other Illustrations of Handguns** 492 pp., illus. $56.75.
Vol. III **Data on Rifling Characteristics of Handguns and Rifles** 730 pp., illus. $88.00.
Firearms Investigation, Identification and Evidence, by J. S. Hatcher, Frank J. Jury and Jac Weller. Stackpole Books, Harrisburg, PA, 1977. 536 pp., illus. $26.95.
Reprint of the 1957 printing of this classic book on forensic ballistics. Indispensable for those interested in firearms identification and criminology.
Game Loads and Practical Ballistics for The American Hunter, by Bob Hagel, Alfred A. Knopf, NY, NY, 1978. 315 pp., illus., hardbound. $14.95.
Everything a hunter needs to know about ballistics and performance of commercial hunting loads.
The Gun Digest Black Powder Loading Manual, by Sam Fadala, DBI Books, Inc., Northfield, IL, 1982. 244 pp., illus. Paper covers. $11.95.
Covers 450 loads for 86 of the most popular black powder rifles, handguns and shotguns.
Gun Digest Book of Popular Sporting Rifle Cartridges, by Clay Harvey, DBI Books, Inc., Northfield, IL, 1984. 320 pp., illus. Paper covers. 13.95.
Provides the hunter/shooter with extensive information on the most popular cartridges introduced during this century.
Handbook for Shooters and Reloaders, by P.O. Ackley, Salt Lake City, UT, 1970, *Vol. I,* 567 pp., illus. $12.50. *Vol. II,* a new printing with specific new material. 495 pp., illus. $12.50.
Handbook of Metallic Cartridge Reloading, by Edward Matunas, Winchester Press, Piscataway, NJ, 1981. 272 pp., illus. $18.95.
Up-do-date, comprehensive loading tables prepared by four major powder manufacturers.
Handloader's Digest, 10th Edition, edited by Ken Warner, DBI Books, Inc., 1985. 320 pp., illus. Paper covers. $12.95.
The big book on handloading with dozens of "how to" features, covering everything from tools and materials to techniques and tips.
Handloading, by Bill Davis, Jr., NRA Books, Wash., D.C., 1980. 400 pp., illus. Paper covers. $15.95.
A complete update and expansion of the NRA Handloader's Guide.
Handloading for Handgunners, by Geo. C. Nonte, DBI Books, Inc., Northfield, IL, 1978. 288 pp., illus. Paper covers. $11.95.
An expert tells the ins and outs of this specialized facet of reloading.
Handloading for Hunters, by Don Zutz, Winchester Press, Piscataway, NJ, 1977. 288 pp., illus. Paper covers. $11.95.
Precise mixes and loads for different types of game and for various hunting situations with rifle and shotgun.
Hodgdon Data Manual No. 24, Hodgdon Powder Co., Shawnee Mission, KS 1984. 400 pp., illus. $14.95.
Has a new silhouette section and complete data on new H4350 powder.
The Home Guide to Cartridge Conversions, by Maj. George C. Nonte Jr., The Gun Room Press, Highland Park, NJ, 1976. 404 pp., illus. $19.95.
Revised and updated version of Nonte's definitive work on the alteration of cartridge cases for use in guns for which they were not intended.
Hornady Handbook of Cartridge Reloading, Hornady Mfg. Co., Grand Island, NE, 1981. 650 pp., illus. $14.00.
New edition of this famous reloading handbook. Latest loads, ballistic information, etc.
Lyman Cast Bullet Handbook, 3rd Edition, edited by C. Kenneth Ramage, Lyman Publications, Middlefield, CT, 1980. 416 pp., illus. Paper covers. $16.95.
Information on more than 5,000 tested cast bullet loads and 19 pages of trajectory and wind drift tables for cast bullets.
Lyman Black Powder Handbook, ed. by C. Kenneth Ramage, Lyman Products for Shooters, Middlefield, CT, 1975. 239 pp., illus. Paper covers $11.95.
The most comprehensive load information ever published for the modern black powder shooter.
Lyman Pistol & Revolver Handbook, edited by C. Kenneth Ramage, Lyman Publications, Middlefield, CT, 1978. 280 pp., illus. Paper covers. $11.95.
An extensive reference of load and trajectory data for the handgun.
Lyman Reloading Handbook No. 46, edited by C. Kenneth Ramage, Lyman Publications, Middlefield, CT, 1982. 300 pp., illus. $16.95.
A large and comprehensive book on reloading. Extensive list of loads for jacketed and cast bullets.
Manual of Pistol and Revolver Cartridges, Volume 1, Centerfire and Metric Calibers, by Hans A. Erlmeier and Jakob H. Brandt, Journal-Verlag, Weisbaden, Germany, 1967. 271 pp., illus. $29.95.
Specifications for each cartridge cataloged; tells bullet and case type with important case dimensions.
Master Index to Handloader and Rifle Magazine, compiled by the staff of Wolfe Publishing Co., Prescott, AZ, 1983. Unpaginated. Paper covers. $8.50.
Covers issues #1-#100 of the *Handloader*; issues #1-#84 of the *Rifle.*
Metallic Cartridge Reloading, edited by Robert S.L. Anderson, DBI Books, Inc., Northfield, IL, 1982. 320 pp., illus. Paper covers. $13.95.
A true reloading manual with a wealth of invaluable technical data provided by outstanding reloading experts. A must for any reloader. Extensive load tables.
Metallic Reloading Basics, edited by C. Kenneth Ramage, Lyman Publications, Middlefield, CT, 1976. 60 pp., illus. Paper covers. $1.95.
Provides the beginner with loading data on popular bullet weights within the most popular calibers.
Military Ballistics, by C.L. Farrar and D.W. Leeming, Pergamon Press, Oxford, England, 1983. 200 pp., illus. Paper covers. $22.50.
Principles of ballistics, illustrated by reference of military applications.
Modern Handloading, by Maj. Geo. C. Nonte, Winchester Press, Piscataway, NJ, 1972. 416 pp., illus. $15.00.
Covers all aspects of metallic and shotshell ammunition loading, plus more loads than any book in print.
Nosler Reloading Manual Number Two, Nosler Bullets, Inc., Bend, OR, 1981. 308 pp., illus. $8.95.
Thorough coverage of powder data, specifically tailored to the well known Nosler partition and solid base bullets.
Pet Loads, by Ken Waters, Wolfe Publ. Co., Inc., Prescott, AZ, 1979. Unpaginated. In looseleaf form. $29.50.
A collection of the last 13 years' articles on more than 70 metallic cartridges. Most calibers featured with updated material.
Practical Handgun Ballistics, by Mason Williams, Charles C. Thomas, Publisher, Springfield, IL, 1980. 215 pp., illus. $29.50.
Factual information on the practical aspects of ammunition performance in revolvers and pistols.
Reloading for Shotgunners, 2nd Edition, edited by Robert S.L. Anderson, DBI Books, Inc., Northbrook, IL, 1985. 256 pp., illus. Paper covers. $11.95.
The very latest in reloading information for the shotgunner.
Sierra Bullets Reloading Manual, Second Edition, by Robert Hayden et al, The Leisure Group, Inc., Santa Fe Springs, CA, 1978. 700 pp., illus. Looseleaf binder. $16.95.
Includes all material in the original manual and its supplement updated, plus a new section on loads for competitive shooting.
Speer Reloading Manual Number 10, Omark Industries, Inc., Lewiston, ID, 1979, 560 pp., illus. Paper covers. $12.00.
Expanded version with facts, charts, photos, tables, loads and tips.
Why Not Load Your Own? by Col. T. Whelen, A. S. Barnes, New York, 1957, 4th ed., rev. 237 pp., illus, $10.95.
A basic reference on handloading, describing each step, materials and equipment. Loads for popular cartridges are given.
Yours Truly, Harvey Donaldson, by Harvey Donaldson, Wolfe Publ. Co., Inc., Prescott, AZ, 1980. 288 pp., illus. $19.50.
Reprint of the famous columns by Harvey Donaldson which appeared in "Handloader" from May 1966 through December 1972.

American Handguns & Their Makers, compiled by J.B. Roberts, Jr. and Ted Bryant, NRA Books, Wash., DC, 1981. 248 pp., illus. Paper covers. $11.95.
First in a series of manuals on gun collecting and the history of firearms manufacturing.
". . . And Now Stainless", by Dave Ecker with Bob Zwirz, Charter Arms Corp., Bridgeport, CT, 1981. 165 pp., illus. $15.00.
The Charter Arms story. Covers all models to date.
Arms & Accoutrements of the Mounted Police 1873-1973, by Roger F. Phillips and Donald J. Klancher, Museum Restoration Service, Ont., Canada, 1982. 224 pp., illus. $49.95.
A definitive history of the revolvers, rifles, machine guns, cannons, ammunition, swords, etc. used by the NWMP, the RNWMP and the RCMP during the first 100 years of the Force.

Arms & Equipment of the Civil War, by Jack Coggins, Outlet Books, New York, NY, 1983. 160 pp., illus. $7.98.

Lavishly illustrated guide to the principal weapons and equipment of the Civil War used by the forces of the Blue and the Gray.

Arms Makers of Maryland, by Daniel D. Hartzler, George Shumway, York, PA, 1975. 200 pp., illus. $40.00.

A thorough study of the gunsmiths of Maryland who worked during the late 18th and early 19th centuries.

Ballard Rifles in the H.J. Nunnemacher Coll., by Eldon G. Wolff. Milwaukee Public Museum, Wisc., 2nd ed., 1961. Paper, 77 pp. plus 4 pp. of charts and 27 plates. $5.00.

A thoroughly authoritative work on all phases of the famous rifles, their parts, patent and manufacturing history.

Basic Documents on U.S. Marital Arms, commentary by Col. B. R. Lewis, reissue by Ray Riling, Phila., PA., 1956 and 1960. *Rifle Musket Model 1855.* The first issue rifle of musket caliber, a muzzle loader equipped with the Maynard Primer, 32 pp. $2.50. *Rifle Musket Model 1863.* The Typical Union muzzle-loader of the Civil War, 26 pp. $1.75. *Breech-Loading Rifle Musket Model 1866.* The first of our 50 caliber breechloading rifles, 12 pp. $1.75. *Remington Navy Rifle Model 1870.* A commercial type breech-loader made at Springfield, 16 pp. $1.75 *Lee Straight Pull Navy Rifle Model 1895.* A magazine cartridge arm of 6mm caliber. 23 pp. $3.00. *Breech-Loading Arms* (five models)-27 pp. $2.75. *Ward-Burton Rifle Musket 1871*-16 pp. $2.50. *U.S. Magazine Rifle and Carbine (cal. 30) Model 1892*(the Krag Rifle) 36 pp. $3.00.

British Military Pistols 1603-1888, by R.E. Brooker, Jr., The Gun Room Press, Highland Park, NJ, 1983. 139 pp., illus. $29.95.

Covers flintlock and percussion pistols plus cartridge revolvers up to the smokeless powder period.

California Gunsmiths 1846-1900, by Lawrence P. Sheldon, Far Far West Publ., Fair Oaks, CA, 1977. 289 pp., illus. $29.65.

A study of early California gunsmiths and the firearms they made.

Carbines of the Civil War, by John D. McAulay, Pioneer Press, Union City, TN, 1981. 123 pp., illus. Paper covers. $7.95.

A guide for the student and collector of the colorful arms used by the Federal cavalry.

Cartology Savalog, by Gerald Bernstein, Gerald Bernstein, St. Louis, MO, 1976. 177 pp., illus. Paper covers. $8.95.

An infinite variations catalog of small arms ammunition stamps.

The Cartridge Guide, by Ian V. Hogg, Stackpole Books, Harrisburg, PA, 1982. 160 pp., illus. $24.95.

The small arms ammunition identification manual.

Catalogue of the Enfield Pattern Room: British Rifles, Herbert Wooden, Her Majesty's Stationery Office, London, England, 1981. 80 pp., illus. Paper covers. $14.95.

The first exhaustive catalog of a specific section of the collection in the Pattern Room at the Royal Small Arms Factory at Enfield Lock.

Civil War Carbines, by A.F. Lustyik. World Wide Gun Report, Inc., Aledo, Ill, 1962. 63 pp., illus. Paper covers. $3.50.

Accurate, interesting summary of most carbines of the Civil War period, in booklet form, with numerous good illus.

Civil War Guns, by William B. Edwards, Castle Books, NY, 1976. 438 pp., illus. $15.00.

Describes and records the exciting and sometimes romantic history of forging weapons for war and heroism of the men who used them.

A Collector's Guide to Air Rifles, by Dennis E. Hiller, London, England, 1980. 170 pp., illus. Paper covers. $15.95.

Valuations, exploded diagrams and many other details of air rifles, old and new.

The Collector's Handbook of U.S. Cartridge Revolvers, 1856 to 1899, by W. Barlow Fors, Adams Press, Chicago, IL, 1973. 96 pp., illus. $10.95.

Concise coverage of brand names, patent listings, makers' history, and essentials of collecting.

Colonel Colt London, by Joseph G. Rosa, Arms & Armour Press, London, England, 1983. 218 pp., illus. $24.95.

The standard reference volume on the London activities of Samuel Colt.

Colt Engraving, by R.L. Wilson, The Gun Room Press, Highland Park, NJ, 1982. 560 pp., illus. $69.95.

New and completely revised edition of the author's original work on finely engraved Colt firearms.

Colt Firearms from 1836, by James E. Serven, new 8th edition, Stackpole Books, Harrisburg, PA, 1979. 398 pp., illus. $29.95. Deluxe ed. $49.95.

Excellent survey of the Colt company and its products. Updated with new SAA production chart and commemorative list.

The Colt Heritage, by R.L. Wilson, Simon & Schuster, 1979. 358 pp., illus. $75.00.

The official history of Colt firearms 1836 to the present.

Colt Pistols 1836-1976, by R.L. Wilson in association with R.E. Hable, Jackson Arms, Dallas, TX, 1976. 380 pp., illus. $100.00.

A magnificently illustrated book in full-color featuring Colt firearms from the famous Hable collection.

Colt's SAA Post War Models, George Garton, Gun Room Press, Highland Park, NJ, 1979. 166 pp., illus. $21.95.

Details all guns produced and their variations.

Colt's Variations of the Old Model Pocket Pistol, 1848 to 1872, by P.L. Shumaker. Borden Publishing, Co., Alhambra, CA, 1966, a reprint of the 1957 edition. 150 pp., illus. $8.95.

A useful tool for the Colt specialist and a welcome return of a popular source of information that had been long out-of-print.

Confederate Longarms and Pistols, "A Pictorial Study", by Richard Taylor Hill and Edward W. Anthony, Taylor Publishing Co., Dallas, TX, 1978. $29.95.

A reference work identifying over 175 Confederate arms through detailed photography, and a listing of information.

Contemporary Makers of Muzzleloading Firearms, by Robert Weil, Screenland Press, Burbank, CA, 1981. 300 pp., illus. $39.95.

Illustrates the work of over 30 different contemporary makers.

Early Indian Trade Guns: 1625-1775, by T.M. Hamilton, Museum of the Great Plains, Lawton, OK, 1968. 34 pp., illus. Paper covers. $7.95.

Detailed descriptions of subject arms, compiled from early records and from the study of remnants found in Indian country.

Fifteen Years in the Hawken Lode, by John D. Baird, The Gun Room Press, Highland Park, NJ, 1976. 120 pp., illus. $17.95.

A collection of thoughts and observations gained from many years of intensive study of the guns from the shop of the Hawken brothers.

Firearms in Colonial America: The Impact on History and Technology 1492-1792, by M.L. Brown, Smithsonian Institution Press, Wash., D.C., 1980. 449 pp., illus. $55.00.

An in-depth coverage of the history and technology of firearms in Colonial North America.

Firearms of the Confederacy, by Claud R. Fuller & Richard D. Steuart, Quarterman Publ., Inc., Lawrence, MA, 1977. 333 pp., illus. $25.00.

The shoulder arms, pistols and revolvers of the Confederate soldier, including the regular United States Models, the imported arms and those manufactured within the Confederacy.

The Firearms Price Guide, 2nd Edition, by D. Byron, Crown Publishers, New York, NY, 1981. 448 pp., illus. Paper covers. $9.95.

An essential guide for every collector and dealer.

Flayderman's Guide to Antique American Firearms . . . And Their Values, Third Edition, by Norm Flayderman, DBI Books, Inc., Northfield, IL, 1983. 624 pp., illus. Paper Covers. $19.95.

Updated and expanded third edition of this bible of the antique gun field.

The .45-70 Springfield, by Albert J. Frasca and Robert H. Hall, Springfield Publishing Co., Northridge, CA, 1980. 380 pp., illus. $39.95.

A carefully researched book on the trapdoor Springfield, including all experimental and very rare models.

The 45/70 Trapdoor Springfield Dixie Collection, compiled by Walter Crutcher and Paul Oglesby, Pioneer Press, Union City, TN, 1975. 600 pp., illus. Paper covers. $9.95.

An illustrated listing of the 45-70 Springfields in the Dixie Gun Works Collection. Little known details and technical information is given, plus current values.

Gas, Air, and Spring Guns of the World, by W.H.B. Smith, Arms & Armour Press, London, England, 1983. 288 pp., illus. Paper covers. $17.50.

The standard work of its kind, invaluable to serious students, gunsmiths, developers, and collectors.

Gun Digest Book of Modern Gun Values, 5th Edition, by Jack Lewis, ed. by Harold A. Murtz, DBI Books, Inc., Northfield, IL, 1985. 432 pp., illus. Paper covers. $14.95.

All-new expanded edition covers the current values of all non-military guns in production from 1900-1983.

The Gun Collector's Handbook of Values, 1983-84, by C.E. Chapel, G.P. Putnam and Son, East Rutherford, NJ, 1984. 462 pp., illus. $19.95.

The 14th revised edition of the best-known price reference for collectors of firearms.

The Gunsmiths and Gunmakers of Eastern Pennsylvania, by James B. Whisker and Roy Chandler, Old Bedford Village Press, Bedford, PA, 1982. 130 pp., illus. Limited, numbered edition. Paper covers. $17.50.

Locates over 2,000 gunsmiths practicing before 1900, with references and documentation.

The Gunsmiths and Gunmakers of Western Pennsylvania, by James B. Whisker and Vaughn E. Whisker, Old Bedford Village Press, Bedford, PA, 1982. 103 pp., illus. Limited, numbered and signed edition. Paper covers. $17.50.

Lists over 650 names of gunsmiths practicing before 1900.

Gunsmiths of Ohio—18th & 19th Centuries: Vol. I, Biographical Data, by Donald A. Hutslar, George Shumway, York, PA, 1973. 444 pp., illus. $35.00.

An important source book, full of information about the old-time gunsmiths of Ohio.

The Hand Cannons of Imperial Japan, 1543-1945, by Harry Derby, Harry Derby, Charlotte, NC, 1982. 300 pp., illus. $37.00.

Superb, comprehensive and definitive study of Japanese handguns beginning with the introduction of the matchlock in Japan and continuing into the post-WW II period.

The Hawken Rifle: Its Place in History, by Charles E. Hanson, Jr., The Fur Press, Chadron, NE, 1979. 104 pp., illus. Paper covers. $6.00.

A definitive work on this famous rifle.

Hawken Rifles, The Mountan Man's Choice, by John D. Baird, The Gun Room Press, Highland Park, NJ, 1976. 95 pp., illus. $17.95.

Covers the rifles developed for the Western fur trade. Numerous specimens are described and shown in photographs.

High Standard Automatic Pistols, 1932-1950, by Charles E. Petty, American Ordnance Publications, Charlotte, NC, 1976. 124 pp., illus. $12.95.

Describes and illustrates the early history of the company and many details of the various popular pistols. Includes dates and serial numbers.

Historical Hartford Hardware, by William W. Dalrymple, Colt Collector Press, Rapid City, SD, 1976. 42 pp., illus. Paper covers. $5.50.

Historically associated Colt revolvers.

A History of the Colt Revolver, by Charles T. Haven and Frank A. Belden, Outlet Books, New York, NY, 1978. 711 pp., illus. $25.00.

A giant of a book packed with information and pictures about the most cherished American revolver.

A History of the John M. Browning Semi-Automatic .22 Caliber Rifle, by Homer C. Tyler, Jefferson City, MO, 1982. 58 pp., illus. Paper covers. $10.00.

All models and variations are shown. Includes engraved guns.

The History and Development of Small Arms Ammunition, Vol. 1, by George A. Hoyem, Armory Publications, Tacoma, WA, 1981. 230 pp., illus. $27.50.

Describes and illustrates ammunition from military long arms—flintlock through rimfire.

The History and Development of Small Arms Ammunition, Vol. 2, by George A. Hoyem, Armory Publications, Tacoma, WA, 1982. 303 pp., illus. $45.00.

Small arms and ammunition of 31 nations and dominions covered in detail together for the first time.

History of Modern U.S. Military Small Arms Ammunition, Vol. 2, 1940-1945, by F.W. Hackley, W.M. Woodin and E.L. Scranton, The Gun Room Press, Highland Park, NJ, 1976. 300 pp., illus. $35.00.

A unique book covering the entire field of small arms ammunition developed during the critical World War II years.

The Kentucky Rifle, by Merrill Lindsay, Arma Press, NY/the Historical Society of York County, York, PA, 1972. 100 pp., 81 large colored illustrations. $17.95.

Presents in precise detail and exact color 77 of the finest Kentucky rifles ever assembled in one place. Also describes the conditions which led to the development of this uniquely American arm.

Kentucky Rifles and Pistols 1756-1850, compiled by members of the Kentucky Rifle Association, Wash., DC, Golden Age Arms Co., Delaware, OH, 1976. 275 pp., illus. $35.00.

Profusely illustrated with more than 300 examples of rifles and pistols never before published.

Know Your Ruger Single Action Revolvers 1953-1963, by John C. Dougan, edited by John T. Amber, Blacksmith Corp., Southport, CT, 1981. 199 pp., illus. $35.00.

A definitive reference work for the Ruger revolvers produced in the period 1953-1963.

The Krag Rifle Story, by Franklin B. Mallory and Ludwig Olson, Springfield Research Service, Silver Spring, MD, 1979. 224 pp., illus. $20.00.

Covers both U.S. and European Krags. Gives a detailed description of U.S. Krag rifles and carbines and extensive data on sights, bayonets, serial numbers, etc.

Krag Rifles, by William S. Brophy, The Gun Room Press, Highland Park, NJ, 1980. 200 pp., illus. $29.95.

The first comprehensive work detailing the evolution and various models, both military and civilian.

The Krieghoff Parabellum, by Randall Gibson, Randall Gibson, Midland, TX, 1980. 280 pp., illus. $35.00.

A definitive work on the most desirable model Luger pistol.

Lever Action Magazine Rifles Derived from the Patents of Andrew Burgess, by Samuel L. Maxwell Sr., Samuel L. Maxwell, Bellevue, WA, 1976. 368 pp., illus. $29.95.

The complete story of a group of lever action magazine rifles collectively referred to as the Burgess/Morse, the Kennedy or the Whitney.

Levine's Guide to Knife Values, by Bernard R. Levine, DBI Books, Inc., Northbrook, IL, 1985. 480 pp., illus. Paper covers. $19.95.

An important guide to today's knife values.

Manual of Pistol and Revolver Cartridges, Volume 2, Centerfire U.S. and British Calibers, by Hans A. Erlmeier and Jakob H. Brandt, Journal-Verlag, Weisbaden, Germany, 1981. 270 pp., illus. $35.00.

Catalog system allows cartridges to be traced either by caliber or alphabetically.

Mauser Bolt Rifles, by Ludwig Olson, F. Brownell & Son, Inc., Montezuma, IA, 1976. 364 pp., illus. $29.95.

The most complete, detailed, authoritative and comprehensive work ever done on Mauser bolt rifles.

The Metric FAL, by R. Blake Stevens and Jean E. Van Rutten, Collector Grade Publications, Toronto, Canada, 1981. 372 pp., illus. Paper covers. $50.00.

Volume three of the FAL series. The free world's right arm.

Military Pistols of Japan, by Fred L. Honeycutt, Jr., Julin Books, Lake Park, FL. 1982. 167 pp., illus. $24.00.

Covers every aspect of military pistol production in Japan through WWII.

Military Rifles of Japan, by Fred L. Honeycutt Jr. and F. Pratt Anthony, Julin Books, Lake Park, FL, 2nd edition, 1983. 206 pp., illus. $29.00.

Limited, signed and numbered edition. Includes the early Murata period, markings, etc.

Military Small Arms Ammunition of the World, 1945-1980, by Peter Labbett, Presidio Press, San Rafael, CA, 1980. 129 pp., illus. $18.95.

An up-to-date international guide to the correct identification of ammunition by caliber, type, and origin.

M1 Carbine, Design, Development and Production, by Larry Ruth, The Gun Room Press, Highland Park, NJ, 1983. 300 pp., illus. Paper covers. $17.95.

The complete history of one of the world's most famous and most produced military firearms.

Modern Guns, Fred Adolph Catalog, reprinted by Armory Publications, Tacoma, WA, 1983. 67 pp., illus. Paper covers. $10.95.

Reprint of a scarce American gun catalog of the early 1900s.

More Single Shot Rifles, by James C. Grant, The Gun Room Press, Highland Park, NJ, 1976. 324 pp., illus. $25.00.

Details the guns made by Frank Wesson, Milt Farrow, Holden, Borchardt, Stevens, Remington, Winchester, Ballard and Peabody-Martini.

The New England Gun, by Merrill Lindsay, David McKay Co., NY, 1976. 155 pp., illus. Paper covers, $12.50. Cloth, $20.00.

A study of more than 250 New England guns, powder horns, swords and polearms in an exhibition by the New Haven Colony Historical Society.

Simeon North: First Official Pistol Maker of the United States, by S. North and R. North, The Gun Room Press, Highland Park, NJ, 1972. 207 pp., illus. $9.95.

Reprint of the rare first edition.

The Northwest Gun, by Charles E. Hanson, Jr., Nebraska State Historical Society, Lincoln, NB, 1976. 85 pp., illus., paper covers. $6.

Number 2 in the Society's "Publications in Anthropology." Historical survey of rifles which figured in the fur trade and settlement of the Northwest.

The P-08 Parabellum Luger Automatic Pistol, edited by J. David McFarland, Desert Publications, Cornville, AZ, 1982. 20 pp., illus. Paper covers. $6.00.

Covers every facet of the Luger, plus a listing of all known Luger models.

Paterson Colt Pistol Variations, by R.L. Wilson and R. Phillips, Jackson Arms Co., Dallas, TX, 1979. 250 pp., illus. $35.00.

A tremendous book about the different models and barrel lengths in the Paterson Colt story.

Peacemaker Evolutions & Variations, by Keith A. Cochran, Colt Collectors Press, Rapid City, SD, 1975. 47 pp., illus. Paper covers. $10.00.

Corrects many inaccuracies found in other books on the Peacemaker and gives much new information regarding this famous arm.

The Pennsylvania-Kentucky Rifle, by Henry J. Kauffman, Crown Publishers, New York, NY 1981. 293 pp., illus. $9.98.

A colorful account of the history and gunsmiths who produced the first American rifle superior to those brought from the Old Country.

Pennsylvania Longrifles of Note, by George Shumway, George Shumway, Publisher, York, PA, 1977. 63 pp., illus. Paper covers. $6.95.

Illustrates and describes samples of guns from a number of Pennsylvania rifle-making schools.

The Pinfire System, by Gene P. Smith and Chris C. Curtis, The Pinfire System, San Francisco, CA, 1983. 216 pp., illus. $50.00.

The first attempt to record the invention, development and use of pinfire cartridge arms and ammunition.

The Plains Rifle, by Charles E. Hanson, Jr., The Gun Room Press, Highland Park, NJ, 1977. 171 pp., illus. $19.95.

Historical survey of popular civilian arms used on the American frontiers, their makers, and their owners.

The Radom Pistol, by Robert J. Berger, Robert J. Berger, Milford, CT, 1981. 99 pp., illus. Paper covers. $10.00.

The complete story of the VIS (Radom) pistol.

The Rare and Valuable Antique Arms, by James E. Serven, Pioneer Press, Union City, TN, 1976. 106 pp., illus. Paper covers. $4.95.

A guide to the collector in deciding which direction his collecting should go, investment value, historic interest, mechanical ingenuity, high art or personal preference.

Reloading Tools, Sights and Telescopes for Single Shot Rifles, by Gerald O. Kelver, Brighton, CO, 1982. 163 pp., illus. Paper covers. $10.00.

A listing of most of the famous makers of reloading tools, sights and telescopes with a brief description of the products they manufactured.

Rifles in Colonial America, Vol. I, by George Shumway, George Shumway, Publisher, York, PA, 1980. 353 pp., illus. $49.50.

An extensive photographic study of American longrifles made in the late Colonial, Revolutionary, and post-Revolutionary periods.

Rifles in Colonial America, Vol. II, by George Shumway, George Shumway, Publisher, York, PA, 1980. 302 pp., illus. $49.50.

Final volume of this study of the early evolution of the rifle in America.

Ruger Rimfire Handguns 1949-1982, by J.C. Munnell, G.D.G.S. Inc., McKeesport, PA, 1982. 189 pp., illus. Paper covers. $12.00.

Updated edition with additional material on the semi-automatic pistols and the New Model revolvers.

Samuel Colt's New Model Pocket Pistols; The Story of the 1855 Root Model Revolver, by S. Gerald Keogh, S.G. Keogh, Ogden, UT, 1974. 31 pp., illus., paper covers. $5.00.

Collector's reference on various types of the titled arms, with descriptions, illustrations, and historical data.

Savage Automatic Pistols, by James R. Carr. Publ. by the author, St. Charles, Ill., 1967. A reprint. 129 pp., illus. with numerous photos. $30.00.

Collector's guide to Savage pistols, models 1907-1922, with features, production data, and pictures of each.

Scottish Arms Makers, by Charles E. Whitelaw, Arms and Armour Press, London, England, 1982. 363 pp., illus. $29.95.

An important and basic addition to weapons reference literature.

Sharps Firearms, by Frank Seller, Frank M. Seller, Denver, CO, 1982. 358 pp., illus. $39.95.

Traces the development of Sharps firearms with full range of guns made including all martial variations.

Small Arms of the Sea Services, by Robert H. Rankin. N. Flayderman & Co., New Milford, CT, 1972. 227 pp., illus. $14.50.

Encyclopedic reference to small arms of the U.S. Navy, Marines and Coast Guard. Covers edged weapons, handguns, long arms and others, from the beginnings.

Southern Derringers of the Mississippi Valley, by Turner Kirkland. Pioneer Press, Tenn., 1971. 80 pp., illus., paper covers. $2.00.

A guide for the collector, and a much-needed study.

Still More Single Shot Rifles, by James J. Grant, Pioneer Press, Union City, TN, 1979. 211 pp., illus. $17.50.

A sequel to the author's classic works on single shot rifles.

The 36 Calibers of the Colt Single Action Army, by David M. Brown. Publ. by the author at Albuquerque, NM, new reprint 1971. 222 pp., well-illus. $65.00.

Edited by Bev Mann of *Guns Magazine*. This is an unusual approach to the many details of the Colt S.A. Army revolver. Halftone and line drawings of the same models make this of especial interest.

The Trapdoor Springfield, by M.D. Waite and B.D. Ernst, The Gun Room Press, Highland Park, NJ, 1983. 250 pp., illus. $29.95.

The first comprehensive book on the famous standard military rifle of the 1873-92 period.

Underhammer Guns, by H.C. Logan. Stackpole Books, Harrisburg, PA, 1965. 250 pp., illus. $10.00.

A full account of an unusual form of firearm dating back to flintlock days. Both American and foreign specimens are included.

U.S. Enfield, by Ian Skennerton, Ian Skennerton, Margate, Australia, 1983. 190 pp., illus. $21.50.

Covers both the British pattern and the U.S. Model 1917 rifles.

U.S. Military Small Arms 1816-1865, by Robert M. Reilly, The Gun Room Press, Highland Park, NJ, 1983. 270 pp., illus. $35.00.

Covers every known type of primary and secondary martial firearms used by Federal forces.

The Virginia Manufactory of Arms, by Giles Cromwell, University Press of Virginia, Charlottesville, VA, 1975. 205 pp., illus. $29.95.

The only complete history of the Virginia Manufactory of Arms which produced muskets, pistols, swords, and cannon for the state's militia from 1802 through 1821.

Walther P-38 Pistol, by Maj. George Nonte, Desert Publications, Cornville, AZ, 1982. 100 pp., illus. Paper covers. $7.50.

Complete volume on one of the most famous handguns to come out of WWII. All models covered.

Walther Models PP and PPK, 1929-1945, by James L. Rankin, assisted by Gary Green, James L. Rankin, Coral Gables, FL, 1974. 142 pp., illus. $20.00.

Complete coverage on the subject as to finish, proof marks and Nazi Party inscriptions.

Walther Volume II, Engraved, Presentation and Standard Models, by James L. Rankin, J.L. Rankin, Coral Gables, FL, 1977. 112 pp., illus. $20.00.

The new Walther book on embellished versions and standard models. Has 88 photographs, including many color plates.

Walther, Volume III, 1908-1980, by James L. Rankin, Coral Gables, FL, 1981. 226 pp., illus. $24.50.

Covers all models of Walther handguns from 1908 to date, includes holsters, grips and magazines.

The Whitney Firearms, by Claud Fuller. Standard Publications, Huntington, W. Va., 1946. 334 pp., many plates and drawings. $40.00.

An authoritative history of all Whitney arms and their maker. Highly recommended. An exclusive with Ray Riling Arms Books Co.

The William M. Locke Collection, compiled by Robert B. Berryman, et al, The Antique Armory, Inc., East Point, GA, 1973. 541 pp., illus. $40.00.

A magnificently produced book illustrated with hundreds of photographs of guns from one of the finest collection of American firearms ever assembled.

The Winchester Book, by George Madis, Art & Reference House, Lancaster, TX, 1980. 638 pp., illus. $39.50.

A greatly enlarged edition of this most informative book on these prized American arms.

The Winchester Handbook, by George Madis, Art & Reference House, Lancaster, TX, 1982. 287 pp., illus. $19.95.

The complete line of Winchester guns, with dates of manufacture, serial numbers, etc.

Winchester—The Gun That Won the West, by H.F. Williamson. Combat Forces Press, Washington, D.C., 1952. Later eds. by Barnes, NY. 494 pp., profusely illus., paper covers. $20.00.

A scholarly and essential economic history of an honored arms company, but the early and modern arms introduced will satisfy all but the exacting collector.

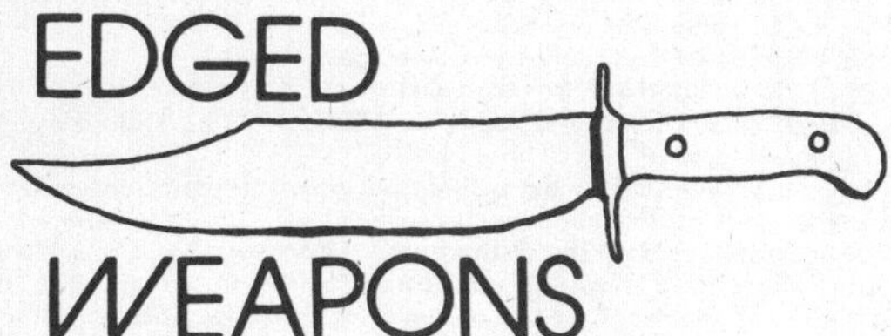

The Robert Abels Collection of Bowie Type Knives of American Interest, by Robert Abels, Robert Abels, Hopewell Junction, NY, 1974. 20 pp., illus. Paper covers. $1.95.

A selection of American Bowie-type knives from the collection of Robert Abels.

American Axes, by Henry Kauffman, The Stephen Green Press, Brattleboro, VT, 1972. 200 pp., illus. $25.00.

A definitive work on the subject. Contains a roster of American axe makers, glossary and notes on the care and use of axes.

American Knives; The First History and Collector's Guide, by Harold L. Peterson, The Gun Room Press, Highland Park, NJ, 1980. 178 pp., illus. $15.00.

A reprint of this 1958 classic. Covers all types of American knives.

American Polearms 1526-1865, by Rodney Hilton Brown, H. Flayderman & Co., New Milford, CT, 1967. 198 pp., illus. $14.50.

The lance, halbred, spontoon, pike and naval boarding weapons used in the American military forces through the Civil War.

American Primitive Knives 1770-1870, by G.B. Minnes, Museum Restoration Service, Ottawa, Canada, 1983. 112 pp., illus. $14.95.

Origins of the knives, outstanding specimens, structural details, etc.

The American Sword, 1775-1945, by Harold L. Peterson, Ray Riling Arms Books, Co., Phila., PA, 1980. 286 pp. plus 60 pp. of illus. $29.95.

1977 reprint of a survey of swords worn by U.S. uniformed forces, plus the rare "American Silver Mounted Swords, (1700-1815)."

The Art of Blacksmithing, by Alex W. Bealer, Funk & Wagnalls, New York, NY, revised edition, 1976. 438 pp., illus. $21.95.

Required reading for anyone who makes knives or is seriously interested in the history of cutlery.

The Best of Knife World, Volume I, edited by Knife World Publ., Knoxville, TN, 1980. 92 pp., illus. Pater covers. $3.95.

A collection of articles about knives. Reprinted from monthly issues of Knife World.

Blacksmithing for the Home Craftsman, by Joe Pehoski, Joe Pehoski, Washington, TX, 1973. 44 pp., illus. Paper covers. $3.50.

This informative book is chock-full of drawings and explains how to make your own forge.

Blades and Barrels, by H. Gordon Frost, Wallon Press, El Paso, TX, 1972. 298 pp., illus. $17.95.

The first full scale study about man's attempts to combine an edged weapon with a firearm.

Bowie Knives, by Robert Abels, Robert Abels, NY, 1960. 48 pp., illus. Paper covers. $3.00.

A booklet showing knives, tomahawks, related trade cards and advertisements.

Custom Knife...II, by John Davis Bates, Jr., and James Henry Schippers, Jr., Custom Knife Press, Memphis, TN, 1974. 112 pp., illus. $20.00.

The book of pocket knives and folding hunters. A guide to the 20th century makers' art.

For Knife Lovers Only, by Harry K. McEvoy, Knife World Publ., Knoxville, TN, 1979. 67 pp., illus. Paper covers. $4.95.

A fascinating and unusual approach to the story of knives.

The German Bayonet, by John Walter, Arms and Armour Press, London, England, 1982. 128 pp., illus. $19.95.

A comprehensive history of the regulation patterns 1871-1945.

A Guide to Handmade Knives, edited by Mel Tappan, The Janus Press, Inc., Los Angeles, CA, 1977. No paper covers. Deluxe hardbound. $19.50.

The official directory of the Knifemakers Guild.

Gun Digest Book of Knives, 2nd Edition, by Jack Lewis and Roger Combs, DBI Books, Inc., Northfield, IL, 1982. 288 pp., illus. Paper covers. $10.95.

Covers the complete spectrum of the fascinating world of knives.

How to Make Knives, by Richard W. Barney & Robert W. Loveless, Beinfield Publ., Inc., No. Hollywood, CA, 1977. 178 pp., illus. $15.00.

A book filled with drawings, illustrations, diagrams, and 500 how-to-do-it photos.

Inscribed Union Swords, 1861-1865, by David V. Stroud, Pinecrest Publishing Co., Kilgore, TX, 1984. 192 pp., illus. Limited, numbered, and signed edition. $27.50.

A definitive work on presentation Union swords.

Kentucky Knife Traders Manual No. 6, by R.B. Ritchie, Hindman, KY, 1980. 217 pp., illus. Paper covers. $10.00.

Guide for dealers, collectors and traders listing pocket knives and razor values.

Knives '86, 6th Edition, edited by Ken Warner, DBI Books, Inc., Northbrook, IL, 1985. 256 pp., illus. Paper covers. $11.95.

Covers trends and technology for both custom and factory knives.

Knife Digest, Second Annual Edition, edited by William L. Cassidy, Knife Digest Publ. Co., Berkeley, CA, 1976. 178 pp., illus. $15.00.

The second annual edition of the internationally known book on blades.

Knife Throwing, Sport...Survival...Defense, by Blackie Collins, Knife World Publ., Knoxville, TN, 1979. 31 pp., illus. Paper covers. $3.00.

How to select a knife, how to make targets, how to determine range and how to survive with a knife.

Knife Throwing a Practical Guide, by Harry K. McEvoy, Charles E. Tuttle Co., Rutland, VT, 1973. 108 pp., illus. Paper covers. $3.95.

If you want to learn to throw a knife this is the "bible".

Knifecraft: A Comprehensive Step-by-Step Guide to the Art of Knifemaking, by Sid Latham, Stackpole Books, Harrisburg, PA, 1978. 224 pp., illus. $24.95.

An exhaustive volume taking both amateur and accomplished knifecrafter through all the steps in creating a knife.

Knives and Knifemakers, by Sid Latham, Winchester Press, Piscataway, NJ, 1973. 152 pp., illus. $17.50.

Lists makers and suppliers of knife-making material and equipment.

Levine's Guide to Knife Values, by Bernard R. Levine, DBI Books, Inc., Northbrook, IL, 1985. 480 pp., illus. Paper covers. $19.95.

An important guide to today's knife values.

Light But Efficient, by Albert N. Hardin, Jr. and Robert W. Hedden, Albert N. Hardin, Jr., Pennsauken, NJ, 1973. 103 pp., illus. $7.95.

A study of the M1880 Hunting and M1890 intrenching knives and scabbards.

Marble Knives and Axes, by Konrad F. Schreier, Jr., Beinfeld Publ., Inc., No. Hollywood, CA, 1978. 80 pp., illus. Paper covers. $5.95.

The first work ever on the knives and axes made by this famous old, still-in-business, manufacturer.

The Modern Blacksmith, by Alexander G. Weygers, Van Nostrand Reinhold Co., NY, 1977. 96 pp., illus. $10.95.

Shows how to forge objects out of steel. Use of basic techniques and tools.

Nathan Starr Arms Maker 1776-1845, by James E. Hicks, The Restoration Press, Phoenix, AZ, 1976. 166 pp., illus. $12.95.

Survey of the work of Nathan Starr of Middletown, CT, in producing edged weapons and pole arms for the U.S., 1799-1840, also some firearms.

Naval Swords, by P.G.W. Annis, Stackpole Books, Harrisburg, PA, 1970. 80 pp., illus. $12.50.

British and American naval edged weapons 1660-1815.

A Photographic Supplement of Confederate Swords with Addendum, by William A. Albaugh III, Moss Publications, Orange, VA, 1979. 259 pp., illus. $24.95.

A new updated edition of the classic work on Confederate edged weapons.

Pocket Knife Book 1 & 2—Price Guide, by Roy Ehrhardt, Heart of America Press, Kansas City, MO, 1974. 96 pp., illus. Spiral bound stiff paper covers. $6.95.

Reprints from the pocket knife sections of early manufacturers and sporting goods catalogs.

Pocket Knife Book 3—Price Guide, by Roy and Larry Ehrhardt, Heart of America Press, Kansas City, MO, 1974. Spiral bound stiff paper covers. $6.95.

Compiled from sections of various product sales catalogs of both Winchester and Marble Co. dating from the '20s and '30s.

The Pocketknife Manual, by Blackie Collins, Blackie Collins, Rock Hill, SC, 1976. 102 pp., illus. Paper covers. $5.50.

Building, repairing and refinishing pocketknives.

Practical Blacksmithing, edited by J. Richardson, Outlet Books, NY, 1978. four volumes in one, illus. $9.98.

A reprint of the extremely rare, bible of the blacksmith. Covers every aspect of working with iron and steel. from ancient uses to modern.

Rice's Trowel Bayonet, reprinted by Ray Riling Arms Books, Co., Phila., PA, 1968. 8 pp., illus. Paper covers. $3.00.

A facsimile reprint of a rare circular originally published by the U.S. Government in 1875 for the information of U.S. Troops.

The Samurai Sword, by John M. Yumoto, Charles E. Tuttle Co., Rutland, VT, 1958. 191 pp., illus. $11.00.

A must for anyone interested in Japanese blades, and the first book on this subject written in English.

Scottish Swords from the Battlefield at Culloden, by Lord Archibald Campbell, The Mowbray Co., Providence, RI, 1973. 63 pp., illus. $5.00.

A modern reprint of an exceedingly rare 1894 privately printed edition.

Step-by-Step Knifemaking, by Davis Boye, Rodale Press, Emmous, PA, 1978. 288 pp.,illus. $12.95.

Gives the fundamentals of knifemaking and shows how to make knives either as a hobby or as a business.

The Sword in the Age of Chivalry, by R. Ewar Oakeshott, Arms & Armour Press, London, England, 1982. 160 pp., illus. $32.50.

A classic work—the result of 25 years of research by an authority whose work is acknowledged by scholars all over the world.

Swords and Other Edged Weapons, by Robert Wilkinson-Latham, Arco Publishing Co., New York, NY, 1978. 227 pp., illus. $8.95.

Traces the history of the "Queen of Weapons" from its earliest forms in the stone age to the military swords of the Twentieth century.

Tomahawks Illustrated, by Robert Kuck, Robert Kuck, New Knoxville, OH, 1977. 112 pp., illus. Paper covers. $10.00.

A pictorial record to provide a reference in selecting and evaluating tomahawks.

U.S. Military Knives, Bayonets and Machetes, Book III, by M. H. Cole, M.H. Cole, Birmingham, AL, 1979. 219 pp., illus. $25.00.

The most complete text ever written on U.S. military knives, bayonets, machetes and bolo's.

GENERAL

Advanced Muzzleloader's Guide, by Toby Bridges, Stoeger Publishing Co., So. Hackensack, NJ, 1985. 256 pp., illus. Paper covers. $11.95.

The complete guide to muzzle-loading rifles, pistols and shotguns—flintlock and percussion.

American Gunsmiths, by Frank M. Sellers, The Gun Room Press, Highland Park, NJ, 1983. 349 pp. $39.95.

A comprehensive listing of the American gun maker, patentee, gunsmith and entrepreneur.

American Tools of Intrigue, by John Minnery & Jose Ramos, Desert Publications, Cornville, AZ, 1981. 128 pp., illus. Paper covers. $10.00.

Clandestine weapons which the Allies supplied to resistance fighters.

Black Powder Gun Digest, 3rd Edition, edited by Jack Lewis, DBI Books, Inc., Northfield, IL, 1982. 256 pp., illus. Paper covers. $11.95.

All new articles, expressly written for the black powder gun buff.

Buckskins and Black Powder, by Ken Grissom, Winchester Press, Piscataway, NJ, 1983. 224 pp., illus. $15.95.

A mountain man's guide to muzzleloading.

Carbine; The Story of David Marshall "Carbine" Williams, by Ross E. Beard, Jr., The Sandlapper Store, Inc., Lexington, SC, 1977. 315 pp., illus. Deluxe limited edition, numbered and signed by the author and "Carbine". $25.

The story of the man who invented the M1 Carbine and holds 52 other firearms patents.

Colonial Frontier Guns, by T.M. Hamilton, The Fur Press, Chadron, NE, 1980. 176 pp., illus. Paper covers. $12.00.

French, Dutch, and English trade guns before 1780.

Colonial Riflemen in the American Revolution, by Joe D. Huddleston, George Shumway Publisher, York, PA, 1978. 70 pp., illus. $18.00.

This study traces the use of the longrifle in the Revolution for the purpose of evaluating what effects it had on the outcome.

The Complete Black Powder Handbook, by Sam Fadala, DBI Books, Inc. Northfield, IL, 1979. 288 pp., illus. Paper covers. $11.95.

Everything you want to know about black powder firearms and their shooting.

Complete Book of Shooting: Rifles, Shotguns, Handguns, by Jack O'Connor, Stackpole Books, Harrisburg, PA, 1983. 392 pp., illus. $24.95.

A thorough guide to each area of the sport, appealing to those with a new or ongoing interest in shooting.

The Complete Book of Target Shooting, by Wes Blair, Stackpole Books, Harrisburg, PA, 1984. 416 pp., illus. $24.95.

The encyclopedia of up-to-date shooting information.

The Complete Book of Thompson Patents, compiled by Don Thomas, The Gun Room Press, Highland Park, NJ, 1981. 482 pp., illus. Paper covers. $15.95.

From John Blish's breech closure patented in 1915 to Charles W. Robin's automatic sear release of 1947. Includes all other firearm patents granted to the developers of the famed "Tommy gun."

The Complete Book of Trick & Fancy Shooting, by Ernie Lind, The Citadel Press, Secaucus, NJ, 1977. 159 pp., illus. Paper covers. $6.00.

Step-by-step instructions for acquiring the whole range of shooting skills with rifle, pistol and shotgun.

The Complete Encyclopedia of Arms and Weapons, by Leonid Tarassuk and Claude Blair, Charles Scribner's Sons, New York, N.Y., 1983. 560 pp., illus. $41.50.

Describes armor, crossbows, swords, daggers, cannon, pistols, rifles, bayonets, etc. Comprehensive and arranged alphabetically.

The Complete Guide to Game Care and Cookery, by Sam Fadala, DBI Books, Inc., Northfield, IL, 1981. 288 pp., illus. Paper covers. $11.95.

A step-by-step journey beginning with meat-hunting philosophy and tactics through what to do with the game once you've brought it down. Includes many recipes.

The Complete Shooter, by Sam Fadala, DBI Books, Inc., Northfield, IL, 1984. 480 pp., illus. Paper covers. $17.95.

Covers nearly every aspect of shooting, from how to choose the right cartridge/rifle, recoil, defense, varmint, black powder guns, sights, reloading wildcats—nearly everything.

The Complete Survival Guide, edited by Mark Thiffault, DBI Books, Inc., Northfield, IL, 1983. 256 pp., illus. Paper covers. $10.95.

Covers all aspects of survival from manmade and natural disasters—equipment, techniques, weapons, etc.

Dead Aim, by Lee Echols, Acme Printing Co., San Diego, CA, a reprint, 1972. 116 pp., illus. $9.95.

Nostalgic antics of hell-raising pistol shooters of the 1930's.

Eli Whitney and the Whitney Armory, by Merrill Lindsay, Arma Press, North Branford, CT, 1979. 95 pp., illus. Paper covers. $4.95. Cloth $9.95.

History of the Whitney Armory 1767-1862, with notes on how to identify Whitney flintlocks.

The Encyclopedia of Infantry Weapons of World War II, by Ian V. Hogg, Harper & Row, New York, NY, 1977. 192 pp., illus. $15.95.

A fully comprehensive and illustrated reference work including every major type of weapon used by every army in the world during World War II.

Encyclopedia of Modern Firearms, Vol. 1, compiled and publ. by Bob Brownell, Montezuma, IA, 1959. 1057 pp. plus index, illus. $50.00. Dist. by Bob Brownell, Montezuma, IA 50171.

Massive accumulation of basic information of nearly all modern arms pertaining to "parts and assembly". Replete with arms photographs, exploded drawings, manufacturers' lists of parts, etc.

The FP-45 Liberator Pistol, 1942-1945, by R.W. Koch, Research, Arcadia, CA, 1976. 116 pp., illus. $15.00.

A definitive work on this unique clandestine weapon.

Famous Guns & Gunners, by George E. Virgines, Leather Stocking Press, West Allis, WI, 1980. 113 pp., illus. $12.95.

Intriguing and fascinating tales of men of the West and their guns.

Firearms of the American West, 1803-1865, by Louis A. Garavaglia and Charles G. Worman, University of New Mexico Press, Albuquerque, NM, 1983. 300 pp., illus. $35.00.

An encyclopedic study tracing the development of uses of firearms on the frontier during that period.

The German Sniper, 1914-1945, by Peter R. Senich, Paladin Press, Boulder, CO, 1982. 468 pp., illus. $49.95.

The development and application of Germany's sniping weapons systems and tactics traced from WW I through WW II.

Great Sporting Posters, by Sid Latham, Stackpole Books, Harrisburg, PA, 1980. 48 pp., illus. Paper covers. $14.95.

Twenty-three full-color reproductions of beautiful hunting and fishing poster art, mostly of the early 1900s.

Gun Digest 1986, 40th Edition, edited by Ken Warner, DBI Books, Inc., Northbrook, IL, 1985. 496 pp., illus. Paper covers. $15.95.

All-new articles in this most famous of gun annuals.

Gun Digest Book of Holsters and Other Gun Leather, edited by Roger Combs, DBI Books, Inc., Northfield, IL, 1983. 256 pp., illus. Paper covers. $11.95.

An in-depth look at all facets of leather goods in conjunction with guns. Covers design, manufacture, uses, etc.

Gun Digest Book of Metallic Silhouette Shooting, by Elgin Gates, DBI Books, Inc., Northfield, IL, 1979. 256 pp., illus. Paper covers. $11.95.

Examines all aspects of this fast growing sport including history, rules and meets.

Gun Digest Book of Modern Gun Values, 5th Edition, by Jack Lewis, ed. by Harold A. Murtz, DBI Books, Inc., Northfield, IL, 1985. 432 pp., illus. Paper covers. $14.95.

All-new expanded edition covers the current values of all non-military guns in production from 1900-1983.

Gun Digest Book of Scopes and Mounts, by Bob Bell, DBI Books, Inc., Northfield, IL, 1983. 224 pp., illus. Paper covers. $11.95.

Traces the complete history, design, development of scopes and mounts from their beginnings to the current high-tech level of today. Covers the various uses and applications for the modern shooter/hunter.

Gun Digest Book of Sporting Dogs, by Carl P. Wood, DBI Books, Inc., Northbrook, IL, 1985. 256 pp., illus. Paper covers. $11.95.

Investigates various training philosophies, problem dogs, training for versatility, kenneling, etc. Covers most all hunting/sporting dogs.

Gun Talk, edited by Dave Moreton, Winchester Press, Piscataway, NJ, 1973. 256 pp., illus. $9.95.

A treasury of original writing by the top gun writers and editors in America. Practical advice about every aspect of the shooting sports.

The Gun That Made the Twenties Roar, by Wm. J. Helmer, rev. and enlarged by George C. Nonte, Jr., The Gun Room Press, Highland Park, NJ, 1977. Over 300 pp., illus. $17.95.

Historical account of John T. Thompson and his invention, the infamous "Tommy Gun."

The Gunfighter, Man or Myth? by Joseph G. Rosa, Oklahoma Press, Norman, OK, 1969. 229 pp., illus. (including weapons). Paper covers. $9.95.

A well-documented work on gunfights and gunfighters of the West and elsewhere. Great treat for all gunfighter buffs.

The Gunfighters, by Dale T. Schoenberger, The Caxton Printers, Ltd., Caldwell, ID, 1971. 207 pp., illus. $17.95.

Startling expose of our foremost Western folk heroes.

Guns of the Gunfighters, by the editors of Guns & Ammo, Crown Publishing Co., New York, NY, 1982. 50 pp., illus. Paper covers. $6.98.

A must for Western buffs and gun collectors alike.

Guns Illustrated, 1986, 18th Edition, edited by Harold A. Murtz, DBI Books, Northbrook, IL, 1985. 344 pp., illus. Paper covers. $13.95.

Packed with timely interesting articles and solid field testing on a wide variety of firearms.

The Gunsmith in Colonial Virginia, by Harold B. Gill, Jr., University Press of Virginia, Charlottesville, VA, 1975. 200 pp., illus. $11.95.
The role of the gunsmith in colonial Virginia from the first landing at Jamestown through the Revolution is examined, with special attention to those who lived and worked in Williamsburg.

Guns & Shooting: A Selected Bibliography, by Ray Riling, Ray Riling Arms Books Co., Phila., PA, 1982. 434 pp., illus. Limited, numbered edition. $75.00.
A limited edition of this superb bibliographical work, the only modern listing of books devoted to guns and shooting.

Hatcher's Notebook, by Maj. Gen. J. S. Hatcher. Stackpole Books, Harrisburg, Pa., 1952. 2nd ed. with four new chapters, 1957. 629 pp., illus. $19.95.
A dependable source of information for gunsmiths, ballisticians, historians, hunters, and collectors.

Hit the White Part, by Massad Ayoob, Concord, NH, 1982. 107 pp., illus. Paper covers. $7.95.
Second Chance, the art of bowling pin shooting.

Home Guide to Muzzle Loaders, by George C. Nonte, Jr., Stackpole Books, Harrisburg, PA, 1982. 224 pp., illus. Paper covers. $14.95.
From the basics of muzzleloading, to the differences between the modern and replica muzzle loader, plus how to make one.

How to Make Practical Pistol Leather, by J. David McFarland, Desert Publications, Cornville, AZ. 1982. 68 pp., illus. Paper covers. $8.00.
A guide for designing and making holsters and accessories for law enforcement, security, survival and sporting use.

The Identification and Registration of Firearms, by Vaclav "Jack" Krcma, C. C. Thomas, Springfield, IL, 1971. 173 pp., illus. $25.00.
Analysis of problems and improved techniques of recording firearms data accurately.

Kill or Get Killed, by Col. Rex Applegate, new rev. and enlarged ed. Paladin Press, Boulder, CO, 1976. 421 pp., illus. $19.95.
For police and military forces. Last word on mob control.

Law Enforcement Bible, No. 2, edited by Det. Robert A. Scanlon, Stoeger Publishing Co., So. Hackensack, NJ, 1984. 368 pp., illus. Paper covers. $11.95.
World's standard law enforcement reference.

The Law Enforcement Book of Weapons, Ammunition and Training Procedures, Handguns, Rifles and Shotguns, by Mason Williams, Charles C. Thomas, Publisher, Springfield, IL, 1977. 496 pp., illus. $40.00.
Data on firearms, firearm training, and ballistics.

Law Enforcement Handgun Digest, 3rd Edition, by Jack Lewis, DBI Books, Inc., Northfield, IL, 1980. 288 pp., illus. Paper covers. $10.95.
Covers such subjects as the philosophy of a firefight, SWAT, weapons, training, combat shooting, etc.

L'Incisione Delle Armi Sportive (Engraving of Sporting Arms), by Mario Abbiatico, Edizioni Artistiche Italiane, Famars, Brescia, Italy, 1983. 536 pp., illus. Italian text. $125.00.
An encyclopedia of Italian engraving on sporting arms, with 1,000 black and white and 200 full-color photos.

Lyman Muzzleloader's Handbook, 2nd Edition, edited by C. Kenneth Ramage, Lyman Publications, Middlefield, CT, 1982. 248 pp., illus. Paper covers. $11.95.
Hunting with rifles and shotguns, plus muzzle loading products.

The Machine Gun: Book 2, by Col. George M. Chinn, USMC (Ret.), Bureau of Ordnance, Dept. of the Navy, 1952, reprinted by Col. Chinn, 1982. 236 pp., illus. Limited signed and numbered edition. $29.95.
History, evolution and development of manual, auto, and airborne repeating weapons by the Soviet Union and her satellites.

The Machine Gun: Book 3, by Col. George M. Chinn, USMC (Ret.), Bureau of Ordnance, Dept. of the Navy, 1951, reprinted by Col. Chinn, 1982. 717 pp., 407 illus. $49.95.
Development during WW II and the Korean conflict by the U.S. and their Allies of full-auto machine gun systems.

The Machine Gun: Book 4, by Col. George M. Chinn, USMC (Ret.), Bureau of Ordnance, Dept. of the Navy, 1955, reprinted by Col. Chinn, 1982. 662 pp., illus. Signed and numbered edition. $49.95.
Graphs and schematic line drawings of mechanisms and their operation.

Medicolegal Investigation of Gunshot Wounds, by Abdullah Fatteh, J.B. Lippincott Co., Phila., PA, 1977. 272 pp., illus. $35.00.
A much-needed work, clearly written and easily understood, dealing with all aspects of medicolegal investigation of gunshot wounds and deaths.

Military Small Arms of the 20th Century, 5th Edition, by Ian V. Hogg and John Weeks, DBI Books, Inc., Northfield, IL, 1985. 304 pp., illus. Paper covers. $14.95.
Fully revised and updated edition of the standard reference in its field.

Modern Airweapon Shooting, by Bob Churchill & Granville Davis, David & Charles, London, England, 1981. 196 pp., illus. $20.00.
A comprehensive, illustrated study of all the relevant topics, from beginnings to world championship shooting.

No Second Place Winner, by Wm. H. Jordan, publ. by the author, Shreveport, LA (Box 4072), 1962. 114 pp., illus. $12.50.
Guns and gear of the peace officer, ably discussed by a U.S. Border Patrolman for over 30 years, and a first-class shooter with handgun, rifle, etc.

Old Time Posters from the Great Sporting Days, Stackpole Books, Harrisburg, PA, 1982. 48 pp., illus. Paper covers. $19.95.
Quality reproductions of 22 fine sporting posters in full color. 11"x16".

Olympic Shooting, by Colonel Jim Crossman, NRA, Washington, DC, 1978. 136 pp., illus. $12.95.
The complete, authoritative history of U.S. participation in the Olympic shooting events from 1896 until the present.

Pistols of the World, Revised Edition, by Ian V. Hogg and John Weeks, DBI Books, Inc., Northfield, IL, 1982. 304 pp., illus. Paper covers. $12.95.
Revised, single-volume encyclopedia begins in 1870 and follows the development of the hand-held weapon through today. 2000 handguns are described.

E.C. Prudhomme, Master Gun Engraver, A Retrospective Exhibition: 1946-1973, intro. by John T. Amber, The R.W. Norton Art Gallery, Shreveport, LA, 1973. 32 pp., illus., paper covers. $5.00.
Examples of master gun engraving by Jack Prudhomme.

The Quiet Killers II: Silencer Update, by J. David Truby, Paladin Press, Boulder, CO, 1979. 92 pp., illus. Paper covers. $8.00.
A unique and up-to-date addition to your silencer bookshelf.

Sam Colt: Genius, by Robt. F. Hudson, American Archives Publ. Co., Topsfield, MA, 1971. 160 pp., illus. Plastic spiral bound. $6.50.
Historical review of Colt's inventions, including facsimiles of patent papers and other Colt information.

The Shooter's Workbench, by John A. Mosher, Winchester Press, Piscataway, NJ, 1977. 256 pp., illus. $15.95.
Accessories the shooting sportsman can build for the range or shop, for transport and the field, and for the handloading bench.

Small Arms of the World, 12th Edition, by W.H.B. Smith, revised by Edward C. Ezell, Stackpole Books, Harrisburg, PA, 1983. 1,024 pp., illus. $49.95.
An encyclopedia of global weapons—over 3,500 entries.

Sporting Arms of the World, by Ray Bearse, Outdoor Life/Harper & Row, N.Y., 1977. 500 pp., illus. $15.95.
A mammoth, up-to-the-minute guide to the sporting world's favorite rifles, shotguns, handguns.

Street Survival Tactics for Armed Encounters, by Ronald J. Adams, et al, Calibre Press, Northbrook, IL, 1983. 403 pp., illus. $25.95.
Positive tactics to employ on the street to effectively use firearms to defeat assailants.

Survival Guns, by Mel Tappan, The Janus Press, Inc., Los Angeles, CA, 1976. 458 pp., illus. Paper covers. $9.95.
A guide to the selection, modification and use of firearms and related devices for defense, food gathering, etc. under survival conditions.

Thompson Guns 1921-1945, Anubis Press, Houston, TX, 1980. 215 pp., illus. Paper covers. $10.00.
Facsimile reprinting of five complete manuals on the Thompson submachine gun.

The Trapper's Handbook, by Rick Jamison, DBI Books, Inc., Northfield, IL, 1983. 224 pp., illus. Paper covers. $11.95.
Gives the ins and outs of successful trapping from making scent to marketing the pelts. Tips and solutions to trapping problems.

A Treasury of Outdoor Life, edited by William E. Rae, Stackpole Books, Harrisburg, PA, 1983. 520 pp., illus. $24.95.
The greatest hunting, fishing, and survival stories from America's favorite sportsman's magazine.

Triggernometry, by Eugene Cunningham. Caxton Printers Lt., Caldwell, ID, 1970. 441 pp., illus. $12.95.
A classic study of famous outlaws and lawmen of the West—their stature as human beings, their exploits and skills in handling firearms. A reprint.

Weapons of the American Revolution, and Accoutrements, by Warren Moore. A & W Books, NY, 1974. 225 pp., fine illus. $15.
Revolutionary era shoulder arms, pistols, edged weapons, and equipment are described and shown in fine drawings and photographs, some in color.

The Winchester Era, by David Madis, Art & Reference House, Brownsville, TX, 1984. 100 pp., illus. $14.95.
Story of the Winchester company, management, employees, etc.

You Can't Miss, by John Shaw and Michael Bane, John Shaw, Memphis, TN, 1983. 152 pp., illus. Paper covers. $9.95.
The secrets of a successful combat shooter; tells how to better your defensive shooting skills.

Gunsmithing

The Art of Engraving, by James B. Meek, F. Brownell & Son, Montezuma, IA, 1973. 196 pp., illus. $24.95.
A complete, authoritative, imaginative and detailed study in training for gun engraving. The first book of its kind—and a great one.

Artistry in Arms, The R.W. Norton Gallery, Shreveport, LA., 1970. 42 pp., illus. Paper, $5.00.
The art of gunsmithing and engraving.

Basic Gunsmithing, by John E. Traister. Tab Books, Inc., Blue Ridge Summit, PA, 1983. 288 pp., illus. Paper covers. $9.95.
An owner's guide to repairing, remodeling, cleaning, and restoring rifles, shotguns, and handguns.

Building the Kentucky Pistol, by James R. Johnston, Golden Age Arms Co., Worthington, OH, 1974. 36 pp., illus. Paper covers. $4.00.
A step-by-step guide for building the Kentucky pistol. Illus. with full page line drawings.

Building the Kentucky Rifle, by J.R. Johnston. Golden Age Arms Co., Worthington, OH, 1972. 44 pp., illus. Paper covers. $5.00.
How to go about it, with text and drawings.

Checkering and Carving of Gun Stocks, by Monte Kennedy. Stackpole Books, Harrisburg, PA, 1962. 175 pp., illus. $27.95.
Rev., enlarged clothbound ed. of a much sought-after, dependable work.

Clyde Baker's Modern Gunsmithing, revised by John E. Traister, Stackpole Books, Harrisburg, PA, 1981. 530 pp., illus. $24.95.
A revision of the classic work on gunsmithing.

The Complete Rehabilitation of the Flintlock Rifle and Other Works, by T.B. Tyron. Limbo Library, Taos, NM, 1972. 112 pp., illus. Paper covers. $6.95.
A series of articles which first appeared in various issues of the *American Rifleman* in the 1930s.

Contemporary American Stockmakers, by Ron Toews, The Dove Press, Enid, OK, 1979. 216 pp., illus. $80.00.
The only reference book on its subject. Over 200 detailed photographs of fine rifle stocking.

Do-It-Yourself Gunsmithing, by Jim Carmichel, Outdoor Life-Harper & Row, New York, NY, 1977. 371 pp., illus. $16.95.
The author proves that home gunsmithing is relatively easy and highly satisfying.

Firearms Assembly 3: The NRA Guide to Rifle and Shotguns, NRA Books, Wash., D.C., 1980. 264 pp., illus. Paper covers. $11.50.

Text and illustrations explaining the takedown of 125 rifles and shotguns, domestic and foreign.

Firearms Assembly 4: The NRA Guide to Pistols and Revolvers, NRA Books, Wash., D.C., 1980. 253 pp., illus. Paper covers. $11.50.

Text and illustrations explaining the takedown of 124 pistol and revolver models, domestic and foreign.

Firearms Blueing and Browning, by R.H. Angier. Stackpole Books, Harrisburg, PA, 151 pp., illus. $12.95.

A useful, concise text on chemical coloring methods for the gunsmith and mechanic.

First Book of Gunsmithing, by John E. Traister, Stackpole Books, Harrisburg, PA, 1981. 192 pp., illus. $18.95.

Beginner's guide to gun care, repair and modification.

Gun Care and Repair, by Monte Burch, Winchester Press, Piscataway, NJ, 1978. 256 pp., illus. $15.95.

Everything the gun owner needs to know about home gunsmithing and firearms maintenance.

Gun Digest Book of Exploded Firearms Drawings, 3rd Edition edited by Harold A. Murtz, DBI Books, Inc., Northfield, IL, 1982. 480 pp., illus. Paper covers. $14.95.

Contains 470 isometric views of modern and collector's handguns and long guns, with parts lists. A must for the gunsmith or tinkerer.

The Gun Digest Book of Firearms Assembly/Disassembly Part I: Automatic Pistols, by J.B. Wood, DBI Books, Inc., Northfield, IL, 1979. 320 pp., illus. Paper covers. $12.95.

A thoroughly professional presentation on the art of pistol disassembly and reassembly. Covers most modern guns, popular older models, and some of the most complex pistols ever produced.

The Gun Digest Book of Firearms Assembly/Disassembly Part II: Revolvers, by J. B. Wood, DBI Books, Inc., Northfield, IL, 1979. 320 pp., illus. Paper covers. $12.95.

How to properly dismantle and reassemble both the revolvers of today and of the past.

The Gun Digest Book of Firearms Assembly/Disassembly Part III: Rimfire Rifles, by J. B. Wood, DBI Books, Inc., Northfield, IL, 1980. 288 pp., illus. Paper covers. $12.95.

A most comprehensive, uniform, and professional presentation available for disassembling and reassembling most rimfire rifles.

The Gun Digest Book of Firearms Assembly/Disassembly Part IV: Centerfire Rifles, by J. B. Wood, DBI Books, Inc., Northfield, IL, 1980. 288 pp., illus. Paper covers. $12.95.

A professional presentation on the disassembly and reassembly of centerfire rifles.

The Gun Digest Book of Firearms Assembly/Disassembly, Part V: Shotguns, by J.B. Wood, DBI Books, Inc., Northfield, IL, 1980. 288 pp., illus. Paper covers. $12.95.

A professional presentation on the complete disassembly and assembly of 26 of the most popular shotguns, new and old.

The Gun Digest Book of Firearms Assembly/Disassembly Part VI: Law Enforcement Weapons, by J.B. Wood, DBI Books, Inc., Northfield, IL, 1981. 288 pp., illus. Paper covers. $12.95.

Step-by-step instructions on how to completely dismantle and reassemble the most commonly used firearms found in law enforcement arsenals.

Gun Digest Book of Gun Care, Cleaning and Refinishing, Book One: Handguns, by J.B. Wood, DBI Books, Inc., Northfield, IL, 1984. 160 pp., illus. Paper covers. $8.95.

The how, when and why of proper maintenance: revolvers, autoloaders, blackpowder handguns.

Gun Digest Book of Gun Care, Cleaning and Refinishing, Book Two: Long Guns, by J.B. Wood, DBI Books, Inc., Northfield, IL, 1984. 160 pp., illus. Paper covers. $8.95.

The care and maintenance of long guns with meticulous detail and step-by-step, illustrated, clearly written text.

Gun Digest Book of Gunsmithing Tools and Their Uses, by John E. Traister, DBI Books, Inc., Northfield, IL, 1980. 256 pp., illus. Paper covers. $10.95.

The how, when and why of tools for amateur and professional gunsmiths and gun tinkerers.

The Gun Digest Book of Pistolsmithing, by Jack Mitchell, DBI Books, Inc., Northfield, IL, 1980. 288 pp., illus. Paper covers. $11.95.

An expert's guide to the operation of each of the handgun actions with all the major functions of pistolsmithing explained.

Gun Digest Book of Riflesmithing, by Jack Mitchell, DBI Books, Inc., Northfield, IL, 1982. 256 pp., illus. Paper covers. $11.95.

The art and science of rifle gunsmithing. Covers tools, techniques, designs, finishing wood and metal, custom alterations.

Gun Digest Book of Shotgun Gunsmithing, by Ralph Walker, DBI Books, Inc., Northfield, IL, 1983. 256 pp., illus. Paper covers. $11.95.

The principles and practices of repairing, individualizing and accurizing modern shotguns by one of the world's premier shotgun gunsmiths.

Gun Owner's Book of Care, Repair & Improvement, by Roy Dunlap, Outdoor Life-Harper & Row, NY, 1977. 336 pp., illus. $12.95.

A basic guide to repair and maintenance of guns, written for the average firearms owner.

Guns and Gunmaking Tools of Southern Appalachia, by John Rice Irwin, Schiffer Publishing Ltd., 1983. 118 pp., illus. Paper covers. $9.95.

The story of the Kentucky rifle.

Gunsmith Kinks, by F.R. (Bob) Brownell. F. Brownell & Son, Montezuma, IA, 1st ed., 1969. 496 pp., well illus. $12.95.

A widely useful accumulation of shop kinks, short cuts, techniques and pertinent comments by practicing gunsmiths from all over the world.

Gunsmith Kinks 2, by Bob Brownell, F. Brownell & Son, Publishers, Montezuma, IA, 1983. 496 pp., illus. $14.95.

An incredible collection of gunsmithing knowledge, shop kinks, new and old techniques, short-cuts and general know-how straight from those who do them best—the gunsmiths.

Gunsmithing, by Roy F. Dunlap. Stackpole Books, Harrisburg, PA, 714 pp., illus. $27.95.

Comprehensive work on conventional techniques, incl. recent advances in the field. Valuable to rifle owners, shooters, and practicing gunsmiths.

Gunsmithing: The Tricks of the Trade, by J.B. Wood, DBI Books, Inc., Northfield, IL, 1982. 256 pp., illus. Paper covers. $11.95.

How to repair and replace broken gun parts using ordinary home workshop tools.

Gunsmiths and Gunmakers of Vermont, by Warren R. Horn, The Horn Co., Burlington, VT, 1976. 76 pp., illus. Paper covers. $5.00.

A checklist for collectors, of over 200 craftsmen who lived and worked in Vermont up to and including 1900.

The Gunsmith's Manual, by J.P. Stelle and Wm.B. Harrison, The Gun Room Press, Highland Park, NJ, 1982. 376 pp., illus. $12.95.

For the gunsmith in all branches of the trade.

Gunstock Finishing and Care, by A. Donald Newell, Stackpole Books, Harrisburg, PA, 1982. 512 pp., illus. $22.95.

The most complete resource imaginable for finishing and refinishing gun wood.

Home Gun Care & Repair, by P.O. Ackley, Stackpole Books, Harrisburg, PA, 1969. 191 pp., illus. Paper covers. $6.95.

Basic reference for safe tinkering, fixing, and converting rifles, shotguns, handguns.

Home Gunsmithing Digest, 3rd Edition, by Tommy L. Bish, DBI Books, Inc., Northfield, IL, 1984. 256 pp., illus. Paper covers. $11.95.

The know-how supplied by an expert.

How to Build Your Own Wheellock Rifle or Pistol, by George Lauber, The John Olson Co., Paramus, NJ, 1976. Paper covers. $9.95.

Complete instructions on building these arms.

How to Build Your Own Flintlock Rifle or Pistol, by Georg Lauber, The John Olson Co., Paramus, NJ, 1976. Paper covers. $9.95.

The second in Mr. Lauber's three-volume series on the art and science of building muzzle-loading black powder firearms.

"How to Build Your Own Percussion Rifle or Pistol", by Georg Lauber, The John Olson Co., Paramus, NJ, 1976. Paper covers, $9.95.

The third and final volume of Lauber's set of books on the building of muzzle-loaders.

Learn Gunsmithing, by John Traister, Winchester Press, Piscataway, NJ, 1980. 202 pp., illus. $16.95.

The troubleshooting method of gunsmithing for the home gunsmith and professional alike.

Lock, Stock and Barrel, by R.H. McCrory. Publ. by author at Bellmore, NY, 1966. Paper covers. 122 pp., illus. $6.00.

A handy and useful work for the collector or the professional with many helpful procedures shown and described on antique gun repair.

Mr. Single Shot's Gunsmithing Idea Book, by Frank DeHaas, Tab Books, Inc., Blue Ridge Summit, PA, 1983. 168 pp., illus. $18.95.

A must-have manual for anyone interested in collecting, repairing, or modifying single-shot rifles.

The Modern Gunsmith, by James V. Howe, Bonanza Books, NY, 1982. 415; 424; 68 pp., illus. $14.95.

Two volumes and the supplement in one. The most authoritative work ever written on gunsmithing and gunmaking.

The Modern Kentucky Rifle, How to Build Your Own, by R.H. McCrory. McCrory, Wantagh, NY, 1961. 68 pp., illus., paper bound. $6.00.

A workshop manual on how to fabricate a flintlock rifle. Also some information on pistols and percussion locks.

The NRA Gunsmithing Guide—Updated, by Ken Raynor and Brad Fenton, National Rifle Association, Wash., DC, 1984. 336 pp., illus. Paper covers. $15.95.

Material includes chapters and articles on all facets of the gunsmithing art.

Pistolsmithing, by George C. Nonte, Jr., Stackpole Books, Harrisburg, PA, 1974. 560 pp., illus. $27.95.

A single source reference to handgun maintainence, repair, and modification at home, unequaled in value.

Professional Care and Finishing of Gun Metal, by John E. Traister, Tab Books, Inc., Blue Ridge Summit, PA, 1982. 303 pp., illus. Paper covers. $12.95.

Restore old and antique firearms into handsome workable possessions.

Professional Gunsmithing, by W.J. Howe, Stackpole Books, Harrisburg, PA, 1968 reprinting. 526 pp., illus. $24.95.

Textbook on repair and alteration of firearms, with detailed notes on equipment and commercial gunshop operation.

Recreating the American Longrifle, by William Buchele, et al, George Shumway, Publisher, York, PA, 1983. 175 pp., illus. Paper covers. $20.00; Cloth $27.50.

Includes full-scale plans for building a Kentucky rifle.

Respectfully Yours H.M. Pope, compiled and edited by G.O. Kelver, Brighton, CO, 1976. 266 pp., illus. $16.50.

A compilation of letters from the files of the famous barrelmaker, Harry M. Pope.

The Trade Gun Sketchbook, by Charles E. Hanson, The Fur Press, Chadron, NB, 1979. 48 pp., illus. Paper covers. $4.00.

Complete full-size plans to build seven different trade guns from the Revolution to the Indian Wars and a two-thirds size for your son.

The Trade Rifle Sketchbook, by Charles E. Hanson, The Fur Press, Chadron, NB, 1979. 48 pp., illus. Paper covers. $4.00.

Includes full scale plans for ten rifles made for Indian and mountain men; from 1790 to 1860, plus plans for building three pistols.

Troubleshooting Your Rifle and Shotgun, by J.B. Wood, DBI Books, Inc., Northfield, IL, 1978. 192 pp., illus. Paper covers. $6.95.

A gunsmiths advice on how to keep your long guns shooting.

American Pistol and Revolver Design and Performance, by L. R. Wallack, Winchester Press, Piscataway, NJ, 1978. 224 pp., illus. $19.95.
How different types and models of pistols and revolvers work, from trigger pull to bullet impact.

American Police Handgun Training, by Charles R. Skillen and Mason Williams, Charles C. Thomas, Springfield, IL, 1980. 216 pp., illus. $21.50.
Deals comprehensively with all phases of current handgun training procedures in America.

Askins on Pistols and Revolvers, by Col. Charles Askins, NRA Books, Wash., D.C., 1980. 144 pp., illus. Paper covers. $9.95.
A book full of practical advice, shooting tips, technical analysis and stories of guns in action.

The Black Powder Handgun by Sam Fadala, DBI Books, Inc., Northfield, IL, 1981. 288 pp., illus. Paper covers. $11.95.
The author covers this oldtimer in all its forms: pistols and six-shooters in both small and large bore, target and hunting.

Blue Steel and Gun Leather, by John Bianchi, Beinfeld Publishing, Inc., No. Hollywood, CA, 1978. 200 pp., illus. $12.00.
A complete and comprehensive review of holster uses plus an examination of available products on today's market.

Browning Hi-Power Pistols, Desert Publications, Cornville, AZ, 1982. 20 pp., illus. Paper covers. $6.00.
Covers all facets of the various military and civilian models of this gun.

Colt Automatic Pistols, by Donald B. Bady, Borden Publ. Co., Alhambra, CA, 1974. 368 pp., illus. $18.50.
The rev. and enlarged ed. of a key work on a fascinating subject. Complete information on every automatic marked with Colt's name.

The Colt .45 Auto Pistol, compiled from U.S. War Dept. Technical Manuals, and reprinted by Desert Publications, Cornville, AZ, 1978. 80 pp., illus. Paper covers. $5.95.
Covers every facet of this famous pistol from mechanical training, manual of arms, disassembly, repair and replacement of parts.

Combat Handgun Shooting, by James D. Mason, Charles C. Thomas, Springfield, IL, 1976. 256 pp., illus. $27.50.
Discusses in detail the human as well as the mechanical aspects of shooting.

Combat Handguns, edited by Edward C. Ezell, Stackpole Books, Harrisburg, PA, 1980. 288 pp., illus. $19.95.
George Nonte's last great work, edited by Edward C. Ezell. A comprehensive reference volume offering full coverage of automatic handguns vs. revolvers, custom handguns, combat autoloaders and revolvers—domestic and foreign, and combat testing.

Combat Shooting for Police, by Paul B. Weston. Charles C. Thomas, Springfield, IL, 1967. A reprint. 194 pp., illus. $20.00.
First publ. in 1960 this popular self-teaching manual gives basic concepts of defensive fire in every position.

The Complete Book of Combat Handgunning, by Chuck Taylor, Desert Publications, Cornville, AZ, 1982. 168 pp., illus. Paper covers. $12.95.
Covers virtually every aspect of combat handgunning.

Defensive Handgun Effectiveness, by Carroll E. Peters, Carroll E. Peters, Manchester, TN, 1977. 198 pp., charts and graphs. $15.00.
A systematic approach to the design, evaluation and selection of ammunition for the defensive handgun.

The Defensive Use of the Handgun for the Novice, by Mason Williams, Charles C. Thomas, Publisher, Springfield, IL, 1980. 226 pp., illus. $20.00.
This book was developed for the home owner, housewife, elderly couple, and the woman who lives alone. Basic instruction for purchasing, loading and firing pistols and revolvers.

Flattops & Super Blackhawks, by H.W. Ross, Jr., H.W. Ross, Jr., Bridgeville, PA, 1979. 93 pp., illus. Paper covers. $9.95.
An expanded version of the author's book "Ruger Blackhawks" with an extra chapter on Super Blackhawks and the Mag-Na-Ports with serial numbers and approximate production dates.

The Gun Digest Book of Autoloading Pistols, by Dean A. Grennell, DBI Books, Inc., Northfield, IL, 1983. 288 pp., illus. Paper covers. $11.95.
History, operating principles and firing techniques for rimfire, military/police, competition, hunting, assault autos, value trends.

The Gun Digest Book of Combat Handgunnery, by Jack Lewis and Jack Mitchell, DBI Books, Inc., Northfield, IL, 1983. 288 pp., illus. Paper covers. $11.95.
From the basics to competition, training and exercises.

Gun Digest Book of Firearms Assembly/Disassembly Part I: Automatic Pistols, by J.B. Wood, DBI Books, Inc., Northfield, IL, 1979. 320 pp., illus. Paper covers. $12.95.
A thoroughly professional presentation on the art of pistol disassembly and reassembly. Covers most modern guns, popular older models, and some of the most complex pistols ever produced.

Gun Digest Book of Firearms Assembly/Disassembly Part II: Revolvers, by J.B. Wood, DBI Books, Inc., Northfield, IL, 1979. 320 pp., illus. Paper covers. $12.95.
How to properly dismantle and reassemble both the revolvers of today and of the past.

Gun Digest Book of Gun Care, Cleaning and Refinishing, Book One: Handguns, by J.B. Wood, DBI Books, Inc., Northfield, IL, 1984. 160 pp., illus. Paper covers. $8.95.
The how, when and why of proper maintenance: revolvers, autoloaders, blackpowder handguns.

The Gun Digest Book of Pistolsmithing, by Jack Mitchell, DBI Books, Inc., Northfield, IL, 1980. 288 pp., illus. Paper covers. $10.95.
An expert's guide to the operation of each of the handgun actions with all the major functions of pistolsmithing explained.

Gun Digest Book of Single Action Revolvers, by Jack Lewis, DBI Books, Inc., Northfield, IL, 1982. 256 pp., illus. Paper covers. $11.95.
A fond, in-depth look at the venerable "wheelgun" from its earliest days through today's latest developments.

Hallock's .45 Auto Handbook, by Ken Hallock, The Mihan Co., Oklahoma City, OK, 1981. 178 pp., illus. Paper covers. $11.95.
For gunsmiths, dealers, collectors and serious hobbyists.

A Handbook on the Primary Identification of Revolvers & Semi-automatic Pistols, by John T. Millard, Charles C. Thomas, Springfield, IL, 1974. 156 pp., illus. Paper covers. $15.00.
A practical outline on the simple, basic phases of primary firearm identification with particular reference to revolvers and semi-automatic pistols.

Handguns for Self Defence, by Gerry Gore, Macmillan South Africa, Johannesburg, South Africa, 1981. 164 pp., illus. Paper covers. $15.00.
Choosing the gun, basic skills, the draws, stopping power, etc.

Handguns of the World, by Edward C. Ezell, Stackpole Books, Harrisburg, PA., 1981. 704 pp., illus. $39.95.
Encyclopedia for identification and historical reference that will be appreciated by gun enthusiasts, collectors, hobbyists or professionals.

Handloading for Handgunners, by Geo. C. Nonte, DBI Books, Inc., Northfield, IL, 1978. 288 pp., illus. Paper covers. $9.95.
An expert tells the ins and outs of this specialized facet of reloading.

High Standard Automatic Pistols 1932-1950, by Charles E. Petty, American Ordnance Publ., Charlotte, NC, 1976. 124 pp., illus. $12.95.
A definitive source of information for the collector of High Standard pistols.

The Illustrated Book of Pistols, by Frederick Wilkinson, Hamlyn Publishing Group, Ltd. London, England, 1979. 192 pp., illus. $10.98.
A carefully researched study of the pistol's evolution and use in war and peace.

Know Your 45 Auto Pistols—Models 1911 & A1, by E.J. Hoffschmidt, Blacksmith Corp., Southport, CT, 1974. 58 pp., illus. Paper covers. $5.95.
A concise history of the gun with a wide variety of types and copies.

Know Your Walther P.38 Pistols, by E.J. Hoffschmidt, Blacksmith Corp., Southport, CT, 1974. 77 pp., illus. Paper covers. $5.95. variations.
Covers the Walther models Armee, M.P., H.P., P.38—history and variations.

Know Your Walther P.P. & P.P.K. Pistols, by E.J. Hoffschmidt, Blacksmith Corp., Southport, CT, 1975. 87 pp., illus. Paper covers. $5.95.
A concise history of the guns with a guide to the variety and types.

Law Enforcement Handgun Digest, 3rd Edition, by Jack Lewis, DBI Books, Inc., Northfield, IL, 1980. 288 pp., illus. Paper covers. $9.95.
Covers such subjects as the philosophy of a firefight, SWAT, weapons, training, combat shooting, etc.

The Luger Pistol (Pistole Parabellum), by F.A. Datig. Borden Publ. Co., Alhambra, CA, 1962. 328 pp., well illus. $14.95.
An enlarged, rev. ed. of an important reference on the arm, its history and development from 1893 to 1945.

Luger Variations, by Harry E. Jones, Harry E. Jones, Torrance, CA, 1975. 328 pp., 160 full page illus., many in color. $35.00.
A rev. ed. of the book known as "The Luger Collector's Bible".

Lugers at Random, by Charles Kenyon, Jr. Handgun Press, Chicago, IL. 1st ed., 1970. 416 pp., profusely illus. $22.50.
An impressive large side-opening book carrying throughout alternate facing-pages of descriptive text and clear photographs. A new boon to the Luger collector and/or shooter.

Mauser Pocket Pistols 1910-1946, by Roy G. Pender, Collectors Press, Houston, TX, 1971. 307 pp. $25.00.
Comprehensive work covering over 100 variations, including factory boxes and manuals. Over 300 photos. Limited, numbered ed.

The Mauser Self-Loading Pistol, by Belford & Dunlap, Borden Publ. Co., Alhambra, CA. Over 200 pp., 300 illus., large format. $18.50.
The long-awaited book on the "Broom Handles", covering their inception in 1894 to the end of production. Complete and in detail: pocket pistols, Chinese and Spanish copies, etc.

Modern American Centerfire Handguns, by Stanley W. T. Trzoniec, Winchester Press, Piscataway, NJ, 1981. 260 pp., illus. $24.95.
The most comprehensive reference on handguns in print.

The New Handbook of Handgunning, by Paul B. Weston, Charles C. Thomas, Publisher, Springfield, IL, 1980. 102 pp., illus. $20.00.
A step-by-step, how-to manual of handgun shooting.

The Pistol Book, by John Walter, Arms & Armour Press, London, England, 1983. 176 pp., illus. $19.95.
A concise and copiously illustrated guide to the handguns available today.

The Pistol Guide, by George C. Nonte, Stoeger Publ. Co., So. Hackensack, NJ, 1980. 256 pp., illus. Paper covers. $10.95.
A unique and detailed examination of a very specialized type of gun: the autoloading pistol.

Pistol & Revolver Digest, 3rd Edition, by Dean A. Grennell, DBI Books, Inc., Northfield, IL, 1982. 288 pp., illus. Paper covers. $11.95.
The latest developments in handguns, shooting, ammunition, and accessories, with catalog.

Pistol & Revolver Guide, 3rd Ed., by George C. Nonte, Stoeger Publ. Co., So. Hackensack, NJ, 1975. 224 pp., illus. Paper covers. $6.95.
The standard reference work on military and sporting handguns.

The Pistols of Germany and its Allies in Two World Wars, by Jan C. Still, Douglas, AK, 1983. 145 pp., illus. Paper covers. $12.95.
Military pistols of Imperial Germany and her World War I Allies and postwar military, paramilitary and police reworks.

Pistols of the World, Revised Edition, by Ian V. Hogg and John Weeks, DBI Books, Inc., Northfield, IL, 1982. 306 pp., illus. $12.95.
A valuable reference for collectors and everyone interested in guns.

Quick or Dead, by William L. Cassidy, Paladin Press, Boulder, CO, 1978. 178 pp., illus. $12.95.
Close-quarter combat firing, with particular reference to prominent twentieth-century British and American methods of instruction.

Report of Board on Tests of Revolvers and Automatic Pistols. From the *Annual Report* of the Chief of Ordnance, 1907. Reprinted by J.C. Tillinghast Marlow, NH, 1969. 34 pp., 7 plates, paper covers. $5.00.

A comparison of handguns, including Luger, Savage, Colt, Webley-Fosbery and other makes.

Revolver Guide, by George C. Nonte, Jr., Stoeger Publishing Co., So. Hackensack, NJ, 1980. 288 pp., illus. Paper covers. $10.95.

Fully illustrated guide to selecting, shooting, caring for and collecting revolvers of all types.

Ruger Automatic Pistols and Single Action Revolvers, Book 3, by Hugo A. Lueders, Blacksmith Corp., Southport, CT, 1983. 95 pp., illus. Paper covers. $17.50.

A key reference for every Ruger enthusiast, collector and dealer.

Target Pistol Shooting, by K.B. Hinchliffe, David and Charles, London, 1981. 235 pp., illus. $25.00.

A complete guide to target shooting designed to give the novice and expert guidance on the correct techniques for holding, aiming, and firing pistols.

The Walther P-38 Pistol, by Maj. Geo. C. Nonte, Paladin Press, Boulder, CO, 1975. 90 pp., illus. Paper covers. $5.00.

Covers all facets of the gun—development, history, variations, technical data, practical use, rebuilding, repair and conversion.

The Walther Pistols 1930-1945, by Warren H. Buxton, Warren H. Buxton, Los Alamos, NM, 1978. 350 pp., illus. $29.95.

Volume I of a projected 4 volume series "The P.38 Pistol". The histories, evolutions, and variations of the Walther P.38 and its predecessors.

The Women's Guide to Handguns, by Jim Carmichel, Stoeger Publishing Co., So. Hackensack, NJ, 1984. 190 pp., illus. Paper covers. $8.95.

For women interested in learning how to select, buy, store, carry, care for and use a handgun.

hunting

NORTH AMERICA

Advanced Wild Turkey Hunting & World Records, by Dave Harbour, Winchester Press, Piscataway, NJ, 1983. 264 pp., illus. $19.95.

The definitive book, written by an authority who has studied turkeys and turkey calling for over 40 years.

After Your Deer Is Down, by Josef Fischl and Leonard Lee Rue, III, Winchester Press, Piscataway, NJ, 1981. 160 pp., illus. Paper covers. $10.95.

The care and handling of big game, with a bonus of venison recipes.

All About Deer in America, edited by Robert Elman, Winchester Press, Piscataway, NJ, 1976. 256 pp., illus. $15.95.

Twenty of America's great hunters share the secrets of their hunting success.

All About Small-Game Hunting in America, edited by Russell Tinsley, Winchester Press, Piscataway, NJ, 1976. 308 pp., illus. $16.95.

Collected advice by the finest small-game experts in the country.

All About Varmint Hunting, by Nick Sisley, The Stone Wall Press, Inc., Wash., DC, 1982. 182 pp., illus. Paper covers. $8.95.

The most comprehensive up-to-date book on hunting common varmints found throughout North America.

All About Wildfowling in America, by Jerome Knap, Winchester Press, Piscataway, NJ, 1977. 256 pp., illus. $13.95.

More than a dozen top writers provide new and controversial ideas on how and where to hunt waterfowl successfully.

All-American Deer Hunter's Guide, edited by Jim Zumbo and Robert Elman, Winchester Press, Piscataway, NJ, 1983. 320 pp., illus. $29.95.

The most comprehensive, thorough book yet published on American deer hunting.

All Season Hunting, by Bob Gilsvik, Winchester Press, Piscataway, NJ, 1976. 256 pp., illus. $14.95.

A guide to early-season, late-season and winter hunting in America.

Bear Hunting, by Jerry Meyer, Stackpole Books, Harrisburg, PA, 1983. 224 pp., illus. $14.95.

First complete guide on the how-to's of bear hunting. Information on every type of bear found in the U.S. and Canada.

The Best of Nash Buckingham, by Nash Buckingham, selected, edited and annotated by George Bird Evans, Winchester Press, Piscataway, NJ, 1973. 320 pp., illus. $17.95.

Thirty pieces that represent the very cream of Nash's output on his whole range of outdoor interests—upland shooting, duck hunting, even fishing.

The Best of Jack O'Connor, by Jack O'Connor, Amwell Press, Clinton, NJ, 1984. 192 pp., illus. $27.50.

A collection of Jack O'Connor's finest writings.

Big Game of North America, Ecology and Management, by Wildlife Management Institute, Stackpole Books, Harrisburg, PA, 1983. 512 pp., illus. $29.95.

An outstanding reference for professionals and students of wildlife management.

Big Rack, Texas All-Time Largest Whitetails 1892-1975, by Robert Rogers, et al, Outdoor Worlds of Texas, Inc., 1980. 167 pp., illus. $19.95.

Pictures and stories of all classifications of Texas trophy whitetail deer.

Bird Hunting Know-How, by D.M. Duffey. Van Nostrand, Princeton, NJ, 1968. 192 pp., illus. $9.95.

Game-getting techniques and sound advice on all aspects of upland bird hunting, plus data on guns and loads.

Black Powder Hunting, by Sam Fadala, Stackpole Books, Harrisburg, PA, 1978. 192 pp., illus. $10.95.

The author demonstrates successful hunting methods using percussion firearms for both small and big game.

The Bobwhite Quail Book, Compiled by Lamar Underwood, Amwell Press, Clinton, NJ, 1981. 442 pp., illus. $25.00.

An anthology of the finest stories on Bobwhite quail ever assembled under one cover.

Bobwhite Quail Hunting, by Charley Dickey, printed for Stoeger Publ. Co., So. Hackensack, NH, 1974. 112 pp., illus., paper covers. $3.95.

Habits and habitats, techniques, gear, guns and dogs.

The Book of the Wild Turkey, by Lovett E. Williams, Jr., Winchester Press, Piscataway, NJ, 1981. 204 pp., illus. $21.95.

A definitive reference work on the wild turkey for hunter, game manager, conservationist, or amateur naturalist.

Bowhunter's Digest, 2nd Edition, by Chuck Adams, DBI Books, Inc., Northfield, IL, 1981. 288 pp., illus. Paper covers. $11.95.

All-new edition covers all the necessary equipment and how to use it, plus the fine points to improve your skills.

The Complete Book of Hunting, by Rober Elman, Abbeville Press, New York, NY, 1982. 320 pp., illus. $29.95.

A compendium of the world's game birds and animals, handloading, international hunting, etc.

The Complete Book of the Wild Turkey, by Roger M. Latham, Stackpole Books, Harrisburg, Pa., 1978. 228 pp., illus. $12.95.

A new revised edition of the classic on American wild turkey hunting.

The Complete Guide to Bird Dog Training, by John R. Falk, Winchester Press, Piscataway, NJ, 1976. 256 pp., illus. $16.95.

How to choose, raise, train, and care for a bird dog.

The Complete Guide to Bowhunting Deer, by Chuck Adams, DBI Books, Inc., Northfield, IL, 1984. 256 pp., illus. Paper covers. $11.95.

Plenty on equipment, bows, sights, quivers, arrows, clothes, lures and scents, stands and blinds, etc.

The Complete Guide to Game Care and Cookery, by Sam Fadala, DBI Books, Inc., Northfield, IL., 1981. 288 pp., illus. Paper covers. $9.95.

How to dress, preserve and prepare all kinds of game animals and birds.

The Complete Turkey Hunt, by William Morris Daskal, El-Bar Enterprises Publishers, New York, NY, 1982. 129 pp., illus. Paper covers. $7.95.

Covers every aspect of turkeys and turkey hunting, by an expert.

Confessions of an Outdoor Maladroit, by Joel M. Vance, Amwell Press, Clinton, NJ, 1983. $20.00.

Anthology of some of the wildest, irreverent, and zany hunting tales ever.

Covey Rises and Other Pleasures, by David H. Henderson, Amwell Press, Clinton, NJ, 1983. 155 pp., illus. $17.50.

A collection of essays and stories concerned with field sports.

Coveys and Singles: The Handbook of Quail Hunting, by Robert Gooch, A.S. Barnes, San Diego, CA, 1981. 196 pp., illus. $11.95.

The story of the quail in North America.

Death in the Silent Places, by Peter Hathaway Capstick, St. Martin's Press, New York, NY, 1981. 243 pp., illus. $14.95.

The author recalls the extraordinary careers of legendary hunters such as Corbett, Karamojo Bell, Stigand and others.

Deer Hunting, by R. Smith, Stackpole Books, Harrisburg, PA, 1978. 224 pp., illus. Paper covers. $10.95.

A professional guide leads the hunt for North America's most popular big game animal.

Deer Hunter's Guide to Guns, Ammunition, and Equipment, by Edward A. Matunas, an Outdoor Life Book, distributed by Stackpole Books, Harrisburg, PA, 1983. 352 pp., illus. $24.95.

Where-to-hunt for North American deer. An authoritative guide that will help every deer hunter get maximum enjoyment and satisfaction from his sport.

The Deer Book, edited by Lamar Underwood, Amwell Press, Clinton, NJ, 1982. 480 pp., illus. $25.00.

An anthology of the finest stories on North American deer ever assembled under one cover.

Deer in Their World, by Erwin Bauer, Stackpole Books, Harrisburg, PA, 1984. 256 pp., illus. $29.95.

A showcase of more than 250 natural habitat deer photographs. Substantial natural history of North American deer.

The Desert Bighorn, edited by Gale Monson and Lowell Sumner, University of Arizona Press, Tucson, AZ, 1980. 392 pp., illus. $35.00.

Life history, ecology and management of the Desert Bighorn.

The Dove Shooter's Handbook, by Dan M. Russell, Winchester Press, Piscataway, NJ, 1974. 256 pp., illus. $12.95.

A complete guide to America's top game bird.

Dove Hunting, by Charley Dickey, Galahad Books, NY, 1976. 112 pp., illus. $6.00.

This indispensable guide for hunters deals with equipment, techniques, types of dove shooting, hunting dogs, etc.

Drummer in the Woods, by Burton L. Spiller, Stackpole Books, Harrisburg, PA, 1980. 240 pp., illus. $15.95.

Twenty-one wonderful stories on grouse shooting by "the Poet Laureate of Grouse".

The Duck Hunter's Book, edited by Lamar Underwood, Amwell Press, Clinton, NJ, 1983. 650 pp., illus. $25.00.

Anthology of the finest duck hunting stories ever written.

The Duck Hunter's Handbook, by Bob Hinman, Winchester Press, Piscataway, NJ, 1974. 252 pp., illus. $14.95.

Down-to-earth, practical advice on bagging ducks and geese.

The Duck-Huntingest Gentlemen, by Keith C. Russell et al, Winchester Press, Piscataway, NJ, 1980. 284 pp., illus. $17.95.

A collection of stories on waterfowl hunting.

Ducks of the Mississippi Flyway, ed. by John McKane, North Star Press, St. Cloud, MN, 1969. 54 pp., illus. Paper covers. $6.95.

A duck hunter's reference. Full color paintings of some 30 species, plus descriptive text.

Expert Advice on Gun Dog Training, edited by David M. Duffey, Winchester Press, Piscataway, NJ, 1977. 256 pp., illus. $16.95.

Eleven top pros talk shop, revealing the techniques and philosophies that account for their consistent success.

For Whom the Ducks Toll, by Keith C. Russell, et al, Winchester Press, Piscataway, NJ, 1984. 288 pp., illus. Slipcased, limited and signed edition $30.00. Trade edition. $16.95.
A select gathering of memorable waterfowling tales by the author and 68 of his closest friends.

A Gallery of Waterfowl and Upland Birds, by Gene Hill, with illustrations by David Maass, Pedersen Prints, Los Angeles, CA, 1978. 132 pp., illus. $44.95.
Gene Hill at his best. Liberally illustrated with fifty-one full-color reproductions of David Maass' finest paintings.

Game in the Desert Revisited, by Jack O'Connor, Amwell Press, Clinton, NJ, 1984. 306 pp., illus. $27.50.
Reprint of a Derrydale Press classic on hunting in the Southwest.

The Game Trophies of the World, edited and compiled by G. Kenneth Whitehead, Paul Parey, Hamburg, W. Germany. 215 pp., illus. Paper covers. $29.00.
Covers all the game trophies of the world using the Boone & Crockett method of scoring. Text in English, French and German.

Getting the Most out of Modern Waterfowling, by John O. Cartier, St. Martin's Press, NY, 1974. 396 pp., illus. $17.95.
The most comprehensive, up-to-date book on waterfowling imaginable.

Goose Hunting, by Charles L. Cadieux, A Stonewall Press Book, distributed by Winchester Press, Piscataway, NJ, 1979. 197 pp., illus. $16.95.
Personal stories of goose hunting from Quebec to Mexico.

Great Whitetails of North America, by Robert Rogers, Texas Hunting Services, Corpus Christi, TX, 1981. 223 pp., illus. $24.95.
Pictures and stories of over 100 of the largest whitetail deer ever taken in North America.

Grizzly Country, by Andy Russell. A.A. Knopf, NYC, 1973, 302 pp., illus. $13.95.
Many-sided view of the grizzly bear and his world, by a noted guide, hunter and naturalist.

Grizzlies Don't Come Easy, by Ralph Young, Winchester Press, Piscataway, NJ, 1981. 200 pp., illus. $15.95.
The life story of a great woodsman who guided famous hunters such as O'Connor, Keith, Fitz, Page and others.

The Grizzly Book/The Bear Book, two volume set edited by Jack Samson, Amwell Press, Clinton, NJ, 1982. 304 pp.; 250 pp., illus. Slipcase. $37.50.
A delightful pair of anthologies. Stories by men such as O'Connor, Keith, Fitz, Page, and many others.

Grouse Magic, by Nick Sisley, Nick Sisley, Apollo, PA, 1981. 240 pp., illus. Limited edition, signed and numbered. Slipcase. $30.00.
A book that will enrich your appreciation for grouse hunting and all the aura that surrounds the sport.

Gun Digest 1986 Hunting Annual, 3rd Edition edited by Robert S.L. Anderson, DBI Books, Inc., Northbrook, IL, 1985. 256 pp., illus. Paper covers. $12.95.
Well-rounded, fully illustrated collection of expert hunting tips and techniques.

Gun Digest Book of the Hunting Rifle, by Jack Lewis, DBI Books, Inc., Northfield, IL, 1983. 256 pp., illus. Paper covers. $11.95.
A thorough and knowledgeable account of today's hunting rifles.

Gun Digest Book of Sporting Dogs, by Carl P. Wood, DBI Books, Inc., Northbrook, IL, 1985. 256 pp., illus. Paper covers. $11.95.
Investigates various training philosophies, problem dogs, training for versatility, kenneling, etc. Covers most all hunting/sporting dogs.

Grouse and Woodcock, An Upland Hunter's Book, by Nick Sisley, Stackpole Books, Harrisburg, PA, 1980. 192 pp., illus. $13.95.
Latest field techniques for effective grouse and woodcock hunting.

Hal Swiggett on North American Deer, by Hal Swiggett, Jolex, Inc., Oakland, NJ, 1980. 272 pp., illus. Paper covers. $8.95.
Where and how to hunt all species of North American deer.

Handgun Hunting, by Maj. George C. Nonte, Jr. and Lee E. Jurras, Winchester Press, Piscataway, NJ, 1975. 245 pp., illus. $10.95.
A book with emphasis on the hunting of readily available game in the U.S. with the handgun.

Hard Hunting, by Patrick Shaughnessy and Diane Swingle, Winchester Press, Piscataway, NJ, 1978. 200 pp., illus. $15.95.
A couple explores a no-frills, low-cost, highly successful, adventurous approach to wilderness hunting.

The History of Wildfowling, by John Marchington, Adam and Charles Black, London, England, 1980. 288 pp., illus. $27.50.
Covers decoys, punting, and punt guns.

Horns in the High Country, by Andy Russell, Alfred A. Knofp, NY, 1973. 259 pp., illus. $15.50.
A many-sided view of wild sheep and their natural world.

How to Hunt, by Dave Bowring, Winchester Press, Piscataway, NJ, 1982. 208 pp., illus. Paper covers. $10.95; Cloth. $15.00.
A basic guide to hunting big game, small game, upland birds, and waterfowl.

The Hunter's Book of the Pronghorn Antelope, by Bert Popowski and Wilf E. Pyle, Winchester Press, Piscataway, NJ, 1982. 376 pp., illus. $16.95.
A comprehensive, copiously illustrated volume and a valuable guide for anyone interested in the pronghorn antelope.

A Hunter's Fireside Book, by Gene Hill, Winchester Press, Piscataway, NJ, 1972. 192 pp., illus. $14.95.
An outdoor book that will appeal to every person who spends time in the field—or who wishes he could.

The Hunter's Shooting Guide, by Jack O'Connor, Outdoor Life Books, New York, NY, 1982. 176 pp., illus. Paper covers. $5.95.
A classic covering rifles, cartridges, shooting techniques for shotguns/rifles/handguns.

The Hunter's World, by Charles F. Waterman, Winchester Press, Piscataway, NJ, 1983. 250 pp., illus. $29.95.
A classic. One of the most beautiful hunting books ever produced.

Hunting the American Wild Turkey, by Dave Harbour, Stackpole Books, Harrisburg, PA, 1975. 256 pp., illus. $14.95.
The techniques and tactics of hunting North America's largest, and most popular, woodland game bird.

Hunting America's Game Animals and Birds, by Robert Elman and George Peper, Winchester Press, Piscataway, NJ, 1975. 368 pp., illus. $16.95.
A how-to, where-to, when-to guide—by 40 top experts—covering the continent's big, small, upland game and waterfowl.

Hunting America's Mule Deer, by Jim Zumbo, Winchester Press, Piscataway, NJ, 1981. 272 pp., illus. $16.95.
The best ways to hunt mule deer. The how, when, and where to hunt all seven sub-species.

Hunting Dog Know-How, by D.M. Duffey, Winchester Press, Piscataway, NJ, 1983. 208 pp., illus. Paper covers. $8.95.
Covers selection, breeds, and training of hunting dogs, problems in hunting and field trials.

Hunting Moments of Truth, by Eric Peper and Jim Rikhoff, Winchester Press, Piscataway, NJ, 1973. 208 pp., illus. $15.00.
The world's most experienced hunters recount 22 most memorable occasions.

Hunting the Rocky Mountain Goat, by Duncan Gilchrist, Duncan Gilchrist, Hamilton, MT, 1983. 175 pp., illus. Paper covers. $10.95.
Hunting techniques for mountain goats and other alpine game. Tips on rifles for the high country.

Hunting and Stalking Deer Throughout the World, by Kenneth G. Whitehead, Batsford Books, London, 1982. 336 pp., illus. $35.00.
Comprehensive coverage of deer hunting areas on a country-by-country basis, dealing with every species in any given country.

Hunting Trophy Deer, by John Wootters, Winchester Press, Piscataway, NJ, 1983. 265 pp., illus. $12.95.
All the advice you need to succeed at bagging trophy deer.

Hunting the Uplands with Rifle and Shotgun, by Luther A. Anderson, Winchester Press, Piscataway, NJ, 1977. 224 pp., illus. $12.95.
Solid practical know-how to help make hunting deer and every major species of upland game bird easier and more satisfying.

Hunting Wild Turkeys in the Everglades, by Frank P. Harben, Harben Publishing Co., Safety Harbor, FL, 1983. 341 pp., illus. Paper covers. $8.95.
Describes techniques, ways and means of hunting this wary bird.

Hunting the Woodlands for Small and Big Game, by Luther A. Anderson, A. S. Barnes & Co., New York, NY, 1980. 256 pp., illus. $12.00.
A comprehensive guide to hunting in the United States. Chapters on firearms, game itself, marksmanship, clothing and equipment.

In Search of the Wild Turkey, by Bob Gooch, Greatlakes Living Press, Ltd., Waukegan, IL, 1978. 182 pp., illus. $9.95.
A state-by-state guide to wild turkey hot spots, with tips on gear and methods for bagging your bird.

The Market Hunter, by David and Jim Kimball, Dillon Press Inc., Minneapolis, MN, 1968. 132 pp., illus. $10.00.
The market hunter, one of the "missing chapters" in American history, is brought to life in this book.

Matching the Gun to the Game, by Clair Rees, Winchester Press, Piscataway, NJ, 1982. 272 pp., illus. $26.95.
Covers selection and use of handguns, black-powder firearms for hunting, matching rifle type to the hunter, calibers for multiple use, tailoring factory loads to the game.

Mixed Bag, by Jim Rikhoff, National Rifle Association of America, Wash., DC, 1981. 284 pp., illus. Paper covers. $9.95.
Reminiscences of a master raconteur.

Modern Pheasant Hunting, by Steve Grooms, Stackpole Books, Harrisburg, PA, 1982. 224 pp., illus. $8.95.
New look at pheasants and hunters from an experienced hunter who respects this splendid gamebird.

Modern Turkey Hunting, by James F. Brady, Crown Publ., N.Y.C., NY, 1973. 160 pp., illus. $30.00.
A thorough guide to the habits, habitat, and methods of hunting America's largest game bird.

Modern Wildfowling, by Eric Begbie, Saiga Publishing Co., Ltd., Surrey, England, 1980. 171 pp., illus. $27.50.
History of wildfowling, guns and equipment.

More Grouse Feathers, by Burton L. Spiller. Crown Publ., NY, 1972. 238 pp., illus. $15.00.
Facsimile of the original Derrydale Press issue of 1938. Guns and dogs, the habits and shooting of grouse, woodcook, ducks, etc. Illus by Lynn Bogue Hunt.

More Than a Trophy, by Dennis Walrod, Stackpole Books, Harrisburg, PA, 1983. 256 pp., illus. Paper covers. $12.95.
Field dressing, skinning, quartering, and butchering to make the most of your valuable whitetail, blacktail or mule deer.

More Stories of the Old Duck Hunter, by Gordon MacQuarrie, Willow Creek Press, Oshkosh, WI, 1983. 200 pp., illus. $15.00.
Collection of 18 treasured stories of The Old Duck Hunters originally published in major magazines of the 1930s and '40s.

Mostly Tailfeathers, by Gene Hill, Winchester Press, Piscataway, NJ, 1975. 192 pp., illus. $14.95.
An interesting, general book about bird hunting.

Murry Burnham's Hunting Secrets, by Murry Burnham with Russell Tinsley, Winchester Press, Piscataway, NJ, 1984. 244 pp., illus. $17.95.
One of the great hunters of our time gives the reasons for his success in the field.

The Muzzleloading Hunter, by Rick Hacker, Winchester Press, Piscataway, NJ, 1981. 283 pp., illus. $19.95.
A comprehensive guide for the black powder sportsman.

My Lost Wilderness: Tales of an Alaskan Woodsman, by Ralph Young, Winchester Press, Piscataway, NJ, 1983. 193 pp., illus. $15.95.
True tales of an Alaskan hunter, guide, fisherman, prospector, and backwoodsman.

The Nash Buckingham Library, compiled by Douglas C. Mauldin, Delta Arms Sporting Goods, Indianola, MS 1980. 7 volume set in slipcase. $150.00.
Seven outdoor hunting classics by Nash Buckingham, the 20th century's greatest sporting writer.

New England Grouse Shooting, by William Harnden Foster, Willow Creek Press, Oshkosh, WI, 1983. 213 pp., illus. $45.00.
A new release of a classic book on grouse shooting.

North American Elk: Ecology and Management, edited by Jack Ward Thomas and Dale E. Toweill, Stackpole Books, Harrisburg, PA, 1982. 576 pp., illus. $39.95.
The definitive, exhaustive, classic work on the North American Elk.

The North American Waterfowler, by Paul S. Bernsen, Superior Publ. Co., Seattle, WA, 1972. 206 pp., Paper covers. $4.95.
The complete inside and outside story of duck and goose shooting. Big and colorful, illus. by Les Kouba.

On Target for Successful Turkey Hunting, by Wayne Fears, Target Communications, Mequon, WI, 1983. 92 pp., illus. Paper covers. $5.95.
Professional turkey hunting advice.

The Old Pro Turkey Hunter, by Gene Nunnery, Gene Nunnery, Meridian, MS, 1980. 144 pp., illus. $12.95.
True facts and old tales of turkey hunters.

1001 Hunting Tips, by Robert Elman, Winchester Press, Piscataway, NJ, 1983. 544 pp., illus. Paper covers. $14.95.
New edition, updated and expanded. A complete course in big and small game hunting, wildfowling and hunting upland birds.

The Old Man's Boy Grows Older, by Robert Ruark, Holt, Rinehart and Winston, New York, NY, 1961. 302 pp., illus. $35.00.
A classic by a big-game hunter and world traveler.

One Man's Wilderness, by Warren Page, Holt, Rinehart and Winston, NY, 1973. 256 pp., illus. $30.00.
A world-known writer and veteran sportsman recounts the joys of a lifetime of global hunting.

Opening Shots and Parting Lines: The Best of Dickey's Wit, Wisdom, and Wild Tales for Sportsmen, by Charley Dickey, Winchester Press, Piscataway, NJ, 1983. 208 pp., illus. $14.95.
Selected by the writer who has entertained millions of readers in America's top sporting publications—49 of his best pieces.

The Outdoor Life Bear Book, edited by Chet Fish, an Outdoor Life book, distributed by Stackpole Books, Harrisburg, PA, 1983. 352 pp., illus. $26.95.
All-time best personal accounts of terrifying attacks, exciting hunts, and intriguing natural history.

The Outlaw Gunner, by Harry M. Walsh, Tidewater Publishers, Cambridge, MD, 1973. 178 pp., illus. $12.50.
A colorful story of market gunning in both its legal and illegal phases.

Pinnell and Talifson: Last of the Great Brown Bear Men, by Marvin H. Clark, Jr., Great Northwest Publishing and Distributing Co., Spokane, WA, 1980. 224 pp., illus. $20.00.
The story of these famous Alaskan guides and some of the record bears taken by them.

Popular Sporting Rifle Cartridges, by Clay Harvey, DBI Books, Inc., Northfield, IL, 1984. 320 pp., illus. Paper covers. $12.95.
Provides the hunter/shooter with extensive information on most of the cartridges introduced during this century.

The Practical Hunter's Handbook, by Anthony J. Acerrano, Winchester Press, Piscataway, NJ, 1978. 224 pp., illus. Paper covers. $11.95.
How the time-pressed hunter can take advantage of every edge his hunting situation affords him.

The Practical Wildfowler, by John Marchington, Adam and Charles Black, London, England, 1977. 143 pp., illus. $21.95.
Advice on both the practical and ethical aspects of the sport.

Predator Caller's Companion, by Gerry Blair, Winchester Press, Piscataway, NJ, 1981. 280 pp., illus. $18.95.
Predator calling techniques and equipment for the hunter and trapper.

Ralf Coykendall's Duck Decoys and How to Rig Them, revised by Ralf Coykendall, Jr., Winchester Press, Piscataway, NJ, 1983. 128 pp., illus. Slipcased. $21.95.
For every discriminating book collector and sportsman, a superb new edition of a long out-of-print classic.

Ranch Life and the Hunting Trail, by Theodore Roosevelt, Readex Microprint Corp., Dearborn, MI. 1966 186 pp. With drawings by Frederic Remington. $15.00.
A facsimile reprint of the original 1899 Century Co., edition. One of the most fascinating books of the West of that day.

Records of Exotics, Volume 2, 1978 Edition, compiled by Thompson B. Temple, Thompson B. Temple, Ingram, TX, 1978. 243 pp., illus. $15.00.
Lists almost 1,000 of the top exotic trophies bagged in the U.S. Gives complete information on how to score.

Ringneck! Pheasants & Pheasant Hunting, by Ted Janes, Crown Publ., NY, 1975. 120 pp., illus. $8.95.
A thorough study of one of our more popular game birds.

Sheep and Sheep Hunting, by Jack O'Connor, Winchester Press, Piscataway, NJ, 1983. 320 pp., illus. Paper covers. $13.95.
Memorial edition of the definitive book on wild sheep hunting.

Charles Sheldon Trilogy, by Charles Sheldon, Amwell Press, Clinton, NJ, 1983. 3 volumes in slipcase. **"The Wilderness of the Upper Yukon,"** 363 pp., illus.; **"The Wilderness of the North Pacific Coast Islands,"** 246 pp., illus.; **"The Wilderness of Denali,"** 412 pp., illus. Deluxe edition. $205.00.
Custom-bound reprinting of Sheldon's classics, each signed and numbered by the author's son, William G. Sheldon.

Shooting Pictures, by A.B. Frost, with 24 pp. of text by Chas. D. Lanier, Winchester Press, Piscataway, NJ, 1972. 12 color plates. Enclosed in a board portfolio. Ed. limited to 750 numbered copies. $200.00.
Frost's 12 superb 12" by 16" pictures have often been called the finest sporting prints published in the U.S. A facsimile of the 1895-6 edition printed on fine paper with superb color fidelity.

Shots at Mule Deer, by Rollo S. Robinson, Winchester Press, Piscataway, NJ, 1970. 209 pp., illus. $15.00.
Description, strategies for bagging it, the correct rifle and cartridge to use.

Small Game Hunting, by Tom Brakefield, J.B. Lippincott Co., Phila., PA, 1978. 244 pp., illus. $10.
Describes where, when, and how to hunt all major small game species from coast to coast.

Squirrels and Squirrel Hunting, by Bob Gooch. Tidewater Publ., Cambridge, MD, 1973. 148 pp., illus. $6.
A complete book for the squirrel hunter, beginner or old hand. Details methods of hunting, squirrel habitat, management, proper clothing, care of the kill, cleaning and cooking.

Strayed Shots and Frayed Lines, edited by John E. Howard, Amwell Press, Clinton, NJ, 1982. 425 pp., illus. $25.00.
Anthology of some of the finest, funniest stories on hunting and fishing ever asembled.

Successful Deer Hunting, by Sam Fadala, DBI Books, Inc., Northfield, IL, 1983. 288 pp., illus. Paper covers. $11.95.
Here's all the dope you'll need—where, why, when and how—to have a successful deer hunt.

Successful Turkey Hunting, by J. Wayne Fears, Target Communication, Corp., Mequon, WI, 1983. 92 pp., illus. Paper covers. $5.95.
How to be more successful and get more enjoyment from turkey hunting.

Successful Waterfowling, by Zack Taylor, Crown, Publ., NY, 1974. 276 pp., illus. Paper covers. $15.95.
The definitive guide to new ways of hunting ducks and geese.

Through the Brazilian Wilderness, by Theodore Roosevelt, Greenwood Press, Westport, CT, 1982. Reprinting of the original 1914 work. 370 pp., illus. $22.50.
An account of a zoogeographic reconnaissance through the Brazilian hinterland.

Timberdoodle, by Frank Woolner, Crown Publ., Inc., NY, 1974. 168 pp., illus. $15.95.
A thorough, practical guide to the American woodcock and to woodcock hunting.

Topflight; A Speed Index to Waterfowl, by J.A. Ruthven & Wm. Zimmerman, Moebius Prtg. Co., Milwaukee, WI, 1968. 112 pp. $8.95.
Rapid reference for specie identification. Marginal color band of book directs reader to proper section. 263 full color illustrations of body and feather configurations.

The Trophy Hunter, by Col. Allison, Stackpole Books, Harrisburg, 1981. 240 pp., illus. $24.95.
Action-packed tales of hunting big game trophies around the world—1860 to today.

Turkey Hunting with Charlie Elliot, by Charles Elliot, David McKay Co., Inc., New York, NY 1979. 275 pp., illus. $14.95.
The old professor tells all about America's big-game bird.

Turkey Hunting, Spring and Fall, by Doug Camp, Outdoor Skills Bookshelf, Nashville, TN, 1983. 165 pp., illus. Paper covers. $12.95.
Practical turkey hunting, calling, dressing and cooking, by a professional turkey hunting guide.

Turkey Hunter's Guide, by Byron W. Dalrymple, et al, a publication of The National Rifle Association, Washington, DC, 1979. 96 pp., illus. Paper covers. $9.95.
Expert advice on turkey hunting hotspots, guns, guides, and calls.

Where the Grizzly Walks, by Bill Schneider, The Mountain Press, Missoula, MT, 1983. 204 pp., illus. Paper covers. $8.95.
The survival of the grizzly is discussed by the author.

The Whispering Wings of Autumn, by Gene Hill and Steve Smith, Amwell Press, Clinton, NJ, 1982. 192 pp., illus. $17.50.
A collection of both fact and fiction on two of North America's most famous game birds, the Ruffed Grouse and the Woodcock.

The Whitetail Deer Hunter's Handbook, by John Weiss, Winchester Press, Piscataway, NJ, 1979. 256 pp., illus. Paper covers. $11.95.
Wherever you live, whatever your level of experience, this brand-new handbook will make you a better deer hunter.

Whitetail: Fundamentals and Fine Points for the Hunter, by George Mattis, World Publ. Co. New York, NY, 1976. 273 pp., illus. $9.95.
A manual of shooting and trailing and an education in the private world of the deer.

Whitetail Hunting, by Jim Dawson, Stackpole Books, Harrisburg, PA, 1982. 224 pp., illus. $14.95.
New angles on hunting whitetail deer.

The Wild Sheep of the World, by Raul Valdez, Wild Sheep and Goat International, Mesilla, NM, 1983. 150 pp., illus. $45.00.
The first comprehensive survey of the world's wild sheep written by a zoologist.

The Wild Turkey Book, edited and with special commentary by J. Wayne Fears, Amwell Press, Clinton, NJ, 1982. 303 pp., illus. $22.50.
An anthology of the finest stories on wild turkey ever assembled under one cover.

20 Great Trophy Hunts, by John O. Cartier, David McKay Co., Inc., New York, NY, 1981. 320 pp., illus. $22.50.
The cream of outstanding true-life hunting stories.

AFRICA/ASIA

African Rifles & Cartridges, by John Taylor. The Gun Room Press, Highland Park, NJ, 1977. 431 pp., illus. $21.95.
Experiences and opinions of a professional ivory hunter in Africa describing his knowledge of numerous arms and cartridges for big game. A reprint.

African Hunting and Adventure, by William Charles Baldwin, Books of Zimbabwe, Bulawayo, 1981. 451 pp., illus. $75.00.
Facsimile reprint of the scarce 1863 London edition. African hunting and adventure from Natal to the Zambesi.

Bell of Africa, by Walter (Karamojo) D. M. Bell, Neville Spearman, Suffolk, England, 1983. 236 pp., illus. $35.00.
Autobiography of the greatest elephant hunter of them all.

Big Game Hunting Around the World, by Bert Klineburger and Vernon W. Hurst, Exposition Press, Jericho, NY, 1969. 376 pp., illus. $30.00.
The first book that takes you on a safari all over the world.

Jim Corbett's India, edited by R. E. Hawkins, Oxford University Press, London, England, 1979. 250 pp., illus. $35.00.

A selection of stories from Jim Corbett's big game hunting books.

Death in the Long Grass, by Peter Hathaway Capstick, St. Martin's Press, New York, NY, 1977. 297 pp., illus. $13.95.

A big game hunter's adventures in the African bush.

The Elephant Hunters of the Lado, by Major W. Robert Foran, Amwell Press, Clinton, NJ, 1981. 311 pp., illus. Limited, numbered, and signed edition, in slipcase. $175.00.

From a previously unpublished manuscript by a famous "white hunter."

Elephant Hunting in East Equatorial Africa, by Arthur H. Neumann, Books of Zimbabwe, Bulawayo, 1982. 455 pp., illus. $85.00.

Facsimile reprint of the scarce 1898 London edition. An account of three years ivory hunting under Mount Kenya.

Encyclopedia of Big Game Animals of Africa, by Pierre Fiorenza, Larousse and Co., Inc., New York, NY, 1983. $85.00.

Detailed information on the life and habitat of each species. 120 full-color photographs.

Green Hills of Africa, by Ernest Hemingway. Charles Scribner's Sons, NY, 1963. 285 pp., illus. Paper covers. $7.95.

A famous narrative of African big-game hunting, first published in 1935.

A Hunter's Wanderings in Africa, by F. C. Selous, Books of Zimbabwe, Bulawayo, 1981. 455 pp., illus. $85.00.

A facsimile reprint of the 1881 London edition. A narrative of nine years spent among the game of the interior of South Africa.

Hunting in Africa, by Bill Morkel, Howard Timmins, Publishers, Capetown, South Africa, 1980. 252 pp., illus. $25.00.

An invaluable guide for the inexperienced hunter contemplating a possible safari.

Hunting the Big Cats, two volume set, edited by Jim Rikhoff, Amwell Press, Clinton, NJ, 1981. Total of 808 pp., illustrated by Bob Kuhn. Limited, numbered, and signed edition. In slipcase. $175.00.

The most definitive work on hunting the world's largest wild cats ever compiled. A collection of 70 articles on hunting in Africa, Asia, North and South America.

Hunting on Safari in East and Southern Africa, by Aubrey Wynne-Jones, Macmillan South Africa, Johannesburg, S. Africa, 1980. 180 pp., illus. $42.50.

Every aspect of hunting in East and Southern Africa is covered, from the early planning stages of the hunt itself.

The Recollections of an Elephant Hunter 1864-1875, by William Finaughty, Books of Zimbabwe, Bulawayo, 1980. 244 pp., illus. $85.00.

Reprint of the scarce 1916 privately published edition. The early game hunting exploits of William Finaughty in Matabeleland and Nashonaland.

Tanzania Safari, by Brian Herne, Amwell Press, Clinton, NJ, 1982. 259 pp., illus. Limited, signed and numbered edition. Slipcase. $75.00.

The story of Tanzania and hunting safaris, professional hunters, and a little history, too.

The Wanderings of an Elephant Hunter, by W.D.M. Bell, Neville Spearman, Suffolk, England, 1981. 187 pp., illus. $35.00.

The greatest of elephant books by perhaps the greatest elephant hunter of all times, 'Karamojo' Bell.

RIFLES

The Accurate Rifle, by Warren Page, Winchester Press, Piscataway, NJ, 1973. 256 pp., illus. $15.95.

A masterly discussion. A must for the competitive shooter hoping to win, and highly useful to the practical hunter.

The AK-47 Assault Rifle, Desert Publications, Cornville, AZ, 1981. 150 pp., illus. Paper covers. $7.50.

Complete and practical technical information on the only weapon in history to be produced in an estimated 30,000,000 units.

American Rifle Design and Performance, by L.R. Wallack, Winchester Press, Piscataway, NJ, 1977. 288 pp., illus. $20.00.

An authoritative, comprehensive guide to how and why every kind of sporting rifle works.

The Bolt Action: A Design Analysis, by Stuart Otteson, edited by Ken Warner, Winchester Press, Piscataway, NJ, 1976. 320 pp., illus. Paper covers. $14.95; Cloth. $20.00.

Precise and in-depth descriptions, illustrations and comparisons of 16 bolt actions.

Bolt Action Rifles, revised edition, by Frank de Haas, DBI Books, Inc., Northfield, IL, 1984. 448 pp., illus. Paper covers. $14.95.

A revised edition of the most definitive work on all major bolt-action rifle designs.

The Book of the Garand, by Maj.-Gen. J.S. Hatcher, The Gun Room Press, Highland Park, NJ, 1977. 292 pp., illus. $15.00.

A new printing of the standard reference work on the U.S. Army M1 rifle.

The Commerical Mauser '98 Sporting Rifle, by Lester Womack, Womack Associates, Publishers, Prescott, AZ, 1980. 69 pp., illus. $20.00.

The first work on the sporting rifles made by the original Mauser plant in Oberndorf.

The Deer Rifle, by L.R. Wallack, Winchester Press, Piscataway, NJ, 1978. 256 pp., illus. $15.95.

Everything the deer hunter needs to know to select and use the arms and ammunition appropriate to his needs.

F.N.-F.A.L. Auto Rifles, Desert Publications, Cornville, AZ, 1981. 130 pp., illus. Paper covers. $7.50.

A definitive study of one of the free world's finest combat rifles.

The Fighting Rifle, by Chuck Taylor, Paladin Press, Boulder, CO, 1983. 184 pp., illus. Paper covers. $12.95.

The difference between assault and battle rifles and auto and light machine guns.

The First Winchester, by John E. Parsons, Winchester Press, Piscataway, NJ, 1977. 207 pp., illus. $35.00.

The story of the 1866 repeating rifle.

A Forgotten Heritage; The Story of a People and the Early American Rifle, by Harry P. Davis, The Gun Room Press, Highland Park, NJ, 1976. 199 pp., illus. $9.95.

Reprint of a very scarce history, originally published in 1941, the Kentucky rifle and the people who used it.

The German Rifle, by John Walter, Arms and Armour Press, London, England, 1982. 160 pp., illus. $16.95.

A comprehensive illustrated history of the standard bolt-action design, 1871-1945.

The Golden Age of Single-Shot Rifles, by Edsall James, Pioneer Press, Union City, TN, 1975. 33 pp., illus. Paper covers. $2.75.

A detailed look at all of the fine, high quality sporting single-shot rifles that were once the favorite of target shooters.

The Gun Digest Book of Firearms Assembly/Disassembly Part III: Rimfire Rifles, by J.B. Wood, DBI Books, Inc., Northfield, IL, 1980. 288 pp., illus. Paper covers. $12.95.

A most comprehensive, uniform, and professional presentation available for disassembling and reassembling most rimfire rifles.

The Gun Digest Book of Firearms Assembly/Disassembly Part IV: Centerfire Rifles, by J.B. Wood, DBI Books, Inc., Northfield, IL, 1980. 288 pp., illus. Paper covers. $12.95.

A professional presentation on the disassembly and reassembly of centerfire rifles.

Gun Digest Book of Gun Care, Cleaning and Refinishing, Book Two: Long Guns, by J.B. Wood, DBI Books, Inc., Northfield, IL, 1984. 160 pp., illus. Paper covers. $8.95.

The care and maintenance of long guns with meticulous detail and step-by-step, illustrated, clearly written text.

Gun Digest Book of the Hunting Rifle, by Jack Lewis, DBI Books, Inc., Northfield, IL, 1983. 256 pp., illus. Paper covers. $11.95.

Covers all aspects of the hunting rifle—design, development, different types, uses, and more.

Gun Digest Book of Riflesmithing, by Jack Mitchell, DBI Books, Inc., Northfield, IL, 1982. 256 pp., illus. Paper covers. $11.95.

Covers major and minor gunsmithing operations for rifles—locking systems, triggers, safeties, rifling, crowning, scope mounting, and more.

Know Your M1 Garand, by E. J. Hoffschmidt, Blacksmith Corp., Southport, CT, 1975, 84 pp., illus. Paper covers. $5.95.

Facts about America's most famous infantry weapon. Covers test and experimental models, Japanese and Italian copies, National Match models.

The M-14 Rifle, facsimile reprint of FM 23-8, Desert Publications, Cornville, AZ, 50 pp., illus. Paper $5.95.

In this well illustrated and informative reprint, the M-14 and M-14E2 are covered thoroughly.

The Modern Rifle, by Jim Carmichel, Winchester Press, Piscataway, NJ, 1975. 320 pp., illus. $15.95.

The most comprehensive, thorough, up-to-date book ever published on today's rifled sporting arms.

North American FALS, by R. Blake Stevens, Collector Grade Publications, Toronto, Canada, 1979. 166 pp., illus. Paper covers. $20.00.

NATO's search for a standard rifle.

100 Years of Shooters and Gunmakers of Single Shot Rifles, by Gerald O. Kelver, Brighton, CO, 1975. 212 pp., illus. Paper covers $10.00.

The Schuetzen rifle, targets and shooters, primers, match rifles, original loadings and much more. With chapters on famous gunsmiths like Harry Pope, Morgan L. Rood and others.

The '03 Springfields, by Clark S. Campbell, Ray Riling Arms Books Co., Phila., PA, 1978. 320 pp., illus. $29.95.

The most authoritative and definitive work on this famous U.S. rifle, the 1903 Springfield and its 30-06 cartridge.

The Pennsylvania Rifle, by Samuel E. Dyke, Sutter House, Lititz, PA, 1975. 61 pp., illus. Paper covers. $5.00.

History and development, from the hunting rifle of the Germans who settled the area. Contains a full listing of all known Lancaster, PA, gunsmiths from 1729 through 1815.

The Revolving Rifles, by Edsall James, Pioneer Press, Union City, TN, 1975. 23 pp., illus. Paper covers. $2.50.

Valuable information on revolving cylinder rifles, from the earliest matchlock forms to the latest models of Colt and Remington.

The Rifle Book, by Jack O'Connor, Random House, NY, 1978. 337 pp., illus. Paper covers. $10.95.

The complete book of small game, varmint and big game rifles.

Rifle Guide, by Robert A. Steindler, Stoeger Publishing Co., South Hackensack, NJ, 1978. 304 pp., illus. Paper covers. $9.95.

Complete, fully illustrated guide to selecting, shooting, caring for, and collecting rifles of all types.

Rifles AR15, M16, and M16A1, 5.56 mm, by D.B. McLean. Normount Armament Co., Wickenburg, AZ, 1968. Unpaginated, illus., paper covers. $10.00.

Descriptions, specifications and operation of subject models are set forth in text and picture.

Rifle Shooting as a Sport, by Bernd Klingner, A.S. Barnes and Co., Inc., San Diego, CA, 1980. 186 pp., illus. Paper covers. $15.00.

Basic principles, positions and techniques by an international expert.

The Rifleman's Rifle: Winchester's Model 70, 1936-63, by Roger C. Rule, Alliance Books, Inc., Northridge, CA, 1982. 368 pp., illus. $59.95.

The most complete reference book on the Model 70, with much fresh information on the Model 54 and the new Model 70s.

Ned H. Roberts and the Schuetzen Rifle, edited by Gerald O. Kelver, Brighton, CO, 1982. 99 pp., illus. $10.00.

A compilation of the writings of Major Ned H. Roberts which appeared in various gun magazines.

The Ruger No. 1, by J.D. Clayton, edited by John T. Amber, Blacksmith Corp., Southport, CT, 1983. 200 pp., illus. $39.50.

Covers this famous rifle from original conception to current production.

Schuetzen Rifles, History and Loading, by Gerald O. Kelver, Gerald O. Kelver, Publisher, Brighton, CO, 1972. Illus. $10.00.

Reference work on these rifles, their bullets, loading, telescopic sights, accuracy, etc. A limited, numbered ed.

The Sporting Rifle and Its Projectiles, by Lieut. James O Forsyth, The Buckskin Press, Big Timber, MT, 1978. 132 pp., illus. $10.00.

Facsimile reprint of the 1863 edition, one of the most authoritative books ever written on the muzzle-loading round ball sporting rifle.

The Springfield Rifle M1903, M1903A1, M1903A3, M1903A4, Desert Publications, Cornville, AZ, 1982. 100 pp., illus. Paper covers. $6.95.

Covers every aspect of disassembly and assembly, inspection, repair and maintenance.

The .22 Rifle, by Dave Petzal, Winchester Press, Piscataway, NJ, 1972. 244 pp., illus. $12.95.

All about the mechanics of the .22 rifle. How to choose the right one, how to choose a place to shoot, what makes a good shot, the basics of small-game hunting.

U.S. Rifle M14, from John Garand to the M21, by R. Blake Stevens, Collector Grade Publications, Toronto, Canada, 1983. 400 pp., illus. $34.95.

The complete history of the M14 rifle.

The American Shotgun, by David F. Butler, Lyman Publ., Middlefield, CT, 1973. 256 pp. illus. Paper covers. $15.00.

A comprehensive history of the American smoothbore's evolution from Colonial times to the present day.

American Shotgun Design and Performance, by L.R. Wallack, Winchester Press, Piscataway, NJ, 1977. 184 pp., illus. $16.95.

An expert lucidly recounts the history and development of American shotguns and explains how they work.

The Golden Age of Shotgunning, by Bob Hinman, Wolfe Publishing Co., Inc., Prescott, AZ, 1982. $17.95.

A valuable history of the late 1800s detailing that fabulous period of development in shotguns, shotshells and shotgunning.

The Gun Digest Book of Firearms Assembly/Disassembly, Part V: Shotguns, by J.B. Wood, DBI Books, Inc., Northfield, IL, 1980. 288 pp., illus. Paper covers. $12.95.

A professional presentation on the complete disassembly and assembly of 26 of the most popular shotguns, new and old.

Gun Digest Book of Gun Care, Cleaning and Refinishing, Book Two: Long Guns, by J.B. Wood, DBI Books, Inc., Northfield IL, 1984. 160 pp., illus. Paper covers. $8.95.

The care and maintenance of long guns with meticulous detail and step-by-step, illustrated, clearly written text.

Gun Digest Book of Shotgun Gunsmithing, by Ralph Walker, DBI Books, Inc., Northfield, IL, 1983. 256 pp., illus. Paper covers. $9.95.

The principles and practices of repairing, individualizing and accurizing modern shotguns by one of the world's premier shotgun gunsmiths.

Gun Digest Book of Trap and Skeet Shooting, by Art Blatt, DBI Books, Inc., Northfield, IL, 1984. 288 pp., illus. Paper covers. $11.95.

Valuable information for both beginner and seasoned shooter.

How to be a Winner Shooting Skeet & Trap, by Tom Morton, Tom Morton, Knoxville, MD, 1974. 144 pp., illus. Paper covers. $8.95.

The author explains why championship shooting is more than a physical process.

L.C. Smith Shotguns, by Lt. Col. William S. Brophy, The Gun Room Press, Highland Park, NJ, 1979. 244 pp., illus. $29.95.

The first work on this very important American gun and manufacturing company.

A Manual of Clayshooting, by Chris Cradock, Hippocrene Books, Inc., New York, NY, 1983. 192 pp., illus. $24.95.

Covers everything from building a range to buying a shotgun, with lots of illustrations and diagrams.

The Mysteries of Shotgun Patterns, by George G. Oberfell and Charles E. Thompson, Oklahoma State University Press, Stillwater, OK, 1982. 164 pp., illus. Paper covers. $25.00.

Shotgun ballistics for the hunter in non-technical language, with information on improving effectiveness in the field.

The Parker Gun, by Larry L. Baer, The Gun Room Press, Highland Park, NJ, 1983. 240 pp., illus. $29.95.

The only comprehensive work on the subject of America's most famous shotgun.

Plans and Specifications of the L.C. Smith Shotgun, by Lt. Col. William S. Brophy, USAR Ret., F. Brownell & Son, Montezuma, IA, 1982. 247 pp., illus. $19.95.

The only collection ever assembled of all the drawings and engineering specifications on the incomparable and very collectable L.C. Smith shotgun.

The Police Shotgun Manual, by Robert H. Robinson, Charles C. Thomas, Springfield, IL 1973. 153 pp., illus. $21.50.

A complete study and analysis of the most versatile and effective weapon in the police arsenal.

Reloading for Shotgunners, 2nd Edition, edited by Robert S.L. Anderson, DBI Books, Inc., Northbrook, IL, 1985. 256 pp., illus. Paper covers. $11.95.

The very latest in reloading information for the shotgunner.

Score Better at Skeet, by Fred Missildine, with Nick Karas. Winchester Press, NY 1972. 160 pp., illus. $10.00.

The long-awaited companion volume to *Score Better at Trap*.

Score Better at Trap, by Fred Missildine, Winchester Press, Piscataway, NJ, 1976. 159 pp., illus. $10.00.

An essential book for all trap shooters.

75 Years with the Shotgun, by C.T. (Buck) Buckman, Valley Publ., Fresno, CA, 1974. 141 pp., illus. $10.00.

An expert hunter and trapshooter shares experiences of a lifetime.

The Shotgun Book, by Jack O'Connor, Alfred A. Knopf, New York, NY, 2nd rev. ed., 1981. 341 pp., illus. Paper covers $9.95.

An indispensable book for every shotgunner containing authoritative information on every phase of the shotgun.

The Shotgun in Combat, by Tony Lesce, Desert Publications, Cornville, AZ, 1979. 148 pp., illus. Paper covers. $8.00.

A history of the shotgun and its use in combat.

Shotgun Digest, 2nd Edition, edited by Jack Lewis and Jack Mitchell, DBI Books, Inc., Northfield, IL 1980. 288 pp., illus. Paper covers. $11.95.

All-new look at shotguns by a double-barreled team of writers.

Shotgunners Guide, by Monte Burch, Winchester Press, Piscataway, NJ, 1980. 208 pp., illus. $18.95.

A basic book for the young and old who want to try shotgunning or who want to improve their skill.

Shotgunning: The Art and the Science, by Bob Brister, Winchester Press, Piscataway, NJ, 1976. 321 pp., illus. $15.95.

Hundreds of specific tips and truly novel techniques to improve the field and target shooting of every shotgunner.

The Sporting Shotgun: A User's Handbook, by Robin Marshall-Ball, Stonewall Press, Wash., DC, 1982. 176 pp., illus. $23.95.

An important international reference on shotgunning in North America and Europe, including Britain.

Sure-Hit Shotgun Ways, by Francis E. Sell, Stackpole Books, Harrisburg, PA, 1967. 160 pp., illus. $15.00.

On guns, ballistics and quick skill methods.

Skeet Shooting with D. Lee Braun, edited by R. Campbell, Grosset & Dunlap, NY, 1967. 160 pp., illus. Paper covers $5.95.

Thorough instructions on the fine points of Skeet shooting.

Trapshooting with D. Lee Braun and the Remington Pros., ed. by R. Campbell. Remington Arms Co., Bridgeport, CT. 1969. 157 pp., well illus., Paper covers. $5.95.

America's masters of the scattergun give the secrets of professional marksmanship.

Winchester Shotguns and Shotshells, by Ronald W. Stadt, Armory Publications, Tacoma, WA, 1984. 200 pp., illus. $29.50.

From the hammer double to the Model 59.

Wing & Shot, by R.G. Wehle, Country Press, 167. 190 pp., illus. $12.

Step-by-step account on how to train a fine shooting dog.

The World's Fighting Shotguns, by Thomas F. Swearengen, T. B. N. Enterprises, Alexandria, VA 1979. 500 pp., illus. $29.95.

The complete military and police reference work from the shotgun's inception to date, with up-to-date developments.

ARMS ASSOCIATIONS IN AMERICA AND ABROAD

UNITED STATES

ALABAMA

Alabama Gun Collectors Assn.
Dick Boyd, Secy., P.O. Box 5548, Tuscaloosa, AL 35405

ARIZONA

Arizona Arms Assn.,
Clay Fobes, Secy., P.O. Box 17061, Tucson, AZ 85731

CALIFORNIA

Calif. Hunters & Gun Owners Assoc.
V.H. Wacker, 2309 Cipriani Blvd., Belmont, CA 94002
Greater Calif. Arms & Collectors Assn.
Donald L. Bullock, 8291 Carburton St., Long Beach, CA 90808
Los Angeles Gun & Ctg. Collectors Assn.
F.H. Ruffra, 20810 Amie Ave., Apt. #9, Torrance, CA 90503

COLORADO

Pikes Peak Gun Collectors Guild
Charles Cell, 406 E. Uintah St., Colorado Springs, CO 80903

CONNECTICUT

Ye Conn. Gun Guild, Inc.
Robert L. Harris, P.O. Box 8, Cornwall Bridge, CT 06754

FLORIDA

Florida Gun Collectors Assn., Inc.
John D. Hammer, 5700 Mariner Dr., 304-W, Tampa, FL 33609
Tampa Bay Arms Collectors' Assn.
John Tuvell, 2461 — 67th Ave. S., St. Petersburg, FL 33712
Unified Sportsmen of Florida
P.O. Box 6565, Tallahassee, FL 32314

GEORGIA

Georgia Arms Collectors
Cecil W. Anderson, P.O. Box 218, Conley, GA 30027

HAWAII

Hawaii Historic Arms Assn.
John A. Bell, P.O. Box 1733, Honolulu, HI 96806

IDAHO

Idaho State Rifle and Pistol Assn.
Tom Price, 3631 Pineridge Dr., Coeur d'Alene, ID 83814

ILLINOIS

Fox Valley Arms Fellowship, Inc.
16 S. Bothwell St., Palatine, IL 60067
Illinois State Rifle Assn.
520 N. Michigan Ave., Room 615, Chicago, IL 60611
Illinois Gun Collectors Assn.
195 So. Schuyler Ave., Bradley, IL 60915
Mississippi Valley Gun & Cartridge Coll. Assn.
Lawrence Maynard, R.R. 2, Aledo, IL 61231
NIPDEA
c/o Phil Stanger, 1029 Castlewood Lane, Deerfield, IL 60015
Sauk Trail Gun Collectors
Gordell M. Matson, P.O. Box 1057, Milan, IL 61264
Wabash Valley Gun Collectors Assn., Inc.
Eberhard R. Gerbsch, 416 South St., Danville, IL 61832

INDIANA

Indiana Sportsmen's Council-Legislative
Maurice Latimer, P.O. Box 93, Bloomington, IN 47402
Indiana State Rifle & Pistol Assn.
Thos. Glancy, P.O. Box 552, Chesterton, IN 46304
Southern Indiana Gun Collectors Assn., Inc.
Harold M. McClary, 509 N. 3rd St., Boonville, IN 47601

IOWA

Central States Gun Collectors Assn.
Avery Giles, 1104 S. 1st Ave., Marshtown, IA 50158

KANSAS

Four State Collectors Assn.
M.G. Wilkinson, 915 E. 10th, Pittsburg, KS 66762
Kansas Cartridge Coll. Assn.
Bob Linder, Box 84, Plainville, KS 67663
Missouri Valley Arms Collectors Assn.
Chas. F. Samuel, Jr., Box 8204, Shawnee Mission, KS 66208

KENTUCKY

Kentuckiana Arms Coll. Assn.
Tony Wilson,Pres., Box 1776, Louisville, KY 40201
Kentucky Gun Collectors Assn., Inc.
Ruth Johnson, Box 64, Owensboro, KY 42302

LOUISIANA

Washitaw River Renegades
Sandra Rushing, P.O. Box 256, Main St., Grayson, LA 71435

MARYLAND

Baltimore Antique Arms Assn.
Stanley I. Kellert, E-30, 2600 Insulator Dr., Baltimore, MD 21230

MASSACHUSETTS

Bay Colony Weapons Collectors, Inc.
Ronald B. Santurjian, 47 Homer Rd., Belmont, MA 02178
Massachusetts Arms Collectors
John J. Callan, Jr., P.O. Box 1001, Worcester, MA 01613

MICHIGAN

Royal Oak Historical Arms Collectors, Inc.
Nancy Stein, 25487 Hereford, Huntington Woods, MI 48070

MINNESOTA

Minnesota Weapons Coll. Assn., Inc.
Box 662, Hopkins, MN 55343

MISSISSIPPI

Mississippi Gun Collectors Assn.
Mrs. Jack E. Swinney, P.O. Box 1332, Hattiesburg, MS 39401

MISSOURI

Mineral Belt Gun Coll. Assn.
D.F. Saunders, 1110 Cleveland Ave., Monett, MO 65708

MONTANA

Montana Arms Collectors Assn.
Lewis E. Yearout, 308 Riverview Dr. East, Great Falls, MT 59404
The Winchester Arms Coll. Assn.
Lewis E. Yearout, 308 Riverview Dr. East, Great Falls, MT 59404

NEW HAMPSHIRE

New Hampshire Arms Collectors, Inc.
Frank H. Galeucia, Rte. 28, Box 44, Windham, NH 03087

NEW JERSEY

Englishtown Benchrest Shooters Assn.
Michael Toth, 64 Cooke Ave., Carteret, NJ 07008
Experimental Ballistics Associates
Ed Yard, 110 Kensington, Trenton, NJ 08618
Jersey Shore Antique Arms Collectors
Joe Sisia, P.O. Box 100, Bayville, NJ 08721
New Jersey Arms Collectors Club, Inc.
Angus Laidlaw, 230 Valley Rd., Montclair, NJ 07042

NEW YORK

Empire State Arms Coll. Assn.
P.O. Box 2328, Rochester, NY 14623
Hudson-Mohawk Arms Collectors Assn., Inc.
Bennie S. Pisarz, 6 Lamberson St., Dolgeville, NY 13329
Iroquois Arms Collectors Assn.
Kenneth Keller, club secy., (Susann Keller, show secy.) 214 - 70th St., Niagara Falls, NY 14304
Mid-State Arms Coll. & Shooters Club
Jack Ackerman, 24 S. Mountain Terr., Binghamton, NY 13903

NORTH CAROLINA

Carolina Gun Collectors Assn.
Jerry Ledford, 3231 - 7th St. Dr. NE, Hickory, NC 28601

OHIO

Central Ohio Gun and Indian Relic Coll. Assn.
Coyt Stookey, 134 E. Ohio Ave., Washington C.H., OH 43160
Ohio Gun Collectors, Assn.
P.O. Box 24 F, Cincinnati, OH 45224
The Stark Gun Collectors, Inc.
William I. Gann, 5666 Waynesburg Dr., Waynesburg, OH 44688

OKLAHOMA

Indian Territory Gun Collector's Assn.
P.O. Box 4491, Tulsa, OK 74159

OREGON

Oregon Cartridge Coll. Assn.
Richard D. King, 3228 N.W. 60th, Corvallis, OR 97330
Oregon Arms Coll. Assn., Inc.
Ted Dowd, P.O. Box 25103, Portland, OR 97225

PENNSYLVANIA

Presque Isle Gun Coll. Assn.
James Welch, 156 E. 37 St., Erie, PA 16504

SOUTH CAROLINA

Belton Gun Club, Inc.
J.K. Phillips, Route 1, Belton, SC 29627

SOUTH DAKOTA

Dakota Territory Gun Coll. Assn., Inc.
Curt Carter, Castlewood, SD 57223

TENNESSEE

Memphis Antique Weapons Assn.
Jan Clement, 1886 Lyndale #1, Memphis TN 38107
Smoky Mountain Gun Coll. Assn., Inc.
Hugh W. Yarbro, P.O. Box 286, Knoxville, TN 37901
Tennessee Gun Collectors Assn., Inc.
M.H. Parks, 3556 Pleasant Valley Rd., Nashville, TN 37204

TEXAS

Houston Gun Collectors Assn., Inc.
P.O. Box 741429, Houston, TX 77274
Texas State Rifle Assn.
P.O. Drawer 710549, Dallas, TX 75371

UTAH

Utah Gun Collectors Assn.
Nick Davis, 5676 So. Meadow Lane #4,Ogden, UT 84403

WASHINGTON

Washington Arms Collectors, Inc.
J. Dennis Cook, P.O. Box 7335, Tacoma, WA 98407

WISCONSIN

Great Lakes Arms Coll. Assn., Inc.
Edward C. Warnke, 2913 Woodridge Lane, Waukesha, WI 53186
Wisconsin Gun Collectors Assn., Inc.
Lulita Zellmer, P.O. Box 181, Sussex, WI 53089

WYOMING

Wyoming Gun Collectors
Bob Funk, Box 1805, Riverton, WY 82501

NATIONAL ORGANIZATIONS

Amateur Trapshooting Assn.
P.O. Box 458, Vandalia, OH 45377
American Association of Shotgunning
P.O. Box 3351, Reno, NV 89505
American Defense Preparedness Assn.
Rosslyn Center, Suite 900, 1700 N. Moore St., Arlington, VA 22209
American Police Pistol & Rifle Assn.
1100 N.E. 125th St., No. Miami, FL 33161
American Single Shot Rifle Assn.
L.B. Thompson, 987 Jefferson Ave., Salem, OH 44460
American Society of Arms Collectors, Inc.
Robt. F. Rubendunst, 6550 Baywood Lane, Cincinnati, OH 45224
Association of Firearm and Toolmark Examiners
Eugenia A. Bell, Secy., 7857 Esterel Dr., LaJolla, CA 92037
Boone & Crockett Club
205 South Patrick, Alexandria, VA 22314
Cast Bullet Assn., Inc.
Ralland J. Fortier, 14193 Van Doren Rd., Manassas, VA 22111
Citizens Committee for the Right to Keep and Bear Arms
Natl. Hq.: Liberty Park, 12500 N.E. Tenth Pl., Bellevue, WA 98005
Deer Unlimited of America, Inc.
P.O. Box 509, Clemson, SC 29631
Ducks Unlimited, Inc.
One Waterfowl Way, Long Grove, IL 60047
Experimental Ballistics Associates
Ed Yard, 110 Kensington, Trenton, NJ 08618
Handgun Hunters International
J. D. Jones, Dir., P. O. Box 357 MAG, Bloomingdale, OH 43910
International Benchrest Shooters
Evelyn Richards, 411 N. Wilbur Ave. Sayre, PA 18840
International Cartridge Coll. Assn., Inc.
Victor v. B. Engel, 1211 Walnut St., Williamsport, PA 17701
International Handgun Metallic Silhouette Assoc.
Box 1609, Idaho Falls, ID 83401
International Military Arms Society
David M. Armstrong, P.O. Box 122, Williamstown, WV 26187
International Quail Foundation
P.O. Box 550, Edgefield, SC 29824-0550
The Mannlicher Collectors Assn.
Rev. Don L. Henry, Secy., P.O. Box 7144, Salem, OR 97303
Marlin Firearms Coll. Assn., Ltd.
Dick Paterson, Secy., 407 Lincoln Bldg., 44 Main St., Champaign, IL 61820
Miniature Arms Collectors/Makers Society Ltd.
Joseph J. Macewicz, Exec. Secy., 104 White Sand Lane, Racine, WI 53402
National Assn. of Federally Licd. Firearms Dealers
Andrew Molchan,2801 E. Oakland Park Blvd., Ft. Lauderdale, Fl 33306
National Automatic Pistol Collectors Assn.
Tom Knox, P.O. Box 15738, Tower Grove Station, St. Louis, MO 63163
National Bench Rest Shooters Assn., Inc.
Stella Buchtel, 5735 Sherwood Forest Dr., Akron, OH 44319
National Muzzle Loading Rifle Assn.
Box 67, Friendship, IN 47021
National Reloading Mfrs. Assn.
4905 S.W. Griffith Dr., Suite 101, Beaverton, OR 97005
National Rifle Assn. of America
1600 Rhode Island Ave., N.W., Washington, DC 20036
National Shooting Sports Fdtn., Inc.
Arnold H. Rohlfing, Exec. Director, P.O. Box 1075, Riverside, Ct 06878
National Skeet Shooting Assn.
Ann Myers, Exec. Director, P.O. Box 28188, San Antonio, TX 78228
National Varmint Hunters Assn. (NVHA)
P.O. Box 17962, San Antonio, TX 78217
National Wild Turkey Federation, Inc.
P.O. Box 530, Edgefield, SC 29824
North American Hunting Club
7901 Flying Cloud Dr., P.O. Box 35557, Minneapolis, MN 55435
North-South Skirmish Assn., Inc.
T.E. Johnson, Jr., 9700 Royerton Dr., Richmond, VA 23228
Remington Society of America
Fritz Baehr, 3125 Fremont Ave., Boulder, CO 80302
Ruger Collector's Assn., Inc.
Nancy J. Padua, P.O. Box 211, Trumbull, CT 06611
SAAMI, Sporting Arms and Ammunition Manufacturers' Institute, Inc.
P.O. Box 218, Wallingford, CT 06492
Safari Club International
Holt Bodinson, 5151 E. Broadway, Suite 1680, Tucson, AZ 85711
Sako Collectors Assn., Inc.
Mims C. Reed, Pres., 313 Cooper Dr., Hurst, TX 76053
Second Amendment Foundation
James Madison Building, 12500 N.E. 10th Pl., Bellevue, WA 98005
Slug Shooters International
P.O. Box 402, McHenry, IL 60050
Southern California Schuetzen Society
Rick Van Meter, P.O. Box 11152, Phoenix, AZ 85061
U.S. Revolver Assn.
Chick Shuter, 96 West Union St., Ashland, MA 01721
Winchester Arms Collectors Assoc.
Lewis E. Yearout, 308 Riverview Dr., E., Great Falls, MT 59404
World Fast Draw Assn.
Bob Arganbright, 4704 Upshaw, Northwoods, MO 63121

AUSTRALIA

Sporting Shooters' Assn. of Australia Inc.
Mr. K. MacLaine, P.O. Box 210, Belgrave, Vict. 3160, Australia

CANADA

Alberta

Canadian Historical Arms Society
P.O. Box 901, Edmonton, Alb., Canada T5J 2L8
National Firearms Assn.
Natl. HQ: P.O. Box 1779, Edmonton, Alta. T5J 2P1, Canada

BRITISH COLUMBIA

Historical Arms Collectors Society of B.C.
Ron Tyson, Box 80583, Burnaby, B.C. Canada V5H 3X9

NEW BRUNSWICK

Canadian Black Powder Federation
Mrs. Janet McConnell, P.O. Box 2876, Postal Sta. "A", Moncton, N.B. E1C 8T8, Can.

ONTARIO

Ajax Antique Arms Assn.
Monica A. Wright, P.O. Box 145, Millgrove, Ont., L0R 1V0, Canada
The Ontario Handgun Assn.
1711 McCowan Rd., Suite 205, Scarborough, Ont., M1S 2Y3, Canada
Oshawa Antique Gun Coll. Inc.
Monica A. Wright, P.O. Box 145, Millgrove, Ont., L0R 1V0, Canada
Tri-County Antique Arms Fair
P.O. Box 122, R.R. #1, North Lancaster, Ont., K0C 1Z0, Canada

EUROPE

ENGLAND

Arms and Armour Society of London
A.R.E. North. Dept. of Metalwork, Victoria & Albert Museum, South Kensington, London SW7 2RL
British Cartridge Collectors Club
Peter F. McGowan, 15 Fuller St., Ruddington, Nottingham
Historical Breechloading Smallarms Assn.
D.J. Penn, M.A., Imperial War Museum, Lambeth Rd., London SE1 6HZ, England.Journal and newsletter are $8 a yr. seamail; surcharge for airmail
National Rifle Assn. (British)
Bisley Camp, Brookwood, Woking, Surrey, GU24 0PB, England

FRANCE

Syndicat National de l'Arquebuserie du Commerce de l'Arme Historique
B.P. No 3, 78110 Le Vesient, France

GERMANY (WEST)

Deutscher Schützenbund
Lahnstrasse, 6200 Wiesbaden-Klarenthal, West Germany

NEW ZEALAND

New Zealand Deerstalkers Assn.
Mr. Shelby Grant, P.O. Box 6514, Wellington, New Zealand

SOUTH AFRICA

Historical Firearms Soc. of South Africa
P.O. Box 145, 7725 Newlands, Republic of South Africa
South African Reloaders Assn.
Box 27128, Sunnyside, Pretoria 0132, South Africa

Directory of the Arms Trade

AMMUNITION (Commercial)

Activ Industries, Inc., P.O. Box 238, Kearneysville, WV 25430/304-725-0451 (shotshells only)
Alberts Corp., 519 East 19th St., Paterson, NJ 07514/201-684-1676
BBM Corp., 221 Interstate Dr., West Springfield, MA 01089/413-737-3118 (45 ACP shotshell)
Bingham Ltd., 1775-C Wilwat Dr., Norcross, GA 30093
C.W. Cartridge Co., 71 Hackensack St., Wood-Ridge, NJ 07075/201-438-5111 (Sharps combustible cartridges)
Cascade Cartridge Inc., (See Omark)
Dynamit Nobel of America, Inc., 105 Stonehurst Court, Northvale, NJ 07647/201-767-1660(RWS)
Eley-Kynoch, ICI-America, Wilmington, DE 19897/302-575-3000
Estate Cartridge Inc., P.O. Box 3702, Conroe, TX 77305 (shotshell)
Federal Cartridge Co.; 2700 Foshay Tower, Minneapolis, MN 55402/612-333-8255
Fisher Enterprises, 655 Main St. #305, Edmonds, WA 98020/206-776-4365 (Prometheus airgun pellets)
Frontier Cartridge Division-Hornady Mfg. Co., Box 1848, Grand Island, NE 68801/308-382-1390
Hansen Cartridge Co., 244 Old Post Rd., Southport, CT 06490/203-259-7337
ICI-America, Wilmington, DE 19897/302-575-3000(Eley-Kynoch)
Midway Arms, Inc., 7450 Old Hwy. 40 West, Columbia, MO 65201/314-445-9521
Nevins Ammunition, Inc., 7614 Lemhi Ave., Suite #1, Boise, ID 83709/208-322-8611 (centerfire handgun)
Omark Industries, Box 856, Lewiston, ID 83501/208-746-2351
Precision Prods. of Wash., Inc., N. 311 Walnut Rd., Spokane, WA 99206/509-928-0604 (Exammo)
RWS, (See Dynamit Nobel of America)
Remington Arms Co., 939 Barnum Ave., P. O. Box #1939, Bridgeport, CT 06601
Service Armament, 689 Bergen Blvd., Ridgefield, NJ 07657
Super Vel, FPC, Inc., Hamilton Rd., Rt. 2, P. O. Box 1398, Fond du Lac, WI 54935/414-921-2652
Ten-X Mfg., 2410 East Foxfarm Rd., Cheynne, WY 82001
United States Ammunition Co. (USAC), Inc., 1476 Thorne Rd., Tacoma, WA 98421/206-627-8700
Weatherby's, 2781 E. Firestone Blvd., South Gate, CA 90280
Winchester, Shamrock St., East Alton, IL 62024

AMMUNITION (Custom)

Accuracy Systems Inc., 15203 N. Cave Creek Rd., Phoenix, AZ 85032/602-971-1991
Beal's Bullets, 170 W. Marshall Rd., Lansdowne, PA 19050/215-259-1220 (Auto Mag Specialists)
Bell's Gun & Sport Shop, 3309-19 Mannheim Rd., Franklin Park, IL 60131
Brass Extrusion Labs. Ltd., 800 W. Maple Lane, Bensenville, IL 60106
C.W. Cartridge Co., 71 Hackensack St., Wood-Ridge, NJ 07075 (201-438-5111)
Russell Campbell Custom Loaded Ammo, 219 Leisure Dr., San Antonio, TX 78201/512-735-1183
Cumberland Arms Rt. 1, Shafer Rd., Blantons Chapel, Manchester, TN 37355
Denali Bullet Co., P.O. Box 82217, Fairbanks, AK 99701/907-479-8227
Eagle Cap Custom Bullets, P.O. Box 659, Enterprise, OR 97828/503-426-4282
E.W. Ellis Sport Shop, RFD 1, Box 315, Corinth, NY 12822
Ellwood Epps Northern Ltd., 210 Worthington St. W., North Bay, Ont. PIB 3B4, Canada
Estate Cartridge Inc., P.O. Box 3702, Conroe, TX 77305/409-539-9144 (shotshell)
Jack First Distributors, Inc., 44633 Sierra Hwy., Lancaster, CA 93534/805-945-8961
Ramon B. Gonzalez, P.O. Box 370, Monticello, NY 12701/914-794-4515
R.H. Keeler, 817 "N" St., Port Angeles, WA 98362/206-457-4702
K.K. Arms Co., Star Route Box 671, Kerrville, TX 78028/512-257-4718
KTW Inc., 710 Foster Park Rd., Lorain, OH 44053 216/233-6919 (bullets)
Dean Lincoln, Custom Tackle & Ammo, P.O. Box 1886, Farmington, NM 87499/505-632-3539
Lindsley Arms Cartridge Co., Inc., P.O. Box 5738, Lake Worth, FL 33466/305-968-1678 (inq. S.A.S.E.)
Lomont Precision Bullets, 4236 West 700 South, Poneto, IN 46781/219-694-6792 (custom cast bullets only)
McConnellstown Reloading & Cast Bullets, Inc., R.D. 3, Box 40, Huntingdon, PA 16652/814-627-5402
North American Arms, 1800 North 300 West, Spanish Fork, UT 84660/801-798-9891
Numrich Arms Corp., 203 Broadway, W. Hurley, NY 12491
Olsen Development Lab., 307 Conestoga Way #37, Edgeville, PA 19403/215-631-1716 (Invicta)
Pearl Armory, Revenden Springs, AR 72460
Robert Pomeroy, Morison Ave., Corinth, ME 04427/207-285-7721 (custom shells)
Precision Ammo Co., P.O. Box 63, Garnerville, NY 10923/914-947-2720
Precision Prods. of Wash., Inc., N. 311 Walnut Rd., Spokane, WA 99206/509-928-0604 (Exammo)
Anthony F. Sailer-Ammunition, 707 W. Third St., P. O. Box L, Owen, WI 54460/715-229-2516
Sanders Cust. Gun Serv., 2358 Tyler Lane, Louisville, KY 40205
Senica Run, Inc., P.O. Box 3032, Greeley, CO 80633
George W. Spence, 115 Locust St., Steele, MO 63877/314-695-4926 (boxer-primed cartridges)
The 3-D Company, Box J, Main St., Doniphan, NE 68832/402-845-2285 (reloaded police ammo)
Zero Ammunition Co., Inc., P.O. Box 1188, Cullman, AL 35055/205-739-1606

AMMUNITION (Foreign)

Action Arms Ltd., P. O. Box 9573, Philadelphia, PA 19124/215-744-0100
Beeman Inc., 47-GDD Paul Drive, San Rafael, CA 94903/415-472-7121
Dan/Arms, 275 Commerce Dr., Suite 300, Fort Washington, PA 19034/215-635-3511
Dynamit Nobel of America, Inc., 105 Stonehurst Court, Northvale, NJ 07647/210-767-1660(RWS, Geco, Rottweil)
FFV Norma, Inc., 300 S. Jefferson, Suite 301, Springfield, MO 65806
Fiocchi of America, Inc., 1308 Chase, Springfield, MO 65803/417-864-6970
Hansen Cartridge Co., 244 Old Post Rd., Southport, CT 06490/203-259-7337
Norma, (See Outdoor Sports Headquarters, Inc.)
Hirtenberger Patronen-, Zündhütchen- & Metallwarenfabrik, A.G., Leobersdorfer Str. 33, A2552 Hirtenberg, Austria
Paul Jaeger, Inc., P.O. Box 449, 1 Madison Ave., Grand Junction, TN 38039 (RWS centerfire ammo)
Kendall International Arms, Inc., 501 East North, Carlisle, KY 40311/606-289-7336 (Lapua)
Lapua (See Kendall International, Inc.)
PMC (See Patton and Morgan Corp.)
Patton and Morgan Corp., 5900 Wilshire Blvd., Suite 1400, Los Angeles, CA 90036/213-938-0143 (PMC ammo)
RWS (Rheinische-Westfälische Sprengstoff) [See Dynamit Nobel of America; Paul Jaeger, Inc.]
Sports Emporium, 1414 Willow Ave., Philadelphia, PA 19126 (Danarms shotshells)

AMMUNITION COMPONENTS—BULLETS, POWDER, PRIMERS

Accurate Arms Co., Inc., (Propellents Div.), Rt. 1, Box 167, McEwen, TN, 37101/615-729-5301 (powders)
Acme Custom Bullets, P.O. Box 380304, San Antonio, TX 78280/512-680-4828
Alaska Bullet Works, P.O. Box 54, Douglas, AK 99824 (Alaska copper-bond cust.)
Alberts Corp., 519 E. 19th St., Paterson, NJ 07514/201-684-1676 (swaged bullets)
Ammo-O-Mart Ltd., P.O. Box 125, Hawkesbury, Ont., Canada K6A 2R8/613-632-9300 (Nobel powder)
Ballistic Prods., Inc., Box 488, 2105 Shaughnessy Circle, Long Lake, MN 55356
Ballistic Research Industries (BRI), 2825 S. Rodeo Gulch Rd. #8, Soquel, CA 95073/408-476-7981 (12-ga. Sabo shotgun slug)
Barnes Bullets, P.O. Box 215, American Fork, UT 84003/801-756-4222
Bell's Gun & Sport Shop, 3309-19 Mannheim Rd., Franklin Pk., IL 60131/312-678-1900
Bergman and Williams, 2450 Losee Rd., Las Vegas, NV 89030/702-642-1091 (copper tube 308 cust. bull.; lead wire i. all sizes)
Bitterroot Bullet Co., Box 412, Lewiston, ID 83501/208-743-5635 (Coin or stamps) f.50¢ U.S.; 75¢ Can. & Mex.; intl. $3.00 and #10 SASE for lit.
Black Mountain Bullets, Rte. 3, Box 297, Warrenton, VA 22186/703-347-1199 (cust.)
B.E.L.L., Brass Extrusion Laboratories, Ltd., 800 W. Maple Lane, Bensenville, IL 60106
Milton Brynin, 214 E. Third St., Mount Vernon, NY 10550/914-664-1311 (cast bullets)
Buffalo Rock Shooter Supply (See Chevron Bullets)
CCI, (See: Omark Industries)
CheVron Bullets, R.R. 1, Ottawa, IL 61350/815-433-2471
Kenneth E. Clark, 18738 Highway 99, Madera, CA 93637/209-674-6016 (Bullets)
Clete's Custom Bullets, RR 6, Box 1348, Warsaw, IN 46580
Cooper-Woodward, P.O. Box 972, Riverside, CA 92502/714-683-4295
Corbin Mfg. & Supply, Inc., P.O. Box 2659, White City, OR 97503/503-826-5211 (bullets)
Cor-Bon Custom Bullets, P.O. Box 10126, Detroit, MI 48210/313-894-2373 (375, 44, 45 solid brass partition bull.)

Custom Bullets by Hoffman, 2604 Peconic Ave. Seaford, NY 11783 (7mm, 308, 257, 224, 270)
Denali Bullet Co., P.O. Box 82217, Fairbanks, AK 99701/907-479-8227 (bullets)
Division Lead, 7742 W. 61 Pl., Summit, IL 60502
DuPont, Explosives Dept., Wilmington, DE 19898
Dynamit Nobel of America, Inc., 105 Stonehurst Court, Northvale, NJ 07647/201-767-1660 (RWS percussion caps)
Eagle Bullet Works, P.O. Box 2104, White City, OR 97503 (Div-Cor 375, 224, 257 cust. bull.)
Eagle Cap Custom Bullets, P.O. Box 659, Enterprise, OR 97828/503-426-4282
Eldora Plastics, Inc., P.O. Box 127, Eldora, IA 40627/515-858-2634 (Lage Uniwad)
Elk Mountain Shooters Supply Inc., 1719 Marie, Pasco, WA 99301 (Alaskan bullets)
Excaliber Wax, Inc., P.O. Box 432, Kenton, OH 43326/419-673-0512 (wax bullets)
Federal Cartridge Co., 2700 Foshay Tower, Minneapolis, MN 55402/612-333-8255 (nickel cases)
FFV Norma, Inc., 300 S. Jefferson, Suite 301, Springfield, MO 65806 (powder)
Fisher Enterprises, 655 Main St. #305, Edmonds, WA 98020/206-776-4365
Forty Five Ranch Enterprises, 119 S. Main, Miami, OK 74354/918-542-9307
Glaser Safety Slug, 711 Somerset Lane, P.O. Box 8223, Forest City, CA 94404
Godfrey Reloading Supply, Hi-Way 67-111, Brighton, IL 62012 (cast bullets)
Lynn Godfrey, (See: Elk Mtn. Shooters Supply)
GOEX, Inc., Belin Plant, Moosic, PA 18507/717-457-6724 (black powder)
Green Bay Bullets, P.O. Box 10446, 1486 Servais St., Green Bay, WI 54307-54304/414-469-2992 (cast lead bullets)
Grills-Hanna Bulletsmith Co., Lt., Box 655, Black Diamond, Alb. TOL OHO Canada/403-652-4393 (38, 9mm, 12-ga.)
GTM Co., George T. Mahaney, 15915B E. Main St., La Puente, CA 91744 (all brass shotshells)
Hansen Custom Bullets, 3221 Shelley St., Mohegan, NY 10547
Hardin Specialty Distr., P. O. Box 338, Radcliff, KY 40160/502-351-6649 (empty, primed cases)
Hepplers Gun Shop, 6000 B Soquel Ave., Santa Cruz, CA 95062/408-475-1235 (BRI 12-ga. slug)
Hercules Inc., Hercules Plaza, Wilmington, DE 19894 (smokeless powder)
Hodgdon Powder Co. Inc., P.O. Box 2932, Shawnee Mission, KS 66201/913-362-9455
Hornady Mfg. Co., P.O. Drawer 1848, Grand Island, NE 68802/308-382-1390
Illinois Custom Bullet Mfg., R.R. 1, Dunlap, IL 61525/309-685-1392 (handgun, heavy game, silhouette)
Kendall International Arms, Inc., 501 East North, Carlisle, KY 40311/606-289-7336 (Lapua bull.)
NORMA (See FFV Norma)
N.E. House Co., 195 West High St., E. Hampton, CT 06424/203-267-2133 (zinc bases in 30, 38, 44 and 45-cal. only)
Jaro Manuf., P.O. Box 6125, 206 E. Shaw, Pasadena, TX 77506/713-472-0471 (bullets)
J&J Custom Bullet, 1210 El Rey Ave., El Cajon, CA 92021 (Power-Pak)
J&P Enterprises, SR 80219, Fairbanks, AK 99701/907-488-1534 (Grizzly 4-cal. ogive 32&49 mil. bonded core tubing bull.)
Ka Pu Kapili, P.O. Box 745, Honokaa, HI 96272 (Hawaiian Special cust. bullets)
Kodiak Custom Bullets, 8261 Henry Circle, Anchorage, AK 99507
L.L.F. Die Shop, 1281 Highway 99 North, Eugene, OR 97402/503-688-5753
Lage Uniwad Co., 1102 Washington St., Eldora, IA 50627/515-858-2634
Ljutic Ind., Inc., Box 2117,Yakima, WA 98902 (Mono-wads)
Lomont Precision Bullets, 4236 West 700 South, Poneto, IN 46781/219-694-6792 (custom cast bullets)
Lyman Products Corp., Rte. 147, Middlefield, CT 06455
Mack's Sport Shop, Box 1155, Kodiak, AK 99615 (cust. bull.)
Michael's Antiques, Box 233, Copiague, L.I., NY 11726 (Balle Blondeau)
Miller Trading Co., 20 S. Front St., Wilmington, NC 28401/919-762-7107 (bullets)
Morrison Custom Bullet Corp., P.O. Box 5574 Sta. Edmonton, Alb. T6C 3T5 Canada (9mm, 357 handgun)
Non-Toxic Components, Inc., P.O. Box 4202, Portland, OR 97208 (steel shot kits)
Nosler Bullets Inc., 107 S.W. Columbia, Bend, OR 97702/503-382-5108
Ohio Shooters Supply, 7532 Tyler Blvd., Mentor, OH 44060 (cast bullets)
Old Western Scrounger, 12924 Hwy A-12, Montague, CA 96064/916-459-5445
Omark Industries, Box 856, Lewiston, ID 83501/208-746-2351
The Oster Group, 50 Sims Ave., Providence, RI 02909 (alloys f. casting bull.)
PMC Ammunition, 5400 Wilshire Blvd., Suite 1400, Los Angeles, CA 90036/213-938-3201
Pepperbox Gun Shop, P.O. Box 922, East Moline, IL 61244 (257, 224 rifle cal. cust. bull.)
Pyrodex, See: Hodgdon Powder Co., Inc. (black powder substitute)
Robert Pomeroy, Morison Ave., East Corinth, ME 04427/207-285-7721 (empty cases)
Power Plus Enterprises, 6939 Macon Rd. #15, Columbus, GA 31907/404-561-1717 (12-ga. shotguns slugs; 308, 45 ACP, 357 cust. bull.)
Precision Swaged Bullets, Rte. 1, Box 93H, Ronan, MT 59864/406-676-5135 (silhouette; out-of-prods. Sharps)
Professional Hunter Supplies, P.O. Box 608, Ferndale, CA 95536/707-786-9460 (408, 375, 308, 510 cust. bull.)
Prospect Bullet Co., 1620 Holmes Ave., Prospect Park, PA 19076/215-586-6240 (9mm, 38 cust.)
Redwood Bullet Works, 3559 Bay Rd., Redwood City, CA 94063 (cust.)
Remington-Peters, 939 Barnum Ave., P.O. Box #1939, Bridgeport, CT 06601
S&S Precision Bullets, 22965 La Cadena, Laguna Hills, CA 92653/714-768-6836 (linotype cast bull.)
Sansom Bullets, 2506 Rolling Hills, Dr., Greenville, TX 75401 (custom)
Sierra Bullets Inc., 10532 So. Painter Ave., Santa Fe Springs, CA 90670
Speer Products, Box 856, Lewiston, ID 83501
Supreme Products Co., 1830 S. California Ave., Monrovia, CA 91016/800-423-7159/818-357-5395 (rubber bullets)
Swift Bullet Co., Quinter, KS 67752/913-754-3959 (375 big game, 224 cust.)
Tallon Bullets, 1194 Tidewood Dr., Bethel Park, PA 15102/412-471-4494 (dual. diam. 308 cust.)
Taracorp Industries, 16th & Cleveland Blvd., Granite City, IL 62040/618-451-4400 (Lawrence Brand lead shot)
Traft Gunshop, P.O. Box 1078, Buena Vista, CO 81211/303-395-6034 (cust. bull.)
Trophy Bonded Bullets, 7704 Kingsley, Houston, TX 77087/713-645-4499 (big game 458, 308, 375 cust.)
Vitt & Boos, 2178 Nichols Ave., Stratford, CT 06497/203-375-6859 (Aerodynamic shotgun slug, 12-ga. only)
Winchester, Shamrock St., East Alton, IL 62024
Worthy Products, Inc., Box 88 Main St., Chippewa Bay, NY 13623/315-324-5450 (slug loads)
Zero Bullet Co. Inc., P.O. Box 1188, Cullman, AL 35055/205-739-1606

ANTIQUE ARMS DEALERS

AD Hominem, R.R. 3, Orillia, Ont., L3V 6H3, Canada/705-689-5303
Antique Arms Co., David F. Saunders, 1110 Cleveland, Monett, MO 65708/417-235-6501
Antique Gun Parts, Inc., 1118 S. Braddock Ave., Pittsburgh, PA 15218/412-241-1811
Armsport, Inc., 3590 N.W. 49th St., Miami, FL 33142/305-635-7850
Beeman Inc., 47 Paul Dr., San Rafael, CA 94903/415-472-7121 (airguns only)
Wm. Boggs, 1243 Grandview Ave., Columbus, OH 43212
Century Arms, Inc., 5 Federal St., St. Albans, VT 05478/802-524-9441
Dave Chicoine, d/b/a Liberty A.S.P., 19 Key St., Eastport, ME 04631/207-853-2327
Peter Dyson Ltd., 29-31 Church St., Honley, Huddersfield, W. Yorksh. HD7 2AH, England/0484-661062 (acc. f. ant. gun coll.; custom-and machine-made)
Ed's Gun House, Box 62, Rte. 1, Minnesota City, MN 55959/507-689-2925
Ellwood Epps Northern Ltd., 210 Worthington St. W., North Bay, Ont. PIB 3B4 Canada
William Fagan, 126 Belleview, Mount Clemens, MI 48043/313-465-4637
Jack First Distributors, Inc., 44633 Sierra Hwy., Lancaster, CA 93534/805-945-8961
N. Flayderman & Co., Squash Hollow, New Milford, CT 06776/203-354-5567
Chet Fulmer, P.O. Box 792, Rt. 2, Buffalo Lake, Detroit Lakes, MN 56501/218-847-7712
Robert S. Frielich, 396 Broome St., New York, NY 10013/212-254-3045
Garcia National Gun Traders, Inc., 225 S.W. 22nd Ave., Miami, FL 33135
Herb Glass, Bullville, NY 10915/914-361-3021
James Goergen, Rte. 2, Box 182BB, Austin, MN 55912/507-433-9280
Griffin's Guns & Antiques, R.R. 4, Peterboro, Ont., Canada K9J 6X5/705-745-7022
The Gun Shop, 6497 Pearl Rd., Parma Heights (Cleveland), OH 44130/216-884-7476
Hansen & Company, 244 Old Post Rd., Southport, CT 06490/203-259-7337
Holbrook Antique Militaria, 4050 S.W. 98th Ave., Miami, FL 33165/305-223-6500
Jackson Arms, 6209 Hillcrest Ave., Dallas, TX 75205/214-521-9929
Lever Arms Serv. Ltd., 572 Howe St., Vancouver, B.C., Canada V6C 2E3/604-685-6913
Lone Pine Trading Post, Jct. Highways 61 and 248, Minnesota City, MN 55959/507-689-2922
Charles W. Moore, R.D. #1, Box 276, Schenevus, NY 12155/607-278-5721
Museum of Historical Arms, 1038 Alton Rd., Miami Beach, FL 33139/305-672-7480 (ctlg $5)
Muzzleloaders Etc. Inc., 9901 Lyndale Ave. So., Bloomington, MN 55420/612-884-1161
New Orleans Arms Co., 5001 Treasure St., New Orleans, LA 70186/504-944-3371
O.K. Hardware, Westgate Shopping Center, Great Falls, MT 59404
Old Western Scrounger, 12924 Hwy A-12, Montague, CA 96064/916-459-5445 (write for list; $2)
Pioneer Guns, 5228 Montgomery, (Cincinnati) Norwood, OH 45212/513-631-4871
Pony Express Sport Shop, Inc., 16606 Schoenborn St., Sepulveda, CA 91343/818-895-1231
Martin B. Retting, Inc., 11029 Washington, Culver City, CA 90230/213-837-6111
Ridge Guncraft, Inc., 125 E. Tyrone Rd., Oak Ridge, TN 37830/615-483-4024
San Francisco Gun Exch., 124 Second St., San Francisco, CA 94105/415-982-6097
Santa Ana Gunroom, P.O. Box 1777, Santa Ana, CA 92701/714-541-3035
Don L. Shrum's Cape Outfitters, 412 So. Kingshighway, Cape Girardeau, MO 63701/314-335-4103
S&S Firearms, 74-11 Myrtle Ave., Glendale, NY 11385/212-497-1100
Steves Gun House, Rte. 1, Minnesota City, MN 55959
James Wayne, 308 Leisure Lane, Victoria, TX 77904/512-578-1258
Ward & Van Valkenburg, 114-32nd Ave. N., Fargo, ND 58102
M.C. Wiest, 125 E. Tyrone Rd., Oak Ridge, TN 37830/615-483-4024
J. David Yale, Ltd., 2618 Conowingo Rd., Bel Air, MD 21014/301-838-9479
Lewis Yearout, 308 Riverview Dr. E., Great Falls, MT 59404

APPRAISERS, GUNS, ETC.

Ahlman's, Rt. 1, Box 20, Morristown, MN 55052/507-685-4244
Dave Chicoine, dba Liberty Antique Sixgun, 19 Key St., Eastport, ME 04631/207-853-2327

D.O.C. Specialists (D.A. Ulrich), 2209 So. Central Ave., Cicero, IL 60650/312-652-3606
Ellwood Epps (Orillia) Ltd., R.R. 3, Hwy. 11 No., Orillia, Ont. L3V 6H3, Canada/705-689-5333
N. Flayderman & Co., Inc., RFD 2, Squash Hollow, New Milford, CT 06776/203-354-5567
Griffin & Howe, 589 Broadway, New York, NY 10012/212-966-5323
Dean Lincoln's Custom Tackle & Ammo, Inc., P.O. Box 1886, Farmington, NM 87499/505-632-3539
Orvis Co. Inc., Rte. 7A, Manchester, VT 05254/802-362-3622
PM Airservices Ltd., P.O. Box 1573, Costa Mesa, CA 92628/714-968-2689
Pony Express Sport Shop, Inc., 16606 Schoenborn St., Sepulveda, CA 91343/818-895-1231
John Richards, Rte. 2, Bedford, KY 40006/502-255-7222
Lewis Yearout, 308 Riverview Dr. East, Great Falls, MT 59404/406-761-0589

AUCTIONEERS, GUNS, ETC.

Alberts Corp., 519 East 19th St., Paterson, NJ 07514/201-684-1676
Richard A. Bourne Co. Inc., Corporation St., Hyannis, MA 02647
Christies-East, 219 E. 67th St., New York, NY 10021
Tom Keilman, 12316 Indian Mount, Austin, TX 78758
Harold Kelley, Box 125, Woburn, MA 01801
"Little John's" Antique Arms, 777 S. Main St., Orange, CA 92668
Parke-Bernet (see Sotheby's)
Sotheby's, 1334 York Ave. at 72nd St., New York, NY 10021
James C. Tillinghast, Box 19GD, Hancock, NH 03449

BOOKS (ARMS), Publishers and Dealers

Armory Publications, P.O. Box 44372, Tacoma, WA 98444/206-531-4632
Arms & Armour Press, 2-6 Hampstead High Street, London NW3 1QQ, England
Beeman Inc., 47 Paul Dr., San Rafael, CA 94903/415-472-7121 (airguns)
Blacksmith Corp., P.O. Box 424, Southport, CT 06490/203-367-4041
Blacktail Mountain Books, 42 First Ave. West, Kalispell, MT 59901/406-257-5573
Brownlee Books, Box 489, Hooks, TX 75561
DBI Books, Inc., 4092 Commercial Ave., Northbrook IL 60062/312-272-6310
Dove Press, P.O. Box 3882, Enid, OK 73702/405-234-4347
Fortress Publications Inc., P.O. Box 241, Stoney Creek, Ont. L8G 3X9, Canada/416-662-3505
Guncraft Books, Div. of Ridge Guncraft, Inc., 125 E. Tyrone Rd., Oak Ridge, TN 37830/615-483-4024
Gunnerman Books, P.O. Box 4292, Auburn Hills, MI 48057/313-879-2779
Handgun Press, 5832 S. Green, Chicago, IL 60621
Jackson Arms, 6209 Hillcrest Ave., Dallas, TX 75205
Long Survival Publications, P.O. Box 163-GD, Wamego, KS 66547/913-456-7387
Lyman, Route 147, Middlefield, CT 06455
Paladin Press, P.O. Box 1307, Boulder, CO 80306/303-443-7250
Personal Firearms Record Book Co., P.O. Box 2800, Santa Fe, NM 87501/505-983-2381
Petersen Publishing Co., 84990 Sunset Blvd., Los Angeles, CA 99069
Gerald Pettinger Arms Books, Route 2, Russell, IA 50238/515-535-2239
Ray Riling Arms Books Co., 114 Greenwood Ave., Box 135, Wyncote, PA 19095/215-438-2456
Rutgers Book Center, Mark Aziz, 127 Raritan Ave., Highland Park, NJ 08904/201-545-4344
Small Arms Press, Box 1316, St. George, UT 84770
Stackpole Books, Cameron & Kelker Sts., Telegraph Press Bldg., Harrisburg, PA 17105
Stoeger Publishing Co., 55 Ruta Court, South Hackensack, NJ 07606
Ken Trotman, 2-6 Hampstead High St., London, NW3, 1QQ, England
Winchester Press, 220 Old New Brunswick Rd., Piscataway, NJ 08854/201-981-0820
Wolfe Publishing Co., Inc., Box 30-30, Prescott, AZ 86302/602-445-7810

BULLET & CASE LUBRICANTS

Chopie Mfg. Inc., 700 Copeland Ave., La Crosse, WI 54601/608-784-0926 (Black-Solve)
Clenzoil Corp., P.O. Box 1226, Sta. C, Canton, OH 44708/216-833-9758
Cooper-Woodward, Box 972, Riverside, CA 92502/714-683-4295 (Perfect Lube)
Corbin Mfg. & Supply Inc., P.O. Box 2659, White City, OR 97503/503-826-5211
Green Bay Bullets, 1486 Servais St., Green Bay, WI 54304/414-469-2992 (EZE-Size case lube)
Hodgdon Powder Co., Inc., P.O. Box 2932, Shawnee Mission, KS 66201/913-362-9455
Javelina Products, Box 337, San Bernardino, CA 92402/714-882-5847 (Alox beeswax)
Jet-Aer Corp., 100 Sixth Ave., Paterson, NJ 07524
LeClear Industries, 1126 Donald Ave., Royal Oak, MI 48073/313-588-1025
Lyman Products Corp., Rte. 147, Middlefield, CT. 06455 (Size-Ezy)
Marmel Prods., P.O. Box 97, Utica, MI 48087/313-731-8029 (Marvellube, Marvelux)
Micro-Lube, P.O. Box 117, Mesilla Park, NM 88047/505-524-4215
Mirror Lube, American Specity. Lubricants, P.O. Box 693, San Juan Capistrano, CA 92693/714-496-1098
M&N Bullet Lube, P.O. Box 495, 151 N.E. Jefferson St., Madras, OR 97741/503-475-2992
Northeast Industrial, Inc., P.O. Box 249, 405 N. Canyon Blvd., Canyon City, OR 97820/503-575-2513 (Ten X-Lube; NEI mold prep)
Pacific Tool Co., P.O. Box 2048, Ordnance Plant Rd., Grand Island, NE 68801/308-384-2308
RCBS, Inc., Box 1919, Oroville, CA 95965
Radix Research & Marketing, Box 247, Woodland Park, CO 80863/303-687-3182 (Magnum Dri-Lube)
SAECO Rel, 2207 Border Ave., Torrance, CA 90501/213-320-6973
Shooters Accessory Supply (SAS) (See Corbin Mfg. & Supply)
Tamarack Prods., Inc., P.O. Box 224, Barrington, IL 60010/312-526-9333 (Bullet lube)

BULLET SWAGE DIES AND TOOLS

C-H Tool & Die Corp., 106 N. Harding St., Owen, WI 54460/715-229-2146
Lester Coats, 416 Simpson Ave., North Bend, OR 97459/503-756-6995 (lead wire core cutter)
Corbin Mfg. & Supply Inc., P.O. Box 2659, White City, OR 97503/503-826-5211
Hollywood, 7311 Radford Ave., No. Hollywood, CA 91605/213-875-1131
Huntington Die Specialties, P.O. Box 991, Oroville, CA 95965/916-534-1210
Independent Machine & Gun Shop, 1416 N. Hayes, Pocatello, ID 83201/208-232-1264 (TNT bullet dies)
MSS Industries, P.O. Box 6, River Grove, IL 60171 (tool)
L.L.F. Die Shop, 1281 Highway 99 North, Eugene, OR 97402/503-688-5753
Rorschach Precision Products, P.O. Box 151613, Irving, TX 75015/214-790-3487
SAS Dies, (See Corbin Mfg. & Supply)
Sport Flite Mfg., Inc., 2520 Industrial Row, Troy, MI 48084/313-280-0648
TNT (See Ind. Mach. & Gun Shop)
Whitney Sales, P.O. Box 875, Reseda, CA 91335/818-345-4212 (tungsten carbide rifle dies)

CARTRIDGES FOR COLLECTORS

AD Hominem, R.R. 3, Orillia, Ont., Canada L3V 6H3/705-689-5303
Ida I. Burgess, Sam's Gun Shop, 25 Squam Rd., Rockport, MA 01966/617-546-6839
Cameron's, 16690 W. 11th Ave., Golden CO 80401/303-279-7365
Chas. E. Duffy, Williams Lane, West Hurley, NY 12419
Tom M. Dunn, 1342 So. Poplar, Casper, WY 82601/307-237-3207
Ellwood Epps (Orillia) Ltd., Hwy. 11 North, Orillia, Ont. L3V 6H3, Canada/705-689-5333
Jack First Distributors, Inc., 44633 Sierra Hwy., Lancaster, CA 93534/805-945-8961
Glaser Safety Slug, Inc., P.O. Box 8223, Foster City, CA 94404/415-345-7677
"Gramps" Antique Cartridges, Box 341, Washago, Ont., Canada L0K 2B0
Griffin's Guns & Antiques, R.R. #4, Peterboro, Ont. K9J 6X5, Canada/705-745-7022
Hansen and Hansen, 244 Old Post Rd., Southport, CT 06490/203-259-7337
Idaho Ammunition Service, 410 21st Ave., Lewiston, ID 83501
San Francisco Gun Exchange, 124 Second St., San Francisco, CA 94105/415-982-6097
James C. Tillinghast, Box 405, Hancock, NH 03449/603-525-6615 (list $1)
Lewis Yearout, 308 Riverview Dr. E., Great Falls, MT 59404

CASES, CABINETS AND RACKS—GUN

Alco Carrying Cases, 601 W. 26th St., New York, NY 10001/212-675-5820 (aluminum)
Bob Allen Sportswear, 214 S.W. Jackson, Des Moines, IA 50315/515-283-1988/800-247-8048 (carrying)
Amacker Products Inc., P.O. Box 1432, Tallulah, LA 71282/318-574-4903
The American Import Co., 1453 Mission St., San Francisco, CA 94103/415-863-1506
Armes de Chasse, 3000 Valley Forge Circle, King of Prussia, PA 19406/215-783-6133
Art Jewel Ltd., 421A Irmen Dr., Addison, IL 60101/312-628-6220
Assault Systems of St. Louis, 869 Horan, St. Louis, MO 63026/314-343-3575 (canvas carrying case)
Beeman Precision Arms, Inc., 47-GDD Paul Dr., San Rafael, CA 94903/415-472-7121
Morton Booth Co., Box 123, Joplin, MO 64801
Boyt Co., Div. of Welsh Sportg. Gds., Box 220, Iowa Falls, IA 50126
Brenik, Inc., 925 W. Chicago Ave., Chicago, IL 60622
Browning, Rt. 4, Box 624-B, Arnold, MO 63010
Cap-Lex Gun Cases, Capitol Plastics of Ohio, Inc., 333 Van Camp Rd., Bowling Green, OH 43402
Chipmunk Mfg. Co., 114 E. Jackson, Medford, OR 97501/503-664-5585 (cases)
Dara-Nes Inc., see: Nesci
Dart Mfg. Co., 4012 Bronze Way, Dallas, TX 75237/214-333-4221
Detroit-Armor Corp., 2233 No. Palmer Dr., Schaumburg, IL 60195/312-397-4070 (Saf-Gard steel gun safe)
Doskocil Mfg. Co., Inc., P.O. Box 1246, Arlington, TX 75010/817-467-5116 (Gun Guard carrying)
East-Tenn Mills, Inc., 3112 Industrial Dr., Skyline Industrial Park, Johnson City, TN 37601/615-928-7186 (gun socks)
Ellwood Epps (Orillia) Ltd., R.R. 3, Hwy, 11 North, Orillia, Ont. L3V 6H3, Canada/705-689-5333 (custom gun cases)
Norbert Ertel, P.O. Box 1150, Des Plaines, IL 60018/312-825-2315 (cust. gun cases)
Flambeau Plastics Corp., 801 Lynn, Baraboo, WI 53913
Fort Knox Security Products, 1051 N. Industrial Park Rd., Orem, UT 84057/801-224-7233 (safes)

Gun-Ho Case Mfg. Co., 110 East 10th St., St. Paul, MN 55101
Hansen and Hansen, 244 Old Post Rd., Southport, CT 06490/203-259-7337
Marvin Huey Gun Cases, P.O. Box 22456, Kansas City, MO 64113/816-444-1637 (handbuilt leather cases)
Jumbo Sports Prods., P.O. Box 280-Airport Rd., Frederick, MD 21701
Kalispel Metal Prods. (KMP), P.O. Box 267, Cusick, WA 99119/509-445-1121 (aluminum boxes)
Kane Products Inc., 5572 Brecksville Rd., Cleveland, OH 44131/216-524-9962 (GunChaps)
Kolpin Mfg., Inc., Box 231, Berlin, WI 54923/414-361-0400
Marble Arms Corp., 420 Industrial Park, Gladstone, MI 49837/906-428-3710
Bill McGuire, 1600 No. Eastmont Ave., East Wenatchee, WA 98801 (custom cases)
Merchandise Brokers, P.O. Box 491, Lilburn, GA 30247/404-923-0015 (GunSlinger portable rack)
Nesci Enterprises, Inc., P.O. Box 119, Summit St., East Hampton, CT 06424/203-267-2588 (firearms security chests)
Nortex Industrial Fan Co., 2821 Main St., Dallas TX 75226/214-748-1157 (automobile gun rack)
Paul-Reed, Inc., P.O. Box 227, Charlevoix, MI 49720
Penguin Industries, Inc., Airport Industrial Mall, Coatesville, PA 19320/215-384-6000
Precise, 3 Chestnut, Suffern, NY 10901
Protecto Plastics, Div. of Penquin Ind., Airport Industrial Mall, Coatesville, PA 19320/215-384-6000 (carrying cases)
Randall Manufacturing, 12826 Pierce St., Pacoima, CA 91331
Red Head Brand Corp., 4949 Joseph Hardin Dr., Dallas, TX 75236/214-333-4141
Richland Arms Co., 321 W. Adrian, Blissfield, MI 49228
Saf-T-Case Mfg. Co., 104 S. Rogers, Irving, TX 75060/214-679-8827
San Angelo Co. 1841 Industrial Ave., San Angelo, TX 76904/915-655-7126
Buddy Schoellkopf, 4949 Joseph Hardin Dr., Dallas, TX 75236/214-333-2121
Schulz Industries, 16247 Minnesota Ave., Paramount, CA 90723/213-636-7718 (carrying cases)
Sealine Enterprises, 821 So. 3rd, Kent, WA 98032/206-852-1784 (vaults)
Se-Cur-All Cabinet Co., K-Prods., P.O. Box 2052, Michigan City, IN 46360/219-872-7957
Security Gun Chest, (See Tread Corp.)
Stearns Mfg. Co., P.O. Box 1498, St. Cloud, MN 56301
Tread Corp., P.O. Box 13207, Roanoke, VA 24032/703-982-6881 (security gun chest)
Trik Truk, P.O. Box 3760, Kent, WA 98301 (P.U. truck cases)
Weather Shield Sports Equipm. Inc., Rte. #3, Petoskey Rd., Charlevoix, MI 49720
Wilson Case Co., 906 Juniata Ave., Juniata, NE 68955/402-751-2145 (cases)
Woodstream Corp., Box 327, Lititz, PA 17543

CHOKE DEVICES, RECOIL ABSORBERS & RECOIL PADS

Action Products Inc., 22 N. Mulberry St., Hagerstown, MD 21740/800-228-7763 (rec. shock eliminator)
Bob Allen Companies, 214 S.W. Jackson St., Des Moines, IA 50302/515-283-2191
Arms Ingenuity Co., Box 1; 51 Canal St., Weatogue, CT 06089/203-658-5624 (Jet-Away)
Armsport, Inc., 3590 N.W. 49th St., Miami, FL 33142/305-635-7850 (choke devices)
Baer Custom Guns, 1725 Minesite Rd., Allentown, PA 18103/215-398-2362 (compensator syst. f. 45 autos)
Stan Baker, 5303 Roosevelt Way NE, Seattle, WA 98105/206-522-4575 (shotgun)
Briley Mfg. Co., 1085-A Gessner, Houston, TX 77055/713-932-6995 (choke tubes)
C&H Research, 115 Sunnyside Dr., Lewis, KS 67552/316-324-5445 (Mercury recoil suppressor)
Vito Cellini, Francesca Inc., 3115 Old Ranch Rd., San Antonio, TX 78217/512-826-2584 (recoil reducer; muzzle brake)
Clinton River Gun Serv. Inc., 30016 S. River Rd., Mt. Clemens, MI 48045 (Reed Choke)
Dahl Gun Shop, 6947 King Ave. West, Billings, MT 59106/406-652-3909
Defense Technology Associates, 3333 Midway Dr., Suite 104, San Diego, CA 92110/619-223-5339 (Muzzle-Mizer rec. abs.)
Edwards Recoil Reducer, 269 Herbert St., Alton, IL 62002/618-462-3257
Emsco Variable Shotgun Chokes, 101 Second Ave., S.E., Waseca, MN 56093/507-835-1779
Griggs Recreational Prods. Inc., P.O. Box 789, Bountiful, UT 84010/801-295-9696 (recoil director)
La Paloma Marketing, 4500 E. Speedway Blvd., Suite 93, Tucson, AZ 85712/602-881-4750 (Action rec. shock eliminator)
Lyman Products Corp., Rte. 147, Middlefield, CT. 06455 (Cutts Comp.)
Mag-na-port International, Inc., 41302 Executive Drive, Mt. Clemens, MI 48045/313-469-6727 (muzzle-brake system)
Mag-Na-Port of Canada, 1861 Burrows Ave., Winnipeg, Manitoba R2X 2V6, Canada
Don Mitchell Corp., 19007 S. Reyes Ave., Compton, CA 90221/714-964-3678 (muzzle brakes)
Multi-Gauge Enterprises, 433 W. Foothill Blvd., Monrovia, CA 91016/818-357-6117/358-4549 (screw-in chokes)
Pachmayr Gun Works, Inc., 1220 So. Grand Ave., Los Angeles, CA 90015/213-748-7271 (recoil pads)
P.A.S.T. Corp., 210 Park Ave., P.O. Box 7372, Columbia, MO 65205/314-449-7278 (recoil reducer shield)
Poly-Choke Div., Marble Arms, 420 Industrial Park, Gladstone, MI 49837/906-428-3710
Pro-Port Ltd., 41302 Executive Dr., Mt. Clemens, MI 48045/313-469-7323
Purbaugh, see: Multi-Gauge Enterprises
Supreme Products Co., 1830 S. California Ave., Monrovia, CA 91016/800-423-7159/818-357-5395 (recoil pads)

CHRONOGRAPHS AND PRESSURE TOOLS

B-Square Co., Box 11281, Ft. Worth, TX 76110/800-433-2909
Custom Chronograph Co., Rt. 1, Box 98, Brewster, WA 98812/509-689-2004
H-S Precision, Inc., 112 N. Summit St., Prescott, AZ 86302/602-445-0607 (press. barrels)
Paul Jaeger, Inc., P.O. Box 449, 1 Madison Ave., Grand Junction, TN 38039
Oehler Research, Inc., P.O. Box 9135, Austin, TX 78766/512-327-6900
Telepacific Electronics Co., Inc., P.O. Box 1329, San Marcos, CA 92069/714-744-4415
Tepeco, P.O. Box 342, Friendswood, TX 77546/713-482-2702 (Tepeco Speed-Meter)
M. York, 5508 Griffith Rd., Gaithersburg, MD 20760/301-253-4217 (press. tool)

CLEANING & REFINISHING SUPPLIES

A.C. Enterprises, P.O. Box 448, Edenton, NC 27932/919-482-4992
American Gas & Chemical Co., Ltd., 220 Pegasus Ave., Northvale, NJ 07647/201-767-7300 (TSI gun lube)
Armite Labs., 1845 Randolph St., Los Angeles, CA 90001/213-587-7744 (pen oiler)
Armoloy Co. of Ft. Worth, 204 E. Daggett St., Ft Worth, TX 76104/817-461-0051
Beeman Inc., 47 Paul Dr., San Rafael, CA 94903/415-472-7121
Belltown, Ltd., P.O. Box 74, Route 37, Sherman, CT 06784/203-354-5750 (gun clg. cloth kit)
Birchwood-Casey, 7900 Fuller Rd., Eden Prairie, MN 55344/612-927-7933
Blacksmith Corp., P.O. Box 424, Southport, CT 06490/800-531-2665 (Arctic Friction Free gun clg. equip.)
Blue and Gray Prods., Inc., R.D. #6, Box 362, Wellsboro, PA 16901/717-724-1383
Break-Free, a Div. of San/Bar Corp., 9999 Muirlands Blvd., Irvine, CA 92714/714-855-9911 (lubricants)
Jim Brobst, 299 Poplar St., Hamburg, PA 19526/215-562-2103 (J-B Bore Cleaning Compound)
GB Prods. Dept., H & R, Inc., Industrial Rowe, Gardner, MA 01440
Browning Arms, Rt. 4, Box 624-B, Arnold, MO 63010
J.M. Bucheimer Co., P.O. Box 280, Airport Rd., Frederick, MD 21701/301-662-5101
Burnishine Prod. Co., 8140 N. Ridgeway, Skokie, IL 60076/312-583-1810 (Stock Glaze)
Call 'N, Inc., 1615 Bartlett Rd., Memphis, TN 38134/901-372-1682 (Gunskin)
Chem-Pak, Inc., 11 Oates Ave., P.O. Box 1685, Winchester, VA 22601/703-667-1341 (Gun-Savr.protect. & lubricant)
Chopie Mfg. Inc., 700 Copeland Ave., La Crosse, WI 54601/608-784-0926 (Black-Solve)
Clenzoil Corp., Box 1226, Sta. C, Canton, OH 44708/216-833-9758
Clover Mfg. Co., 139 Woodward Ave., Norwalk, Ct. 06856/800-243-6492 (Clover compound)
J. Dewey Mfg. Co., 186 Skyview Dr., Southbury, CT 06488/203-264-3064 (one-piece gun clg. rod)
Diah Engineering Co., 5177 Haskell St., La Canada, CA 91011/213-625-2184 (barrel lubricant)
Dri-Slide, Inc., 411 N. Darling, Fremont, MI 49412/616-924-3950
The Dutchman's Firearms Inc., 4143 Taylor Blvd., Louisville, KY 40215/502-366-0555
Forster Products, 82 E. Lanark Ave., Lanark, IL 61046/815-493-6360
Fountain Prods., 492 Prospect Ave., W. Springfield, MA 01089/413-781-4551
Forty-Five Ranch Enterpr., 119 S. Main St., Miami, OK 74354/918-542-9307
Frank C. Hoppe Division, Penguin Ind., Inc., Airport Industrial Mall, Coatesville, PA 19320/215-384-6000
J-B Bore Cleaner, 299 Poplar St., Hamburg, PA 19526
Ken Jantz Supply, Rt. 1, Sulphur, OK 73086/405-622-3790
Jet-Aer Corp., 100 Sixth Ave., Paterson, NJ 07524 (blues & oils)
Kellog's Professional Prods., Inc., P.O. Box 1201, Sandusky, OH 44870
K.W. Kleinendorst, R.D. #1, Box 113B, Hop Bottom, PA 18824/717-289-4687 (rifle clg. cables)
Terry K. Kopp, Highway 13, Lexington, MO 64067/816-259-2636 (stock rubbing compound; rust preventative grease)
LPS Chemical Prods., Holt Lloyd Corp., 4647 Hugh Howell Rd., Tucker, GA 30084/404-934-7800
LaPaloma Marketing, Inc., 4500 E. Speedway Blvd., Suite 93, Tucson, AZ 85712/602-881-4750 (Amer-Lene solution)
Mark Lee, 2333 Emerson Ave. No., Minneapolis, MN 55411/612-521-0673 (rust blue solution)
LEM Gun Spec., Box 31, College Park, GA 30337/404-761-9054 (Lewis Lead Remover)
Liquid Wrench, Box 10628, Charlotte, NC 28201 (pen. oil)
Lynx Line Gun Prods. Div., Protective Coatings, Inc., 20626 Fenkell Ave., Detroit, MI 48223/313-255-6032
MJL Industries, P.O. Box 122, McHenry, IL 60050/815-344-1040 (Rust Free)
Marble Arms Co., 420 Industrial Park, Gladstone, MI 49837/906-428-3710
Marksman Inc., P.O. Box 598, Chesterland, OH 44026/216-729-9392 (bore cleaner & conditioner)
Micro Sight Co., 242 Harbor Blvd., Belmont, CA 94002/415-591-0769 (bedding)
Mirror-Lube, American Specity. Lubricants, P.O. Box 693, San Juan Capistrano, CA 92693/714-496-1098
Mount Labs, Inc., see: LaPaloma Marketing, Inc.
New Method Mfg. Co., P.O. Box 175, Bradford, PA 16701/814-362-6611 (gun blue; Minute Man gun care)
Northern Instruments, Inc., 6680 North Highway 49, Lino Lake, MN 55014 (Stor-Safe rust preventer)
Numrich Arms Co., West Hurley, NY 12491 (44-40 gun blue)
Old World Oil Products, 3827 Queen Ave. No., Minneapolis, MN 55412
Omark Industries, Box 856, Lewiston, ID 83501/208-746-2351
Original Mink Oil, Inc., P.O. Box 20191, 11021 N.E. Beech St., Portland, OR 97220/503-255-2814

Outers Laboratories; see: Omark Industries
Parker-Hale/Precision Sports, P.O. Box 708, Cortland, NY 13045
RBS Industries Corp., 1312 Washington Ave., St. Louis, MO 63103/314-241-8564 (Miracle All Purpose polishing cloth)
Reardon Prod., 103 W. Market St., Morrison, IL 61270 (Dry-Lube)
Rice Protective Gun Coatings, 235-30th St., West Palm Beach, FL 33407/305-845-2383
Richards Classic Oil Finish, John Richards, Rt. 2, Box 325, Bedford, KY 40006/502-255-7222 (gunstock oils, wax)
Rig Products, 87 Coney Island Dr., Sparks, NV 89431/703-331-5666
Rusteprufe Labs., Rte. 5, Sparta, WI 54656/608-269-4144
Rust Guardit, see: Schwab Industries
San/Bar Corp., Break-Free Div., 9999 Muirlands Pkwy., Irvine, CA 92718/714-855-9911 (lubricants)
Saunders Sptg. Gds., 338 Somerset, No. Plainfield, NJ 07060 (Sav-Bore)
Schwab Industries, Inc., P.O. Box 1269, Sequim, WA 98382/206-683-2944 (Rust Guardit)
Secoa Technologies, Inc., 3915 U.S. Hwy. 98 So., Lakeland, FL 33801/813-665-1734 (Teflon coatings)
Silver Dollar Guns, P.O. Box 475, 10 Frances St., Franklin, NH 03235/603-934-3292 (Silicone oil)
TDP Industries, Inc., 603 Airport Blvd., Doylestown, PA 18901/215-345-8687
Taylor & Robbins, Box 164, Rixford, PA 16745 (Throat Saver)
Texas Platers Supply Co., 2453 W. Five Mile Parkway, Dallas, TX 75233 (plating kit)
Totally Dependable Products; See: TDP
Treso Inc., P.O. Box 4640, Pagosa Springs, CO 81157/303-264-2295 (mfg. Durango Gun Rod)
C. S. Van Gorden, 1815 Main St., Bloomer, WI 54724/715-568-2612 (Van's Instant Blue)
WD-40 Co., P.O. Box 80607, San Diego, CA 92138-9021/619-275-1400
Williams Gun Sight, 7389 Lapeer Rd., Davison, MI 48423 (finish kit)
Winslow Arms Inc., P.O. Box 783, Camden, SC 29020 (refinishing kit)
Wisconsin Platers Supply Co., (See Texas Platers Supply Co.)
Woodstream Corp., P.O. Box 327, Lititz, PA 17543 (Mask)
Zip Aerosol Prods., See Rig

CUSTOM GUNSMITHS

Accuracy Systems Inc., 15203 N. Cave Creek Rd., Phoenix, AZ 85032/602-971-1991
Ahlman's Inc., R.R. 1, Box 20, Morristown, MN 55052/507-685-4244
Don Allen Inc., HC55, Box 322, Sturgis, SD 57785/605-347-4686
American Custom Gunmakers Guild, 3507 Red Oak Lane, Plainview, TX 79072/806-293-9042
Amrine's Gun Shop, 937 Luna Ave., Ojai, CA 93023
Antique Arms Co., D. F. Saunders, 1110 Cleveland Ave., Monett, MO 65708/417-235-6501 (Hawken copies)
Armament Gunsmithing Co., Inc., 525 Route 22, Hillside, NJ 07205/201-686-0960
John & Mary Armbrust, John's Gun Shop, 823 S. Union St., Mishawaka, IN 46544/219-255-0973
Armurier Hiptmayer, P.O. Box 136, Eastman, Que. J0E 1P0, Canada/514-297-2492
Armuriers Liegeois-Artisans Reunis "ALAR," rue Masset 27, 4300 Ans, Belgium
Atkinson Gun Co., P.O. Box 512, Prescott, AZ 86301
Ed von Atzigen, The Custom Shop, 890 Cochrane Crescent, Peterborough, Ont., K9H 5N3 Canada/705-742-6693
Creighton Audette, 19 Highland Circle, Springfield, VT 05156/802-885-2331
Richard W. Baber, Hanson's Gun Center, 1440 N. Hancock Ave., Colorado Springs, CO 80903/303-634-4220
Bain and Davis Sptg. Gds., 307 E. Valley Blvd., San Gabriel, CA 91776/213-573-4241
Baer Custom Guns, 1725 Minesite Rd., Allentown, PA 18103/215-398-2362 (rifles)
Stan Baker, 5303 Roosevelt Way NE, Seattle, WA 98105/206-522-4575 (shotgun specialist)
Joe J. Balickie, Rte. 2, Box 56-G, Apex, NC 27502/919-362-5185
Barta's Gunsmithing, 10231 US Hwy., #10, Cato, WI 54206/414-732-4472
Donald Bartlett, 16111 S.E. 229th Pl., Kent, WA 98031/206-630-2190
R. J. Beal, Jr., 170 W. Marshall Rd., Lansdowne, PA 19050/215-259-1220
Behlert Custom Guns, Inc., RD 2 Box 36C, Route 611 North, Pipersville, PA 18947/215-766-8680
George Beitzinger, 116-20 Atlantic Ave., Richmond Hill, NY 11419/718-847-7661
Bell's Custom Shop, 3309 Mannheim Rd., Franklin Park, IL 60131/312-678-1900 (handguns)
Bennett Gun Works, 561 Delaware Ave., Delmar, NY 12054/518-439-1862
Gordon Bess, 708 River St., Canon City, CO 81212/303-275-1073
Al Biesen, 5021 Rosewood, Spokane, WA 99208/509-328-9340
Roger Biesen, W. 2039 Sinto Ave., Spokane, WA 99201
Stephen L. Billeb, Box 219, Philipsburg, MT 59858/406-859-3919
Bob's Gun & Tackle Shop, 746 Granby St., Norfolk, VA 23510/804-627-8311
Boone Mountain Trading Post, 118 Sunrise Rd., Saint Marys, PA 15857/814-834-4879
Victor Bortugno, Atlantic & Pacific Arms Co., 4859 Virginia Beach Blvd., Virginia Beach, VA 23462
Charles Boswell (Gunmakers), Div. of Saxon Arms Ltd., 1166 Kapp Dr., Clearwater, FL 33575/813-461-4989
Art Bourne, (See Guncraft)
Kent Bowerly, 1213 Behshel Hts. Rd., Kelso, WA 98626/206-636-2859
Larry D. Brace, 771 Blackfoot Ave., Eugene, OR 97404/503-688-1278
Breckheimers, Rte. 69-A, Parish, NY 13131
A. Briganti, 475 Rt. 32, Highland Mills, NY 10930/914-928-9816
Brown Precision Inc., P.O. Box 270W, 7786 Molinos Ave., Los Molinos, CA 96055 (rifles)
Lenard M. Brownell, (See Billingsley & Brownell)
Buckhorn Gunsmithing, Larry Matthews, 341 W. 17th St. Coquille, OR 97423/503-396-5998
Ted Buckland, 361 Flagler Rd., Nordland, WA 98358/206-385-2142 (ML)
David Budin, Main St., Margaretville, NY 12455/914-568-4103
George Bunch, 7735 Garrison Rd., Hyattsville, MD 20784
Ida I. Burgess, Sam's Gun Shop, 25 Squam Rd., Rockport, MA 01966/617-546-6839 (bluing repairs)
Leo Bustani, P.O. Box 8125, W. Palm Beach, FL 33407/305-622-2710
Cache La Poudre Rifleworks, 168 No. College Ave., Ft. Collins, CO 80524/303-482-6913 (cust. ML)
Cameron's Guns, 16690 W. 11th Ave., Golden, CO 80401
Lou Camilli, 4700 Oahu Dr. N.E., Albuquerque, NM 87111/505-293-5259 (ML)
Dick Campbell, 1198 Finn Ave., Littleton, CO 80124/303-799-0145
Ralph L. Carter, Carter's Gun Shop, 225 G St., Penrose, CO 81240/303-372-6240
Shane Caywood, P.O. Box 321, Hwy. 51 So., Minocqua, WI 54548/715-356-9631
R. MacDonald Champlin, P.O. Box 693, Manchester, NH 03105/603-483-8559 (ML rifles and pistols)
Mark Chanlynn, Rocky Mtn. Rifle Wks. Ltd., 1704-14th St., Boulder, CO 80302/303-443-9189
Dave Chicoine, d/b/a Liberty A.S.P., 19 Key St., Eastport, ME 04631/207-853-2327
Claude Christopher, 1606 Berkley Rd., Greenville, NC 27834/919-756-0872
Classic Arms Corp., P.O. Box 8, Palo Alto, CA 94302/415-321-7243
John Edward Clark, R.R. #4, Tottenham, Ont. L0G 1W0 Canada/416-936-2131 (ML)
Kenneth E. Clark, 18738 Highway 99, Madera, CA 93637/209-674-6016
Clinton River Gun Serv. Inc., 30016 S. River Rd., Mt. Clemens, MI 48045/313-468-1090
Charles H. Coffin, 3719 Scarlet Ave., Odessa, TX 79762/915-366-4729
Jim Coffin, 250 Country Club Lane, Albany, OR 97321/503-928-4391
John Corry, 628 Martin Lane, Deerfield, IL 60015/312-541-6250 (English doubles & repairs)
Crest Carving Co., 14849 Dillow St., Westminster, CA 92683
Crocker, 1510 - 42nd St., Los Alamos, NM 87544 (rifles)
J. Lynn Crook, P.O. Box 654, Lebanon, TN 37087/615-449-1930
Cumberland Knife & Gun Works, 5661 Bragg Blvd., Fayetteville, NC 28303/919-867-0009 (ML)
The Custom Gun Guild, 5091-F Buford Hwy., Doraville, GA 30340/404-455-0346
D&D Gun Shop, 363 Elmwood, Troy, MI 48083/313-583-1512
Dahl Gunshop, 6947 King Ave. West, Billings, MT 59106/406-652-3909
Homer L. Dangler, Box 254, Addison, MI 49220/517-547-6745 (Kentucky rifles; brochure $3)
Davis Co., 2793 Del Monte St., West Sacramento, CA 95691/916-372-6789
Jack Dever, 8520 N.W. 90, Oklahoma City, OK 73132/405-721-6393
R. H. Devereaux, D. D. Custom Rifles, 475 Trucky St., St. Igance, MI 49781/906-643-8625
Dominic DiStefano, 4303 Friar Lane, Colorado Springs, CO 80907
Dixon Muzzleloading Shop, Inc., RD #1, Box 175, Kempton, PA 19529/215-756-6271 (ML)
William Dixon, Buckhorn Gun Works, Rt. 4 Box 200, Rapid City, SD 57701/605-787-6289
C. P. Donnelly-Siskiyou Gun Works, 405 Kubli Rd., Grants Pass, OR 97527/503-846-6604
Charles Duffy, Williams Lane, W. Hurley, NY 12491
Duncan's Gunworks Inc., 1619 Grand Ave., San Marcos, CA 92069/619-727-0515
David R. Dunlop, Rte. 1, Box 199, Rolla, ND 58367
Jere Eggleston, P.O. Box 50238, Columbia, SC 29250/803-799-3402
Elko Arms, Dr. L. Kortz, 28 rue Ecole Moderne, B-7400 Soignies, H.T., Belgium
William A. Emick, P.O. Box 741, Philipsburg, MT 59858/406-859-3280
Bob Emmons, 238 Robson Rd., Grafton, OH 44044/216-458-5890
Bill English, 4411 S.W. 100th, Seattle, WA 98146/206-932-7345
Englishtown Sporting Goods, Inc., David J. Maxham, 38 Main St., Englishtown, NJ 07726/201-446-7717
Armas ERBI, S. coop., Avda. Eulogio Estarta, Elgoibar (Guipuzcoa), Spain
Ken Eyster, Heritage Gunsmiths Inc., 6441 Bishop Rd., Centerburg, OH 43011/614-625-6131
Andy Fautheree, P.O. Box 863, Pagosa Springs, CO 81147/303-264-2892 (cust. ML)
Ted Fellowes, Beaver Lodge, 9245-16th Ave., S.W., Seattle, WA 98106/206-763-1698 (muzzleloaders)
Jack First Distributors Inc., 44633 Sierra Highway, Lancaster, CA 93534/805-945-8961
Clyde E. Fischer, P.O. Box 1437, Three Rivers, TX 78071/512-786-4125
Marshall F. Fish, Rt. 22 North, Westport, NY 12993/518-962-4897
Jerry A. Fisher, 1244-4th Ave. West, Kalispell, MT 59901/406-755-7093
Flaig's Inc., 2200 Evergreen Rd., Millvale, PA 15209/412-821-1717
Flynn's Cust. Guns, P.O. Box 7461, Alexandria, LA 71306/318-445-7130
John Fordham, Box 9 Dial Star Rt., P.O. Box 1093, Blue Ridge, GA 30513/404-632-3602
Larry L. Forster, Box 212, 220-1st St. N.E., Gwinner, ND 58040/701-678-2475
Fountain Products, 492 Prospect Ave., West Springfield, MA 01089/413-781-4651
Jay Frazier, S.R. Box 8644, Bird Creek, AK 99540/903-653-8302
Freeland's Scope Stands, 3737—14th Ave., Rock Island, IL 61201/309-788-7449
Fredrick Gun Shop, 10 Elson Drive, Riverside, RI 02915/401-433-2805
Frontier Arms, Inc., 420 E. Riding Club Rd., Cheyenne, WY 82001
Frontier Shop & Gallery, Depot 1st & Main, Riverton, WY 82501/307-856-4498
Fuller Gunshop, Cooper Landing, AK 99572
Karl J. Furr, 76 East 350 No., Orem, UT 84057/801-225-2603
Gander Mountain, Inc., P.O. Box 248, Wilmot, WI 53192/414-862-2331
Garcia Natl. Gun Traders, Inc., 225 S.W. 22nd Ave., Miami, FL 33135
Jim Garrett, P.O. Box 8563, Fort Collins, CO 80524

Gentry's Bozeman Gunsmith, David O. Gentry, 2010 No. 7th, Bozeman, MT 59715/406-586-1405 (cust. Montana Mtn. Rifle)
Gentry's Bluing & Guns Shop, Box 984, Belgrade,MT 59714
Edwin Gillman, R.R. 6, Box 195, Hanover, PA 17331/717-632-1662
Gilman-Mayfield, 1552 N. 1st, Fresno, CA 93703/209-237-2500
Dale Goens, Box 224, Cedar Crest, NM 87008
Dave Good, 14906 Robinwood St., Lansing, MI 48906/517-321-5392
A. R. Goode, 4125 N.E. 28th Terr., Ocala, FL 32670/904-622-9575
Goodling's Gunsmithing, R.D. #1, Box 1097, Spring Grove, PA 17362/717-225-3350
Gordie's Gun Shop, Gordon Mulholland, 1401 Fulton St., Streator, IL 61364/815-672-7202
Charles E. Grace, 10144 Elk Lake Rd., Williamsburg, MI 49690/616-264-9483
Griffin & Howe, 589 Broadway, New York, NY 10012/212-966-5323
H. L. "Pete" Grisel, 61912 Skyline View Dr., Bend, OR 97701/503-389-2649 (rifles)
Karl Guenther, 43-32 160th St., Flushing, NY 11372/212-461-7325
Gun City, 504 Main Ave., Bismarck, ND 58501/701-223-2304
Guncraft, Inc., 117 W. Pipeline, Hurst, TX 76053/817-282-6481
Guncraft (Kamloops) Ltd., 127 Victoria St., Kamloops, B.C. V2C 1Z4, Canada/604-374-2151
Guncraft (Kelowna) Ltd., 1771 Harvey Ave., Kelowna, B.C. V1Y 6G4, Canada/604-860-8977
The Gun Works, Joe Williams, 236 Main St., Springfield, OR 97477/503-741-4118 (ML)
The Gunworks Inc., 3434 Maple Ave., Brookfield IL 60513/312-387-7888
H-S Precision, Inc., 112 N. Summit, Prescott, AZ 85302/602-445-0607
Martin Hagn, Genl. Del., Cranbrook, B.C. VIC 4H5, Canada (s.s. actions & rifles)
Fritz Hallberg, The Outdoorsman, P.O. Box 339, Ontario, OR 97914/503-889-3135
Charles E. Hammans, P.O. Box 788, Stuttgart, AR 72160/501-673-1388
Dick Hanson, Hanson's Gun Center, 1440 No. Hancock, Colorado Springs, CO 80903/303-634-4220
Harkrader's Cust. Gun Shop, 825 Radford St., Christiansburg, VA 24073
Rob't W. Hart & Son Inc., 401 Montgomery St., Nescopeck, PA 18635/717-752-3481 (actions, stocks)
Hartmann & Weiss KG, Rahlstedter Bahnhofstr. 47, 2000 Hamburg 73, W. Germany
Hubert J. Hecht, Waffen-Hecht, 724 K St., Sacramento, CA 95814/916-448-1177
Edw. O. Hefti, 300 Fairview, College Station, TX 77840/409-696-4959
Stephen Heilmann, P.O. Box 657, Grass Valley, CA 95945/916-272-8758
Iver Henriksen, 1211 So. 2nd St., Missoula, MT 59801 (Rifles)
Heppler's Gun Shop, 6000 B Soquel Ave., Santa Cruz, CA 95062/408-475-1235
Wm. Hobaugh, The Rifle Shop, Box M, Philipsburg, MT 59858/406-859-3515
George Hoenig, 6521 Morton Dr., Boise, ID 83705/208-375-1116
Dick Holland, 422 N.E. 6th St., Newport, OR 97365/503-265-7556
Hollis Gun Shop, 917 Rex St., Carlsbad, NM 88220/505-835-3782
Bill Holmes, Rt. 2, Box 242, Fayetteville, AR 72701/501-521-8958
Steven Dodd Hughes, P.O. Box 11455, Eugene, OR 97440/503-485-8869 (ML)
Al Hunkeler, Buckskin Machine Works, 3235 So. 358th St., Auburn, WA 98001/206-927-5412 (ML)
Huntington's, P.O. Box 991, Oroville, CA 95965/916-534-1210
Hyper-Single Precision SS Rifles, 520 E. Beaver, Jenks, OK 74037/918-299-2391
Independent Machine & Gun Shop, 1416 N. Hayes, Pocatello, ID 83201
Paul Jaeger, Inc. P.O. Box 449, 1 Madison Ave., Grand Junction, TN 38039
R. L. Jamison, Jr., Route 4, Box 200, Moses Lake, WA 98837/509-762-2659
J. J. Jenkins Ent. Inc., 375 Pine Ave. No. 25, Goleta, CA 93017/805-967-1366
Jerry's Gun Shop, 9220 Ogden Ave., Brookfield, IL 60513/312-485-5200
Neal G. Johnson, Gunsmithing Inc., 111 Marvin Dr., Hampton, VA 23666/804-838-8091
Peter S. Johnson, The Orvis Co., Inc., Manchester, VT 05254/802-362-3622
Joseph & Associates, 4810 Riverbend Rd., Boulder, CO 80301/303-332-6720
Jos. Jurjevic, Gunshop, 605 Main St., Marble Falls, TX 78654/512-693-3012
Ken's Gun Specialties, K. Hunnell, Rt. 1 Box 147, Lakeview, AR 72642/501-431-5606
Kennedy Gun Shop, Rte. 12, Box 21, Clarksville, TN 37040/615-647-6043
Kennon's Custom Rifles, 5408 Biffle, Stone Mtn., GA 30088/404-469-9339
Stanley Kenvin, 5 Lakeville Lane, Plainview, NY 11803/516-931-0321
Kesselring Gun Shop, 400 Pacific Hiway No., Burlington, WA 98233/206-724-3113
Benjamin Kilham, Kilham & Co., Main St., Box 37, Lyme, NH 03768/603-795-4112
Don Klein Custom Guns, P.O. Box 277, Camp Douglas, WI 54618/608-427-6948
K. W. Kleinendorst, R.D. #1, Box 113B, Hop Bottom, PA 18824/717-289-4687
Terry K. Kopp, Highway 13, Lexington, MO 64067/816-259-2636
J. Korzinek, R.D. #2, Box 73, Canton, PA 17724/717-673-8512 (riflesmith) (broch. $1.50)
Lee Kuhns, 652 Northeast Palson Rd., Paulsbo, WA 98370/206-692-5790
Sam Lair, 520 E. Beaver, Jenks, OK 74037/918-299-2391 (single shots)
Maynard Lambert, Kamas, UT 84036
Harry Lawson Co., 3328 N. Richey Blvd., Tucson, AZ 85716/602-326-1117
John G. Lawson, (The Sight Shop), 1802 E. Columbia, Tacoma, WA 98404/206-474-5465
Mark Lee, 2333 Emerson Ave., N., Minneapolis, MN 55411/612-521-0673
Bill Leeper, (See Guncraft)
LeFever Arms Co. Inc., R.D. #1, Box 31, Lee Center, NY 13363/315-337-6722
Leland Firearms Co., 13 Mountain Ave., Llewellyn Park, West Orange, NJ 07052/201-964-7500 (shotguns)
Al Lind, 7821—76th Ave. S.W., Tacoma, WA 98498/206-584-6363
Max J. Lindauer, R.R. 2, Box 27, Washington, MO 63090
Robt. L. Lindsay, J & B Enterprises, 9416 Emory Grove Rd., P.O. Box 805, Gaithersburg, MD 20877/301-948-2941 (services only)
Ljutic Ind., Box 2117, Yakima, WA 98904 (shotguns)
Llanerch Gun Shop, 2800 Township Line, Upper Darby, PA 19082/215-789-5462
James W. Lofland, 2275 Larkin Rd., Boothwyn, PA 19061/215-485-0391 (SS rifles)
London Guns, 1528—20th St., Santa Monica, CA 90404/213-828-8486
McCann's Muzzle-Gun Works, Tom McCann, 200 Federal City Rd., Pennington, NJ 08534/609-737-1707 (ML)
McCormick's Gun Bluing Service, 609 N.E. 104th Ave., Vancouver, WA 98664/206-256-0579
Stan McFarland, 2221 Idella Ct., Grand Junction, CO 81506/303-243-4704 (cust. rifles)
Bill McGuire, 1600 N. Eastmont Ave., East Wenatchee, WA 98801
Harold E. MacFarland, Route #4, Box 1249, Cottonwood, AZ 86326/602-634-5320
Nick Makinson, R.R. #3, Komoka, Ont. N0L 1R0 Canada/519-471-5462 (English guns; repairs & renovations)
Frank E. Malin, P.O. Box 968, Lambeth, Ont. N0L 1S0, Canada/519-681-6482
Monte Mandarino, 136 Fifth Ave. West, Kalispell, MT 59901/406-257-6208 (Penn. rifles)
Lowell Manley, 3684 Pine St., Deckerville, MI 48427/313-376-3665
Mantzoros Cust. Gunsmith, P.O. Box 795, Cooper Landing, AK 99572/907-595-1201
Dale Marfell, 107 N. State St., Litchfield, IL 62056/217-327-3832
Marquart Precision Co., P.O. Box 1740, Prescott, AZ 86302/602-445-5646
Marsh Al's, 3341 W. Peoria Ave., Suite 401, Phoenix, AZ 85029/602-939-0464
Elwyn H. Martin, Martin's Gun Shop, 937 S. Sheridan Blvd., Lakewood, CO 80226/303-922-2184
Mashburn Arms & Sporting Goods Co., Inc., 1218 N. Pennsylvania, Oklahoma City, OK 73107/405-236-5151
Seely Masker, Custom Rifles, 261 Washington Ave., Pleasantville, NY 10570/914-769-2627
E. K. Matsuoka, 2801 Kinohou Place, Honolulu HI 96822/808-988-3008
Geo. E. Matthews & Son Inc., 10224 S. Paramount Blvd., Downey, CA 90241
Maurer Arms, 2154-16th St., Akron, OH 44314/216-745-6864 (muzzleloaders)
John E. Maxson, 3507 Red Oak Lane, Plainview, TX 79072/806-293-9042 (high grade rifles)
R. M. Mercer, 216 S. Whitewater Ave., Jefferson, WI 53549/414-674-3839
Miller Arms, Inc., Dean E. Miller, P.O. Box 260, St. Onge, SD 57779/605-578-1790
Miller Custom Rifles, 655 Dutton Ave., San Leandro, CA 94577/415-568-2447
Miller Gun Works, S. A. Miller, P.O. Box 7326, Tamuning, Guam 96911
David Miller Co., 3131 E. Greenlee Rd., Tucson, AZ 85716/602-326-3117 (classic rifles)
Tom Miller, c/o Huntington, 601 Oro Dam Blvd., Oroville, CA 95965/916-534-8000
Earl Milliron, 1249 N.E. 166th Ave., Portland, OR 97230/503-252-3725
Bill Monell, Red Mill Road, Pine Bush, NY 12566/914-744-3021
Wm. Larkin Moore & Co., 31360 Via Colinas, Suite 109, Westlake Village, CA 91360/213-889-4160
J. W. Morrison Custom Rifles, 4015 W. Sharon, Phoenix, AZ 85029/602-978-3754
Mitch Moschetti, P.O. Box 27065, Cromwell, CT 06416/203-632-2308
Mountain Bear Rifle Works, Inc., Wm. Scott Bickett, 100-B Ruritan Rd., Sterling, VA 22170/703-430-0420
Larry Mrock, R.F.D. 3, Box 207, Woodhill-Hooksett Rd., Bow, NH 03301/603-224-4096 (broch. $3)
Bruce A. Nettestad, R.R. 1, Box 140, Pelican Rapids, MN 56572/218-863-4301
Newman Gunshop, 119 Miller Rd., Agency, IA 52530/515-937-5775
Paul R. Nickels, Interwest Gun Service, P.O. Box 243, 52 N. 100 W., Providence, UT 84332/801-753-4260
Ted Nicklas, 5504 Hegel Rd., Goodrich, MI 48438/313-797-4493
William J. Nittler, 290 More Drive, Boulder Creek, CA 95006/408-338-3376 (shotgun repairs)
Jim Norman, Custom Gunstocks, 11230 Calenda Rd., San Diego, CA 92127/619-487-4173
Nu-Line Guns, 1053 Caulks Hill Rd., Harvester, MO 63303/314-441-4500
O'Brien Rifle Co., 324 Tropicana No. 128, Las Vegas, NV 89109/702-736-6082 (17-cal. Rifles)
Olympic Arms Inc., 624 Old Pacific Hwy. S.E., Olympia, WA 98503/206-456-3471
Vic Olson, 5002 Countryside Dr., Imperial, MO 63052/314-296-8086
The Orvis Co., Inc., Peter S. Johnson, Rt. 7A, Manchester, VT 05254/802-362-3622
Maurice Ottmar, Box 657, 113 East Fir, Coulee City, WA 99115/509-632-5717
Pachmayr Gun Works, 1220 S. Grand Ave., Los Angeles, CA 90015
Pasadena Gun Center, 206 E. Shaw, Pasadena, TX 77506/713-472-0417
Paterson Gunsmithing, 438 Main St., Paterson, NJ 07501/201-345-4100
John Pell, 410 College Ave., Trinidad, CO 81082/303-846-9406
A. W. Peterson Gun Shop, 1693 Old Hwy. 441, Mt. Dora, FL 32757 (ML)
Eugene T. Plante, Gene's Custom Guns, 3890 Hill Ave., P.O. Box 10534, White Bear Lake, MN 55110/612-429-5105
Ridge Guncraft, Inc., 125 E. Tyrone Rd., Oak Ridge, TN 37830/615-483-4024
Rifle Ranch, Jim Wilkinson, Rte. 10, 3301 Willow Creek Rd., Prescott, AZ 86301/602-778-7501
Rifle Shop, Box M, Philipsburg, MT 59858
J. J. Roberts, 166 Manassas Dr., Manassas Park, VA 22111/703-361-4513
Wm. A. Roberts Jr., Rte. 4, Box 75, Athens, AL 35611/205-232-7027 (ML)
Don Robinson, Pennsylvania Hse., 36 Fairfaix Crescent, Southowram, Halifax, W. Yorkshire HX3 9SQ, England (airifle stocks)
Bob Rogers Guns, P.O. Box 305, Franklin Grove, IL 61031/815-456-2685
Carl Roth, 4728 Pine Ridge Ave., Cheyenne, WY 82001/307-634-3958 (rust bluing)
Royal Arms, 1210 Bert Acosta, El Cajon, CA 92020/619-448-5466
R.P.S. Gunshop, 11 So. Haskell, Central Point, OR 97502/503-664-5010
Russell's Rifle Shop, Route 5, Box 92, Georgetown, TX 78626/512-778-5338 (gunsmith services)
SSK Industries, Rt. 1, Della Dr., Bloomingdale, OH 43910/614-264-0176

Sanders Custom Gun Serv., 2358 Tyler Lane, Louisville, KY 40205
Sandy's Custom Gunshop, Rte. #1, Box 20, Rockport, IL 62370/217-437-4241
Saratoga Arms Co., 1752 N. Pleasantview Rd., Pottstown, PA 19464/215-323-8326
Roy V. Schaefer, 965 W. Hilliard Lane, Eugene, OR 97404/503-688-4333
SGW, Inc. (formerly Schuetzen Gun Works), see: Olympic Arms
Schumaker's Gun Shop, Rte. 4, Box 500, Colville, WA 99114/509-684-4848
Schwartz Custom Guns, 9621 Coleman Rd., Haslett, MI 48840/517-339-8939
David W. Schwartz Custom Guns, 2505 Waller St., Eau Claire, WI 54701/715-832-1735
Schwarz's Gun Shop, 41-15th St., Wellsburg, WV 26070/304-737-0533
Butch Searcy, 15, Rd. 3804, Farmington, NM 87401/505-327-3419
Shane's Gunsmithing, P.O. Box 321, Hwy. 51 So., Minocqua, WI 54548/715-356-9631
Shaw's, Finest in Guns, 9447 W. Lilac Rd., Escondito, CA 92025/619-728-7070
George H. Sheldon, P.O. Box 475, Franklin, NH 03235 (45 autos only)
Lynn Shelton Custom Rifles, 1516 Sherry Court, Elk City, OK 73644/405-225-0372
Shell Shack, 113 E. Main, Laurel, MT 59044/406-628-8986 (ML)
Shilen Rifles, Inc., 205 Metro Park Blvd., Ennis, TX 75119/214-875-5318
Harold H. Shockley, 204 E. Farmington Rd., Hanna City, IL 61536/309-565-4524 (hot bluing & plating)
Shootin' Shack, 1065 Silverbeach Rd. #1, Riviera Beach, FL 33403/305-842-0990 ('smithing services)
Shootin' Shop, Inc., 225 Main St., Springfield, OR 97477/503-747-0175
Walter Shultz, 1752 N. Pleasantview Rd., Pottstown, PA 19464
Silver Dollar Guns, P.O. Box 475, 10 Frances St., Franklin, NH 03235/603-934-3292 (45 autos only)
Simmons Gun Spec., 700 So. Rogers Rd., Olathe, KS 66062/913-782-3131
Simms Hardware Co., 2801 J St., Sacramento, CA 95816/916-442-3800
Steve Sklany, 566 Birch Grove Dr., Kalispell, MT 59901/406-755-4527 (Ferguson rifle)
Jerome F. Slezak, 1290 Marlowe, Lakewood (Cleveland), OH 44107/216-221-1668
John Smith, 912 Lincoln, Carpentersville, IL 60110
Snapp's Gunshop, 6911 E. Washington Rd., Clare, MI 48617/517-386-9226
Fred D. Speiser, 2229 Dearborn, Missoula, MT 59801/406-549-8133
Spencer Reblue Service, 1820 Tupelo Trail, Holt, MI 48842/517-694-7474 (electroless nickel plating)
Sportsmen's Equip. Co., 915 W. Washington, San Diego, CA 92103/619-296-1501
Sportsmen's Exchange & Western Gun Traders, Inc., P.O. Box 111, 560 S. "C" St., Oxnard, CA 93032/805-483-1917
Jess L. Stark, Stark Mach. Co., 12051 Stroud, Houston, TX 77072/713-498-5882
Ken Starnes, Rt. 1, Box 269, Scroggins, TX 75480/214-365-2312
Steelman's Gun Shop, 10465 Beers Rd., Swartz Creek, MI 48473/313-753-4884
Keith Stegall, Box 696, Gunnison, CO 81230
Date Storey, 1764 S. Wilson, Casper, WY 82601/307-237-2414
Victor W. Strawbridge, 6 Pineview Dr., Dover Point, Dover, NH 03820/603-742-0013
W. C. Strutz, Rifle Barrels, Inc., P.O. Box 611, Eagle River, WI 54521/715-479-4766
Suter's House of Guns, 332 N. Tejon, Colorado Springs, CO 80902/303-635-1475
A. D. Swenson's 45 Shop, P.O. Box 606, Fallbrook, CA 92028
Talmage Ent., 43197 E. Whittier, Hemet, CA 92344/714-927-2397
Target Airgun Supply, P.O. Box 428, South Gate, CA 90280/213-569-3417
Taylor & Robbins, Box 164, Rixford, PA 16745
James A. Tertin, c/o Gander Mountain, P.O. Box 128 - Hwy. W, Wilmot, WI 53192/414-862-2344
Larry R. Thompson, Larry's Gun Shop, 521 E. Lake Ave., Watsonville, CA 95076/408-724-5328
Gordon A. Tibbitts, 1378 Lakewood Circle, Salt Lake City, UT 84117/801-272-4126
Daniel Titus, 872 Penn St., Bryn Mawr, PA 19010/215-525-8829
Tom's Gunshop, Tom Gillman, 4435 Central, Hot Springs, AR 71913/501-624-3856
Todd Trefts, 217 W. Koch, Bozeman, MT 59715/406-587-3817
Trinko's Gun Serv., 1406 E. Main, Watertown, WI 53094
Dennis A. "Doc" Ulrich, 2511 S. 57th Ave., Cicero, IL 60650
Upper Missouri Trading Co., Inc., Box 181, Crofton, MO 68730
Chas. VanDyke Gunsmith Service, 201 Gatewood Cir. W., Burleson, TX 76028/817-295-7373 (shotgun & recoil pad specialist)
Milton Van Epps, Rt. 69-A, Parish, NY 13131/313-625-7498
Gil Van Horn, P.O. Box 207, Llano, CA 93544
John Vest, 473-550 Audrey Dr., Susanville, CA 96130/916-257-6702
Vic's Gun Refinishing, 6 Pineview Dr., Dover, NH 03820/603-742-0013
Walker Arms Co., Rt. 2, Box 73, Hiwy 80 West, Selma, AL 36701/205-872-6231
Walker Arms Co., 127 N. Main St., Joplin, MO 64801
R. D. Wallace, Star Rt. Box 76, Grandin, MO 63943
R. A. Wardrop, Box 245, 409 E. Marble St., Mechanicsburg, PA 17055
Weatherby's, 2781 Firestone Blvd., South Gate, CA 90280/213-569-7186
Weaver Arms Co., P.O. Box 8, Dexter, MO 63841/314-568-3800 (ambidextrous bolt action)
J. S. Weeks & Son, 4748 Bailey Rd., Dimondale, MI 48821 (custom rifles)
Terry Werth, 1203 Woodlawn Rd., Lincoln, IL 62656/217-732-3870
Cecil Weems, P.O. Box 657, Mineral Wells, TX 76067/817-325-1462
Wells Sport Store, Fred Wells, 110 N. Summit St., Prescott, AZ 86301/602-445-3655
R. A. Wells, 3452 N. 1st Ave., Racine, WI 53403/414-639-5223
Terry Werth, 1203 Woodlawn Rd., Lincoln, IL 62656/217-732-9314
Robert G. West, 27211 Huey Lane, Eugene, OR 97402/503-689-6610
Western Gunstocks Mfg. Co., 550 Valencia School Rd., Aptos, CA 95003
Whitefish Sportsman, Pete Forthofer, 711 Spokane Ave., Whitefish, MT 59937/406-862-7252
Duane Wiebe, P.O. Box 497, Lotus, CA 95651/916-626-6240
M. Wiest & Son, 125 E. Tyrone Rd., Oak Ridge, TN 37830/615-483-4024
Dave Wills, 2776 Brevard Ave., Montgomery, AL 36109/205-272-8446
Williams Gun Sight Co., 7389 Lapeer Rd., Davison, MI 48423
Bob Williams, P.O. Box 143, Boonsboro, MD 21713
Williamson-Pate Gunsmith Service, 117 W. Pipeline, Hurst, TX 76053/817-268-2887
Thomas E. Wilson, 644 Spruce St., Boulder, CO 80302 (restorations)
Robert M. Winter, P.O. Box 484, Menno, SD 57045/605-387-5322
Lester Womack, 512 Westwood Dr., Prescott, AZ 86301/602-778-9624
J. David Yale, Ltd., 2618 Conowingo Rd., Bel Air, MD 21014/301-838-9479 (ML work)
Mike Yee, 4700-46th Ave. S.W., Seattle, WA 98116/206-935-3682
York County Gun Works, RR 4, Tottenham, Ont., LOG 1WO Canada (muzzle-loaders)
Russ Zeeryp, 1601 Foard Dr., Lynn Ross Manor, Morristown, TN 37814

CUSTOM METALSMITHS

Don Allen, Inc., HC55, Box 322, Sturgis, SD 57785/605-347-4686
Alley Supply Co., P.O. Box 848, Gardnerville, NV 89410/702-782-3800
Baer Custom Guns, 1725 Minesite Rd., Allentown, PA 18103/215-398-2362
Al Biesen & Assoc., West 2039 Sinto Ave., Spokane, WA 99201/509-328-6818
Ross Billingsley & Brownell, Box 25, Dayton, WY 82836/307-655-9344
Ted Blackburn, 85 E., 700 South, Springville, UT 84663/801-489-7341 (precision metalwork; steel trigger guard)
Gregg Boeke, Rte. 2, Box 149, Cresco, IA 52136/319-547-3746
Larry D. Brace, 771 Blackfoot Ave., Eugene, OR 97404/503,688-1278
A. Briganti, 475 Rt. 32, Highland Mills, NY 10930/914-928-9816
Leo Bustani, P.O. 8125, W. Palm Beach, FL 33407/305-622-2710
Clinton River Gun Serv. Inc., 30016 S. River Rd., Mt. Clemens, MI 48045/313-468-1090
Dave Cook, 5831-26th Lane, Brampton, MI 49837/906-428-1235
Crandall Tool & Machine Co., 1540 N. Mitchell St., Cadillac, MI 49601/616-775-5562
The Custom Gun Guild, Frank Wood, 5091-F Buford Highway, Doraville, GA 30340/404-455-0346
D&D Gun Shop, 363 Elmwood, Troy, MI 48083/313-583-1512
Ken Eyster Heritage Gunsmiths Inc., 6441 Bishop Rd., Centerburg, OH 43011/614-625-43031
Phil Fischer, 7333 N.E. Glisan, Portland, OR 97213/503-255-5678
Flaig's Inc., 2200 Evergreen Rd., Millvale, PA 15209/412-821-1717
Fountain Prods., 492 Prospect Ave., W. Springfield, MA 01089/413-781-4651
Fredrick Gun Shop, 10 Elson Dr., Riverside, RI 02915/401-433-2805 (engine turning)
Geo. M. Fullmer, 2499 Mavis St., Oakland, CA 94601/415-533-4193 (precise chambering—300 cals.)
Roger M. Green, P.O. Box 984, 315 S. 2nd St., Glenrock, WY 82637/307-436-9804
Gentry's The Bozeman Gunsmith, 2010 N. 7th, Bozeman, MT 59715/406-586-1405
Griffin & Howe, 589 Broadway, New York, NY 10012/212-966-5323
Harkrader's Custom Gun Shop, 825 Radford St., Christiansburg, VA 24073
Hubert J. Hecht, Waffen-Hecht, 724 K St., Sacramento, CA 95814/916-448-1177
Stephen Heilmann, P.O. Box 657, Grass Valley, CA 95945/916-272-8758
Klaus Hiptmayer, P.O. Box 136, R.R. 112 #750, Eastman, Que. JOE1PO, Canada/514-297-2492
Hollis Gun Shop, 917 Rex St., Carlsbad, NM 88220/505-885-3782
Huntington's, P.O. Box 991, Oroville, CA 95965
Paul Jaeger, Inc., P.O. Box 449, 1 Madison St., Grand Junction, TN 38039
Ken Jantz, Rt. 1, Sulphur, OK 73086/405-622-3790
Neil A. Jones, RD #1, Box 483A, Saegertown, PA 16433/814-763-2769
Kennons Custom Rifles, 5408 Biffle Rd., Stone Mountain, GA 30088/404-469-9339
Benjamin Kilham, Kilham & Co., Main St., Box 37, Lyme, NH 03768/603-795-4112
Terry K. Kopp, Highway 13, Lexington, MO 64067/816-259-2636
Ron Lampert, Rt. 1, Box 61, Guthrie, MN 56461/218-854-7345
Mark Lee, 2333 Emerson Ave., N., Minneapolis, MN 55411/612-521-0673
J. W. Morrison Custom Rifles, 4015 W. Sharon, Phoenix, AZ 85029/602-978-3754
Bruce A. Nettestad, Rt. 1, Box 140, Pelican Rapids, MN 56572/218-863-4301
Vic Olson, 5002 Countryside Dr., Imperial, MO 63052/314-296-8086
Pasadena Gun Center, 206 E. Shaw, Pasadena, TX 77506/713-472-0417
Penrod Precision, 126 E. Main St., P.O. Box 307, No. Manchester, IN 46962/219-982-8385
Precise Chambering Co., 2499 Mavis St., Oakland, CA 94601/415-533-4193
Dave Talley, Rt. 4, Box 366, Leesville, SC 29070/803-532-2700
Herman Waldron, Box 475, Pomeroy, WA 99347/509-843-1404
R. D. Wallace, Star Rt. Box 16, Grandin, MO 64943
Fred Wells, Wells Sport Store, 110 N. Summit St., Prescott, AZ 86301/602-445-3655
Terry Werth, 1203 Woodlawn Rd., Lincoln, IL 62656/217-732-3870
John Westrom, Precise Firearm Finishing, 25 N.W. 44th Ave., Des Moines, IA 50313/515-288-8680
Dick Willis, 141 Shady Creek Rd., Rochester, NY 14623

DECOYS

Carry-Lite, Inc., 5203 W. Clinton Ave., Milwaukee, WI 53223
Deer Me Products Co., Box 34, 1208 Park St., Anoka, MN 55303/612-421-8971 (Anchors)
Ted Devlet's Custom Purveyors, P.O. Box 886, Fort Lee, NJ 07024/201-886-0196
Flambeau Prods. Corp., 15981 Valplast Rd., Middlefield, OH 44062/216-632-1631
G & H Decoy Mfg. Co., P.O. Box 1208, Henryetta, OK 74437/918-652-3314

Penn's Woods Products, Inc., 19 W. Pittsburgh St., Delmont, PA 15626/412-468-8311
Royal Arms, 1210 Bert Acosta, El Cajon, CA 92020/619-448-5466 (wooden, duck)
Woodstream Corp., P.O. Box 327, Lititz, PA 17543

ENGRAVERS, ENGRAVING TOOLS

Abominable Engineering, P.O. Box 1904, Flagstaff, AZ 86002/602-779-3025
John J. Adams, P.O. Box 167, Corinth, VT 05039/802-439-5904
American Derringer Corp., 127 N. Lacy Dr., Waco, TX 76705/817-799-9111
Paolo Barbetti, c/o Stan's Gunshop, 5303 Roosevelt Way N.E., Seattle, WA 98105/206-522-4575
Robert Barnard, P.O. Box 93, Fordyce, AR 71742/501-352-5861
Billy R. Bates, 2905 Lynnwood Circle S.W., Decatur, AL 35603/205-355-3690
Joseph C. Bayer, 439 Sunset Ave., Sunset Hill Griggstown, RD 1, Princeton, NJ 08540/201-359-7283
Angelo Bee, 10703 Irondale Ave., Chatsworth, CA 91311/213-882-1567
Sid Bell Originals Inc., R.D. 2, Box 219, Tully, NY 13159/607-842-6431
Weldon Bledsoe, 6812 Park Place Dr., Fort Worth, TX 76118/817-589-1704
Rudolph V. Bochenski, 318 Sweet Ave., Buffalo, NY 14212/716-897-5148
Carl Bleile, Box 11464, Cincinnati, OH 45211/513-662-0802
C. Roger Bleile, Box 5112, Cincinnati, OH 45205/513-251-0249
Erich Boessler, Gun Engraving Intl., Am Vogeltal 3, 8732 Münnerstadt, W. Germany/9733-9443
Henry "Hank" Bonham, 218 Franklin Ave., Seaside Heights, NJ 08751/201-793-8309
Boone Trading Co., 562 Coyote Rd., Brinnon, WA 98320/206-796-4330 (ivory, scrimshaw tools)
Bryan Bridges, 6350 E. Paseo San Andres, Tucson, AZ 85710
Frank Brgoch, 1580 So. 1500 East, Bountiful, UT 84010/801-295-1885
Dennis B. Brooker, RR #3, Indianola IA 50125/515-961-8200
Burgess Vibrocrafters (BVI), Rt. 83, Grayslake, IL 60030
Byron Burgess, 1631 "C" St., Eureka, CA 95501/707-445-8251
Brian V. Cannavaro, Gun City U.S.A., 573 Murfreesboro Rd., Nashville, TN 37210/615-256-6127
Winston Churchill, Twenty Mile Stream Rd., RFD Box 29B, Proctorsville, VT 05153/802-226-7772
Clark Engravings, P.O. Box 80746, San Marino, CA 91108/818-287-1652
Frank Clark, 3714-27th St., Lubbock, TX 79410/806-799-3838
Crocker Engraving, 1510 - 42nd St., Los Alamos, NM 87544
W. Daniel Cullity, 209 Old County Rd., East Sandwich, MA 02537/617-888-1147
Art A. Darakis, RD #2, Box 350, Fredericksburg, OH 44627/216-695-4271
Tim Davis, 230 S. Main St., Eldorado, OH 45321/513-273-4611
Ed Delorge, 2231 Hwy. 308, Thiboudaux, LA 70301/504-447-1633
James R. DeMunck, 3012 English Rd., Rochester, NY 14616/716-225-0626 (SASE)
C. Gregory Dixon, RD 1, Box 175, Kempton, PA 19529/215-756-6271
Howard M. Dove, 52 Brook Rd., Enfield, CT 06082/203-749-9403
Michael W. Dubber, 3107 E. Mulberry, Evansville, IN 47714/812-476-4036
Henri Dumoulin & Fils, rue du Tilleul 16, B-4411 Milmoret (Herstal), Belgium
Robert Evans, 332 Vine St., Oregon City, OR 97045/503-656-5693
Ken Eyster, Heritage Gunsmiths Inc., 6441 Bishop Rd., Centerburg, OH 43011/614-625-6131
John Fanzoi, P.O. Box 25, Ferlach, Austria 9170
Jacqueline Favre, 3111 So. Valley View Blvd., Suite B-214, Las Vegas, NV 89102/702-876-6278
Armi FERLIB, 46 Via Costa, 25063 Gardone V.T. (Brescia), Italy
L. R. Fliger, 3616 78th Ave. N., Brooklyn Park, MN 55443/612-566-3808
Firearms Engravers Guild of America, Robert Evans, Secy., 332 Vine St., Oregon City, OR 97045/503-656-5693
Fountain Prods., 492 Prospect Ave., W. Springfield, MA 01089/413-781-4651
Henry Frank, 210 Meadow Rd., Box 984, Whitefish, MT 59937/406-862-2681
Leonard Francolini, 56 Morgan Rd., Canton, CT 06019/203-693-2529
GRS Corp., P.O. Box 748, 900 Overland St., Emporia, KS 66801/316-343-1084 (Gravermeister tool)
Donald Glaser, 1520 West St., Emporia, KS 66801
Eric Gold, Box 1904, Flagstaff, AZ 86002
Howard V. Grant, P.O. Box 396, Lac Du Flambeau, WI 54538/715-588-3586
Griffin & Howe, 589 Broadway, New York, NY 10012/212-966-5323
Gurney Engraving Method, #513-620 View St., Victoria, B.C. V8W 1J6 Canada/604-383-5243
John K. Gwilliam, P.O. Box 26854, Tempe, AZ 85282/602-894-1739
Hand Engravers Supply Co., 4348 Newberry Ct., Dayton, OH 45432/513-426-6762
Jack O. Harwood, 1191 S. Pendlebury Lane, Blackfoot, ID 83221/208-785-5368
Frank E. Hendricks, Master Engravers, Inc., P.O. Box 95, Bergheim, TX 78004/512-336-2665
Heidemarie Hiptmayer, R.R. 112, #750, P.O. Box 136, Eastman, Que. J0E 1P0, Canada/514-297-2492
Harvey Hoover, 1263 Nunneley Rd., Paradise, CA 94969/916-872-1154
Ken Hunt, c/o Hunting World, Inc., 16 E. 53rd St., New York, NY 10022/212-755-3400
Jim Hurst, 4537 S. Irvington Ave., Tulsa, OK 74135/918-627-5460
Ken Hurst/Firearm Engraving Co., P.O. Box 249, Route 501, Rustburg, VA 24588/804-332-6440
Ralph W. Ingle, #4 Missing Link, Rossville, GA 30741/404-866-5589 (color broch. $3)
Paul Jaeger, Inc., P.O. Box 449, 1 Madison Ave., Grand Junction, TN 38039
Ken Jantz Supply, Rt. 1, Sulphur, OK 73086/405-622-3790 (tools)
Bill Johns, 1113 Nightingale, McAllen, TX 78501/512-682-2971
Joseph, 301 E. 6th St., P.O. Box 638, Joseph, OR 97846/503-432-3585
Steven Kamyk, 9 Grandview Dr., Westfield, MA 01085/413-568-0457
T. J. Kaye, Rocksprings St. Rt., Box 277, Junction, TX 76849/915-446-3091
Lance Kelly, 1824 Royal Palm Dr., Edgewater, FL 32032/904-423-4933
Jim Kelso, Rt. 1, Box 5300, Worcester, VT 05682/802-229-4254
Kleinguenther's, P.O. Box 1261, Seguin, TX 78155
E. J. Koevenig, Engraving Service, P.O. Box 55, Hill City, SD 57745/605-574-2239
John Kudlas, 622-14th St. S.E., Rochester, MN 55901/507-288-5579
Ben Lane, Jr., 2118 Lipscomb St., Amarillo, TX 79109/806-372-3771
Beth Lane, Pontiac Gun Co., 815 N. Ladd, Pontiac, IL 61764/815-842-2402
Herb Larsen, 35276 Rockwell Dr., Abbotsford, B.C. V2S 4N4, Canada/604-853-5151
Terry Lazette, 142 N. Laurens Dr., Bolivar, OH 44612/216-874-4403
Franz Letschnig, Master-Engraver, 620 Cathcart, Rm. 422, Montreal, Queb. H3B 1M1, Canada/514-875-4989
W. Neal Lewis, 9 Bowers Dr., Newnan, GA 30263/404-251-3045
Frank Lindsay, 1326 Tenth Ave., Holdrege, NE 68949/308-995-4623
Steve Lindsay, P.O. Box 1413, Kearney, NE 68847/308-236-7885
London Guns, 1528-20th St., Santa Monica, CA 90404/213-828-8486
Harvey McBurnette, Rt. 4, Box 337, Piedmont, AL 36272
Lynton S.M. McKenzie, 6940 N. Alvernon Way, Tucson, AZ 85718/602-299-5090
Wm. H. Mains, 3111 S. Valley View Blvd., Suite B-214, Las Vegas, NV 89102/702-876-6278
Robert E. Maki, P.O. Box 947, Northbrook, IL 60062/312-724-8238
George Marek, P.O. Box 213, Westfield, MA 01086/413-568-5957
Frank Mele, P.O. Box 361, Somers, NY 10589
S. A. Miller, Miller Gun Works, P.O. Box 7326, Tamuning, Guam 96911
Cecil J. Mills, 2265 Sepulveda Way, Torrance, Ca 90501/213-328-8088
Frank Mittermeier, 3577 E. Tremont Ave., New York, NY 10465
Mitch Moschetti, P.O. Box 27065, Denver, CO 80227/303-936-1184
Gary K. Nelson, 975 Terrace Dr., Oakdale, CA 95361/209-847-4590
NgraveR Co., 879 Raymond Hill Rd., Oakdale, CT 06370/203-848-8031 (engr. tool)
New Orleans Arms Co., P.O. Box 26087, New Orleans, LA 70186/504-944-3371
New Orleans Jewelers Supply, 206 Chartres St., New Orleans, LA 70130/504-523-3839 (engr. tool)
Hans Obiltschnig, 12. November St. 7, 9170 Ferlach, Austria
Oker's Engraving, 365 Bell Rd., Bellford Mtn. Hts., P.O. Box 126, Shawnee, CO 80475/303-838-6042
Gale Overbey, 612 Azalea Ave., Richmond, VA 23227
Pachmayr Gun Works, Inc., 1220 S. Grand Ave., Los Angeles, CA 90015/213-748-7271
Rex C. Pedersen, 2717 S. Pere Marquette, Ludington, MI 49431/616-843-2061
Marcello Pedini, 5 No. Jefferson Ave., Catskill, NY 12414/518-943-5257
E. L. Peters, P.O. Box 1927, Gibsons, B.C. V0N 1V0, Canada/604-886-9665
Paul R. Piquette, 40 Royalton St., Chicopee, MA 01020/413-592-1057
Eugene T. Plante, Gene's Custom Guns, 3890 Hill Ave., P.O. Box 10534, White Bear Lake, MN 55110/612-429-5105
Jeremy W. Potts, 912 Poplar St., Denver, CO 80220/303-355-5462
Wayne E. Potts, 912 Poplar St., Denver, CO 80220/303-355-5462
Ed Pranger, 1414-7th St., Anacortes, WA 98221/206-293-3488
E. C. Prudhomme, 513 Ricou-Brewster Bldg., Shreveport, LA 71101/318-425-8421
Puccinelli Design, P.O. Box 2222, San Anselmo, CA 94960/415-382-1464
Martin Rabeno, Spook Hollow Trading Co., Box 37F, RD #1, Ellenville, NY 12428/914-647-4567
Jim Riggs, 206 Azalea, Boerne, TX 78006/512-249-8567 (handguns)
J. J. Roberts, 166 Manassas Dr., Manassas Park, VA 22111/703-361-4513
John R. and Hans Rohner, Sunshine Canyon, Boulder, CO 80302/303-444-3841
Bob Rosser, 162 Ramsey Dr., Albertville, AL 35950/205-878-5388
Richard D. Roy, 87 Lincoln Way, Windsor, CT 06095/203-688-0304
Joe Rundell, 6198 Frances Rd., Clio, MI 48420/313-687-0559
Robert P. Runge, 94 Grove St., Ilion, NY 13357/315-894-3036
Shaw-Leibowitz, Rt. 1, Box 421, New Cumberland, WV 26047/304-564-3108 (etchers)
Shaw's "Finest In Guns," 9447 W. Lilac Rd., Escondido, CA 92025/619-728-7070
George Sherwood, Box 735, Winchester, OR 97495/503-672-3159
Ben Shostle, The Gun Room, 1201 Burlington Dr., Muncie, IN 47302/317-282-9073
W. P. Sinclair, 36 South St., Warminster, Wiltsh. BA12 8DZ, England
Ron Skaggs, 2433 Coach Dr., Spring Valley, CA 92077/619-698-8582
Mark A. Smith, 200 N. 9th, Sinclair, WY 82334/307-324-7929
R. Spinale, 3415 Oakdale Ave., Lorain, OH 44055/216-246-5344
Ray Swan, 885 French Rd., Cheektowaga, NY 14227/716-668-3430
Robt. Swartley, 2800 Pine St., Napa, CA 94559
George W. Thiewes, 1846 Allen Lane, St. Charles, IL 60174/312-584-1383
Denise Thirion, Box 408, Graton, CA 95444/707-829-1876
Anthony Tuscano, 1473 Felton Rd., South Euclid, OH 44121
Robert B. Valade, 931-3rd. Ave., Seaside, OR 97138/503-738-7672
John Vest, 473550 Audrey Dr., Susanville, CA 96130/916-257-6702
Ray Viramontez, 4348 Newberry Ct., Dayton, OH 45432/513-426-6762
Vernon G. Wagoner, 2325 E. Encanto, Mesa, AZ 85203/602-835-1307
R. D. Wallace, Star Rt. Box 76, Grandin, MO 63943
Terry Wallace, 385 San Marino, Vallejo, CA 94590
Floyd E. Warren, 1273 State Rt. 305 N.E., Cortland, OH 44410/216-638-4219
Kenneth W. Warren, Mountain States Engraving, 8333 E. San Sebastian Dr., Scottsdale, AZ 85258/602-991-5035
David W. Weber, 1421 East 4th, North Platte, NE 69101/308-534-2525
Rachel Wells, 110 N. Summit St., Prescott, AZ 86301/602-445-3655
Sam Welch, Box 2152, Kodiak, AK 99615/907-486-5085
Claus Willig, c/o Paul Jaeger, Inc., P.O. Box 449, 1 Madison Ave. Grand Junction, TN 38039
Mel Wood, Star Route, Box 364, Elgin, AZ 85611/602-455-5541

GAME CALLS

Black Duck, 1737 Davis Ave., Whiting, IN 46394/219-659-2997
Burnham Bros., Box 669, 912 Main St., Marble Falls, TX 78654/512-693-3112

Call'N, Inc., 1615 Bartlett Rd., Memphis, TN 38134/901-372-1682
Faulk's, 616 18th St., Lake Charles, LA 70601
Lohman Mfg. Co., P.O. Box 220, Neosho, MO 64850/417-451-4438
Mallardtone Game Calls, 2901 16th St., Moline, IL 61265/309-762-8089
Phil. S. Olt Co., Box 550, Pekin, IL 61554/309-348-3633
Penn's Woods Products, Inc., 19 W. Pittsburgh St., Delmont, PA 15626
Scotch Game Call Co., Inc., 6619 Oak Orchard Rd., Elba, NY 14058/716-757-9958
Johnny Stewart Game Calls, Box 7954, Waco, TX 76710/817-772-3261
Sure-Shot Game Calls, Inc., P.O. Box 816, Groves, TX 77619
Thomas Game Calls, P.O. Box 336, Winnsboro, TX 75494
Weems Wild Calls, P.O. Box 7261, Ft. Worth, TX 76111/817-531-1051

GUN PARTS, U.S. AND FOREIGN

American Derringer Corp., 127 N. Lacy Dr., Waco, TX 76705/817-799-9111
Armsport, Inc., 3590 N.W. 49th St., Miami, FL 33142/305-635-7850
Badger Shooter's Supply, 106 So. Harding, Owen, WI 54460/715-229-2101
Behlert Custom Guns, Inc., Box 227, Monmouth Junction, NJ 08852/201-329-2284 (handgun parts)
Cherokee Gun Accessories, 830 Woodside Rd., Redwood City, CA 94061/415-572-3266
Dave Chicoine, d/b/a Liberty A.S.P., 19 Key St., Eastport, ME 04631/207-853-2327 (S&W only; ctlg. $5)
Crown City Arms, Inc., P.O. Box 550, Cortland, NY 13045/607-753-8238 (rifle, handgun)
Charles E. Duffy, Williams Lane, West Hurley, NY 12491
Christian Magazines, P.O. Box 184, Avoca, PA 18641
Federal Ordnance Inc., 1443 Potrero Ave., So. El Monte, CA 91733/213-350-4161
Jack First Distributors Inc., 44633 Sierra Highway, Lancaster, CA 93534/805-945-8961
Forster Products, 82 E. Lanark Ave., Lanark, IL 61046/815-493-6360
Gun City, 504 Main, Bismarck, ND 58501/701-223-2304 (magazines, gun parts)
Gun-Tec, P.O. Box 8125, W. Palm Beach, FL 33407 (Win. mag. tubing; Win. 92 conversion parts)
Hansen and Hansen, 244 Old Post Rd., Southport, CT 06490/203-259-7337
Walter H. Lodewick, 2816 N.E. Halsey, Portland, OR 97232/503-284-2554 (Winchester parts)
Marsh Al's, 3341 W. Peoria Ave., Suite 401, Phoenix, AZ 85029/602-939-0464 (Contender rifle)
Michigan Armament Marketing, Inc., 135 Sumner, Lake Elsinore, CA 92330/714-674-5750 (handgun parts; magazines)
Morgan Arms Co., Inc., 2999 So. Highland Dr., Las Vegas, NV 89109/702-737-5247 (MK-I kit)
Numrich Arms Co., West Hurley, NY 12491
Pacific Intl. Merch. Corp., 2215 "J" St., Sacramento, CA 95816/916-446-2737 (Vega 45 Colt mag.)
Potomac Arms Corp. (See Hunter's Haven)
Pre-64 Winchester Parts Co., P.O. Box 8125, West Palm Beach, FL 33407 (send stamped env. w. requ. list)
Martin B. Retting, Inc., 11029 Washington Blvd., Culver City, CA 90230/213-837-6111
Rock Island Armory, Inc., 111 E. Exchange St., Geneseo, IL 61254/309-944-2109
Royal Ordnance Works Ltd., P.O. Box 3245, Wilson, NC 27893/919-237-0515
Sarco, Inc., 323 Union St., Stirling, NJ 07980
Sherwood Intl. Export Corp., 18714 Parthenia St., Northridge, CA 91324
Simms, 2801 J St., Sacramento, CA 95816/916-442-3800
Clifford L. Smires, R.D. 1, Box 100, Columbus, NJ 08022/609-298-3158 (Mauser rifle parts)
Springfield Sporters Inc., R.D. 1, Penn Run, PA 15765/412-254-2626
Triple-K Mfg. Co., 568-6th Ave., San Diego, CA 92101/619-232-2066 (magazines, gun parts)

GUNS (Foreign)

Abercrombie & Fitch, 2302 Maxwell Lane, Houston, TX 77023 (Ferlib)
Action Arms, P.O. Box 9573, Philadelphia, PA 19124/215-744-0100
Aimpoint U.S.A., 201 Elden St., Suite 302, Herndon, VA 22070/703-471-6828
Allen Firearms Co., 2879 All Trades Rd., Santa Fe, NM 87501/505-471-6090 (ML)
American Arms Inc., P.O. Box 27163, Salt Lake City, UT 84127/801-972-5006
Anschutz (See PSI)
AYA (Aguirre y Aranzabal) See IGI Domino or Wm. L. Moore (Spanish shotguns)
Armoury Inc., Rte. 202, New Preston, CT 06777
Armes de Chasse, 3000 Valley Forge Circle, Suite 1051, King of Prussia, PA 19046/215-783-6133 (Merkel)
Armsource Inc., 6 Donald Dr., Orinda, CA 94563/415-254-2767 (Manufrance)
Armsport, Inc., 3590 N.W. 49th St., Miami, FL 33142/305-635-7850
Armurier Liegeois-Artisans Reunis (A.L.A.R.), 27, rue Lambert Masset, 4300 Ans, Belgium
Baikal International, 12 Fairview Terrace, Paramus, NJ 07652/201-845-8710 (Russian shotguns)
Pedro Arrizabalaga, Eibar, Spain
Beeman, Inc., 47-GDD Paul Dr., San Rafael, CA 94903/415-472-7121 (FWB, Weihrauch, FAS, Unique, Korth, Krico, Agner, Hammerli firearms)
Benelli Armi, S.p.A., via della Stazione 50, 61029 Urbino, Italy
Beretta U.S.A., 17601 Indian Head Highway, Accokeek, MD 20607/301-283-2191
Bingham Ltd., 1775-C Wilwat Dr., Norcross, GA 30093/404-448-1440
Charles Boswell (Gunmakers), Div. of Saxon Arms Ltd., 1166 Kapp Dr., Clearwater, FL 33575/813-461-4989
M. Braun, 32, rue Notre-Dame, 2240 Luxemburg, Luxemburg (all types)
Britarms/Berdan (Gunmakers Ltd.), See: Action Arms
British Guns, P.O. Box 1924, Corvallis, OR 97339/503-752-5886 (Agent for W.&C. Scott)
Bretton, 21 Rue Clement Forissier, 42-St. Etienne, France
Browning (Gen. Offices), Rt. 1, Morgan, UT 84050/801-876-2711
Browning, (parts & service), Rt. 4, Box 624-B, Arnold, MO 63010/314-287-6800
Caprinus U.S.A., Inc., 100 Prospect St., Stamford, CT 06901/203-359-3773 (stainl. steel shotguns)
Century Arms Co., 3-5 Federal St., St. Albans, VT 05478
Champlin Firearms, Inc., Box 3191, Enid, OK 73701
Christopher & Associates, 5636 San Fernando Rd., Glendale, CA 91202/213-725-7221 (SAM 180 rifle)
Clayco Sports Ltd. See: Frigon Guns
Conco Arms, P.O. Box 159, Emmaus, PA 18049/215-967-5477 (Larona)
Connecticut Valley Arms Co., 5988 Peachtree Corners East, Norcross, GA 30092/404-449-4687 (CVA)
Walter Craig, Inc., Box 927, Selma, AL 36701/205-875-7989
Davidson Supply, 2703 High Point Rd., Greensboro, NC 27403/800-367-4867
Des Moines Imports, 21 Glenview Dr., Des Moines, IA 50312/515-279-1987 (Spanish Gorosabel shotguns)
Diana Import, 842 Vallejo St., San Francisco, CA 94133
Charles Daly (See Outdoor Sports HQ)
Dikar s. Coop. (See Connecticut Valley Arms Co.)
Dixie Gun Works, Inc., Hwy 51, South, Union City, TN 38261/901-885-0561 ("Kentucky" rifles)
Double M Shooting Sports, 462 S. Hoop Pole Rd., Guilford, CT 06437
Dynamit Nobel of America, Inc., 105 Stonehurst Court, Northvale, NJ 07647/201-767-1660 (Rottweil)
E.M.F. Co. Inc. (Early & Modern Firearms), 1900 E. Warner Ave. 1-D, Santa Ana, CA 92705/714-966-0202
Ernest Dumoulin-Deleye, see: Midwest Gun Sport
Henri Dumoulin & Fils, rue du Tilleul 16, B-4411 Milmort (Herstal), Belgium
Peter Dyson Ltd., 29-31 Church St., Honley, Huddersfield, Yorkshire HD7 2AH, England (accessories f. antique gun collectors)
Elko Arms, 28 rue Ecole Moderne, 7400 Soignes, Belgium
Euroarms of American, Inc., P.O. Box 3277, 1501 Lenoir Dr., Winchester, VA 22601/703-661-1863 (ML)
Excam Inc., 4480 E. 11 Ave., P.O. Box 3483, Hialeah, FL 33013
Exel Arms of America, 14 Main St., Gardner, MA 01440/617-632-5008
FTL Marketing Corp., 12421 Oxnard St., No. Hollywood, CA 91606/818-985-6039 (Valmet auto rifle)
J. Fanzoj, P.O. Box 25, Ferlach, Austria 9170
Armi FERLIB di Libero Ferraglio, 46 Via Costa, 25063 Gardone V.T. (Brescia), Italy
Fiocchi of America, Inc., 1308 W. Chase, Springfield, MO 65803/417-864-6970 (Antonio Zoli)
Firearms Imp. & Exp. Corp., (F.I.E.), P.O. Box 4866, Hialeah Lakes, Hialeah, FL 33014/305-685-5966
Flaig's Inc., 2200 Evergreen Rd., Millvale, PA 15209/412-821-1717
Auguste Francotte & Cie, S.A., rue de Trois Juin 109, 4400 Herstal-Liege, Belgium
Frankonia Jagd, Hofmann & Co., Postfach 6780, D-8700 Wurzburg 1, West Germany
Freeland's Scope Stands, Inc., 3737 14th Ave., Rock Island, IL 61201/309-788-7449
Frigon Guns, 627 W. Crawford, Clay Center, KS 67432/913-632-5607
Renato Gamba, S.p.A., Gardone V.T. (Brescia), Italy (See Steyr Daimier Puch of America Corp.)
Armas Garbi, Urki #12, Eibar (Guipuzcoa) Spain (shotguns, See W. L. Moore)
Gastinne Renette, P.O. Box 3395, College Sta.; 225 Industrial Dr., Fredericksburg, VA 22401/703-898-1524
George Granger, 66 Cours Fauriel, 42 St. Etienne, France
Griffin & Howe, 589 Broadway, New York, NY 10012/212-966-5323 (Purdey, Holland & Holland)
Gun South, Dept. Steyr, Box 6607, 7605 Eastwood Mall, Birmingham, AL 35210/205-592-7932 (Steyr, FN)
Heckler & Koch Inc., 14601 Lee Rd., Chantilly, VA 22021/703-631-2800
Heller & Levin Associates, Box 456, 2322 Grand Ave., Baldwin, NY 11510/516-868-6300
Heym, Friedr. Wilh., see: Paul Jaeger, Inc.
HOWCO Dist. Inc., 122 Lafayette Ave., Laurel, MD 20707/301-953-3301
Hunting World, 16 E. 53rd St., New York, NY 10022
IGI Domino Corp., 200 Madison Ave., New York, NY 10016/212-889-4889 (Breda)
Incor, Inc., P.O. Box 132, Addison, TX 75001/214-931-3500 (Cosmi auto shotg.)
Interarmco, See Interarms (Walther)
Interarms Ltd., 10 Prince St., Alexandria, VA 22313 (Mauser, Valmet M-62/S)
Paul Jaeger Inc., P.O. Box 449, 1 Madison Ave., Grand Junction, TN 38039 (Heym)
Jenkins Imports Corp., 462 Stanford Pl., Santa Barbara, CA 93111/805-967-5092 (Gebrüder Merkel)
John Jovino Co., 5 Centre Market Pl., New York, NY 10013/212-925-4881 (Terminator)
Kassnar Imports, 5480 Linglestown Rd., Harrisburg, PA 17110
Kawaguchiya Firearms, c/o La Paloma Marketing, 4500 E. Speedway Blvd., Suite 93, Tucson, AZ 85712/602-881-4750
Kendall International, Inc., 501 East North, Carlisle, KY 40311/606-289-7336
Kimel Industries, Box 335, Matthews, NC 28105/704-821-7663
Kleinguenther's, Distinctive Firearms, Inc., 2485 Hwy 46 No., Seguin, TX 78155/512-379-8141
Kleinguenther Firearms, P.O. Box 2020, Seguin, TX 78155
Knight & Knight, 302 Ponce de Leon Blvd., St. Augustine, FL 32084/904-829-9671 (Bernardelli shotguns)
Krico-North America, P.O. Box 266, Bolton, Ont. LOP 1AO, Canada/416-880-5267
L. A. Distributors, 4 Centre Market Pl., New York, NY 10013

Lanber Arms of America, Inc., 377 Logan St., Adrian, MI 49221/517-263-7444 (Spanish o-u shotguns)
Lanchester U.S.A., Inc., P.O. Box 47332, Dallas, TX 75247/214-688-0073 (Sterling)
La Paloma Marketing, 4500 E. Speedway Blvd., Suite 93, Tucson, AZ 85712/602-881-4750 (K.F.C. shotguns)
Morris Lawing, 150 Garland Court, Charlotte, NC 28202/704-375-1740
Leland Firearms Co., 13 Mountain Ave., Llewellyn Park, West Orange, NJ 07052/201-325-3379 (Spanish shotguns)
Liberty Arms Organization, Box 306, Montrose, CA 91020/213-248-0618
Llama (See Stoeger)
MRE Dist. Inc., 19 So. Bayles Ave., Pt. Washington, NY 11050/516-944-8200 (IGI Domino)
Magnum Research, Inc., 7271 Commerce Circle West, Minneapolis, MN 55432/612-574-1868 (Israeli Galil)
Mandall Shtg. Suppl. 3616 N. Scottsdale Rd., Scottsdale, AZ 85252/602-945-2553
Mannlicher (See Steyr Daimler Puch of Amer.)
Manu-Arm, B.P. No. 8, Veauche 42340, France
Manufrance, See: Armssource, Inc.
Manurhin, See: Matra-Manurhin
Marocchi USA Inc., 5939 W. 66th St., Bedford Park, IL 60638
Marathon Products Inc., 1331 Silas Deane Highway, Wethersfield, CT 06109/203/563-0222
Matra-Manurhin International, Inc., 631 S. Washington St., Alexandria, VA 22314/703-836-8886
Mauser-Werke Oberndorf, P. O. Box 1349, 7238 Oberndorf/Neckar, West Germany
Mendi s. coop. (See Connecticut Valley Arms Co.)
Merkuria, FTC, Argentinska 38, 17000 Prague 7, Czechoslovakia (BRNO)
Midwest Gun Sport, Belgian HQ, 1942 OakWood View Dr., Verona, WI 53593/608-845-7447 (E. Dumoulin-Deleye)
Mitchell Arms Corp., 116 East 16th St., Costa Mesa, CA 92627/714-548-7701 (Uberti pistols)
Wm. Larkin Moore & Co., 31360 Via Colinas, Suite 109, Westlake Village, CA 91360/213-889-4160 (AYA, Garbi, Ferlib, Piotti, Lightwood Perugini Visini)
Navy Arms Co., 689 Bergen Blvd., Ridgefield, NJ 07657
O&L Guns Inc., P.O. Box 1146, Seminole, TX 79360/915-758-2933 (Wolverine rifle)
Odin International, Ltd., 818 Slaters Lane, Alexandria, VA 22314/703-339-8005 (Valmet/military types; CETME; Zastava)
Osborne's, P.O. Box 408, Cheboygan, MI 49721/616-625-9011 (Hammerli; Tanner rifles)
Outdoor Sports Headquarters, Inc., 967 Watertower Lane, Dayton, OH 45449/513-865-5855 (Charles Daly shotguns)
PM Air Services Ltd., P.O. Box 1573, Costa Mesa, CA 92626/714-968-2689
Pachmayr Gun Works, 1220 S. Grand Ave., Los Angeles, CA 90015
Pacific Intl. Merch. Corp., 2215 "J" St., Sacramento, CA 95816/916-446-2737
The Parker Gun, Div. of Reagent Chemical & Research, Inc., 1201 N. Watson Rd., Suite 224, Arlington, TX 76011/817-649-8781
Parker-Hale, Bisleyworks, Golden Hillock Rd., Sparbrook, Birmingham B11 2PZ, England
Perazzi U.S.A. Inc., 206 S. George St., Rome, NY 13440/315-337-8566
E. F. Phelps Mfg., Inc., 700 W. Franklin, Evansville, IN 47719 (Heritage 45-70)
Precise, 3 Chestnut, Suffern, NY 10901
Precision Sales Intl. Inc., PSI, P.O. Box 1776, Westfield, MA 01086/413-562-5055 (Anschutz)
Precision Sports, P.O. Box 708, Kellogg Rd., Cortland, NY 13045/607-756-2851 (BSA CF rifle; AYA side-by-side shotgun)
Puccinelli Co., P.O. Box 2222, San Anselmo, CA 94960/415-382-1464 (I.A.B., Rizzini, Bernardelli shotguns of Italy)
Quality Arms, Inc., Box 19477, Houston, TX 77224/713-870-8377 (Bernardelli shotguns)
Quantetics Corp., Imp.-Exp. Div., 582 Somerset St. W., Ottawa, Ont. K1R 5K2 Canada/613-237-0242 (Unique pistols-Can. only)
RG Industries, Inc., 2485 N.W. 20th St., Miami, FL 33142/305-635-5311 (Erma)
L. Joseph Rahn, Inc., 134 E. Main St., Manchester, MI 48158/313-428-7014 (Garbi, Astra shotguns)
Ravizza Carlo Caccia Pesca, s.r.l., Via Melegnano 6, 20122 Milano, Italy
Richland Arms Co., 321 W. Adrian St., Blissfield, MI 49228
Rottweil, (See Dynamit Nobel of America)
Sarco, Inc., 323 Union St., Stirling, NJ 07980/201-647-3800
Savage Industries, Inc., Springdale Rd., Westfield, MA 01085/413-562-2361
Thad Scott, P.O. Box 412; Hwy 82 West, Indianola, MS 38751/601-887-5929 (Perugini Visini; Bertuzzi s/s dble. shotguns)
Service Armament, 689 Bergen Blvd., Ridgefield, NJ 07657 (Greener Harpoon Gun)
Sherwood Intl. Export Corp., 18714 Parthenia St., Northridge, CA 91324
Shore Galleries, Inc., 3318 W. Devon Ave., Chicago, IL 60645
Shotguns of Ulm, P.O. Box 253, Millitown, NJ 08850/201-297-0573
Don L. Shrum's Cape Outfitters, 412 So. Kingshighway, Cape Girardeau, MO 63701/314-335-4103
Sigarms, Inc., 8330 Old Courthouse Rd., Suite 885, Tysons Corner, VA 22180/703-893-1940
Sile Distributors, 7 Centre Market Pl., New York, NY 10013/212-925-4111
Simmons Gun Specialties, Inc., 700 S. Rogers Rd., Olathe, KS 66062/913-782-3131
Sloan's Sprtg. Goods, Inc., 10 South St., Ridgefield, CT 06877
Franz Sodia Jagdgewehrfabrik, Schulhausgasse 14, 9170 Ferlach, (Kärnten) Austria
Steyr-Daimler-Puch, Gun South, Inc., Box 6607, 7605 Eastwood Mall, Birmingham, AL 35210/800-821-3021 (rifles)
Stoeger Industries, 55 Ruta Ct., S. Hackensack, NJ 07606/201-440-2700
Taurus International Mfg. Inc., P.O. Box 558567, Ludlam Br., Miami, FL 33155/305-662-2529
Thomas & Barrett, North Frost Center, 1250 Northeast Loop 410, Suite 200, San Antonio, TX 78209/512-826-0943
Loren Thomas Ltd., P.O. Box 18425, Dallas, TX 75218 (Bruchet)
Toledo Armas, S.A., 302 Ponce de Leon Blvd., St. Augustine, FL 32084/904-829-9671
Tradewinds, Inc., P.O. Box 1191, Tacoma, WA 98401
Uberti, Aldo. See: Allen Firearms Co.
Ignacio Ugartechea, Apartado 21, Eibar, Spain
Valmet Sporting Arms Div., 7 Westchester Plaza, Elmsford, NY 10523/914-347-4440 (sporting types)
Valor of Florida Corp., 5555 N.W. 36th Ave., Miami, FL 33142/305-633-0127 (Valmet)
Ventura Imports, P.O. Box 2782, Seal Beach, CA 90740 (European shotguns)
Verney-Carron, B.P. 72, 54 Boulevard Thiers, 42002 St. Etienne Cedex, France
Perugini Visini & Co. s.r.l., Via Camprelle, 126, 25080 Nuvolera (Bs.), Italy
Waffen-Frankonia, see: Frankonia Jagd
Waverly Arms Inc., Box 4202, Columbia, SC 29240/803-736-2821 (Armurerie Vouzelaud)
Weatherby's, 2781 Firestone Blvd., So. Gate, CA 90280/213-569-7186
Whittington Arms, Box 489, Hooks, TX 75561
Winchester, Olin Corp., 120 Long Ridge Rd., Stamford, CT 06904
Fabio Zanotti di Stefano, Via XXV Aprile 1, 25063 Gardone V.T. (Brescia) Italy
Zavodi Crvena Zastava, 29 Novembra St., No. 12, Belgrade, Yugosl.
Antonio Zoli & Co., See: Fiocchi of America, Inc.

GUNS & GUN PARTS, REPLICA AND ANTIQUE

Antique Arms Co., David E. Saunders, 1110 Cleveland, Monett, MO 65708/417-235-6501
Antique Gun Parts, Inc., 1118 S. Braddock Ave., Pittsburgh, PA 15218/412-241-1811 (ML)
Armoury Inc., Rte. 202, New Preston, CT 06777
Armsport, Inc., 3590 N.W. 49th St., Miami, FL 33142
Artistic Arms, Inc., Box 23, Hoagland, IN 46745 (Sharps-Borchardt replica)
Beeman Precisions Arms, Inc., 47-GDD Paul Dr., San Rafael, CA 94903/415-472-7121
Bob's Place, Box 283J, Clinton, IA 52732 (obsolete Winchester parts only)
Cache La Poudre Rifleworks, 168 No. College Ave., Fort Collins, CO 80524/303-482-6913
Dave Chicoine, d/b/a Liberty A.S.P., 19 Key St., Eastport, ME 04631/207-853-2327(S&W only; ctlg. $5)
Collector's Armoury, Inc., 800 Slaters Lane, Alexandria, VA 22314/703-339-8005
Dixie Gun Works, Inc., Hwy 51, South, Union City, TN 38261/901-885-0561
Federal Ordnance Inc., 1443 Portrero Ave., So. El Monte, CA 91733/213-350-4161
Jack First Distributors, Inc., 44633 Sierra Hwy., Lancaster, CA 93534/805-945-6981
Fred Goodwin, Goodwin's Gun Shop, Silver Ridge, Sherman Mills, ME 04776/207-365-4451 (Winchester rings & studs)
Hansen & Hansen, 244 Old Post Rd., Southport, CT 06490/203-259-7337
Terry K. Kopp, Highway 13, Lexington, MO 64067/816-259-2636 (restoration & pts. 1890 & 1906 Winch.)
The House of Muskets, Inc., 120 N. Pagosa Blvd., Pagosa Springs, CO 81147/303-264-2295 (ML guns)
Log Cabin Sport Shop, 8010 Lafayette Rd., Lodi, OH 44254/216-948-1082 (ctlg. $30)
Edw. E. Lucas, 32 Garfield Ave., East Brunswick, NJ 08816/201-251-5526 (45/70 Springfield parts; some Sharps, Spencer parts)
Lyman Products Corp., Middlefield, CT 06455
Tommy Munsch Gunsmithing, Rt. 2, Box 248, Little Falls, MN 56345/612-632-5835 (Winchester parts only; list $1.50)
Numrich Arms Co., West Hurley, NY 12491
Ram Line, Inc., 406 Violet St., Golden, CO 80401/303-279-0886
Replica Models, Inc., 800 Slaters Lane, Alexandria, VA 22314/703-339-8005
S&S Firearms, 88-21 Aubrey Ave., Glendale, NY 11385/212-497-1100
Sarco, Inc., 323 Union St., Stirling, NJ 07980/201-647-3800
C. H. Stoppler, 1426 Walton Ave., New York, NY 10452 (miniature guns)
Upper Missouri Trading Co., Box 191, Crofton, NE 68730/402-388-4844
C. H. Weisz, Box 311, Arlington, VA 22210/703-243-9161
W. H. Wescombe, P.O. Box 488, Glencoe, CA 95232 (Rem. R.B. parts)

GUNS (Pellet)

Barnett International, Inc., P.O. Box 934, 1967 Gunn Highway, Odessa, FL 33556/920-2241
Beeman Precision Airguns, 47 Paul Dr., San Rafael, CA 94903/415-472-7121
Benjamin Air Rifle Co., 3205 Sheridan Rd., Racine, WI 53403/414-633-5424
Collector's Armoury, Inc., 800 Slaters Lane, Alexandria, VA 22314/703-339-8005
Crosman Airguns, 980 Turk Hill Rd., Fairport, NY 14450/716-223-6000
Daisy Mfg. Co., P.O. Box 220, Rogers, AR 72756/501-636-1200 (also Feinwerkbau)
Dynamit Nobel of America, Inc., 105 Stonehurst Ct., Northvale, NJ 07647/201-767-1660 (Dianawerk)
Great Lakes Airguns, 6175 So. Park Ave., Hamburg, NY 14075/716-648-6666
Harrington & Richardson Arms Co., Industrial Rowe, Gardner, MA 01440 (Webley)
Gil Hebard Guns, Box 1, Knoxville, IL 61448
Interarms, 10 Prince, Alexandria, VA 22313 (Walther)
Kendall International Inc., 501 East North, Carlisle, KY 40311/606-289-7336 (Italian Airmatch)
Mandall Shooting Supplies, Inc., 3616 N. Scottsdale Rd., Scottsdale, AZ 85252/602-945-2553 (Cabanas line)
Marathon Products Inc., 1331 Silas Deane Highway, Wethersfield, CT 06109/203-563-0222
Marksman Products, see: S/R Industries

McMurray & Son, 109 E. Arbor Vitae St., Inglewood, CA 90301/213-412-4187 (cust. airguns)
Paragon Sales & Services, Inc., P.O. Box 2022, Joliet, IL 60434/815-725-9212
Phoenix Arms Co., Phoenix House, Churchdale Rd., Eastbourne, East Sussex BN22 8PX, England (Jackal)
Power Line (See Daisy Mfg. Co.)
Precise, 3 Chestnut, Suffern, NY 10901
Precision Sports, P.O. Box 708, Kellogg Rd., Cortland, NY 13045/607-756-2851 (B.S.A.)
S/R Industries, Inc., 5622 Engineer Dr., Huntington Beach, CA 92649/714-898-7535 (Marksman)
Service Armament, 689 Bergen Blvd., Ridgefield, NJ 07657 (Webley)
Sheridan Products, Inc., 3205 Sheridan, Racine, WI 53403
Smith & Wesson, 2100 Roosevelt Ave., Springfield, MA 01104
Target Airgun Supply, P.O. Box 428, South Gate, CA 90280/213-569-3417

GUNS, SURPLUS—PARTS AND AMMUNITION

Can Am Enterprises, Fruitland, Ont. LOR ILO, Canada/416-643-4357 (Enfield rifles)
Century Arms, Inc., 3-5 Federal St., St. Albans, VT 05478
Walter Craig, Inc., Box 927, Selma, AL 36701/205-875-7989
Eastern Firearms Co., 790 S. Arroyo Pkwy., Pasadena, CA 91105
J. M. Emringer, Armurier, 3A, rue de Bettembourg, L-3346 Leudelange, Grand-Duchy of Luxemburg
Federal Ordnance, Inc., 1443 Potrero Ave., So. El Monte, CA 91733/818-350-4161
Garcia National Gun Traders, 225 S.W. 22nd, Miami, FL 33135
Hansen and Hansen, 244 Old Post Rd., Southport, CT 06490/203-259-7337
Lever Arms Serv. Ltd., 572 Howe St., Vancouver, B.C., Canada V6C 2E3/604-685-6913
Paragon Sales & Services, Inc., P.O. Box 2022, Joliet, IL 60434 (ammunition)
Sarco, Inc., 323 Union St., Stirling, NJ 07980/201-647-3800 (military surpl. ammo)
Service Armament Co., 689 Bergen Blvd., Ridgefield, NJ 07657
Sherwood Intl. Export Corp., 18714 Parthenia St., Northridge, CA 91324/818-349-7600
Springfield Sporters Inc., R.D. 1, Penn Run, PA 15765/412-254-2626

GUNS, U.S.-made

AMT (Arcadia Machine & Tool), 536 N. Vincent Ave., Covina, CA 91722/818-915-7803
Accuracy Systems, Inc., 15203 N. Cave Creek Rd., Phoenix, AZ 85032/602-971-1991
Advantage Arms USA, Inc., 840 Hampden Ave., St. Paul, MN 55114/612-644-5197
Alpha Arms, Inc., 12923 Valley Branch, Dallas, TX 75234/214-243-8124
American Arms (Eagle 380 auto pistol), See: Wilkerson Firearms Corp.
American Derringer Corp., 127 N. Lacy Dr., Waco, TX 76705/817-799-9111
ArmaLite, 118 E. 16th St., Costa Mesa, CA 92627
Armament Systems and Procedures, Inc., Box 356, Appleton, WI 54912/414-731-8893 (ASP pistol)
Arminex Ltd., 7882 E. Gray Rd., Scottsdale Airpark, Scottsdale, AZ 85260/602-998-0443 (Excalibur s.a. pistol)
Arm Tech, Armament Technologies Inc., 240 Sargent Dr., New Haven, CT 06511/203-562-2543 (22-cal. derringers)
Armes de Chasse, 3000 Valley Forge Circle, King of Prussia, PA 19406/215-783-6133
Arnett Guns (See Gary DelSignore Weaponry)
Artistic Arms, Inc.,Box 23, Hoagland, IN 46745 (Sharps-Borchardt)
Artistic Firearms Corp., John Otteman, 4005 Hecker Pass Hwy., Gilroy, CA 95020/408-842-4278 (A.F.C. Comm. Rifle 1881-1981)
Auto Nine Corp., see: FTL Marketing Corp.
Auto-Ordnance Corp., Box GD, West Hurley, NY 12491/914-679-7225
Barrett Firearms Mfg., Inc., 312 S. Church St., Murfreesboro, TN 37130/615-896-2938 (Light Fifty)
Bighorn Rifle Co., P.O. Box 215, American Fork, UT 84003/801-756-4222
Bren Ten (See Dornaus & Dixon Ent.)
Brown Precision Co., P.O. Box 270W; 7786 Molinos Ave., Los Molinos, CA 96055/916-384-2506 (High Country rifle)
Browning (Gen. Offices), Rt. 1, Morgan, UT 84050/801-876-2711
Browning (Parts & Service), Rt. 4, Box 624-B, Arnold, MO 63010/314-287-6800
Bushmaster Firearms Co., 803 Forest Ave., Portland ME 04103/207-775-3324 (police handgun)
Challanger Mfg. Corp., 118 Pearl St., Mt. Vernon, NY 10550 (Hopkins & Allen)
Champlin Firearms, Inc., Box 3191, Enid, OK 73701
Charter Arms Corp., 430 Sniffens Ln., Stratford, CT 06497
Chipmunk Manufacturing Inc., 114 E. Jackson, Medford, OR 97501/503-664-5585 (22 S.S. rifle)
Classic Arms, 815-22nd St., Union City, NJ 08757/201-863-1493
Colt Firearms, P.O. Box 1868, Hartford, CT 06102/203-236-6311
Commando Arms, Inc., Box 10214, Knoxville, TN 37919
Coonan Arms, Inc., 830 Hampden Ave., St. Paul, MN 55114/612-646-6672 (357 Mag. Autom.)
Cumberland Arms, Rt. 1, Shafer Rd., Blanton Chapel, Manchester, TN 37355
The Custom Gun Guild, 5091-F Buford Highway, Doraville, GA 30340/404-455-0346
Davidson Supply, 2703 High Point Rd., Greensboro, NC 27403/800-367-4867
Davis Industries, 13748 Arapahoe Pl., Chino, CA 91710/714-591-4727 (derringer)
Leonard Day & Co., P.O. Box 723, East Hampton, MA 01027/413-527-7990 (ML)
Gary DelSignore Weaponry, 3675 Cottonwood, Cedar City, UT 84720/801-586-2505 (Arnett Guns)
Demro Products Inc., 372 Progress Dr., Manchester, CT 06040/203-649-4444 (Wasp, Tac guns)
Detonics Mfg. Corp., 13456 S.E. 27th Pl., Bellevue, WA 98005/206-747-2100
Dornaus & Dixon Enterprises, Inc., 15896 Manufacture Lane, Huntingdon Beach, CA 92649/714-891-5090
DuBiel Arms Co., 1724 Baker Rd., Sherman, TX 75090/214-893-7313
Excalibur (See Arminex)
FTL Marketing Corp., 12521 Oxnard St., No. Hollywood, CA 91606/818-985-6039 (Pocket Partner)
Falling Block Works, P.O. Box 3087, Fairfax, VA 22038/703-476-0043
Feather Enterprises, 2500 Central Ave., Boulder, CO 80301/303-442-7021
Federal Eng. Corp., 3161 N. Elston Ave., Chicago, IL 60618/312-267-4151 (XC-220 carbine)
Firearms Imp. & Exp. Corp., P.O. Box 4866, Hialeah Lakes, Hialeah, FL 33014/305-685-5966 (FIE)
Fraser Firearms Corp., 34575 Commerce Rd., Fraser, MI 48026/313-293-9545
Freedom Arms Co., P.O. Box 1776, Freedom, WY 83120 (mini revolver, Casull rev.)
Freedom Arms Marketing (See: L.A.R. Mfg. Co.)
Frontier Shop & Gallery, Depot 1st & Main, Riverton, WY 82501/307-856-4498
Garrett Accur-Light Inc., P.O. Box 8563, Fort Collins, CO 80524/303-224-3067
Golden Age Arms Co., 14 W. Winter St., Delaware, OH 43015
HJS Industries, Inc., P.O. Box 4351, Brownsville, TX 78520/512-542-3340 (22 4-bbl.; 38 S&W SS derringers)
Harrington & Richardson, Industrial Rowe, Gardner, MA 01440
Hatfield Rifle Works, 2028 Frederick Ave., St. Joseph, MO 64501/816-279-8688 (squirrel rifle)
A.D. Heller, Inc., Box 268, Grand Ave., Baldwin, NY 11510
Holmes Firearms Corp., Rte. 6, Box 242, Fayetteville, AR 72701
Hopkins & Allen Arms, 3 Ethel Ave., P.O. Box 217, Hawthorne, NJ 07507/201-427-1165 (ML)
Lew Horton, 175 Boston Rd., Southboro, MA 01701
Hyper-Single Precision SS Rifles, 520 E. Beaver, Jenks, OK 74037/918-299-2391
Ithaca Gun Co., Ithaca, NY 14850
Jennings-Hawken, 326½-4th St. N.W., Winter Haven, FL 33880 (ML)
Iver Johnson, 2202 Redmond Rd., Jacksonville, AR 72076/501-982-9491
Jennings Firearms, 4510 Carter Ct., Chino, CA 91710/714-591-3921
KK Arms Co., Karl Kash, Star Route, Box 671, Kerrville, TX 78028/512-257-4441 (handgun)
Kimber of Oregon, Inc., 9039 S.E. Jannsen Rd., Clackamas, OR 97015/503-656-1704
Kimel Industries, Box 335, Matthews, NC 28105/704-821-7663
L.A.R. Manufacturing Co., 4133 West Farm Rd., West Jordan, UT 84084/801-255-7106 (Grizzly Win Mag pistol)
Ljutic Ind., Inc., P.O. Box 2117, 918 N. 5th Ave., Yakima, WA 98902/509-248-0476 (Mono-Gun)
M & N Distributors, 23535 Telo St., Torrance, CA 90505/213-530-9000 (Budischowsky)
MS Safari Arms, P.O. Box 23370, Phoenix, AZ 85062/602-269-7283
Magnum Sales, Subs. of Mag-na-port, 41302 Executive Drive, Mt. Clemens, MI 48045/313-469-7534
Marlin Firearms Co., 100 Kenna Drive, New Haven, CT 06473
Matteson Firearms Inc., Otsego Rd., Canajoharie, NY 13317/607-264-3744 (SS rifles)
Merrill Pistol, see: Rock Pistol Mfg.
Michigan Armament, Marketing Inc., 135 Sumner Ave., Lake Elsinore, CA 92330/714-674-5750 (pistols)
Michigan Arms Corp., 363 Elmwood, Troy, MI 48084/313-583-1518 (ML)
Military Armament Corp., P.O. Drawer 1358, 1481 So. Loop-Suite 4, Stephensville, TX 76401/817-968-7543 (Ingram submach. gun)
Mitchell Arms of California, Inc., 19007 S. Reyes Ave., Compton, CA 90221/714-964-3678 (AR-50 survival rifle)
The M.O.A. Corp., 110 Front St., Dayton, OH 45402/513-223-6401 (Maximum pistol)
O.F. Mossberg & Sons, Inc., 7 Grasso St., No. Haven, CT 06473
Mowrey Gun Works, Inc., 800 Blue Mound Rd., Saginaw, TX 76131/817-281-5996
Navy Arms Co., 689 Bergen Blvd., Ridgefield, NJ 07657
North American Arms, 1800 North 300 West, Spanish Fork, UT 84660/801-798-9891
North Georgia Armament, 5265 Jimmy Carter Blvd., Suite 1442, Norcross, GA 30093/404-446-3504
Numrich Arms Corp., W. Hurley, NY 12491
ODI, Inc., 124A Greenwood Ave., Midland Park, NJ 07432/201-444-4557
Oregon Trail Riflesmiths, Inc., P.O. Box 45212, Boise, ID 83711/208-336-8631 (ML)
Ozark Mountain Arms, Inc., P.O. Box 397, 141 Byrne St., Ashdown, AR 71822/501-989-2345 (ML)
Pecos Valley Armory, 1022 So. Canyon, Carlsbad, NM 88220/505-887-6023 (ML)
Pennsylvania Arms Co., Box 128, Duryea, PA 18642/717-457-4014
Phillips & Bailey, Inc., P.O. Box 219253, Houston, TX 77218/713-392-0207 (357/9 Ultra, rev. conv.)
Power Custom, Inc., P.O. Box 1604, Independence, MO 64055 (Power Custom Combat handgun)
Precision Small Parts, 155 Carlton Rd., Charlottesville, VA 22901/804-293-6124
Provider Arms, Inc., 261 Haglund Dr., Chesterton, IN 46304/219-879-5590 (ML Predator rifle)
R.B. Industries, Ltd. (See Fraser Firearms Corp.)
R G Industries, 2485 N.W. 20th St., Miami, FL 33142/305-635-5311
Randall Manufacturing, 12826 Pierce St., Pacoima, CA 91331
Raven Arms, 1300 Bixby Dr., Industry, CA 91745/213-961-2511 (P-25 pistols)
Remington Arms Co., 939 Barnum Ave., P.O. Box #1939, Bridgeport, CT 06601
Rock Pistol Mfg., Inc., 150 Viking, Brea, CA 92621/714-990-2444 (Merrill pistol)
Ruger (See Sturm, Ruger & Co.)
Savage Industries, Inc., Springdale Rd., Westfield, MA 01085/413-562-2361

B. Searcy Co., 15, Rd. 3804, Farmington, NM 87401/505-327-3419 (mountain rifle)
L.W. Seecamp Co., Inc., P.O. Box 255, New Haven, CT 06502/203-877-3429
Serrifile, Inc., P.O. Box 508, Littlerock, CA 93543/805-945-0713 (derringer; single shot))
C. Sharps Arms Co., Inc., P.O. Box 885, Big Timber, MT 59011/406-932-4353
Shiloh Products, 181 Plauderville Ave., Garfield, NJ 07026 (Sharps)
The Silhouette, 1409 Benton, Box 1509, Idaho Falls, ID 83401/208-524-0880 (Wichita International pistol)
Six Enterprises, 6564 Hidden Creek Dr., Dan Jose, CA 95120/408-268-8296 (Timberliner rifle)
Smith & Wesson, Inc., 2100 Roosevelt Ave., Springfield, MA 01101
Sokolovsky Corp., Box 70113, Sunnyvale, CA 94086/408-245-9268 (45 Automaster pistol)
Sporting Arms, Inc., 12923 Valley Branch, Dallas, TX 75234/214-243-8124 (Snake Charmer II shotgun)
Springfield Armory, Inc., 420 W. Main St., Geneseo, IL 61254/309-944-5138
SSK Industries, Rt. 1, Della Dr., Bloomingdale, OH 43910/614-264-0176
Steel City Arms, Inc., 1883 Main St., Pittsburgh, PA 15215/412-784-9400 (d.a. "Double Deuce" pistol)
Sterling Arms Corp., 211 Grand St., Lockport, NY 14094/716-434-6631
Sturm, Ruger & Co., Southport, CT 06490
Tennessee Valley Arms, P.O. Box 2022, Union City, TN 38261/901-885-4456
Texas Longhorn Arms, Inc., P. O. Box 703, Richmond, TX 77469/713-341-0775 (S.A. sixgun)
Thompson-Center Arms, P.O. Box 2426, Rochester, NH 03867/603-332-2394
Traders International, Inc., P.O. Box 595, Indian Trail, NC 28105/704-821-7684
Trail Guns Armory, 1634 E. Main St., League City, TX 77573 (muzzleloaders)
Trapper Gun, Inc., 18717 E. 14 Mile Rd., Fraser, MI 48026/313-792-0133 (handguns)
The Ultimate Game Inc., P.O. Box 1856, Ormond Beach, FL 32075/904-677-4358
Ultra Light Arms Co., P.O. Box 1270, Granville, WV 26534/304-599-5687
United Sporting Arms, Inc, 2021 E. 14th St., Tucson, AZ 85719/602-623-4001 (handguns)
U.S. Repeating Arms Co., P.O. Box 30-300, New Haven, CT 06511/203-789-5000
Universal Firearms, 2202 Redmond Rd., Jacksonville, AR 72076/501-982-9491
Weatherby's, 2781 E. Firestone Blvd., South Gate, CA 90280
Weaver Arms Corp., 115 No. Market Pl., Escondido, CA 92025/619-746-2440
WSI, P.O. Box 66, Youngstown, OH 44501/216-743-9666 (9mm Viking)
Dan Wesson Arms, 293 So. Main St., Monson, MA 01057
Wichita Arms, 444 Ellis, Wichita, KS 67211/316-265-0661
Wildey, 28 Old Route 7, Brookfield, CT 06804/203-775-4261
Wildey Firearms, 299 Washington St., Newburgh, NY 12550/1-800-243-GUNS
Wilkerson Firearms Corp., P.O. Box 157, Westminster, CA 92684/714-891-1441 (Eagle 380 d.a. auto)
Wilkinson Arms, Rte. #2, Box 2166, Parma, ID 83660/208-722-6771
Winchester, (See U.S. Repeating Arms)
York Arms Co., 50 W. State St., Hurricane, UT 84737/801-635-4867

GUNSMITHS, CUSTOM (see Custom Gunsmiths)

GUNSMITHS, HANDGUN (see Pistolsmiths)

GUNSMITH SCHOOLS

Colorado School of Trades, 1575 Hoyt, Lakewood, CO 80215/303-233-4697
Lassen Community College, P.O. Box 3000, Hiway 139, Susanville, CA 96130/916-257-6161
Modern Gun Repair School, 2538 No. 8th St., Phoenix, AZ 85006/602-990-8346 (home study)
Montgomery Technical College, P.O. Drawer 487, Troy, NC 27371/919-572-3691
Murray State College, Gunsmithing Program, 100 Faculty Dr., Tishomingo, OK 73460/405-371-2371
North American School of Firearms, Curriculum Development Ctr., 4401 Birch St., Newport Beach, CA 92663/714-546-7360 (correspondence)
North American School of Firearms, Education Service Center, Oak & Pawnee St., Scranton, PA 18515/717-342-7701
Penn. Gunsmith School, 812 Ohio River Blvd., Avalon, Pittsburgh, PA 15202/412-766-1812
Piedmont Technical School, P.O. Box 1197, Roxboro, NC 27575
Pine Technical Institute, 1100 Fourth St., Pine City, MN 55063/612-629-6764
Police Sciences Institute, 4401 Birch St., Newport Beach, CA 92660/714-546-7360 (General Law Enforcement Course)
Shenandoah School of Gunsmithing, P.O. Box 300, Bentonville, VA 22610/703-743-5494
Southeastern Community College, Admissions "TF" Gear Ave., West Burlington, IA 52655/319-752-2731
Trinidad State Junior College, 600 Prospect, Trinidad, CO 81082/303-846-5631
Yavapai College, 1100 East Sheldon St., Prescott, AZ 86301/602-445-7300

GUNSMITH SUPPLIES, TOOLS, SERVICES

A.C. Enterprises, P.O. Box 448, Edenton, NC 27932/919-482-4992
Albright Prod. Co., P. O. Box 1144, Portola, CA 96122 (trap buttplates)
Don Allen, Inc., HC55, Box 322, Sturgis, SD 57785/605-347-4686 (stock duplicating machine)
Alley Supply Co., Carson Valley Industrial Park, P.O. Box 848, Gardnerville, NV 89410/702-782-3800 (JET line lathes, mills, etc.)
Ametek, Hunter Spring Div., One Spring Ave., Hatfield, PA 19440/215-822-2971 (trigger gauge)
Anderson Mfg. Co., Union Gap Sta., P.O. Box 3120, Yakima, WA 98903/509-453-2349 (tang safe)
Answer Stocking Systems, 113 N. 2nd St., Whitewater, WI 53190/414-473-4848 (urethane hammers, vice jaws, etc.)
Armite Labs., 1845 Randolph St., Los Angeles, CA 90001/213-587-7744 (pen oiler)
B-Square Co., Box 11281, Ft. Worth, TX 76110/800-433-2909
Jim Baiar, 490 Halfmoon Rd., Columbia Falls, MT 59912 (hex screws)
Behlert Custom Guns, Inc., RD 2 Box 36C, Route 611 North, Pipersville, PA 18947/215-766-8680
Dennis M. Bellm Gunsmithing, Inc., dba P.O. Ackley Rifle Barrels, 2376 S. Redwood Rd., Salt Lake City, UT 84119/801-974-0697 (rifles only)
Al Biesen, W. 2039 Sinto Ave., Spokane, WA 99201 (grip caps, buttplates)
Roger Biesen, 5021 W. Rosewood, Spokane, WA 99208/509-328-9340 (grip caps, buttplates)
Billingsley & Brownell, Box 25, Dayton, Wy 82836/307-655-9344 (cust. grip caps, bolt handle, etc.)
Blue Ridge Machine and Tool, P.O. Box 536, 2806 Putnam Ave., Hurricane, WV 25526/304-562-3538 (machinery, tools, shop suppl.)
Bonanza Sports Mfg. Co., 412 Western Ave., Faribault, MN 55021/507-332-7153
Briganti Custom Gun-Smithing, P.O. Box 56, 475-Route 32, Highland Mills, NY 10930/914-928-9816 (cold rust bluing, hand polishing, metal work)
Brownells, Inc., 222 W. Liberty, Montezuma, IA 50171/515-623-5401
Lenard M. Brownell (See Billingsley & Brownell)
W.E. Brownell Co. Checkering Tools, 3356 Moraga Place, San Diego, CA 92117/619-276-6146
Buehler Scope Mounts, 17 Orinda Way, Orinda, CA 94563/415-254-3201
Burgess Vibrocrafters, Inc. (BVI), Rte. 83, Grayslake, IL 60030
M.H. Canjar, 500 E. 45th, Denver, CO 80216/303-295-2638 (triggers, etc.)
Chapman Mfg. Co., P.O. Box 250, Rte. 17 at Saw Mill Rd., Durham, CT 06422/203-349-9228
Chase Chemical Corp., 3527 Smallman St., Pittsburgh, PA 15201/412-681-6544 (Chubb Multigauge for shotguns)
Chicago Wheel & Mfg. Co., 1101 W. Monroe St., Chicago, IL 60607/312-226-8155 (Handee grinders)
Dave Chicoine, d/b/a Liberty A.S.P., 19 Key St., Eastport, ME 04631/207-853-2327 (spl. S&W tools)
Chopie Mfg., Inc., 700 Copeland Ave., LaCrosse, WI 54603/608-784-0926
Classic Arms Corp., P.O. Box 8, Palo Alto, CA 94302/415-321-7243 (floorplates, grip caps)
Clover Mfg. Co., 139 Woodward Ave., Norwalk, CT 06856/800-243 6492 (Clover compound)
Clymer Mfg. Co., Inc., 14241 W. 11 Mile Rd., Oak Park, MI 48237/313-541-5533 (reamers)
Dave Cook, 720 Hancock Ave., Hancock, MI 49930 (metalsmithing only)
Dayton-Traister Co., 9322-900th West, P.O. Box 593, Oak Harbor, WA 98277/206-675-5375 (triggers)
Dem-Bart Hand Checkering Tools, Inc., 6807 Hiway #2, Snohomish, WA 98290/206-568-7356
Dremel Mfg. Co., 4915-21st St., Racine, WI 53406 (grinders)
Chas. E. Duffy, Williams Lane, West Hurley, NY 12491
The Dutchman's Firearms Inc., 4143 Taylor Blvd., Louisville, KY 40215/502-366-0555
Peter Dyson Ltd., 29-31 Church St., Honley, Huddersfield, West Yorksh. HD7 2AH, England/0484-661062 (accessories f. antique gun coll.)
Edmund Scientific Co., 101 E. Gloucester Pike, Barrington, NJ 08007/609-547-3488
Emco-Lux, 2050 Fairwood Ave., P.O. Box 07861, Columbus, OH 43207/614-445-8328
Jack First Distributors, Inc., 44633 Sierra Hwy., Lancaster, CA 93534/805-945-8961
Forster Products, Inc., 82 E. Lanark Ave., Lanark, IL 61046/815-493-6360
Francis Tool Co., (f'ly Keith Francis Inc.), P.O. Box 7861, Eugene, OR 97401/503-746-4831 (reamers)
G. R. S. Corp., P.O. Box 748, 900 Overlander St., Emporia, KS 66801/316-343-1084 (Gravermeister; Grave Max tools)
Gilmore Pattern Works, P.O. Box 50084, Tulsa, OK 74150/918-245-9627 (Wagner safe-T-planer)
Glendo Corp., P.O. Box 1153, Emporia, KS 66801/316-343-1084 (Accu-Finish tool)
Grace Metal Prod., 115 Ames St., Elk Rapids, MI 49629 (screw drivers, drifts)
Gunline Tools, Box 478, Placentia, CA 92670/714-528-5252
Gun-Tec, P.O. Box 8125, W. Palm Beach, Fl 33407
Half Moon Rifle Shop, 490 Halfmoon Rd., Columbia Falls, MT 59912/406-892-4409 (hex screws)
Henriksen Tool Co., Inc., P.O. Box 668, Phoenix, OR 97535/503-535-2309 (reamers)
Huey Gun Cases (Marvin Huey), P.O. Box 22456, Kansas City, MO 64113/816-444-1637 (high grade English ebony tools)
Ken Jantz Supply, Rt. 1, Sulphur, OK 73086/405-622-3790
Jeffredo Gunsight Co., 1629 Via Monserate, Fallbrook, CA 92028 (trap buttplate)
Kasenit Co., Inc., P.O. Box 726, Mahwah, NJ 07430/201-529-3663 (surface hardening compound)
Terry K. Kopp, Highway 13, Lexington, MO 64067/816-259-2636 (stock rubbing compound; rust preventive grease)
J. Korzinek, RD#2, Box 73, Canton, PA 17724/717-673-8512 (stainl. steel bluing; broch. $1.50)
John G. Lawson, (The Sight Shop) 1802 E. Columbia Ave., Tacoma, WA 98404/206-474-5465
Lea Mfg. Co., 237 E. Aurora St., Waterbury, CT 06720/203-753-5116
Lock's Phila. Gun Exch., 6700 Rowland Ave., Philadelphia, PA 19149/215-332-6225
Longbranch Gun Bluing Co., 2455 Jacaranda Lane, Los Osos, CA 93402/805-528-1792

McIntrye Tools, P.O. Box 491/State Road #1144, Troy, NC 27371/919-572-2603 (shotgun bbl. facing tool)
Meier Works, Steve Hines, Box 328, 2102-2nd Ave., Canyon, TX 79015/806-655-9256 (European acc.)
Michaels of Oregon Co., P.O. Box 13010, Portland, OR 97213/503-255-6890
Miller Single Trigger Mfg. Co., R.D. 1, Box 99, Millersburg, PA 17061/717-692-3704
Frank Mittermeier, 3577 E. Tremont, New York, NY 10465
Moderntools, 1671 W. McNab Rd., Ft. Lauderdale, FL 33309/305-979-3900
N&J Sales Co., Lime Kiln Rd., Northford, CT 06472/203-484-0247 (screwdrivers)
Karl A. Neise, Inc., 1671 W. McNab Rd., Ft. Lauderdale, FL 33309/305-979-3900
Olympic Arms Inc., dba SGW, 624 Old Pacific Hwy. S.E., Olympia, WA 98503/206-456-3471
Palmgren Steel Prods., Chicago Tool & Engineering Co., 8383 South Chicago Ave., Chicago, IL 60617/312-721-9675 (vises, etc.)
Panavise Prods., Inc., 2850 E. 29th St., Long Beach, CA 90806/213-595-7621
Pilkington Gun Co., P.O. Box 1296, Muskogee, OK 74402/918-683-9418 (Q.D. scope mt.)
Redman's Rifling & Reboring, Route 3, Box 330A, Omak, WA 98841/509-826-5512 (22 RF liners)
Richland Arms Co., 321 W. Adrian St., Blissfield, MI 49228
Riley's Inc., 121 No. Main St., P.O. Box 139, Avilla, IN 46710/219-897-2351 (Niedner buttplates, grip caps)
Roto/Carve, 6509 Indian Hills Rd., Minneapolis, MN 55435/800-533-8988 (tool)
A.G. Russell Co., 1705 Hiway 71 North, Springdale, AR 72764/501-751-7341 (Arkansas oilstones)
Schaffner Mfg. Co., Emsworth, Pittsburgh, PA 15202 (polishing kits)
SGW, Inc. (formerly Schuetzen Gun Works), See: Olympic Arms
Shaw's, 9447 W. Lilac Rd., Escondido, CA 92025/619-728-7070
James R. Spradlin, Jim's Gun Shop, 113 Arthur, Pueblo, CO 81004/303-543-9462 (rust blues; stock fillers)
L.S. Starrett Co., 121 Crescent St., Athol, MA 01331/617-249-3551
Texas Platers Supply Co., 2453 W. Five Mile Parkway, Dallas, TX 75233 (plating kit)
Timney Mfg. Inc., 3106 W. Thomas Rd., Phoenix, AZ 85017/602-269-6937
Stan de Treville, Box 33021, San Diego, CA 92103/619-298-3393 (checkering patterns)
Turner Co., Div. Cleanweld Prods., Inc., 821 Park Ave., Sycamore, IL 60178/815-895-4545
Twin City Steel Treating Co., Inc. 1114 S. 3rd, Minneapolis, MN 55415/612-332-4849 (heat treating)
Walker Arms Co., Rt. 2, Box 73, Hwy. 80 W, Selma, AL 36701/205-872-6231 (tools)
Will-Burt Co., 169 So. Main, Orrville, OH 44667 (vises)
Williams Gun Sight Co., 7389 Lapeer Rd., Davison, MI 48423
Wilson Arms Co., 63 Leetes Island Rd., Branford, CT 06405/203-488-7297
Wisconsin Platers Supply Co. (See Texas Platers)
W.C. Wolff Co., P.O. Box 232, Ardmore, PA 19003/215-647-1880 (springs)
Woodcraft Supply Corp., 313 Montvale, Woburn, MA 01801

HANDGUN ACCESSORIES

Ajax Custom Grips, Inc., 12229 Cox Lane, Dallas, TX 75244/214-241-6302
Bob Allen Companies, 214 S.W. Jackson St., Des Moines, IA 50302/515-283-2191
American Gas & Chemical Co., Ltd., 220 Pegasus Ave., Northvale, NJ 07647/201-767-7300 (clg. lube)
Armson, Inc., P.O. Box 2130, Farmington Hills, MI 48018/313-478-2577
Armsport, Inc., 3590 N.W. 49th St., Miami, FL 33142/305-635-7850
Assault Accessories, P.O. Box 8994 CRB, Tucson, AZ 85738/602-791-7860 (pistol shoulder stocks)
Baramie Corp., 6250 E. 7 Mile Rd., Detroit, MI 48234 (Hip-Grip)
Bar-Sto Precision Machine, 73377 Sullivan Rd., Twentynine Palms, CA 92277/619-367-2747
Behlert Custom Guns, Inc., RD 2 Box 36C, Route 611 North, Pipersville, PA 18947/215-766-8680
Bingham Ltd., 1775-C Wilwat Dr., Norcross, GA 30093 (magazines)
C'Arco, P.O. Box 308, Highland, CA 92346/714-862-8311 (Ransom Rest)
Central Specialties Co., 200 Lexington Dr., Buffalo Grove, IL 60090/312-537-3300 (trigger lock)
Dave Chicoine, d/b/a Liberty A.S.P., 19 Key St., Eastport, ME 04631/207-853-2327 (shims f. S&W revs.)
D&E Magazines Mfg., P.O. Box 4876, Sylmar, CA 91342 (clips)
Doskocil Mfg. Co., Inc, P.O. Box 1246, Arlington, TX 75010/817-467-5116 (Gun Guard cases)
Essex Arms, Box 345, Island Pond, VT 05846/802-723-4313 (45 Auto frames)
Frielich Police Equipment, 396 Broome St., New York, NY 10013/212-254-3045 (cases)
R. S. Frielich, 211 East 21st St., New York, NY 10010/212-777-4477 (cases)
Terry K. Kopp, Highway 13, Lexington, MO 64067/816-259-2636
Lee's Red Ramps, 7252 E. Ave. U-3, Littlerock, CA 93543/805-944-4487 (ramp insert kits; spring kits)
Lee Precision Inc., 4275 Hwy. U, Hartford, WI 53027 (pistol rest holders)
Kent Lomont, 4236 West 700 South, Poneto, IN 46781 (Auto Mag only)
Lone Star Gunleather, 1301 Brushy Bend Dr., Round Rock, TX 78664/512-255-1805
Los Gatos Grip & Specialty Co., P.O. Box 1850, Los Gatos, CA 95030 (custom-made)
MTM Molded Prods. Co., 3370 Obco Ct., Dayton, OH 45414/513-890-7461
No-Sho Mfg. Co., 10727 Glenfield Ct., Houston, TX 77096/713-723-0966
Harry Owen (See Sport Specialties)
Pachmayr, 1220 S. Grand, Los Angeles, CA 90015 (cases)
Pacific Intl. Mchdsg. Corp., 2215 "J" St., Sacramento, CA 95818/916-446-2737 (Vega 45 Colt comb. mag.)
Poly-Choke Div., Marble Arms Corp., 420 Industrial Park, Gladstone, MI 49837/906-428-3710 (handgun ribs)
Randall Manufacturing, 12826 Pierce St., Pacoima, CA 91331 (magazines, carrying rugs)
Sile Distributors, 7 Centre Market Pl., New York, NY 10013
Sport Specialties, (Harry Owen), Box 5337, Hacienda Hts., CA 91745/213-968-5806 (.22 rimfire adapters; .22 insert bbls. f. T/C Contender, autom. pistols)
Sportsmen's Equipment Co., 415 W. Washington, San Diego, CA 92103/619-296-1501
Turkey Creek Enterprises, Rt. 1, Box 10, Red Oak, CA 74563/918-754-2884 (wood handgun cases)
Melvin Tyler, 1326 W. Britton, Oklahoma City, OK 73114/800-654-8415 (grip adaptor)
Whitney Sales, P.O. Box 875, Reseda, CA 91335/818-345-4212

HANDGUN GRIPS

Ajax Custom Grips, Inc., 12229 Cox Lane, Dallas, TX 75234/214-241-6302
Art Jewel Enterprises Ltd., 421A Irmen Dr., Addison, IL 60101/312-628-6220
Barami Corp., 6250 East 7 Mile Rd., Detroit, MI 48234/313-891-2536
Bear Hug Grips, P.O. Box 9664, Colorado Springs, CO 80909
Beeman Inc., 47 Paul Dr., San Rafael, CA 94903/415-472-7121 (airguns only)
Bingham Ltd., 1775-C Wilwat Dr., Norcross, GA 30093
Boone's Custom Ivory Grips, Inc., 562 Coyote Rd., Brinnon, WA 98320/206-796-4330
Dave Chicoine, d/b/a Liberty A.S.P., 19 Key St., Eastport, ME 04631/207-853-2327 (orig. S&W 1855-1950)
Fitz Pistol Grip Co., Box 171, Douglas City, CA 96024
Gateway Shooters' Supply, Inc., 10145-103rd St., Jacksonville, FL 32210/904-778-2323 (Rogers grips)
Herrett's , Box 741, Twin Falls, ID 83301
Hogue Combat Grips, P.O. Box 2038, Atascadero, CA 93423/805-466-6266 (Monogrip)
Paul Jones Munitions Systems, (See Fitz Co.)
Russ Maloni, 604 Hillside Dr., Colleyville, TX 76034/817-656-4449
Millett Industries, 16131 Gothard St., Huntington Beach, CA 92647/714-842-5575 (custom)
Monogrip, (See Hogue)
Monte Kristo Pistol Grip Co., Box 171, Douglas City, CA 96024/916-778-3136
Mustang Custom Pistol Grips, see: Supreme Products Co.
Pachmayr Gun Works, Inc., 1220 S. Grand Ave., Los Angeles, CA 90015/213-748-7271
Robert H. Newell, 55 Coyote, Los Alamos, NM 87544/505-662-7135 (custom stocks)
Rogers Grips (See Gateway Shooters' Supply)
A. Jack Rosenberg & Sons, 12229 Cox Lane, Dallas, TX 75234/214-241-6302 (Ajax)
Royal Ordnance Works Ltd., P.O. Box 3254, Wilson, NC 27893/919-237-0515
Russwood Custom Pistol Grips, 604 Hillside Dr., Colleyville, TX 76034/817-656-4449 (cust. exotic woods)
Jean St. Henri, 6525 Dume Dr., Malibu, CA 90265/213-457-7211 (custom)
Sile Dist., 7 Centre Market Pl., New York, NY 10013/212-925-4111
Sports Inc., P.O. Box 683, Park Ridge, IL 60068/312-825-8952 (Franzite)
Supreme Products Co., 1830 S. California Ave., Monrovia, CA 91016/800-423-7159/818-357-5359
Sergeant Violin, P.O. Box 25808, Tamarac, FL 33320/305-721-7856 (wood pistol stocks)
R. D. Wallace, Star Rte. Box 76, Grandin, MO 63943
Wayland Prec. Wood Prods., Box 1142, Mill Valley, CA 94942/415-381-3543

HEARING PROTECTORS

AO Safety Prods., Div. of American Optical Corp., 14 Mechanic St., Southbridge, MA 01550/617-765-9711 (ear valves, ear muffs)
Bausch & Lomb, 635 St. Paul St., Rochester, NY 14602
Bilsom Interntl., Inc., 11800 Sunrise Valley Dr., Reston, VA 22091/703-620-3950 (ear plugs, muffs)
David Clark Co., Inc., 360 Franklin St., Worcester, MA 01604
Marble Arms Corp., 420 Industrial Park, Gladstone, MI 49837/906-428-3710
North Consumer Prods. Div., 16624 Edwards Rd., P.O. Box 7500, Cerritos, CA 90701/213-926-0545 (Lee Sonic ear valves)
Safety Direct, 23 Snider Way, Sparks, NV 89431/702-354-4451 (Silencio)
Smith & Wesson, 2100 Roosevelt Ave., Springfield, MA 01101
Willson Safety Prods. Div., P.O. Box 622, Reading, PA 19603 (Ray-O-Vac)

HOLSTERS & LEATHER GOODS

Active Leather Corp., 36-29 Vernon Blvd., Long Island City, NY 11106
Alessi Custom Concealment Holsters, 2465 Niagara Falls Blvd., Tonawanda, NY 14150/716-691-5615
Allen Firearms Co., 2879 All Trades Rd., Santa Fe, NM 87501/505-471-6090
Bob Allen Companies, 214 S.W. Jackson, Des Moines, IA 50315/515-283-2191
American Sales & Mfg. Co., P.O. Box 677, Laredo, TX 78040/512-723-6893
Andy Anderson, P.O. Box 225, North Hollywood, CA 91603/213-877-2401 (Gunfighter Custom Holsters)
Armament Systems & Procedures, Inc., P.O. Box 356, Appleton, WI 54912/414-731-8893 (ASP)
Rick M. Bachman (see Old West Reproductions)
Barami Corp., 6250 East 7 Mile Rd., Detroit, MI 48234/313-891-2536
Beeman Inc., 47-GDD Paul Dr., San Rafael, CA 94903/415-472-7121
Behlert Custom Guns, Inc., RD 2 Box 36C, Route 611 North, Pipersville, PA 18947/215-766-8680

Bianchi International Inc., 100 Calle Cortez, Temecula, CA 92390/714-676-5621
Ted Blocker's Custom Holsters, Box 821, Rosemead, CA 91770/213-442-5772 (shop: 4945 Santa Anita Ave., Temple City, CA 91780)
Bo-Mar Tool & Mfg. Co., Rt. 12, Box 405, Longview, TX 75605/214-759-4784
Boyt Co., Div. of Welsh Sptg., P.O. Box 220, Iowa Falls, IA 51026/515-648-4626
Brauer Bros. Mfg. Co., 2012 Washington Blvd., St. Louis, MO 63103/314-231-2864
Browning, Rt. 4, Box 624-B, Arnold, MO 63010
J.M. Bucheimer Co., P.O. Box 280, Airport Rd., Frederick, MD 21701/301-662-5101
Buffalo Leather Goods, Inc., Rt. 4, Box 187, Magnolia, AR 71753/501-234-6367
Cathey Enterprises, Inc., 9516 Neils Thompson Dr., Suite 116, Austin, TX 78759/512-837-7150
Cattle Baron Leather Co., P.O. Box 100724, San Antonio, TX 78201/512-697-8900 (ctlg. $2)
Chace Leather Prods., Longhorn Div., 507 Alden St., Fall River, MA 02722/617-678-7556
Cherokee Gun Accessories, 830 Woodside Rd., Redwood City, CA 94061/415-572-3266
Cobra Ltd., 1865 New Highway, Farmingdale, NY 11735/516-752-8544
Colt, P.O. Box 1868, Hartford, CT. 06102/203-236-6311
Daisy Mfg. Co., P.O. Box 220, Rogers, AR 72756/501-636-1200
Davis Leather Co., G. Wm. Davis, 3930 "F" Valley Blvd., Walnut, CA 91789/714-598-5620
Eugene DeMayo & Sons, Inc., 2795 Third Ave., Bronx, NY 10455/212-665-7075
DeSantis Gunhide, 140 Denton Ave., New Hyde Park, NY 11040/516-354-8000
Ellwood Epps Northern Ltd., 210 Worthington St. W., North Bay, Ont. P1B 3B4, Canada (custom made)
GALCO Gun Leather, 4311 W. Van Buren, Phoenix, AZ 85043/602-233-0596
Gunfighter (See Anderson)
Ernie Hill Speed Leather, 3128 S. Extension Rd., Mesa, AZ 85202
Hoyt Holster Co., Inc., P.O. Box 69, Coupeville, WA 98239/206-678-6640
Don Hume, Box 351, Miami, OK 74354/918-542-6604
Hunter Corp., 3300 W. 71st Ave., Westminster, CO 80030/303-427-4626
John's Custom Leather, 525 S. Liberty St., Blairsville, PA 15717/412-459-6802
Jumbo Sports Prods., P.O. Box 280, Airport Rd., Frederick, MD 21701
Kane Products, Inc., 5572 Brecksville Rd., Cleveland, OH 44131/216-524-9962 (GunChaps)
Kirkpatrick Leather Co., P.O. Box 3150, Laredo, TX 78044/512-723-6631
Kolpin Mfg. Inc., P.O. Box 231, Berlin, WI 54923/414-361-0400
Morris Lawing, 150 Garland Ct., Charlotte, NC 28202/704-375-1740
George Lawrence Co., 306 S. W. First Ave., Portland, OR 97204/503-228-8244
Liberty Organization Inc., P.O. Box 306, Montrose, CA 91020/213-248-0618
Lone Star Gunleather, 1301 Brushy Bend Dr., Round Rock, TX 78664/512-255-1805
Mixson Leathercraft Inc., 1950 W. 84th St., Hialeah, FL 33014/305-820-5190 (police leather products)
Nordac Mfg. Corp., Rt 12, Box 124, Fredericksburg, VA 22405/703-752-2552
No-Sho Mfg. Co., 10727 Glenfield Ct., Houston, TX 77096/713-723-5332
Kenneth L. Null-Custom Concealment Holsters, R.D. #5, Box 197, Hanover, PA 17331 (See Seventrees)
Arvo Ojala, 3960 S.E. 1st, Gresham, OR 97030
Old West Reproductions, R. M. Bachman, 1840 Stag Lane, Kalispell, MT 59901/406-755-6902 (ctlg. $3)
Pioneer Prods, P.O. Box G, Magnolia, AR 71753/501-234-1566
Pony Express Sport Shop Inc., 1606 Schoenborn St., Sepulveda, CA 91343/818-895-1231
Red Head Brand Corp., 4949 Joseph Hardin Dr., Dallas, TX 75236/214-333-4141
Red River Outfitters, P.O. Box 241, Tujunga, CA 91042/213-352-0177
Rogers Holsters Co., Inc., 1736 St. Johns Bluff Rd., Jacksonville, FL 32216/904-641-9434
Roy's Custom Leather Goods, Hwy, 1325 & Rawhide Rd., P.O. Box G, Magnolia, AR 71753/501-234-1566
Safariland Leather Products, 1941 So. Walker Ave., Monrovia, CA 91016/818-357-7902
Safety Speed Holster, Inc., 910 So. Vail, Montebello, CA 90640/213-723-4140
Buddy Schoellkopf Products, Inc., 4949 Joseph Hardin Dr., TX 75236/214-333-2121
Schulz Industries, 16247 Minnesota Ave., Paramount, CA 90723/213-636-7718
Seventrees Systems Ltd., R.D. 5, Box 197, Hanover, PA 17331/717-632-6873 (See Null)
Sile Distr., 7 Centre Market Pl., New York NY 10013/212-925-4111
Smith & Wesson, 2100 Roosevelt Ave., Springfield, MA 01101
Milt Sparks, Box 187, Idaho City, ID 83631/208-392-6695 (broch. $2)
Robert A. Strong Co., 105 Maplewood Ave., Gloucester, MA 01930/617-281-3300
Torel, Inc., 1053 N. South St., P.O. Box 592, Yoakum, TX 77995/512-293-2341 (gun slings)
Triple-K Mfg. Co., 568 Sixth Ave., San Diego, CA 92101/619-232-2066
Viking Leathercraft, Inc., P.O. Box 2030, 2248-2 Main St., Chula Vista, CA 92012/619-429-8050
Whitco, Box 1712, Brownsville, TX 78520 (Hide-A-Way)
Wildlife Leather, P.O. Box 339, Merrick, NY 11566/516-379-3440 (lea. gds. w. outdoor themes)
Wyman Corp., P.O. Box 8644, Salt Lake City, UT 84104/801-359-0368 (Cannon Packer f. rifle, shotgun)

HUNTING AND CAMP GEAR, CLOTHING, ETC.

Bob Allen Sportswear, P.O. Box 477, Des Moines, IA 50302/800-247-8048
Eddie Bauer, 15010 NE 36th St., Redmond, WA 98052
L. L. Bean, Freeport, ME 04032
Bear Archery, R.R. 4, 4600 Southwest 41st Blvd., Gainesville, FL 32601/904-376-2327 (Himalayan backpack)
Big Beam, Teledyne Co., 290 E. Prairie St., Crystal Lake, IL 60014 (lamp)
Big Buck, Brazell Mfg. & Distr. Co., 5645 S. Waterbury Plaza, Suite D, Salt Lake City, UT 84121/801-272-4471 (game bag, hoist, etc.)
Browning, Rte. 1, Morgan, UT 84050
Brush Hunter Sportswear, Inc., NASCO Ind., 3 NE 21st St., Washington, IN 47501/812-254-4962
Camp-Ways, 1140 E. Sandhill Ave., Carson, CA 90746/213-604-1201
Challanger Mfg. Co., Box 550, Jamaica, NY 11431 (glow safe)
Chippewa Shoe Co., P.O. Box 2521, Ft. Worth, TX 76113/817-332-4385 (boots)
Coleman Co., Inc., 250 N. St. Francis, Wichita, KS 67201
Converse Rubber Co., 55 Fordham Rd., Wilmington, MA 01887 (boots)
Danner Shoe Mfg. Co., P.O. Box 22204, Portland, OR 97222/503-653-2920 (boots)
DEER-ME Prod. Co., Box 34, Anoka, MN 55303/612-421-8971 (tree steps)
Dunham Co., P.O. Box 813, Brattleboro, VT 05301/802-254-2316 (boots)
Durango Boot, see: Georgia/Northlake
Frankonia Jagd, Hofmann & Co., Postfach 6780, D-8700 Wurzburg 1, West Germany
Freeman Ind., Inc., 100 Marblehead Rd., Tuckahoe, NY 10707 (Trak-Kit)
French Dressing Inc., 15 Palmer Heights, Burlington, VT 05401/802-658-1434 (boots)
Game-Winner, Inc., 2625 Cumberland Parkway, Suite 205, Atlanta, GA 30339/404-434-9210 (camouflage suits; orange vests)
Gander Mountain, Inc., P.O. Box 248, Hwy. "W", Wilmot, WI 53192/414-862-2331
Georgia Boot Div., U.S. Industry, 1810 Columbia Ave., Franklin, TN 37064/615-794-1556
Georgia/Northlake Boot Co., P.O. Box 10, Franklin, TN 37064/615-794-1556 (Durango)
Gokeys, 84 So. Wabasha, St. Paul, MN 55107/612-292-3933
Gun Club Sportswear, Box 477, Des Moines, IA 50302
Gun-Ho Case Mfg. Co., 110 E. 10th St., St. Paul, MN 55101
Himalayan Industries, Inc., P.O. Box 7465, Pine Bluff, AR 71611/501-534-6411
Bob Hinman Outfitters, 1217 W. Glen, Peoria, IL 61614
Hunting World, 16 E. 53rd St., New York, NY 10022
Kap Outdoors, 1704 Locust St., Philadelphia, PA 19103/215-723-3449 (clothing)
Kelty Pack, Inc., 9281 Borden Ave., Sun Valley, CA 91352/213-768-1922
Kenko Intl. Inc., 8141 West I-70 Frontage Rd. No., Arvada, CO 80002/303-425-1200 (footwear & socks)
La Crosse Rubber Mills Co., P.O. Box 1328, La Crosse, WI 54601/608-782-3020 (boots)
Langenberg Hat Co., P.O. Box 1860, Washington, MO 63090/314-239-1860
Peter Limmer & Sons Inc., Box 66, Intervale, NH 03845 (boots)
Marathon Rubber Prods. Co. Inc., 510 Sherman St., Wausau, WI 54401/715-845-6255 (rain gear)
Marble Arms Corp., 420 Industrial Park, Gladstone, MI 49837
Nelson Recreation Prods., Inc., Fuqua Industries, 14760 Santa Fe Trail Dr., Lenexa, KS 66215/800-255-6061
The Orvis Co., Manchester, VT 05254/802-362-3622 (fishing gear; clothing)
PGB Assoc., 310 E. 46th St., Suite 3E, New York, NY 10017/212-867-9560
Quabaug Rubber Co./Vibram U.S.A., 17 School St. N. Brookfield, MA 01535/617-867-7731 (boots)
Quoddy Moccasins, Div. R. G. Barry Corp., 67 Minot Ave., Auburn, ME 04210/207-784-3555
Ranger Mfg. Co., Inc., P.O. Box 3676, Augusta, GA 30904
Ranger Rubber Co., 1100 E. Main St., Endicott, NY 13760/607-757-4260 (boots)
Red Ball, P.O. Box 3200, Manchester, NH 03105/603-669-0708 (boots)
Red Head Brand Corp., 4949 Joseph Hardin Dr., Dallas, TX 75236/214-333-4141
Refrigiwear, Inc., 71 Inip Dr., Inwood, Long Island, NY 11696
Reliance Prod. Ltd., 1830 Dublin Ave., Winnipeg 21, Man. R3H 0H3 Can. (tent peg)
W. R. Russell Moccasin Co., 285 S.W. Franklin, Berlin, WI 54923
Safariland Hunting Corp., P.O. Box NN, McLean, VA 22101/703-356-0622 (camouflage rain gear)
Safesport Mfg. Co., 1100 West 45th Ave., Denver, CO 80211/303-433-6506
Saf-T-Bak, see: Kap Outdoors
SanLar Co., Rte. 2, Box 123, Sullivan, WI 53178/414-593-8086 (huntg. sweat-suits)
Servus Rubber Co., 1136 2nd St., Rock Island, IL 61201 (footwear)
Spruce Creek Sportswear, see: Kap Outdoors
Stearns Mfg. Co., P.O. Box 1498, St. Cloud, MN 56301
Teledyne Co., Big Beam, 290 E. Prairie St., Crystal Lake, IL 60014
10-X Mfg. Products Group, 2828 Forest Lane, Suite 1107, Dallas, TX 75234/214-243-4016
Thermos Div., KST Co., Norwich, CT 06361 (Pop Tent)
Norm Thompson, 1805 N.W. Thurman St., Portland, OR 97209
Trim Unlimited, 2111 Glen Forest, Plano, TX 75023/214-596-5059 (electric boat)
Utica Duxbak Corp., 1745 S. Acoma St., Denver, CO 80223/303-778-0324
Waffen-Frankonia, see: Frankonia Jagd
Walker Shoe Co., P.O. Box 1167, Asheboro, NC 27203-1167/919-625-1380 (boots)
Weinbrenner Shoe Corp., Polk St., Merrill, WI 54452
Wenzel Co., 1280 Research Blvd., St. Louis, MO 63132
Wolverine Boots & Shoes Div., Wolverine World Wide, 9341 Courtland Dr., Rockford, MI 49351/616-866-1561 (footwear)
Woods Inc., 90 River St., P.O. Box 407, Ogdensburg, NY 13669/315-393-3520
Woodstream Corp., Box 327, Lititz, PA 17543 (Hunter Seat)
Woolrich Woolen Mills, Mill St., Woolrich, PA 17779/717-769-6464
Yankee Mechanics, RFD No. 1, Concord, NH 03301/603-225-3181 (hand winches)

KNIVES AND KNIFEMAKER'S SUPPLIES—FACTORY and MAIL ORDER

A.C. Enterprises, P.O. Box 448, Edenton, NC 27932/919-482-4992
Alcas Cutlery Corp., 1116 E. State St., Olean, NY 14760/716-372-3111 (Cutco)
Atlanta Cutlery, Box 839, Conyers, GA 30207/404-922-3700 (mail order, supplies)
Bali-Song, see: Pacific Cutlery Corp.
L. L. Bean, 386 Main St., Freeport, ME 04032/207-865-3111 (mail order)
Benchmark Knives (See Gerber)
Crosman Blades™, The Coleman Co., 250 N. St. Francis, Wichita, KS 67201
Boker, The Cooper Group, 3535 Glenwood Ave., Raleigh, NC 27612/919-781-7200
Bowen Knife Co., Box 1929, Waycross, GA 31501/912-287-1200
Browning, Rt. 1, Morgan, UT 84050/801-876-2711
Buck Knives, Inc., P.O. Box 1267; 1900 Weld Blvd., El Cajon, CA 92022/619-449-1100 or 800-854-2557
Camillus Cutlery Co., 52-54 W. Genesee St., Camillus, NY 13031/315-672-8111 (Sword Brand)
W. R. Case & Sons Cutlery Co., 20 Russell Blvd., Bradford, PA 16701/814-368-4123
Charlton, Ltd., P.O. Box 448, Edenton, NC 27932
Charter Arms Corp., 430 Sniffens Lane, Stratford, CT 06497/203-377-8080 (Skatchet)
Chicago Cutlery Co., 5420 N. County Rd. 18, Minneapolis, MN 55428/612-533-0472
Collins Brothers Div. (belt-buckle knife), See Bowen Knife Co.
Colonial Knife Co., P.O. Box 3327, Providence, RI 02909/401-421-1600 (Master Brand)
Custom Knifemaker's Supply, P.O. Box 308, Emory, TX 75440/214-473-3330
Custom Purveyors, Ted Devlet's, P.O. Box 886, Fort Lee, NJ 07024/201-886-0196 (mail order)
Dixie Gun Works, Inc., P.O. Box 130, Union City, TN 38261/901-885-0700 (supplies)
Eze-Lap Diamond Prods., Box 2229, 15164 Weststate St., Westminster, CA 92683/714-847-1555 (knife sharpeners)
Gerber Legendary Blades, 14200 S.W. 72nd St., Portland, OR 99223/503-639-6161
Golden Age Arms Co., 14 W. Winter St., Delaware, OH 43015/614-369-6513 (supplies)
Gutmann Cutlery Co., Inc., 900 S. Columbus Ave., Mt. Vernon, NY 10550/914-699-4044
H & B Forge Co., Rte. 2 Geisinger Rd., Shiloh, OH 44878/419-895-1856 (throwing knives, tomahawks)
Russell Harrington Cutlery, Inc., Subs. of Hyde Mfg. Co., 44 River St., Southbridge, MA 01550/617-764-4371 (Dexter, Green River Works)
J. A. Henckels Zwillingswerk, Inc., 9 Skyline Dr., Hawthorne, NY 10532/914-592-7370
Imperial Knife Associated Companies, 1776 Broadway, New York, NY 10019/212-757-1814
Indian Ridge Traders, Box 869, Royal Oak, MI 48068/313-399-6034 (mostly blades)
J.A. Blades, Inc., an affiliate of E. Christoper Firearms Co., State 128 & Ferry Street, Miamitown, OH 45041/513-353-1321 (supplies)
Ken Jantz Supply, Rt. 1, Sulphur, OK 73086/405-622-3790 (supplies)
Jet-Aer Corp., 100 Sixth Ave., Paterson, NJ 07524/201-278-8300
KA-BAR Cutlery Inc., 5777 Grant Ave., Cleveland, OH 44105/216-271-4000
KA-BAR Knives, Collectors Division, 434 No. 9th St., Olean, NY 14760/716-372-5611
Keene Corp., Cutting Serv. Div., 1569 Tower Grove Ave., St. Louis, MO 63110/314-771-1550
Kershaw Knives/Kai Cutlery USA Ltd., Stafford Bus. Pk., 25300 SW Parkway, Wilsonville, OR 97070/503-636-0111
Knifeco, P.O. Box 5271, Hialeah Lakes, FL 33014/305-635-2411
Knife and Gun Finishing Supplies, P.O. Box 13522, Arlington, TX 76013/817-274-1282
Koval Knives, 822 Busch Ct. GD, Columbus, OH 43229/614-888-5159 (supplies)
Lamson & Goodnow Mfg. Co., 45 Conway St., Shelburne Falls, MA 03170/413-625-6331
Lansky Sharpeners, P.O. Box 800, Buffalo, NY 14221/716-634-6333 (sharpening devices)
Al Mar Knives, Inc., P.O. Box 1626, 5755 SW Jean Rd., Suite 101, Lake Oswego, OR 97034/503-635-9229
Matthews Cutlery, P.O. Box 33095, Decatur, GA 30033/404-636-3970 (mail order)
R. Murphy Co., Inc., 13 Groton-Harvard Rd., Ayer, MA 01432/617-772-3481 (StaySharp)
Nordic Knives, 1643-C Copenhagen Dr., Solvang, CA 93463 (mail order)
Normark Corp., 1710 E. 78th St., Minneapolis, MN 55423/612-869-3291
Ontario Knife, Queen Cutlery Co., P.O. Box 500, Franklinville, NY 14737/716-676-5527 (Old Hickory)
Pacific Cutlery Corp., 3039 Roswell St., Los Angeles, CA 90085/213-258-7021 (Bali-Song)
Parker Cutlery, 6928 Lee Highway, Chattanooga, TN 37415/615-894-1782
Plaza Cutlery Inc., 3333 Bristol, #161, South Coast Plaza, Costa Mesa, CA 92626/714-549-3932 (mail order)
Queen Cutlery Co., 507 Chestnut St., Titusville, PA 16354/800-222-5233
R & C Knives and Such, P.O. Box 32631, San Jose, CA 95152/408-923-5728 (mail order; ctlg. $2)
Randall-Made Knives, Box 1988, Orlando, FL 32802/305-855-8075 (ctlg. $1)
Rigid Knives, P.O. Box 816, Hwy. 290E, Lake Hamilton, AR 71951/501-525-1377
A. G. Russell Co., 1705 Hiwy. 71 No., Springdale, AR 72764/501-751-7341
Bob Sanders, 2358 Tyler Lane, Louisville, KY 40205 (Bahco steel)
San Diego Knives, P.O. Box 326, Lakeside, CA 92040/619-561-5900 (mail order)
Schrade Cutlery Corp., 1776 Broadway, New York, NY 10019/212-757-1814
Sheffield Knifemakers Supply, P.O. Box 141, Deland, FL 32720/904-734-7884
Smith & Wesson, 2100 Roosevelt Ave., Springfield, MA 01101/413-781-8300
Jesse W. Smith Saddlery, N. 307 Haven St., Spokane, WA 99202/509-534-3229 (sheathmakers)
Swiss Army Knives, Inc., P.O. Box 846, Shelton, CT 06484/203-929-6391 (Victorinox; folding)
Tekna, 1075 Old County Rd., Belmont, CA 94002/415-592-4070
Thompson/Center, P.O. Box 2426, Rochester, NH 03867/603-332-2394
Tommer-Bordein Corp., 220 N. River St., Delano, MN 55328/612-972-3901
Tru-Balance Knife Co., 2155 Tremont Blvd., N.W., Grand Rapids, MI 49504/616-453-3679
Utica Cutlery Co., 820 Noyes St., Utica, NY 13503/315-733-4663 (Kutmaster)
Valor Corp., 5555 N.W. 36th Ave., Miami, FL 33142/305-633-0127
Washington Forge, Inc., Englishtown, NJ 07727/201-446-7777 (Carriage House)
Wenoka Cutlery, P.O. Box 8238, West Palm Beach, FL 33407/305-845-6155
Western Cutlery Co., 1800 Pike Rd., Longmont, CO 80501/303-772-5900 (Westmark)
Walt Whinnery, Walts Cust. Leather, 1947 Meadow Creek Dr., Louisville, KY 40218/502-458-4351 (sheathmaker)
J. Wolfe's Knife Works, Box 1056, Larkspur, CA 94939 (supplies)
Wyoming Knife Co., 101 Commerce Dr., Ft. Collins, CO 80524/303-224-3454

LABELS, BOXES, CARTRIDGE HOLDERS

Milton Brynin, 214 E. Third St., Mount Vernon, NY 10550/914-667-6549 (cartridge box labels)
Del Rey Products, P.O. Box 91561, Los Angeles, CA 90009/213-823-0494
E-Z Loader, Del Rey Products, P.O. Box 91561, Los Angeles, CA 90009
Hunter Co., Inc., 3300 W. 71st Ave., Westminster, Co 80030/303-472-4626 (cartridge holders)
Peterson Label Co., P.O. Box 186, 23 Sullivan Dr., Redding Ridge, CT 06876/203-938-2349 (cartridge box labels; Targ-Dots)

LOAD TESTING and PRODUCT TESTING, (CHRONOGRAPHING, BALLISTIC STUDIES)

Accuracy Systems Inc., 15203 N. Cave Creek Rd., Phoenix, AZ 85032/602-971-1991
Hutton Rifle Ranch, P.O. Box 45236, Boise, ID 83711/208-343-9841
Kent Lomont, 4236 West 700 South, Poneto, IN 45781/219-694-6792 (handguns, handgun ammunition)
Plum City Ballistics Range, Norman E. Johnson, Rte. 1, Box 29A, Plum City, WI 54761/715-647-2539
Russell's Rifle Shop, Rte. 5, Box 92, Georgetown, TX 78626/512-778-5338 (load testing and chronographing to 300 yds.)
John M. Tovey, 4710 - 104th Lane NE, Circle Pines, MN 55014/612-786-7268
H. P. White Laboratory, Inc., 3114 Scarboro Rd., Street, MD 21154/301-838-6550

MISCELLANEOUS

Action, Mauser-style only, Crandall Tool & Machine Co., 1540 N. Mitchell St., Cadillac, MI 49601/616-775-5562
Action, Single Shot, Miller Arms, Inc., P.O. Box 260, St. Onge, SD 57779 (deHaas-Miller)
Activator, B.M.F. Activator, Inc., P.O. Box 262364, Houston, TX 77207/713-477-8442
Adapters, Sage Industries, P.O. Box 2248, Hemet, CA 92342/714-925-1006 (12-ga. shotgun; 38 S&W blank)
Adapters for Subcalibers, Harry Owen, P.O. Box 5337, Hacienda Hts., CA 91745/818-968-5806
Airgun Accessories, Beeman Precision Arms, Inc., 47 Paul Dr., San Rafael, CA 94903/415-472-7121 (Beeman Pell seat, Pell Size, etc.)
Air Gun Combat Game Supplies, The Ultimate Game Inc., P.O. Box 1856, Ormond Beach, FL 32075/904-677-4358 (washable pellets, marking pistols/rifles)
Archery, Bear, R.R. 4, 4600 Southwest 41st Blvd., Gainesville, FL 32601/904-376-2327
Arms Restoration, J. J. Jenkins Ent. Inc., 375 Pine Ave. No. 25, Goleta, CA 93017/805-967-1366
Assault Rifle Accessories, Cherokee Gun Accessories, 830 Woodside Rd., Redwood City, CA 94061/415-572-3266
Assault Rifle Accessories, Choate Machine & Tool Corp., P.O. Box 218, Bald Knob, AR 72010 (folding stocks)
Assault Rifle Accessories, Feather Enterprises, 2500 Central Ave., Boulder, CO 80301/303-442-7021
Assault Rifle Accessories, Ram-Line, Inc., 406 Violet St., Golden, CO 80401/303-279-0886 (folding stock)
Barrel Band Swivels, Phil Judd, 83 E. Park St., Butte, MT 59701
Bedding Kit, Fenwal, Inc., Resins Systems Div., 400 Main St., Ashland, MA 01721
Belt Buckles, Bergamot Brass Works, 820 Wisconsin St., Delavan, WI 53115/414-728-5572
Belt Buckles, Herrett's Stocks, Inc., Box 741, Twin Falls, ID 83303/800-635-9334 (laser engr. hardwood)
Belt Buckles, Just Brass Inc., 121 Henry St., P.O. Box 112, Freeport, NY 11520/516-379-3434 (ctlg. $2)
Belt Buckles, Pilgrim Pewter Inc., R.D. 2, Tully, NY 13159/607-842-6431
Benchrest & Accuracy Shooters Equipment, Bob Pease Accuracy, P.O. Box 787, Zipp Road, New Braunfels, TX 78130/512-625-1342
Benchrest Rifles & Accessories, Robert W. Hart & Son Inc., 401 Montgomery St., Nescopeck, PA 18635/717-752-3481
Blowgun, PAC Outfitters, P.O. Box 56, Mulvane, KS 67110/316-777-4909
Bulletproof Clothing, EMGO USA Ltd., 115 E. 57th St., Suite 1430, New York NY 10022/212-772-3444
Cannons, South Bend Replicas Ind., 61650 Oak Rd., S. Bend, IN 44614/219-289-4500 (ctlg. $5)

Cartridge Adapters, Kestmati, 23011 Moulton, Suite G-6, Laguna Hills, CA 92653
Cartridge Adapters, Sport Specialties, Harry Owen, Box 5337, Hacienda Hts., CA 91745/213-968-5806 (ctlg. $3)
Case Gauge, Plum City Ballistics Range, Rte. 1, Box 29A, Plum City, WI 54761/715-647-2539
Cased, high-grade English tools, Marvin Huey Gun Cases, P.O. Box 22456, Kansas City, MO 64113/816-444-1637 (ebony, horn, ivory handles)
Cherry Converter, Amimex Inc., 2660 John Montgomery Dr., Suite #3, San Jose, CA 95148/408-923-1720 (shotguns)
Clips, D&E Magazines Mfg., P.O. Box 4876, Sylmar, CA 91342 (handgun and rifle)
CO_2 Cartridges, Nittan U.S.A. Inc., 4901 Morena Blvd., Suite 307, San Diego, CA 92117/714-272-6113
Computer & PSI Calculator, Hutton Rifle Ranch, P.O. Box 45236, Boise, ID 83711/208-343-9841
Crossbows, Barnett International, 1967 Gunn Highway, Odessa, FL 33552/813-920-2241
Deer Drag, D&H Prods. Co., Inc., 465 Denny Rd., Valencia, PA 16059/412-898-2840
Defendor, Ralide, Inc., P.O. Box 131, Athens, TN 37303/615-745-3525
Dehumidifiers, Buenger Enterprises, P.O. Box 5286, Oxnard, CA 93030/805-985-0541
Dryer, Thermo-Electric, Golden-Rod, Buenger Enterprises, Box 5286, Oxnard, CA 93030/805-985-0541
E-Z Loader, Del Rey Prod., P.O. Box 91561, Los Angeles, CA 90009/213-823-04494 (f. 22-cal. rifles)
Ear-Valve, North Consumer Prods. Div., 16624 Edwards Rd., Cerritos, CA 90701/213-926-0545 (Lee-Sonic)
Embossed Leather Belts, Wallets, Wildlife Leather, P.O. Box 339, Merrick, NY 11566/516-379-3440 (outdoor themes)
Farrsight, Farr Studio, 1231 Robinhood Rd., Greenville, TN 37743
Flares, Colt Industries, P.O. Box 1868, Hartford, CT 06102
Flares, Smith & Wesson Chemical Co., 2399 Forman Rd., Rock Creek, OH 44084
Frontier Outfitters, Red River Outfitters, P.O. Box 241, Tujunga, CA 91042/213-352-0177 (frontier, western, military Americana clothing)
Game Hoist, Cam Gear Ind., P.O. Box 1002, Kalispell, MT 59901 (Sportsmaster 500 pocket hoist)
Game Hoist, Precise, 3 Chestnut, Suffern, NY 10901
Game Scent, Buck Stop Lure Co., Inc., 3015 Grow Rd. N.W., R. #1, Stanton, MI 48888/517-762-5091
Game Scent, Pete Rickard, Inc., Rte. 1, Cobleskill, NY 12043/518-234-2731 (Indian Buck lure)
Game Scent, Safariland Hunting Corp., P.O. Box NN, McLean, VA 22101/703-356-0622 (buck lure)
Gargoyles, Pro-tec Inc., 11108 Northrup Way, Bellevue, WA 98004/306-828-6595
Gas Pistol, Penguin Ind., Inc., Airport Industrial Mall, Coatesville, PA 19320/215-384-6000
Grip Caps, Classic Arms Corp., P.O. Box 8, Palo Alto, CA 94301/415-321-7243
Gun Bedding Kit, Fenwal, Inc., Resins System Div., 400 Main St., Ashland, MA 01721/617-881-2000
Gun Jewelry, Sid Bell Originals, R.D. 2, Box 219, Tully, NY 13159/607-842-6431
Gun Jewelry, Pilgrim Pewter Inc., R.D. 2, Box 219, Tully, NY 13159/607-842-6431
Gun Jewelry, Al Popper, 6l4 Turnpike St., Stoughton, MA 02072/617-344-2036
Gun Jewelry, Sports Style Assoc., 148 Hendricks Ave., Lynbrook, NY 11563
Gun photographer, Mustafa Bilal, 727 Bellevue Ave. East, Suite 103, Seattle, WA 98102/206-322-5449
Gun photographer, Art Carter, 818 Baffin Bay Rd., Columbia, SC 29210/803-772-2148
Gun photographer, John Hanusin, 3306 Commercial, Northbrook, IL 60062/312-564-2706
Gun photographer, Int. Photographic Assoc., Inc., 4500 E. Speedway, Suite 89, Tucson, AZ 85712/602-326-2941
Gun photographer, Charles Semmer, 7885 Cyd Dr., Denver, CO 80221/303-429-6947
Gun photographer, Jim Weyer, 224½ Huron St., Toledo, OH 43604/419-241-5454
Gun photographer, Steve White, 1920 Raymond Dr., Northbrook, IL 60062/312-564-2720
Gun Sling, La Paloma Marketing, 4500 E. Speedway Blvd., Suite 93, Tucson, AZ 85712/602-881-4750 (Pro-sling system)
Gun Slings, Torel, Inc., 1053 N. South St., Yoakum, TX 77995
Hand Exerciser, Action Products, Inc., 22 No. Mulberry St., Hagerstown, MD 21740/301-797-1414
Horsepac, Yellowstone Wilderness Supply, P.O. 129, West Yellowstone, MT 59758/406-646-7613
Horsepacking Equipment/Saddle Trees, Ralide West, P.O. Box 998, 299 Firehole Ave., West Yellowstone, WY 59758/406-646-7612
Hugger Hooks, Roman Products, Inc., 4363 Loveland St., Golden, CO 80403/303-279-6959
Insect Repellent, Armor, Div. of Buck Stop, Inc., 3015 Grow Rd., Stanton, MI 48888
Insert Chambers, GTM Co., Geo. T. Mahaney, 15915B E. Main St., La Puente, CA 91744 (shotguns only)
Insert Barrels, Kestmati, 23011 Moulton, Suite G-6, Laguna Hills, CA 92653
Insert Barrels and Cartridge Adapters, Sport Specialties, Harry Owen, Box 5337, Hacienda Hts., CA 91745/213-968-5806 (ctlg. $3)
Kentucky Rifle Drawings, New England Historic Designs, P.O. Box 171, Concord, NH 03301/603-224-2096
Knife Sharpeners, Lansky Sharpeners, P.O. Box 800, Buffalo, NY 14221/716-634-6333
Light Load, Jacob & Tiffin Inc., P.O. Box 547, Clanton, AL 35045
Locks, Gun, Bor-Lok Prods., 105 5th St., Arbuckle, CA 95912
Locks, Gun, Master Lock Co., 2600 N. 32nd St., Milwaukee, WI 53245
Magazines, San Diego Knives, P.O. Box 326, Lakeside, CA 92040/619-561-5900 (auto pist., rifles)
Magazines, Mitchell Arms of California, Inc., 19007 S. Reyes Ave., Compton, CA 90221/714-964-3678 (stainless steel)
Magazines, Ram-Line, Inc., 406 Violet St., Golden, CO 80401/303-279-0886
Miniature Cannons, Karl J. Furr, 76 East, 350 North, Orem, UT 84057/801-225-2603 (replicas)
Miniature Guns, Charles H. Stoppler, 5 Minerva Place, New York, NY 10468
Monte Carlo Pad, Hoppe Division, Penguin Ind., Airport Industrial Mall, Coatesville, PA 19320/215-384-6000
Old Gun Industry Art, Hansen and Hansen, 244 Old Post Rd., Southport, CT 06490/203-259-7337
Pell Remover, A. Edw. Terpening, 838 E. Darlington Rd., Tarpon Springs, FL 33589
Powderhorns, Frontier, 2910 San Bernardo, Laredo, TX 78040/512-723-5409
Powderhorns, Kirk Olson, Ft. Woolsey Guns, P.O. Box 2122, Prescott, AZ 86302/602-778-3035
Powderhorns, Tennessee Valley Mfg., P.O. Box 1125, Corinth, MS 38834
Powderhorns, Thomas F. White, 5801 Westchester Ct., Worthington, OH 43085/614-888-0128
Practice Ammunition, Hoffman New Ideas Inc., 821 Northmoor Rd., Lake Forest, IL 60045/312-234-4075
Pressure Testg. Machine, M. York, 5508 Griffith Rd., Gaithersburg, MD 20760/301-253-4217
Ram Line, Inc., 406 Violet St., Golden, CO 80401/303-279-0886 (accessories)
Ransom Handgun Rests, C'Arco, P.O. Box 308, Highland, CA 92346/714-862-8311
Reloader's Record Book, Reloaders Paper Supply, Don Doerkson, P.O. Box 556, Hines, OR 97738/503-573-7060
Rifle Magazines, Butler Creek Corp., Box GG, Jackson Hole, WY 83001/307-733-3599 (30-rd. Mini-14)
Rifle Magazines, Condor Mfg. Co., 418 W. Magnolia Ave., Glendale, CA 91204/213-240-1745 (25-rd. 22-cal.)
Rifle Magazines, Miller Gun Works, P.O. Box 7326, Tamuning, Guam 96911 (30-cal. M1 15&30-round)
Rifle Slings, Bianchi International, 100 Calle Cortez, Temecula, CA 92390/714-676-5621
Rifle Slings, Chace Leather Prods., Longhorn Div., 507 Alden St., Fall River, MA 02722/617-678-7556
Rifle Slings, John's Cust. Leather, 525 S. Liberty St., Blairsville, PA 15717/412-459-6802
Rifle Slings, Kirkpatrick Leather Co., P.O. Box 3150, Laredo, TX 78044/512-723-6631
Rifle Slings, Schulz Industr., 16247 Minnesota Ave., Paramount, CA 90723/213-636-7718
RIG, NRA Scoring Plug, Rig Products, 87 Coney Island Dr., Sparks, NV 89431/702-331-5666
Rubber Cheekpiece, W. H. Lodewick, 2816 N.E. Halsey, Portland, OR 97232/503-284-2554
Saddle Rings, Studs, Fred Goodwin, Sherman Mills, ME 04776
Safeties, William E. Harper, The Great 870 Co., P.O. Box 6309. El Monte, CA 91734/213-579-3077 (f. Rem. 870P)
Safeties, Williams Gun Sight Co., 7389 Lapeer Rd., Davison, MI 48423
Safety Slug, Glaser Safety Slug, 711 Somerset Lane, P.O. Box 8223, Forest City, CA 94404/415-345-7677
Salute Cannons, Naval Co., R.D. 2, 4747 Cold Spring Creamery Rd., Doylestown, PA 18901
Sav-Bore, Saunders Sptg. Gds., 338 Somerset St., N. Plainfield, NJ 07060
Scrimshaw Engraving, C. Milton Barringer, 244 Lakeview Terr., Palm Harbor, FL 33563/813-785-0088
Scrimshaw, G. Marek, P.O. Box 213, Westfield, MA 01086/413-568-9816
Sharpening Stones, A. G. Russell Co., 1705 Hiway 71 North, Springdale, AR 72764/501-751-7341 (Arkansas Oilstones)
Shell Catcher, Auto Strip Pak, 419 W. Magnolia Ave., Glendale, CA 91204/213-240-1745
Shooter's Porta Bench, Centrum Products Co., 443 Century, S.W., Grand Rapids, MI 49503/616-454-9424
Shooting Coats, 10-X Products Group, 2828 Forest Lane, Suite 1107, Dallas, TX 75234/214-243-4016
Shooting Glasses, Bilsom Intl., Inc., 11800 Sunrise Valley Dr., Reston, VA 22091/703-620-3950
Shooting Glasses, Willson Safety Prods. Division, P.O. Box 622, Reading, PA 19603
Shotgun Barrel, Pennsylvania Arms Co., Box 128, Duryea, PA 18642/717-457-0845 (rifled)
Shotgun bore, Custom Shootg. Prods., 8505 K St., Omaha, NE 68127
Shotgun Case Accessories, AC Enterprises, P.O. Box 448, Edenton, NC 27932/919-482-4992 (British-made Charlton)
Shotgun Converter, Amimex Inc., 2660 John Montgomery Dr., Suite #3, San Jose, CA 95148/408-923-1720
Shotgun Ribs, Poly-Choke Div., Marble Arms Corp., 420 Industrial Park, Gladstone, MI 49837/906-428-3710
Shotgun Sight, bi-ocular, Trius Prod., Box 25, Cleves, OH 45002
Shotgun Specialist, Moneymaker Guncraft, 1420 Military Ave., Omaha, NE 68131/402-556-0226 (ventilated, free-floating ribs)
Shotshell Adapter, PC Co., 5942 Secor Rd., Toledo, OH 43623/419-472-6222 (Plummer 410 converter)
Shotshell Adapter, Jesse Ramos, Box 7105, La Puente, CA 91744 (12 ga./410 converter)
Snap Caps, Edwards Recoil Reducer, 269 Herbert St., Alton, IL 62002/618-462-3257
Sportsman's Chair, Ted Devlet's Custom Purveyors, P.O. Box 886, Fort Lee, NJ 07024/201-886-0196
Springfield Safety Pin, B-Square Co., P.O. Box 11281, Ft. Worth, TX 76110/800-433-2909
Springs, W. C. Wolff Co., Box 232, Ardmore, PA 19003/215-647-1880
Stock Duplicating Machine, Don Allen, Inc., HC55, Box 322, Sturgis, SD 47785/605-347-4686
Supersound, Edmund Scientific Co., 101 E. Gloucester Pike, Barrington, NJ 08007/609-547-3488 (safety device)

Swivels, Michaels, P.O. Box 13010, Portland, OR 97213/503-255-6890
Swivels, Sile Dist., 7 Centre Market Pl., New York, NY 10013/212-925-4111
Swivels, Williams Gun Sight Co., 7389 Lapeer Rd., Davison, MI 48423
Tomahawks, H&B Forge Co., Rt. 2, Shiloh, OH 44878/419-896-2075
Tree Stand, Portable, Advanced Hunting Equipment Inc., P.O. Box 1277, Cumming, GA 30130/404-887-1171 (tree lounge)
Tree Stand, Climbing, Amacker Prods., P.O. Box 1432; 602 Kimbrough Dr., Tallulah, LA 71282/318-574-4903
Tree Steps, Deer Me Products Co., Box 34, 1208 Park St., Anoka, MN 55303/612-421-8971
Trophies, Blackinton & Co., P.O. Box 1300, Attleboro Falls, MA 02763
Trophies, F. H. Noble & Co., 888 Tower Rd., Mundelein, IL 60060
Walking Sticks, Lifeline Industries, P.O. Box 771, Santa Monica, CA 90406
Warning Signs, Delta Ltd., P.O. Box 777, Mt. Ida, AR 71957
World Hunting Info., Jack Atcheson & Sons, Inc., 3210 Ottawa St., Butte, MT 59701
World Hunting Info., J/B Adventures & Safaris, Inc., 5655 So. Yosemite St., Suite 200, Englewood CO 80111/303-771-0977
World Hunting Info., Wayne Preston, Inc., 3444 Northhaven Rd., Dallas, TX 75229/214-358-4477

MUZZLE-LOADING GUNS, BARRELS or EQUIPMENT

Luther Adkins, Box 281, Shelbyville, IN 46176/317-392-3795 (breech plugs)
Allen Firearms Co., 2879 All Trades Rd., Santa Fe, NM 87501/505-471-6090
Anderson Mfg. Co., Union Gap Sta. P.O. Box 3120, Yakima, WA 98903/509-453-2349 (Flame-N-Go fusil; Accra-Shot)
Antique Arms Co., David F. Saunders, 1110 Cleveland, Monett, MO 65708/417-235-6501
Antique Gun Parts, Inc., 1118 S. Braddock Ave., Pittsburgh, PA 15218/412-241-1811 (parts)
Armoury, Inc., Rte. 202, New Preston, CT 06777
Armsport, Inc., 3590 N.W. 49th St., Miami, FL 33142/305-635-7850
Arm Tech, Armament Technologies Inc., 240 Sargent Dr., New Haven, CT 06511/203-562-2543 (22-cal. derringers)
Bauska Rifle Barrels, Inc., 105-9th Ave. West, Box 511, Kalispell, MT 59901/406-755-2635
Beaver Lodge, 9245 16th Ave. S.W., Seattle, WA 98106/206-763-1698
Beeman Precision Arms, Inc., 47-GDD Paul Dr., San Rafael, CA 94903/415-472-7121
Blackhawk East, C2274 POB, Loves Park, IL 61131/815-633-7784 (black powder)
Blackhawk West, Box 285, Hiawatha, KS 66434 (blck powder)
Blue and Gray Prods., Inc. RD #6, Box 362, Wellsboro, PA 16901/717-724-1383 (equipment)
Jim Brobst, 299 Poplar St., Hamburg, PA 19526/215-562-2103 (ML rifle bbls.)
Ted Buckland, 361 Flagler Rd., Nordland, WA 98358/206-385-2142 (custom only)
Butler Creek Corp., Box GG, Jackson Hole, WY 83001/307-733-3599 (poly & maxi patch)
C.N.S. Co., P.O. Box 238, Mohegan Lake, NY 10547
Cache La Poudre Rifleworks, 168 N. College, Ft. Collins, CO 80521/303-482-6913 (custom muzzleloaders)
Challanger Mfg. Co., 118 Pearl St., Mt. Vernon, NY 10550
R. MacDonald Champlin, P.O. Box 693, Manchester, NH 03105/603-483-8557 (custom muzzleloaders)
Chopie Mfg. Inc., 700 Copeland Ave., LaCrosse, WI 54601/608-784-0926 (nipple wrenches)
Connecticut Valley Arms Co. (CVA), 5988 Peachtree East, Norcross, GA 30092/404-449-4687 (kits also)
Earl T. Cureton, Rte. 2, Box 388, Willoughby Rd., Bulls Gap, TN 37711/615-235-2854 (powder horns)
Homer L. Dangler, Box 254, Addison, MI 49220/517-547-6745
Leonard Day & Co., P.O. Box 723, East Hampton, MA 01027/413-527-7990
Dixie Gun Works, Inc., P.O. Box 130, Union City, TN 38261
Dixon Muzzleloading Shop, Inc., RD #1, Box 175, Kempton, PA 19529/215-756-6271
Peter Dyson Ltd., 29-31 Church St., Honley, Huddersfield, W. Yorksh. HD7 2AH, England/0484-661062 (acc. f. ML shooter replicas)
EMF Co., Inc., 1900 E. Warner Ave. 1-D, Santa Ana, CA 92705/714-966-0202
Euroarms of America, Inc., P.O. Box 3277, 1501 Lenoir Dr., Winchester, VA 22601/703-662-1863
Excam, Inc., 4480 E. 11th Ave., Hialeah, FL 33012
Andy Fautheree, P.O. Box 863, Pagosa Springs, CO 81147/303-264-2892 (cust. ML)
Ted Fellowes, Beaver Lodge, 9245 16th Ave. S.W., Seattle, WA 98106/206-763-1698
Firearms Imp. & Exp. Corp., (F.I.E.), P.O. Box 4866, Hialeah Lakes, Hialeah, FL 33014/305-685-5966
Marshall F. Fish, Rt. 22 N., Westport, NY 12993/518-962-4897 (antique ML repairs)
The Flintlock Muzzle Loading Gun Shop, 1238 "G" So. Beach Blvd., Anaheim, CA 92804/714-821-6655
Forster Prods., 82 E. Lanark Ave., Lanark, IL 61046/815-493-6360
Frontier, 2910 San Bernardo, Laredo, TX 78040/512-723-5409 (powderhorns)
C. R. & D. E. Getz, Box 88, Beavertown, PA 17813 (barrels)
GOEX, Inc., Belin Plant, Moosic, PA 18507/717-457-6724 (black powder)
Golden Age Arms Co., 14 W. Winter St., Delaware, OH 43015 (ctlg. $2.50)
A. R. Goode, 4125 N.E. 28th Terr., Ocala, FL 32670/904-622-9575 (ML rifle barrels.)
Green Mountain Rifle Barrel Co., Inc., RFD 1, Box 184, Center Ossipee, NH 03814/603-539-7721
Guncraft Inc., 117 W. Pipeline, Hurst, TX 76053/817-282-6481
The Gun Works, 236 Main St., Springfield, OR 97477/503-741-4118 (supplies)
Hatfield Rifle Works, 2028 Frederick Ave., St. Joseph, MO 64501/816-279-8688 (squirrel rifle)
Hopkins & Allen, 3 Ethel Ave., P.O. Box 217, Hawthorne, NJ 07507/201-427-1165
The House of Muskets, Inc., 120 N. Pagosa Blvd., Pagosa Springs, CO 81147/303-264-2295 (ML bbls. & supplies)
Steven Dodd Hughes, P.O. Box 11455, Eugene, OR 97440/503-485-8869 (cust. guns)
JJJJ Ranch, Wm. Large, Rte. 1, State Route 243, Ironton, OH 45638/614-532-5298
Jennings-Hawken, 326½-4th St. N.W., Winter Haven, FL 33880
Jerry's Gun Shop, 9220 Odgen Ave., Brookfield, IL 60513/312-485-5200
LaChute Ltd., Box 48B, Masury, OH 44438/216-448-2236 (powder additive)
Morris Lawing, 150 Garland Ct., Charlotte, NC 28202/704-375-1740
Leding Loader, R.R. #1, Box 645, Ozark, AR 72949 (conical ldg. acc. f. ML)
Les' Gun Shop (Les Bauska), 105-9th West, P.O. Box 511, Kalispell, MT 59901/406-755-2635
Lever Arms Serv. Ltd., 572 Howe St., Vancouver, BC V6C 2E3, Canada
Log Cabin Sport Shop, 8010 Lafayette Rd., Lodi, OH 44254/216-948-1082 (ctlg. $3)
Lyman Products Corp., Rte. 147, Middlefield, CT 06455
McCann's Muzzle-Gun Works, 200 Federal City Rd., Pennington, NJ 08534/609-737-1707
McKeown's Sporting Arms, R.R. 4, Pekin, IL 61554/309-347-3559 (E-Z load rev. stand)
Mike Marsh, 6 Stanford Rd., Dronfield Woodhouse, Nr. Sheffield S18 SQJ, England (accessories)
Maurer Arms, 2154-16th St., Akron, OH 44314/216-745-6864 (cust. muzzleloaders)
Michigan Arms Corp., 363 Elmwood, Troy, MI 48084/313-583-1518
Mountain State Muzzleloading Supplies, Inc., Box 154-1, State Rt. 14 at Boaz, Williamstown, WV 26187/304-375-7842
Mowrey Gun Works, Inc., 800 Blue Mound Rd., Saginaw, TX 76131/817-281-5996
Muzzleloaders Etc., Inc., Jim Westberg, 9901 Lyndale Ave. S., Bloomington, MN 55420/612-884-1161
Numrich Corp., W. Hurley, NY 12491 (powder flasks)
Kirk Olson, Ft. Woolsey Guns, P.O. Box 2122, Prescott, AZ 86302/602-778-3035 (powderhorns)
Olde Pennsylvania, P.O. Box 17419, Penn Hills, PA 15235 (black powder suppl.)
Oregon Trail Riflesmiths, Inc., P.O. Box 45212, Boise, ID 83711
Ox-Yoke Originals, 130 Griffin Rd., West Suffield, CT 06093/203-668-5110 (dry lubr. patches)
Ozark Mountain Arms Inc., P.O. Box 397, 141 Byrne St., Ashdown, AR 71822/501-989-2345 (rifles)
Pecos Valley Armory, 1022 So. Canyon, Carlsbad, NM 88220/505-887-6023
A. W. Peterson Gun Shop, 1693 Old Hwy. 441 N., Mt. Dora, FL 32757 (ML guns)
Phyl-Mac, 609 N.E. 104th Ave., Vancouver, WA 98664/206-256-0579 (cust. charger)
Provider Arms, Inc., 261 Haglund Rd., Chesterton, IN 46304/219-879-5590 (Predator rifle)
R.V.I., P.O. Box 1439 Stn. A, Vancouver, B.C. V6C 1AO, Canada (high grade BP acc.)
Richland Arms, 321 W. Adrian St., Blissfield, MI 49228
Salish House, Inc., P.O. Box 383, Lakeside, MT 55922/406-844-3625
H. M. Schoeller, 569 So. Braddock Ave., Pittsburgh, PA 15221
Shiloh Products, 181 Plauderville Ave., Garfield, NJ 07026 (4-cavity mould)
Shore Galleries, Inc., 3318 W. Devon Ave., Chicago, IL 60645/312-676-2900
Sile Distributors, 7 Centre Market Pl., New York, NY 10013/213-925-4111
C. E. Siler Locks, 7 Acton Woods Rd., Candler, NC 28715/704-667-2376 (flint locks)
C. Sharps Arms Co., Inc., P.O. Box 885, Big Timber, MT 59011/406-932-4353
Ken Steggles, see: Mike Marsh
The Swampfire Shop, 1693 Old Hwy. 441 N., Mt. Dora, FL 32757/904-383-0595
Tennessee Valley Arms, P.O. Box 2022, Union City, TN 38261/901-885-4456
Tennessee Valley Mfg., P.O. Box 1125, Corinth, MS 38834 (powderhorns)
Ten-Ring Precision, Inc., 1449 Blue Crest Lane, San Antonio, TX 78232/512-494-3063
Traditions, Inc., Saybrook Rd., Haddam, CT 06438 (guns, kits, accessories)
Treso Inc., P.O. Box 4640, Pagosa Springs, CO 81157 (accessories)
Upper Missouri Trading Co., Box 191, Crofton, NE 68730/402-388-4844
J. S. Weeks & Son, 4748 Bailey Rd., Dimondale, MI 48821/517-636-0591 (supplies)
Fred Wells, Wells Sport Store, 110 N. Summit St., Prescott, AZ 86301/602-445-3655
W. H. Wescomb, P.O. Box 488, Glencoe, CA 95232/209-293-7010 (parts)
Thos. F. White, 5801 Westchester Ct., Worthington OH 43085/614-888-0128 (powder horn)
Williamson-Pate Gunsmith Serv., 117 W. Pipeline, Hurst, TX 76053/817-268-2887
Winchester Sutler, Siler Route, Box 393-E, Winchester, VA 22601/703-888-3595 (haversacks)
York County Gun Works, R.R. #4, Tottenham, Ont. LOG 1WO, Canada (locks)

PISTOLSMITHS

Armament Gunsmithing Co., Inc., 525 Route 22, Hillside, NJ 07205/201-686-0960
Armson, Inc., P.O. Box 2130, Farmington Hills, MI 48018/313-478-2577
Baer Custom Guns, 1725 Minesite Rd., Allentown, PA 18103/215-398-2362 (accurizing 45 autos and Comp II Syst.; cust. XP100s, P.P.C. rev.)
Bain and Davis Sptg. Gds., 307 E. Valley Blvd., San Gabriel, CA 91776/213-573-4241
Lee Baker, 7252 East Ave. U-3, Littlerock, CA 93543/805-944-4487 (cust. blue)
Bar-Sto Precision Machine, 73377 Sullivan Rd., Twentynine Palms, CA 92277/619-367-2747(S.S. bbls. f. 45 ACP)
Barta's Gunsmithing, 10231 US Hwy. #10, Cato, WI 54206/414-732-4472
R. J. Beal, Jr., 170 W. Marshall Rd., Lansdowne, PA 19050/215-259-1220 (conversions, SASE f. inquiry)

Behlert Custom Guns, Inc., RD 2 Box 36C, Route 611 North, Pipersville, PA 18947/215-766-8680 (short actions)
Bell's Custom Shop, 3309 Mannheim Rd., Franklin Park, IL 60131/312-678-1900
Bob's Gun & Tackle Shop, 746 Granby St., Norfolk, VA 23510/804-627-8311
F. Bob Chow, Gun Shop, Inc., 3185 Mission, San Francisco, CA 94110/415-282-8358
Brown Custom Guns, Inc., Steven N. Brown, 8810 Rocky Ridge Rd., Indianapolis, IN 46217/317-881-2771 aft. 5 PM
Leo Bustani, P.O. Box 8125, W. Palm Beach, FL 33407/305-622-2710
Dick Campbell, 1198 Finn Ave., Littleton, CO 80124/303-799-0145 (PPC guns; custom)
Cellini's, Francesca Inc., 3115 Old Ranch Rd., San Antonio, TX 78217/512-826-2584
D&D Gun Shop, 363 Elmwood, Troy, MI 48083/313-583-1512
Dave Chicoine, d/b/a Liberty A.S.P., 19 Key St., Eastport, ME 04631/207-853-2327 (rep. & rest. of early S&W prods.)
Davis Co., 2793 Del Monte St., West Sacramento, CA 95691/916-372-6789
Day Arms Corp., 2412 S.W. Loop 410, San Antonio, TX 78227/512-674-5220
Dominic DiStefano, 4303 Friar Lane, Colorado Springs, CO 80907/303-599-3366 (accurizing)
Duncan's Gunworks Inc., 1619 Grand Ave., San Marcos, CA 92069/619-727-0515
Dan Dwyer, 915 W. Washington, San Diego, CA 92103/619-296-1501
Englishtown Sptg. Gds. Co., Inc., David J. Maxham, 38 Main St., Englishtown, NJ 07726/201-446-7717
Jack First Distributors, Inc., 44633 Sierra Hwy., Lancaster, CA 93534/805-945-8961
John Fordham, Box 9 Dial Star Rte., P.O. Box 1093, Blue Ridge, GA 30513/404-632-3602
Fountain Prods., 492 Prospect Ave., W. Springfield, MA 01089/413-781-4651
Frielich Police Equipment, 396 Broome St., New York, NY 10013/212-254-3045
Giles' 45 Shop, 8614 Tarpon Springs Rd., Odessa, FL 33556/813-920-5366
Gilman-Mayfield, 1552 N. 1st., Fresno, CA 93703/209-237-2500
The Gunworks Inc., John Hanus, 3434 Maple Ave., Brookfield, IL 60513/312-387-7888
Gil Hebard Guns, Box 1, Knoxville, IL 61448
Paul Jaeger, Inc., P.O. Box 449, 1 Madison Ave., Grand Junction, TN 38039
J. D. Jones, Rt. 1, Della Dr., Bloomingdale, OH 43910/614-264-0176
L. E. Jurras & Assoc., P.O. Box 680, Washington, IN 47501/812-254-7698
Kart Sptg. Arms Corp., 1190 Old Country Rd., Riverhead, NY 11901/516-727-2719 (handgun conversions)
Ken's Gun Specialties, Rt. 1 Box 147, Lakeview, AR 72642/501-431-5606
Benjamin Kilham, Kilham & Co., Main St., Box 37, Lyme, NH 03768/603-795-4112
Terry K. Kopp, Highway 13, Lexington, MO 64067/816-259-2636 (rebblg., conversions)
John G. Lawson, The Sight Shop, 1802 E. Columbia Ave., Tacoma, WA 98404/206-474-5465
Kent Lomont, 4236 West South, Poneto, IN 46781/219-694-6792 (Auto Mag only)
Mag-na-port International, Inc., 41302 Executive Drive, Mt. Clemens, MI 48045/313-469-6727
Robert A. McGrew, 3315 Michigan Ave., Colorado Springs, CO 80910/303-636-1940
Rudolf Marent, 9711 Tiltree, Houston, TX 77075/713-946-7028 (Hammerli)
Elwyn H. Martin, Martin's Gun Shop, 937 So. Sheridan Blvd., Lakewood, CO 80226/303-922-2184
Conley E. Morris, 2135 Waterlevel Hwy., Cleveland, TN 37311/615-476-3984
Robert L. Nassenstein, 4304 - 6th Ave., Tacoma, WA 98406/206-752-3107 (accurizing, custom 45 parts)
Nu-Line Guns, 1053 Caulks Hill Rd., Harvester, MO 63303/314-441-4501
Pachmayr Gun Works, 1220 S. Grand Ave., Los Angeles, CA 90015
Paterson Gunsmithing, 438 Main St., Paterson, NJ 07502/201-345-4100
RPS Gunshop,11 So. Haskell St., Central Point, OR 97502/503-664-5010
Bob Rogers Gunsmithing, P.O. Box 305, Franklin Grove, IL 61031/815-456-2685 (custom)
SSK Industries (See: J. D. Jones)
L. W. Seecamp Co., Inc., Box 255, New Haven, CT 06502/203-877-3429 (DA Colt auto conversions)
Hank Shows, dba The Best, 1078 Alice Ave., Ukiah, CA 95482/707-462-9060
Silver Dollar Guns, P.O. Box 475, 10 Frances St., Franklin, NH 03235/603-934-3292 (45 ACP)
Spokhandguns Inc., Vern D. Ewer, P.O. Box 370, 1206 Fig St., Benton City, WA 99320
Sportsmens Equipmt. Co., 915 W. Washington, San Diego, CA 92103/619-296-1501 (specialty limiting trigger motion in autos)
Irving O. Stone, Jr., 73377 Sullivan Rd., Twentynine Palms, CA 92277/619-367-2747
Victor W. Strawbridge, 6 Pineview Dr., Dover Pt., Dover, NH 03820
A. D. Swenson's 45 Shop, P.O. Box 606, Fallbrook, CA 92028
Trapper Gun, 18717 East 14 Mile Rd., Fraser, MI 48026/313-792-0134
Dennis A. "Doc" Ulrich, 2209 So. Central Ave., Cicero, IL 60650/312-652-3606
Vic's Gun Refinishing, 6 Pineview Dr., Dover, NH 03820/603-742-0013
Walters Industries, 6226 Park Lane, Dallas, TX 75225/214-691-5150

REBORING AND RERIFLING

P.O. Ackley (See Dennis M. Bellm Gunsmithing, Inc.)
Atkinson Gun Co., P.O. Box 512, Prescott, AZ 86301
Dennis M. Bellm Gunsmithing Inc., 2376 So. Redwood Rd., Salt Lake City, UT 84119/801-974-0697 (price list $3; rifle only)
Mark Chanlynn, Rocky Mtn. Rifle Works, Ltd., 1707-14th St., Boulder CO 80302/303-443-9189
Dave Chicoine, d/b/a Liberty A.S.P., 19 Key St., Eastport, ME 04631/207-853-2327 (reline handgun bbls.)
A. R. Goode, 4125 N.E. 28th Terr., Ocala, FL 32760/904-622-9575
H-S Precision, Inc., 112 N. Summit, Prescott, AZ 85302/602-445-0607
Terry K. Kopp, Highway 13, Lexington, MO 64067/816-259-2636 (Invis-A-Line bbl.; relining)
Les' Gun Shop, (Les Bauska), 105-9th West, P.O. Box 511, Kalispell, MT 59901/406-755-2635
Matco, Inc., 126 E. Main St., No. Manchester, IN 46962/219-982-8282
Nu-Line Guns, 1053 Caulks Hill Rd., Harvester, MO 63303/314-441-4500 (handguns)
Redman's Reboring & Rerifling, Route 3, Box 330A, Omak, WA 98841/509-826-5512
Siegrist Gun Shop, 8752 Turtle Rd., Whittemore, MI 48770/517-873-3929
Snapp's Gunshop, 6911 E. Washington Rd., Clare, MI 48617
J. W. Van Patten, P.O. Box 145, Foster Hill, Milford, PA 18337/717-296-7069
Fred Wells, Wells Sport Store, 110 N. Summit St., Prescott, AZ 86301/602-445-3655
Robt. G. West, 27211 Huey Lane, Eugene, OR 97402/503-689-6610

RELOADING TOOLS AND ACCESSORIES

Activ Industries, Inc., P.O. Box 238, Kearneysville, WV 25430/304-725-0451 (plastic hulls, wads)
Advance Car Mover Co., Inc., Rowell Div., P.O. Box 1181, 112 N. Outagamie St., Appleton, WI 54912/414-734-1878 (bottom pour lead casting ladles)
Accessory Specialty Co., 2711 So. 84th St., West Allis, WI 53227/414-545-0879 (Reload-a-stand)
Advanced Precision Prods. Co., 5183 Flintrock Dr., Westerville, OH 43081/614-895-0560 (case super luber)
American Wad Co., P&P Tool, 125 W. Market St., Morrison, IL 61270/815-772-7618 (12-ga. shot wad)
Ammo Load Inc., 1560 E. Edinger, Suite G, Santa Ana, CA 92705/714-558-8858
Anderson Mfg. Co., R.R.1, Royal, IA 51357/712-933-5542 (Shotshell Trimmers)
C'Arco, P.O. Box 308, Highland, CA 92346/714-862-8311 (Ransom "Grand Master" progr. loader)
Colorado Sutler Arsenal, 6225 W. 46th Pl., Wheatridge, CO 80033/303-420-6383
Creighton Audette, 19 Highland Circle, Springfield, VT 05156/802-885-2331 (Universal Case Selection gauge)
B-Square Eng. Co., Box 11281, Ft. Worth, TX 76110/800-433-2909
Ballistic Prods., P.O. Box 488, 2105 Shaughnessy Circle, Long Lake, MN 55356/612-473-1550
Ballistic Research Industries (BRI), 2825 S. Rodeo Gulch Rd. #8, Soquel, CA 95073/408-476-7981 (shotgun slug)
Bear Machine Co., 2110 1st Natl. Tower, Akron, OH 44308/216-253-4039
Belding & Mull, Inc., P.O. Box 428, 100 N. 4th St., Philipsburg, PA 16866/814-342-0607
Berdon Machine Co., Box 483, Hobart, WA 98025/206-392-1866 (metallic press)
Blackhawk East, Dowman Greene, C2274 POB, Loves Park, IL 61131/815-633-7784
Blackhawk West, R. L. Hough, Box 285, Hiawatha, KS 66434/303-366-3659
Bonanza Sports, Inc., 412 Western Ave., Faribault, MN 55021/507-332-7153
Gene Bowlin, Rt. 1, Box 890, Snyder, TX 79549/915-573-2323 (arbor press)
Brown Precision Co., P.O. Box 270W, 7786 Molinos Ave., Los Molinos, CA 96055/916-384-2506 (Little Wiggler)
C-H Tool & Die Corp., 106 N. Harding St., Owen, WI 54460/715-229-2146
Camdex, Inc., 2228 Fourteen Mile Rd., Warren, MI 48092/313-977-1620
Carbide Die & Mfg. Co., Inc., 15615 E. Arrow Hwy., Irwindale, CA 91706/213-337-2518
Carter Gun Works, 2211 Jefferson Pk. Ave., Charlottesville, VA 22903
Cascade Cartridge, Inc., (See: Omark)
Cascade Shooters, 60916 McMullin Dr., Bend, OR 97702/503-389-5872 (bull. seating depth gauge)
Central Products f. Shooters, 435 Route 18, East Brunswick, NJ 08816 (neck turning tool)
Chevron Case Master, R.R. 1, Ottawa, IL 61350
Lester Coats, 416 Simpson Ave., No. Bend, OR 97459/503-756-6995 (core cutter)
Container Development Corp., 424 Montgomery St., Watertown, WI 53094
Continental Kite & Key Co., (CONKKO) P.O. Box 40, Broomall, PA 19008/215-356-0711 (primer pocket cleaner)
Cooper-Woodward, Box 972, Riverside, CA 92502/714-683-4295 (Perfect Lube)
Corbin Mfg. & Supply Inc., P.O. Box 2659, White City, OR 97503/503-826-5211
Custom Products, RD #1, Box 483A, Saegertown, PA 16443/814-763-2769 (decapping tool, dies, etc.)
J. Dewey Mfg. Co., 186 Skyview Dr., Southbury, CT 06488/203-264-3064
Dillon Precision Prods., Inc., 7442 E. Butherus Dr., Scottsdale, AZ 85260/602-948-8009
Division Lead Co., 7742 W. 61st Pl., Summit, IL 60502
Eagle Products Co., 1520 Adelia Ave., So. El Monte, CA 91733
Edmisten Co. Inc., P.O. Box 1293, Hwy 105, Boone, NC 28607/704-264-1490 (I-Dent-A Handloader's Log)
Efemes Enterprises, P.O. Box 122M, Bay Shore, NY 11706 (Berdan decapper)
Eldora Plastics, Inc., P.O. Box 127, Eldora, IA 50627/515-848-2634 (Lage Uniwad)
W. H. English, 4411 S. W. 100th, Seattle, WA 98146 (Paktool)
Fitz, Box 171, Douglas City, CA 96024 (Fitz Flipper)
Flambeau Prods. Corp., 15981 Valplast Rd., Middlefield, OH 44062/216-632-1631
Forster Products Inc., 82 E. Lanark Ave., Lanark IL 61046/815-493-6360
Francis Tool Co., P.O. Box 7861, Eugene, OR 97401/503-746-4831 (powder measure)
Freechec' (See: Paco)
Geo. M. Fullmer, 2499 Mavis St., Oakland, CA 94601/415-533-4193 (seating die)
Gene's Gun Shop, Rt. 1, Box 890, Snyder, TX 79549/915-573-2323 (arbor press)

Gopher Shooter's Supply, Box 278, Faribault, MN 55021
Hart Products, Rob W. Hart & Son Inc., 401 Montgomery St., Nescopeck, PA 18635
Hensley & Gibbs, P.O. Box 10, Murphy, OR 97533/503-862-2341 (bullet moulds)
Richard Hoch, The Gun Shop, 62778 Spring Creek Rd., Montrose, CO 81401/303-249-3625 (custom Schuetzen bullet moulds)
Hoffman New Ideas Inc., 821 Northmoor Rd., Lake Forest, IL 60045/312-234-4075 (spl. gallery load press)
Hollywood Loading Tools, Inc., 7311 Radford Ave., No. Hollywood, CA 91605/213-875-1131
Hornady Mfg. Co., P.O. Drawer 1848, Grand Island, NE 68802/308-382-1390
Hulme see: Marshall Enterprises (Star case feeder)
Huntington, P.O. Box 991, Oroville, CA 95965/916-534-1210 (Compact Press)
Independent Mach. & Gun Shop, 1416 N. Hayes, Pocatello, ID 83201/208-232-1264
Javelina Products, Box 337, San Bernardino, CA 92402 (Alox beeswax)
Neil Jones, RD #1, Box 483A, Saegertown, PA 16433/814-763-2769 (decapping tool, dies)
Paul Jones Munitions Systems (See Fitz Co.)
King & Co., Edw. R. King, Box 1242, Bloomington, IL 61701/309-473-3558
Lage Uniwad Co., 1102 N. Washington St., Eldora, IA 50627 (Universal Shotshell Wad)
Leding Loader, R.R. #1, Box 645, Ozark, AR 72949 (conical loadg. acc. f. ML)
Lee Custom Engineering, Inc. (See Mequon Reloading Corp.)
Lee Precision, Inc., 4275 Hwy. U, Hartford, WI 53027/414-673-3075
L. L. F. Die Shop, 1281 Highway 99 N., Eugene, OR 97402/503-688-5753
Dean Lincoln, Custom Tackle & Ammo, P.O. Box 1886, Farmington, NM 87401 (mould)
Ljutic Industries, 918 N. 5th Ave., Yakima, WA 98902/505-632-3539
Lock's Phila. Gun Exch., 6700 Rowland, Philadelphia, PA 19149/215-332-6225
Lyman Products Corp., Rte. 147, Middlefield, CT 06455
McKillen & Heyer Inc., 37603 Arlington Dr., Box 627, Willoughby, OH 44094/216-942-2491 (case gauge)
Paul McLean, 2670 Lakeshore Blvd., W., Toronto, Ont. M8V 1G8 Canada/416-259-3060 (Universal Cartridge Holder)
MEC, Inc. (See Mayville Eng. Co.)
MSS Industries, P.O. Box 6, River Grove, IL 60171
MTM Molded Products Co., 3370 Obco Ct., P.O. Box 14117, Dayton, OH 45414/513-890-7461
Magma Eng. Co., P.O. Box 161, Queen Creek, AZ 85242
Marmel Prods., P.O. Box 97, Utica, MI 48087/313-731-8029 (Marvelube, Marvelux)
Marquart Precision Co., P.O. Box 1740, Prescott, AZ 86302/602-445-5646 (precision case-neck turning tool)
Marshall Enterprises, 792 Canyon Rd., Redwood City, CA 94062/415-365-1230 (Hulme autom. case feeder f. Star rel.)
Mayville Eng. Co., 715 South St., Mayville, WI 53050/414-387-4500 (shotshell loader)
Mequon Reloading Corp., P.O. Box 253, Mequon, WI 53092/414-673-3060
Merit Gun Slight Co., P.O. Box 995, Sequim, WA 98382/206-683-6127
Multi-Scale Charge Ltd., P.O. Box 309 LPO, Niagara Falls, NY 14304/416-276-6292
Normington Co., Box 6, Rathdrum, ID 83858 (powder baffles)
Northeast Industrial Inc., N.E.I., P.O. Box 249, 405 N. Canyon Blvd., Canyon City, OR 97820/503-575-2513 (bullet mould)
Ohaus Scale, (See RCBS)
Omark Industries, Box 856, Lewiston, ID 83501/208-746-2351
P&P Tool Co., 125 W. Market St., Morrison, IL 61270/815-772-7618 (12-ga. shot wad)
Pacific Tool Co., P.O. Box 2048, Ordnance Plant Rd., Grand Island, NE 68801/308-384-2308
Paco, Box 17211, Tucson, AZ 85731 (Freechec' tool for gas checks)
Pak-Tool Co., 4411 S.W. 100th, Seattle, WA 98146
Pitzer Tool Mfg. Co., RR #3, Box 50, Winterset, IA 50273/515-462-4268 (bullet lubricator & sizer)
Plum City Ballistics Range, Norman E. Johnson, Rte. 1, Box 29A, Plum City, WI 54761/715-647-2539
Marian Powley, Petra Lane, R.R.1, Eldridge, IA 52748/319-285-9214
Precise Alloys Inc., 406 Hillside Ave., New Hyde Park, NY 11040/516-354-8860 (chilled lead shot; bullet wire)
Quinetics Corp., P.O. Box 29007, San Antonio, TX 78229/516-684-8561 (kinetic bullet puller)
RCBS, Inc., Box 1919, Oroville, CA 95965/916-533-5191
Redding Inc., 114 Starr Rd., Cortland, NY 13045
Reloaders Paper Supply, Don Doerksen, P.O. Box 556, Hines, OR 97738/503-573-7060 (reloader's record book)
Rifle Ranch, Rte. 10, 3301 Willow Creek Rd., Prescott, AZ 86301/602-778-7501
Rochester Lead Works, 76 Anderson Ave., Rochester, NY 14607/716-442-8500 (leadwire)
Rorschach Precision Prods., P.O. Box 151613, Irving, TX 75015/214-790-3487 (carboloy bull. dies)
Rotex Mfg. Co. (See Texan)
SAECO Rel. 2207 Border Ave., Torrance, CA 90501/213-320-6973
SSK Industries, Rt. 1, Della Drive, Bloomingdale, OH 43910/614-264-0176 (primer tool)
Sandia Die & Cartridge Co., Rte. 5, Box 5400, Albuquerque, NM 87123/505-298-5729
Shannon Associates, P.O. Box 32737, Oklahoma City, OK 73123
Shooters Accessory Supply, (See Corbin Mfg. & Supply)
Jerry Simmons, 715 Middlebury St., Goshen, IN 46526/219-533-8546 (Pope de- & recapper)
J. A. Somers Co., P.O. Box 49751, Los Angeles, CA 90049 (Jasco)
Sport Flite Mfg., Inc., 2520 Industrial Row, Troy, MI 48084/313-280-0648 (swaging dies)
Star Machine Works, 418 10th Ave., San Diego, CA 92101/619-232- 3216
Texan Reloaders, Inc., 444 So. Cips St., Watseka, IL 60970/815-432-5065
Trico Plastics, 590 S. Vincent Ave., Azusa, CA 91702
Tru Square Metal Products, P.O. Box 585, Auburn, WA 98002/206-833-2310 (Thumler's tumbler case polishers; Ultra Vibe 18)
Vibra-Tek, 1022 So. Tejon, Colorado Springs, CO 80903/303-634-8611 (brass polisher; Brite Rouge)
WAMADET, Silver Springs, Goodleigh, Barnstaple, Devon, England
Weatherby, Inc., 2781 Firestone Blvd., South Gate, CA 90280/213-569-7186
Weaver Arms Corp., 115 No. Market St., Escondido, CA 92025/619-746-2440 (progr. loader)
Webster Scale Mfg. Co., P.O. Box 188, Sebring, FL 33870/813-385-6362
Whits Shooting Stuff, P.O. Box 1340, Cody, WY 82414
L. E. Wilson, Inc. P.O. Box 324, 404 Pioneer Ave., Cashmere, WA 98815/509-782-1328
Zenith Enterprises, 5781 Flagler Rd., Nordland, WA 98358/206-385-2142

RESTS—BENCH, PORTABLE, ETC.

B-Square Co., P.O. Box 11281, Ft. Worth, TX 76109/800-433-2909 (handgun)
Jim Brobst, 299 Poplar St., Hamburg, PA 19526/215-562-2103 (bench rest pedestal)
Bullseye Shooting Bench, 6100 - 40th St. Vancouver, WA 98661/206-694-6141 (portable)
C'Arco, P.O. Box 308, Highland, CA 92346/714-862-8311 (Ransom handgun rest)
Centrum Products Co., 443 Century S.W., Grand Rapids, MI 49503/616-454-9424 (Porta Bench)
Philip Cooley, 34 Bay Ridge Ave., Brooklyn, NY 11220/212-745-9311
Cravener's Gun Shop, 1627 - 5th Ave., Ford City, PA 16226/412-763-8312 (portable)
Decker Shooting Products, 1729 Laguna Ave., Schofield, WI 54476 (rifle rests)
Garbini Loga Systems, St. Galler Str. 72, CH-9325 Roggwill TG, Switzerland
The Gun Case, 11035 Maplefield, El Monte, CA 91733
Joe Hall's Shooting Products, Inc., 443 Wells Rd., Doylestown, PA 18901/215-345-6354 (adj. portable)
Harris Engineering, Inc., Barlow, KY 42024/502-334-3633 (bipods)
Rob. W. Hart & Son, 401 Montgomery St., Nescopeck, PA 18635
Tony Hidalgo, 12701 S.W. 9th Pl., Davie, FL 33325/305-476-7645 (adj. shooting seat)
J. B. Holden Co., 295 W. Pearl, Plymouth, MI 48170/313-455-4850
Hoppe's Div., Penguin Industries, Inc., Airport Industrial Mall, Coatesville, PA 19320/251-384-6000 (bench rests and bags)
North Star Devices, Inc., P.O. Box 2095, North St. Paul, MN 55109 (Gun Slinger)
Progressive Prods., Inc., P.O. Box 67, Holmen, WI 54636/608-526-3345 (Sandbagger rifle rest)
Protektor Model (see Tuller & Co.)
San Angelo Mfg. Co., 1841 Industrial Ave., San Angelo, TX 76904/915-655-7126
Suter's, Inc., House of Guns, 332 N. Tejon, Colorado Springs, CO 80902/303-635-1475
Tuller & Co., Basil Tuller, 29 Germania, Galeton, PA 16922/814-435-2442 (Protektor sandbags)
Turkey Creek Enterprises, Rt. 1, Box 65, Red Oak, OK 74563/918-754-2884 (portable shooting rest)
Wichita Arms, 444 Ellis, Wichita, KS 67211/316-265-06612

RIFLE BARREL MAKERS

P.O. Ackley Rifle Barrels (See Dennis M. Bellm Gunsmithing Inc.)
Atkinson Gun Co., P.O. Box 512, Prescott, AZ 86301
Jim Baiar, 490 Halfmoon Rd., Columbia Falls, MT 59912/406-892-4409
Bauska Rifle Barrels, Inc., 105-9th Ave. West, Kalispell, MT 59901/406-755-2635
Dennis M. Bellm Gunsmithing Inc., 2376 So. Redwood Rd., Salt Lake City, UT 84119/801-974-0697; price list $3 (new rifle bbls., incl. special & obsolete)
Leo Bustani, P.O. Box 8125, West Palm Beach, FL 33407/305-622-2710 (Win.92 take-down; Trapper 357-44 mag. bbls.)
Ralph L. Carter, Carter's Gun Shop, 225 G St., Penrose, CO 81240/303-372-6240
Mark Chanlynn, Rocky Mtn. Rifle Works, Ltd., 1707-14th St., Boulder, CO 80302/303-443-9189
Charles P. Donnelly & Son, Siskiyou Gun Works, 405 Kubli Rd., Grants Pass, OR 97527/503-846-6604
Douglas Barrels, Inc., 5504 Big Tyler Rd., Charleston, WV 25313/304-776-1341
Douglas Jackalope Gun & Sport Shop, Inc., 1048 S. 5th St., Douglas, WY 82633/307-358-3854
Federal Firearms Co., Inc., P.O. Box 145, Thoms Run Rd., Oakdale, PA 15071/412-221-0300
C. R. & D. E. Getz, Box 88, Beavertown, PA 17813
A. R. Goode, 4125 N.E. 28th Terr., Ocala, FL 32670/904-622-9575
Green Mountain Rifle Barrel Co., Inc., RFD 1 Box 184, Center Ossipee, NH 03814/603-539-7721
Half Moon Rifle Shop, 490 Halfmoon Rd., Columbia Falls, MT 59912/406-892-4409
H-S Precision, Inc., 112 N. Summit, Prescott, AZ 85302/602-445-0607
Hart Rifle Barrels, Inc., RD 2, Lafayette, NY 13084/315-677-9841
H&H Barrels Works, Inc., 1520 S.W. 5th Ave., Ocala, FL 32674/904-351-4200
Wm. H. Hobaugh, The Rifle Shop, Box M, Philipsburg, MT 59858/406-859-3515
Terry K. Kopp, Highway 13, Lexington, MO 64067/816-259-2636 (22-cal. blanks)
Les' Gun Shop, (Les Bauska), 105-9th West, P.O. Box 511, Kalispell, MT 59901/406-755-2635
Marquart Precision Co., P.O. Box 1740, Prescott, AZ 86302/602-445-5646
Matco, Inc., Box 349, 126 E. Main St., No. Manchester, IN 46962/219-982-8282
McMillan Rifle Barrel U.S. International, 3604 Old College Rd., Bryan, TX 77801/409-846-3990
Nu-Line Guns, 1053 Caulks Hill Rd., Harvester, MO 63303/314-441-4500
Numrich Arms, W. Hurley, NY 12491

Olympic Arms Inc. dba SGW, 624 Old Pacific Hwy. S.E., Olympia, WA 98503/206-456-3471
John T. Pell Octagon Barrels, (KOGOT), 410 College Ave., Trinidad, CO 81082/303-846-9406
Pennsylvania Arms Co., Box 128, Duryea, PA 18642/717-457-0845 (rifled shotgun bbl. only)
Redman's Rifling & Reboring, Rt. 3, Box 330A, Omak, WA 98841/509-826-5512
Sanders Cust. Gun Serv., 2358 Tyler Lane, Louisville, KY 40205
Gary Schneider, 12202 N. 62d Pl., Scottsdale, AZ 85254/602-948-2525
SGW, Inc., D. A. Schuetz, 624 Old Pacific Hwy. S.E., Olympia, WA 98503/206-456-3471
E. R. Shaw, Inc., Prestley & Thoms Run Rd., Bridgeville, PA 15017/412-221-3636
Shilen Rifles, Inc., 205 Metro Park Blvd., Ennis, TX 75119/214-875-5318
W. C. Strutz, Rifle Barrels, Inc., P.O. Box 611, Eagle River, WI 54521/715-479-4766
Fred Wells, Wells Sport Store, 110 N. Summit St., Prescott, AZ 86301/602-445-3655
Bob Williams, P.O. Box 143, Boonsboro, MD 21713
Wilson Arms, 63 Leetes Island Rd., Branford, CT 06405/203-488-7297

SCOPES, MOUNTS, ACCESSORIES, OPTICAL EQUIPMENT

A.R.M.S. (Atlantic Research Marketing Systems), 230 W. Center St., West Bridgewater, MA 02379/617-584-7816
Action Arms Ltd., P.O. Box 9573, Philadelphia, PA 19124/215-744-0100
Aimpoint U.S.A., 201 Elden St., Suite 302, Herndon, VA 22070/703-471-6828 (electronic sight)
Alley Suppl. Co., P.O. Box 848, Gardnerville, NV 89410/702-782-3800
The American Import Co., 1453 Mission, San Francisco, CA 94103/415-863-1506
Anderson Mfg. Co., Union Gap Sta. P.O. Box 3120, Yakima, WA 98903/509-453-2349 (lens cap)
Apollo Optics (See Senno Corp.)
Armsport, Inc., 3590 N.W. 49th St., Miami, FL 33122/305-635-7850
Armson, Inc., P.O. Box 2130, Farmington Hills, MI 48018/313-478-2577 (O.E.G.)
B-Square Co., Box 11281, Ft. Worth, TX 76109/800-433-2909 (Mini-14 mount)
Bausch & Lomb Inc., 1400 Goodman St., Rochester, NY 14602/716-338-6000
Beeman Inc., 47-GDD Paul Dr., San Rafael, CA 94903/415-472-7121
Bennett, 561 Delaware, Delmar, NY 12054/518-439-1862 (mounting wrench)
Lenard M. Brownell (See Billingsley & Brownell)
Browning Arms, Rt. 4, Box 624-B, Arnold, MO 63010
Buehler Scope Mounts, 17 Orinda Highway, Orinda, CA 94563/415-254-3201
Burris Co. Inc., 331 E. 8th St., Box 1747, Greeley, CO 80631/303-356-1670
Bushnell Optical Co., 2828 E. Foothill Blvd., Pasadena, CA 91107
Butler Creek Corp., Box GG, Jackson Hole, WY 83001/307-733-3599 (lens caps)
Kenneth Clark, 18738 Highway 99, Madera, CA 93637/209-674-6016
Clearview Mfg. Co., Inc. 20821 Grand River Ave., Detroit, MI 48219/313-535-0033 (mounts)
Colt Firearms, P.O. Box 1868, Hartford CT 06102/203-236-6311
Compass Instr. & Optical Co., Inc., 104 E. 25th St., New York, NY 10010
Conetrol Scope Mounts, Hwy 123 South, Seguin, TX 78155
Cougar Optics, P.O. Box 115, Groton, NY 13071/607-898-5754
D&H Prods. Co., Inc., 465 Denny Rd., Valencia, PA 16059/412-898-2840 (lens covers)
Davis Optical Co., P.O. Box 6, Winchester, IN 47934/317-584-5311
Del-Sports Inc., Main St., Margaretville, NY 12455/914-586-4103 (Kahles scopes; EAW mts.)
Dickson (See American Import Co.)
Flaig's, Babcock Blvd., Millvale, PA 15209
Fontaine Ind., Inc., 11552 Knott St., Suite 1, Garden Grove, CA 92641/714-898-9163
Freeland's Scope Stands, Inc., 3737 14th, Rock Island, IL 61201/309-788-7449
Griffin & Howe, Inc., 589 Broadway, New York, NY 10012/212-966-5323
Heckler & Koch, Inc., 14601 Lee Rd., Chantilly, VA 22021/703-631-2800
H.J. Hermann Leather Co., Rt. 1, Skiatook, OK 74070 (lens caps)
J.B. Holden Co., 295 W. Pearl, Plymouth, MI 48170/313-455- 4850
The Hutson Corp., 105 Century Dr., No., Mansfield, TX 76063/817-477-3421
Import Scope Repair Co., P.O. Box 2633, Durango, CO 81301/303-247-1422
Interarms, 10 Prince St., Alexandria, VA 22313
Paul Jaeger, Inc., P.O. Box 449, 1 Madison Ave., Grand Junction, TN 38039 (Schmidt & Bender; EAW mts., Noble)
Jason Empire Inc., 9200 Cody, P.O. Box 14930, Overland Park, KS 66214/913-888-0220
Jennison TCS (See Fontaine Ind., Inc.)
Kahles of America, Div. of Del-Sports, Inc., Main St., Margaretville, NY 12455/914-586-4103
Kenko Intl. Inc., 8141 West I-70 Frontage Rd. No., Arvada, CO 80002/303-425-1200
Kowa Optimed, Inc., 20001 S. Vermont Ave., Torrance, CA 90502/213-327-1913
Kris Mounts, 108 Lehigh St., Johnstown, PA 15905
Kwik-Site, 5555 Treadwell, Wayne, MI 48185/313-326-1500 (rings, mounts only)
T.K. Lee, 2830 S. 19th St., Off. #4, Birmingham, AL 35209/205-871-6065 (reticles)
E. Leitz, Inc., 24 Link Dr., Rockleigh, NJ 07647/201-767-1100
Leupold & Stevens Inc., P.O. Box 688, Beaverton, OR 97075/503-646-9171
Jake Levin and Son, Inc., 9200 Cody, Overland Park, KS 66214
W.H. Lodewick, 2816 N.E. Halsey, Portland, OR 97232/503-284-2554 (scope safeties)
Lyman Products Corp., Route 147, Middlefield, CT. 06455
Mandall Shooting Supplies, 7150 E. 4th St., Scottsdale, AZ 85252
Marble Arms Co., 420 Industrial Park, Gladstone, MI 49837/906-428-3710
Marlin Firearms Co., 100 Kenna Dr., New Haven, CO 06473
Robert Medaris, P.O. Box 309, Mira Loma, CA 91752/714-685-5666 (side mount f. H&K 91 & 93)
Millet Industries, 16131 Gothard St., Huntington Beach, CA 92647/714-842-5575 (mounts)
O.F. Mossberg & Sons, Inc., 7 Grasso Ave., North Haven, CT 06473
Nikon Inc., 633 Stewart Ave., Suite 1006, New York, NY 10022/212-605-0325
Nite-Site, Inc., P.O. Box O, Rosemount, MN 55068/612-890-7631
Numrich Arms, West Hurley, NY 12491
Nydar, (See Swain Nelson Co.)
Orchard Park Enterprise, P.O. Box 563, Orchard Park, NY 14127/716-662-2255 (Saddleproof mount)
Oriental Optical Co., 605 E. Walnut St., Pasadena, CA 91101/213-792-1252 (scope & binocular repairs)
Pachmayr Gun Works, 1220 S. Grand Ave., Los Angeles, CA 90015/213-748-7271
Ken Patable Enterprises, P.O. Box 19422, Louisville, KY 40219 (det. shotgun scope mount)
Pilkington Gun Co., P.O. Box 1296, Muskogee, OK 74402/918-693-9418 (Q. D. mt.)
Pioneer Marketing & Research Inc., 216 Haddon Ave. Suite 522, Westmont, NJ 08108/609-854-2424 (German Steiner binoculars; scopes)
Precise, 3 Chestnut, Suffern, NY 10901
Ram Line, Inc., 406 Violet St., Golden, CO 80401/303-279-0886 (see-thru mt. f. Mini-14)
Ranging, Inc., 90 Lincoln Rd. North, East Rochester, NY 14445/716-385-1250
Ray-O-Vac, Willson Prod. Div., P.O. Box 622, Reading, PA 19603 (shooting glasses)
Redfield Gun Sight Co., 5800 E. Jewell Ave., Denver, CO 80222/303-757-6411
S & K Mfg. Co., Box 247, Pittsfield, PA 16340/814-563-7808 (Insta-Mount)
SSK Industries, Rt. 1, Della Dr., Bloomingdale, OH 43910/614-264-0176 (bases)
Sanders Cust. Gun Serv., 2358 Tyler Lane, Louisville, KY 40205 (MSW)
Schmidt & Bender, see: Paul Jaeger, Inc.
Seattle Binocular & Scope Repair Co., P.O. Box 46094, Seattle, WA 98146
Senno Corp., 505 E. 3d, P.O. Box 3506, Spokane, WA 99220/800-541-5689
Sherwood Intl. Export Corp., 18714 Parthenia St., Northridge, CA 91324/818-349-7600 (mounts)
W.H. Siebert, 22720 S.E. 56th St., Issaquah, WA 98027
Simmons Outdoor Corp., 14205 S.W. 119 Ave., Miami, FL 33186/305-252-0477
Singlepoint (See Normark)
Southern Precision Inst. Co., 3419 E. Commerce St., San Antonio, TX 78219
Spacetron Inc., Box 84, Broadview, IL 60155(bore lamp)
Stoeger Industries, 55 Ruta Ct., S. Hackensack, NJ 07606/201-440-2700
Supreme Lens Covers, Box GG, Jackson Hole, WY 83001 (lens caps)
Swain Nelson Co., Box 45, 92 Park Dr., Glenview, IL 60025 (shotgun sight)
Swarovski Optik,Div. of Swarovski America Ltd., One Kenny Dr., Cranston, RI 02920/401-463-6400
Swift Instruments, Inc., 952 Dorchester Ave., Boston, MA 02125
Tasco, 7600 N.W. 26th St., Miami, FL 33122/305-591-3670
Tele Optics, 5514 W. Lawrence Ave., Chicago, IL 60630/312-283-7757 (repair services only)
Thompson-Center Arms, P.O. Box 2426, Rochester, NH 03867/603-332-2394 (handgun scope)
Tradewinds, Inc., Box 1191, Tacoma, WA 98401
John Unertl Optical Co., 3551-5 East St., Pittsburgh, PA 15214
United Binocular Co., 9043 S. Western Ave., Chicago, IL 60620
Vissing (See Supreme Lens Covers)
Wasp Shooting Systems, Box 241, Lakeview, AR 72642/501-431-5606 (mtg. system f. Ruger Mini-14 only)
Weatherby's, 2781 Firestone, South Gate, CA 90280/213-569-7186
W.R. Weaver, Omark Industries, Box 856, Lewiston, ID 83501 (mounts & bases only)
Weaver Scope Repair Service, P.O. Box 20010, El Paso, TX 79998/915-593-1005
Wide View Scope Mount Corp., 26110 Michigan Ave., Inkster, MI 48141
Williams Gun Sight Co., 7389 Lapeer Rd., Davison, MI 48423
Boyd Williams Inc., 8701-14 Mile Rd. (M-57),Cedar Springs, MI 49319 (BR)
Willrich Precision Instrument Co., 95 Cenar Lane, Englewood, NJ 07631/201-567-1411 (borescope)
Carl Zeiss Inc.,Consumer Prods. Div., Box 2010, 1015 Commerce St., Petersburg, VA 23803/804-861-0033

SIGHTS, METALLIC

Accura-Site Co., Inc., P.O. Box 114, Neenah, WI 54956/414-722-0039
Alley Supply Co., P.O. Box 848, Gardnerville, NV 89410/702-782-3800
Armson, Inc., P.O. Box 2130, Farmington Hills, MI 48018/313-478-2577
B-Square Eng. Co., Box 11281, Ft. Worth, TX 76110/800-433-2909
Beeman Inc., 47 Paul Dr., San Rafael, CA 94903/415-472-7121 (airguns only)
Behlert Custom Sights, Inc., RD 2 Box 36C, Route 611 North, Pipersvifile, PA 18947/215-766-8680
Bingham Ltd., 1775-C Wilwat Dr., Norcross, GA 30093/404-448-1440
Bo-Mar Tool & Mfg. Co., Rt. 12, Box 405, Longview, TX 75605/214-759-4784
Buehler Scope Mounts, 17 Orinda Highway, Orinda, CA 94563/415-254-3201
Burris Co., Inc., 331-8th St., P.O. Box 1747, Greeley, CO 80632/303-356-1670
Farr Studio, 1231 Robinhood Rd., Greeneville, TN 37743/615-638-3825 (sighting aids)
Andy Fautheree, P.O. Box 863, Pagosa Springs, CO 81147/303-264-2892 ("Calif. Sight" f. ML)
Freeland's Scope Stands, Inc., 3734-14th Ave., Rock Island, IL 61201/309-788-7449
Paul Jaeger, Inc., P.O. Box 449, 1 Madison Ave., Grand Junction, TN 38039
Lee's Red Ramps, 7252 E. Ave. U-3, Littlerock, CA 93543/805-944-4487 (white outline rear sight)
James W. Lofland, 2275 Larkin Rd., Boothwyn, PA 19061/215-485-0391
Lyman Products Corp., Rte. 147, Middlefield, CT 06455
Mag-na-port International, Inc., 41302 Executive Drive, Mt. Clemens, MI 48045/313-469-6727

Marble Arms Corp., 420 Industrial Park, Gladstone, MI 49837/906-428-3710
Merit Gunsight Co., P.O. Box 995, Sequim, WA 98382/206-683-6127
Micro Sight Co., 242 Harbor Blvd., Belmont, CA 94002/415-591-0769
Millet Industries, 16131 Gothard St., Huntington Beach, CA 92647/714-842-5575
Miniature Machine Co., 210 E. Poplar, Deming, NM 88030/505-546-2151 (MMC)
Omega Sales, Inc., P.O. Box 1066, Mt. Clemens, MI 48043/313-469-6727
Poly Choke Div., Marble Arms Corp., 420 Industrial Park, Gladstone, MI 49837/906-428-3710
Redfield Gun Sight Co., 5800 E. Jewell St., Denver, CO 80222
S&M Tang Sights, P.O. Box 1338, West Babylon, NY 11704/516-226-4057
Schwarz's Gun Shop, 41-15th St., Wellsburg, WV 26070
Simmons Gun Specialties, Inc., 700 S. Rodgers Rd., Olathe, KS 66062/913-782-3131
Slug Site Co., Ozark Wilds, Versailles, MO 65084/314-378-6430
Tradewinds, Inc., Box 1191, Tacoma, WA 98401
Wichita Arms, 444 Ellis, Wichita, KS 67211/316-265-0661
Williams Gun Sight Co., 7389 Lapeer Rd., Davison, MI 48423

STOCKS (Commercial and Custom)

Accuracy Products, 9004 Oriole Trail, Wonder Lake, IL 60097
Advanced Stocking Systems, see: Answer Stocking Systems
Ahlman's Inc., R.R. 1, Box 20, Morristown, MN 55052
Don Allen Inc., HC55, Box 322, Sturgis, SD 57785/605-347-4686
Answer Stocking Systems, 113 N. 2nd St., Whitewater, WI 53190/414-473-4848 (synthetic f. shotguns)
Anton Custom Gunstocks, 7251 Hudson Heights, Hudson, IA/319-988-3941
Creighton Audette, 19 Highland Circle, Springfield, VT 05156/802-885-2331 (custom)
Jim Baiar, 490 Halfmoon Rd., Columbia Falls, MT 599123
Joe J. Balickie, Custom Stocks, Rte. 2, Box 56-G, Apex, NC 27502/919-362-5185
Bartas Gunsmithing, 10231 U.S.H.#10, Cato, WI 54206/414-732-4472
Donald Bartlett, 16111 S.E. 229th Pl., Kent, WA 98031/206-630-2190 (cust.)
Beeman Inc., 47 Paul Dr., San Rafael, CA 94903/415-472-7121 (airguns only)
Dennis M. Bellm Gunsmithing, Inc., 2376 So. Redwood Rd., Salt Lake City, UT 84119/801-974-0697
Al Biesen, West 2039 Sinto Ave., Spokane, WA 99201
Roger Biesen, 5021 W. Rosewood, Spokane, WA 99208/509-328-9340
Stephen L. Billeb, Box 219, Philipsburg, MT 59858/406-859-3919
E.C. Bishop & Son Inc., 119 Main St., Box 7, Warsaw MO 65355/816-438-5121
Gregg Boeke, Rte. 2, Box 149, Cresco, IA 52136/319-547-3746 (cust.)
John M. Boltin, 2008 Havens Dr., North Myrtle Beach, SC 29582/803-272-6581
Kent Bowerly, 1213 Behshel Hts. Rd., Kelso, WA, 98626/206-636-2859 (custom)
Larry D. Brace, 771 Blackfoot Ave., Eugene, OR 97404/503-688-1278 (custom)
Garnet D. Brawley, P.O. Box 668, Prescott, AZ 86301/602-445-4768 (cust.)
Frank Brgoch, #1580 South 1500 East, Bountiful, UT 84010/801-295-1885 (cust.)
A. Briganti, 475 Rt. 32, Highland Mills, NY 10930/914-928-9816
Brown Precision Co., P.O. Box 270W; 7786 Molinos Ave., Los Molinos, CA 96055/916-384-2506
Lenard M. Brownell, (See Billingsley & Brownell)
W. E. Brownell, 3356 Moraga Pl., San Diego, CA 92117/619-276-6146
Jack Burres, 10333 San Fernando Road, Pacoima, CA 91331/818-899-8000 (English, Claro, Bastogne Paradox walnut blanks only)
Calico Hardwoods, Inc., 1648 Airport Blvd., Windsor, CA 95492/707-546-4045 (blanks)
Dick Campbell, 1198 Finn Ave., Littleton, CO 80124/303-799-0145 (custom)
Shane Caywood, 321 Hwy. 51 So., Minocqua, WI 54548/715-356-9631 (cust.)
Claude Christopher, 1606 Berkley Rd., Greenville, NC 27834/919-756-0872 (rifles)
Winston Churchill, Twenty Mile Stream Rd., RFD, Box 29B, Proctorsville, VT 05153
Clinton River Gun Serv., Inc., 30016 S. River Rd., Mt. Clemens, MI 48045/313-468-1090
Charles H. Coffin, 3719 Scarlet Ave., Odessa, TX 79762/915-366-4729
Jim Coffin, 250 Country Club Lane, Albany, OR 97321/503-928-4391
Reggie Cubriel, 14206 Indian Woods, San Antonio, TX 78249/512-492-9825 (cust. stockm.)
The Custom Gun Guild, 5091-F Buford Highway, Doraville, GA 30340/404-455-0346
D&D Gun Shop, 363 Elmwood, Troy, MI 48083/313-583-1512 (cust.)
Dahl's Custom Stocks, Rt. 4, Box 558, Lake Geneva, WI 53147/414-248-2464 (Martin Dahl)
Dahl Gun Shop, 6947 King Ave. West, Billings, MT 59106/406-652-3909
Homer L. Dangler, Box 254, Addison, MI 49220/517-547-6745
Sterling Davenport, 9611 E. Walnut Tree Dr., Tucson, AZ 85715/602-749-5590 (custom)
Jack Dever, 8520 N.W. 90, Oklahoma City, OK 73132/405-721-6393
Charles De Veto, 1087 Irene Rd., Lyndhurst, OH 44124/216-442-3188
Duncan's Gunworks Inc., 1619 Grand Ave., San Marcos, CA 92069/619-727-0515 (cust.)
David R. Dunlop, Rte. 1, Box 199, Rolla, ND 58367
D'Arcy A. Echols, 1309 Riverview Ave., Colorado Springs, CO 81601/303-945-0465 (custom)
Jere Eggleston, 400 Saluda Ave., Columbia, SC 29205/803-799-3402 (cust.)
William A. Emick, P.O. Box 741, Philipsburg, MT 59858/406-859-3280 (custom)
Bob Emmons, 238 Robson Road, Grafton, OH 44044 (custom)
Englishtown Sporting Goods Co., Inc., David J. Maxham, 38 Main St., Englishtown, NJ 07726/201-446-7717 (custom)
Ken Eyster Heritage Gunsmiths Inc., 6441 Bishop Rd., Centerburg, OH 43011/614-625-6131 (cust.)
Reinhart Fajen, Box 338, Warsaw, MO 65355/816-438-5111
Ted Fellowes, Beaver Lodge, 9245 16th Ave. S.W., Seattle WA 98106/206-763-1698
Phil Fischer, 7333 N.E. Glisan, Portland, OR 97213/503-255-5678 (cust.)
Clyde E. Fischer, P.O. Box 1437, Three Rivers, TX 78071/512-786-4125 (Texas Mesquite)
Jerry A. Fisher, 1244-4th Ave. W., Kalispell, MT 59901/406-755-7093
Flaig's Inc., 2200 Evergreen Rd., Millvale, PA 15209/412-821-1717
Flynn's Cust. Guns, P.O. Box 7461, Alexandria, LA 71301/318-455-7130 (cust.)
Donald E. Folks. 205 W. Lincoln St., Pontiac, IL 61764/815-844-7901 (custom trap, Skeet, livebird stocks)
Larry L. Forster, P.O. Box 212, Gwinner, ND 58040/701-678-2475
Fountain Prods., 492 Prospect Ave., W. Springfield, MA 01089 (cust.)
Frank's Custom Rifles, 10420 E. Rusty Spur, Tucson, AZ 85749/602-749-4563
Freeland's Scope Stands, Inc., 3737 14th Ave., Rock Island, IL 61201/309-788-7449
Game Haven Gunstocks, 13750 Shire Rd., Wolverine, MI 49799/616-525-8238 (Kevlar riflestocks)
Jim Garrett, Garrett Accur-Light Inc., P.O. Box 8563, Fort Collins, CO 80524/303-224-3067 (fiberglass)
Dale Goens, Box 224, Cedar Crest, NM 87008
Gordie's Gun Shop, Gordon Mulholland, 1401 Fulton St., Streator, IL 61364/815-672-7202 (cust.)
Gary Goudy, 263 Hedge Rd., Menlo Park, CA 94025/415-322-1338 (cust.)
Gould's Myrtlewood, 341 W. 17th St., Coquille, OR 97423/503-396-5998 (gun blanks)
Charles E. Grace, 10144 Elk Lake Rd., Williamsburg, MI 49690/616-264-9483
Roger M. Green, 315 S. 2d St., P.O. Box 984, Glenrock, WY 82637/307-436-9804
Griffin & Howe, 589 Broadway, New York, NY 10012/212-966-5323 (custom)
Karl Guenther, 43-32 160th St., Flushing, NY 11372/212-461-7325
Guncraft, Inc., 117 W. Pipeline, Hurst, TX 76053/817-282-6481
The Gunworks Inc., John Smallwood, 3434 Maple Ave., Brookfield, IL 60513/312-387-7888 (cust.)
Half Moon Rifle Shop, 490 Halfmoon Rd., Columbia Falls, MT 59912
Rick J. Halstead, 1100 W. Polk Ave., Lovington, NM 88260/505-396-3746
Harper's Custom Stocks, 928 Lombrano St., San Antonio, TX 78207/512-732-5780
Hubert J. Hecht, Waffen-Hecht, 724K St., Sacramento, CA 95814/916-448-1177
Edward O. Hefti, 300 Fairview, College Station, TX 77840/409-696-4959
Warren Heydenberk, 187 W. Sawmill Rd., Rt. 4, Quakertown PA 18951/215-536-0798 (custom)
Doug Hill, 4518 Skyline Place, Enid, OK 73701/405-242-4455 (cust.)
Klaus Hiptmayer, P.O. Box 136, Eastman, Que., J0E 1P0 Canada/514-297-2492
Hoenig & Rodman, 6521 Morton Dr., Boise, ID 83705/208-375-1116 (stock duplicating machine)
George Hoenig, 6521 Morton Dr., Boise, ID 83705/208-375-1116
Hollis Gun Shop, 917 Rex St., Carlsbad, NM 88220
Paul Jaeger, Inc., P.O. Box 449, 1 Madison Ave., Grand Junction, TN 38039
Robert L. Jamison, Rt. 4, Box 200, Moses Lake, WA 98837/509-762-2659 (cust.)
J. J. Jenkins Enterprises, Inc., 375 Pine Ave. #25, Goleta, CA 93117/805-967-1366 (custom)
Johnson Wood Products, I.D. Johnson & Sons, Rte. #1, Strawberry Point, IA 52076/319-933-4930 (blanks)
David Kartak, SRS Box 3042, South Beach, OR 97366/503-867-4951 (custom)
Stanley Kenvin, 5 Lakeville Lane, Plainview, NY 11803/516-931-0321 (custom)
Don Klein, P.O. Box 277, Camp Douglas, WI 54618/608-427-6948
Harry Lawson Co., 3328 N. Richey Blvd., Tucson, AZ 85716/602-326-1117 (cust.)
LeFever Arms Co., Inc., R.D.#1, Box 31, Lee Center, NY 13363/315-337-6422
Al Lind, 7821 76th Ave. S. W., Tacoma, WA 98498/206-584-6361 (cust. stockm.)
G. Little, No. 4026 Sargent, Spokane, WA 99212/509-928-3003 (blanks only)
Ron Long, 81 Delta St., Denver, CO 80221
Earl K. Matsuoka, 2801 Kinohou Pl., P.O. Box 61129, Honolulu, HI 96822/808-988-3008 (cust.)
Bill McGuire, 1600 N. Eastmont Ave., East Wenatchee, WA 98801/509-884-6021
Maurer Arms, Carl R. Maurer, 2154-16th St., Akron, OH 44314/216-745-6864
John E. Maxson, 3507 Red Oak Lane, Plainview, TX 79072/806-293-9042 (custom)
R. M. Mercer, 216 S. Whitewater Ave., Jefferson, WI 53549/414-674-3839 (custom)
Robt. U. Milhoan & Son, Rt. 3, Elizabeth, WV 26143
Miller Arms, Inc., D. E. Miller, P.O. Box 260, St. Onge, SD 57779/605-578-1790
Earl Milliron Custom Guns & Stocks, 1249 N.E. 166th Ave., Portland, OR 97230/503-252-3725
Bill Monell, Red Mill Road, Pine Bush, NY 12566/914-744-3021 (custom)
Ted Nicklas, 5504 Hegel Rd., Goodrich, MI 48438/313-797-4493 (custom)
Paul R. Nickels, Interwest Gun Service, P.O. Box 243, Providence, UT 84332/801/753-4260
Jim Norman, Custom Gunstocks, 11230 Calenda Road, San Diego, CA 92127/619-487-4173
Oakley and Merkley, Box 2446, Sacramento, CA 95811 (blanks)
Vic Olson, 5002 Countryside Dr., Imperial, MO 63052/314-296-8086 (custom)
Maurice Ottmar, Box 657, 113 E. Fir, Coulee City, WA 99115/509-632-5717 (cust.)
Pachmayr Gun Works, 1220 S. Grand Ave., Los Angeles, CA 90015 (blanks and custom jobs)
Pasadena Gun Center, 206 E. Shaw, Pasadena, TX 77506/713-472-0417 (cust.)
Paulsen Gunstocks, Rte. 71, Box 11, Chinook, MT 59523/406-357-3403 (blanks)

Don Robinson, Pennsylvania Hse., 36 Fairfax Crescent, Southowram, Halifax, W. Yorksh. HX3 9SW, England (blanks only)
Carl Roth, Jr., 4728 Pineridge Ave., Cheyenne, WY 82001/309-634-3958
Matt Row, Lock, Stock 'N Barrel, 8972 East Huntington Dr., San Gabriel, CA 91775/818-287-0051
Royal Arms, 1210 Bert Acosta, El Cajon, CA 92020/619-448-5466
Sage International Ltd., 1856 Star Batt Dr., Rochester, MI 48063/313-852-8733 (telescoping shotgun stock)
Sanders Cust. Gun Serv., 2358 Tyler Lane, Louisville, KY 40205 (blanks)
Saratoga Arms Co., 1752 N. Pleasantview RD., Pottstown, PA 19464/215-323-8386
Roy Schaefer, 965 W. Hilliard Lane, Eugene, OR 97404/503-688-43333 (blanks)
Schwartz Custom Guns, 9621 Coleman Rd., Haslett, MI 48840/517-339-8939
David W. Schwartz, 2505 Waller St., Eau Claire, WI 54701/715-832-1735 (custom)
Shaw's, The Finest in Guns, 9447 W. Lilac Rd., Escondido, CA 92025/619-728-7070
Dan A. Sherk, 1311-105th Ave., Dawson Creek, B.C. V1G 2L9, Canada/604-782-3720 (custom)
Hank Shows, The Best,1078 Alice Ave., Ukiah, CA 95482/707-462-9060
Walter Shultz, 1752 N. Pleasantview Rd., Pottstown, PA 19464
Sile Dist., 7 Centre Market Pl., New York, NY 10013/213-925-4111 (shotgun stocks)
Six Enterprises, 6564 Hidden Creek Dr., San Jose, CA 95120/408-268-8296 (fiberglass)
Ed Sowers, 8331 DeCelis Pl., Sepulveda, CA 91343/818-893-1233 (custom hydro-coil gunstocks)
Fred D. Speiser, 2229 Dearborn, Missoula, MT 59801/406-549-8133
Sport Service Center, 2364 N. Neva, Chicago, IL 60635/312-889-1114 (custom)
Sportsmen's Equip. Co., 915 W. Washington, San Diego, CA 92103/714-296-1501 (carbine conversions)
Keith Stegall, Box 696, Gunnison, CO 81230
Stinehour Rifles, Box 84, Cragsmoor, NY 12420/914-647-4163
Talmage Enterpr., 43197 E. Whittier, Hemet, CA 92344/714-927-2397
James C. Tucker, 205 Trinity St., Woodland, CA 95695/916-662-3109 (cust.)
Milton van Epps, Rt. 69-A, Parish, NY 13131
Gil Van Horn, P.O. Box 207, Llano, CA 93544
John Vest, 473-550 Audrey Dr., Susanville, CA 96130/916-257-6702 (classic rifles)
R. D. Wallace, Star Rt. Box 76, Grandin, MO 63943 (cust.)
Weatherby's, 2781 Firestone, South Gate, CA 90280/213-569-7186
Cecil Weems, P.O. Box 657, Mineral Wells, TX 76067/817-325-1462
Frank R. Wells, 10420 E. Rusty Spur, Tucson, AZ 85749/602-749-4563 (custom stocks)
Fred Wells, Wells Sport Store, 110 N. Summit St., Prescott, AZ 86301/602-445-3655
Terry Werth, 1203 Woodlawn Rd., Lincoln, IL 62656/217-732-9314 (cust.)
Western Gunstocks Mfg. Co., 550 Valencia School Rd., Aptos, CA 95003
Duane Wiebe, P.O. Box 497, Lotus, CA 95651
Bob Williams, P.O. Box 143, Boonsboro, MD 21713
Williamson-Pate Gunsmith Service, 117 W. Pipeline, Hurst, TX 76053/817-268-2887
Jim Windish, 2510 Dawn Dr., Alexandria, VA 22306/703-765-1994 (walnut blanks)
Dave Wills, 2776 Brevard Ave., Montgomery, AL 36109/305-272-8446
Robert M. Winter, P.O. Box 484, Menno, SD 57045/605-387-5322
Mike Yee, 4700-46th Ave. S.W., Seattle, WA 98116/206-935-3682
Russell R. Zeeryp, 1601 Foard Dr., Lynn Ross Manor, Morristown, TN 37814

TRAP & SKEET SHOOTERS EQUIP.

A.C. Enterprises, P.O. Box 448, Edenton, NC 27932/919-482-4992
Bob Allen Companies, 214 S.W. Jackson, Des Moines, IA 50315/515-283-2191
The American Import Co., 1453 Mission St., San Francisco, CA 94103/415-863-1506 (Targetthrower)
Anton Custom Gunstocks, 7251 Hudson Heights, Hudson, IA 50643/319-988-3941
C&H Research, 115 Sunnyside Dr., Lewis, KS 67552/316-324-5445 (Mercury recoil suppressor)
D&H Prods. Co., Inc., 465 Denny Rd., Valencia, PA 16059/412-898-2840 (snap shell)
Frigon Guns, 627 W. Crawford, Clay Center, KS 67432/913-632-5607
Griggs Recreational Prods. Inc., P.O. Box 789, Bountiful, UT 84010/801-295-9696 (recoil redirector)
Ken Eyster Heritage Gunsmiths, Inc., 6441 Bishop Rd., Centerburg, OH 43011/614-625-6131 (shotgun competition choking)
Hoppe Division, Penguin Inds. Inc., Airport Mall, Coatesville, PA 19320/215-384-6000 (Monte Carlo pad)
Hunter Co., Inc., 3300 W. 71st Ave., Westminster, CO 80030/303-427-4626
MCM (Mathalienne de Construction de Mecanique), P.O. Box 18, 17160 Matha, France (claybird traps)
Meadow Industries, P.O. Box 450, Marlton, NJ 08053/609-953-0922 (stock pad, variable; muzzle rest)
Wm. J. Mittler, 290 Moore Dr., Boulder Creek, CA 95006 (shotgun choke specialist)
Moneymaker Guncraft, 1420 Military Ave., Omaha, NE 68131/402-556-0226 (free-floating, ventilated ribs)
Multi-Gauge Enterprises, 433 W. Foothill Blvd., Monrovia, CA 91061/213-358-4549; 357-6117 (shotgun specialists)
William J. Nittler, 290 Moore Dr., Boulder Creek, CA 95006/408-338-3376 (shotgun barrel repairs)
Outers Laboratories, Div. of Omark Industries, Route 2, Onalaska, WI 54650/608-783-1515 (trap, claybird)
Purbaugh & Sons (See Multi-Gauge) (shotgun barrel inserts)
Remington Arms Co., P.O. Box 1939, Bridgeport, Ct. 06601 (trap, claybird)
Daniel Titus, Shooting Specialties, 872 Penn St., Bryn Mawr, PA 19010/215-525-8829 (hullbag)
Trius Products, Box 25, Cleves, OH 45002/513-941-5682 (can thrower; trap, claybird)
Winchester-Western, New Haven, CT 06504 (trap, claybird)

TARGETS, BULLET & CLAYBIRD TRAPS

Amacker Products Inc., P.O. Box 1432, Tallulah, LA 71282/318-574-4903
Beeman Inc., 47-GDD Paul Dr., San Rafael, CA 94903/415-472-7121 (airgun targets, silhouettes and traps)
Bulletboard Target Systems Laminations Corp., Box 469, Neenah, WI 54956/414-725-8368
Caswell Equipment Co., Inc., 1221 Marshall St. N.E., Minneapolis, MN 55413/612-379-2000 (target carriers; commercial shooting ranges)
J.G. Dapkus Co., P.O. Box 180, Cromwell, CT 06416/203-632-2308 (live bullseye targets)
Data-Targ, (See Rocky Mountain Target Co.)
Detroit-Armor Corp., Detroit Bullet Trap Div., 2233 N. Palmer Dr., Schaumburg, IL 60195/312-397-4070
The Dutchman's Firearms Inc., 4143 Taylor Blvd., Louisville, KY 40215/502-366-0555
Electro Ballistic Lab., 616 Junipero Serva Blvd., Stanford, CA 94305 (Electronic Trap Boy)
Ellwood Epps Northern Ltd., 210 Worthington St., W., North Bay, Ont. P1B 3B4, Canada (hand traps)
Hunterjohn, P.O. Box 477, St. Louis, MO 63166 (shotgun patterning target)
Jaro Manuf., 206 E. Shaw, Pasadena, TX 77506/713-472-0417 (paper targets)
Laminations Corp. ("Bullettrap"), Box 469, Neenah, WI 54956/414-725-8368
MCM (Mathalienne de Construction Mecanique), P.O. Box 18, 17160 Matha, France (claybird traps)
MTM Molded Prods. Co., 3370 Obco Ct., Dayton, OH 45414/513-890-7461
Millard F. Lerch, Box 163, 10842 Front St., Mokena, IL 60448 (bullet target)
National Target Co., 4960 Wyaconda Rd., Rockville, MD 20852
Outers Laboratories, Div. of Omark Industries, Rte. 2, Onalaska, WI 54650/608-783-1515 (claybird traps)
Peterson Label Co., P.O. Box 186, 23 Sullivan Dr., Redding Ridge, CT 06876/203-938-2349 (paste-ons; Targ-Dots)
Remington Arms Co., Bridgeport, CT 06602 (claybird traps)
Rocky Mountain Target Co., P.O. Box 700, Black Hawk, SD 57718/605-787-5946 (Data-Targ)
Sheridan Products, Inc., 3205 Sheridan, Racine, WI 54303 (traps)
South West Metallic Silhouettes, Rt. 7, Box 82, Abilene, TX 79605/915-928-4463
Trius Prod., Box 25, Cleves, OH 45002/513-914-5682 (claybird, can thrower)
U.S. Repeating Arms Co., P.O. Box 30-300, New Haven, CT 06511/203-789-5000 (claybird traps)
Winchester, Olin Corp., 120 Long Ridge Rd., Stamford, CT 06904

TAXIDERMY

Jack Atcheson & Sons, Inc., 3210 Ottawa St., Butte, MT. 59701
Dough's Taxidermy Studio, Doug Domedion, 2027 Lockport-Olcott Rd., Burt, NY 14028/716-625-8377 (deer head specialist)
Jonas Bros., Inc., 1037 Broadway, Denver, CO 80203 (catlg. $2)
Kulis Freeze-Dry Taxidermy, 725 Broadway Ave., Bedford, OH 44146
Mark D. Parker, 1233 Sherman Dr., Longmont, CO 80501/303-772-0214

TRIGGERS, RELATED EQUIP.

Ametek, Hunter Spring Div., One Spring Ave., Hatfield, PA 19440/215-822-2971 (trigger gauge)
NOC, Cadillac Industrial Park, 1610 Corwin St., Cadillac, MI 49601/616-775-3425 (triggers)
M.H. Canjar Co., 500 E. 45th Ave., Denver, CO 80216/303-295-2638 (triggers)
Central Specialties Co., 200 Lexington Dr., Buffalo Grove, IL 60090/312-537-3300 (trigger lock)
Crown City Arms, Inc., P.O. Box 550, Cortland, NY 13045/607-753-8238
Custom Products, Neil A. Jones, RD #1, Box 483A, Saegertown, PA 16433/814-763-2769 (trigger guard)
Dayton-Traister Co., 9322-900th West, P.O. Box 593, Oak Harbor, WA 98277/206-675-5375 (triggers)
Electronic Trigger Systems, 4124 Thrushwood Lane, Minnetonka, MN 55345/612-935-7829
Flaig's, 2200 Evergreen Rd., Millvale, PA 15209/412-821-1717 (trigger shoes)
Bill Holmes, Rt. 2, Box 242, Fayetteville, AR 72701/501-521-8958 (trigger release)
Neil A. Jones, see: Custom Products
Mad River Metalcraft Inc., 1524 Winding Trail, Springfield, OH 45503/513-399-0948 (bolt shroud safety)
Michaels of Oregon Co., P.O. Box 13010, Portland, OR 97213/503-255-6890 (trigger guards)
Miller Single Trigger Mfg. Co., R.D. 1, Box 99, Millersburg, PA 17061/717-692-3704
Bruce A. Nettestad, Rt. 1, Box 140, Pelican Rapids, MN 56572/218-863-4301 (trigger guards)
Ohaus Corp., 29 Hanover Rd., Florham Park, NJ 07932 (trigger pull gauge)
Pachmayr Gun Works, 1220 S. Grand Ave., Los Angeles, CA 90015 (trigger shoe)
Pacific Tool Co., P.O. Box 2048, Ordnance Plant Rd., Grand Island, NE 68801 (trigger shoe)
Richland Arms Co., 321 W. Adrian St., Blissfield, MI 49228 (trigger pull gauge)
Serrifile Inc., P.O. Box 508, Littlerock, CA 93543/805-945-0713
Timney Mfg. Co., 3106 W. Thomas Rd., Suite 1104, Phoenix, AZ 85017/602-269-6937 (triggers)
Melvin Tyler, 1326 W. Britton Rd., Oklahoma City, OK 73114/800-654-8415 (trigger shoe)
Williams Gun Sight Co., 7389 Lapeer Rd., Davison, MI 48423 (trigger shoe)

Highlights of This Issue

This French 75 fired our first cannonshot in the Great War. **Page 26.**

In the real dirty world of waterfowling, the pump gun is tops. **Page 80.**

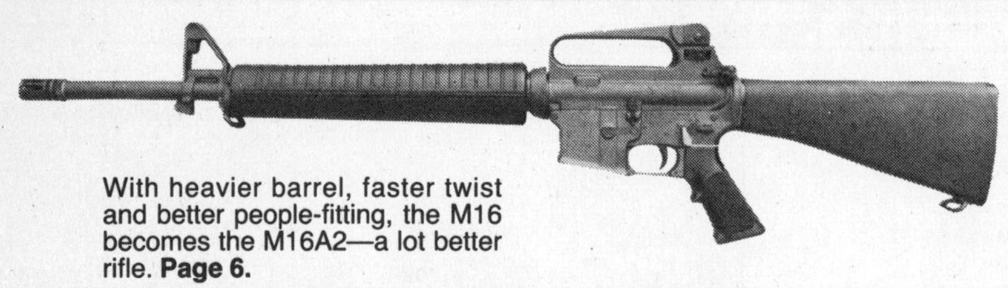

With heavier barrel, faster twist and better people-fitting, the M16 becomes the M16A2—a lot better rifle. **Page 6.**

Both these are 12-gauge tubes, but the big one offers much, much more. **Page 18.**

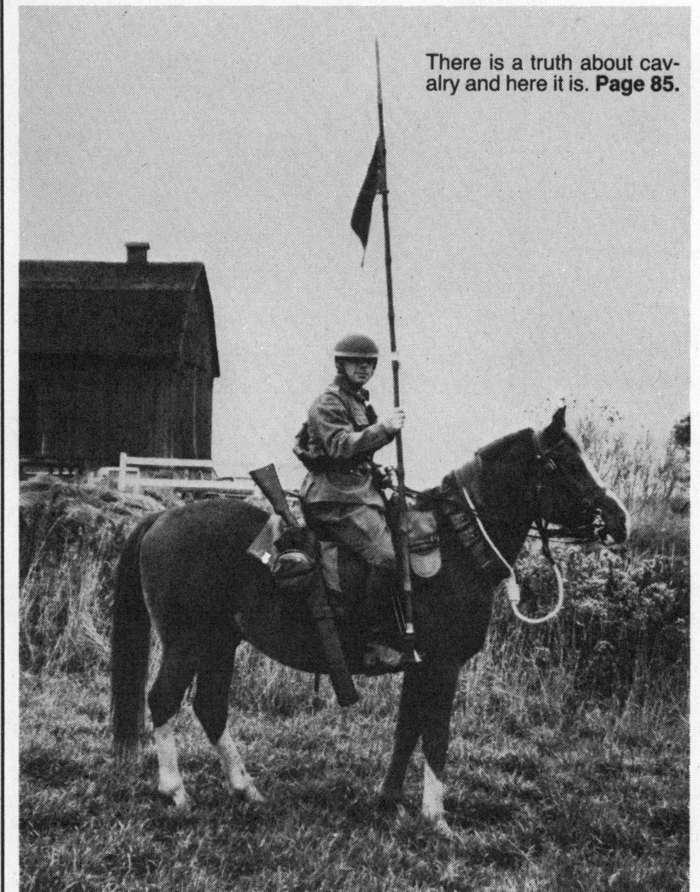

There is a truth about cavalry and here it is. **Page 85.**

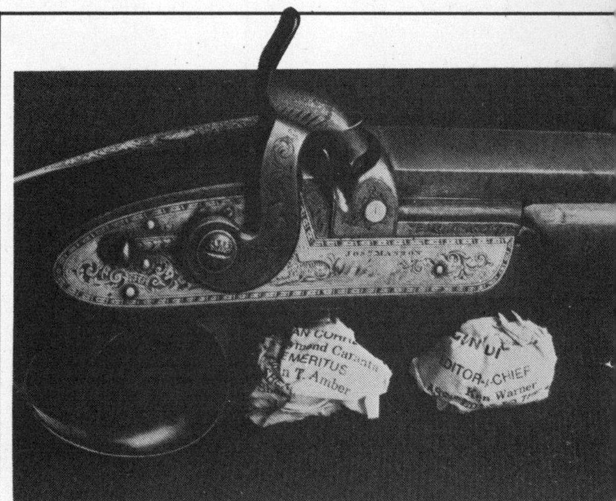

Roger Barlow shoots editorial wads. **Page 23.**

Highlights of This Issue Cont'd.

This is a Burgess of Conyers. **Page 211.**

The Model 94 and the 30-30 may not have been born together, but they certainly grew up a pair. **Page 33.**

Here's a recount on 20 years that changed gunleather for good. **Page 47.**

The editor tries out Wolf Ears. **Page 218.**

Here's a gun to go along most anywhere. **Page 118.**

These are the guns that replaced the double guns. **Page 68.**